VICTIMS OF POLITICS

VICTIMS OF POLITICS

The State of Human Rights

Kurt Glaser
Stefan T. Possony

DISCARD

New York   Columbia University Press   1979

PUBLIC LIBRARY
EAST ORANGE, NEW JERSEY

323.4
G548
cop.1

Library of Congress Cataloging in Publication Data

Glaser, Kurt, 1914–
    Victims of politics.

    Bibliography: p. 557
    Includes index.
    1. Civil rights. 2. Discrimination.
    3. Oppression (Psychology) I. Possony, Stefan Thomas,
    1913–   joint author. II. Title.
JC571.G55   301.5'92   78-5591
ISBN: 0-231-04442-9

Kurt Glaser is Professor of Government, Southern Illinois University at Edwardsville

Stefan T. Possony is Senior Fellow, Hoover Institution on War, Revolution and Peace, Stanford University

Columbia University Press
New York   Guildford, Surrey

Copyright © 1979 by Columbia University Press
All Rights Reserved
Printed in the United States of America

35.00
5/3/79

IN MEMORIAM

Drawing by Rhoda Gralnick,
Pegasus Studios Ltd.

WENZEL JAKSCH

1896 - 1966

Wenzel Jaksch was born of German parents near the linguistic border in Southern Bohemia, where the quarrels of nationalist intellectuals had never penetrated, and where Czechs and Germans were united by religion far more than they were divided by language. "I remember thankfully," he once wrote, "that I never heard a derogatory word about another people in my home or in our school." After working in the building trade in polyglot Vienna and serving in the Austro-Hungarian army in World War I, he returned to the German part of Bohemia after it had been forced into the new state of Czecho-Slovakia against the will of its inhabitants. The communists were threatening to seize power over all Bohemia, and Jaksch joined the struggle for democracy as a full-time organizer and news writer with the Sudeten German labor movement. As a Social Democratic member of the Czecho-Slovak parliament from 1929 to 1938, he was an "activist": a German who cooperated with the Czechs in the effort to persuade them to abandon discrimination against the Sudeten Germans. Convinced that the very imperfect democracy of Czecho-Slovakia was far better than the totalitarianism of Hitler's Third Reich, Jaksch and the Social Democrats urged President Beneš not to yield to Hitler in 1938. After Munich, Jaksch stayed in Prague, helping Jews and others on the Gestapo's wanted list to escape to the still-free parts of Europe. As the Wehrmacht marched into Prague on March 15, 1939, Jaksch skied over the snow-clad Beskide Mountains into Poland, from where he made his way to London.

Throughout World War II, Jaksch served as the principal spokesman for the democratic Sudeten Germans in London. He made a valiant effort to dissuade Dr. Beneš from his plan to expel the entire Sudeten German population. This plan was carried out with Stalin's approval—and the reluctant consent of Truman and Attlee—at the close of World War II. There is little doubt that it contributed greatly to the ease with which the communists gained total power in Czecho-Slovakia in 1948. While in London, Jaksch met and married his wife,

Joan, the former Research Secretary of the Fabian Society, who gave him essential support in his ongoing struggle for human rights.

As an administrator of expellee affairs in the state government of Hesse, and later as a deputy of the Social Democratic Party of Germany in the *Bundestag*, Jaksch became a prominent advocate of the rights of expellees, particularly *Heimatrecht:* a person's right to his original home. But his assertion of German expellee rights was always tempered by full regard for the rights of others. He was deeply convinced that restoration of the rights Germans had lost through Hitler's excesses depended on German–Slavic reconciliation. He took the lead in organizing German–Polish and German–Czech conferences, as well as a still continuing series of German-American conferences designed to raise the level of information about Eastern Europe. Wenzel Jaksch's dedication to human rights was universal: he carried within him the vision of a better world in which people of all nations and races would enjoy these rights to the fullest. He was a world citizen in every sense of the term. In grateful remembrance of the privilege of counting Wenzel Jaksch among our close friends, and with affectionate thoughts for his widow, we dedicate this book to his memory.

KURT GLASER
STEFAN T. POSSONY

CONTENTS

PART IV. FUNCTIONAL AREAS OF DISCRIMINATION

LIST OF ILLUSTRATIONS

PREFACE

Political theorists are fond of labeling the nineteenth century the Age of Ideology. It was during the long and relatively peaceful era symbolized by Queen Victoria that the doctrines of free market economics and classical liberalism reached full development; that elements of St. Simonian industrialism, Comtean positivism, utilitarianism, Hegelian dialectic, and Feuerbachian materialism were compounded into the ideology of revolutionary communism and its supporting "science"; and that nationalism emerged in both its liberal and authoritarian variants—the latter laced with racial notions that became the core of national socialism. It was the twentieth century, however, in which these ideologies became the major grounds of conflict. World War I was, in essence, about nations and nationalism; the conflicts that followed it were about communism and authoritarian as well as totalitarian nationalism versus modern liberalism and democratic socialism as upholders of a shaky status quo. World War II was about nationalism, both traditional and totalitarian, and later (without timely recognition in the West) about communism. Most struggles, political, military, and guerrilla, since World War II have been about nationalism, communism, and democratic liberalism—the latter often misused to mask authoritarian or totalitarian goals of Third World politicians. Every one of these ideologies for which people have fought and killed one another has promised the betterment

of the human race—or at least that segment of it to which ideological propaganda is targeted.

The present study was motivated by the perception that, while wars and political struggles about ideologies have shaped the lives of Americans and of most other peoples in the world, there has been little or no analysis of their human consequences. Much has been written about the processes and strategies of politics, but what of the victims? What impact do the various ideologies and their protagonists have on people's everyday lives? What about the rights of human beings to life, liberty, and the pursuit of happiness—including the right to labor and to enjoy the yield thereof? After a revolution in the name of national independence or majority rule, what is the payoff, positive or negative, for the citizen who wants to exercise his or her rights to free speech, freedom of assembly and democratic political action, freedom of religion, and his or her right to provide for family economic security?

All too often, United States and United Nations policies have been dedicated to the pursuit of abstractions. After noble principles such as decolonization, self-determination, or liberation have been hailed as victorious, innocent people frequently find themselves persecuted, driven from their homes, starved, or slaughtered. These tragedies are reported at length in newspapers and magazines and briefly (when pictures are available) in television newscasts. As social scientists we must ask whether such phenomena reflect an essential chaos of human existence and hence can only be deplored, or whether rational analysis is possible and can lead to a body of theory and practice that might aid in preventing and resolving conflicts. We cannot expect social science to come up with total solutions to all problems: That would be compounding a new ideology. We think most readers will come to agree with us that humankind has suffered enough from ideologies in and of this century.

Those writing a book about a phase of history not tucked comfortably into the past but continuing to happen must sometimes be forcefully reminded that they are not creating a daily newspaper. Obviously, updating takes place during the writing, editing, and final preparation of the manuscript, but there comes a day when the book is sent to the printery— just as a prototype automobile or airplane is placed on the production line. A book about current world problems is necessarily obsolescent when it arrives in the bookstores. We know that some of the situations described in the pages that follow have been changed by recent events. The most we can hope is that we have succeeded in presenting the facts correctly as far as they go and that the generalizations drawn from them are valid.

It nevertheless seems permissible to survey briefly a few major developments affecting human rights during the months since the manuscript received its final editing (June 1977 through March 1978).

For one thing, Western silence about the genocide in Cambodia has been definitely broken, though disagreement on details persists. In July 1977, the *Washington Post* (as reprinted in *The Guardian* of July 31) reported that Cambodia watchers in Thailand now set the death total at "several hundred thousand"—a downward revision of earlier estimates. Disease and starvation, however, had begun to take a greater toll than communist executions. But an exhaustive and well-documented study that

appeared in mid-1977 (John Barron and Anthony Paul, *Murder of a Gentle Land*, New York: Readers' Digest Press–Thomas Y. Crowell) re-established the figure of 1.2 million fatalities in two years as more accurate. Confirming an earlier finding that the Angka Loeu, the Cambodian communist party, trusts only the *peuple de base*, the mountain and forest dwellers in the North and Northeast (Jean Morice, *Cambodge, du Sourire à l'Horreur*, Paris: Editions France-Empire, 1977), Barron and Paul estimate that about 4 million urbanites were relocated. They were driven into the jungle, wilderness, or thinly populated areas, without regard to health, sex, age, creed, class, ethnicity, education, profession, or political membership. Of these, at least 400,000 died from exhaustion or stress, disease without medical treatment, famine, punishment, violence, torture, executions, massacres, and suicide.

The other deaths—more than one-half the total—resulted from mass executions, killings, and drownings, in which terror and cruelty as well as slow death techniques were utilized. There were public and televised executions, including those in which masses of victims were mowed down by machine guns. Occasionally "courts" were improvised to convict suspects of invented charges, but most executions and killings were at random. In this highly uniform state the majority of victims were necessarily Khmers.

Survivors quoted in newspaper and magazine articles reported unanimously that soldiers had apparent freedom to kill arbitrarily whenever and whomsoever they felt like killing. They were allowed to strike as often as they lusted for blood and atrocities. Illiterate and ignorant juveniles were masters over life and death, and no ceiling was placed on the numbers to be dispatched: the more the better. Indeed, a popular slogan of the Angka Loeu holds that "One or two million young people are quite enough to build the new Cambodia" (*Der Spiegel*, No. 11/1977, p. 123).

Other reports have dealt with the plight of

refugees who escape in boats or across the border into Thailand. A pitiful story tells of 249 Indo-Chinese who boarded the 1,570-ton oil tanker *Leap Dai*, chartered by the World Conference on Religion and Peace, in January 1977. They reached the outskirts of Singapore, where they remained six months later, since no country was willing to take them (*Evening Bulletin*, Providence, Rhode Island, June 29, 1977). The current American refugee program provides 15,000 places for about 100,000 refugees from Cambodia, Laos, and Vietnam now in camps outside Indo-China. Their number is constantly augmented by those who flee in row boats, rubber rafts, or whatever will float, or who make their way through the jungle.

In October 1977 a new wave of killings was reported in Cambodia—this time by a pro-Chinese faction of Angka called the "new Khmer Rouge" which undertook to purge the "old Khmer Rouge," the traditional party bureaucrats. Finally, in January 1978, the Department of State took official notice of human rights violations in Cambodia. Acting Secretary of State Warren M. Christopher accused its communist regime of "the most flagrant and massive abuses of human rights to be found in the world today." But little or nothing has been done to move the refugees out of camps or other forms of marginal existence.

Massacres of genocide magnitude in Uganda have already been recorded in the appropriate chapters of this book. Additional documentation, however, became available throughout 1977. In May, the International Commission of Jurists made public (under the title *Uganda and Human Rights*, Geneva: ICJ) a series of reports it had submitted to the United Nations Commission on Human Rights—where the Afro-Asian bloc succeeded in preventing any action. The Jurists' report, drawn up by senior officials who are or have been Attorney-General, Lord Chancellor, Chief Justice, or Supreme Court President in their various countries, lists hundreds of cases of shooting, skull-smashing, torture, beating, and cannibal-

ism at gun point. A memorandum from a former Minister of Education, written in 1973 but published for the first time in 1977 by the ICJ, indicated that President Idi Amin had a list of 2,000 people, the educated elite of Uganda, who were scheduled to be killed. Recent reports confirm that a large portion of the qualified people of Uganda—civil servants, judges, professional soldiers, police, doctors, and businessmen—have indeed been exterminated (*The Guardian*, May 29, 1977). The practice of forcing prisoners to kill one another was confirmed several months later by an escapee who told how he had been made to bludgeon over twenty men to death in the Naguru death camp (Associated Press dispatch from Nairobi, *Stanford Daily*, October 5, 1977). The autumn of 1977 saw the publication of *A State of Blood: The Inside Story of Idi Amin*, by Henry Kyemba (New York: Ace Books), Amin's Minister of Health, who did not defect until May 1977. As Minister of Health, Kyemba had access to Mulago Hospital, including its busy morgue; he saw the bullet-riddled bodies of Archbishop Janani Luwum and two cabinet ministers who, Amin announced to the world, had died in a motor accident. As Kyemba describes it, Amin's rule rests "upon simple unbridled terror, enforced by fifteen thousand thugs, mostly Nubians and southern Sudanese, spread through three separate security organizations. Their loyalty is bought with a license to plunder and with provision of luxury items ferried on the twice weekly flight to England, the 'whiskey run' " (John Darndon in the *New York Times Book Review*, November 6, 1977, p. 50). While Kyemba's factual account seems entirely credible, it remains a mystery why he served Amin so long—especially after the dictator had had his own brother liquidated in 1972.

A close competitor of Idi Amin is President Macias Nguema of Equatorial Guinea, whose victims—typically clubbed to death—number tens of thousands. No significant changes are reported in the latter country, but only a continuation of systematic killings, torture, and forced labor, against which Amnesty International and the Anti-Slavery Society of London have protested repeatedly. Ethiopia, on the other hand, is a relative newcomer to the group of countries practicing mass executions. Quite apart from the efforts of Muslim Eritreans and the Somali tribesmen in the Ogaden Desert to achieve self-determination—issues on which the USSR is now projecting its power *against the rights of people to make their own political decisions*—the Dergue, the Marxist junta that overthrew Emperor Haile Selassie, finds itself challenged by several parties within Ethiopia proper. At least one of these, the Ethiopian People's Revolutionary Party, claims to stand to the left of the Dergue.

The exposure of Ethiopians to higher education abroad and at home, beginning in the 1950s, created a new intelligentsia numbering about 30,000. The Dergue has never been able to capture the loyalty of this stratum, which provides the cadres of the opposition parties. In the absence of constitutional means of conflict resolution—such as free elections—the political struggle is carried on with reciprocal violence. A student demonstration in Addis Ababa in May 1977 was broken up by government troops who were reported to have shot 1,000 students to death. Guerrilla warfare between the Dergue and the opposition smoldered throughout the summer of 1977 and flared up in the fall. In November, for instance, soldiers dismounted from four Land-Rovers and opened fire with machine guns on junior high school pupils singing anti-government songs as they left school. The number of victims was not recorded, but the firing was sustained. Shortly thereafter, a high member of the Dergue, the mayor-designate of Addis Ababa, and a policeman were shot to death in broad daylight (*New York Times*, November 6, 1977). Violence escalated on both sides; an African diplomat stated that in late December 1977 and early 1978 he frequently saw bodies on the street and heard gunfire. Expressing the

government's point of view, Mayor Alemu Abebe of Addis Ababa blamed the state of insecurity on "counterrevolutionaries." It was, he said, "impossible for people to walk the streets. There were daily assassinations in which five or six comrades were killed. We have seen our comrades dropping one by one." Mounting what a spokesman for the Dergue called "justifiable terror" (a category unknown in legal philosophy or social science), the regime hunted down members of the EPRP throughout December. Diplomats set the figures at 700 killed and 5,000 arrested—an estimate an official spokesman called "ridiculous" (AP story in *St. Louis Post-Dispatch*, February 9, 1978). The *New York Times* (February 10, 1978) cited a figure of 1,000 killed and 10,000 arrested from mid-December to the date of its dispatch. The official Ethiopian press agency has published no overall figures but announced that 19 underground leaders were executed and 279 arrested in a single January operation (*St. Louis Post-Dispatch*, January 16, 1978).

Border warfare between Cambodia and Vietnam, causing renewed suffering of civilian populations, as well as occasional Cambodian raids into northeast Thailand, were noted by the world press in late 1977 and early 1978. A simultaneous happening that attracted little attention was a major genocide conducted in 1977 by the Pathet-Lao government of Laos, supported by communist Vietnam, against the Meo hill tribes numbering about 100,000 people. The Meos, whose only crime from a Western point of view is growing opium, fiercely resist any attempt to control them—for which reason most fought on the United States side in the recent war. Some groups, however, sided with the pro-communist Pathet-Lao. The present campaign, using numerically superior forces armed with sophisticated equipment, was launched in April 1977. In Sayabouri Province, in northern Laos, at least 200 Meos were killed, according to refugees who had crossed the Mekong River into Thailand. The genocidal drive reached full force in early November, when Soviet-made jets bombed out Meo villages in Xieng Khousang Province, and a Vietnamese artillery barrage opened the way for invasion by five Vietnamese regiments. According to Meo Colonel Yong Kwang, who commanded a group that fled to Thailand, the Vietnamese bombardment caused as many as 1,000 deaths and injuries in two villages. The invading troops fired lethal gas grenades into caves where they suspected Meos were hiding. The *Bangkok Post* cited a ranking Thai intelligence source as stating that Lao-Viet forces had killed at least 1,300 Meos, wounded over 800, and captured some 5,400 others in the Phou Bia district alone. Following the communist custom of projecting guilt, Radio Vientiane boasted that "we have successfully confronted fierce opposition and sabotage by imperialism and reactionary powers. . . . we have finally smashed the enemy schemes and acts of sabotage." As of this writing, approximately 50,000 to 60,000 Meos still control a small jungle area of three or four hundred square kilometers in northern Laos. But Lao and Viet troops are advancing in a pincer movement in an apparent effort to annihilate the Meos as an ethnic entity.

On the subject of slavery, to which a chapter of this book is devoted, there is little to report save the abuse of diplomatic immunity by two United Nations officials, whom the Anti-Slavery Society accused of holding servants in slave-like conditions in New York. One servant, according to the Society's chairman, Colonel Patrick Montgomery, "worked a minimum of fourteen hours and often as long as nineteen hours a day, seven days a week, for 2½ years without any time off or vacation. She was compelled to labor . . . by threats of imprisonment, deprivation of future employment and deportation if she tried to run away" (*St. Louis Post-Dispatch*, August 14, 1977). The Anti-Slavery Society was the particular target of USSR and Ukrainian wrath at a meeting of the Social Committee of ECOSOC, held on May 2, 1977, to debate a report by the Committee on Non-Governmental Organizations (NGOs), which examines at two-year intervals the merits and demerits of NGOs in consultative relationship with ECOSOC. Not only had the Anti-Slavery Society "slandered certain member states," but Amnesty International and the International League for Human Rights engaged in "propaganda activities . . . aimed exclusively at poisoning international relations and spreading false information about the socialist states." It seems evident that the Soviet bloc would like to muzzle the NGOs in their appearances before United Nations bodies—an attitude shared to a limited extent by Chile (supplement to *Anti-Slavery Society Newsletter*, June 1977).

Torture, likewise the subject of a chapter, remains an active issue. The 1977 report of Amnesty International (AI) mentions cases of torture in a number of countries on several continents. The organization's concern was reflected in several publications of AI's Campaign for the Abolition of Torture, including medical studies on the effects of torture and a major report on the first trial of torturers in Greece. A report submitted by AI to the Inter-American Commission on Human Rights cited 19 affidavits of torture in Uruguay, as well as mistreatment of prisoners bordering on torture in several other states. In the case of the Philippines, AI submitted to the government the names of 88 military men identified by prisoners as having used torture. Subsequently, four of them were brought to trial. In Argentina, a report compiled by church sources named 47 torture centers in rural areas and sixty men charged with applying torture. They included police officers, a police doctor, and two former judges. The report also claimed that in December 1976 there were 29 prisoners massacred during an alleged "prison transfer" although the official version was that they had been shot "while trying to escape." In Israel, on the other hand, the government was able to produce evidence disproving charges of torture of Arabs in the occupied territories that had been raised in the London *Sunday Times* (*Boston Globe*, July 3, 1977). The Israeli government promised to prosecute any case of alleged torture in which genuine evidence might be submitted. In a case brought by the Republic of Ireland under the European Convention on Human Rights, the government of the United Kingdom admitted having tortured suspected IRA terrorists to extract information. But it declared that the practice had been discontinued and would not be resumed.

During her 1977 trip to Latin America, Mrs. Rosalynn Carter spoke with two American missionaries who said they were unjustly imprisoned, beaten, and starved in a Brazilian jail. After being arrested for no apparent reason other than having grown beards not shown on their identification photographs, they were stripped and placed in a tiny cell with 34 other naked men. They were kicked and beaten daily; a typical meal consisted of a handful of damp flour and a piece of dried meat "the size of a nickel or a quarter." The United States filed a note of concern with the Brazilian government, which had already rejected U.S. military aid because of a critical report by the Department of State citing oppressive administration of the National Security Law and occasional cases of torture—notwithstanding recent steps to reduce abuses. But despite the continued efforts of the Geisel administration to reform the political structure and ease arbitrary laws, cases of torture continued to surface, typically in a document published in February 1978 by 22 political prisoners in São Paulo. According to Edward M. Mezvinsky, United States representative on the United Nations Commission on Human Rights, torture remains a challenge to the integrity of the United Nations, since "torture and other cruel forms of intimidation are increasingly being used as the leading edge of oppression to intimidate the leaders for the oppressed" (*St. Louis Post-Dispatch*, June 9 and December 6, 1977; *New York Times*, February 19, 1978). A word of caution is in order, however, since charges of

torture are sometimes trumped up. Defenders or the Baader-Meinhof gang in Germany alleged that white painted and soundproofed cells constituted "sensory deprivation." They even objected to the searching of visitors for weapons—searches that in retrospect were wholly insufficient, since Andreas Baader and Jan-Carl Raspe committed suicide with pistols.

Terrorism is another major form of human rights violation. It operates directly, by denying people secure enjoyment of their rights to life, liberty, and property, and indirectly by providing the reason or pretext for government policies that are at best inconvenient and which have the potential for becoming oppressive. It is always open to debate whether government measures to control or stamp out terrorism (e.g. in Rhodesia, South Africa, Argentina, or Uruguay) represent an overreaction or a prudent concern for public order. This book contains no chapter devoted specifically to terrorism, but if we were starting it again today, we would almost certainly write one.

A chronology of terrorist events is unnecessary here. Suffice it to note that since World War II it has appeared mainly as a regional phenomenon. Its first important theater was Southeast Asia, where the collapse of Japanese hegemony had left a partial power vacuum. A second regionally based terrorist campaign is that of Al Fatah against Israel, which has extended into many parts of the world and has been continuous for more than 20 years. The massacre of the Israeli Olympic team in Munich in 1972, and a series of airplane hijackings, slowed but by no means stopped by the Israeli rescue at Entebbe (Uganda) and the German commando operation at Mogadishu (Somalia), are emanations from this theater. In March 1977 members of the Hanafi Muslim sect attacked the B'nai B'rith headquarters, a mosque, and the city hall in Washington, D.C., killing two and holding one hundred under threat of death for 39 hours. Only after mediation by Arab ambassadors were the hostages released, the *quid pro quo*, approved by

Attorney General Griffin Bell, being the release of Hanafi leader Hamaas Abdul Khaalis on his own recognizance pending indictment (*St. Louis Post-Dispatch*, March 10, 13, and 17, 1977).

The third major theater of terrorism has been Northern Ireland, where the state of insecurity has made normal economic and social life almost impossible. Late 1977 and early 1978 saw a resurgence of attacks against civilians in the Six Counties, a typical exploit being the bombing of crowded restaurants. A fourth important theater of terrorism has developed in recent years in Southern Africa. There, terrorism is employed as an adjunct to guerrilla warfare—an aspect to be treated presently. We have already noted the appearance of terrorism in a fifth theater: the Horn of Africa—a region in strategic proximity to the oil route from the Persian Gulf.

A sixth center of terrorism has arisen in Italy. Rome was recently described as "the capital of terrorism" where gangs of trigger-happy youths roam the nocturnal streets ready to kill in defense of extreme ideologies—mostly ultra-leftist. In 1977 alone there were more than 2,000 assassinations, woundings, kidnappings, shootouts with police, bombings, and arson incidents. From January 1 to late March 1978 there were 11 political murders and 13 kidnappings, the most noteworthy being the kidnapping and subsequent murder of former Premier Aldo Moro (*U.S. News & World Report*, March 27, 1978, p. 92). This action of the Red Brigades, in the opinion of Deputy Assistant Secretary of State Steve R. Pieczenik, was aimed at destabilizing not only the governing Christian Democratic Party but the entire state of Italy. To demonstrate that the government could function effectively in a crisis, it was necessary to demonstrate that Mr. Moro was not indispensable. Dr. Pieczenik, a psychiatrist and political scientist whose consulting services the Italian government had requested, said in an interview that the Italians were now developing hitherto lacking crisis-management

techniques (*New York Times*, April 23, 1978). The Italian Communist Party finds itself in an embarrassing position. While it shares with the Red Brigades the ultimate objective of social revolution and hopes like them to profit from the discontent of the younger generation, the self-identification with communism and the Marxist-Leninist jargon employed by the Red Brigades are causing many Italians to turn away from the Communist Party (*U.S. News & World Report*, May 1, 1978, p. 34).

A seventh theater, where terrorism seems (as of this writing) to be on the decline after a peak, is in southern South America, Argentina, and Uruguay in particular. The situation in Argentina might be characterized as a standoff between anti-government leftist terrorism (including the killing or kidnapping of executives of American business firms and American consular officials), and repressive terrorism by the government, which is reported to have detained several thousand people under a State of Siege (U.S. Department of State, *Human Rights Reports*, March 1977, pp. 106–7; *Le Monde*, January 8, 1977). Terrorism in Uruguay was made notorious by the leftist Tupamaros, an urban guerrilla group that during the 1960s and 1970s totally frustrated attempts to maintain public order and indeed prepared the way for replacement of democracy by a military dictatorship. It is doubtful, however, that anti-government terrorism, though still latent, justifies the torture and terrorism currently employed by the Uruguayan government, reported by Amnesty International to hold about five thousand political prisoners for whom "the use of torture has become routine" (*Human Rights Reports*, p. 142).

Recent events in Puerto Rico suggest that an eighth regional theater of terrorism may emerge in the Caribbean. In Cuba, however, terrorism is a monopoly of the Castro government, which is reported to have thrown between 10,000 and 20,000 actual and suspected dissidents into concentration camps, where some 4,000 have died. Those who refuse communist "rehabilitation," consisting of forced labor with brain washing, are denied food and medicines, resulting in numerous deaths from disease as well as those from torture, beating, and shooting (*Das Da*, Hamburg, February 1977; Frances R. Grant, "What of Cuba and Human Rights?" *Freedom at Issue*, November–December, 1977, pp. 9–11). The Inter-American Commission on Human Rights, on the basis of detailed information concerning arbitrary arrest, lack of due process of law, forced labor, forced indoctrination, and terrorizing of prisoners with real and simulated executions, concluded that "absolute disregard for human dignity" is the state of affairs in Cuba (*Neue Zürcher Zeitung*, July 31, 1977).

From time to time, terrorist actions take place outside the main theaters. One series of incidents, related to Southeast Asia insofar as they involve a country in that region, has its locale in the Netherlands. In May 1977, South Moluccan terrorists, hoping to force the Dutch government to press for independence of their Indonesian-controlled island homeland, seized a train and a school and held them for several days. Their threats against the school children and train passengers provoked the danger of violent Dutch reaction against the 40,000 South Moluccans living in Holland, most of whom had no connections with the terrorists. Violent acts by South Moluccan extremists continue: an attack on a provincial administration took place in March 1978.

Terrorism is frequently employed as an adjunct to guerrilla warfare. Guerrilla strategy is embraced by revolutionary movements unable to achieve a broad mass base through persuasion or propaganda—sometimes because the supposedly "downtrodden" feel they would be worse off without their "oppressors" and prefer the lower rungs of a modern economy, with some hope of upward mobility, rather than a reversion to primitivism. The goal of guerrilla terrorism is to create a mass base through fear and to paralyze those groups and institutions among the native masses that

collaborate with the regime to be overthrown or driven out. At the same time the supposedly (and to varying extents actually) oppressive power is compelled to spend increasing portions of its resources on security; economic growth is slowed or halted and demoralization may set in.

Guerrilla warfare in the strict sense attacks the enemy's military personnel and installations and his power apparatus. Guerrilla terrorism concentrates on unarmed citizens devoted to peaceful pursuits as well as on their property, with the object of tearing apart the fabric of society. Its perpetrators do not shrink from extreme cruelty; in fact the more gruesome the deed the better it serves the aim of terrorism—to instill terror. Guerrilla terrorism was a standard practice of the Viet Cong during the Vietnam war. Unable to assure security in outlying areas, the Saigon government had to move large numbers of peasants into protected villages. Such terrorism is the central *modus operandi* of the so-called Patriotic Front attempting to gain power in Rhodesia from bases in Zambia and Mozambique. The Front has demanded that power be handed to it before any election, since it is evident that its leaders Joshua Nkomo and Robert Mugabe fear they will lose in the free elections planned by the new interracial Executive Council. The Rhodesian Ministry of Information has published a chronology of 112 terrorist attacks between May 1974 and October 1976 (*Harvest of Fear*, Salisbury, 1976); about 90 percent of the victims are black. With few exceptions, these acts of murder and mayhem, the gory details of which are spared the reader, were directed against unarmed civilians.

Terrorism has forced a major curtailment of the education of Africans, especially in outlying districts. Between January and August 1977, 356 primary and 11 secondary schools were forced to close and 58,758 pupils were deprived of schooling.

It is to interdict guerrilla terrorism that Rhodesian forces, under Ian Smith's largely white government and more recently under the inter-racial transitional regime, have raided terrorist bases in Mozambique and Zambia. After a June 1977 raid into Mozambican territory entirely controlled by the "Zimbabwe Liberation Army," in which the Rhodesians overran four bases, killing 32 terrorists and destroying much equipment, the British Foreign Secretary, the U.S. Department of State, and Secretary-General Waldheim of the United Nations joined in declaring the operation illegal. This did not deter the Rhodesian government from a larger raid in late November 1977, in which the Rhodesian forces claimed they inflicted massive losses on Robert Mugabe's Zimbabwe African National Union (ZANU) army.

The international law of the matter is that a state is prohibited from allowing its territory to be used for staging attacks on another state—a principle recognized in 1871 in the settlement of the *Alabama* claims (see Charles G. Fenwick, *International Law*, New York: Appleton-Century-Crofts, 1965, pp. 743–45). Should a state fail to meet this international obligation, the injured state is entitled to take direct action for its own security. The same rule applies to Israeli reprisals after terrorist raids from neighboring states.

SWAPO, the "South West Africa People's Organization," a largely Ovambo group that has gained recognition in the United Nations as a spokesman for the (doubtfully existent) Namibian people, combines guerrilla warfare (attacks against South African forces) with guerrilla terrorism (attacks against black and white civilians). SWAPO even terrorizes its own people; members who object to its policies or discipline are sent to a "corrective camp" in Zambia, where more than one thousand South West Africans of various ethnic groups are reported held in starvation conditions. SWAPO guerrillas seldom operated in groups larger than 10 or 12 men; their main activities are planting landmines, attacking villages, and sometimes abducting entire settlements and schools. Since January 1978, SWAPO operatives assassinated Toiva Shiyagaya, Minister of Health and Welfare of Ovambo, and Chief Clemence Kapuuo of the Herero, both moderate black leaders involved in the internal settlement of South West Africa/Namibia's problems.

Behind the terrorist fronts in the various theaters are the manipulators. One of the remote-control centers is in the USSR; another is Palestinian. There are other Arab promoters in Libya, Iraq, Algeria, Syria, and South Yemen, which is a major staging area. Libya's General Qaddafi is reported to have paid $5 million to Black September for the massacre of the Israeli Olympic team in Munich. It is believed that a similar sum financed the December 1975 kidnapping of Arab oil ministers from the Vienna meeting of the Organization of Petroleum Exporting Countries (OPEC). Cuba plays a major role and Czecho-Slovakia furnishes weapons, notably to the Irish Republican Army. Terrorist groups in the different theaters are interlinked, providing personnel for joint operations, exchanging information, and sharing training facilities, weapons, and explosives.

Before its military venture in Africa, Cuba acted mainly through the Tricontinental Organization, within which modern urban guerrilla tactics were developed. Algeria, North Korea, and communist Vietnam were also members of Tricontinental, the communist linkage of which is a matter of record. Soviet influence, however, is exercised indirectly, and the Kremlin's control over certain terrorist groups, such as the Red Brigades in Italy, is to say the least doubtful. Yet all terrorist groups share an essential mission of creating and maintaining psychological traumata and chaos, as well as recruiting for extremist pseudo-Marxist ideologies. Terrorism is in essence a form of genocide because it kills and maims innocent civilians, and because it destroys the framework within which self-determination can be exercised. Russian support of terrorism in the name of "national Liberation" is thus contradictory (see Possony and Bouchey, 1978).

The state of human rights in the world has not changed markedly since the manuscript of this book was sent to press. The use of repressive psychiatry and the imprisonment of dissidents for political "offenses" in the USSR seem to be increasing, yet the disposal of prominent critics of the regime by exile and cancellation of citizenship rather than execution might be considered a positive development. Seven psychiatrists refused to certify that political dissidents are mentally ill and were fired from their jobs; two of them were jailed (according to Amnesty International, quoted in *Die Welt*, March 8, 1978). In mainland China, the camp population appears to have been reduced, but there is no evidence that the brainwashing and re-education system, as described in chapter 26, have been abolished. In Vietnam, the "re-education" program is continuing with full momentum.

The annual survey of freedom published by Freedom House (*Freedom at Issue*, no. 44 [1978], pp. 3–19) shows that India and Spain have moved into the "free" column, as well as newly independent Djibouti—which Somalia would like to annex on grounds of ethnic affinity. Kuwait, Syria, Ghana, Madagascar, and Nepal moved from "not free" to "partly free." Conversely, the Congo Republic (Brazzaville) fell from "partly free" to "not free" and Seychelles from "free" to "partly free," while Angola, Equatorial Guinea, and Ethiopia dropped to the worst category. Freedom House registered "a serious decline—but with no change in category" in South Africa.

President Carter has continued his human rights policy. Within its limitations as an essentially verbal policy, it has achieved a modicum of success. "It is not coincidental," writes Professor Raymond D. Gastil of Freedom House, that 1977 has been "a year in which many more gains than losses have been made in political and civil freedoms." While governments that have liberalized would hardly be likely to acknowledge United States pressure, "the change of attitude of the U.S. government

toward freedom has again and again been cited as one among a number of contributing factors—Iran, Thailand, and China (Taiwan) particularly come to mind, and there may even have been some moral assistance in India or Sri Lanka" (*ibid.*, p. 18). A similar assessment was reached by Deputy Secretary of State Warren Christopher, who, in addressing the American Bar Association, disclaimed credit for particular improvements but stated his belief that "the almost geometric increase in world awareness of human rights issues is perhaps the major accomplishment of our human rights diplomacy."

On the minus side, it must be admitted that the Carter administration's human rights policy has been invoked selectively. It has been stated emphatically as applied to Western countries, such as South Africa, Chile, Brazil, and Uruguay; in muffled tones where military allies or suppliers of oil are concerned, such as Iran or Saudi Arabia; and incoherently with regard to communist regimes. On the subjects of continuing though diminishing human rights violations in mainland China, terrorism by Rhodesian and SWAPO guerrillas, operation of concentration camps by East Germans in South Yemen, and government terror in Ethiopia—not to mention the dictatorial practices of a score of African heads of government, among whom only Amin has been criticized—the administration has been wholly silent. Evidently, human rights must give way to the exigencies of *Weltpolitik*, but current American policy is incoherent even from that point of view.

It appears that the United States delegation was instructed to maintain a low profile at the Belgrade conference to review execution of the Final Act agreed at Helsinki in 1975, lest the already precarious détente with the USSR and its satellites be irreparably derailed. This conference, which opened in June 1977, was marked by profound disagreement throughout. If it accomplished nothing, it had some value as an exercise in communication. "The

Russians had to listen to very detailed discussion of their internal practices and found very little support for their claim, which is anyway contrary to the text of the Final Act, that this amounted to impermissible interference in their internal affairs. The right of mutual criticism emerged strengthened, as did the connection between internal policies and external relations. The Russians showed up the weakness of their case by refusing any serious discussion in this area." (*The Times*, London, March 10, 1978.) Although the Western delegations had hoped that Belgrade would produce a meaningful statement about human rights and some concrete measures of liberalization, these were not forthcoming. All the conference could do was to reaffirm the Final Act and agree to meet again at Madrid in November 1980.

On the surface, it would appear that Cuba has emerged as the major imperialist power of the decade, with military and technical personnel in at least 19 African countries. Closer analysis, however, shows that the Castro regime is merely serving as a proxy for the Kremlin. The latter intervenes openly when opportunity offers, as in the case of Ethiopia.

Once we dispense with the rule that political boundaries once established—no matter how—are sacred and may never be disturbed, it seems evident that successful revolts in Eritrea and the Ogaden region against Ethiopia would have been gains for self-determination. The Muslim Eritreans and Somali of the Ogaden are ethnically very different from the Coptic Amharas, the *Staatsvolk* (ruling nation) of Ethiopia. In this struggle we find the USSR and Cuba on the side of Amhara (and their own) imperialism—a test of Leninist ability to digest ideological contradiction.

In Angola, the anti-Marxist UNITA led by Jonas Savimbi has regained control of much of the southern half of the country, and is waging a war of attrition against the MPLA and the Cubans. The most interesting development in 1977, however, was the revealing of what really happened in Angola. It now appears that

the South African expedition into Angola in late 1975 took place at the specific (though unannounced) request of the United States, and that South African and UNITA forces could have defeated the Luanda regime and the Cubans had not Congress imposed a reversal of United States policy. The reasons why President Ford and Secretary Kissinger did not fight for an active anti-communist policy in Africa are multiplex and have to do with the state of mind of the American people, its state of disinformation, the Vietnam defeat, and the *problématique* of Presidential re-election.

In Rhodesia/Zimbabwe and South West Africa/Namibia, the United States has joined with Great Britain (and Canada, France, and West Germany in the case of SWA) in proposing political arrangements in the name of democracy. Given the ethnic structure of these countries and the actual and self-evident goals of contenders for power, it is clear that instant dismantling of white regimes in favor of unmodified territorial democracy would produce, not liberal democratic systems conforming to the image projected in Washington and London, but one-party dictatorships reflecting tribal hegemony and, in Rhodesia, a likely civil war between the supporters of two would-be dictators. After much fumbling and bumbling in Washington, London, and New York, moderate black and white leaders in both Rhodesia and South West Africa have agreed on transitional arrangements combining majority rule with guarantees for ethnic rights. The only parties dissatisfied are the largely external ZANU, ZAPU, and SWAPO, who have now revealed themselves to be *against majority rule*, because they know they would be defeated in free elections.

Since Russian logistic aid and ideological as well as technical training provided to ZANU, ZAPU, and SWAPO are a matter of record beyond any need for demonstration here, and since their particiation in international terrorism is notorious, continued insistence in Washington and London that these groups "must be included" in the new political structures is counterproductive for U.S. and British interests as well as human rights. Support of these organizations by the World Council of Churches raises a question of religious ethics as well as a legal question of tax exemption.

As will be seen in the opening chapters of this book, a world consensus on human rights is developing but has by no means reached definitive form. Permanent and transcendent norms need to be separated from culturally conditioned and hence mutable precepts—a task requiring sociological, political and scientific, as well as philosophical analysis. It is self-evident that a person has the right to life, but when does a person begin and end? Is the right to vote conditional on ability to understand the issues involved in the vote? What of social and economic rights to employment, education, health care, and a basically sufficient standard of living: do they conflict with rights of liberty and property and are they rights at all rather than desiderata? And what of the contradictions between individual and group rights, especially in multi-ethnic societies? As will be seen in the body of this book, there are cases where total fulfillment of clashing rights is a logical impossibility.

This book is a study of the social data involved in human rights, discrimination, and oppression. The authors hope they have provided reasonable answers to some questions, but in so doing they have had to ask new questions and leave other existing questions open. If this book provides an impetus for further study and analysis it will have served its purpose.

Kurt Glaser
Stefan T. Possony

St. Louis, Missouri and
Los Altos, California
March 1978

ACKNOWLEDGMENTS

The authors gratefully acknowledge the following publishers, institutions, and individuals who have kindly permitted us to reprint material here.

The University of California Press for the extracts from *Society in India: Community and Change*—Volume 1, by David G. Mandelbaum. Copyright © 1970 by David G. Mandelbaum.

The Dorsey Press, A Division of Richard D. Irwin, Inc., for the extracts from *Ethnic Dynamics: Patterns of Intergroup Relations in Various Societies*, by Chester L. Hunt and Lewis Walker, Originally published in 1974.

The Economist of London for the maps of the Turkish invasion of Cyprus.

Mr. Phillip Goodhart, M.P. for the extracts from *The Double Exodus: A Study of Arab and Jewish Refugees in the Middle East*, by Terence Prittie and Bernard Dineen. Originally published in 1974.

The Houghton Mifflin Company for the extracts from *Race and Ethnic Relations* by B. Berry. Copyright © 1965 by the Houghton Mifflin Company.

The McGraw-Hill Book Company and Jonathan Cape Ltd. for the poem "Soul on Ice" by Eldridge Cleaver. Copyright © 1968 by Eldridge Cleaver. Used by permission of the McGraw-Hill Book Company and Jonathan Cape, Ltd.

The Minority Rights Group for the extracts from *The Biharis in Bangladesh*, Report No. 11, by Ben Whitaker, originally published in 1972; and *Canada's Indians* by James Wilson, originally published in 1974.

Oxford University Press for the extracts from *The Immigrant Workers and Class Structures in Western Europe* by Stephen Castles and Godula Kosack. Used by permission of the Oxford University Press. Originally published in 1973.

Prentice-Hall, Inc. for the extracts from *Strangers Next Door: Ethnic Relations in American Communities* by Robin M. Williams, Jr. Copyright © 1964. Reprinted by permission of Prentice-Hall, Inc., Englewood Cliffs, New Jersey.

Prentice-Hall, Inc. and Ina Corinne Brown for the extracts from *Understanding Race Relations*. Copyright © 1973. Reprinted by permission of Prentice-Hall, Inc., Englewood Cliffs, New Jersey and Ina Corinne Brown.

Sidgwick & Jackson, Ltd. for the extracts from *The Fourth World: Victims of Group Oppression* edited by Ben Whitaker. Copyright © Sidgwick & Jackson 1972 and Minority Rights Group.

Sudentendeutscher Rat, Munich, for the extracts from *Documents on the Expulsion of the Sudeten Germans*, edited by W. K. Turnwald. Originally published in 1951 and 1953.

Swets Publishing Service, a Division of Swets & Zeitlinger, B. V., for the extracts from *The Israeli Dilemma: Essays on a Warfare State* by Georges R. Tamarin. Originally published in 1973.

Dr. W. A. Veenhoven for extracts from his *Case Studies on Human Rights and Fundamental Freedoms*. Originally published in 1975.

PART ONE

ETHICAL AND LEGAL PERSPECTIVES

1

INTRODUCTION:
THE HUMAN CONDITION

The human condition is characterized by an unending series of man-made catastrophes. History is often interpreted as a sequence of class struggles, but the "classes" have never been simply groups of people who are rich or poor but alike in other respects; they have constituted any number of distinct or not so distinct groups hostile to one another for a wide variety of reasons. There are struggles—and wars—between states, religious groups, political parties, ethnic groups, races, generations, the sexes, economic enterprises, and competing criminal organizations. There are perennial conflicts between criminals and the police, feuds and fights between families, clans, elites and would-be elites, and sometimes power struggles between individuals affecting large numbers of people. Struggle and conflict, violence and war, have marked every society in historical memory, with the possible exception of a few isolated tribal groups. Human life is strife, and *Homo sapiens* is *Homo pugnans*.

The phenomenon has been recognized by conservatives like Thomas Hobbes with his *bellum omnium contra omnes* as well as by leftist revolutionaries like Marx with his class struggle and Lenin with his analysis of imperialism. Marx wrote in 1852: "No credit is due to me for discovering the existence of classes in mod-

ern society, nor yet the struggle between them. Long before, the bourgeois historians had described the historical development of the class struggle." (in McLellan, 1971, p. 152).

The liberal philosopher Bertrand Russell ascribed to power, and hence to power struggles, the same dominant role that energy has in physics. Others who recognized the inevitability or at least the omnipresence of conflict include right-wing theoreticians like Carl Schmitt, who regarded the "friend-foe" constellation as the essence of politics, as well as left-wing practitioners like Joseph Stalin, who thought that everything turns around the question: *"Kto kogo?"* ("who does what to whom?")—not to mention psychoanalysts like Sigmund Freud, who contended that people are naturally aggressive, and behaviorists like Harold D. Lasswell, who gave one of his books the suggestive title: *Politics: Who Gets What, When, How?* (1936).

A. *Explanations of Human Perversity*

There are conflicting viewpoints about the fundamental causes of this ravaged human condition. Believers in Judeo-Christian religions tend to ascribe all wretchedness to sin. Hindus will charge it to negative karma left over from past incarnations. Moralists attribute man's dedication to quarrelsomeness to lack of ethics and inability in critical moments to live up to principles. Social phenomena such as differences between rich and poor, the circulation of elites, and the anonymity of institutions are supposed to explain violence. Power, the *libido dominandi*, and the urge to expand, the need of states and political regimes to preserve themselves against foreign and domestic threats, as well as political and economic competition, have been held responsible for the apparent impossibility of lasting peace. Psychologists search for the roots of violence in psychological traumas, such as envy, fear, hatred, the lust for revenge, sadomasochism, mental diseases like paranoia, brain dysfunction, and advanced stages of syphilis, and also in a universally though unevenly distributed trait of aggressiveness which humans share with animals and which is, according to Lorenz (1966), part of the essential mechanism whereby the herd, clan, or tribe perpetuates itself.

B. The Role of Ideology

Much of the human suffering reported in this book is caused accidentally or even deliberately by governments. Court philosophers have developed for the latter a doctrine to explain and even justify deeds of rapine and slaughter that would make the individual doing the same a candidate for the gallows or the firing squad. The doctrine is that of *sovereignty*, summed up in the thesis "The King can do no wrong." Use of sovereign power in disregard of human rights is justified on grounds of *raison d'état*. As Frederick the Great understood in later years, it was *raison d'état* that moved his father Frederick William, creator of the Prussian Army, to overrule the clemency recommendation of a court martial and order the execution, in Fred-

erick's presence, of his closest friend Katte, with whom the young prince hoped to flee from his father's cruelty and the drabness of a Prussian barracks. "In that moment Frederick ceased to be a human being. . . . This experience led to the eruption and discovery of his most frightful strength, the strength that shaped his life: to send other human beings to die for him" (Schmid, 1933, pp. 84–85). Napoleon's arbitrary death sentence against the Duke of Enghien in 1804 could likewise be charged to *raison d'état*.

Jean Bodin (1530–96), who formulated the political theory for Bourbon absolutism, defined sovereignty as "the supreme power over citizens and subjects, unrestrained by law." According to a standard American textbook:

Sovereignty was identified from the outset with royal absolutism; and the sovereign monarch, whose power was absolute and unlimited, restrained by no human authority whatsoever, was equipped to resist the universalist claims of the Papacy and the Empire on the one hand and the decentralizing, almost anarchic tendencies of feudalism on the other. (Palmer and Perkins, 1957, p. 25)

Bossuet, elaborating on the Grand Monarch's "*l'état, c'est moi*," commented: "The entire state is incorporated in him, in him is the power, in him is the will of the entire people" (Prélot, 1948, p. 65). These absolutist dicta were faithfully echoed by Lenin, who in rebuking Kautsky (who had complained about the reign of terror) explained: "The revolutionary dictatorship of the proletariat is power won and maintained by the violence of the proletariat against the bourgeoisie, power that is unrestricted by any laws" (Lenin, 1918, p. 19).

Royalists never had a monopoly of *raison d'état*: the Roundheads were as proficient liquidators as the Cavaliers. Rousseau and his followers transferred unlimited sovereignty, unrestrained by law, from the monarch to the nation. The formula now became: The Nation (in practice the dictator, junta, assembly, committee of public safety, or politbureau) can do no wrong. Sovereignty, under Jacobin democracy, finds expression in the *general will*, the operation of which Rousseau describes as follows:

> The social compact . . . tacitly includes the understanding, which alone can give force to the rest, that whoever refuses to obey the general will shall be compelled to do so by the whole body. This means nothing less than that he will be *forced to be free;* for this is the condition which, by giving each citizen to his country, secures him against all personal dependence. In this lies the key to the working of the political machine; this alone legitimizes civil undertakings which, *without it,* would be absurd, tyrannical, and liable to the most frightful abuses. (*Social Contract*, Book II, ch. 3, emphasis supplied)

What happens to people when they are "forced to be free" is described in some detail in the chapters that follow.

In accordance with various schools of philosophy and tastes for theory, strategies have been invented to root out the causes of man's inhumanity to man and to put an end to the resulting misery. Such strategies usually aim at abolishing a particular political, social, ethnic, religious, or constitutional factor and replacing it with a new institution through which conflicts are supposedly to be assuaged, controlled, or even eliminated. Alas, some of the ideas and crusades advanced for bettering the human condition have only compounded the disaster. And in modern times the conflict between ideologies—"creeds" are nowadays concerned with ideas for the salvation of political and social life—is one of the main reasons why people kill each other in large numbers.

There are potent reasons why political ideologies, and other creeds for which implicit belief is demanded, augment rather than reduce human conflict. An ideology that has superficial plausibility and is easily sloganized lends itself to use as a weapon in power struggles. The ideology serves to conquer, preserve, and legitimize power, but is not—and cannot be—employed for any serious effort to improve the lot of man. It is possible that an ideology may provide good and correct insights, allow the valid diagnosis of social ills, and point the way to therapeutic correction. Nevertheless, all ideologies lack general validity and must lead to disaster whenever they are applied in circumstances where they do not fit. Furthermore, ideologies are reductionist and treat problems they cannot master as though they did not exist. This is why they are so easily sloganized.

However we may yearn for simple explanations, there is no reason to assume that a whole complex of human woes can be attributed to one prime cause or even to a limited number of causes. It is far more likely that each major catastrophe is rooted in multiple specific causes and conditions, and that it must be explained through a particular "mix" of interrelationships. Sometimes one factor dominates, sometimes another, and oftentimes several factors interact. The "factors" themselves are by no means static but vary with time and place. Expressions like "economic causes," "racial differences," or "power struggles" denote more or less empty generalities which must be filled up with concrete data to become meaningful.

Hence the ideologization of thinking about human misery leads to unwarranted though firmly held convictions, which if acted upon result in even worse misery. In the ideological perspective, states can be grouped according to their constitutional formulas, while economies are neatly classified according to their "systems" of management and property distribution. Yet a cursory glance at political and socioeconomic structures will show that systems which conform to abstract "ideal types" simply do not exist. Instead, democracies, for example, involve aristocratic and authoritarian-dictatorial aspects, while democratic aspects are seldom missing from dictatorships and even tyrannies. "Capitalism" is always mixed with "socialism," just as "socialism" and "communism" cannot avoid elements of "capitalism." Ideology is a pattern of thinking in which abstraction predominates and through which the ability to perceive reality is atrophied.

Similarly, miseries also are mostly of a mixed type and involve conflicts between groups which themselves contain various kinds of people and which never conform to ideal types. What is typically called a "class struggle," for instance, usually has ethnic, religious, historical, psychological, and geographic aspects. Businessmen, factory workers, and farmers each have many characteristics not limited to the economic classes to which they are supposed to belong. They continue to share these characteristics in common, even if they find themselves on opposite sides of a barricade. (The term "class" itself reflects the mental operation of grouping people by specific characteristics. E.g., people who wear glasses and people over two meters tall are classes.) A "class struggle" is usually seen as a conflict between two groups, yet most societies have more than two classes. On their part, ethnic struggles cannot possibly take place in isolation from social antagonisms. Struggles between religions are interwoven with social and ethnic cleavages. And conflicts between states and societies involve all phases of human life.

C. The Activation of Conflict

Struggles and conflicts become acute if and when they are incited and conducted by organized groups. Necessarily, such action groups must be far smaller than social or ethnic "classes" such as the "poor," "the farmers," the "Basques." A class of whatever nature can be led into struggle only if a small number of persons from within the class or even from outside it (Lenin!) establish themselves as a leadership cadre for the purpose of carrying out a particular political program.

Conflict usually breaks out when relationships between social groups (of whatever type) degenerate from one of coexistence or cooperation into one of hostility. Such a deformation of the "normal" relationship takes one of three typical forms: (a) a power struggle between competing groups of more or less equal strength, (b) a rebellion by the weak against the strong, or (c) oppression by the strong of the weak. The struggle embroils a ruling group with one or more groups of ruled individuals whose activation proceeds as the gradual paralyzation of the rulers progresses. Should this reach a point where the initially "weak" become stronger than their rulers, revolution takes place and the new ruling class proceeds to persecute its erstwhile oppressors. Both activation and paralyzation tend to be stimulated by outside events such as changes in the prevailing ideology, technological advances, economic crises, foreign domination or conquest, and political dynamism through which the preexisting arrangements become outdated.

Thus, human catastrophes may result in situations ripe for historical change through a shift in intergroup relationships and the emergence of new goals. These are never entirely spontaneous, but are brought about by the deliberate action of organized leadership groups pursuing antagonistic objectives. In this process, the old "ruling classes" regard self-preservation as their main goal, though they may agree to reforms that do not endanger them. Their opponents strive to overthrow the rulers and assume power and domination themselves. A human catastrophe does *not*, however, *necessarily* result in historical change. The group afflicted must have a potential for cohesion and conflict: they must not, as Spengler would put it, be ahistorical (1923, 2, pp. 57–58). Lacking the essential "historical energy," the victims will suffer in silence. As shown in later chapters, millions of people are starving to death in Africa and Asia, and the rest of the world is going about its business as usual. In some cases they are victims of circumstance, including overpopulation in relation to resources. In other cases, as in Cambodia, they have been deliberately deprived of the means of subsistence.

In a normal situation (which in modern times is characterized by internal and external accelerated dynamism in such fields as technology, communications, incomes, migrations, and power constellations) hostility between groups is always latent—not between all groups but between some of them. Hence, low-intensity confrontations are taken for granted. Yet there is always the expectation that latent conflicts may erupt and turn into confrontations of high intensity and frequency. The actions of all leadership groups are strongly influenced by such anticipations, either in the sense that battles are being prepared or precautions taken to prevent the aggravation of latent crises. Some of those latter actions, especially when they are born of fear, may be counterproductive.

It goes without saying that the strategies of the various types of leadership are interrelated with the strategies of foreign groups which, for reasons of their own, support this or that side in an emerging conflict. Under modern conditions, furthermore, most local conflicts are influenced by ideologies of a universal type, as well as the availability of foreign resources, such as money and weapons (Beilenson, 1972, *passim.*).

All in all, the catastrophic aspects of human history cannot be gainsaid. Yet it would be wrong to say that history has been exclusively destructive. Such an interpretation would be patently wrong for two reasons. One is that episodes involving violence or the application of force, such as wars and revolutions, have not always, on balance, been destructive in their effects. The other is that a population greater than a century ago is living longer and healthier lives at a higher material standard. Unfortunately, there is another population that is living a marginal or submarginal existence, for reasons that will be examined in chapter 21 (on economic discrimination) and in the final part of the book (dealing with extreme forms of discrimination).

These are the two sides of the human condition: the series of destructive acts and policies is continuing, as is the series of constructive actions. Destructiveness, however, could not be sustained unless it were based upon creative work accomplished in the areas of science and culture as well as material welfare.

2

BASIC CONCEPTS OF HUMAN RIGHTS

There never was a time when people stopped worrying about good government, good laws, human and political rights, and peace. Sometimes they worried too much, and sometimes too little. Sometimes they were too idealistic, sometimes too cynical. Neither freedom nor equality, let alone national independence, are modern ideals; all central political ideas current today can be traced back to ancient philosophers such as those of Israel, Greece, India, and China. These ideas assumed different forms and expressed different meanings among peoples of distinctive cultures and civilizations, but there seems never to have been any society without a more or less elaborate legal system recognizing and protecting human rights as such. The content of these rights was of course variable, and only a few legal systems extended them to all inhabitants. These systems reflected central and perennial ideas about the best ways to regulate human relationships in order to minimize quarrels, crises, feuds, and civil wars.

The systematic development of international law began in earnest during the seventeenth century, but it was at first limited to relations among states and their duties to one another in peace and war. Explicit formulations of human rights made their appearance at the end of the seventeenth century and were elaborated during the eighteenth century, but they remained essentially within the purview of municipal rather than international law. Milestones along this road were the English Bill of Rights (1689); Locke's *Civil Government* (1690), which set forth the concept of unalienable human rights to life, liberty, and property and justified the Glorious Revolution as a struggle to safeguard them; Montesquieu's *L'Esprit des Lois* (Geneva, 1748); the American Declaration of Independence (1776) and Bill of Rights (1788–91); and the French Declaration of the Rights of Man and the Citizen (1789), which was more authoritarian than the Anglo-Saxon documents but did assert the right to property—which the government could take only for public necessity and with prior and equitable indemnity—the inviolability of free speech, religious toleration, and freedom of the press; and the right to equal treatment in the courts and due process of law.

A. *Human Rights as an International Concern*

Human rights began to be an issue of international politics in the nineteenth century, notably in connection with the Greek Revolution (1821–29) and in the ideology of the German *Vormärz* and the Italian *Risorgimento*, which proclaimed the right of nations to self-determination—a claim that was bound to change the map of Europe and indeed to precipitate two world wars. Human rights were supposedly at issue in World War I, but it turned out that most of the atrocities attributed to the Germans had been fictional, while the Allies ventured onto questionable ground in continuing the blockade after the armistice so as to starve Germany into signing the Treaty of Versailles.

Human rights were a genuine issue in World War II. It can be argued with some cogency that the essential psychological stimulus which made the British and later the Americans ready to do battle with Germany again was the Hitler regime's manifest injustice to its opponents, and to Jewish people. Whatever their views on National Socialism, the Anglo-Saxons intervened because human rights were being trampled upon rather than because of the attack against Poland, whose government was hardly angelic in its domestic or foreign policy. It may perhaps have been forgotten that the Polish delegate to the League declared in Geneva in 1930 that his country wished to be rid of 2.5 million Jews (Lloyd George, 1938, pp. 1393ff.; see chapter 22, C2).

The League of Nations concerned itself with human rights in limited areas. One of them was slavery, in which organs of the League attempted to replace the International Slavery Bureau created by the act of Brussels in 1890, which, ironically, was *abolished* by the 1919 St. Germain treaty that dismantled the Austrian Empire. The other was the protection of national minorities left by the 1919 boundaries, a field in which the League proved singularly ineffective, since the governments complained against—Poland in particular—were as members of the Council judges in their own case (Jaksch, 1967, p. 253). It was only after World War II that comprehensive efforts were taken to build a body of international law dealing with human rights. These efforts culminated in the Universal Declaration of Human Rights, adopted and proclaimed by the General Assembly of the United Nations on December 10, 1948. This document states a large number of specific rights, of which only a few will be enumerated here:

(a) life, liberty, and security of person (Art. 3);

(b) freedom from slavery or servitude (Art. 4);

(c) equality before the law and equal protection of the law (Art. 7);

(d) freedom from arbitrary arrest, detention, or exile (Art. 9);

(e) a fair and public hearing by an impartial Tribunal on any criminal charges; no punishment until proof of guilt in a public trial with all guarantees necessary for defense (Arts. 10 and 11);

(f) freedom of movement within each state; the right to leave any country including one's own and to return to one's own country (Art. 13);

(g) the right to a nationality (citizenship)—the right not to be arbitrarily deprived of it nor denied the right to change it (Art. 15);

(h) ownership of property free of arbitrary deprivation (Art. 17);

(i) freedom of thought, conscience, and religion (Art. 18);

(j) freedom of opinion and expression (Art. 19);

(k) the right to work, to free choice of employment, and to equal pay for equal work (Art. 23);

(l) the right to an adequate standard of living (Art. 25);

(m) the right to education, including free elementary education; the right of parents to choose the education for their children (Art. 26).

Since the General Assembly has only advisory powers, the Universal Declaration did not create positive law directly binding on states. What it did do was to register international consensus as to the essential minimum of human rights and the moral obligation of all member states of the United Nations to realize these rights in their municipal law.

It was intended that the Universal Declaration should be supplemented by conventions creating positive international law binding on states ratifying them. Several conventions were adopted and have come into force prohibiting discrimination; the Convention for the Prevention and Punishment of the Crime of Genocide has taken effect—though a number of major powers including the United States have not ratified; and there are conventions on slavery and the protection of indigenous and tribal populations. They will be discussed in the chapters on these subjects.

Efforts to create positive law on human rights in general, however, have been less successful. After lengthy preparation, the General Assembly adopted the International Covenant on Economic, Social, and Cultural Rights and the International Covenant on Civil and Political Rights, on December 16, 1966. The preambles of both declare that "the ideal of free human beings enjoying freedom from fear and want can only be achieved if conditions are created whereby everyone may enjoy his economic, social and cultural rights, as well as his civil and political rights." The implication is that while technology and material resources are factors in the prevention of hunger and catastrophe, effectively defined and applied rights of universal validity are needed to avoid the misuse of resources for destructive purposes. Accordingly, major efforts have been undertaken within the UN to elaborate extensive catalogues of the various human rights and to provide practical formulations so that individual states could be guided in improving their domestic laws and their judicial and administrative practices.

So far, however, only a few members of the UN have pursued human rights legislation with any enthusiasm. Ratifications for the two human rights Covenants came in so slowly that it was not until 1975 that the necessary 35 were received in both cases, not including, up to this writing (early 1978), ratification by the United States. A reading of the Covenants suggests that many states may fear that adherence would afford the United Nations too much leverage to interfere in their domestic affairs. Their final effect is, like that of the Universal Declaration, hortatory: they state what their authors felt *ought to be* the law.

The UN documents are unclear, even confused, about the differences between rights, fundamental and inherent rights, principles and rules, and the interrelationships of those rights with political ideals. The absence of definitions of freedom, equality, liberty, justice, democracy, etc., is striking and leaves ample room for divergent interpretation. For example, the human rights Covenants state that "all peoples have the rights of self-determination," whereas Article 1/2 of the UN Charter regards self-determination of peoples as a "principle." The Covenants explain that the people "by virtue of that right . . . freely determine their political status and freely pursue their economic, social and cultural development." Self determination thus is proposed as a right, but it also remains a principle, because the Covenants do not alter the Charter.

B. Rights, Norms, and Super-Norms

Some clarity might be attained if we divide this entire complex into norms, rights, and procedural principles or rules. To illustrate: The UN documents state in their preamble that all members of the human family have equal and inalienable rights and that these rights derive from the inherent dignity of the human person. These two points may be regarded as *super-norms,* but, like Immanuel Kant's categorical imperative, they are philosophical rather than legal principles. Rights such as freedom of movement or due process of law can be viewed as applications of the norms of liberty and justice, respectively.

The Covenant on Civil and Political Rights lays out, in Article 9, some specific rights derived from the norm of justice—for example, that an arrested or detained person is entitled "to trial within a reasonable time" and that anyone who has been "the victim of unlawful arrest or detention shall have an enforceable right to compensation." The documents stipulate, *inter alia*, that no torture should be applied, that anyone has the right to be recognized "as a person" before the law, that everybody is equal before the law, that the law must provide equal protection, that there is a right to presumed innocence, to defense, and to remedy, etc.

On a lower level, there are procedural stipulations dealing with such matters as examination of witnesses, the assistance of interpreters, the double-jeopardy rule, and the rule, taken over from Roman law but replicated in the United States Constitution, that no one shall be held guilty of an offense "which did not constitute a criminal offense . . . at the time when it was committed" (Article 15).

The list of norms in the Covenants has grown longer since the Declaration of Independence, the Bill of Rights, and the Declaration of the Rights of Man. It now includes life, liberty, pursuit of happiness (freedom of choice), equality, personal freedom, justice, property, the right to a nationality and a domicile, the right to order, safety, progress, brotherhood between peoples, education, and peace, and indeed nearly all the rights set forth in the Universal Declaration. There are also some significant restrictions. Article 20 provides that "any propaganda for war" and "any advocacy of national, racial, or religious hatred that constitutes incitement to discrimination, hostility or violence" shall be prohibited by law.

The implementing rights of the norm of liberty include representation and liberty; those of the norm of personal freedom the rights to religious, ethnic, and cultural freedom, the freedoms of information, association, speech, and belief, freedom from fear and want, and freedom to move and migrate; and those of the norm of property the rights to lawful acquisition, employment, and social welfare.

These various norms and rights must be balanced according to the *super-norm* intended by Article 30 of the Universal Declaration of Human Rights, December 10, 1948, which provides that no state, group, or person has "any right to engage in any activity or to perform any act aimed at the destruction of any rights and freedoms" set forth in the Declaration. This clearly means that none of the norms and the derivative rights must be disregarded.

Another super-norm is contained in Article 29/11 of the Universal Declaration, which stipulates that "in the exercise of his rights and freedoms, everyone shall be subject only to such limitations as are determined by law, solely for the purpose of securing due recognition and respect for the rights and freedoms of others and of meeting the just requirements of morality, public order and the general welfare in a democratic society." Article 4 of the Covenant on Economic, Social, and Cultural Rights enlarges on this point and states that rights may be limited as determined by law, but "only insofar as this may be compatible with the nature of these rights and solely for the purpose of promoting the general welfare in a democratic society." Considering the elasticity of the general welfare clause of the United States Constitution, it is difficult to imagine a case in which the Human Rights Committee would rule a law of a member state did *not* promote the general welfare. The Committee, charged with enforcing the Covenant, might in theory have to decide whether the society of the member state was "democratic," thus venturing into a political thicket (Felix Frankfurter in *Colegrove v. Green*) which the United Nations has hitherto eschewed. Article 5 of both Covenants repeats Article 30 of the Universal Declaration but adds that no state, group, or person is entitled to limit rights or freedoms recognized in the Covenant "to a greater extent than is provided for in the present Covenant."

Without trying to give a full interpretation of these texts, it is enough to state that no one is entitled to push his claims to the extreme, and that one is allowed to implement his rights only to the extent that he does not trespass on the rights of others. In practice, a person can claim only these rights vouchsafed to him by positive municipal law—supportive international conventions being helpful but not decisive.

Finally, there is the *super-norm* that no single norm or right may prevail to the extent that it invalidates any of the other norms or rights, but that the whole set of norms and rights should be respected and implemented. In other words, the norms and rights are mutually limiting and in their implementation must be balanced against one another. For example, order must be balanced with life, liberty, equality, justice, etc., while freedom must be balanced with order, equality, justice, or equality with liberty and progress. This type of balancing is typical of politics rather than jurisprudence, though courts may have to deal with such questions, especially if charged (as in the United States) with judicial review of legislation.

That the various provisions bearing on a particular set of problems are interrelated and that each stipulation must be interpreted in the context of the other stipulations is set forth repeatedly in UN documents—for example, in the Definition of Aggression adopted on December 14, 1974. A particularly impressive case is provided by the Declaration on Principles of International Law concerning Friendly Relations and Cooperation among States in accordance with the Charter of the United Nations, adopted on October 24, 1970. This declaration contains seven principles: no threat or use of force; settlement of disputes by peaceful means; nonintervention in domestic affairs; interstate cooperation; equal rights and self-determination of peoples; sovereign equality of states; and fulfillment in good faith of the obligations assumed through the Charter. This declaration also contains an acknowledgement of the principle of the territorial integrity and political independence of any state. Some of these principles are mutually contradictory, at least potentially so. The principle of equal rights and self-determination of peoples, for instance, can in many instances be implemented only if the territorial integrity of a state and the nonintervention rule are disregarded.

Nevertheless, the Declaration ends with the injunction that in interpreting and applying the seven principles all must be regarded as interrelated and "each principle should be construed in the context of the other principles." Furthermore, none of those principles should be interpreted as prejudicing the provisions of the Charter, the rights and duties of member states, and the rights of peoples. It also was declared that the principles of the Charter and of this particular declaration "constitute basic principles of international law." According to Article 38 of the Statute of the International Court of Justice, this means that the provisions are to be considered in the light of international conventions and the rules established by them, "international custom, as evidence of a general practice accepted as law," the general principles of law recognized by civilized nations, judicial decisions, and the teachings of "the most highly qualified publicists."

Hence no norm, no right, and no principle is strong enough to exclude other norms, rights, and principles, regardless of how much importance is attributed, rightly or wrongly, to a particular claim in a particular case. Where rights or principles conflict, a reasonable compromise must be found, reflecting the total needs and resources of each contesting party.

A compromise is likewise in order when two or more groups assert *the same right* in a conflicting manner: typically in the form of claims to the same piece of real estate. As has been noted, the Conventions enacting the right of self-determination as positive law have not yet taken effect and the practice of states—as described in later chapters, notably in the cases of the Kurds and of Eritrea—would hardly suggest its reception as customary law. Similarly the right of homeland (*Heimatrecht*) claimed by German expellees has attracted some sympathy, but has hardly achieved the status of an enforceable legal tenet. Both, however, have achieved wide recognition as ethical principles of interethnic and international relations. They enter into policy and might even be arbitrable as principles of political equity under Article 38 of the Statute of the International Court. What is to be done, however, when two groups assert self-determination and *Heimatrecht* with respect to the same territory or to overlapping territory, as is the case with the Israeli and the Palestinian Arabs? Here is a case where purely legal norms are inadequate and too vague. For instance, what exactly is the "people" that is to enjoy self-determination? Does the Russian text use the word "*narod*" (closer to [French] *nation* or *Volk*)? Would the Arabic translation be "*umma*" or "*sha'ab*"? The Palestinians consider themselves a *sha'ab* or ethnic subgroup within the *umma* or greater Arab nation. Their leaders have made quite clear their desire for an Arabic state in Palestine, and this would even apply to the "secular" state with which they would replace Israel. Equity must therefore take into account that the Arab *umma* already embraces a number of self-determining states which occupy some 95 percent of the Near East south of Turkey, whereas there is only one Jewish state.

C. Problems of Practical Application

It would be a miscarriage of justice for a norm with its derivative to be interpreted and applied mechanically or in disregard of common sense and the facts of the case. For example, Article 13 of the Covenant of Economic, Social and Cultural Rights grants everyone the right to education, which is to be directed "to the full development of the human personality and the sense of its dignity." Primary education shall be "compulsory" and "available free to all": there is no freedom of choice whether to accept it. North Americans and Europeans will probably take this to mean that everybody, except the incapacitated, must acquire elementary reading, writing, and mathematical skills. Suppose, however, that in a particular nomadic society the essential skills for survival are shooting with a bow and riding a horse—or recognizing edible and poisonous plants. Does not the child have a right, as his *primary* education, to learn the arts without which he would perish, before culturally foreign techniques are thrust upon him?

The Convention specifies that secondary education should be provided in different forms (corresponding to choices and aptitudes). "Higher education shall be made equally accessible to all, on the basis of capacity." At the same time, individuals and (social) "bodies" are free to establish and direct their own educational institutions.

The various rights enumerated in the Covenants, but also in many other UN documents, are stated in considerable detail. For example, the Declaration of the Rights of the Child of November 19, 1959, stipulates, *inter alia*, that a child, wherever possible, should grow up in the care and under the responsibility of its parents and that mentally or socially handicapped children should be given special treatment, education, and care. Children should not be "admitted to employment before an appropriate minimum age." In this particular case, ten rights are stated as "principles." Principle 8 is strongly preferential: "The child shall in all circumstances be among *the first* to receive protection and relief."

The overall objective of education is to enable the child, "on a basis of equal opportunity, to develop his abilities, his individual judgement, and his sense of moral and social responsibility. . . . The best interests of the child shall be the guiding principle. . . ."

Thus, as a statement of general ideals about education the UN declaration of 1959 seems to reflect universal standards fairly. A general prescription is laid down which applies to the normal requirement of nearly the whole population, and special prescriptions are set forth to fit a variety of educational tasks and human differences. This does not mean, however, that the majority of states are prepared to turn over the supervision of their educational policies to UN bureaucrats.

It is obvious that some "rights" exist only in the form of ideals far beyond early realization. "Adequate food, clothing and housing" cannot always be provided and "the continuous improvement of living conditions" is not practical everywhere, despite Article 11 of the Covenant on Economic, Social and Cultural Rights. The same is true with respect to Article 12/1, which insists on the "right of everyone to the enjoyment of the highest attainable standard of physical and mental health." Ratification of the Convention by enough states to bring it into force has in no way bridged the gap between hope and reality.

Some inequalities are explicitly sanctioned. For example, Article 2/3 of the same Covenant authorizes "developing countries" to "determine to what extent they would guarantee the economic rights recognized in the present Covenant to non-nationals." This means that some countries are permitted to discriminate economically against aliens, whereas others are held to higher standards. In practice, sovereign states have always insisted on their right to make and enforce any policies they please about aliens, including deportation if they become an economic burden. The potential interference in domestic policy implied by such articles of the Covenant as 2/3 may indeed be a reason why so few states have seen fit to ratify it.

A less than absolute commitment to political

freedom is implied by Article 4 of the Covenant on Civil and Political Rights. Its language authorizes the signatories during emergencies threatening the life of the nation to derogate "from their obligations under the present Covenant to the extent strictly required by the exigencies of the situation." Since some countries live under quasi-permanent emergency legislation, the practical result of this authorization is to accept wide variations in human rights legislation and practices. There are certain rights from which *no* derogations are allowed, namely, the "inherent right to life," the prohibition on "torture or . . . cruel, inhuman or degrading treatment or punishment," the interdiction of slavery and servitude, the rule against *ex post facto* law, the rule that everybody must be recognized "as a person before the law," and "the right to freedom of thought, conscience, and religion." Whether or not this particular choice between firmness and flexibility is sound is not relevant for our purpose. The main point is that human rights can be realized only through firmness in principle and adaptability to concrete circumstances.

Restrictions on the exercise of rights, provided they are prescribed by law, are recognized if limitations are "necessary in a democratic society in the interests of national security or public order or for the protection of the rights and freedoms of others." This particular type of restriction may be used against the free functioning of trade unions. Article 12 of the Covenant on Civil and Political Rights is concerned with the right of *everyone* to "liberty of movement and freedom to choose" a residence within the territory of a state, and with the right to leave any country, including his own. These rights may be subject to restrictions provided by law "to protect national security, public order, public health, or morals or the rights and freedom of others . . . consistent with the other rights recognized in the present Covenant." These restrictions could be interpreted so as to emasculate the right which the Convention so nobly proclaims.

Article 19 of the same Covenant deals with

the right to hold opinions, freedom of expression, and with the freedom to seek, receive, and impart information and ideas of all kinds. It states that the exercise of this right "carries with it special duties and responsibilities. It may therefore be subject to certain restrictions, but these shall only be such as are provided by law and are necessary (a) for respect of the rights or reputations of others; (b) for the protection of national security or of public order (*ordre public*), of public health or morals." The notion that rights should be paired with responsibilities and duties has not been applied to other rights, which the Convention would grant unconditionally. The problems raised by the exercise of those responsibilities—does a censor decide?—are not tackled. The *ordre public* clause is somewhat nebulous but could be used to justify suppression of free speech for as long as a particular *ordre public* (or political system) lasts.

Finally, the proclamation of Teheran on Human Rights, of May 13, 1968, recognizes that the "existence of over 700 million illiterates throughout the world is an enormous obstacle to all efforts at realizing the aims and purposes of the Charter of the United Nations and the provisions of the Universal Declaration of Human Rights." This expresses the view that full human rights are practicable only in literate populations. But there are many societies where systems of writing are unknown and have no social or cultural utility. To say flatly that members of such societies do not and cannot have full human rights is an attitude of cultural chauvinism akin to that of missionaries (discussed in chapter 27, B) who feel impelled to get the "naked savages" into clothes as rapidly as possible.

Some readers may be disposed to ask at this point: Why dwell on United Nations pronouncements at such length, since some are General Assembly declarations with advisory rather than legislative character, while others are Conventions that the United States and other major powers have not ratified? The answer is twofold. First, these documents express a certain consensus among people of good will on what human rights are, or in any case *ought to be*. Secondly, they show differences between theory and practice. The many qualifications and restrictions suggest that many governments are loath to commit themselves to guarantee human rights. Others, such as the United States, protect human rights quite fully in their domestic law but refuse to accept international supervision. While there are some who urge such acceptance (e.g. through United States ratification of the Genocide Convention), others fear that international control might abridge the freedoms and guarantees of due process enjoyed by United States citizens, as well as the imposition of alien sets of priorities where rights conflict.

D. The Limitations of International Law

The body of customs, provisions, rules, principles, agreements, treaties, etc., which make up international law do not by themselves constitute an international legal order or system; they are merely one of its integral parts. International law is essentially a body of case law, supplemented in specific areas by international legislation. Some of its sources are listed in Article 38 of the Statute of the International Court, which directs that tribunal to apply:

(a) international conventions, whether general or particular, establishing rules expressly recognized by the contesting states;

(b) international custom, as evidence of a general practice accepted as law;

(c) the general principles of law recognized by civilized nations;

(d) subject to the provisions of Article 59, judicial decisions and the teachings of the most highly qualified publicists of the various nations, as subsidiary means for the determination of rules of law.

From all these "sources" of international law, the particular rules applicable to a given situation are to be drawn.

For any particular case, all pertinent provisions must be applied concurrently and their meaning, which is usually ambiguous if not contradictory, must be elucidated. Such exegesis follows rules, many of which were codified in the law of treaties. Hence the rules of interpretation must be regarded as a part of the *corpus juris*.

International law is self-enforcing only to the extent that it is voluntarily observed. To find out whether its rights or those of its citizens have been violated, an aggrieved state must file a complaint to activate whatever international legal machinery is available. It will normally first complain directly to the supposed violator. The two states may reach a compromise or an agreement, regardless whether or not the protested act was legal. If the complaint is rejected, a dispute arises. The stronger state may at this point impose its will by force or the threat of force. Otherwise, the processes of peaceful settlement are set in motion.

In diplomatic negotiation, with or without a mediating third power, both sides will utilize legal arguments derived from the international *corpus juris* or they may agree to submit the dispute to arbitration by a third state. In this case the arbitrator (usually a state) performs as judge. He will listen to the legal arguments of both sides and issue an award. The case also can be referred to the International Court for an advisory opinion, which is not binding, or for a judgment which, theoretically, is binding. There are additional ways of settling international disputes, including actions by the political bodies of the United Nations and regional organizations, but these are the basic legal procedures.

International jurisprudence involves determining the nature of the alleged violation and establishing that it is governed by international law, identifying the relevant rules of law, and interpreting these provisions as they apply to the violation. The incriminating acts must be precisely described and their actual occurrence must be proved. The plaintiff government must show the deed to have been perpetrated by the respondent government upon its orders or in the form of legislation, or by persons for whom it carries responsibility. Conversely, the respondent government may show that the violation did not take place or that it happened without the respondent's initiation or participation.

Such questions must be cleared up by evidence and counter-evidence on the facts and by arguments and counter-arguments on the law. In international disputes the facts are often hard to determine because governments do not find it difficult to conceal, to confuse, and to deceive. Legal arguments can be stretched, and no rule is free of ambiguity. Since it must be applied in the context of the circumstances in which the violation occurred, there is wide room for entirely logical divergent interpretations. The prerogatives of sovereignty which often contradict international law have not been abolished. Hence many actions charged as violations are defended as legitimate uses of sovereignty, including vital interest, self-defense, and self-preservation.

The ambiguities of the law and the limitations on accurate fact-finding require adjudication by a judge or a court of judges. The judge is expected to be entirely uninvolved in the dispute and to base his verdict on the most reasonable construction of the law and the factual evidence.

The triad—legal rules, adversary pleadings, and judgment—works very well in municipal law. In international law, the adversary pleadings are highly competent; the *corpus* of legal rules is unfinished and to the extent that it exists, it remains ambiguous, sometimes questionable. It often fails to bind a supposedly transgressing state (which may have never accepted a particular rule).

The key weakness, however, lies in the judicial function: those who are called upon to decide international litigations, including the judges of the International Court, cannot be reliably objective. In each case, some—but not all—of the judges will be disinterested. A few judges may be jurists first and foremost, and decide the case on purely legal grounds, even to the extent of opposing their government's policy; but no one has yet voted against his own country. International judges usually have a political background and may have strong political interests in a given case; but it is up to them whether they voluntarily disqualify themselves. Sometimes they stay on a case against a litigant's objection. Thus, international justice often tends to lead to political verdicts.

True, the International Court has historically leaned toward political empiricism and sometimes even wisdom, and it has been a master in Solomonic *Realpolitik*. But in allowing for political realities, international law can be tempered and distorted.

No one knows the international law with respect to a given issue until the dispute has been litigated and a proper verdict been rendered and accepted by both litigants. Often it is never established, since only a very small percentage of international disputes are adjudicated. Most disputes are settled through political compromise or through force, and many disputes are not settled at all.

International law deals, in some of its most essential parts, with political conflicts and, therefore, is qualitatively different from municipal law. Its provisions are aids to the resolution of a conflict, and its norms are designed to guide the behavior of governments. But international law, as conceived at present, is no substitute for sovereignty or power.

3

DISCRIMINATION
AND NONDISCRIMINATION

The concept of discrimination is defined in some detail in chapter 8, D, and forms the central subject of parts III and IV of this book. There, facts are reported and analyzed to show who discriminates against whom, and how discriminatory practices operate in specific functional areas, such as law, politics, and economics. Here, we shall examine the international norms against which these facts may be measured. At this point Milton Yinger's definition of discrimination in the American context will suffice: "differential treatment solely on the grounds of race, religion, national origin, ethnic group, class, age or sex." To internationalize this definition, a few additional categories such as "caste" might be added. The term "discrimination" is usually employed and will be used in this book in the negative sense of deprivation or denial of rights, privileges, or property a person or group might otherwise enjoy. Positive discrimination, in the sense of granting special privileges or benefits to a person or group, will be called "preferment."

A. The United Nations Texts

For authoritative statements of international norms, we turn again to the enactments and pronouncements of the United Nations, bearing in mind the *caveat* already stated regarding their validity as international law.

Article 2/3 of the United Nations Charter commits the organization—and presumably in a general way its members—to "achieve international cooperation in solving international problems of an economic, social, cultural, or humanitarian character, and in promoting and encouraging respect for human rights and for fundamental freedoms for all *without distinction as to race, sex, language, or religion* . . ." (emphasis supplied). The group right of "equal rights and self-determination *of peoples*" is stated in article 1/2. Those are confirmed as objectives to be *promoted* by the United Nations in Article 55, paragraph c of which calls for "universal respect for, and observance of, human rights and fundamental freedoms for all without distinction as to race, sex, language, or religion." A similar wording, with the same catalogue of four categories, is repeated in Article 76c.

The three Charter stipulations have the identical meaning that human rights and fundamental freedoms apply to all humans without distinction. In Article 1/3, the promotion and encouragement of respect for rights and freedoms is listed as one of the purposes of the United Nations. Article 55 is mainly concerned with standards of living, full employment, social progress and development, and more generally with economic, social, medical, cultural and educational problems. Article 76 restates the purposes of the UN in connection with the international trusteeship system. In addition to the individual rights confirmed in 76c, attention should be paid to the group right indicated in 76b, which calls for "progressive development towards self-government or independence as may be appropriate to the *particular circumstances of each territory* and its peoples and the *freely expressed wishes of the peoples concerned . . .*" (emphasis supplied). The point here is that more than one people may inhabit a territory, and use of the plural indicates that the wishes of each people must be respected. If several peoples inhabit a territory, the one with a numerical majority may claim its particular homeland, but not the entire territory if the other peoples desire otherwise. Where the peoples interlock or overlap so as to preclude territorial division, they are mutually obligated to grant one another political rights.

According to Article 2 of the Universal Declaration of Human Rights, everyone is entitled to all rights and freedoms without distinction of any kind. The Declaration lengthened the catalogue from the four categories mentioned in the Charter to twelve: "race, color, sex, language, religion, political or other opinion, national or social origin, property, birth or other status."

Since the various rights and freedoms as formulated in UN documents do not state any exclusions, it is self-evident that all are meant to be applicable to all persons. Article 7 of the Universal Declaration applies the nondiscrimination rule to the law and does so in several propositions: all are equal before the law; all "are entitled without any discrimination to equal protection against any discrimination . . . and against any incitement to such discrimination." By forbidding discrimination against persons, the language *ipso facto* forbids discrimination against any *class of* persons, such as women, political opponents, workers, peas-

ants, members of a particular race or ethnic group, agnostics or believers—or even capitalists. Aside from the protection against incitement, which has remained a matter of pure rhetoric, equality before the law dates back at least to the formal abolition of aristocratic privilege. This type of equality is at least the implicit basis of modern legal codes. Discrimination is, however, frequently implicitly or explicitly envisaged in legal texts whereby dictatorial governments define their own authority. Use of state power by one class (e.g. the proletariat) to liquidate another, as advocated by Lenin in *State and Revolution*, is a clear violation of the nondiscrimination principle.

Article 16/1 of the Universal Declaration deals with the right of men and women to marry and found a family "without any limitation due to race, nationality or religion." Whether the omission of other pertinent categories such as political opinion, social origin, property and birth could be construed as a derogation from the full rule is arguable. But why was a short catalog used here? Such inconsistencies suggest the unfinished nature of the UN texts. Interesting sociolegal possibilities are raised by the second sentence, which provides that men and women "are entitled to equal rights as to marriage, during marriage, and at its dissolution." A number of signatories of the Declaration have not seen fit to abolish Muslim or tribal polygamy (polygyny). Were the Declaration accepted as positive law, women in such countries would acquire the right to practice polyandry and to banish their husbands by saying the proper words three times, if the equivalent right is granted to men (Amelunxen, 1975b). Non-discrimination in marriage would also benefit men by eliminating the requirement that they pay bride-money—the *mahr* of Arab countries or the *lobola* of tribal Africa.

Article 23/2 sets forth the "right to equal pay for equal work" which is to be applied "without any discrimination."

Article 2/2 of the Covenant on Economic,

Social and Cultural Rights, which, as already noted, has not taken effect for lack of ratifications, restates the relevant Charter provisions. In this Covenant, the "states parties . . . guarantee that the rights . . . will be exercised without discrimination of any kind." The criteria consist of the twelve categories enshrined in the Universal Declaration.

Article 11/1 recognizes "the right of every one to an *adequate* standard of living" (Italics added), but in this context, nothing is stated concerning discrimination or equality. Instead, the text calls for "continuous improvement of living conditions." Thus, the nondiscrimination rule does *not* imply economic equality. Rather the implication seems to be that the negative effects of inequality could be negated through steady economic progress. The pertinent norms appear to be satisfied as long as basic needs—food, clothing, and housing—are covered in an "adequate" manner. There is thus an equal floor but no equal ceiling.

The "right to work, to free choice of employment, to just and favorable conditions of work and to protection against unemployment" is guaranteed by Article 23/1 of the Universal Declaration of Human Rights. The right to work and the right to fair and equal wages are confirmed in Article 7 of the Covenant on Economic, Social and Cultural Rights. Neither document, however, states an obligation to work. Whether a person who deliberately chooses not to work nevertheless remains fully entitled to an "adequate standard of living" might have to be settled in court—if the contents of these documents should become positive law.

Article 2/1 of the Covenant on Civil and Political Rights restates the customary provision that the rights recognized in the particular document apply to all without distinction, but it states further that the signatories undertake to respect and ensure to all individuals within their territories and jurisdictions the rights granted by the Covenant. If in force and rigorously interpreted, the Covenant might require governments that have ratified to purge their legislations of all provisions creating or resulting in discriminatory treatment. However, no real duties are imposed on states party to the Covenant.

Article 4/1 deals with emergencies and permissible derogations from the obligations. It states that such derogations must not exceed the limits required by the exigencies and must not "involve discrimination *solely* on the ground of race, color, sex, language, religion or social origin" (emphasis added). Here two points are of interest: first, political or other opinion, national origin, property, birth and other status are omitted, presumably because "emergencies" often relate to factors of this kind; second, for the rest of the criteria discrimination is—at least implicitly—accepted, provided it is not *exclusively* exercised on the basis of differences in race, color, sex, etc. Yet why should discrimination on the basis of national origin be allowed in emergency situations but be prohibited on the basis of race, color, language, or religion—all of them factors which time and again have caused political emergencies?

Article 24 of the same Covenant deals with the right of children to measures of protection, which measures should be applied without any discrimination as they "are required" by the child's "status as a minor." In the catalogue of this article, political or other opinion and "other status" are eliminated. It seems superficially plausible that children have no political or other opinions, yet children may be—and have been—judged according to the political position of their parents. Article 24/3 provides that "every child has the right to acquire a nationality"—a right which the convention does not grant to adults, although it is proclaimed in Article 15 of the Universal Declaration. Without a procedure for determining which state is obliged to grant the nationality, however, such provisions are meaningless.

Article 26 repeats the point about equality before the law without discrimination, but states additionally that the law shall "prohibit any discrimination and guarantee to all persons equal and effective protection against discrimination on any ground." The customary twelve categories are then given as examples. Hence the implication is left that the twelve-item catalogue is still incomplete. Moreover, this article calls upon the signatories to enact antidiscriminatory statutes. No general practice, however, has emerged from this stipulation.

Point 8 of the Proclamation of Teheran upholds the "principle of nondiscrimination" and condemns "all ideologies based on racial superiority and intolerance." Thus, it defines nondiscrimination as a principle, but instead of connecting this principle with problems arising from multiraciality, it places it in contradiction to a particular ideology, which as of 1968, when the proclamation was issued, was not professed by any state though there are still a few that practice it. In point 11, however, the proclamation refers to discrimination "on grounds of race, religion, belief or expression of opinion" and asserts that from such discrimination there arise "gross denials of human rights." The latter phrase is a good definition of discrimination, but the expression appears only seldom in UN documents. Point 15 of the Teheran Proclamation calls for eliminating discrimination against women. The Proclamation, it should be noted, has no legal standing as positive law, but might conceivably be used as a subsidiary source to determine legal meanings.

The Declaration on the Elimination of all Forms of Racial Discrimination, of November 20, 1963, and the International Convention on the Elimination of all Forms of Racial Discrimination, of December 21, 1965, are formal United Nations documents and illustrate the emphasis which the General Assembly has been placing on this particular type of discrimination. The convention against racial discrimination has been in force among ratifying states since January 1969.

The preamble of the Declaration refers back to the Charter with its four-item catalogue and to the Universal Declaration of Human Rights, but it does not quote the twelve standard categories of discriminations. Instead, it says that "everyone is entitled to all the rights and freedoms . . . without distinction of any kind, *in particular*, as to race, color or national origin" (emphasis added). Thus, some forms of discrimination are declared more urgent than others. The preamble goes on to link these problems to colonialism "and all practices of segregation and discrimination associated therewith." It criticizes the doctrine of racial superiority, affirms "that there is no justification for racial discrimination either in theory or in practice," and confesses alarm about "legislative, administrative or other measures in the form, *inter alia*, of *apartheid*, segregation and separation." There are, however, many more forms of racial discrimination that are not listed, of which unequal schools, employment bias, peonage, and slavery are only a few. The fact that they were omitted suggests that the political purposes of the Declaration may have overshadowed its humanitarian aims. The preamble tends to equate discrimination with segregation and separation but shies away from making this point explicit. Nor does it spell out the precise meaning of these terms and the objections to practices criticized.

Article 1 rules that discrimination, on the ground of race, color, or ethnic origin, is an offense to human dignity. Article 2/1 states the customary position that there should be no discrimination "in matters of human rights and fundamental freedoms" in the treatment of "persons, groups of persons, or institutions." Article 2/3 calls for "special concrete measures" to secure "adequate development or protection of individuals" belonging to what in clear language could be called endangered racial groups. Article 3/1 seeks to prevent discrimination "in the field of civil rights, access to citizenship, education, religion, employment, occupation and housing." Article 6 calls for "election through universal and equal suffrage" and for participation in the government. Article 7/1 deals with equality before the law and protection by the state against violence or bodily harm, while Article 7/2 establishes the "right to an effective remedy" for any discrimination a person may have suffered "on the grounds of race, color, or ethnic origin with respect to his fundamental rights and freedoms." Why remedies should be called for only in case of three rather than twelve instances of discrimination remains unexplained.

The preamble to the Convention on the Elimination of All Forms of Racial Discrimination reiterates that the promotion and encouragement of universal respect and observance of human rights and fundamental freedoms for all without distinction as to race, sex, language or religion is one of the purposes of the United Nations. Article 1/1 defines racial discrimination as "any distinction, exclusion, restriction or preference based on race, color, descent or national or ethnic origin which has the purpose or effect of nullifying or impairing the recognition, enjoyment or exercise, on an equal footing, of human rights and fundamental freedoms in the political, economic, social, cultural or any other field of public life." Article 1/2, however, states that the Convention does not apply to exclusions, restrictions or preferences between citizens and noncitizens.

Article 1/4 permits reverse discrimination to overcome deprived status:

Special measures taken for the sole purpose of securing adequate advancement of certain racial or ethnic groups or individuals requiring such protection . . . to ensure . . . equal enjoyment or exercise of human rights and fundamental freedoms shall not be deemed racial discrimination, provided, however, that such measures do not, as a consequence, lead to the maintenance of separate rights for different racial groups and that they shall not be continued after the objectives for which they were taken have been achieved.

Article 2/2 calls specifically for "special and concrete measures to ensure the adequate development and protection of certain groups or individuals." By contrast, Article 2/1e obligates the signatories to encourage "integrationist multi-racial organizations and movements and other means of eliminating barriers between races," but prudently adds a qualification: "where appropriate."

Article 5 restates the fundamental rights which should not be disturbed by any discriminatory measures, notably the right to equal treatment before the tribunals and all other organs administrating justice, the right to security of person and protection by the state against violence or bodily harm, and various political rights, as well as nine civil rights and six economic, social, and cultural rights. The catalogue was thereby expanded to such a point where, for all practical purposes, the concept of discrimination or nondiscrimination was tied to all human rights enumerated in United Nations documents.

Nondiscrimination has been stated to be a principle but it has not, in the UN texts, become a right, let alone a fundamental or inherent right. It cannot be regarded as a legal norm but it clearly is a policy rule valid for the enforcement of rights and freedoms. Since, as pointed out, all of the formulated rights and freedoms apply to everyone, to all individuals and to all groups, nondiscrimination neither adds nor detracts from the body of substantive UN prescriptions. The principle of nondiscrimination is essentially redundant. Yet the writers of the Fourteenth Amendment found it necessary to state it in the United States Constitution, despite the amplitude of the Bill of Rights. Internationally, members of the United Nations have proved singularly loath to accept any controls that would infringe their right to do as they please with their citizens or subjects.

B. The Quest for Nondiscrimination in the Real World

International concern about discrimination became active during World War II; before that time the term was hardly ever used, except in connection with commercial and some minority treaties.*

The National Socialists treated the concept of human rights with contempt. While they sometimes loudly asserted the rights of Germans, they denied all rights to certain ethnic groups. They also denied key rights to religious and political groups, many of which were composed of German nationals. The toll the Germans paid to Hitlerism and through the effects of World War II was of the same general magnitude as that paid by the Poles and perhaps (absolutely though not proportionately) even the Jews.

Preoccupation with the norm of equality has been another major root of the concern about discrimination, notably equality before the law, which was specifically rejected by the Third Reich. The principle of nondiscrimination is not tied solely to the norm of equality or the obverse notion that there should be no privileges, however, but also to virtually all other norms, such as freedom, liberty, property, or security. Discrimination becomes serious when it reaches the point of "gross denials of human rights." For example, a denial of freedom to groups of persons may imply detention, forced labor, serfdom, or slavery; a denial of property rights may lead to confiscations; and a denial of the inviolability of life may result in genocide.

The interest in discrimination is an intellectual heritage of the war against the National Socialists' ideology of racial superiority. But to emphasize that aspect while overlooking many current problems is equivalent to beating a dead horse. Perhaps this particular approach was chosen by the General Assembly because it was trying to avoid choosing between communist and liberal societies. In any event, the *Ersatz* ideology propagated by Hitler and Goebbels was opposed, *post mortem*, by the nondiscrimination creed as an *Ersatz* of the original *Ersatz*. The psychoideological confusions and dissemblance of this substitution have harmed the cause of human rights and fundamental freedoms.

The practical and potentially useful meaning of the principles of nondiscrimination is that they provide criteria to evaluate legislation and policy from the point of view of whether, by intent or as byproduct, arbitrary, unfair, unjust, unreasonable, vicious, destructive, or even deadly treatment is meted out to certain groups of persons. The Declaration on Racial Discrimination states in its preamble that "racial discrimination harms not only those who are its objects but also those who practice it." The point is well-taken, as recent examples in Cyprus and Uganda have confirmed.

But in order to act upon discrimination intelligently—and to show to the discriminator that he is harming himself—the phenomenon must be understood and not be confused with other phenomena. Furthermore, the problem must be handled without self-righteousness and with ample humility. For no one is innocent.

The data to be examined in this book will make it evident that the various UN declarations and covenants dealing with discrimination and nondiscrimination have not come to grips with reality. The major aspect of this reality is that discrimination is not practiced on homogenous, or "equal," populations. All populations, even if at first they look ethnically or religiously uniform, are composed of groups differing in one or more factors which their members think very important. The principle of nondiscrimination cannot, therefore, be aimed at restoring a mythical "sameness" which was maliciously disrupted. On the contrary, it is aimed at making it possible for groups with major differences to live together. It also is aimed at ensuring that the disparate

---

* On the history of the term and the concept, see Wilhelm Kewenig, *Der Grundsatz der Nichtdiskriminierung im "Völkerrecht der internationalen Handelsbeziehungen*, vol. 1, "Der Begriff der Diskriminierung," Frankfurt, Athenäum, 1972, pp. 24f. The concept was formulated clearly in the 14th Amendment of the U.S. Constitution (1868): "No state shall make or enforce any law which shall abridge the privileges or immunities of citizens. . . ."

groups can all enjoy equal rights and freedoms in a fashion suitable to their differing cultural styles and aspirations.

After years of rhetorical exercises, the Convention on Racial Discrimination finally came around to recognizing that special measures are needed to ensure the adequate development of "certain racial or ethnic groups or individuals" lest they be unable to enjoy rights and freedoms. But such special measures are not just needed for tribal societies lacking the resources to advance on their own, but to many groups within the most advanced countries. Governments take from some and give to others under the heading of "social welfare," while the more recent "affirmative action" is a system of preferment (positive discrimination) in favor of groups hitherto discriminated against.

For that matter, the principle of equality before the law applies to taxation, but in this case a different type of equality must be invoked than that used before criminal courts. Equal taxes could hardly be levied on poor and rich; while there can be equality in tax rates (in the sense of equal percentages of income or of the ratable value of real property), "equality" is usually invoked in advocacy of systems adjusted to the taxpayers' "ability to pay." This particular variant of "equality" has led to progressive tax rates, which, by definition, charge some persons higher percentages of their incomes than others. "A heavy progressive or graduated income tax" was one of ten program points advocated by Karl Marx and Friedrich Engels in *The Communist Manifesto* (1848) as steps toward abolishing bourgeois conditions of production. The damaging effects of progressive income taxation on economic growth are common knowledge; it is significant that the highest tax rate in the USSR is 13 percent. The inequalities in the progressive system as applied in the United States are such that it is modified by different schedules for single and married people, exemptions for homeowners and for medical expenses, mineral depletion allowances and a host of other "loopholes"—

which in their turn provoke new charges of discrimination.

To return to intergroup relations: it is easy to agree that barriers between races and racial divisions are undesirable and in real life all too frequently entail denials of rights. But it does not follow that "integration" would remove the trouble. The United Nations has never issued a rationale explaining why human rights are better protected by integrationist multiracial organizations and movements than by those representing the interests of specific groups. Experience belies the claim that barriers between the races must fall in multiracial societies. Nor is it sound to assume that simply because antidiscrimination laws are enacted, racial strife is thereby prevented or terminated. This, obviously, is a question of fact: in some areas integration may work, in others it may lead to intensified conflict—to escape which people resort to new patterns of spontaneous segregation. Consequently, if it is desired to reduce racial tensions, policies must be designed to conform with real problems at a real place and a real time.

But suppose desegregation could be enforced: if coercion is needed, there must be resistance—one or more of the groups concerned must be opposed. Hence the group rights of self-determination and self-government, also espoused by the United Nations, would be violated. These rights have never, by definition, been limited to peoples living in compact or contiguous territories—a scattered group might claim them. When rights conflict, recourse must be had to the UN rule that the several rights must be realized concurrently. In practice, this means compromise: the alternative to perennial warfare is acceptance of partial solutions.

International discussion about segregation and separation is reflected in the Declaration but not in the Convention on the Elimination of Racial Discrimination. In the Convention—which to some extent constitutes positive law, while the declaration is purely hortatory with subsidiary juridical effect—the argument centers on distinction, exclusion, restriction, or preference. But the Convention, too, ignores the many different ways by which multiracial, multicolor, multiethnic, and multinational states are organized and are functioning. The General Assembly uncritically accepted the myth of the monolithic nation-state and therefore failed to see that it should have recognized—and necessarily left member states to solve for themselves—the many unsolved problems of structured or unstructured federalism.

The UN prose disregards the fact that, while racial cleavages may be dominant issues in some states, ethnic or religious cleavages can be just as devastating in others. Actually, the ethnic problem is downgraded in Conventions which speak merely of ethnic or national *origin*. The Convention on Discrimination in Employment and Occupation (effective 1960) groups national origin with social origin. Either formulation ignores the fact of persistent ethnicity (which is discussed at length in chapter 7,C2). Language is handled as a distinct category and appears divorced from ethnicity. On the other hand, race and color are treated as distinct categories, although the two factors relate to the same basic phenomenon. All this bespeaks sloppiness or manipulation. In any case there has been little progress toward solving the serious problems which aroused the General Assembly's interest.

This analysis, which could be pushed much further, shows that UN "legislation" on discrimination, whatever its precise legal standing, is imperfect. The political perspective must include the fact that many of the votes in the General Assembly which brought these documents into existence were cast by governments which would not and could not possibly apply the provisions of those treaties to their own regimes and populations.

1. UNSOLVED SEMANTIC PROBLEMS

The principle of nondiscrimination must be concerned mainly with discriminatory treatment of groups. There is no way to prevent discrimination in relationships between individuals, all of whom discriminate between kin and stranger, friend and foe, persons they like and dislike, people with whom they enter into professional relationships and people they marry or jilt. The UN draftsmen made no attempt to legislate aesthetic standards of physical appearance—somatic norm images (about which more in chapters 11,A, and 13,B2)—or to rule that unwashed persons with halitosis should be treated as though they were clean. The distinctions and discriminations which are to be eliminated are those between groups, such as races and religions, men and women, or persons who speak different languages. Yet the various rights proposed to eliminate discriminatory treatment refer mainly to treatment given to individuals, while problems related to group treatment are rarely taken up. The right of self-determination is granted "to all peoples," but no definition of "people" is provided. True, such definitions are difficult to draft and the best may remain controversial and even confusing. But the human rights covenants surely should have dealt with the fact that a large number of peoples in the sense of nations, nationalities, and ethnic groups (see chapters 6,A, and 7,C), do not at present exercise self-determination because they are under the *de facto* and often the *de jure* rule or domination of peoples "foreign," at least in the ethnic sense. In varying degrees this is the case in virtually every country on the globe. The UN also should have addressed itself to the far more pressing problem that the very existence of some peoples is being denied.

The Universal Declaration of Human Rights, in Article 15, states that everyone has the right to a "nationality," that no one should be arbitrarily deprived of it or denied the right to change it. This article is confused. If the term "nationality" is interpreted to mean "citizenship," in the sense of belonging to a state (*Staatsangehoerigkeit*), the "national" must be given the right to live and work within a particular territory and be provided with the relevant identification documents. Furthermore if he is to enjoy the right to become a citizen of another state, the article is incomplete since it does not specify what states shall grant these rights. Shall the United Nations have authority to compel members to admit stateless persons and those expelled by their states of origin in violation of their rights—such as the Asians of East Africa? Would not such compulsion be a derogation of sovereignty and self-determination? The peoples of the United Kingdom and the United States did not accept the recent influx of Asian and Vietnamese refugees, respectively, with entire good grace—how would they have reacted had the admission of these people been ordered by an international authority?

The term "nationality" has another meaning: that a person has a particular ethnic origin, in the sense of having parents of a particular ethnic group and having been brought up with a particular language and ethnic culture. Given this alternate meaning, it would be difficult to see how a person could change his or her "nationality," even if granted the right to do so. Ethnicity is a rather permanent set of characteristics, even though each ethnos contains a whole range of personality types, while persons of mixed ancestry or those who travel or live abroad extensively absorb the influences of several ethnicities. It is possible to change language, up to a degree, but ethnicity is a context with remarkable durability, especially in the case of sedentary groups, but also in the case of people who migrate or are expelled and yet retain their group cohesion. Since many states, including the United States, indulge in efforts to "de-ethnicize" ethnic groups, the UN should have made clear that *all peoples have the right to preserve their ethnicity*. The subject is ignored, though contemporary mass migrations,

including those of "guest workers," raise enormous difficulties on this score.

Article 29 of the Declaration, in still another confused sentence, ascribes to the "community" the exclusive role of making possible the free and full development of the personality. But if this is the case, the nature of the "community" must be defined in terms of ethnicity, language, religion, and even race if relevant, and the rule of nondiscrimination must be explicitly extended to such communities as entities as well as to individuals. Article 23 of the Covenant on Political and Civil Rights states that the family is the "natural and fundamental group unit of society" and therefore "is entitled to protection by society and the state." The elaboration of this point is incomplete. Does this mean only the nuclear families found, for instance, in northern Europe, the United States, and the Anglo-Saxon dominions? Or does it include extended families, polygamous families, and experimental types of families? Nor do the documents say anything about the relationship between the family and the broader community of which it is a part, especially within states without a uniform population.

The Covenant on Civil and Political Rights, Article 27, refers to "those states in which ethnic, religious or linguistic minorities exist." Persons belonging to minorities "shall not be denied the right, in community with the other members of their group, to enjoy their own culture, to progress and practice their own religion, or to use their own language." This is a surprisingly weak rendering of the principle of nondiscrimination, restricting it, so far as minorities are concerned, to only three instead of twelve factors.

The concept of "minority" was inherited from the League of Nations, which stated it clearly. An attempt to give it a precise sociological meaning is made in chapter 9. In one sense, virtually every person belongs to a particular minority in one way or the other; to designate only particular groups in a society as "minorities" invites discrimination. In the United States, for instance, Portuguese-Americans desired the preferment accorded Spanish-surnamed persons, whereupon New England Senators prevailed upon the Department of Health, Education and Welfare to recognize them as an additional "minority." Now the Italians are wondering . . . and the Greeks . . . and perhaps the Armenians? Is it not sounder to say that an ethnic or religious group is entitled to the full range of human rights regardless of its size and therefore regardless of the ratio of its size to the size of other groups? A particular group may be smaller than other groups within the same state territory, but it may be a numerical majority within its own habitat. Or it could be a numerical minority everywhere. Should its rights change if through intention or circumstances it should outbreed larger ethnic or racial groups? What is most serious is that this particular article, through omission, grants "minorities" social and cultural rights only but denies them their political rights. It also implies that an ethnic minority is not a people and therefore does not enjoy the right of self-determination which is guaranteed elsewhere to "all peoples."

2. CONFLICTING CONCEPTS OF EQUALITY

Let us return to the principle that rules about nondiscrimination must refer to groups rather than individuals. This is clear enough, but insight into a generality fails to indicate what legislative practice should be followed. For example, how can the ideal of nondiscriminatory employment be achieved? there have been experiments with quota systems, but it turned out—as should have been foreseen—that this practice easily degenerates into "reverse discrimination" which, in the United States, has been challenged in court. Furthermore, quota systems tend to contradict Article 7c of the Covenant on Economic, Social and Cultural Rights which provides for "equal opportunity for everyone to be promoted in his employment . . . subject to no considerations

other than those of seniority and competence." Persons are in fact preferred or discriminated against when their competence is *not* the decisive element in a decision for or against hiring. No one must be denied a job for which he is qualified because his race, color, sex, religion, ethnicity, etc., are "overrepresented" in an enterprise or office. Yet this rule is frequently modified, with justification, where job requirements are minimal and where one of the main purposes of a project is to provide employment for groups suffering particularly high rates of unemployment. The Covenant texts do not address practical problems of this type, but it is self-evident that standards intended to be authoritative should leave individual states the flexibility to find pragmatic solutions to problems of this kind.

A similar question arises with respect to the principle of equality before the law, even though it is the most strongly based antidiscrimination rule. The law classifies crimes by categories and in general prescribes equal punishments for equal delicts. This is a case of subtle equality. Both homicide and manslaughter are forms of killing. Still, they are different in their legal nature and therefore they are handled as distinct crimes. In addition, of three persons charged with homicide, two may receive different penalties because of aggravating or attenuating circumstances, while a third may be acquitted on grounds of "insanity." And even if two criminals are given identical sentences for identical crimes, the length of their incarceration actually depends upon their subsequent behavior.

In multiethnic societies equality before the law may be complicated if several ethnic and religious groups live under different legal systems. For example, one group may be monogamous, another polygamous. What is murder in one culture may be justifiable homicide in another. Group A may have a system of corporal punishments, and group B may not even have the death sentence. In situations of this type, states usually are wise enough not to impose a unified legal code, but instead try defendants according to the codes observed by their particular groups. But complications may arise if the defendant lives outside his group's habitat or offends against a member of another group, even though innocently following the rule of his own system.

Complications of this type may not be too meaningful to citizens of developed countries. But they are important in multiethnic and multitribal societies, in countries that employ large numbers of foreign migrant workers or "guest workers" (see chapter 19,D), and they are involved in race relations in the United States. The point is that the Covenants presumed to "legislate" for the entire world before the problems were solved intellectually. Consequently, many of the solutions they suggest are defective. This does not mean that the Covenants do not contain useful formulations, nor that the thrust of the effort is misdirected. But the Covenants are premature. It is thus only natural that they run into troubles with ratification and that few states have incorporated the UN prescriptions into their national codes. The Declarations have not accomplished much in diminishing discrimination the world over. But the agitation about discrimination, which as we shall see in subsequent chapters has been highly selective, has exacerbated international tensions.

4

CRIMES AGAINST HUMANITY

The Nuremberg Trials have gone down in history as a questionable legal experiment because of their one-sided "victor's justice" and their use of *ex post facto* law. The International Military Tribunal (IMT) acquired, nevertheless, a limited credibility—the degree of which will be left open here—as a source of future international law. The built-in bias of the IMT became manifest when it made haste to drop the Katyn Forest massacre charge after it became clear that a trial of Germans on this count would convict the Kremlin. But the charge was not withdrawn, nor were the Germans acquitted: the whole matter was quietly dropped. Hence it is necessary that any principles elucidated at Nuremberg be confirmed by an impartial international legal forum before being accepted as valid.

Crimes against humanity, which are gross denials of human rights, are nevertheless real happenings that are still taking place. That is why a discussion of the law dealing with them, defective though it may be, is relevant to an understanding of the total problem.

The charges at Nuremberg were grouped under three counts: crimes against peace, war crimes, and crimes against humanity. Under the heading of "extermination," the crimes against humanity included genocide. "Crimes against humanity" were defined in 1945 to supplement the customary concept of "war crimes"; the two categories overlap in Article 6 (b) and (c) of the IMT Charter. New language seemed necessary to deal legally with the mass crimes which seemed to be novel during World War II and were committed by military or paramilitary forces acting under orders. As finally written, the Nuremberg Charter was designed to handle all crimes against humanity—all mass crimes ordered from the top, regardless of whether they were committed in times of peace or in times of war; and regardless also whether they were perpetrated by soldiers or civilians. Inclusion of crimes "against any civilian population" made it possible to prosecute government officials for crimes against their own citizens.

In fact, the Tribunal did not handle crimes against humanity which were committed or alleged to have been committed before World War II. Nor did it try all the crimes committed during the war. Some were tried by individual allies under IMT precedent; many more were and are still being prosecuted by the Germans. The IMT limited its attention to crimes related to the war and, indeed, it treated war itself as the capital crime. That was not only legally questionable but politically dangerous, since it left the Allies open to "conviction" by historical revisionists.

Furthermore, the International Military Tribunal was limited by its terms of reference to "trial and punishment of the major war criminals of the European Axis" (Art. 1) and crimes (as enumerated) committed "in the interests of the European Axis countries" (Art. 6). Any crimes charged against Allied personnel, such as the liquidation of Polish resistance fighters, terror bombing of civilians such as the Allied attacks on Dresden and Hamburg, and—as some contend—the atomic bombing of Hiroshima, were to go untried and unpunished. A Charter referring to suspects and defendants as "war criminals" *before* they were tried and convicted is wholly at odds with the legal principles of civilized nations.

The United Nations adopted its first genocide resolution in December 1946, when the tribunal had already pronounced judgment and the sentences were being executed.

Genocide is merely one in a long catalog of crimes against humanity. But it was singled out because of its comprehensive nature. Unlike specific crimes such as massacres, withholding of food, and deliberate infection, genocide (as elaborated in section C) is defined in terms of intent to destroy a national, ethnic, racial, or religious group. There was considerable pressure, especially in the United States, to legislate promptly on this most massive crime. However, it was not the original intent of the UN to deal only with the part and forget the whole.

A. Codification of the Nuremberg Principles

In 1947, the General Assembly asked the International Law Commission (ILC)—whose function it is to codify international law—to put the Nuremberg Principles into generally acceptable legal form. The ILC presented its draft in 1950 and proposed the following definition of crimes against humanity:

Murder, extermination, enslavement, deportation and other inhuman acts done against any civilian population, or persecutions on political, racial or religious grounds, when such acts are done or such persecutions are carried on in execution of, or in connection with any crime against peace or any war crime.

The General Assembly failed to act on this text, which subsequently was merged with the drafts devoted to the definition of aggression.

The crime against the peace—aggressive war—was created *ex post facto* for use by the International Military Tribunal of Nuremberg. Hence there was an inclination to provide belated sanction to this doubtful procedure—not to mention the questionable and, in the view of some, invalid legal principle involved (see Tucker, 1960; Possony, 1968; and Glaser, 1971). The United States had been largely responsible for preaching that, as of 1939, offensive war was legally forbidden, and for persuading the IMT to accept this notion as the basis for its jurisprudence.

Crimes against humanity, as defined by the ILC, are not necessarily connected with aggression and war; even when they are, a "defending" force could commit them. Nor is there any reason why rules forbidding crimes against humanity should be limited to outrages against civilians. Military personnel, especially prisoners of war, are often subjected to abuse. Many crimes against humanity, such as manhunts against and enslavement of primitive tribespeople, are committed through sheer sadism or cupidity unrelated to war. More often than not, massacres, deportations, and the like hamper rather than further the war effort. Be that as it may, no mention was made of any crime against humanity in the definition of aggression as it emerged in 1974.

Accordingly, except for genocide, which was outlawed by international convention, this particular class of crimes has no legal standing in the sense that it was legislated upon by General Assembly declarations or UN covenants. However, the crimes in question are proscribed, in one way or the other, in most or all domestic legal codes and by implication (though with moral rather than positive-law effect) in the various UN human rights documents discussed in chapter 2. Even though the United States has not ratified the Genocide Convention, because of fears that it might infringe on constitutional rights, the moral force of that document is generally recognized by American scholars.

Nevertheless, there is an important distinction. A stipulation like that of the International Covenant on Civil and Political rights, Article 7, that "no one shall be subjected to torture," falls short of outlawing torture as a widespread and systematic practice and does not condemn this outrage as an international crime. Yet in the reality of today—which is far worse than that of a half-century ago—torture and related crimes are being perpetrated on a large scale and by governments of diverse political colorations. Since this type of criminality is clearly on the rise, the failure of the General Assembly to deal with it signifies the weakness of the UN as a world organization and the irrelevance of many of its current concerns. It also suggests strongly that the high-sounding UN declarations do not reflect general practice or international custom and therefore cannot seriously be held to be sources of international law. In 1974, eight nations called for UN action to stop the torture of war prisoners. Whether and how this matter will be treated is not known at this writing.

Crimes against humanity constitute extreme forms of discrimination and persecution against political, racial, or religious groups, as was recognized in the ILC draft. By ignoring the fact that such crimes may occur outside the context of aggression and war, the ILC left out of consideration the sum and substance of group persecution. An adequate draft would also protect national, social, and cultural groups, as well as all ages and both sexes.

The human rights documents prohibit discrimination on the grounds of political opinion. If interpreted literally, this wording would exclude discrimination or persecution because of political action beyond "the right to freedom of peaceful assembly and association" guaranteed in the Universal Declaration, Article 20. The limits of political and oppositional activity are not clearly defined; indeed, the issue has been avoided. Unfortunately, political activity, real or potential, is the most frequent cause (or stimulant) of criminal repression.

With respect to the criminal acts themselves—murder, extermination, enslavement, deportation, and inhumane treatment—major categories are left out, such as systematic killing through assignment to particular hazardous missions in punitive or special military or forced labor units, forced recruitment into an enemy's military service, inhumane treatment of prisoners of war, the deliberate creation of conditions of starvation and freezing, shooting of hostages, mass rapes, forced marches, plunder and confiscations, detention of civilian prisoners under inhumane conditions, refusal of medical services, the application of foreign and martial law to citizens of occupied territories outside zones of combat or civil disorder, denial of due process and equality before the law, refusal to accept international humane help such as provided by the Red Cross, disruption of families, reprisal actions against civilian populations, killings of civilian hostages, forced repatriation and denial of desired repatriation, as well as forced labor. Actual cases of many of these crimes are described in the chapters that follow, especially chapters 22 through 28.

B. Specification of Crimes Against Humanity

Crimes against humanity may be grouped in six categories, corresponding to the specific rights they violate:

1. *Crimes Against the Right to Life:* These include deliberate and (by generally accepted

standards) unnecessary killings, especially of elites of peoples marked for subjugation, political opponents, and "unwanted" ethnic or racial groups. They also include crippling, torture, deprivation of food, denial of medical help, and imposing of conditions which result in debilitation and disease, as well as stunting the growth of children. Specific war-connected crimes include military overkill (killing designed to terrorize the enemy rather than to secure a specific military result), massacres, killing of hostages, atrocities and terroristic warfare, the withholding of food, inhumane treatment of prisoners and civilians, evacuations, deportations, and forced labor designed to create fatalities. Guerrilla-war-connected crimes would include terror bombing of schools, hospitals, theaters, airplanes, etc.

Crimes against the right to life also include certain extreme measures designed to produce psychological effects—including those forms of fear, suspicion, rage, depersonalization, and desocialization that could be classified clinically as mental disorders. Given the reality of psychomatic disease, measures of this type must be regarded as a particular form of torture. As will be seen, they are often practiced as mass torture, e.g. in the "special" Soviet mental hospitals. Psychological torture is, however, to be distinguished from legitimate psychological warfare, which leaves the target free to accept or reject propaganda or other communications directed at him.

The application of drugs which produce physical or psychological harm, or the practice of medical torture, also must be regarded as a crime against humanity, just as the employment of narcotics to weaken an enemy is a criminal method of warfare. (This was practiced by the British and Japanese against China, and probably also by China and North Vietnam against the U.S.)

2. *Crimes Infringing Rights to Freedom:* These include slavery, serfdom, captivity without due legal process or for reasons unconnected with any offense, detention in camps under inhumane conditions, long prison or camp sentences for trivial crimes or actions not criminal by international standards (such as criticizing a government or its policies), the incarceration of healthy persons in mental institutions, and the nonreturning of prisoners of war or civilian prisoners or, conversely, their forced repatriation. Under this heading, forced labor plays a significant role, especially if it causes a high mortality. Mistreatment of women in the form of arranged or forced marriages, or their exploitation under conditions resembling serfdom, must also be mentioned. Mass mistreatments of children also occur, especially in countries so near the starvation level that parents are forced to sell their children as household servants or into farm or factory peonage.

It must be pointed out that conditions similar to those created by crimes against humanity often occur through neglect, collision of economic interests, war, catastrophe, dysfunctional ideology, or sheer circumstances. Conditions are often unsatisfactory in orphanages, reform schools, jails, and mental hospitals—perhaps because the public does not care, because administrators are incompetent, or because governments lack funds for improvement. Or the OPEC raises the price of oil, causing a shortage of fertilizer, leading to food shortfalls in marginal countries where millions starve to death. Such conditions are often called "criminal," but that is inexact usage. Crime, as distinguished from accident, presupposes an *intention to inflict injury* or (in the case of criminal neglect) intentional disregard of safety or health risks to others. Our enumeration continues:

3. *Crimes Infringing Rights to Security:* These include all forms of government-directed terrorism such as racial and ethnic pogroms, coercive measures in disregard of proper legal procedure and of the principle of equal treatment before the law, systematically improper application of laws to cripple certain groups of people, the dispersal of groups, the denial of cul-

tural rights, and government-sponsored or tolerated incitement to intergroup violence. This category also includes crimes of deliberate neglect such as government-tolerated crime waves (especially against groups whose departure is desired), the denial of police protection, and the freeing of dangerous criminals or lunatics—whether through corruption or mistaken ideology.

4. *Crimes Against the Right to Property:* They include ideologically motivated mass expropriations (when combined with expulsions freedom, security, and sometimes life are lost), confiscation of property without compensation or without the right of appeal before an impartial court of law, punitive taxation, and denial of the right to earn a livelihood. Whether economic coercion falls in this category depends on its degree and motivation. A good case has been made (e.g. by Banfield in *The Unheavenly City*) that minimum-wage laws hurt the people they are intended to help: they force workers of low marginal productivity into unemployment. Even "free" economies abound with coercive legislation, such as price and interest fixing or forcing workers to accept bargaining agents they do not want. Yet because such laws are usually motivated by the sincere belief they will help the downtrodden, they are not criminal even when manifestly counterproductive.

5. *Crimes Against the Group Right of Self-Preservation and Self-Determination:* These include measures that make it impossible for a group to carry forward its culture, its language, and its social institutions. Forced assimilation, forced language change, and educational policies that denigrate the group fall in this category. Denial of effective political representation violates self-determination, but a group may not rightfully demand representation in the body politic of another group if it would deprive the latter of the right to manage its own affairs. Denial of freedom of association and of religion overlaps this category and that of crimes against freedom.

6. Genocide: This, the *non plus ultra* crime against humanity, combines elements of any of the foregoing, as well as measures not listed and which might not be criminal in themselves, when undertaken for the specific purpose of "liquidating" or "exterminating" groups, or the "final solution" of ethnic, social, religious or political "problems."

Some of the enumerated crimes against humanity are less serious than others. A particular transgression may result from severe but traditional discrimination rather than from criminal intent. Whether a repressive measure is or is not criminal depends less on fine theoretical distinctions than on the brutality and frequency of certain acts, their effect on individuals and groups, and the perpetrator's purpose. *Oppression*—which is a *governmental* policy and activity—marks the crime against humanity and distinguishes it from discrimination and barbarous custom. For example, in a traditional society where wives constitute an economic asset for the male, payment of a bride price may not be oppressive or, in any event, may not be so experienced by the women who are subjected to this practice. When society changes, however, the bride price may suddenly be experienced as oppressive. In Niamey, the capital of Niger, a mass protest against bride price took place in 1968. Young men and women claimed the prices demanded by parents delayed marriage intolerably and had bad social effects. The Government agreed. (Anti-Slavery Society, 1973, p. 6.) Egypt is currently trying to stop the traffic in brides, who are shipped out to the Persian Gulf countries and Libya at about $500 per head.

Similarly, the denial of medical help may be related to a shortage of doctors and medicines. Where these are in short supply, gross discriminations, though they inevitably entail fatalities, would seem to be preferable to an "egalitarian" solution which would withhold medical help from *all*, on the ground that not everybody can be helped. If large numbers of people must be treated, the ancient egalitarian solution of drawing lots is impractical. However, denial of medical help may be derived from an oppressive intent, in which case a crime is being committed. Social customs which once found wide approval and which necessarily were sanctioned and prescribed by political authority, such as the killing of female babies, cripples, albinos, sick and old people, or human sacrifice, must in modern times be regarded as crimes against humanity.

Some of the specific acts that figure in crimes against humanity may not be criminal under all circumstances. Each act must be evaluated on the basis of the full evidence and tested as to whether it was justifiable or not. There is justifiable homicide, permissible in self-defense or group-defense, or in order to prevent a larger crime or a catastrophe, provided these and other "adequate reasons" are "sufficiently supported by credible evidence, when weighed by unprejudiced mind, guided by common sense and by correct rules of law." A crime against humanity must be treated according to the same rules which apply to all other crimes. Homicide may be accidental, culpable, excusable, felonious, justifiable, necessary, or negligent. Hence, "the term 'homicide' is neutral; while it describes the act, it pronounces no judgment on its moral or legal quality" (*Black's Law Dictionary*, pp. 867f. and 1004). "Genocide," however, despite its analogous derivation, has been defined from the outset in a criminal context. Mass killings resulting from legitimate acts of war are not considered genocide, even though their probability is considered in command decisions. In any case, persons or governments accused of genocide are, like other defendants, entitled to their day in court.

It should be the task of the United Nations to formulate standards for governmental behavior in emergency and crisis situations.

Under modern conditions, crimes against humanity can be practiced most easily by op-

pressive regimes. Conversely, such crimes define the nature of oppression and characterize what is truly objectionable about an oppressive regime. The fact that a regime is monarchical or dictatorial does not automatically make it oppressive: the benevolent autocrat may be a rare phenomenon nowadays but they still exist here and there. It is obvious that an autocrat, crowned or uncrowned, can afford to be benevolent only so long as whatever political opposition exists poses no serious threat to his or her rule. Such was the case before the spread of democratic ideology in Europe: Maria Theresa and Joseph II of Austria, for instance, were benevolent autocrats. But as soon as a serious threat arises, the autocrat must choose: abandon autocracy and give the *frondeurs* at least a share of power, or abandon benevolence and clap them in prison or chop off their heads. A tyranny or totalitarian state is defined as a regime that denies free expression to the political opposition—a denial that provokes more opposition and ultimately demoralization within the ruling party. Such a regime must commit crimes against humanity to stay in power. Experience shows, however, that most modern totalitarian dictatorships—those of Hitler and Stalin being typical—indulge in overkill.

A benevolent autocracy, should it exist, would show a low score on political rights but a high score on civil rights in the Annual World Freedom Survey published by Freedom House, New York, which rates countries on a 7-point scale. The only countries with civil rights rated 3 points higher than political rights in 1975 were Honduras and Liberia, though others that approached the model (civil rights 2 points higher) include Cameroon, Liechtenstein, Monaco, Nigeria, and Swaziland— countries at opposite ends of the per-capita GNP scale. Benevolent autocracy, it would appear, is not a matter of *pane et circenses*.

Unfortunately, democratic government, as the record shows, also can become guilty of oppressive crimes. Perhaps it is true to say (as we would hope) that crimes against humanity can nowhere be committed on a systematic basis *unless* they are perpetrated in secrecy. If mass repression can be exposed and documented, and if its true nature as a criminal act, and usually as a senseless act, comes to be fully understood, it cannot be continued.

In the real world such understanding is prevented not only by naïve belief that such events cannot really happen, but also by political passion, deception, secrecy, and propaganda, and by conspiracy of silence. The worst crimes of history have found eager apologists, and have often been promoted by intellectuals bemused by the abstractions of airy cloud-castles. Silence about mass-criminal events is an essential ingredient of government criminality; and those who keep silence when they know, those who fail to disclose the information when they can, and those who whitewash the misdeeds or fraternize with their perpetrators are accomplices of any crime against humanity thereby protected. The studied indifference of a President who toasts with champagne the ruler of the world's largest concentration-camp system but refuses to attend the AFL-CIO dinner for the man who risked his life to publish the facts about these camps is a signal that the executive branch of the United States Government, at least, does not care very much what crimes are committed against the democratic opposition in the USSR.

Since the matter of governmental criminality has rarely, if ever, been properly treated, its grim reality is widely ignored. When it happens, it is usually not recognized. By contrast, existential inequalities and minor discriminations, practical difficulties in reconciling conflicting human rights, divergent structural concepts, and measures undertaken to maintain order or oppose aggression are easily misinterpreted, and often are maliciously misrepresented as crimes against humanity. There is a need for formal and internationally binding definitions of crimes against humanity. They must be based on rigorous logic and must distinguish crimes, as offenses against universal morality, from ideologies and policies. To provide such definitions is a proper function of the United Nations, but one unlikely to be fulfilled as long as the General Assembly is swayed by political emotionalism.

C. Genocide

The Convention on Punishment of the Crime of Genocide, of December 9, 1948, deals with the most extreme form of discrimination which can be directed against national, ethnic, racial, or religious groups, namely, measures taken against a group or its members with a view to exterminating the group.

The first Draft Convention, prepared by the UN Secretariat, declared genocide to be "in violent contradiction with the spirit and aims of the United Nations." It declared the purpose of the Convention to be "to prevent the destruction of racial, national, linguistic, religious or political groups of human beings."

Genocide was defined as "a criminal act directed against any of the aforesaid groups of human beings, with the purpose of destroying it in whole or in part, or of preventing its preservation or development." Such acts were listed as the causing of death, injuring of health, group massacres, individual executions, imposing lethal conditions of life, excessive work or physical exertion likely "to result in the debilitation or death of the individuals," mutilation and biological experiments, deprivation of the means of livelihood, restrictions on births, destroying the specific characteristics of the groups by transfer of children, forced and systematic exile of individuals, prohibition of the use of the national language, etc., and preparatory acts to commit genocide. "Those committing genocide shall be punished, be they rulers, public officials or private individuals." The competent organs of the UN will be called upon "to take measures for the suppression or prevention of such crimes."

The signatories "shall do everything in their power to give full effect to the intervention of the United Nations."

This draft envisaged in Article 13 that genocide may be committed by a ruling government, or by sections of the population, or else the government may fail to resist genocide successfully, in which case the survivors of the victimized group should be granted "redress of a nature and in an amount to be determined by the United Nations."

The ad hoc committee which wrote the next version of the Convention defined genocide as an act "committed with the intent to destroy a national, racial, religious or political group": the linguistic group no longer was mentioned. A shorter list of physical acts mentioned killings, impairing physical integrity, "inflicting . . . conditions of life aimed at causing . . . deaths," birth prevention, and acts of cultural genocide. Genocide itself, conspiracy to commit genocide, direct incitement to commit genocide, attempt to commit genocide, and complicity were declared to be punishable acts, whether committed by heads of states, public officials, or private individuals. The weak provisions for enforcement by the United Nations were weakened further.

On December 11, 1946, the General Assembly adopted a Declaration in which genocide was defined as "a denial of the right of existence of entire human groups" and was deemed to be directed against "racial, religious, political and other groups"; now the national group was dropped. The General Assembly reiterated that genocide is a crime for the commission of which private individuals, public officials, or statesmen are punishable, and it recommended that "international co-operation be organized between states with the view to facilitating the speedy prevention and punishment of the crime of genocide. Member states were invited to enact the necessary legislation for the prevention and punishment of this crime.

The preamble to the Convention, which was approved by the General Assembly on December 9, 1948, and entered into force among ratifying states on January 12, 1951, declared genocide "a crime under international law, contrary to the spirit and aims of the United Nations and condemned by the civilized world." It recognized that genocides inflicted great losses on humanity at all periods of history and stated the conviction that international cooperation is required "to liberate mankind from such an odious scourge."

Accordingly, in Article I, the contracting parties undertook to prevent and punish genocide. In Article II, the victim groups were described as "national, ethnical, racial, or religious"; national groups were again mentioned. Criminal acts involved killing, causing serious bodily or mental harm, deliberately bringing about physical destruction through conditions of life, birth prevention, and forcible transfer of children. (The latter point was largely a reaction to the abduction of 28,000 Greek children whom various communist governments refused to return home after the termination of the Greek civil war.) Article IV holds constitutionally responsible rulers, public officials, or private individuals to be liable for punishment. The proviso about UN action was weakened to the point of insignificance.

1. WEAKNESSES OF THE GENOCIDE CONVENTION

The Convention itself has many shortcomings. For example, the clause about "incitement" is the main reason why, as of this writing, the United States Senate has not approved the Convention. It is feared that this proviso could interfere with freedom of speech and lead to foreign interference and meddling. Protection from slander and libel is a difficult problem, since a law strong enough to be effective is likely to be abused by those who would deter investigative reporting. The truth, in any case, is better served by a free and competitive press than by national or international regulation.

The crime of genocide itself is inadequately defined, both as to intent and specific acts, in Articles II and III of the Convention. How, for instance, is "intent to destroy" to be proved? Administrators of Soviet slave-labor camps would probably claim that dissident non-Russian nationalists are in camp to be "reeducated" rather than liquidated. Conversely, proponents of birth-control programs might be charged with "intent to destroy" by preventing births. The psychological aspect of genocide also requires exploration: the crime is of such a nature that it presupposes, almost necessarily, "normal" human attitudes such as fear, anger, hatred, fury, and aggressiveness, as well as autistic and hostile thoughts. It is most likely to involve mental disorders ranging from neuroses and phobias via obsessive-compulsive reactions, delusions, and paranoia to brain dysfunction, disease, and damage. These may impair or destroy the culprit's mental capacity to judge genocidal acts and deprive him of the moral freedom to abstain from committing the genocidal crime (see *Black's Law Dictionary*, pp. 929ff.), so that an international court would have to judge him insane. The point is that the Convention aims at prevention as well as punishment, and therefore the structure of the crime must be clearly understood.

Genocide in the form of criminal acts carried out repeatedly and frequently over a long time is usually undertaken by a dictator or ruling group. Whether or not the perpetrators of genocide are subsequently ruled insane, they are legally responsible for their acts as are all those who aided and abetted the crime. But it is also possible—considering the nature of the crime, it is even highly probable—that persons who order, direct, or conduct genocide are mentally deranged. Perhaps as a "chief who no more in bloody fight engages" (Homer, *Iliad*, Book III) or as a "desk criminal" or *Schreibtischtäter*, the genocidist has become excessively autistic and thinks only in abstractions; or he suffers from an extreme form of paranoia or cerebral dysfunction, or both. In this case it would seem to be the duty of the authorities to remove him from office lest *other* top officials become responsible. This may be a purely platonic obligation because the mad ruler may be all-powerful. Crimes and punishments, however, are defined without assurance that the criminal can be brought to justice.

The force of world public opinion in preventing genocide is most effective when knowledge of genocidal measures is made public. At times, however, states find it expedient to keep such knowledge secret, acquiescing in the crime through their silence. That is what the U.S. and the U.K., as well as most other states, did with regard to Hitler's crimes until they were actually at war with Germany, and about Stalin's crimes until Soviet-Western relations deteriorated in 1948. Under-the-rugmanship is still practiced intermittently with regard to the crimes of Brezhnev, Mao, and other communist rulers, not to mention a few right-wing dictators.

Effects similar to those of genocide have occurred without anyone's deliberately intending to wipe out a people or ethnic group. There come to mind in this connection the million Irish who died during the potato famine of the 1840s, the Indians in the United States during the nineteenth century, and the Indians of Brazil, Colombia, and Peru today. The causes of these decimations (which are considered at length in chapters 11,H4, and 27,A and B) were largely economic. They included trade policy, colonization and development, and nonrecognition of native land tenure so as to facilitate land grabs. Such genocide by negligence stands in relation to genocide *sensu proprio* as manslaughter does to murder. The Convention should be strengthened to make policies causing massive "incidental" deaths punishable as "second-degree genocide."

The Convention regards as an act of genocide the forcible transfer of children from one to another group. The implication is that the bloodless reduction or elimination of an ethnic or religious group is to be regarded as genocide. We agree. But the transfer of children is just one of the requisite methods, and a very rare one at that. The usual method is that of cultural and linguistic transformation of a population within a given territory (*Umvolkung*), a process not included as genocide, because it does not necessarily involve physical extermination. *Umvolkung* is what happened to the Elbe Slavs, who were Germanized, and the Slavs along the lower Vistula, who were Polonized. It has also been the fate of most immigrant groups in the United States to the extent that they have lost their original languages, the entire population of the West Indies, the Cossacks in the Russian area, the Visigoths in North Africa, the Arabs and Jews in Spain (except those who emigrated) and, to a large extent, the Occitans and Bretons in France.

Umvolkung is accompanied by group conflict which sometimes leads to bloody repression, but essentially it is restricted to dispersal and resettlement, imposition of language and culture, the redrawing of political boundaries, denial of autonomy and self-government, and assimilation. If the disappearance of a particular *genus* is to be avoided, because each group enjoys the inherent right of self-preservation, measures of forced cultural transformation should be outlawed by international law. If a particular group should wish to dissolve, this is sanctioned by the writ of self-determination, but other groups remain free to judge whether they can assimilate its members without jeopardizing *their* identity. The problem, as will become evident in subsequent chapters, is difficult and complex; it would be better not to legislate than to legislate in a blundering fashion.

The provisions in the Convention for international action to prevent and suppress acts of genocide (Article 8) are utterly vague and almost meaningless. No attempt was made to tie this task to the authority of the Security Council under Chapter VII of the Charter dealing with threats to the peace, breaches of the peace, and acts of aggression. Thus, genocide is a crime which, according to this Convention, need only be punished after the event. Since no effective procedures were outlined for prevention and suppression, the crime of genocide—which is a crime of extreme discrimination—is in effect being tolerated, contrary to the intent of the Convention itself.

The provisions for redress and restitution in the early drafts do not reappear in the Convention. Hence, no provisions are made for the victims, or their heirs, to get compensation for their losses and sufferings. In this connection, it may be mentioned that East Germany, and to a lesser extent Austria, which are co-responsible for some of the genocidal acts committed during World War II, have not been asked by the UN to live up to their responsibilities. Austria made only inadequate restitution, while the GDR, a new member of the UN, refused to make any restitution at all. By contrast, the Federal Republic of Germany went to considerable lengths to right some of the wrongs committed by the Hitler regime. This unilateral assumption of responsibility reflects the FRG's claim to be the sole legitimate successor and the trustee of the German Reich.

2. THE PROBLEM OF POLITICAL GENOCIDE

The Convention deals with genocidal acts perpetrated against national, ethnic, racial, or religious groups. This wording excludes concerns with acts of mass murder or inhuman treatment directed against political groups. Slave labor camps and even extermination camps are not deemed to fall under the purview of this international agreement. As Senator Brien McMahon put it in 1950, "the maintenance of the slave labor camps in any country if it wasn't done for the purpose of destroying that particular race, would not come within the four corners of this Convention" (Genocide Hearings, 1950, p. 137).

Through the dropping of political groups from the victim list, the most severe form of discrimination currently practiced is, in effect, tolerated and, in a sense, "legalized" by omission.

Yet there is no doubt that mass slaughter and the imposition of conditions that kill (e.g. in concentration and slave-labor camps) has been aimed mainly at political groups. Hence, the Convention should have included political groups; and it might have been broadminded and realistic enough to recognize that some groups may very well be hostile and threaten the security of the state, in which case the threatened state should be allowed to protect itself, albeit by *nongenocidal* means. Once again, a real problem was ignored.

For that matter, the catalogue of the Convention reflects historical oversimplification. Hitler did not limit his genocide to extermination camps and not all his victims fell under the four categories subsequently laid down in the Convention. For example, in 1934, Hitler killed both a number of political opponents and numerous members of his own party, an act which Stalin emulated on a much larger scale: he exterminated a considerable portion of the party and the military high command. These crimes were praised by the U.S. ambassador to Moscow as an act of self-defense against the "fifth column."

Hitler ordered the killing of substantial numbers of mentally sick and retarded patients, and he meted out inhuman and genocidal treatment to forced labor brought in from abroad. Captured communist political commissars were exterminated and prisoners of war of "inferior" nationalities were mistreated. The Hitler regime also practiced *Sippenhaft* (imprisonment of family members) and farmed out children of political opponents to nonrelated and spiteful families, in the same way that the Dauphin, Louis XVI's son, was assigned to the tender killing cares of Monsieur Simon, a cobbler. If the Convention had been in force during World War II, and if Hitler had been held to compliance with it, he would have argued—as indeed he did argue from time to time—that he was not persecuting anyone on racial or ethnic grounds, but simply was protecting Germany from its enemies. The Convention should have made it clear to him that he was entitled to protect his country but also that he was obligated as chief of state to ensure the observance of human rights and of the German legal codes, which explicitly forbade any genocidal measures against native or foreign groups. (These same codes, as *they existed during the Third Reich*, have been used to convict perpetrators of atrocities in a long series of trials conducted by the Federal Republic of Germany.)

The thesis that the term "genocide" does not apply to the phenomenon now known as Gulag Archipelago is a piece of sophistry that must be rejected. It is true that in communist countries opponents of the regime have been repressed merely because of political reasons; they were and still are regarded as "enemies of the people." It is also true that, at least during Stalin's time, large numbers of people were killed who engaged in no political activity at all but were regarded as *potential* political opponents. Many others were repressed because prisoners were forced to give names; the innocent individuals denounced under duress may have made up the largest number of victims. Torture was authorized by a decree of the CPSU's Central Committee of January 20, 1939. In other contexts, hostages were shot *en masse*, wounded prisoners were shot in the civil war, and famines were organized, especially in Ukraine, Kazakhstan, North Caucasus, and Middle Volga (see Conquest, 1971). The term "political genocide" is thus a logical application of the basic concept.

A major campaign was waged for the "liquidation of the Kulaks as a class" after the "bourgeoisie" and the "capitalists" had been liquidated. This raises the question why *social class* is not included in the categories of people who must be protected against genocide. Lenin and Stalin were open advocates of "class genocide."

Just as National Socialist genocide was not

exclusively ethnic or racial, so communist genocide is not exclusively social or political. Members of *all* ethnic groups and believers of all religions have been victimized by the terror machine, but various groups were victims of ethnic genocide in the proper sense, among them the Balts, Chechen, Chinese, Crimean Tatars, Finish Ingrians, Greeks, Ingush, Jews, Kalmyks and eastern Mongolians, Koreans, Meskhetians, Poles (e.g. the Katyn murders), Ukrainians, Volga and other Germans— citizens of the USSR and of annexed territories—as well as foreigners who happened to be in their midst.

3. UNRESOLVED PROBLEMS

The text of the Convention is disingenuous insofar as it conceals the brutal fact that genocide is necessarily a crime committed or at least tolerated by governments. To be sure, private individuals may act as accomplices, low level or provincial government officials may be acting on their own, and occasional "spontaneous" riots may be provoked against a disliked element of the population. Mass crimes can happen everywhere and should not really be the subject of an international convention lest meddling in other countries' domestic affairs become the rule. But the *systematic* and repeated killing of members of publicly proscribed groups and the imposition of intolerable conditions of life through specially designed institutions and major policies must necessarily be caused, and in many ways must even be legislated, by governments. At the very least such measures cannot possibly be carried out for any length of time against substantial numbers of victims unless the top levels of government tacitly approve the atrocities. Consequently, and by definition, genocide must be deemed to be undertaken by governments which have become criminal. It is to this gruesome reality of the *criminal government* that the Convention should have directed its attention.

This reality is addressed to some extent, in the Declaration on Principles of International Law concerning Friendly Relations and Cooperation among States in Accordance with the Charter of the United Nations, of October 24, 1970. In this document we read that "every state has the duty to refrain from any forcible action which deprives peoples . . . of their right to self-determination and freedom and independence." But a government which turns criminal will not live up to its duties. If genocide is to be stopped, the spirit of the Charter should prompt the search for a solution under Chapter VI dealing, within the context of the Security Council's activities, with the pacific settlement of disputes. Failing in such attempts, enforcement actions could be contemplated as laid down in Chapter VII. In the latter case, enforcement against a major power or over such a power's objections would be paralyzed by the veto. In addition, Article 51 upholds "the inherent right of individual or collective self-defense." In its present version, this article applies only to armed attack against a state, but if the UN were serious with its opposition to genocide, Article 51 should be rewritten, or reinterpreted, to apply to groups which are under attack through genocidal measures.

A more recent UN document, the Definition of Aggression of 1974, calls for support to peoples struggling for liberation from "colonialist or racist regimes or other forms of alien domination." In point of fact, the UN directs its attention to *European* colonialism, ignoring colonialism as practiced by African peoples against one another (e.g. Sudan, Nigeria-Biafra), or by Russia, China, or India and other non-European and non-North American powers. Thus self-determination in the context of "colonialism" is regarded as a more important objective than self-determination *in general*, and the achievement of self-determination (i.e. political independence, in the current and wrong interpretation) is given higher priority than protection against genocide. The lower value has been given precedence over the higher value.

Whatever the defects of the Genocide Convention might be, this document could have had a moral impact. Yet the sad truth is that during the first 25 years of its existence, after ratification, the Convention has had no impact whatever and genocidal behavior has not ceased. The USSR, where many of the genocidal acts perpetrated under Stalin were admitted and repudiated, *socially* rehabilitated many of the victims, though not all of them; but rehabilitation fell short of full redress and in many cases the victims were dead. In some instances, rehabilitation led to new wrongs. For example, the Crimean Tatars who were expelled from their habitat were "rehabilitated," but they were not allowed to return home and repossess the properties taken away from them and given to other people. Similarly, the Volga Germans have not been permitted to return to their historic area of settlement. In other instances, ethnic groups (or rather their remnants) which had been subjected to genocidal persecution were reinstated in the *status quo ante*. In effect, then, there was massive discrimination between those groups which were persecuted and those which were not; and there continues to be very serious discrimination between groups given some degree of remedy (for some, such as the Ukrainians, Georgians, and Baltic peoples, the only full remedy would be independence from Russia) and those who, like the massacred Poles, were given no redress at all.

In summary, some forms of discrimination are less important, whereas others are of overriding gravity. UN legal texts, while voluminous and in many ways valuable, have not succeeded in sorting out and solving the complex legal problems involved. The UN policies, far from pursuing a systematic quest for higher justice and from providing any semblance of protection, have overplayed some of the real or supposed cases of discrimination, while they ignored life-or-death issues. It goes without saying that war is not an attractive remedy against genocide and that even if it were, the UN would be able to coerce a criminal government only if it could mobilize superior military force and if its action were not blocked by the veto of a permanent member of the Security Council. The power of the UN is that of moral persuasion, but there can be no such moral power if the UN—through omissions and tergiversations—covers up for the criminal immorality of genocide and fails to define the standards which its member states are obligated to observe. Human rights can only prosper in a *Rechtsstaat*—a state based on legal norms and principles and ruled by a government of laws, not arbitrary and passionate men. Unfortunately, not all members of the UN can be regarded as lawful states or even profess commitment to the norms of justice.

There is a danger, moreover, that a forum such as the UN General Assembly will be miscontrued—even by its delegates—as being vested with legislative powers, and that it will bring forth pseudo-law, of which its pronouncements about South West Africa and Israel are typical. The General Assembly is not, of course, the only source of pseudo-law. It is also present in advisory opinions of the International Court, as well as in showpieces intended to dazzle the public, such as the Kellogg-Briand Pact and the more recent "Final Act" signed at Helsinki.

5

THE BODY COUNT

Gil Elliot made a valiant effort to count "the number of man-made deaths in the twentieth century." He arrived at a total of 110 million, which he regards as "a reasonable conservative estimate" (1972, pp. 155, 212). Elliot's rough figures cover the years up to the late 1950s, and they are conservative. He underestimated the losses through combat and epidemics in World War I, the losses in the interethnic struggles in multinational Yugoslavia, the numbers slain in the revenge against real collaborators and anticommunists falsely accused of collaborating carried out in Italy, France, and Czecho-Slovakia between 1944 and 1947, and the casualties in clashes between oppressors and resisters in Eastern Europe between the wars and after World War II (including casualties in connection with the explusion of 18 million Reich and ethnic Germans and the *razvod* of the Baltic elites). He also understated the casualties in Vietnam (where Ho Chi Minh conducted large massacres in the north before the communists ever invaded the south), and especially in China, about which his information is insufficient. Although he discussed man-made famines, he did not notice certain famines which took place in the USSR and China. Elliot said little about Cuba. He ignored the use of narcotics as a tool of conflict, and he failed to report on the human toll taken by Latin American development facilitated by extermination of the Amerindians. He is quite aware of the impact of mass violence on population growth, but since he did not study the problem specifically, he vastly underrated the demographic impact, especially on the USSR and China. We shall not undertake a demographic analysis, because reductions in the birth rate may be indirect consequences of crimes against humanity or may be results of population policies dealing with overcrowding and overstraining of resources (but see chapter 28).

Given these qualifications, Mr. Elliot's data, which reflect considerable study, are extremely useful. Since the executioners fail to keep book, there are no "body counts" of exterminations, artificial or tolerated famines and epidemics, or even wars (save for claims of own and enemy casualties distorted for propaganda reasons). The statistical information on such disasters is often withheld or not even collected, so that data are fragmentary and conflicting. Those who prefer a realistic to a conservative estimate may assume that the toll of violence, minus demographic losses, could easily have been 50 percent higher. Robert Conquest estimated the total human cost of soviet communism to be between 35 and 45 million lives, while Richard L. Walker assayed the cost of communism in China, between 1927–1970, as between 34 and 64 million (Human Cost, 1971, p. iv). Alexander Solzhenitsyn reiterated in April 1975, in a press conference at Paris, his earlier estimate that 40 million persons were killed in the Gulag camps and that 26 million died from (man-made) famine, the collectivization of agriculture, and through massacres (*Die Welt*, April 12, 1975, p. 15). Thus, in the USSR and China alone, and only counting the toll that must be attributed to crimes against humanity committed by communists, 135 to 175 million persons may have been killed, according to carefully calculated and documented estimates.

In judging criminal violations of human rights, however, it makes little difference whether the victims of a particular crime number 50, 500, 5000, or 5 million. Regardless how many victims, the criminals can be punished only once, and the *lex talionis* (retribution principle) simply cannot be made to work in the case of mass murder. Civilized courts will condemn even a multiple murderer to almost painless death by shooting, the guillotine, or properly conducted hanging: they will no longer order that one be boiled in oil or tied down, smeared with honey, and left to be eaten by army ants.

Credibility can be gained by accepting Mr. Elliot's figure precisely because he understates the toll. On this basis of 110 million man-made deaths between 1900 and 1970, worldwide, it can be calculated, according to Elliot's data, that about 7 percent of those deaths were due to massacres and political violence.

The 110 million fatalities include 38 million soldiers, or slightly more than one-third of the total. Since these losses result from war and civil war, they cannot properly be attributed to crimes against humanity. Even if the Nuremberg indictment and the UN 1974 Definition of Aggression were legally valid, self-defense against aggression, according to Article 51 of the UN Charter, is an inherent right. There is, of course, always a question who is acting legitimately in self-defense. Construing Article 51 of the UN Charter retroactively *à la* Nuremberg, it may be doubted whether the

right of collective defense is exercised legitimately when action is taken to retaliate against capture of a forward pawn—such as Poland became for Britain through the unilateral guarantee of March 31, 1939, and the formal alliance of August 25 of that year. It cannot be argued that Britain seriously hoped to defend Poland, a country Churchill found it necessary to sacrifice for reasons of state in 1944. It seems therefore most logical to assume that the 45 to 50 million fatalities, or up to 45 percent of the total loss, caused by World War II do not fall under the rubric of crimes against humanity, except as they involved unnecessary taking of life.

The Definition of Aggression, Article 6, acknowledges that there are legitimate uses of force. In some instances, within the very framework of human rights and the need to protect them, the use of military force might be necessary and legitimate, even if operations have to be initiated. Experience indicates in any case that states will fight when their vital interests are at stake and not otherwise; there is nothing international law can do to change this fact. Furthermore, while this may be deplorable, war can never be fought in such a way that civilians will escape entirely unscathed.

Accordingly, we calculate from the data which Mr. Elliot provided that at a minimum 35 percent of the losses were caused by noncriminal applications of force. Another 25 percent—including World War II losses from such episodes as the saturation bombing of Rotterdam, Coventry, Hamburg, and Dresden and the sinking of refugee ships such as the *Lancastria* and the *Wilhelm Gustloff*—are in a doubtful category: that is, a portion may be charged to criminal decisions, the actual amount depending on standards applied. A final 40 percent, or about 45 million deaths, such as killings in camps, executions, massacres, repression, forced labor, famine, etc. resulted without question from crimes against humanity.

To put this differently, about 3 percent of all the deaths, from whatever causes, that occurred anywhere in the world during the twentieth century are attributable to criminal behavior of governments or subordinate government agencies. This does not include the toll exacted by private criminals, routine crime-fighting by the police, and legitimate death penalties.

To repeat, those are conservative figures and it is entirely possible, even probable, that deliberate crimes against humanity cost the lives of substantially more than 100 million. That means that during the twentieth century, one out of every 30 inhabitants of the earth was killed through government criminality.

It would be foolish to argue that force and violence can be wholly eliminated from political life. Since no one has yet shown how this miracle might be performed, or even that such a miracle would necessarily be beneficial, positive international law cannot reflect the impractical notion that violence is unlawful and criminal under all conditions, and there can be no law for a nonexistent society.

If self-defense is an inherent right, and this is the minimal position that can be taken on the propriety of using force, except by a doctrinaire pacifist, the problem is to define the full content of what self-defense might be. For example, self-defense cannot be restricted to merely striking back after one has already been hit. The right to prevent an attack which is being prepared must necessarily fall under the purview of self-defense. (For a discussion of the limits of this right see Tucker, 1960, pp. 142–45.) Nor can force be restricted to defense of one's own country. If a person is walking down the street, and sees someone on the other side being attacked, he is morally obligated to come to the victim's defense. Despite the talk about the illegality of aggression, in the sense of initial use of force, this moral obligation would seem to exist also in international life, at least in the case of unprovoked attacks. Perhaps the perpetration of a crime against hu-

manity, which is an illegal act of force, could be construed as an act of aggression even though not directed at another state. Thus, the state engaged in murder is the aggressor, not his victim, let alone the state which comes to the victim's rescue.

Among the self-determining nations, though some have disarmed almost completely and some have never really armed, not a single one has ever redefined its claim to sovereignty as not extending to the right of self-defense or even to the right of war. The general understanding among "peace-loving" sovereign nations, however, has been that war should be viewed as a last resort, when no other solution is feasible and any further delay would be highly dangerous. In communist thinking, however, revolutionary wars and wars of national liberation are always permissible, so that to this extent peace takes a lower priority even though "peace" is a propaganda tool.

There is general agreement among statesmen that war should not be counterproductive or "self-defeating" in the sense that the objectives pursued are unattainable or too costly to attain. War and violence can be functional or dysfunctional. They can stabilize or destabilize a society, increase or decrease a threat, or, from the point of view of human rights, enlarge or reduce human satisfaction. How force is to be applied when the need arises is for the strategist to decide. To avoid defeating his own purposes, the strategist must not place himself above the law and he must not willfully transgress the limitations dictated by accepted legal norms and by human rights.

In *The Pathology of Politics* (1972), Carl J. Friedrich demonstrated that politics "cannot be managed without violence, betrayal, corruption, secrecy, and propaganda. The moralist will be asking in vain for a moral politics, but he may reasonably ask for *a more moral* politics. . . . When acting thus, the moralist is highly functional." Agreed, except that Friedrich's understanding of violence is too academic: he views it too narrowly and fails to emphasize its necrophilic and criminal dimensions. The point is that if it is to be functional, force must be applied not unrestrictedly, but reasonably and according to rules of civilized conduct.

By the same token, the framers of legal provisions must address themselves to reality. For example, it would be foolish to decree that, in case of war, certain elements of the hostile population in an occupied country or even in the belligerent's own country must not be interned. Other necessities may arise: France, for instance, interned the anti-Franco Spanish soldiers who fled from Spain after the end of the Civil War. A short while later France, which had declared war on Germany in September 1939, to help Britain "save" Poland, was invaded and occupied by Hitler's armies. The Spaniards had a hard life, and some blamed the Vichy government, which enjoyed only limited freedom of action (Montseny, 1950). But this criticism was not entirely fair.

Be that as it may, it is legitimate to insist that the conditions of internment be humane and do not in any manner reflect sentiments of revenge, hatred, and punishment. Standards in food, housing, heat, clothing, and medical aid exist and should be observed, whether or not the internees are regarded as hostile. Situations of necessity may require drastic action but coercion beyond internment can only be justified by compelling reasons (see chapter 25,B1). Internment camps, like prisoner-of-war camps but unlike forced labor and extermination camps (see chapter 24), are not evil or criminal institutions *per se*.

Necessity of this kind, however, has never been defined in international law and the limits of permissible actions have not been set. Until this is done, decision-makers have no real yardstick to guide them in emergencies. One simple rule would protect against most abuses of emergency measures: camps and similar institutions should be subject to constant international inspection.

Aside from extreme actions undertaken under the dispensation of necessity, crimes against humanity may result from deliberate decisions by a government or from a government's failure to prevent activities or events (such as famines and epidemics) harmful to certain groups. UN documents often refer to the duties of states—a subject which easily activates allergies. But surely it is a governmental duty not only to act against discrimination caused by unequal treatment, but also to protect victims against extreme and lethal discrimination executed through unlawful detention, physical harm, and mass murder.

The distinction between *crimes against humanity*, which are by definition intentional, and *unintentional injury*, or harm occurring as a byproduct of noncriminal activities and policies, can usually be made without much difficulty. One major criterion is that mass crimes are, almost invariably, accompanied by scapegoating and diabolization, and by propaganda inciting to violence against the victims. Unintentional injuries against humanity usually are unconnected with pathology or criminality but, in the main, must be attributed to ignorance, lack of communications, and bureaucratic autism.

There are several techniques which allow the formulation of substantial suspicion about the psychiatric component of mass crimes from afar. However, a legally valid determination of psychiatric impairment requires clinical examination which is feasible only after the miscreants are apprehended.

PART TWO

GROUPS AND THEIR INTERACTION

6

THE DYNAMICS OF GROUP BEHAVIOR

A society without groups, consisting of an infinite number of persons, all in symmetrical relation to the state, is theoretically conceivable. Rousseau gives us a glimpse of such an atomistic nation in his *Social Contract*, in which he inveighs against "partial societies" as obstacles to the General Will. Aldous Huxley divides his *Brave New World* into five biological castes, designated by the letters alpha to epsilon, but all the members of each caste are expected to have uniform chromosomes, abilities, and opinions. Rousseau's modern disciple, B. F. Skinner, advocates a system of "operant conditioning," in which he hopes to shape human personalities by manipulating their environment (Skinner, 1971); a technique that leads a critic to complain that "Skinner has effectively abolished personality and hence man." (Arnold, 1971)

A. Functional and Total Groups

But even Rousseau's, Huxley's, and Skinner's utopias must necessarily contain occupational groups as well as groups defined by age, IQ, and state of health. None of them proposed abolishing males and females, even though that was the dream of certain medieval philosophers (Molnar, 1972). In practice, every country and every society contains a multiplic-

ity of overlapping groups defined by a wide variety of criteria: bankers, preachers, and bus drivers; black, white, and brown people; Catholics, Protestants, Jews, and Muslims; young, middle-aged, and old; ambulant and cripples, and so forth. Generally speaking, these groups fall into two main categories: *functional groups*, defined by a particular and limited aspect of life such as occupation, educational background, state of health, and other factors that shape interests but do not control or define the personality; and *total groups*, so-called because their doctrines or essences tend to define, shape, and limit the personalities of their members. A Parent-Teacher's Association is a typical functional group; a religious order, to the extent that purported commitments are real, is a total group. What groups are total groups at any period in history is determined by the prevailing ideology (Lemberg, 1974).

Like the societies of particular countries, international society also contains a variety of groups. The most prominent among these are *nations:* large aggregations of people that have their own national states or aspire to them, except when they have achieved full partnership in multinational states. It must be noted that a nation is not identical with all the citizens or inhabitants of a national state; a nation may be divided among several states (as are the Kurds in the contemporary Middle East), while a state (such as the old Austro-Hungarian Empire or the USSR today) may contain a number of nations. *Nationalities* are groups with the characteristics generally identified with nations (see chapter 10), but which are too small or too scattered to have their own national states. The Jews have been a nationality since the diaspora and are counted as a nationality in the USSR; with the founding of modern Israel some of them, at least, have become a nation. *Ethnic groups* are groups within a society having a particular cultural and emotional attachment to their land or people of origin or peoples of cultural or racial affinity. In countries of immigration, they take the form of "hyphenated groups," such as German-Americans, Italian-Argentines, or Ukrainian-Canadians, owing political allegiance to their country of citizenship but maintaining inherited cultural roots. Finally, we have the *pseudo-nation:* the group that lacks the distinctiveness, the cultural and linguistic cohesiveness, or the common history to become a nation, but inhabits or claims a territory (usually one hitherto governed by a colonial power). Pseudo-nations are promoted as nations by ambitious politicians, swelling the ranks of the marginal or submarginal ministates and political monstrosities in the General Assembly of the United Nations.

Nations, nationalities, and ethnic groups live in the realm of language, culture, tradition, and political allegiance—all factors that impinge directly on the personality and its identity. For this reason they all have the potential to become total groups and intolerant of competing allegiances: each such group has a built-in tendency to channelize the aggressive instincts of its members. The extent to which such totality is achieved, and to which clashes of interest result in conflict, depends on the overall constellation in which these groups find themselves at a given point in history. Not the least of the factors dictating the degree of totality is the prevailing ideology, which is subject to change. Two nations, for instance, may coexist peacefully within the same territory and as subjects of the same monarch for centuries. Suddenly, an ideology becomes prevalent which dictates that every nation must have its own independent state, and the result is civil war (Lemberg, 1974).

Two other categories that are competitors for totality on the international scale are races and religions. Racially, mankind is divided into five or six macrogroups: Australids, Europids, Negrids, Khoisanids (Cape peoples), Mongolids, and Indianids (Eickstedt, 1937, Peters, 1937, and Garn, 1971). The latter two are classified as a single group by Coon (1963), who speculates that the ancestors of American Indians migrated from Asia before the breakthrough of the Bering Strait. Each macrogroup is subdivided into anthropological types, such as the Nordics, Alpines, and Arabs among the Europids and the Sudanese and Zambesian among the Negrids, as well as into cultural-linguistic groups (e.g., Celts, Basques, Nguni, and Sotho) with attributes capable of crystalizing into nationality. The world religions are similarly grouped: each major religion has its subreligions (Catholic and Protestant, Sunnite and Shi'ite, etc.) and its sects, most of which overlap political boundaries. The extent to which race and religion assert claims to totality and become provocations for conflict is, again, a question of prevailing ideology. In an age when churches seemed the only repositories of truth, people were more ready to exterminate (if they could not convert) nonbelievers than in an era when religions are fighting rear-guard actions against the inroads of science and of materialist philosophies. It is, indeed, the adherents of the latter who have taken the place of the early caliphs and the crusaders in asserting totality on a world scale: communism, whether of Muscovite or Peking orientation, demands total commitment and tolerates no competing authority.

There are, of course, numerous functional groups that operate across national boundaries. The international business community contains generalized organizations such as Rotary International and its competitors, specialized trade and technical associations, and a large number of multinational corporations. The labor movement is represented in the International Federation of Free Trade Unions (which split off from the World Federation of Trade Unions when the latter came under communist control), in the intergovernmental International Labor Office (from which the United States withdrew in 1977), and in various formal and informal committees. Specialized fields of interest present a myriad of functional groups, each asserting partial claim to the loyalties of its members, ranging from the International Political Science Association to the International Naturists Federation.

B. *Integrators and Differentiators*

Every group, whether functional or total, is characterized by one or more features that are integrators, identifiers indicating membership in the group, and also by differentiators, distinguishing its members from those of other groups. The essential thing about an integrator is that members of the group in question have it, whereas persons outside the group do not.

In the case of functional groups, the integrator is an interest or set of interests which the group represents; with regard to other characteristics, such as race, age, sex, etc., the group is indifferent—except insofar as such characteristics also function as differentiators. In the case of total groups, or those with the potential of becoming total, the integrators are more closely related to the personalities of the members. The integrator in this case may be a set of physical characteristics, a typical mental makeup, adherence to a religion or a political movement, or it may be expressed in language, dialect, or cultural style. A visible integrator will be a signal whereby members recognize one another and are also recognized by others—such as the distinctive appearance of certain races. Intentional visible signals include headgear such as the fez and the yarmulke, and costumes such as the "plain" clothing of conservative Quakers and Amish in the United States. Or the signal may be audible: a language, dialect, or manner of speech.

Groups subject to persecution or extermination will endeavor to avoid giving visible signals to those not of their group. In the days of Ferdinand and Isabella, many Spanish Jews and Muslims went through the ritual of conversion, but continued to practice their faith secretly. Suspecting the devoutness of new "believers," the Holy Inquisition sent forth dust inspectors to paw through the offal of convert families. Failure to find pork bones raised a presumption of false conversion, confession of which was then extracted on the torture wheel. Analogously, a group with a negative self-image will tend to hide or mitigate its visible signals, as manifested by the former popularity of whiteners and hair straighteners among American Negroes. The current prevalence of "natural" hairdress and African or pseudo-African costume is clear evidence that the black self-image has become positive.

Integrators and differentiators, and hence the composition of groups, are determined in three alternative ways:

Internally, by the will of individual members. A typical case is the decision to join or maintain membership in a church, fraternity, political party, or other voluntary organization. Membership in ethnic groups is acquired through the claim of ancestry—sometimes involving a choice in the case of persons of mixed parentage—combined with learning of or improving fluency in the language of the group if not the mother language of the person concerned. A desire to shift political allegiance on the part of immigrants is manifested in their application for citizenship in the new country. In all these cases, the members consciously and intentionally apply the integrators of the group to themselves.

Externally, when the integrator is initially

a differentiator: a signal for exclusion from another group or from a larger group believed to embrace both. Whether or not that larger group exists or can exist as a functioning community is irrelevant to the psychological situation. Insofar as American Negroes have sought total assimilation into white society and hence their own extinction as a group, the unity of the black community—indeed acceptance of the word "black" as an honorable name rather then an epithet—was forged through the common experience of rejection. To the extent that a group is defined through external (involuntary) identification of its members, that group—particularly those within it who wish they belonged to some other group—will be afflicted with a negative self-image.

Objectively, by such factors as sex, visible physical characteristics, cultural and linguistic inheritance, age, wealth, occupation, and other data that can be registered statistically. As a rule, the determination of integrators and groups proceeds in all three ways, the relative weight of which shifts with changing circumstances. Objectively, the term "Afro-American" refers to an American citizen who is wholly or partly of African descent. This heritage is usually signalled by physical characteristics, but there are cases in which a person who appears "white" chooses to be identified as black. Conversely, people of partial African descent but without pronounced African physical characteristics frequently succeed in "passing," in which case they have excluded themselves from the black group. Within the total American society, the black group is defined externally by exclusion from white society and by traditional discriminations against blacks, as well as by the dictum of white racial purists that anyone with the least trace of African ancestry is black. It is significant that this definition, which is basically prejudicial, has been accepted almost without exception by persons so classified—whereas it would seem more logical to give persons of mixed ancestry a choice. In its inception, therefore, the black segment of American society was an externally defined and involuntary group: people were not asked whether they wanted to belong to it. Accepting their group as thus defined, an increasing number of black intellectuals have further defined themselves and their people internally by developing distinctive cultural styles and by asserting black superiority and exclusiveness in various respects. Such counterclaims to "white superiority" are indeed necessary if the negative self-image of American blacks is to be transformed into a positive one.

C. Group Interests and Preferences

Each group, functional or total, has definable interests related to its integrators and differentiators. Dairy farmers, for instance, want higher milk prices; clothing workers' unions want tariffs and quotas against cheap Asian garments; sick people want improved medical care; while Seventh Day Adventists and Orthodox Jews want the right to close their shops on their Sabbath and keep them open Sunday. Such group interests may or may not conflict with the interests of other groups. Where conflicts exist or threaten, the statesman's task is to find a compromise that, if not wholly satisfactory, is the least unsatisfactory to all parties.

Groups not only formulate their interests in the shape of goals and programs, but they also range them in a rank order of priority. For interests of highest priority, the group will expend maximum efforts; if it is a total group, it is usually prepared to fight for them. It should be observed, however, that interests thought vital at one point may turn out to be less so in the light of experience. The viability of a political society depends on the ultimate reconciliation of group interests. Should such reconciliation prove impossible, separation may be the price of peace.

Group interests normally include survival of the group and, in the case of total and quasi-total groups, development as a cultural and political entity. When the history of a group has been marked by discrimination and deprivation, however, its members may seek assimilation into or merger with the regionally dominant group, so that the prime goal of the group becomes its own extinction. This has been the case with immigrant groups in the United States—including blacks (who have been described as "internal immigrants")—until a recent shift in ideology brought about a resurgence of ethnic awareness and pride.

When group interests appear irreconcilable, or when one group thinks that competing groups are not willing to make concessions, violence may result. Its effects sometimes make all groups concerned aware that compromise, however uncomfortable, is better than the alternative of mutual destruction and slaughter.

Group membership normally entails a natural preference for members of the in-group—at least in matters relevant to the interests of the group. This preference is reflected in the composition of group organizations, which are normally limited to persons exhibiting the integrator of the group concerned. You cannot, for instance, join the Knights of Columbus unless you are a Catholic, while a black student's association at a university is in practice (though sometimes not in theory) closed to whites. Members of total groups, and of ethnic groups to the extent that they approach totality, also exhibit a tendency to discriminate in social and cultural matters: to associate with members of the in-group and to prefer its cultural style. The one exception that comes to mind is the case of the sexes, on whose symbiotic life the future of mankind depends. Women may frequently prefer the company of men and vice versa.

D. Group Salience and Identification

The human personality is more than a construction of protoplasm and far more than an assortment of impressions and perceptions generated by haphazard sensory inputs. Without committing ourselves to a particular theological view, we can assert that the human person is a *Gestalt*, characterized by autonomy vis-à-vis his or her environment. According to Gehlen, human beings differ from animals in exhibiting a hiatus between perception and action. Instead of reacting immediately, they reflect on the meaning of sensory inputs and the most expedient action to deal with the facts such inputs seem to indicate (Gehlen, 1950).

While much routine human behavior, like that of animals, is guided by inherited and conditioned reflexes, there is a difference in the way the latter are acquired. Conditioned reflexes in animals are created through experience, which is registered but not analyzed—the classic example is Pavlov's dog experiment. In human beings, conditioned reflexes are usually learned intentionally through repeated acts of will; the person acquires useful reflexes and related motor dexterity, as in learning to drive a car, sail a boat, or play the violin. Psychoanalysis has shown that subconsciously acquired conditioned reflexes are often dysfunctional, and it sometimes takes long and expensive therapy to get rid of them.

The human person does not, however, live in a vacuum. His character is formed through autonomous response to his life experiences, especially those involving interpersonal relations. To quite an extent, people make themselves. What they make—like the work of any artist or artisan—depends on the material they receive and what they do with it. The experiential material that shapes the human personality tends to place its recipient in categories or groups in which his membership is determined internally, externally, or objectively as the case may be. A given subject, for instance, has the experience of growing up white and male in a lower-middle-class Protestant family. He is afflicted with myopia and asthma—factors that would propel him toward a bookish life, unless he deliberately sets out to overcome them as did Theodore Roosevelt. At 35 we find him a professor, a member of sev-

eral learned societies, an ardent social re-
former, and a member of a new and exotic
church. The essential point is this: the elements that have become parts of our subject's
personality are all expressed in terms of iden-
tifications and categories.

As soon as we pass beyond the primordial
drives for survival, food, sex, and (as Freud
believed) destruction and death, we find a
drive basic to the formation of cultures. This is
the *identification drive:* the urge to grow beyond
oneself, to integrate one's personality in a
larger cause or movement, and to perpetuate
oneself by belonging to a community that continues in space and time. This drive is by no
means limited to Europeans: it is especially
strong in African society (Mbiti, 1970). Its negative side is *Weltangst:* the fear of isolation and
annihilation that overwhelms the individual
lacking the social and cultural reinforcement of
"belonging." When the impersonality of modern society prevents someone from satisfying
his identification drive, that person is described as suffering *anomie*—lacking norms or
guidance systems.

The search for the self is correctly described
as the search for *identity*. This identity is
always described in terms of categories extending beyond the individual. To say, "I am myself and I do my own thing" is inadequate,
since the self can only be defined in terms of
cultural time and space.

The many groups to which a person belongs
are of unequal importance in shaping the personality and fixing a rank-order of values. The
power of a category to determine loyalties and
the cohesive strength of the group so identified
are a function of the *salience* of the integrator–
differentiator. To illustrate: national patriotism and religion are generally high-salience integrators. A man will die for his country or his
God, but hardly for his Chamber of Commerce or his cricket team. The advertising
slogan "Us Tareyton smokers would rather
fight than switch" is delightful in its absurdity,
since it raises a low-salience identifier—smoking a particular cigarette—to artificially high

status. If Tareyton smokers were as belligerent
as the advertisement suggests, they would be
most likely to fight one another.

When a person belongs to two groups with
conflicting interests, the side he chooses reflects his judgment of the salience of these
groups in his personal life, and only secondarily the merits of the issue. "My country right
or wrong" states a resolution to ignore the
merits of the issue altogether in favor of a high-
salience loyalty. The salience of a group has
two aspects: *internal*, as perceived by members
of that group, and *external*, as perceived by outsiders. An effective group leader succeeds in
raising the internal salience of his group and its
identifiers; a corresponding increase in external
salience usually follows.

The salience of integrators and discriminators and of the groups designated thereby is
the product of a number of factors, including:

1. Specific interests and goals of the
group in question, distinguishable from the
interests of other groups and the "public interest" of the larger society.
2. Incompatibility, real or imagined, between the goals of the group and the interests of other groups, of the larger society,
or—in a plural society—the interests of the
group or coalition in political control.
3. Assignment of a distinctive economic
or social role to the group and its members
through the operation of traditions, customs, or laws. As a rule, such distinctive
roles involve occupations regarded as menial, servile, or unclean (such as leather
workers in Japan). But they may in some
cases involve special privileges (such as the
right of Jews during the Middle Ages to lend
money at interest, which was forbidden to
Christians).
4. Discrimination of legal, social, economic, or political character or a combination of these, or real or imagined persecution
practiced against the group. The salience of
the group naturally increases with the severity and duration of the discrimination: a relation that explains the cohesiveness of Jews in
the diaspora.

Groups suffering the latter two discriminations are sometimes called "minorities"—A term referred to below and explained in more detail in chapter 9. The term "minority" will be used throughout this book in a sociological, not a statistical sense.

It must be observed in this connection that opposite policies of dominant groups may be perceived as discriminatory in varying circumstances—depending on the specific goals of deprived groups. If such a group seeks assimilation into the dominant group, it will contend that policies designed to maintain its separateness as a group—such as parallel school systems—are discriminatory, and that the concept "separate but equal" is a cloak for discrimination. If, however, the goals of the deprived group center around its survival, progress, and achievement of power, its members may regard efforts to assimilate them as discriminatory: as a denial of their right to maintain their distinctive language and culture. Afro-Americans have, until very recently, sought integration and assimilation, whereas the Germans in Bohemia made every effort to resist assimilation by the Czechs during the last few decades of the Habsburg empire and under the first Czecho-Slovak Republic.

The goals of a deprived group may center around abolishing existing or perceived discrimination, and escaping from an inferior social or economic role. These goals may be resisted by groups from whom concessions are demanded, and to that extent salience of identification will increase on both sides. Such an increase in salience may, however, lead to a shift in the goals of the deprived group. Policies hitherto resented as discriminatory may become acceptable, particularly if accompanied by goal-satisfaction in other respects. Afro-Americans, for instance, are becoming much more interested in upward mobility than in integration, while black leaders in South Africa are looking to see what advantages they can secure for their peoples from the government's policy of separate development.

Ethnic groups, nations, and proto-nations vary in salience and hence in their ability to survive and compete. Such salience is reflected in ethnic awareness, centering on the cherishing of a distinctive culture—and normally a language or dialect. Such a growth in salience may be accompanied by a shift from assimilationism to cultural or even political separatism: a development that seems to be at the root of the current difficulties on Cyprus.

The salience of a group also reflects the quality of its leadership. Whereas highly charismatic leaders generate the greatest short-term rise in salience, long-term gains are better consolidated by leaders who can develop doctrines and programs as well as formulate the "mission" of the group.

An increase in the salience of groups with competing interests, including ethnic groups as well as economic groups (such as employers and trade unions), brings with it an increased potential for conflict. Such conflict can, however, be averted by tradeoffs yielding improved goal-satisfaction.

As Eugen Lemberg has pointed out (1974), the relative salience of groups and their integrators is greatly influenced by changes in the prevailing ideology. Every ideology includes a rank order of important and unimportant human characteristics, biological and acquired, and a shift in this order may dictate a rearrangement of salient groups. Thus, during the religious and dynastic wars of the sixteenth and seventeenth century, it was unimportant what language you spoke and what nationality you professed: what was wanted was loyalty to a monarch and not conformity with a national culture. It was, on the other hand, of the highest importance whether you were a Catholic or a Protestant. After the Peace of Augsburg, many German princes invoked the rule of *cuius regio eius religio* to prescribe the religion of their subjects. A German who belonged to the "wrong" church for his locality had the choice of converting or moving. This arrangement did not prevent the Thirty Years War (1618–1648), in which more than half the people of Germany slaughtered one another in the name of

God—in which occupation they were encouraged by statesmen on the periphery (such as Richelieu and Gustavus Adolphus) with national axes to grind. The Peace of Westphalia (1648) left Germany religiously divided. With the advent of the Enlightenment, however, religion dwindled in importance and both rulers and subjects became more tolerant. By the end of the eighteenth century, Europeans were no longer ready to kill one another for religious reasons, a symptom of the growing "secularism" some conservatives deplore.

The French Revolution and the military expeditions it generated spread the new doctrine of nationalism, which in Central Europe took a form elaborated in the writings of Johann Gottfried Herder: the idea that each ethnic-linguistic *Volk* was an entity having its own personality and being entitled to its own independent state. Coreligionists of different tongues who had lived together peaceably for centuries suddenly found they could not stand each other and demanded political divorce (Lemberg, 1964, 1, pp. 171–74). The resulting tensions precipitated two world wars and major changes in the map of Europe.

While criteria for dividing a society in many alternate ways are always present in the abstract, it is ideology that gives them salience to become operative and to integrate conscious, goal-directed, and at least potentially conflicting groups. A political society may, for instance, consist of two or more different races, but its unity will not be disturbed without the spread of an ideology that asserts race to be a central factor in human identity (Lemberg, 1974). Analogously, religious quarrels and class warfare are motivated more by ideology than by religion or class as such. There are many countries where Catholics and Protestants as well as employers and workers manage to resolve their differences.

E. The Propensity to Discriminate

It has already been observed that, with few exceptions, members of any group tend to show preference for members of their own group—usually called the "in-group." The strength of preference varies directly with the salience of the group, and of groups with which it may come in conflict. Partial groups, such as professional societies, trade unions, and business associations, tend to limit preference to matters relevant to the specific interests of such groups. Groups that approach totality in their involvement of the personality, such as nations and ethnic groups that purport to define the whole identity of their members, exhibit a far stronger degree of preference.

The stronger the in-group preference, the greater the tendency to form an "enemy image." Such images figure prominently in the ideology of deprived groups seeking relative as well as absolute upward mobility, and also in groups who fear that goal-fulfillment of such deprived groups would threaten their status or existence. This "enemy image" will arise in the minds of members, will be communicated and expanded by word of mouth, and will figure prominently in its literature. Even when the official policy of group leadership is to seek accommodation with competing groups, the "enemy image" may nevertheless flourish. It becomes a target for hostility which, in its turn, generates defensive reactions on the part of the group cast in the role of "enemy."

The "enemy image" is not always pure fiction: it may have a factual basis in experienced discrimination, cruelty, or behavior suggesting inferiority. But once formed, it has a tendency to become exaggerated. When a deprived group seeks assimilation into or merger with a dominant group that is the subject of an "enemy image," the feelings of its members become psychologically ambiguous, reflecting a dialectic of fascination and hostility. Intergroup relations are then hard to stabilize, because any solution will prove emotionally unsatisfying in one way or another.

In relations among ethnic groups, in-group preference evokes a natural tendency to discriminate: to prefer members of the in-group as employees, business associates, and neighbors. The group occupying an inferior socioeconomic status will tend to demand legislation prohibiting intergroup discrimination, and will seek the support of allies in dominant groups for "equal opportunity employment" and "open housing" policies. American experience indicates wide acceptance of "equal opportunity" and even limited acceptance of "affirmative action"—that is, compensatory discrimination in favor of the deprived group. "Open housing" policies, on the other hand, are frequently opposed, circumvented, or exploited by real-estate speculators. Employment represents a partial aspect of life, whereas housing patterns may involve total groups and their cultures.

In an asymmetrical socioeconomic relationship, intergroup encounters are frequently marked by misunderstandings or even conflicts having their roots in class differences rather than characteristics of ethnic groups as such. Class friction reinforces the discriminatory tendencies of ethnic groups.

Situations may arise in which the members, if not the leadership of ethnic groups consider discrimination necessary for the preservation of the way of life, culture, and in extreme cases the existence of such groups. When ethnic groups are ranged in order of socioeconomic rank, those in the middle may find themselves jeopardized by demands and behavior of groups lower on the ladder, especially when the latter are directed toward "integration" rather than autonomous development. Members of Slavic ethnic groups in the United States, themselves victims of discrimination by WASP's and assimilated North Europeans, resist black invasion of their residential areas. The success of "blockbusters" and the "tipping" mechanism that transforms neighborhoods almost overnight are indications that American working-class whites are not willing to live in black-dominated areas (Grodzins, 1958).

The upper class and the intellectuals show far less resistance to integration, since blacks who can afford expensive housing or who have qualified for intellectual or artistic occupations—with the partial exception of ethnic chauvinists—tend to move into the same cosmopolitan culture. Those white liberals in the United States whose income and lifestyle protects them from association with "lower class" people of whatever group, tend to be ardent integrationists, since they can afford to advocate integration without jeopardizing their own way of living or personal safety. Socioeconomic groups that are economically marginal, on the other hand, including ethnic groups concentrated above—but not too far above—the poverty line, are the most sensitive to clashes of interest with groups both above and below them. Americans of Slavic or South European descent are thus commonly accused of racial bias, and some may indeed have acquired such bias through traumatic experiences. The stereotyped television bigot Archie Bunker is given the style of an "ethnic" although his identity is discreetly kept secret.

F. Group Leadership and the Problem of Salience

Group leaders normally find it advantageous to raise the salience of their group in the eyes of its own members. The ability of the group to pursue its goals and, more importantly, to support a hierarchy or even a bureaucracy, correlates positively with the internal salience of the group. The latter, in turn, is supported by the external salience of competing groups, especially those thought to be obstacles to attainment of group goals, and even more those that are the subjects of "enemy images." The external salience of a group thought—rightly or wrongly—to endanger the survival or culture of another group will, naturally, reinforce the internal salience of the group thinking itself jeopardized.

The internal salience needed to defend a status quo, to block political or social change, is logically less than that required to generate effective pressure for such change. The more revolutionary the desired change, the greater the group salience required to overcome resistance. Increased internal salience of the defending group will reflect the seriousness of the perceived threat to its survival.

Insofar as a group's identifiers and differentiators, its leaders, its goals, and its internal communications are generally known, a rise in its internal salience will usually be reflected in greater external salience. The increased capacity for action evoked by energetic leadership may then be offset by greater militancy and hostility of competing groups—a reaction to increased external salience of the first group.

When the goals of a group conflict with those of other groups in the same society, the ideal situation is to enjoy high internal salience while that of competing groups remains relatively low. In raising the internal salience of their group by emphasizing integrators, goals, and the "enemy image" when conflict is expected, the leadership must therefore decide whether to adopt a low profile, curbing external salience, or a high profile, amplifying external salience.

Increased external salience may prove a disadvantage in the long run, since it generates greater internal salience and solidarity in competing groups. In the short run, however, high external salience—especially if manifested in demonstrations or riots—may exact concessions from competing groups—especially if the latter are too disorganized to react effectively.

The strategy of goal-oriented group leaders will therefore be directed toward raising the internal salience of their own group, while avoiding acts that unnecessarily raise the internal salience of competing or conflicting groups. The specific plan will depend on whether a functional or a total group is involved.

Functional groups tend to seek their goals through bargaining, compromise, and political arrangement. Such transactions sometimes involve competing or related groups in the same general area (such as transport, education, or public health). At other times they involve totally unrelated groups, which may pool their influence to get legislation enacted, to elicit favorable administrative measures, or to shape public opinion for the joint benefit of all groups concerned. For total groups, however, the options of bargaining and compromise are not always open. When they are available, they may require major modifications of goals by one or more parties to a conflict. If A and B, for instance, are ethnic groups, and B seeks assimilation into A while A adheres to a doctrine of cultural or racial purity, it is clear that total goal satisfaction for both groups is out of the question. Seeking a solution other than a crusade, jihad, or civil war may therefore be a problem of mutual modification of goals rather than attempting maximum goal satisfaction at the expense of the other group.

G. Tactics and Manipulative Devices

The range of tactics that a group may effectively employ in carrying out its strategy necessarily is determined by its size, socioeconomic status, and political position in relation to other groups with which it competes or conflicts. While the ideal model of a plural society is more or less symmetrical—with its ethnic, religious, and economic groups in approximate balance, and none of them dominating or monopolizing state power—the typical real situation is characterized by the inequality of groups. Groups are found in various rank orders: large–small, powerful–weak, rich–poor, culturally central–culturally deviant, etc. Generally, the political system is the institutional expression of the group or coalition of groups forming a majority of the society, but there are important exceptions:

1. The state may be the expression of an ethnic, cultural, or racial group that forms a numerical minority, as is the case in South Africa—a situation being changed, however, by the creation of black governments and the subtraction of their citizens from the political system of the Republic.

2. The state may be controlled by a disciplined and closed party containing but a small fraction of the population—even though it purports to govern in the name of the proletariat or the people as a whole.

3. The state may be controlled by a military-charismatic dictator and the elite surrounding him, as is the case in most African and some Latin-American and Asian countries.

4. Political power, including the molding of public opinion, may be concentrated to a greater or lesser degree in the hands of an "establishment" representing particular regions, economic groups, cultural styles, or tribes. Such was the case in Czecho-Slovakia before the expulsion of its minorities, and there are those who claim that "establishment" rule exists in the United States.

The bureaucracy will as a rule cooperate with the controlling group, however defined, but it may generate a power base sufficient for it to survive or even initiate changes in political rule.

1. THE STAATSVOLK

A tactic available to a dominating group is to identify its particular interest with that of the larger society. A crude example of this tactic involving a partial group is found in the remark attributed to Charles E. Wilson, a Detroit executive appointed Secretary of Defense under President Eisenhower: "What is good for General Motors is good for America." Among total groups, a common phenomenon of this sort is that of the ethnic group which,

having secured control of territory containing a plurality of groups, assumes the role of a *Staatsvolk*. A *Staatsvolk* (there being, significantly, no English equivalent for this Central Eruopean term) shapes the state to fit its particular traditions and goals, treating other groups as "foreign" elements to be assimilated or, if that proves impossible, segregated or even expelled (Glaser, 1973c). The *Staatsvolk* makes its own language "official" and limits education in other languages. Proficiency in the official language, and more broadly conformity to the culture of the *Staatsvolk*, becomes a requirement for public employment, in which members of the *Staatsvolk* receive automatic preference. The classic example of this pattern before World War I was given by the Magyars, who tried to "Magyarize" their Slovaks, Serbs, Croats, Rumanians, and Ukrainians. After the war their precept was emulated by the Czech, Polish, and Rumanian elites, who evaded the minority treaties of the League of Nations.

Insofar as ethnic groups resist assimilation—which is generally the case with those that do not have a negative self-image—the policy of identifying the state with a particular dominating group is usually counterproductive. Groups that resist assimilation, or those that seek assimilation and find themselves denied it, become disaffected. Ethnic groups linked to majorities in neighboring states, such as the Sudeten Germans and the Poles in Czecho-Slovakia, usually want to join those states.

In a territory with a multiethnic and particularly a multiracial population, the *Staatsvolk* may conclude that assimilation of certain other groups—especially if large—could only be accomplished at the cost of demographic, cultural, and political adjustments that would extinguish its own life. The decision may therefore be made to exclude the out-group or groups from the body politic. Such a separation can only be stabilized, however, if the groups so excluded are permitted their own forms of political expression—their own bodies politic with formal status equivalent to that of the *Staatsvolk*. In this case the politics of the total area assumes the form of accommodation among a plurality of politically organized groups. This is the model toward which current South African policy is pointed.

2. THE CULTURAL STEAMROLLER

There is, however, a more subtle version of the *Staatsvolk* tactic. A state ideology is formulated that explicitly denies the relevance of ethnicity, national origin, race, or religion to membership in the body politic or participation in the cultural "mainstream." The dominant group nevertheless proceeds to impose its particular cultural pattern under the label of universality. This is the pattern in the United States, in which acculturation is defined as "joining the American mainstream," that is, getting rid of ethnic idiosyncrasies. It is typified by the fact that some Americans but not others are considered "hyphenated." Those of Anglo-Saxon descent never are. Cultural dominance is ensured by a monolingual education system, in which the study of "foreign" languages and cultures is postponed until the secondary level—when children's language-absorbing ability has already passed its peak. Strong pressure is brought on immigrant parents to speak and teach the children the national language rather than their own "foreign" speech: a concept that in itself contradicts the denial of ethnicity as a criterion of nationality.

Such a cultural steamroller may or may not be consciously directed. The United States' "melting pot" is stirred by many who, for want of breadth, sincerely believe the rump culture they represent is "the" American culture—to which nonconforming cultures have no contribution to make.

When the "common" culture of a complex society is dominated by a particular group and its cultural-linguistic heritage, the effect is to establish a hierarchy of ethnic groups in which social acceptability corresponds to resemblance to the preferred group. Thus, among those Americans who have openly vaunted the "superiority" of the Anglo-Saxon race, North Europeans are preferred because they are "most easily assimilable," followed by Northern Slavs, Southern Slavs, and—at some distance—Italians and Greeks (Adams, 1900; Robertson, 1972). The U.S. Department of State requires a Foreign Service Officer who marries a foreigner to submit a resignation, but the officer can usually arrange to have the resignation refused if the woman is British or French and of good family. The speech patterns of the dominant group become "standard," others being classified as dialects, and hence as signals of social inferiority. Since scholastic and academic tests, civil service examinations, and selection procedures in business and government all reflect the content of the "common" culture—which turns out to be the culture of the dominant group—they become automatic discriminators against members of other groups.

Elevation of the dominant-group culture to the status of a "common" culture affords a way to blunt intergroup conflict, since it is always coupled with protestations of absolute nondiscrimination (discrimination being automatic and invisible). But it also makes the dominant-group culture vulnerable to dilution and distortion by artists who actually belong to other cultures, but have particular gifts for simulation and adaptation. Such a culture loses its flavor of specific ethnicity and becomes dull and sterile: certain aspects, such as the American entertainment industry, may be dominated by cultural immigrants and hence an instrument of alienation rather than cohesion. Because the assimilants have alienated themselves from their own ethnic groups and cultures, without truly absorbing that of the host society, their art becomes inauthentic and neurotic (Robertson, 1972, pp. 229ff.). The assimilationists' tactic also reduces the internal salience of the dominant group so that its heritage becomes obscured, and it loses its capacity to formulate and pursue group-specific goals. Hence, concealment of dominant-group hegemony may be soothing in the short run, but it may also pave the way to cultural fragmentation and disintegration.

Deprived or oppressed groups, as well as those low on the socioeconomic ladder, find a different set of tactical alternatives available to them. In a constitutional system characterized by formal guarantees (such as the British and American Bills of Rights), deprived groups will usually find it advantageous to invoke and seek the broadest interpretation of their constitutional rights. This policy may lead to identification of and legislative action to prohibit hitherto unrecognized forms of discrimination, which is the main theme of recent Civil Rights legislation in the United States. (Specific cases will be further explored in chapters 20 and 21 on political and economic discrimination.)

3. TACTICS AVAILABLE TO DEPRIVED GROUPS

There are also several tactics which the leaders and communicators of a deprived group can employ to raise the internal saliency and militancy of their group. One of these is imputing to the dominant group or aggregation greater saliency and goal-directedness than it in fact possesses. In the United States, for instance, many discriminatory effects of the "common" culture in education, business, and public affairs are automatic and unintentional. Black political militants and a number of popular black writers, however, interpret them as evidence that all whites are involved in a massive conspiracy to keep the blacks deprived and subordinate.

A corollary tactic is to treat all other groups as though they formed a single monolithic majority. This tactic can also be observed in the United States, whose citizens of European descent are scattered among a wide variety of ethnic groups with major cultural, linguistic, and even physical differences. Many of these groups have experienced, and some still experience, discrimination, especially social and cultural, analogous to (though usually not so severe or protracted as) that suffered by blacks. But the prevailing tendency of black and, to some extent, Mexican-American and Indian radical writers is to treat the white community as essentially monolithic. They construct an "enemy image" of a universally privileged white society dedicated to maintaining its superior position over other racial groups. Because this image is so far from reality, it is hardly likely to evoke a "white front" against the blacks. The "echo effect" of black awareness and militancy has been the self-assertion of particular groups, especially those that diverge from the Anglo-Saxon model—such as German-Americans, Italian-Americans, Polish-Americans, and the like. Circumstances may at time propel such groups into tactical alliances with blacks, Mexican-Americans, and Indians.

Such policies, which raise the internal salience of deprived groups, improve their abilities to formulate and pursue goals and programs designed to widen economic, cultural, and educational opportunity. They also help to create awareness of group problems and needs among members of other groups. But such tactics may also narrow the choice of strategic options. By raising the salience of the integrators that unify the group and distinguish it from others, and by assigning these integrators positive rather than negative values, the militant tactic contitutes an option for autonomous or even separate development, closing the door on assimilation and integration. The apostles of *négritude* have outlined a culture rooted in the African somatic norm image: a culture that is inherently exclusive and in which whites are racially incapable of participating (Mphahlele, 1974, ch. 4). To the extent that non-Anglo-Saxon groups in the United States, and groups other than *Staatsvölker* in other countries, assert and win acceptance for the goal of autonomous cultural development—an inevitable corollary of a positive self-image—they create a situation calling for differentiation rather than amalgamation of school systems. Viewed in this perspective, interschool busing for "racial balance" appears as an exercise in absurdity. Who is going to balance whom and for what purpose?

The tactic of militant self-assertion involves the additional hazard of making intergroup co-operation more difficult to achieve. Assertion of goals and programs on the part of the de-prived group leads other groups to consider their own objectives—which may make those of the deprived group more difficult to achieve unless accommodation can be reached. Asser-tion of group identity and purpose, therefore, must always be coupled with due regard for the dignity and rights of other groups. While a denigrating "enemy image" clearly serves short-range tactical needs, it is likely to prove counterproductive—even to its authors—in the long run.

H. Manipulation of Ideology and Institutions

A tactic available to both functional and total groups but used to particular advantage by leaders and communicators of deprived ethnic groups is the manipulation of ideology and po-litical institutions. Those of liberal Western so-ciety can be easily manipulated because they were not designed for the social complex in which they must function today. The British and American Constitutions and those mod-eled after them were designed for what was thought, at least, to be a homogenous society. John Locke's political man was a merchant, barrister, or perhaps a scholar who frequented London coffee houses in the decades after the Glorious Revolution: a Tory or Whig capable of political revolution to preserve traditional liberties, but not of blueprinting massive social change, of machine politics in the style made famous in Jersey City, Chicago, and Memphis, or of directing media messages to the subli-minal.

The eighteenth-century political scheme of Western Europe and America, which liberal political institutions were designed to fit, did not contemplate a plurality of distinct groups demanding political expression. Nor did it in-clude masses susceptible to direct manipula-tion of their collective subconscious by charis-matic leaders. Where such masses and leaders appeared, as in the French and Russian Revo-lutions, liberals (such as the Girondists, Ca-dets, and even the Mensheviks) were routed by the revolutionary terror. Western democracy envisions political decision-making as the sum-mation of rational choices by individuals. This ideal is achieved only to the extent that voters and their parliamentary representatives are open to rational argument and not subject to orders by bosses or ideologues.

The obvious way to profit from this situa-tion is to demand for members of one's group the democratic rights of individuals while welding them into a centrally controlled bloc. In the United States, for instance, demo-graphic movement has placed blacks in stra-tegic positions in several large states. At times when other groups are evenly divided, black leaders with the authority to mobilize votes command a bargaining power beyond the pro-portionate size of their constituency. Similar leverage is at times exercised by Polish-Americans and Italian-Americans, while German-Americans—perhaps because of their traumatic experiences during the two World Wars—tend to resist mobilization (Lane, 1969; Levy and Kramer, 1972).

1. MINORITIES AND THE DOUBLE STANDARD

Another ideological tactic that can be in-voked within the framework of liberal democ-racy is to establish a concept of "minorities," permitting special privileges for members of groups so defined. The term "minority" is used with a variety of meanings and implications, and is therefore unscientific, but the concept has attracted a body of literature and therefore cannot be avoided. In the United States it has become a political concept. Blacks, American Indians, and Spanish-surnamed persons, many of whom have indeed experienced severe discrimination and deprivation, have been classed as "minorities"—to the exclusion of other persons who may be equally deprived but do not fit into these categories. Going beyond the concept of "equal opportunity employment," an "affirmative action" program mandated by national law calls for preference for its beneficiaries until certain quotas are reached. It is contended that such reverse discrimination is needed to compensate past discrimination against the "minorities." The possibility that hitherto undiscovered "minorities" might have equally serious complaints (e.g. in the area of cultural and linguistic discrimination) has not been explored.

The ideal competitive situation for an ethnic group or a nation, within a plural society or internationally, is a double standard for permissible and forbidden ideology and activities—which opens to the beneficiary group a wider range of options and narrows those of its competitors. Such an advantage has to some extent been achieved by the leaders of non-European groups and nations, both in the United States and in the United Nations.

In the United States, the nonethnic and nonracial base of American nationalism (see chapter 10,C) is invoked to express liberal disapproval of white exclusiveness in social and recreational activities—a disapproval that can be disarmed by the admission of "token" blacks. Any organization proclaiming as a purpose the protection of the interests of Americans of European descent—except particular groups identified as targets of discrimination, such as Portuguese and perhaps Italians and Poles—falls under the automatic taboo of "fascism." (This is a self-fulfilling criticism: because of the taboo, only persons with fascist tendencies or strong racial antipathies are likely to start or join such organizations.) Analogously, anthropologists who find genetic inheritance relevant to ability and performance

in American society are likely to be denounced as "racists" and sometimes even hooted off the academic platform. Because the tests used to select industrial employees measure ability to function within a European-based culture, it is contended that they should be dropped in favor of culturally neutral tests—as though such tests could be devised or, if they could, would be relevant to the needs of European-style technology and industry.

In short, action to raise the salience or assert group-specific goals for the ethnic spectrum loosely defined as the "American majority" is prohibited by the current liberal dispensation (Robertson, 1972, esp. ch. 23). Through the differentiation of "minority rights," however, such salience and goal-directedness is explicitly encouraged in certain groups, among whom Blacks, Mexican-Americans, and Indians, whether or not they are individually deprived, are the beneficiaries of government programs limited to their groups. Unofficially, the "minority" dispensation is also extended to groups firmly ensconced in the establishment such as American Jews. While the Jews have no government programs for their explicit benefit (and clearly do not need any), they do have several organizations exercising overt group-specific political pressure—on behalf of Israel, for instance—of a type that would be unacceptable if manifested by Germans or Anglo-Saxons.

The same double standard dominates the international arena. African and Asian nations, or more exactly the elites who purport to speak for them, are conceded unquestioned rights to self-determination and political power, while Europeans in those areas are denied—through the dogmatic application of territorial majoritarianism—the autonomy necessary for their own survival. Tribal and regional groups that fail to qualify for the magic title of "nation" are likewise denied self-determination: having supported the independence of Zaïre and Nigeria, the United Nations connived in the reconquest of Katanga and Biafra on the ground that the

larger political communities "needed their resources." Both the Security Council and the
General Assembly remained silent when India
seized Goa without a referendum to see
whether the Goans, who had been linked to
Portugal centuries before a unified India ever
existed, really wanted to join the Indian federation. Evidently, Africans and Asians are still
permitted to indulge in a kind of imperialism
long since prohibited to Europeans.

Hence, when confrontations take place on
the domestic and international levels, the prevailing ideology is managed so as to justify
groups and nations defined *a priori* as "deprived" in making and enforcing demands of
the broadest character. Violence is frequently
supported or condoned in the name of "popular revolution" or "national liberation." The actions of groups and nations defined *a priori* as
privileged, however, are held unjustified even
if they are defensive. The gains and losses to
the *individuals* involved are seldom considered
in such ideological judgment.

While criteria based on racial or somatic factors are taboo for European and American society, they are explicitly admitted by those
blacks who have committed themselves to African or Afro-American cultures. Julius M.
Waiguchu (1971, pp. 66–75) declares flatly that
the African heritage is genetically transmitted,
that the person of African descent who denies
it must pay the price of self-hatred and alienation, and that the Afro-American can never
be successfully assimilated into the "definitely
European" American culture. Conversely,
apostles of *négritude* hold that Europeans (a category that includes White Americans) can
never progress beyond a superficial understanding of black culture, and agitate for a

purge of black education from "corrupting"
white influences (Mphahlele, 1974, ch. 1).

2. SELF-DENIGRATION OF "PRIVILEGED" GROUPS

Ideological manipulation by or on behalf of
deprived groups reaches its apex when it leads
"privileged" groups to adopt a negative self-
image. The psychological effect may be so
strong that the paralyzation referred to in
chapter 1 ensues and the deprived groups find
themselves in a revolutionary position. The extent to which this has happened in the United
States is suggested by the title of a popular
book: *The Decline of the WASP* (Schrag, 1970).

As a result of ideological manipulation, deprived groups or coalitions of such groups may
have a higher degree or even a monopoly of
goal-directedness in a plural society. Politics of
dominant groups are then concerned with ap-
peasing and propitiating these goal-directed
"deprived" groups; assertion of goals by other
groups endangered thereby is placed under
taboo—a subtle form of political discrimination. A reason why many American blacks
have a particular animus against South Africans is that the latter provide an example of
goal-directedness on the part of European ethnic groups—an example that Americans of European descent might conceivably be tempted
to follow.

Ultimately, the tactics of any deprived
group will depend on whether it decides to
seek its goals through accommodation or conflict. If the latter, it should not count on the
prevailing ideology remaining manipulated to
its advantage, since in the long run any
group—deprived, privileged, or in between—
will shape ideology to suit its own interests.

7

SPECIFIC CHARACTERISTICS OF GROUPS

The previous chapter dealt with groups in general and the ways in which they interact. This chapter describes in some detail the specific characteristics of groups that figure throughout this book. Five main categories are examined: citizenship, race, ethnic, class, and caste.

Chapter 9 deals with the minority syndrome. A minority is not a particular kind of group in terms of membership, nor is it necessarily smaller in numbers than the group or groups that dominate a society. Minority status is rather a situation of deprivation and powerlessness in which a group of any composition may find itself. Because the minority syndrome has been the subject of extensive sociological analysis it is introduced and explained, although one of the authors would have preferred to omit the term minority from this book as methodologically inexact.

A. Citizenship Groups

This kind of group requires little explanation since it is defined as the body of people who owe allegiance to and enjoy the protection of a particular state. Citizenship is acquired at birth under one of two traditional rules. The first is *ius soli*, the principle that persons born within a state are birthright citizens of that state. The other is *ius sanguinis*, the principle that a child inherits the citizenship of his parents, or of one of them, regardless of where he or she is born. Most states employ a combination of these rules, with the result that many persons have dual citizenship or are able to choose upon coming of age.

Citizenship can be acquired by naturalization, usually after a required period of residence. It is generally lost if one becomes a citizen of another country or performs an act symbolic of such citizenship—such as voting in a foreign election or serving in foreign armed forces without permission of one's own government. Traditionally, a woman has acquired the citizenship of her husband upon marriage, and this rule is still followed by many countries. Some years ago, the United States abandoned this principle: a woman neither gains nor loses American citizenship through marriage. Foreign spouses of either sex are given preference for immigration visas and enjoy shorter waiting periods for naturalization than other aliens.

Political, social, and usually economic life within a country is dominated by the citizens of that country. As they are normally far more numerous than aliens, their intergroup behavior vis-à-vis aliens tends to be relaxed except where political conflicts are involved. So far as personal behavior is concerned, little spontaneous discrimination takes place on the basis of citizenship in the formal sense. Where discrimination against foreigners occurs, it is far more likely to be evoked by nationality or ethnicity as manifested by perceivable characteristics such as language or accent, manners and attitudes, dress, or somatic appearance. Such discrimination by no means disappears when the alien obtains his or her naturalization papers; conversely, it is usually not felt by aliens having the characteristics of citizens. In Japan, for instance, American students of Japanese descent find themselves treated as though they were or at any rate ought to be Japanese, even though their knowledge of the language is faulty or nonexistent. Americans with high linguistic proficiency and thorough knowledge of Japanese manners and attitudes, on the other hand, are seldom or never really accepted into Japanese society (Suzuki and Sakamoto, 1975).

Discrimination against aliens is essentially a matter of public policy expressed in legislation and regulations. An alien entering a country may be required to obtain an entry visa, or if he belongs to a group accorded visa-free entry (such as Americans in Western Europe), he must obtain a sojourn or residence permit to outstay the time allowed for tourists and business visitors. If he wishes to accept employment he must obtain a work permit, which some countries—depending on the labor market—are quite reluctant to grant. In many countries, foreigners are restricted in business activity, practice of professions, ownership of real estate, and the like. They may be deported if they become public charges or—in some countries—if they manifest objectionable behavior or opinions. Some of these strictures against aliens are considered in the chapters on functional types of discrimination.

As a rule, citizens within a country enjoy preferred status and greater access to wealth and power than noncitizens. There are exceptions to this rule. One is the case of Less Developed Countries (LDCs), especially former colonies, which are dependent upon expatriate

personnel to fill out the higher echelons of business and government. In this case, aliens from the developed countries who have usable skills or business acumen tend to enjoy preferred economic and social status. Such privilege often arouses hostility among the native masses, with the result that the expatriates may find themseves under physical attack (as has happened in Zaïre and Zambia) even though their sudden departure would leave economic and administrative chaos and even though they remain highly paid—sometimes, in part, to compensate for personal insecurity. It is the policy of most LDCs to replace expatriate technical and administrative personnel with their own citizens as rapidly as possible, and to require varying proportions of domestic participation in business undertakings.

Another situation in which at least certain aliens enjoy a preferred status is in countries under military or political occupation. In such countries (for instance, in Germany following World War II and in most of Eastern Europe today) members of the military occupation or the political apparatus of hegemony enjoy a privileged status with preferential living facilities, although they may be restricted in their activities and contacts by their own governments.

A further distinction, important in countries such as the United States and the United Kingdom, which are goals of immigrants, is that between aliens legally and illegally within the host state. While most states extend to aliens equality before the law and in the benefits of labor and social legislation, the illegal immigrant is normally unable to seek redress for wrongs suffered. Those who misuse the illegal alien can threaten to denounce him to authorities, which they do if he complains. This problem, particularly as it exists in the United States, is discussed at some length in the chapter on legal discrimination.

Generally speaking, the group behavior of aliens within a country is a set of responses to the situation in which they find themselves. If they are threatened, they will join forces to seek protection; if they are culturally isolated, they will congregate with their own kind. In the United States and Canada, immigrants from each country, insofar as they become organized, tend to merge into associations which are essentially ethnic ("hyphenated" rather than foreign) in character and in which they remain after they become citizens.

B. Racial Groups

1 THE TERM "RACE" IN POPULAR AND SCIENTIFIC USAGE

The term "race" is often used loosely in popular literature and political speech, especially in referring to groups that turn out on closer examination to be ethnically or linguistically defined and limited. We thus hear about the "Jewish race," the "Irish race," or the "French race"—despite the great variations in physical features within any of these categories—and even Lord Runciman used the term "race" with reference to the Czechs in his 1938 report, which became a prelude to the Munich Agreement. There are, on the other hand, the racial groups recognized by anthropologists as listed in the preceding chapter.

If the term "race" (or any other term) is to be of use in this book, it must be used with an exact and consistent meaning. Two central meanings, however, are present to a greater or lesser extent in practically all uses of the concept: first the idea of common descent, or concentrated biological relationship; secondly, the idea of inherent, genetically determined, characteristics.

Physical anthropologists, geneticists, and biologists use the concept race when they refer to an *inbreeding population* (or a cluster of inbreeding populations) whose biological history has produced a distinctive gene pattern. In the popular sense, however, races are defined in terms of social and political relationships. Racial characteristics are by scientific definition genetically determined characteristics associated with the physical identity of the inbreeding population concerned and consequently valid criteria for race differentiation. Race characteristics in the social sense are those mainly physical (somatic) characteristics in terms of which specific inbreeding populations are identified and individuals' biogenetic relationships with these populations are deduced.

2. RACE AS A BIOLOGICAL AND AS A SOCIAL CATEGORY

Where groups differentiated in terms of race as defined above live together and interact, race becomes a social category. It then refers to the way groups define one another's social positions in terms of certain physical or other characteristics which are believed to be genetically determined. The operative factor in this case is *belief*—one or both parties define the interaction as between groups with different biological histories and thus as groups with different inherent characteristics. Whether this idea agrees with biological facts is irrelevant. Biological descent (real or imagined) and consequently any characteristic considered to be genetically determined can thus become a criterion for social differentiation. This differentiation can result in the hierarchical ranking of the groups in respect to status, power, and prestige. Both somatic and sociocultural characteristics can be relevant in this connection. One group can even classify another group as a separate race because of that group's different lifestyle, as long as this categorization rests on the belief that the different lifestyle is determined by the group's different biological descent and biological history. Such a belief is supported by C. J. Jung's concept of "archetypes"—inherited building blocks of cultural content. The clearest examples of racial categorization are, however, based on somatic (bodily) criteria, of which skin color is by far the most common.

A relationship can therefore be defined as

racial when at least one of the groups in a contact situation views the differentiating factors
as determined by biological descent. The differences need not only be of somatic nature:
they can include lifestyle, level of development, national identity, etc., *as long as the parties concerned believe and accept that these nonphysical differences are also genetically determined*. In
this case, visible somatic differences may serve
as a signal for divergent culture patterns. Race
as a social category is thus a matter of belief
rather than objective biological fact.

3. SUBJECTIVITY IN ASSESSING "RACIAL" PROBLEMS

Historical and comparative anthropology
provides many cases in which social status is
ascribed, rightly or wrongly, to biological descent. In many such cases, status is related to
inbreeding within a particular lineage such as a
royal family rather than the inbreeding of entire groups having divergent norm images—
a term explained in C3, below. In prerevolutionary France, for instance, the aristocracy rationalized their privilege in terms of heredity
(Barzun, 1965, ch. 2). The socioeconomic deprivation inflicted on the lower castes in India
and Japan is likewise justified by supposedly
inferior descent, and much the same could be
said of the gypsies in much of Europe, the
Cholo in Peru, and the Negroes in northern
Brazil.

In South Africa, the social cleavage between
English- and Afrikaans-speakers is frequently
ascribed to differentiated "races." Sir Arthur
Conan Doyle, the creator of Sherlock Holmes,
described the Afrikaners as follows:

Take a community of Dutchmen (Hollanders) of
the type of those who defended themselves for fifty
years against all the power of Spain at a time when
Spain was the greatest power in the world. Intermix
with them a strain of those inflexible French Huguenots who gave up home and fortune and left their
country forever at the time of the revocation of the
Edict of Nantes. The product must obviously be
one of the most rugged, virile, unconquerable races
ever seen upon earth.

It must be observed at this point that much
discrimination that appears racial at first glance
may actually reflect rejection of incompatible
ethnic or class cultures. If two groups look different, the relatively deprived group is likely to
assign rejection by the relatively privileged
group to race prejudice, whereas race may
serve as a signal of expected (and desired) behavior rather than as a value in itself.

4. HOW THE TERM "RACE" WILL BE USED IN THIS BOOK

Unless otherwise qualified, the term race is
used here in its social meaning. Race in common usage means a group of persons who
regard themselves as constituting a genetically
related distinct group, regardless whether this
genetic interrelatedness is biologically true or
not. A group can also be defined and treated as
a separate race by others even though its own
members do not define themselves as such.
Race is only one of the five components of ethnicity in popular usage.

C. Nations, Nationalities, and Ethnic Groups

Ethnic diversity is and always has been one of
mankind's outstanding characteristics. The
course of contemporary history has been
largely determined by the way ethnic groups
arrange their mutual relationships (see chapter
12). Persistent conflict in most of the developing countries of Asia and Africa reflects the
fact that their peoples still spontaneously identify themselves in terms of ethnic character
rather than membership in political states.
What then is the nature of ethnicity, which
plays such a key role in the history of human
relationships?

1. CONTENT AND DEFINITIONS OF ETHNICITY

Ethnicity is made up of five basic components, namely the cultural, social, racial (biological), psychological, and historical. The *cul-*

tural component refers to the lifestyle, norms, value-system, and communication symbols (predominantly language) of a group. The *social* component involves the structuring of relationships between the members of the group—between parents and children, between the sexes, marriage partners, business groups, power groups, etc. The *racial* component refers to the biological history of the group—its objective biological affinity, as well as the way in which the group members define their heredity and genetic character vis-à-vis other groups. The *psychological* component has to do with the way the individual identifies with the group, his emotional involvement with it, as well as the process whereby group values and norms are internalized so that they become part of the individual's personality. The *historical* component integrates those shared experiences of the past which bind the group physically and emotionally, such as the persecutions and massacres visited on the Jews, the perennial struggle of the Kurds in Iraq for their independence, and the Boer-Afrikaners' military confrontation with Britain, to mention three examples among many. These components determine the group's ethos, particular lifestyles, values, tastes, and collective traits that make its culture different from those of other groups.

A few generally accepted definitions of the concept ethnic group will show what social scientists regard as the basic characteristics of such a group. According to Shibutani and Kwan (1965, p. 47), "an ethnic group consists of those who conceive of themselves as being alike by virtue of their common ancestry, real or fictitious, and who are so regarded by others." In his well-known work, *Race and Ethnic Relations*, Berry (1965, pp. 46–47) describes an ethnic group as follows:

> The ethnic group is a human group bound together by ties of cultural homogeneity. Complete uniformity, of course, is not essential; but there does prevail in an ethnic group a high degree of loyalty and adherence to certain basic institutions, such as family patterns, religion, and language. The ethnic group often possesses distinctive folkways and

mores, customs of dress, art and ornamentation, moral codes and value systems and patterns of recreation. There is usually some sort of object to which the group manifests allegiance, such as a monarch, a religion, a language or a territory. Above all, there is a consciousness of kind, a we-feeling. The ethnic group may even regard itself as a race, a people with a common ancestry; but the fact of such common descent is of much less significance than the *assumption* that there is a blood relationship and the *myths* which the group develops to substantiate such an assumption. Ethnic groups, of course, are not all alike, and none would embody all the features enumerated above. Some will emphasize certain of these characteristics to the exclusion of others. Religion may serve as an important object of allegiance to one and be of little import to another. Furthermore, ethnic groups are dynamic; the folkways may change, the institutions become radically altered and the object of allegiance shift from one trait to another, but the sentiment of loyalty to the group and the consciousness of belonging remain as long as the group exists. The ethnic group may not have its own political unit, it may have had one in the past, it may aspire to have one in the future, or its members may be scattered through existing states. Political unification is not an essential feature of the group. The term, accordingly, would include such groups as Arabs, French Canadians, British Canadians, Welsh, English, Flemish, Walloons, Scots, Jews and Pennsylvania Dutch. The Soviet Union itself is composed of more than a hundred ethnic groups, including, for example, Polish, Kazak, German, Armenian, Georgian, Tartar and Ukrainian.

Some social scientists, such as Milton Gordon, with reference to ethnic groups in North America (in Isajiw, 1974, p. 113), consider a sense of peoplehood (*Volkstum*) based on race, religion, or national origin, alone or in combination, the essential motor of ethnicity. Deutsch, in defining a "people" (1970, p. 85), emphasizes the storage, recall, and transmission of a common bank of information, as well as compatible symbols and habits in combining and processing information. All, however, seem agreed that consciousness of identity is of prime importance and often at the root of demands for political institutions. Wallerstein (1973, p. 168) sums up the matter:

By ethnic consciousness I mean the sentiment, shared by a group of people who define their boundaries in cultural terms (a common language, religion, colour, history, style of life, and the like, or a combination of these), that they must seek to assert or extend their rights in the political arena in order to defend possibilities for their continued existence as a group and/or to maintain or improve their material conditions.

2. ETHNIC ASSOCIATION—SOMATIC NORM IMAGES

Despite variations in the specific characteristics of ethnic groups—which lead some scientists to consider them imaginary since they cannot be exactly measured—they remain one of the most stable and persistent groupings in the world. They emerge through centuries of human association. They are not formed by contracts or organization meetings, and unlike the companies or clubs formed that way they cannot be dissolved or placed in bankruptcy. Ethnic groups are historical realities that cannot be stifled even by political cataclysms. Two world wars put an end to many states and brought forth new ones, but no ethnic groups vanished and no new groups appeared. Even in the United States, home of the proverbial "melting pot," a recent survey by the Bureau of the Census showed that more than half the population identify themselves with one of eight white ethnic groups—a survey that left out the smaller white groups and the non-white groups (*U.S. News and World Report*, June 4, 1973, p. 46).

Artificial ethnic integration usually involves forcing certain groups to abandon their lifestyles and adopt those of others—usually those of the dominant group or coalition (see chapters 17 and 18). Policies of this kind fly in the face of ethnic categories, which are "objective in that they are well established beliefs held in common by a great many people, and they are objective in that they exist independently of the desires of any particular individual. The classification of people in any community is a matter of consensus, and as far as any given individual is concerned, it is part of the external world to which he must adjust" (Shibutani and Kwan, 1965, p. 47).

Although ethnicity always includes a cultural component, a physical component can be present, especially where group members associate their ethnic identity with a specific physical appearance. Even members of a group lacking external features distinguishing it from all other groups will usually entertain an image, however vague, of the way they should look.

After analyzing 27 definitions of "ethnic group," Isajiw found the most common integrators to be ancestry, culture, religion, race (including physical traits), and language (1974, p. 117). He observes that race can function as a cultural trait if it is a subjective part of the individual's self-definition. Such self-definitions are cultural: the blond, nordic images of Brunhilde and Siegfried belong to the phase of German culture of which Wagner, Houston Stewart Chamberlain, and Hitler were exponents; they do not reflect German biology. In any case, each person is socialized into the cultural traits of his/her ancestors, whether or not these are biologically inherited.

Members of a group do not all look alike. Within any group, such as Zulus, Scots, Basques, or Mongols, there is a wide range of physical variation. Many people, however, have in mind clusters of physical features which represent the typical physical appearance of their ethnic group. In other words, what we find here is a sort of *physical norm*, a specific physical image which is perpetuated as a mental construct. The average Zulu has, for example, a vague, undefined image of what a typical Zulu should look like. In his paintings and illustrations of American life, Norman Rockwell has created a somatic norm image which many Americans have accepted. Actually, relatively few Americans (who may look WASP but actually be Polish or Italian) look like Rockwell's people.

Somatic norm images, which function to a

large extent subconsciously, are usually sufficient to identify macrogroups and their members. A Zulu can distinguish Europeans, Asians, and Africans, but he often cannot tell whether a European is German, English, or Italian or whether an African is a Tswana, a Xhosa, or a Zulu until he hears him speak. The subject of norm images is explored further in chapter 13,B2.

3. OVERLAPPING OF ETHNIC AND OTHER GROUPS

Ethnic group and minority are also not synonymous: The Afrikaners, for example, are a distinct ethnic group in the Republic of South Africa, but they have become the dominant sociopolitical group in a country containing various ethnic groups. Most of the latter (for example the Xhosas and the Zulus) constitute minorities in the generally acceptable sociopolitical sense in the white areas of South Africa, though they are achieving dominant status in their own homelands. It would thus not be wrong to describe the latter as *ethnic minorities* as long as it is realized that not all ethnic groups are minorities or vice versa. Marden and Meyer (1968, p. 24) have the following to say in this connection:

Ethnic is an increasingly popular term in the writing about minorities and in the vocabulary of those engaged in action on behalf of minorities. Often it is used popularly as equivalent to the term *minority*. This is, of course, inaccurate. *Ethnic* is a term which emphasizes the cultural ethos (values, expectations and behavior) of a group and formerly, quite properly, was limited in reference to groups whose cultural characteristics are their prime distinguishing factor. Dominants as well as minorities are ethnic groups. An ethnic group, unlike a nationality group, is a population which has preserved visible elements of a tradition without primary reference to former loyalties to a nation-state. The French emigrés who came to New Orleans after the French Revolution were a nationality group. The present French-Canadians are an ethnic group. Minority status may strengthen ethnicity, just as ethnicity may contribute to minority status.

Class and caste are basically power, prestige, and status hierarchies and the dividing lines between them can cut across ethnic boundaries. In the United States, for instance, the entrepreneurial and managerial class still contains a strong WASP element, but many non-WASPs have entered it and some have reached the top. Moreover, ethnic groups often have their internal class or caste stratification; their elites and their occupational castes. An attempt in the late 1930s by Rexford Guy Tugwell's Resettlement Administration to move Jewish garment workers from Manhattan slums to a model city in New Jersey failed because the garment workers formed socially distant caste-like groups differentiated by the price ranges of the clothing they made. Conversely, in multi-ethnic Hindu society, major caste lines cut across ethnic and linguistic boundaries.

Various countries having a plurality of ethnic groups find various structural arrangements to avoid or settle interethnic conflict (see chapter 12). In some cases there is a gap between theory and practice: in the USSR, for instance, ethnic pluralism serves as a cloak for russification. In the Republic of South Africa, the policy of the dominant whites is to provide each major nonwhite group its territorial base or homeland, with administrative autonomy that can evolve into political independence. The groups lacking a territorial base (Coloured and Asians) will associate with the white group in a plural system based on personal rather than territorial autonomy. In the United States, on the other hand, the concept of assimilation via the "melting pot" still dominates official thinking, though it is today increasingly challenged.

D. Classes, Social and Economic

Class is a form of group differentiation found in all countries and in all societies. In its widest meaning it refers to the stratified structure of a society in which groups have different shares of wealth and property, power, income, prestige, and status. Beyond this generalization, however, there is disagreement. Sociologists tend to see classes in terms of a clear rank order, classifying people in terms of their socioeconomic level rather than their function. Economists, on the other hand, view classes in terms of their relationship to the means of production; a small and not particularly successful entrepreneur might have a lower income than a highly skilled worker, yet the first would still be technically a "capitalist," the second a "proletarian." People who occupy identical or similar positions in the economic system, however, tend to crystallize into classes in both the sociological and economic sense.

Before the definitions of classes to be used throughout this book are introduced, some enlightenment may be drawn from the ideas of Karl Marx, Max Weber, and Talcott Parsons about classes. As summarized by David R. Weeks:

Marx saw classes as aggregates of people who are in the same relationship to the means and relationships of production—the way in which things are produced and the system of exchange and distribution. And the most important feature of any system of production is who owns and controls it. Marx saw capitalist society as ultimately divided into two mutually opposed groups whose interests were *irreconcilably divergent:* the bourgeoisie or owners and the proletariat or non-owners. . . .

Max Weber . . . sees classes in terms of their relationship to economic power, to their "amount and kind of power, or lack of such, to dispose of goods or skill for the sake of income in a given economic order." . . . "Property" and lack of "property" are therefore, the basic categories of all class situations." . . . "In our terminology, 'classes' are not communities; they merely represent possible, and frequent, bases for communal action." . . .

Talcott Parsons describes social class as a reflection of social position and social prestige: "A class may then be defined as a plurality of kinship units which, in those respects where status in a hierarchical context is shared by their members, have approximately equal status. The class status of an indi-

vidual, therefore, is that which he shares with the other members in an effective kinship unit." (Weeks, 1972, pp. 44–46)

While Parsons does not subscribe to Marx's doctrine of inevitable class conflict, he does consider that class membership is hereditary. Differential access to opportunity and pressures exerted on young people tend to limit interclass mobility.

Although social scientists often differ in their definition of classes, if can be generalized that a class is a large category of people who have the same socioeconomic status in relation to other segments of their community or society. The most important objective criteria for class differentiation are types of occupation, income, material possessions, educational level, and political power—not necessarily in this sequence. Classes tend to overlap and merge, especially in high-mobility countries such as the United States. There may be pronounced variations within classes; certain unionized workers in the United States have achieved wages providing middle-class incomes through the power of their unions to manipulate the market. The result is to deny employment to or lower the wages of other workers not so organized. Insofar as classes represent a continuum, however, the upper pole consists of the landed or moneyed aristocracy plus the upper reaches of the bourgeoisie—the financiers, managers of large companies and a few top professionals—while the bottom pole consists of the unemployable *lumpenproletariat* and next to them the mass of casual, unskilled, slum-dwelling laborers.

People show their awareness of class membership by self-classification when asked by field investigators and by joining political parties and associations that defend class interests. Bottomore (1969, p. 526) is probably right when he states:

Social surveys have shown plainly that most people are familiar with the class structure of their society, and are aware of their own positions within it.

Equally, it has been shown that class membership is still the strongest single influence upon a person's social and political attitudes; and that the major political parties in most countries represent preeminently class interests.

It would be impossible to devise a taxonomy of classes to which some objection could not be raised. To avoid confusing the reader, however, it is necessary that a single set of meanings be followed throughout this book. The following five-class system has therefore been adopted with no pretensions of infallibility:

1. *The Aristocracy:* This is the remnant of the old royalty and nobility, whose traditional functions were to govern and to lead forces in battle. In countries with feudal or semifeudal landholding systems the aristocracy persists in the class of *Junkers, haciendados, fazendeiros,* or however the landed proprietors may be called. In more modern countries the aristocrat is a *rentier*, perhaps with a title or predicate, who lives from inherited wealth—though he may have a profession or some business directorships. Such an aristocrat may devote his energies to public service, as did the Pitts, the Palmerstons, and Winston Churchill; Theodore and Franklin Roosevelt, and several Rockefellers, Harrimans, and Vanderbilts. Or he may achieve notoriety through conspicuous consumption, like the "jet setters" Tommy Manville, Ali Kahn (whom his father excluded from the Aghaship), and the deposed monarchs Farouk and Bao Dai (quondam "emperor" of Vietnam).

2. *The High Bourgeoisie* or entrepreneurial and managerial class. This group includes those who have created or who have inherited and actively manage large businesses. It also includes managerial personnel who started at middle-class levels and have risen to the highest echelons of corporate structures and—in view of the increased role of government—the highest ranks of the civil service and the military, who frequently slip into corporate jobs upon leaving government service. Professionals who achieve the highest levels of material reward (such as fashionable surgeons and

psychiatrists, lawyers with corporate or society practices, stage and screen stars, and writers of best-sellers) may move up into the high bourgeoisie, often to drop out of it if they lack business ability or prudence. In modern corporate society, the key to climbing the organizational ladder may be skill in bureaucratic politics rather than knowledge, originality, or inspiration. The high bourgeois, in other words, may be a bureaucratic rather than enterprising type: a conservator rather than an innovator. Since conspicuous consumption is almost a categorical imperative of high bourgeois behavior and progressive taxation discourages capital accumulation, only the richest can relieve their children of the need to earn a living, thereby opening to them the option of joining the aristocracy—or, alternately, one of the several radical movements, "parking their sports cars and marching to the barricades," as was said of the youthful demonstrators at the 1968 Democratic Convention in Chicago.

3. *The Middle Class.* Traditionally, this was the class of small merchants, professionals, shopkeepers, artisans, and independent farmers. But, as Ralf Dahrendorf has pointed out (1959), these groups have been gradually replaced by a "new middle class" of salaried employees and officials, first in industry and then in public administration and commerce. These employees and officials, including many professionals in group practice, do not own the capital with which they work (except indirectly, if they accumulate share holdings) and are thus proletarians in the strictly economic sense. But they are wholly bourgeois in outlook. They distinguish themselves and observe social distance from the working class, and hope to rise toward the high bourgeoisie or at least hope that their children may do so. Because of the status difference between white-collar and manual work, the more conventional would rather accept—or see their wives and children accept—low-paid clerical positions than engage in manual trades producing considerably higher income. The conformism of the middle class in America, West Germany, and elsewhere is such that many of its

young people revolt and experiment with alternative lifestyles.

4. *The Working Class, or Proletariat.* It was once universally and is still common thought that everyone below the middle class belongs to a single "lower class," to which middle class people have often attributed vulgarity and lack of culture. Under the influence of sociologists such as Gans and Hollingshead and writers ideologically as far apart as Banfield and Herbert Marcuse, a distinction is made between the working class and the lower class. The working class includes all skilled industrial and agricultural manual workers, people in service occupations (cooks, waiters and waitresses, bus drivers, mail carriers, etc.), and unskilled workers insofar as they are normally steadily employed.

5. *The Lower Class.* The relation of the lower class to the productive system is essentially marginal. In some countries, including the United States and Brazil, it contains heavy concentrations of racial and cultural minorities, though it is not defined racially as a class. Being to a large extent frozen out of more lucrative jobs—often because they have no chance to qualify—its members take the menial jobs no one else will do. Or they may subsist on welfare doles when these are available. A lower class person may achieve considerable short-range wealth through illegal activities such as making book, prostitution, the drug trade, or even larceny or robbery. But he or she necessarily remains within the lower class, the essential characteristic of which is lack of a stable relationship to the economic system (see chapter 15, C5).

Marx to the contrary, the classes within a capitalist society are not necessarily antagonistic, though they can become so if persuaded by ideologists that their interests are contradictory. Classes are, indeed, an inevitable reflection of the division of labor in a managerial-technocratic society. The experience of socialist societies shows that they too develop classes: different from those in capitalist society but quite as clearly defined (see Djilas,

1974, *The New Class*). A class system necessarily entails inequalities of wealth and power, but these inequalities are not invidious so long as they reflect the relative valuation of occupations in a free and competitive market, and so long as all members of the society have the *opportunity* to achieve upward social mobility.

Of the five classes, only the lower class presents a social problem in its mode of existence. Public policy should be directed toward helping lower-class people to move out of that class through education and economic opportunity. But it is probably utopian to expect to abolish it altogether, whether under capitalism or under socialism, since some people will always be unable to fulfill their own material needs.

E. Castes

The caste system is a complex structure of social ranking and hierarchial status gradation, the largest example being that of the Hindu society in India. Caste systems are also found in Japan, Ceylon (Sri Lanka), Burma, and Pakistan. Some social scientists claim that even the American white–black differentiation, as well as the European–native relationships of colonial societies, exhibit certain typical caste characteristics. But the Hindu caste system of India is regarded as the archetype. Egon Bergel (1962, p. 35) observes that "the caste system represents a logical extreme, approaching the ideal type of absolutely inflexible order." George and Achilles Theodorson (1969, p. 38) define the caste system as follows:

A closed social stratum based on heredity that determines its members' prestige, occupation, place of residence, and social relationships. The castes of a society form a hierarchy of superior-subordinate ranks and relationships that is justified by religion, law, and magic. Each caste is endogamous, and social relations between members of different castes are severely limited and formalized.

The caste system is usually described as a system of stratification; extremely rigid, birth-ascribed (with status assigned according to group descent and not individual achievement), and with a minimum of individual mobility. According to Berreman (1967, pp. 48–67),

That a caste system is comprised of groups implies that each rank in the hierarchy is shared by socially distinct aggregates of people. These people recognize that they comprise discrete, bounded ranked entities. The size and degree of corporateness of such groups vary widely. The members usually share a group name; always they interact with one another in characteristic ways; always there are symbols of group membership ranging from skin colour to cultural features such as language, occupation, dress, place of residence, and the like. Only members of the group are one's peers. Where group affiliation is relevant, individual attributes are irrelevant. . . . That membership in castes is determined by birth means that an individual is assigned his lifelong and unalterable status according to his parentage. . . . That a caste system is hierarchy implies that it is a system of differential evaluation, differential power and rewards, and differential associations; in short, a system of institutionalized inequality. . . . Castes are ranked, ultimately, in terms of differential 'intrinsic worth' ascribed to those who comprise them. . . . Rank is expressed and validated in interaction between persons; . . . Who may be one's friend, one's wife, one's neighbour, one's master, one's servant, one's client, one's competitor, is largely a matter of caste. Every relevant other is a superior, a peer, or an inferior, depending upon caste. Only within the caste is status equally found.

Surajit Sinha believes "that the stability of the caste system cannot be attributed decisively to a single set of factors like the mode of production, cultural pluralism, the doctrine of karma and the like." He points out that instead of the perfect coordination of roles among interacting groups, which is the ideal objective of the Hindu caste system, recorded studies show much evidence of jostling for power, prestige, and economic advantage among the castes.

The status hierarchy of the caste system depends less on rituals and religious beliefs than on the distribution of land-holding and power (Sinha, 1967, p. 97).

The caste system is basically a religious institution which has evolved over more than 2500 years. Aryan-speaking groups that conquered India used it to perpetuate their dominance over the non-Aryan natives. The names of the four classic or main castes appear for the first time in the late Vedic hymns: Kshatriyas, Brahmins, Vaishyas, and Sudras. They correspond roughly to aristocratic warriors, priests, commoners and slaves. The Brahmins gradually rose to the top, displacing the Kshatriyas. The Vaishyas became predominantly traders and the Sudras servants and agricultural workers. The Sudra caste later absorbed the skilled workers. The hierarchical structure of Hindu society contains a fifth basic component, namely the untouchables (*Harijans*). The latter are not a fifth caste but literally an outcaste, traditionally treated as a pariah group.

The four main caste groups, or *varnas*, as well as the Harijans, are divided into specific castes or *jatis*. About 25 of these are general, being found throughout India; the number of local castes has been estimated as high as 3000 (Hutton, 1946, p. 128). There are Hindu as well as non-Hindu castes, the latter being forced to accept a status of inferiority.

The essential operative unit in the Hindu caste society is not the major group—the *varna*, or the "untouchable" group—but rather the *jati*: a small endogamous group which practices a traditional occupation, is of close common descent, and enjoys a certain measure of cultural, ritual, and juridical autonomy. *Jatis* are mostly locally defined communities consisting of a number of families living in the same village or complex of villages. Collectively the *jatis* form a social system with an extremely complex structure. The larger divisions are subdivided both vertically and horizontally with lines crisscrossing from all angles. Philip Mason refers to a recent study in

South India by André Beteille describing a village of 349 households.

It is a village in which some generations ago a ruling sovereign endowed a community of Brahmins, whose duties were to study the scriptures and pray; until lately the Brahmins owned most of the land. At first sight, there are three groups in the village—92 Brahmin households, 168 non-Brahmins (or, as the Brahmins would say, *Sudras*, people of the fourth *varna*), and 89 Harijan, or "untouchable" households. But on examination, each of these main groups is divided, the 92 Brahmin households into no less than twelve *jatis*—groups who marry within the group—the 168 Sudras into 25 *jatis*, and the 89 "untouchables" into four *jatis*. Something of the kind would be found in most Indian villages. (Mason, 1970a, p. 142)

The fixing of a person's status for his or her entire life through the incident of birth into a particular major group and *jati* is reinforced by Hindu theological notions such as *karma* and *dharma*. The idea of karma teaches a Hindu that he is born in a particular subcaste because he deserves to be born there, as a reward or punishment for his deeds in a previous incarnation. Had he behaved better during his previous incarnation he would have been born in a higher caste. The caste hierarchy thus registers the state of each individual's soul. Dharma has many meanings, one of which is "that which is right or moral." A person who accepts the caste system and the rules of his or her particular subcaste is living according to dharma, while anyone who questions them is violating dharma. In addition to rewards and punishments in his life, the person who fulfills dharma will in his or her next incarnation be born in a high caste, rich, whole and well endowed. The violator will be reborn in a low caste, poor, deformed, and ill endowed. Caste therefore, indicates the kind of life a person led in his or her previous incarnation.

Because the so-called Untouchables or *Harijans* form the lowest stratum in traditional Hindu society they suffer a large variety of disabilities and discriminatory practices. This group originated when Aryan-speaking peoples settled in Northern India more than 2000 years ago and downgraded the less developed natives to a class of servants and slaves. Mahatma Gandhi named them Harijans (literally children of Hari or God). Since 1935 they have been referred to as "scheduled castes." The Harijans include a large number of separate castes and *jatis*. As more than 85 percent of the Harijans live in rural areas, where the caste system remains most rigid, it is obvious that they are destined to suffer disabilities, disqualifications, and inequalities for a long time to come.

Egon Bergel (1962, p. 65) summarizes the Hindu caste system in an eight-point model, on which it would be difficult to improve:

1. The caste system rests on religious grounds; castes are ordained by divine decision.
2. Also for religious reasons a person must remain in his caste and carefully fulfill the caste obligations or he will be punished by being reborn into a lower caste; correct ritual behavior leads to his reincarnation in a higher caste (double religious sanction).
3. Intermarriage or breach of ritual obligations leads to loss of caste; in extreme cases the person becomes an outcast, an untouchable (social sanction).
4. Caste status is inherited and cannot be changed.
5. Members of a caste (or better, subcaste) have approximately equal status.
6. A specific occupation is assigned to each caste; members of other castes cannot engage in the same trade.
7. The castes are hierarchically stratified in the same way as classes in a class system.
8. The caste system is recognized as valid by all castes, including the underprivileged.

The operational aspects of the caste system are discussed in chapter 16,B.

The concept of caste is often extended to group-differentiated situations outside India, especially where a rigid system of social stratification based on heredity is found. There are numerous societies that exhibit one or more features of Bergel's eight-point model. Some researchers have seen castelike elements in black–white relations in the American South, though it would be inaccurate to speak of the American social system as a whole as a caste society. In this connection a well-known Indian social scientist, Surajit Sinha, has written:

One may agree with Berreman that there are indeed some parallels between the relationship of the Negro and White Americans in the United States and of the upper castes and "Untouchables" in India. Besides endogamy and status stratification, the concept of pollution in sexual relations, commensality and residence, and belief in the inheritance of the bio-physical qualities along racial or ethnic lines, are common properties of the two sets of relationships. In other words, it makes some sense to say that the Negroes are the "Untouchables" of American society. However, a Hindu villager from India will in vain look for jatis with hereditary occupations such as pottery, basketry, weaving, smithing, leather-work and the priesthood in the American environment. He will also find that within his "varna" rank of white or Negro, his social status is guided mainly by his personal attainments in wealth, occupation, education and the like and not by the ascribed status of his extended kin or jati group. (1967, pp. 98–99)

Sinha further contrasts modes of integration. A non-Hindu tribe in prolonged contact with the Hindu peasantry evolves into a caste with specific economic functions and social rank. Yet even when "fully" integrated the tribe retains its corporate identity and cultural uniqueness. This is very different from the "melting pot" integration in the United States, where ethnic groups face social pressures that tend to fragment them into nuclear families competing within a mobile, impersonal, and atomistic open-class society.

On balance, the differences between the Indian and American systems outweigh the similarities. The religious sanction that lends the 2500-year-old Indian system its stability is lacking in the United States, where few believe in reincarnation and hardly any of these in a karma expressed in caste. While deprived groups in India, except for modernizing leaders and their following, accept institutional inequality, those in America are united in fighting social stratification. The identity of caste with occupation does not exist in America; formerly typically Negro occupations such as redcaps (luggage porters) and sleeping-car attendants have almost disappeared. There is a concentration of blacks in low-paid occupations, but no absolute barrier to their advancement: Blacks work as unskilled laborers and skilled craftspeople, as white-collar employees, government officials, artists, teachers, and administrators. The socioeconomic variation within ethnic and racial groups is generally greater than that between groups.

The traditional Hindu caste system, characterized by rigid segmentation and social immobility based on ascription by birth, has been described as one pole on a scale of mobility and equality. The other pole is a completely "open" society free from ascriptive structuring, stratification, or ranking, in which every person enjoys an equal opportunity to rise according to his or her abilities in the power, status, and reward structure.

The extremes on any linear scale are theoretical: nowhere in the world will a society be found corresponding to either polar model. The caste system in India still exists, but it has lost the rigidity and unyielding grip on the peoples of India that it had as recently as two generations ago. It is of interest to us as a model, since castelike relations can be found in a number of countries. The Aborigines of Australia, the Maoris of New Zealand, the Burakumin of Japan, the Gypsies of Western Europe, the Coloureds of South Africa, the Negroes in South America, the Jews in Russia, American Indians in North and South America and the Jamaicans in Britain are only a few of the deprived groups exhibiting aspects of caste status, though they are also racial or ethnic groups.

Thus, while there are various kinds of

groups having characteristics that can be described and compared, these categories are overlapping rather than mutually exclusive. For this reason a particular group may be discussed in several chapters. It may be a group of citizens or aliens, a racial group limited to or concentrated in a particular class, or a caste or quasi-caste, in almost any combination.

8

BEHAVIOR OF GROUPS IN INTERACTION

Having considered the behavioral dynamics of groups as such and the characteristics of several kinds of groups, we shall now turn to the way groups behave when in contact with one another, particularly in situations of competition and conflict. Most of the case material, in this chapter and those that follow, involves the interaction of nations, nationalities, and ethnic groups (as defined in chapter 6) as well as racial groups as a social category (as explained in chapter 7). The behavior patterns observed in these groups are, as might be expected, also found in other groups such as tribes, clans, classes, and castes.

Four fundamental psychosocial forces are found in nations, nationalities, and ethnic groups and in racial groups insofar as the latter acquire ethnicity and thus become internally rather than externally defined. They are: 1. *consciousness of kind*, that is, of a distinctive sociocultural identity; 2. a *sense of historicity*, an idea of common origin and destiny, exemplified by heroes and epics and, frequently, a sense of mission; 3. the *primacy of self-interest*, and 4. the claim to *self-determination* and to *perpetuation of the group* (these claims have been recognized as human rights, particularly group perpetuation, denial of which constitutes the crime of genocide (see chapter 4, C).

Knowledge of these forces, which are closely linked with the components of ethnicity

(chapter 7) and the national integrators (chapter 10), should aid understanding of the typical intergroup behavior patterns (section B). Such knowledge helps us to see why social groups in contact are ethnocentric, why they are prejudiced about one another, why they maintain social distance, and why their concepts of other groups are often stereotypes. It will also help us to understand phenomena such as separatism, segregation, inequality, discrimination, racism and racialism, pluralism, and the ranking and stratification of people in classes, castes, and minorities. At the same time light will be thrown on the integrative processes of group interaction, especially those of assimilation and amalgamation. Hence, a sound knowledge of these psychosocial forces will enable us to understand better why groups in contact are attracted or repelled, and the way groups seek and find compromises between their conflicting interests.

A. The Universality of Group Differentiation

The mass media sometimes seem to suggest that group conflict, discrimination and inequality, social deprivation, and group prejudice are social ills limited to the United States and South Africa. Closer examination of the 150-odd states that belong to the United Nations, however, should make it clear that these negative aspects of group contact and group differentiation exist almost everywhere. The human and social characteristics that produce these phenomena with universal regularity could hardly be explained by mere coincidence. Analysis of propaganda that encourages these types of negative behavior suggests that the propensity toward it springs from certain basic, biologically rooted human needs and drives. It may be granted that many cases of discrimination, prejudice, and unequal treatment reflect culturally induced (i.e. learned) behavior. But why do so many people "learn" so easily and why can people apparently never be "induced" to relinquish these practices altogether? One will also seek in vain for established peoples and tribes who in dealing with other peoples and tribes exhibit no sign of ethnocentrism and prejudice. Consciousness of kind and of identity is a universal social imperative, the emotional wellspring of group self-respect as well as group differentiation.

The history of discrimination and inequality revolves around a basic theme: people's unequal positions in the competition for scarce goods and thus in society's reward, status, and opportunity structure. No normal person can stay very long out of this competition, on the outcome of which the quality of life greatly depends. Where families and clans or larger groups such as classes, castes, tribes, ethnic groups, and nations depend for their existence on the same material and nonmaterial resources, group differentiation and some degree of competition and conflict are unavoidable.

Intergroup differentiation and discrimination are observed in a continuum ranging from mild or even harmless forms to extreme practices such as slavery, forced labor, and genocide. Certain forms of discrimination and inequality are formally institutionalized in laws, proclamations, regulations, and adminis-

trative decisions. Others, although less formally institutionalized, are interwoven in the social, economic, and political structure and thus exert a stronger hold on persons than legal measures.

A visitor from another planet could not fail to be impressed with the complex way mankind is segmented. Our visitor would soon note barriers separating social groups called class, tribe, caste, community, ethnic group, and nation, as well as categories based on sex, age, and race. A prominent social scientist has the following to say about segmentation:

> All societies are differentiated along class lines, communal lines, or both. (Class divisions refer to objective group differences in wealth, income and occupation. Communal divisions refer to ascriptive criteria, including racial, tribal, religious, linguistic, and ethnic differences.) At least one such socially differentiating characteristic is found in all societies. . . . when a sizeable proportion of individuals who share some class or communal characteristic become subjectively aware of their similarity to other such individuals, value that similarity positively, and attribute some importance to it in defining their relations with individuals who do not share that social characteristic—then these social differences may be said to draw people into segmental division or segments. (Nordlinger, 1972, pp. 6–7)

1. EQUALITY AS A UTOPIAN CONCEPT

It would take a very naive utopian to believe that our segmented world, peopled by human beings involved in ceaseless competition for wealth, honor, and prestige, will ever rise above intergroup competition and tension. Equally slim is man's chance of creating societies free from one or other form of individual or group ranking, stratification, inequality, and discrimination, and where all occupy the same vertical position on the socioeconomic totem pole. On the contrary, an observer of the current scene (Ina C. Brown, 1973, pp. 1–2) argues that there is less threat of a nuclear holocaust than of social disintegration. She fears "a breakdown of consensus within national boundaries. The groups involved sometimes differ in race, but more often in nationality, religion, language, class, or ideology, and sometimes in a combination of two or more of these."

A fact often unnoticed, because we are so used to it, is that the average person's life is dominated by differences and conflicts between the groups to which he belongs and those to which he is an outsider: those called in-groups and out-groups by sociologists. So long as interpersonal and intergroup competition persists there must be winners and losers. Consequently, members of the society will find themselves, individually and collectively, in unequal positions in the power, status, reward, and opportunity structure. Such inequality always implies a form of ranking, stratification, and social hierarchy. As Melvin Tumin observes: "The fact that social inequality is found everywhere suggests that there are univeral features in social structures that generate inequality" (Tumin, 1967, p. v.).

The total elimination of social inequality remains an illusive dream unlikely ever to become a reality. Leonard Reissman (1973) has pointed out that revolutions in the name of equality usually produce new social hierarchies with newer brands of inequalities and a different, but unequal, redistribution of rewards and privileges. Attempts at perfect equality in nineteenth-century utopian colonies and some of the present-day "communes" are minuscule short-lived exceptions that prove the rule. Theoretically egalitarian states such as the United States, the USSR, and Israel are characterized by the rhetoric rather than the substance of equality.

Dennis Wrong (1972, p. 101), in an observation that calls to mind an ancient Greek method of choosing public officials, argues that "equality of opportunity could literally be achieved in full only by a method of allocating individuals' to social positions that was strictly random, such as drawing lots." A society with guaranteed social equality has no more chance of materializing than distribution of power or wealth by lottery has of being accepted in any society.

2. PATTERNS OF STRATIFICATION

Social inequality is expressed in social stratification, a phenomenon that is apparently universal in social life. Don Martindale (1972, p. 209) points out that:

No human group has been known in which differential influence by some members over others has been completely absent and in which differential claims on the prizes of social life have been unknown. Human stratification is endlessly varied: it may be provisional and subject to change or relatively fixed and unchanging; it may form people into a low broad-based or a steep narrow-based pyramid of importance. The theory of stratification is concerned with the formation and destruction of hierarchies of human influence and reward.

Melvin M. Tumin, a social scientist of considerable authority in the United States, describes the way in which differential power, status, wealth, and prestige result in social stratification as follows:

[A] society consists of various strata arranged in a hierarchical order based on the amount of power, property, evaluation and psychic gratification that the strata characteristically receive. This is the general picture of a stratified society, and all societies are stratified in this way to some degree. The word "social" is an important qualifier, since the strata consist of *socially defined* statuses that receive *socially prescribed* quotas of power, property, and prestige. . . .

Today, serious expression of discontent with the prevailing modes of distributing goods and services marks the entire world. The discontent is, of course, eloquent testimony to its presence. On one level the nations of the world constitute a world-wide system of stratification: the haves versus the have-nots. And *within every* nation, including all the so-called socialist countries, stratification is also to be found.

Tumin then emphasizes the *universality* of socially structured and sanctioned inequality of power, property, and prestige (1967, pp. 13 and 17).

The connection between social differentiation and stratification is also explained by Yinger as follows:

Most human groups, whether they have two members or many millions, are characterized by *social differentiation*. The members hold different positions, have different rights and responsibilities, and possess different kinds of influence over group action. In many instances this variation expresses a ranking system; individuals are not only different, but higher and lower, lords and peasants, chiefs and Indians. If this *ranking system persists* over a period of time, so that *there is opportunity for it to be built into institutional* patterns and to influence significantly the personalities of the individuals involved, we speak *of a particular kind of social differentiation: stratification*. (1965, p. 8)

The relationships between distinguishable castes and classes, as well as the dominant group–minority relationship discussed in chapter 9, create types of social differentiation which, in a larger society, are patterned on the stratification model.

The main shortcoming of the stratification concept lies in its implicit assumption that social groups are neatly divided by horizontal lines. Empirical data show, however, that classes, castes, and socially ranked ethnic groups are not compartmentalized in mutually exclusive and rigidly drawn horizontal strata but overlap and spill over into adjoining groups. They are not separated by impenetrable physical boundaries. A member of one group may therefore acquire the privileges, status, economic well-being, or prestige typical of the group above, or he may sink to the level of the group below. A more realistic conception is that of a rank order of *overlapping concentrations of persons*, each with a different share of political and economic power, privileges, and prestige. The original stratification model is nevertheless used by many authors to illustrate social inequality.

The universality of ethnic and race discrimi-

nation as a specific form of social inequality (or social stratification) is strikingly illustrated in countries which suddenly experience an influx of foreign ethnic groups and racially alien elements. Chester Hunt and Lewis Walker (1974) refer in this context to the position of the Chinese in Mexico and black immigrants in Britain. They state:

The Chinese suffered not only from discriminatory legislation but also from occasional riots and even massacres. One such incident at Torreon in 1911 caused the death of 300 Chinese. The virulence of anti-Chinese feeling contrasts with the supposedly more benign pattern of ethnic relations in Latin countries and indicates that, with groups outside of their traditional orbit, Mexicans are subject to the same tensions as are people of other areas.

They then quote Magnus Morner's comments on the position of the Chinese:

Thus the Chinese, a hard-working, only partly assimilated group, faced almost identical kinds of persecution in the United States and Northern Mexico. Such episodes show that, under certain conditions, latent ethnic prejudice may produce discrimination and racial violence in any ethnic environment. It is not a phenomenon unique to Anglo-Saxons, Germans and South Africans.

Hunt and Walker characterize the situation in Great Britain as follows:

The United Kingdom is thus a country without a strong tradition of open racial discrimination, in which no major group espoused a racist ideology and which some of the colored immigrants regarded as their cultural homeland. Nevertheless, the ethnic conflicts and adjustments which have taken place appear strikingly similar to those in countries which have known a history of slavery and a racist ideology. The problems of ethnic adjustment seem strikingly similar regardless of the disparity of historical background. (Hunt and Walker, 1974, pp. 149 and 316)

B. Typical Behavior Patterns in Intergroup Relations

A certain standardization can be seen in the behavior patterns of groups that have been in continuous interaction over a wide front for a reasonable length of time. The typical case involves at least two clearly differentiated groups competing within a single political state for the most advanced, lucrative, and prestigious positions. All groups depend for their existence and livelihood on limited available resources as well as the power and the means to utilize and control them. Although the specific sequences of events are unique in each case, a cross-cultural and cross-national analysis of intergroup competition will show that certain actions occur over and over again. These universal behavior patterns can be grouped into two main categories—associative and dissociative processes. The associative processes include behavior patterns that bring people closer together and are grouped under the concepts of assimilation and amalgamation. Dissociative processes involve behavior patterns that pull people apart. They are conceptualized as segregation, discrimination, and separatism. While pluralism is often interpreted as dissociative, pluralist structures offer the only non-violent alternative to outright separation where groups are too different to be merged into a homogeneous body.

Both associative and dissociative processes can function as means of accommodation, though they sometimes appear as forms of conflict. Accommodation can be defined as some sort of working arrangement between competing groups aimed at obviating and neutralizing the more excessive forms of group conflict by means of relatively stable social structures. Accommodation appears in a large variety of forms, including patterns of segregation, differentiation, stratification, and pluralism (see chapter 12).

Four types of behavior patterns found overtly or latently in all intergroup contact situations and closely interwoven with the above-mentioned associative and dissociative processes, are ethnocentrism, prejudice, social distance, and stereotyping (including labelling). These four phenomena are very closely interrelated, and knowledge of their function and meaning is a key to the psychosocial dynamics of in- and out-group differentiation. In other words, these four psychosocial behavior patterns combine to cause some persons or groups to be treated as insiders and others as outsiders by other persons or groups competing for power, status, reward, and opportunity.

1. ETHNOCENTRISM

Ethnocentrism will be used here to denote the attempt to universalize the values of one's own particular tribe, ethnic group, nationality, or nation. It is expressed in the slogan: "Everybody else ought to be like us." Ethnocentrism may relate to any of the five components of ethnicity (chapter 7, C1) singly or in combination. It may thus relate to politics, social customs and manners, religion, or even aesthetics—including racially oriented concepts of what are beautiful or ugly people.

Here are some examples of typical ethnocentric attitudes, either expressed or implicit in ethnic or national policy:

God is an Englishman.

Non-Chinese are barbarians; they should be made to show their respect for civilization by kowtowing to the Emperor.

Everybody will be white when they get to Heaven.

People with flat noses are ugly.

People with long noses are ugly.

The Anglo-Saxons have a mission to civilize the rest of the world.

A child who cannot speak English has a learning problem and should be placed with other retarded children.

Russian is the language of socialism.

Bohemia (Čechy) is the homeland of the Czechs (Český); Germans who live in Bohemia are therefore foreigners.

German is a language for horses.

It is unclean and indecent to eat . . . (pork, beef, horse, dog, etc., etc.).

Note that while some of these attitudes refer to the biological or somatic aspect of race, others are cultural in content. Since ethnocentric attitudes are a product of emotive feelings rather than rational thought, racial and cultural aspects are frequently mixed. Comparing their own preferred ethnic group or nation with others—generally viewed in an unfavorable light—ethnocentrists tend to use the term "race" where it does not belong: to refer to nations or to groups integrated more by cultural and historical than by somatic characteristics (see Chapter 12).

Doubtlessly aware of the political hazards inherent in loose usage of descriptors, Ashley Montagu (1963) suggested that the concept of race be dropped in favor of that of ethnic group because racial categories encourage prejudice. The ethnic group, Montagu pointed out, shares a common culture, with racial features playing a secondary role. Members of the Caucasian race, for instance, may belong to Spanish or German ethnic groups, which in turn may have some non-Caucasian members. Members of the Negroid race belong to numerous ethnic groups, usually called tribes but manifesting in some cases the behavior of European-type nations, including the desire to form national states—such as the Ibo, the Yoruba, the Bemba, the Swazi, and the Zulu. Black and white English-speaking Americans are sometimes cited as an example of people of different races belonging to the same ethnic group, but it seems better to leave open at this point the question whether they are one ethnic group, two, or many. As for Montagu's suggestion, its value to scholars hinges not on whether it helps to calm prejudice but on whether it more accurately describes what is

observed. If, as much of the evidence analyzed in this book suggests, human behavior is motivated more strongly by cultural variations than by physical differences, then it is useful to follow Montagu's advice and concentrate on interethnic relations. It is necessary, of course, to take account of the extent to which race plays a role in shaping such relations and as a signal of ethnic membership or nonmembership (chapter 6,B).

There is no evidence that the shift of emphasis Montagu suggests will actually reduce prejudice: it may only shift it from one rubric to another. Race prejudice may be replaced by ethnic prejudice, which can be quite as destructive in its effects, as evident in Canada, Cyprus, and the Middle East.

Subjective identification with social groups occurs everywhere and is indeed a psychological necessity, since pathologies of the personality are found where the process is disturbed. Almost any observable cultural, behavioral, or physical trait may be useful in forming social identity: as a signal or integrator. But because social organization is immensely variable and subject to constant change, there is no objective reason why the social boundaries of a group must remain constant or fixed into posterity—except in the tradition of the group itself. Change is indeed a characteristic of social limits. The modern mind acknowledges this by being amazed that the Lapps of Scandinavia or the Bushmen of the Kalahari have refused the benefits of "civilization" with such inordinate resistance.

Does this also mean that prejudice and stereotypes, which represent the reverse side of ethnocentrism, are social-psychological necessities? A German social psychologist, Hofstätter (1954), stated that prejudice must be accepted as a normal phenomenon of human social life and that no one is free from it. Support for this point of view is also discerned in classical writings on ethnocentrism by W. G. Sumner (1906), on "we-feeling" by Cooley (1912), and on "consciousness of kind" by

Giddings (1922). The argument may be summarized by saying that human nature involves a dislike of the unlike, or that in-group feelings will always be accompanied by some degree of dislike for the out-group. Civilized behavior requires the control of such feelings; they cannot be abolished outright.

The essential minimum of ethnocentrism is a preference for the in-group, which need not be rational in itself, but should not be so fanatical as to eclipse rationality. If people dislike the social group to which they belong, they will leave it and join other groups. But if they are held within their group by the refusal of other groups to admit them (as has been the case with American blacks and South African Coloured), that group becomes externally defined and a source of political unrest. Enlightened ethnocentrism seeks the self-interest of the in-group with due regard for the parallel interests of out-groups.

Benevolent ethnocentrism, however, is not always beneficial in its effects. A *Staatsvolk* or culturally dominant group may feel morally obliged to share its way of life with others it thinks culturally deprived because they speak and live differently. If forced assimilation or suppression of the out-group language ensues, the result is cultural impoverishment for the assimilators and alienation and frustration for the assimilatees (see chapters 17 and 18). The same misplaced benevolence can be observed in encounters beyond national borders. Christian missionaries decree that naked "savages" must be clothed; deprived of their normal vitamin intake through the skin, they become prey to respiratory diseases. Converted to "the one true path to salvation," chieftains and warriors abandon polygamy, and the surplus wives end up in brothels.

Benevolent ethnocentrism also leads to the export of political institutions. The departing British bequeathed each of their former African dependencies a Westminster-style democracy, which all except Botswana have since abolished. Soviet and Maoist ideologists are no doubt prepared to argue that the export of communism is benevolent. But in view of the mass murders, imprisonments, and degradations of human dignity employed to accomplish this end, it would take extreme dedication to Lenin's view that "our morality is wholly subordinated to the interests of the class-struggle of the proletariat" (speech to Young Communist League, October 2, 1920) to make this contention credible.

Ethnocentrism becomes pernicious when a social group, a nation, or an ideological movement rides roughshod over the rights and interests of others to attain its objectives. Cases in point include Hitler's extermination camps, the expulsion of 18 million Germans from their traditional homelands at the close of World War II, expropriation and expulsion of Asians in East Africa, crushing of the Kurd nation's struggle for independence, and the proclaimed desire of Arab extremists to "throw Israel into the sea."

2. PREJUDICE

When a person has and acts on subjective opinions about someone else—opinions that are usually negative and that would not stand up under objective investigation—we say that person is prejudiced. It should hardly need demonstrating that entire groups, or substantial parts thereof, can have prejudices against other groups. Modern social science has developed quantitative techniques for measuring the extent and intensity of such prejudices. The question arises: are intergroup prejudices inevitable? Are they an unavoidable consequence of essential ethnocentrism? Does it follow as a matter of course that a Chosen People cannot believe itself to be "chosen" without harboring a prejudice toward or a stereotype of others who are not so divinely endowed? These questions touch upon some of the central issues in social science and will take us to the roots of social solidarity if answered fully and fairly.

In social science prejudice is treated as a special type of attitude displaying the usual components of attitudes in a particular combination. The first of these components is called *cognitive* (or conceptual) and refers to our ideas, opinions, beliefs, or "knowledge" about an object. In the case of prejudice these cognitions refer to social objects—i.e. individuals or social groups. The essence of a prejudice is that it is based on *unsubstantiated* opinions, as distinguished from a conclusion drawn from substantiated opinions or beliefs.

The second component of attitudes can be called the *affective* or emotional aspect. Thus an attitude may involve a feeling for or against, a favorable or an unfavorable disposition toward the object in question. This is also the case with prejudice, although on the whole social sciences has paid little attention to favorable prejudices while concentrating on the unfavorable. The emotional aspect of attitudes, depending on the strength of the emotions involved, may reinforce or distort the cognitive component. That is why a simple presentation of "the facts" to a prejudiced individual will not necessarily remedy the prejudice.

The third component is usually called the *conative* or behavioral, and refers to readiness or willingness to express in action the beliefs and feelings experienced. A person's behavior is treated as interdependent with and illustrative of his or her beliefs and feelings about the stimulus-object. The behavior patterns of a group toward others—including the rules or customs applied to intergroup contacts, patterns of integration, segregation, or discrimination, as well as distances maintained in various situations—are all indicative of the extent and kind of prejudices entertained by the group in question.

Prejudices, therefore, predispose the individual or group having them to act accordingly. They differ from other attitudes in that their cognitive element consists of unsubstantiated—often false—opinions rather than substantiated opinions or facts.

Prejudice is a specific case of what we call categorization: the tendency to group things or people that look alike. Categorization in general, however, is a necessary part of human thought, enabling a person to discern differences and likenesses among objects confronted. Cognitively speaking, it is a normal process in which every human being indulges. Allport wrote that "The human mind must think with the aid of categories. . . . Once formed, categories are the basis for normal prejudgment. We cannot possibly avoid this process. Orderly living depends upon it" (1954, p. 20). A philosopher might warn at this point, however, that the normality of the process is no warrant at all of either the adequacy of a set of categories or the correct assignment of cases to the categories themselves.

Most people find that their cultures present them with ready-made sets of categories. If they live in a relatively stable environment, they find that these categories solve most daily problems. The critical question is of course how a particular classification becomes part of a culture. Taking a pragmatic view, we may say that a culture institutionalizes a particular categorization because it works. But when circumstances change, categories may cease to work, partially or altogether. The bearers of the culture will then have to experiment with new ones or experience a "decline and fall."

Occasionally, ingenious members of a culture may experiment with new systems without significant changes in the environment; some cultures even encourage it. If the new system is accepted, its author will be hailed as an innovator. If it is only accepted a generation later, the originator is considered to have lived before his or her time. If the new system is rejected altogether, the innovator is likely to be denounced or even arrested as a radical. Acceptability of the new system depends less on its objective merit than on its conformity with prevailing prejudices or the possibility of modifying these.

The social categories in common use remain fairly simplistic and undifferentiated, if not mediocre, compared to scientific classifications. They function as time-savers in a busy world. A million events befall every human being every day. The complexities of living somehow make it impossible to treat every event on individual merit. We therefore invent categories and simply generalize. It is a regrettable but useful short cut. To the extent that we discount individual differences among members of a class we treat them as essentially alike. The application of a uniform prejudgment to cases falling in a single class is, in fact, valued as an element of judicial fairness.

Cognition, however, is followed by affect (emotion) and conation (action). Having generalized about an object, rightly or wrongly, we are likely to have beliefs and feelings about it (especially if it is a social object), and these beliefs and feelings are likely to be expressed in some sort of action. Differences in personality and social structure will, however, determine the degree to which classifications become rigid. The relevant personality differences were made the subject of study by Rokeach in his pioneering work *The Open and the Closed Mind* (1960). Here the open-minded individual is one who is free to discard his dogmatic categories in the light of new evidence, whereas the closed-minded person is unable to do so. This argument is to some extent circular, since a person able to free himself from prejudice would probably not be prejudiced to begin with.

While prejudice appears to be universal and spontaneous, the evidence indicates that specific prejudices are learned. Acquired prejudices are transmitted from one person to another and from group to group through communication, interaction, and social memory. Particular prejudices, furthermore, are by no means immutable. Otherwise it would, for instance, be almost impossible to account for the fusion of ethnic groups such as occurred among the Dutch, German, and French in the formation of the Afrikaners in South Africa, or to account for the interracial mating that has occurred throughout history. Similarly, to believe that prejudice is unchangeable would be tantamount to saying that religious conversion is impossible. Political campaigns and programs of advertising, sensitivity-group training, indoctrination, and brainwashing are implicitly aimed at the reduction, change, or maintenance of prejudice. The principle underlying all these efforts is that anything that may be learned may also be unlearned, although the latter is accomplished with a little more difficulty in the absense of appropriate reinforcements.

Prejudice, in its broadest sense, is not necessarily destructive. Quite a number of our modern social institutions are actually designed to be "prejudiced" at the level of institutionalized values. So, for example, we want the press to be on guard against censorship in order to remain free; we want the courts to be fair even if a "murderer" is acquitted on a technical point.

Prejudice, whether constructive or destructive in impact, is a widespread phenomenon. We would certainly be hard put to trace an individual who is completely free from prejudice in the technical sense. In a world where there is perpetual competition for scarce resources, including power and prestige, prejudices will inevitably develop, especially when groups compete. Even if we grant that prejudice is a variable, that some individuals display more of it than others, that some societies have made it more legal than others, and that measures to combat it vary in speed and permanence, it is most unlikely that prejudice can ever by completely eradicated. It will always be available for manipulation by unscrupulous politicians.

For a final word on prejudice, we turn to William J. Wilson (1973, p. 38):

While it is meaningful to speak of positive attitudes, including positive prejudices, the concept of prejudice generally implies a negative orientation. This is particularly true in the interethnic attitude toward the members of a specific group solely because they are members of that group. In contrast to ethnocentrism, with its in-group focus and derivative generalized rejection of out-groups, prejudice is focused on and directed toward a specific out-group.

The logical behavioral outcome of prejudice is discrimination. That subject, however, is reserved for the final section of this chapter.

3. SOCIAL DISTANCE

Every social group draws a distinction between the in-group and the out-group. The distinction is supposedly drawn by all the members of the in-group, and in this sense they can be said to share a norm. In the application of this norm they then define and treat out-groups in a different way from that applicable to the in-group. In rejecting the different culture, manners, politics, or somatic appearance of out-groups they are said to be applying normative discrimination.

A problem in the use of this concept is that an in-group may be almost anything. For Sumner and for many other anthropologists it was a primitive society, which in most cases is culturally homogeneous. But in modern societies organized as relatively large political units, there will be a plurality of in-groups. Normative discrimination as a legitimate basis for public policy is therefore limited to distinctions shared by all in-groups. When distinctions are drawn by some group against other groups, the discriminatory actions resulting therefrom lack general validity, even when the local majority supports them. This is the case in most societies where ethnic minorities are present. Discrimination against Jews in Eastern Europe or against Indians in Kenya may gain public support, particularly from those who benefit, but is regarded as invidious by the world at large.

Distinctions may be self-imposed, as in the case of religious groups that observe dietary laws not common to the society as a whole, or who have their Sabbath on a different day. If the validity of the norms in question is intentionally undefined in public policy—as in a society that permits people to eat what they please, except other human beings—it means that this kind of intergroup discrimination is permissible, since it does not endanger the society as a whole.

When subgroups are consciously or unconsciously excluded from full participation in social life, they are usually designated "minority groups." Although mostly ethnic groups, minority groups may include any subgroup that is disqualified *de jure* or *de facto* from roles in business or public affairs corresponding to individual abilities. Some subgroups, however, are disqualified through normative discrimination, in which case they cannot properly be called minority groups. The legal distinction between adult and child, and the seniority rule giving precedence to those with longer records of service, are cases in point.

The concept of social distance became popular after Bogardus (1933) had developed a research format which could be applied with relative ease and with only minor modifications in a wide variety of social settings. In its most general form, respondents are asked whether they would accept members of indicated groups in a series of relationships. These relationships are graded from very intimate (e.g. marriage) through intermediate (e.g. colleague in job or profession) to remote (visitor to respondent's country) or rejection (no entry to respondent's country).

Results showed a remarkable consistency. Different populations of respondents showed constant and distinctive patterns of preferences despite the lapse of time between interviews. The concept of social distance was mainly applied in the fields of race and ethnic relations, but it was also used in studies of other social groups and categories including the sexes as well as age, occupational, class, and religious groups. Social distance must, of course, be interpreted in the light of other factors such as genetic, somatic, or linguistic distance. It may result from conflict or confrontation, or reflect widely held beliefs and stereotypes.

Social distance data may be used in a number of ways. They are clearly relevant in any attempt to understand the pattern of relationships in a given society. They also show that behavior may not conform to the current official ideology—resistance to busing of school pupils in American cities being a case in point. In any planned program to increase (e.g. in war) or to decrease (e.g. in peace) the prejudice toward a given group, the success or failure of the campaign may be measured in social distance units. The scale alone does not provide a reliable prediction of actual behavior, but it remains a widely used technique for the measurement of a behavioral component of prejudice. It shows, as could have been expected, that in most cases in-groups are preferred to out-groups.

The question whether a given degree of social distance represents normative or social discrimination cannot be settled in advance, but only with reference to the standards of evaluation prevailing in the particular society. As societies adopt the standards embodied in the Declaration of Human Rights, the result is a more critical examination of normative discriminations hitherto accepted as legitimate.

Social distance is closely related to differences in status, and a few observations are now in order about status. In achievement-oriented societies, status is allocated on the basis of what a person or group has done. An achieved status is that of a medical doctor. An ascribed status, on the other hand, is held irrespective of what a person can do or how he performs, but simply on the basis of certain qualities or characteristics. These usually include sex, age, kinship, race, and ethnic group membership. Such characteristics are largely biologically determined or remain unchangeable for the lifespan of most individuals. Societies differ in the extent to which they emphasize achievement or ascription in the allocation of status. No achievement-oriented society, however, has yet succeeded in completely eliminating status ascription.

Certainly the most important, salient, and tangible structure to result from ascriptive structure is kinship. Almost every status that exists in the traditional societies of Africa,

Asia, and Oceania is meshed with the kinship system. In this sense ethnic solidarity may be viewed as an extension of the ascriptive ties of kinship. In the large, advanced societies of modern times, the economic, political, religious, and other social spheres have severed their ties with and their subordination to kinship—so that the relative importance of kinship is clearly diminished. In order to function as a unified political entity they develop a national identity as an alternative or substitute for particularist ethnic solidarity. But kinship has never been completely replaced by an alternative arrangement in any known society. Indeed, some sociologists argue that kinship systems have become more specialized in shedding some of their functions to other social spheres and therefore have become more irreplaceable.

In most cases, ascriptive status is allocated at the birth of the individual. This is possible because the characteristics used in assigning status are present and observable at birth and cannot willfully be changed. (Exceptions exist but are rare and traumatic.) After birth the socialization of the individual is set in motion. The purpose of this process is to teach the individual to play a role appropriate to the status allocated to him. Immediate relatives are the most important agents of socialization, but role-playing continues and is reinforced and presumably rewarded throughout the life of the individual. If status is hereditary, the social structure will be relatively stable, if not rigid.

The important question about differential treatment as a consequence of ascription, is whether all or most members of the society involved agree with the distinctions. If so, we have a case of normative discrimination; if not, we have a case of social discrimination. A case of normative discrimination based mainly on ascription though with an element of achievement is the traditional Kikuyu society, which Goldthorpe (1974) describes as follows:

traditional Kikuyu society was based on a differentiation, according to age, in which each man had much the same chance of becoming an elder with prestige and power.

From an early age boys set up informal groups who played and herded goats and, later, cattle together while girls also formed neighbourhood groups. Such one-sex peer groups are probably to be found in all societies. Kikuyu society was unusual in formalizing them and making them, along with descent groups, the most important groups in the social structure. Both boys and girls were circumcised, traditionally at the age of about 18–20, and initiated into an age-set, that is a group of those initiated together, who remained a group with rights and duties to one another as they passed successively through the different states of life. Some time after initiation the young men were (so to speak) called up into a military organization, forming warrior bands under the leadership of one of their own number.

. . . After his time in the warrior grade the next stage in a man's life, when he settled down to marry, cultivate, and bring up children, was a comparatively humdrum one and his ambitions would no doubt turn to the time when he might become one of the elders, whose fire he tended and whose errands he ran. Entry to the grades of elder (there were more than one) was not an automatic matter of attaining the requisite age. The acceptance of one's age-mates had to be gained by personal qualities shown throughout life. This system ensured, therefore, that those who eventually served as judges and priests had the requisite qualities but it also meant that they were relatively old. It was not just a matter of waiting one's turn but everyone had much the same chance to prove himself. There was, that is, equality of opportunity. The system was also intensely conservative, for one proved one's self by conforming to traditional values, and might have the opportunity in old age to ensure that everyone else did so too.

It is the professed ideal of modern societies, especially Western societies, to become achievement-oriented, at least in the more important areas of social relationships such as employment, education, and politics. Modernizing societies limit the operation of birth-ascription so as to facilitate "the circulation of the elites" (Pareto, 1923, §§2027–36).

There are some who would do away with ascription altogether. In public affairs, and in the employment policies of business firms interested in government contracts or in a progressive image, the code phrases are "equal opportunity" and "regardless of race, color, or creed," which are shorthand for "absence of restrictions on individual achievement." "Affirmative action," on the other hand—despite denials from the U.S. Department of Health, Education, and Welfare—is a code phrase for employment quotas for women, blacks, and Spanish-surnamed persons: an effort to operate the ascription system in reverse. Modern societies reject the caste-system of traditional India, and where castelike distinctions occur, as with ethnic or religious minorities, they are rejected as anachronisms. As modernization proceeds, ascriptive distinctions become increasingly controversial.

It would be rash, however, to assume that ascription is about to disappear altogether as a principle of social organization. Even the Labour governments of Great Britain, for instance, have not attempted to abolish the House of Lords. Instead, the powers of that body have been further limited (by the Parliament Act of 1949) and mobility into the Upper Chamber has been enhanced by the appointment of life peers and peeresses. J. S. Mill, the father of modern liberalism, was well aware of the weaknesses and dangers of pure representative government with universal suffrage; he noted that a hereditary king may sometimes serve (as in Greece) as a check against democratic abuses (1861, pp. 220, 281). Effective representation is not tied to any particular method of selection, but reflects the attitudes of the representative and the represented. In societies with tribal traditions, representation through heredity and ascription may be better understood and accepted than representation by ballots: the latter, being culturally foreign, is subject to manipulation and is all too often a cloak for hegemony of particular tribes over others. The fact that the ties of the extended family link almost the entire population to tribal leaders even lends ascriptive systems a democratic quality—though not in the European sense—since almost every member of the community has his or her particular chief or councilor whose traditional obligation includes defending the interests of his relatives. Some of the most stable African systems combine elements of ascriptive and electoral representation.

4. STEREOTYPES

Stereotypes are an aspect of the cognitive component of prejudice, and are unsubstantiated and usually sloganized beliefs about a person, a category of persons, or a group. The term has been used in very different contexts, however, ranging from the above to "pictures in our heads" (Lippmann, 1944) and to "somatic norm types" which Hoetink (1962) described as the ideal or actual physiognomy and behavior of a particular group or "race." Despite varying definitions there is no doubt that stereotyping is a basic attitudinal component of in-group–out-group differentiation. According to Robin Williams:

Stereotypes constitute a part of culture, a part of an organized aggregate of shared symbols, beliefs, and values. Considered as part of a system or prejudice, stereotypes are operative in defining both the objects of action and the evaluative standards applied to social objects. Indeed, the maintenance of established stereotypes over long periods of time is possible partly because there are systems of action primarily devoted to their maintenance. These systems range from processes of inculcation within the family to the incorporation of stereotypes in song and story and to society-wide dissemination through media of mass communication. Stereotypes are also components of social and personality systems: as summaries of and rationalizations for past experiences, they have sociological implications; as predictions of the behavior of others they give direction to psychological energies. The function of stereotypes as far as social systems are concerned is that the sharing of stereotypes reassures the holders and helps maintain systems of group privileges and power. In situations of competition and conflict, stereotypes simplify the alignments, sharpen group boundaries, and facilitate ingroup consensus. . . . Thus stereotypes emerge as distillations of the political, economic, and cultural alignments of nations as interpreted by leaders and intellectuals, especially through mass media and in reference to dramatic public events. What one person or one group believes about another is usually expressed without any immediate confrontation of evidence. Stereotypes may contain a core of truth, but the amount of truth may be very little indeed. . . .

Stereotypes that refer to social categories, statuses, groups, or collectivities are usually stated in terms of qualities (traits, properties, characteristics) conceived as if somehow inherent in the objects: Americans are materialistic; Italians are excitable; Orientals are inscrutable; professors are absent-minded; women are flighty; white people are cruel. Such imputations of qualities very easily become expectations of behavior; and these stereotypes have the same overgeneralized and rigid character as those of physical appearance or psychological states. (Williams, 1973, pp. 481, 483)

The typical research instrument is a paper-and-pencil questionnaire developed by Katz and Braly (1933) giving a long list of adjectives from which respondents are asked to select a limited number they think descriptive of an indicated group. Thus white American students stereotyped Negroes with strong agreement as superstitious, lazy, happy-go-lucky, ignorant, etc. With somewhat less agreement the Turks were thought to be cruel, very religious, treacherous, etc. The many repetitions of this procedure have showed that student populations have remarkably definite and consistent ideas about the "nature" of at least some of the more conspicuous groups or nationalities. As it cannot reasonably be assumed that respondents have had representative contact with or experience of the groups they stereotype so consistently, it must be inferred that the "information" was picked up from other individuals, parents, teachers, the mass media, or the culture in general.

Some interesting variations were observed. Prothro and Melikian (1954) found that Arab students, for example, had much the same opinion as American students about the Negroes, but thought quite differently of the Turks, whom they found strong, militaristic, nationalistic, courageous, etc. The question whether these stereotypes contain a "kernel of truth" because of their consistency will clearly not be settled unless consensus is reached on a procedure to determine the true distribution of these characteristics in a particular group. There is, however, an upsetting quality to social life which makes it almost impossible to separate fact from fiction. A good example of this occurs in the area of sex-role socialization.

The distinction between male and female social roles is made in all societies; sex is clearly an ascriptive status allocated at birth. In all societies very definite beliefs are held about the rights, duties, and expected behavior of the sexes. These beliefs guide the process of socialization from birth. Observation has shown that differential treatment of the sexes starts as soon as the sex of the baby is announced and continues throughout the period of primary socialization. When a baby of three months exercises its limbs, Granny may imagine the little boy as an athlete, but if it is a little girl she may conjure up a ballerina. These differences in role expectations are verbalized on countless occasions by persons significant in the child's social world and—what is more important—the child eventually learns to respond and play his or her allotted role in ways which elicit rewards.

As long as everybody remains happy with differential sex roles, we have a case of normative discrimination. Only when the distinction is called into the area of controversy will the disadvantaged (women, in most cases) point out that sex-role stereotypes are prejudiced in order to preserve male privilege. The problem is how to decide whether the stereotyped roles cause or result from differences in physique and behavior. Research to answer this question would require a control group of unsocialized males and females—a technical if not moral impossibility. Some help may be found in W. I. Thomas's well-known theorem: "If men [meaning people] define situations as real they are real in their consequences." Social scientists have documented sexual bias in nursery tales, schoolbooks, folklore, etc., and some careful research on reputed differences between men and women has been published. The evidence does not, for instance, support the popular belief that women have lower IQ's (D. Wright, 1972).

Under the pressure of feminists, especially in Western countries, sex discriminations are clearly losing their normative character. In some cases differential roles persist (for instance in Spain and Latin America a young lady consorting with a young man must be accompanied by her dueña). In others they are, in theory, outlawed, as in employment in the United States after discrimination by sex became illegal. Even in Switzerland, where the franchise was historically associated with the bearing of arms, women finally gained the vote in 1971.

C. Stratification: Process and Effect

A final social process whereby intergroup relationships become structured in differentiated societies is *ranking*. This is the process that places individuals and groups at different levels in the power, reward, and opportunity system. Its result is stratification, which appears in many shapes and configurations. Stratification always implies social inequality despite its wide range of behavioral manifestations.

The stratification produced by ranking usually differentiates people in at least one of three ways: by class, by status, and by power. As described in section A2, the strata are not rigidly separated units but rather groups overlapping along a continuum between two extremes which can, for convenience, be called the haves and the have-nots. Melvin Tumin, who has studied social stratification in depth, points out that this type of structure always reflects four major processes: differentiation, ranking, evaluation, and reward. He states:

Essentially we mean by social stratification the arrangement of any social group or society into a hierarchy of positions that are unequal with regard to power, property, social evaluation and/or psychic gratification. . . . Power refers to the ability to secure one's end in life, even against opposition. Property may be defined as rights over goods and services. Evaluation refers to a societal judgement that a status or position is more prestigeous and honourable than others, or more popular, or preferable for one or another reason. Psychic gratification includes all sources of pleasure and contentment that are not otherwise classifiable as property, power or evaluation. (1967, p. 12)

Tumin describes the driving force behind the stratification process:

Ultimately, the argument for stratification . . . rests upon premises regarding human motivation. These premises, usually left unstated, maintain that one can't get people to do unequally difficult or unequally skilled tasks without distributing evaluations and rewards unequally. The unequal compensation serves as the motivating force. (ibid., p. 27)

Tumin illustrates social stratification in the context of the differentiation-ranking-evaluation-reward process by pointing out that in American society one is generally considered better, superior or more worthy if one is

White rather than Negro
male rather than female
Protestant rather than Catholic or Jewish
educated rather than uneducated
rich rather than poor
white-collar rather than blue-collar
of good family background rather than undistinguished family origin
young rather than old
urban or suburban rather than rural dwelling
of Anglo-Saxon origin rather than any other
native-born rather than of foreign descent
employed rather than unemployed

married rather than divorced
(ibid., p. 107)

Even the smallest group—including a group of two such as a couple—is characterized by differentiation in one form or another. Ranking is always present in larger groups. Their members are not only different but lower and higher, less and more powerful, poor and rich—the omnipresent gradation sloganized as haves and have-nots. The differences in levels occupied by persons and groups reflect a relatively stable pattern of interpersonal and intergroup relationships.

Inequality can become a structural characteristic of a society only if it becomes institutionalized—built into the social fabric of the group in the form of relatively permanent social behavior patterns. We can distinguish between three dimensions of social inequality (stratification) in the areas of class, status, and power—an analytical approach generally credited to the German sociologist Max Weber. A person's class position is his economic function (e.g. as entrepreneur, manager, or worker) in the process of production, distribution, and exchange. People's relationships to the means of production are inherently unequal: there is no such thing as a "classless society," even in communist countries. Status, as distinguished from class, refers to social honor, prestige, and esteem. Status inequality reflects the higher or lower prestige accorded different social attributes and lifestyles. Finally, power involves political power: being in position to manage, control, or manipulate the institutions and processes that shape public policy. Depending on the political and economic system, access to power is obtained through ascription, political skill, wealth, sycophancy, or chutzpah. But as W. G. Runciman rightly states "The most difficult question however is not how many dimensions of stratification there are, but where the dividing line should be drawn within each" (1972, p. 53).

D. Discrimination

Although discrimination may be favorable or unfavorable, the word is used mostly in its negative sense and will be so used here: positive discrimination will be called "preferment." Discrimination, then, means subjecting a person or a group to diminished enjoyment of social, economic, civil, political, or legal rights. Victims of discrimination have reduced access to society's resources and occupy the lower positions in the societal power, status, reward and opportunity structure. Their life-chances (in the sense of the chance to survive; to enjoy adequate food, clothing, and shelter; as well as education, physical and mental health, and vocational fulfillment) are thus inferior to those of the dominant group. Discrimination also involves laws, customs, and arrangements that block entry into the dominant group or power system through marriage, employment, or intersocialization. In other words, discriminatory practices and systems can be used as ways and means of preventing the out-group from becoming assimilated into and amalgamated with the dominant group. Discrimination (in the sociopolitical context) is not primarily directed against individuals *per se*, but against groups. Although it is the individual member of such a group who suffers the impact of discrimination as a personal experience, this happens because of his membership in a particular group.

The difference between prejudice and discrimination should be recalled at this point. Prejudice is a negative attitude based on unverified (and frequently false) data. Discrimination is behavior reflecting the attitude of rejection: it withholds advantages from and imposes disabilities on its victim. Discriminatory behavior is often seen as the objective parallel of prejudice or as action growing out of prejudiced attitudes (Gould and Kolb, 1964, p. 203).

Discrimination in its original sense means the drawing of a distinction: it is morally neutral in itself. To accommodate the moral relevance of discrimination, categories proposed by Milton Yinger (1968, p. 448) will be invoked:

> With reference to human interaction we can think of the dictionary meanings of discrimination . . . as falling along a continuum. Although no sharp lines can be drawn, it is useful to divide this continuum into three sectors on the basis of the extent to which norms are shared. Thus, at one end of the continuum is the type of differential treatment that is based on generally accepted standards of excellence or appropriateness. . . . The second type is discrimination that is deemed invalid—that is, based on unacceptable criteria—by many members of a society because it violates primary customs and laws yet is regarded as acceptable by significant subgroups and supported by secondary norms. . . . Third, there are the distinctions drawn by individuals in violation of the established standards, customs, or laws, without subgroup support and lacking even secondary normative sanctions.

The case material discussed in subsequent chapters requires insertion of a fourth type of discrimination between Yinger's first and second, giving the following four categories:

(1) *Normative discrimination:* legal or customary application of standards of differential treatment.

(2) *Permissible social discrimination:* application of standards of differential treatment not declared either valid or invalid.

(3) *Social discrimination:* application of invalid standards of differential treatment with subgroup support.

(4) *Individual discrimination:* application of invalid standards of differential treatment without subgroup support.

This classification is not exhaustive, nor does it eliminate subjective judgment—how is "validity," for instance, to be decided? It is, however, a useful classification for the purpose at hand.

To test Yinger's scheme as thus modified, the place of ethnocentrism may be considered.

The meaning of the term has remained essentially unchanged since Sumner defined it (1906, pp. 12–13) as the "view of things in which one's own group is the center of everything, and all others are scaled and rated with reference to it." This definition takes for granted a more or less integrated in-group, differentiated from all others, the out-group. Sumner adds that: ". . . the most important fact is that ethnocentrism leads a people to exaggerate and intensify everything in their own folkways which is peculiar and which differentiates them from others. It therefore strengthens the folkways."

Other authors link ethnocentrism with the existence of peace in the in-group, matched by hostility toward the out-group. According to Noel:

From this perspective the values of the in-group are equated with abstract, universal standards of morality and the practices of the in-group are exalted as better or more "natural" than those of any out-group. Such an orientation is essentially a matter of in-group glorification and not of hostility toward any specific out-group. Nevertheless, an inevitable consequence of ethocentrism is the rejection or downgrading of all out-groups to a greater or lesser degree as a function of the extent to which they differ from the in-group. The greater the difference the lower will be the relative rank of any given outgroup. (1968, pp. 157–58)

The legends, sagas, songs, and historical records of many ancient civilizations abound in clear examples of ethnocentric behavior. As Ina C. Brown relates:

The best documented of the older records are those of Egypt. The Egyptians made captives or vassals of the various neighboring peoples they conquered. They spoke scornfully of the Negroes to the South of them and at one point erected a barrier which they forbade the Negroes to pass. This barrier is often cited as proof of the Egyptians' prejudice against the blacks. But the Egyptians erected a similar barrier against the Bedouin, and they spoke with equal scorn of the "troglodytes," the Asiatic sand dwellers, and the blue-eyed Lib-

yans. The Egyptian artists pictured their miserable war captives being brought home and, apparently for color effect or contrast, the artist sometimes painted a black Negro, a mulatto, a hook-nosed Hittite, a bearded Hebrew, and a fair Libyan chained together. The evidence suggests that the whole complex of dress, weapons, the way of wearing the hair or beard, were quite as important as color or other physical features in distinguishing the various peoples with whom the Egyptians had contact. Apparently they made no distinction in their neighbors except in terms of their strength or weakness as enemies, or their usefulness as allies or tributaries. (1973, pp. 63–64)

Yinger defines discrimination in the American context as "differential treatment *solely on the grounds of race, religion, national origin, ethnic group, class, age or sex*." He distinguishes discrimination thus defined from differentiation on the basis of objective qualifications, e.g. for licenses or jobs (1965, p. 27, emphasis added).

Although discrimination involves overt behavior expressing the complex of feelings, attitudes, and sentiments we describe as prejudice, the latter need not necessarily lead to discrimination. Many white Americans are prejudiced against blacks, but they stop short of translating their prejudice into overt acts of discrimination; in fact they often endeavor to eliminate them because they think them morally wrong. Discrimination never occurs without an ideological thrust that has its roots in the beliefs, value systems, and needs of the discriminators. Thus, prejudice may exist without discrimination, but discrimination cannot occur without prejudice.

As shown in part I, uniform international criteria for discrimination as yet exist only in embryo and then only in respect of the most extreme forms of oppression, such as slavery and genocide. An international norm against mass expulsions has not been agreed upon, since too many members of the United Nations still indulge in that practice. Were the Universal Declaration of Human Rights and the antidiscrimination Conventions to be applied literally, virtually all countries of the world would fail to pass the test of non-discrimination. Such international legislation fails to take into account the manifold subtle forms of discrimination built into social, political, and economic systems. Because these are seldom directly and formally institutionalized (e.g. by legislation), they often escape the attention of the many self-appointed adjudicators of international morality.

Discrimination is relative in the sense that it appears along a continuum, with extreme forms on one end and situations where it is insignificant or nonexistent on the other. Whether a given situation involves discrimination or preferment is a matter of perspective. As S. J. Makielski significantly asks:

Is a housewife living in a $40,000 home, surrounded by labor-saving devices, with the best medical care on call, whose primary nutritional problem is one of losing weight, by any standard deprived? A Navajo Indian living on a reservation might emphatically say no. A member of an organization dedicated to the liberation of women would say, as emphatically, yes.

At any given point in time, every person is confronted with what can be called his "opportunity structure," which is the set of alternatives available to him—in other words, his options. Each person's opportunity structure is shaped by a number of limitations, such as psychological predisposition, physical assets or handicaps, social status, economic standing, geographic location, range of social contacts, age and sex. Generally, opportunity structures change through time, the number of choices available increasing as one passes from infancy into childhood and adulthood and then usually decreasing at the onset of old age. (1973, pp. 14, 19)

Analysis of discrimination involves searching for answers to the following questions: Who discriminates against whom, why, how, and to what effect? The *who* will be the dominant groups and the *whom* the subordinate. The *why* of the matter relates to the needs, prejudice, fears, rationalizations, and belief systems of the discriminators. The *hows* in-

volve areas and techniques of discrimination; they are described in part IV. They include not only instruments such as laws and institutions, but also social position when it functions as a differentiator. The effects of discrimination include inequities and barriers in areas such as employment, housing, education, credit, political and civil rights, social and spatial mobility, marriage, religion, entertainment, and recreation. Discrimination lowers its victims' status, prestige, power rating, and access to reward and opportunity; their life chances are diminished or depreciated.

While integration is widely viewed as a path to equality, it may also be a means of discrimination. Smaller ethnic groups have lost language and culture by being stirred into the "melting pot" of some dominant group and being forced to conform to the latter's cultural and somatic norm images. Later we shall deal with negative effects of and protests against "melting pot" processes in both Europe and the United States.

Nor are constitutions a guarantee against discrimination. As Duchaček observes (1973a, pp. 12–13), totalitarian dictatorships often have the most elaborate bills of rights. It is his view that:

The people and the nation will always suggest a mosaic of individuals and groups with conflicting goals and different concepts of how to attain them. Even when men agree on such general goals as the "pursuit of happiness," they are likely to disagree on their precise meaning and how best to pursue them. The conflicts which result pit individuals against individuals, groups against individuals, and groups against each other. Constitutions are primarily political documents which reflect the core meaning of politics by identifying conflicting values and interests and provide for their solution by compromise and coercion. . . . Bills of rights create, rather than resolve, dilemmas, by listing conflicting rights and liberties and promising constitutional protection for all of them. Consequently, the search for appropriate compromises and balance among desirable yet conflicting values is left to the subsequent working and evolution of a given national system. Therefore, bills of rights, either explicitly or implicitly, treat rights and liberties as relative, not absolute. (*Ibid.*, pp. 250–52)

As will be seen from the case material presented in subsequent chapters, disparate groups in contact seldom if ever establish a relationship of true equality. In the light of human weaknesses, such a dispensation would indeed be a historical oddity. Nor, as Leonard Reissman writes, is the degree of equality that some societies achieve final in any way:

[Equality] is a process in the sense that its definitions necessarily keep changing, thereby reflecting changing circumstances, including better social knowledge and understanding. Obviously, what seemed like a definitive statement of equality to the designers of the Declaration of Independence could not be accepted as adequate today; we know more about society and its structure than the signers ever could have known. Jefferson and his cosigners clearly did not mean to include their slaves when they declared that "all men are created equal." Even later we learned that legal equality was not being enforced in the courts, let alone in the more informal social relationships of daily life, although we somehow assumed that enforcement would follow the law exactly. Recent court decisions, for example, have revealed the various ways by which the poor have been denied their legal rights (for example, by not being informed about them), as well as how Blacks are denied equal treatment in the courts (for example, by underrepresentation on jury panels). (1973, pp. 23–24)

As Reissman further suggests, "Martin Luther King's classic phrase that he had climbed the mountain and seen the promised land, is only relatively true; more than likely, the promised land was only a plateau from which new mountains would become visible as we approach them." The path to these further mountains is however, beset with paradoxes and pitfalls. Like any other principle, that of equality becomes self-defeating if carried to its logical extreme. Income redistribution to achieve equality would make the rich poorer, but it would also make the poor poorer since investment would stop and managers would seek jobs without risk or responsibility. Furthermore, in a society where groups are differentiated by objective factors such as language, culture, and race, measures taken in the name of equality but not attuned to the distinctive needs of individuals and groups may produce new inequalities without eliminating causes of conflict.

9

THE MINORITY SYNDROME

The term "minority" is bothersome because it is used with a great variety of meanings. To illustrate only two: much is said about "minority governments" in Southern Africa without consideration of the fact that the principle of majority rule rests upon a prior social contract (Locke, 1690, II, §95). In a territory with several ethnic groups whether or not of different races, the terms "majority" and "minority" are politically meaningless unless these groups have first entered into an explicit or implicit social contract creating a single body politic—which is not the case in South Africa, Southwest Africa, or Rhodesia. The concepts "majority" and "minority" clearly imply a larger whole to which both belong.

If you are an American Indian or have a Spanish surname in the United States, you belong to a recognized minority and enjoy special protection of the law. If you are an Italian, a Turk, or a Basque, or a recently arrived Russian, you may have equal problems of cultural adaptation and economic survival and yet not enjoy "minority" treatment. Clearly, the term "minority" is used in the two cases with vastly different meanings.

In this book the term "minority" is used in one sense only: to indicate a deprived and subordinate group subjected to discrimination of legal, social, economic, or political character and/or assigned a servile or menial economic or social role through the operation of traditions, customs, or laws. The concept of "minority" is relatively recent and only became established in social science after World War II when the American Louis Wirth defined it in sociologically meaningful terms. (For further definitions see also Simpson and Yinger, 1972; Marden and Meyer, 1968, chapters 2 and 19; Arnold and Caroline Rose, 1972, pp. 3–7; and Biegel, 1972, pp. 13–22).

Since the outbreak of World War I, and for reasons connected with the ideology of that war, the Western world has revealed a particular sensitivity about groups who are victims of persistent unequal treatment in their countries of permanent residence. Attention was, from the beginning, directed at discriminatory treatment of *groups* rather than persons. Yinger stresses the group aspect of what we shall describe as the minority syndrome when he writes:

But discrimination occurs when all members of a group are treated in a manner that is in violation of accepted standards no matter what characteristics they possess as individuals. The origin of this practice is to be found in the appearance of heterogeneous societies. Through most of man's history—the first several hundred thousand years of it—he lived in small, homogeneous societies. All members spoke the same language, practiced the same religion, were of the same physical type, and followed the same customs. A few thousand years ago this situation began to change as a result of migration and conquest. Groups which were different in important ways came into continuous contact. Under some circumstances they were formed into larger structures—nations and empires. Their former identities, however, frequently remained. There were conquerors and conquered; tribes clung to their own customs and religions—the sacred ways of their fathers; racial lines remained; memories of an earlier day when they had been independent stood as barriers against loss of group identity. . . . Today, both migration and the process of forging larger societies continue to create minorities. There is scarcely a society in the world today that does not have within it one or more groups, different in language, religion, race, or culture, which are in some measure disprivileged. (1965, p. 24)

It is in this context that the concept "minority," as used here, acquired its specific sociological meaning.

A. *The Concept of "Minority"*

Before World War II the term "minority" was mainly used to denote nationalities and ethnic groups whom the drawing of political boundaries had placed in subordinate positions in states controlled by other *Staatsvölker*. Professors E. C. and H. M. Hughes observed in this connection: "For the term minority was historically applied in Europe to a group of people living on soil which they had occupied from time immemorial, but who, through change of boundaries, have become politically subordinate. They are strangers, though at home" (Quoted in Schermerhorn, 1967, p. 6). Schermerhorn refers to this period as follows:

The power relations between people in Europe have been largely those of military conquest. The continuous shifting of boundary lines as one people after another became dominant has occurred for centuries; the uncertain vicissitudes of war have led at times to the engulfing of whole peoples in the territory of another, and at other times to the incorporation of mere fragments. . . . Each new treaty created a new crop of minorities; and the Versailles Treaty, which probably came closest to the realization of the nationalistic norm, perhaps orginated the largest number of minorities. (*Ibid.*, pp. 5–6)

1. EFFORTS TOWARD PRECISE DEFINITION

Until the early 1930s it was a widespread practice in social science to group all problems of relationships between differentiated groups—whether they involved variant races, classes, castes, or nationalities; or language, religious or ethnic groups—under the umbrella concept of "intergroup relations." This language did not permit adequate analysis of the kind of differentiation involved. There were, in particular, discriminatory situations which the socioeconomic terms *class* and *caste* did not exactly cover, even though elements of these relationships might be involved. A term was needed to deal with cases in which groups differing in cultural or physical characteristics were unequally treated. A case in point frequently cited was the position of various nationalities in the former Austro-Hungarian Empire. It must be added, however, that some of the discrimination charged by spokesmen of non-German groups was imaginary, so that sociologists, when dealing with the situation *before* World War I (especially in the Austrian half of the Empire), often based their analysis on fictitious premises.

The position of the German-Austrians, Magyars, Croats, Czechs, Poles, Serbs, Slovaks, and other nationalities in the Dual Monarchy was in no way comparable to that of classes or castes, even though there were differences among the socioeconomic profiles of the various groups. Their differences were ethnic and linguistic: each group had its own language, each had experienced a national *risorgimento*, and each had leaders with high political aspirations. Propaganda originated by Slavic separatists during World War I and echoed by the French, who were otherwise unsure why they were fighting the war (Masaryk, 1927, p. 94), pictured Austria-Hungary as "the prison of nations" with the German-Austrians as *Staatsvolk*-jailer and the other peoples in various stages of deprivation. Western sociologists in many cases accepted the propaganda as true and developed the "minority" concept to fit what they thought was the case. Actually, the Germans enjoyed only a weak predominance in the Austrian half of the Empire; they had lost their majority in the Reichsrat several decades before World War I, and the non-German groups were well represented in the central civil service and the officers' corps. The Slavic areas shared fully in the 69 percent growth in real Gross National Product between 1903 and 1913—a growth rate never again reached in the succession states after the breakup of the empire (Hertz, 1947, pp. 38ff.).

The situation described in this chapter as the minority syndrome did exist in Austria-Hungary, but it existed locally and the Germans were by no means the only villains. Under the 1867 Basic Law wide legislative powers were vested in the Crown Lands, whose traditional boundaries did not match the settlement areas of major ethnic groups. Hungary was granted almost total self-government in 1867; the Czechs in Bohemia and Moravia wanted the same but objected to a division of their Lands along nationality lines. By force of numbers they achieved the role of *Staaatsvolk* in Bohemia. The Poles did likewise in Galicia, where they used their power to Polonize the schools. In both these Lands Germans, and in Galicia Ukrainians as well, found themselves at a cultural and political disadvantage (Hantsch, 1953, ch. 5). Basically, however, Austria was committed to a policy of ethnic equality. This was unfortunately not true in Hungary, where the Magyar regime in Budapest unwisely attempted to impose a linguistic-cultural state on a multinational country.

Extreme differentiation in the political, cultural and economic status of ethnic groups became prevalent in Central Europe after the Paris Peace Treaties of 1919, which redrew the map in the name of self-determination. The nationalities south and east of Germany are so scattered that it is geographically impossible to draw boundaries placing each ethnic unit in a national state. As a result, each so-called "succession state" had a *Staatsvolk* determined to shape a centralized cultural-linguistic state in its own image, and a variety of smaller and some larger ethnic groups equally determined to maintain their cultural and linguistic integrity but lacking the political power to enact school laws and budgets. It was at this point that the term "minority" came into common usage, particularly in connection with the Minority Protection Treaties administered by the Council of the League of Nations. Through the discriminations heaped upon them, these statistical minorities soon qualified as sociological minorities. Jaksch (1967, pp. 255–56), who devotes an entire chapter to the ineffectiveness of the Minority Treaties, quotes the *Manchester Guardian Weekly* of October 17, 1930, on the treatment of the Ukrainian minority in Poland as follows (retranslated from the German):

The Polish terror in the Ukraine is now worse than anything else happening in Europe. Ukraine had become a country of desperation and devastation, which seem all the more tragic since the rights of the Ukrainians were guaranteed by international treaties. But the League of Nations is totally deaf to all appeals and arguments, and the outside world knows nothing of the situation or does not care. . . .

On the 22nd and 23rd [of September, 1930] divisions of armed police burst into the village of Kupcznce (near Tarnopol), destroyed the cooperative shop as well as the library, and smashed the instruments of the village band. Many inhabitants were beaten. . . .

In the village of Zurow the dairy was totally destroyed; even the machines, the chemicals, and the glass bottles were made unusable. The people working in the dairy were mercilessly beaten. . . . The Ukrainian cooperative reading room, the library, and the equipment were vandalized: tables, chairs, books, china, stoves, and the piano were smashed or torn to fragments, the flooring was torn up, and clothing and bedding were shredded with knives. In Tarnopol the library with 40,000 volumes was destroyed. . . . It is actually a complete and highly developed civilization that has been destroyed during the last three weeks. The cooperative schools, libraries, and institutions were built through years of work, sacrifice, and enthusiasm on the part of the Ukrainians. They were almost entirely financed by the Ukrainians with their own resources regardless of the greatest difficulties. The Ukrainians are as pained by the loss of these things as by the inhuman physical suffering.

Increasingly, researchers began to feel that the tension between a dominant group and a deprived group required its own conceptual scheme and theoretical system. As Donald Young remarked: "There is, unfortunately, no word in the English language which can with philological propriety be applied to all these groups which are distinguished by biological features, alike national traits, or a combination of both" (1932, p. xiii). Although it was Young who suggested the term "minority," it was more than a decade later when Louis Wirth produced a comprehensive definition of the new concept:

We may *define a minority* as a group of people who, because of their physical or cultural characteristics, are singled out from the others in the society in which they live for differential and unequal treatment, and who therefore regard themselves as objects of collective discrimination. The existence of a minority in a society implies the existence of a corresponding dominant group enjoying higher social status and greater privileges. Minority status carries with it the exclusion from full participation in the life of the society. Though not necessarily an alien group the minority is treated and regards itself as a people apart. (1945, p. 347)

A minority, Wirth continues, "must be distinguishable from the dominant group by physical or cultural marks. In the absence of such identifying characteristics it blends into the rest of the population in the course of time." He then points out that minorities suffer objective disadvantages, being denied certain economic, social, and political opportunities. Their members are looked down upon and may be targets of contempt, hatred, ridicule, and violence. They are likely to be socially isolated, spatially segregated, and economically insecure. As a result, "Minorities tend to develop a set of attitudes, forms of behavior, and other subjective characteristics which tend further to set them apart" (*Ibid.*, pp. 347–48).

A question that may occur to the reader at this point is, *why* do majority groups feel the compulsion to discriminate against or persecute smaller groups of people whose only offense is that they are different physically or culturally? As our case material makes evident, motivations are complex. A clue to human perversity, however, is provided by an early prophet of Aryan superiority, Vacher de Lapouge, who remarked during the 1880s: "I am convinced that in the next century millions of men will cut each other's throats because of one or two degrees more or less of cephalic index" (in Benedict, 1945, p. 3). The bitter fate of many minorities since then is dramatic proof of de Lapouge's remarkable prophetic insight into the weaknesses of his fellow beings. The intensity of people's feelings about human biology is illustrated by the care that rich Japanese parents take in choosing their sons- and daughters-in-law so as not to devalue their own status or that of their children through marriages to persons lacking the correct genealogical qualifications. Koreans and members of the Burakumin, the lowest Japanese caste, are the worst status risks.

2. THE MINORITY AS EXPERIENCED BY ITS MEMBERS

Psychological tension in minority group members is a response to the discrepancy between a person's perceived situation, and his or her personal and group aspirations. The tension is aggravated when the goals are contradictory, as are those of assimilation and preserving group identity in the absence of a pluralist institutional structure that can accommodate this dialectic. The ranking black philosopher W. E. B Dubois wrote rather early in his career (1897):

One ever feels his twoness,—an American, a Negro; two souls, two thoughts, two unreconciled strivings; two warring ideals in one dark body, whose dogged strength alone keeps it from being torn asunder.

The history of the American Negro is the history of this strife,—this longing to attain self-conscious manhood, to merge his double self into a better and truer self. In this merging he wishes neither of the old selves to be lost. He would not Africanize America, for America he would not bleach his Negro soul in a flood of white Americanism, for he knows that Negro blood has a message for the world. He simply wishes to make it possible for a man to be both a Negro and an American without being cursed and spit upon.

American Blacks are still to a large extent an externally defined group. Exclusion from white society is thrust on most black children before their *négritude* is internally asserted. St. Clair Drake observes that the ghetto forces a Black "to identify as a Negro first, an American second, and it gives him geographical 'roots.' " The white middle class, Drake continues, is the reference group for those who are mobile; yet the entire system reinforces racial identity, since defensive solidarity must be maintained against the white world. Drake quotes Ann Pettigrew to the effect that "the perception of relative deprivation, the discrepance between high aspirations and actual attainment . . . is a critical psychological determinant of mental disorder. And certainly racial discrimination acts to bar the very achievements which the society encourages individuals to attempt" (Drake, 1971, pp. 44–45).

Apart from the specific physical violence visited on American Blacks by Klansmen and lynching mobs and continued by characters such as Bull Connor and Jim Clark, whose function was to guard the *status quo* with dogs and police clubs, many American blacks feel that the atmosphere in which they have to live is inherently violent. The Reverend Ralph David Abernathy, who has experienced enough specific violence (his home and his church were bombed in 1957 after the Montgomery bus boycott had ended segregated seating), expresses this attitude:

There is violence in the land. The violence that is present, and of which I speak, takes on various forms. It is inflicted mainly upon poor and black people. There is the violence of an unjust war perpetuated upon a tiny nation of brown people 10,000 miles away from the United States mainland. There is also the violence of racism, which manifests itself in many forms. The violence is seen in the practice of denying decent human survival to the masses, only to give large sums of unnecessary resources to the classes. The violence of racism is seen in police brutality; exploitation of the ghetto, the plantation, the colony, or whatever you choose to call that area where poor and black people struggle to live or exist. Violence is evident in an unjust educational system, which pollutes the mind because it is not honest and truthful; in unemployment, underemployment, poor housing, inadequate medical and dental care, and the many other forms of repression and oppression imposed by the power structure upon the black and poor people. This violence is seen so clearly in our country, the United States of America—the wealthiest and most prosperous of all nations—a nation that preaches one thing and practices another. This is the most destructive form of violence. (Abernathy, 1971, p. 181)

Although Abernathy makes it clear that, like his friend and mentor Dr. Martin Luther King, Jr., he wants the revolution fought and won by "soul force" rather than physical violence, he projects a continuum of violence embracing the physical, economic, social, and psychological. His less sophisticated followers may be inclined to see the continuum as morally horizontal—nonphysical violence as equivalent to physical violence. There is danger of a logical short-circuit, in which economic injustice becomes an excuse for crime. It might even be surmised that for some, the crime and toughness glorified in Black *machismo* films play the ideological role of piecemeal revolution.

Another aspect of the minority experience is failure to fit the prevailing somatic norm image—a discrepancy that may result in self-rejection (see chapter 13, B2).

Attitudes reflecting an intermediate level in the stratification system are expressed by Mexican-Americans. The following are excerpts from statements collected by Hirsch (1973, pp. 10 and 18):

Case No. 1: "By admitting to being Chicano, to being this new person, we lose nothing, we gain a great deal. Any Mexican American afraid to join the Chicano cause can only be afraid for himself and afraid of the Gringo. The Black has faced this truth and found that he must make his way as a Black or as nothing, certainly not as the White man's "nigger." We can no longer be the Anglo's "Pancho." . . . The United States has been anything but a melting pot, because the Gringo has purposely segregated, separated, and relegated the non-Anglo to an inferior and degraded status. Melting pot has meant surrender of one's past and culture to something euphemistically called American society or culture. The melting pot worked only for immigrants with a white skin who came to America. Regardless of nationality, these were willing to sacrifice a discrete identity in order to succeed and enter the polluted mainstream of American 'can-doism'—can cheat, can swindle, can steal, can discriminate, can invade, can kill." (From Armando B. Rendon, *Chicano Manifesto*, p. 14.)

Case No. 2: "The meskun's not a White man, but he is a hell of a lot whiter than a nigger."

Case No. 3: "I think like an Anglo and I act like an Anglo but I will never look like an Anglo. Just looking at me, no one could tell if I am an American or one of those blasted Mexicans from across the river. It's hell to look like a foreigner in your own country."

B. Characteristics of the Minority Situation

Ethnic, racial, and religious groups assigned to low status or deprived of opportunities can be found in all regions of the world. Some of these minorities, each associated with a well-known problem situation, are listed in table 9.1, which does not pretend to be exhaustive.

Table 9.1. TYPICAL MINORITIES IN VARIOUS PARTS OF THE WORLD

Country	Minority	Type of Discrimination
Afghanistan	Baluchis	S
	Pathans	S
	Sindhis	S
Algeria	Berbers, including Kabyls	E, S
Australia	Aborigines	E
Burma	Indians	C, L
Canada	French-speaking	C
	(American) Indians	C, E, S
Cyprus	Turks	S
Czechoslovakia	Germans	P
Europe (East and West)	Romani (Gypsies)	C, E
Fiji	Indians	E, L
Great Britain	Blacks	C
	U.K. citizens of non-U.K. descent	L
India	Kashmiri	E, S
Indonesia	Japanese	C, L
Iraq	Kurds	C, P, S
Israel	Arabs	C
Japan	Ainu	C
	Burakumin	C
Kenya	Masai	E
Malaysia	Chinese	C, L
Nigeria	Ibos	P, S
Northern Ireland	Catholics	C, E
Pakistan	Bengalis	C, P
	Pathans	S
Philippines	Indians	E, L
Poland	Germans	P
	Jews	P
Rwanda	Tutsi	P
South Africa	Coloured, Asians	C, L, E
South America	Indians (tribal)	E, some P
Spain	Basques	C, S
Sri Lanka (Ceylon)	Tamils	C, E
Sudan (intermittently)	Nilo-Hamites	C, S
Uganda	Indians	E, L, P
	Acholi, Langi	P
USSR	Crimean Tartars	P, S
	Jews	E, P
	Volga Germans	P
	Other non-Russian nationalities	C, S

Table 9.1. *(Continued)*

Country	Minority	Type of Discrimination
United States	Blacks	C, E
	Indians	C, E, S
	Mexican-Americans	C, E
	Orientals	C
	Puerto Ricans	C, E
Yugoslavia	Croats	P, S
	Moslems	E
	Turks	E
Zanzibar	Arabs	E, P

Key to Types of Discrimination

C: cultural and social, including linguistic

E: economic, including access to education and employment; extreme economic discrimination includes seizure of property and denial of subsistence resources

L: legal, including limitation of citizenship and political rights

P: persecution, especially of leadership; interference with freedom of movement

S: denial of self-determination or autonomy, if demanded. (An "S" has not been entered for American blacks, because there is no significant black autonomy movement. Autonomy is, however, a major demand of most Indian groups.)

The reader will probably recognize some of the situations and groups listed, but not others. He or she should not rush to condemn a country because it happens to be listed. There are often urgent reasons for minority treatment; a *Staatsvolk* may not be able to grant a minority equality in all respects without destroying its own ethnic integrity or losing its territorial base. No nation or nationality ever has a moral obligation to self-destruct.

Because of structural complexity, a full listing of minorities was not attempted for countries such as Angola, Lebanon, Mozambique, Rhodesia, and the USSR. The status of Bantu-speaking peoples in South Africa is ambivalent: they are minorities in the white area, yet at least in the process of becoming *Staatsvölker* in their Homelands.

All these 48 cases, and the many more that might have been listed, exhibit the structural components of a minority situation. At least some of the following eight elements come into play:

(1) A situation involves socially differentiated groups or categories in asymmetrical relationship.

(2) The groups are differentiated by specific criteria of a cultural or racial nature, as defined in chapter 7.

(3) The socially differentiated groups or categories are arranged in a rank-order of differential status, prestige, privileges, opportunities, and power. Some groups enjoy superior positions and opportunities in the competition for scarce goods, some inferior.

(4) The criteria for group differentiation are assigned relative values, at least by the dominant group or groups. In a given society, for instance, positions on the upper rungs of the economic ladder may be restricted to people of particular ethnic groups, tribes, or religions.

(5) The criteria for group differentiation are also the criteria for ranking of groups.

(6) The valuation of group differentiators and the consequent ranking of groups having particular characteristics are stable, since they reflect a consensus, at least among the dominant groups. (There may be disagreement on particular points—no one is likely to admit that another religion is superior to his own. The rank order may also vary for different factors—the richest people are not necessarily the best educated or even the most powerful.)

(7) Individuals are ranked, not because of their personal qualities, but because of their membership (mainly through birth) in or stable association with a specific group or category. Members of a low-ranking group inherit the disqualifications of their group. Extreme cases of this kind include the Jews during the Third Reich and in the USSR today, as well as the Asian community of Uganda.

(8) The ranking process as described takes place within a specific political unit. (Disagreement may arise as to whether a

political unit exists or whom it includes: all people living within a given territory do not necessarily form a single political unit.)

Where a minority situation exists, the society contains one or more dominant groups. Subordinate groups have less power, privileges, and prestige than the dominant group, and the inequality is directly related to distinctive cultural or somatic characteristics of the subordinate group.

To summarize, the eight elements of a typical minority situation in a national society can be grouped under three main headings: (a) a superior-subordinate relationship pattern; (b) the cultural or somatic differentiation of the groups concerned; (c) the lesser status, power, and opportunities of the subordinate group.

C. Definition and Identification of Minorities

On the basis of these structural elements, the following definition of minorities can be formulated:

A minority is a group or category of persons within a specific political unit who are differentiated from a dominant group through one or more cultural or somatic factors such as lifestyle, language, religion, genealogy, physical characteristics, nationality, ethnicity, or historicity and who because of this differentiation are subjected to discrimination, disqualifications, limitations, inequalities, or disabilities in respect of opportunities, power, status, and prestige.

This definition agrees in broad outline with Louis Wirth's previously discussed definition. It also conforms generally to the very well-known model formulated by Wagley and Harris (1958, pp. 4 and 10) to typify minority situations, which consists of five points:

(1) minorities are subordinate segments of complex state societies;
(2) minorities have special physical or cul-

tural traits which are held in low esteem by the dominant segments of the society;
(3) minorities are self-conscious units bound together by the special traits which their members share and by the special disabilities which these bring;
(4) membership of a minority is transmitted by a rule of descent which is capable of affiliating generations even in the absence of readily apparent special cultural or physical traits;
(5) minority peoples, by choice or necessity, tend to marry within the group.

Minority situations are always found within specific political systems. Regulation of the relationships, rights, and obligations of groups and individuals within the borders of a national state is the prerogative of that state, subject of course to international norms and treaties, such as the Treaty of Rome which provides for free movement of labor throughout the European Common Market and for transfer of work credits for social security purposes. Within each national state or closely knit region, the dominant group or groups set political and cultural norms and social standards. Groups defined as alien are normally subjected to discrimination and denied equal access to social standing and economic gain, as well as political and civil rights.

A society's cultural standards always include an aesthetic standard of physical appearance (somatic norm image). This concept may be defined here briefly as a synthesis of visible characteristics, particularly with regard to skin color, hair color and type, facial features, and in some cases physique (see Hoetink, 1967, ch. 4; also, below, chapter 13, B2).

The concept "minority," therefore, has a sociocultural and political rather than a statistical meaning. It is, however, a fact that most sociological minorities are also numerical minorities. Barron explains the relationship as follows:

Numerical size undoubtedly has played an important role in the struggle for power between interacting ethnic groups. It is not surprising, therefore, to find that in most societies of the world, statistically smaller groups are, in fact, sociological minorities and the larger ones are usually dominant. But social power is not dependent solely upon the variable of size of numbers; other variables such as weapons, organizational skill, leadership, resources and literacy can offset numerical strength so that statistical majorities can become sociological minorities and some statistical minorities become sociological majorities. (1967, p. 3)

1. THE STATUS CONTINUUM, STRATIFICATION, AND MINORITIES

The levels of rights and privileges must not be viewed as discrete horizontal layers separated by watertight floors and ceilings. The more likely pattern is a continuum with shadings of prestige, status, opportunities, and power. It is seldom true in real life that a dominant group commands all privileges while a minority commands none. Rather, they spill over in diminishing extent from the dominant group into the ranks of the minority.

It is exactly this idea of a status continuum which has resulted in partial obsolescence of the once-popular stratification model for socially differentiated societies. Stratification, however, still remains a popular conceptual tool, and will be used here whenever it fits the facts of the society under scrutiny.

Today minority situations are mostly studied in terms of overlapping status concentrations using the status-continuum model. It is then easier to explain why a person can belong simultaneously to both a minority and a dominant group, which often happens in societies where groups are differentiated by noncongruent criteria. So, for instance, Roman Catholic Slovaks in the U.S.A. can, in religious and cultural orientation, form a minority group vis-à-vis the dominant White-Anglo-Saxon-Protestant (WASP) segment of the population, and even in relation to blacks insofar as the latter seek and achieve integration in the Anglo-Saxon cultural community (see Hare, *The Black Anglo-Saxons*, 1965). At the same time, Slovaks form part of the white racial majority.

2. COMPETITION FOR SCARCE GOODS

A group in a minority situation is at a disadvantage in the competition for scarce goods. These, as we have seen, include non-material goods such as prestige and political power. As Yinger observes,

"If stratification means unequal distribution of things that are prized and scarce, we need to know what those things are. There are three basic types: *Income* (control over economic goods and services), *prestige* (control over social honor), and *power* (control over the activities of other persons). (1965, p. 10)

The distribution of these goods is not stable: the competition is ongoing.

Whenever a group finds itself in a minority position, its members, individually and collectively, attempt, by competing with the dominant group, to secure the privileges, prestige, opportunities, and economic and political power denied them. The dominant group discriminates against the minority because of somatic or cultural characteristics its members dislike. Should the minority, however, challenge the dominant group's monopoly or preponderant possession of the scarcest and most valued social good—political and economic power—the dominant group will employ every legal and political strategy to defend the status quo. Should the sociological minority also be a statistical minority, the most productive strategy may be a compromise: cession of a share (albeit a minority share) of power. Where the sociological minority is a statistical majority, however, experience suggests that the deprived group, once it has attained "majority rule," will impose its own pattern of discrimination, jeopardizing the existence of the former dominating group. Facing this threat the dominating group, unless totally decadent and demoralized, will man the barricades or the trenches rather than commit political suicide.

D. Cultural and Racial Minorities

Minorities can be divided into two main categories: cultural and racial. The term "racial" is defined here as indicating a social category, as explained in chapter 7, B2. "Culture" is used in its widest meaning—"the way of life of a social group; the group's total man-made environment, including all the material and non-material products of group life that are transmitted from one generation to the next." (Theodorson and Theodorson, 1969, p. 95.)

Unless otherwise qualified the term cultural minorities is used in its extensive meaning. Where necessary the recognized subcategories (linguistic, religious, ethnic, and national minorities), will be indicated clearly. In practice so-called national minorities are usually differentiated socially according to one or more cultural characteristics. The same is true of most ethnic minorities, but there are some who are largely identified by biological (racial) factors.

The adjective *national* is usually an indicator of a group's political history. At the present time it is always applied to groups within a "nation-state" or ideological state expressing the aspirations of nationality alien to or persecuted by the regime. Status as a national minority may result from migration, colonialism, or annexation, or simply from not being a large enough group to maintain a national state. Among the latter are the Magyars in Slovakia, the Germans and Magyar Szeklers in Rumanian-ruled Transylvania, and the Turks in Yugoslavia. Among groups with the size and ability to maintain national states, but who are forcibly prevented from doing so and are therefore classified as "captive nations," are the Tibetans in communist China, the non-Russian nationalities in the USSR, and the Kurds divided between Iraq, Iran, Syria, and Turkey—about whom more in later chapters.

In most cases linguistic and religious minorities can also be described as cultural minorities. In deciding whether to discriminate against a person, members of the dominant group take note of his or her language (or accent in speaking the dominant-group language) or any indication of religion. A bigoted Protestant, for instance, might not hire an applicant wearing a Star of David. Usually, groups whose minority treatment is signaled by their language or faith are also differentiated from the dominant groups in other cultural characteristics such as lifestyles and value systems. The Indian Constitution, for example, makes provision for language and religious minorities but not for cultural, ethnic, or national ones. This is not because there are no such minorities but because the Indian government considers language and religion to be sufficiently accurate indicators of ethnicity, culture, and nationality.

A racial minority may be defined formally as a socially differentiated group or category within a complex political community which, identified by somatic and cultural criteria, occupies a subordinate position and whose restricted political and economic power, life-chances and status ranking are defined and rationalized by the dominant group mainly in terms of biogenetic differences. Since there is today, for all practical purposes, no minority defined exclusively in terms of biological determinism, any analytical model of such a group would be academic. In the case of most racial minorities, significant elements of cultural difference are also perceived.

1. SOMATIC AND CULTURAL CRITERIA

A racial group does not become a target for discrimination (and hence a minority) only because it varies from the dominant somatic norm image. Rather, its visible physical characteristics must be thought to signal social, cultural, or inherent human characteristics subjectively defined as inferior or undesirable by the dominant group. The physical norm image of the minority thus symbolizes its supposed social, cultural, or inherent human inferiority.

On closer analysis, much behavior thought

at first to be racially determined turns out to be ascriptive: people tend to live up to role expectations. Aunt Jemima will produce the expected pancakes unless she takes the drastic (and for her revolutionary) step of throwing over that role altogether. The roles assigned to the minority group and which its members usually play—to make a living if for no better reason—are largely prescribed by the dominant group to fit its own subjective definition of the minority group's proper status and power. Differentiated roles within a national society are not determined mainly by what individuals achieve but by the groups to which they belong. The unequal opportunities, status, and power of American Negroes, Australian Aborigines, Canadian Red Indians, Ugandan Asians, Sudanese Blacks, South African Coloureds (to mention a few examples) are not determined primarily by their personal and individual achievements and qualifications but in each case by their membership in a specific group ascriptively assigned a low status and largely excluded from power.

2. MINORITIES AS EXTERNALLY DEFINED GROUPS

It follows from the foregoing that the minority status of a racially differentiated group is, in the final analysis, determined by the subjective way in which the dominant group defines the minority group. Its members will not be able to overcome their low status even if it is shown that the dominant group follows criteria which, objectively, do not indicate socially or culturally undesired traits or are not even present to any great degree in the minority. Of decisive importance is the dominant group's subjective definition of the situation, which in many cases rests on ideas having little if any objective content.

Racial minorities are thus decisively defined by the way the dominant group interprets somatic and cultural criteria believed to be hereditary. Where clearly somatic characteristics are present they are taken as signals of nonsomatic traits such as lifestyle, historicity, and socio-

economic level of development. What then happens is that a measure of objective knowledge about the role of heredity, so far as bodily traits such as skin color and hair texture are concerned, is transferred to characteristics which are exclusively or mainly culturally determined, such as language, life style, religion, and behavior. Through this sleight of hand, objective knowledge is replaced by subjective ideas, belief systems, ideologies, and even myths, which ultimately determine whether certain persons are to be treated as a minority or not.

3. STEREOTYPING OF MINORITIES—THE SELF-FULFILLING PROPHECY

Stereotyping plays an undeniable role in the process by which dominant groups categorize persons as "different" and therefore as members of minorities. A stereotype can be based predominantly on somatic characteristics such as the slanting eyes of the Chinese or the hooked noses of the Jews (either of which provides a basis for caricature), or it may be cultural, like the Sambo image of the American black. Robert Penn Warren describes Sambo's personality: "He was the supine, grateful, humble, irresponsible, unmanly, banjo-picking, servile, grinning, slack-jawed, docile, dependent, slow-witted, humorous, child-loving, childlike, watermelon-stealing, spiritual-singing, blamelessly fornicating, happy-go-lucky, hedonistic, faithful black servitor who sometimes might step out of character long enough to utter folk wisdom or bury the family silver to save it from the Yankee" (quoted by Boskin, 1972, p. 154).

Stereotyping is usually also accompanied by labelling: the bestowing of derogatory nicknames. Many racial epithets change from decade to decade or even from year to year; a list of them would be beside the point. It may be observed, however, that terms considered offensive in one language may be quite acceptable in another. The terms "yid" (for a Jew) and "goy" (for a Gentile) are treated as epithets in English dictionaries, but they are perfectly correct in Yiddish. The term "goy" (pl. goyim) is derived from the Hebrew *goi*, people— equivalent to *gens*, the Latin root of Gentiles.

The dominant group's image of a minority often develops as a self-fulfilling prophecy. During the 1930s National Socialist propaganda built up a stereotype of the Jewish community which caused a large part of the German population to see the Jews as unscrupulous userers who enriched themselves at other people's expense and who had only a superficial loyalty toward their country. As Hitler's vendetta against the Jews progressed, they were compelled to seek safety in increasing solidarity, isolation, and even emigration. In this way millions of Jews became disaffected from the regime and increasingly alienated from other Germans. The definition of the Jewish situation propounded by ideologists such as Rosenberg and Streicher was in essence a "prophecy," some aspects of which eventually came true. R. K. Merton embodied a refinement of Thomas's previously mentioned theorem, "if men define situations as real, they are real in their consequences," in his well-known *Self-Fulfilling Prophecy* (1957, pp. 421–36).

In the case of racial minorities the self-fulfilling prophecy usually starts as a predominantly subjective process. Specific persons are defined as a separate category or group on the basis of certain cultural or somatic characteristics. Although some of these characteristics are undoubtedly real, such as a specific language, lifestyle, religion, or clearly observable physical features, there are others which exist only subjectively in the minds of the dominant group. The meaning the dominant group attaches to visible characteristics is particularly important. Language and religion, for instance, usually innocuous in themselves (unless the latter involves female circumcision or human sacrifices), are taken as signals of traits believed to be inherited and to be inferior and undesirable.

Even a slight shading in skin color can serve as this signal. In such a case negative sociocultural characteristics (e.g. poverty, family disorganization, low educational level, and backward lifestyle), considered to be inherent in the subordinate group, may actually be present in varying degrees but as results of the treatment meted out to the group. In this way, characteristics attributed to a group are actually acquired. Subjective characteristics can therefore result in objective facts. If, for instance, certain persons are defined subjectively as a racial minority by a dominant group—regardless how false the definition may be—then the inequalities they suffer are actually experienced. Through the inferior status thrust upon it, the group develops an acquired inferiority by the standards of the dominant culture. That is why the self-fulfilling prophecy serves as an important perception in the study of racial minorities.

The mere fact that social differentiation (regardless by what criteria) results in groups and categories does not mean that these groups will necessarily become involved in a minority situation. Social differentiation based on race (characteristics assumed to be genetic in origin) can result in group formation without a clear superior-subordinate structure developing. A minority situation appears only if the differentiation places some groups above others in the power and status hierarchy. The disqualifications, incompetencies, poorer life-chances and reduced rewards concomitant with this status and power differentiation determine the essential character of minority status.

E. Special Problems of Racial Minorities

The central psychosocial process that makes a minority specifically racial is that other groups attribute to it social, cultural, and other non-physical characteristics which they associate with biological inheritance. Whether the minority actually has the characteristics attributed to it, and whether the association with hereditary traits is valid, are irrelevant to the process. As Ina C. Brown points out, "this attributing of class, religious, social, linguistic, or economic difference to inborn physical qualities serves an important function in justifying discriminatory practices." She quotes Robert Redfield's observation that "in so doing you push the problems out of the social category for which man is responsible into the biological category where God can be held responsible" (Brown, 1973, p. 19).

American blacks are a minority whose subordinate status has been defined in racial terms by other groups. The fact that, as their socioeconomic situation improves, this external definition is being replaced by internal definition (reflected in black exclusiveness) does not alter the point of departure. Many individual blacks have successfully entered the middle class and have thus risen above the economic level of the minority. But insofar as discrimination persists, it is triggered by the somatic differential. Thus within our definition American blacks form a classic example of a racial minority. Brown has written in this connection:

> The separation of black and white in churches, schools, community and recreational facilities, civic affairs, business, and government has meant that Negroes were in, but not of, the community. . . . The most far-reaching aspect of the black experience lies in the fact that Negroes were robbed of any cultural identification with their African heritage yet denied the right to become Americans in the fullest sense of the word. Other immigrant groups usually came in families with cultural and linguistic patterns relatively intact. Moreover, most of them were from European backgrounds. As time went on they moved from the status of hyphenated-Americans into full integration into the national life. Although they might maintain sentimental ties with the country of their origin or that of their ancestors, they ceased to be Italian- or Polish- or Irish-Americans. They belonged. . . . The Negroes were not only brought in chains, but they came for

the most part as individuals cut off from family ties and even from others of their own language and cultural community. So completely were they shut off from their original homelands that only in recent years have many Negroes thought of themselves or their ancestors in this country as Afro-Americans. Yet they were never allowed to forget that they did not belong and were really a different order of being. (1973, pp. 146–47)

While exception could hardly be taken to Brown's statements about segregation and socioeconomic deprivation, some black writers might feel that she is underrating black culture and perpetuating what Vansertima (1971) calls the "cultural deprivation myth." In view of resurgent ethnic awareness among groups of European descent, it would appear that she interprets integration too much in terms of dehyphenization.

A minority can also be conceptualized as racial, however, without noteworthy differences in somatic norm images. English- and Afrikaans-speaking South Africans, for instance, are both white and of West European ancestry; they have several merging and overlapping social and cultural interests and characteristics. Yet both groups tend to interpret differences in language and lifestyle in terms of divergent cultural and biological backgrounds. After the Anglo-Boer War which ended the independence of the Transvaal and the Orange Free State (1899–1902), the Afrikaners interpreted their subordinate socioeconomic and political position in a British-dominated economic and (for some years) political system in a way typical of racial minorities. For the average Afrikaner, the English "conqueror" was more than merely culturally strange: he was also a foreigner who was predisposed, because of his different biological history, to be unlike the Afrikaner. Even today the Afrikaans-English differentiation is, to a greater or lesser extent and notwithstanding some mobility between the two groups, attributed to biological as well as cultural determinants.

Another category of the South African population, the Coloureds, has been conceptualized by the whites mainly as a separate *racial* category. Whether the Coloured will achieve a degree of *ethnic* identification as a result of being provided with separate political institutions remains to be seen. Their socioeconomic status, however, is related to a racial rather than a cultural differential. They are West European in culture and, despite economic retardation, have the same lifestyle and aspirations as the whites. Had the Coloureds' subordinate position not been rationalized in racial terms, they might still have tended to concentrate in the lower ranks of the working and farm-labor classes, but they would not have formed a minority.

If groups are traditionally associated with specific signs such as clothes or ritual objects that can be worn or displayed, these signs will serve as indicators of group affiliation and thus of social status. In the past it has often happened that the visibility of specific minorities—racial, cultural, or religious—has been raised by means of artificial symbolization. Shibutani and Kwan mention some interesting examples:

Soon after the spread of Islam, Christians and Jews living under the Caliphs were required to dress in ways that would make them easy to recognize. The practices varied, but in many locales they wore girdles. In some parts of Spain Jews were required to dress in yellow and were not allowed to wear turbans. In 1215, Pope Innocent III ordered that all Jews and Moslems be required to wear badges on their outermost garment, ostensibly to prevent intermarriage and concubinage. The size, shape, and color of the badge was left to the discretion of local authorities. In England the badges were yellow; in Austria Jews were forced to wear different clothing as well. This practice was revived in Nazi Germany, where Jews again had to wear yellow badges. After the Manchu conquest of China the new rulers decreed that any person found wearing clothes of Chinese design, retaining Chinese coiffure, or binding the feet of their female children would be severely punished. Thus, from 1644 Chinese men were forced to wear Manchu dress and a queue—the

"pigtail"—as a symbol of their submission to Manchu rule. This practice continued until the 1911 revolution. Through such symbols barriers may be perpetuated between ethnic groups that have been in contact so long that they have no other differentiating marks. (1965, pp. 77–78)

In the case of racial minorities, clearly visible physical characteristics tend to stabilize and perpetuate group differentiation more than do insignificant physical differences. In the contemporary world, however, where external group definition begets a reactive internal definition, cultural and race differences have become interwoven to the point where it is difficult to find a minority whose lower status and life chances are interpreted entirely in biological terms. The mixture of cultural and biological components in intergroup relations is never static; the two ebb and flow, merge, and overlap. In times of acute tension and conflict of interest people are inclined to attach more importance to biological determinism. Differences in historicity, culture, and lifestyle are then regarded as "unbridgeable." As has been seen, relationships between groups are defined to a large extent by what people *believe*, and this is certainly true of race relations.

Minorities are found in practically all countries; those that can claim to be free of minority problems are few and far between. Some countries admit to having minorities but deny that they have any minority *problems*. This is a contradiction in terms since the existence of a minority by definition implies a problem situation. Indonesian political leaders, for instance, allege that their country experiences no minority problems: if one, however, analyzes the position of the Indians, Christians, Chinese, and Japanese—not to mention the Papuans in Irian Jaya—it soon becames clear that empirical investigation will not support the Indonesian claim.

Like the poor, minorities will always be with us. Countries which concede that they have minority problems are merely admitting that their people are real people and not soulless, emotionless and senseless zombies. Those who protest their innocence are, on the other hand, often motivated by guilt feelings that can usually be traced to skeletons in the national closet. It also does not become countries with few and small minorities to adopt holier-than-thou attitudes toward their less fortunate neighbors. Some countries have problems that are objectively larger and more complex than others. In each case, the question is: What are leaderships doing to reach a peaceful and just accommodation? Countries such as Canada, Australia, New Zealand, and Japan have minority problems statistically smaller though no less serious than those of Israel, Brazil, the United States, or South Africa. Hence, accomplishment should be judged by relative effort rather than by the degree to which problems still remain partly unsolved.

The mere existence of minorities does not mean that dominant groups act cruelly and unjustly or that the minorities are automatically the victims of blatant exploitation and suppression. Some people think that the concept of minority contains by definition an indictment of the dominant groups: a polarization of guilt versus innocence. This simplistic distortion of complex social structures is as naive as it is dangerous. On this point the words of Ben Whitaker, the Director of the London based Minority Rights Group, should be called to mind:

Some minorities are far from faultless (liberals tend to forget that people do not become virtuous merely by reason of their predicament); and of course majorities too have their rights as well as their responsibilities. One of the most interesting questions raised by group stigmatization is why some minorities are seen as a threat or a scapegoat while others are tolerated. Psychologists at Bristol University have found evidence that people, as soon as they are divided into groups, automatically begin to discriminate against outsiders. Many species besides humans fear and attack non-conformity; indeed it has been argued that all people need a pecking-order and a group to look down upon—until in turn they are united by a new enemy. Perhaps it is in order to avoid facing up to the less pleasant parts of ourselves, or through failure to realize the real roots of our frustration, that we project our aggression and fear on to other safer targets—of whom visibly distinct groups, such as immigrants, women or policemen, are often the most easily available. This anti-social re-direction of violence and anger is likely to continue until we are able to recognize and come to terms with the aggressive emotions that are in all of us, and learn to channel them into some constructive and relevant outlets. Even in the field of human rights, it is easy to be aroused by cruelties, as long as they are not our own: but only when we stop blaming other people for what we are, can we hope to begin to attain maturity. (1972a, pp. 10–11)

PART THREE

KTO KOGO:
GROUPS INVOLVED IN DISCRIMINATION
AND OPPRESSION

10

NATIONALISM AND NATIONAL IDENTITY

Since Germany lost its colonies in World War I, the (not always willing) godfathers of colonial independence have been the powers of Western Europe, with the United States as a benevolent bystander. The political theory employed in "nation building" therefore came from the coastal states on both sides of the Atlantic—not from Germany, Austria, or points east. This fact has led to much confusion and quite a few unpleasant surprises— such as the civil war in Nigeria and the mutual slaughter of Greek and Turkish Cypriots—the causes of which have seldom been fathomed. The confusion has its root in failure to recognize two fundamentally different types of nationalism: territorial, reflecting a rationally conceived model of a nation corresponding to a geographic state; and ethnic-linguistic, typified by Johann Gottfried Herder's romantic idea of the *Volk* as a collective personality. French, British, and American political science tends to take the territorial model for granted, whereas the political feelings and behavior of most Asian and African peoples correspond more closely to Herder's romantic picture.

For historical reasons that will be noted in the following section, Western political thinkers from Hobbes to Locke and Burke and from Bodin and Bossuet to Rousseau and St. Simon accepted as a "nation" the people living under a particular government, without asking *why* they were living under that government. When royal marriages, wars, and treaties caused boundary changes, nationality shifted with territorial allegiance. Many Poles thought partition of their country made them into Russians, Prussians, and Austrians, and only abandoned this belief when they rejected the rational, territorial concept of the nation (Lemberg, 1964, 1, p. 170).

The rationalist political model, which formed the conceptual basis for the British constitutional monarchy and for the American and French revolutions, found its dialectical answer in the romantic idea of the *Volk*. The concept given definitive form by Herder (especially in his *Ideas on the Philosophy of Human History*) was echoed by Goethe, Schiller, and other German writers of the *Sturm und Drang* era. The essence of Herder's teaching, which became the starting point for nationalist thought through central and eastern Europe, is explained by the German sociologist Eugen Lemberg as follows:

The revolutionary principle of the romantic world image, to which the new nations owed their birth, was precisely the single basic thought formulated by Herder . . . : that all these phases of life previously considered separately and studied for their own sakes, such as language, poetry, music, law, philosophy, politics, economics, religion, etc., are expressions of a people and therefore radiations of a principle of life, which may be called the national soul, national spirit, or simply nation (*Volk*).

The nation thus acquired the character of an individual, or a personality. It had become that superindividual individuality that lived in the teachings of national prophets, not only of nineteenth century Europe, but also of twentieth century Asia and Africa. (*Ibid.*, p. 172)

The same totality, as well as a feedback of European nationalist ideas, is observable in the thoughts of Arab reformers like Afghani (1837–1897), Mohammed Abduh (1848–1905), and Mustafa Kamil (1874–1908), the Hindu nationalists Chatterjee (1838–1894) and Gandhi, and apostles of *négritude* such as Azikiwe, Leopold Senghor, and Aimé Césaire.

A. *The Emergence of Modern Nationalism*

The common people of medieval Europe were scattered in regional tribes speaking divergent dialects. The area of each tribe contained a number of local fiefs, each centering upon the castle of its local lord. Peasants were bound to the soil and seldom traveled beyond the fiefs where they were born. The fief was the major culture-forming unit, and often developed its distinctive folkways and costumes. Political integrators of wider range were comparatively weak but were universal and Christian; indeed it was a "European nation" that launched the Crusades and stopped the Saracens at the Pyrenees. The body politic of this nation was the nobility and its intelligentsia was the clergy—the custodians of religion and learning and, above all, the common liturgical and political language. So long as the governance of Europe and its major regions was limited to an elite, the fact that the masses could communicate only with difficulty was of small moment.

The division of Charlemagne's empire and the struggle between the Papacy and the Hohenstaufen Emperors dashed all hopes of restoring a unified political system. The more enterprising regional rulers, such as the Carolingians and Capetians in France, William of Normandy and his successsors in England, the Houses of Castile and Aragon in Spain, and somewhat later the Hohenzollerns in Brandenburg-Prussia and the Hapsburgs in Austria, succeeded in creating dynastic-territorial states that (with the exception of Austria) evolved into modern national states. Needing a legitimizing ideology, these rulers took over as best they could the integrators of the Empire and the Papacy: each king styled himself "Defender of the Faith." They added new integrators of their own: loyalty to and pride in the dynasty, and in some cases a sense of regional function such as that of the Hapsburg Empire—Europe's shield against the Turks (Lemberg, 1964, 1, pp. 64–73, 86–87).

With the growth of market towns and cities as craft and trade centers, the bourgeois and the linguistic-cultural nation made their appearance. As Lemberg has pointed out, the nobility and the bourgeoisie had very different relations to language. For the nobleman, language was a way to communicate and perhaps a political symbol—not a criterion of identity. William ("The Silent") of Orange—of German descent and a champion of *Nederlands* nationalism against Spain—thought in French: when stabbed by an assassin, he spoke his last words in that language. As modernization progressed, French replaced Latin as the language of diplomacy and the *lingua franca* in which noble and cultured Europeans (with the partial exception of the British) could communicate. The bourgeoisie, on the other hand, acquired its literacy in the regional vernacular and remained stubbornly monolingual. From the beginning, its members identified with others of like tongue and tradition: they were local and particularist more than European (*ibid.*, 1:100). Whether the emergence of potential *Staatsvölker* with their roots in the bourgeoisie strengthened or weakened the dynastic-territorial states depended mainly on whether linguistic-cultural boundaries coincided with or overlapped political borders.

1. LINGUISTIC NATION BUILDING IN FRANCE AND SPAIN

Monarchs and their governments undertook with varying success to guide the process of nation-making, using language as a political weapon. France, for instance, is admired as the classic model of a unified nation, and many are inclined to assume that it arose spontaneously, like Venus from the deep. The fact is that the French cultural nation was created through dynastic politics—*à coups d'épée*, as Richelieu once put it. At the height of the Middle Ages, France was a territorial state with various regional dialects and even languages. Apart from the non-Latin districts where the medieval forms of Basque, Breton, Flemish, and German were spoken, the two major linguistic regions were that of the Langue d'Oïl, containing 30 million French people today, and that of the Langue d'Oc, the southern half of France, with a present day population of 15 million. Despite over four centuries of linguistic discrimination, about 8 million of these people retain some knowledge of the Occitan language, as it is called, and 2 million speak it daily. Those who spoke only Occitan appear to have died out about 1930.

Like other Latin languages, Occitan resulted from a mixture of the speech of the Roman invaders with that of the local people. Phonetically, Occitan has more in common with Catalan, Castilian, and Italian than with French: Occitan and Catalan only separated after the thirteenth century. Occitan had become a literary language in the eleventh century, and a state of Occitania was emerging along the Mediterranean seaboard: it would have extended from Nice to Barcelona had not the French part been annexed by the Capetians in the thirteenth century. As a growing nation, Occitania was characterized by urbanity and tolerance, and its Jews were exempt from the persecution typical of the Middle Ages in much of Europe. Unfortunately, however, Occitania was also the home of the heretical Albigenses, which gave the kings in Paris an excuse to mount a crusade against them and to annex the entire area northeast of the Pyrenees to their growing kingdom. The royal government in Paris did not undertake immediate linguistic conversion, but waited until 1532, when an edict of Francis I "abolished" Occitan in favor of French (Fougeyrollas, 1968, pp. 131–41).

The people of the Langue d'Oïl, inhabiting the Parisian basin and its tributaries, including Lyon, Savoy, French Switzerland, and Wallonia, are Francians—so named by Robert Lafont. The Francian language, the ancestor of modern French, is characterized by a German impact left by Frankish invasions. This impact was not strong enough to convert the Francians into speakers of Low German (*Plattdeutsch*), but it did serve to shift the phonetics to a pattern totally different from any other Latin language. The distinctive feature of French, as compared with Spanish or Italian, is precisely the Germanic influence.

The policy of the Capetians, and their successors, the Valois and the Bourbons, was to make the speech of the Île de France (the region immediately surrounding Paris) the standard speech of the whole kingdom, to the detriment of regional languages and cultures. Like the Basque and Breton languages, the Langue d'Oc was "extinguished" as a respectable language and removed from the school curriculum. They and the various regional dialects of Francian became the province of private societies, which studied them as archaic curiosities to be consigned to the archives and forgotten. Whether the net result was cultural impoverishment or enrichment depends upon the answer to a question of cultural morphology: was destruction of the regional languages a necessary condition for the development of classic French and the literary age of Ronsard, Montaigne, Racine, Corneille, Voltaire, and Rousseau?

Linguistic nation-building in Spain followed a similar pattern. National integrative forces proceeded from culturally poor Castile rather than the more civilized Aragon or Andalusia. But the same integration that unified most of Iberia alienated the Spanish subjects in the Netherlands, for whom the leap from *Hollands* to *Castellano* was too far (Lemberg, 1964, 1:123–29). Burgundy, once an important regional power, had run afoul of the problem even earlier. Its nobility stood united behind its dukes, but its bourgeoisie disintegrated into *welsche* and *dietsche* nations, and Burgundy disappeared from the map.

Brought up in a narrow linguistic community and viewing speakers of other languages as "foreigners," the awakening bourgeoisie demanded expression in "pure" national states. Early evidences of this tendency were the deuniversalizing of the Sorbonne in 1381, when antiforeign measures forced the German professors to leave the university, and the Kuttenberg Decree of 1409, which provoked a similar exodus from the University of Prague. But once the religious wars of the Reformation had been settled under the rule of *cuius regio, eius religio*, the danger that Europe might fly into fragments remained abated throughout the age of absolutism, since the nobility and the classically trained civil servants were territorialists, not ethnic nationalists. The economic base of bourgeois nationalism, however, continued to expand—most rapidly in Western Europe, Germany, and German Austria, as well as Scandinavia, and more slowly but still appreciably in the eastern lands of the Hapsburg Empire, in Italy, the Balkans, and in Russia.

The nation of France, which even today remains the prototype for nations in general, was without doubt the legitimate child of the *ancien régime*, but this fact in no way deterred it from devouring its parent. Even secondary school pupils learn about the French Revolution as the event that unleashed the forces of bourgeois democracy and modern nationalism.

But they are not told about a dialectic that is central to understanding why nationalism both in Europe and in Europe's former colonies operates the way it does. This dialectic derives from the fact that nationalism not only integrates but also differentiates: it expresses not only objective differences but, more importantly, *the need to feel different*. It thus follows that reactive nationalism—that which integrates an awakening or even a mature nation against "foreign" domination or oppression—tends to adopt a political style as nearly opposite as possible to that of the state or nation seen as the oppressor.

2. HERDER'S VOLK IN CENTRAL EUROPE

The French Revolution was conducted in the language of the Enlightenment. Robespierre's Reign of Terror was, so to speak, rationalism carried *à l'outrance*. When Napoleon invaded Germany and set up puppet states on the Rhine and in Westphalia, he did so in the name of *liberté, egalité, et fraternité*. German nationalism, which found expression in the Stein-Hardenburg reforms and the Wars of Liberation that eliminated Napoleonic hegemony, naturally sought a model opposite to that of French rationalism—that model was the *Volk*.

The German reformers of the *Befreiungskriege* (wars of liberation), having embraced Herder's doctrine of national distinctiveness and having experienced democracy as foreign occupation, sought their political character in the Prussian *ständisch* (status-group representation) tradition, which was authoritarian in conception but also insisted on a rule of law that guaranteed every citizen due process. A feature of Freiherr vom Stein's reform that historians often forget was his decentralization of administrative decision-making to Prussian cities, which enjoyed a tradition of *Selbstverwaltung* (self-administration) radically different from the *tutelle* (tutelage) by the Prefect that characterizes French local government.

Herder's ideas soon became popular among

the peoples of Central Europe, and the early part of the nineteenth century was marked by a linguistic renaissance. Following the example of Jacob Grimm, who laid down the basis of modern literary German, Father Josef Dobrovský, Samuel Linde, Vuk Karadžič, and Bartholemew Kopitar provided modern grammars for the Czech, Polish, Serbo-Croatian, and Slovene languages. The Slovak scholars Jan Kollár and Pavel Šafárik promoted the development of Slovak as an independent literary language and a sense of Slovak nationhood. Safárik joined the historian Palacký in sponsoring the 1848 Slav congress in Prague.

Although the early leaders of Czech national revival sought accommodation rather than conflict with the German-Austrians, the movement was consistently anti-German in tone. Upon experiencing their national awakening, a process known by the generic term of the *risorgimento*, the Czech bourgeois began to feel they had been deliberately Germanized and thereby nationally alienated, even though the intent of the linguistic decrees of the Josephine era was to establish a language of communication, not a language of identity. Through neglect rather than deliberate suppression, Czech had sunk to the level of a peasants' and workers' dialect, so that the initial phases of the Czech cultural revival had to be conducted in German, in which language Palacký wrote the first version of his *History of Bohemia*. The Czechs, showing a symptom typical of cultures in early stages of development confronting those that have reached maturity, were seized by a massive inferiority complex, typified by the pathetic effort of the archivist Hanka to "discover" a Slavic *Nibelungenlied*. An inferiority complex, no less than actual oppression or cultural imperialism, gives rise to reactive or defensive nationalism, which instinctively seeks the style opposite to that of the real or fancied oppressor.

The Czech revivalists could hardly reject the German Herder's concept of the linguistic-cultural nation, since Herder had formulated their

raison d'être. But they could and did reject the Prussian style represented by Stein, Hardenberg, Fichte, and Hegel, choosing instead the French rational-democratic style against which the Germans had revolted. Palacký's history pictured the Czech nation as the eastern pioneer of western democracy and assembled a gallery of democratic heroes including Zižka, Hus, Chelčicky, and Komensky—later expanded to include Palacký himself, Havliček, and Masaryk. This democratic image had nothing to do with the actual behavior of Czech politicians, especially in their relations with other national groups. It was, in fact, demolished by modern Czech positivist historians such as Jaroslav Goll and Josef Pekař (Lemberg, 1964. 1, p. 138). But it had, in the meantime, fulfilled its internal function of creating a self-image for the Czech people, and its external function of enlisting United States support for a Czech—nominally a Czecho-Slovak—nation-state (Glaser, 1973d, pp. 305–8). The essential point is that the integrators of a modern state, and the signals whereby it attracts outside support, are likely to contain a good deal of hyperbole if not outright mythology.

B. Nationalism as a Cause of Conflict

The young Italian nationalist Guiseppe Mazzini, whose idealism inspired liberals across Europe and even in the United States, pictured the rising age of nationalism as one of the brotherhood of equal peoples. His "Brotherhood Pact of Young Europe," which he drafted in 1834, contains the following thoughts:

16. By right of divine law, vouchsafed by God to humanity, all peoples are free—they are brothers and united to one another in equality.

17. Each people has its own distinctive mission, and must contribute toward fulfilling the general

task of humanity. Its mission lies in its ethnicity [*nazionalità*, equivalent to German *Volkstum*]. Ethnicity is holy. (cited by Rabl, 1963, p. 40)

This idealistic perspective, which persists even today, as the myth underlying the Charter of the United Nations, might be realized on a continent where the territories of ethnic-linguistic nations correspond to political boundaries. Western Europeans believed, at least, that they had achieved such a state of affairs, but in central and eastern Europe the situation was entirely different. Here, as was later to be the case in Africa and parts of Asia, kingdoms and empires were created through dynastic territorial politics without regard to ethnic settlement areas, which were scattered across the map of central and eastern Europe without regard to political boundaries. There were literally hundreds of larger and smaller ethnic enclaves and exclaves, and there were cities, towns, and even villages where two or three languages were spoken.

Two liberal models for solving the problems of multiethnicity with a large territorial state were proposed during the revolutionary years of 1848 and 1849. One emanated from the German National Assembly in St. Paul's Church at Frankfurt, the other from the Austrian *Reichstag* at Kroměříž (Kremsier).

On May 31, 1848, the National Assembly in Frankfurt adopted the so-called "Declaration for the Protection of Nationalities," which a cynic might be disposed to interpret as the generosity of a majority *Staatsvolk* secure in its hegemony. The idea that rising nationalities could find political fulfillment within the existing state was expressed in this document as follows:

The henceforth united and free Germany is large and powerful enough to grant those tribes that have grown up within it and that speak other languages without jealousy and to the full extent, the rights accorded them by Nature and History. No German citizen on German soil . . . who speaks a foreign language should have cause to complain that his tribal ethnicity is condemned to wither or that the

German hand of brotherhood is withdrawn where it should be extended. (cited, *ibid.*, p. 41: author's translation)

The Austrian draft was the handywork of the Czech historian František Palacký, who had declined an invitation to the German National Assembly because he did not want his nation to join an empire in which another ethnic-linguistic nation would be in the majority. Instead, Palacký wanted to keep Bohemia (which the Czechs, incidentally, call Čechy, the land of the Czechs) within an Austria reorganized as a federation of equal "nationalities and confessions." "We must construct Austria in such a way that the peoples are glad to live in it," Palacký told the Constitutional Committee of the *Reichstag* on January 23, 1849. The Kroměříž constitution contained the important sentence: "All national tribes [*Volksstämme*] of the empire are endowed with equal rights." Palacký's Austrian model contemplated a territorial state in which no one nationality would have a majority or constitute itself a *Staatsvolk* at the expense of the others. The political loyalty of the citizen would then be directed toward two objects: his ethnic-linguistic nation (*Volk* or *Volksstamm*) as well as the territorial federation in which his nationality, along with others, found political fulfillment. It should be apparent that in this construction loyalty to the territorial federation is secondary, and is dependent on the rights accorded the ethnic-linguistic nationality.

The self-expression of nationalities theoretically possible under the Austrian model was only partly realized in practice. The so called October Diploma of 1860, which decentralized many legislative powers from the Vienna Parliament to the Crown Lands, purported to guarantee nationality rights but contained no specific rules for their observance (Hantsch, 1953, pp. 50–51). Its principle was confirmed throughout Austria (but not Hungary) in the Basic Law of December 21, 1867, which guaranteed "the equality of all regionally customary languages (*landesübliche Sprachen*) in schools, administration, and public life" (Jaksch, 1963, pp. 26f). But Austria consisted of historic Crown Lands, each containing an ethnic-linguistic majority and one or more minorities; the Basic Law did not prevent local majorities from creating monopolies for their particular languages. The Poles in Galicia, for instance, closed Ukrainian schools; the Slovenes in Carniola closed German schools, while the Czechs and Germans in Bohemia engaged in a bitter *Kulturkampf*. In the Hungarian half of the Empire, the total decentralization of internal affairs to Budapest permitted the Magyars to commit what history must record as the cardinal political sin—the wages of which are always national tragedy (*ibid.*, pp. 39–45). This is the attempt to found a linguistic-cultural state embracing the aspirations of a particular *Staatsvolk* in a multinational or multitribal region.

A significant effort to maximize the rights of nationalities within a multinational territorial state was made by the Social Democratic parties of Austria at their Brno Congress in 1899. They adopted a program drafted by the German Bohemian Josef Seliger and his Czech colleague Antonín Němec, the essential points of which were:

1. Austria is to be restructured as a democratic federation of nationalities.

2. In the place of the historic Crown Lands, nationally limited self-administrative bodies shall be formed. Their legislation and administration shall be entrusted to national chambers elected by universal, equal, and direct suffrage.

3. All self-governing areas of one and the same nation constitute a unified national body, which administers its national affairs with full autonomy.

4. The rights of national minorities shall be guaranteed by a special law to be enacted by the Imperial Parliament.

5. We recognize no primacy of any nationality, and therefore reject the demand for a state language. The Imperial Parlia-

ment shall determine the extent to which a language for communication (*Vermittlungssprache*) is required. (in Wierer, 1960, p. 105—author's translation)

To adapt federalism to a country where ethnic groups were not settled in compact blocks but were scattered and intermixed, Dr. Karl Renner, the most original jurist among the Austrian Social Democrats, developed what was then called combined territorial and personal autonomy but might be more clearly described as two-track federalism. Under Renner's plan, the central government would be limited to defense, foreign affairs, and national economic and social policy. Noncultural public functions such as highway maintenance, police, and tax collection would be delegated to eight self-administering regions with limited legislative power. The operation of schools and universities, libraries, theaters, and other cultural facilities, however, would be in the hands of democratically elected "national governments," representing the eight ethnic nations of Austria. They would all have their headquarters in Vienna, and would serve their members wherever they might be located within the Empire (*ibid.*, p. 107). The term "personal autonomy" meant that each adult citizen could choose freely among the ethnic communities. Renner's plan was given a partial and successful trial in Moravia, where the Equalization of 1905 helped ease tensions between Czechs and Germans (Jaksch, 1963, pp. 73–74).

The historian Rudolf Wierer gives two reasons why the plans of Renner and other Austrian federalists remained largely on paper and failed to rescue the Dual Monarchy from ultimate destruction. For one thing, most of the projects excluded Hungary, and those that did not were sternly resisted by the government in Budapest—which employed a wide variety of oppressive measures in the effort to "Magyarize" its minorities. More importantly, however, Renner and other Social Democrats were wrong in assuming that the industrial working class was basically international in outlook. Austrian experience showed that the workers were even more prone to indulge in national extremism and interethnic conflict than the economically "secure" middle class (Wierer, 1960, p. 109).

Efforts to achieve ethnic equality within a federalized Austria-Hungary were, as things turned out, eclipsed by the increasingly popular notion that each ethnic-linguistic nation or nationality group was entitled to found its own independent state. This idea was given legal form by Dr. Pasquale Stanislao Mancini in his 1851 inaugural lecture at the University of Turin on "Ethnicity (*nazionalità*) as a Basis of International Law." Mancini argued that, since law springs from humanity's moral needs, it was not the historical monarchies but rather the living national communities—each unified by genetics, language, and ideological awareness—that formed the natural subjects of the law of nations. Individual freedom in constitutional law had its international-law counterpart in the *sovereignty of the nation* within its territory limited by natural boundaries (Rabl, 1963, p. 46—his emphasis). The trouble, of course, is that nations and nationalities often disagree about where their "natural boundaries" are to be found.

In Bohemia, the Austro-Slav federalism of Palacký and his friends was progressively pushed aside by the separatist nationalism of the Gregr brothers and their "Young Czech" disciples. These were soon emulated by Magyar, South Slav, Polish, Rumanian, and other nationalists in East-Central Europe. Ideologically, this separatism reflected a *mésalliance* between the Declaration of Independence—in a distortion few Americans understood—and Herder's romantic doctrine of the linguistic-cultural *Volk*. Each nation or nationality invoked the theory to gain as much real estate as possible, regardless of other peoples' rights. Operationally, maximal nationalism could be summarized in these propositions:

(a) My ethnic-linguistic nation, large or small, has a right to its sovereign national state.

(b) This national state must contain the entire ethnic-linguistic nation, wherever settled.

(c) My language shall be the official state language. Speakers of other tongues shall be assimilated, expelled, or in any case prevented from diluting or subverting the national culture. (Glaser, 1973d, p. 311)

Central Europe is not the only region where nations, nationalities, and tribes are scattered, interlocked, and intermingled. The same is true of most of Africa and much of Asia and Latin America. Where regionally dominant nations or ethnic groups set themselves up as *Staatsvölker*, denying political expression to other peoples with *Staatsvolk* aspirations of their own, oppression and bloodshed are the most likely results. This is true even when—in fact precisely when—forced assimilation is practiced under the liberal mantle of territorial nation-building. In a region where nationalist ideology has sown the dragon's teeth of interethnic conflict, only two political systems are capable of maintaining or restoring peace:

1. Control by a dominant power *within* the region. While this power might or might not have an ethnic-linguistic base, it would have to function as a territorial power, curbing excesses of ethnic nationalism rather than pitting one nationalism against the other.

2. Control by a great power *outside* the region. This is a role that Great Britain, France, Germany, Russia, and even the United States have undertaken or attempted at various times and places.

C. National Integrators and Differentiators

Most groups have specific integrators or combinations thereof. In many cases, the integrators themselves suffice to describe the group and suggest its needs (e.g. left-handed golf players). Nations, unlike most functional and total groups, have a variety of alternate integrators that may appear singly or in combination. Or, looking at things the other way, groups identified and differentiated by wholly divergent characteristics or sets of characteristics may, under the right circumstances, exhibit the behavior we commonly associate with nationalism. But they do not necessarily exhibit that behavior.

Lemberg groups the factors that may serve to integrate nations in five main categories: language, genetic background, cultural community, concept of history, and citizenship (1964, 2, pp. 34–50). Within each category, a wide range of specific forms is possible.

1. LANGUAGE

Language is the most commonly cited integrator in both the rational-territorial and ethnic-cultural models of the nation, as they have evolved in Europe. One of the earliest cultural anthropologists, Wilhelm von Humboldt, pointed out the effect of language structure on mental development. "A people lives in its language," was the judgment of Count Széchenyi, a leader of the Magyar *risorgimento*. With the shift of economic decision-making from the nobles and merchant princes to the bourgeoisie, language assumed a stronger differentiating function; while the old elite spoke one or more languages of communication (such as Latin, French, or German in Central Europe), the bourgeoisie did not. Where a monolingual bourgeoisie found itself at odds with a cosmopolitan elite, as in Bohemia and other lands of the Hapsburg crown and in the Baltic countries, language became a class as well as national differentiator (*ibid.*, pp. 34–36).

There are authors who, in agreement with Stalin (Marxism and the National Question, 1913), insist that language is one of the essential features of a nation—the others being terri-

tory,* economic life, and psychic formation expressed in a community of culture. Following this reasoning, the French federalist Fougeyrollas contends that Belgium (where the problems of Burgundy persist in the form of linguistic struggles) is not a nation but a state superimposed on two peoples. Switzerland, by the same token, is not a nation but a state federating cantons of four languages (Fougeyrollas, 1968, p. 33).

Without a community of language, Fougeyrollas argues, a nation does not or does not yet exist: where a language other than the official one is spoken, the national question is not sufficiently resolved. Nation-building to fit the rational-territorial model—creating a cultural nation to fit politically determined boundaries—then becomes a matter of planned linguistic discrimination. Such was indeed the policy of French education, which used a centrally controlled school system to spread a standardized and classical speech—that of the political center as "purified" by court scholars. Fougeyrollas's judgement is that the cost has been too high in cultural impoverishment. He pleads for a sharing of resources so that the regional tongues will be revitalized as vehicles of popular culture; French people would be enabled to "return to their roots" and to find a regional as well as a national identity (*ibid.*, pp. 131–41).

While Fougeyrollas's views are significant as indicators of a possible shift in French cultural policy, it must be observed that he does not distinguish clearly enough between the identifying and communicative functions of language. The two often intermingle, as when members of an in-group take pleasure in being

---

* Strict application of this reasoning would suggest that a nation expelled or deported from its territory would thereby cease to be a nation. While Stalin decreed several deportations, it is doubtful that he or latter-day Stalinists would contend that people lost a right *because* they were deported. Rather, they were deported because they were alleged to have commited acts that negated their right of settlement.

overheard but not understood by "out-groupers." But the two factors are discrete and often contradictory. Speech patterns that best reflect ethnic character and that radiate strong feelings of community are often limited to natives of particular landscapes and are in many cases difficult or impossible for "out-groupers" to understand. This is true, for instance, of Gullah (spoken by rural blacks in the coastal areas of Georgia and South Carolina), Cockney, *Plattdeutsch*, Sardinian, and many tribal dialects in Africa.

Fougeyollas confirms Lemberg's account of the historical role played by the bourgeoisie as the agent of national—and hence linguistic—aggregation and segregation. The national education system, staffed by teachers who are bourgeois in outlook if not in economic status, spreads and consolidates the national language by making it the medium in which things are learned and remembered. In countries lacking a bourgeoisie, because they have not yet undergone a commercial revolution or because they are passing directly from precapitalism to socialism, its nation-building role may be played by government bureaucrats or party functionaries.

Structurally, linguistic nation-building may assume alternate forms. Fougeyrollas's enumeration of these forms merits brief comment, not as a definite classification, but because it illustrates the inadequacy of much Western thinking about political linguistics. His first case is that of a single language spoken over a wide area, exemplified by the use of Arabic from Iraq to Morocco and Swahili in several East African states. This grouping overlooks an essential difference. Arabic is the unifying tongue of the *Umma* or Arab nation, and the language of the Holy Koran: a language of identity *par excellence*. Swahili, on the other hand, developed as a trading language along the East African coast through the interaction of Arabic and native languages of the Bantu group. It is widely spoken, and was carried to areas remote from the coast (such as the Congo)

by caravans, but it has always served as a language of communication among speakers of different African languages. There is no such thing as a Swahili people, and hence there can be no Swahili identity. The original languages of identity in East Africa are the tribal tongues, and the fact that circumstances have caused certain population groups (about 10 percent of the people of Tanzania, for instance) to use Swahili as their family speech does not give it identifying status—any more than English becomes a language of identity for linguistically alienated Polish-Americans or Italian-Americans. President Nyerere's goal of making Swahili the language of identification for Tanzanians can only be accomplished through deliberate *linguistic conversion* (see chapter 18, A3).

In Fougeyrollas's second case, a political territory contains major linguistic groups with protonational characteristics and often with aspirations to become nations in their own right. He mentions the Hausa, Yoruba, and Ibo of Nigeria, but the same could be said of the Hindi, Tamil, and other language groups in India. In neither case can the language of *one* of these groups serve as a language of identity for *all*, and—as India found out—it may even be unacceptable as a language of communication. There are 14 languages spoken within the Republic of India. Ten of these are based on Sanskrit, with an admixture of Arab-oriented Urdu: a legacy of the Moghul occupation. The other four are based on the Dravidian language of Tamil, and all except Tamil itself have absorbed a large content of Sanskrit words. A radical differentiation of structure with resulting near-total noncommunicability separates the Sanskrit-based languages from the Tamil group; within each group various degrees of noncommunicability—and hence mutual aversion—separate the distinct language communities. This results in economic discrimination based on linguistic localism: the demand that scarce jobs in developing industries be given "sons of the soil," and the use of violence to enforce this preference (Mohan Das, 1975, p. 175). Clearly, India needs a language of communication if the Indian political system is not to fall apart.

Among the peoples of India, the political identification of individuals is primarily local and secondarily regional. An all-embracing Indian nationalism, with its accompanying attitude of "Indian-ness" rather than particularism, developed most fully among the Hindi-speaking leadership of the Congress Party. As in the United States, the culturally dominant group assumed the role of model for the larger society, and the ability of Indian nationalism to transcend regional and linguistic identity has varied with the similarity of cultural (and to some extent racial) patterns: greatest in the North, least in the South.

Indian leaders realized even before independence that Hindi, the language of the largest plurality, could never be made a language of identity for speakers of other tongues. They hoped, however, that it would be accepted as a language of communication, thus making possible the phasing out of English, which is still resented as the language of the colonial power.

As things turned out, however, the non-Hindi-speaking states were inclined to object to any preferred status for Hindi, even as a language of communication. The Madras Legislature passed a resolution opposing the use of Hindi as a national language, and in this found the support of West Bengal, which shares the Sanskrit-based Bengali language with Bangla Desh. The linguistic states became bastions of ethnocentricity, and those in the South have yielded to the pressure of "sons of the soil" movements and effectively though quietly deny employment to (and thus drive away) speakers of languages other than that of the region (*ibid.*).

In Fougeyrollas's third case, the language of one ethnic group (such as Wolof in Senegal) is understood by speakers of other languages and thus emerges as the language of a multiethnic nation. Such an evolution is acceptable only if the language in question is not perceived as a cultural threat by the groups who speak other languages. This condition, in turn, is likely to exist if the language in question has acquired currency as a trading language—a role that Wolof shares with Hausa and Swahili. As already indicated, this model proved unworkable in India—a country where language riots are as frequent as those about food or jobs.

In the fourth and last case described by Fougeyrollas, the multiplicity of local languages—or, it may be added, their mutual power of repulsion—leads to the choice of the colonial language as a medium of communication. The use of French by the Ivory Coast is Fougeyrollas's case in point, but the same tendency, with English, has been observed in Nigeria. There, the leaders of the government (which is a coalition of tribes that joined to defeat the Ibo in the recent civil war) have talked at length about the need for an African national language but have been unable to agree on one. Structurally, Nigeria is characterized by a delicate intertribal balance of power and by marked differences in cultural styles—especially between the Moslem, Sudanic, stock raising, largely traditional Hausa and Fulani in the North and the European-influenced, widely Christianized tribes in the Southeast and West, with their agricultural and handicrafts economies and higher degree of modernization. It should be noted that the use of Hausa as a trading language is basically limited to the semi-desert along the southern fringe of the Sahara, and does not extend into the coastal regions of Nigeria. The major peoples of that state may be called protonations: each is large enough to form a national state in its own right and one of them, the Ibo, fought an unsuccessful war of independence. Such a protonation shares with nations in the full sense a tendency to indulge in political and cultural imperialism: to impose its rule and, whenever possible, its culture and language over as wide an area as possible—in short, to discriminate against other ethnic groups. It is therefore understandable that each of the pro-tonations of Nigeria fears that raising the lan-guage of one of its rivals to a federation-wide status—even if only as a language of com-munication—would work to its political or cul-tural disadvantage (Fougeyrollas, 1968, pp. 39–53).

The situation in Nigeria is thus structurally similar to that prevailing in India. In both countries the language of the former colonial power survives as an instrument of com-munication—not because it is positively de-sired but because parts of the population enter-tain much stronger objections to each indigenous language that is a candidate for na-tional status.

While the USSR remains theoretically com-mitted to multilinguality, the Russian language plays a central role in efforts to shape a "Soviet nation" peopled by "new Soviet persons." The model reflected in this intended all-embracing nationality is, however, essentially Russian. The preferred status of the Great Russians is reflected in Soviet historiography, which lauds the Czars' imperialist conquests as "progres-sive" because they opened a broader area to so-cialism. The non-Russian nations of the USSR are unanimous in resisting Russification, and this resistance is reflected in their litera-tures—even in works written with an eye cocked at the Soviet censor. The Party literary hacks fulminate regularly against non-Russian literatures as "instruments of bourgeois-national propaganda"—their pre-revolutionary epics are condemned and suppressed, whereas equivalent Russian epics are glorified as "clas-sics."

The effectiveness of language as a national or ethnic integrator is confirmed by the frequency with which it figures in policies intended to frustrate, or conversely to foster, ethnic iden-tification and cultural development. In the Moslem parts of the USSR, for instance, Ara-bic writing is being replaced with the Latin alphabet—which in the Western USSR is re-jected in favor of Cyrillic. The official reason is that the Latin alphabet is simpler, but the real

reason is to detach the Turkic peoples of Cen-tral Asia from the Islamic tradition (Dushnyck, 1975b, pp. 516f.). In the areas annexed from Rumania after World War II, the Soviet gov-ernment is busily trying to create a "Moldavian language" (Rumanian written in Cyrillic with an admixture of Russian words) for the pur-pose of alienating the population from their loyalty to the Rumanian nation and state. In both Eastern and Western Europe, educational and cultural policies as well as budgets are managed so as to withhold resources from lan-guages and cultures having political implica-tions central governments would rather not confront. Thus, the Transylvania Saxons who remain in Rumania and the Magyars in that state and in Slovakia are held culturally to short rations, while contacts with the main German and Magyar language communities are deliberately made difficult. The linguistic minorities of France are likewise educationally deprived and to some extent linguistically alienated, since the Paris government has doggedly resisted demands for bilingual educa-tion. Conversely, however, a national govern-ment may elect to develop a pluralist base of support. The British have in recent years given particular support to Welsh education with the result that the number of Welsh speakers, hav-ing shrunk steadily for a century or more, is again on the increase.

2. HEREDITY

As a national integrator, heredity operates in both a formal-juridical and a social-psychological manner. In the first case, appli-cation of *ius sanguinis* confers on a person the citizenship of his parents. Offspring of mixed marriages may have a choice, as do children of U.S. citizens born abroad, or the citizenship of the father may be controlling (as in Indonesia). In the case of Israel, a matrilineal rule applies: a person whose mother was a Jew is considered Jewish. This does not automatically confer Israeli citizenship, but it entitles the person to claim it under *aliyah*, the law of return.

Citizenship acquired by birth does not automatically evoke in the individual the loyalty needed to make a nation or its nation-state function effectively under stress. But it does create a predisposition toward such loyalty, just as denial or revocation of such citizenship will normally be met with feelings of alienation.

The more important national integrating function of heredity is not via citizenship—which is membership in a *state*, not necessarily a nation—but direct, operating in the areas of individual and group identity. The operating factor is the *belief*, whether biologically realistic or not, that members of the nation are descended from common ancestors (e.g. Abraham, or Romulus and Remus) or from a clearly identified biological group. Insofar as race plays a role as an integrator or differentiator, it does so as a *social* category (as defined in chapter 7).

Analysis of the sociology of European history suggests that that heredity as such—as distinguished from an ideology of heredity (such as doctrine about "Nordic purity")—has played at most a secondary role in the integration of modern nations (Lemberg, 1964, 2, pp. 40–42). Even the *Stamm* or tribe, the primary unit of identification beyond local fiefs, was unified mainly by language, costume, and manners rather than descent.

Belief in common heredity may, however, assume the status of a myth, and as such become an effective integrator. The relationship of a believed myth to objective truth is wholly irrelevant to its sociopsychological efficacy: the Zion Community, founded on the Illinois prairie by the late Wilbur Voliva, was integrated by the conviction that the earth is flat. As Lemberg observes (1964, 1, pp. 195ff.), racial ideologies have figured most prominently in extreme types of nationalism that emerged in crises—such as the integral nationalism of Barrès and Déroulède, which became popular in France after the defeat of 1870. French integral nationalists not only created a cult around Joan of Arc but also adopted the race theories of Gobineau and Vacher de Lapouge.

A similar phenomenon took place in Germany after its 1918 defeat and imposition of the punitive Treaty of Versailles.

3. CULTURAL COMMUNITY

The function of cultural community as a national integrator is typified by the fact that a viable nation has its national literature and art based on tradition, myth, and experience. Out of the literature and art emerge characters—real, idealized, or imaginary—with whom members of the nation identify. Fiction, poetry, music, and the graphic and plastic arts likewise foster the visualization and fixation of national aspirations.

A paradoxical fact, to which Lemberg draws attention (2, pp. 42–44), is that while national culture is often urged as an essential criterion of nationality, that culture is often limited to a small educated class. The working masses that represented August Bebel's Germany knew nothing of Goethe or Bach. Efforts to spread German culture to the masses in the 1920s encountered an obstacle: the specific and centrifugal cultural forces of sectarian and political groups were stronger than the unifying force of the still-emerging German national cutlure, while German nationalism and the cultural matrices that supported it were fragmented along class lines. Bismarck's policies, which culminated in foundation of the *Reich* in 1871, had their base in an unstable alliance of feudal Junkers and business magnates, but there was also the democratic—essentially petty-bourgeois—nationalism that had been in evidence at the National Assembly at the Frankfurt Paulskirche in 1848–49 and the working-class nationalism of Bebel and even Karl Marx. It may surprise some readers to learn that editor Charles A. Dana of the *New York Tribune* once reprimanded Marx, who was writing about European politics from London, for "too much emphasis on the German point of view" (Jaksch, 1967, pp. 53–58, 475).

Although Catholic–Protestant antagonism in Germany exhausted its potential for violence in the Thirty Years' War, it remained as a powerful social force and motivator of discrimination until quite recently: Bismarck's *Kulturkampf* of 1872–86 reflected sentiments widespread among German Protestants. Political parties had sectarian orientations: nationalists tended to be Lutheran and anti-Catholic; there was a Catholic Center Party; and socialists were strongly anticlerical and in their left (and later communist) wing, antireligious. German culture could, until World War I and even during the interwar period, be described as a bundle of particular cultures—a fact that doubtlessly contributed to the downfall of both the Empire and the Weimar Republic.

Until rather recently, participation in national cultures—as distinguished from regional or class-oriented subcultures—was limited to those enjoying a bourgeois standard of living. Even within that privileged stratum, culture in more than a superficial sense is often jeopardized by specialization (Gehlen, 1953). While television has replaced the Colt 45 as "the great equalizer," programs designed for mass consumption must necessarily be reduced to the lowest cultural denominator. Modern sociological analyses of adult education students and of radio and television publics, however, have shown that a modern national society such as West Germany consists of very different cultural groups which have less to do with one another than with the corresponding groups across state boundaries (Schulenberg, 1957, cited by Lemberg, 2, p. 44).

Lemberg (*ibid.*) observes that "the member of a nation, even though he knows nothing and understands nothing of its high culture, is nevertheless a contributor to and a substrate of that culture. This culture would be impossible without him; it focuses upon him in many respects." Hauptmann's weavers and the working-class characters evoked by Molnar, D. H. Lawrence, and Brecht come to mind in this connection.

Michael Novak's *The Rise of the Unmeltable Ethnics* (1973) is essentially a protest against American mass culture, with its tendency to homogenize all ethnic groups according to an Anglo-Saxon norm. Novak (pp. 188ff.) addresses himself specifically to the need for authentic high culture to have roots in the people. He writes:

Ordinary people are not *merely* a "mass." Their instincts and needs are prostituted, not expressed, by "mass culture." . . . The intellectual is the servant of wisdom insofar as he helps to discriminate, to clarify, and to articulate the human situation. His sensitivities lead him to aspects of experience the experts are liable to neglect. He serves people, against the experts.

The intellectual, then, is not in principle alienated from the people. He lives among them, and makes their experience a major focus of his empathy and intuition.

Citing Dwight Macdonald, Novak warns against the emergence of a "middlebrow culture," patronized by the rich but preserving the essential characteristics of mass culture. Middlebrows like "the formula, the built-in reaction, the lack of any standard except popularity." Midcult, with which Macdonald identifies several prominent literary magazines and the authors of quite a few best-selling novels, "pretends to respect the standards of High Culture while in fact it waters them down and vulgarizes them."

Because Anglo-Saxon literature in America continues to exude nineteenth-century optimism, Novak feels (perhaps he should have limited his stricture to Yankee literature), it is incapable of effective social criticism. This function has fallen to non-Anglo-Saxon "ethnics," particularly the Jewish intellectuals clustered around Columbia University, the *Partisan Review* and *Commentary*. It is not necessary to endorse Novak's literary judgment to see the sociological point involved: that in a plural society intellectual leadership and hence long-range control over ideology may slip from the hands of a hitherto dominant group and be taken over by others. To sum up: cultural community may be recognized as a national integrator, but it is not static and it is subject to alienation.

4. HISTORY AND IDEOLOGY

Lemberg's category of concept of history (*Geschichtsbild*) as a national integrator is expanded here to include ideology: the two factors interact closely. The way people interpret political and economic situations involving them is in large part derived from their understanding of how these situations came about; conversely, prophets of an ideology create history to fit. Marx, for instance, projected a philosophy of historical materialism to match his economic beliefs.

Lemberg introduces the subject (2, pp. 45–46) by observing that emerging nations—which could not use language as a criterion of nationality, perhaps because their elites belonged to another linguistic culture—have sometimes invoked a concept of history as a national integrator. As the Czech upper classes spoke German in the early nineteenth century, Palacký—the historian of the Czech *risorgimento*—distinguished the Czechs by picturing them as champions of liberal democracy against the Germans, who were supposed to represent feudal reaction. This polarization was far from the fact, which was that both the Czech and German groups in Bohemia had their feudal nobles, their chauvinist nationalists, and their liberal democrats (Jaksch, *passim.*). It might be noted in passing that Palacký's *History of Bohemia* was written in German and later translated under the title "History of the *Czech* people."

Such fictionalized history, replicated in the Prussian particularism of Treitschke and the chauvinism of Stalinist historians (who pictured Russian imperialism in Central Asia as progressive because it prepared the matrix for socialism), is tailored to fit its integrating purpose. Concerned for national purity, it treats periods of weakened national consciousness and foreign influence as times of decay, even if they were periods of prosperity and high inter-national culture. Eschatological myths such as those of Christianity and Marxism-Leninism exercise a similar nation-building function.

Much is said elsewhere in this book about efforts to create a new "Soviet nation" peopled by a new breed of "Soviet men and women." Suffice it here to say that the blend of Marxism-Leninism and Russian nationalism that supports this concept is the ingenious concoction of Stalin, who must be created with restoring total dedication to the Fatherland to the apex of the Soviet scale of values. This process could not be accomplished without excommunicating the Marxist historian Pokrovsky and rehabilitating the entire gallery of Czarist heroes including Ivan the Terrible (Lemberg, 1, pp. 232–38). Whatever Khrushchev may have said about Stalin, he was the essential architect of the Soviet system as it exists today: a genuinely anti-Stalinist communism is unthinkable.

The American republic, which had its beginning in a revolt of the colonists to secure their rights as *Englishmen* (Gorer, 1948, p. 28), lacked the national integrators and differentiators employed by the awakening nations of Europe. It therefore turned to a motive looked at suspiciously by nations that have suffered the consequences of nationalism and imperialism, and one that has embroiled it in foreign adventures not necessarily to its own interest (Glaser, 1973b): a belief in mission, an electness gained through suffering and struggle, and a special duty to humanity at large. Lemberg, one of the few Europeans to understand how the integrators and hence the behavior of the American nation differs from those of European nations, believes that this sense of mission was necessary to give the new nation the attraction and integrating force which other nations had gained from language, ethnic character, and history (1, pp. 253).

Lemberg calls the Declaration of Independence "a catechism of this messianism," expressing the freedoms of the English Constitution in universal terms. Such universalizing, he writes, reflects a frequently encountered "compensation ideology": to make up for inferiority feelings toward the older culture, a new nation asserts that its forerunner has been untrue to its mission, which the new nation now takes up. Poland, for instance, has been pictured as a martyr for the freedom betrayed by Western Europe, and black Africans often assert that they are better Christians than secularized Europeans. If Lemberg is correct, American messianism is not merely a harmful aberration, obstructing realistic formulation of the national interest, but represents the polarization of forces that holds the United States together. It is not necessary at this point to pass judgment on Lemberg's theory, but it does help to explain why disillusionment with America's idealist ventures overseas has been accompanied by a breakdown of national morale—a phenomenon observed in milder form in the early 1920s.

5. CITIZENSHIP

There are schools of social science that consider the state the only sufficient criterion for existence of a nation—without the state, only ethnic groups, but no nations in the true sense, can exist. Even Max Weber places the nation organized as a state on a higher level than the ethnic group. Few would deny, however, that the Polish nation continued to exist throughout more than a century of partition, even though some Poles may initially have thought otherwise.

Citizenship is membership in a state. A state is a political entity: as the term is used in this book, it is a group of people occupying a definite territory and organized under a government independent, or at least largely independent, of any other government. A *constituent* state of a federation may have all the characteristics of a state in its internal affairs, but is not regarded as a state in international law. The Charter of the Organization of American States (1948) indicates that a state, to qualify as a person of international law, must have: (a)

permanent population, (b) a defined territory, (c) government, and (d) capacity to enter into relations with other states. Kalijarvi, on the other hand, defines a nation as "a group of people connected not by legal but by psychological or cultural ties based on such influences as history, community of language, race, religion, and customs (1954, p. 79). While the majority of countries represent both a nation and a state, the two are distinct and should not be confused. The term "nationality" will therefore be used here in the sense of belonging to a nation, and never in the sense of citizenship, even though the latter usage is common among international lawyers.

The United States was a territorial state in origin and development; it was not the expression of a linguistic-cultural nation. Americans have explicitly rejected race, creed, color, or national origin as criteria of national identity and they disdain European particularism. Citizenship therefore assumes a greater role as a national integrator than in most other countries. Hardly anywhere else is the naturalization ceremony treated as such a serious occasion, on a par with weddings and funerals. Americans therefore have a tendency, shared to some extent by the British, to confuse states and nations. Americans unversed in the complexities of European politics are inclined to assume that homogenous nations of "Czechoslovaks" and "Yugoslavs" live in the corresponding states of East-Central Europe, that only Rumanians live in Rumania, and that all other states have long since reached the uniformity that the American melting pot is supposed to have achieved.

In the American context, and in other countries of European settlement such as Canada, Brazil, and South Africa, citizenship is an important integrating force. This is probably because its acquisition represents an act of will on the part of the individual or his forebears. In all countries of immigration, the intent to make a new life, of which naturalization is a formal expression, is an important integrator.

D. Interchangeability of National Integrators

The integrators that hold nations together, and the reasons why people feel they belong to one nation rather than another, are by no means static. Analysis of their history shows that they are interchangeable, each functioning at particular times and places. The French language was historically a major engine of political integration and it remains the backbone of the French cultural nation. But if the recent resurgence of cultural pluralism and the revival of regional tongues such as Occitan and Breton continues, its role as an integrator may very well be assumed by an ideology of civic loyalty based on federalism, pluralism, and multilevel integration. Such an ideology is being invoked in Belgium, where its success remains uncertain.

Lemberg's list of integrators is not exhaustive. He did not include religion, the political effects of which might be subsumed under culture or ideology. There is also the possibility that other group-forming characteristics may exercise a nation-building function in the future. What makes nationalism a force and binds the individual to the nation is not so much the existence of specific integrators but rather a total system of concepts, values, and norms: an ideology. Nationalism is the integrating and differentiating ideology of the large groups into which most of humanity (but by no means all) falls during the present century.

A word remains to be said about the integrating function of ideology. While post-Enlightenment social science has tended to brand ideology as fiction, its necessity has gradually been recognized—for instance by Ernst Bloch, who accepts Marxism as a value system but recognizes scientific truth independent of Marxism. All social groups, including families, tribes, nations, and states, need ideologies to justify their existence, and the denigration or "debunking" of ideology therefore causes social or political disintegration (Lemberg, 2, pp. 54ff.).

Observation indicates, however, that ideologies do not usually create nations, but rather that nations form ideologies. The important thing is not that all people think alike, but that they perceive the national group as a unity, differentiated from and implicitly better than analogous "foreign" unities. Under the influence of Napoleon's conquest, German philosophers such as Fichte, Schelling, and Hegel asserted that the individual can be free only if the people is free—an idea that today dominates Black African politics. Nations are personalized and symbolized by flags, coats of arms, and animal totems (ibid., pp. 58–59).

The ideological function of religion is illustrated by the legend of Vladimir of Kiev, who supposedly sent out messengers to see which great religion would be most suitable for his kingdom: Judaism, Islam, Roman Catholicism, or Eastern Orthodoxy. The splendid ceremony in the Hagia Sophia at Constantinople induced him to choose the last. Later, the Ottoman empire integrated only its ruling caste through Islam, since the non-Muslims were its taxpayers and it could not afford to eliminate them. As a result, the Christian peoples were integrated by anti-Turk ideologies that finally destroyed the empire. The essential problem is that an integrating ideology must reach all the people within the state: if it does not, it will prove to be a disintegrator. In that case, either the ideology must be changed or a structural innovation corresponding to the ideology must be sought.

11

OPPRESSION OF NATIONALITY GROUPS AND PROTO-NATIONS

Ethnicity is common to the linguistic-cultural nation, the nationality (like a nation but too small or scattered to have its own state), and the ethnic group linked by historical and cultural identity. It is also shared by the proto-nation: the nationality or ethnic group struggling for political and cultural self-determination and having the potentiality of becoming a nation in its own right. Proto-nations are groups that have never succeeded in establishing their own states but whose nationalism is clearly expressed.

It will also be remembered that ethnicity is a compound of cultural, social, racial (biological), psychological, and historical components. Their relative importance varies from case to case. Although race may serve as a signal of ethnicity, it is not a reliable test of ethnicity and it is in no way identical with ethnicity itself. Shibutani and Kwan differentiate between ethnic and (biological) racial groups as follows:

> To avoid confusion with the scientific concept of race we shall use another term altogether. . . . What is needed is a technical term to designate the popular distinctions without accepting the false beliefs on which they rest. Ideally suited for this purpose is the term ethnic, which corresponds roughly to what German scholars mean by Volk; the term is used by anthropologists to refer to a "people." An ethnic group consists of people who conceive themselves as being of a kind. They are united by emotional bonds and concerned with the preservation of their type. With very few exceptions they speak the same language, or their speech is at least intelligible to each other, and they share a common cultural heritage. Since those who form such units are usually endogamous, they tend to look alike. Far more important, however, is their belief that they are of common descent, a belief usually supported by myths or a partly fictitious history. A people do not necessarily constitute a nation; although men who regard themselves as being of a kind tend to move in that direction, they are not necessarily united under a single government. (1965, pp. 40–41)

A. Ethnic Norm Images

While many ethnic groups in various parts of the world define themselves wholly or partly in terms of biological descent, language is consistently the central ethnic integrator and therefore the most reliable signal of ethnic identity. Language is always an integral part of culture; it is the vehicle for communication among members of a people and the principal means for transmitting culture from one generation to the next. The proliferation of languages illustrates mankind's cultural diversity. As Philip L. Wagner points out,

> Linguistic heterogeneity is one of the most obvious, most absolute and most fixed of the categories of diversity that apply to human populations. The sharp discontinuities and relatively uniform blocs that characterize modern linguistic communities strongly influence human behavior, and particularly the association of people and their interaction. Political, social and economic structures are often closely related with linguistic usage. (1958, p. 86)

Each ethnic group, over the course of its history, develops a norm image which symbolizes the concentrated essence (synthesis) of its character and identity. The norm images of ethnic groups always contain a cultural nucleus; a somatic element is also present when a group is strongly conscious of physical traits associated with its total identity. While the norm image is difficult to measure since it is basically a subjective *mental construct*, it nevertheless represents the way a group defines itself culturally, and sometimes physically as well. The norm images of ethnic groups play a key role in the development of in-group–out-group relations. They also determine to a considerable extent the emergence of ethnocentrism, prejudice, discrimination, and intergroup conflicts.

The word "oppression" in the title of this chapter is justified by the fact that few governments or dominant groups that control them seem inclined to let diverse groups develop according to their own lights and manage their own affairs. Such groups must fight to maintain their ethnic integrity, which the facts recited show they do, despite the threats and inducements employed to coax them into melting pots. Despite a growing awareness that we are becoming "one world," the population of this planet speaks more than 6000 languages (including 27 major languages, each spoken by at least 40 million people) and is composed of more than 10,000 ethnic units (some of which can trace their genesis to the very dawn of history). The persistence of ethnicity is, indeed, the theme of what follows.

Table 11.1. MAJOR NATIONALITY GROUPS IN THE USSR

Armenians	3,559,151	Latvian	1,429,844
Azerbaijani	4,379,937	Lithuanian	2,664,944
Bashkir	1,239,681	Moldavian	2,697,994
Byelorussian	9,051,775	Mordvinian	1,262,670
Chechen	612,674	Polish	1,167,523
Chuvash	1,694,351	Russian	
Estonian	1,007,356	(Great)	129,015,140
Georgian	3,245,300	Tadzhik	2,135,883
German	1,846,317	Tatar	5,930,670
Jewish	2,150,707	Turkmenian	1,525,284
Kazakh	5,298,818	Ukrainian	40,753,246
Kirghiz	1,452,222	Uzbek	9,195,093

(SOURCE: USSR census of January, 1970, as reported in UN Demographic Yearbook, 1971, pp. 504–5.)

B. *Oppression of Nationalities in the USSR*

The USSR, despite its claim to be the world's most peaceful multinational and multiethnic state, is ruthlessly attempting to assimilate its ethnic minorities in a socialist melting pot. More than 200 languages are spoken in Russia, and the census of 1959 lists 111 established ethnic units, several of which comprised more than 5 million people each. The populations of the larger groups according to the 1970 census are shown in table 11.1. These ethnic minorities, or "nationalities" as the Russians call them, are determined to preserve their cultural integrity, despite strenuous efforts to russify them. A number of them qualify as nations—including the Azerbaijani, Estonians, Georgians, Latvians, Lithuanians, and Ukrainians—having established their independent states in 1917 or 1918 and having suffered reannexation through military conquest.

1. "NATIONAL IN FORM, SOCIALIST IN SUBSTANCE"

Ostensibly, the Russian–controlled Communist Party has adopted a tolerant attitude toward demands for autonomy by the ethnic minorities. With important exceptions (notably the Jews, the Germans, and the Poles) each ethnic unit is concentrated in an autonomous, geographically delineated enclave, and local self-determination is the official slogan. In fact, this is the basis on which the 15 Union Republics of the USSR have been organized. Groups too small to have Union Republics have so-called Autonomous Republics or Autonomous Regions. Within each Union Republic or Autonomous Republic, the official major ethnic group·is supposedly dominant in social customs, culture, language, and lifestyle.

The Russians, who numbered 129 million in 1970, have a deep-rooted historical fear that the 113 million non-Russians, of whom more than half are of Mongoloid-Asian stock, may challenge their leading position in the Russian imperium or even overthrow it altogether. To maintain their political dominance they follow a policy of divide and rule, ruthlessly exploiting the ethnic diversity of the non-Russians. While the larger ethnic groups are lulled with superficial self-determination, the cultural identity of the smaller ethno-linguistic groups is progressively eroded. But both the larger and smaller nationalities are targets of a ruthless Great Russian campaign to undermine their ethnic identity through systematic russification. As Goldhagen writes:

In exalting things Russian and in glorifying Russian nationalism, Stalin and successive Soviet leaders were moved not by chauvinistic impulses, but by consideration of totalitarian *raison d'état*. They appealed to Russian national feelings, because the Russians were the most numerous and the most important of all the nations of the Soviet Union and their support was necessary if communism was to succeed. Moreover, it is easier to rule an ethnically homogenous state than a multinational realm, which is a perpetual breeding ground of recalcitrant national feelings and aspirations. Also, insofar as the Soviet leaders were still needful of Marxian rationalizations, they could justify to themselves their policy to make the minorities surrender to Russian culture in the process they euphemistically call the "fusion of nations," or "internationalization" as a progressive endeavor: the undoing of

Kleinvölkerei as a step towards the creation of a universal socialist society. . . . Whatever the motives of the Soviet leaders, it is clear that for them the preservation of the separate identities of the ethnic minorities is not a desirable goal, and that their aim is to bring about the "fusion of the nations." (1968, p. xi)

2. LINGUISTIC AND CULTURAL CONFLICT

Although the Russians account for 53 percent of the USSR's population, the 14 major non-Russian ethnic units ("nationalities"), each with a Soviet republic of its own, are growing at rates considerably faster than that of the USSR as a whole—especially the central Asians. Between 1959 and 1970, for instance, while the total population of the USSR expanded by 15.7 percent, population growth of typical nationalities was as shown in table 11.2. The low growth rates of Latvians and Estonians doubtless reflect severity of oppression—a subject treated in subsequent chapters.

Table 11.2. POPULATION GROWTH OF TYPICAL NATIONALITIES
(in percent)

Tadzhiks	52.9	Georgians	20.5
Uzbeks	52.9	Lithuanians	14.6
Turkmenians	52.2	Russians	
Azerbaijani	49.0	(Great)	13.1
Kazakhs	46.3	Latvians	2.1
Armenians	27.7	Estonians	1.8

(SOURCE: *Conflict Studies*, No. 30, 1972)

A major instrument of Russification is, of course, the Russian language. It is a required subject in schools throughout the USSR and may be used in the proceedings of local authorities. The role that linguistic Russification plays in the fusion policy is frankly stated in an article by P. Rogachev and M. Sverdlin in the party journal *Kommunist:*

In the spiritual rapprochement of nations, the spread of the international language plays a great role. In effect, as is noted in the program of the Communist Party of the Soviet Union, Russian has become that language. This is the tongue of a majority, or 54.7 percent of the population of the USSR. . . . The rapprochement [*sblidzheniye*] of the Socialist nations is already evident now, when we can only speak of fusion [*sliyaniye*] as a relatively distant prospect. On the other hand, it is just as incorrect to undermine these processes. The rapprochement of nations in the period of the advanced building of Communism is creating the conditions for their future fusion. (No. 9 [1963]:19)

The main thrust of Russification is undoubtedly aimed at those groups which racially, culturally, and linguistically differ most markedly from the Russians. Examples are the Jews, the Ukrainian Catholics, Armenians, Mongol-Buddhists (e.g. the Kalmyks) and the many Turko-Muslim groups of the North-Caucasian, Central, and Eastern Asiatic regions of the USSR. The numerically and politically weaker groups, especially those that lack a territorial base, are suffering the worst plight (see chapter 18,A6). Resistance is strongest among the Turkic peoples of Central Asia. Only 1 to 2 percent of the Turkic inhabitants of Central Asia and Azerbaidzhan consider Russian to be their native language, while over 90 percent of the Tatars still claim Tatar as theirs.

A sure sign of the persistence of ethnicity in the USSR is substantial evidence of separatist movements in some of the more established ethnic enclaves. Not all separatists strive for sovereign independence, as do the Ukrainians, but all seek genuine ethnic self-determination in their own homelands. It is remarkable how often the concept of the homeland is found in non-Russian poems and stories. For instance:

Men were always transformed to dust, it seems.
The homeland is the remains of our forefathers
Who turned into dust for this precious soil
(Choltan Ergash: "Recognizing the Homeland")

A young Kyrgyz poet, Turar Kojomberdiev, wrote the following significant lines:

Remember, even before your mother's milk—
you drank the milk of the homeland.

Another contemporary author, the poet Gulriukhsor, expresses the intimate feelings of a Tajik for his *Vatan* (homeland). He writes:

I don't remember the
first time I said *Vatan*,
with affection I called
my land, my country
"my soul" . . .
(Quoted in Allworth, 1973, pp. 15–16, 71)

The Communist Party has reason to believe that many of the Ukrainians—numerically the greatest ethnic minority in the USSR—want more than mere attachment to a separate Union Republic in the USSR. Russians as well as Ukrainians remember the independent Ukrainian Republic, which rejected both Czarism and communism, and which was conquered by military force. The struggle for an independent Ukraine is kept alive by a broadly based Ukrainian intelligentsia in the United States and Canada.

3. ISLAMIC AWAKENING IN SOVIET
   CENTRAL ASIA

A resurgence of Turkic and Islamic nationalism is also reported from Soviet Central Asia. In Tadzhikistan, for instance, there is still a powerful movement for a greater Islamic brotherhood encompassing all Islamic groups—an ideal with geopolitical undertones that fan Russian suspicion. In a fairly recent Tazhik play about World War II, a Tazhik tries to persuade a fellow prisoner of war to "help the Germans free our homeland from the Bolshevik *kaffirs*" (unbelievers).

Central Asian cultural life today is marked by reawakened interest in the past and concern to preserve national legacies. There is also a sense of religious, linguistic, and cultural kinship among the several nationalities. That, however, is balanced by particular nationalisms which the Great Russian communists have encouraged under their "divide and rule" policy. Sheehy describes the political situation as follows:

For lack of *samizdat* material, it is impossible to be sure along what lines the Central Asians are thinking. From the Soviet Press, however, one gains the impression that the authorities fear the possible attractions of Asian communism and pan-Turkism, both of which would answer the Muslim peoples' cultural particularism. The danger of pan-Turkism, from the Russian point of view, is that it encourages the Turkic peoples to think that their natural place is not in the predominantly Slav "fraternal family of the peoples of the Soviet Union." If the right circumstances arose, it would also very likely lead to the Turkic peoples of the Soviet Union forming a common front against Russian domination. But it seems unlikely today that the individual Turkic nationalities are dreaming of merging into a single Turkic state. (1972, pp. 22–23)

On this score, Sheehy observes:

It is very possible that national consciousness in Central Asia might have developed along different lines if the present republics had not been arbitrarily set up by Moscow in 1924. But now, thanks to the Party policy of fostering distinctive national languages and cultures, of building up native intelligentsias and promoting native participation in the conduct of republican affairs, the peoples after whom the republics were named have clearly come to identify themselves with their republics, producing what Professor Pipes has called "the psychological reality of statehood." "It does not matter," he writes, "that the Uzbek republic is a Soviet creation and that its government enjoys no meaningful authority. For many Uzbeks it is a reality, and as such it serves as a powerful stimulant to national sentiment." (p. 21)

As Sheehy suggests, political recognition of these ethnonational units is not a sign of Russian magnanimity but a divide and rule strategy to forestall an Islamic Central Asian separatist movement which might become unstoppable. Resurgent concern for the restoration and preservation of ethnic heritage and cultural life will make it extremely difficult for the Russians to denationalize these peoples. Soviet nationality policy has in effect sowed the dragon's teeth by promoting the crystallization of specific ethno-linguistic groups,

including the Kazakh, the Kirgiz, and Tajik, the Turkmen, and the Uzbek. They have all become intensely aware of and attached to their national identities. It seems evident that the Communist Party fears that these *risorgimenti*, which have now gained their own momentum, will hamper the merging of nations into a single Soviet nationality.

Ethnic persistence in the USSR is demonstrated by eight ethnic groups who were deported from their homelands and scattered to the far corners of Central and East Asiatic Russia during World War II. They are the Volga Germans and seven Muslim-Turkic peoples (the Meskhetians, Chechen, Ingush, Crimean Tatars, Balkars, Karachai, and Kalmyks). Despite a series of tribulations, they are all still engaged in a continuous struggle to maintain their ethnic identity (see also Conquest, 1970, Sheehy, 1972). Zbigniew Brzezinski, in his forward to the Chornovil Papers (1970), forecast: "It is not inconceivable that in the next several decades the nationality [ethnic] problem will become politically more important in the Soviet Union than the racial issue has in the United States." Differential birth rates, which favor growth of the non-Slavic nations, may well bring this prophecy to pass.

C. National Conflict and Oppression in South Asia

Ethnic persistence is also manifest on the Indian subcontinent. The linguistic struggles resulting from this fact are described in chapter 18, A1, while population movements and genocide are treated in chapters 22 and 28, respectively. Attention is focused here on several cases of particular oppression related to interethnic conflict.

1. THE BIHARIS: A PEOPLE CONDEMNED TO EXTINCTION

A tragic example of ethnic persistence and its sometimes bitter rewards is that of the Muslim and Urdu-speaking Biharis of Bihar and Bangladesh. Their situation is concisely described by Ben Whitaker, Director of the Minority Rights Group in London, from whose Report No. 11 the following is quoted:

Prior to partition, in the state of Bihar in India—the original homeland of the Biharis—Moslems constituted a minority of four million (about 13 percent) of the population of nearly thirty million. Although they formed an important element in the urban community, except in the administrative district of Purnea, they were greatly outnumbered by Hindus. When therefore Bihar was assigned to India at the time of partition in 1947, although many Bihari Moslems stayed put, large numbers migrated to East Bengal which became the eastern wing of Moslem Pakistan. Another considerable community who, because of unemployment in Bihar, had gone to Calcutta in search of work, moved on to East Bengal when they began to feel insecure. The first exodus was precipitated by communal massacres of some thirty thousand of them by Bihari Hindus between 30 October and 7 November 1946, in retaliation for the slaughter of Hindus by Moslems at Noakhali in East Bengal. The Bihari massacre was widely reported in the press and this provoked the killing of Moslems in West Bengal and elsewhere. As a result other Urdu-speaking Moslems from several states fled to East Pakistan at the same time, but all these fugitives came to be known collectively as Biharis, because the majority of them came from Bihar. . . .

The number of Moslems who moved to East Pakistan was approximately 1,300,000, of whom one million came from Bihar and its neighborhood. . . . Although Biharis never played an active part in politics . . . their general loyalty remained towards the continuance of a united Pakistan, mainly from a feeling of self-preservation.

After Yahya Khan on March 1, 1971, postponed the promised National Assembly, Bengalis turned on the Biharis . . . as symbols of the Pakistani domination. Over 300 of them were killed by extremist mobs at Chittagong in early March 1971. There were other attacks at Jessore, Khulna, Rangpur and Saidpur. A further slaughter at Mymensingh caused a large influx of Biharis into the Mirpur suburb of Dacca. The Urdu-speaking community claim that, in all, several thousands of their people were killed by pro-Bengali supporters of secession prior to the Pakistani army's ruthless intervention on 25 March 1971. . . .

On Bangladesh's independence in December 1971, most of the West Pakistani civilians there were evacuated to India, along with the defeated army. But the Biharis were left behind as castaways.

In enclaves on the outskirts of *Dacca* there are approximately 278,000 Biharis. The two principal enclaves are some six miles to the north of the capital, not far from the airport, at *Mirpur*, a traditional Bihari area (where there are now some 150,000, of whom 10,000 are living in tents), and at *Mohammedpur* (where there are 95,000, of whom 44,000 are living in eight camps). The camps provide only some psychological protection, since they are unguarded and easily entered. Those at Mohammedpur are the worst in Bangladesh, especially the central reception camp, which is overcrowded with new arrivals of refugees and dispossessed families. Here 10,000 people are living ten or more to a tent, many of them in makeshift erections perched on roofs which are likely to be swept away into a sea of muddy excrement during the monsoon. (20 inches of rain can fall in a storm, accompanied by high winds.) (Whitaker, 1972b, pp. 7–9, 13)

The Biharis, of whom Whitaker estimated 735,180 living in enclaves in 1972, are the largest group among some 1.5 million non-Bengalis in Bangladesh. Their theoretical options are migration back to India, exodus to Pakistan or another Islamic country, or integration into the Bengali community. Ideally each Bihari should be able to choose, but prospects for the realization of any of these options look dismal.

Under the Delhi agreement of August 1971, Pakistan agreed to receive a substantial number of Biharis. But it now appears that Pakistan, in the throes of a major economic crisis, is no longer able to help its former loyal citizens and will eventually accept fewer than 50,000 Biharis. It is safe to guess that they will be the Biharis who can bid the highest prices of admission: those least in need. India, likewise, is bursting at the seams and can accept few reimmigrants.

The Biharis made the fatal mistake of being on the losing side in a war. They are so exposed that Whitaker regretfully concludes that the only way they can escape persecution is by abandoning their identity as Biharis—giving up their language and culture, and becoming full-fledged Bangladeshi. This means becoming Bengali, since Bangladesh is a linguistic-ethnic, not a territorial state.

2. AUTONOMIST AND SEPARATIST MOVEMENTS

West Pakistan, or what is now simply Pakistan, is by no means homogenous in language. Urdu, the official language, is spoken by only 15 percent of the population as a language of identity, though many more speak it as a language of communication. Four established ethnolinguistic and cultural segments can be distinguished: the Sindhis of Sind, the Pathans of the northwest frontier, the Baluchis of Baluchistan, and the Punjabis of the Punjab, the last mentioned being the dominant ethnic group in West Pakistan. The non-Punjabi ethnolinguistic segments reject domination by the Punjabis and harbor separatist movements having as their objective at least greater local autonomy. Both the Baluchis and the Pathans, who are ethnically linked to Iran and Afghanistan, make no bones about their desire for independence. In an effort to stem the tide of national separatism the government of West Pakistan has divided the area into four provinces, one for each of the four major ethnolinguistic groups. Whether this dispensation goes far enough to allay ethnic nationalism beyond the Punjabi borders is doubtful.

In the border areas between Pakistan and Afghanistan, the Pathans are currently engaged in a dramatic battle to establish their own ethnic homeland (to be known as Paktoonistan), comprising a territory now divided between these two states. Generations of minority status and discrimination have failed to erode the ethnic identity of this proud people. Afghanistan has strong ethnic and historical ties with the Pathans. It maintains that for its part it would be prepared to grant land for an autonomous homeland for this Pushto-speaking people but that Pakistan is not prepared to cooperate by yielding its Pathan-dominated northwest frontier areas.

To the south, in India, live 33 million members of 414 disparate indigenous communities, generally known as the Scheduled Tribes (Girijans). Despite their primitive lifestyle, their social and economic backwardness, and their weak bargaining position, these people have so far had remarkable success in preserving their unique ethnic character. By creating separate scheduled areas for the tribal people and grouping them in a separate administrative category, the Indian government has unwittingly promoted the development of a strong pan-tribal movement. The tribal people call themselves *Adivasis* (original inhabitants), a name that strengthens the tribes' sentiment of intercommunal brotherhood—despite the ethnic and racial differences separating them.

The 500,000-strong Naga people of Nagaland in Northeast India—the first and only state in India with a Christian majority and English as official language—has won international renown for its struggle to win greater autonomy (see chapter 21,G2). Equally strong separatist movements center around the ethnolinguistic aspirations of the southern Hindus of Dravidian stock. Their four principal languages (Telugu, Tamil, Kannada, and Malayalam) belong to the Dravidian language family and are spoken by more than 100 million people. The strongest resistance to Hindi as the official language of the Union comes from the Dravidian speakers, who argue that their languages as cultures are at least as ancient as those based upon Sanskrit. Tamil in particular has an ancient classical literature to rival that of Sanskrit (Le Page, 1973–74, p. 55).

Particularly in the states known today as Mysore, Andhra/Pradesh, Kerala, Tamil Nadu (Madras State), and Maharashtra, a strong sentiment in favor of the creation of autonomous states based on language areas has existed since 1947. The protagonists of linguistic separatism say they fear creeping subjugation by the northern Aryan Hindus. An Indian authority, Dr. Krishna Kodesia, writes:

The problem is certainly not a new one. It made its first appearance as early as 1905 at the time of the partition of Bengal under Lord Curzon and since then it has been the product of different forces at work at different times and places and still remains unsolved. With the creation of the Andhra state in 1953 as a separate unit, the demand became more insistent. The cry for linguistic redistribution and regrouping of the states has arisen firstly from the fact that the states in India had not been organized on any scientific basis during the British regime and secondly, because the monopoly of power and patronage of some powerful groups in certain areas has created difficulties for the minority groups. . . . The decision to allow the Andhras to separate from Madras became the signal for linguistic groups all over India to increase their agitation. New organizations and pressure groups, dedicated to the linguistic idea, sprang up all over India. In order to appease public opinion, the Indian government set up a reorganization committee which submitted a report on November 1st, 1956. On the basis of this report 14 states and six union territories were established. (Kodesia, 1969, Preface and pp. 13–14)

In the case of Tamil Nadu in particular, where the four Dravidian languages are firmly established, local citizens argue cogently in favor of partitioning the state into four separate units. Kodesia quotes a prominent Indian leader, Dr. Radha Kumud Mukerji, who as early as 1947 called for "cultural autonomy of each linguistic unit to enable it to make its complete contribution not merely to South India but also to the culture of India as a whole" (*ibid.*, p. 23).

A strong regional separatism is found in the four southern states—Andhra Pradesh, Kerala, Mysore, and Tamil Nadu. Important groups in these areas demand a separate Dravidian state on historical, linguistic, and cultural grounds. Their most powerful mouthpiece is the Dravida Munnetra Kazhagam (DMK) which has a particularly strong following in Madras. Nothing short of a separate Dravidian homeland will ever satisfy the more extreme members of this movement.

Although these separatist movements are largely defined in terms of linguistic divisions, it appears upon careful examination that language is to a great extent an indicator of other cultural differences as well, including lifestyle and social norms.

Even in cosmopolitan urban areas it is not at all uncommon to find people of different religions or languages concentrated in specific occupations or particular residential areas.

The map of Calcutta thus shows a highly differentiated texture. *Ethnic groups tend to cluster together in their own quarters.* They are distinguished from one another not only by language and culture but also by broad differences in the way they make their living. Naturally there is a considerable amount of overlap, but this does not obscure the fact that each ethnic group tends to pursue a particular range of occupations. . . . It can be said, therefore, that the diverse ethnic groups in the population of the city have come to bear the same relation to one another as do the castes in India as a whole. (Bose, 1965, p. 102, emphasis added)

Such urban clustering is a major factor preserving the traditional ethnic, linguistic, and religious cleavages in India. Altogether, the casualties of ethnolinguistic and ethnoreligious conflicts in the Indian subcontinent must be calculated not in hundreds of thousands but in millions.

D. Malay–Chinese Relations in Malaysia

When the Federation of Malaysia was founded in 1963, more than one million Chinese of Singapore became citizens of the new state. Almost immediately, they sensed the real danger that their cultural as well as their economic interests would be submerged in the larger Malay-dominated community. When Singapore left the Federation in 1965 to become an independent state, Malaysian political planners had to pay the price for treating ethnicity as a factor of secondary importance.

Although they paid the usual lip-service to national unity, the Malays never really trusted the Chinese. The latter were often called money-grabbers who refused to cut the ethnic umbilical cord with either Nationalist or Communist China, "hiding Chinese passports under their pillows just in case." After the bloody Malay–Chinese riots of 1969 the Malaysian leaders began to dissociate themselves from the Chinese. According to Cynthia Enloe:

Malay leaders loosened their ties with the Chinese elite and pledged to Malayanise developmental programs. What Arend Lijphart (1969) has called "consociational democracy," in which social fragmentation is papered over by elite co-operation, had come apart at the seams. Although Chinese are still in parliament and the ministries, the Kuala Lumpur regime is more Malay than it has ever been since independence. . . . The bloodshed of 1969 is not forgotten, but there appears to be less obsession with caution and ambiguity in governmental actions. At home this has meant clearer ethnic priorities favouring Malays, while abroad it has meant greater independence from the West. In other words, Malay militancy has limited local Chinese influence internally and raised Chinese influence externally. (1974, p. 229)

After Singapore had been established as an independent state, some 3.5 million Chinese stayed behind in Malaysia—about 34 percent of the total population. Their exclusiveness arouses Malay suspicion that the Chinese are not altogether loyal; they are sometimes called a "foreign fifth column." This sentiment is nurtured by the determination of the Chinese not to allow their lifestyle, language, religion, and culture to be undermined by Malayanization.

The large numbers of Indians and Chinese found in enclaves elsewhere in the Far East are further examples of groups whose ethnic identity has survived many generations of life in foreign countries and a bewildering variety of discriminatory practices to remain a primary sociocultural reality.

E. Ethnic Conflict and Oppression in Africa

Africa has a larger variety of nations, ethnic groups, tribes, languages, and cultures than any other region. More than 800 different languages and dialects have been identified on the continent. South of the Sahara more than 15 culture and language groups may be distinguished: Hamites, Semites, Negroes, Nilo-Hamites, Nilotes, Southern Bantu, Western Bantu, Eastern Bantu, Hottentot, Pigmies, Damaras, Asian-Indians, Caucasians, and Coloureds.

The three most important religious groupings are tribal (135 million), Islamic (115 million), and Christian (72 million). Each of the main religious groups consists of larger and smaller sects and cults.

In this context the price of maintaining ethnic identity is sometimes more than discrimination. It is often expulsion and total loss of property. During the past decade the East African states of Kenya, Tanzania, and Uganda have expelled many of the Asians (mostly Indians and Pakistani) who constituted their small business class. The extent of these expulsions is shown in table 11.3.

Table 11.3.   ASIANS IN EAST AFRICA, 1969–1972

	Total Population (millions)	Asians 1969	Asians 1972
Kenya	11.0	139,000	105,000
Tanzania	13.6	85,000	52,000
Uganda	10.0	74,300	1,000

(SOURCE: Minority Rights Group Report No. 16, London, 1973, p. 7; 1972 figures estimated.)

It was argued that the Asians "resisted Africanization." But as will be shown (chapter 12, E2), the Africanization of Asians is a cultural impossibility. Ethnic persistence can be observed in virtually every one of Africa's 44 independent states. Ethnicity, especially tribal rivalry, has played a role in practically every one of the approximately 30 successful coups carried out since 1960. Colin Legum has stated (1970, p. 102) that "tribalism is Africa's natural condition, and is likely to remain so for a long time."

1. TRIBALISM, ETHNICITY, AND MODERNIZATION

The boundaries of colonies in Africa—later to be frozen as borders of new states—were drawn in the late nineteenth century with no regard for ethnic patterns of settlement. Tribes and linguistic groups were divided and highly diversified people were placed together. Secondary processes of intercultural contact and culture change through urbanization, migration, religious conversion, and education tended to create further divisions within Africa's modern societies.

It should be stressed that ethnic loyalties are not necessarily eroded by social and cultural change. Colin Legum, for instance, writes that "tribalism is not inherently anti-modern. Tribalism must be distinguished from traditionalism. Traditional systems may pass away while tribal affiliations remain strongly entrenched in defence of ethnocentric interests." Not detribalization and territorial nationalism but the rise of modern ethnic nationalism should be anticipated in Africa. This could lead to "scrambles for opportunity and the struggle to get one tribe or another into power" (Legum, 1970, p. 102; see also Wolstenholme and O'Connor, 1965, p. 119).

In Africa, trade unions are not so well developed as are political parties. The best developed trade unions in Black Africa are those in Zambia, Kenya, and Ghana. Labor action in Ghana and Kenya went hand in hand with political aspirations, and labor discontent was

therefore an inherent ingredient of the rising tide of nationalism. The Trade Union Congress of Ghana was, for instance, taken over by Dr. Nkrumah's Convention Peoples Party. For the time being, nationalism superseded local and tribal loyalties.

Where labor movements became separated from political protests, as in Zambia, ethnic factors tended to play a much greater role in shaping industrial relations. The copperbelt strikes between 1935 and 1940, when grievances were not political but economic, were led by a particular ethnic group, the Bembas. That tribe tended to dominate the trade unions, whereas the rival Lozi tended to monopolize administrative offices. Other tribes, such as the Nyakuza and the Lunda, resisted both Bemba and Lozi leadership on the Copperbelt and pursued secessionist policies.

2. PARTY POLITICS AS ETHNIC POLITICS

Ethnicity plays an even greater role, however, in the formation of political associations and parties. This factor often threatens the social and political stability of African states. An early case of the secularization of ethnic loyalties was the formation of the *Egbe Omo Ududwa* (Association of the Children of Odudwa) movement among the Yoruba in western Nigeria. This movement sought to cultivate a modern Yoruba nationalism and in so doing laid the foundation for an almost exclusively Yoruba political party: the Action Group (AG), led by Chief Awolowo. All the other political parties in Nigeria also had their distinctive ethnic support bases. Membership in the Northern Peoples Congress (NPC) was primarily Hausa-Fulani and that of the National Convention for Nigerian Citizens (NCNC) predominantly Ibo.

Similar delicate ethnic relationships exist in Kenya, where national integration is hampered by the fact that many tribes have not reached the stage of coalescence or even compromise. It was the Kikuyu who took the lead in the political decolonization of Kenya. Kenyan independence was therefore not the product of a comprehensive Kenyan nationalism, but rather of a Kikuyu nationalism (see chapter 20). Since then, the Luo have also "awakened" politically and the outcome of Kikuyu–Luo relationships will in all probability determine Kenya's future leadership. President Kenyatta, a Kikuyu, has particularly tried to meet the demands of the Luo and Kalenji. The Kikuyu and Luo were never neighbors and first met during colonial times. This contact tended to intensify their ethnic consciousness rather than to lessen it. The same can be said of the Bemba and Lozi in Zambia who had little, if any, contact with each other before colonization. But once they met on the Copperbelt they fell into intense power struggles.

Probably the most intense and even violent example of interethnic power struggle, reaching the point of denial of the right to exist is that in Rwanda and Burundi. Unlike the former Belgian Congo, where tribal loyalties have produced demands for independent tribal states or for a loose form of federation, Rwanda and Burundi are countries where traditional rule by a minority of about 14 percent, the Tutsi, over the rest of the population, the Hutu, has been increasingly opposed by the latter. The cattle-herding Tutsi invaded the area before the fifteenth century and, after subjugating the Hutu, established a highly organized political, social, and economic hierarchy, at the apex of which was the Mwami or King. In this order the position of the Hutu, a farming people, was similar to that of the serfs in medieval Europe.

In 1946 the area became a UN Trust Territory under Belgian administration; it was then called Ruanda-Urundi. The 1950s witnessed growing opposition of the Hutu to indirect Belgian and direct Tutsi rule and the gradual introduction of partly democratic nontraditional institutions by the Belgians. The first political parties appeared in the late 1950s. The most important party in Rwanda was the *Parti du Mouvement de l'Émancipation Hutu* (Parme-hutu), which, under its leader, Mr. Kayibanda, became the chief Hutu party. In Burundi, the two chief parties were the *Parti de l'Unité et du Progrès National du Burundi* (UPROMA) and the *Parti Democrate-Chrétien du Burundi* (PDC). Both professed loyalty toward the Tutsi monarchy.

The tension between the Tutsi and the Hutu in Rwanda led to violence in November 1959. Some hundreds of people were killed and many thousands of huts were burned. Many Tutsi chiefs and subchiefs were killed or driven from their posts, and in many cases the Belgian administration appointed Hutu to fill the vacancies until municipal elections could be held. The Rwanda elections resulted in a smashing victory for Parmehutu, which won 70 percent of the seats, and Gregoire Kayibanda (a Hutu) became Prime Minister of the provisional government. In Burundi a coalition led by PDC won the communal elections in November and December 1960 and a provisional government led by Tutsi was formed shortly afterward.

The Hutu thereupon became the rulers of Rwanda, where they follow a deliberate policy of genocide against the Tutsi. In Burundi, however, the Tutsi consolidated their position and instituted large-scale massacres of Hutu tribesmen (see chapter 19, F1).

3. ETHNIC WARFARE BETWEEN
   ARABS AND NEGROES

In Sudan, the Arabs of the north have for some years conducted a "race war" against the numerically larger but less developed Negro* population of the south. The civil war began in 1955 when a southerner, William Deng of the Sudan African National Union, led a rebellion against Khartoum.

---

* The term "Negro" will be used in this book in its exact sense to mean a person belonging to the Negrid macrogroup (Congoid in Carleston S. Coon's terminology). It will not be used for Australids, Khoisanids, or persons of mixed ancestry, even though these might classify themselves socially as "black."

At the outset, civilians joined southern troops and police in an onslaught against northerners, and 1000 people were killed. The war continued, and in September 1963, the northern military leaders launched an all-out campaign to crush the rebellion. They were unsuccessful, and turned their wrath on the clergy, who were persecuted and then deported. Renewed rebellion broke out. Southern guerrilla groups formed a coalition called Anyanya (a dialect name for a fatal poison) and began attacking government posts. Government reprisals on villagers soon followed, and this pattern continued for eight years unaffected by the overthrow of the army regime in 1964 and the countercoup of 1969. Deaths ran to hundreds of thousands, particularly on the southern side, since the north possessed superior weapons and logistics. Southern intellectuals who fell into the hands of northern forces were systematically liquidated (interview with a Sudanese informant, June 1973).

Southern leaders pressed repeatedly for some kind of federal structure that would loosen the Arab stranglehold. The government of Gaafar Nemeiri, who seized power in May 1969, offered local autonomy within a united "socialist" Sudan, but only after the rebellion had been crushed (Kabara, 1971, pp. 261–63). After diplomatic intervention of other African states, however, an agreement was signed at Addis Ababa in 1972. An autonomous South Sudan Region was created, with its own Assembly and High Executive Council. The region enjoys wide legislative power, and is even empowered to engage in diplomacy with neighboring states on matters within its jurisdiction. The Southern Command of the Sudanese Army, specified in the Addis Ababa agreement, is fixed at 12,000 men, of whom 6000 must be citizens of the Southern Region.

Not only has Sudan as a whole adopted a pluralist political structure, but the Southern Region is plural within itself. The Addis Ababa agreement provides for English-language schools with Arabic as a second language. Village elementary schools are started in the local language—of which there are close to a hundred, Nilotic and Bantu—with English the first foreign language. After the fourth grade, instruction is in English, with Arabic the first foreign language. Both are used as languages of communication in South Sudan. Any attempt to impose either as a language of identity would be fiercely resisted.

A similar struggle not yet resolved is found in the Islamic Republic of Mauritania, which occupies the southwest corner of the Sahara and adjacent territory. The majority of the population are nomadic Moors of Arab-Berber origin but there is a Negro minority in the south. France, which became active in Mauritania in the middle of the nineteenth century, gradually achieved its administrative unity while respecting the Moors' spiritual tradition and social structure. Mauritania became independent in 1960, and the Negroes who live in its southern parts still do not enjoy any significant share of the political power wielded by the Islamic rulers in the North.

Although domination of blacks by Muslims is the general pattern in Africa, the situation is occasionally reversed. In Chad, for instance, a Negro political monopoly was created by François Tombalbaye, a black Protestant from the south. Muslims in that country are fighting for "national identity"—not secession but recognition as a separate cultural group. In 1963 Tombalbaye launched a "purification" campaign during which most of the leading Muslims in government service were arrested. In 1965 another massive campaign was launched, which for the northern Muslims was the last straw. They launched a revolt, forming the *Front de liberation nationale* (FROLINAT) in June 1966. In August 1971, Tombalbaye accused Libya of fomenting a plot to overthrow his government.

These power struggles in the Sudan, Mauritania, and Chad are, despite their religious overtones, basically fired by ethnic animosities between Arabs and Hamites, on the one hand,

and Negroes on the other. They reflect social distance and ethnic differentiation, as well as a lack of understanding across cultural barriers.

4. ETHNIC OBSTACLES TO "NATION BUILDING"

Ethnic differences also inhibit the concerted campaign employing the entire range of political-guerrilla-military tactics against the white regimes of Southern Africa projected by the Organization of African Unity (OAU). The anti-white aspect is superficial rather than basic; Black nationalism can be, and usually is, directed against competing black groups. President Julius Nyerere of Tanzania once said:

We have artificial "nations" carved out at the Berlin Conference; we are struggling to build these nations into stable units of human society. And these weaknesses, too, are being exploited. We are being reminded daily of these weaknesses. We are told that tribalism will not allow us to build nations. But when we take measures to deal with tribalism, we are accused of dictatorship. (In Sigmund, 1961, p. 209)

President Nyerere was not exaggerating, since tribalism is Africa's natural condition—a condition that produces ethnic contestants in the scramble for resources and opportunities.

Ethnicity, which in Africa and many other areas is tribal in form, is a normal phenomenon of plural societies. Loyalty is directed toward the family, the tribal community, the tribal authorities, and the tribal chief. Tribalism is found in both rural and urban areas. It is a dynamic concept which can assume different forms and integrate at different levels.

Processes of change have eroded traditional systems, but not necessarily tribal loyalties, because tribalism—as we have seen—is not inherently antimodern. Wallerstein illuminates this problem:

Often what a writer means by detribalization is simply a decline in chiefly authority. It does not necessarily follow that an individual who is no longer loyal to his chief has rejected as well the tribe as the community to which he owes certain duties

and from which he expects a certain security. (1970, p. 10)

National integration at the expense of tribal loyalties is desired by modernizing leaders in a number of African states. There are two ways to achieve this goal: the pluralist model and the assimilationist model. Most African governments choose assimilation, which implies attaining a common identity and value consensus. Tribalism has caused this model to fail in Africa. National coalescence remains obstructed by ethnic separatism in fields such as trade unions, voluntary organizations, and residential districts. Contacts and conflicts in the industrial society cause tribalism to crystallize rather than to disappear.

Massive tribal conflicts have occurred in Zaire, Rwanda, Burundi, Nigeria, Uganda, Sudan, Mauritania, Chad, Somalia, and Kenya. The three largest conflicts—in Rwanda-Burundi, Nigeria, and Sudan—exacted a total death toll of over 1 million. "Minor" conflicts have brought death to thousands of people and driven even greater numbers to flight. It may therefore be asked why African governments continue to pursue assimilationist policies in the face of these disasters. Could it be that European and American political scientists are exporting the wrong ideologies? The pluralist model, which is gaining some currency in the United States and which is applied in the black homelands of South Africa, has proved to be more realistic. Not only does it permit the modernization of tribes, but it also places coexistent tribalisms on an equal footing, thereby minimizing inter-tribal exploitation.

5. TENSION AND ACCOMMODATION IN SOUTH AFRICA

The Republic of South Africa is located within what until 1910 was called British South Africa—a territory including now-independent Botswana, Lesotho, and Swaziland. It contains four major population segments:

whites; the Coloured, people of mixed Europid-Khoisanid stock plus the remaining Khoisanids; Asians, mostly Indians, with a few Chinese; and the black (Bantu-speaking) nations of which there are nine. The whites have two linguistic subcultures: Afrikaners and English-speakers. Among themselves, the black peoples manifest significant differences in ethnicity, language, historical background, and lifestyle.

The policy of "separate development" proclaimed by the South African government is in fact a policy of *multinational* development. It envisages the accommodation of varying ethnic interests in a pattern of political independence, taking into account a high degree of economic and technical interdependence. Recent election results suggest that the majority of the white population supports this plan for a multinational commonwealth, consisting of separate territorial states for the main ethnic groups, economically interlocked in a common market. Leaders of some of the non-white groups are not so enthusiastic, and some would frankly prefer a policy of assimilation. But the South African *Staatsvolk* is not about to embrace a policy in which it would be assimilated by groups ethnically (even though not territorially) foreign.

Multinational development is complicated by the fact that South Africa's ethnic groups do not live in compact territories. Many are scattered in exclaves and urban townships, and several groups, such as the Coloured and Asians, lack a territorial base at all. Yet despite these problems, the process of accommodation takes place through argument and negotiation—through continuous even though sometimes heated dialogue—and violent confrontations such as those of 1976 are the exception, not the rule. The Republic of South Africa has had in this century no ethnic conflicts that even by the wildest stretch of the imagination could be compared with those in other parts of Africa, not to mention the intercommunal struggles on the Indian subcontinent.

Each Black ethnohistorical group in South Africa is treated as a nation on its way to statehood and each already enjoys a considerable degree of self-government. The Transkei, homeland of the largest Xhosa-speaking population group, received its independence in October 1976. Because each disparate people has its distinctive language and culture, and is no less ethnocentric than European nations of equivalent size, any attempt to integrate all blacks in a single state would be doomed to failure.

F. Ethnic Oppression in the Middle East and the Maghreb

The ethnic feelings of Arabs are oriented on two levels: toward the greater Arab nation, (*'amm* or *umma*) and toward the specific homeland (*watan*) and its regional people (*khāss* or *sha'ab*). This distinction needs to be kept clearly in mind in thinking about the Arab-Israeli dispute. According to Y. Harkabi (1974, 47n):

Arab ideologues tend now to distinguish between the one Arab "nation" and the many Arab "peoples," such as the Egyptians, Iraqis and so on. They call attachment to the nation *qawmiyya*, "nationalism," whereas attachment to the people, and especially its land, they call *wataniyya*, which recently took on the sense of "patriotism." Correspondingly, there are those who distinguish between the general homeland of all Arabs, *al-watan al-'amm*, and the homeland of a specific people, which is called *al-watan al-khāss*.

The leaders and intellectuals of the Palestinian Arabs take advantage of the discrepancy in categories between the Arabic and English (and most other European) languages to perpetrate a semantic deception, which is explained in chapter 22,C2.

Less well known are the grievances of some of the non-Arab ethnic groups that live in Arab lands. In Iraq the local Ba'athist regime is confronted with the separatist claims of the 1.25 million Kurds, a historically established ethno-linguistic group that has been waging a virtually continuous battle for greater independence since 1961. The anti-Kurdish offensive in Kurdistan forced more than 80,000 Kurdish refugees to seek asylum in Iran. The latter country also has about 2 million Kurds, and is therefore in an ambiguous position. Iranians, as non-Arabs although Muslims, have tended to sympathize with Iraqi Kurds; the Shah's government is distrustful of Russian influence in Iraq and has therefore welcomed developments that weaken Baghdad. Yet Teheran does not wish to encourage its own Kurds to secede. It has therefore always limited military support to the Iraqi Kurds, and recent events suggest that Teheran regards them as expendable.

Background information on the Kurdish question is supplied by Professor Emmanuel Sivan of Jerusalem, from whose article on the Kurds (1975a) the following is extracted:

The Kurds are the only minority in the Middle East possessing its own language, enjoying a geographical concentration, and having a substantial number of people (ca. six million). . . . Racially the Kurds are Aryans, of a branch akin to the Iranians. . . . Up until the seventh century the Kurdish religion was Zoroastrian, but with the Islamic conquests a process of Islamization was begun which ultimately spread to all tribes (though some of them still maintain some Zoroastrian mores and customs). Most Kurds are Orthodox (Sunni) Muslims and only a minority are heterodox (Shi'ite).

. . . the Kurdish tribes enjoyed a very extensive autonomy in Iran as well as in the Ottoman empire until the nineteenth century and even later, and semi-independent Kurdish principalities flourished from time to time in these regions. The national states, established on the ruins of the multi-national Ottoman Empire, constituted a severe challenge to the Kurdish minorities living in them. Moreover, their centralist character stood in open contradiction to the autonomous structure of the Kurdish tribes. . . .

Ever since the end of the First World War, the Kurdish question has been centered more and more in Iraq. Here the Kurds found themselves in an almost endless conflict with the central government. . . . The driving force behind the 1961 insurrection was undoubtedly the Kurdish demand for self-determination: a demand for political, administrative and cultural autonomy in the Iraqi framework—perhaps as a first phase towards complete political independence.

The rebels' seizure of control over mountainous northern Iraq in 1962 created a situation of *de facto* Kurdish autonomy. This was given formal expression in 1964 when the rebels established independent governmental organs: parliament, senate, government and administration. These institutions ruled the Kurdish region and even levied taxes. In all of these developments the Kurdish Democratic Party played a central role. It integrated into the rebel army and exerted itself in order to bolster national consciousness in its ranks as well as among the rural and tribal population. Mulla Mustafa Barzani, the prime Minister, was elected Party President.

Recent history of the Kurd struggle may be summarized as follows. In July 1966, Prime Minister Al-Bazzaz of Iraq published a program granting wide autonomy to the Kurds: it would have recognized their nation and language; decentralized administration; granted amnesty and freedom of publication; and included Kurds in the General Staff and the civil service. His successor, Nadji Taleb, refused to carry it out. Hostilities broke out again in the summer of 1968, and—when Baghdad found itself unable to win the war—an agreement was concluded on March 11, 1970. It again provided broad autonomy; recognition of the Kurdish language; an autonomous Kurd administration and proportional participation in the central legislature. The agreement seemed generous, but there were six secret clauses, and these may have provoked the renewed fighting that broke out March 12, 1974.

This time, the fortunes of war turned against the Kurds. Faced with a better trained and equipped Iraqi Army, Barzani and his *Peshmerga* troops were forced to flee into the mountains; They acquitted themselves well, but were no match for Russian-supplied T–22 supersonic bombers, Zukhoi–20 bombers, and T–62 tanks. (Taubinger, 1975a, pp. 253–59.) With planes and bombs supplied by that self-proclaimed champion of the right of self-determination, the USSR, the Baghdad government mounted a series of air raids that forced thousands of people to flee from Kurdistan across the border into Iran. By August, the number of Kurdish refugees in Iran was estimated at 72,000 (*The Times*, London, August 31, 1974).

David Hirst reported in *The Guardian* after a personal visit to Barzani that the Baghdad government was using aircraft to kill civilians as well as military personnel: "A whole quarter—shops, houses, a school, and part of a hospital—was demolished. They [the aircraft] came back and did it a second time. At least 130 people died. They included 80 children and one soldier. When I left Kurdistan they were still digging for bodies." (May 9, 1974.)

It was, finally, the Shah who administered the fatal blow. Barzani's meager supplies came through the mountain passes from Iran; the American CIA, rightly or wrongly, was rumored to have a hand in the matter (*Daily Telegraph*, October 10, 1974; *The Times*, London, October 16, 1974 and January 1, 1975). On March 6, 1975, however, the Iraqi and Iranian foreign ministers met in Algiers under the good offices of President Boumedienne. They signed an agreement whereby Iraq made a territorial concession in the Shatt al Arab estuary, enabling tankers to reach an Iranian refinery, in return for an end of all aid from or via Iran to the Kurd rebels (*The Times* and *The Guardian*, London, March 7, 1975). The aid cutoff put an end, at least for the time being, to Kurdish plans for an independent state. The Algiers agreement supposedly provides for "self-rule" for the Kurds, but the extent of such autonomy remains to be seen.

In the Maghreb (Arab North Africa) there is another important ethnolinguistic group determined to maintain its identity and culture in the face of Arab pressure, the Kabyls, who number 1.5 million and live in Algeria. Again we turn to Professor Sivan for background (1975b, pp. 263 ff.).

The Berbers are the ancient inhabitants of the Maghreb, established there long before the Phoenician and Roman conquests. . . . The Berbers in Algeria number three to four million: one-fourth to one-third of the population. Estimates vary because of lack of a clear linguistic census in mixed areas. Yet it is greater Kabylia which surpasses each of the other concentrations in size and in level of cultural-political consciousness. It is, moreover, very near to the capital, Algiers, and thus perceived as potentially dangerous to the government, and hence is more systematically muzzled and oppressed. Greater Kabylia remained more staunchly hostile to the Arab conquerors than any other part of the Central Maghreb. Even after the Kabyls had finally embraced Islam, they managed to remain particularist. Worship was held in Arabic and Kabyl (a rare dispensation from the use of Arabic alone); Kabyl customary law continued to exist alongside Moslem written law (*Shari'a*). . . . While preserving their distinctive culture, the Kabyls became converted to Algerianhood in the late nineteenth century; they spearheaded the nationalist struggle against the French.

Since the war of independence (1954–1962) the Kabyl problem has been mainly that of cultural-racial particularism *within* the Algerian framework. Kabyl continues to be the major spoken language of Greater Kabylia; Kabyl folklore retains astonishing vitality; rural social structures remain intact (though their political role is secondary and unofficial); and even in Islamic practice Kabyl customs (some of pagan origin) persist *de facto*. Cultural concessions, however, are refused by the government, which sees ethnic or cultural particularism as a mortal danger to Algerian unity.

Arab-Kabyl conflict has centered on economic policy and the sharing of power. The ban on smoking imposed by the *Front de Libération Nationale* (FLN) ruined the Kabyl tobacco growers, and the development budgets of Presidents Ben Bella (1962–1965) and Boumedienne (who overthrew Ben Bella in 1965) have emphasized industry at the expense of agriculture, the mainstay of the Kabyl economy.

Armed revolt, spearheaded by the *Front des Forces Socialistes* (FFS), essentially a Kabyl ethnic political movement, broke out in the summer of 1963. It failed because of Kabyl disunity and because Ben Bella took advantage of border warfare with Morocco to enlist the Kabyl army contingent in the name of "Sacred Union." Boumedienne's efficient secret police has wiped out the local cadre of the FFS, which remains a movement of intellectuals abroad (Sivan, 1975b, pp. 273, 275–76).

A newer opposition group with a broader mass base among Kabyls at home is the *Mouvement Democratique du Renouveau Algérien* (MDRA), founded by Krim Belkassem in October 1967. The MDRA, which eschews Marxist doctrine in favor of economic and social conservatism, tried to launch several operations within Algeria. But an attempt to kill an unpopular minister, Kaid Ahmed, failed and a betrayal led to liquidation of the local network and imprisonment of its leaders. Boumedienne offered Belkassem a chance to return to Algeria as a minister, but the MDRA leader feared a trap and rejected it. Algerian secret agents assassinated Belkassem in November 1970, in Frankfurt, but Mourad Terbouche soon succeeded in taking command and reorganizing the movement (*ibid.*, p. 278).

The MDRA concentrates on long-term educative work among migratory Kabyl workers in France and Germany. The Kabyls are far from permanently "pacified": whether they turn from the quest for autonomy within Algeria to outright separatism depends largely on whether the government grants them ethnic fulfillment within the Algerian state.

G. Ethnicity in the United States

In terms of physical appearance, Americans can be divided into five main groups: whites, blacks, chicanos and other Hispanic-Americans, Orientals, and American Indians. Many people would, of course, not fit neatly into any of these categories. Traditionally, the American melting pot had three root ingredients: West European (especially Anglo-Saxon) origin and culture, a white somatic norm image stereotyped to match West European culture, and Protestant (mainly nonconformist) religion. The Catholics remained a minority, except locally, and their churches became centers for the preservation of ethnic cultures—typically Polish, Czech and Slovak, Lithuanian, and Italian. After 150 years of immigration, the West Europeans in general and the WASPs in particular have lost much of their predominance; their role as literary mentors is being challenged by Jews, Italians, Slavs, and even Armenians. Meanwhile, the black slaves have been emancipated and their descendants are asserting group rights with increasing militancy; Indians are claiming what they feel is their patrimony; and the Chicanos are in full revolt against Anglo-Saxon culture. Obviously, the United States is going through a stage of ethnic transformation and group reidentification.

1. ETHNIC REPRESSION AND RENAISSANCE

The melting pot was never impartial; it was managed so as to recast people in the Anglo-Saxon mold—or, to use another metaphor—people were flattened by the "cultural steamroller." Conflict arises when people refuse to be melted or culturally flattened.

The Anglo-Saxons, however, and the monolingual and monocultural educators who administer their tradition, do not give up so easily. Among other things, it is too much effort to expand the school curriculum to include non–Anglo-Saxon content. As Dinnerstein and Jaher put it:

Because of a predominantly English heritage in the colonial period, the United States, a country of many peoples, often has evaluated its varied citizenry by a single standard: White, Anglo-Saxon, middle-class Protestantism. Although popular rhetoric glorified the country as a melting pot of different peoples, in actuality this has meant melting diversity into conformity with Anglo-Saxon characteristics. Those unable or unwilling to accomplish the transformation have suffered varying degrees of abuse and ostracism because middle-class America demands conformity before it gives acceptance. (1970, p. 3)

Nevertheless, after over three centuries of WASP domination, the ethnic identity of other major European groups has not eroded to the point where their members identify themselves simply as Americans. According to information compiled by the U.S. Bureau of the Census, 25.5 million American citizens call themselves Germans. The other main groups are English, 29.5 million; Irish, 16.5 million; Hispanic, 9.5 million; Italian, 8.75 million; French (including French-Canadian), 5.5 million; Polish, 5 million; and Russian, 2.25 million.

Recent in-depth studies of the "melting pot" in operation have confirmed the persistence of ethnic identification over several generations. This trend is borne out by the number of publications in languages other than English. While far less numerous than half a century ago, there are still enough Americans who read languages other than English to support 254 foreign-language newspapers in 35 languages—a figure that only includes those with substantial circulations. They include 13 each in Chinese and Italian, 15 Armenian, 17 Polish, 31 German, 10 Czech, 6 Yiddish, 11 French, 10 Japanese, 4 Bulgarian, and 10 Arabic.

Ethnic heritages were neglected in the nineteenth century, because immigrants were too busy trying to climb the economic ladder. Since social stratification reflected conformity with Anglo-Saxon norms, many accepted "Americanization" as the price of getting ahead. Recent years, however, have seen an "ethnic renaissance." Much credit for it goes to black leaders and intellectuals and their wakening to their own cultural heritage. Isajiw has remarked:

Too often it has been assumed that ethnic identity in North America is a temporary matter, i.e. that in time all "ethnics" assimilate and the ethnic group

boundaries disappear. . . . Much evidence indicates that in North America ethnic identities persist beyond cultural assimilation and that persistence of ethnic identity is not necessarily related to the perpetuation of traditional ethnic culture. Rather, it may depend more on the emergence of ethnic "rediscoverers," i.e. persons from any consecutive ethnic generation who have been socialized into the culture of the general society but who develop a symbolic relation to the culture of their ancestors. Even relatively few items from the cultural past, such as folk art, music, can become symbols of ethnic identity. . . . and rather than accepting the entire baggage of ethnic tradition persons from consecutive ethnic generations show a degree of freedom in choosing such items . . . which correspond to their needs created perhaps by the specific character of relations in society as a whole. (1972, p. 121)

Even in New York, the melting pot and the arrival of millions of "internal migrants" from the South and from Puerto Rico have shifted, but not changed the basic multiethnic character of the city. Definite concentrations of Jews, WASPs, Irish Catholics, Germans, blacks, and Puerto Ricans can be observed—a configuration that leaves its stamp on New York politics.

The revival of ethnicity is clearly echoed in a growing demand for ethnic studies in higher education. It was formulated in these terms by a prominent non-Anglo-Saxon scholar:

I stand before you an unabashed advocate of ethnic studies. I do not believe that ethnic studies are a panacea, but I do think that properly taught ethnic studies can help to cure the sickness of America. It is a sickness born of the historic attempt to impose one standard of Americanism upon a population composed of many diverse cultural groups. It is a sickness which has its origins in the disparagement of anyone who deviated in speech, manners, and, of course, skin color, from the model of the ideal America. . . . *American history could be told as a story of cultural genocide.* . . . the psyche of ethnic Americans (and who is not an ethnic today?) bears the *scars of this effort to fit us all into the Procrustean bed of Anglo-American conformity. The cure for this sickness, I contend, is a healthy pluralism:* an acceptance of cultural and group differences as legitimate expressions of our diversity. Ethnic studies, I suggest, are essential for us to gain such an acceptance. . . . Which of us would wish to return to the Eisenhower years of consensus, to that era of self-deception when we (the intelligentsia) had persuaded ourselves that the Melting Pot had done its work? Were we not all middle class All-Americans? Then the blacks rioted, youth rebelled, and the white ethnics raged, and we discovered that beneath the surface placidity roiled turbulent and frightening social forces. . . . We are engaged in nothing less, I suggest, than yet another redefinition of America. Many of our cherished beliefs about this society have been shattered. We need to devise *a new conception of a pluralistic America* and to invent the institutional and social policies appropriate to such a society. Such a conception and such policies must be based upon a truer reading of the American past than we have purveyed heretofore. This is, as I see it, the task of ethnic studies. (Vecoli, 1972)

The obstinate persistence of ethnicity in America has prevented the melting pot from producing a culturally homogenous mass. After reading Novak's (1973) account of homogenized culture, Americans must be rather glad this is so. In language reminiscent of C. G. Jung, Richard Kolm refers to the unconscious and irrational elements of people's commitment to their groups. The strength of this "collective subconscious" explains the persistence of ancient cultures and their vitality in the struggle for existence and identity. Actual intergroup relations, including the racial crises and their repercussions, Kolm writes, have exploded the myth that ethnic groups other than racial are about to disappear from the American scene. The wholly homogenized society, in which each person relates directly to the totality "without the mediation of the intervening groups (cultural, religious, occupational and others)" likewise belongs in the trash heap of exploded myths (Kolm, 1971, pp. 59, 62). This view is confirmed by the social psychologist Gordon Allport, who writes: "We should improve human relations only by learning to live with racial and cultural pluralism for a long time to come" (Allport, 1952, pp. 67–68).

2. THE EMERGENCE OF BLACK ETHNOCENTRISM

The ancestors of today's generation of blacks were the only group of immigrants brought to the New World against their wishes. Cut off from their ethnic origin in Africa, and denied full participation in the mainstream of American life, they were destined to be a marginal people—at least for a while. A myth that remains widespread, although refuted by Herskovits (1941) and other writers, is that blacks arrived "culturally naked" compared with European immigrants. Black writers such as Vansertima (1971) and Waiguchu (1971), however, offer proof that the continuity of African culture in the Americas has been far broader and deeper than generally thought. The problem was that many whites, especially those who compiled school curricula, did not recognize black culture. Waiguchu (pp. 82–83) thinks the most deprived people are black intellectuals, because they "are still very much in the man's bag" and are trying to adapt themselves to a cultural and conceptual system for which they are genetically unfitted.

Not so much a lack of ethnic identity but rather confusion about it has seriously curtailed the socioeconomic and political bargaining power of American blacks. Color seemed to be the only basis on which they could unite for bargaining. By doing so they incurred the stigma of black racism; they were, in many cases, less successful than white groups who engaged in social, economic, and political bargaining on an ethnic basis. These factors contributed to an identity crisis in the Negro— one that proved important in shaping the black struggle for social and political equality.

Thus the cult of "Black Is Beautiful" was born. Black militants rejected the term "Negro" which, while a correct descriptor for persons of Congoid/Negrid ancestry, suggested a servile role in American society and compliance with "the man's" scheme of things. A growing tendency to use the term "Afro-American" indicated that blacks were preparing to confront the WASP-dominated establishment, not just as a racial group with dark skins, but as a unit of the American population with its own cultural identity. Jerome Skolnick, in the National Commission on Violence Staff Report, quotes from a paper prepared by the Student Nonviolent Coordinating Committee (SNCC):

The sytematic destruction of our links to Africa, the cultural cut-off of blacks in this country from blacks in Africa are not situations that conscious black people in this country are willing to accept. Nor are conscious black people in this country willing to accept an educational system that teaches all aspects of Western Civilization and dismisses our Afro-American contribution . . . and deals with Africa not at all. Black people are not willing to align themselves with a Western culture that daily emasculates our beauty, our pride and our manhood.

Skolnick comments: "In addition to demanding recognition of a rich cultural heritage, militant blacks resented the policy implications of the rejection of that heritage by whites" (1972, p. 558).

Many blacks—especially so-called militants—have accepted and even sought status as a separate ethnic group. Hoetink observes that: "the militant Blacks are precisely trying to *create* a culture of their own—which might be called an emancipatory culture—so as to emphasize *also* in linguistic expression, dress, hairdos, etc., the distinction which somatically already exists between them and the White group" (1974, p. 32).

The social rejection symbolized by residential segregation has also stimulated identification with the segregated group. Black students at several universities have demanded all-black dormitories. It is the subculture of the all-black community that finds expression in an emotional state sometimes described as "soul." Two leading tacticians of Black Power, Carmichael and Hamilton, warned specifically (1967) against any coalition in which blacks might share control over their own group.

To many Negro leaders in the late 1960s, a cultural revolution implanting a new value system and cultural personality seemed a prerequisite for creating an autonomous black community. At the height of black nationalism, extreme separatists were said to constitute less than 15 percent of the adult black population. Many others, however, supported demands that could be classed as communal pluralism: integration in the mainstream of American life as well as developing a distinctive sociocultural identity. Carmichael and Hamilton, writing in 1973 (p. 288), called for group solidarity and identity, so that black people could bargain from a position of strength—though not necessarily for the same kind of rewards obtained by white society. "The ultimate values and goals," they argued, "are not domination or exploitation of other groups, but rather an effective share in the total power of the society." Singham, however, thought that for most black leaders assimilation rather than distinctive identity had always remained the main objective (1972, p. 111).

The basic structural problem—whether American blacks are or should become a single cultural community with American whites or whether America's destiny is to nurture a series of parallel cultural communities—is too complex to be treated in the present context. Suffice it to register the fact that the problem exists, and that opinion about it is both divergent and subject to pendulum swings as political fashions change.

3. THE CHICANO IDENTITY: LA RAZA

A second group experiencing a strong ethnic renaissance consists of 12 million Spanish-speaking Americans, among them the seven million Mexican-Americans (or Chicanos) of the Southwestern states: California, New Mexico, Texas, Arizona, and Colorado. It has been predicted that by the end of the century there will be more Spanish-Americans than Black Americans. The Spanish-American population growth rate is more than 500,000 a year, and may very well reach one million a year, including new arrivals and births, by 1980.

More than 60 percent of all Spanish-Americans coming into the United States are from Mexico; almost half arrive illegally. Another 15 percent are from Puerto Rico and are U.S. citizens by birth. Roughly 7 percent are from Cuba, settling chiefly in Florida. About as many are migrants from Central and South America. Among California's population three in 20 are Mexican Americans. In Texas the figure is one in four and many demographers predict that before long all South Texas will be Mexican. Large Chicano populations are also to be found in Illinois, Indiana, Iowa, Kansas, Michigan, Oregon, Utah, and Washington. Greater Los Angeles, with about 1.1 million Chicanos, has the greatest concentration of Mexican Americans in the United States—only Mexico City and Guadalajara are larger. In the greater Chicago area there are more than 350,000 Chicanos.

The new ethnic consciousness among Mexican Americans is strongest in the five Southwestern states. To the Chicano his *mestizo* status (the result of Spanish-Indian interbreeding) has become a source of pride as well as identity. Unlike the Negro, he identifies with his fellows in ethnohistorical terms and defines his community as a distinct people. In his well-known *Chicano Manifesto* Armando Rendon exalts this proud historical creation.

We must explore and exploit the heritage of the Spaniards, a thousand-of-years-old history and culture, with ties going back to the Phoenicians, the Greeks, the Romans, and the Arabs. We must give honor to the Spanish father, as Wilfredo Sedillo insists, and I with him. We have hardly begun to investigate the fathomless inheritance that is ours from our Indian forebears, the Nahúas, the Toltecs, the Aztecs, and the North American Indians. José Angel Gutiérrez once spoke of the Indian heritage as "our better half," that is, our Indian mother. We are the offspring, the mestizo, who finds himself in an alien culture, but who is finding himself able to

adapt to both culture sources and become the modern Chicano. (1971, Introduction and chapter 14)

Chicano ideologues visualize their people as embracing all Spanish-speaking mestizos—*La Raza* (the Spanish-Indian race) of the New World—of which the Chicanos in the United States form a specific segment. The *Chicano Manifesto* explains this wider geopolitical perspective:

The current revolt of Chicanos against the Anglo system of life and thought is essentially a prophetic statement of purpose. We Chicanos are convinced that it is our destiny to carry out a major role in the coming decades, not only in the United States but in all the Americas. Los Chicanos hope to participate in the creation of a new world. Few, if any, Chicanos hope personally to enjoy that future. Nevertheless, with the promise of a new day for our children in mind and heart, we strive to bring the tomorrows of social and economic equality, of creative and intellectual opportunity, closer to today.

The manifesto also proclaims ethnohistorical virility: outbreeding the Gringos as a road to political power. Any leader, however, who thinks the population explosion a suitable weapon for *improving* the status of his group (as does Rejes Tijerina) should visit India and spend a few days roaming the streets of Calcutta.

Although all Chicanos are of Mexican descent, Chicano culture is not identical to that of Mexico. Chicanoism focuses on a separate cultural and sociopolitical identity for the Mexican-American community of the American Southwest, which does not seek to rejoin Mexico. This double marginality (involving both Mexico and the United States) forms the important driving power behind the Chicanos' struggle for ethnic self-determination in their own geographically defined community. Chicano leaders maintain that historically the greatest part of this area belongs to the Mexican-Americans. They regard the area (Aztlán) as their ethnohistorical fatherland and demand that it be restored as an autonomous Chicano region. "We Mexican-Americans did not come to the United States," they explain, "it came to us." As two leading Mexicanos put it:

It is a moving experience to most Mexican Americans to stand in front of an old adobe building in Sante Fe, New Mexico, the Governor's Palace, and note that it was built in 1610. In 1610, ten years before the landing of the Pilgrims on Plymouth Rock, Sante Fe's Spanish population had a government and schools, was engaged in agriculture and commerce.

The Spanish could, indeed, have sent welcoming parties to Jamestown and Plymouth (Casavantes and Leiva, 1973, p. 409).

In June 1967, a group of Spanish-speaking Americans who call themselves the *Alianza Federal de Mercedes* (Federal Alliance of Land Grants) and claim to be the legal and rightful owners of millions of acres of land, revolted (unsuccessfully) against the Governments of the United States of America, the State of New Mexico, and Rio Arriba (Up River) County, formally proclaiming the Republic of Rio Chama in that area (Love, 1969 p. 35). The rationale is suggested by Armando Rendon in his *Chicano Manifesto:*

The Mexican American, it should be recalled, is a fusion of two revolutionary well-springs (the United States and Mexico, both born in rebellion against Old World despotism), with a Mexican Indian people who had developed one of the most highly civilized and complex cultures of the Western hemisphere.

. . . What is essential to recognize and understand is that a revolution is now in progress in the Southwest. It . . . reaches into many states outside the Southwest, involving the lives and futures of perhaps six million Mexican-Americans today, and some 15 million by the year 2000.

The Chicano revolt strikes at the myths of Anglo supremacy, discards the Anglo-or-nothing value system, and seeks the creation of a meaningful and sensitive balance between the dominant Anglo way of existence and the Chicano way of life.

Unlike the efforts of the Negro people in America—who in past decades sought equality of treatment and opportunity in an Anglo-dominated world on the Anglo's terms and only recently sought anew a black identity and cultural separateness—the Chicano from the earliest phases of his uprising in the 1960's has sought equality and respect for his way of life, his culture, and his language.

The Chicano perceives that he cannot be a whole man if he forfeits these birthrights for the Anglo pot of atole (porridge) euphemistically called equality. He knows that the dominant society has sought to castrate him (cortarle los *huevos*) culturally and psychologically by offering him social and economic success if he only eschews his heritage, his *Chicanismo.* This the true Chicano refuses to do, the price is too high. . . .

The Anglo should realize that the loyalty the Chicano nurtures for a language, a culture, and a history that on the surface seem to pertain to a foreign land is not disloyalty to this nation but rather a special bond to the land, another source of inspiration and a channel of communication with the brown peoples of the world. It is this mixed heritage that has thrust the Chicano into a nationwide movement, a national search, individual by individual, to reassess our role as Mexican Americans and to achieve fully the guarantees of the United States Constitution and the Treaty of Guadalupe Hidalgo. . . . (Rendon, 1971, p. 18)

Because of their numbers, the Mexicans are in a much stronger bargaining position than the 1.8 million Puerto Ricans and 800,000 Cubans, who are comparative newcomers on the American scene. It was only after World War I that Puerto Ricans came to the continental United States in significant numbers, especially to New York. Cuban emigration reached its peak after the takeover of Cuba by Fidel Castro at the end of the 1950s, when more than 300,000 Cubans entered via Miami. The Puerto Ricans soon discovered that they were somatically and racially as well as culturally unacceptable to most American whites. Cultural differences also led to friction between them and American blacks. Caught between hostile elements, they developed a strong feeling of solidarity and a sense of community, emerging as a separate ethnic group. The Cuban exiles, belonging for the most part to wealthier strata who could afford the high cost of fleeing, were better educated and occupationally qualified. They have for the most part adjusted well economically, and with a resident theater and an opera they lead Miami's cultural life. Many Cubans, despite considerable economic and a lesser degree of cultural assimilation, are intent on maintaining their ethnic identity. In this they are aided by Florida laws providing for bilingual education wherever there are a sufficient number of non-anglophone children.

4. NATIVE AMERICANS: THE INDIANS

As the oldest native Americans, the Indians (Indianids) have probably lost the most after more than three centuries of contact with the whites. Until fairly recently it seemed as though their folk pride were fast being eroded by the onslaughts of American urban-industrial life and by a welfare system that gave reservation Indians a dole rather than the means to become economically self-sustaining. Since the late 1960s, however, there have been signs that the American Indians were, like a Phoenix, rising from the ashes of defeatism and disintegration.

The more than 850,000 Indians are scattered and isolated. More than half are settled on or near the more than 300 reservations; the rest are in cities and small communities throughout the U.S.A. About one-third are Navajo, Cherokee, Sioux, or Chippewa. Roughly half live in the West. Oklahoma, Arizona, California, New Mexico, and North Carolina have the largest Indian populations. During the 1960s small groups of Indians staged minor confrontations to protest their deprived status. One of these demonstrations, in 1969, received much publicity because of its target—Alcatraz Island, the former Federal prison in San Francisco Bay. It was, however, the American Indian Movement (AIM), whatever may be thought of the political wisdom of its leaders, that made the Indian cause known to the public.

U.S. Government policy toward native Americans was characterized by the Indian Removal Act of 1830, which authorized resettlement of eastern Indians west of the Mississippi. The following year Chief Justice Marshall's majority Supreme Court decision (*Cherokee Nation v. Georgia*, 5 Peters 1, 1831) held that Indians were not properly foreign nations but "domestic dependent nations . . . in a state of pupilage." The 140 million acres originally ceded by treaty to Indian tribes were reduced to 50 million acres under the Indian Allotment Act of 1887, which gave each surviving Indian family 160 acres and made the 90 million acres left over available to white homesteaders. Assimilationism was compounded with bureaucratic paternalism: the Bureau of Indian Affairs generated a 33-volume administrative manual containing over 2000 regulations, 389 treaties (many broken), 5000 statutes, and 500 Attorney-General's opinions (Feaver, 1975, 2:19–20).

The assimilationist policy was reversed by Franklin D. Roosevelt's Indian Reorganization Act of 1934, shaped by Commissioner of Indian Affairs John Collier, an anthropologist who led the fight for Indian cultural survival. The Act moved toward "the rudiments of reservation self-government and economic development" (*ibid.*, p. 20). In 1946, Congress created the Indian Claims Commission, which has entertained some 800 claims and made a number of awards—mostly in cash rather than land. In 1971, however, the Commission awarded 40 million acres as well as $962 million in cash to the Indians and Eskimos of Alaska in return for oil lands to which they held traditional claims. Without the opportunity and a plan for investment, however, money payments may prove disruptive rather than beneficial to families living in a primitive economy.

Meanwhile, however, apparent improvement in the Indians' situation had led public opinion toward the view that Federal care for Indians should be ended—a view reflected in

Congress. But the phaseout policy, too, was reversed, and the Indians became beneficiaries of Kennedy's "New Frontier" and Johnson's "War on Poverty." Millions of dollars were poured into reservation schools and community services—but without creating a structure for economic self-sufficiency. On July 8, 1970, President Nixon announced a new policy of "self-determination without termination . . . to strengthen the Indian's sense of autonomy without threatening his sense of community. We must assure the Indian that he can assume control of his own life without being separated involuntarily from the tribal group. And we must make it clear that Indians can become independent of federal control without being cut off from Federal concern and Federal support" (*Dialogue*, U.S. Information Agency, Washington, no. 2 [1973], p. 44).

The history of revolutions, however, suggests that initial concessions to a deprived group do not quiet things down but encourage the deprived group and its leaders to ask for more and to ask more vigorously. In any event, Nixon's conciliatory speech was followed by the AIM-staged takeover of the headquarters of the Bureau of Indian Affairs in 1972 and the widely publicized 71-day siege at Wounded Knee in South Dakota (where hundreds of Indians had been killed by U.S. soldiers in 1890).

The new mood of the Indians was surveyed, somewhat impressionistically, by *U.S. News and World Report* (April 2, 1973, p. 26) in these words:

From the brown, rolling hills of the Sioux Nation in South Dakota to the Atlantic and Pacific coasts, America's Indians are heading for a showdown with Federal authority over old grievances and new hopes. . . .

The conflict also is going on in courthouses, in State legislatures, and in Federal offices in Washington as Indian militants fight with a vigor rarely displayed since battles with U.S. cavalry a century ago.

After pointing out the growing demand for fuller autonomy and civil and political rights among Indians in Oklahoma and Arizona, the magazine continues:

A cultural and political renaissance is sweeping through the Indian tribes of Oklahoma. Indians who have attempted to merge into the dominant white society suddenly are taking new pride in the color of their skin and their heritage. Their children are learning tribal languages and attending ceremonial "pow-wows" to dance and sing as their ancestors did. There is a revival of interest in Indian arts and handicraft.

Politically, Indians are demanding an end to discrimination, better education for their children, more jobs and the right to preserve their cultural identity.

The Navajo, the largest tribe, comprising 13 percent of all Indians, have determined to take full charge of their own reservation—larger than West Virginia. "What is rightfully ours, we must protect," says Navajo chairman Peter MacDonald. "What is rightfully due us, we must claim" (in *ibid.*, p. 29).

Although the Indian tribes have never formed a nation or group of nations in the European sense, there are some indications that a new American Indian "nation" is emerging. A new cohesiveness is shown by the expanding Affiliated Tribes of the Northwest, which cooperatively defends Indian rights in Idaho, Montana, Oregon, and Washington. Indian efforts are resulting in major revisions of Federal policies (*ibid.*, February 25, 1974, p. 60).

"We are an emerging nation," says Navajo leader MacDonald (*ibid.*, June 3, 1974, p. 53). The same sentiment, but referring to Indians generally, is echoed by Vine Deloria, Jr., the chief ideologist of AIM, who combines insight and tactical realism with flights of utter romanticism. The former is apparent in his awareness of the cultural inchoateness of the so-called American "mainstream" and of the need for ethnic groups to identify themselves within a territorial nation. Only minority groups, he consideres, have the necessary resistance to "the tidal waves of the electric world" and "the potential for exercise of power" (1970, p. 116).

Deloria's tactical skill is evident in his manipulation of liberal guilt feelings. As Feaver comments (1975, 3, p. 45), the Indian movement "heralded a renaissance of 'radical chic'; and practised the technique of manipulating the media in its staging of a revolution-*manqué* in the by now well-worn politics-as-street-theatre style." Deloria is romantic in his call for an immediate return to tribalism:

the white man must drop his dollar-chasing civilization and return to a simple, tribal, game-hunting, berry-picking life if he is to survive. He must quickly adopt not just the contemporary Indian world view but the ancient Indian world view to survive. (in *ibid.*, p. 39.)

The calling forth of a new American Indian nation, or even several such nations, faces major obstacles. One is low resistance to assimilation: while only 1 percent of all American marriages is interracial, the 1970 census showed that at least one-third of the American Indians who had married during the preceding decade had taken non-Indian partners.

The language problem is more fundamental. Would not a nation that explicitly rejects European culture and technology (as Deloria wants the Indians to do) be corrupted by a European language? Yet of the 760,572 American Indians enumerated by language in the 1970 census, only 244,666 professed an Indian mother tongue, including Aleut and Eskimo. There were, on the other hand, 383,764 English speakers, while 24,621 indicated Spanish—more than any one Indian language except Navajo. A crumb of comfort might be had from the fact that 20,954 *white* people indicated an Indian mother tongue.

But even if Indians were to relearn Indian languages, what would they learn? According to a ranking linguist, "the North American Indian tribes, instead of speaking related dialects, originating in a single parent language, in reality speak many languages belonging to distinct families, which have no apparent unity of origin" (Powell, 1891, p. 120). Powell lists 56 different linguistic *families;* Franz Boas (1911, pp. 78–79) enumerates 55. Their distribution is indicated in table 11.4. Among the smaller linguistic families enumerated by Powell in 1891 are the Chinook with 600 speakers, Chumashan with 40, and Mariposan with 145. Many of the linguistic families and languages belonging to them have probably become extinct since 1891. The fact remains, however, that for a group of their size, the American Indians show a linguistic dispersion unequaled anywhere else in the world.

Table 11.4. MOTHER TONGUE OF AMERICAN INDIANS BY LINGUISTIC FAMILIES (1970—Principal Tribes Only)

Language *Indian Mother Tongue*	*Number of Speakers*
Algonquin [a]	18,079
Athapaskan [b]	106,566
Iroquois [c]	17,571
Muskogee	16,507
Piman	11,311
Pueblo	11,289
Sioux [d]	20,221
Others and not specified	41,423
Total	242,967
Other Mother Tongues	
English	383,764
Spanish	24,621
French	8,387
Aleut and Eskimo	1,699
Other	47,520
Total	465,991
Language Not Recorded	51,614
Grand Total	760,572

SOURCE: U.S. Bureau of the Census, 1970 Census; Supplemental Report, American Indians. Table 18, Abridged.
[a]Includes Delaware, Kickapoo, Massachuset, Menominee, and Shawnee
[b]Includes 89,749 Navajo
[c]Includes Cherokee, Mohawk, Oneida, and Tuscarora
[d]Includes Dakota, Omaha, Iowa, Missouri, Winnebago, and Crow

H. Ethnic Problems in Canada

Ethnic persistence in Canada is usually associated with the French-English cleavage. The history of Canada is largely the history of accommodation between these two dominant ethnolinguistic segments. Today no Dominion government can deal with national issues without considering their interests and identities.

The French–English problem tends to obscure the struggle for ethnic self-preservation waged by other Canadian minorities, such as the Indians. According to the Minority Rights Group in London:

There are something over five hundred thousand people in Canada today who are identifiably of native ancestry, and they fall, legally, into three separate categories: Inuit (Eskimos), "Status" Indians and "Non-Status" Indians. . . . The "status" group, numbering about 250,000, comprises those native people defined as Indian under the Indian Act, which makes them the direct responsibility of the Federal Government. This special legal standing gives them some privileges, such as exemption from certain taxes, but it also heavily restricts their freedom in other areas; for example, their land, education and economic enterprises are controlled by the administration. About half the status group are known as "treaty Indians" because their ancestors signed treaties direct with the Crown, by which they surrendered huge tracts of land in return for reserves, gifts and the promise of services. Each status Indian is registered as a member of an Indian band and lives, or is entitled to live, on a reserve. In all there are some 560 bands who have the use of 2,300 reserves with a total area of just over six million acres. About a quarter of the status Indians now live off reserve. . . . A status Indian may, if he wishes, renounce his special legal standing, receive his share of the band's resources and give up his right to a home on the reserve to live as an ordinary Canadian citizen. When he has made this choice he, his wife and children under the age of twenty-one automatically become "non-status" Indians; the decision is irrevocable and will apply to his descendants as well as to his immediate family. Indian status may also be lost or gained through marriage; if a status man marries a non-status woman, white or native, both she and any subsequent children become Indians under the law. If a status woman marries a nonstatus man, then she and her children are not legally Indians. . . . There are probably more than 260,000 non-status native people who have not been totally absorbed into the mainstream of Canadian society. (James Wilson, 1974, p. 6).

For more than a century the Canadian Indians have generally been regarded as a spiritually demolished people—a dying race. It is only recently that they have shown signs of a serious endeavor to rehabilitate themselves and recover their cultural-historical identity. According to the Minority Rights Group, rebuff and failure in attempts at integration led to a change in mood among the Indians during the 1960s. Indian organizations increased rapidly in number and effectiveness. The first countrywide native body, the National Indian Council, was formed to represent both status and nonstatus people throughout Canada. Because of the radically different legal situation of the two groups, the Council dissolved in 1967 and two successor organizations were formed: the Native Council of Canada for the nonstatus people and the National Indian Brotherhood for the status Indians. Regional and provincial associations also proliferated after 1965. The Minority Rights Group attributes this development to impatience with Canadian Indian policies and their administration as well as "a resurgence of pride and interest in Indian culture and a growing determination that the Indians should resume control over their own destinies."

The prominent Indian leader, Harold Cardinal, sums up the demands of native Canadians:

What the Indian wants is really quite simple. He wants the chance to develop the resources available to him on his own homeland, the reserve. What he needs to make this possible includes financial assistance, enough money to do the job properly so that he does not fail for lack of adequate financing; training in the precise skills he will need to develop the resources . . . and, finally, access to expert advice and counsel throughout the stages of development so that he will not fail because he was given the wrong advice or no advice at all. With the money, know-how, and expert guidance, then if the Indian fails, at least it will not be because he didn't try to succeed, and at least it will not be because he was not allowed to try. . . . One key factor remains, Indian involvement. Our people want the right to set their own goals, determine their own priorities, create and stimulate their own opportunities and development. (in *ibid.*, p. 27)

On another occasion Cardinal reiterated:

It is necessary to emphasize that the question of *establishing a positive Indian identity does not mean political separatism—not yet, at least not if the white man will agree to be reasonable*. . . . our most basic problem is gaining respect, respect on an individual basis that would make possible acceptance for us as an ethnic group. Before this is possible, the dignity, confidence and pride of the Indian people must be restored. No genuine Indian participation in the white world can be expected until the Indian is accepted by himself and by the non-Indian as an Indian person, with an Indian identity. As long as Indian people are expected to become what they are not—white men—there does not and there will not exist a basis upon which they can participate in Canadian society. (in Elliott, 1971, 1, pp. 141–42, 149)

The Minority Rights Group report points out the conviction with which Canadian Indians feel they can and must retain their "Indianness." Chief Dave Courchene, President of the Manitoba Indian Brotherhood, spoke eloquently on this point at Treaty Centennial celebrations in 1971:

We are gathered here with the spirits of our ancestors to commemorate one hundred years of struggle; to commemorate the tragedies in the lives of the victims; to celebrate our survival; to reaffirm our identity and to reassert that our treaties as fact and as symbol will be retained and respected; and to honour our magnificent young people, who will assure that we will never be dishonoured.

For in this way, we will reassert that God was right in making us Chipewyan, Cree, Ojibway and Sioux as part of the North American Indian nation and that man is wrong in trying to make us white.

For in the ultimate end, we will stand before Him

and say proudly, but humbly, Lord I am one of those men you made in *your world. I am an Indian!* (in James Wilson, 1974, pp. 29–30)

I. Ethnicity and Ethnic Oppression in the World at Large

It is only possible to mention a few of the many other countries where ethnicity plays a key role in political and demographic policy or intergroup friction.

Switzerland is ethnolinguistically segmented into speakers of German, French, Italian, and Romanch, with a Protestant–Catholic division cutting across these groups. Many experts regard Switzerland as the world's most successful exercise in democratic pluralism. The crux of the matter is, however, that the ethnic factor finally determines the sociopolitical structure of modern Switzerland from canton to canton. Preserving the heritage of many centuries of sovereign independence, the Swiss Cantons still retain important political powers, and they remain sharply differentiated in customs, dialect, and outlook. As viable political units, the cantons, not the central government, have jurisdiction over all educational, religious, intellectual, and artistic matters (Rabushka and Shepsle, 1972, p. 209).

More than eight million Gypsies are struggling not to be engulfed by the slums of European cities. Claiming to be "the oldest people on earth," they still try to retain their distinctive historical character and lifestyle. The World Romany Congress, whose first postwar assembly was held in London in 1971, is mobilizing its people for a campaign to eliminate discrimination and social inequality.

The two million Basques of Northern Spain are a good example of a small group who manifest surprisingly strong ethnic solidarity and sense of community despite their minority status over generations. Most politically conscious Basques identify with the *Euzkadi Ta*

Azkatasuna movement (ETA). Their main aim is an autonomous homeland (*Euzkadi*) composed of the four Basque provinces of Spain: Navarra, Guipuzcoa, Vizcaya, and Alava. A young Basque rebel told a correspondent of *Newsweek:* "We're not sentimentalists. We will continue to kill civil guards and Spanish secret police who are repressing Euzkadi. And we seek freedom for Basques under both French and Spanish rule. There's no reason why we should be under two different flags. We have a flag—and our own nation" (April 23, 1973, p. 15). (See also chapter 12,B.)

The part played by ethnicity in the history of modern Cyprus is common knowledge. The recent Greek-Turkish confrontation there involved a clash between Turkish Cypriots seeking regional autonomy and the Greek-controlled administration of a unitary state (see chapter 22,C3).

Yugoslavia, reorganized as a "peoples' federation" in 1946, was itself the product of ethnic strife within the Hapsburg monarchy: its birth process was World War I. Conceived as a "Greater Serbia," it is itself rent by ethnic cleavages: ethnically there is no such thing as a "Yugoslav." Five distinct major Slav ethnic groups are officially recognized: Serbs, Croats, Slovenes, Macedonians, and Montenegrins. Eight smaller ethnic groups also live in the country, among them the 750,000 Muslim Slavs who maintain a strong sense of ethnicity. The present unrest among the 4 million Croats (numerically the second strongest group after the 7 million Serbs) is rooted in a deep-seated urge for greater ethnic self-determination— which caused the Croats to take the German side in World War II. Even a national hero like Marshal Tito—whose past injustices and atrocities, like those of his mentors in the Kremlin, tend to be forgotten—cannot afford to ignore ethnic divisions. Yugoslav structural politics revolve around the question of legislative and administrative centralization versus decentralization to the member republics that represent its major nationalities.

Finally, the one ethnohistorical group universally recognized as the best example of ethnic continuity are the more than 20 million Jews scattered across the world—almost 6 million in the United States alone. The Jewish population in New York City is bigger than that of Jerusalem. Paradoxically, anti-Semitism has been an important motivator in the perpetuation of the Jewish culture and ethos. The well-known Jewish author Lewis Browne has on occasion said that the Jews would soon disappear if they were not continually hounded and reminded that they were Jews. In 1968, in a letter to the Communist Party leader Leonid Brezhnev, the young Soviet Jewish engineer Boris Kochubiyevsky elucidated this aspect:

Why is it that the most active sector of Jewish youth, raised and educated in the U.S.S.R., still retains a feeling of Jewish national unity and national identity? How is it possible that Jewish boys and girls who know nothing about Jewish culture and language, who are mostly atheists, continue to feel so acutely and be so proud of their national affiliation? . . . The answer is simple: Thanks for that, in large measure, can be given to anti-Semitism—the new brand which was implanted from above and, as a means of camouflage, is called anti-Zionism; and the old anti-Semitism which is still alive among the more backward sectors of Soviet society. It is precisely this anti-Zionism and anti-Semitism which prevents us from relaxing and welds us closer together (In Barghoorn, 1974, p. 128).

The vast majority of Jews are quite willing to remain in their countries of settlement—provided their identity can be accommodated in a system of ethnic and cultural pluralism. Those strongly motivated by Jewish nationalism and those persecuted by the states where they live—frequently the same people— migrate or seek migration to Israel. Most other Jews believe (though a small but vocal minority dissents) that Zionism is a viable and justifiable historical development, and that an independent Jewish state in Palestine lends strength and permanence to Jewish culture in other parts of the world. It is comforting to have a place of refuge in case of renewed anti-Semitism, and under the rule of *Aliyah* (the law of return) any Jew may claim Israeli citizenship.

The salience of ethnicity is aptly characterized by Andrew Greeley:

> . . . ethnic differences, even in the second half of the twentieth century, proved far more important to men than did the differences in philosophy or economic system. Many who would not die for a premise or a dogma or a division of labor, would more or less cheerfully die for a difference rooted in ethnic origins. Chinese and Malay fight each other in Southeast Asia; Ibo and Hausa in Nigeria; Greek and Turk on Cyprus; Czech and Slovak in Czechoslovakia; Arab and Jew in the Middle East; black (at least so-called) fight white (at least relatively) in the United States; and the French and the English, running out of colonial peoples with which to contend, now renew the feud that the Hundred Years' War never did settle. (1971, p. 3)

Ethnicity becomes operational through the emotional ties created among people, the consciousness of community which motivates people into associating with their own kind and identifying as "in-group" members. As far as can be seen, ethnicity will continue into the future as one of the primary evolutionary powers in the history of man. This was recognized clearly during a June 1965, seminar in Ljubljana, Yugoslavia, on the problems of multiethnic societies. At the close of the seminar, organized by the UN, the delegates resolved by acclamation:

> . . . The right to develop their own traditions and characteristics autonomously . . . the free choice by nations of their own social and political systems as well as of the form of government best suited to their needs and the right to form new independent states, to federate into multi-national states or to form national regions within independent states. . . . all countries must refrain from any action designed to change frontiers by force on the pretext of protecting a kindred group in an adjoining state. . . . Integration should never mean the suffocation of the minority concerned. . . . all Governments should promote and protect the rights of ethnic, religious, linguistic or national groups not only through the adoption of constitutional and legislative provisions, but also through the promotion of all forms of activities consistent with political, economic and social conditions of the state or country concerned. (Multinational, 1965, pp. 6–9, 35)

12

INTERGROUP CONFLICT
AND ACCOMMODATION

On March 21, 1960, about 5000 blacks massed in front of the Sharpeville police station near Vereeniging, South Africa. They were protesting at being required to carry reference books; the objective of the Pan-African Congress, which organized the assembly, was to hold a peaceful demonstration. The crowd eventually grew to 20,000; some of its members became unruly and stones were thrown at the police. Three shots were fired from within the crowd at the police and some policemen opened fire, without authorization. Sixty-seven people were killed in the affray.

Since then, this incident is commemorated every year as the "Sharpeville Massacre" by groups who picture that tragic event as the major atrocity of the century. More recently, one of General Idi Amin's banned ministers remarked cynically that Sharpeville was still recalled annually but that the world remained blind to conflict still raging throughout Africa and the world.

Conflict between divergent groups coming into contact has occurred throughout human existence; the Old Testament is replete with such strife, as are the records of ancient, medieval, and modern history. Conflict takes place not only between groups but within groups when opposing parties or factions compete for power and possessions, and in the process seek to neutralize or eliminate other groups. Racial conflict is the most highly publicized form of conflict, but ethnic, religious, and language quarrels can also erupt into violence. In recent years they have cost more human lives than fighting between races.

A. *Major Ethnic Conflicts Since World War II*

One of the most gruesome cases of genocide, about which the civilized world wrung its collective hands but took no concrete measures, was mass slaughter in East Pakistan, later known as Bangladesh (see also chapter 28,C). East Pakistani grievances against rule by the geographically larger but less populous West exploded on March 1, 1971, when President Yahya Khan cancelled a promised session of the National Assembly. East Pakistan was swept by revolt, and the entire city of Dacca went on strike. The leaders in West Pakistan responded by sending the Army to "solve the problem." There followed an orgy of murder and carnage seldom recorded in modern history. Hundreds of students and lecturers were cut down in their hostels. In Shankripatti, the Army cordoned off an entire street and systematically entered the houses to murder men, women, and children. It is estimated that 8000 people were slain in this way.

The bloodbath soon engulfed the entire country. An eyewitness, Mascarenhas, testified:

Horrified Bengalis suddenly became aware that the West Pakistan army had launched a campaign of genocide in East Bengal. The systematic pattern of the murders throughout the province matches exactly the dictionary definition of genocide. . . . During my sojourn with the army in Comilla area I was to see at first hand the screaming terror of the "kill and burn missions" as Hindus and other target types were systematically hunted from village to village and house to house. (1971, pp. 116–17)

More than 500,000 people were killed and another 8 million Bengalis fled across the frontier to India. They would quite likely have stayed there indefinitely, had not the Indian government intervened on behalf of Bengali independence. That event did not, however, put an end to persecution in the country henceforth known as Bangladesh. The half million Muslim Biharis sided with the Urdu-speaking West Pakistani because of ethnolinguistic affinity. After 1971, they found themselves on the receiving end of oppression (see chapter 19).

There are a number of African states that need not bow to West Pakistan in the matter of genocide, especially when internal political strife based on ethnic differences is involved. The interethnic hostility that racks Rwanda and Burundi, two ministates in the heart of Africa with a population of around four million each, has already been described. A few further details of the resulting genocide will be added here. In post-independence Rwanda, Hutu university students, with the silent approval of the authorities, began driving Tutsi students from the University campus. Stanley Meisler, in a report in *The Times* (London,

April 12, 1973), stated: "Hutu students formed tribunals to check the blood line of other students and determine who was really Tutsi. Bands of Hutus then roamed the campus and town looking for Tutsi students, attacking those they found with iron bars."

In Tutsi-ruled Burundi, the Hutu, who account for 84 percent of the total population of 3.7 million, have sought from time to time to overthrow the Tutsi minority. An open Hutu revolt began on April 29, 1972, with an organized attack on the eastern frontier and an incursion from the south via Tanzanian territory. Jeremy Greenland, who was in Burundi at that time, described the scene as follows: "They [the Hutu] made their policy clear by killing every Tutsi in their path" (*Pretoria News*, January 8, 1974).

The Government retaliated by arresting every prominent Hutu. Persecution of Hutus blanketed the country. Hutu schoolteachers, church leaders, nurses, traders, and civil servants were loaded into Land Rovers at gunpoint by Tutsi and taken away. Gangs of Tutsi went through the suburbs of Bujumbura with a fine comb in search of Hutu and took them away by the truckload. "Throughout May and half of June 1972, the excavators were busy every night in Gitega and Bujumbura burying the dead in mass graves" (*ibid*).

Hutu students at the University were murdered and the same fate awaited many scholars at the country's secondary schools. Greenland provides a somber report of the foreign attitude toward these murders: "French pilots, supplied under a programme of military assistance, kept Burundi's planes on a steady course while Burundi soldiers machinegunned Hutu rebels out of the side-windows. . . . The United Nations says little, even when its own vehicles are requisitioned and used to take Hutu to their death. It was ironic to see Land-Rovers marked UNICEF being used for this purpose" (*ibid*).

The picture in nearby Uganda, where tribal differences are compounded by religious dissension, is hardly any better under the current dictator, General Idi Amin. Political observers of the African scene estimate that tribal murders and unpublicized assassinations in the three years up to and including 1974 have seen General Amin's opponents and suspected opponents murdered by tens of thousands.

Ethiopia, on the eastern horn of Africa, long occupied a unique position in the African political structure. As the ruler of one of the world's oldest monarchies, Emperor Haile Selassie was a respected and venerated figure among his fellow African rulers. This is perhaps why the Organization of African Unity chose Addis Ababa for its headquarters.

Recent political developments, however, have suggested that the "Father of Africa" had little time for the problems of his own people. In a country where the Coptic Christian Church occupied a privileged position, religion played a decisive role in civil service appointments. Of the 14 provincial governors in Ethiopia, not one was a Muslim. Thousands of Ethiopian Muslims staged the biggest protest in the country's history and handed a 13-point petition to Premier Makonnen protesting against discrimination. The Islamic community represents 35 percent of the country's total population of 25 million. As a reporter said in a dispatch from Addis Ababa: "The Muslims have always felt second-class citizens, gravely under-represented in positions of responsibility" (*Pretoria News*, September 23, 1974).

For 12 years, with events carefully concealed from the outside world, Haile Selassie fought the guerrillas in the northern province of Eritrea, annexed in 1962 and inhabited by groups ethnically different from the rest of Ethiopia. When independence became the watchword in Africa, Selassie interpreted it to mean independence from European states only. Guerrilla action and bloody reprisals have spread in recent years. Two provincial ministers were murdered, Ethiopia's Japanese-operated copper mine was devastated, and four American oil prospectors were kidnapped.

These actions were taken by the freedom fighters of Eritrea to demonstrate to the outside world that a bitter internal conflict, approaching the stage of a war of independence, was in existence. Since the overthrow of the Emperor, the new government has sought to crush Eritrean resistance, but has succeeded only in occupying the larger cities.

The Arab-Negro conflict in Ethiopia's western neighbor, Sudan, has already been described in chapter 11,F3. At its base is the fact that the 4 million people living in the three southern provinces are of Negrid origin, are mostly Christians or adherents of African religions, and speak indigenous languages while using English as an official *lingua franca;* the 11 million inhabitants of the North, on the other hand, are Muslims, speak Arabic, and are of Arab and mixed descent but culturally Arabic.

The blacks in the South have resisted domination from the North since the days when Arab slave traders came south on slaving raids. According to a report:

Southern resistance was fundamentally, a protest against the bland northern conviction (prevalent even in the most enlightened circles) that the views of the southerners need not be taken seriously in determining the structure, ethos and political behaviour of an independent Sudan. To northerners it seemed only natural that northern officials should replace the British in the south and that Sudan should commit itself fully to the Arab political world. That southerners might have different views seemed unimportant. (*The Times*, London, March 27, 1972)

Conflict between different races and ethnic groups is not a phenomenon confined to Africa, however. In Malaysia, the Malay-Chinese plural society is often rocked by clashes between the two groups. In one such Malay-Chinese clash in 1959 on Pangkor Island (on the Malaysian west coast), 2000 of the 6000 Chinese on the island (which has a total population of 8000) had to be evacuated.

It was during the Penang crisis, however, that Malaysia experienced its worst bloodshed resulting from racial conflict. Penang Island is situated on the northwestern coast of Malaysia and has a population consisting mainly of Chinese, Malays, and Indians, with the Chinese in the majority. Economic problems on the mainland resulting from the devaluation of the Malaysian dollar toward the end of 1967 filtered through to Penang and on November 24, 1967, a strike took place on the island. Five people were killed and 92 injured on the first day. What had started as an economic protest soon degenerated into a racial clash, which was intensified by the proximity of racial groups in urbanized and crowded Penang. The racial friction spread from Penang to the neighboring coastal belt of the mainland itself. When order was restored the official casualty figures were 29 killed, more than 200 injured, and about 1300 arrested.

B. Ethnic Conflicts That Remain Unresolved

The most active guerrilla movement on the European continent is the Basque ETA movement, whose activities are concentrated in Spain. Conflict between the Basques and the regime of General Franco dates from the Spanish Civil War, when three of the provinces remained loyal to the republican cause. Toward the end of the war the regime consequently ruled the Basques with an iron hand, imposing heavy taxation on their provinces and seeking to destroy all traces of the traditional language and culture that express Basque identity.

One of the most sensational murders in Spain occurred when four members of the ETA blew up the car of the Prime Minister, Admiral Carrero Blanco, causing his death. According to the authoritative *Annual of Power and Conflict:* "In 1973 the ETA posed the greatest problem for the security forces, partly because it recruits and operates in the Basque

country where discontent among the clergy and labour force combine with a traditional sturdy independence that fosters separatism" (Crozier, 1974, p. 24). Strike action has been used to obtain better employment opportunities for Basque workers. The ETA kidnapped a prominent industrialist, Felipe Huarte, and forced his company to pay it ransom of $800,000 and conclude a model labor agreement with strikers at one of his factories.

It has always been Moscow's propaganda strategy to depict the non-Russian nations of the USSR as autonomous republics which voluntarily joined the Union and voluntarily remain therein. This image is strengthened, for example, by Ukraine's membership in the United Nations and its own flag and national anthem: all symbols of a sovereign independent state. Behind this façade, however, lies the true Russian political scene:

> But the main objective of the Kremlin has always been the creation of a "uniform Soviet nation," a homo Sovieticus, who in essence would be Russian-speaking and Russian-thinking with all ultimately comprising a Russian nation. Towards this end, since 1965, the Soviet government has stepped up its oppression and persecution in Ukraine, as well as in the other captive countries. . . . in Ukraine the KGB imprisons hundreds of Ukrainian intellectuals for their defense of the Ukrainian language, Ukrainian national traditions and, in short, Ukrainian identity. *Ukrainian Quarterly* [New York], Autumn 1972, p. 231)

In January 1972, the Kremlin again launched a massive purge amongst the intellectuals of Ukraine with the purpose of destroying that nation's cultural revival. The action taken against authors particularly shocked the world. Vyacheslav Chornovil, 36, author of *The Chornovil Papers*, was sentenced to seven years hard labor and banishment (assignment to forced labor away from his home) for five years. Urily Shukhevych, 40, the son of General Roman Shukhevych who had already spent 20 years in prison for refusing to disavow his father, was sentenced to a further five years and another five years of banishment. Svyatoslav Karavansky, 53, translator of Charlotte Brontë's *Jane Eyre* into Ukrainian, and who had already spent 18 years in prison, was sentenced to a further eight years and seven months. In numerous cases the Kremlin has condemned Ukrainian nationalists to jail for the rest of their lives (see also chapter 18,B6).

The expulsion of ethnic groups charged by the Kremlin with being "pro-German" during World War II is described in chapter 22. Discussion here is limited to the interethnic aspect of the deportation of the Crimean Tatars, who are being held in exile in central Asia. According to Walter Dushnyck:

One can only speculate as regards the unwillingness of the Soviet government to allow the return of the Tartars to the Crimea. Fears undoubtedly exist in Moscow that the Tartars, under certain circumstances and in view of their historical aversion to the Russians, may be more loyal to their ethnic and cultural brethren in Turkey than to the USSR, thereby menacing the security of the strategic Crimea (Dushnyck, 1975b, p. 519).

Suppression of the non-Russian peoples under the Soviet government is evoking growing reaction. In February 1972, more than 17,000 Lithuanians protested at the suppression of their religion and confronted Brezhnev and the United Nations on this issue. Some time later four Lithuanians burned themselves to death; three of them were laborers. In both Latvia and Estonia, communists have revolted openly against russification of their homelands. The Kremlin finds itself unable to suffocate the national feelings of the Balts.

The murder of a French bus driver by a young Algerian in Marseilles focused attention anew on the conflict between the various ethnic groups in France. Foreign migrant laborers in France have made an important contribution to economic growth. The French, like other Europeans, having "risen above" menial labor, leave unpleasant tasks to be done mainly by migrant workers. Road construction, un-

derground work, street cleaning, and dangerous work in all kinds of weather are usually done by the migrants, of whom there are currently more than 3 million, with their families, in France. One out of every five laborers in France is a foreigner.

This one murder was apparently enough to ignite smoldering racial hatred. Anti-Arab violence soon spread throughout the country. Gilbert Sedbon reported from Paris:

Ten Algerians were murdered for apparently racial motives. In Marseilles gunmen in a speeding car shot down a 16-year-old boy. In Toulouse, 50 soldiers of the crack 9th paratroop regiment rampaged the streets beating up any Arab they could see. Similar incidents followed in Toulon, in Nice and other French Riviera towns. . . . Racial hatred is now smouldering through much of France, where nearly a million Arabs live and work, often in miserable conditions. (*Pretoria News*, South Africa, September 13, 1973)

In nearby Belgium, the national conflict is not between locals and foreigners as in France but between different language groups. Since the beginning of the century, Dutch-speaking Flemings and French-speaking Walloons have been involved in intense strife. Many of the 19 postwar governments have fallen because of the language problem, and the conflict has frequently erupted in violence. The Walloons in southern Belgium fear that they will be dominated by the more prolific Flemish. The major economic revival after World War II was concentrated in Flanders; Europe's second largest harbor, Antwerp, is located in that region. Although speakers of French continue to dominate the higher corporate levels, the economic position of the Walloon masses has deteriorated. Hence, the language conflict between the two groups has been intensified by economic disparities.

Canada, too, is plagued by a language conflict. In commenting on the new Language Act adopted by the Province of Quebec, granting French precedence over English, *The Citizen* (Ottawa, February 21, 1974) observed: "More than 100 years after Confederation, almost five years after passage of the Dominion Official Languages Act, bilingualism continues to be one of the most controversial topics in Canada." The Premier of Quebec, Robert Bourassa, said after the passing of the Act: "Henceforth, there is an officially French state in North America. It is a moment of great pride for all of us." This evoked negative reaction throughout Canada and emotional protest marches were staged by the English minority in Quebec, which represents 13 percent of the total population of the province.

Language conflict is not the only source of disunity in Canada, however; other ethnic minorities are also beginning to press for political rights. Anthony Astrachan of the Times-Post News Service reports that Canadians who are neither of British nor of French origin have joined forces to overthrow three provincial governments in the past five years. These Canadians form a third of Canada's population of 22 million, a fact which the Government has largely ignored. The resulting dissatisfaction has reinforced the alienation of the Canadian West, where Ukrainians, Germans, Poles, and Scandinavians are concentrated. Ethnic feelings are likely to complicate the already difficult federal-provincial relations in the key central provinces of Ontario and Quebec as well.

In Australia the public became sharply aware that an "Aborigine problem" existed when the Queen arrived to open Parliament in late February, 1974. She was confronted with a bitter and insulting demonstration by several hundred Aborigines who had converged on Canberra from various parts of Australia. The Aborigines form a minority group of 45,000 with another 120,000 being of mixed descent. As such they have one black representative in the white-controlled Department of Aboriginal Affairs in the person of Charles Perkins, the only senior black civil servant. According to Perkins the white officials act in a high-handed manner, giving the impression that they alone

know what is best for the Aborigines. The only representative body of blacks, the National Aboriginal Congress, complains of being rebuffed and abused by the Minister when it sought to obtain some administrative and statutory rights (*Rand Daily Mail*, Johannesburg, March 29, 1974, p. 23). (For more on Australia, see chapter 13,F2.)

In Australia's neighbor, New Zealand, the Maoris have also started voicing protest at their woeful lot. One of the most powerful and most radical Maori groups, the Nga Tamatoa Council, has embarrassed the Government on a number of occasions by staging demonstrations at state functions. The Maoris are a minority of about 240,000 in a total population of 3 million, and although their economic level is considerably more advanced than that of the Australian aborigines they are particularly sensitive to discrimination in respect of house leasing, employment, and social intercourse (Western, 1975, pp. 330, 335). According to a recent report, New Zealand officials, both white and Maori, agreed that intergroup relations had deteriorated to the point of open conflict; groups of Maoris would occasionally attack whites in the streets of Auckland or Wellington (*To The Point*, South Africa, April 5, 1974). The question arises whether, in New Zealand and elsewhere, uncontrolled urbanization may not be a factor aggravating intergroup conflict.

Since the situation of blacks in the United States involves several aspects of intergroup relations, it appears in a number of chapters. Inasmuch as responsible leaders of all American racial groups are sincerely concerned with reaching an accommodation—though they differ as to structure and priorities—this topic hardly belongs in the category of unresolved ethnic conflicts. At the height of the civil-rights struggle in 1963, however, when there were 930 demonstrations and sit-ins in 115 cities in 11 states within 12 months, and again in 1968 when riots erupted after the murder of Dr. Martin Luther King, black–white relations presented aspects of unresolved conflict. But they never involved those intractable elements of hostility that characterize many other conflicts reviewed in this book.

In contrast to the major conflicts in the United States, those of Northern Ireland are more of a religious and ethnic nature. The six counties, plagued by a breakdown of law and order, are so often in the news that the intensity of the conflict is not always realized. A new assassination is all too often just another casualty figure. In 1970 there were 14 killings traceable to religious conflict. In 1971 this figure rose to 123, and in 1972 to 467, according to a report by Sir Graham Shillington. This progression continued into 1973 and 1974, and casualties have continued at a high rate to the time of this writing.

C. Minorities in Conflict Situations

Intergroup conflicts in the Far East tend to involve ethnic, religious, and linguistic minorities. The government of the Philippines, for instance, finds itself involved in guerrilla warfare with Muslim rebels. Its army launched a full-scale offensive in 1973 in an effort to suppress the rebellion. During this campaign a Philippine unit was trapped and its members summarily decapitated in an ambush at Tungawan, 60 miles from Zamboanga.

The objective of the Muslims is to break completely with the Philippines and establish their own independent state in Mindanao and Sulu, the traditional homeland of their ancestors. The culture of the 3 million Muslims—representing about 8 percent of the population—differs greatly from that of the Christians in the north. Mochtar Lubis put his finger on the nub of the conflict when he wrote in *Newsweek*:

To a degree, the present strife in the southern Philippines was probably inevitable. The Muslims

there have remained outside the mainstream of the Philippine Christian society by their own choice. Unwilling to modernize their political and economic structures, they continue to maintain their old feudal patterns of life. And now this indigenous population, wedded to its traditional ways, feels its very existence threatened by aggressive outsiders, of different religion, who legitimately or illegitimately are taking over lands the Muslims have always considered their own. (May 28, 1973, p. 23)

Widespread fighting and ambushes have made several provinces unsafe. Almost 100,000 people have fled or have been resettled by the government in an attempt to pacify rebel territory.

A Muslim minority group is also causing the government of Thailand concern. It is in the south, on the Malay peninsula, that Muslim separatist activity is rampant. Police posts had to be strengthened in this area in August 1974. The Governor of Yala Province reported that 10 policemen and about an equal number of guerrillas were killed in one month in his province alone.

The southern part of Thailand is exceptionally fertile and is also of great strategic value, as its coastal belt is the scene of oil exploration. Discontent amongst Muslims in this area surfaced in the mid-1960s, when many arrests were made and charges of high treason were lodged. Those arrested were set free in 1971, but the area has been plagued since by terrorist activity.

The South is inhabited mostly by Malay Muslims whose dress, customs, language, and religion differ from those of the Buddhist Thais who are dominant in Bangkok. The government claims to have killed more than 150 of the separatists since 1970 and to have arrested at least 2000. Newspaper reports speak of more than 3000 Muslims fleeing into the jungle to escape the harsh treatment of officialdom. The matter is complicated by the fact that the guerrillas are receiving communist support. This does not bespeak any love for Islam in Moscow or Peking, both of which persecute it in their own domains. It merely illustrates the way in which communists exploit religious and ethnic conflict to create trouble for "bourgeois" governments.

The minority problems of Japan, the economic miracle of the East, were pertinently highlighted when a time bomb blew up a statue in a park in Hokkaido. The statue depicts a group of five people, four Japanese and one an Ainu, the latter in a subservient position, according to Ainu spokespeople. About 210 Ainu assembled in Hokkaido in January 1973 to protest their low economic status and condition. According to the *Daily Yomiuri*, January 24, 1973, the theme of the meeting was: "Why should the Ainu, the aborigines of Japan, be subject to racial discrimination and prejudice in Japan?"

The Japanese colonized the Ainu toward the end of the nineteenth century and for a while placed them on reservations. Most of them have subsequently assimilated with the Japanese, but it is estimated that about 60,000 Ainu retain their ethnic identity.

The Ainu are not the only ones in a subservient position in Japan, however. The million or more Burakumin found mainly in western Japan are traditionally regarded as being of the lowest order and origin. Their situation is described in chapter 16,C.

When the state of Israel is mentioned in a discussion of minorities and ethnic conflicts, images of Jews and Arabs in confrontation arise in many people's minds. What is less known is that the Jewish population itself consists of two distinct elements—the Jews of European descent, mostly East Europeans or *Ashkenazim*, who have provided the model for the *Sabras* or Israeli-born, and the Sephardic "Orientals" who come from Muslim countries in North Africa and the Middle East. The two groups are quite different in educational and economic levels and in cultures. While a substantial number of "Oriental" Jews were already present when Israel was founded in 1948, the majority came between 1951 and 1954, at a time when Arab countries, reacting

to the Israeli-Arab conflict, made life unbearable for their Jewish inhabitants. As of 1970, the 650,000 "Oriental" migrants constituted 26 percent of Israel's Jewish population, while their children make up another quarter (Friendly, 1972, pp. 3–4).

In contrast to the urbanized European Jews, who brought with them a variety of occupational skills, the Jews living in Arab countries were typical members of underdeveloped societies. Many were illiterate or nearly so and all were extremely poor. The difference in educational levels is illustrated in table 12.1. The "Oriental" Jews are noted for their higher birth rate and larger families. Among "Orientals," 50.7 percent of the families have five or more members, as contrasted with 12.0 percent for European and American immigrants and 24.7 percent among the Israeli born. The average number of children born by an "oriental" Jewish woman in her lifetime is 4.22, while European-American women bear an average of 2.78, and Israeli-born women 2.95. The characteristic "Oriental" family contains six to nine persons.

Since most North African Jews who had achieved middle-class status moved to Europe, particularly France, those who came to Israel occupied the lower rungs of the economic ladder. Their per capita income is estimated to be as low as 54 percent of that of European Jews (*ibid.*, p. 7). Comparatively few occupy white-collar jobs, while a majority perform manual production and service tasks. Economic and

Table 12.1.   ISRAELI JEWS AGED 14 AND ABOVE, BY NUMBER OF YEARS OF SCHOOLING

Origin	Number of Years of Schooling (in percent)			
	0	1–4	5–8	9+
Europe and America	2.6	8.2	33.3	55.9
Africa and Asia	23.6	8.4	38.3	29.7
Israeli born	1.1	1.2	21.6	76.1

Source: Friendly, 1972, pp. 3–4.

social inequality tend to be perpetuated. While educational levels are improving and majority of "Oriental" families now have television sets, electric refrigerators, and washing machines, their school dropout rate remains nine times higher than for their European counterparts (Tamarin, 1975, p. 133).

Many Israelis doubtlessly shared the surprise of the outside world when the *Pantherim Schechorim* (Black Panthers: no connection with the American group of that name) made their appearance in March 1971, in the first of a series of riots that was to last until August of that year. According to Friendly,

> The group coalesced in the Musrara section of Jerusalem, a mid-town slum area. The members were Moroccan youths, aged 19 to 22, who came to realize more sharply than most the disabilities they suffered and the bleakness of their prospects. School drop-outs long since, they began to see how intimately education and future income were linked; they felt they had missed their chance forever. Most of them were juvenile offenders and graduates of one sort or another of reform schools where they had been committed for petty crime, and had not been admitted into the army: in Israel anyone not performing the standard three years of military service is stigmatized as close to leprous. Accordingly, they could not find jobs or even obtain driver's licenses and saw themselves as caught in a vicious circle. (1972, p. 8)

As Friendly indicates, the Black Panthers were a marginal group, and their movement soon broke up. While it lasted, however, it focused public attention on the problems of the "Orientals" and provided the impetus for a series of measures designed to better their lot. These have included a massive expansion of public housing, occupational upgrading, and a variety of educational programs for parents as well as children. A degree of success in these programs is suggested by the fact that income of "Oriental" families is growing at a rate 20 percent higher than the income of Western Jewish families.

D. Religious Conflict: The Case of India

India probably provides the classic and most massive example of religious conflict. Two independent states, conceived respectively as Muslim and Hindu in character, were established when the British withdrew from the Indian subcontinent in 1947. Despite population exchanges involving millions, and massacres in which tens of thousands perished, a residual Muslim population remained in the Republic of India. The 1961 census reported that 83 percent of Indians were Hindus, 10 percent Muslims, the remaining 7 percent being scattered among other religions.

The removal of most Indian Muslims to Pakistan has not prevented periodic outbreaks of interfaith violence. The powder keg was ignited in 1961 by a small incident that, in many countries, would attract but scant attention. A young woman college student from a Hindu family was raped one night by several young Muslims. In shame and humiliation she poured kerosene over herself and set it alight. Immediate and widespread reaction followed. Shops were closed as students marched through the streets calling for retribution. Shops were looted and several were burned. Ninety-four people were arrested on the first day after the rape and another 272 were arrested the second day. Violence continued for a week; 12 people were killed and 38 injured on February 7 and 8 alone. Newsmen described the scene in Jabalpur, where the girl had been raped, as follows: "Charred and burned houses and looted shops bore grim witness to the havoc caused by arsonists and hooligans. . . . There were very few houses which escaped the fury of the miscreants in South Mellonigunj. Destruction was almost complete in the Humamantal locality" (Ghurye, 1968, p. 332).

Hindu-Muslim hostility reached another peak in 1964. The cause this time lay in violence against Hindus in Muslim Kashmir and in Pakistan. It was reported during the last week of December 1963, that a hair of the Prophet Muhammad had been stolen from the Hazratbal Mosque in Srinagar, the capital of Kashmir. The situation there was already explosive because Kashmir had been joined to India by its Hindu ruler despite the Islamic faith of three-quarters of its population. Pakistan claimed the province, but India doggedly refused (and still refuses) to permit the United Nations to conduct a plebiscite there. As a result, the report of the theft—the truth or the lack of it being irrelevant—sufficed to set off 10 days of demonstrations in Srinagar. Comment emanating in Pakistan hinted in a subtle manner that the Hindu minority was responsible for the theft, and Hindus were promptly assaulted and their houses burned. Refugees fled across the frontier into India, and as soon as they had told their grim tales retribution began in that country. A total of 1034 huts were destroyed in the 24th Parganas District. In Calcutta 88 people had been killed and 508 injured by January 1964. According to the official figures, 5271 Indian Muslims fled across the frontier into (then) East Pakistan.

The brutal nature of religious conflict in India is illustrated by this account quoted from the *Times of India*:

Are we never to see the end of communal violence in this country? The incidents in Ferozabad conform to a pattern which is as familiar as it is sickening. A Hindu procession playing music passes by a Mosque and violence erupts. This is the beginning of a grim chain reaction. In Ferozabad on Sunday there was only a slight but significant variation in the pattern. A bomb was hurled at the passing procession. This fact suggests that the violence was not spontaneous but premeditated. . . . People going about their business peacefully continue to be attacked with knives solely because they profess a religious faith other than that of the assailant. (In Ghurye, 1968, p. 328)

The bomb in the incident described killed six persons and injured 40.

Conflict within the Indian community is not confined to that provoked by religion, however. There is also considerable tension between the upper and lower classes and castes. Unrest among rural laborers protesting against their treatment by landlords has spread swiftly throughout the country since 1967, when the famous Naxalbari revolt broke out. As Hari Sharma points out:

The other side—landlords, rich peasants, rentiers, paymasters—responded differently, depending on their strength and organization. Sometimes they fled to the cities, to return only when their allies in the state apparatus (the police, the army) made it safe for them to do so. At other times they retaliated with force. In the village of Venmani in East Thanjavur, for example, they attacked the landless laborers' hamlet at midnight. Shooting into the air, they forced everybody out of his or her house, pushed as many as they could into a single hut, and set fire to it. Forty-four people—men, women, and children—were burnt alive while jubilant landlords stood guard to prevent anyone from escaping. (In Gough and Sharma, 1973, p. 81)

A similar incident took place in the Putnea District of Bihar, where all 45 houses belonging to a community of sharecroppers were razed. At least 14 people were killed and 35 injured (*ibid.*, p. 97).

The preceding analysis of conflict situations in various parts of the world is selective rather than comprehensive. Its purpose is to show that conflict is not confined to one or two countries or to specific political systems and that no political system is immune to conflict. The empirical problem is therefore less that of avoiding conflict than of overcoming it through accommodation.

E. Intergroup Accommodation

In any society with distinctive groups, whether identified by ethnicity, race, religion, or any other factor, a certain amount of friction is bound to be present. A society that would give each group full satisfaction of its needs and wants is utopian; we can only speak of various forms of accommodation. Analytically, the forms of accommodation in a heterogenous society fall into two main categories—those which reject diverse groups altogether (or at best restrict their right to exist), and those which recognize these groups and grant them existence and the right to group identity. Based on Milton M. Gordon's classification (Yetman and Steele, 1972, p. 256), the division is represented in Figure 12.1.

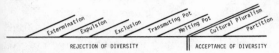

REJECTION OF DIVERSITY ‖ ACCEPTANCE OF DIVERSITY

FIGURE 12.1.

At one extreme is extermination, which occurs when a dominant group expresses its total rejection of diversity by genocide. At the other extreme, partition may take place when two groups recognize each other's identity, but decide they would be happier in separate states. But it may also take place when only one of the two groups asserts a separate identity but succeeds—through war, revolution, or political pressure—in winning its independence.

Expulsion is obviously less extreme than extermination. Certain minorities within the society can be classified as nondesirable and can be expelled from the country through pressure or by direct government action. The right of the minority to exist within the society is denied, but not necessarily the right to live elsewhere. In the case of exclusion, a certain minority group is not expelled from the national territory but is denied all political, social, and economic rights. Members of this group who remain in the country—sometimes because they are not permitted to emigrate—become second-class citizens. A classic example of expulsion is the case of the ethnic Germans of Czecho-Slovakia. When World War II ended and the Sudetenland was returned to Czecho-Slovak control, the "National Front" government expelled the entire German-speaking population, regardless whether they had supported or opposed the Hitler regime, except

for a small residue who were overlooked. Ironically, even a few surviving Jews were expelled, since—reflecting the maxim *"Čo žid to němec"* (A Jew is a German)—the Czecho-Slovak census treated Yiddish as a dialect of German. The most striking case of exclusion is the treatment of Jews in the USSR.

The "transmuting pot" demands that minority groups dissociate themselves from their specific ethnic and cultural characteristics and background, and then associate themselves with those of the dominant group. The diversity of groups is therefore again denied, and the result is cultural assimilation or integration. A more symmetrical relation between groups, in theory at least, is found in the melting pot. In the United States, "the 'melting pot' idea envisaged a biological merger of the Anglo-Saxon peoples with other immigrant groups and a blending of their respective cultures into a new indigenous American type" (Yetman and Steele, 1972, p. 255). The melting pot is conceived as producing a new unit which would absorb all the smaller ones. Since human interbreeding results from individual decisions, it is clear that groups will only "melt" to the extent that they are mutually acceptable.

At the other end of the scale are accommodation models based on the acceptance of divergent groups. In the structure known as cultural pluralism the goal of each group is to preserve its language, its religion, its institutions, and cultural possessions within the broader framework of the political society. Public policy based on cultural pluralism allocates resources so that each divergent group receives its appropriate share of public revenue with which to operate its own schools, theaters, cultural institutions, and in many cases welfare facilities.

Where differences between groups are fundamental, where a reasonably symmetrical relationship seems unlikely, and where geography permits, political separation may be the form of accommodation most conducive to intergroup peace. This has been the consideration underlying the separation of Singapore from Malaysia, that of Bangladesh from Pakistan, and most cases of decolonization. Partition does not always, however, bring the political and economic bliss promised by its promoters.

1. POLICIES THAT REJECT DIVERSITY AND DIVERSE PEOPLE

Genocide is defined by the United Nations Convention of 1946 as: "acts committed with intent to destroy, in whole or in part, a national, ethnic, racial or religious group." History offers us numerous examples of such acts. Genesis 34:14–29 tells how the Israelites, having persuaded the Hivite males to be circumcised on the promise of merging the tribes, slew them to the last man, taking over the Hivite women as additional wives. The Romans rose above sex preference; they killed all the inhabitants of Carthage. More recent genocides include the Turkish massacres of Armenians after World War I, and the slaughter of Jews by the Hitler regime during World War II.

The conduct of the West Pakistani army in East Pakistan, which resulted in the death of more than half a million people and the flight of 8 million Bengalis into India, can also be classified as genocide (see chapter 28, C). Genocide is likewise a frequent outcome of ethnic and religious conflicts in Africa. The mutual slaughter of Tutsi and Hutu in Rwanda and Burundi, already noted, is dealt with in its legal aspects in chapter 19,F1, under the heading: "Denial of the Right to Exist." It is significant that the United Nations, despite its brave pretensions and despite the Genocide Convention, has done exactly nothing about these massacres.

The struggle between Muslims and Lugbara Christians in Uganda likewise ended in genocide. General Amin, who emphasizes his Islamic identity by adding *Al Hadj* (one who has made the pilgrimage to Mecca) to his titles, has systematically removed Christians from gov-

ernment posts, although half the population belong to Christian churches. The number of tribal murders and political killings since Amin seized power has been estimated between 80,000 and 90,000; Amin's brother-in-law Wanume Kibedi, a former foreign minister living in exile, calls these figures too low (Sempangi, 1975).

Expulsions. As a "solution" to the problem of heterogeneous groups, expulsion is in essence less barbarous than deliberate genocide. But it is almost as tragic in its effects and is often genocidal in the way it is carried out. Forced population movements frequently involve mass deaths caused by cruelty or neglect. The major mass expulsion of the twentieth century, that of 18 million Reich and ethnic Germans at the close of World War II, is discussed at length in chapter 22. It is to be observed here, however, that this expulsion is hardly to be classified as a "solution" to a problem of interethnic compatibility. While political and cultural quarrels between Germans and Slavs cannot be erased from history, that same history also records long periods of peaceable coexistence. The notion that Slavs and Germans cannot live together was partly a result of war propaganda and partly an amalgam of Pan-Slav ideas concocted initially by the exile cabinet of Dr. Beneš in London and the pro-Communist underground in Prague. It was later taken up with some enthusiasm by the Kremlin, which saw in the uprooting of 18 million people the opportunity to create social chaos in Germany (making that country ripe for communism) and to cast Czecho-Slovakia and Poland in the role of permanent clients of Moscow.

The most striking example of expulsion in more recent years has been that of the Asians from East Africa. A study by Rothchild and Marris of the Asians in Kenya shows that they doubt the value of Kenyan citizenship.

From the way the government is handling the matter, I don't think there is any advantage in citizenship for non-Africans. . . . The biggest disadvantage is that a non-African can be deprived of his citizenship—but not an African. There is no promise of getting jobs, and if they are thrown out, they will be stateless. Even citizens are deported. . . . The people are not treated according to their citizenship, but according to their colour. There is no future. The government prefers BLACK Africans only (in Hunt and Walker, 1974, p. 121).

The significant point here is that race and culture override citizenship as criteria of sociopolitical compatibility. The term African is limited to persons of Negrid (Congoid) ancestry, and no matter how much an Asian may try to conduct himself as a law-abiding, tax-paying Kenyan, Tanzanian, or Ugandan, he will always be an "outsider," subject to expropriation or expulsion whenever the politicians need a scapegoat.

The Asians, mostly of Indian and Pakistani origin, have contributed decisively to the economic development of East Africa, and as traders they occupied the key positions in the economy. When Africa obtained independence and "Africanization" became a policy, the Asians began to be pictured as strangers who were exploiting the black population. Demonstrations took place; Tanzania was the first country to introduce work permits which gave preference to blacks rather than to Asians, who for the most part had chosen to retain their British citizenship. In August 1972, General Amin expelled 50,000 Asians from Uganda. They were not allowed to take anything with them except the sum of £55 (reduced from £2500). These people were scattered all over the world. Just over 27,000 went to Britain, 10,000 to India, 6000 to the United States, and 1000 to Canada; 4000 became inmates of United Nations camps, and smaller groups were divided up among other countries.

At least 200,000 Asians are estimated to have fled to Britain from East and Central Africa (Tandon, 1973, p. 25). The influx reached such proportions that the British government imposed restrictions on the entry of persons who possess United Kingdom passports but lack British "patriality." A "patrial" is a person who has lived in the U.K. as a citizen, or whose parent or grandparent did so (Crum Ewing, 1975, p. 520).

Exclusion, milder in its effects than expulsion but often a cause of violence nevertheless, may be based on racial, caste, religious, ethnic, or other criteria. The treatment of blacks in the United States exhibits significant elements of exclusion. A case of exclusion by religious membership is that found in Northern Ireland. When the island was divided, the Republic of Ireland acquired 84 percent of the territory and 66 percent of the population. Its dominant religion is Roman Catholic; there is a 5 percent Protestant minority and a small Jewish community. But in the far more densely populated counties of Northern Ireland, the Protestant majority is only two-thirds and the other third of the population is Catholic. The religious division in Northern Ireland has become decisive in socioeconomic affairs. Both Catholics and Protestants have a tendency to form communities limited to their own kind, as reflected in the distinction—unknown in England— between "a Protestant pub" and "a Catholic pub." When there are jobs to be filled, preference is given to people of the same faith. Since the Protestants were traditionally better off and formed most of the middle class, better work opportunities and business prospects were to be found in the Protestant sector.

"Northern Ireland was to be a protestant enclave. This did not mean that Roman Catholics were hindered from engaging in worship, but it did mean that the Protestant majority was determined to maintain its dominance in all areas of life, so that it would retain its separation from the much larger Irish Free State [now the Republic of Ireland] and guarantee that, within the enclave, Protestant rule would never be threatened" (Hunt and Walker, 1974, p. 32).

In the Republic of Ireland, the Protestant minority is in turn being excluded. For example: "The real problems of discrimination, however, come from the practices of the community rather than from legally defined areas. Both in the Supreme Court and in the High Court it was an unwritten understanding that at least one judge in each would be a Protestant. This has been quietly dropped, and all the judges are now Catholics" (Jackson, 1972, p. 211).

The Protestants are especially handicapped in education. Secondary schools are privately owned, and the state pays £25 annually per pupil to the school. The Roman Catholic schools are integrated with a religious order, whose vows of poverty ease the financial burden. The Protestants have to hire teachers, and since their numbers are small, the cost of keeping a child in school is very much higher than the subsidy paid by the state. Therefore, the parents must pay their own educational costs, whereas the Catholics pay nothing. This has caused a crisis in the Protestant schools, which are slowly being strangled. There is also discrimination against Protestants in mixed marriages in the Republic of Ireland (see chapter 18,B7). Its effect of forcing children into the Catholic faith is a form of long-term cultural assimilation.

As in the case of the Asians of East Africa, exclusion may be precipitated by too much success. This has happened in the Philippines, where the Chinese established themselves firmly in commerce during the years of American control between 1898 and 1946. By 1932 they controlled between 70 and 80 percent of the retail trade, and also pocketed a large share of the gross domestic product. When American control came to an end there was already widespread Filipino resentment against the Chinese. The reaction came with independence in 1946. The Philippine government immediately passed laws tending to push the Chinese out of retail trade. Special taxes were levied on foreigners (Chinese), and at the same time it was made much more difficult to obtain citizenship. Ten years' residence was required, followed by a special investigation by the po-

lice, the National Bureau of Investigation, and the health authorities. Applicants had to be able to speak and write English and Spanish, they were required to have some knowledge of a "native language," and they had to pay 5000 pesos.

Foreigners are not allowed to own agricultural land, minerals, or "forests." The Chinese may not purchase land, they are not permitted to own markets in the towns, and their activities in the import-export field are curtailed. Having forced the Chinese into trade by barring them from owning land, controlling natural resources, or joining the professions, the Philippine government has imposed severe restrictions which threaten to force the Chinese out of Commerce and into the ranks of the destitute (see Eitzen, 1968, *passim*).

Exclusion is also felt by the Aborigines of Australia. It is likewise the lot of the Tamils of Sri Lanka, who are victims of a hostile ethnic and language policy applied by the Singhalese majority.

2. POLICIES THAT REJECT DIVERSITY
   BUT ACCEPT DIVERSE PEOPLE

Cultural Assimilation. American Indians offer interesting examples of resistance to assimilation. Two contrasting tendencies are pointed out by Alexander Lesser:

[The Indians] have survived the exterminations which depleted and destroyed the Indian peoples of the Atlantic seaboard and of California; the forced evacuations which took many from their homes into alien country; and the concentration of tribal groups in restricted areas, stripped of their traditional land base. Most important of all, they have survived despite the generations of national effort to force assimilation upon them, for our dominant Indian policy from the beginning has been assimilation. Their existence today reflects the voluntary decision of their members, as citizens of the United States, to maintain traditional group life, in many cases on the homelands of their ancestors. (1972, pp. 335–37)

The Indians who left their homes and moved to the cities and towns lost some of the bonds with their traditional societies in the course of time. These Indians were systematically assimilated in two or three generations. But despite this drain, Indian societies have kept their identity and have shown new determination to maintain their distinctive culture. Indians want economic integration but not at the cost of cultural alienation and they demand a voice in determining their own future. Lesser continues:

the community is still there, as strong in numbers and as viable and unassimilated as ever. Some members have left and chosen assimilation, but an increase of the population at home has usually more than made up for the loss. It has become increasingly probable that many of the communities that have endured, are likely to be with us for a long and indefinite future unless radical or brutal measures are taken to disorganize and disperse them, We may have to come to terms with a people who seem determined to have a hand in shaping their own destiny. (*Ibid.*, p. 337)

There is no clear American policy in the matter of assimilating the Indians, nor does the Federal government have any clear jurisdiction over the subject. Certainly the Bureau of Indian Affairs has in recent years recognized Indian cultures as values to be preserved and has sought to develop bicultural approaches to education. But Indians who move to cities and towns find themselves in a society whose schools, libraries, theaters, and social clubs are geared to perpetuate an essentially European-derived and, as ethnic spokesmen claim, mainly Anglo-Saxon culture. If Poles and Italians find themselves alienated and under pressure to "Americanize," how much more true this must be for Indians and other non-Europeans. Should the Indian reaction against educational and cultural homogenization prove successful and should they gain—from the states as well as the Federal government—a measure of cultural, socioeconomic, and in some cases even territorial autonomy, then it is possible that in their case assimilation will make way for cultural pluralism.

Unlike Indians, who are still approaching the stage of organization where they are capable of generating a policy, American blacks have long had a policy, championed by their "establishment" organizations, the NAACP and the Urban League. It is the policy of "integration," meaning the overthrow of racial barriers and the achievement of equal access to education, jobs, housing, and public facilities and services. While black leaders have always emphasized the voluntary nature of social relations, social amalgamation and ultimately racial mixing are implicit in this policy.

Since the landmark Supreme Court decision of 1954, major changes have taken place. Official segregation in schools, colleges, restaurants, hotels, and (theoretically) in housing has come to an end, though a wide degree of voluntary segregation persists. Only where racial mixing is asserted as a primary value, overriding considerations of educational quality and the school–neighborhood relationship does resistance continue, and this should probably be interpreted as objection to uprooting rather than racial antagonism. But in the meantime many black intellectuals have begun to question the value of cultural assimilation—one of the promised "payoffs" of integration. As Hunt and Walker observe:

The emergence of a militant separatist black group was confusing both to integrationist blacks, who felt they were leading the wave of the future into a color-blind society, and to whites of almost all persuasions. . . . At this juncture in the development of race relations in the United States, many black Americans find themselves at the crossroads wondering which way to go. Which will provide a richer and less oppressive life, the road of social integration or cultural assimilation, or the path leading toward separatism? . . . These are some of the major questions facing black America in its search for freedom, equality and liberation. (1974, p. 329)

The USSR pretends to offer a model of cultural pluralism but practices cultural assimilation. The Union Republics and the smaller units representing various nationalities cannot levy their own taxes except as empowered to do so by the central government. They control their economic affairs only through delegated powers and within a centrally conceived plan. They retain a certain degree of cultural autonomy, manifested in the use of the ethnic language in government offices, as the language of instruction in the school system, in the production of literature, in programmes of mass communication, and in the performing arts. The content of such expression is, however, controlled by the Party under the principle: "national in form, socialist in content" (Dushnyck, 1975b, p. 56).

Although the Kremlin poses as a guardian of regional and ethnic political and cultural autonomy, many of its policies endanger the survival of local units and nationality groups. Industrialization has tended to break up ethnic groups. Perpetuating the old Czarist practice of *razvod* (scattering ethnic groups thought sources of potential trouble), the central ministries dispatch scientists, managers, and workers all over the USSR, and bring groups from rural areas to work in towns and industry complexes. Since Russians are to be found in every locality, the Great Russian nation is strengthened at the expense of minorities.

National diversity in the USSR is seen by communist leaders as a transitional phase which will later disappear in socialist uniformity. Khrushchev envisaged the end-result as follows: "Communism will not conserve and perpetuate national distinctions. We will support the objective process of increasingly closer rapprochement of nations and nationalities, proceeding under the conditions of communist construction on a voluntary and democratic basis. It is essential that we stress the education of the masses in the spirit of proletarian internationalism and soviet patriotism" (*ibid.*, p. 64). Soviet patriotism, however, requires that Russian be an obligatory subject in all minority schools. Other languages are tolerated, but Russian is the medium that makes communication possible between all the nationalities.

It may be granted that a multilingual state needs a language of communication; but when that language is identified with the dominant majority and its history, is taught by members of that majority, and becomes the vehicle for indoctrination in state-oriented patriotism as well as the linguistic key to rise in status, it is difficult to avoid imposing it as a language of identity, even if such avoidance is intended. Ostensible cultural pluralism may therefore become a cloak for cultural assimilation.

Amalgamation. The melting pot idea has received a great deal of attention since the 18th century, when the writer J. Hector John Crevecoeur wrote in his *Letters from an American Farmer:* "Here individuals of all nations are melted into a new race of men, whose labours and posterity will one day cause great changes in the world" (Gordon, 1971, p. 269). The theory is that the various groups will melt into a new unit, the culture of no one group will remain dominant, and the whole process will be accompanied by cross-breeding. The ideal is amalgamation. However, non–Anglo-Saxons in the United States complain with growing vehemence that they have been served up a diluted (because supposedly universalized) Anglo-Saxon culture, to which their own groups have had little or no input. To the extent this is true, the American melting pot is really a transmuting pot.

One of the few examples of successful amalgamation can be found in Mexico, not as the result of planning, but as a product of unplanned social evolution. There is little ethnic conflict among Mexicans, because the Spaniards imported black slaves to do the work, and they intermarried with the Indians. The result was a new Mestizo group which rapidly came to outnumber the other groups. As Hunt and Walker put it, "The proportion which can be identified as other than mestizo is rapidly shrinking" (1974, p. 150). Then the revolution of 1910 brought the Mestizo to the fore as the true representatives of Mexican nationalism, which indicates that the amalgamation between the various groups had created a new majority.

Assimilation and amalgamation depend on the availability of a dominant or common culture which all groups concerned can accept. Such a culture was provided in Mexico by the Catholic Church, which was flexible enough to adapt native styles in art and music and to hallow a few local saints, headed by Nuestra Señora de Guadalupe. A commonly acceptable culture was not available in East Africa, where failure of the Asians to integrate with African society is often mentioned by African politicians as a pretext for their expulsion (Tandon, 1973, p. 13).

But how can Asians become Africans? Being an African means belonging to a tribe, in which membership can be acquired only through rites and rituals such as President Kenyatta describes in his *Facing Mount Kenya*. Tribal councils, however, seldom admit outsiders, particularly if they are of other races. The anomaly lies in the fact that Africans observe tribal pluralism among themselves: Kikuyu, Luo, Hutu, and Baganda recognize one another's identity. Yet they refuse to accept Asians as a tribe parallel with those native to Africa.

Nor is intermarriage a solution. As Tandon observes:

It cannot be, for even if intermarriage were to be encouraged or forced (as Sheikh Aboud Karume did in Zanzibar), it would—if it were 100 percent successful—dissolve Asian ethnic distinctiveness but give birth to a yet new community of hybrid population. The problem of the Asians is thus not solved; it is only transformed into a new problem. The accusation that "Asians do not allow their daughters to marry us" must, therefore, be seen for its symbolic importance. As Justin O'Brien wrote: ". . . it is reflective of the simple folks' feeling that Asians must somehow be brought down from the pedestal. . . . It is not that many Africans would have wanted to marry Asian girls—but to have got some of them in sexually subordinate position would have served the same purpose as getting their male protectors to soil their hands on land." (*Ibid.*, p. 13)

General Amin, in any case, not only preaches but practices national integration through intermarriage. His four wives come from different regions of Uganda, and it was thought at one time that he might take an Asian wife.

3. POLICIES THAT ACCEPT DIVERSITY

Cultural Pluralism. As a policy, cultural pluralism recognizes and accepts ethnic and other group differences within the society. As Hunt and Walker describe it:

In a situation of cultural pluralism all groups, theoretically, have equal rights. It is a system which flourishes best when each ethnic group in a society has a specific territory in which it is a numerical majority, and when there is at least an approximate equality of economic development between groups. . . . A basic premise of cultural pluralism is that there is no need to sacrifice ethnic identity. . . . cultural pluralism is an attractive pattern, as it offers the hope of combining the preservation of ethnic distinctiveness with the advantages of coordination in a larger state. (1974, pp. 7–8)

Canada can be considered an example of cultural pluralism. There, the basic differences between the English- and French-speaking populations have been confronted, partly by territorial separation, partly by personal autonomy—choice of ethnic-linguistic group in mixed areas. English and French enjoy equal status in Dominion affairs, but the provinces give some preference to their majority languages. Recent legislation has granted French the preferred position in Quebec.

Another state which is trying to solve the problem of ethnic differences by means of cultural pluralism is Yugoslavia. There are five major national groups in this country and more than nine smaller recognized ethnic groups which can be identified. These ethnic differences are compounded by diversity of religion and language.

The northern republics of Yugoslavia—Croatia and Slovenia—were formerly Hapsburg territories and inherited the Roman Catholic religion as well as the Latin alphabet. The Serbs, on the other hand, were heirs of the Byzantine tradition: their religion was Orthodox and they used the Cyrillic alphabet. The third largest religious group in Yugoslavia are the Muslims, who are found in Bosnia-Herzegovina and Kossovo.

Although Yugoslavia is a communist country, its revolution was largely local rather than a Red Army operation. While its first postwar constitution was almost a verbatim copy of the 1936 Stalin Constitution of the USSR, Tito's government appears to have carried out to a large extent the decentralization which the Soviet document promises in theory. As Hunt and Walker note:

In June, 1950 . . . Tito launched the workers' self-management movement which ultimately led to the decentralization of the entire system and the abolition of most central planning. . . . The reforms were based on the premise that the Soviet state had developed into an over-centralized bureaucracy where the working class was more an object of manipulation than a dominant force. The Yugoslav system proposed to reverse this trend by making the workers in their enterprises the dominant force within society. (*Ibid.*, p. 376)

Tito's decentralization was not conceived as a strengthening of the ethnic republics but rather a shifting of economic decision-making to the enterprise level. The change had, however, a profound effect on interethnic relations in Yugoslavia. The more industrialized northern areas were able to attract larger investments and to pay larger salaries to their workers. The southern agricultural regions lacked an adequate infrastructure and fell behind in economic development. This had a negative influence on the feelings of the various nationalities toward one another.

It appears that the various ethnic languages in Yugoslavia are guaranteed, although the ideological content of instruction remains under communist control. Children of any national group are taught in their mother tongue wherever there are enough to form a class—15 being the minimum in Serbia. Equal rights are guaranteed to all ethnic groups in government and representative organs—in theory. Doubts are raised from time to time as to how effectively this principle is carried out, for instance

by Dr. Savka Dabčević-Kučar in the Croat Executive Committee (*Vjesnik*, February 13, 1971) and more recently by the Federation of Socialist Youth of Yugoslavia (*Mladost*, December 5, 1974). Under the 1974 Constitution, each of the six national republics has 30 members in the Federal Council and 12 delegates in the Council of Republics and Provinces. Each of the eleven Provinces has 20 members in the first-named body and 8 in the second. The structure of the Yugoslav federal organs thus expresses the equal representation of ethnic units and flies in the face of the one-man-one-vote principle.

A historical example of successful pluralism in a Central European context was the Moravian Equalization (*Mährischer Ausgleich*) of 1905, which regulated cultural relations between a Czech majority and a German minority. Each national group was assured proportionate representation in the diet and separate Czech and German administrations for schools and cultural institutions were created. Progress toward a similar arrangement in Bohemia was interrupted by World War I (Glaser, 1961, p. 16). As recently as July 1975, Major Zděnek Sladeček, reaffirming the principles of Right of Homeland (*Heimatrecht*) and self-determination at a rally of expelled German South Moravians, declared that

all Europe must, if it is to become a federation of free peoples and ethnic groups, adhere to the principles that we worked out as a model in the Moravian Equalization. The Moravian Equalization is therefore not only a historical document but also a charter for the solution of European nationality problems. (*Sudetendeutsche Zeitung*, Munich, July 11, 1975)

A different form of political and cultural pluralism is emerging in the Republic of South Africa in relations between the white, Coloured, and Indian populations. When the National Party came to power in 1948, the accent was on segregation and political, social, and cultural contacts between the three groups were discouraged. The Coloured had formerly enjoyed the right to vote together with the whites, but were removed from the common roll—a step many people thought retrograde. But as separation proceeded it gradually became apparent that the National Party was moving toward greater autonomy for the Coloured in their own affairs. The Council for Coloured Affairs was established in 1959, and the old policy of simple segregation (apartheid) was modified to become "parallel development." The latter is "community-directed in that it aims at the retention of the Coloured group's ethnic identity and the promotion of its socio-economic development as a coherent, self-contained community, managing its own affairs" (Vosloo, 1972, p. 370).

In 1961 Prime Minister Verwoerd prophesied that the Coloured population would obtain full control of their own affairs with their own parliamentary, executive, and administrative bodies within a decade. This was partly achieved in July 1969, when the Council for Coloured Affairs was replaced by the Coloured Representative Council, with authority to deal with matters such as finance, local government and administration, social welfare, and rural settlements. Coloured development, however, is still in its beginning stages, and political, social, and economic goals have not yet been clearly defined. As Vosloo puts it: "For the Coloureds it meant parallel development in some form of association with the Whites in the same homeland. At the moment there is a great deal of uncertainty as to the form this association might take" (*Ibid.*, p. 382).

An outside observer might wonder why it would not be fairer and less discriminatory to restore the Coloured to the common voters' roll as some of the group's leaders demand. This proposal, however, would involve not merely an act of accommodation on the part of the South African nation but actually a merger of that nation into a differently defined nation, the stability of which cannot be assumed. The structural aspects of this problem are discussed

in chapter 20,C4. Suffice it to say here that political self-rule in one form or another is definitely in the future of the Coloured in South Africa.

The Indian community, numbering some 600,000 and concentrated in and around Durban, is likewise moving toward self-determination. A Department of Indian Affairs was created in 1961 and an Indian National Council in 1964. The latter was replaced in 1968 with the South African Indian Council, a body nominated by the Minister of Indian Affairs and consisting of fifteen members from Natal, seven from the Transvaal, and three from the Cape Province. According to an Indian author: "The council has no more than advisory powers, but it is serving the important purpose of being a channel through which the Indian community can bring its needs and grievances to the attention of the government" (Joosub, 1972, p. 423).

Although South African governments before and after the National Party took power in 1948 sought to repatriate the Indians to India and the so-called Joint Commission recommended economic pressure to induce repatriation in the late 1950s, that policy has been changed. The National Party and the government now view the Indians as a South African people entitled to their own identity and autonomous development. Indians remain subject to apartheid, especially in the matter of housing, but at least some see advantages therein. As Joosub points out: "Our customs and religion differ from those of the other racial groups, and we prefer to live with our own kind. We would, for example, not want our children to attend school with children of other racial groups, nor would we want our young people to belong to white or black groups, and acquire their ways of life or adopt their habits" (*ibid.*, p. 431).

As in the case of the Coloureds, it is not yet clear what kind of institutions will manage relations between Whites and Indians. The important point is that the basis for political and cultural pluralism has now been laid in South Africa.

In the meantime, some of the irritating features of apartheid are being removed, such as separate elevators and post-office windows. Coloured are now included on certain statutory boards and higher levels in the Post Office and Railways are being opened to them. The Government is now committed to eliminating the White-Coloured wage gap for jobs in each category. Coloured also benefit from a rapid increase in the number of hotels licensed to serve guests of all races.

Switzerland is often cited as a model of the successful accommodation of ethnic diversity with democratic stability. There are four language groups in Switzerland—German, French, Italian, and Rhaeto-Romanic (Romansch). The Catholic and Protestant religious groups are about evenly balanced, although in some localities (such as Basel) the Roman Catholic Church has been disestablished in favor of the Old Catholics, who refuse to recognize the infallibility of the Pope or the bodily ascension of Mary. While language differences cause major structural problems in Belgium and provoke riots in India, their role in Switzerland is no longer significant.

For a series of unique historical reasons, language is not salient in Swiss national politics. Unlike most European countries, Switzerland did not originate as a nation-state. Rather, the Swiss confederation grew out of a mutual alliance of Swiss cantons in their common struggle against feudal rulers and the German emperor; this confederation possessed no constitution, no central government, no national army, nor even a capital city. The Swiss cantons were all sovereign for mutual advantage. (Rabushka and Shepsle, 1972, p. 209)

The Swiss Civil War (*Sonderbundskrieg*) of 1847 was not about language but about religion, particularly the privileges and power of religious orders. The victorious Protestant and liberal Catholic forces were led by a French-speaking General, Guillaume Henri Dufour, whose marching orders to the troops issued

November 5, 1847, contained a message of reconciliation comparable to Lincoln's second inaugural address (Thürer, 1948, pp. 47–50).

It was after this war that the Swiss decided that they needed an effective central government—a decision strengthened by the turbulence of 1848. But the new government's powers were limited and the new constitution recognized German, French, Italian, and Rhaeto-Romanic as national languages. It also prohibited any activity by the Jesuits, who, the Swiss felt rightly or wrongly, had been instigators of dissension. Since 1848, the cantons have maintained jurisdiction over all matters affecting religion, education, the arts and culture, as well as a wide range of social and economic affairs. Political life has remained largely centered in the cantons, so that problems are usually solved within that forum rather than at the level of the central government. The only canton with serious internal problems is Bern, where the French-speaking Jura is the center of a separatist movement demanding its own canton within the Swiss federation (Paul, 1974). It is significant that when Swiss newspapers mention "the state," the reference is to the canton, not the central government.

A factor that has prevented factionalism at the national level is the overlapping of language and religious lines. There are German- and French-speaking Protestants, and the same is true of the Roman Catholics. Language and religious affiliations which divide the groups act as a balance between them, a phenomenon which is unique to Switzerland and which has helped cultural pluralism to find full expression there.

Partition, political and geographical separation, is a form of coexistence analogous to divorce. It is adopted by groups of diverse ethnicity, race, language, or religion who find they cannot enjoy full political rights within one political system without a collision of vital interests. In the extreme case, the two groups are unable to keep the peace in close proximity.

Partition may be conditional, leaving the separated units in a confederation or some other form of political association. Or it may be absolute, leaving separate sovereign states. Frequently, only one group or region desires partition, while other members of the political system are determined to prevent it. Sometimes the issue is decided by civil war.

Separatist movements in the United States since the defeat of the Confederacy have been marginal and limited to fractions of minorities. Makielski tells us:

In the state of New Mexico, a Mexican-American leader, Rejes Lopez Tijerina, offered what was a full separatist programme. For a period of time the movement attracted support, but imprisonment and legal counter-attacks successfully suppressed the movement by the mid-1970's, a suppression that was assured when Tijerina was killed in a gun battle. The black orientated Republic of New Africa movement followed a similar pattern. . . . Its announced goal was to create a full-fledged separate nation for American blacks. . . . Besides these two prominent efforts there were within the Indian-American, Mexican-American, and Black American protest movements various separatist-oriented leaders and spokesmen. (1973, p. 56)

Any proliferation of serious separatism among deprived groups in the United States is probably excluded by the fact that these groups depend heavily on government largesse. The general thrust of their organizations is to agitate for greater benefits (e.g. "Operation Breadbasket" and the "Welfare Rights" movement) and their leadership tends to be neo-Keynesian in economic belief. Were the opportunity to secede offered, it would hardly be accepted without the promise of generous "foreign aid." This is also true of Puerto Rico, which has seen a recent resurgence of independentist agitation.

Separatism among Canadian Indians is to be taken a little more seriously, and has caused Prime Minister Trudeau to express concern. Perhaps one reason is that Canada does not have a paternalist bureaucracy like the U.S.

Bureau of Indian Affairs. In any case, the Indians are no longer satisfied with their position in Canadian society, and separatism may be the final outcome. As the Indian leader Harold Cardinal pointed out (as quoted, chapter 11,I), Indians demand acceptance as Indians. Otherwise there is no basis for their participation in Canadian society. This is a clear indication that the Indians reject the prospect of cultural assimilation with the Canadians, and that they will look for another alternative—even if this should turn out to be partition, which would probably be conditional rather than absolute.

French-speaking Canadians have for a long time been dissatisfied with their cultural situation, and this discontent has recently assumed a separatist aspect, particularly since the Parti Quebecois gained a majority in the Quebec assembly on November 15, 1976. Speculation as to possible outcomes seems premature at the time of writing. Note can be taken, however, of several obstacles to Quebec independence. Aside from the entrenched provisions of the British North America Act, which the British government might not be willing to amend without a clear mandate from English-speaking Canada, a separate Quebec could hardly be economically viable, while aid from the United States would not be forthcoming. (See *U.S. News and World Report*, November 29, 1976, pp. 20–21, and December 13, 1976, pp. 48–52; also Eric Kierans in *The Guardian*, weekly edition, March 13, 1977, p. 17.)

Nigeria is a territorial state, and there is no such a thing as a Nigerian nation, despite the efforts of various leaders to create one. There are almost 250 languages and dialects, and several of the peoples of Nigeria are large enough to constitute independent nations in their own right. Obafemi Awolowo, a leading politician belonging to a minority people, once remarked: "Nigeria is not a nation. It is a mere geographical expression. There are no 'Nigerians' in the same sense as there are 'English,' 'Welsh,' or 'French.' The word

'Nigerian' is merely a distinctive appellation to distinguish those who live within the boundaries of Nigeria from those who do not" (Hunt and Walker, 1974, p. 277).

The ethnic balance in Nigeria is such that the Hausa-Fulani—a group of closely related Muslim tribes concentrated in the north and numbering 35 million—have been able to play a politically dominant role, even though they account for less than half the total population. In politics and in the army—categories that overlap in Nigeria and in several other African states—leaders of the Hausa-Fulani usually work in alliance with those of the Yoruba, a large tribal nation in the West, many of whose members are also Muslims. The Ibo, on the other hand, the largest of several tribes in the southeast, have generally found themelves in the position of outsiders.

A Minorities Commission, set up by Britain three years before independence, tried to persuade Nigerian political leaders to include certain human rights clauses (based on the UN's Convention on Human Rights) in the constitution so that members of minority groups would be protected by guarantees affirming the rights of individual citizens. Some of these rights were written into the constitution, but the riots of the 1960s and the open discrimination practiced by the Hausa-Fulani made them a mockery. Furthermore, certain fundamental rights—such as the right to education and the right to work—were not even included in the formal Bill of Rights, to the detriment of minority communities. Hunt and Walker point out that the Nigerian Bill of Rights never really protected minorities, since it emphasized *individual rights* rather than the structural adaptations needed to protect the *group rights* of minorities.

The Commission evidently proceeded by analogy with the American and the British practice which was to guarantee not group rights, but individual rights, on the theory that a Government committed to the protection of individual rights would also be committed to the protection of minorities. . . . In

effect, the Minorities Commission sought to protect Nigeria from the slashing wounds of ethnic conflict by applying the Band-Aid of constitutional guarantees of individual rights. It was a remedy directed to individual privileges when major structural changes in the Government were required. (*Ibid.*, pp. 276–77)

A potential for conflict existed in the fact that the Ibo, a coastal people who had been longest in contact with Europeans and who had profited from missionary education, had reached a stage of development more advanced than the other tribes, particularly the Hausa-Fulani masses. They had spread over much of Nigeria, occupying a more than proportional share of positions in the army and civil service, and assuming a role in business somewhat akin to that of the Asians in East Africa. The acute phase of interethnic relations in Nigeria began with the overthrow of Prime Minister Sir Abubakar Tafawa Balewa and his government in January 1966. Although the coup reflected nearly universal dissatisfaction with the corruption and favoritism of the Balewa regime, it was led by Ibo officers and was misrepresented as an Ibo attempt to seize control of Nigeria. The regime of General Ironsi that had emerged from the January coup was overthrown in a countercoup on July 29, 1966. The northern and western officers who organized it massacred all the Ibo and other eastern officers they could lay their hands on, and many Ibo enlisted men as well (Uwechue, 1971, pp. 27–42). The July coup was followed by anti-Ibo riots. Many Ibos were killed and an estimated 2 million fled to the eastern region, including many who had never been there as they had been born in the north (Rubin and Weinstein, 1974, p. 171). After the breakdown of conciliation, Colonel Ojukwu, who had emerged as Ibo leader after the death of General Ironsi, proclaimed the independent state of Biafra on May 30, 1967.

Biafra's bid for independence was crushed in a civil war that lasted until January, 1970. Estimates of the death toll vary greatly, but some run to 1 million or more. It is beyond the scope of this inquiry to enter into a post-mortem, but two factors that contributed to the central government's victory may be mentioned here. One is the weapons and supplies furnished the central government by the United Kingdom and, competing for influence, the USSR. Uwechue (1971, pp. 91–93) attributes this British intervention to lack of understanding of Nigeria's ethnic problems and expediency. Lest "perfidious Albion" be judged too harshly, it is well to apply game theory to the situation in which Whitehall found itself. If the values seven and three are assigned to Nigeria (less Biafra) and Biafra respectively—corresponding to their resources rather than their populations—the payoff matrix confronting the British is as shown in table 12.2. The other factor that helped the central government is the fact that Biafra itself was multiethnic. Its smaller peoples—the Efik, Ibibio, and Ejaw—did not like the idea of Ibo hegemony. The tendency to conceive the new state as an expression of Ibo nationality undermined the support these tribes might have given a more pluralistically structured Biafra.

Events in the Nigerian civil war were in some respects a replication of what happened in the former Belgian Congo (now Zaïre) when Katanga tried to secede. Other attempted secessions may be mentioned here in passing: those of the Basques and the Kurds, for instance, against which the governments of Spain and Iraq, respectively, apply the harshest of repressive measures. The leaders of southern Sudan (whose struggle was described in chapter 11,F3) would have preferred independence but accepted a compromise which created an autonomous Southern Region. Its fragility is suggested by the remark of a Sudanese diplomat, a southerner, to one of the authors: "My chief is a northerner. Last year we were out in the jungle, trying to kill each other. Today we confront each other across a desk." In July 1975, it was reported that fighting had broken out again and that a new rebel army was being formed to struggle for the "total independence" of southern Sudan (*San Jose Mercury*, July 29, 1975).

The struggle between Christians and Muslims in the Philippines also has separatist characteristics. The Muslims in the South are a mi-

Table 12.2. BRITISH OPTIONS IN NIGERIAN CIVIL WAR

	Available Options		
	Aid Central Government	Stay Neutral: Aid Neither	Aid Biafra
Outcome of War	Consequences for the British		
A. If Central Government wins	British retain influence in all Nigeria [+10]	British lose part of influence to USSR in all Nigeria [+5]	British lose all influence to USSR in all Nigeria [0]
B. If Biafra wins	British retain influence in rump Nigeria; lose it in Biafra [+7]	British lose part of influence; to USSR in rump Nigeria, to France in Biafra [+5]	British lose influence to USSR in rump Nigeria; retain it in Biafra [+3]
Mean payoff (on assumptions given in each column)	(on assumption outcome A twice as likely as outcome B) [+9]	(on assumption outcomes A and B equally likely) [+5]	(on assumption outcome B twice as likely as outcome A) [+2]

nority group totally different in culture and background from the Christians in the developed northern regions. The Muslims want to make their traditional homeland an independent state. Like many other colonies, the Philippines were not politically unified when the colonizers undertook that task. Even they never succeeded in subduing the "Moros," whom the history books call "wild" because they would have none of either Spanish rule or Christianity.

Thailand has a problem not unlike that of the Philippines. The southern part of the country, close to Malaysia, contains Muslim separatists who rebel against the Bhuddist Thais in the North. The problem in southern Thailand is complicated by the fact that the region is also infested with communist-supported guerrillas who operate back and forth across the Thailand–Malaysia frontier.

The major instance of partition at the close of World War I was the carving up of Austria-Hungary among seven successor states—an event that reflected Allied policy rather than the proven inability of the peoples of the Hapsburg Empire to find a *modus vivendi*. The partition of Germany and Korea after World War II resulted from differences among the occupying powers, not any divisiveness within the German or Korean people. Partition, therefore, can be imposed from without. When this happens, the partitioners are usually pursuing their own interests, not those of the people or peoples they divide. The major partition since World War II based on the desire of those separated was the division of British India into separate Hindu and Muslim states at the time of independence. We have seen that the geographical and religious boundaries did not altogether coincide so that religious clashes are still frequent.

Generally negative attitudes toward partition are therefore a possible reason for antagonism toward South African policies involving or suggesting partition. Such a policy

was advocated by Edward Tiryakian, who despaired of successful integration. "His plan for partition would divide the present Republic of South Africa into two countries. One would be a nation ruled by Africans and the other a nation ruled by a combination of Europeans, Indians and Coloureds, with the Europeans dominant. The African nation would include the present Bantustans and reserves along with a good deal of land not included in these categories" (Hunt and Walker, 1974, p. 199).

At first sight Tiryakian's suggestion seems plausible. The possibility that whites, Coloureds and Indians might eventually share the power cannot be excluded. But the creation of a black state presents a problem, because there is no "African Nation." There are great ethnic differences between the Bantu peoples of South Africa. Their cultural background is different and their languages are as different as European languages. On more than one occasion white intervention has kept black peoples from exterminating one another. Nor is a single black state geographically possible. For example, the Tswanas live traditionally in Northwest Transvaal, the Zulus in Natal, and the Xhosas in Transkei and in the Ciskei in the eastern Cape Province. To divide the Republic into two would necessitate the large scale resettlement of many peoples, which would be an impossibility. This is why the homelands policy of the South African government is designed to lead the black nations to sovereign independence within the areas where they have traditionally lived and where many of them still live. In this way the South African homelands policy offers the various ethnic groups something in the subjects of many other countries are denied—self-government in their own territories. No one in South Africa contends, of course, that partition is a total solution to a complex of problems that require action on a broad front. It is, however, gaining increasing acceptance as an essential element of any future *modus vivendi*.

13

RACIAL DISCRIMINATION

As pointed out in chapter 7, B2, the term "race" has both a biological and a social usage, which are often only loosely related. This chapter, concerned with discriminatory behavior of racial groups, will have mostly to do with the latter.

A. Rational and Irrational Classifications

Although it was once thought that human beings might belong to more than one species, scientists are today agreed that the entire population of the planet belongs to a single species, *Homo sapiens*, regional sectors of which made the transition from the previous stage of evolution, *Homo erectus*, at different times in prehistory. A species is "a breeding unit or population, which has a gene pool of its own," all members of which are capable of interbreeding and will do so given the opportunity (Coon, 1963, pp. 12–13).

Homo sapiens is polytypic, and is divided into subspecies, or major racial groups, five or six in number. The enumeration given in chapter 6, A, is repeated here for the sake of convenience. Human populations are further differentiated into regional and local races (such as the Nordic, Alpine, Mediterranean, Dinaric and Indo-

MAJOR HUMAN RACIAL GROUPS

Eickstedt, 1937, and Peters, 1937	*Carleton S. Coon, 1963*
Europids	Caucasoids
Mongolids	Mongoloids (includes American Indians)
Indianids	
Negrids	Congoids
Khoisanids	Capoids (Cape Peoples)
Australids	Australoids

European types among the Europids; or the Forest Negroes, Nilotics, and Pygmies among the Congoids). Where divergent populations meet, racial patterns take the form of a *mosaic* (where the minority lives in enclaves, as in India) or a *clinal zone* (where one macrogroup merges into another, as do Caucasoids and Mongoloids among the Turkic peoples of Central Asia—Coon, p. 18).

The criteria employed in classifying races include visible features such as hair, shape and skin-folds of the eye, skin color, and facial profile, as well as medical factors such as frequency of blood types, pulse and metabolic rates and temperatures, and reactions to diseases and drugs (Shapiro, 1958, p. 344). The psychological and mental characteristics of races are a matter of academic dispute. While differences have been observed and measured, scientists differ as to the influence of heredity and of cultural and socioeconomic environment.

When the term "race" is used in its social context, particularly in describing or expressing racial antagonism, the concept is seldom defined in any biologically consistent way. Physically similar individuals or groups may be classified and treated differently in different countries or regions. A person who is "Black" in the United States might well be a "Mestizo" in Mexico and a "Crioulo" in Brazil.

Popular usage of the term "race" is an expression of the need felt by most human beings to identify themselves with groups more specific than *Homo sapiens*. In ordinary social intercourse the immediate need is not for an objective classification but rather for a subjective one to perform the social function of setting "us" apart from "them."

B. The Dimensions of Racial Discrimination

No form of social stratification arouses more emotion than that involving groups defined (rightly or wrongly) as racial. In today's intellectual climate, discrimination perceived as racial evokes instant condemnation far more intense than that aroused by discriminatory practices based on language, religion, ethnicity, nationality, or sex.

It is tempting to speculate why this should be so. Why do so many people become livid when they read or hear of a black in South Africa being refused accommodation in a white hotel, or a Negro being denied apprenticeship to a trade in America, or a West Indian being refused an apartment in England, when they take little notice of the death of more than a million people in the Third World every year from starvation or malnutrition, and continue their breakfasts undisturbed when their morning papers tell about mass killings in Bangladesh, Iraq, Nigeria, Uganda, Ethiopia, Rwanda and Burundi; the expulsion of Asians; or the refusal of exit visas to Jews? In these

latter cases religion and ethnicity—and not race—are the integrators and differentiators of the groups concerned.

If mortality statistics since World War II are compared, it is seen that those who have lost their lives in so-called racial conflicts are only a small fraction of the number killed in clashes between disparate ethnic, national, linguistic, and religious groups. And the number slain in black–white confrontations is an even smaller fraction. If the number of racial victims in the United States, the United Kingdom, and South Africa since 1960 are added together, including the Sharpeville massacre and the riots following the murder of Dr. Martin Luther King, Jr., the total is hardly more than 500. These losses are to be compared with the tens and hundreds of thousands of deaths in the genocides mentioned in the previous chapter; national struggles such as those of the Kurds, Eritreans, and Lebanese; and more recently the forced evacuation of the entire urban population of Cambodia. Chairman Leo Cherne of Freedom House, in urging an investigation, pointed out that the Cambodian operation could hardly have been accomplished without hundreds of thousands of casualties, seeing that hospital patients were forced to rise from their beds and walk, and those who could not move thrown out the windows, while operations in progress were stopped at gunpoint and the patients left to die on the tables (Cherne, 1975, *passim*.).

All this leaves us with the question: Why are opinion leaders and the media in many countries hypersensitive about *racial* discrimination and yet indifferent to atrocities committed for ideological, religious, or nationalist reasons? Is it a genuine concern—or the result of manipulative propaganda? And—since protest is always against noncommunist Western countries (the massacres of blacks in the Sudan being a typical case of *un*concern)—what political forces might benefit from such manipulation?

1. RACIAL MINORITIES AND RACIAL DISCRIMINATION

In chapter 8, it was pointed out that in all societies the competition for scarce goods, tangible and intangible, leads to an unequal distribution of power, status, rewards, and opportunities. The result is a hierarchical system of group differentiation, i.e. a stratification or ranking system in which various groups are unequally positioned. In chapter 9 it was noted that the so-called racial problem is today studied chiefly in the context of *racial minorities*, i.e. those groups whose inferior status is socially defined in terms of biological descent, with visible physical (somatic) characteristics serving as the main signals for assignment to groups and differential status ascription. Racial differences, however, are not limited to the physical; they may include lifestyle, level of socioeconomic development, national or ethnic identity, or language, *provided* these nonsomatic differences are defined, justified, and rationalized chiefly as results of biological descent. Racial discrimination encompasses the disqualifications, disabilities, taboos, restrictions, and deprivations which reflect the minority group's lower socioeconomic status and which are justified by the dominant group as rational responses to biogenetic differences.

2. SOMATIC IMAGES AND DISCRIMINATION

It need hardly be argued that each individual's physical appearance (somatic image) is an integral part of her or his personality and unique human identity. Even without the reinforcement provided by advertising, physical appearance would play a major role in the choice of sex and marriage partners. One's physical appearance can never be entirely divorced from one's social life; in fact, throughout life the somatic image will have a *social significance*, tending to shape social relationships. When an ethnic group has a relatively long history of inbreeding (biological isolation), physical characteristics (for instance, the high cheek bones of Slavs) may become an integral component of its total identity.

While not all members of a racial or ethnic group look alike, it can be empirically verified that members of most groups accept certain physical characteristics as typical, despite physical variation within the group itself. Despite the great variation within the Caucasoid (Europid) macrogroup, for instance, there is a somatic image that enables instant (and with few exceptions correct) identification of that group's members and nonmembers. Subgroups, such as the Nordics of Scandinavia, the Dravidians of India, and the Berbers of Northern Africa, also have their somatic images, conceptualized by members of the groups as well as outsiders. But here caution is in order: the blonde "Swedish" maiden may turn out to be Italian and a person who looks "Chinese" may be a Thai or a Filipino. In most cases, identification is aided by cultural norms, expressed in language, manners, or costume—Thais and Vietnamese, for instance, can be distinguished by their hats. Many groups, however, can be identified in terms of somatic norms alone, despite widely varying physical traits.

To summarize: the average member of each historically established biocultural group carries a mental image, in terms of which he visualizes and defines the physical appearance of his group. This somatic typology is an integral part of the group's subjective identity, and as such plays an important role in separating in- and out-groups.

Racial differences are commonly symbolized in terms of skin color. Major color types that serve as indices of biocultural affiliation include the "white" of the Europeans and their transoceanic descendants, the "yellows" and "browns" of the Mongoloids (including Chinese, Malays, and American Indians), and the "black" of Congoid and Australoid peoples. Yet within each group there is a wide range of pigmentation, and these ranges overlap. There are "white" Americans and South Africans who are darker than some of their "colored" compatriots. Where there is a discrepancy between skin color and facial features, the latter are usually controlling; an albino Negro is recognized as "black," whereas very dark Mediterranean types are still "white."

Harmannus Hoetink, a prominent Dutch sociologist, describes the way in which somatic traits, especially skin color, are *socially defined* as a norm of biocultural affiliation:

I suggest the term "somatic norm image," which I would define as follows: the complex of physical (somatic) characteristics which are accepted by a group as its norm and ideal. Norm, because it is used to measure aesthetic appreciation; ideal, because usually no individual ever in fact embodies the somatic norm image of his group.

It is clear that this somatic norm image is a sociopsychological concept. It belongs to the *spiritual* heritage of the group, and is comparable with such concepts as that of a norm of behavior. . . . In the same way the somatic norm image is the yardstick of aesthetic evaluation and ideal of the somatic characteristics of the members of the group. . . .

It is only continued social contact between groups with different somatic norm images which results in consciousness of a group's own, socially determined somatic norm image. This is why I consider that the process whereby the individual becomes aware of his somatic norm image can be studied most successfully (perhaps even exclusively) in a segmented society.

The individual's consciousness of the somatic norm image is a social property; it is, like any other group property, transmitted to the young individual in the course of socialization, it is "taught" by the group. (1967, pp. 120–22)

The largest measure of somatic distance is found between the Caucasoids of European origin and the Congoids or Negrids. Where aesthetic standards are based on racial somatic images, which is the case throughout Europe, North America, and European settlements, persons not conforming, to some degree at least, to the somatic norm image of the racial majority may suffer devastating psychological wounds.

3. DISCRIMINATION IN ISLAMIC CULTURE

Racial differentiation was long prevalent in the Middle East. Mural drawings in old Egyptian tombs show clear distinctions between the red-faced Egyptians and those of other hues: "whites" to the north, "yellow" people to the east and "blacks" to the south (Rose, 1968, p. 12). Physical traits such as skin color were treated not only as indexes of descent and group membership but also as marks or symbols of inferiority, backwardness, or ugliness and repulsiveness.

Bernard Lewis, who has made a thorough study of the social significance of race (biological descent) and color in the world of Islam, concludes that the supposed absence of color prejudice and discrimination in the Muslim world is a myth. He points out, *inter alia*, that the *Arabian Nights* shows blacks almost invariably in menial roles: slaves, bath attendants, household servants, and the like. "Perhaps even more revealing in its way is the story of the good black slave who lived a life of virtue and piety, for which he was rewarded by turning white at the moment of his death" (1971, p. 5). Early pre-Islamic poetry and historical records contain many verses suggesting contempt and hatred for persons of (black) African origin. Lewis tells of a meeting between a black-skinned Arab leader (Ubāda) and a Christian functionary during the Arab conquest of Egypt. On seeing the black Ubāda the Christian said: "Get this black man away from me and bring another to talk to me." When the Arabs insisted that the Ubāda was the wisest and noblest among them, the Christian asked: "How can you be content that a black man should be foremost among you? It is more fitting that he should be below you." In one poem (660 A.D.) a black slave poet unburdens himself as follows: "If my color were pink, women would love me; but the Lord hath marred me with blackness." The famous black poet Nusyab remarked to Umayyad Caliph Abd Al-Malik: "My color is pitch-black, my hair is wooly, my appearance repulsive." In 750 A.D. the black poet Daub Ibn Salm and an Arab were arrested and brought before a judge in Mecca on a charge of flaunting luxurious clothes. According to the chronicler the Arab was released; the black was flogged. "The judge said: 'I can stand this from Ibn Ja'far, but should I stand it from you? Because of your base origin or your ugly face? Flog him, boy'— and he flogged him" (ibid., pp. 10, 11, and 14).

The following story from the early eighth century reveals the social distance obtaining between Arabs and black Africans in the sphere of intimate personal relations. The famous singer Said Ibn Misjah, invited to accompany a number of Arabs to a singing girl's house, offered to withdraw when lunch was served, saying: "I am a black man. Some of you may find me offensive. I shall therefore sit and eat apart." They were embarrassed but arranged for him to take his food (and later his wine) separately (ibid.). As the Muslims expanded their sphere of control in Africa, the growing frequency of personal contact between Arabs and blacks led to a corresponding increase in Arab racism. Several historical narratives point to the fact that black Africans were regarded as people destined by their very nature to be slaves.

The following pronouncement of Ibn Al-Faqih (902–903 A.D.) is typical of anti-black prejudice in classical Muslim Arab society. Of his own people he says: "Nor are they overdone in the womb until they are burnt, so that the child comes out something between black and murky, malodorous, stinking, wooly-haired, with uneven limbs, deficient mind and depraved passions, such as the Zanj, the Ethiopians, and other Blacks who resemble them" (ibid., p. 34). The Arab writer Ma'sūdi (956 A.D.) comments on blacks in general, quoting Galen who "mentions ten specific attributes of the Black man which are all found in him and in no other: frizzy hair, thin eyebrows, broad nostrils, thick lips, pointed teeth, smelly skin, black eyes, furrowed hands and feet, a long

penis and great merriment. Galen says that merriment dominates the Black man because of his defective brain, whence also the weakness of his intelligence" (ibid.). Similar scriptures are found in ancient Persian treatises, which describe blacks as naked and as animals except for their manner of walking.

The prevalent Islamic view that blacks are born to slavery was expressed by Ibn Khaldūn in the fourteenth century: "The only people who accept slavery are the Negroes . . . owing to their low degree of humanity and their proximity to the animal stage." A strong race bias minimized intermarriage between Muslim Arabs and black Africans. It is even said that the Prophet forbade intermarriage with blacks with the words: "Do not bring black into your pedigree." According to Lewis, "to the present day, in North Africa, a man with Negroid features, even of the highest social status, is described contemptuously as Ould Khadem, 'the son of a slave-woman' " (ibid.).

4. THE SYMBOLISM OF COLOR

In many cultures white and black have positive or negative connotations—some ancient, some recent—when used to symbolize people, actions, and values. Harold Isaacs points out that these contextual references to black and white are deeply implanted in the Bible, in the language of Milton and Shakespeare, and "indeed are laced into almost every entwining strand of the arts and literature in which our history is clothed" (1972a, pp. 12–15). Black, he notes, is used in a negative sense throughout, denoting sin, ignorance, wickedness and evil. "My skin is black upon me," cries Job, bemoaning his sufferings (Job 30:30). White, in contrast, indicated virginity, purity, virtue, and beauty. The lack of adequate scientific explanation of differences in skin pigmentation led to resurrection of the myth of Ham. To punish Ham, commented a scholar more than 400 years ago, God willed that "a sonne should bee born whose name was Chus, who note onely it selfe, but all his posteritie after him should bee so blacke and lothsome, that it might remain a spectacle of disobedience to all the worlde. And of this blacke and cursed Chus came all these blacke Moores which are in Africa" (Kovel, 1971, p. 64).

Melvin Tumin makes a most important point:

> The student must also take into account the way in which certain superficial physical differences such as skin color are used as hooks on which to hang cultural distinctions and differentiations. That is where and how skin color becomes relevant: as a trait to which other traits are ascribed, or from which it is assumed other traits may be inferred. The belief is that knowledge of a man's skin color implies something as well about his native intelligence, musical capacity, capacity for passion and love, or some such thing. These beliefs are either indisputably false or undemonstrable by any evidence. But they are believed in—and that is what gives them their power. For men act on what they believe to be real, often regardless of any scientific evidence to the contrary. (in *ibid.*, pp. 6–7)

Wagatsuma writes that long before any sustained contact with either Caucasoid Europeans or dark-skinned Africans, the Japanese, for instance, valued a "white" skin as beautiful and deprecated a "black" skin as ugly. "During the Nara period (710–793), court ladies made ample use of cosmetics and liberally applied white powder to the face. . . . The whiteness of an untanned skin was the symbol of . . . privileged class which was spared any form of outdoor labor." Wagatsuma mentions that for many Japanese in the United States the white skin of the Caucasian women symbolizes the biosocial gap between the Western and Oriental worlds. One Japanese expressed himself this way: "Sometimes I feel that the white skin of the Caucasians tells me that, after all, I am an Oriental and cannot acquire everything Western, however Westernized I might be. It is like the last border I cannot go across, and it is symbolized by the white skin" (1967, p. 133). In sharp contrast to their feelings

about whiteness, Japanese generally react negatively to Negroid features, particularly the black skin. Their "basic feelings are repulsion and disgust towards Negro features"; and these feelings are often justified as a "physiological reaction, which one's reasoning cannot control." (*ibid.*, p. 137).

Nor can there be any doubt that in India a light skin color enjoys a higher social status than a dark skin. Many northern Indians have a vague prejudice against their darker southern compatriots. Members of the higher castes are generally also fairer-skinned than the untouchable outcasts. In the upper castes a dark-skinned girl will find her complexion a handicap in the marriage market, while a fair skin will boost a girl's bargaining power (Béteille, 1969, p. 42). Air India was accused of favoring light-skinned hostesses in a parliamentary discussion in March 1975. Even the Anglo-Indians, despite their *ethnically* insecure status, value their relatively fair complexions. In the words of an Indian interviewee, "the fairer ones proudly proclaim themselves to be of British origin, whereas the darker ones reluctantly admit that they are Indians" (Gist and Wright, 1973, p. 41).

Among the so-called "Indian Jews" in Cochin and Bombay a lighter skin color generally bestows greater social bargaining power than a dark complexion. In 1687 visiting Dutch Jews from Amsterdam found that the Cochin Jews were divided into higher and lower *jatis* (endogamous subcastes): the White Jews and the Black Jews. The Black Jews resemble the Indian population of the region, whereas the White Jews claim to be "original and genuine" Jews and maintain that the Black Jews are merely the descendants of their converted slaves (Strizower, 1971, p. 5). Like the Cochin Jews, but quite independently of them, the Bombay Jews (Bene Israel) were separated into two *jatis*, the higher called the Gora ("fair ones"), and the lower Kala ("dark ones"). According to Mandelbaum, "they too did not interdine or intermarry, though they did worship in the same synagogues. Those of the higher *jati* claimed purer Jewish ancestry; the lower, they alleged, were of mixed origin." (1972, Volume 2, p. 563.)

C. *Psychological Aspects of Discrimination*

1. THE FACTOR OF VISIBILITY

For several years the Social Psychiatry Center of the École Pratique des Hautes Études in France has been studying the pathology of minority acculturation. The researchers were struck by the importance of skin color for both failure and success in the adaptive responses of out-groups (Raveau, 1975, p. 353). Black migrant workers throughout Europe soon become aware of their high physical visibility, and find particularly that it (their skin color in particular) also makes them socially visible and pegs them at a low social level. The discrimination experienced by the four million Rom (Gypsies) of Europe, most of them in the eastern half, has its roots in clashing lifestyles, but their darker skin serves as one of the signals by which they are identified. In an article in *Soviet Studies*, Otto Ulč (1969) describes discriminatory patterns comparable to those in Western countries. A gypsy orphan, for instance, would not readily find adoptive parents; interracial marriages are rare; parents reject integrated education, forbid their children to fraternize with Romany children and petition school principals to introduce segregated classes. Further on, Ulč describes a "backlash" similar to that sometimes observed against blacks in the United States. "The danger of racial pollution of a white neighborhood is prone to turn a Czech liberal into an unqualified bigot" (1969, p. 141).

As for color prejudice in the United States, enough has been said in other chapters. Mention may be made, however, of the so-called "doll tests" conducted thirty years ago by two black sociologists, Kenneth and Mamie Clark. The Clarks presented black children with four dolls, which were identical in all respects save the color of their skin—two were white and two brown. More children rejected the brown and preferred the white doll. This test showed that even at a very early stage of their lives black children were being socialized by the white-dominated culture to accept, among other things, the negative significance of their own skin color.

2. PREJUDICE AS INFLUENCED BY RELATIVE SIZE OF GROUPS

Nonwhites account for less than 3 percent of the population in the United Kingdom. Yet where nonwhite immigrants have concentrated, color prejudice has arisen. In most European-Caucasoid communities there is a "tipping point," at which the proportion of "outsiders"—especially outsiders who are physically visible—reaches a level where parents see a threat to their children and their lifestyle. A survey carried out by PEP (1966–67) showed that physically nonidentifiable outsiders experience far less discrimination than colored outsiders. Asians with Caucasoid or Mongoloid features and skins varying between white and brown face far less opprobrium than the unmistakably Negroid West Indians (see Banton, 1972, pp. 96–97). Addressing himself to white Britons, Michael Banton writes:

If they ask what difference the prejudice of White English people would make to their personal lives if their skin turned brown, they may like to reflect on the case of a Welshman, an ex-commando and former Services boxing champion living in a Dorset town. He suffered from a kidney disease which meant that he had to seek lighter work. The disease also darkened his skin so that he was mistaken for a coloured man. As a result, he has experienced colour prejudice. "It is not as if it happened just once. It might happen ten times a week. I have known it to happen three times a day. Sometimes I have been stopped in the street by a stranger, who says something like: 'You bloody wog, why don't you go back to the palm trees?' " (1972, pp. 97–98)

A factor aggravating race prejudice in the United Kingdom is the higher birth rate among blacks. In Cardiff, a typical center of nonwhite concentration, Bloom found that more than 25 percent of coloreds who had lived in the UK more than 20 years wished they had been born white—"And why not? You get a better deal in this world if you are white" (1971, pp. 103–4). A 1967 *Sunday Times* poll revealed that only 1 percent of the respondents thought there was no color discrimination in Britain.

3. THE EXPERIENCE OF DISCRIMINATION

Freeman and his co-researchers have found that Negro college students tend to conform to the traditional social stratification based on color gradations within the black American community (1966, pp. 86–87). Skin color often influences the selection of a marriage partner. Freeman's team concludes:

Certainly, from the data presented here, it is difficult to reach any other conclusion than that skin color is at least a concomitant, if not a determinant, of social status in terms of prestige attributes typically employed within the larger American society. . . . In both groups (white collar and blue collar), with occupation controlled, middle class self-identification is correlated with having light skin. Thus, the data rather clearly indicates that skin color is a status variable, or at least a correlate of more general status variables, among this study group. . . . the husband's skin color, like his occupation, represents a status characteristic by which he and his family are judged. In the same sense in which skin color is a predictor of choice of a marital partner, it also serves as a screening variable with respect to current status position. (1966, pp. 92, 97 and 100).

Equally, it is highly unlikely that St. Clair Drake exaggerates when he writes:

Both Negroes and Whites are "victims" of one persisting legacy of the slave trade—the derogation of "negroidness." The idea that a dark skin indicated

intellectual inferiority is rapidly passing, but at the esthetic level derogatory appraisal of thick lips, kinky hair, and very dark skin is still prevalent. That many Negroes reject their own body image is evident from advertisements for skin lighteners in the major Negro publications, and Negro children in experimental situations begin to reject brown dolls for white ones before the age of five. The ever present knowledge that one's negroid physiognomy is evaluated as "ugly" lowers self-esteem and, therefore, weakens self-confidence. The rise of the new African states has given a psychological "lift" to those American Negroes who still look more African than *métis*, but extreme Negro physical traits are still a source of inner disquiet—especially for women. (There is no equivalent in America of the African cult of *négritude* whose poets idealize the black woman.) These negative esthetic appraisals are part of a larger stereotype-complex which equates Africa with primitiveness and savagery and considers Negro ancestry a "taint." (1971, p. 45)

The self-deprecation felt by American blacks as a result of external definition of their group, and their anger at their own craving for whiteness, are well expressed by Eldridge Cleaver in his autobiographical *Soul on Ice* (1968). The following passages are taken from his account of his experiences in Folsom prison (1966):

One afternoon, when a large group of Negroes was on the prison yard shooting the breeze, I grabbed the floor and posed the question: which did they prefer, white women or black? Some said Japanese women were their favorite, others said Chinese, some said European women, others said Mexican women—they all stated a preference, and they generally freely . admitted their dislike for black women.

"I don't want nothing black but a Cadillac," said one.

"If money was black I wouldn't want none of it," put in another. . . .

From our discussion, which began that evening and has never yet ended, we went on to notice how thoroughly, as a matter of course, a black growing up in America is indoctrinated with the white race's standard of beauty. Not that the whites made a conscious, calculated effort to do this, we thought, but since they constituted the majority the whites brainwashed the blacks by the very processes the whites employed to indoctrinate themselves with their own group standards. It intensified my frustrations to know that I was indoctrinated to see the white woman as more beautiful and desirable than my own black woman.

Cleaver tells how he was aroused by the killing in Mississippi of a young Chicago Black, Emmett Till, allegedly for flirting with a white woman. Cleaver found the woman's picture in the paper sexually stimulating. *"I was disgusted and angry with myself. . . . I flew into a rage at myself, at America, at white women, at the history that had placed those tensions of lust and desire in my chest."* The conflict so unhinged Cleaver that he was "treated" by a psychiatrist who told him he hated his mother. "At the moment I walked out of the prison gate," Cleaver tells, "my feelings toward white women in general could be summed up in the following lines:

TO A WHITE GIRL

I love you
Because you're white,
Not because you're charming
Or bright.
Your whiteness
Is a silky thread
Snaking through my thoughts
In redhot patterns
Of lust and desire.
I hate you
Because you're white.
Your white meat
Is nightmare food.
White is
The skin of Evil.
You're my Moby Dick,
White Witch,
Symbol of the rope and hanging tree,
Of the burning cross.

Loving you thus
And hating you so,
My heart is torn in two.
Crucified.

Cleaver embarked on a career of rape, conceiving that crime as an insurrectionary act, defying and trampling on the White man's law. He took to heart LeRoi Jones' poem urging antiwhite violence and "I know that if I had not been apprehended I would have slit some white throats."

Again in prison, Cleaver admitted he was wrong, that he "had gone astray—astray not so much from the white man's law as from being human, civilized—for I could not approve the act of rape. . . . I lost my self-respect. My pride as a man dissolved and my whole fragile moral structure seemed to collapse, completely shattered." He then had to work his way through a traumatic identity crisis.

I had to find out who I am and what I want to be, what type of man I should be, and what I could do to become the best of which I was capable. I understood that what had happened to me had also happened to countless other blacks and it would happen to many, many more.

Negroes are adamant that no white person can ever really fathom a black person's social experience of rejection and alienation.

"Passing," or joining a socially preferred group, is a form of upward mobility found in all stratified societies. In South America, where several gradations of skin color between the polar black and white serve as criteria for corresponding status levels, passing is far easier than in countries where the basic dividing line is drawn between all whites and all (known) nonwhites. The less visible a complex of inherited traits, the less it will block passing. Buraku outcasts in Japan with high socioeconomic and educational credentials find it far easier to pass as middle-class Japanese than do the offspring of Japanese women and black U.S. servicemen, mainly because the latter out-group is physically visible while the Burakumin are not.

D. Racism and Color Prejudice in the Guise of Class Differentiation

Segregation of castes and races is justified and rationalized by socially defined differences in biological descent, with social status fixed ascriptively at birth. In a class system, on the other hand, status depends on income, occupation, and lifestyle—qualities that a person has some possibilities of changing. Hence a class system is more flexible. Whereas class differentiation is based chiefly on economic and social criteria, cultural minority status is determined mainly by such factors as ethnicity, historicity, language, and religion. These are characteristics which the individual may acquire, learn, or discard. Ranking systems structured in terms of class and cultural criteria thus generally show greater intergroup mobility than ranking systems based on caste and race.

It is only natural that citizens of a country with a history of discrimination will attempt to justify, explain, or rationalize it in order to minimize disapproval. A study of UN debates about discrimination shows that *class discrimination*, if not approved, is the *least disapproved*. It is followed by *cultural discrimination* (based on ethnicity, lifestyle, nationality, historicity, language, or religion); *caste discrimination* (often disguised as simply a more extreme form of class differentiation); and, finally, *racial discrimination* (especially white–black), which is the most abhorred. In view of this "rating system," it is obvious that a dominant group accused of racial discrimination will attempt to minimize the censure of the world community by claiming that the discrimination is based on *class* or *culture*.

Caste remains an unpopular disguise or euphemism because of its universal association with untouchability and deprivation, and because its central feature of descent necessarily has a "racial" component. In the Bengali language the concept of *jati* not only signifies

caste, "but also comes closer to the meaning of 'race' than perhaps any other word in popular usage" (Beteille, 1969, p. 454).

Because of the opprobrium attached to racial discrimination, politicians, business people, and civic leaders of white-dominated national societies will often concede that their organizations and social groups condone and participate in what appears to be race discrimination based on color prejudice but which is actually class differentiation: rejection of lower class lifestyles. In the United States, in particular, it is argued that the deprivation of many blacks is no different from that experienced by white ethnic groups who have found themselves in the lower socioeconomic stratum—and have for the most part managed to rise above it. In many cases, however, investigation will show that race rather than class is the actual differentiator.

The problem in the United States, and perhaps elsewhere, is complicated by the fact that many blacks, especially recent migrants from the South and their children, do belong to the lower class (as defined in chapter 7), and indulge in a lifestyle that is anathema to the next higher group, the working class. Banfield explains the relation between race and class differences in these terms:

Much of what appears (especially to Negroes) as race prejudice is really *class* prejudice or, at any rate, class antipathy. Similarly, much of what appears (especially to Whites) as "Negro" behavior is really lower-class behavior. The lower class is relatively large among Negroes; it appears even larger than it is to those whites who fail to distinguish a Negro who exhibits outward signs—lack of skill, low income, slum housing, and so on—which in a white would mark him as lower class, from one whose culture is working, middle, or even upper class but whose opportunities have been limited by discrimination and whose income is low (1974, p. 87).

For many whites, blackness is a visible signal of lower-class personality. Cultural distance and lack of personal contact makes it difficult for whites to classify blacks by socioeconomic level; the problem is compounded when blacks affect distinctive clothing, speech, and manners that cut across class lines. Insofar as housing is concerned, the rent and purchase subsidies granted by the Department of Housing and Urban Development (HUD) tend to project lower-class people into working- and middle-class neighborhoods. In many cases they lack the resources or the interest to keep up the property in which they are installed. White homeowners, therefore, often feel that their investment can best be safeguarded by keeping blacks out of their neighborhoods altogether as long as it can be managed. A typical attitude is: "I don't mind well-bred Negroes, but if they move in, undesirable types are likely to follow."

Unlike European immigrants of various ethnic, national, and religious backgrounds, the children of black, Indian, Mexican, and Oriental Americans cannot assimilate with the supposed "mainstream" by adopting "nonethnic" names, consumption patterns, and manners. Thousands of black families who have attained levels of socioeconomic sophistication comparable with those of middle-class whites, have remained within predominantly black neighborhoods. "White flight" seems to indicate that socioeconomic class is not the great leveler in white–black relations that it is among the various white ethnic groups. Nathan Kantrowitz's research in the New York metropolitan area has confirmed the truism that money does not necessarily decrease segregation. "If . . . one begins by calculating the segregation levels between poor Blacks and poor Whites and then goes on to calculate segregation levels between rich Blacks and rich Whites, one finds that segregation levels remain high in both cases. Thus, increasing incomes for Blacks, whatever its other benefits, does not lead to the integration of wealthier Blacks and Whites" (1973, p. 35).

According to Karl and Alma Taeuber: In recent decades, Negroes have been much more successful in securing improvements in eco-nomic status than in obtaining housing on a less segregated basis. Continued economic gains by Negroes are not likely to alter substantially the prevalent patterns of residential segregation (in Wilson, 1973, p. 143).

Robert Blauner points out:

There is still much in the northern ghettos today that resembles the life conditions of the ethnic immigrants. All this is true and it might shatter my argument except for one fact. A continuing racist theme, with powerful social structural consequences, has served to consolidate rather than to erase the distinctive experience of the past. There is no other lower class group in America's pluralistic society that has met in the past or meets in the present the systematic barriers of categorical exclusion, blockage, and discrimination based on race and colour. This has been such an omnipresent reality for Afro-Americans that just as the way in which black individuals have confronted the patterns of exclusion and denigration are central themes of their personal biographies, so the direct and indirect struggle against racism is the core of the history of the Negro group in this country. (1972, p. 588)

In his analysis of occupational mobility among Negro men, Otis Duncan concludes that certain facets of white–black occupational discrepancy can be explained only in terms of racial discrimination.

Although it is not as yet possible to assemble all the components into a single quantitative representation of the stratification process, it is virtually certain that the entire configuration of family background factors, educational levels and occupation achievement is insufficient to account for differences between Negroes and non-Negroes in earnings and family income. There is a residual effect for "race," whether it can legitimately be taken to be a measure of "discrimination" in some strict sense of the term or not. (Duncan, 1972, p. 235)

Other countries dominated by Europids or Caucasoids also contain blacks who are concentrated in the lower socioeconomic strata, and whose race is evidently a factor that tends to keep them there. In South Africa, Australia, New Zealand, Canada, and the Common Market (EEC) countries, the situation resembles that in the United States: all other things being equal, members of outsider groups socially defined as "nonwhites" are exposed to more prolonged and more severe deprivation than Whites in comparable socioeconomic class positions. In Britain, the PEP survey already mentioned showed that better qualified nonwhite immigrants suffered more discrimination than unskilled nonwhites. "As [nonwhite] immigrants and their children acquire better qualifications and higher expectations, they may experience not greater acceptance, but more rebuffs" (Banton, 1972, p. 72). The PEP report (1968) concluded that "the experiences of White immigrants, such as Hungarians and Cypriots, compared with Black or Brown immigrants, such as West Indians and Asians, leave no doubt that the major component in the discrimination is color" (Bloom, 1971, p. 110).

The research of Leonard Bloom in Bute Town, Cardiff, Wales, revealed that whereas Greek and Italian immigrants were scattered throughout the city, the colored immigrants were concentrated in what was virtually an enclave. By 1970 not a single colored inhabitant of Bute Town had reached a university. The Greek and Italian immigrants find employment easily; for the coloreds there are but a few jobs outside the dockland area of Cardiff. "The colored people have to face so complicated a pattern of rejection and acceptance that they have little basis on which to make a rational prediction about their future" (Field and Haiken, 1971, p. 100).

As distinguished from the Irish migrant worker in Britain, the colored person remains a "nonbelonger." Hugh Tinker, Director of the Institute of Race Relations, London, has remarked: "We have the paradox that a child born in England of parents who come from the Caribbean or South Asia will still be referred to as an 'immigrant' " (Tinker, 1972, p. 66).

E. Racism and Color Prejudice in South America and the Caribbean

In all South American and Caribbean countries, with a few exceptions such as black-ruled Guyana, social stratification is based on conformity with a Europid-Caucasoid somatic norm image. The association of class and race is so close that class differences are often indicated in racial terms. Today, as three centuries ago, the upper classes and ruling elites are predominantly white and the lower classes predominantly black. It is still considered a social step downward to marry someone much darker than oneself.

In a typical Latin-American society the class system will be polarized between persons obviously rich, influential, educated, West European in lifestyle and white at one extreme, and persons obviously economically deprived, poorly educated (if at all), socially backward, powerless and black at the other. The *Jornal da Bahia* (August 1–2, 1971) concedes that racism is indeed a factor in the Brazilian class system, as reflected in expressions such as "He is black but intelligent," "A black man with a white soul," etc. As in the United States and Western Europe, blacks in most Latin-American countries cannot fail to notice the speed with which white immigrants move to the higher classes and the ease with which they acquire the material symbols of success and wealth (see Dzidzienyo, 1972, p. 181). Nor does it take a great deal of perception on the part of a so-called "pure" or polar black to notice that lower class mestizos without Negroid features are not exposed to the same prejudice and discrimination as "pure" blacks in comparable socioeconomic positions. They also notice that lower class mulattoes (persons of Caucasian-Negro descent with some visible Negroid somatic features) occupy an intermediate level on the socioeconomic ladder. As Dzidzienyo points out (1972, p. 169), even the attainment of professional rank and economic status by a black does not bring him the social acceptance enjoyed by white and light-skinned people at the same economic level.

1. PATTERNS OF RACIAL STRATIFICATION

South American and Caribbean countries, however, do not exhibit a single color barrier dividing all the whites from all the nonwhites, but a number of color gradations between the poles of black and white—each with its own status rating. This continuum makes possible a process of racial upgrading ("passing") which is difficult or impossible in a simple two-category racial system. Individuals with clearly Negroid features, however, are left on the lowest rung of the status ladder.

The social distance between the contiguous racial shadings is also smaller than that between polar white and black. Color alone does not prevent a Negro, for instance, from rising to the next rung of the status ladder by personal achievement. Similarly, a mulatto or mestizo, trading on a combination of wealth and Caucasoid features, can buy "white" status through worldly success. Indians accultured to white lifestyles are usually defined as mestizo or mixed blood. For individuals with highly visible Negroid features, however, the chances for upward social mobility remain minimal— no matter what the individual achievement. According to Hoetink:

While there is no need to dispute the fact of serious discrimination against the darkest strata in virtually all Afro-Latin societies, it does make a difference, both for the self-perception and the image of the future of the groups involved, that in these countries there does exist an inclusionist ideology of interracial mixing and that it *can* legitimately exist because there is indeed a socio-racial continuum. That in such an ideology emphasis is placed on the "whitening" of the population is virtually unavoidable in a multiracial society where a racist ingredient in the mechanisms of social selection operates by definition. (1974, p. 40)

That the practice of status promotion across a color spectrum reduces the conflict potential in race relations is reflected in the absence of racial clashes such as occurred in the United States in the mid-1960s. There is, however, a dividing line in countries such as Brazil between whites and "people of color," with mulattoes gravitating to one category or the other (Dzidzienyo, 1962, p. 167).

As shown typically by Georg Maier (1975) in the case of Peru, race and class remain intimately linked in many Latin-American countries. Indians and Blacks are still distinguished socially by their appearance, even though they were assimilated centuries ago into the national societies of Latin America and form the numerical majority in many countries. Clothing, speech, and culture are losing force as status indicators in the context of expanding cities, but color is becoming even more crucial (Pitt-Rivers, 1969, pp. 386–87). As both social mobility and class consciousness increase, so does color consciousness, because of the close linkage of color and class (See Hoetink, 1967, p. 36). It is thus understandable why blacks and darker coloreds endeavor to marry "upward" in the color hierarchy. Most countries of the continent "would bleach themselves snow white if they could, no matter how much they speak out against United States racism" (Rivera, 1971, p. 159). At the top of the social ladder, the white *criollos* are extremely sensitive about their class position and extremely jealous of their white lineage.

The social significance of the color spectrum is reflected in the two dominant languages of South America, Spanish and Portuguese. Hoetink (1967, pp. 166f.) lists the following terms:

Portuguese (State of Bahia, Brazil)

CABRA: Slightly lighter in skin color than the "pure" Negro, with somewhat longer, although frizzy, hair and somewhat less Negroid nose and lips

CABO-VERDE: Very dark-skinned but with long straight hair and European facial features

ESCURO: Dark, with European features

MULATO ESCURO and MULATO CLARO: Dark-colored and light-colored, with clearly "hybrid" facial features

PARDO: Used sometimes for a very light *mulato claro*

SARARA: Albino-like, with frizzy or very curly hair

MORENO: Light brown, with long, black but not necessarily straight hair

Because of the endless varieties of hybridization, not every colored individual can be placed in a category without further qualification. An individual can, for instance, be described as a *moreno*, but with *cabelo ruim*, "bad" hair.

Spanish

TRIGUENO
MORENO
MORENO CLARO : Very light-colored individuals with frizzy, "bad" hair
GRIFO
PARDO

JABAO (Puerto Rico): One who has a "white" skin but "bad" fair hair, and Negroid facial features

The number of distinctions between types of hair is legion: hair which is "bad" (*pelo malo*), i.e. very frizzy and therefore short, is *pasu, pimienta, colchon,* or *jonjo;* while hair which is long but nevertheless frizzy is *pasa;* "half"-bad hair is *media-pasa.*

2. BRAZIL: SLIDING-SCALE DISCRIMINATION

Brazilians make much of the fact that their country is free from color prejudice based on racial origin, such as exists in the United States. But as Dzidzienyo points out (1972, p. 168) Brazilians exhibit equal prejudice against people who look black, and in any case origin and appearance cannot meaningfully be separated.

Brazilian color prejudice is clearly revealed in the low status rating of the *mulata* (female of

white-black parentage). "The term *mulata* is now used so loosely that it means any non-white woman who is relatively dark; it is even used to describe a near-black woman and is a polite way of avoiding the term 'Black' (prêta or negra), which is considered uncomplimentary" (*ibid.*, p. 171). Dzidzienyo provides the following case history:

In 1960 when a "people of color" club in Rio de Janeiro decided to enter a girl for the "Miss Rio de Janeiro" contest—the winner of which competes in the "Miss Brazil" contest—some other clubs threatened to withdraw from the competition. They seemed to fear that if a *Mulata* were allowed to enter the contest that year, then before long really black girls might compete as well. It is clear from this that while *Mulatas* may be considered suitable as dancers during carnival time, they are not thought to be proper representatives of Brazilian beauty. (*Ibid.*)

The expression *boa aparência* (good appearance) often crops up in advertisements for employees whose positions and activities involve contact with the public, particularly with upper class Brazilians. This expression is code, meaning that applicants are more likely to be successful if white or, to put it negatively, not too dark.

Superficially, Brazil follows a liberal racial policy. But an increase in the number of blacks with moderately high educational qualifications has led to increased dislike for blacks. The official Brazilian ideology of non-discrimination, by camouflaging rather than reflecting reality, achieves without tension the same results as do overtly racist policies (*ibid.*, p. 178). The greater tolerance of whites for Indians, and the consequent greater upward mobility of the latter, are all too obvious to the blacks. Roger Bastide found that 93 percent of white students in Bahia said they would not marry a Negro; 87 percent said they would not marry even a light-skinned *mulato*. Florestan Fernandes, writing about São Paulo, maintains that "mixed marriages meet with almost insurmountable resistance as things now stand" (see Mason, 1970a, p. 310).

3. RACIAL DISCRIMINATION IN THE CARIBBEAN

Recent research by Solaun and Kronus (1973) in Cartagena, Colombia (population 300,000) reveals a picture similar to that in Brazil. Racial "upgrading" with its attendant social mobility emphasizes the deprivation of the Negroes and darker hybrids more than the gains of those who "pass." Mestizos of mixed white–Indian parentage experience less discrimination than blacks or mulattoes. There are virtually no Negroes at the elite level, and practically no whites in the lower class. Less than 5 percent of law school graduates of the University of Cartagena between 1943 and 1964 were physically identifiable Negroes. By contrast, the bulk of the lower class slum dwellers are somatically Negro (*ibid.*, pp. 114, 118). Few white men marry darker persons. The researchers found "there are virtually no *negras* in the brothels attended by *blancos*. Thus the bulk of the miscegenation process occurs between racially close individuals" (*ibid.*, p. 126).

Situations similar to that in Colombia are found in most of the island countries and littoral states of the Caribbean: Blacks are concentrated at the lowest levels of the status pyramid, the apex of which is dominated by people mainly Caucasoid in appearance. As in countries further south, upward mobility can be attained through "bleaching." And the higher the economic level of "mixed bloods," the more important racial considerations seem to be (see Hoetink, 1967, p. 42). Marriages between whites and nonwhites with predominantly Negroid features are rare.

Broadly, the Caribbean presents a common scale of color values couched in terms of a polar distinction of black and white.

Around this polar distinction the social classes crystallize. The coloured group, in which both physical and "objective" status criteria are important, is in a very real sense the "middle class" *vis-à-vis* either the white or the black groups, which are the "upper" and "lower" classes respectively. . . .

[T]he acceptance of new members in the upper stratum of all Caribbean societies is determined by physical characteristics, in fact by sufficient whiteness of skin, in addition to criteria of prosperity and education. . . .

While the white, coloured and Negro categories may each be internally subdivided into socioeconomic classes, some of which may wholly or partly overlap, the *chances* of upward mobility as well as the maximum *distance* of this mobility are unequal for the members of each of the categories. This inequality is determined by physical characteristics. The membership of the highest white "class" is in principle closed to non-whites on the grounds of their physical characteristics, and it is therefore not a class in sociological sense. (*Ibid.*, pp. 45, 50)

In Haiti, the white colonists were eliminated by Toussaint l'Ouverture's revolution at a time when Napoleon I was unable to divert sufficient forces from Europe to hold either Haiti or Louisiana. The vacuum was filled by a racially mixed group that had adopted much of the European culture. Even today, whiteness and educational attainment correlate positively and a lighter-skinned elite constituting 4 percent of the population controls over 70 percent of the country's wealth. In Jamaica, as in many South American societies, color, including conformity with Caucasoid somatic norms, was formerly both a determinant and indicator of social status. In Guyana, on the other hand, the situation is reversed: it is the East Indians rather than the blacks who are the main victims of discrimination. Lowenthal (1969, p. 311) summed up the situation in the Caribbean as follows:

The lot of the great majority of West Indians does not remotely resemble the ideal. At the bottom of the social hierarchy the top is too far away to see or to enjoy, except vicariously. The success of the few who have stormed the portals of the elite has little meaning to those who struggle every day for a bare living. The black masses deem it no accident that those who are better off have lighter skins than they do, and they remember the long history of colored advance at their expense. The free-colored alliance with whites against the slaves has endured, socially if not politically, down to the present. (*Ibid.*, p. 311)

Since 1969, there has been some loosening of stratification; black and brown groups have acquired political power, even though much wealth remains in the hands of Whites.

F. Racism and Color Prejudice in Developed Western Countries

The survey that follows will show that behavioral and attitudinal patterns identified as racism and color prejudice and commonly associated with South Africa and with other countries containing large nonwhite populations are replicated to various degrees in a number of developed western countries. Countries that have only recently experienced racial tensions, such as the United Kingdom and West Germany, are now beginning to realize that countries such as the United States, South Africa, Rhodesia, Australia, and New Zealand have long been grappling with the same problems they now encounter.

1. THE UNITED STATES

The relative quiet at the moment—after the *Sturm und Drang* of the 1960s—can easily be misinterpreted as a sign that interracial tension and color prejudice have become secondary problems in American society. For millions of ghetto blacks, Chicanos, Puerto Ricans and Indians, however, white racism and color prejudice remain permanent facets of their man-made environment. A few years ago, while the Kerner Commission was warning that "Our nation is moving into two societies, one black, one white—separate and unequal," Angus Campbell and Howard Schuman (1970a and 1970c) were conducting research in 15 American cities. They found that while most whites endorsed "equal opportunities for all," the majority would not agree that white racism might

be responsible for the disadvantages suffered by blacks at virtually all levels of life. More than half the respondents saw the difficulty in "something about Negroes themselves," thus placing "the whole burden of Black disadvantage on Blacks themselves" (Schuman, 1972, pp. 385 and 389). The same year 67 percent of white respondents interviewed by William Brink and Lewis Harris agreed with the propositions: "Negroes have less ambition than Whites" and "Negroes are asking for more than they are ready for" (Quoted, Burkey, 1971, p. 81).

Research also shows that theoretical acceptance of racial equality is no guarantee that it will be achieved in practice. While "affirmative action" is an attractive slogan, only a minority of Americans want it legally enforced (*ibid.*, p. 84). Despite a burgeoning of legal instruments and bureaucracies intended to enforce equal opportunity, few informed white Americans would claim that blacks really enjoy equal opportunities in employment and upward mobility. According to Alan Pifer, president of the Carnegie corporation (1973, p. 39) educated whites tend to earn $2400 more per year than educated blacks at each degree level. This difference remained constant even after accounting for the quality of the institution attended, age, field of specialization, and the level of the degree.

In 1970 a third of all black families were living below the poverty line and more than 8 percent of the Negro labor force was unemployed. The corresponding figures for Mexican Americans were 35 percent and 8 percent. By January, 1975, black unemployment had increased to more than 1.4 per million or 13.4 percent of the 10,460,000-strong black labor force. Among black teenagers the unemployment rate had risen to 14.1 percent, as compared with 8.2 percent for teenagers generally. The depressed economic, educational, and social status of American Indians has already been noted. It might be added that reservation Indians have one of the highest infant mortality rates in the world, and their illiteracy is still estimated as at least 40 percent.

2. CANADA, AUSTRALIA, AND NEW ZEALAND

The presence of considerable numbers of blacks, Indians, Eskimos, and nonwhite immigrants from Asia and the Caribbean in Canada is a potential source of racial friction. Basically, white Canadians share the feelings of their southern neighbors on "color," but they are less frequently aroused. Although the black community of Toronto, for instance, does not suffer the poverty endemic in United States ghettos, Negroid appearance is nevertheless a status depressant, as is a tribal-oriented Indian or Eskimo lifestyle. The mobility potential of decultured Indians is, however, larger than that of blacks, because the former do not have Negroid features. Whites generally also manifest stronger resistance to biological amalgamation with blacks than with Indians. Yet, Canadian Indians experience their status as that of a subordinate group denied its rightful heritage.

Canada had little experience with black–white relations before 1960, but by 1970 its black population had reached 100,000. If the current rate of growth continues, Toronto alone will have 500,000 blacks by 1980. The lessons being learned are illuminating. Here are some examples:

In the mid-1960s the city of Halifax, Nova Scotia, decided to demolish its black neighborhood called Africville. By 1969 its several hundred families had all been resettled in public housing projects among whites. By 1972 there was general disenchantment with this move. A spokesman for the Africville people declared: "Black and White, like oil and water, just don't mix." A three-year study conducted by Dalhousie University pronounced the project a social failure. It found that whites moved away as quickly as they could from their new black neighbors and that the folk of Africville had been deprived of their sense of community and autonomy.

In March 1970 a seminar on black education was held at Toronto University. One delegate observed: "The Black child in Ontario schools operates in an environment that takes no account of his blackness." Another said: "Colour *does* matter. We don't want teachers to say Blacks and Whites are the same." The consensus of the teachers, psychologists, and social workers at the seminar was that black children suffered psychological harm by being treated as though they were no different from white children. According to a study by York University in March 1972, racial discrimination in Toronto was spreading rapidly and had been checked only by the smallness of the city's black and other ethnic minorities. In August 1973, a Toronto seminar on race relations was told by a West Indian delegate: "We are sitting on a powder keg in Montreal and Toronto." In February 1975, the Canadian government tabled in Parliament a report warning that any significant increase in immigration from Asia and the Caribbean would lead to social tension. It would be astonishing, the report said, if there were no public concern about the country's ability to absorb large numbers of immigrants "possessing novel and distinctive features."

In two other Commonwealth countries—Australia and New Zealand—Anglo-Saxon-dominated establishments are finding out that color prejudice and racism are not confined to academic research programs. Both countries have indigenous communities whose position resembles that of the Indians in Canada.

In Australia, sophisticated Aborigines realize that assimilation is no unqualified invitation to black-white fusion, but that the physical distance between the two races is matched by social distance, especially in intimate, personal associations. They mistrust the so-called "special measures" introduced to emancipate Aborigines from their stone-age backwardness (Rowley, 1972a, p. 400). That white immigrants from Western Europe are more easily assimilated in the white Australian society than themselves or Asians has a racist implication quite clear to the perceptive Aborigine. And even though the "White Australia" Policy has been officially dropped, the country's social and political structure is such that White Australia will remain. One Australian scholar says unequivocally: "Few, if any, Australians want to 'open the floodgates,' or to include non-Europeans in the immigration programme on the same basis as that of Europeans" (Palfreeman, 1971, p. 142). Moderate Australians admit to ethnocentrism, in the sense of preference for the characteristics of one's own group, but deplore racism, which they define as the active persecution of other groups. Pragmatic management, they claim, has kept the number of Asians to a level where racism has not emerged. Such Australians warn against "the misguided compulsions of moralism." They rejoice in being able to walk city streets alone at night, and would like to keep it that way.

One of the early moves of Gough Whitlam's Labor government was to reverse previous policy and to grant assisted passages to migrants regardless of color. Yet there was no increase in the proportion of colored people admitted. Assisted migrants in the first six months of 1973 coming from Asia, Commonwealth countries in Africa, or the Caribbean totaled 110 out of 26,013 arrivals. The number born in these countries totaled 269. Proportionately, there were no more Asians and Africans than in 1971–72 under the previous government.

The traditional and implicit racial biases in Australia's immigration policy were never reversed. Large numbers of unskilled and semiskilled workers from Europe have no difficulty in getting assisted passages because relatives and community groups can guarantee them jobs. But many professional Asians and some Africans are not recognized by their professional bodies in Australia. According to the *Johannesburg Star* (November 29, 1973) the Immigration Minister, Al Grasby, "explained the limited number of non-European migrants by saying that the right sort of people did not apply in non-European countries." One reason

might be that advertisements for immigrants were placed in European papers only.

The minority status of the Australian Aborigines resembles that of American Indians in several respects. In both cases the native communities claim that European settlers have robbed them of their best land; that they have been denied any meaningful social, economic, and political power by means of institutionalized discrimination; and that social deprivation has confined them to an impoverished subculture. To the average Australian the "Abo" is still a socially inferior person, someone to be helped to his feet economically, educationally, and vocationally—provided this rehabilitation is not done in "my house, school, club or circle of friends." Through laws that classify the Aborigines as "protected" persons or "government wards," the authorities themselves contribute to the perpetuation of a negative stereotype and emphasize unnecessarily the black–white differences. The status of the blacks is thus determined more by ascription than by personal achievement. In this connection Colin Tatz states:

By ascription I mean the act of assigning, imputing or attributing a characteristic or status to a person. In Australia we have at least thirty current statutes which ascribe certain characteristics to a considerable proportion of the Aboriginal race, mainly the "tribal" Aborigines in Queensland, West Australia, the Northern Territory and South Australia. These attributes are usually negative: such as inability to manage their own affairs and property, unworthiness for inclusion in industrial awards, inability to handle liquor, inability in relation to certain rules of evidence in courts, inability to govern their own communities and so on. The ascriptions are blanket ones, applying to these particular racial groups as a whole—from which the individual has to seek "exemption." (1972, p. 99)

Until quite recently most white Australians denied that the Aborigines were subjected to discrimination. Living in the largest population centers, they came into contact with relatively few of them. As recently as the beginning of 1974, for instance, there were fewer than 12,000 Aborigines in Sydney, Australia's largest city—or less than 0.4 percent of the total population of 2.8 million. The rude awakening came only after relatively large numbers of Aborigines began to migrate to the larger urban industrial areas. For the first time the whites of these areas were brought face to face with Aborigines and became acutely aware of the enormous gap in all spheres of life between themselves and the new arrivals. The social distance between them was no longer perceived as something abstract; it became concrete and took shape in a rigid system of social ranking.

For many white Australians the "noble" and dispossessed "savage" of school-age picture books had become a social burden overnight. "Stories" and rumors began to proliferate. In 1974 a member of the Western Australian Parliament complained that Aborigines "showed little motivation or drive, little will to achieve and little dignity, and were being kept in idleness and drink by social welfare money that came from white taxpayers. We are creating a select class in society, a group which does not have to work. These Aborigines are people who have gone beyond the bounds of society's traditions and rules, and who are degraded and degenerated by drink" (*Pretoria News*, August 27, 1974).

Aborigines find themselves forced to struggle continually against a feeling of inferiority caused by their underclass position in Australian society. Part-Aboriginal Pastor David Kirk maintains: "We have a massive inferiority complex"—a feeling that generates almost universal hatred for whites (Lippman, 1972, p. 27). This hatred is continually reinforced by the ways whites communicate to Aborigines that they will never really "belong." Bruce McGuinness charges that even in the sphere of sexual relations Aborigines are merely used but never openly admitted to the "inner temples" of whites (1972, p. 155).

Wage discrimination was still common in the early 1970s, as were limitations on the per-

sonal freedom and legal rights of Aborigines in Queensland and the Northern Territory (where the majority live). More than a third of the Aboriginal labor force in Northern Australia is unemployed. According to Pittock,

Effective discrimination in the administration of justice on the courts is also common in such centres as Darwin and Alice Springs. Illiterate Aborigines, often unable to understand and speak ordinary English, let alone legal jargon, are frequently brought before courts in these centres without interpreters or legal representation. (1972, pp. 243–44)

In central Australia, the registered infant mortality rate is 208 per 1000 live births—one of the highest in the world. In the Northern Territory, one child in six dies in its first four years. The age structure of the part-Aboriginal population as well as the living conditions suggest that Aborigines and part-Aborigines have similar death rates throughout Australia. Pittock concludes:

Whatever rationalizations we can offer in these various instances of institutional racism, certain cold facts remain. One is that, whatever the reason or historical context, Aborigines today suffer many handicaps which truly make them, as a race, underprivileged citizens. A second is that were a comparable number of non-Aborigines suffering in the same way, it would be regarded as a major political issue which would threaten to bring down governments. (1972, pp. 244–245)

Recent research surveys underscore the fact that white color prejudice is more prevalent and the social gap between whites and Aborigines much larger than many people thought or hoped. Ronald Taft found in 1970 that more than 75 percent of an urban test group were opposed to interracial marriages. More than half favored some form of segregation for certain public facilities (McConnochie, 1973, p. 123). Three years later Lorna Lippman reported in four country towns "an inherent belief in the inferiority of the Aboriginal position (a belief constantly bolstered by reference to low material and social standards) which is sometimes transferred as belief in the inferiority of Aborigines themselves. All stereotypes mentioned pertaining to Aborigines were derogatory and Aborigines were both felt and seen to be in a continuously subordinate position" (*ibid.*, p. 125). At about the same time J. S. Western summed up his own research as follows: "The overall results are unequivocal. White Australians, whether in large cities, in smaller centres or in small country towns, show extensive prejudice towards Aborigines. They show a reluctance to enter into social relationships with them, they use derogatory stereotypes as explanations for Aboriginal social status, and they accept no personal responsibility for the tension which exists between Aborigines and the social order" (*ibid.*, p. 172).

In his report on *Aborigines in Australia Today*, written for the National Aboriginal Forum in 1974, Chris Mullard, a black British sociologist, is overtly skeptical about the motives behind the latest policy shift of the Australian government. Government policy, he says, has evolved from "physical extermination in the nineteenth century to extermination through excessive and paternal welfarism; from genocide and cultural rape to the 'smoothing of the dying pillow' approach" (1974, p. 9). Mullard rejects self-determination as paternalistic, escapist, and a stratagem to avoid ultimate responsibility. "In essence it is a piece of political camouflage, a con trick, a palliative for a guilt-based societal neurosis, and it has only slight relevance to the demands of Aboriginal society. It was conceived for the benefit of Whites and . . . it was not grounded in the social realities which face the majority of Aborigines" (*ibid.*, p. 13). Mullard concludes that the Aborigines believe they are victims of institutionalized white racism and white social, economic, and political domination, and that they are socialized to believe in their own social and cultural inferiority. "Aborigines are living in a racist pressure chamber. . . . not only have the Whites taken his land, but they are now beginning to make claims on his soul" (*ibid.*, pp. 47f.).

This view corresponds in large measure with the assessment two years earlier of Australian race relations by another black academic, Sekai Holland:

The most common question asked of me, as a black by white Australians, is whether Australian society is as racist as either Rhodesian or South African society. I think they expect that, having come to Australia as a student and having been treated well in that regard, I will naturally say that of course it is not. But any honest reply, although it evokes much anger from white Australians must always be the same: Australia, for the Aborigines, (and they are the prime measure of racism here) is worse than either South Africa or Rhodesia for the Africans.

The reason why white Australians can believe that Australia is not a racist country, while at the same time acknowledging that South Africa is one, is that the ideology adopted by South Africa, with its complex set of racist laws and the open practice of segregation as a policy, is more obvious. They are satisfied that South Africa has to have racist laws because it has a colour problem, and believe that separation is the best way to avoid conflict and exploitation. Australia, they believe, would have to do the same thing if Europeans were outnumbered four to one by tribal Aborigines. Yet they insist that this is just hypothetical because Australia does not have a colour problem! People like this are simply not aware of the magnitude of the problem which already exists in Australia.

The Aborigines have been completely dispossessed of their land and relegated to an insignificant role in Australian society. Unfortunately, the facts of this accomplishment serve to delude many Australians that there is no problem of racism in Australia. The significance of their position is not that they are unable to recognize the complete triumph of racist ideology—the supplementation and dispossession of one race by another. There can be little doubt that this has been achieved in Australia. South Africa, however, still has a long way to go. (1972, pp. 187–188, 211)

Finally, an organ of the white establishment, *The Australian* (May 18, 1972), has this to say:

This is a racist country—not a white heat racist but largely racist by default. A stream of intolerance lies beneath the national geniality: a basic intolerance of diversity.

This does not explode in factory fights, pub brawls, football riots. It surfaces mainly in the squalor and unemployment among Aboriginals and in the blunt . . . or oblique rejection of migrants.

Australian racism is not a blow in the face. It is a back turned, a pious face averted to a hungry kid without homework space in a tin shanty—and with no bus to the distant school (or change of clothes when it pours).

3. SOUTH AFRICA

As a result of the historical linkages connecting national origin, racial heritage, language, culture, economic development, and size of population groups in South Africa, the lines between these groups are more clearly drawn than in Australia, Canada, or the United States. Color and race are only two among a number of differentials that mark the South African ethnopolitical spectrum.

The Dutch, French, German, and English settlers who laid the foundations of the modern white South African nation in the seventeenth and eighteenth centuries came from what were then the greatest economic and military powers in the world. Their first contact was with Capoid (Hottentot and Bushman) tribes at the southernmost tip of the continent. Later, in the interior, they encountered the more numerous Congoid (Bantu-speaking) tribes, with which their relations were sometimes warlike, sometimes peaceful.

From the very outset the disparity in lifestyle, culture, language, economic development, and physical appearance was so obvious and striking that ethnoracial separation fast became one of the whites' most important investments in survival. Color became the outward symbol of group differentiation, a somatic barrier that grew into a physical watershed. The polarization process was essentially the same that operated in South America, the Caribbean, the United States, and Australia; but the color line was drawn more rigidly in South Africa because of the whites' great numerical inferiority to the blacks. Elementary demographic arithmetic shows that biological

merger would eliminate the white south African nation as a distinctive ethnoracial group.

South Africans argue that color is not the reason for the policy that has come to be known as apartheid, but merely a signal of the real ethnic differences between the white nation and the various black peoples. Even if the color difference had not existed, they claim, the deep-rooted cultural and historical contrasts would have aroused the same resistance to assimilation on the part of the whites, and (as has happened) on the part of many blacks in positions of cultural or political leadership. They point out that many of the most bitter struggles of our time, such as the clashes between Hindus and Muslims, the ideological wars in China and Indo-China, the confrontation of Semitic nations (Jews and Arabs) in the Near East, the reciprocal terrorism in Northern Ireland and Cyprus, and even the European phases of the two World Wars, and the associated boundary shifts and mass expulsions, were expressions of political, cultural, and ideological differences within single racial macrogroups.

Traditional stereotyped categories are reflected in the popular grouping of the Republic's inhabitants into white, Coloured, Asian, and Bantu (black) South Africans. This oversimplification is particularly misleading with regard to the black peoples, who are highly differentiated and can in no way be described as a homogeneous group.

Each of the nine main Bantu-speaking South African peoples constitutes a distinctive society, at least some of whose leaders are committed to maintaining its separate identity as an established ethnopolitical unit. Despite a limited measure of cross-cultural assimilation, the major national groups retain their distinctive language and cultures, which are in process of adaptation to modern conditions but without loss of their individuality. Each of the main black nations has a traditional homeland, which does not contain the entire population of that group but nevertheless serves as the geopolitical nucleus of its national development.

Black intellectuals opposed to the South African government's objective of separate nation-states for the whites and the main black ethnic groups question the feasibility of the policy. They call attention to their low status in the South African reward and opportunity system and claim that it is largely the result of color prejudice and racism. They are particularly exasperated by what is called "petty apartheid"—officially enforced segregation in buses, trains, restaurants and hotels, theaters, and recreation facilities, and even post offices and bottle stores. In particular, they see the legal prohibition of "mixed" marriages and sex relations as a fundamentally racist measure. They resent the negative stereotypes associated with their Negroid appearance and their low level of socioeconomic development. There is a tendency to blame black poverty on the white man's color barrier.

The importance of race and color differences as a motivational force in the policy of separate development is a subject of debate. The fact is that cultural and sociopolitical differences between the two main racial groups of South Africa have always clearly corresponded with color, which is the visible signal. This is a psychosocial reality which will not disappear overnight.

Every nation decides for itself whom it wishes to assimilate sociopolitically and whom it wishes to absorb into its power structure. This explains why the United States, Great Britain, Canada, Australia, and New Zealand refuse to open their doors to millions of Asians—despite pressure on these countries to do so for humanitarian reasons. No nation pursues foreign policy primarily attuned to furthering the interests of other nations or ethnonational groups.

The crux of the matter is assimilability. It happens that in South Africa color differences are a convenient signal for sociocultural disparity. The greater the vulnerability of a nation in terms of its survival, the stricter the selective processes involved in cross-cultural assimilation. There is no historical precedent for a nation's voluntarily giving up the right to determine who should be assimilated.

It is therefore naive to expect white South Africans to manage ethnic relations with mechanical objectivity or become indifferent and nondiscriminatory in pursuing their basic group interests. A nation incapable of acting upon intelligent self-interest is a nation incapable of assuring its own survival. In any case, the prejudices of white South Africans are hardly any stronger than others which the world has been conditioned to accept as unchangeable if uncomfortable realities: the mutual feelings of Arabs and Jews, of Hindus and Muslims, and indeed of Communists and anti-Communists.

South Africa recognizes the black peoples within its borders as distinct national units or protonations. These emerging nations are becoming politically disengaged from the white nation. This process is designed to culminate in separate self-determining ethno-national states within the historical homelands of the peoples concerned. Meaningful political independence, however, must be coupled with economic independence, or at least some symmetry of bargaining power within a common market. It is for this reason that the *development* side of "separate development" assumes particular importance. More is said on this subject in chapter 20, C4.

4. GREAT BRITAIN

A surge of colored immigration to the United Kingdom in the late 1950s led to increasing attention to "race relations," about which a considerable literature has appeared. Investigators found that along with successive waves of Commonwealth immigrants, color prejudice and racism had acquired a firm foothold in Great Britain. Despite the Race Relations Act of 1968 and a continuous refrain of appeals by both church and state that the public should expiate their racist sins, color prejudice does not seem likely soon to lose its dubious status as one of Britain's most thorny social problems (Banton, 1972, p. 97).

All researchers find that color prejudice is at its worst on the level of intimate personal relations. After a survey in Bristol, Richmond concludes:

Despite the physical proximity of immigrants and native-born living in the survey area, there was a minimum of face-to-face interaction between them and an absence of primary group relationships that cut across ethnic boundaries. The barriers were most evident in the case of coloured immigrants in their relations with white neighbours. . . . Although coloured immigrants lived in close physical proximity to other residents and there was a good deal of face-to-face interaction on the street and at work, primary group relationships within the area were almost entirely confined to others of the same racial, national and religious group. Except in the case of some Irish and European males, marital relationships rarely crossed ethnic boundaries and almost all close friendships and recreational activities were with others of the same cultural background. (1973, pp. 185–88)

In this domain of primary associations, a predominantly Negroid appearance remains the final disqualification. The research of C. J. Hill showed that 90 percent of his respondents were against "mixed" marriages. The preferment of Hungarians and Cypriots over West Indians has already been noted (Richmond, 1973, p. 96). According to Bloom (1971, p. 115) racism is "the remnants of the arrogance of a colonial period, given a peculiar power by the insularity and imperviousness of the British social system and its severely hierarchical structure."

Like the *Gastarbeiter* in Germany, France, and Switzerland, the colored worker in Britain can find only the most menial and unattractive type of job. The PEP report points out: "It is fair to say that coloured immigrants were often employed in only one type of job as regards remuneration, level of skill and interest, dirtyness and heaviness, and hours of work or type of shift; and where this was true it was the most menial and unattractive type of job, for which it had been impossible to attract white labour" (Quoted in Castles and Kosack, 1973, p. 109). Of the 36 private agencies for the recruitment of office staff interviewed, all agreed that the majority of their clients would not take colored applicants (*ibid.*, p. 110). According to the largest agency in Croydon, only three out of one thousand firms would take colored applicants (Patterson, 1968, p. xviii). And those who did find work were compelled to take jobs below their level of qualification. The 1971 census revealed that only a tiny proportion of colored workers were employed in so-called white-collar work. Coloreds earn less than whites with comparable skills and training. Color prejudice and racism are also responsible for the problems colored immigrants have in finding suitable accommodation. Landlords who let to immigrants know that they can charge them far higher rents than local people for the same accommodation. Authorities on this situation refer to the "newcomers' tax" and the "foreigners' levy" imposed on the colored people in particular (*ibid.*, p. 277).

Britain's so-called Commonwealth Immigrants Acts (1962 and 1968) and the Immigration Act of 1971 all have a racist component which clearly reflects the prejudice of the ordinary Briton against nonwhite "foreigners." Race riots in Nottingham and Notting Hill in 1958 and the rapid influx of colored immigrants from Commonwealth countries made the British public sensitive to growing racial friction. The Commonwealth Immigrants Act of 1968 was designed to close loopholes in the 1962 law, which could have permitted an unmanageable surge of nonwhite immigrants holding British passports (Rothchild, 1973, p. 390). Its enactment was hastened by the sudden escalation of Asian immigration from East Africa, where the Africanization drive of newly emancipated black nations triggered a mass exodus of Asians. As a result of the new restrictions, the number of colored immigrants decreased from more than 57,000 in 1967 to fewer than 27,000 in 1970. The Immigration Act of 1971 radically altered the position of most Commonwealth citizens, bringing it more into line with that of aliens. The automatic right of Commonwealth citizens to register as U.K. citizens after five years' residence was also abrogated.

However limited Great Britain's capacity to provide new arrivals with jobs and housing, these statutory restrictions on Commonwealth immigrants with U.K. passports are racist in their *effect*, for the simple reason that the vast majority of these immigrants come from non-European countries where out-migration is often the ultimate escape from massive poverty and social deprivation. In sharp contrast to this are the so-called White Dominions which, having dynamic economies, each year gain a surplus of *white* migrants from European countries. The new immigration curbs have now locked the door to all but a favored few entrants: the only colored Commonwealth citizens admitted into the U.K. now are doctors, nurses and certain other trained professionals. As Hugh Tinker, Director of the Institute of Race Relations, London, has commented, the Immigration Act of 1971 created for the first time a legal distinction between "belongers" and "non-belongers" based "almost explicitly on race." Tinker continues: "In future, any coloured immigrant who can obtain entry into Britain in order to work—and the number will be small—will be treated as a transient, and as a second-class citizen" (1972, p. 68).

G. Color Prejudice and Racism as Universal Phenomena

We have already noted the temptation to evade international censure by converting a race problem to a "class" or "ethnic" issue—or, as is the mode in the European Common Market, a "problem of migrant labor." A careful analysis of the class structure of South America and the Caribbean, the *Gastarbeiter* problem of the EEC countries, the caste systems of India, Sri Lanka, and Japan and the ethnic problems of other countries, however, will make it evident that nearly all of these situations have racial components.

Racial motivations also lurk behind supposedly ethnic differences in a number of black African and Asian countries. In Liberia, for instance, a person must belong to the Congoid (Negrid) macrogroup to qualify for civic rights—yet President Tolbert of that country demands that South Africa jettison its racist policies. A racial factor is also evident in the expulsion of Indians from Uganda, Kenya, and other African countries. Leo Kuper found that in bloody revolutions in Rwanda (1962) and Zanzibar (1964), the hostile camps (Tutsi and Hutu in Rwanda and Arabs and Blacks in Zanzibar) rationalized their disparate interests largely in racial terms (Kuper, 1973). The same is true of many other intergroup conflicts in Africa where no white presence played any role whatever.

It is a peculiar tendency of our times that the world community will witness without much emotion large-scale suppression if it is defined in an ethnic or ideological context, but will condemn with much passion a far milder case of suppression which is defined as racism. We have already noted that racial casualties are far outweighed by losses in struggles where race is not an issue. The 500,000 Ibos and the many Hausa, Fulani, Yorubas, and others opposing them killed in the Biafra war all belonged to the Congoid macrogroup. Likewise, General Amin's slaughter of fellow Ugandans has involved tribal loyalties but hardly racial ones. The slaughter in East Pakistan in 1971 and in Kurdistan from 1970 to 1974 involved national and linguistic quarrels, not differences in race. Yet these tragedies are quickly forgotten while far smaller clashes in South Africa are remembered.

Speaking during the 31st session of the United Nations Commission on Human

Rights, United States delegate Philip Hoffman said in Geneva on March 1, 1973, that "racial discrimination is found in many and varied forms, some blatant, others more subtle," and "is not a simple question of Black and White. . . . Tribalism continues to be a stubborn problem in many areas," Mr. Hoffman added. "The world has recently witnessed several grave instances of gross violation of human rights as a matter of official policy directed against members of different ethnic or tribal groups." He emphasized that racial discrimination "exists everywhere in one form or another—and this applies to North and South America, Europe (West and East), all of Africa and Asia. No continent, country or people is free of some form of racial discrimination. Violations of human rights can be found today in discrimination not only of whites against blacks, but blacks against whites, whites against whites and blacks against blacks."

For this reason the U.S. delegate expressed concern that the UN decade for action against racism and racial discrimination might fall short of its objectives if countries maintained that discrimination was practiced only "somewhere else" and made Southern Africa the sole preoccupation of the decade. He called for "frank and critical self-examination by all governments" on this issue.

It would take psychological research beyond the scope of this book to determine conclusively why national groups are usually supported in efforts to protect their religious, linguistic, cultural, or historical identities through separatist policies, but condemned whenever they try to entrench their *racial* identities. A partial explanation may be offered: first, many people confuse racial differentiation with racial discrimination; secondly, it suits certain factions involved in the international power struggle to induce people to believe that racial separation can only be achieved through racial oppression. There is no reason, however, why racial differentiation (in the sense of avoiding amalgamation with other

groups) need necessarily involve discrimination and suppression.

The presence of a white or European ingredient is no prerequisite at all for the existence of racism. There was a clear racial factor in the 16-year civil war (1956–1972) between blacks and Arabs in the Southern Sudan, even though no European party was involved in the struggle. The same is true of the expulsion by blacks of the ruling Arab minority in Zanzibar in early 1964. Since Arabs are a Semitic people, closely related to the Jews, those in whom original Arab stock predominates belong to the Caucasoid macrogroup. Yet Arabs, as the victims of European discrimination, have tended to identify with the nonwhite peoples—except where their interests happen to clash. Other racial conflicts where Europeans are not involved include the confrontations between the Chinese and Turkic peoples of Sinkiang province; Chinese and Tibetans; Taiwanese and mainland Chinese; Malays and Chinese in Malaysia and Indonesia; Koreans and Japanese; Lao speakers and Karens in Thailand; Burmese, Kachins, and Karens in Burma; Hindus and Nagas in India; and Papuan and non-Papuan people in New Guinea. None of these conflicts has been generally recognized as racial. Yet any of them would immediately be so classified if one of the groups involved happened to be white.

The point is, that when two groups within the same macrogroup fall out, their differences may be ethnic or racial or a combination of both. The same is true when the contestants belong to different macrogroups; it is possible for nationalities belonging to different macrogroups to have a conflict that is essentially ethnic and national rather than racial.

Conflicts that are specifically racial, however, abound not only in South Africa, but in many other parts of the world. The physical white-black polarization may not jibe with the noble concept of the Brotherhood of Man, but it remains a universal social and hence political fact that affects the behavior of the members of all macrogroups involved. From Australia, for instance, white–Aborigine strife is reported in the West Australian town of Laverton, whose mayor believes that Aborigines—who "should never have been given drinking rights"—get involved in racial incidents because they can't hold their liquor. Social apartheid between whites and Aborigines, including residential segregation, is a fact of Australian life. In February 1974, a crowd of 300 Aborigines demonstrated their disenchantment with Australia's racism by booing first Prime Minister Whitlam, and then the Queen when she arrived to open Parliament. In Queensland, where most of the Aborigine tribesmen live, rampant discrimination has led commentators to compare that state with the United States South.

In nearby New Zealand, the self-styled Polynesian Panther Party has called the country a "white male club." The Panthers mark the increasing militancy among New Zealand's 240,000 Maoris and 70,000 other Pacific indigenes who make up about 10 percent of the country's total population. The New Zealand government has tightened entry rules for Pacific islanders, prompting Fijian charges that the immigration policy was a manifestation of feelings of white superiority. The Rev. Peter McCormack, director of Roman Catholic social services for the archdiocese of Wellington, has said that "behind their talk of racial equality the whites have an inbred distrust, contempt and, at best, social disapproval, of the Polynesians." The Maoris demand better educational opportunities and additional seats in Parliament. White New Zealanders, on the other hand, are beginning to see Maori particularism as a threat to their own security. Further strains have ensued through the influx of large numbers of Polynesians during the past decade—six suburbs in Auckland are virtually Polynesian ghettos. Economic conditions have transformed the Polynesians into competitors for white jobs—a development with potentially explosive implications.

Meanwhile, in the United Kingdom, Enoch Powell, known for his opposition to black immigration and currently a United Ulster Unionist M.P., has raised afresh the specter of racial conflict in Britain and has demanded a drastic program to repatriate thousands of colored immigrants. In a February 1975 speech he warned that nonwhite immigration was creating an explosive situation in several urban centers. "Those who imagine that it can be defused and normalized by race relations boards and community relations commissions have not begun to comprehend how deep are the fundamentals involved."

At a 1973 conference in Birmingham, British trade unions were accused of "aiding and abetting racialism." A year later the Community Relations Commission reported that "color discrimination in employment is widespread, despite the Race Relations Act" (*Daily Telegraph*, June 10, 1974). Two months later, the complaint was repeated in Parliament. In a recent report on "racial disadvantage" in employment, PEP disclosed after an investigation of 27 of Britain's 40 largest employers that more than half the plants allowed "some form of discrimination." But employers were not the only ones at fault. PEP found several instances where trade unions were involved in discrimination. In one case, a union district official admitted that his union had connived to keep Asian bus conductors from rising to inspector jobs. Despite a plethora of laws, boards, and bureaucrats, Britain's black people are, in the words of Sir Geoffrey Wilson, Chairman of the Race Relations Board, "second-class citizens, locked into second-class jobs and living in second-class accommodations."

And so we can go on—from continent to continent—and find that most people everywhere value their descent (biological history), often base insider-outsider distinctions predominantly on differences in biological history, assign descent a primary role in shaping each group's overall identity, tend partly to rationalize and justify differences in status and level of development as biologically dictated, and tend to demonstrate the primacy of race in intergroup relations. There is much to substantiate the conclusion drawn by a black sociologist, William J. Wilson: "In actual fact, however, there are no known cases of racial groups in advanced nation states having established egalitarian relationships. By the same token, there are no known cases in which the relationships between racial groups have been based on complete equality of power" (1973, p. 18). Pierre van den Berghe thinks that multiracial societies are almost invariably hierarchized in terms of prestige, wealth, and power (1972, p. 257). Whether a nonhierarchical multiracial society can be created and stabilized remains to be tested.

14

PATTERNS OF DISCRIMINATION IN A STRATIFIED SOCIETY

While individuals experience the effects of stratification, the phenomenon always occurs in a group context. The individual is not ranked because of his personal characteristics, but because he belongs to (or is thought to belong to) a particular group. Ranking is always multidimensional, since the individual who belongs to several groups can be ranked on various levels simultaneously, depending upon the status, prestige, power, etc, which each group affiliation confers upon the individual. A person may, for instance, be within a religious majority, but at the same time be held within a deprived lower class because of his race (somatic image and descent), language, or nationality.

A. Stratification and Social Discrimination

Social discrimination and social deprivation result from the stratification and ranking within a society of its various groups, however these groups may be defined and integrated. Such discrimination may take place in different spheres—social, cultural, linguistic, legal, economic, or even political. It may be multidimensional: a group may experience general and brutal discrimination in one sphere and fairly superficial, almost token, discrimination in another.

Status is of two kinds: *ascribed*, resulting from group membership (e.g. male or female, black or white, Protestant or Catholic); and *achieved*, through the individual's own efforts. Taken as a whole, the individual's social position (status) and social behavior (interaction with other people) are largely determined by his descent, occupation, income, level of education, residential area, language, religion, lifestyle, ethnic association, race, age, and sex: a combination of ascribed and achieved factors. Status, as well as economics, determines the social rewards an individual receives. Doctors and lawyers, for instance, earn well, not only because of the cost of their training and the market for their services, but also because Western societies accept their high status. In the USSR, on the other hand, medical doctors have lower status and earnings and are mostly female.

The differential status resulting from stratification leads to unequal life chances: that is, to unequal opportunities to survive, to enjoy good health and proper housing and food, to rise in social and economic status—particularly through education—and to arrange one's own associations with other people, such as in marriage or friendships. Typical victims of this unequal status are the black *Gastarbeiter* (migrant workers) in Western Europe, who are kept out of the intimate and personal spheres of white Europeans, and thereby miss many chances, economic as well as social, since jobs and apartments are often obtained through friends and relatives.

The main points at this stage are that people can be the victims of social discrimination and deprivation because they are of the "wrong" race, lifestyle, value system, descent, religion, language, age, or sex; social discrimination is linked with people's life chances and their position in society. Social discrimination and deprivation vary in intensity, ranging from total rejection to superficial and mild forms of social disapproval or avoidance. The devices used to produce specific discriminatory effects include marriage restrictions; school, residential and club segregation; selective immigration; job segregation and discrimination; discriminatory language practices in school or factory; and culturally biased selection devices. All these operate to limit the upward mobility of deprived groups.

B. Social Relationships and Status Stratification

Dislike for the lifestyle, language, religion or nationality of a minority is not the only reason for social discrimination. Often a dominant group sees the deprived group as a threat to its position of power and privilege. Social discrimination is thus intimately linked with a national society's power structure, particularly in the sense of access to and control of those resources capable of producing material and nonmaterial values. In this connection John Goldthorpe propounds the following hypothesis:

Social inequality in all its manifestations can be thought of as involving differences in social power and advantage; power being defined as the capacity to mobilize resources (human and non-human) and advantage as the possession of, or control over whatever in society is valued and scarce. Power can be used to secure advantage, while certain advantages constitute the resources that are used in the exercise of power. Moreover, different forms of power and advantage tend in their very nature to be convertible; economic resources can be used to gain status or to establish authority; status can help to reinforce authority or to create economic opportunities; positions of authority usually confer status and command high economic rewards, and so on (1974, p. 218).

Goldthorpe also emphasizes that systems of social stratification are inherently highly resistant to change. "The members of the highest strata have the motivation and, in general, the resources to hold on to their position and to transmit it to their children, while the members of the lowest strata are often caught up in vicious circles of deprivation." He concludes that social stratification, with its consequent social deprivation, is a structural component of British society which will not disappear very soon.

1. THE HIGH COST OF DISCRIMINATION

Violence, crime and other sociopathological phenomena among deprived groups are often generated by the frustrations caused by social discrimination. Dealing with violence and riots in the United States, Leonard Bloom writes:

One example suffices. During *the three years 1965–7 in the USA, rioting and racialism cost the deaths of 130 citizens and the injury of over 3,600. Nearly 29,000 arrests were made*, and the estimated damage to property and the economic loss was about *714 millions.* This period included major riots at Watts, Newark and Detroit. After the murder of Martin Luther King in April 1968, rioting and looting broke out across the USA from Washington, D.C. to Oakland, California; from Denver to Tallahassee; and in Washington, D.C. alone more than 20 people were killed.

The *intangible concealed costs were* the civic disruption and insecurity, the hardening of misunderstanding between whites and non-whites and the cutting short of social and political dialogue. The encouraging of a tough frontier philosophy of attempting to suppress social distress with violence is matched by a counter-philosophy that only violence will bring about social improvements. When the expression of social distress is effectively suppressed the processes of estrangement and rebellious despair may be hastened. (1971, p. 141, emphasis added)

The fact that the riots and violence were not limited to a small band of extremists points to the probability that acute frustration must have been fairly general among American blacks. Fogelson and Hill suggest that the proliferation of riots would hardly have been possible without the tacit support of at least a sizable minority of the black community (1968, p. 243).

Any sudden spreading of the gap between expectations and gratification will produce tension. Hence, a limited improvement in the status and chances of a deprived group may aggravate rather than appease social conflict. The revolution of rising expectations among black Americans is an obvious fact. The emergence of the Black Power movement in 1966 reflects a refusal to accept the stratification existing in the United States as an unchangeable fact of life. The disorders of the 1960s were, as the writings of Bayard Rustin suggest (1971, *passim.*), more than purely local riots, yet less than a full-scale rebellion.

A significant improvement in educational, political, and vocational opportunities appears to have aroused a level of expectation among the black masses which most whites thought quite unrealistic. Improvement has continued, though it is limited by structural factors that hamper the efficient functioning of the American labor market as a whole (see chapter 21,B2).

2. STRATIFICATION IN THE WESTERN HEMISPHERE

In Canada there is a distinct danger that the erosion of Eskimo culture may lead to serious social disorganization within the ranks of this remote minority community. Ferguson comments:

The values of Eskimo culture are being constantly undermined, and its content pauperized. This seems not only ethically wrong, but unrealistic in planning for the future. For there will always be a small population of Eskimo who will prefer to follow traditional life despite the hardships. The traditional values of their culture can only be preserved by placing a positive worth on their language, mythology, socialization pattern and other cultural features which define and give meaning to being an Eskimo. It is not satisfactory to turn the Canadian Eskimo into Arctic Hillbillies, but that is what is happening. (1971, pp. 27–8)

In the United States the victims of the worst social discrimination are not the blacks or the Chicanos but the nonassimilated Indians. Indian life expectancy is only two-thirds the national rate; one-third of all adult Indians are illiterate, and the unemployment rate is over 60 percent on most reservations (Strauss and Clinton, 1973, p. 153). The detribalized and urbanized Indians have the least social bargaining power and are cut off from standard Indian services. They are largely ignored by the establishment and by other minorities. "In Tucson, Arizona, the United Fund Drive budgets zero dollars for the Tucson Indian Center. Other cities like Chicago, with a respectable Indian population, allocate negligible amounts of community funds for urban Indians ($43,000 in 1970), compared to traditional middle-class boy scout activities, which received $401,200" (Chaudhuri, 1973, p. 110).

In Latin America, unassimilated Indians are not much better off. Those who have been completely absorbed by the middle-class white-mestizo society are the sophisticates who were in any event moving away from traditional Indian life. In Mexico, for instance, Indians are today working as unskilled laborers on land which used to be their own but which has gradually been taken over by the Europeanized Ladinos.

It is chiefly individual sophisticated Chicanos who are assimilated in the mainstream of American society on a basis of social equality. "The claim that Mexican-Americans . . . are sharing in the benefits or modernization, is demonstrably false, despite the existence of a fair percentage of assimilated middle-class Mexican-Americans (the self-styled Spanish). . . . Even Albuquerque, the most modern city of the State, evidences social inequalities that are as dramatic as those in rural counties" (Merkx and Griego, 1971, p. 602).

3. RANKING SYSTEMS IN AFRICA AND ASIA

The broad social cleavage between whites and blacks in South Africa has emerged from over two centuries of contact between a modernizing white nation and a number of black nations that share the characteristics of lesser developed countries to the north. The same type of stratification system has developed in Rhodesia, even though the whites moved into that country nearly two and a half centuries after the Dutch settlements in South Africa. In many Black African states the sociocultural disparity between tribes and nations is far deeper and more far-reaching than the black–white gap in Southern Africa.

In most Asian countries, various forms of social discrimination and deprivation are intimately linked to the almost bewildering variety of cultures, languages, religions, ideologies, and ethnic identities. The mind boggles at the pervasiveness, persistence, and complexity of India's caste system (see chapter 16,B). Where people of different groups compete for scarce jobs or business concessions, the dominant group does not shy at the grossest forms of discrimination to preserve its privileged position. The luckless Indians of postwar Burma are a case in point. Because social deprivation

made their daily lives more and more intolerable, nearly 500,000 accepted "repatriation" between 1945 and 1970. The 250,000 (mostly stateless) who have remained behind are still the victims of social discrimination, as shown by their scavenger existence. Chakravarti notes, "Indians who are still in Burma are mostly hewers of wood and drawers of water and most of them desire to return to India due to the difficult conditions in Burma" (1971, p. 181). The rigid and persistent pattern of social ranking in Japan (see Section D1 below and chapter 16,C) resembles in many respects the Hindu caste system of India.

C. Migrant Workers and Gypsies

The plight of migrant workers in Europe has already been mentioned. These *Gastarbeiter* put up with grossest forms of social deprivation (further analyzed in chapters 15,F and 21) only because the economic hardships they endured in their homelands are even worse than the social ostracism and discrimination they encounter in Europe.

Before the oil crisis, immigrants in Common Market Europe peaked at over 10 million: UN experts predicted they would reach 22 million by 1980. France alone had 3.4 million migrant workers; some 175,000 newcomers a year entered the country until the gates were lowered. Even Spain, essentially a labor export country, felt the burden of thousands of illegal migrant workers who could not fit into the economy or social order. The *Gastarbeiter* phenomenon resulted from the rapid expansion of a modern economy having on its fringe a series of lesser developed economies such as those of Spain and Portugal, Southern Italy, Greece, Turkey, and North Africa, as well as the non-white members of the British Commonwealth. This coexistence of disparate economies, which is duplicated in Southern Africa, results in massive labor migration from the less developed nations to the developed region. In none of the

European host countries has an adequate infrastructure been built to provide the migrant workers and their dependents with proper housing, schools, transport, medical, and social services. Strong social resistance to close personal relations with migrant workers blocks assimilation beyond the marginal and superficial. *Gastarbeiter* fill the most menial jobs and exhibit all the classic characteristics of a deprived subculture.

Turks will submit to the most wretched social deprivation merely to escape the crowds of unemployed thronging the recruitment offices in their homeland. "In Turkey unemployment is so high that recruitment officers are faced in Turkish market places with 500 people for 50 jobs at a time. These men have traveled for days to try and get a job and when they find that the recruitment officer can only take on 50 people, then it happens sometimes that some of the recruiting people are heavily injured, because the other 450 needed jobs too" (Van Houte and Melgert, p. 39).

Opinion polls in all European countries confirm a mounting displeasure with the *Gastarbeiter*. Writing in *Encounter* (London), Jonathan Power comments: "For most Europeans they are here to take advantage of our wealth-creating system, to compete for our scarce housing, and to partake of our social services. When social reality and psychological prejudice are so far apart, and when the culprit is so easily identifiable and locatable, there before us is the best recipe in the sociological book for turbulence" (no. 3, September 1974, pp. 8–9).

According to a recent study of *Gastarbeiter* in West Germany:

Vocational contacts between the West German population and the guest workers are limited to the necessary minimum. Non-vocational relations during leisure time and in human associations are few and far between—and almost non-existent among neighbors.

The more fragmentary the German citizens' knowledge of their guest workers, the stronger their prejudice against them. These prejudices, in turn, hamper people getting closer together and thus getting to know each other better—so that a vicious circle results. The feeling of "being different" with which the nation delimits itself determines the discrimination. The inner attitude of a majority of the Germans, particularly those of the older generation, swings in a significant way between haughty arrogance on the one hand and feelings of envy and hate on the other. Where positive attitudes are to be found, they tend to emphasize the "utility" of the alien as a "useful servant."

Ethnic chauvinism is expressed in the stereotype that guest workers are dirty, unkempt, underdeveloped, stupid and lazy. Order and cleanliness, still a typical German idol, is generally denied as an attribute of guest workers. Guest workers are spoken to in the familiar form and by their first names. Their difficulties in adjusting to an industrial society are ignored. Since they do not understand the German language correctly, the Germans talk with them in a kind of primitive "Pidgin-German" thereby hampering them in gaining a better knowledge of the language. According to their nationality, they are labeled with discriminatory nicknames and derogatory appellations, such as "sheep thieves, camel drivers, Hottentots (North Africans), Mohammeds, Caraway Turks, Musselmen (Turks), Partisans, bear trainers (Yugoslavs), spaghetti eaters, Macaronis, lemon shakers (Italians)." (Amelunxen, 1975a, pp. 127–28)

The many factors which prevent *Gastarbeiter* in the EEC countries from having their wives and children with them exacerbate the feeling of isolation, ostracism, and rejection which characterizes their general social position. In fact, the workers' separation from their families often aborts their marriages. Gilles Verbunt describes the tragic sequence of events which usually lead to such a family crisis:

This lasting separation from his family from every point of view has a harmful influence on the worker. In the end he becomes a stranger to his wife and there are often cases of desertion. The number of divorces (official or in practice) is great, and it is difficult to ensure that alimony is paid from one country to another. . . .

The husband is usually there several years before he is joined by his family. All the steps he is called upon to take . . . his way of organizing his timetable and his leisure within the framework of his new life, the concepts of city life by which he is gradually affected, mean that the immigrant worker changes during his early years abroad, not only in habits but in mentality. This creates a cultural gap between him and his wife. (1969, pp. 7, 9).

On the same subject, Amelunxen adds:

In West Germany more than one million foreign workers, who have conducted themselves without reproach for between five and eight years, would meet the qualifications for a permanent sojourn permit (the so-called "little naturalization"). But only 7,000 of these have achieved this more or less assured status. Non-European aliens usually do not receive a permanent sojourn permit, even after marriage with a German woman. Not infrequently this situation causes the break-up of families. (1975a, p. 117)

It is during his leisure hours, in particular, that the single migrant worker feels his isolation most acutely. An article in the Swiss *National-Zeitung* of March 2, 1968, has thrown some light on this problem:

The difficulties begin when he awakes on Saturday morning. From then on he is in a state of mind which may turn into a severe depression. . . . During the week the Italian does not think about his lot as an emigrant. If he is unfairly treated, if he has, against his will, to eat Swiss food or to prepare his own food, this does not affect him much. He hardly has time to be bothered about it. It does not upset him much that his bed is uncomfortable and that he has to share his room with others. He is tired from his work and has no desire to chew over the tiresomeness of the day and thus experience it all over again.

From the cursed free Saturday on, matters are different. Many a worker passes through an unquiet 48 hours full of bitterness and dissatisfaction. There is nothing that he wants to do and he does not know how to kill the time. He has no desire to rest but neither does he want to expend energy unnecessarily; he becomes keyed up. For 48 hours he is sick . . . a sort of three-day fever, which does not disappear until Monday, when, on foot or on his bike, he makes his way to work. Only now does the Italian

worker feel at ease and like a normal human being again; alert and dynamic.

Even the tolerance of the liberal Dutch is being strained by immigration of out-groups exhibiting high sociocultural and physical disparity. Fredericus Willems, Secretary of the Dutch Federation of Trade Unions, refers to "a rather cool attitude, a certain degree of aloofness. . . . One may be different in the Netherlands, but one is at the same time excluded." Even the Jews, Willems adds, were not accepted in certain cirlces before the Second World War. Floods of immigrants and ghettos, Willems points out, are new problems and, he implies, a potential threat to the country (1972, pp. 71–72). He lists several episodes, which he calls xenophobia rather than discrimination:

—inhabitants of the Zaanstreek who pretend that they dare not let their daughters pass the foreign workers' houses on their way to school;
—the local population in Brabant which is opposed to the conversion of an empty monastery (of which there are many in the area) into housing for foreign workers;
—the burgomaster of a small town in Friesland who is willing to lodge some foreign workers but immediately withdraws his offer as soon as he learns that they are twenty in number: "My people cannot bear that many." (*Ibid.*, p. 73)

Attention has also been drawn to the social discrimination visited upon Gypsies. A report published by the Minority Rights Group in London (Puxon, 1973), observes that they have long been a rejected and neglected minority, lacking education and work opportunities and often even a place to live. Deprivation has indeed become hereditary. While the largest Gypsy communities are in Southeast Europe, the most acute intolerance is found in Western Europe. After citing a Council of Europe document alleging discrimination in violation of the

European Convention on Human Rights, the Minority Rights Group report gives these details:

Besides nomadic and settled Rom, the existence of the Romani migrant workers, mostly from Jugoslavia, Turkey and Spain, seeking employment in western and northern Europe, has added a new factor. The migrant workers number about 66,000—the largest groups being in France, West Germany and Italy. . . .
Since the War, a generation has been growing up illiterate and unprepared to compete in modern society. Now by numbers alone they are compelling adjustment in official policy. Some states, among them West Germany, Belgium and the Netherlands, have reacted by trying to close their frontiers to foreign Rom, and deporting those on their territory, in order to reduce the scale of the problem. They have then concentrated on harassing their Romani citizens in the belief that if the so-called free life on the road becomes intolerable they will be forced to settle and sink unnoticed into the new urban slums.

The hostility of established middle-class residents becomes acute as soon as these "outsiders" try to reduce the "social distance" between themselves and their host communities, for example, by coming to live in the same street. The following incidents occurred in Britain and are typical backlash reactions:

Members of Havering Council in Essex advocated using dogs to evict twelve Gypsy caravans from a public park. . . . Gypsies were eventually removed from Oldchurch Road in Romford after a battle with fifty police. . . . Epsom and Walton Downs conservators declared their intention of having security corps men to help the police repel the hundreds of gypsy caravans visiting their traditional camping place on Epsom Downs, where they come the week before Derby Day. . . . In the face of continuing resistance from local authorities, Gypsies have been fighting increasingly steadfast battles for their rights. One of the first of these battles was at St. Mary Cray where after attempts to evict them, thirty families barricaded themselves in, defending themselves with five-foot railway lines embedded in concrete. There was much fighting, and at least five attempts were made to remove them. . . . At Hil-

lingdon the council was employing a full-time "ranger" whose job it was to move on the Gypsies. It is said that the council was planning to take on a second ranger. There were about 80 families there. After being harassed by rangers, many families moved on to a site called Coln Park Caravan Site, at West Drayton. The response of the council was to send in towing vehicles, bulldozers and police. But the travellers received a tip-off, and barricaded the gate. The council got a bulldozer to smash down the gate. A caravan was brought up to the gate and set on fire. Behind this, a second caravan was filled with concrete and made immovable. Chaos followed. (Sandford, 1973, pp. 75, 79–80)

D. Discrimination in Personal Relationships

The sphere of personal relationships involves close association and intimate social contact, such as family life, marriage, friendship, personal recreation, housing, and social and personal privacy generally. The consensus of social scientists is that these so-called primary relationships are the main area of discrimination in societies having a rank order of social groups, regardless whether this stratification is based on socioeconomic criteria or on race, ethnicity, language, religion, lifestyle, or nationality.

1. MINORITIES IN JAPAN

Though Japanese "boosters" contend that their country is free from serious social discrimination, review of a few well-documented studies makes clear that this industrial giant of Asia is home to several identifiable minorities who most certainly would not confirm the myopic denials of the dominant Japanese. Each of the minority groups in Japan—defined both culturally and biologically—has a distinctive history of separation and deprivation. Each group has its own heritage of cultural and physical features that are judged as unacceptable by the majority community.

Ethnic minority groups in Japan—defined in terms of separate national origins, different genetic attributes, or a history of outcaste status based on ritual pollution—account for about four percent or 4,500,000 of Japan's 110,000,000 residents as of 1974). . . . Some 2,000,000 of these minorities are indigenous *burakumin* (citizens of outcaste communities). About 1,000,000 Okinawans—residing on the Ryūkyū Islands—constitute the second largest minority group in Japan. An estimated 500,000 other Japanese citizens suffer minority status for allegedly genetic and cultural differences, including *hibakusha* (atom-bomb survivors), *konketsuji* (mixed-blood citizens) mainly of Japanese with Korean or American parentage, *kikajin* (naturalized citizens) mainly of Korean or Japanese ancestry, *Ainu* (aboriginals) on the northern island of Hokkaidō, and a number of Japanese who have returned to their homeland after once emigrating or spending formative years abroad. In addition to 109,000,000 Japanese citizens, nearly 1,000,000 foreign nationals live in Japan. Over 600,000 of these resident aliens are Koreans, who thus form the third largest ethnic minority group in Japan—after Burakumin and Okinawans (Wetherall and DeVos, 1975, pp. 336–37).

However much the Burakumin are disdained, the situation of the Ainu is even worse. They are the survivors of the aboriginal inhabitants of Japan, antedating the settlement of Mongoloids from mainland Asia. Their anthropological classification is obscure; they exhibit Caucasoid features as well as some traces of Mongoloid and Australoid admixture.

They are distinguished by an abundance of hair on the head, face, and body, a condition never found in Mongoloids (Shapiro, 1958). Because of their greater physical visibility, the 16,000 surviving Ainu are more vulnerable to discrimination than the Burakumin.

The present attitude of Majority Japanese towards Ainu is one of condescending quaintness. Many Japanese tourists visit Ainu reservations to see professionals perform traditional dances at Bear Festivals and produce native crafts. Like Native American culture, the remnants of Ainu culture have been commercialized in the face of majority cultural oppression. Resident Ainu have reported being ver-

bally abused by majority Japanese. Ainu are sometimes called *gaijin* (foreigners) by majority Japanese despite the legal status of Ainu as Japanese nationals. Ainu tell also of being irritated by tourists who express surprise that "Ainu speak pretty good Japanese," and wonder "How do Ainu walk?" The word for "dog" in Japanese is *inu*. Using the exclamatory "ah," majority Japanese are known to convert *Ainu da* (It's an Ainu) to *Ah, inu da!* (Ah, a dog!). (Asahigawa 1971:178–179, 181, 202.) Ainu youth, like Native American youth, are determined to reverse the directions of majority oppression, but as yet they face enormous social barriers in the majority community, not the least of which—as for other minorities in Japan—is the pervasive Japanese sense of racial if not cultural purity and superiority. (Wetherall and DeVos, 1975, p. 346)

Even a trace of Ainu blood in the children of mixed marriages results in their treatment as Ainu by majority Japanese.

In the case of the *Konketsuju*, or Caucasoid–Mongoloid mixed-bloods, physical visibility is a signal for social deprivation. Nearly 18,000 have been fathered by U.S. servicemen since the end of World War II, and there are also 2000 offspring of black–Japanese unions. Middle-class Japanese society views this biosocially marginal group as second-class Japanese and they are thus to a large extent socially ostracized. One of the most tragic and pitiable minorities in the world, however, are the so called *Hibakusha* ("persons who have experienced the Atom Bomb"). According to Wetherall and DeVos:

The bombings of Hiroshima and Nagasaki in 1945 created a new ethnic minority in Japan that shows every sign of perpetuating itself and being perpetuated into future generations. The variety of physical and psychological problems that plagued survivors in the weeks, months and years following the two holocausts generated widespread doubts among Hibakusha and non-Hibakusha alike concerning the genetic wholesomeness of Hibakusha parents and their descendants. Conspicuous atom-bomb afflictions gave rise to the kinds of discrimination commonly suffered by maimed and scarred individuals around the world. But the ailment most alarmingly imputed to persons even remotely exposed to the flashes was "invisible" in the darkest recesses of the body.

Hibakusha . . . are popularly believed to carry defective genetic mutants expected to manifest in subsequent generations. This fear of contamination has placed considerable psychological stress on Hibakusha identity and has raised difficult barriers for Hibakusha seeking marriages with nonhibakusha majorities. Atom-bomb survivors are sometimes described as nuclear outcastes, and Hibakusha communities have been called *genbaku buraku* (atom-bomb settlements). The comparison with Burakumin is not without a tragic irony, however. Hiroshima has traditionally had large Burakumin communities, and not a few Hibakusha carry a double burden that tends to make them minorities within their own minority group. (*Ibid.*, p. 353)

2. INTERGROUP PERSONAL RELATIONSHIPS IN WESTERN COUNTRIES

Characteristic of social discrimination is the resistance of groups, however defined, to sharing their streets, houses, clubs, and friendships with members of other groups whose cultural or racial differences are highly visible. The deeper and more obvious the gap between groups, the stronger each group's out-group antipathy and the more determined its resistance to assimilating or being assimilated by the out-group.

Dominant groups frequently form negative stereotypes of deprived groups. Public opinion surveys in Australia, for instance, have shown that whites tend to think Aborigines "dirty," "drunken," "irresponsible," or "wasteful." One such survey showed that whites had very little contact with Aborigines living in the same town (51 percent had none) and that 60 percent of Whites had unfavorable attitudes of varying intensity about them (Lippman, 1972, p. 31). Segregation of bars and restaurants is also observed.

When an Aboriginal family achieves a degree of economic security and acceptance by white neighbors, it is subject to "attack from the rear." Some such families have had to move

repeatedly to free themselves of dirty and drunken fellow-Aborigines. They live in fear that endless "relations" will arrive by the carload and, following tribal custom, demand that the integrated family share everything it has gained. The newcomers' behavior is often such as to outrage the white neighbors.

The United States has only recently emerged from institutional segregation. As Ina Corinne Brown writes:

Until the Public Accommodation Acts of the 1960s, the question of where to stay when travelling, where to eat, or even where one might find a drink of water or toilet facilities, were daily problems to Negroes. In many areas social and cultural opportunities were equally restricted. As late as 1953 two-thirds of the Negro population in thirteen states were without access to library facilities of any kind. Throughout the States where separate schools were required, museums, parks, playgrounds, theatres and concert halls were also generally closed to Negroes. In many Northern areas such facilities were technically open, but were located so far from the poorer Negro residential areas as to put them completely out of reach. Until 1968 South Carolina law required separate work rooms, doors and stairways for Black and White textile workers. (1973, p. 153)

Surveys in the United States indicate a persistence of racial exclusiveness: as late as 1971, 44 percent of urban and 55 percent of suburban whites indicated they would feel at least a little disturbed if a Negro family of similar status moved next door. But there is a shift toward greater interracial acceptance. Between 1964 and 1970 the number of respondents favoring desegregation rose from 27 percent to 35 percent (an additional 44 percent supported partial desegregation), while the number of whites stating they had only white friends dropped from 81 to 68 percent (Campbell, 1971, pp. 124, 136, 147).

Interracial relations in the urban-suburban community of University City, Missouri, were studied by Gelfand and Lee (1973, pp. 258–59). "Although secondary contacts in shopping areas naturally became more common as the number of blacks in the city increased, socializing on any personal level remained intermittent and relatively infrequent. The teas and parties that were held in an attempt to extend interracial contacts failed to promote lasting interracial friendships." It is typical of inter-ethnic relations in many American cities that people of various ethnic groups mingle and work together during the day in offices, banks, factories, department stores, and universities. But in the evening each ethnic group returns to its own neighborhood, as do the "assimilated" suburbanites. Neighborhoods of pronounced ethnic character have their own schools (except as diluted by busing), their own little shops, their own doctors, and their own festivals. Integration is limited to work and does not extend into social life. Richmond's research in Bristol, England, revealed the same tendency to exclusivism in the sphere of primary social relations. Although there was no formal color bar in places open to the public, there was comparatively little mixing among the different ethnic groups in social and recreational activities (1973, p. 195).

3. GROUP ENDOGAMY AND EXOGAMY

Marriage still provides the most accurate index of social discrimination. Middle-class Japanese parents, for instance, will go to great lengths to investigate the genealogy of prospective in-laws. Special agents or intermediaries are often employed for this purpose. Members of so called outcaste communities (such as Burakumin) are viewed as the major danger for social contamination and are therefore ruled out as prospective spouses. In East Africa the greatest fear on the part of Asian Indians is that their daughters may officially be forced to marry blacks. Yash and Dharam Ghai write: "The Zanzibar government comes nearest to demanding complete assimilation. . . . Vice President Karume, who rules Zanzibar (now a part of Tanzania) with an autonomy bordering on independence, has brought pressure on the Asian community in an attempt to promote the

marriage of its daughters to Africans and a decree passed in 1970 dispenses with the necessity for the consent of both parties to the marriage" (1970, pp. 68–69). Karume threatened to deport any parent who sent his daughter abroad to get married or who stood in the way of his child's marriage to a member of another race. In the spring of 1970 Karume attempted to force the marriages of four Persian girls, arresting and holding for deportation their fathers and brothers, who had objected. Although Tanzania's President Nyerere failed to persuade Karume to reverse this order, a protest by the Anti-Slavery Society brought assurance from the Tanzanian High Commissioner in London that those detained had been released and the expulsion orders withdrawn. On September 9, however, it was reported that four young Persian girls had been forced to marry members of the Tanzanian Revolutionary Council. When their male relatives protested, they were sentenced to jail and whipping. A People's Court found them guilty of acting against a Presidential Decree which forbids any person from stopping an intended marriage "unless one of the partners has been convicted of theft, suffers from venereal disease, tuberculosis or leprosy or is a mental defective." A report from Zanzibar stated that 30 more girls had been chosen for forced marriages (Rothchild, 1973, p. 303; *Daily Telegraph*, London, September 30 and October 10, 1970).

Marriages between groups may be discouraged by discriminatory treatment of the offspring. The Muslim and Judaic rules are opposite: in mixed marriages, children of a Muslim father are Muslims, whereas children of a Jewish mother are Jews. Within Israel, Jews of European origin have tended to regard marriages with "Afro-Asians" as status-depressing though there is today an increasing number of intercommunal marriages. In South Africa, social disapproval of racially mixed marriages is reinforced by laws forbidding them. Conversely, efforts of the Pakistan government to promote East–West marriages proved a complete failure. Although New Zealand has no laws forbidding mixed marriages, Richard Thompson found that Maoris and Pacific Islanders, along with blacks, were the least preferred marriage partners for white New Zealanders (1969, p. 181). Social distance was least in the case of Northwestern European groups, and greatest in the case of Asians, such as Chinese, Hindus, and Japanese.

In Latin America, which has no single race barrier but a hierarchy of color (see Chapter 13, E1) marriages tend to be limited to persons of the same group or groups that are socioculturally and somatically not too far apart.

E. Social Deprivation and Restricted Life Chances

Social deprivation means reduced life chances *in relation to the life chances of others*. The term may be applied to poor people in relation to the more affluent within a country, or it may be used in comparing poor with rich countries. Deprivation has two aspects: *objective* and *perceptual*. The first refers to the person's relative situation by objective standards such as income, education, housing, and social services. The second indicates the way the person perceives his situation, which may be better or worse than the objective standard.

Awareness of relative social deprivation among disadvantaged groups grows especially fast when their expectations are stimulated by an increase in their standard of living (particularly through educational and occupational advancement). The revolution of rising expectations among American blacks after World War II is now being duplicated in South Africa. A rapid improvement in the living standards of nonwhites is generating an equally rapid escalation of expectations. Because actual advancement obviously cannot keep pace with expectations, some nonwhite opinion leaders have a

far more acute sense of deprivation than they had when their standard of living was far lower and their life chances, relative to those of the whites, were far more restricted than they are today.

W. G. Runciman, an acknowledged authority on social inequality, points out that precisely because of the expectations-fulfillment gap, revolutions are likely to occur at times of rising prosperity. He cites the French and Russian revolutions as examples and quotes de Tocqueville's observation: "Patiently endured so long as it seemed beyond redress, a grievance comes to appear intolerable once the possibility of removing it crosses men's minds. . . . At the height of its power feudalism did not inspire so much hatred as it did on the eve of its eclipse" (1972, p. 24).

The historical record suggests that perceptual rather than objective deprivation is the decisive motor of revolutionary action. What matters is that people are *aware* they are unjustly deprived, relative to other persons or groups. In the United States, improved education and jobs, faster upward mobility into the middle class, and more effective political bargaining power fired the conviction among the Negro masses that spectacular advancement was in the offing. Since this expectation was not fulfilled, a crisis resulted.

Social deprivation is common in multiethnic countries and is by no means limited to discrimination across macroracial lines. In Uganda, for instance, leaders of the smaller tribes accused the politically and economically dominant Baganda of using deliberate social discrimination to entrench their own preferred position. "They watched the Baganda consolidate their . . . advantage by becoming the educational and economic elite as well. By demanding an equal share of the benefits of development, they necessarily intensified the ethnic basis of Ugandan politics" (Nelson Kasfir, in Olorunsola, 1972, p. 80). Baganda dominance was curbed by President Obote, and suppressed—at least for the time being—by

General Amin. Both were supported by coalitions of smaller tribes (see chapter 20, D3).

In Kenya, members of smaller tribes speak of "Kikuyuization" of the country's social, cultural, economic, and political institutions. Tribal imbalances play a major role in the Kikuyus' success in maintaining the leading position in Kenya's social hierarchy. It was the Kikuyu-dominated Kenya African National Union which launched the policy of deliberate socioeconomic discrimination against Asians (see chapter 21). A black M.P., Mr. J. K. Gataguta, defended in Parliament the Nairobi City Council's replacement of Asians with Africans in the municipal market stalls as follows: "Again here, Mr. Speaker, Sir, I must make it quite clear that it is very wrong for anybody to think that this is discrimination. It is not. If the government thinks that some section of the community has advanced so far in commerce and industry and that something should be done to remove the imbalance, that is not discrimination" (House of Representatives Debates, X, 4th Session, December 14, 1966, cols. 2784–85). A year later an M.P. said: "So it is useless although we are all citizens, to talk in terms of fair competition against the people who have been established for a long time and who have the money and the know-how, just because they happen to be citizens. I reject this, we must discriminate, Mr. Speaker" (*Ibid.*, XIII, 5th Session, November 6, 1967, col. 1765).

Enough is said elsewhere about social deprivation of black Americans to make a recapitulation unnecessary here. Suffice it to say that *absolute* improvement in Black standards of living has been accompanied by only *limited relative improvement*, which has become retrograde since the economic dislocation induced by the oil crisis. Allen Pifer, President of the Carnegie Corporation of New York, has said:

The most important result of the northward migration, however, was that it transformed what was once "the Southern problem" into a national issue. As long as nearly all blacks lived in the South,

Northerners and Westerners could put the issue of black freedom low on their list of priorities. Once blacks began to move North and West in large numbers, however, the nation as a whole had to face squarely the questions of prejudice and discrimination. It was quickly discovered that racial prejudice was not limited to the South. Though blacks in the North and West did not face the kind of legally enforced repression they did in the South, they encountered social prejudice and economic discrimination of enormous magnitude. The movement of blacks to the cities outside the South was accompanied by race riots, discrimination in housing, which caused the growth of black ghettos, in turn resulting in *de facto* segregated schooling for blacks, and prejudice on the job market. As a result of these factors, only the meanest and lowest paid forms of employment were available to most black migrants and their children (1973, p. 6).

The effects of social discrimination on black incomes in the United States are discussed in chapter 21.

The USSR purports to be a classless society—or at least on the way there. But insofar as incomes are an index of stratification, the similarity with capitalist economies is more striking than the difference. As David Lane points out:

There is a system of inequality closely related to occupation. Workers who have skills requiring training and education and who are in short supply tend to receive a greater financial reward than those who have little or no skill. . . .

The rising level of skill and education associated with advanced industrialization would appear to be creating a system of social inequality which, save for its ownership class component, is very similar to that of Western capitalist states. Literacy is universal and an increasing but relatively privileged part of the population is receiving higher education. The relative number of unskilled jobs is falling and that of highly skilled categories is rising but both groups are likely to persist in the near future. Finally, even though the wage differential previously enjoyed by "white-collar" workers is gradually giving way to greater equality of income . . . , differential incomes are very much part of the Soviet social structure. Even in the Soviet view of the foreseeable future, it would appear that though social differences are planned to decline, the structure of social inequality is to remain (1971, pp. 69–70).

Other indicators of social deprivation include longevity, health, and mortality. In India, for instance, the different life expectancies between castes and between various ethnic and racial groups are significant. In Canada today an Indian baby has as much chance of living past the age of one year as a white child has of living beyond the age of 60. In 1970 the average life expectancy for white men in the United States was three years more than that for blacks, and in the case of women there was a five-year difference in favor of whites. The average life expectancy of reservation Indians was nearly twenty years less than that of whites. Testifying before a Senate Committee in 1967, Dr. Alan C. Nermann summarized the sociomedical deprivation of Negroes in Lowndes County, Alabama, as follows:

According to the 1960 US census, 15,500 people live in the county, of whom 81 percent are Negroes. While the median income for White families is $4,400 a year, that of the Negro is $935. Of the 3,768 housing units in the county, 3,000 have no sewage disposal, 2,700 have no piped water supply and 1,053 are considered dilapidated. Only 0.4 percent of White babies are delivered by midwives in Alabama; 31.9 percent of Negro babies are so delivered, and these have an infant mortality rate of 9 percent, three and one-half times the national average. (In Bromley and Longino, 1972, p. 491)

Some 90 percent of the black school children had never seen a doctor. "Concepts of child care, community sanitary facilities, public water supply, milk pasteurization, family planning, nutrition, dental care and prophylaxis, insect vectors of disease, proper soil use for growing food and all the other basic health concerns are essentially missing in Lowndes County and, I would hazard to guess, in much of rural America" (ibid., pp. 493–94).

Medical deprivation, however, is not con-

fined to rural America. Los Angeles has a ghetto death rate 22 percent higher than the rest of the city (Jacobs, 1972, pp. 526, 549), and in Chicago it has been reported that medical neglect causes an unnecessary death toll of 600 black babies a year. Those who survive are often permanently crippled by the effects of malnutrition and childhood disease (Dr. Pierre deVise, quoted in Hill et al., 1973, pp. 185–86).

In the United Kingdom, West Germany, France, and Switzerland foreign workers have a higher incidence of deficiency diseases and tuberculosis and a higher mortality rate for all ages than the indigenous population. To a large extent this disadvantage can also be traced to their poorer living conditions and social deprivation in the host country. For black Africans in France the TB rate has been estimated as high as 10 to 15 percent in some workers' hostels, compared with 0.3 percent for the French population as a whole. In the U.K. a national survey conducted by the British Tuberculosis Association in 1956 showed that TB rates were 12 times higher for people born in India and 26 times higher for natives of Pakistan than for those born in Britain (IRR, 1968, p. 22). Even allowing for higher susceptibility owing to differences in climate, the link between tuberculosis and deprivation is undeniable.

The infant mortality rate is likewise higher for migrants than for natives in most West European countries. This is seen in British districts where Africans, West Indians, and Asians live. In France, the 1966 infant mortality rate was twice as high for Algerian as for French children. Proportionately three times as many Algerian as French workers are patients in French hospitals.

Social discrimination and deprivation, considered broadly, include cultural, legal, political, and economic aspects. These, however, are sufficiently complex so that separate chapters have been devoted to each.

15

DISCRIMINATORY PRACTICES OF SOCIAL AND CULTURAL GROUPS

No racially and culturally diverse country is free from unequal and discriminatory practices in those spheres of man's existence which collectively constitute his social and cultural life. These are irrevocably bound to each individual's language and to the ethnic group with which he or she identifies and whose culture pattern provides standards for judging events and people in daily life. Sociocultural behavior also includes the way people work, the way they spend their leisure time, their way of acquiring education and training, their relations with the opposite sex, and their ways of communicating with their own and other people. The psychological aspect of sociocultural behavior embraces intangibles like attitudes, acceptance or rejection of authority, ideas about respect, honor, and prestige, as well as a sense of historicity, consciousness of kind, and above all a feeling of "belonging." Where interacting groups diverge in these social and cultural factors, they become important criteria for group differentiation.

A. How Social and Cultural Discrimination Operates

The quality of social and cultural life is usually measured in terms of the human rights dis-cussed in part I. In a situation of diversity, their application involves the right to associate with one's own people, or with others if they also want to associate; the right to communicate with one's own and other people; the right of each group to develop its culture; the right to equal economic opportunity; the right to rise in wealth and status; the right to choose one's own religion and practice it freely; the right to move freely in public; equal access to public services and facilities; the right to privacy; and recognition of human dignity. These rights are most effective where their observance rests less on legislation than on being embedded in the mores of a society and thus historically sanctioned. In practice, however, the realities of social stratification ensure that social and cultural "rights" and "liberties" within a national society can never actually be or become "equal" in an absolute sense. As long as people in society differentiate groups by their characteristics, interest, or needs, some people will enjoy their social and cultural rights "more equally" than others.

What, then, do social and cultural discrimination mean? Victims of discrimination are subject to unequal treatment, disqualifications, disabilities or deprivation compared to others within the same national society (see Chapter 8). To the extent a group is a target of discrimination, it finds itself in a low stratum in the national or regional society, with few opportunities for social and occupational mobility. Discrimination tends to bar members of the deprived group from voluntary assimilation in the dominant culture, which pictures them with negative stereotypes. Discrimination and inequality are determined by two interacting processes: the way in which groups in a society become differentiated through specific criteria like race, language, or religion; and the ranking of groups in a stratified reward, opportunity, power and status structure. Discrimination and deprivation are not aimed at any particular person; they are encountered by virtue of membership in a group occupying a low position in a stratification system.

Our point of departure is the question: *Kto Kogo?*—who discriminates against whom, and in what way and to what effect? And at what points in society can the effects of discrimination be perceived?

There are people who, because of their low caste and class position, are subject to discrimination in the form of inadequate education, limited mobility, poor housing, social ostracism, and denial of human dignity. Whether they are to be classified as minorities depends on social structure and policy. Thus, the Harijans (untouchables) of India are clearly a minority, as are the remnants of the bourgeoisie and the *Kulaks* in the USSR. Industrial workers in the United States, on the other hand, are not a minority, even though individual workers may belong to minorities otherwise defined. Many minorities experience discriminatory acts aimed at their language, religion, lifestyle, and values, and even their whole physical existence as a separate group.

If discrimination could be ranked on a continuum with insignificant or nominal discrimination at one end and extreme discrimination at the other, then slavery and genocide could be regarded as the most extreme forms of discrimination.

B. The Universality of Sociocultural Discrimination

The data reported in this book suggest strongly that there is no country in the world where discrimination and the resultant social inequality—however slight or superficial—do not constitute a permanent part of the man-made environment of certain people or groups. This pessimistic view of the prospects of social equality is shared by Ralf Dahrendorf who has written:

If it is true that inequalities among men follow from the very concept of societies as moral communities, then there cannot be, in the world of our experience, a society of absolute equals. Of course, equality before the law, equal suffrage, equal chances of education and other concrete equalities are not only possible but in many countries real. But the idea of a society in which all distinctions of rank betwen men are abolished transcends what is sociologically possible and has a place only in the sphere of poetic imagination. Wherever political programs promise societies without class or strata, a harmonious community of comrades who are all equals in rank, the reduction of all inequalities to functional differences, and the like, we have reason to be suspicious, if only because political promises are often merely a thin veil for the threat of terror and constraint. Wherever ruling groups or their ideologists try to tell us that in their society all men are equal, we can rely on George Orwell's suspicion that "some are more equal than others." (1972, p. 40)

1. GROUP INEQUALITY AS A NATURAL CONDITION

Many social scientists are moving reluctantly toward the conclusion that inequality is an inevitable condition of humanity. In primitive societies with access to abundant natural resources, and with no or extremely limited technology, equality was possible if not usual. Engels believed that communist villages with perfect equality existed in prehistoric times (1886), but no modern anthropologist has ever found one. According to Rousseau, inequality originated when one man fenced off a piece of land and claimed it as his inalienable posses-sion and found his claim credited by others. For arch-pragmatist Niccoló Machiavelli there was no problem: he saw inequality among men as an implicit and fundamental condition of social life.

Today there are even social scientists who consider inequality a necessity for modern complex societies because occupational dif-ferentiation and role specialization depend on it. Differentiation without inequality is the promise of "full communism," pending which millennium the CPSU has accepted a "perfor-mance principle" suspiciously like that of capi-talism. The relation of inequality to occupa-tional differentiation is well illustrated by the situation of the 8 million migrant workers in Western Europe. They move into the lowest positions with the smallest pay and the lowest prestige. This inequality is not entirely dys-functional, because it allows redundant work-ers from poor countries to do needed menial jobs that North Europeans are no longer will-ing to perform. Equality in this regard would sharpen competition in higher occupational categories and lead to trade-union pressure on governments either to prohibit migrant work-ers or to limit their occupational and class mo-bility.

The migrant workers, on the other hand, re-alize that they will be kept on the lowest stra-tum in the host country. But they would rather accept the worst jobs in Europe than subsist on the verge of starvation at home. Through in-equality the host countries can therefore ac-quire enough workers to man the lowest jobs in the labor structure without an economic threat to the local workers. From the migrant work-ers' point of view, inequality actually affords them a limited upward mobility they would not enjoy if forced to remain at home.

By providing differential rewards to the oc-cupants of different social positions, modern complex societies in fact create a selective pro-cess whereby better-qualified persons gravitate to the top and the least qualified to the lowest

positions in the socio-economic hierarchy. Those who reach the top, however, are in-clined to use the power they have acquired to maintain their privileged positions at the ex-pense of the merit principle.

Inequality maintained by power rather than free competition usually leads to situations of conflict. The direction and nature of changes will then depend largely on the bargaining power of interacting groups. Inequality of op-portunity can only be maintained as long as some members of a society are capable of using force or pressure to keep other members in lower positions. The strategies, techniques, and procedures applied to this effect may vary from direct political and legal coercion to sub-tle forms of class, race, or ethnic discrimi-nation.

In most countries where group differentia-tion is pronounced and complex, a complex ranking and stratification system will emerge. Although the lines between strata are invaria-bly blurred, and the differential status, rights, and power of each stratum actually fuse into one another on a continuum, there is usually no doubt about who definitely occupies the lowest and the highest positions. The rank order in the middle echelons is more doubtful.

2. A CASE STUDY: A CITY IN VERMONT

A study of Burlington, Vermont, under-taken by E. L. Anderson in the 1930s forms a real-life scenario of complex and subtle inequalities. Anderson's most significant ob-servations are summarized by Brewton Berry:

In this community of 25,000 there are no less than 35 distinct ethnic groups; and, while status is an elusive social phenomenon and its measurement ex-tremely baffling, it is very real and enters promi-nently into the consciousness of everyone. At the top of the status hierarchy stand the Old Yankees. They, of course, regard themselves as the best peo-ple; and Anderson says that newcomers "accept the Old Americans at their own evaluation." . . . *There is widespread agreement about which groups* occupy the opposite position in the *system of rank—the Negroes and the Chinese vie for that unenviable position.* And it is interesting to note that there are very few of either, so the prejudice against them does not arise from any fear that they may some day dominate the community. English and English-speaking Canadians enjoy a high status, being more acceptable to the Yankees than other ethnic groups. The Irish have witnessed a great change in their position within the space of a century. When they first came to the city in 1849, they took a position on the lowest rung of the social ladder. Today, however, their status is much higher. . . . The French Canadians are the largest group, being 10,000 strong; but their status is very low. They are among the oldest groups in the community, too, having been represented there almost as long as the Yankees. . . . Even so, they are poor, docile, unaggressive, and concerned primarily with maintaining their customs, language, and religion. As one of their own number expressed it, "The French don't stick together; they act as if they felt inferior and ashamed of their nationality." There are many other peoples represented in Burlington's population—Jews (mostly Polish and Russian), Germans, Italians, Syrians, Greeks, Norwegians, Swedes, Finns, Armenians, Turks, and others—and each ethnic group has a certain position in the status hierarchy which, though not rigid and permanent, is nevertheless apparent to all. . . . Certain occupations, for example, are highly regarded, and others are held in low esteem. Labor in mills and factories carries little prestige, and it is in this area that the French Canadians have well-nigh a monopoly. At the other extreme are the professions, in which Old Americans take the lead. Thirty-one of the 44 lawyers are Old Americans, which is far more than their proportionate share. The medical profession is almost entirely in the hands of the Yankees, the Irish, and the English Canadians. The Old Americans have to a large extent retreated from the commercial life of the city, but they still control the banks, most of the city's manufacturing, and the University. . . . Status differences, too, are seen in residential locations. Most desirable is the hilltop in the vicinity of the University, and here the Yankees predominate. Least desirable is the waterfront, and it is there that the most recent arrivals settle, and there also remain the failures when the more successful in their group move on. . . . Thus, the meeting of racial and ethnic groups in Burlington has resulted in a pattern of stratification; though the lines between the various levels are not sharply drawn, the strata themselves are neither permanent nor precise, and vertical mobility is not utterly precluded. (Berry, 1965, pp. 173–75.)

A visitor to Burlington or any similar New England town today would still find stratification, but with less vertical range and rigidity than that described by Anderson. There are several reasons. First, World War II brought about extensive social mixing, since the strata of officers, NCOs, and enlisted men correlated only moderately with class origins. Secondly, the Yankees have taken in increasing numbers to liberalism and "radical chic," so that, to many, socializing with "the great unwashed" seems almost a civic duty. Finally, and most importantly, in the period of prosperity and moderate inflation that followed World War II, the wages of industrial workers caught up with and in many cases overtook white-collar salaries. Increasing numbers of non-WASPs have, to use Norman Podhoretz's phrase, "made it" in business or the professions, and neither the University or Vermont or any other state university is in any sense a WASP sanctuary.

C. Discrimination and Inequality as Social Realities

A study based solely on acts of the legislature and official regulations and decisions would represent a totally false and incomplete picture of a country's discrimination pattern. Formally prescribed discrimination and inequality are only the tip of the iceberg. In most countries, essential mechanisms of discrimination are informal but in complex and subtle ways built into the social, cultural, economic, and political structure of society.

An in-depth cross-national analysis shows very quickly that there are numerous countries where discrimination and inequality are permanent facts of life. Yet most have not one single measure in their statute books that sanctions discrimination or inequality. Many countries of the Third World and the Russian and Chinese communist blocs, where discrimination and inequality are rife in practice, even have constitutional provisions against discrimination and inequality. A number were enthusiastic signatories of the Universal Declaration of Human Rights.

Overt statutory or legal discrimination is often less onerous in its effects than the informal kind. No country legally enforces poverty, to which discrimination is often, though by no means always, a major contributing cause. Yet many countries do nothing to abolish or eliminate those types of discrimination and inequality which directly or indirectly create or perpetuate poverty. These are often disguised as "protective" trade union rules or laws, in which discrimination is not even mentioned. The view is gaining currency that the so-called "poverty syndrome" or "poverty culture" is a vicious circle, largely created and sustained by discrimination and inequality not in the statute books but deeply seated in the social structure of the community. Those who think (or would like to believe) that social inequality is the doubtful monopoly of countries with complex population compositions, such as the United States and South Africa, should consider Dahrendorf's assessment of inequality as a universal condition of social life:

Even in the affluent society, it remains a stubborn and remarkable fact that men are unequally placed. There are children who are ashamed of their parents because they think that a university degree has made them "better." . . . There are firms that build their offices with movable walls because the status of their employees is measured in square feet and an office has to be enlarged when its occupant is promoted. . . . Of course, such differences are no longer directly sustained by the force of legal sanction, which upholds the system of privilege in a caste or estate society. Nevertheless, our society—quite apart from the cruder gradations of property and income, prestige and power—is characterized by a multitude of differences of rank so subtle and yet so penetrating that one cannot but be skeptical of the claim one sometimes hears that a leveling process has caused all inequalities to disappear. . . . Throughout our society, social inequality is still turning men against men. (1972, p. 16)

1. DISCRIMINATION IN IMMIGRATION SYSTEMS

Both Canada and Australia have recently made considerable changes in their immigration policies, purportedly jettisoning the last vestiges of racial or ethnic discrimination. Would-be immigrants are now selected on a colorblind and ethnically neutral basis. In Canada, age, education, skills, and adaptive qualities form the final criteria for the selection of applicants, with a strong bias in favor of persons in the managerial, professional, or technical occupations. This shift of emphasis has brought about an immediate and drastic reduction in immigration of unskilled workers. As R. A. Jenness, a former Director in the Planning and Evaluation Branch of the Canadian Department of Manpower and Immigration, puts it:

During the 1946–1962 period, only 10 percent of the immigrants were destined to managerial or professional or technical occupations, while 30 percent were destined to primary or unskilled work. Obviously, a policy of bringing in unskilled and primary workers made little sense in an economy that was shifting rapidly away from primary occupations, and placing greater demands on human skills and ingenuity. Unemployment levels among the primary and unskilled workers were already high, and immigration of more of this kind of labour merely aggravated the situation. In 1972, however, under the new selection criteria, close to 33 percent of all immigrants were destined to higher skilled occupations, and only 6 percent were going to primary or unskilled pursuits. (1974, p. 15)

In practice, criteria calling for "adaptive qualities" and "skill" most decidedly favor the white immigrant. Millions of nonwhites from Africa and Asia (where emigration might be the only alternative to starvation) are kept out

of Canada for the simple reason that relatively
few people on these continents (except in countries such as India, which have surpluses of
university graduates), can meet the Canadian
selection requirements. The tens of thousands
of Asians forced from East Africa in the past
five years have subjected Canada to a test in
which it has not, according to Yash and
Dharan Ghai, exactly distinguished itself:

Many of the Asians who are equipped for a life in
the U.K. could also fit into Canadian society, and
most of them would be willing to emigrate there
despite their greater ignorance of conditions in Canada. A certain amount of emigration to Canada does
take place (approximately 5,000 went in 1968 alone),
but immigration regulations are stringent, being related basically to Canada's man-power requirements,
and it is unlikely that many Asians who do qualify
tend to be those with professional or commercial
skills or with considerable financial means, groups
which are very mobile in any case. So Canada cannot really be looked to for alleviation of hardship
cases unless there is significant change of policy.
(1970, p. 198)

By insisting on skills and education, Canada
discriminates in fact against nonwhite immigrants without explicit measures to that effect.

In 1973 the Labor Government in Australia
officially bid farewell to its White Australia immigration policy with great fanfare. But just as
in Canada, the *de facto* selection criteria operate
strongly in favor of whites. Immigrants must
(a) be economically viable, and (b) have personal qualities that will enable them to fit into
the Australian community. In addition they
must (c) be medically fit; (d) have a satisfactory
character record, and (e) have a sincere intention of making a permanent home in Australia.
Obviously, millions of hunger-ridden Asians
would like to move to Australia, but few could
meet all five criteria. India alone is saddled
with more than 25 million unemployed, 10
million beggars, and more than 250 million
people poor by the most conservative standard.
Ten million immigrants would swamp Austra-

lia without measurably alleviating the situation
on the Asian continent. H. I. London of New
York University concludes that "despite the
enlightened rulings of the past six years, the
government still pursues a policy designed to
preserve racial homogeneity and overtly favor
European as opposed to Asian immigrants"
(*International Migration Review*, No. 27, 1974,
p. 440). The Australians are not to be criticized
for protecting their own vital interests, but
they are out of order in pointing the finger of
righteous indignation at others who do likewise.

2. STRUCTURAL INEQUALITY IN THE
   UNITED STATES

Discrimination and inequality are so deep-
seated in the social, economic, and political
structures of most countries that no legislation
or official approval is needed to perpetuate
them. There are societies where the roots of inequality date back thousands of years, such as
the Hindu caste system. In many other societies inequality has become systemic in the context of dominant-group–minority relations.
One of the latter is the United States, where
the behavior of large sectors of the white population toward blacks is dominated by a syndrome linked to the historical belief that blacks
are inherently inferior. S. Freedman defines
this condition as "structural racism"—a pattern
of social action culminating in discriminatory
treatment:

Structural racism is a pattern of action in which
one or more of the institutions or organizations of
society have the power to throw more burdens on
and less benefits to the members of one race than
another on an ongoing basis, or to support another
institution or organization in so doing, and use the
power in this manner. It should be emphasized that
in this definition the intentions of the actors, or the
formal statement of the relevant norms, laws, values
are irrelevant to the question of whether an institution is acting in a structurally racist manner. What
counts is whether its actions *in fact* distribute burdens and rewards in a racially biased fashion (1969).

This definition is supported by Ina Brown, who considers the United States a "racist society," racially divided and with a structural organization that promotes racial distinctions. "The way our cities are set up and the whole pattern of segregation that long had the sanction of law as well as custom, have all combined to separate whites and blacks and to keep them ignorant of one another, but especially to keep whites ignorant of blacks. *These patterns are an outgrowth of slavery*" (1973, p. 8). As Brown points out, segregation and discrimination shape learned behavior. As mentioned in chapter 9, role-playing takes place: the victim of discrimination expects and actually plays the inferior role.

Stokely Carmichael and Charles Hamilton, known for their advocacy of Black Power, distinguish between two levels of racism:

Racism is both overt and covert. It takes two closely related forms: individual whites acting against individual blacks, and acts by the total white community against the black community. We call these individual racism and institutional racism. The first consists of overt acts by individuals, which cause death, injury or the violent destruction of property. This type can be reached by television cameras; it can frequently be observed in the process of commission. The second type is less overt, far more subtle, less identifiable in terms of specific individuals committing the acts. But it is no less destructive of human life. The second type originates in the operation of established and respected forces in the society, and thus receives far less public condemnation than the first. (1967, p. 4)

The black ghetto is the symbol of a discrimination conceived as entirely racial in motivation. Judge J. Skelly Wright of the District of Columbia Supreme Court, noted for several decisions protecting the rights of inner-city poor, describes the ghetto subculture in these words:

The twin problems of racism and poverty have converged in our society to become the problem of the inner city itself. Where once our cities were cultural meccas, they are now miserable slums. Where once the immigrants to our cities came from abroad with hopes for a better, happier life, now they come from the South, despairing if not desperate. And after they arrive they find no escape from the cycle of poor health, substandard housing, disorientated family relationships, interrupted schooling and joblessness. There are *35 million hard-core poor who, in the richest nation* the world has ever known, earn less than $3,000 a year, the income level defined by the Federal Government as constituting poverty by American standards. And, particularly in the inner city, a vastly disproportionate number of the poor are Negroes; in addition to the misery of poverty, they must bear the psychic brunt of the white racism that is eating away our society.

Ignorance, discrimination, slums, poverty, disease and unemployment—these are the conditions that breed despair and violence. Is it any wonder that our cities, once melting pots, are now powder kegs? (1969, pp. 430–31)

3. SOCIAL EFFECTS OF STRUCTURAL INEQUALITY

The recently arrived migrant from the South or the young person who has grown up in the atmosphere described by Judge Wright finds himself an unskilled worker in a district where such workers are in surplus and in an economy where public policy tends to raise the price of labor, thus reducing the demand for unskilled workers. The statistical unemployment rate for blacks remains persistently above that for whites, even though the effect of *present* discrimination was diminishing even before recent "equal opportunity" legislation (Gilman, 1965; Killingsworth, 1969). Black unemployment tends, however, to remain concentrated in the ghetto, where its effect on family life is reflected in the number of black households headed by women and the supportive role of extended families.

Blaming the Victim. American public policy intended to help the victim of poverty is frequently characterized by an ideological process which William Ryan characterizes as "blaming the victim." Educationally, the shorthand phrase is "culturally deprived," which is the assigned reason why a child in a slum school fails to learn to read and write, persists in speaking a lower-class (usually black) dialect, and squirms and looks out of the window rather than paying attention to the lessons. Ryan writes:

> In pursuing this logic, no one remembers to ask questions about the collapsing buildings and torn textbooks, the frightened, insensitive teachers, the six additional desks in the room, the blustering, frightened principals, the relentless segregation, the callous administrator, the irrelevant curriculum, the bigoted or cowardly members of the school board, the insulting history book, the stingy taxpayers, the fairy-tale readers, or the self-serving faculty of the local teacher's college. We are encouraged to confine our attention to the child and to dwell on all his alleged defects. (1971, p. 172)

Analogously, the anomie and more frequent criminality of young black males in America are blamed on the supposedly deviant Negro family with its absent father and domineering and frequently promiscuous mother. This approach distracts attention from structural factors that make it more difficult for black males, especially recent migrants and ghetto youth lacking marketable skills, to play their traditional role as breadwinners. One of these is political interference in the labor market, mainly in these forms:

1. Anti-Black discrimination by trade unions, whose monopoly position as bargaining agents is entrenched in federal law.

2. Wage contracts reflecting rates above the market level that will sustain full employment, the result being labor-saving automation at a faster pace than would occur in a free market; again, federal (and parallel state) labor law encourages such contracts by preventing price competition by workers which would bring wages down to a full-employment level (but no lower).

3. The minimum-wage law, which stripped of its misleading verbiage bars from employment anyone whose marginal utility (gain to the prospective employer from hiring him) is less than his cost (the statutory minimum wage and fringe benefits and overhead).

4. Increasingly complex regulations which make compliance and paperwork relatively more difficult for the small business than the giant corporation.

Another factor that perpetuates the matriarchal Black family is the Aid to Dependent Children (ADC) system which in many states *penalizes the father who stays home* by providing benefits only to families with no adult male present. Unemployed fathers have to sneak in back doors at night to visit their wives, evading the Welfare Department sleuths who will stop payments if it becomes evident that they have *not* deserted their families.

Instead of making structural changes in education and economic policy, however, most bureaucrats and ideologues of the American welfare establishment visualize the poverty syndrome as a self-perpetuating vicious circle. Its effects are treated as though internalized in the victims; the "poverty culture" is accepted as an excuse for deviant behavior.

As Ryan observes, the modern version of "blaming the victim" is free of the moral onus of old-fashioned racism:

> Victim-blaming is cloaked in kindness and concern, and bears all the trappings and statistical furbelows of scientism; it is obscured by a perfumed haze of humanitarianism. . . . those who practice this art display a deep concern for the victims that is quite genuine. . . . Its adherents include sympathetic social scientists with social consciences in good working order and liberal politicians with a genuine commitment to reform. They are very careful to dissociate themelves from vulgar Calvinism or crude racism. . . . "The Negro is *not born* inferior," they shout apoplectically. "Force of circumstance," they explain in reasonable tones, "has *made* him inferior." And they dismiss with self-righteous contempt any claims that the poor man in America is plainly unworthy or shiftless or enamored of idleness. No, they say, he is "caught in the cycle of poverty." The stigma that marks the victim and accounts for his victimization is an acquired stigma, a stigma of social, rather than genetic, origin. But the stigma, the defect, the fatal difference—though derived in the past from environmental forces—is still located within the victim, inside his skin. With

such an elegant formulation, the humanitarian can have it both ways. He can, all at the same time, concentrate his charitable interest on the defects of the victim, condemn the vague social and environmental stresses that produced the defect (some time ago), and ignore the continuing effect of victimizing social forces (right now). It is a brilliant ideology for justifying a perverse form of social action designed to change, not society, as one might expect, but rather society's victim. (1971, pp. 173–74)

Given the victim-blaming view of poverty, there are no cures, only palliatives. Instead of structural changes that would open opportunities to blacks and other minorities, we have educators proposing elaborate programs of "compensatory education," public-housing bureaucrats calling for bigger and better concentrations of poverty or else moving "low income families" (shorthand for welfare recipients) into the suburbs, and welfare dispensers demanding bigger and bigger appropriations. These demands are echoed by so-called Welfare Rights organizations, whose members have been seduced into embracing the very system that keeps them locked into poverty. The alternative policy—that of freeing American business from the restraints that prevent it from hiring the poor at their market wage, and increasing their productivity through employment and training—is not even explored.

Some Are Poorer Than Others. Governments very seldom set out to make people poor by laws or decrees imposing an obligation of poverty. Poverty usually occurs through economic and social evolution leading to unequal distribution of resources or through catastrophes (such as floods, droughts, and wars) that deprive people of their means of subsistence. More often than not, however, the poorest people turn out to have (or be reputed to have) specific characteristics regarded by a dominant group as inferior or undesirable.

4. SPONTANEOUS SEGREGATION: "WHITE FLIGHT"

A mass exodus of middle-class whites, and even not so middle-class whites, from central city neighborhoods to quieter (and whiter) suburbs has been a major sociodemographic trend in the United States during the past twenty-five years. This white outflow amounted to almost 6 million between 1950 and 1960. It then accelerated; passing 5 million during the first six years of the 1960s. The white population of central city neighborhoods dropped by more than 2 million in the 1960s, whereas blacks in these areas increased by at least the same number. These shifts have brought new patterns of *de facto* ethnic and racial inequality in housing and residential choice.

After 1948, when the Supreme Court ruled that racial and religious covenants were unenforceable in the Courts, minority groups began to find it somewhat less difficult to obtain access to neighborhoods on the basis of financial status and preference. Still, neighborhood exclusiveness remained a commonly accepted value, widely enforced by the real estate, home-building, and lending industries. It served as the final factor in the constellation which created the nation's new patterns of residential segregation. (Bromley and Longino, 1972, p. 77)

These authors join many others in arguing that the concentration of poor blacks is a direct cause of poor education. In racially mixed schools, they feel, the "deficiencies" of culturally disadvantaged Negro children would be "leavened through contact with children more fortunate in background and home environment." They consider busing an attempt to equalize educational quality but fear it will acerbate white flight, making the situation even worse in the long run (*ibid.*, pp. 82–83).

5. SEGREGATION AS A CLASS PHENOMENON

It does not follow, however, that busing ghetto children to a supposedly "better" school will give them much of value. If Bromley and Longino's contention that they need "intensive programs" (a circumlocution for remedial classes) is granted, it seems clear that these can best be given by teachers familiar with the environment where the children live. Nor is the "leavening" by the "more fortunate" children and their middle-class curriculum likely to be appreciated. As a young black militant girl put it: "I realized I was born black when I went to elementary school and they told me about Dick and Jane and Bow Wow and Spot and all that crap and I knew that wasn't me" (in Burkey, 1971, p. 81). As Eldridge Cleaver once pointed out, American school curricula are based on European standards of aesthetics.

While the integrated school may provide satisfactory or even superior education for middle-class and upper-working-class black children whose families have made satisfactory socioeconomic adjustment—and who frequently are able to move outside the ghetto—the child of the ghetto subculture is likely to find his sense of inferiority reinforced by contact with culturally foreign material and peers two or three grades ahead in achievement.

Ghettos are not the result of any conspiracy of white bankers, industrialists, or real-estate tycoons. Their formation has been stimulated, however, by real-estate practices, including the racial covenants that were legal until 1948. The persistence of slum conditions in black and mixed neighborhoods is in large part a result of "red lining" by banks and insurance companies. While concentrated black settlements have always existed, in the North as well as the South, the occupation of entire inner-city districts by blacks has taken place largely during the three decades since World War II. A wave of migration of poor blacks from the rural South, and a lesser wave of poor whites from the South and from Appalachia, absorbed all available cheap housing. The housing shortage was then further intensified by government-financed "urban renewal" projects, which demolished thousands of "substandard" but occupied houses and replaced them with new housing at rents the migrants could not afford or—typically in St. Louis, East St. Louis, and New Haven—with fields full of weeds.

More importantly, the migrants, with hardly any exception, belonged to the *lower* class—the class *below* the industrial proletariat or working class whose lot Karl Marx sought to better. This is Class V in the five-class stratification model developed in *Elmtown's Youth* (1940) by A. B. Hollingshead, who found that nearly one-fourth of the population in a "typical" Midwestern county seat belonged to this substratum. In language recalling descriptions of ghetto life, Hollingshead observes that the Class V families, among whom only one was black

are excluded from the two leading residential areas . . . employers do not like to hire them unless labor is scarce or they can be induced to work for low wages . . . Class V persons are almost totally isolated from organized community activities . . . They knew that their children were discriminated against in the school system by both the teachers and the pupils. The Class V's get the bad jobs, such as helping in the junk yards and hauling garbage and ashes . . . Class V persons give the impression of being resigned to a life of frustration and defeat in a community that despises them for their disregard of morals, lack of "success" goals, and dire poverty (1949, *passim.*, cited by Banfield, 1974, p. 88).

Banfield writes of the typical lower-class individual:

Impulse governs his behavior, either because he cannot discipline himself to sacrifice a present for a future satisfaction or because he has no sense of the future. He is therefore radically improvident; whatever he cannot use immediately he considers valueless. His bodily needs (especially sex) and his taste for "action" take precedence over everything else—and certainly over any work routine. He works only as he must to stay alive, and drifts from one unskilled job to another, taking no interest in his work. (1974, p. 61)

Banfield concludes that lower-class culture as a whole is pathological.

It should be obvious at this point that, when many members of a race *happen to belong* to a particular class, race and class differences become confused. We have already quoted Banfield's observation that much apparent race prejudice is really class prejudice.

Because lower-class people are the most physically active and the least considerate, even a minority of them will determine the character of a neighborhood and turn it into a slum, where the fear of physical violence is pervasive. Because a large percentage of urban blacks are lower-class, a largely black neighborhood (unless quite expensive) is likely to be dominated by lower-class elements. Since lower-class activism is compounded with racial antagonism, such a neighborhood is not safe for whites. Observers have estimated the "tipping point," after which a neighborhood or village will become entirely black, occurs when blacks constitute 30 percent of the total population. A few integrated communities have managed to stabilize themselves below the tipping point through voluntary agreement or rigid enforcement of occupancy limits—forms of limited or disguised discrimination. It is an anomaly that American law, which has been interpreted to mandate residential integration, is at the same time interpreted to prohibit the one device that would assure such integration—"systems adopted and enforced by local authorities."

D. Social Discrimination as Social Practice

Lack of upward mobility may have accumulative causes. These include past deprivations caused by minority status or lower-class status that prevents the acquisition of marketable skills; unsophisticated lifestyle; or lack of opportunity caused by poverty. As the deprived person grows older, he may encounter continuing discrimination, much of it rationally motivated by a lack of educational background or job skills and experience. As Makielski observes (1973, p. 19), most minority members land in dead-end jobs and many are unable to find any job at all. Where continuing opportunities are missing, an employee reaches a peak

in his career sooner, thus losing the economic benefits of a higher income level, and he may be subject to the "last hired, first fired effect."

1. MIGRANT WORKERS AS A DEPRIVED SOCIAL GROUP

As indicated in the previous section, the legal rights granted in theory to migrant workers in Europe do not protect them against unequal treatment. Stephen Castles and Godula Kosack point out that "even the rights which are guaranteed to foreigners by law are often eroded by administrative practices, or simply by illegal police actions" (1973, p. 125). They describe housing practice as follows:

Access to public housing for families not affected by slum clearance through registration on the waiting list is possible in all four countries. Here too, certain problems arise for immigrants. Firstly *there is direct discrimination*, due to reluctance to house immigrants when indigenous people are also waiting. For instance the French Social and Economic Council found that: "Although they may in theory have equality of access to [public] housing, *discrimination remains in practice because of the de facto priority given to indigenous populations.*" In some cases such discrimination is council policy. The Lyon study mentions a case in which a local council grants to a housing society only on the condition that no Algerians should be housed in a new estate. Other councils wanted the proportion of Algerians to be lower than the 15 per cent maximum. In Britain, Wolverhampton Council operated a rule which required immigrants to be in the town two years to go on the housing list, compared with one year for people born in the United Kingdom.
. . . Moreover, immigrants are usually more mobile than the indigenous population, due to their difficulties in finding reasonable jobs and housing, so that they often lack long residence qualifications in any one town, even if they have been in the country for many years. (*Ibid.*, pp. 309–10)

There is also a disturbing gap between equality in theory and discrimination in practice in the field of education. A research fellow of the Max Planck Institute, Berlin (Hüfner, 1972, p. 141) points out that children of migrant workers are often not receiving the basic education to which they are entitled. In the West German state of North Rhine-Westphalia, for instance, unofficial 1969 statistics showed that 60 percent of the migrant children did not complete elementary schools. As Sjef Theunis observes (1972, p. 162), conditions are very much the same in the Netherlands.

2. SOCIOCULTURAL DISCRIMINATION IN COMPLEX SOCIAL SYSTEMS

Latin America provides a variety of interesting cases in which group differentiation based on class, caste, political, and economic power, create inequalities and discrimination despite official egalitarian ideologies. In his highly readable book on Latin-America, Julius Rivera stresses that the inequalities to which peasants are subjected are rooted directly in societal structures.

Elementary education is compulsory in every country, in theory although not in practice; enforcing the law is beyond any government's power. Very few countries have integrated their ethnic societies, certainly not in the rural areas. . . . Moreover, if thousands of families can hardly eat, it is simply unthinkable to expect that their children would go to school. (1971, pp. 33, 75–76)

The following assessment by the London-based Minority Rights Group on the situational realities in Brazil shows that discrimination still occurs in countries who can boast of long traditions of legally enshrined "color blind" equality.

In a society where social control mechanisms have traditionally been used with great effect to ensure that one group remains dominant and the other dominated it has not been found necessary to enact rigid rules in order to ensure the continuance of the dominant-dominated relationship. Were legal precepts alone proof that racial justice and harmony exist, it would be a completely different story. The distinction between theory and practice is very important in an assessment of the black Brazilian's position, because there are no legal provisions which force him to remain in a disadvantaged position;

there is, in fact, no need for them because the economic, social and political structures of Brazil are such that, by their very nature, they operate against the interest of the blacks. This kind of politico-socioeconomic structure can effectively handle the rare black person who manages to succeed despite all the odds against him, because his example does not threaten to upset the fixed nature of existing unequal relationships. If anything, because he has managed to "make it," he will be used by the society as a "pin-up" to support the contention that Brazil is indeed a racial democracy. In fact a certain few names are often cited to show that some "people of colour" have been successful—the implication being of course that the rest could follow suit if they would only try harder. Ignored here is the fact that had these few black Brazilians not been exceptionally gifted or fortunate, they would not have attained success. (Whitaker, 1972a, pp. 116–67)

Situations similar to that in Brazil are found in most other South American countries.

Despite legal prohibitions, the caste system in India persists as a pattern of organized inequality that pervades the daily lives of several hundred million people on the subcontinent. The fact that the Indian Constitution affords special protection ("positive discrimination"?) to the more than 100 million Harijans (untouchables, officially designated as the scheduled castes) perpetuates rather than eliminates their outcaste status. Their legally guaranteed position—reflected in separate voting lists, job reservation in government service, and the like—actually helps to preserve the inequalities which form the traditional way of life for millions of people. Lelah Dushkin challenges the value of protective discrimination:

The evidence suggests that, at best, the benefits can reduce the disabilities only indirectly and in the long run; in the short run they may have the opposite effect. The "stigma of pollution" is not removed by forcing people to call attention to it every time they apply for a job or run for office. If "untouchability" is a set of disabilities traditionally imposed on certain castes, then "removing untouchability" means ending the exclusions and humiliations practised by others. It has nothing to do with granting benefits to individual members of those castes. (1972, p. 175)

The main problem is that the removal of legal disabilities does not automatically remove social disabilities. As Philip Mason points out, the Indian Constitution makes it illegal to refuse, for example, entry to a temple, or the use of a well, on account of caste. But it is a very different matter to ensure tht a Harijan can use these facilities without suffering insult or even attack (1970a, p. 185). More than 80 percent of Scheduled Castes members are still illiterate. In spite of *de jure* equality the "Untouchables" can acquire pathetically few marketable assets and skills; hence they remain at the bottom of the socioeconomic ladder.

E. Attitude and Emotions in Sociocultural Discrimination

In relations between nations, ethnic and racial groups (irrespective of cultural or somatic integrators), castes and in some cases classes competing for scarce goods, certain emotional processes take place. They were described in chapter 8,B under the headings of ethnocentrism, prejudice, and social distance stereotyping. All these processes are closely interwoven and together present a psychosocial phenomenon known as the *insider-outsider syndrome*.

Ethnocentrism and prejudice provide the psychoemotional fuel for the negative group-stereotyping and social distancing that result in discrimination and inequality. They form integral components of the human personality. No community can destroy prejudice by a proclamation in the government gazette, nor can the United Nations compel a nation by resolution not to be ethnocentric. Peter Rose summarizes the process of in- and out-differentiation as follows:

Throughout human history men have set themselves apart from others, making clear distinctions between "us" and "them." The ties of kinship, faith, politics, culture and tradition, and real or imagined racial differences, separately or in combination, have always served as bases for in-group solidarity, ethnocentric pride, and claims of superiority. Such facts of social life have often been responsible for the instigation and perpetuation of conflicts and cleavages within societies and between them.

Ethnocentrism. A group with a strong ethnocentric character considers itself unique—the center of the social universe. Its values and norms (including the somatic image) are the criteria by which people are judged as normal or strange in appearance, manners, and behavior. Ethnocentrism is evident in varying degrees among all nations and ethnic groups—in fact a certain minimum is necessary for group survival. But in exaggerated form it provokes discrimination and inequality, which can assume even pathological proportions as they did among the Germans under Hitler. Anthropological research has shown that the names many peoples give to their own group embody the assumption that they are "*the* people." Ethnocentrism in a racial sense means that one's own racial identity becomes the point of departure when "distance" between groups is "measured." Note the clear ethnocentric undertones in the following little verse by Robert Louis Stevenson:

Little Indian, Sioux or Crow,
Little frosty Eskimo
Little Turk or Japanee,
Oh! don't you wish that you were me?

(Quoted in Rose, 1968, p. 26)

To Stevenson, the "me" represented the only normal lifestyle and appearance: the English.

Non-European ethnic and racial groups in the United States, as well as the less-favored European groups, attribute their inferior positions largely to a strong ethnocentric inner core in the dominant culture, which they construe—perhaps to a degree no longer realistic—as WASP-dominated. WASP norms and standards are applied in the school system with such rigor that many non-WASP children are diagnosed as having learning disabilities and in most cases actually acquire them. These disabilities then set off a vicious circle of deprivation that hampers those afflicted in securing the education and training needed to rise in socioeconomic status. A large number of Negro and Mexican-American children in public schools are classified as retarded (according to WASP standards). As Mercer concludes:

Disproportionately large numbers of children of Negro and Mexican-American heritage are labeled mentally retarded by the public schools and placed in special education classes. This phenomenon appears to be true throughout the United States in communities with a sizable Mexican-American or Negro population. . . .

When these statistics are presented as rates per thousand, the disproportions are more readily interpreted in terms of children. In one county, 51.8 Spanish-surname children in every thousand were in special education classes compared to 15.1 English-speaking Caucasian children (henceforth called Anglos). Comparable rates for some other counties with 12,000 or more Spanish-surname children enrolled were 21.2 to 7.1; 45.3 to 13.0; 49.1 to 16.0; 25.5 to 8.8; and 32.4 to 9.9. The rates of placement for Spanish-surname children are consistently two to three times higher than Anglo rates. . . . In one county, 108 Negro children per 1,000 were in special education classes compared to 16 Anglo children per 1,000. Other high rate counties had 51.3 Negro children to 13.0 Anglo children; 72.2 to 13.2; 62.2 to 15.1; 74.1 to 15.7. In every case, Negro rates of labeled mental retardates per 1,000 in the public schools ran more than three times higher than Anglo rates. (1971, pp. 315–17)

Several comments on Mercer's data seem in order. First, blacks and Chicanos may well have higher clinical retardation rates, since retardation is often caused by birth defects or accidents, some of which can be prevented by adequate prenatal and obstetrical care. While a "culturally neutral" test probably does not exist, since any human communication involves culture, it should be possible to distinguish between clinical retardation and appar-

ent retardation caused by cultural discrepancy. In the latter case a further distinction must be made between ethnic and class factors in the culture of the children. It is the task of the school to cherish and, within available resources, to develop the ethnic heritage of each child—including its language. Lower-class culture, on the other hand, is not an object of school care; it needs to be supplemented and in many cases modified if the child is not to remain in the lower-class. Since the culture of poor Afro-Americans is not only a lower-class culture, a teacher of their children must have considerable knowledge of the African heritage and be able to distinguish Africanisms worth preserving from lower-class mannerisms of no cultural value. It would appear that preservation of cultural heritage should take precedence over any "leavening" that might be gained through intercultural mixing.

Prejudice. Ethnocentrism and prejudice are intimately linked. Group prejudice is basically a complex of negative attitudes directed at persons classed as members of out-groups. Many sociologists and psychologists believe that outgroup antipathy is not necessarily pathological, but a normal product of group differentiation. Henry Pratt Fairchild represents this point of view:

From time immemorial it has been inherent in the very nature of human group identification that the members of any particular group should feel more warmly attracted to other members of their own group than to outsiders. It is the very essence of human association that persons who live together continuously in more or less intimate bonds of society should be characterized by many similarities of thought, feeling, and action, and moreover that they should regard their own ways as right and good and preferable to those of strangers. Moreover, if the members of a particular group also possess distinctive observable physical traits of skin, hair, eyes, or other features, it is also in the established order of things that these particular endowments should be regarded as correct, admirable, and beautiful. . . . Feelings of loyalty, devotion, and approbation, along with a comfortable sense of "belonging," are characteristic of practically everyone's sentiments toward the "in-groups" of which he is a member. . . . For the aggregate of these sentiments there is probably no better comprehensive word than "sympathy." . . . The obverse is "antipathy," and this is the typical attitude toward the "out-group" and its members. . . . All of these things have been accepted without question from time immemorial, and it has been ordinarily taken as a matter of course that one's attitude toward the stranger should be one of dislike, suspicion, and hostility. (In Berry, 1965, pp. 313–14)

Inequality and discrimination are always associated with prejudice. In fact prejudice is an emotional prerequisite for discriminatory behavior, which is its operational or behavioral aspect. Whether prejudice is expressed in overt discrimination will be determined by many factors, such as relative power position of groups, intensity of ethnocentrism and out-group antipathy, and levels of sociocultural and political sophistication. The targets of prejudice are therefore very frequently groups of persons perceived as *strangers* in a cultural or racial sense. The early Chinese, for example, distinguished between themselves and a yellow-haired and green-eyed people in a distant province "who greatly resemble monkeys from whom they are descended" (Rose, 1968, p. 11).

A particularly illuminating example of the roles which ethnocentrism and prejudice play in the evaluation of in- and out-group behavior can be found in a survey which Professor Georges Tamarin undertook among Israeli school children:

We selected the most extreme form of prejudice: the extermination of the out-group. We asked the pupils, in direct confrontation, to comment on the following text:

G-Form-1. You are well acquainted with the following passages of the Book of Joshua: "So the people shouted when the priests blew with the trumpets: and it came to pass, when the people heard the sound of the trumpet, and the people shouted with a great shout, that the wall fell down flat, so that the people went up into the city, every man straight before him, and they took the city. And they utterly destroyed all that was in the city, both man and woman, young and old, and ox, and sheep, and ass, with the edge of the sword." (VI, 20, 21) "And that day Joshua took Makkedah, and smote it with the edge of the sword, and the king thereof he utterly destroyed, them, and all the souls that were therein; he let none remain: and he did unto the king of Makkedah as he did unto the king of Jericho. Then Joshua passed from Makkedah, and all Israel with him, unto Libnah, and finally against Libnah. And the Lord delivered Lachish into the hand of Israel, which took it on the second day, and smote it with the edge of the sword, and all the souls that were therein, according to all that he had done in Libnah." (X, 28–32)

Please anwer the following two questions:

1. Do you think Joshua and the Israelites acted rightly or not? Explain why you think as you do.

2. Suppose that the Israeli Army conquers an Arab village in battle. Do you think it would be good or bad to act towards the inhabitants as Joshua did towards the people of Jericho and Makkedah? Explain why.

As an additional exploration of the influence of ethnocentrism on moral judgment, another (control) group was presented with the G-Form-2 text. This group consisted of two sub-groups, parallel classes of the 7th and 8th grades of another Tel Aviv school (N = 168; 86 boys, 82 girls). The first sub-group was presented with the above-mentioned biblical text (asking only the first question), and the second group with a text analogous to Joshua, but presented in a 'Chinese' version:

The story of General Lin:

General Lin, who founded the Chinese Kingdom 3000 years ago, went to war with his army to conquer a land. They came to some great cities with high walls and strong fortresses. The Chinese War-God appeared to General Lin in his dream and promised him victory, ordering him to kill all living souls in the cities, because those people belonged to other religions. General Lin and his soldiers took the towns and utterly destroyed all that was therein, both man and woman, young and old, and ox, and sheep, and ass, with the edge of the sword. After destroying the cities, they continued on their way, conquering many countries.

Please answer the question: Do you think that General Lin and his soldiers acted rightly or not? Explain why? . . .

The answers were classified in the following way: "A" represents total approval, "B" represents partial approval or disapproval, "C" represents total disapproval, and "X" represents confused or irrelevant answers (which were eliminated from the statistical calculations). . . .

An analysis of the answers revealed the following:

1. The striking difference in the approval of the genocide by Joshua (A—60%, B—20%, C—20%), as compared to that of General Lin, leader of an outgroup (A—7%, B—18%, C—75% on G-Form-2), unequivocally proves the influence of chauvinism and nationalist-religious prejudices on moral judgment;

2. The answers to G-Form-1 (A—66%, B—8%, C—26% to the first question and A—30%, B—8%, C—62% to the second) indicate the existence of a highly prejudiced attitude among a considerable number of the respondents, despite some differences in the nuances of the responses, justifying the discriminatory tendencies (religious, racial-nationalist, strategic justification of the extermination, etc.). (Tamarin, 1973, pp. 185–89)

The advent of an important nonwhite population in the United Kingdom and of racial prejudice and discrimination in that country has already been described. It remains here to cite two recent accounts that throw further light on the social psychology of this development. Anthony Richmond reports on his research in Bristol:

The Coloured immigrant group as a whole was allocated to a position of low prestige within the status hierarchy. However, it will be shown . . . that the Bristol-born and other English residents saw the differences between them and the immigrant population not only as a question of status, in a hierarchal sense, but also of distinct cultural val-

ues. There was wide-spread feeling that the Coloured immigrant simply did not "belong" there. The indigenous population saw the Coloured immigrants not only as a threat to their social position, but also as an alien element who brought with it attitudes, values, and patterns of behavior that were strange. The immigrant population, particularly the Coloured immigrants, were seen as a threatening element because they disturbed the familiar sub-culture of the area. (1973, p. 102)

The reactions of three of Richmond's respondents are quoted because they show how a prejudiced person rationalizes his out-group antipathy in general and his racial prejudice in particular:

(1) There are too many of them. It is all right when there are only one or two, but if a lot moved in they will be ruling us soon.—They should all be sent home. Otherwise there will be no jobs for us Whites. . . .

(2) I don't like it at all. There are thousands of them in the old area. Immigration ought to be stopped. There's a family down the road and I don't want anything to do with them. . . .

(3) They don't live the same. Squalid isn't the word for their houses! You see them down City Road and Ashley Road areas. How they live! That used to be a nice area, but look at it now and it's only since them Coloureds have come into it. (pp. 152–53)

Two-thirds of the adult sample in Bristol, especially English-born, agreed with the statement, "English people keep themselves to themselves and don't really accept strangers for a long time" (p. 184).

Today prejudice against foreign ethnic groups in Britain is general in spite of subtle and sophisticated attempts to camouflage or to rationalize it. By redefining social attitudes in neutral-sounding language, the average Briton has tried to escape admitting that racial and ethnic prejudice in the U.K. is fast becoming socially institutionalized. Professor C. Eric Lincoln, a sociologist specializing in American race relations, showed the new attitude in Britain to be the same old race prejudice which all

Americans know. He quotes a remark a London taxi-driver made to him:

They're not like you, sir. You're an American. It's not that they're Black, so much—they can't help that, I suppose. But if you'll pardon me, sir, they're filthy dirty. Most of them have tuberculosis. They spit in the street and they have venereal disease. Up in Birmingham and some other places, why, they're taking over the country. (Lincoln, 1964, p. 113)

Lincoln continues:

A few days later I had lunch with a young M.P. at the House of Commons. "How do you assess the color problem in Britain?" I asked him.

"Well, first of all," he assured me, "it isn't at all like the racial problem in America. The British people, as you no doubt know, have absolutely no history of racialism. Our problem is primarily a physical problem—a problem of space and housing—particularly of housing. Many of our own people have been waiting years for housing. It's a matter of housing and jobs and trying to physically absorb a million immigrants into a situation that is already overcrowded."

Six months later, the same M.P. was reluctant to discuss the problem at all. In the interim the Labor Government had published a white paper on the subject and clamped down on the number of Commonwealth immigrants to be allowed into the country. . . .

Again and again throughout my visits in Britain I was to hear variations of the same theme: "We aren't prejudiced. We just don't have the facilities." (*Ibid.*, p. 114)

Many Britons, Lincoln concludes, rationalize their prejudice as love of country. They "want to keep Britain White not because they hate other races, but because they love Britain."

Despite a manifest effort to set aside prejudice, the purveyors of American culture have managed to aggravate the identity crisis that afflicts many American blacks and is, in fact, a recurrent theme in black literature. Not so much through Anglo-Saxon chauvinism as through sheer intellectual laziness and lack of imagination, the U.S. education establishment seeks to universalize its monolingual and monoethnic curriculum, based on an essentially WASP cultural model. The entertainment industry likewise creates an image of a society homogenized into an Anglo-Saxon culture, ethnic variations generally being erased except for a special dispensation to Jewish identity and occasional explorations of black, Indian, and other ethnic subsocieties which—while nearly always sympathetic—tend to emphasize their alien character. The universality of the Anglo-Saxon culture, therefore, has limits and American Blacks find themselves outside these limits. The resulting dilemma has been summarized as follows:

Negroes in the U.S.A. are integrated into a society dominated by whites, and tend to introject the social attitudes of whites, including the white self-concept. *The ideal personality type is that of the middle-class white Protestant.* Nevertheless, despite his introjection of white values, the Negro remains a Negro within a hostile white society out of which he cannot contract and at the same time retain his mental stability. He is therefore born into, and lives throughout his life, within a society that employs double standards. His behaviour, values and idea of selfhood are continually fluctuating between conflicting, irreconcilable, and tempting loyalties and their consequent behaviour patterns. *The Negro wants to be a Negro. But he also wants to be white. Society permits him to be neither*, and his sense of identity is unstable and unrewarding. (Bloom, 1971, p. 145)

Despite long range economic gains (see chapter 21), blacks as a group remain in a subordinate status, and it is natural that many suspect a white conspiracy to keep them there. Their socioeconomic disadvantages are typical of marginal groups who cannot be assimilated in the dominant culture. The reasons again are not conspiratorial but evolutionary. Any national culture is necessarily content-specific, and the prevailing Anglo-Saxon-dominated culture has evolved with a set of norms and images that define the Negro as a foreigner. Frantic efforts are made to redesign the culture—e.g., by redrawing the pictures in the children's readers to include some black faces, by consigning Little Black Sambo, Doctor Doolittle, and most Stephen Foster songs to the scrapheap, and by re-naming Johnny "Chico." But viable cultures are not designed and engineered; they must grow spontaneously. And when they do, they are usually ethnocentric, as is the evolving black culture.

1. THE CASE OF THE JEWS IN THE USSR

In strength of feeling and proneness to violence, anti-Semitism is surpassed only by color prejudice. The term was reputedly coined during the 1870s by Wilhelm Marr, who called Bismarck's Reich "a new Palestine" (Bracher, 1970, p. 36); it was intended to denote the genetic inferiority of the Jewish "race." As a social tendency, anti-Semitism dates from the Middle Ages; the *Merchant of Venice*, notwithstanding its literary merit, is clearly anti-Semitic.

Anti-Semitism in Russia dates back to the eighteenth century. Coincident with the rise of revolutionary movements, the number of pogroms—mass attacks on Jewish shops and homes, usually culminating in killings—increased markedly after 1870. As the Jews formed a convenient scapegoat to distract the population from the economic problems, pogroms were tolerated and even encouraged by the *Okhrana* (Czarist secret police), which translated an obscure French satire and resurrected it as *The Protocols of the Elders of Zion*—supposedly documenting a Jewish conspiracy to seize control of the world. Pogroms reached a climax during the 1919–21 civil war when more than 200,000 Jews were killed. In Ukraine alone more than 1300 pogroms took place in some 700 places. Western abhorrence of this massive slaughter of innocent people brought an end to the pogroms, but not to Russian anti-Semitism. The Russian-dominated Communist Party (CPSU) set about "noiselessly" denationalizing the Jews by refusing them the wherewithal for national existence.

The present upsurge in Jewish group awareness, stimulated by Israel's life-and-death struggle against the Arabs, has shown the utter failure of the CPSU's policy of national liquidation through assimilation. And the more strongly the Jews assert their ethnohistorical identity, the more draconic the oppression heaped upon them and on their language, religion, and culture. During the decade of tension from 1956 to 1965 the number of synagogues dropped from an estimated 450 to fewer than 70. By the late 1960s there was not a single Yiddish school or class left in the USSR, and most Jewish theaters had to close down for fear of official vendettas. Practicing Jews are excluded from all higher administrative posts, while students are barred from the universities by a quota moving rapidly toward zero. Jews who speak out in public against anti-Semitism are branded as reactionary Zionist racists and frequently sent to prison or forced labor on trumped-up charges of "anti-Soviet agitation."

The obstinate resistance of the Jews to cultural or biological Russification has exacerbated Russian anti-Semitism. The Soviet delegation to the UN even tried to have an anti-discrimination convention amended to equate Zionism with "Nazism" (*Jewish Chronicle*, London, October 22, 1965). This identification is attempted by the Soviet anti-Semite Trofim Kichko in his book *Judaism and Zionism* (Kiev, 1968). His chief target is the so-called Jewish bourgeoisie, activated by:

the chauvinistic idea of the god-chosenness of the Jewish people, the propaganda of messianism and the idea of ruling over the peoples of the world. . . . Such ideas of Judaism were inculcated into the Jews first by the priests and later by the rabbis for centuries and are inculcated today by Zionists, educating the Jews in the spirit of contempt and hatred towards other peoples. . . . Judaism teaches that Jews should force the subjugated peoples in the invaded lands to work for them as for a people of priests. . . . If, however, the subjugated should not want to submit, the Torah solves the problem shortly, clearly, and in a particularly inhuman way: "For the nation and Kingdom that will not serve

Thee shall perish." (Isaish, 60:12) (In Kochan, 1972, pp. 323–24)

Anti-Jewish feelings of rank-and-file CPSU members are encouraged by the Party leaders: on the 50th anniversary of the October Revolution, Secretary Brezhnev extolled the many nationalities of the USSR—but never mentioned the Jews. Nor are they represented in the Council of Nationalities, the branch of the Supreme Soviet that supposedly represents the various peoples. Byelorussia, Ukraine, and Lithuania, where Jews are concentrated, have only six Jewish deputies among 1073 in that rubber-stamp chamber, while the 835-strong Russian delegation includes only one Jew. And the 5312 members of Union Republic Supreme Soviets include only 14 Jews—elected as individuals and not to represent the Jewish nation. As Kochan observes, the Jews of the USSR are shown as such on their internal passports, but are not allowed to have any internal communal structure, or any elected or appointed organ to represent them. Such large Jewish communities as those of the Ukraine and White Russia, with their centuries of tradition, have no educational or cultural institutions.

Russian anti-Semitism escalated sharply during the Israeli–Arab hostilities in May–June 1967, especially during the Six-Day War. "Having treacherously attacked the Arab countries and capitalized on the advantages of their sudden blow," declared *Izvestia* (June 15, 1967), "the Israeli forces seized territory almost four times as large as the entire size of Israel [true, but most of it was desert]. The invaders are killing prisoners of war and defenseless peasants, driving the inhabitants from their homes and publicly executing men, women, and children. Even Western correspondents compare these crimes with what the Nazis did in the occupied countries during World War II."

It seems evident that the Russians wish to liquidate the Jews of the USSR as a group, and that as long as they identify themselves with

Judaism and with Israel they will be branded as racists and enemies of the Russian nation. This became evident again during the Yom Kippur War of October 1973. The obvious thing would be to let these "disloyal" people emigrate. But that would displease the Arabs and obstruct the Kremlin's plan for Middle Eastern domination. Truly, the Jews in the USSR are hostages to Russian foreign policy.

2. STEREOTYPING AS AN ATTITUDINAL COMPONENT OF DISCRIMINATION

Stereotypes are identities ascribed to people, based on popular belief about various groups (see chapter 8,B4). Out-group stereotypes are usually negative, but sometimes they are positive—e.g., British are good seamen, Southerners are courtly, Frenchmen are the best lovers. Stereotyping has been called the assignment of a "social identity"—usually a combination of several stereotypes (Williams, 1973, pp. 480f.).

In his classic work on ethnic relations in American communities, Robin M. Williams, Jr., elucidated the vocabulary of stereotyping as follows:

> Stereotypes are part of a whole way of talking about outgroups. This special universe of discourse has its own distinctive vocabulary, its own idiom, its own peculiar style. . . . We may define the language of prejudice as an aggregate of words and phrases applied (accidentally or intentionally, directly or indirectly) to express contempt, derision, stereotypic assumptions, or, at least, a belief that there are generalized group differences, to another social category or to an individual because of his membership in that category. (*Ibid.*, p. 484)

Accidental-Indirect Stereotyping

Phrases Pertaining to Color   These phrases follow an historical tradition of equating whiteness with purity or desirability and blackness with evil. Examples are: "That's darn white of you," "Free, white, and twenty-one," "He treated me white," or "Your face may be black, but your heart's as white as mine."

Disparagement of Other Minorities This behavior may take the form of whites telling Negroes jokes about Jews, Italians, Catholics, etc. or confidential statements such as "you Negroes are all right with me, but it's those Jews I don't like."

Accidental-Direct Stereotyping

Racial Testimonials In many cases, Hometown Negroes reported that whites seek to establish rapport by making favorable categorical statements of their preference for Negroes or by making assertions that Negroes are not inferior to whites; for example, "I like Negro people," "What the hell—you're as good as I am," or the statement sometimes referred to by Negroes as the "black mammy speech": "I've loved the colored ever since I was rocked to sleep in the arms of my black mammy." . . .

The Racial Slip To the Negroes of Hometown, the most noticeable and disturbing of all the elements of the language of prejudice, despite its accidental nature, is the racial slip. This involves unintentional phrases. . . . for example, "I worked like a nigger," "I jewed him down," "There's a nigger in the wood-pile," or . . . reference to Brazil nuts as "nigger-toes," or reference to a type of garden weed as "nigger-heads."

Intentional-Indirect Stereotyping

Stereotyped Preconceptions of Negroes Many Negroes know the stereotypes about them held by whites, and they express disapproval of white people who expect all Negroes to be able to dance and sing, or who assume that each Negro knows thoroughly all aspects of Negro life in the South and in Africa, or who think that each Negro knows all other Negroes, or who believe that Negroes are lazy, ignorant, and happy-go-lucky, or who believe that all Negroes are sexually immoral. . . .

Caricatures of the Negro Negroes also express disapproval at the way Negro life is parodied in the media of communication; they often cite the examples of the former radio shows of "Amos 'n' Andy" and "Beulah," the "Little Black Sambo" children's fable, and certain cinema characters. The annoyance is more extreme when in interracial contacts, they are addressed by whites in imitations of Negro dialect . . . or called names drawn from derogatory stories, like "Sambo," "Nicodemus," or "Rastus."

Intentional-Direct Stereotyping

Jokes, Songs, and Stories Disparaging Negroes Embedded in American culture are a number of so-called darky jokes, comic stories in pseudo-Negro dialect, stories ridiculing the stereotyped traits of the Negro, or songs that contain racial epithets. These are intentional to the extent that the white person is usually aware that they have racial implications; . . .

Intentional Use of Racial Epithets Situations of interracial tension often involve purposive words of contempt on the part of whites, like "smoke," "jig," "coon," or "shine." Some Negroes have been able to recall as many as twenty of these epithets. However, as far as Negro reactions are concerned, the one most negatively evaluated term is the word "nigger"—a word so intensely disliked that the Negro press generally prints it as "n----r," regardless of the context." (*Ibid.*, pp. 484–86)

Physical stereotyping tends to emphasize extreme traits. A black skin will always be seen "blacker," hooked noses become beaks, fuzzy hair becomes fuzzier, and thick lips thicker. This tendency can be seen clearly in the pictures of Jews that once appeared in the National Socialist periodical *Der Stürmer* and which are replicated in modern Arab propaganda (and, sadly, in certain extremist publications in the United States).

In modern Japan the stereotype of approximately 3 million members of a pariah caste, the Burakumin, embodies both physical and socio-cultural elements. The usual image of this minority emphasizes mental retardation, uncleanliness, laziness, and an appearance projecting social backwardness and intellectual inferiority generally. In Brazil the stereotype of the Polish immigrants is a similar mixture. They are described as inclined to alcoholism, excessively religious, always fair-haired, inclined to take to crude manual tasks and therefore intellectually inferior, and inclined to mate with blacks (Richmond, 1972, p. 247).

The same combination of physical, social and cultural components is found in American stereotypes of the Mexicans.

Latins, especially Mexicans, have been stereotyped as being lazy, constantly taking siestas, speaking with a foreign accent, and being interested in banditry, bull-fights, and guitars. . . . An analysis of American movies would reveal that Blacks have virtually never been depicted as villains and that, in recent years at least, Indians have been cast as perhaps savage but nonetheless sympathetic characters. Rarely, if ever, has a Mexican-American been portrayed as anyone but a bandit (usually incompetent), who is ultimately done in by a heroic Anglo-American cowboy. (Makielski, 1973, p. 63)

In North Africa French colonialism created the stereotype of the ragged and filthy "Arab," who has been described as an illiterate person who speaks pidgin French, sleeps on the floor, eats couscous, and never washes. Such an "Arab" is lazy, inept at any job, but handy with a knife; he is to be entrusted only with the most menial of labor and paid a minimum, since he needs next to nothing. Actually, as Valabrègue (1973) found in a thorough investigation, the typical Arab or other African in France is strongly motivated, works hard for low wages, and is no more inclined to rowdy or violent behavior than the French worker. Yet the difference (more cultural than somatic) has evoked stereotypes:

"I find that Algerians are vermin and should be expelled; syphilis is skyrocketing." (Marseilles hotel porter)

"They take our women. They must be really vicious. They have a smell I can't stand and they act like they were in the jungle." (Paris taxi driver)

"Forbidden to dogs and Arabs." (sign on the Riviera)

"As a security measure, we do not serve liquor to Algerians." (sign in a bar at Dijon)

"Any woman who goes to bed with a Black must be a whore." (pp. 61–62)

France, it will be recollected, is the country that has long taken credit for "abolishing" race prejudice.

One of the most complex stereotypes to unravel is the American idea of Chinese, including Chinese-Americans. As Yee observes

(1973, pp. 103–11), it consists of sharply conflicting notions. He quotes Isaacs (1962):

American images of the Chinese tend largely to come in jostling pairs. The Chinese are seen as a superior people and an inferior people; devilishly exasperating heathens and wonderful humanists; wise sages and sadistic executioners; thrifty and honorable men and sly and devious villains; comic opera soldiers and dangerous fighters. (pp. 70–71)

In the Broadway play *Chickencoop Chinaman*, the Chinese American hero identifies himself as follows:

Chinamen are made, not born—out of junk-imports, lies, railroad scrap iron, dirty jokes, broken bottles, cigar smoke, Cosquila Indian blood, wine spit and lots of milk of amnesia. I am the natural born ragmouth speaking the motherless bloody tongue. I talk the talk of orphans. . . . I was no more born than nylon or acrylic. For I am a Chinaman, a miracle of synthetic, drip dry and machine washable. (Cited in Yee)

The undeserved image became a perceptual anomaly as "for decades American traders, diplomats, and Protestant missionaries had developed and spread conceptions of Chinese deceit, cunning, idolatry, despotism, xenophobia, cruelty, infanticide, and intellectual and sexual perversity" (Miller, 1969, p. 201). According to a Chinese American professional man in St. Louis, however, social discrimination of the kind described by Yee is rapidly disappearing. Chinese Americans, he said, are worried less about obstacles to assimilation than about preserving their culture and language.

The exploitation of stereotypes for political gain belongs to the stock in trade of political parties throughout the world. Shortly before the election of June 1961, in Zanzibar, the African newspaper *Sauti Ya Afro-Shirazi*, included the following in its comment on an Afro-Shirazi Party meeting:

Today we would like to . . . remind our African brethren who are insisting on helping the Arabs . . . [of] the actions done by the Arabs during their time alone. The Arabs made the people sweep with their breasts; the Arabs pierced the wombs of the women who were pregnant so that the wives could see how a baby was placed. The Arabs shaved the people's hair and then used their heads as places for knocking their toothbrushes. The Arabs had the people castrated like cows so that they might converse with their wives without wanting them. The Arabs made the African old men chew palm nuts without breaking them in order that they may laugh.

The persistence of stereotypes is well epitomized in our concluding quotation, from an American writer, William L. Smith:

There is still a cowboy and Indian world, where the good guys—whether they are following the political trail or riding into the sunset—wear White skins under their white hats, speak standard English (unless it is a cowboy drawl), and most important of all, never lose a fight. There is still a strong tradition that equates Anglo-American origin and Anglo-American ways with virtue, with goodness, even with political purity. (1973, p. 142)

3. SOCIAL DISTANCE AS A MEASURE OF TOLERANCE OF OUTSIDERS

Ultimately, all these psychological factors add up to social distance—the closeness of relationship that one group will tolerate with another. In Israel, for instance, the greatest social distance within the Jewish population is between those of European (mostly Ashkenazi) and of oriental origin. In 1967 Tumin measured social distance in the United Kingdom and found that West Indians were less acceptable than Americans, Germans, or Jews as sons-in-law or neighbors but slightly more acceptable than Germans as workmates. A survey made in the United States in 1963 shows that "whereas 88% of the White informants would not object to working next to a Negro, 80% would not object to sitting next to a Negro at a lunch counter, and about 80% would not mind using the same 'rest room' as a Negro; nearly all *would* object to their own teenage daughter marrying a Negro" (Bloom, 1971,

p. 152). In a 1968 survey in 15 American cities, 48 percent of the respondents felt that "there should be some limit" on the number of black families moving into a neighborhood, while 40 percent did not favor restrictions. It may be observed, however, that a vote for a limit may be a vote for integration, since unlimited black entry often leads to "White flight" and resegregation. Forty-nine percent said that they would not mind at all if a black family with about the same income and education as themselves moved next door to them, but 33 percent indicated that they would prefer their small children to have white playmates only (Campbell and Schuman, 1970c, pp. 275–77).

In 1968, W. H. Ferry published in *The Center Magazine*, issued by the Ford-Foundation–funded Center for the Study of Democratic Institutions, an essay in which he reluctantly concludes "that racial integration in the United States is impossible." He elaborates:

I set forth this proposition without qualification. There are no hidden unlesses, buts, or ifs in it. I shall not deny that in some remote future integration may come about. But I do not see it resulting from the present actual trends in American society. It can only be produced by some event overturning these trends. There is no denial in this proposition that there will be a steady betterment in the material situation of blacks. . . .

My proposition is sad. Like tens of thousands of other Americans I have supported, organized, and taken part in reformist projects, with integration always beckoning at the end of weary labors. Now such activities must be seen as nothing more than acts of good-will, rather like Peace Corps expeditions into an undeveloped country that look toward the welfare and material progress of the natives but not to their integration with the homeland.

After commenting on the possibility that blacks may become a separate political community, and observing that improvements for them are "primarily aimed at the prevention of civic commotions," Dr. Ferry continues:

The United States is a white man's country, conducted according to white customs and white laws for white purposes. And it must be acknowledged that 89 per cent of Americans are non-black. I would not even make the argument that whites should not run the country for their own interests. I would argue that whites do not see, except in perilous self-deceit, that racial integration is one of these interests. . . . Whites have little objection to bettering the condition of black lives as long as it does not cost much, and as long as it leads to the continuance of blacktowns and so does not present the threat of genuine integration at any level. The white condition for black betterment is, to put it simply, separation. (1968, *passim*.)

Whether integration is a feasible strategy to overcome discrimination in the United States thus emerges as a pragmatic question rather than a test of faith in a categorical imperative.

16

CLASS, CASTE, AND SEX DISCRIMINATION

A. *Deprivation Relating to Class*

A class is a group of people within a society who perform a particular economic function or range of functions. Theoretically, two or more classes may enjoy equal status, but they are usually found in a rank order corresponding to the scarcity of the goods or services provided by each class and of the resources it controls. If oil, for instance, becomes scarcer, oil producers as a class will gain in status.

In modern urban industrial society, there is a tendency to define classes in terms of income, education, and lifestyle rather than specific economic function. Classes are not, of course, rigidly separated; they merge into one another and their rank order is unstable. A trade in great demand today may be redundant tomorrow. Class discrimination is said to take place when access to education, employment, and social amenities is granted or denied on the basis of class origin rather than individual ability.

1. INTERCLASS MOBILITY— THE CIRCULATION OF ELITES

Class members are not entrapped from birth in socioeconomic strata; mobility across class boundaries is characteristic of the class system. Achievement today plays a greater part than one's origins; many born into low socioeco-

nomic groups succeed in moving upward. Frank Parkin describes this aspect of class mobility:

> The political implications of upward social mobility seem apparent enough. Mobility provides an escape route for large numbers of the most able and ambitious members of the underclass, thereby easing some of the tensions generated by inequality. Elevation into the middle class represents a *personal* solution to the problems of low status, and as such tends to weaken collectivist efforts to improve the lot of the underclass as a whole. . . .
>
> Most social mobility, however, is of a relatively short-range kind and so does not necessarily involve sharp changes in political identity. The children of manual workers who cross the class line tend to assume fairly modest white-collar positions—as clerks, salesmen, shop assistants, schoolteachers, and the like. Recruitment to established middle-class professions requiring long periods of training and education is far less common. (1971a, pp. 49–51)

Referring to lower- and working-class people of superior talents, Pareto coined the concept of "the circulation of elites, blocking of which stimulates revolutionary activity."

2. AMBIGUITIES IN THE CLASS STRUCTURE— CONFLICT BETWEEN AND WITHIN CLASSES

People with approximately the same bargaining capacity in the market form socioeconomic clusters we call classes. This creates the economic foundations of the three-class system in capitalist society comprising an upper, middle, and working class. To these must be added the "lower" class—with no stable relation to economic processes. They have nothing to offer but unskilled labor, yet they sometimes achieve collective bargaining power by rioting to enforce their demands. (See chapter 15,C5)

Each class has its status, and the quota of prestige and power each group enjoys is ascribed socially. Consensus develops as to upper-, middle-, and working-class lifestyles, and the hierarchical perception of power, status, and prestige becomes part of the ordinary person's "social" personality. As Parkin observes "the more completely the subordinate class comes to endorse and internalize the dominant value system, the less serious will be the conflicts over existing inequalities" (*ibid.*, p. 84).

Class inequality has two aspects. One is the difference in income and other rewards enjoyed by the various classes; the other lies in the way people are recruited for middle- and upper-class positions. Stratification is said to exist when upward mobility is blocked. Common economic interests make a group a class in the objective sense. "But they can act as a class only when they come to realize their common interests, and that there are other classes with different—usually opposing—interests. The development of class consciousness is the precondition for true class existence. . . . Classes do not exist independently, but only in relation to each other" (Castles and Kosack, 1973, p. 466).

In urban industrial Western society, the occupational structure forms the backbone of the class structure. Parkin (1971a, p. 19) pictures the backbone of the reward system as a hierarchy of broad occupational categories, running from high to low:

Professional, managerial and administrative
Semiprofessional and lower administrative
Routine white collar
Skilled manual
Semiskilled manual
Unskilled manual

Through trade unions, skilled and semiskilled manual workers often obtain incomes higher than most routine white-collar people earn.

The out-migrating Europeans who formed most of the national population of the United States took with them the norms, lifestyles, and prejudices of their classes. No sociologist will believe that the so-called "upper-class" residents of Boston are less class-conscious than their counterparts in London, Paris, or Madrid or any more ready to accept upward mobility from "below." As in Latin America, class and race have become so interwoven in the American social structure that it is not always easy to distinguish the specific roles of each.

More particularly, it is the relatively large share of blacks in lower occupational income and educational categories which helps to perpetuate their low class status. The downtown poverty that has developed in American cities (see chapters 9; 13,D; and 21,E) has created a stratum of people not comparable to the European working class but rather a lower one. They could be equated with the *Lumpenproletariat*, to which Herbert Marcuse would assign the historical role Marx denied it. In the American context, Herbert Gans distinguishes between the working class and the lower class as follows:

The former is distinguished by relatively stable semi-skilled or skilled blue-collar employment and a way of life that centres on the family circle, or extended family. The lower class is characterised by temporary, unstable employment in unskilled—and the most menial—blue-collar jobs and by a way of life equally marked by instability. Largely as a result of a man's instability, the lower-class family is often matrifocal or female-based. This is most marked among the Negro population. . . . Although this type of family organisation had some stable and positive features, especially for its female members, the hypothesis has been suggested that it raises boys who lack the self-image, the aspiration, and the motivational structure that would help them to develop the skills necessary to function in the modern job market. . . . These conditions are, of course, exacerbated by racial and class discrimination, low incomes, slum and overcrowded housing conditions, as well as illness and other deprivations which bring about frequent crises. (In Wedderburn, 1973, p. 128)

Some theorists believe that the European working (manual-labor) class is losing its traditional character as a result of technological progress, economic prosperity, and better education. Manual workers are not disappearing, but rather growing into the middle class—a process called *embourgeoisement*. Supporters of the *embourgeoisement* theory claim that manual workers are increasingly adopting middle-class values and life styles and that Western-European society is evolving a new social structure. Figure 16.1 shows the difference.

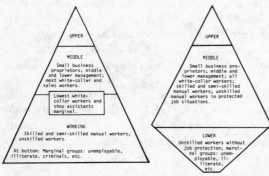

FIGURE 16.1.

Through the confluence of formerly antagonistic classes, *embourgeoisement* theorists proclaim, class conflict in the traditional sense will disappear. Opponents of the theory concede that it contains elements of truth, but do not agree that the metamorphosis will mean the end of class discrimination. As Castles and Kosack point out (1973, pp. 470f.), advanced technology has tended to reduce work to a mere repetition of monotonous tasks and thus

to confirm the worker's subordinate position and his feeling of alienation.

3. CLASS STRATIFICATION IN NON-COMMUNIST EUROPE

It is generally conceded that fluidity between classes has increased, especially in borderline cases. The new mobility, however, involves consumption patterns and material lifestyles (with everybody wanting luxury holidays, overseas trips, stylish motor cars, gourmet food, and the latest clothes). Merging of value and belief systems is far less apparent. Manual workers in Western Europe still tend to view society as divided between "us" and "them." It is astonishing how little interclass mobility is to be found in Western Europe, considering its well-developed educational systems and the strong emphasis on achievement-oriented socialization. Working class families often impose class rigidities upon themselves by setting low educational and occupational goals and by neglecting linguistic skills. Finally, the low prestige of manual occupations forms a barrier no worker can cross, no matter how skilled and well-paid he might be (Archer and Giner, 1971, p. 34).

The notion that workers are exploited by the upper classes is part of the ideology of trade unionism as well as socialism. The concentration of wealth in the hands of relatively few remains a fact of life in Western Europe as well as the United States, but progressive income taxes redistribute much of the usufruct and death duties eat into family fortunes. Whether workers *are* exploited and whether unequal distribution of wealth is *ipso facto* inequitable are questions of ideology and beyond the scope of this book. There are students of Western European social structure who contend that the upper-class elites, drawing increasingly from the middle class, together with the "service class" of bureaucrats, managers, and technocrats, are gradually forming a new ruling class.

Bottomore (1971, p. 402) cites a French study which shows that most occupational mobility is *within* classes. Of the 14 percent of manual workers who changed jobs, two-thirds took other manual jobs. The limited interclass movement is usually over short distances: skilled manual workers move into clerical jobs. There is little or no mobility from the working class directly into the upper class or elite.

In the United Kingdom prominent researchers such as Richard Titmus, John Goldthorpe, Dorothy Wedderburn, and John Westergaard have collected an impressive body of data suggesting that social (class) inequalities in Britain have not changed much since World War II. Manual workers point out that they suffer inequities in job situations to a far greater degree than the white-collar non-manual workers. For example whereas 25 percent of all firms had no pension schemes for manual workers, almost all offered this security to white-collar staff. The latter could also count on longer paid holidays in more than 60 percent of the firms studied; they also enjoyed better promotion and career opportunities and greater job stability than the manual workers (Wedderburn and Craig, 1969, pp. 6–8). The rigidity of interclass and interoccupational barriers is confirmed by income, occupational, educational, and social status differences. David Martin and Colin Crouch point out that in the so-called public schools such as Eton and Harrow "an elite still purchases for its children access to segregated, privileged instruction, with a strong probability of it leading to high-status positions." Their alumni continue to dominate industry, the Church, and Conservative Party politics, and to supply about half the incoming Administrative Class appointees (1971, pp. 255f.).

Martin and Crouch also observe that survival in school varies with social class.

At age eleven to thirteen, a professional or managerial family's child has nine times as much chance of entering a grammar school as a manual worker's. At seventeen he would have thirty times as high a chance of being still at school. Among non-manual middle-class families, one in four of their children who go to grammar school go on to university; whereas only one in fifteen or twenty of unskilled workers' children who achieved grammar school do so. (*ibid.*)

Yet even the poorest Briton, the victim of typical class inequalities, must be counted a "have" rather than a "have not" by world standards.

In Scandinavia, too, occupation plays a major role in social identity. The Danish Who's Who, for instance gives three occupational entries for married persons: own occupation, father's occupation, and occupation of father-in-law (Svalastoga and Carlsson, 1971, p. 359). "Low" social origin remains a handicap, especially in schools, where it correlates positively with low grades and failure to graduate (*ibid.*, p. 378).

In Southern- and Mediterranean-European countries, the large peasantry is most vulnerable to social deprivation and class discrimination. Greece, for example, has a dual but interrelated stratification system, in which peasants and unskilled workers share the lowest level (Mouzelis and Attalides, 1971, p. 182). The lower class comprises all those who possess neither property nor education. Although together they represented about 75 percent of the Greek labor force, only 10 percent of urban workers' sons and 14 percent of peasants' sons registered for university education. "Thus, when a sample of Athens University Students were asked, 'Do you think that in our country, genuine ability alone can enable a young man or woman to succeed?' 82% of the men and 86% of the women replied in the negative" (*ibid.*, p. 189). The picture is substantially the same in Spain and Italy, where small upper classes constituting 4 to 6 percent of the population dominate the positions of power, reward, and opportunity to the obvious detriment of the peasantry and the working classes.

This fact, among others, contributes to the virility of Italian and Spanish communism.

4. THE PERSISTENCE OF CLASSES IN THE COMMUNIST "CLASSLESS SOCIETY"

Since human beings in communist-ruled countries also compete for scarce goods, they cannot escape the universal process of ranking and stratification. The prerevolutionary aristocracy, bourgeoisie, and *rentier* class were simply replaced by new elites.

Long-term wage trends in the communist orbit show a clear-cut pattern of built-in inequality. This trend began in the USSR with the first Five-Year Plan, when according to Fainsod, egalitarianism "was repudiated in the search for a system of wage payments and income distribution that would maximize efficiency and stimulate production; mass welfare gave way to capital expansion and the accumulation of armaments" (1963, p. 108). A labor aristocracy of Stakhanovites—named after Alexei Stakhanov, the propaganda model of the efficient worker—began drawing wages far higher than those paid the rank-and-file. Despite an urban minimum wage of 300 rubles per month decreed in 1956, the wage spread between unskilled and skilled labor ranged recently from 1:2 in the clothing industry to 1:3.2 in mining, the average being about 1:2.8. The comparable spread in the United Kingdom was only 1:1.3 (Nove, 1961, p. 386). The spread in Yugoslavia moved from about 1:1.8 in 1951 to as much as 1:4.3 in 1961.

In both the Warsaw Pact states and Yugoslavia there is a dual elite of skilled manual workers and professional intelligentsia, which owes many of its advantages to membership in the Communist Party and skill at rising in that organization. The intelligentsia in particular is given access to better housing, official cars, foreign currency for trips abroad, and other "perks" similar to those enjoyed by capitalist elites. It is from this group that Communist universities recruit most of their students. In 1965, for example, 52 percent of Polish applicants for university enrollment came from the intelligentsia and the managerial elites, compared with 15 percent of peasant and 25 percent of working-class origin. For the medical academies, the respective figures were 57, 14 and 23 percent (Vaughan, 1971, p. 328).

The peasantry of Communist Europe must decidedly be regarded as a socially deprived class. Most peasant workers in the USSR are in fact unskilled manual laborers on collective or state farms, which are always controlled by their Communist Party branches. Their schools, social services, housing, and medical treatment are inferior to those provided city workers. Not having the automatic right to leave the village, collective-farm children are in a particularly invidious position. Peasant workers from collective farms who wish to go anywhere for more than a month, must first obtain a "pass" from the local village Soviet—a privilege which is granted with extreme reluctance. By refusing them a "pass" to seek work elsewhere, the Soviet can force peasant children to perform collective-farm labor. They are not covered by the law prohibiting employment of persons under 16. "No maximum working hours have ever been fixed for collective farmers, but there is no doubt that they are expected to work much longer than workers in non-agricultural institutions" (Mervyn Matthews, 1972, p. 60).

Students of Soviet affairs distinguish broadly four major classes: (a) peasants; (b) unskilled manual and white-collar workers; (c) skilled manual, white-collar, professional, and managerial workers; (d) the real ruling class comprising the elites of the groups listed in (c) plus the top political functionaries and party bureaucrats. The latter, some 3 million in number, constitute the Soviet elite. Any progress toward a classless society has been vitiated by the chasm between Party members and everyone else.

The executive and professional class is overrepresented in the top organs of the CPSU. At the 23rd Congress in 1966 the top level bureaucracy constituted 2.1 percent of total party members but it accounted for 40 percent of the delegates to the Congress and 81.1 percent of the full members of the Central Committee. It is the ruling stratum (consisting of the non-manual, professional, and managerial elites, together with the top political and administrative functionaries) who are today identified as the "new class." Drawing on the analysis of contemporary state socialism by Milovan Djilas, Giddens summarizes the basic characteristics of the "new class" as follows:

The transition to state socialism has abolished legal titles to private property in the means of production, but control of property still remains in the hands of a minority grouping. This new class is composed of those "who have special privileges and economic preference because of the administrative monopoly they hold," and its position derives from the dominant role played by the Communist Party in political and economic life. It is a "bureaucratic class," created out of the monopoly of power exercised by the Party, that increasingly undermines the role of the Party itself; "The once lively, compact Party, full of initiative, is disappearing to become transformed into the traditional oligarchy of the new class, irresistibly drawing into its ranks whose who aspire to join the new class and repressing those who have any ideals."

. . . in the Soviet Union, in 1959, industrial manual workers made up some 48 per cent of the membership of the CPSU, and collective farm peasantry a further 13 per cent; non-manual workers comprised only 20 per cent of the total. By 1968, however, the proportion of manual worker members had declined to 39 per cent, and while the ratio of white collar workers had more than doubled, rising to over 45 per cent of the total membership. The intelligentsia are particularly prominent within the last category. (1974, pp. 238–40)

In terms of control over property and the distribution of goods and services, the "new class" of party bureaucrats, ideologues, and technocrats has in fact taken over the role of the bourgeoisie. For this reason, critics of the Soviet system call it "state capitalism" rather than socialism, since the workers lack effective political and economic power.

5. INTERLOCKING OF CLASS AND RACE IN LATIN AMERICA

The complex interrelations between class and race in Latin America have been described in chapter 13,E. Rank and status are determined by class much more than color in Latin American society; a person with nonwhite physical traits may be classed socially as white. Small elites dominate the institutions of social, economic, and political power. The income, educational, and occupational gap between the elites and the lower classes is enormous (Rivera, 1971, p. 73).

Except in Chile and Mexico, Latin-American aristocracies, encompassing 5 percent of the population at most, have experienced no radical weakening of their power position over the past two generations. Usually they control the largest portions of land as well as the top financial and industrial undertakings. The professional group is the next on the status ladder, (Approximately 5 to 15 percent of the total population), followed by the middle class (10 to 30 percent), the urban proletariat (10 to 30 percent), the unskilled workers and peasantry (20 to 60 percent).

Social deprivation exacts its greatest toll in human want and misery among the peasants and unskilled urban workers, who account for more than 50 percent of the total population in most Latin-American and Caribbean countries. In Haiti, for example, the peasantry and urban proletariat are about 85 percent of the total population; both groups are predominantly illiterate and almost a third of the urban adult males are unemployed. The elites, forming less than 3 percent of the population, control over 70 percent of the production and wealth of the country. In the privacy of their homes, clubs, and intimate friendship-groups, the upper classes still refer to the peasants and unskilled urban workers with pejorative epithets denoting primitiveness, stupidity, and backwardness.

For the peasants of countries like Pakistan, Bangladesh, and India, the centuries-old history of extreme economic destitution is at present culminating in a newly emerging class consciousness. In India, for example, peasant uprisings are already occurring on a massive scale, reflecting the fact that an increasing number of peasants are sinking below a subsistence level. Similar hardships are today being experienced by millions of peasants in Pakistan and Bangladesh.

B. Preferment and Deprivation Based on Caste

There is persuasive evidence that the caste system, at least in its basic form, is about 4000 years old and precedes the Aryan period of India (Segal, 1965, pp. 42f). It is thus one of mankind's oldest institutions, attributed to Brahma himself. It was strongly defended by Manu (first century B.C.) and opposed by Gautama Buddha (500 B.C.) (Majumdar, 1961, p. 294). About 1500 A.D. the Sikhs made efforts to destroy this system, and in 1759 Sultan Akbar tried to unite Muslims and Hindus across caste lines. This attempt failed and the 1901 census disclosed that there were 2378 "main castes" and tribes, including about 293 tribes that had been transformed into castes (Segal, 1965, pp. 74 and 85; Singh, 1964, p. 329).

1. THE HINDU CASTE SYSTEM TODAY

The core of the Hindu caste system remains the four *varnas* or castes—the Brahmins, Kshatriyas, Vaisyas and Sudras—which traditionally have different social functions and are stratified in order of social worth and prestige. Outside and below the four-layer caste struc-

ture are the so-called *Harijans* (Scheduled Castes, previously called "Untouchables") and the indigenous tribes (Scheduled Tribes) who share their outcaste status. The more than 80 million Harijans are ranked still lower than the Sudras who, as unskilled and mostly illiterate menials and laborers, already carry an enormous load of social disabilities. For them, social discrimination remains an everyday fact of life, even though the term "Untouchable" has been formally abolished.

As caste membership is irrevocably determined by descent it is extremely difficult for members to escape their birth-ascribed status. And because the Untouchables are on the wrong side of the so-called "pollution barrier" this custom applies to them with even greater rigidity. The four varnas are subdivided into a great number of subcastes or *jatis*, endogamous and self-recruiting groups differing markedly in lifestyle, customs, and occupation. The jatis, between which mobility is strictly limited, are the basic socioeconomic units.

The Hindu caste system [is] as much a horizontal arrangement as a vertical one with numerous groups everywhere trying to fortify themselves behind self-imposed walls of sub-castes, each seeking to insulate itself (ritually and socially), though not economically, from the others and usually to claim superiority over them. (F. J. K. Hsu, quoted in Van der Veen, 1972, p. 233.)

Where a member of one jati is accepted by another, it will usually be found that the social distance between them is extremely small. Social leapfrogging from, for instance, Untouchable to Brahmin status is practically nonexistent. Though the varna scheme determines the broad social strata of Hindu society, it is the great number of jatis which represent the actual day-to-day group differentiation. The members of each group recognize that they form discrete social units, in which membership is determined by birth. Because of the hierarchical structure of the varna system, education, power, rewards, and opportunities are different among each caste. Collectively, varnas and jatis form a broad system of institutionalized inequality.

Because of their limited opportunities for upward mobility, members of the lower castes have weak socioeconomic bargaining power. Deep-rooted ideas on pollution raise the main barriers. Traditionally, certain occupations are regarded as polluting; caste boundaries are directly related to the desire of the higher castes to prevent contamination by personal contact and association, especially in relation to marriage, food, and physical proximity. Indian sociologist G. S. Ghurye writes: "Ideas of purity, whether occupational or ceremonial, which are found to have been a factor in the genesis of caste are the very soul of the idea and practice of untouchability" (in Kuppuswamy, 1972, p. 138).

2. POLLUTION AND RITUAL PURITY

Concern over ritual purity is the obverse of fear of pollution. Certain occupations involve acts which are regarded as defiling, such as the killing of a cow or the disposal of dead animals. They can be expiated only by ritual purification. Even certain conditions and periods are polluting—for instance, the period after a woman's confinement, the menstrual period, and (for the chief mourner) the period after a death. Morris Opler mentions the following defiling situations:

The kitchen of an orthodox household is considered polluted and the food being prepared in it unfit for household consumption if a child of the family, dirty from play, runs into it by mischance or if a woman of the family begins to cook in it without bathing and putting on fresh garments. Food and water are easily defiled; food boiled in water rather than fried in butter is particularly vulnerable in this respect. Food cooked outside the home by men of the family is less likely to be polluted than the same food cooked inside the home by women of the household. Contact with human or animal filth can pollute; so can the resumption of normal activities after the sacred thread one wears has broken and

before it is replaced. Every place of worship, whether it be a family shrine or a temple, must be purified before ritual can begin. There is incessant use of fire and bathing for ritual purification. The number of ideas and practices which have grown up around this theme is enormous, and their subtleties and refinements are exceedingly intricate. (1972, p. 5.)

Jati rankings are closely tied up with ritual purity and pollution. David Mandelbaum points out the following intricacies of the inter-jati pollution barrier:

The traditional explanation is that people of higher jatis are less defiled and keep themselves more pure for purposes of religious ritual than are those of lower jatis. The lowest jatis are the most polluted and least able to have close relations with the higher gods and the higher jatis. Both pollution and purity are linked to a person's biological and physical acts; they are especially related to the bodily processes of men and animals. . . .

Every secretion and excretion that is separated from the body—as well as any separated growth of hair and nails—becomes a defiling object; by the act of severance a person puts himself in an impure state. . . .

The defilement of death falls heavily upon those who have to do with animal carcasses and with the products of the carcasses. The residues of dead animals, like those of humans, contaminate. . . . Among animals, swine are highly defiling because they will eat excrement; those who keep swine are tarred by that defilement.

Those whose jati occupation is to wash clothes, who handle clothes that are not only soiled but with the exudation of sweat, are therefore consigned to low jati rank. More defiling still than sweat-soiled clothes are clothes that have been stained with menstrual blood; washermen who launder the former may not want to touch the latter.

There are differing degrees of jati pollution. Those villagers who wash clothes usually are ranked above those who remove dead cows, eat their flesh, work with their hides. . . .

. . . Most commonly used for purification are the products of the living cow. Cow dung, usually mixed with water, is applied as a general means of ritual cleansing and prophylaxis. The housewife cleans her kitchen regularly, using that mixture.

With it the priest purifies the places where he performs his rites. Such use of cow dung entails the respect—which we have noted above.

Here lies what, to a Westerner, must seem a paradox of Hindu culture. Not only is cow dung ritually "clean," but it is so clean that a Brahmin priest will use it to wash away his impurities (Harper, 1964, p. 184). "The most potent personal purification of all is the ingestion of a mixture containing five products of the cow, namely milk, curds, ghee, dung, and urine" (Mandelbaum, 1972, 1, pp. 184–203).

It is in the context of pollution that the socially depressed status and restricted life-chances of the Harijans can be fully comprehended. According to Philip Mason, former Director of the British Institute of Race Relations:

Ritually, the Brahmin is at the head of the scale. At the other end, beyond the Sudras, outside the pale of the *varnas*, come the people who used to be called the Untouchables, now more politely in Mahatma Gandhi's phrase, the Harijans, or children of God. Their touch, even their shadow, was pollution. They live apart, away from the houses of the twice-born. It is pollution to take a coin from the hand of a Harijan; it must be put on a table. His wages must be thrown on the ground for him to pick up. "When I was the adjutant of an Indian Army battalion in the First World War," a British officer told me, "I was the only person who would give a sweeper his wages or his paybook."
. . . a Harijan as late as 1961 could not walk into the Brahman street of the village to bring the grain he had to pay as rent if he were lucky enough to be tenant of a piece of Brahman land. Not merely his touch but his proximity was still polluting." (1970a, pp. 145–46)

In traditional Hindu society even a physical pollution "distance" was maintained, varying from about 30 feet to about 150 feet.

Traditionally, occupation and caste have always been closely linked, especially among artisan and service groups such as blacksmiths, washermen, barbers and potters. In every village the lowest of the low are the sweepers and scavengers and removers of night soil. It would be hard to find a community worse off in terms of sheer material deprivation and social destitution than this lowest stratum of Untouchable jatis in India.

Intergroup mobility is, as already mentioned, mainly limited to socially contiguous groups. In more intimate personal contacts, the social distance between the main castes (and their constituent clusters of jatis) is still one of the basic structural components of Indian society. As urbanization and industrialization eliminate traditional trades, the corresponding jatis are likely to disappear. But the major castes and the barriers between them will probably persist much longer—barring a major upheaval. Philip Mason illustrates this point in relation to the Brahmin–Non-Brahmin cleavage in Sripuram:

Now that the Brahmins have lost control of both village and state politics, they begin to close their ranks. They are more conscious of their identity as Brahmins, less insistent on the differences between them. Groups who would neither eat nor smoke nor drink together will now sometimes eat at each other's weddings though they will not intermarry; groups who are closer and would eat with each other but still would not marry will now agree that marriage is possible. The Brahmins have drawn together, just as the immense number of non-Brahmins have drawn together against them. But the distance between Brahmin and non-Brahmin is—at this stage—perhaps sharper than ever before. (1970a, p. 155)

Intercaste social distance is also reflected in caste-based residential segregation in rural India. It likewise appears in a multitude of contact situations. David Mandelbaum illustrates this phenomenon:

Thus when men gather to talk, whether in gossip session or serious council meeting, they generally seat themselves with consideration to jati rank. A cot is often used as a bench; some sit on it, others sit on the ground. The upper part of the cot, the part where a sleeper puts his head, is reserved for those of higher rank in the assemblage. The seating order described for a village of Kanput District is this: Brahmins must precede all others on the upper cot, Thakurs precede all but Brahmins. Those of next higher rank sit at the foot of the cot, those of quite inferior status sit on the ground. When only men from the lowest jatis are present, say Chamar leatherworkers and Dhanuk pigkeepers, men of the two jatis may sit on the same cot, but a Chamar will allow a Dhanuk to sit only at the lower part.

Separation in seating is but one detail of the permitted interchange and forbidden contacts among jatis. In some matters, notably marriage, there should be no interchange outside the jati. For other activities, such as smoking together, there may be a larger circle of permissibility. Those in the highest ranks are usually quite rigorous about avoiding close contacts with those of the lowest; they insist that the lowest groups use separate water sources, separate residential areas, and various other means of ensuring physical as well as social distance between the lowest and the highest jatis.

In households that employ full-time servants, as Jyotirmoyes Sarma describes in a Bengal village in Hoogly district, the servants become members of the household even though they must keep to jati avoidances. Such servants of the low Bagdi jati cannot enter the inner rooms, must not touch or handle the water to be used for bathing or drinking, and must observe many other taboos (1972, 1, pp. 481–83).

Common to a number of languages of Northern India, the term jati is derived from the Sanskrit root meaning "to be born," referring to a person's social birthright. Caste is not based on any idea of disparate genetic inheritance. It is, rather, the consequence of behavior in a past life; one need not feel sorry for Untouchables (Mason, 1970a, p. 147).

Traditional restrictions on intercaste marriages block one of the most important avenues toward higher status. According to Isaacs, "marriage remains the most formidable barrier in the path of anyone who wishes to escape his caste. Intercaste marriage among caste Hindus is less infrequent in India now than it was a generation ago, but such marriages involving Scheduled Castes are still extremely rare. . . . ex-untouchables who pass are un-

likely to find mates for their children outside their caste, and if they do, they are unlikely to be able to keep their own caste background hidden" (1972b, p. 401).

Caste endogamy is enforced through fairly rigid restrictions and exclusions; unions between members of different castes and even subcastes are normally not permitted. Marriages are mostly arranged by parents—the typical age being 16 years for boys and 12 years for girls in the higher castes, less in the lower castes—and the horoscopes of the boy and the girl are consulted. The payment of dowry by the parents of the bride or the bridegroom is still widely prevalent among all classes. Marriages involving widely disparate castes or jati clusters are still very exceptional, even among educated people in the urban industrial centers. Mandelbaum observes: "In general, however, the initiatives and negotiations for the marriages of educated young people are largely where they traditionally have been, in the hands of the parents and elder kinsmen." While some matrimonial advertisements in newspapers suggest bold departure in marriage norms, analysis shows that the great majority stipulate the traditional criteria (plus education) and the usual procedures for arranging marriages in urban middle-class society. (1972, 2, p. 653.)

Research in 1969 in Maharashtra showed that more than 60 percent of a student test group (60 percent among the men and 67 percent among the girls) were opposed to intercaste marriage (Kuppuswamy, 1972, p. 133). The intercaste marriages which do occur do not nullify the partners' caste affiliations and status: they cannot convert a Harijan into a Brahmin or vice versa. The higher the caste ranking, the more sensitive are families about the status implications of intercaste marriages. Even in the smaller jatis endogamy is still a common reality. In Gujarat, for instance, the Brahmin varna comprises more than 90 endogamous jatis.

3. THE PERSISTENCE OF UNTOUCHABILITY

The term "untouchable" evokes visions of people plunged into abject poverty and shunned by all other members of society. Although the Scheduled Castes and Scheduled Tribes make up about one-third of the total population, only 15 percent of the seats in the lower house of the Indian Parliament are reserved for them. Roughly 12.5 percent of the Civil Service jobs are assigned to qualified Untouchables (5 percent for Scheduled Tribesmen). The quota system was introduced for 20 years ending in 1980 in hopes that the Harijans would be integrated into the Indian nation by then. But that optimistic prognosis left out of account the durability of the Hindu caste system. As Berreman points out (1973, p. 38) the main concern of Indians is not how to help the less fortunate achieve upward mobility but how to keep power, privilege, and jobs within the family, while assuring the availability of menials to do necessary but unpleasant tasks that are dangerous, dirty, poorly rewarded, or defiling—that is, how to maintain the status quo of inequality.

Quotas for voting rights do not improve people's opportunities in areas such as occupation, education, health, housing and residential status, social prestige, pride of descent, and primary group affiliations (e.g. family and friendship groups). Many upper-caste Indians who supported guaranteed political rights for Untouchables in 1947 did not show the same enthusiasm when it came to cultural and socioeconomic integration of Harijans. When, in 1953, Harijan wrestlers in Mysore State wanted to participate in the wrestling matches in front of the Maharaja, for instance, caste Hindus objected that the Harijans would defile the sacredness of the arena and the caste Hindus would have to touch their bodies (Kuppuswamy, 1972, p. 152).

Social legislation has tended to reinforce rather than weaken the caste system, since it has generally resulted in exclusive and segregated welfare measures such as digging special wells, building special houses and schools, and opening special amenities. Even in the urban areas, educated middle-class Harijans find it difficult to secure houses.

The house owner not only wants to know the ability of the prospective tenant to pay the rent regularly, he also wants to know his caste. Even in a big city like Bombay, one Harijan reported, "In Bombay we live among non-scheduled caste people. The moment I disclosed that I was from a scheduled caste, there would be some sort of noncooperation. They would try to harass us until we left the place." Even in the office the discovery leads to discrimination; particularly in Government offices, the knowledge that one belongs to a scheduled caste spreads quickly. It is not unknown in Government offices for caste Hindus to insist that ex-untouchables keep cups or glasses in a separate place away from the common supply (*ibid.*, pp. 153–54).

Another disadvantage of the quota system is that large numbers of poverty-stricken Indians infiltrate the Scheduled Castes merely to qualify for welfare handouts. Most of India's multitude of castes, however, claimed to be "backward" enough to be counted among the deserving poor and to share in whatever benefits were being handed around. A government commission in 1953 named 2399 such deserving castes and communities with an estimated total population of about 120 million. More and more groups, including some well above the bottom of the socioeconomic ladder, sought "backward" status so as to ride the government gravy train (Isaacs, 1972b, p. 392). As for the quota system, the educational disabilities of the Scheduled Castes are still such that not enough of them qualify to fill their quotas.

A recent study of social change in the Coimbatore District of India (den Ouden, 1975) shows that for the lowest castes the position has shifted very little. They are still refused entry into high-caste rooms and kitchens, may not sell milk directly to high-caste people, are never addressed by respectful verb forms, and have separate wells and graveyards. Although the Kavuntar, a higher caste of farmers, treat their Pallar laborers (who have staged bloody revolts in the past) with a modicum of decency, they still refuse to touch the lowest-caste Paraiyar and Cakkiliyar. The latter two are Untouchable, whereas the touch of the Pallan is not polluting except for Brahmins. For this reason, Pallar women are often taken as prostitutes (not polluting but distant enough to preclude familiarity) by higher-caste men. A Pallan may bring his Kavuntar master his tiffin box in his hands, whereas a Paraiyan or Callikiyan would have to carry it in a basket balanced on his head (*ibid.*, pp. 228–29). A degree of integration, however, has been achieved in the public schools, where pupils and teachers of different castes take their meals and their tea together.

Caste rules, den Ouden summarizes, are being eroded by new norms and values and by the disintegration of regional and village caste *panchayats* that traditionally enforced caste discipline. Caste behavior persists, however, at the highest and lowest levels; in fact, the four lowest castes are tending to draw together as a unit (*ibid.*, pp. 232–33).

Despite the change sampled by den Ouden, the severe social deprivation of the Untouchables today still remains a basic structural characteristic of Indian society. Few are recruited into academic, business and professional circles. More than 80 percent of the Harijans are illiterate; less than 4 percent have had any high-school education and still fewer reach universities. Pathetically few progress as far as the top echelons of their vocation or profession. More than one-third are agricultural laborers—one of the poorest occupational groups in the Indian population, with an average monthly family income of less than $25. More than 75 percent of the Harijan families have an average family income of less than $200 a year.

Actually the Harijans are only one of the three main disadvantaged groups called "Backward Classes." The other two are the indigenous Scheduled Tribes (of which there are 400)

and a large and loosely defined aggregation known as the Other Backward Classes. Although not Untouchables, the Other Backward Classes consist mainly of peasant castes, a socioeconomic category marked by poverty and social destitution. The vast majority of this group are illiterate.

C. Caste Systems as an Obstacle to Social Progress

Growing concern is being expressed in India's parliament and press about the disturbing frequency of atrocities committed by high-caste Hindus against the Harijans. The Indian Government is clearly perturbed at the severity and scope of the backlash. The 1970–71 report of the Commissioner for Scheduled Castes and Scheduled Tribes concludes: "There may be hardly any village in the country which can be termed absolutely free from this evil" (untouchability). The Report is openly skeptical about the progress claimed by many state governments. It points out that the 1955 Act (which legally banned the practice of untouchability) is being widely flouted. The following two newspaper articles report situations which still regularly occur in India:

People in Bombay were horrified by the story of how caste Hindus of Akola district near Bombay gouged the eyes of two untouchable men in September last year. For unknown reasons untouchability has again become a sore on India's body politic. Last year there were riots between the Caste Hindus and untouchables in Bombay followed, a few months later, by more horrifying riots in Ahmedabad. There have been individual incidents of atrocities but nothing as bad as what the two brothers—Gopal and Babhruvahan Gawai—of Akola, have suffered. They belong to the Dhakli village. Gopal's daughter was in love with the village headman's son. She had become pregnant and Gopal decided they should get married to save the family's honour. When he dared to suggest this to the village headman the two brothers were set upon

by the headman's gang who first beat them mercilessly and then gouged their eyes with sticks. (*Pretoria News*, February 12, 1975)

The second report reads:

The Indian caste system cost 78 lives, when passengers on a stranded bus refused to haul themselves
to safety along the same rope. The *Hindustan Times*
reported yesterday that a bus carrying 86 persons
was trapped by flood waters Monday near the town
of Alwar, about 100 miles south-west of Delhi.
Karim Khan, a tea-stall owner, went to the rescue.
He waded out to the bus with a rope he had tied to a
truck standing on high ground. He asked the passengers to haul themselves along the rope to safety.
But the passengers, who belonged to two different
high caste communities refused to share the same
rope and stayed in the bus. The floodwaters rose
higher and the bus was swept away, with the loss of
78 lives (*San Francisco Chronicle*, July 7, 1973).

The caste system has also left its stamp on
the lifestyle and values of many non-Hindu
societies in South Asia. Despite their protestations of innocence there is no doubt that the
caste system is widely spread among the Muslim communities of Pakistan and Bangladesh.
Sri Lanka also has its equivalent of the Indian
pollution barrier. The Gahala Berava, for instance, traditionally a caste of public executioners, were even forbidden to touch the bodies of their victims if the latter belonged to a
high caste. The Rodi, however, are the lowest
of the low: even today their animals share the
odium of their owners and to distinguish them
from the animals of the high caste, their
owners are obliged to hang a coconut shell
from their necks (See Wickramanayake, 1975,
passim.).

The Burakumin are a Japanese pariah group
with some characteristics of an "untouchable"
caste (see chapter 14,D1). "Even today, in
South-Western Japan where one finds 80 percent of the outcastes, there has been only a
light weakening of basic attitudes concerning
the 'biological inferiority' and 'un-Japanese' nature of the outcaste people, although overt behavior toward them is noticeably more cir-
cumspect than before" (DeVos, 1972, pp. 309,

312). In the Osaka area there are quite a
number of companies who have the policy of
not employing any Burakumin. Around the
middle 1960s about half of all unemployed in
Japan were Burakumin, although they account
for only 3 percent of the total population.

It is particularly in the sphere of intimate-
personal relations that the social ostracism of
the Burakumin comes to the fore. Marriage
with an outcaste is regarded as the nadir of
social degradation. Many younger, intelligent,
and ambitious Burakumin resort to "passing,"
but middle-class Japanese employ gobetweens
to avoid mésalliances. For passing outcastes,
the only safe marriage arrangement is one with
someone who is also passing. The revelation
that one family is of outcaste origin may work
like a falling domino, spreading disclosure to
others with whom they are affiliated (*ibid.*,
1972, p. 319).

The following account illustrates the supposed backwardness and defilement of the
Burakumin:

It was customary prior to the turn of the century
for Burakumin to wash the bodies of deceased commoners in return for an offering of *sake*, but after the
outcastes began to realise their emancipation, they
frequently requested money for their services.
Sometimes the demands were exorbitant. When the
sum was refused the Burakumin would threaten the
family by vowing to drink the water used in bathing
the body. The people were usually frightened into
granting the Burakumin demands. (Donoghue,
1973, p. 111)

Most Japanese believe the Burakumin to be
generically polluted and in this respect the latter are treated essentially like untouchables in
India.

D. Discrimination Based on Sex

Sexism means different things to different people. Because of disparate cultural-religious traditions and identities, not to mention differing
levels of development, there is no universally

accepted norm for determining legitimate sex differentiation. It may be taken as generally agreed, however, that in matters of employment, wages, social and economic security, and education, equality should be consciously and purposefully pursued as a matter of public policy. There is also a growing consensus that women should also have access to the top decision-making institutions of business, management, administration, and government.

The term "sexism" will refer here to cases where persons are subjected to prejudice and discrimination mainly because they are women. According to Clarice Stoll (1973, p. 1): "Although the word was coined only recently, its root and meaning are clear. It defines a society's discriminatory ideologies and practices as they are reflected in the opportunities given to individuals for self-expression, with sex being the basis for selective acceptance or rejection." The mere fact of differentiation does not in itself mean or imply discrimination or prejudice. Obvious differences in physical strength have always dictated differences between male and female jobs. Hence, rejecting a woman as a stevedore or ditchdigger can hardly be considered an example of sexism in operation—unless, of course, the woman possesses a physique that is more typical of male laborers.

The importance of sex as a determinant of social stratification varies from community to community. No country in the world, however, can claim truthfully that sex plays no role in the differential allocation of opportunities and rewards in the national society. The basic cause of discrimination against women is to be found in the notions some people have about the genetically determined potentialities (or lack of potentialities!) of the female sex. In a largely male-dominated world there is a deep-seated conviction that woman's subordinate role can be traced to her biological "differentness." It is alleged that God (or Allah, or whatever deity is acknowledged as the highest arbiter) has made women thus and so; and that a sex-differentiated status, power, reward, and opportunity system is therefore in harmony with the "natural" order of things.

1. THE ANALOGY BETWEEN RACISM AND SEXISM

The relationship between racism and sexism is surprisingly close. In both instances, a rationale based on biogenetic determinism plays a decisive role; there is strong institutional support for differential status, power, rewards, and opportunities. Almost from infancy, blacks and women are conditioned to accept subordinate status and restricted opportunities as a normal part of social life. In both situations, group members "inherit" the status of their group, regardless of their individual achievements, and they are socialized to accept the existing ranking system. Particular functions, actions, reactions, needs—even the ways in which emotions are vented and certain needs are fulfilled—are characterized as "typically" feminine. From early childhood, women are socialized in such a way that they spontaneously accept these behavioral patterns and personality attributes. Many behavioral patterns and personality traits considered "typically" and "inherently" feminine are indeed acquired behavior, which with the same stimuli and inducements could just as well be evoked in any boy. Confirming this perception, Clarice Stoll writes:

Honey, Hampson and Hampson (1955) studied 76 ambisexual or hermaphroditic individuals and found that *the best predictor of adult sex role is not physiology*. What mattered more than external appearance, hormones, gonads or chromosomes, was the assignment of sex at birth. They found further that whenever a person designated one sex at birth was reassigned to another in later years, the chances of successful change decreased beyond the first few years of life. Thus sexual identity appears to be socially defined, and its major qualities are imprinted on the child at a quite early age. (1973, pp. 7–8; (emphasis added)

It is thus seen that major features of a normal woman's personality are the result of *nurture*, not *nature*. This fact is very apparent in Japan, where male and female speech patterns are so different that it is difficult for a Japanese to teach the language to a foreigner of the opposite sex.

In combatting sexism, women's liberation leaders emphasize that in male-dominated societies men exploit to their own advantage these stereotypes centering on feminine helplessness, weakness, passivity, and dependence. An analysis initiated by the National Organization for Women (NOW) of 134 books read in three suburban New Jersey towns revealed the following male–female ratios: boy-centered to girl-centered stories 5:2; adult male to adult female (main characters) 3:1; male to female biographies 6:1; male to female animal stories 2:1; and male to female folk or fantasy stories 4:1 (Duchacek, 1973b, p. 93).

The New Jersey study also showed to what extent sexism is reflected in gender. "Soft, delicate, and fluffy kittens are usually female. So is the lazy magpie. Boisterous playful dogs are male. Old people who are mean and ugly are female . . . wise old people are without exception male, and a human being of any stature is male by definition. Thus hieroglyphologists are 'men' who study Egyptian writings and elsewhere we meet 'sayings of Wise Men' " (*ibid.*, p. 104).

2. TRADITIONAL MALE AND FEMALE ROLES

Many female stereotypes involve the woman's home-centered, child-bearing, and child-rearing functions, in contrast to the man's historical dominance in the outside world. They form the basis for rationalizing sex discrimination in employment and earnings, education and training, marriage, and politics. Visible anatomical and sartorial differences between the sexes have also contributed to social stratification, with women in the inferior stratum. "Actually, rural Greek men (and other Mediterranean and Middle Eastern men) with very traditional values often touch their covered genitals in public as if to remind the world of their "tangible' anatomical superiority, while the corresponding gesture for

women would be considered unthinkable most disgusting and dishonoring, and an in dication of immorality and looseness" (Safilios Rothschild, 1974, p. 8). It may be noted tha the original meaning of "testify" was to "swea by one's testicles"—a transaction that only a male could consummate.

The socialization process is so thorough tha even at a very early age children have re hearsed their sex-stereotyped and sex-ascribed roles and act out their later lives accordingly And because woman's role is a group role fixed by birth, society expects a certain perfor mance from her in specific situations, such a being a mother, a grandmother, or a sex part ner.

The first role a person acquires in any society is sex role. This role is ascribed, in that infants are no free to choose one sex role over the other, and is con sidered a basic role, in that it limits and determine other roles that the individual may achieve. . . From the time the pink or blue blanket is placed o the newborn baby, he begins to receive differentia attention and reinforcement from others in his envi ronment. As he matures, these reinforcements grad ually shape an individual's behavior into the appro priate sex role as defined by society. Little boys ar expected to engage in behaviors labeled masculin which train them for male adult roles, while littl girls are expected to display feminine characteristic aligned with adult female roles (Polk and Stein 1972, p. 14).

Each woman struggling for equal rights i marriage, employment, or education will inev itably collide with the sex barrier—that ver strict set of behavioral expectations base solely or mainly on gender.

Leaders of women's liberation movement feel particularly strongly about the way the so called "motherhood" cult inhibits equalizatio of women's rights. A prominent campaigne claims: "The 'motherhood cult' has throughou history enslaved women more than all othe beliefs and values. The idea that only childre brought up with 24 hours per day care by thei natural mother can have a normal develop ment, has cut women off from a large number of educational, occupational, political and social options" (Safilios-Rothschild, 1974, p. 18). In the *Ladies' Home Journal* of June 1970, p. 24, Bruno Bettelheim regretted the fact that "our educational system, while preparing girls for equal occupational life, advocates the value of a now antiquated form of marital life. What school reader ever shows mother working outside the home? Yet millions do."

a large number of social controls built into the educational process, employment, and the entire society help to guarantee that women will restrict themselves to the roles for which they were socialized, and that they will behave according to the appropriate "feminine" norms. Thus, even when women were educated for professional or "masculine" fields such as medicine, law, or engineering, they often felt compelled to behave in a "feminine" manner by choosing pediatrics rather than surgery, domestic rather than criminal law. They had to also avoid any display of roughness, competitiveness or agressiveness if they wanted to escape being labeled "bitches" or "castrating females." And they were not only encouraged but also rewarded for behaving in this way and for accepting the fact that men have to occupy all the top positions. (Safilios-Rothschild, 1974, p. 65).

In perpetuating the traditional sex role stereotypes, the educational system is aided and abetted by the mass media. Fidell and Keith-Spiegel point out that

"television presents several pervasive images of women, each of which denies them adaptive intelligence, creativity, self-reliance, and adult maturity. . . . The standard stereotypic, dependent, housewife-mother character is sometimes less offensive than the snooping sob-sisters, the whimpering neurotics, the childish goofs, the scheming Jezebels, and the mindless sexpots. A "liberated" woman (i.e., the producer's idea of one) is often presented as a cold, sexless, friendless, unattractive person who is basically miserable, or as a flighty, rootless "chick" who has also been liberated from common sense. (1973, p. 449)

3. EMPLOYMENT AND WAGES

Job discrimination and unequal employment conditions are among the most visible evidences of sexism throughout the world. In 1969 a research study initiated by *Redbook Magazine* found that 95 percent of American women employees earned an average of $3600 a year less than men with comparable skills. Yet, only 8 percent of the interviewees thought they were being victimized. According to U.S. Census Bureau figures for 1966, female employees with high-school diplomas and with college education of at least four years earned $1862 and $3964 less than male employees in the two respective categories (See Duchacek, 1973b, p. 92).

The male-female earnings gap in the United States is growing wider. On the basis of mean earnings, the discrepancy between men and women widened from $4713 : $3008 annually in 1957 to $10,202 : $5,903 in 1972. In other words, in 1972 a woman earned only 58 cents for every dollar earned by a male worker, compared with 64 cents on the dollar 15 years earlier (*U.S. News and World Report*, October 8, 1973, pp. 41–42). In each occupational group, men earned substantially more than women. In the professional and technical fields the gap was $4798 in 1972. In the services category (traditionally staffed largely by women) the discrepancy was $3147 in favor of male workers. The discrepancy between the educational level of women and their actual employment shows that the United States, like virtually every other country, underutilizes its trained womanpower. "No matter what sphere of work women are hired for or selected, like sediment in a wine bottle they seem to settle at the bottom" (Epstein, 1972, p. 598).

Although more than 45 percent of American women between the ages of 18 and 64 have entered the labor market, they tend to congregate in the less skilled, lower paid, and less rewarding occupations. In 1965, more than one-fifth of all employed women graduates were service, clerical, factory, or sales workers. Five years later, 12.2 percent of women and 5.1 percent of men working full-time earned less than $3000; 32.5 percent of women and 8.8 percent of men working full-time earned between $3000 and $4999; while 1.1 percent of women and 13.5 percent of men earned $15,000 or more. It is feared that industrial automation and modernization will jeopardize the jobs of an estimated 2.5 million women (See Safilios-Rothschild, 1974, chapter 2).

Women remain concentrated in low-status occupations (such as waitresses, salespersons, and low-skill factory hands); there was a relative decline in the number of women in the professions. Between 1950 and 1970 only seven occupations were added to those in which 100,000 or more women were employed; babysitter, charwoman or cleaner, counter and fountain worker, file clerk, institutional housekeeper, stewardess, musician or music teacher, and receptionist—hardly impressive additions in view of the increased educational attainment of women during this period (Suelzle, 1973, p. 92).

As Jessie Bernard (1971, p. 106) emphasizes, once a job is sex-typed, it tends to attract or be allocated to members of only one sex, regardless of the qualifications of individual members of the other sex. She adds that "regardless of the name of the work [women] do, they end up in service positions or servant roles, no matter what class of job they hold—factory work, technician, secretary, research assistant—they were automatically and *ipso facto* disqualified for the top positions which demanded the aggression forbidden to them by their functional assignment as women" (*ibid.*, pp. 237–38).

Although some women pursue careers as a matter of personal fulfillment, most women enter the labor market because of economic need. Some two-thirds of all women workers in the United States are single, widowed, or divorced, or have husbands who in 1973 earned less than $7000 a year. Women who have to work are, of course, the easiest prey for

discriminatory employment practices and most vulnerable to unemployment. In 1973, for instance, the female unemployment rate was nearly 50 percent higher than that for males. Two-thirds of the female labor force were employed in low-paying jobs. Women accounted for 98 percent of all private household workers, 76 percent of all clerical workers, and 63 percent of all service workers.

But the most vigorous rebellion against sexism in employment comes from women in the professions, where equal professional qualifications and experience have by no means wiped out the pay gap between the two sexes. Until the advent of "Affirmative Action," most American universities were loath to appoint women faculty. In 1973 for instance, Stanford gave 25 of 95 new faculty appointments to women, while Columbia appointed one female tenured professor. In 1971, 2 percent of the full professors at the University of Chicago were women, compared with 8 percent in 1900. Although 30 percent of the Ph.D.'s awarded in sociology were conferred on women only 1 percent of the full professors in sociology in top graduate schools were women. Generally, the salaries paid to married women professors were 70 to 75 percent of those received by men at the same level after attaining a doctorate. And although more women have been achieving professional degrees, the percentage of women entering the high-level occupations has not grown significantly since immediately after World War II. In fact, from 1950 to 1960 the relative share of women in the natural-science professions, where the cult of masculinity is still firmly entrenched, decreased from 11 to 9 percent. In 1973, women accounted for only 2 percent of the engineers, 4 percent of the architects, 5 percent of the attorneys and judges, 9 percent of the physicians and 13 percent of the scientific technicians in the United States.

The Japanese constitution of 1946 guaranteed economic, social, and political equality to all citizens, regardless of "race, creed, sex, social status, or family origin." But a wage gap between men and women at every level of education and skills is the rule rather than the exception in Japan. Women are also the first to be laid off in a recession, such as that precipitated by the December, 1973 oil crisis. The *Japan Christian Activity News* reported on March 8, 1974:

Unlike those of the male work force, women's wages decrease as they age, except in the case of civil servants. In 1971, 32.8 percent of the total labor force was women and of this total 31.1 percent was over 40 years of age, working for private companies and industries, contracting for short periods of time with low wages. As a result, women who were employed full-time earned on an average only one-half of what male workers did in 1971. The equal rights clause of the constitution under which the basic salary of workers cannot be differentiated on the basis of sex, has so far been enforced only in civil service jobs. But even in that situation women's working hours are longer and many complain that their abilities are never really used. A college graduate hired by a Tokyo metropolitan government office is required to clean the whole room 30 minutes before the male workers arrive at the office, and she is expected to serve tea at any time. The whole system is geared so that a women is retired (to the home or part-time jobs) as soon as she reaches her most productive years. Large industries have a strong tendency to set the retirement age for young, full-time women workers at between 30 and 35 years of age. These workers are then forced into low-wage, temporary, part-time work which guarantees both company profit and the continued subjugation of women.

Young unmarried women in particular are subject to severe forms of wage discrimination. The likelihood of an early marriage is considered to absolve employers of the kind of paternal obligation Japanese companies assume when they hire men. In 1972, 9 percent of 500 businesses which employed more than 30 workers demanded that women retire either at marriage or childbirth, and 7 percent actually stipulated a young age for mandatory retirement. Women who take on "part-time" work,

often discover they are working as long or nearly as long as full-time employees, but without the fringe benefits. Because their bargaining power in the labor market is so poor, older married women suffer the worst exploitation. This is why the average wage for women declines after the age of 35.

Half of the women in Great Britain work, but their pay level was recently reported as only 45 percent of male earnings. The Trades Union Congress announced in late 1973 that it was entering the struggle for "equal opportunities." Shortly afterward, the Bow Group of the Conservative Party called for legislation to abolish sexism in employment, education, credit, and housing. In a pamphlet published by the Group, May Colton criticized the exclusion of men as midwives, the prohibition against underground work by women which, she says, prevents a variety of engineering and technical employments, and the "deeply offensive" discrimination against women who would like to become priests (*Daily Telegraph*, London, 10 June, 1974). A report by the General Statistical Office in December 1974, intimated that men would continue to command the top jobs in Britain for at least another 20 years. Kanitkar (1973, p. 404) has pointed out that though women constitute 52 percent of the population there were only 44 women university professors out of a total of 3325 in 1972; only 4 percent of managers were women; there were only two women among 300 Queen's Counsel, and only one High Court judge in a total of 70. The five trade unions which represent the largest numbers of women had only nine women as full-time officials.

An Equal Pay Act has been on the books for several years, but its target of parity did not take effect until December 30, 1975. During the transition period the Government referred three wage agreements to the Industrial Arbitration Board as discriminatory. By March 1975, the Department of Employment was able to report some progress toward equality. Its figures showed that 45 percent of collective wage agreements then gave women between 95 and 99 percent of men's pay, as compared with only 90 percent in March 1974.

The Equal Pay Act has been supplemented by a Sex Discrimination Act, which makes it illegal to discriminate against women in jobs, education, training, housing, facilities, and services; there is a commission to enforce it. But the new act has loopholes and weaknesses. It does not provide maternity leave for unmarried pregnant women, nor does it apply to the clergy or the Armed Forces. Likewise, there is no provision for directly increasing the number of women employed in any occupation (*The Times*, London, May 5, 1975). As of this writing it is too early to comment on the effectiveness of this legislation.

In the Common Market a Commission Study in 1973 found enforcement of equal-pay laws highly inadequate.

The inspectors used by Luxembourg and France to oversee the application of equal rights provisions have too many other responsibilities and are too few in number to be effective. Only Italy employs inspectors responsible solely for supervising equal rights. Germany and the Netherlands have no administrative checks whatsoever. (*European Community*, December, 1973, pp. 7–9)

Several occupations in which large numbers of women work are not covered by minimum wage rules. Among those excluded in France and Luxembourg are caretakers and domestic servants and those employed in farming, gardening, or wine growing. In Italy, some 1.5 million home workers, three-fourths of them women, are not covered by labor laws as they are theoretically "self-employed." Lower wages for women persisted in the Dutch garment, textile, bakery, laundry, ceramic, and shoe industries.

The textile, food, and clothing industries show a variance of 13 percent in Italy, 15 percent in France, 20 percent in Germany, 22 percent in Belgium, and 27 percent in the Netherlands. Differentiation statistics for the electrical equipment industry are 10

per cent in France, 12 per cent in Italy and the Netherlands, 20 per cent in Germany, and 21 per cent in Belgium. Most women still fall at the bottom of the wage hierarchy. The most striking reforms have occurred in government services. (*Ibid.*, p. 8)

It is too early to comment on the results of recent efforts by the EEC to redress the inequality.

4. FEMALE "EQUALITY" IN THE COMMUNIST ORBIT

Communist governments often proclaim that they are eliminating sexism altogether. Persisting employment and wage differentials, they assert, are largely accidental and not the result of direct discrimination.

It is indeed true that many Russian women are admitted to "masculine" occupations, but this does not save them from low status and low pay. In the blue-collar occupations women perform hard physical work, under the supervision of men. It is still common to see women laying brick at Soviet building sites while men operate machines. Soviet women are widely used as miners, shovelers, stevedores, cement workers, drillers, plasterers, ditchdiggers, woodcutters, etc. A Russian writer, Edward Shim, complained that Soviet labor laws concerning women are inadequate and that, for all intents and purposes, women in the USSR have become "beasts of burden" (*Literaturnaya Gazeta*, Moscow, February 1, 1967).

Because women in the USSR are paid far less than men and because they lack other skills, they gravitate to heavy construction to secure adequate wages. At the Saratov Hydroelectric Station site, for instance, women made up 88 percent of the ditchdiggers and 88.5 percent of the carpenters and plasterers. But the foremen of this body of women performing hard physical labor were almost exclusively men (*ibid.*, February 15, 1967).

Wherever women penetrate the traditionally masculine occupations, they seldom reach executive or managerial posts. While 42 percent of all Russian scientists are women, they con stitute less than 1 percent of the members of the prestigious Soviet Academy of Science. Most Soviet medical doctors and about 40 percent of Polish physicians are women, but that is only because this occupation has a lowly status in the communist orbit. And even in medicine, four of every five of managerial positions are occupied by men. In both the USSR and Poland, there are few women lawyers and engineers, though not so few as in some Western countries (for instance, 2.9 percent of lawyers and 1 percent of engineers in the U.K.). According to Dushnyck (1975b, p. 527) the proportions of women in responsible positions in Soviet industry in December, 1963, were:

Enterprise directors, 6%
Chief Engineers, 16%
Shop chiefs and their deputies, 12%
Chiefs of shifts, labs, etc., 22%
Chiefs of sections, 20%
Engineers (except engineer-
     economists), 38%
Technicians, 65%
Forepeople, 20%
Senior bookkeepers, 36%
Statisticians, planners, and engineer-
     economists, 70%

According to a Soviet statistical handbook, women made up 38 percent of the employees of scientific organizations, but only 1300 of 14,700 scientists employed there (8.8 percent).

It also appears that Russian men help their wives less than their "capitalist" counterparts in Western Europe and North America. *Nedelya*, weekly supplement to the government newspaper *Isvestia*, remarked in 1969 that the Soviet Union may have produced a New Woman, but that man has remained very much the same. At a meeting of East European women (reported in *Soviet News*, June 9, 1970) a Czech delegate claimed that women had to spend from four to six hours a day on household chores—the so-called "second shift." In Moscow only 15 percent of all women own washing machines, 37 percent own refriger-

ators, and 20 percent own vacuum cleaners. On October 30, 1969, *Sovetskaya Rossiya* reported that standing in line takes up anything from 30 to 50 percent of all the time that Russian women spend on household chores.

5. EDUCATION AND VOCATIONAL TRAINING

In many developing countries more than 75 percent of all adult women are illiterate and their illiteracy rate is always considerably higher than that of men. Where 20 of every 100 school-age children actually attend school, only five or six will be girls. But even developed countries still harbor prejudices and socioeconomic constraints that effectively confine girls within a narrow range of training and educational options. Learning experiences in schools are to a considerable extent based on traditional sex stereotypes, registered in textbooks and reinforced by sex-stereotyped vocational counseling. The proportion of female secondary school teachers in the United States declined between 1950 (57 percent) and 1965 (46 percent). There was an even sharper decline in the ratio of female elementary school principals—55 percent in 1928 but less than 25 percent in 1970. More males than females are involved in secondary education, and the discrepancy increases as the educational level rises.

Although more women than men graduate from high school, more men complete a college education (*U.S. News and World Report*, October 8, 1973, p. 42). Roughly 75 percent of all intellectually qualified pupils who do not enter college or university are girls—a sure measure of the underutilization of the best female brain power. Many departments apply sex quotas that deny fellowship aid to women with high grade averages in favor of men with lower grades. In awarding fellowships to women, some universities still consider husbands' incomes, whereas the reverse is not the case. As of 1974, there were still a few departments that openly discouraged women from applying for admission to their graduate programs (Safilios-Rothschild, 1974, pp. 38–39). Similar discrimination is found in communist countries: In Russia in the early 1960s, women accounted for less than one-third of all postgraduate students (Lane, 1971, p. 89). In Poland the proportion of women in the higher technical schools between 1951 and 1967 rose only from 10.7 to 12.1 percent.

Sex discrimination is also found in corporate training programs. A typical case is that of Merrill, Lynch, Pierce, Fenner, and Smith, Inc., the largest securities firm in the United States, against which the Equal Employment Opportunity Commission (EEOC) has charged that: "As of May 1973, of 5,197 account executives in Merrill Lynch's branch system, 5,030 or nearly 97%, were white males, while 125 were females, 31 were Spanish-surnamed Americans . . . and 11 were blacks." Account executives with one year's experience are said to earn an average of $25,000 annually; after five years they are in the top 1 percent of Americans in terms of income. Conversely, as of March 31, 1974, 85 percent of all women employees (2598 of 3061), 85 percent of all blacks (1067 of 1259) and 78 percent of Spanish-speaking staff were assigned to "office clerical" jobs—positions which generally are the lowest paying. In the highest paying "professional" home office jobs, however, 85 percent (757 of 895) of the incumbents were white males, as were 79 percent (727 of 915) of the "officials and managers." Not a single woman occupied a management position at a branch office, the EEOC charged, while of 1209 sales persons hired since January 1974, 1137 (94 percent) have been white males, while 42 were females, nine each were blacks or Spanish speaking and the rest were from "other minorities." A further violation of Federal law, the EEOC charged, was involved in the Merrill Lynch maternity-leave policy, which allows managers, at their discretion, to force a pregnant employee to resign or take maternity leave regardless of the opinion of her physician.

6. POLITICAL AND ECONOMIC BARGAINING POWER

Safilios-Rothschild (1974, p. 154) has drawn attention to the fact that only 3.7 million of 28 million working women in the United States are organized in trade unions. Most of the nonunionized women are office workers; the others are domestic workers, farm workers, and retail salespeople. As late as 1973, less than 20 percent of U.S. working women belonged to unions, while only 20 percent of all union members were women. Less than 5 percent of all union officials in leadership positions were women.

In the International Ladies Garment Workers Union and the Communications Workers of America, for example, both of which have a solid female majority, women hold no posts on the national governing bodies. In the Amalgamated Clothing Workers Union, where women comprise 75 percent of the membership, there are only two women on the governing board of twenty-three. There are no women on the Executive Council of the AFL-CIO, the most powerful union federation in the country. The council is made up of union presidents, none of whom is a woman. (*International Socialist Review*, March, 1974, p. 7)

Similar conditions prevail in other industrialized noncommunist countries. Economists have suggested that lack of organization of women workers helps perpetuate the large wage gap between the sexes in Japan. As of 1970, only 29 percent of all women workers belonged to trade unions, compared to nearly 40 percent of all male workers.

Despite verbal commitments to equal opportunity in employment, education, and training—even in marriage—very few women are named to the highest organs of political power. And a late 1973 survey cited by Safilios-Rothschild (1974, p. 144) showed that 63 percent of women (and 63 percent of men) still agreed with the statement: "Most men are better suited emotionally for politics than are most women." Also, 55 percent of women (and 62 percent of men) agreed that: "To be really active in politics, women have to neglect their husbands and children."

An amendment to the United States' Constitution providing that "equality of rights under the law shall not be denied or abridged by the United States or by any state on account of sex" and empowering Congress to pass enforcing legislation is currently several states short of ratification. Opponents of the Equal Rights Amendment point out that if it becomes law, women will lose rights, such as presumption of child custody and indefinite-term alimony in case of divorce as well as social security payments based on a husband's earnings. But the rights so lost are all related to woman's sex-stereotyped role as housewife and mother, as are the husband's rights to set a couple's domicile and to have children bear his surname—which ERA would abolish (see the *Phyllis Schlafly Report*, Alton, Illinois, 1974–1975, *passim.*).

Under the influence of "no-fault" divorce laws (such as that of California) judges are already assuming the ability of women to support themselves and are limiting alimony to transitional retraining periods—typically three years. But a housewife divorced after a long marriage has much lost ground to make up and faces the employment discrimination already described. Furthermore, she has accumulated no social security credits in her own name, since wives' and widows' benefits are based on the husband's earnings. A wife divorced before 10 years of marriage loses all benefits; after 10 years of marriage, the divorcee may receive them, but they may not be combined with benefits earned by the woman as an employee. Bills are currently under consideration in Congress to ease the lot of "displaced homemakers." It would seem obvious that if homemaking is to be regarded as a socially useful function, those performing it—female or male—should accumulate social security benefits in their own names, for which the necessary taxes should be collected.

In the middle 1950s Maurice Duverger made an intensive study of the role of women in the political processes of France, West Germany, Norway, and Yugoslavia. He was struck by the hostility manifested against political activity by women, as well as a significant decline in the influence of women as the upper levels of political power were reached.

The club, the forum, debates, Parliament and political life in general are still considered to be typically masculine activities. . . . The percentage of women members of parliament, for instance, is hardly increasing. On the contrary, it tends to fall after the first elections in which women have had the suffrage, and to become stabilized at a very low level. (1955, p. 45)

Women appear to be enjoying more success at the local level. While only eight women gained seats in the National Assembly and four women became Senators in the 1973 French election, there were 677 women Mayors in France, including the Mayor of Paris (*France Actuelle*, June, 1973, p. 5). In communist countries too, the proportion of women in the party hierarchy decreases in the higher echelons of political power. No woman has ever been a full member of the Politburo in either the USSR or China. While Communist Party membership numbered more than 14 million as of 1970, women members totaled only 2.6 million, or some 20 percent. Although about 30 percent of Supreme Soviet deputies are women, only about 7 percent of these members of the rubber-stamp parliament are *bona fide* officials with political power and influence. The remainder are Party-picked one-term deputies, such as milkmaids, swineherds, and tractor-drivers—types whom Soviet propaganda often acclaims as crowns of Soviet womanhood. Women are conspicuous by their absence in the politically sensitive Soviet professions. Only one woman, Z. Mironova, was among the 97 ambassadors of the USSR. Among 573 Soviet radio, press, and Tass (the Soviet news agency) commentators listed in a Soviet mass communication directory, only eight women were to be found.

E. Marital, Family, and Social Status—The Double Standard

Institutions related to women's social status, legal standing, and marital and family rights are to an increasing extent under attack as instruments for perpetuating of traditional sex-role stereotypes that keep women subordinate. In Spain, for example, the Civil Code until 1972 did not allow women to leave home without parental approval until their 23rd birthday—except to get married or to enter a convent. In countries such as Ireland, Southern Italy, Portugal, Spain, Malta, Tunisia, Greece, and Lebanon, the dogged persistence of the dowry system has reinforced the subordinate social status of women and causes many poor girls without dowries to remain unmarried—one of the worst fates that can befall a woman in a traditional society. Many countries have laws specifically designed to protect women against their own "shortcomings" and "disabilities," but which often prevent qualified women from competing with men on the labor market.

1. SEX-ROLE STEREOTYPES IN LAW AND CUSTOM

Negative sex-role stereotypes are reflected in most legal systems. As Safilios-Rothschild points out, with reference to court treatment of rape cases in the United States:

any degree of previous acquaintance between the woman and the rapist practically always acquits the man. Her lack of consent to sexual intercourse is not considered valid, the implication being that she "provoked" the man or that "she was asking for it." And the raped woman's sexual life prior to the rape plays a very important role in the rapist's conviction—a fact indicating the judges', juries', and lawyers' sexual double standard with regard to women. (1974, p. 138)

In India, the primacy of masculinity permeates most social institutions. Morris Opler relates:

In Indian philosophical thought, the highest manifestation of spirituality—perfect serenity and absence of desire—is considered to be a male attribute. . . .

The female principle is always disturbing; the godlings of disease are invariably goddesses. . . . There is a rite to insure male offspring; the rituals of the sixth and twelfth days after birth are more elaborate if the newborn infant is a boy; the sacred thread ceremony, which formally inaugurates education, is limited to males; there are a number of ceremonies (for which girls and women take responsibility) to promote the health and longevity of males; and in the rituals to honor ancestors, the emphasis is upon aiding the spirits of departed males. At the time of a birth in a family, women of the neighborhood gather to sing songs of rejoicing only if the new family member is a boy. In fact, among the Kshatriyas female infanticide formerly occurred. . . .

In many areas of North India the high castes practice seclusion of women and prohibit the remarriage of widows; no such restrictions are placed on high caste men. A woman's status and acceptance in her husband's family are closely related to her ability to provide healthy sons to perpetuate the line. (1972 p. 6)

In Africa, tribal customs subject many black women to social and legal disabilities. Among certain Bantu-speaking tribes a woman does not inherit her husband's property when he dies. Instead, the inheritance goes to a male descendant. One tribal custom demands that an African widow marry her husband's brother to become, in some cases, his second or third wife. A widowed African woman is always subjected to a man's guardianship. If she wishes to travel overseas, for example, she may have to ask for written permission from her own son.

Most states in the United States apply dual minimum ages for marriage; that for females is usually set lower than for males. Article 767 of the Japanese Civil Code states that a woman must readopt her maiden name when divorced.

Thus, divorced women with school-age children have considerable problems in registering them for school. A twice-elected woman member of the House of Representatives was divorced during her term of office and had to assume her maiden name. For convenience during election campaigns she sued for permission to use her former married name, but she lost her suit. Once a woman is divorced, she cannot remarry for six months. The man, however, can remarry the next day.

In Israel it is explicitly laid down that the Law of Equality of Women (1953) does not apply to marriage and divorce. Hence, Israeli women cannot obtain divorces without the consent of their husbands. A non-Jewish woman, even if converted, may not marry a man belonging to the *Kohanim*, the Jewish rabbinical class. A man may remarry if his wife is declared insane, but the wife remains forever chained to an insane husband (Tamarin, 1973, pp. 33–34). George Tamarin points out that:

In case of marital infidelity, it is not the right but the duty of the husband to divorce (again without alimony) the immoral creature while infidelity on his part is by no means sufficient reason to substantiate the wife's request for divorce.

True, if a man had relations with a *married woman* ("wife of a man"), the couple will be forbidden to marry each other after her (or their) divorce. But the sin on his part was to have spoiled the *property* of another male while a married man has the right to have as many unmarried mistresses as he likes.

In line with the same logic, only the offspring of adulterous relations of a married woman will be considered a *Mamzer* barred to marry pure Jews (but only other bastards or converts) for *ten* generations. . . . Contrarywise, the offspring of the relations of a married man with a free (unmarried) female are pure Jews, enjoying all the rights of full-fledged members of the Chosen People (Tamarin, 1975, p. 19).

In virtually all lesser developed countries the primacy of child-bearing is a sociocultural norm, reinforced by lack of family-planning aids and a cultural bias against birth control, which binds millions of women throughout their adult lives to the never-ending drudgery of domestic servility. Fertility is often directly linked to religious injunctions. Some religions teach that a person without children will never reach heaven or qualify for reincarnation. In Africa, Asia, and South America the number of children a man begets is still a commonly accepted measure of his virility. For millions of women in South America, this cult of virility (machismo) means a much greater exposure to insemination than would occur in socioeconomically more sophisticated communities. In Africa and Asia, too, children are widely valued for their economic worth, chiefly as providers for their parents in old age.

2. WOMEN IN THE ISLAMIC WORLD

Sexism is deeply rooted in the religious and cultural norms of Islam. According to the Koran, feminine names should not be used for angels (Sura 53, v. 29). Al-Tabari's interpretation of Sura 4, v. 38 (sanction of physical punishment in order to force a woman to have sexual intercourse against her will) reads as follows: "Allah the Exalted means by this: admonish the woman . . . if they refuse to repent and perform their duties towards you, then shut them in their homes and beat them, so that they resume their duties." If a rebellious woman does not turn to her husband in repentance, "then Allah permits you to beat her, not too violently. Do not break her bones."

Other basic texts of Islamic law show clearly that women do not enjoy the same status and prestige as men; nor can they claim the same rights. "The Prophet, may Allah pray for him and greet him, said: 'I was shown the fire of hell; most of its inmates were ungrateful women.' It was asked; 'Are they ungrateful to Allah? The Prophet said: 'They are ungrateful to their husbands, ungrateful for kindness.'" On another occasion, Muhammad said: "People who appoint a woman to rule over them will never succeed" (Al-Nasa i, Sunan, Cairo n.d., 8:227). "Lugman said, admonishing his son: 'My son, beware of the bad woman, because they do not call for good; and be wary of the virtuous ones.' Al-Nasan said: 'A man who follows the wishes of his wife—Allah will throw him into the fire. Umar said: Contradict the women; there is blessing in it'" (Al-Damiri, Hayat al-Hayawan, title "ghurah").

Arab society still lives in the Middle Ages, says the Lebanese woman doctor Nawal Sa'dawi. City women are no longer veiled but their education and social role are still fashioned by the past. Conditions are even more backward in the rural and nomadic sectors and in theocracies such as Saudi Arabia, where the veil, polygamy, the harem of the sheikhs, and sequestration of women are the general rule. If the main themes of Arab feminists are similar to those of their Western counterparts, the details are very different, revealing a society steeped in medieval prejudices that disappeared long ago in the West.

"Thus in Egypt," explains women's liberation leader Amina al-Naqqash, "liberal circles have succeeded in pushing through the [President] Sadat bureaucracy a bill giving women for the first time the right to ask for divorce, though only in case the husband marries a second wife." Islamic Law (the Shari'a), hitherto in full force in Egypt, allows husbands to marry up to four wives and gives men the sole right to initiate divorce, which is accomplished simply by repeating three times the words "Thou art divorced." The same bill also brought alimony up to 40 percent of an ex-husband's salary for five years, instead of 25 percent for one year only. Conservative opposition, however, sparked by the students of Al-Azhar, the thousand-year-old religious university, has blocked further action on the bill.

Working in a different atmosphere and for goals more modest than those pursued in Europe and America, Arab women's liberationists are aware of the heavy odds against them. It appears to be their strategy to write

off for the time being the primitive country women as well as the wives of workers and petty bourgeois, all of whom remain in a medieval situation. Arab women's liberation concentrates on university-educated women, hoping to transform these into an avant-garde who will pave the way for the liberation of their sisters. Even here feminists face a difficult task. A recent survey showed that 90 percent of women students at the University of Damascus accepted male supremacy unconditionally, see child-rearing as the primary female role, and will marry subject to the consent of their family. A similar study in Cairo produced similar results for university and high-school women. In his book, *The Contemporary Iraqi Woman* (Dar al Basri Press, Baghdad, 1970), Abd Al-Rahman Al-Darbandi lists some of the precepts that the virtuous Muslim woman should follow:

1. She is forbidden to dance at all times, even if this should be in a private party.
2. She is forbidden to enter bars and other suspect places of entertainment, even if accompanied by her husband, father or brother.
3. She is forbidden to drink hard liquor at all times and in all circumstances.
4. She is forbidden to appear in swimming pools where she mixes with men and where she would be almost naked.
5. She is forbidden to travel in public means of transportation, unless she is accompanied by her father, brother or husband.
6. [Women] must marry at an early age. Governments should encourage this by grants, increases in salary, privileges and various exemptions.
7. Women are housewives; men are providers.
8. A wife should be employed by the government only if she lacks a private source of income, if her family is in dire need of her work, and only if her work outside will not interfere with her duties and obligations at home. (p. 170)

In Egypt, men often divorce their wives if they do not give birth to boys. Also, females inherit less than males (al-Sádāwī, 1972, pp. 110–14). Article 67 of the Egyptian Marriage Law reads:

No alimony is due a wife if she refused to surrender herself (sexually) to her husband, without right, or if she was compelled to do so for any reason unrelated to her husband. Likewise, no alimony is due to her in case she is imprisoned, even if unjustly, or arrested, or raped, or left her husband's house, or was forbidden by her guardian to maintain sexual relations with her husband, or she was in any condition which rendered her useless as a wife.

A phenomenon which is generally known as "mail order marriage" is still quite prevalent in Egypt. Each week some ten girls are sold through marriage contracts to husbands they have never seen. During 1973 and the first half of 1974, 15,000 arranged marriages took place in Egypt's civil courts between Egyptian girls and men from other Arab countries, some in their 60s, 70s and even 80s (see Chapter 23, 32).

Iranians and other Muslims visiting the Federal Republic are quite likely to propose marriage to German women. By marrying a European, a Muslim husband can avoid payment of the *mahr*, the traditional and substantial Islamic wedding gift. German women and their families have usually never heard of this custom and therefore do not demand compliance with it. Yet control over her *mahr*, which is vested neither in her father nor in her husband, is one of the very few rights enjoyed by a Muslim wife.

A woman who marries an Iranian man acquires Iranian citizenship whether she wants it or not. But once she has arrived in Iran, her foreign citizenship is of no avail, since the Iranian authorities hold their own citizenship to be controlling.

Iranian family law is based on the Shari'a: the wife is for all practical purposes the property of her husband. If she tires of the marriage and wishes to return to Europe, she is forbidden to do so without the consent of her husband. In the absence of a West-German–Iranian treaty on mixed marriages, the German embassy is unable to intervene. Furthermore, an exit visa for an Iranian citizen, whether or not he or she possesses dual citizenship, costs a fee currently set at about $300 (Bendix, 1973).

3. THE CULT OF VIRGINITY

The greatest indictment of male chauvinism, however, is to be found in the records of physicians practicing in Muslim countries. In a review of Dr. Ian Young's book, *The Private Life of Islam*, based on medical experiences in Algeria, Edward Behr commented:

Hospital life, in short, reflects the male-dominated Algerian society which uses its Kabyl women as serfs, keeping them in such a state of passivity and ignorance that one patient has to ask her husband what her name is. And Dr. Young's book is an appalling, and largely irrefutable, indictment of the present Algerian government's indifference to those injustices. (*Newsweek*, 18 November, 1974, p. 71)

The following case history recorded by Dr. al-Sádáwí is typical of the traditional obsession of the Muslims with virginity, the loss of which can be literally fatal.

A girl of 20 came to see me with her mother, who was an educational inspector in one of the elementary schools (in Cairo). The mother asked me to examine her daughter and to reassure her about the "safety" of her hymen. I asked the mother why she doubted her daughter's virginity. She answered that she had discovered that her daughter was accustomed, when washing every morning, to put her finger to her hymen in order to feel and size up its opening; and the mother was afraid that her daughter had, in this way, inadvertently damaged her membrane. . . .

I then examined the girl and found that the membrane was intact except for its aperture, which was enlarged, not because of rope-skipping but because of the repeated insertion of her finger which had relaxed the circumference somewhat. . . .

The mother asked in terror: "Will that affect her virginity?"

I told the mother the truth: that if her daughter married, there might not be any blood as a result of her first intercourse with a man. The mother almost crumpled in a nervous breakdown, but I tried to calm and reassure her by giving her a certificate absolving her daughter of responsibility. (1972, pp. 32–34)

In some Arab villages, Dr. al-Sádáwi witnessed marriage traditions that emphasize woman's inferior status. He tells of a nurse who seizes the bride by the legs, tearing out her hymen and wiping off the blood with a towel—which the bride's father exhibits to the wedding party to prove the honor of his daughter. On one occasion, the doctor relates, there was insufficient blood, so the nurse deliberately injured the bride's vagina. This was necessary, she explained, because people measure the bride's honor by the quantity of blood on the towel. Dr. al-Sádáwi also tells of the barbarous practice of clitorectomy:

Hardly a girl reaching nine or ten years of age and still prepubescent, is not brought to a woman called "nurse," who seizes the child by the legs, as she would a hen before slaughter, and with a razor, removes the child's clitoris. This "operation" termed "female circumcision" was common until very lately in our society, and several families insist upon the circumcision of their daughters till this very day.

Often I was called upon to save the life of a girl who was subjected to this ugly operation. For the "nurse" because of her ignorance, was convinced that the deeper she plunged her razor in order to cut out the clitoris at the root, the more virtuous and the more undesirous of sex the girl would become. The sharp razor caused serious hemorrhage and sometimes a girl lost her life before (medical) help could be summoned to save her life. Naturally the "nurse" knows nothing about antiseptics, so that her dirty razor causes inflammation in most cases. The psychological shock caused by this humiliating operation is no doubt considerable and, to a child, indelible, causing her, later in marital life, many problems, of which sexual frigidity is only one, and which reflect themselves upon her husband by way of sexual aberrations and addiction to drugs. (1972, pp. 33–40 and 114–15)

4. EQUALITY OR PREFERENCE?

There are, of course, physical differences between men and women; as of this writing, babies are still being born and nursed by women, since they alone have the biological equipment for these functions. The incubators predicted by Aldous Huxley in his *Brave New World* are, however, at least a technical possibility. Had the courts sustained the original Massachusetts ruling in the Edelin case, making it obligatory for a physician who aborts a live fetus to make every effort to keep that fetus alive, research would have been spurred on the development of incubators that could make Huxley's fantasy come true far sooner than that author would have imagined. It is not unthinkable that some time in the future a professional woman wanting a child without the bother of a nine-month pregnancy will conceive in the usual manner but, after three or four months, visit a special hospital. Here, the fetus will be transferred to an artificial "womb" where it will be nurtured to a stage equivalent to a baby at birth and then returned to the mother.

Equality for women has been made a real issue by the change in the lifestyle wrought by the scientific revolution. Until fairly recently many human occupations—not the least of them that of fighting—required sheer brute strength. This fact dictated a rather natural division of tasks. In the modern industrial society, machines have taken over much of the physical labor—including tasks of destruction—and there is an increasing need for technical skills and manual dexterity: qualities that women can develop as highly as men. More importantly, women have now become able to decide whether or when to bear children—though this right depends on medical services not always available to women of deprived groups.

One of the dangers in trying to overcome discriminations that have persisted for centuries is that of reverse discrimination: *against men.* The effect of "affirmative action" programs in American universities has been to grant a certain preference to women and minority members who meet the minimum qualifications for a position, even though a white male might be more qualified. The administrator who appoints a man when there is a woman applicant is often obliged to prove he did not make the choice on the basis of sex. Since successful personnel selection is not merely a matter of reading test results but involves many intangibles, including sensitivity to both desirable and undesirable personality traits, limitation of selection to factors that can be "proved in court" makes academic or business administration inordinately difficult.

It is a miscarriage of equality to reduce requirements that are actually essential for a job, such as a combination of physical strength and intelligence in a police officer. Yet that is exactly what happened in San Francisco in the wake of a court order requiring increased hiring of minorities and women in the police department. As Phyllis Schlafly relates:

New and less rigorous tests, which are much less demanding, have already been prepared and put into effect. The obvious purpose of the lowered tests is to accept women who could not meet the previous male requirements. Under the new physical tests, height requirements have been abolished. Formerly the height requirement was five feet seven inches, but the San Francisco Police Department has now taken at least two applicants who stand only four feet nine inches. The average height of women applicants is five foot three. The level of the written test has been likewise reduced. How much is indicated by the fact that under the former written tests, about 30 percent of the applicants passed; under the new written tests as many as 80 percent passed.

However, the reduced test levels still don't satisfy the female chauvinists. . . . The attorney for the women has asked the court to order a new lowered physical test for applicants, saying, "It may be necessary to order ratio-hiring of women." (*Report*, February 1975)

Things went even further in Detroit where three militant women persuaded a judge to issue an injunction requiring the police department to hire men and women on a one-to-one ratio. The court order required not only equal hiring but *equal assignment*. "As a result, Detroit policewomen are now regularly answering run-of-the-mill police calls, including domestic quarrels, saloon brawls, civil disturbances, shoot-outs, and other guerrilla-warfare city crises" (*ibid.*). At the same time physical requirements have been reduced and combat training downgraded at the police recruit school. It can hardly be doubted that the Detroit Police Department has been severely impaired in its efficiency.

A possible compromise was pointed out by the Commonwealth Court of Pennsylvania, a state which has adopted an Equal Rights Amendment. In *Commonwealth* v. *Pennsylvania Interscholastic Athletic Association*, handed down March 19, 1975, the court ruled that girls must be admitted to practice and compete with boys in interschool athletics, including contact sports such as football, wrestling, soccer, and lacrosse. But they must meet the same tests as boys, and these tests need not be reduced to accommodate "the fair sex." As the Court said:

The notion that girls as a whole are weaker and thus more injury-prone, if they compete with boys, especially in contact sports, cannot justify the By-Law in light of the EPA. Nor can we consider the argument that boys are generally more skilled. The existence of certain characteristics to a greater degree in one sex does not justify classification by sex rather than by the particular characteristic. Wiegand v. Wiegand, 226 Pa. Superior Ct. 278, 310 A. 2d 426 (1973). If any individual girl is too weak, injury prone, or unskilled, she may, of course, be excluded from competition on that basis but she cannot be excluded solely because of her sex without regard to her relevant qualifications. We believe that this is what our Supreme Court meant when it said in Butler, supra, that "sex may no longer be accepted as an exclusive classifying tool." (in Schafly, *Report*, April 1975)

The most reasonable public policy seems to be, not to accord women any artificial preference, but to treat them as people on the basis of their individual abilities and inclinations. Thus, the woman with the physical stamina and the desire to be a construction worker, a truck driver, or even a professional (American) football player should be admitted if she can keep up with the male competition and is willing to take the same risks of physical injury. The Amazon, as a somatic and psychological type, does exist. If natural physical differences are no longer compounded by cultural conditioning, Amazons may become more frequent.

The question as to how much male-female differences are inborn and how much they are produced by divergent socialization has yet to be studied in depth. So far as intellectual and manipulative skills and occupations and the educational and training programs that lead to them are concerned, any tests other than ability and performance are no longer admissible.

PART FOUR

---◆---

FUNCTIONAL AREAS OF DISCRIMINATION

17

DISCRIMINATION AGAINST ENTIRE CULTURES

Cultural discrimination has two interlocking aspects: discrimination against members of a group because of their culture and discrimination that denies the group an equal opportunity to maintain and develop its culture. Discrimination *because* of culture may involve almost any area of social life, including employment, politics, admission to and treatment in schools and universities, and relative social distance. Discrimination in the *maintenance* of culture involves the use of language in education, government and business, but more particularly the allocation of resources so that—in a multicultural society—one culture or cluster of cultures (normally that of a *Staatsvolk*) is favored at the expense of others.

Where the culture of an ethnic minority is under attack, the objective of the dominant group is usually not the total destruction of the minority culture but rather the entrenchment and advancement of the dominant group's own culture and the extending of preferential treatment to it. Such cultural discrimination expresses the dominant group's ethnocentrism and in-group solidarity. Some degree of cultural preference is inevitable in ethnically heterogeneous national societies; otherwise they would merge into homogeneous cultural communities. Indeed, in many countries some measure of cultural discrimination is the only way in which certain ethnic nations can ensure cultural self-preservation. For example, absolute cultural parity linked to one-man, one-vote elections would cause the culture of the indigenous Fijians to be overwhelmed by that of the more numerous Indian immigrants; the Malays of Malaysia would threaten the Chinese; in Ethiopia the politically dominant Amharas would eventually have to bow to the numerically stronger Gallas; in Iraq the politically dominant Sunnites would be demoted to a subordinate group by the Kurds and Shiites; and in South Africa it would lead to ethnic suicide on the part of the Afrikaners.

A. Discrimination Against Cultures of Entire Ethnic Groups

1. RUSSIFICATION IN THE USSR

As mentioned previously, the 130 million (Great) Russians of the USSR constitute the dominant ethnic group which, through the Communist Party, dominates the top institutions of power and maintains its cultural hegemony entrenched. Insidious Russification, carried out both by open alienation and by subtle forms of cultural erosion, has been employed by the Russians for centuries to neutralize systematically their major ethnic rivals. Their main targets are the Ukrainians (who, notwithstanding their Slavic character, are distrusted because at 42 million they are the second largest nation in the USSR); the Jews (whose firm solidarity with Israel has provoked sharper persecution); and the Muslim-Turkic peoples, numbering more than 70 million (whose cultural identities differ radically from those of the Russians, and whose close historical, ethnic, and religious ties with Asian peoples outside the USSR stoke the fires of Russian suspicion).

Of the 180 million people of Slavic stock, about 50 million are Ukrainians and White Russians (Byelorussians), the remainder being Russian-born Slavs. Some experts feel that the Russians can be regarded as the counterpart of the WASPs in the U.S.A. because of their feeling of superiority over the non-Slav peoples whose lifestyles are considered primitive and whose religions are viewed by the Russian atheists as archaic superstitions.

The Russians appear convinced that *democratic* multinationalism would seriously jeopardize communism in the USSR; hence their policy of progressive "internationalization"—a transparent euphemism for deculturation of the non-Slavic peoples in a Russian-dominated melting pot. Census data already show that large numbers of non-Slavs have surrendered their mother language and adopted Russian. Economic equality is held out as the reward for Russification. But it was brought out at a conference on the nationality question in Soviet Central Asia (Columbia University, April 7–8, 1972) that such equality remains relatively meaningless in the absence of real possibilities for nationalities to make significant independent choices in economic, artistic, cultural, political, and social matters.

Apologists for the Russian dispensation justify it as the authority held by an "elder brother." At the conference mentioned above, several delegates argued that:

the very *"elder brother"* catchword, persistently employed in publicity or propaganda, . . . typifies the nature of pervasive ethnic discrimination currently practiced against non-Russians. *Selective denial of civil* or legal rights to the *Crimean Tatars, Volga Germans, or Meskhetian Turks* deported to Central Asia and still detained there since World War II, as well as the withholding of equal protection for certain other ethnic groups, such as *Jews*, under Soviet nationality policy, has also been cited as evidence of actual discrimination. . . . [it] may be pondered whether the "tyranny of the majority," or even plurality, especially in a country like the USSR where people are divided religiously according to ethnic affiliation, cannot help but inflict political, social, and economic injury upon the minority (notably *when it is fragmented into innumerable units*). Unless that majority erects and rigorously maintains an effective structure of *compensatory devices*, polices its personal contacts constantly to stamp out a "we-they" polarity, and thoroughly denies itself advantages ordinarily accruing to size and power, the actual discrimination suffered by nationalities cannot be largely offset. That this equity has not been achieved in Soviet Central Asia so far . . . is borne out by a great deal of evidence . . . regarding inequality in jobholding, education, real power sharing and the like.

During World War II, eight ethnically distinct peoples in the USSR were deported *en bloc* (see chapter 22, B7). Between 40 percent and 45 percent of the deportees died in conditions of acute misery during the mass expulsion and the first 18 months after their departure. Genocide is a particularly apt word to describe the fate of the Crimean Tatars. According to Ann Sheehy:

Everything was done to destroy all traces of the national life of the Tatars and the very memory of their existence. Houses were demolished, and orchards and vineyards were allowed to become wild and overgrown. The cemeteries of the Tatars were ploughed up, and the remains of their ancestors torn from the earth. . . . Everything written and printed in Crimean Tatar was burnt—from ancient manuscripts to the classics of Marxism-Leninism inclusive. Many of the old Tatar place names in the Crimea were also replaced by Russian ones. (1972, pp. 281–82)

Five of the nations concerned have been "rehabilitated" and returned to their homelands, but the Volga Germans, the Crimean Tatars, and the Meskhetians are still in exile.

On the surface, the non-Russian nations of the USSR enjoy a modicum of local cultural autonomy. But in view of Russian economic domination and infiltration in the local power structures, it is improbable that these ethnic minorities will escape eventual cultural liquidation. William Foltz writes:

> Despite official claims to the contrary, ethnic group status appears to be ranked according to a single scale, with the "elder brother" Great Russians at the top, and the exiled groups, rehabilitated or not, at the bottom. The only way for most individuals to escape this *de facto* group status ranking, is by linguistic and cultural Russification, and beyond that by active service of the political structures that reinforce both the individual and the group status rankings. (1974, p. 109)

The Secretary of the Azerbaijan Communist Party, N. Gadzhiyev, describes the messianic ethnolinguistic goal of the CPSU in the journal *Kommunist:*

> The culture of the Communist Society will come about not by means of a mere fusion of all the national cultures, nor by means of administrative removal of national distinctions and national peculiarities, but in other ways. Gradually all those elements that separate the national cultures will die away, and those features that will form the international base of the culture of Communist society will become stronger. (Goldhagen, 1968, p. 130)

Efforts of Kremlin apologists for Russification to compare the CPSU's ethnic policy with the "melting pot" in the United States have proved unconvincing. The *Ukrainian Quarterly* (1972, no. 3) calls attention to the erroneous theory, accepted by many American writers,

which tends to equate the USSR with America. The average American has come to think that Ukraine and Georgia are as much parts of Russia as Pennsylvania and Texas are parts of the United States. "Caught up by a beatific vision of this 'Promised Land,' they minimized or even denied flatly the phenomenon of Russification of the non-Russian peoples; they compared Siberia to our taming of the West, never seeing the fundamental element of genocide in the Soviet dispersion of nationalities." It was these misguided writers and historians rather than paid Soviet propagandists who helped build a powerful image of the USSR, unified and single-minded, by underplaying the non-Russian nations. This myth has been extremely useful to the Kremlin.

Despite its iron grip on the non-Russian nations, however, Moscow has had to recognize their existence. The *Ukrainian Quarterly* comments:

> . . . Involved in fabricating the "common spiritual face of the Soviet man" are cultural development, way of life, social morality and, above all, language. . . . Proclaiming an integration, however, does not mean that it exists, as attested to by recent official discussion. The regime faces insurmountable difficulties in its struggle against national peculiarities, traditions, cultures and languages. Even in the program of the CPSU it was stated that the "elimination of national differences, especially the linguistic, is a far more protracted matter than the elimination of class differences." (Vol. 27, no. 3 (Autumn, 1972), pp. 254–55)

2. CULTURAL DISCRIMINATION IN THE EASTERN MEDITERRANEAN: CYPRUS, THE KURDS, AND ISRAEL

For nearly two decades the Turkish Cypriots on Cyprus have been complaining that their culture and lifestyle is threatened by the numerically stronger Greeks. They have demanded self-government with a view to autonomous development of their own culture, but the Greek Cypriots have refused this in the name of a unitary state.

The Turkish-Greek clashes in August 1974, underscored the fact that the Turks (supported by mainland Turkey) will not hesitate to use military force to protect their cultural interests. They currently control about 40 percent of the island and all signs point to their being determined to concentrate their cultural influence in specific areas of Cyprus. Differences in language, lifestyle, traditions, and religion make the Turkish-Greek division on Cyprus one for which there is no instant solution (see Chapter 22,C3).

The Turkish-Cypriot counterparts in Iraq are the Kurds. But unlike the former, this Middle East minority has no strong elder brother to whom it can turn for help—unless Iran, with a considerable Kurdish population, decides to resume this role. That, however, is hardly likely, since Teheran does not want to encourage separatism among its own Kurds. The Kurds have long been victims of cultural discrimination. The defeat of their leader Mulla Mustafa Barzani and the consequent shelving of hopes for a genuinely autonomous, or as they would prefer independent, Kurdistan will merely add to their heavy burden.

Farther south, in Israel, non-Jewish communities complain of cultural discrimination. With the partition of Palestine into a Jewish State (Israel) and an Arab State (Jordan) and the Arab attacks against the Jewish community 590,000 Arabs fled or were displaced. They and their children, and additional refugees displaced during the 1967 War, remain semipermanent wards of the United Nations (see chapter 22). In a reciprocal migration, 600,000 or more Jews came to Israel from Arab territories where they and their ancestors had been living for centuries; today fewer than 50,000 Jews, mostly elderly persons, remain in Arab countries. About half a million Palestinian Arabs are living in Israel and they complain of open cultural discrimination by the Israeli

Jews. A prominent Jewish academician (Tamarin) has summed up contempory Israeli-Arab relations as follows:

The most characteristic feature of the coexistence of communities is basic *segregation* in the social domain, with intensive enough economic contacts, accompanied by *hostile* feelings of mistrust, and also hatred on the Arab side and contempt on the Jewish.

. . . In the mid-Sixties, following the abolishment of the Military Government, a short more relaxed period of improved relations ensued. This situation however came to an end with the lightning Israeli victory in 1967, so deeply hurting Arab national pride, and the subsequent contact between Israeli Arabs and their relatives in the occupied territories.

Israeli Arabs do not deny that they achieved tremendous economic progress, concomitant with the transformation (following the sizeable loss of land property) of former *fellahin* into an *urban proletariat*, fully integrated into the country's mostly booming economy, though the first to lose their jobs in case of a recession. They also value the democratic institutions non-existent (except in Lebanon) in the Arab states. But this, in their eyes, is of minor significance in comparison with the hurts endured, discriminations existing in comparing their achievement with that of the Jews, and the absence of a satisfying future for the growing educated stratum. (1975, pp. 124–30)

But there are even Jewish groups in Israel that suffer cultural discrimination because of their background and their physical appearance. The Israeli-born Jews (Sabras) are particularly prone to adopting an attitude of superiority toward the returning diasporic Jews. The victims of the greatest antipathy are the Sephardic Oriental Jews of Africa and Asia. A prominent Jew, Dr. Joseph A. Hasson, wrote in the *New York Times* on August 16, 1972, that the Sephardic Jews were victims of discrimination. He stated:

Ninety percent of important positions in government, the military, the Histadruth (Israel's major labor union), the Jewish Agency, and industry are filled by Ashkenazim, or children of parents born within a six-hundred mile radius of the Minsk-Pinsk area of East Europe. . . . In education, the drop-out rate among Sephardim is high; while they constitute 67% of the primary school population, they represent only 4% of University graduates. The consequence is the evolution in Israel of a caste-class-social order with Sephardim relegated to the unskilled, menial tasks.

Georges Tamarin describes the cultural situation of lower-status Israeli Jews as follows:

amidst general progress, still appallingly large segments of the population, practically in their totality of Afro-Asian descent, live in worst conditions of poverty, backwardness and often crime. Some "Oriental" settlements, especially in the urban slums, threaten to breed pockets of a second and third generation of poverty. . . .

The fact should not be minimized that in social prestige and material welfare there are still marked differences between immigrants and their descendents hailing from Western and those from "Oriental communities." It is equally beyond doubt, that the once reigning and lately much more relaxed "melting pot" ideology, aiming to make "one nation of the ingathered exiles" tended to impose the ideals and norms of the East-European rulers (and not of "truly" Western "too unJewish" groups), at least part of whom did want with missionary zeal to transform the Orientals into "dark skinned Ashkenazim." (1975, pp. 131, 133)

The average Oriental child in Israel consumes only 60 percent as much as a Western child, even though the number of Oriental families with very low education is decreasing and Oriental family incomes are rising 20 percent faster than those of Westerners. Of 200,000 children living "in distress" conditions, between 92 and 94 percent are Oriental, as are all the 45,000 children defined as living in "severe distress" (with regard to housing, education, and parents' income; *ibid.*, p. 133).

3. CULTURAL DISCRIMINATION IN AFRICA

Space permits consideration of only a few of the many cases of cultural discrimination found in Africa. The first involves the civil war in Sudan. Professor G. N. Sanderson identified the root of the conflict as cultural:

Almost all Sudanese communities living north of the 10th Parallel share two characteristics . . . devotion to a recognizably Sudanese style of Islam and a locally acceptable claim to an Arab ancestry. . . .

Southern resistance was fundamentally a protest against the bland northern conviction (prevalent even in the most enlightened circles) that the views of the southerners need not be taken seriously in determining the structure, ethos and political behaviour of an independent Sudan. . . . Northerners were members of a literate and political society which was a province of a world religion and of a major civilization. Southern societies isolated from the outside world until about 1840, seemed by contrast realms of barbarism. Their modes of social organization were incomprehensible; their systems of value seemed absurd or repulsive; their languages, to Arabic-speaking Muslims, were uncouth and contemptible jargons.

Moreover, the circumstances of the opening up of the south in the nineteenth century had led to the dominance of the master-and-slave relationships in contacts between northerners and southerners. This relationship was of course dead; but its earlier existence still subtly affected attitudes and helped to buttress the northerner's profound belief in his own total superiority. (*The Times*, London, March 27, 1972)

The Muslim-Arabs were firmly convinced that forced Arabization of the South would be the easiest shortcut to intercommunity peace. Even the privately owned Christian mission schools in the South were nationalized in 1957 to smother all semblance of anti-Muslim sentiments. As pressures intensified on the South, a growing exodus of the educated elite caused a serious "brain drain" with adverse consequences for the cultural interests of the South. Ali Abdel Rahman, then Minister of the Interior, let the cat out of the bag when he declared in 1958: "The Sudan is an integral part of the Arab world. . . . Anybody dissenting from this view must quit the country" (Wai, 1973,

p. 104). In 1968 the Sudanese Constitution was converted, for all practical purposes, into a legal instrument for Arab-Islamic dominance. As Dunstan Wai has written:

With the Arab revival successfully enshrined in the Islamic constitution, the Southerner would remain an outsider, useful only because his number would add to the prestige and status of his Northern counterpart. Thus the people of the Southern Sudan saw in the Islamic constitution the supreme expression of a way of life, of a culture, of a mystique known as the "Arab Nation." . . . Christian Moslem and pagan Afro-Negro Southerners appeared unanimous in their rejection of such a document. In this situation the Southern representatives, for whom I had the honour to be a spokesman, left the constitution commission at the end of December, 1968. We did not wish to be party to a document that emphasized the Arab race, Islamic religion and Arab culture to the exclusion of other existing races, religions and culture. It would have made nonsense of a regional autonomy anyway. . . . In being told to accept the rule of a constitution based on religion, the Southerners were being told they would become aliens in the Arab world and its cultures, exiles from the negro-African world. They were being told to say goodbye to their cultures and their general way of life. They also saw in the Islamic constitution a legal instrument of state discrimination against non-Moslems." (*Ibid.*, p. 25.)

Not even the appreciable regional autonomy granted to the South in 1972 is regarded by the non-Muslim blacks as an absolute guarantee against encroaching Arabization. The remarks of Premier Sayed Saddiq Lel Mahdi on Islamic hegemony to the Constituent Assembly in October 1966, are still fresh in their memory. He stated: "The dominant feature of our nation is an Islamic one and its overpowering expression is Arab, and this Nation will not have its entity identified and its prestige and pride preserved except under an Islamic revival." The youthful leader of the Islamic Charter Front, Dr. Hassan Turabi, argued that as the South had no culture, the vacuum should be filled by resurging Arab culture (Wai, 1973, p. 24).

The emancipated American slaves who es-

tablished the Republic of Liberia in West Africa lost no time in importing their own formula for out-group discrimination. The "aboriginal" Liberians can today attain cultural equality only at the price of conforming to American Liberian norms and values. To quote Ivo Duchacek:

American black settlers and their descendants openly discriminated against the backward native tribes in government, employment, and social relations for a long time. As a consequence, "The tribal people regard themselves as Bassa or Kpelle rather than Liberians." All twenty presidents of Liberia have been Americo-Liberians. . . . Tolbert is the first president of Liberia who speaks a tribal language (Kpelle) in addition to his mother tongue, English. One of his early statements on the subject of unification between the Americo-Liberians and the aborigines clearly indicated that unification was meant as a process by which the tribes were to absorb Americo-Liberian values and way of life; "The masses of our people must be raised from the mats on the floor to a mattress on every bed." (Duchacek, 1973b, pp. 76–78)

In Ethiopia, where the political and social system is dominated by a numerical minority—the Amhara—the major victims of large-scale cultural discrimination have been the Eritreans in the northeast and especially the Muslims of lowland Eritrea. The separatist Eritrean Liberation Front (ELF) claims on historic and ethnic grounds that the province is a separate entity which should rightly be independent of Ethiopia. Fears among the Muslim Eritreans that their ethnic identity would be smothered were aggravated by the military coup of September 1974, and the assumption of power by a new regime displaying clear anti-Eritrean sentiment.

Rwanda and Burundi provide examples of how mass cultural and ethnic discrimination can be taken to the brink of genocide. In March 1957, intellectuals of the oppressed Hutu majority in Rwanda published the famous *Bahutu* Manifesto, which Lemarchand summarizes as follows:

The heart of the matter, they said, lies in the political monopoly of one race, the Tutsi race, which, given the present structural framework becomes a social and economic monopoly. . . . To remedy the situation they proposed a series of measures designed to achieve "the integral and collective promotion of the Hutu": the abandonment of caste prejudice, the recognition of individual landed property, the creation of a rural Credit Bank . . . to promote agricultural initiatives, the codification of customs, the promotion of Hutu to public office, and the extension of educational opportunities at all levels to Hutu children. (1970, p. 149)

In sharp contrast to this was the arrogant manner in which the Tutsi ruling caste confirmed their claim to ethnic superiority a year later. Again Lemarchand is our source:

To the rising crescendo of Hutu attacks, the ruling oligarchy responded in 1958 by a hardening of its position on the issue of race relations. In May 1958, a group of elderly Tutsi—the Mwami's clients—issued a statement in which they said that the ancestor of the Banyiginya, Kigwa, came to the throne by reducing the indigenous Hutu tribes to a state of servitude, and thus "there could be no basis for brotherhood between Hutu and Tutsi." . . . [The] statement prompted the Hutu to challenge the historical symbols of Tutsi supremacy; and so, by late 1958, the Karinga drum, the supreme symbol of monarchy, became the target of violent criticisms in the Hutu press. More than its symbolic association with the crown, it was attacked for its conjuring up a vision of permanent Hutu inferiority. As the Karinga contained in its external trappings the sexual organs of defeated Hutu kings one can easily see why the emblem of kingship should have caused such deep revulsion among the Hutu elites.

The successful revolt by the Hutu a year later came as no surprise; it was a bloody catharsis accelerated by the Hutu's conviction that only a revolution could right the extreme cultural discrimination practiced by the Tutsi. Today the shoe is on the other foot and the Tutsi are on the receiving end of cultural discrimination. In next-door Burundi, the Hutu revolt of 1972 was crushed; an estimated hundred thousand Hutu were slaughtered.

This bloody vendetta was directed almost solely at the Hutu elite and can thus be classed as selective genocide or aristocide.

B. Cultural Discrimination Against Marginal Groups

1. MARGINAL GROUPS IN SOUTH ASIA: ANGLO-INDIANS AND TAMILS

A lesser-known form of discrimination is revealed in the culturally and socially marginal position of the so-called Anglo-Indians. These descendants of British and Indian parents are predominantly Christian. Numbering a quarter of a million, they have a Western lifestyle and regard English as their mother tongue. According to Noel Gist and Roy Wright,

These cultural attributes have tended to set them apart from the vast majority of the Indian people. Although some of the characteristics such as the Christian faith and the English language are shared in common with a considerable number of other Indians, the Anglo-Indians are the only minority with English as its "mother tongue." Nevertheless, the cultural gap between the Anglo-Indians and other Indian communities—Hindu, Muslim, Sikh, Tribal, Parsee—is wide. The cultural gap, however wide or narrow in specific situations, has its counterpart in the social gap characterizing inter-personal and inter-group relations. (1973, p. 3)

In a preference survey conducted in 1964 among Indian students in Calcutta, involving six ethnic groups (British, Parsees, Egyptians, Anglo-Indians, Jews, and African Negroes), the British group was ranked the most preferred group and the Anglo-Indians the least preferred. Gist and Wright came across the following example of Anti–Anglo-Indian sentiment during their research on this minority:

The "products of British adultery" are once again in the news. The worm that was content to sidle behind the rears of burra sahibs and lick the boots of uncouth British tommies has not turned, and it appears it is no longer in the mood to do the "dirty work" of an "ungrateful administration." . . . this sudden transformation on the part of Anglo-India must be considered more of a case of rats leaving a sinking ship than a sudden love for Mother India.

. . . Let them go back to where they have always wanted to be; in the arms of white soldiers and licking the jack boots of Imperialism.

. . . No, we do not want them. We never did and we never shall. . . . The very fact that they are now willing to change allegiance and come over to the other camp should be enough to betray them for what they really are—a freak section of humanity— opportunists of the first water and traitors to the very core of their halfcaste hearts. (*ibid.*, p. 44)

Little wonder that Frank Anthony, President of the All-India Anglo-Indian Association, once remarked in the Indian Parliament that the "minority peoples of India walk in the shadows of death." (*ibid.*, p. 48).

Discrimination against the Tamil-speaking minority by the dominant Sinhala-speaking community on the island of Sri Lanka (Ceylon) is far more extensive and potentially explosive than that confronting the Anglo-Indians. The Sinhalese—mostly Buddhists—form about 75 percent of the total population. The Tamils— mainly Hindus—only managed to attain equal language status with the Sinhala after bloody riots in the mid-1950s. But not even this advance has prevented the Sinhalese from adopting an even more discriminatory attitude toward the Tamils, especially the descendants of those imported from South India as plantation workers under the British colonial regime. Many Tamil speakers see their only salvation in a separate Tamil state in which they can have full ethnic self-determination. This sentiment was intensified when Prime Minister Bandaranaike's Sri Lanka Freedom Party exploited Sinhala ethnic chauvinism in the 1970 general election and was rewarded by a two to one electoral victory.

During an earlier term of office, Mrs. Bandaranaike had concluded the Indo-Ceylon Agreement of 1964, which settled the citizenship status of 825,000 Tamils of Indian origin in Sri Lanka. Of these, 525,000 were to be returned to India and 300,000 granted Sri Lanka citizenship. The future of an additional 150,000 Tamils was to be settled later. But the government in office from March 1965, to May 1970, took little interest in carrying out the agreement, and by the time Mrs. Bandanaraike returned to office only 15,345 Tamils had been repatriated to India and 5445 granted Sri Lanka citizenship. Her government speeded the pace of repatriation; new procedures made it easy for those moving to take their Provident Fund benefits and other assets with them, and the cooperation of tea estate superintendents was enlisted. A new agreement on January 27, 1974, divided the last group of 150,000 Tamils equally: altogether, 600,000 persons were to be repatriated and 375,000 granted Sri Lanka citizenship. As of June 30, 1976, 172,753 persons had been repatriated to India and 98,716 granted citizenship. It was expected that the agreements would be fully carried out by 1983 (according to information supplied by the Sri Lanka Embassy). The repatriation scheme, however, does not appear to have fully quieted demands for a Tamil state on Sri Lanka.

2. INDIAN MINORITIES ABROAD

Indian and Chinese communities in other countries are often victims of cultural discrimination. In Burma, a centuries-old Indian community has been persecuted systematically since the outbreak of World War II. More than a quarter of a million of these hapless people have been "repatriated" to India since the end of the War. About the same number returned to India and Pakistan on a "voluntary" basis between 1945 and 1968, mainly because discrimination and prejudice had made it impossible for them to protect and promote their established societies as a separate ethnic group. According to Chakravarti,

The Burmese constitution did not recognize Indians as a minority and no special provisions were made either for their representation or for any form of safeguard such as Indians were eligible for under the British. Those who had been in continuous residence in Burma for at least eight years, out of the last ten years, or ten years immediately before the War, were eligible for Burman citizenship. But the naturalization procedure appeared to be so time-consuming, costly and difficult, and future prospects were so uncertain, that only a small number of Indians (estimated between 35,000 and 40,000) ventured to apply. Consequently, only a small number of Indians were offered Burmese citizenship, and a much smaller number (estimated at less than 10,000) accepted it with considerable hesitation (1971, p. 178).

Of about three quarters of a million Indians living in Burma in 1947, less than one-third remain—mostly as "stateless persons" stripped of all meaningful political and civil rights. Chakravarti concludes: "This quarter of a million people, mostly stateless and poor . . . continue to present a human problem, hardly noticed by the civilised world" (*ibid.*, p. 186).

Nor is cultural discrimination unknown in other countries with relatively large Indian minorities such as Malaysia, Singapore, the Philippines, Indonesia and Fiji. In Malaysia, for instance, the Indians (80 percent of them Tamils) have *de jure* equality in most basic political and civil rights. In practice, however, the Malays control the access to education, employment, and business opportunity to such an extent that many Indians have been forced to purchase promotion by accepting cultural alienation. The largest Indian community of South America, in Guyana, is stronger than its counterparts in most Asian countries. Mainly descendants of 240,000 indentured workers imported from India between 1835 and 1917, the so-called East Indians constitute just over half the total population of Guyana. It is, however, the (black) Afro-Guyanese, with the assistance of other small ethnic minorities and more particularly the more than 70,000 so-called "overseas electors" (of whom the overwhelming majority are Africans), who occupy the politically dominant position in Guyana. The East Indians claim that the majority of these overseas Afro-Guyanese are fictitious. According to Rabushka and Shepsle, "Granada Television checked 650 alleged Guyanese residents in Britain and found, on the average, only one name in twenty on the registration list" (1972, p. 103). Little wonder that the Indian-dominated People's Progressive Party (PPP) led by Cheddi Jagan has invoked the electoral slogan of *Apanjaht* (which in Hindu means "vote your race") in an effort to achieve cultural survival through ethnic solidarity.

It is in two East African states, Kenya and Uganda, however, that ethnic discrimination against people of Asian-Indian descent has evoked the greatest media coverage in the West. More than 75,000 Indians "departed" from East Africa between 1960 and 1973 because they were told in no uncertain terms that they were unwanted and unassimilable. In Uganda, President Amin expelled practically the entire Indian community in one fell swoop.

Black Africans were particularly incensed at what they saw as the cultural insularity of the Indians. The latter strongly resisted assimilation with the blacks; they saw Africanization as socioeconomic subordination at best and ethnic annihilation at worst. To protect both their community life and their status, they manifested in-group solidarity and ethnic exclusivism that provoked punitive measures against Indian communalism in East Africa, especially in Uganda. The following letter is typical of the antagonism which Indian resistance to Africanization evoked:

I always wonder why Asians tend to avoid social intercourse with other races. You may work in the same place with an Asian, studying the same institution of learning for many years, but never will you come to know them socially. An Asian will always prove to be a stranger outside his place of work. . . . I am of the opinion that this kind of life is a selfish one in the eyes of true Kenyans and there is no room for it in an independent Kenya. (*Daily Nation*, October 26, 1966)

The attacks on the cultural identity of Indian communities in Burma and East Africa is in strong contrast to the position of their counterparts in the Republic of South Africa. In spite of their weak bargaining power in the most powerful institutions and the considerable cultural and social prejudice they experience at the hands of both the blacks and the whites, the 750,000 Indians in South Africa have their own educational institutions (including the only full-fledged Indian University outside India), at least one autonomous municipal government, a rudimentary group parliament that deals with the white-controlled central parliament, and a wide variety of institutions and facilities guaranteeing a meaningful measure of ethnic autonomy. Only a negligible number have accepted the government's offer of subsidized repatriation (plus compensation) to India.

3. THE OVERSEAS CHINESE

Cultural discrimination against Chinese minorities is on the whole less onerous than that against Indians, but they find themselves in a similar minority status. Although Chinese have lived in the Philippines for more than 5000 years, the Philippine Government follows a systematic policy of depriving the Chinese of any power that could possibly be construed as a threat to the Spanish- and Tagalog-speaking Filipinos. Stringent economic curbs and language qualifications have been invoked to keep the Chinese in a subordinate position. The clannishness, wealth, and visibility of the Chinese provoke strong prejudice and discrimination on the part of the Filipinos. The Chinese react with intensified self-segregation, thus entrenching social and cultural differences.

In Malaysia, Malay-Chinese antagonism and political rivalry has wrecked a partnership. Chinese-dominated Singapore left the Malaysian Federation in 1965. The cultural discrimination experienced by the many Chinese who have remained in Malaysia is clear evidence

that Singapore read the political cards right. The cultural discrimination is reinforced by a biased voting system that favors rural areas where Malays live (see chapter 21,C3), on top of which virtually all municipal councils controlled by Chinese have been suspended. The cultural gap between the two communities was accentuated by the bloody riots between Chinese and Malays in December 1967, and May 1969. As Charles Coppel has written:

Hostility to the Chinese is found in all three countries. Indigenous prejudice against them of various kinds has played its part in determining how many Chinese should have access to citizenship and the rights which that citizenship would bring. One root of that prejudice is economic. The Chinese, envied for their wealth and dominance in various fields of economic life, find that preference is given to indigenous enterprise and that in certain fields alien (read Chinese) capital and skills are totally excluded. What is perceived as the "alienness" of the Chinese provides another theme in anti-Chinese sentiment. In an atmosphere charged with appeals to national unity and nation-building, the Chinese, whether China-born or not, are commonly felt to be "different" from the rest of the population and this difference is held to be of quite a different order from the differences to be found among indigenous ethnic groups. Chinese have not therefore been accorded citizenship as a right in the same sense as indigenous people have. Equal treatment in this regard is something for which Chinese have had to struggle and, when rights have been established, they are often qualified by conditions which do not apply in the case of indigenous people. (1972, p. 19)

4. MARGINAL GROUPS IN THE UNITED STATES

The large-scale out-group antipathy and open cultural, socioeconomic, and political deprivation which have been the Chinese experience in Asia are absent in the United States. But there is a pervasive and perhaps unconscious prejudice on the part of white Americans, as illustrated by an incident related by Albert H. Lee. When the transcontinental railroad celebrated its centennial, the Chinese Historical Society arranged for the dedication of plaques honoring the 12,000 Chinese coolies who had built the Central Pacific. On May 10, 1969, about 20,000 people—including many Chinese—gathered at Promontory Point, where the railroads had met. Secretary of Transportation John A. Volpe, who as an Italian-American should have been sensitive to ethnic feelings, made a bombastic speech lauding the virtues of *Americans*.

Who else but Americans could drill 10 tunnels in mountains 30 feet deep in snow? Who else but Americans could chisel through miles of solid granite? Who else but Americans could have laid 10 miles of track in 12 hours?

Not a word did the Secretary say about the contributions of the Chinese to the railroad or to American life (*Journal of Social Issues*, 1973, pp. 99–100). He seemed to have forgotten that the main reason the Chinese were not Americans, as were most of the Irish who built the Union Pacific, was that Congress had barred them from citizenship.

Pressure to conform to WASP social and cultural standards has fostered a negative self-image among the Chinese in the United States. As Franklin S. Odo has stated:

Like so many distinct ethnic groups in the United States, Asian Americans have been forced into adopting standards developed by a largely white, Anglo-Saxon, Protestant majority. . . . Negative self-image to the point of intense self-hatred is a not-uncommon phenomenon, particularly among the youth, who are especially sensitive about their physical appearance. . . .

Films and TV have a notably pernicious effect, since Asian roles are stereotypes at best and caricatures at worst. Recent works . . . have noted the long history of racism against Asians and the continuing problems encountered by minority actors, playwrights, technicians, and audiences. (1973, pp. 371–90

Greater success in gaining wide cultural recognition in the American mass media in recent years has been achieved by the Chicanos and the native Indians. Chicanos often feel that they suffer WASP out-group prejudice as much as blacks, even in the Southwest where more than 6 million Chicanos live and where Mexican settlements existed before the "Anglos" arrived. Glen Gaviglio observes that the world is becoming a "McLuhanesque global village" in which television, radio, and the press serve up racist stereotypes. One of the worst offenders is the advertising industry. A typical deodorant commercial "shows a Mexican bandito spraying his underarms while a voice says, 'If it works for him, it will work for you.' Do Chicanos stink worse than blacks? Can you envision that same commercial with a sloppy, fat ghetto black wearing a dirty and torn T-shirt? Or is the black movement too powerful (or too violent) to allow that kind of defamation?" (In Duran and Bernard, 1973, p. 402).

"Anglo" prejudice is particularly strong against the more recent migrant workers from Mexico. Gilbert Merkx and Richard Griego comment (in Yetman and Steele, 1972, p. 600) on cultural destruction in New Mexico. Many white Americans believe that the Chicano culture and lifestyle retard the assimilation of Mexican-American children into the mainstream of American life and inhibit the social and educational development of their own children. This view is expressed by Celia Heller, who writes:

The kind of socialization the Mexican-American children receive at home is not conducive to the development of the capacities needed for advancement in a dynamic industrialized society. This type of upbringing creates stumbling blocks to future advancement by stressing values that hinder mobility—family ties, honor, masculinity, and living in the present—and by neglecting the values that are conducive to it—achievement, independence and deferred gratification. (1966, pp. 34–35)

Certain militant Mexican-Americans have even demanded a territorial base to guarantee their integrity—*La Tierra de Aztlan*, the mythical northern land from which the Aztecs came.

Another marginal group is that of the American Indians. White attitudes toward them and the present situation of their communities were molded by two centuries of frontier warfare in which the Indian population was reduced from some 2 million to about 200,000 by 1900. Organizations such as the National Congress of American Indians are endeavoring to maximize solidarity among the 315 different tribal groups to protect Indian historical and cultural rights. It is hoped, in particular, that the reservations can become the geographical base of Indian ethnic self-determination. After more than 140 years, the Bureau of Indian Affairs (BIA) has raised the idea of meaningful autonomy. Patrick Lynch comments:

How does a government agency determine goals for a minority group in America? Does it dissolve the group into the melting pot, protect its members as a unique part of Americana—as a museum piece— does it "modernize" but not "acculturate" them, does it turn them over to the churches, or does it let them make the great decisions about their goals and destiny? The Bureau of Indian Affairs has done all but the latter at various times in its history. There has never been a consistent policy however, that has lasted longer than thirty years. The last policy— that of self-determination—is really just beginning. (In de la Garza et al., 1973, p. 186)

5. AMERICAN INDIANS IN OTHER WESTERN HEMISPHERE COUNTRIES

American Indians have not fared much better in Canada or most South American countries. According to a survey report of the Canadian Corrections Association, entitled *Indians and the Law*, prejudice and discrimination have resulted in "a conviction on the part of the Indians and Eskimo that they are not really a part of a dominant Canadian society and that their efforts to better themselves will fail because they do not have an even chance" (Cardinal, 1971, p. 135). Indian leaders in Canada agree on the need to resist the steady erosion of their culture and historical identity. Increasingly they demand ethnic autonomy in a democratic

plural national community rather than acculturation in a white-dominated melting pot.

Far more pitiful is the state of the Indians in South America (see chapter 27). Writing for the Minority Rights Group in London, Hugh O'Shaughnessy observes that the tradition of Spanish Colonialism is perpetuated in the conviction that lands inhabited by Indians are "free and unoccupied territory open to conquest and colonisation." It is clear that the Iberian-inspired internal culture of South American states does not appreciate competing cultures or values. The result is "not only a false image of Indian society and its historical development, but also a distorted vision of what constitutes the present national society." O'Shaughnessy points to

repeated acts of aggression directed against the aboriginal groups and cultures. There occur both active interventions to "protect" Indian society as well as massacres and forced migrations from the homelands. These acts and policies are not unknown to the armed forces and other government agencies in several countries. Even the official "Indian policies" of the Latin American states are explicitly directed towards the destruction of aboriginal cultures. . . .

As a consequence, we feel the several States, the religious missions and social scientists, primarily anthropologists, must assume the unavoidable responsibilities for immediate action to halt this aggression and contribute significantly to the process of Indian liberation. (*Report* No. 15, pp. 28–29)

In Peru, for example, there are 4000 Quechua-speaking Indian communities, but no attempt is made by the Catholic, Spanish-speaking majority to protect the ethnic identity of the Quechua speakers through communal autonomy. The tribal Indians of Mexico are in an equally unenviable position, especially in the rural areas where the dominant Ladinos openly practice cultural and social discrimination against the Indian tribal communities.

C. The Most Persistent Cultural Discrimination: Anti-Semitism

Anti-Semitism in the United States is, broadly speaking, representative of the problem throughout most of the Western world; the situation is not very different in the United Kingdom, France, or Belgium. A five-year study of anti-Semitism in the 1960s (reported in Selznick and Steinberg, 1971) revealed considerable overt and latent anti-Jewish prejudice. Thirty percent of a representative sample indicated that they felt that "Jews are more loyal to Israel than to America," almost 60 percent thought that "Jews still think of themselves as God's chosen people," whereas 52 percent agreed that "Jews stick together too much." Selznick and Steinberg sum up:

> Over a third of Americans are anti-Semitic as measured by an eleven-item Index of Anti-Semitic Belief. Even the nominally unprejudiced—that third of the population free or virtually free of traditional stereotypes—cannot be said to constitute a solid nucleus of opposition to anti-Semitism. Many give evidence of failing to oppose it in principle, either by answering "don't know" to crucial questions about Jews or by acquiescing in some form of discrimination. (*Ibid.*, p. 184)

Escalation of the Israeli-Arab conflict since 1948 has been paralleled by a surge of anti-Semitism in Eastern Europe and Russia. Undisguised anti-Jewish vendettas and a drastic broadening of anti-Jewish discrimination have been most notable in Poland, Czechoslovakia, and Russia. Poland has seen a transition from covert official prejudice to officially sponsored anti-Semitism disguised as popular rejection of Zionist imperialism and justified resistance to a sinister global Jewish conspiracy. Paul Lendvai, an expert on Jewish affairs in communist countries, illustrates the almost neurotic obsession of the East European communists with the "Jewish danger":

> Television in May 1968 featured at prime viewing time a programme about Israel, "Intolerance," which was warmly praised for exposing the racist atmosphere "permeated with cruelty and hate. This is created both by the fanatically religious element . . . and by the spirit of imitation . . . of the military State machine created by Hitler in the Third Reich, with its storm troopers, its racist laws (including "separate tramways" for Jewish and Arab children), and with its powerful psychological terror directed against its own population. This general "introduction" to Israel, a country ruled by an elite "which is fascinated by Hitler's theory of the Herrenvolk," was embellished by special programs featuring a handful of Polish wives of Jews, who for one or another reason had returned to Poland. . . . In front of the TV cameras they related their martyrdom; how they were tyrannized by rabbis and their Jewish husbands, whose anti-Polish fanaticism burst out in the racist climate of Israel. (1971, p. 167)

Lendvai cites an "Open Letter" to Mrs. Golda Meir (before she became Israel's Prime Minister) in *Glos Robotniczy* (May 12, 1968), charging that the Israeli supreme commander Moshe Dayan was really the SS-official Otto Skorzeny in disguise and that Mrs. Meir—for a consideration—had arranged asylum for Martin Bormann. This nonsense, Lendvai adds, was printed in a paper with a circulation of 250,000 and the author received a prize for "outstanding journalistic work."

Among other things, Poland has introduced racial decrees reminiscent of the Third Reich in order to stigmatize the Jews as a permanent pariah group. As Lendvai writes:

> For the first time since the collapse of Hitler's Germany, the rulers of a nation introduced racialist criteria in the definition of what was actually meant by "Jew." The Polish version of the Nuremberg Laws has never been published, but in practice not only children of mixed marriages, but even "quarter Jews" were considered suspect "Zionists." (*Ibid.*, p. 94)

The Warsaw government's goal is clearly to liquidate the Polish Jews as an ethnic community.

The growth of anti-Semitism in Russia has

been facilitated by the fact that the Jews, despite some degree of cohesion, are not concentrated in any specific geographic area. The Communist Party has consistently refused to acknowledge them as a "nationality" and is trying to destroy their culture, especially since Jewish nationalist sentiment inevitably leads to stronger Jewish identification with Israel. Furthermore, the atheist Russian political system rules out any acknowledgment of Jewish communalism on religious grounds.

Nevertheless, Soviet Jews have their nationality indicated as "Jewish" on the internal identification documents which all USSR citizens are required to carry. Apart from Israel, where circumstances are totally different, the USSR is the only state in the world which obliges every Jew (that is, the son or daughter of two Jewish parents) to register as a Jew under the heading "nationality" (from the ethnic point of view). Registration by nationality has nothing to do with place of birth, language, or culture. It only indicates ethnic origin, and affects over a hundred nationalities, from the Russians, Ukrainians, and Uzbeks to the small tribes in the east and in the far north, including the gypsies. Only a person with parents belonging to two different nationalities can, when he first applies for an "internal passport" at the age of sixteen, choose either his mother's or his father's nationality. He cannot select a third one.

The declared intent of the Soviet Constitution is that every nationality has the same rights, even if it lacks an autonomous Republic or region. Children are to be taught in the National language in "National" Schools, or to learn it in special lessons in the general schools, and nationalities have rights to publications, newspapers, and institutions for the promotion of national culture, art, and history. These rights, are, indeed, granted to some extent to all nationalities, even primitive hunting tribes of only a few hundred souls in the far north—to all nationalities, that is, *except the Jews*, whose population of 3 million outnumbers eight of the fifteen Union Republics.

Technically anti-Semitism is a crime in Russia; anti-Jewish prejudice and discrimination are rampant, however, under the guise of anti-Zionism. Thus, in the state with the third largest number of Jews after the United States and Israel, Jews are denied an opportunity to learn either Hebrew or Yiddish; their voluntary associations are disbanded; their religious practices are discouraged and a request to migrate to Israel is treated as though it were treason (Hunt and Walker, 1974, p. 78).

Ever since the 1967 Six-Day War, Russian Jews have been the target of hate campaigns which have reached almost hysterical levels. As in Poland, open discrimination coupled with humiliation and disparagement of their lifestyle and religion has convinced many that their only hope of escaping the cruel embrace of anti-Semitism is emigration. As 26 Lithuanian Jewish intellectuals protested in a letter dated February 15, 1968, to the First Secretary of the Lithuanian Communist Party:

It is known that if the borders were opened up for emigration today, some eighty per cent of the entire Jewish population would leave Soviet Lithuania and go to Israel. They would leave everything behind, despite the unsettled conditions in the Near East, despite the fact that our people here are used to a damp climate, find it difficult to adjust to the climate there, in the main have no knowledge of Hebrew and do not observe religious traditions, and being mainly employed in services, would not find it easy to become economically integrated into Israeli society. We face a paradoxical attitude. We are not wanted here, we are forcibly denationalized, oppressed and even publicly insulted in the Press—and at the same time we are forcibly detained. As the Lithuanian proverb goes: "He beats and cries with pain at the same time."

Andrei D. Sakharov, the distinguished Soviet physicist and co-creator of the hydrogen bomb, acknowledged in 1968 that "in the highest bureaucratic elite of [the Soviet] government, the spirit of anti-Semitism was never fully dispelled after the 1930's." Russian nationalism as well as communism provided the motivation for the policy, as Jews, character-istically, had family as well as spiritual links with the West. Communist Party policy has reduced the percentage of Jews on the Central Committee from 10.8 in 1939 to almost nil; only one Jew remained in the Central Commit-tee in 1970. There were no Jews in the Polit-buro, the Orgburo, or the top levels of the Sec-retariat. In the sensitive areas of diplomacy, security, foreign trade, and military affairs there were virtually no Jews. There were none at all at the top levels; elsewhere in the hierar-chy there were less than a handful.

It is thus seen that Jews in the USSR suffer both phases of cultural discrimination. They are barred from advancement *because* they are Jews and at the same time hampered in main-taining their Jewish culture. Yet even the Jew who would place personal above group sur-vival cannot abandon his Jewish identity since nationalities are indelibly registered in the So-viet identification scheme.

The worst persecution of Jews since World War II has been in the Arab Middle East since the founding of Israel in 1948. But since its main result has been an exodus to Israel, de-tails are considered in chapter 22 under the rubric of expulsions and forced migration.

This completes the discussion of across-the-board cultural discrimination. The following chapter deals with discrimination in specific areas: language, religion, and education.

18

LANGUAGE, RELIGIOUS, AND EDUCATIONAL DISCRIMINATION

A. Language Discrimination

The most effective way to suppress or destroy the cultural identity of a nation, nationality, or ethnic group is to discriminate against its language. Any such group must struggle to maintain its culture if its language is ignored by the mass media and shunned in the financial, commercial, legal, and administrative professions. There will be a definite degeneration if the language is given a secondary place in school curricula or omitted from them altogether.

The American political scientist Eric Nordlinger has pointed out that in multilingual societies modernization intensifies communal conflicts by propelling language issues into the limelight. It does so by increasing the number, extent, and importance of schools and universities, industries, businesses, and public agencies, as well as intensifying both urbanization and geographic mobility. Which language is spoken in schools and offices becomes an issue of enormous importance. The language conflict becomes central to the competition for governmental and private employment, which is most viciously pursued in the cities. "It is in the national and regional capitals that language issues are decided, it is in the cities that the speakers of different languages compete for

scarce economic rewards, and because of segmental intermingling it is here that slurs upon a man's language are most often (inadvertently or purposefully) made" (1972, pp. 114–15).

Multilingualism within national states is most manageable where established linguistic minorities are concentrated in specific areas. In many countries major ethnolinguistic groups are guaranteed a territorially based autonomy in the national constitution. Examples include the USSR, Yugoslavia, Pakistan, India, Burma, Czechoslovakia (since World War II), and (partially) Canada and Switzerland. The territorial principle is also entrenched by statute in the Republic of South Africa insofar as the language of each major black nation is concerned. In KwaZulu and Lebowa, for example, Zulu and Sotho have legal status as official languages in the respective areas. For the white nation, English and Afrikaans are constitutionally the two official languages of the Republic of South Africa.

In monolingual countries, the national language is usually so obvious that it is not mentioned in the constitution or in fundamental laws. Only where such a language has been explicitly adopted—for instance Hebrew in Israel—is it a matter of legislation.

1. LANGUAGE CONFLICTS: THE CASE OF INDIA

There are more than 720 languages and dialects in India, 24 of them spoken by more than 100,000 people (Duchacek, 1973b, p. 84). The diversity of languages renders acute the problem of a *lingua franca* (language of communication) to be used by the federal government and in interstate communication.

Serious language conflicts figure prominently in the history of modern India, with the smaller ethnolinguistic groups being the main complainants. The Indian government's desire to make Hindi the official federal language is motivated both by Hindi nationalism and by the genuine need for a medium of communication understandable to all. The South, where languages unrelated to the northern Hindi are spoken, has objected all along to imposition of a language sensed as a threat to cultural integrity. It was therefore decided in 1967 that English (which for 15 years had been used alongside Hindi as the second official language of the federal administration, parliament, the judiciary, and official publications) could continue to be used as an "associate language" by the federal authorities until its discontinuance is approved by those states where Hindi is not the official state language (*ibid.*, pp. 86–87). In addition to Hindi and English, 12 other tongues are officially recognized as the main communal languages of specific areas. But it is obvious that many smaller groups face the prospect that their languages will disappear in the absence of official recognition. The bloody riots which occur sporadically over language rights indicate that language differences will for many years remain a salient factor in Indian politics, even though the boundaries of 16 of the 17 states are determined on linguistic grounds.

The creation of Andra Pradesh in 1956 as the first "linguistic" state in India (to accommodate Dravidian Telugu speakers) generated a number of claims for more such states. In some cases specific linguistic concentrations facilitated the creation of new states; in most instances, however, the newly aroused expectations of language groups could not be fulfilled because of economic, political, geographic, historical, or other reasons. Bihar, for example, is torn between Hindi and Bihari. In Assam, where Assamese speakers form 57 percent of the population and Bengali speakers 18 percent, the latter have for many years complained that Assamese is favored at the expense of the Bengali language. In 1960 this linguistic cleavage led to major rioting, resulting in 34 deaths and 10,000 families being rendered homeless. Further riots occurred in 1961 and 1963. Hindi speakers (20 percent) in West Bengal complain that the Bengali-speakers (64 percent) discriminate against Hindi; in Uttar Pradesh, in turn, the Hindi-speakers are accused of discriminating against the Urdu-speaking minority.

Local demands, supported by demonstrations and riots, led in 1960 to the division of the state of Bombay between Gujarati and Marathi speakers and in 1966 to the splitting of Punjab into Punjab State (Punjabi speakers) and Haryana State (Hindi speakers); linguistic nationalism also figured in the Naga rebellion (see chapter 21,G2).

Even before Indian independence, minority leaders had protested against Hindi domination. Speaking in the Constituent Assembly in 1948, T. T. Krishnamachari, an eminent politician from South India, expressed fears that conducting parliament in Hindi

will also mean the enslavement of people who do not speak the language of the legislature, the language of the Centre. . . . There are already elements in South India who want separatism and it is up to us to tax the maximum strength we have to keep those elements down, and my honourable friends in U.P. do not help us in any way by flogging their idea [of] "Hindi Imperialism" to the maximum extent.

A delegate from Madras, T. A. Ramalingam Chettiar, was even more outspoken in expressing his fear of linguistic discrimination:

I have been told by my friends of the North if they were to yield on the question of numerals, they will be twitted by their voters and that they will find their life difficult when they go for elections. What will it be like when we, giving up our own languages, adopt the language of the North, go back to our provinces and face our electorate? . . . I may say that the South is feeling frustrated. . . . Sir, coming here to the capital in the northernmost part of the country, and feeling ourselves as strangers in this land, we do not feel that we are a nation to whom the whole thing belongs, and that the whole country is ours. . . . We have been trying to keep our [Tamil] vocabulary as pure as possible without the admixture of Sanskrit (?). Now we have to go back upon all that. We have to take words from Sanskrit; we have to change our whole course of action. . . . you are permanently handicapping us. Those whose mother-tongue is Hindi, they learn only Hindi. But we in the South, we have got to study not only Hindi but also our mother tongue. . . . the way in which the Hindi-speaking people treat us is more galling than anything which actually is done or is going to be done.

A member of the Indian Senate (*Rajya Sabha*) and leader of the opposition in Madras, C. Annadurai, was quoted in *The Times of India* on May 3, 1961, as warning that "the entire South will revolt" against the imposition of Hindi. Six years later Mr. Annadurai promoted an anti-Hindi cultural union of southern states (Ghurye, 1968, pp. 436–39, 513).

The creation of linguistically defined states has pacified the major ethnolinguistic groups but left the smaller groups at a disadvantage. A group too small to achieve territorial autonomy is faced with the double threat that its language will be submerged both by Hindi (the only official language of India) and by the official language of its own State.

The antagonism against Hindi continues in the four southern states (Andhra, Kerala, Tamil Nadu [Madras], and Mysore) where Dravidian languages prevail and where radical opponents of Hindi seek to ensure full protection of their distinctive ethnolinguistic identity in an independent Dravidian state. Kodesia writes

Language serves as a separatist factor. Withou denying that language binds, it must be admitted that it separates also by erecting speech barriers be tween linguistic states and communities. It acts lik the other two factors in a trio—religion, languag and community. The history of India says hov religion and community have broken us to pieces we cannot reasonably hope that the third factor wi operate in a diffrent way. (1969, p. 33)

2. LANGUAGE PROBLEMS OF OTHER
   MULTILINGUAL STATES IN ASIA

In Sri Lanka discrimination against Tamil speakers has resulted on occasions in bloody clashes with the dominant Sinhalese-speakers especially following the enactment of the "Sin halese Only Act" in 1956. Even the counter vailing Tamil Language Act of 1958 (authoriz ing the "reasonable" use of Tamil i government and education) did little to assuag Tamil fears. On leaving the British Com monwealth in 1972, Sri Lanka promulgated new socialist constitution making Sinhalese th only official language and thus rejecting Tam speakers' demands that Sinhalese and Tamil b given equal status. Disenfranchisement of th so-called Indian Tamils both weakened an embittered the Tamil community. As a conse quence, Sri Lanka's politics are today con ducted on an ethnolinguistic basis. Since 195(no Tamil constituency has returned the can didate of any party other than the exclusivel Tamil ones.

Analogously, the privileged position oc cupied by the Malay language in Malaysia is great affront to the Indians and Chinese of tha country and stimulated the withdrawal (Chinese-dominated Singapore from the Malay sian Federation in 1965. Le Page mentions:

Under the 1957 Constitution the Malays of the Fed eration were given special rights. The Yang di-Per tuan Agong (Head of State) was empowered to safe guard their special position and to ensure th reservation for them of "such proportion as he ma deem reasonable" of positions in the Public Service of scholarships and training facilities and of licence to operate certain trades and businesses. Under thi

Article the rule has been laid down, amongst others, that four-fifths of all Malayan recruits to the Malayan Civil Service must, for the time being, be Malays. (1973–74, p. 68)

Under the constitutional rule, Malay must be taught as a subject in all assisted schools. The official examinations in secondary schools are conducted in either Malay or English, which places the Indian Tamils and Chinese at an obvious disadvantage if their primary schooling was in their own language. Several Chinese secondary schools which taught in Mandarin have now shifted to English in order to continue to qualify for state subsidies. Even in distant Borneo the local communities in Sabah and Sarawak have expressed resentment at Malay domination.

In Indonesia a modernized version of Malay has been elevated to the National language at the expense of the 114 languages (16 of them rated major languages) spoken in this state. A modernized version of another Malay language, Tagalog, is the national language of the Philippines. The viability of various local island vernaculars has suffered as a result. Many Filipinos, however, are lukewarm to Tagalog, as they feel that Spanish and more particularly English are better "investments." Maximo Ramos writes in this connection:

Filipino shoppers in downtown Manila who speak Filipino to the clerk get very little attention or receive haughty stares. One gets prompt service when one speaks English, and prompt, polite service when one speaks Spanish. Some Filipino parents object to their children being taught their mother tongue on the grounds that they have learned the language at home. . . . Tagalog . . . made millions of enemies overnight in 1940 by being imposed on the pupils all over the country without warning (in Le Page, 1971), p. 27).

Pakistan, even since the detachment of Bangladesh, is likewise the scene of acute language conflict. In Sind province, the local legislative assembly made Sindhi the only official language in the face of vehement objections from the 45 percent of the people who speak Urdu. After widespread rioting in 1972, leaders of the two communities agreed on a formula that kept Sindhi as the official language but granted the Urdu speakers 12 years in which to learn it. It seems fair to predict that the rioting will resume in 1984. The dominant position of Sindhi, Urdu, and Punjabi (the chief languages of the politically dominant provinces) is maintained only at the price of discrimination against the 29 languages of smaller ethnolinguistic groups, such as the Baluchis and the Pathans of the North-West Frontier Province, who harbor strong separatist movements. The privileged position occupied by Urdu (the official Pakistani language but spoken by only 15 percent of the population) is being strongly challenged especially by Punjabi speakers whose leaders think themselves the elite of Pakistan.

3. LANGUAGE PROBLEMS IN AFRICA: MOTHER TONGUES VERSUS OFFICIAL LANGUAGES

During the stormy years that preceded decolonization, education in the mother tongue was not a popular idea among Asian and African leaders, who thought it a device whereby the colonial powers would inhibit social, economic, and political development. English or French were regarded as keys to rapid modernization and to personal advancement. South Africa was severely criticized for insisting on mother-tongue education, at least during primary schooling. Since independence, however, many black states have adopted mother-tongue education, at least for the first few school years. Today they consider this system a safeguard against cultural genocide.

But not all ethnic groups enjoy education in their own languages. In Ethiopia, for example, Galla, the language of the numerically strongest people, has a very low prestige value and its use is officially discouraged. Amharic, the official language of Ethiopia, is given preferment in education, government, the judiciary, the mass media, and business in general. Large numbers of Ethiopians who by no means belong to the Amhara ethnic group have had themselves officially listed as Amharic-speaking purely to obtain jobs and benefits.

Some African governments have concluded that the populations of their countries are too diversified to permit national unification around any single African language. Such a policy would, in fact, provoke conflict between the speakers of "unofficial" and "official" languages, and would afford mother-tongue speakers of the official language an advantage in taking civil service tests and in recruitment for managerial positions. Nigeria, therefore, has retained English as its official language, and several of the larger Francophone countries cling to French. Elementary-school curricula begin in the mother tongue in Nigeria, with English as the first learned language, and switch to English medium at Standard Three (5th grade); in Francophone Africa French is the medium from the beginning.

An entirely different policy prevails in Tanzania, where President Nyerere has convinced the members of his Tanganyika African National Union (TANU) to adopt a single African language as an instrument for creating a new Tanzanian national identity. This is a political strategy new to Africa, and it remains to be seen whether it will succeed.

In formulating and directing national policy, Dr. Nyerere is careful to avoid hostility to any of the tribes or their languages. If successful, however, his policy will have the effect of rendering tribal origin irrelevant to personal identity and of transferring ethnic loyalty to a territorial Tanzanian nation. The principal cultural tool in this transformation is the Swahili language (or Kiswahili, as it is called in Tanzania). President Nyerere underlined the importance of a national language by personally translating some of Shakespeare's plays into Swahili. That language has become, to quote Prof. Edwin S. Munger, "a distinct tool for creating a nation and energizing a people" (1974).

The political importance of the shift to Swahili lies in the fact that English, as the language of the former colonial power, and with a structure foreign to African ways of thinking, can only be a language of communication. Swahili, on the other hand, a Bantu language thoroughly African in structure despite its admixture of 15 percent Arabic words (a proportion no greater than that of English and Afrikaans words in Zulu) can become a language of identity for the African peoples in Tanzania. TANU linguistic policy aims at such a conversion. While the speaking of the various tribal languages is in no way prohibited, they will in the long run be culturally "starved to death," since public funds will only support educational and cultural activities conducted in Swahili. Such Swahilization is, of course, a clear case of linguistic discrimination against speakers of other languages who do not choose conversion. Its compulsory nature is suggested by George A. Mhina, Director of the Institute of Kiswahili Research at the University of Dar-es-Salaam, in a seminar paper entitled "The Role of Kiswahili in the Development of Tanzania." Emphasizing the function of language as a central aspect of nationhood, Mhina observes that "an interest in Kiswahili *ceased to be a matter of personal choice* and became a national priority" (Mhina, 1974, p. 8, emphasis supplied).

According to Mhina, the function of Kiswahili is purgative as well as didactic: "the mentality and ideologies inherited from the heavy decades of European domination had to be vigorously swept away and ejected from the mind of the people." "You cannot teach political education in a foreign language. . . . It must be taught in the national language," because only that language contains the terms of economic and social development the people understand.

The instrument of linguistic conversion is the public school system. That system is centrally controlled by the Ministry of Education, which has made Swahili the medium of instruction from grades one to seven in all subjects. English is still the medium of instruction in secondary schools and universities, but teacher training colleges now also conduct their classes in Swahili. As adequate textbooks become available, the use of Swahili will presumably be extended. But English continues to be taught as a subject, and French has been added to the secondary curriculum—largely for the purpose of communicating with Francophone Africans.

4. TERRITORIAL VERSUS PERSONAL AUTONOMY IN BILINGUAL STATES: BELGIUM AND CANADA

Separation of predominantly Catholic Belgium from the mainly Protestant Netherlands in 1830 solved a religious problem but provoked a major linguistic one. The French-speaking Walloons were from the beginning the economically dominant community; their culture was further bolstered by the status of French as an international language. French domination in Brussels is clearly seen in business, trade, and diplomacy. The Dutch-speaking Flemings are extremely sensitive about even the slightest action on the part of the Walloons which even remotely smacks of language discrimination. A Flemish leader was quoted in *The Economist* of July 12, 1963: "In almost any Brussels office, you will find a Flemish speaking porter, a bilingual secretary and a boss who speaks only French. We are going to change all that." Belgian governments have never been able to reconcile the linguistic interests of the two disparate communities. Finally, in 1962, Belgium was divided into two main linguistic areas (North and South); Brussels and some of the villages along the linguistic border were to become mixed areas in which both Flemish and Walloon would be official languages. In 1968 it was agreed, after demonstrations and riots, to move the French-speaking sections of the University of Louvain out of the Flemish area. This step evoked astonishment and dismay among friends of interethnic understanding.

The political crisis which followed the Louvain debacle led to the fall of the Belgian Government, the first time in the country's history that a government had resigned over the language issue. The election which followed was largely a triumph for linguistic extremism. Three nationalist parties, the Volksunie (Flemish) and the French-dominated Democratic Front (Brussels) and Rassemblement Wallon increased their combined representation in the 212-seat Chamber of Reprsentatives from 6 seats in 1961 to 47 in 1974, in addition to causing serious splits in the major parties along language lines. Separate ministries of education, cultural development, and regional economic development were created to satisfy rapidly escalating pressure for more Flemish and Walloon autonomy. In 1973, a plan was put into effect that gave the two regions cultural autonomy and economic decentralization, but stopped short of outright federalism (see van Haegendoren, 1975, *passim.*).

The Flemings and Walloons living in their respective language areas are determined to secure every linguistic advantage. In the Flemish areas, for instance, employers can be compelled by law to use the Dutch language in their dealings with employees and with the local Flemish administration. This law, enacted by the Flanders Region Cultural Council, gave factory inspectors wide powers to make on-the-spot checks at any hour of the day to ensure that all contracts—both written and verbal—are in Dutch. Rivalry between the two linguistic communities is at its height in hybrid Brussels where 50 percent of the population speak French and 20 percent Flemish, with the remaining 30 percent consisting of foreign workers. The Flemings point out that the growing influence of French in the capital jeopardizes Flemish interests, particularly in government and administration. An economic regression in Wallonia in recent years has caused more French-speaking workers to move into Brussels. The many migrant workers, most of whom come from Southern Europe where French is relatively strong, also tend to strengthen the Francophone element. The same preference for French is found in the elite migrants, the "Eurocrats" who work for the European Community. Most of the migrant workers and many Flemish choose to have their children taught in a French-language school. They feel that an education in French is a better investment in a child's advancement. The French-speaking group, particularly in Brussels, exploited this trend by changing the rule that a child is taught in the language spoken in his home to that of free choice by the family head. Many Flemings feel that this 1971 law enlarged the advantage French speakers enjoy in Brussels.

The reverse is true in the case of upper- and middle-class Francophones who move to smaller towns in the region. Most are in Flemish-language territory, where Dutch is the only official language, to which people who move in are expected to adjust (Coppieters, 1971, pp. 15–17). French speakers in Brussels contend that the language boundary stunts the natural growth of a city that is not only the capital of Belgium but of the European Community and NATO as well. In the capital, Flemings are at a disadvantage. There are, for instance, hardly any Dutch-speaking doctors in the hospitals. While Brussels borough councils are supposed to have linguistic equality, the law permits Francophones to be elected to the "Flemish" half of a council (*ibid.*, p. 21).

While Belgium remains theoretically a unitary state, it is actually administered as though it were a federation of two territorially based ethnolinguistic groups. Since 1971 the constitution has required equal numbers of cabinet ministers, with the possible exception of the Prime Minister. Hunt and Walker point out:

Language divisions have cracked the apparent façade of religious unity. For a long time, the Flemish priests were accustomed to denounce the godless French, and the leading Flemish daily carries on its masthead the motto "Alles voor Vlaanderen, Vlaanderen voor Christus" ("All for Flanders, Flanders for Christ"). Catholics do not hesitate to walk out of mass where it is said in the wrong language. . . .

Nearly a hundred thousand Flemish workers commute daily between Brussels, a city in which business is largely conducted in French, and their Flemish homelands. On the other hand, the expansion of adjacent suburbs finds people of French speaking ancestry in zones that have been legally dedicated a Flemish, where they are compelled by law to send their children to Flemish speaking schools. (1974 pp. 29–30)

Meanwhile, natural increase has given the Flemings a preponderance in numbers over the Walloons—a fact of political and cultural significance. As Hunt and Walker point out:

The Flemish are a socially mobile group long considered subordinate, with a memory of ancien grievances aggravated by the fear that world-wide trends are working against the adequacy of their language. The French-speaking Belgians are still a powerful minority, who see their proportions in their country dwindling and their economic power disappearing. Rather than dominating the economy of the country, they are now in need of economic aid, which a non-French majority in Parliament is reluctant to give. (*Ibid.*, p. 31)

More than a hundred years after confederation, bilingualism in Canada is still the most controversial issue of the day. Serious problems are being encountered in administration of the Official Languages Act (1969), establishing the equality of French and English in all activities of the Dominion; linguistic discrimination is constantly being charged by both language communities. The enactment of a new language law in Quebec in 1974, making French the official provincial language with a preferred status over English, has reopened the old question of language rights and minority privileges in the province, where 80 percent of the 6 million inhabitants are Francophone. Many Quebecois feel that, despite the province's French tradition and population, the French language needs special protection if it is not to fall gradually into disuse. On July 3 1974, *The Times* of London remarked of the new language law:

The most explosive feature of the omnibus Bill are provisions that would withdraw the right of parents to determine the language of instruction of their children and make the choice subject to a test administered by the Department of Education. If a child seeking admission to the English language school system does not show adequate proficiency in the English language, he would be streamed into the French system. This section hits particularly hard to new Canadians, who as a rule want to have their children educated in English but whose children, in many cases, haven't yet acquired a grasp of the language.

Many of Quebec's English-speaking Canadians, the most affluent and powerful segment of the population, find that the new act confirms their fears that their days as an elite are numbered. French speakers, on the other hand, maintain that it is only in Quebec that their culture and language are effectively protected, while in the other provinces, and especially in Dominion government administration, it is running a poor second to English. On the whole, the new legislation has deepened the cleavage between the two language communities.

A law recommended in a Quebec Government White Paper of April 1, 1977, and passed by the Provincial Assembly on August 26, 1977, limits English-medium instruction to children already enrolled in English-language schools or having at least one parent who attended an English-language school in Quebec (or elsewhere if the parent was resident in Quebec when the law took effect). A dispensation permits English-language instruction for children of parents assigned to positions in Quebec for three years or less. But all newcomers to Quebec, including both foreign immigrants and English-speaking Canadians who move in from other provinces, must send their children to French-medium schools. Canadians fear an exodus of English-speakers from Quebec as well as economic stagnation in that province, where Anglophones have hitherto been dominant in business. (*New York Times*, July 17 and August 27, 1977; *St. Louis Post-Dispatch*, August 3 and 21, 1977)

5. RESURGENT LINGUISTIC PLURALISM IN SPAIN AND FRANCE

Three groups in Spain complain of linguistic discrimination: the speakers of Catalan, Basque, and Galician (Gallego). Catalan is spoken in Northeast Spain from Valencia to the Pyrenees as well as on the Balearic Islands; the Basques live in Navarre, Alava, Guipuzcoa, and Biscay; the Galicians inhabit Northwest Spain. The three languages have a tenacity and a resilience that have diminished little despite the fact that for five centuries they have had to give way to the dominant Castilian language.

Castilian is the official language of Spain and is mandatory at all levels of education. Most people in Catalonia write in Castilian, and cannot write in their mother tongue. Catalan is not used or recognized in the courts, nor by the administration of the territory. There are no Catalan daily newspapers. Catalan nationalists feel that only decentralization of power in a federal system will prevent the slow but sure demise of their language.

In addition to having a language not known to be related to any other now spoken, the Basques assert a distinctive ethnic identity. But political power struggles, urbanization, industrialization, and the centralism of the late General Franco have eroded the Basque language to such an extent that it has survived significantly only in Navarra and Guipuzcoa, and even then largely in the pastoral areas and fishing villages. Among the upper classes it has been almost entirely supplanted by Castilian. Today, nearly 40 years after the end of the Spanish Civil War, there is clear evidence of a revival of Basque nationalism. A left-wing group (*Euzkadi Ta Askatasuna*—ETA) seeks an independent Basque state comprising the Basque areas of both Spain and France. Since Basque has become a minority language within the region itself, the future of this movement is problematical—though it is possible that middle- and upper-class Basques will return to their language, as many Welsh are doing today.

Galician is more closely related to Portuguese than to Castilian. Had Northwest Spain been attached to Portugal, it would probably be considered a dialect of Portuguese rather than of Spanish. Because the Galicians lack resources and political power, their language has for some generations languished and is no longer taught at school. It is spoken today by peasants and fishermen; among the middle and upper classes it is hardly ever heard. The prospects for a revival of Galician are dim, since it lacks the support of a politicocultural movement such as those supporting Catalan and Basque (see Medina, 1975, *passim.*).

Nation-building in France involved the imposition of the regional tongue of the Île de France or Paris region at the expense of other regional languages and dialects (see chapter 10, A1). As a result, most of them came close to disappearing, though Occitan was perpetuated in modern Catalan. Recently, however, France has seen a revival of regional ethnicity, reflected in growing demand that languages such as Occitan, Breton, Corsican, Basque, and in the Northeast German and Flemish be given a place in school curricula. The extent to which ethnocultural pluralism will revive in France remains to be seen (See Fougeyrollas, 1968, *passim.*).

6. LINGUISTIC RUSSIFICATION IN THE USSR

Non-Russian languages in the USSR are being undermined by the establishment of Russian as the language leading to economic preference. According to the 1959 census, more than 10 million Soviet citizens had abandoned their mother tongue in favor of Russian. Table 18.1, based on the 1970 census, shows a further expansion of Russian at the expense of other languages. In 1959, for instance, 87.7 percent of the Ukrainians spoke Ukrainian as their mother tongue; by 1970 this percentage had dropped to 85.7. For Byelorussians, the ratio decreased from 84.2 percent in 1959 to 80.6 percent in 1970. Russian is spoken as a second language by 36.3 percent of the Ukrainians and 49.0 percent of the Byelorussians, not counting those who reported it as their mother tongue (Sosnowsky, 1972, p. 262).

It is significant what the USSR Foreign Office did not think "fit to print" in the UN publication. In addition to the Jews, the category of "Others" covered some grievous language losses: national languages were spoken by only 66.8 percent of the (mostly Volga) Germans, only 66.2 percent of the Bashkirs, only 67.4 percent of the "peoples of the North, Siberia, and the Far East," and only 63.0 percent of the (Finnish) Karelians.

The case of Moldavia represents an interesting use of language as a political weapon. The Moldavian SSR consists of Western Bessarabia and North Bukovina—territories that Rumania, with Hitler's consent, was forced to yield to the USSR in 1940 and which Stalin seized again in 1945—plus Eastern Bessarabia, previously an autonomous republic within the Ukrainian SSR. The majority of Moldavians are actually Rumanians. To detach them from political loyalty to the Rumanian state, combined Moldavia was raised to Union Republic status and the Soviet Academy of Sciences was commissioned to establish "scientifically" the existence of an independent Moldavian language. According to the Moldavian scholar N. Corlateanu, the new Moldavian language is "developing as a result of interaction with the other languages of the USSR, primarily with the Russian and Ukrainian languages." A grammar, a textbook, and a linguistic atlas are being provided. To distinguish Moldavian from Rumanian, Moscow has decreed that the new language shall be written in the Cyrillic alphabet (Dushnyck, 1975b, pp. 507f.). This is a partial case of genocide by ethnomorphosis: a way of eliminating a nation or nationality by changing national identifiers rather than killing the people (see Possony, 1976, *passim.*).

Colonization is another tool of Russification.

Table 18.1. MAJOR NATIONALITIES AND LANGUAGES IN THE USSR, 1970

Nationality	Membership	% of USSR Pop.	Speakers of Language (Mother-Tongue)	% of USSR Pop.	Ratio: Speakers to Members of Nationality
Armenian	3,559,151	1.47	3,261,053	1.34	.916
Azerbaijani	4,379,937	1.81	4,347,089	1.80	.993
Byelorussian	9,051,755	3.74	7,630,007	.15	.843
Estonian	1,007,356	.42	974,649	.40	.968
Georgian	3,245,300	1.34	3,310,917	1.37	1.020
Jews	2,150,707	.89	380,675 [a]	.15	.177
Kazakh	5,298,818	2.19	5,213,694	2.15	.984
Kirghiz	1,452,222	.60	1,445,213	.60	.995
Latvian	1,429,844	.59	1,390,162	.58	.972
Lithuanian	2,664,944	1.10	2,625,608	1.09	.985
Moldavian	2,697,994	1.12	2,607,367	1.08	.966
Russian	129,015,140	53.37	141,830,564	58.68	1.099
Tadzhik	2,135,883	.88	2,202,671	.91	1.031
Turkmenian	1,525,284	.63	1,514,980	.63	.993
Ukrainian	40,753,246	16.86	35,400,944	14.65	.869
Uzbek	9,195,093	3.80	9,154,704	3.79	.996
Others	22,157,460	9.17	18,429,837 [b]	7.62	.832
Total, USSR	241,720,134		241,720,134		

(SOURCE: Except for speakers of Jewish languages, UN Demographic Yearbook, 1971, pp. 504–05, and 1973, pp. 484–85. Our calculation of percentages and ratios.)
[a] Calculated from percentage given in *Izvestia*, April 17, 1971.
[b] UN figure less Jews.

In Ukraine, for instance, 19 percent of the population (9,126,000 of 47,126,000) are Russians. They, and Russian-speaking Ukrainians, are concentrated in the cities, where 44.9 percent of the people speak Russian as their mother tongue. Considering that cultural and educational life is centered in the cities, the degree of linguistic alienation is alarming.

The Russian language is constantly glorified in the non-Russian press. The November 21, 1973, issue of *Skolotaju Avize* (Teachers' Gazette) in Latvia, for instance, stated: "All peoples of the USSR are allowed to enjoy and enrich their native culture in the mother tongue," but added: "But there is one language which has become dear to all Soviet citizens— the language that was spoken by Lenin . . . the Russian language."

More particularly, Russification aims to purge from the languages of the Turkic peoples the large Arabic and Persian vocabulary inherited from the Muslim conquests. This would, in effect, forestall the development of a single Turkic literary language which might spark a united Muslim-Turkic national movement. Hence, the Kremlin strives to denigrate the Turkic literary and cultural heritage and to replace it with an alien "Soviet" (Russian) heritage emphasizing Soviet patriotism and the "superiority" of Russian language and culture. In a related development, the Latin alphabet was substituted for Arabic scripts.

Garip Sultan, an authority on the Turkic peoples of Central Asia, has pointed out that the influx of Russians into Central Asia, whatever its motivation, constitutes a process of colonialism. He expects this immigration to continue and with it greater diffusion of the Russian language among the Turkic population as well as further proliferation of Russian bureaucrats who would control the economy and the administration of the Turkic republics. Lenin wrote: "The demands of economic turnover always force the nationalities living within one country (as long as they wish to live together) to study the language of the majority."

The spread of Russian is supported by the introduction of Russian grammatical and syntactical features, and by compulsory Russian-language instruction in all schools beginning in the second grade (Wheeler, 1973–74, pp. 36–37). An intensive propaganda campaign is conducted to persuade children to enroll "voluntarily" in Russian-medium classes. Although only about 10 percent of all school children in the Uzbek Republic are of Russian nationality, some 25 percent attend Russian-medium schools. Generally speaking, the higher the grade in Soviet education, the more widespread the use of Russian and the less frequent the use of minority languages.

Even in Ukraine, where the indigenous language is cognate to Russian, it is not a compulsory subject in the Russian-language schools. The latter often do not even teach Ukrainian, and they receive preference in educational budgets. John Kolasky, who in 1962 attended a party school in Kiev on behalf of the Canadian Communist Party and was arrested in 1965, wrote after his return to Canada:

My investigations began to reveal a planned discrimination against Ukraine and Ukrainians and a conspiracy against the Ukrainian language. . . . Russians were everywhere with their arrogant overbearing attitude; their contempt, sometimes veiled but often overt, for the Ukrainian language; their open display of a feeling of Russian superiority. . . . Evidence showing discrimination against Ukraine and Ukrainians, and the campaign of Russification gives conclusive proof of what many have suspected for so long and exposes the falsity of Soviet proclamations of freedom of national development in the USSR and reveals the plight of Ukraine to the public of the democratic world. (In Dushnyck, 1975b, p. 472)

Growing dissidence among the Ukrainian intelligentsia provoked massive reprisals in 1965, when over 100 young writers and poets were rounded up by the KGB. Among those arrested was Vyacheslav Chornovil, a Marxist TV journalist who had been assigned to cover the secret trials. When he refused to testify against his own friends, he was arrested and sentenced to 18 months at hard labor. While attending the trial, he amassed a great many documents proving the illegal arrests and the trumped-up nature of the charges. The manuscript was smuggled out of Ukraine and published by McGraw-Hill under the title *The Chornovil Papers* (1970). Some of the twenty "criminals" described by Chornovil—such as Valentyn Moroz, Panas Zalyvakha, Mykhaylo Osadchy, and Sviatoslav Karavansky—are now internationally known through their writings and their suffering in Soviet jails. All were sentenced to imprisonment.

Despite the ostensible Russian policy of providing children with instruction in their native languages, not a single school in the USSR teaches Hebrew or Yiddish. The Jewish minority has had no state theatre ever since the forcible closure, during the last period of Stalin's life, of the famous Moscow Yiddish State Theatre, together with all Jewish publishing houses, magazines, schools, and cultural institutions (Levenberg, 1972, p. 39). Since 1959 there has been a trickle of books in Yiddish, and a bimonthly Yiddish literary review, *Sovietish Heymland*, was started in 1961 and made a monthly in 1965 (Korey, 1973, p. 86). By the early 1970s, only about 18 percent of the Jewish population spoke Yiddish, compared with 73 percent in 1917.

7. MULTILINGUALISM AND BILINGUAL EDUCATION IN THE UNITED STATES

Mexican-American cultural aspirations center around recognition of the Spanish language and Latin-American culture. Chicanos are embittered by school authorities who punish children for speaking Spanish at school, and by Anglo-Saxon–oriented scholastic tests, administered in English, on which Hispanophone pupils register as mentally retarded. The language problems encountered by American Indians are not very different.

Mexican-Americans can hardly progress through complete educational programs or move ahead in business and professional life until the language obstacle is overcome. That is unlikely as long as educational systems continue to resist bilingual programs, as many still do—despite stimulation by federal encouragement and funding and in a few states (such as Illinois) by progressive state education departments. In general, local school boards have hardly been budged from their long-standing negative orientation to use of "foreign" languages in their schools (Wright et al., 1973, p. 59).

By 1973, only 6.5 percent of the Southwest's schools had bilingual programs and these were reaching only 2.7 percent of the Mexican-American school population—about one student in forty. According to the Civil Rights Commission: "Although an estimated four million persons in the Southwest identify Spanish as their mother tongue, only 25 percent of the elementary and 11 percent of the secondary schools send notices in Spanish to Spanish-speaking parents; 91.7 percent of the Southwest's elementary schools and 98.5 percent of its secondary schools do not use Spanish as well as English in conducting their PTA meetings" (quoted, de la Garza et al., 1973, p. 167).

8. LINGUISTIC DISCRIMINATION IN GERMANY AND ITALY

Linguistic discrimination was never a major issue in the Reich, except in the eastern border provinces. There were complaints about Germanization in Alsace-Lorraine and in the Danish parts of Schleswig, but these were largely resolved by cessions at the end of World War I. The largest ethnic minority in the interior of the Reich was the Polish group that settled in the Ruhr valley, where Germany's largest coal deposits lie, during the rapid industrial growth between 1870 and 1914. They came as miners

and steel workers; most were German citizens although ethnic Poles, and had lived in the areas taken over by Prussia in the three partitions of Poland. By 1905 more than one-third of all miners in the Ruhr were "Prussians of Polish descent." At the Graf Schwerin Mine their percentage rose as high as 51.2; in every case the proportion of Poles working underground was higher, as the Germans reserved the more attractive aboveground jobs for themselves. The *Rheinische-Westfälische Zeitung* of Essen expressed the fear that "the Polish language and race might expand in the Rhenish-Westphalian industrial area and polonize German districts."

In the Ruhr, as elsewhere in the Reich, Poles were victims of the Prussian Germanization policy designed for the eastern provinces, which forbade official use of the Polish language. Even in the Graf Schwerin Mine, the Royal Mining Office refused, for "national reasons," to post the most important safety regulations in the Polish language, despite a high rate of accidents among the Polish workers who could not understand instructions or warnings in German. Paragraph 23 of the *Reichsvereinsgesetz* (Reich Associations Law), directed against the Poles, declared use of the Polish language in public meetings to be a misdemeanor. Thus discriminated against, the Poles founded their own trade union and a large number of clubs and associations to protect their interests and maintain their cultural life (Holzach, 1974).

Linguistic policy was liberalized during the Weimar Republic; Polish associations and schools flourished. Repression during the Third Reich was followed by renewed liberalism under the Federal Republic. In the meanwhile, however, many Poles have become assimilated, and Polish linguistic and cultural activities have withered for lack of interest.

After acquiring considerable non-Italian territory in the 1919 Peace Settlement, Italy embarked on an aggressive Italianization policy, Its best-known victims were the German-Austrians of South Tyrol, where Mussolini settled large numbers of Italians in an attempt to create an artificial majority. A plan to move these ethnic Germans to the Reich was reversed after World War II, and the 1946 Gruber-deGasperi Agreement provided for cultural and limited political autonomy. The Italians, however, were loath to grant meaningful self-government, and it is only recently that a not wholly unsatisfactory *modus vivendi* was reached. The South Tyroleans must still defend their German language and culture vigorously against Italianizing pressures; they need to learn Italian as a language of communication, whereas the reverse is not true for Italians living in the region.

A much smaller and less well-known linguistic minority in Italy is that of the French-speaking people who live in the Aosta Valley in Italy, at the foot of the Alpine range that includes Mont Blanc and the Matterhorn. Since the division of Savoy between France and Italy in 1860, the French-speaking ethnic groups in eastern Savoy has been subjected to Italian assimilationist measures. Instruction in the French language was forbidden in secondary schools in 1879 and in primary schools in 1883. Beginning in 1911, however, permission was given for one hour of French-language instruction per day. Use of French in courts was prohibited in 1880. Under Mussolini, the fascist government attempted to eliminate the French-speaking ethnic group as a cultural entity. French language instruction was abolished altogether; only Italian could be used in court and in dealings with public authorities, and all street and village names as well as personal and family names were Italianized. A number of French-speaking villages were evacuated and their inhabitants resettled in the swamps of the Po Valley.

A group within the embattled minority united to protest its ethnic and cultural interest. Under Joseph Trèves and his pupil Emil Chanoux, agitation was launched for a "Free State of Aosta" within an "Italian Federal Republic." But anti-Italian feeling grew so strong that the group shifted ground and demanded separation from Italy and annexation to France.

The Italian government has made partial concessions, declaring the Aosta Valley a region with "special autonomy." The central government, however, retains the right to revoke acts of the Aosta regional government on the grounds of expediency as well as legality, and differences are adjusted by a "Coordinating Committee" containing two delegates from Rome and only one from Aosta. The Aosta regional government and the local political parties seek support against the centralism of Rome by establishing links with other ethnic groups in Europe, and supporting a new European federalism based on nationality groups rather than existing political states.

B. Religious Discrimination

Religious discrimination is most acute where intertwined with class factors, as in Northern Ireland, or with clashing ethnic identities as in Israel, Sudan, and recently in Lebanon. Yet it is religion rather than class that is the more salient signal of group differences; in a recent survey in Ulster, 42 percent of respondents identified themselves by religion and only 12 percent by class (Nordlinger, 1972, p 98).

Established churches exist in Protestant England and the Scandinavian countries, West Germany, Switzerland, and Italy, Catholic Ireland (until 1972), Spain, Portugal, and most Latin American republics, Orthodox Greece Judaic Israel, Buddhist Burma, Cambodia and Laos (until 1975) and Sri Lanka; Hindu Nepal and Muslim countries from Arab North and West Africa and the Middle East to Afghanistan, Malaysia, and Pakistan in South Asia. The secular countries include the United

States, France, India, and, of course, all communist-ruled states (Duchacek, 1973b, p. 61). Established churches enjoy tax support denied to competing religious communities; discrimination against "nonconformists" in countries having them varies from mild to severe.

1. CONFLICTS BETWEEN RELIGIOUS PRECEPTS AND PUBLIC LAW

Members of minority religions frequently find themselves in conflicts of conscience and obedience concerning what is God's and what is Caesar's. Muslim workers in Europe who wish to obey the Koranic injunction to interrupt their work for prayer complain of discrimination when told they must not hold up assembly lines or administrative routines. Catholics in Zaïre are aggrieved by the law that makes Catholic priests liable to criminal prosecution if they refuse to give African names to children at baptism rather than naming them after Catholic saints (ibid., p. 64).

Protection of religion is not extended to those aspects thought detrimental to public order or social morality. The Swiss Constitution of 1848 guarantees freedom of worship but proscribes the Jesuit Order as well as the founding or refounding of other Catholic orders. It also prohibits the bleeding of slaughter animals which have not been previously stunned—a rule that orthodox Jews claim is designed to forbid Kosher slaughtering. Analogously, article 48 of the Indian constitution prohibits "the slaughter of cows and calves and other milch and draught cattle"—a rule perceived as discriminatory by the 60 million beef-eating Muslims still living in India. A proposal to extend the protection to bulls provoked serious riots in 1967. Only a few countries, including West Germany and the United States, permit conscientious objectors to refuse military service for religious reasons. On the contrary, the Constitutions of Catholic Italy, the Muslim United Arab Republic, and the USSR (!) proclaim the "sacred" duty of defending the fatherland.

2. RELIGIOUS DIVERSITY AS A CAUSE OF CIVIL STRIFE

In southern Thailand and the southern Philippines, Muslim minorities, whose ethnic affinity with the Malays accents their religious divergence, complain of oppression by the dominant Buddhists and Christians, respectively—to such a degree that political separatism is becoming a serious issue. By the end of 1974 the religious cleavage in the Philippines was approaching civil war, illustrating the fact that people fight more bitterly and ruthlessly about religion than almost anything else. Once again, as 300 years ago, the Muslims of Mindanao and the Sulu Archipelago are under attack by Christian Filipino soldiers—no longer mercenaries of the Spanish but servants of the government in Manila. Again, "the cry of jihad is again ringing throughout the islands, winning for Muslim rebels of the Philippines the sympathy of the Muslim populations of Indonesia, Malaysia, the Middle East and as far away as Libya" (Newsweek, 28 May, 1973).

One reason for the conflict was the refusal of the Muslims to join in the modernization of Philippine society and their persistent clinging to feudal patterns of life. Rightly or wrongly, the Muslims feel their existence threatened by "outsiders" who are taking over lands they have always considered their own. The rebellion, directed at creating a Mindanao-Sulu state with 3 million Muslim inhabitants, has already claimed more than 1500 lives. At least 100,000 refugees are herding together in southern towns and cities. The International Herald Tribune of March 25, 1974, commented on "traditional communal distrust—the Muslims because of what they consider centuries-old Christian discrimination in housing, jobs and other areas, and the Christians because they worry that the minority's bitterness will eventually explode against them."

3. THE TRADITION OF "ISLAMIC SUPREMACY"

In countries where Islam's supremacy is unchallenged, its powerful presence in the top institutions of government ensures it a privileged position. In fact, certain Muslim constitutions provide for judicial and religious review of legislation to ensure that it conforms with Islamic law. In Iran, for instance, a court composed of at least five devout doctors of Islamic law and jurisprudence conversant with the exigencies of their age "is empowered to veto any Bill that might contravene the holy principles of Islam." An Advisory Council with the same function exists in Pakistan. Non-Islamic religions, on the other hand, are limited by Muslim standards of "public decency and public peace."

An eminent Indian intellectual, A. B. Shah, has referred to the tendency among Muslims to raise the Islamic religion to the ultimate norm. He concludes that "it would be unrealistic to imagine that the Hindu and the Moslem can live together as equal citizens unless each were willing to dissociate his political from his religious or cultural identity" (In Dalwai, 1969, pp. 20, 23).

Hamid Dalwai, a prominent protagonist of secularism in India, observes that Muslims believe Islam to be the latest and therefore the most perfect religion, and Muhammad the last and final prophet. Islam, which needs no modification, is not only a theology; it has also given its followers a complete social and political system, including rules for dealing with "infidels." Muslim scholars like Maulana Moududi and Maulana Abdul Hassan Nadvi have even discovered an "Islamic economic system" (*ibid.*, p. 73).

Numerous laws give special preference to Islam. In Malaysia it is a punishable offense to persuade a Malay to relinquish his Islamic faith. In Turkey, non-Muslim minorities not deported after the Turko-Grecian War in 1925 found their privileges and rights steadily curtailed, chiefly because non-Muslims came to be viewed as *non-Turks*, as aliens not deserving of

equal treatment. As recently as 1942, a tax on wealth was assessed so as to discriminate heavily against the non-Muslim merchant communities. Those unwilling or unable to pay were summarily condemned to forced labor. The status of Christians and Jews is determined by a few Koranic verses. Allah tells the Muslims: "Ye are the best community that has been raised up for mankind. You enjoin right conduct and forbid indecency; and ye believe in Allah. And if the People of the Scripture [Christians and Jews] had believed it had been better for them. Some of them are believers; but most of them are evil-livers." Another verse says: "Fight against such of those who have been given the Scripture . . . and follow not the religion of truth [Islam] until they pay the tribute readily, being brought down." (Luca, 1975, p. 226). These two verses firmly establish two very important concepts: First, that the Muslims are far superior to any other religious group; secondly, that Christians and Jews who have not accepted Islam should be conquered and "brought down," i.e. humiliated, and made to pay a special tax not payable by Muslims.

Islam has such a strong hold on its adherents that any contradiction between a constitution or law and a sacred text is nearly always resolved in favor of the Shari'a and against the "equality" embodied in the law, especially regarding political rights and appointments. In cases which cannot be "adjusted" by administrative measures, the modern law simply adopts the Koranic text, such as that forbidding the marriage of a Christian or Jew with a Muslim woman. Yet despite his conviction of superiority, the Muslim Arab is painfully aware that Christian societies are far more advanced and that Muslim lands cannot yet be counted among the advanced and industrialized countries.

This apparent contradiction between the word of God and the actual facts bewilders the Arab Moslem. Many try to rationalize the situation by bringing out the worst features of Western culture and civilization. They therefore start with a negative attitude towards the values of modern civilization and remain forever foreign to it and unable to assimilate it. This is especially true of many Arab students who study in the West and who return with a deep feeling of bitterness and frustration. (*Ibid.*, pp. 228–29)

Steeped in the glory of past conquests and culture, modern Arabs seldom achieve the objectivity needed to analyze the internal causes of their present decline and to examine critically the cultural and social values and traditions inherited from a nomadic society built on conquest and exploitation—irrelevant to the modern world for at least the last two centuries.

4. SOCIALIZATION PROBLEMS OF RELIGIOUSLY MIXED COMMUNITIES

In most Muslim-dominated countries local Christian minorities are free to practice their religion, provided it does not conflict with any precept or fiat of Islam. Such toleration is, of course, explained by the fact that these Christian communities are relatively small and pose no serious threat to Muslim dominance. Lebanon is the only exception to the rule; the Christian community accounts for not quite half the country's population.

The Lebanese constitution provides an elaborate system of power-sharing between the Muslim and Christian communities, each of which have their separate political parties. But as these lines are written, Lebanon is still immersed in a religious civil war, in which the Palestinian Arabs (hitherto not recognized as Lebanese) have emerged as the factor that upset the fragile balance. The survival of Lebanon as a state remains doubtful.

The primary loyalties of Lebanese have been to their religious communities, not to the Lebanese state. As early as 1964 Malcolm Kerr (p. 188) pointed to the lack of national consensus: Lebanon does not have the necessary integrators to make it function as a national state.

Yet the Muslim claim for greater representation to match faster population growth is valid only on the premise that an integrated nation exists. Before the demand for majority rule may be asserted, the question must be answered: *majority of what?*

Throughout the Middle East social cohesion across religious lines is lacking: Israeli Arabs, for instance, are drawn increasingly to Muslim-Arab nationalism. Christians in Muslim countries find it difficult to advance in the civil service or the army, despite superior qualifications; advancement beyond a certain officer's grade is often automatically blocked. In Syria, before the 1949 military coup, for example, there was not a single Christian among the eleven district governors; there was one subgovernor among 21; there were three ambassadors out of almost 40 and two general secretaries of the ministries among 17. Egypt, for twenty years under Nasser, never had more than one Christian cabinet member out of 22 and sometimes 28. In Iraq as well as Egypt it is rare for a Christian to rise above the rank of captain or major (Kerr, 1964, pp. 229–30). The occasional Christian personality who has achieved prominence in public life is, of course, always paraded as an example of nondiscrimination.

Since devout Christians can hardly avoid conflict with Islamic law, Christian communities in Arab countries tend to concentrate themselves in socioreligious enclaves. Typical are the Christian Copts in Egypt, whom Edward Wakin (1963) described as the "lonely minority." The Coptic courts have been shorn of most of their powers and subordinated to Egyptian civil courts with Muslim judges. Several thousand Copts convert to Islam each year to escape discrimination. In 1972 alone there were 11 anti-Coptic riots, and many younger Copts feel they have no future whatever in Egypt (*Newsweek*, December 4, 1972, p. 47). Christians in Syria are also victimized by compulsory Islamic religious instruction in all public schools. The Christians in Iraqi Kurdistan were, during the recent revolt, caught between the government (which accused them of collusion with the Kurdish separatists) and the Kurds (who accused them of collaboration with the Baghdad regime).

Conflict between Muslim sects is often quite as serious. A small Sunnite minority (less than 15 percent) rules Iraq by force and subterfuge over the heads of the 60 percent Shiite majority—to say nothing of the Kurds. In Syria, on the other hand, the roles are reversed. There is a 69-percent Sunnite majority, but in 1963 an army coup brought the Shiite-oriented Ba'ath party into power, which the Shiites have since consolidated by destroying the Sunnite economic base.

5. RELIGIOUS PERSECUTION IN AFRICA

Islam has had only qualified success in Africa. Arab-Muslim rule in Zanzibar was overthrown in 1964 in a bloody uprising of Black Africans; Muslim minorities in northern Kenya and Ghana complain of discrimination, and in Ethiopia, oppression by the Christian-Amhara–dominated regime in Addis Ababa is given as the main reason for Eritrean separatism. *The Guardian* (London) of October 19, 1974, reported several massacres of Eritrean Muslims by the Ethiopian army. Toward the end of 1974, thousands of Ethiopian Muslims marched through Addis Ababa to back the 13-point petition they had presented to Premier Makonnen a few weeks earlier. They called for a secular state and equal participation in the administration of the country; they also pointed out that none of the fourteen provincial governors was a Muslim.

In countries such as Sudan and Nigeria, powerful Muslim-oriented regimes hold sway. The Southern Sudan conflict, (see Chapter 11,F3) had a religious aspect, characterized by a campaign to induce public officials to take Arabic names and to embrace Islam. In Nigeria, religious cleavage between the Muslim Hausa-Fulani and the predominantly Christian Ibos was a major cause of the Biafran War. Through the outcome of that war and subsequent political maneuvering, Islam has become the dominating (even though not the majority) religion in Nigeria. In Uganda, many of the 60,000 or more slain under the dictatorship of General Idi Amin were Christian members of the Lugbara tribe, which had dared to oppose him politically. Amin, a Muslim, has removed all Christians from top civil and military posts and has moved to the forefront in the propaganda onslaught against Israel.

An interesting case of religious discrimination occurred in Zambia in the 1960s. It involved the so-called Lumpa sect and Jehovah's Witnesses. The Lumpa Church was founded in 1955 by Alice Mulenga who assumed the surname Lenshina, a corruption of the Latin *regina*. She claimed to have died in 1953 and to have been resurrected; she also announced that God had instructed her to establish a church for Black Africans. The Lumpa Church, which by 1964 had about 30,000 members, came into conflict with the United National Independence Party (UNIP) when the latter demanded that church members buy UNIP membership cards. The Lumpas resisted on the ground that their church could not become involved in party politics. UNIP raiders were sent into Lumpa territory, where they broke up a Lumpa service and eight people died. Lumpa adherents attacked police units and two policemen were killed by Lumpa warriors on July 24, 1964. On the following day police raided the village, killing 14 people, wounding 17, and capturing 36. Thereafter full-scale war erupted: more than 500 people were killed and about 350 wounded; hundreds of huts were burned. Alice Lenshina eventually surrendered to government forces and was detained indefinitely without a trial. According to the (London) *Financial Times*, her crime was to resist the totalitarian claims of UNIP, which had determined to become an all-embracing social as well as political organization. As the (London) *Daily Telegraph* described the situation:

The sect's adherents, followers of the "prophetess" Alice Lenshina, are officially represented as bloodthirsty fanatics whose strange creed has impelled them to rebellion and murder. Yet the only crime of the Lumpa, apart from what they have been driven in desperation to do, was and is that their creed strictly forbids them to engage in politics in any form. They refused to join the ruling United National Independence Party. This soon made them targets for political intimidation. Their huts and crops were burned; they were attacked; some were killed. They built isolated stockaded villages, where they defended themselves against all comers. Party militants persuaded the government to order the Lumpa to disperse from their villages. The Lumpa, fearing that under the new regime they would get no protection at all against the party, refused. Troops and police were sent in and the one-sided battle was on.

Members of Jehovah's Witnesses also came into conflict with the United National Independence Party for refusing to take part in party politics. Witnesses have been evicted from their homes, fired from their jobs, and turned away from shops, markets, and public transport. In a week of violence in March 1969, 45 churches were burned and the houses of 460 Witnesses were destroyed. The situation is not very different in Malawi, from which some 44,000 Jehovah's Witnesses were forced to flee in 1972 after they had refused to accept the supremacy of the Malawi Congress Party.

6. PERSECUTION UNDER MILITANT ATHEISM: THE USSR

The ultimate in religious persecution is that administered by the Kremlin. Under Khrushchev, a special call went out to all party and administrative organs to use the full force of the law against any religious practices which could be regarded as "illegal." On March 2, 1962, *Pravda* wrote:

Now that the building of Communism has been undertaken on a broad front . . . the party has put into its program the task of fully and completely overcoming religious prejudices. . . . The resolution of this problem, as set out by N. S. Khrushchev at the 22nd congress of the CPSU, envisages the elaboration of concrete measures to establish a system of atheist education and in every way to strengthen the program of scientific atheism.

Emphasis was placed on penetrating the family, to prevent "spiritual rape" by fanatically religious parents (*Kommunist*, January, 1964). The penal code was strengthened to root out religious practices. Leaders of groups who encourage "harmful" activities or "incite people to refuse their civic duties" are liable to a maximum prison sentence of five years or exile, with or without confiscation of all their property. In 1966 penalties were extended to cover "the performance of deceitful acts with the aim of arousing religious superstitions among the public" as well as the organization of religious education for the young. The USSR, which in 1962 adopted a UN convention guaranteeing the right of parents to rear their children in their own religion, has expressly denied this right in its domestic legislation. As *Uchitelskaia Gazeta* (Teachers' Gazette) published in Moscow, has stated unequivocally

Communist ideology is irreconcilable with that of religion. . . . [it is the duty of every Soviet teacher] to do everything possible to make atheist education a constitutional part of a Communist education, to root out with finality superstitions and prejudices among children, and to bring up every school child as a militant atheist. (November 13, 1971)

Religious groups are compelled by law to supply lists of their members to the communist authorities. There is a total ban on all relief work; no parish societies, discussion groups, or Sunday schools may be organized. Children of believers are subjected to compulsory instruction in atheism. Those who attempt to continue their religious observances in prison face "special punishments," which in known cases have led to serious physical injury (the Baptist Georgi Vins) or even death under torture (the Baptist Nikolai Khmara; the Orthodox monk Grigori Unka). (Bourdeaux, 1973, pp. 231–32.) Most of the 69 monasteries and convents of the Russian Orthodox Church were closed during the 1960s, along with five of its eight theological seminaries. The Roman Catholic Church is particularly persecuted in the USSR today, not only for its religious steadfastness, but also for its international connections and identification with "separatist" elements among Ukrainians, Byelorussians, Latvians, and above all Lithuanians. It is also reported that outside the Baltic and West Ukraine there are only four Catholic churches open (Gerstenmaier, 1972, p. 238).

The Uniate Eastern-Rite Catholic churches in the Ukraine and Byelorussia have been largely liquidated and their priests deported to Siberia, except for a few who joined the Russian Orthodox Church. Only a few of the 520 monks are still alive and only 30 percent of the 1090 nuns survived. One theological academy, two seminaries, 9900 Catholic primary schools, and 380 Catholic secondary schools have been closed down. In addition 35 Ukrainian Catholic publications and hundreds of Catholic organizations have been banned. Notwithstanding Article 123 of the Stalin Constitution, assuring every Soviet citizen "the right to free religious worship," the January 1965, issue of *Voprosy Istorii* (Problems of History) carried the instruction of the 22nd CPSU Congress "to eradicate completely religious and other superstitions from the consciousness of the people." This responsibility is delegated to local Communist Party organizations. According to documents published in *Christianity Today*, thousands of believers died in prison or exile between 1929 and 1961; over 500, mostly heads of families, were imprisoned in the decade that followed. Homes where meetings had been held were bulldozed, huge fines were levied, and children were snatched from their families and placed in atheist "children's homes."

Islam, the main religion in Turkic Central Asia, is as badly persecuted as Christianity. The Muslim religious hierarchy has been stripped of all effective power and no effort is spared to neutralize its influence by means of compulsory lessons in atheism and materialism. Wheeler points out:

The Soviet authorities make no concealment of their hostility to Islam. Indeed, as a way of life Communism regards Islam as more dangerous and objectionable than any branch of Christendom. It sees it as backward, as militating against material progress. . . . The incompatibility of the Islamic with the Soviet way of life has been stated and restated over and over again, and early attempts by Soviet orientalists to suggest that Communism and Islam have something in common, have been unequivocally condemned. (1973–74, pp. 34–35)

In Turkestan alone the number of mosques decreased from about 12,000 in 1917 to 1200 in 1970. In the whole of the USSR there are no more than 9000 Muslim clergy left, compared with 9000 in Bashkiria alone in 1917. To convince Arabs and other Muslims of Soviet friendship for Islam while continuing to exterminate their religion in the USSR requires a certain amount of ideological acrobatics (Matchett, 1973, p. 256).

Suppression of Judaism in the USSR is a part of the broad campaign to liquidate the Jewish culture as a whole, about which enough has been said in chapter 17.

7. RELIGIOUS DISCRIMINATION IN NORTHERN IRELAND

Since 1969, religious strife in Ulster has come to resemble the Thirty Years' War: the death toll had already reached 1000 by April 1974, and has mounted since. Socioeconomic discrimination by the Protestant majority is compounded by a national issue: Catholic Irishmen do not consider the Protestant Ulstermen as true Irishmen, as they are largely descendants of the Protestant Scots and English settled in the northeastern counties of Ireland. In 1920 these counties were excluded from the Irish Free State and became an integral part of the United Kingdom.

The principal fear of the Ulster Protestants is that the U.K. will abandon them as the price for the normalizing British–Irish relations. This would deliver them as a minority to the mercy of the Catholic majority in Ireland. In his report on *The Two Irelands*, written for the Minority Rights Group, Harold Jackson comments:

> Within their own enclave the Protestants of Ulster, one million strong, outnumber their Catholic brethren by two to one. But in the wider context of Ireland they themselves are easily outnumbered three to one. . . . For its entire fifty years Northern Ireland has been ruled by the Unionist Party and for most of that time there has only been one issue—the preservation of the border with the Catholic Republic. Any real attempt at social, political and economic advance has hit this barrier and bounced back from it. (1972, p. 189)

Parliamentary, regional, and local elections have almost all been fought on the issue of the continuance of Northern Ireland as a separate political entity linked with Great Britain, and virtually all votes have been cast for "Catholic" or "Protestant" candidates (Rabushka and Shepsle, 1972, p. 68).

Religious observance, being highly visible, is not only a source of conflict in itself, but a signal of divergent class and lifestyle. As Jackson observes:

> many Catholics dislike the puritan virtues on which the majority group sets such store—an earnest approach to hard work, a rigid morality and an unforgiving attitude towards the transgression of cultural norms. . . . And the Protestant charges against the Catholics are that they are feckless and lazy and they have too many children, that they expect everything to be handed to them on a plate and they are dirty and smelly. (1972, p. 197)

As pointed out earlier, religion—despite the industrial revolution—has eclipsed class or party as a central identifier for people who live in Ulster. As Richard Rose observes (1971, p. 359), efforts to unite Protestants and Catholics in class-oriented parties have failed, perhaps because of the proximity of the Catholic Irish Republic and the possibility that Ulster might be incorporated therein—a factor that does not operate in England or Scotland.

South of the border the shoe is on the other foot. Article 44 of the Constitution of the Republic of Ireland "recognizes the special position of the Catholic church as the guardian of the faith professed by the great majority of the citizens." Divorce is prohibited and even foreign divorces are not recognized. The manufacture, import, and sale of contraceptive devices is a criminal offense, even if importation is for personal use. Blasphemy (which might include questioning Catholic doctrine) is a crime—a law that has never been invoked directly, although a Protestant sectarian was bound over to keep the peace for saying things "offensive to the listeners' religious views." Although censorship of books and films has been relaxed, it still follows Catholic principles.

There being so few Protestants, it is inevitable that many will choose Catholic marriage partners. A Catholic who marries someone of another religion must conform with the Papal decree *Ne temere*, which requires an agreement to bring up the children in the Catholic faith. Once formalized, that agreement becomes legally binding and enforceable in the courts. As a consequence, the non-Catholic partner in a mixed marriage is reduced to second-class status (Jackson, 1972, pp. 210–12).

C. Cultural Deprivation Through Assimilation

Assimilation is almost always one-sided. One cultural community sets the pattern and absorbs the other(s) (Berry, 1965, p. 254). This process, however, is not always the product of crass cultural discrimination. There is also an insidious, creeping, but nevertheless calculated deculturation of minorities through long-term assimilation—even biological absorption. It is often hard to identify, and there may not be any apparent compulsion; but the minority soon gets the message that the price for advancement is, in fact, deculturation. Today, however, we are witnessing increasing resistance to this tendency among smaller ethnic communities—particularly within multiethnic states. The resurgence of the Basque, Breton, Corsican, Catalan, and Welsh cultures illustrates this trend.

Discrimination by denying assimilation is also possible. There are some ethnic groups who prefer to be absorbed by a dominant culture, but who are then denied assimilation by the dominant group. This type of discrimination usually takes place where a minority is racially different and a competitor for scarce goods.

1. ASSIMILATION AS A FORM OF CULTURAL DISCRIMINATION

The tendency of the Anglo-Saxon group in the United States to assume *Staatsvolk* status has already been noted. It is Anglo-Saxon standards and cultural norms that are to be embraced by the new American emerging from the biological "melting pot." That term, in fact, is derived from the title of Israel Zangwill's drama *The Melting Pot*, produced in 1908, in which the idealistic young hero, David Quixano (a play on Quixote, or a Freudian slip?), declares:

America is God's Crucible, the great Melting Pot where all the races of Europe are melting and reforming. Here you stand, good folk, think I, when I see them at Ellis Island, here you stand in your fifty groups with your fifty languages and histories, and your fifty blood hatreds and rivalries, but you won't be long like that, brothers, for these are the fires of God you've come to—these are the fires of God. A fig for your feuds and vendettas! Germans and Frenchmen, Irishmen and Englishmen, Jews and Russians—into the Crucible with you all. God is making the American. . . . the real American has not yet arrived. He is only in the crucible, I tell you—you will be the fusion of all the races, the coming superman (1909, pp. 37–38).

Zangwill himself did not jump into the "melting pot" he so rapturously described. He remained to the end of his days an ardent Zionist.

The melting pot process has inevitably become associated with so-called Anglo-Saxon conformity, which implies that all minority groups must renounce their distinctive ethnic identities to adopt the sociocultural characteristics and institutions of the dominant group. As Dr. Norman Drachler, Superintendent of Detroit Public Schools, stated to a Congressional Subcommittee:

America, it is true, was a heterogeneous society from our early days, but public education was primarily influenced by a strong Anglo-Saxon, Protestant, rural orientation. Personally, I think this hegemony healthy for a young school system, since it prevented fragmentation and helped to unify our nation. However, after our nation became firmly established, we failed to re-examine our needs and make readjustments in accordance with them. (*Ethnic Heritage*, 1970, p. 117)

The English-language school has been a decisive instrument for implanting WASP norms and values in the children of minority cultural groups. WASP-oriented socialization has even caused many children to develop negative self-images, a form of self-hate as well as a contempt for their own culture. As Dr. Drachler told the Subcommittee, "the so-called 'new immigrants'—the Poles, the Jews, the Russians, the Italians, and others arriving from southern and eastern Europe after 1880—were and often still are referred to [in school texts] in such negative terms as 'hordes,' 'swarms,' 'ignorant,' and the like."

Smith (1973, pp. 141–42) points out that the term "melting pot" refers to a process for recycling junk. "It implied that the broken down and worthless trash from across the seas . . . could be poured into a giant cauldron and under extreme heat and pressure somehow be molded into a shiny new product, something typically American that we could proudly label 'Made in the U.S.A.' " Although the melting-pot theory has fallen into disrepute, Smith continues, the message has not reached all our schools. Indian, black, Chicano, Puerto Rican, and Oriental children are still being stirred, crushed, or pressed into "a uniculture where assimilation . . . is rewarded by the right to wear a white hat and where those who fail to earn that distinction are labeled bad guys."

2. THE REVOLT AGAINST THE MELTING POT

Although the United States Constitution contains and the courts enforce elaborate guarantees of *individual rights*, it says nothing about *group rights*—a distinction elaborated in chapter 19,A2). Since the early 1960s, however, the major minorities have begun to revolt against the melting-pot system, which they view increasingly as culturally equivalent to unconditional surrender. A new ideology has spread: cultural pluralism, calling for curricula and social policies that reconcile the divergent as well as the common interests of various ethnic groups on a basis of peaceful coexistence. Its goal is to preserve ethnic identity without exclusion from the mainstream of American life.

De la Garza et al. consider that the opportunity for assimilation of Mexican-Americans and Indians has passed. They are now "determined to retain their societal structure and cultural identities. Their integration would now occur on a group level rather than on the individual level of immigrant Americans at the turn of the century" (1973, pp. 97–98).

As set forth in section D, below, the immediate grievances of American blacks have stemmed from *non-assimilation* rather than forced assimilation, as in the case of Chicanos and Indians. All these groups, however, suffer from selective assimilation, which robs the cul-

tural minorities of their natural leaders, and consequently of a large portion of their bargaining power. As St. Clair Drake points out (1971, p. 52), integration of middle-class Negroes into neighborhoods, churches, schools, and voluntary associations tends to isolate the Negro masses.

Yetman and Steele (1972, p. 256) quote a former Australian Minister of Immigration: "It is cardinal with us that Australia, though attracting many different people, should remain a substantially homogeneous society, . . . that all whom we admit to reside permanently should be equal here and capable themselves of becoming substantially Australians after a few years of residence, with their children in the next generation wholly so."

Many white Australian liberals favor the assimilation of the Aborigines—an attitude often motivated less by charity than by contempt for and rejection of "Abo" cultural and physical identity. The 1961 Native Welfare Conference accepted "that all Aborigines and part-Aborigines are expected eventually to attain the same manner of living as other Australians and to live as members of a single Australian community enjoying the same rights and privileges, accepting the same responsibilities, observing the same customs and influenced by the same beliefs, as other Australians." But few Aborigines want equal opportunities at the price of ethnic suicide. According to Rowley, one of Australia's most noted experts on the Aborigines,

the Aboriginal does not want to lose his Aboriginal identity. To some extent he is forced into this situation, since what he wants is equality of opportunity now. If he has been cosmetically favoured for "passing," and has made that decision, the Aboriginal spokesman no longer represents him. The demand for immediate equality is often couched in terms of opposition to assimilation; and what is being opposed is, I think, the extreme assimilationist position. (1972a, p. 385)

Rowley also observes that efforts to change social groups deviating from majority standards are psychologically inept, since they tend to emphasize the Australian of European descent as the tutor—and thus to stimulate further opposition.

3. ASSIMILATIONIST AND PLURALIST POLICIES

Increasing numbers of white Australians are beginning to feel that blanket assimilation is discriminatory and to embrace the concept of a plural society with institutions geared to the common as well as the ethnically distinctive interests of whites and Aborigines. In 1974 a Royal Commission of Enquiry into Western Australia's Aboriginal problems recommended separate development for Aborigines who wished to preserve their traditional tribal way of life and integration into the white community for those so desiring. This conflicted with the schemes of the Federal Government, which planned to integrate all Aborigines regardless of their wishes. According to a former Minister of Aboriginal Affairs, Gordon Bryant, however, the overriding principle of government policy is "community self-determination." This he defined as "Aboriginal communities deciding the pace and nature of their future development as significant and respected components within a diverse Australia." As will be seen in chapter 20, the Republic of South Africa's policy of separate development for its major population groups is not so different in concept.

A similar problem exists in Europe, where many educators and social scientists question the policy of educating Gypsies for assimilation in the host society. Grattan Puxon refers pertinently to this problem:

Rom are aware that through state schooling their children are being exposed to a relentless one-way feed-in of the outsider's culture. The child's Romani identity is obliterated, and a generation gap can be artificially opened that hastens the disintegration of the extended family. Creeping assimilation soon becomes a galloping rot. This process is a state monopoly in socialist Eastern Europe. In the West it is assisted by a host of free enterprise reformers and missionaries who, I believe, often trample the children's minds in the rush to rescue them from their "gypsy" upbringing and heritage. (Minority Rights Group Report No. 14, p. 21)

4. FORCED-DRAFT ASSIMILATION

Minorities in Muslim-dominated states have no illusions about the Islamic commitment to brotherhood. As explained in Part B, the Koran commands that infidels be subjugated, not treated as equals. In the case of Sudan, Russell and McCall (1973, p. 108) have drawn attention to the "express policy" of Khartoum to assimilate the Negro tribal cultures into a single Islamic Arabic culture (see chapter 11,F3).

Chinese in Indonesia have likewise come to realize that they can escape discrimination only by assimilating with the dominant Muslim-Indonesian host society. As President Suharto told the Indonesian Parliament on August 16, 1967:

Indonesian citizens of Chinese origin have the same position, rights and responsibilities as other Indonesians. We must prevent discrimination against these Indonesians. . . . we call on all Indonesians of Chinese origin not to delay further their integration and assimilation with the native Indonesians. You must remain aware that you chose Indonesian citizenship voluntarily, without being forced, and that you have not only the same rights, but also the same duties as other citizens. (Minority Rights Group Report No. 10, p. 7)

The choice is clear: remain culturally distinct and socially isolated, or accept deculturation as the price of upward mobility.

In the USSR, the socioeconomic price that non-Russians must pay to preserve their cultural identity is so exorbitant that the sophisticates and elites, in particular, are compelled to seek social, economic, and political advancement through Russification. The CPSU, essentially a Russian party, is particularly afraid of separatist movements which might place the USSR in the position of a colonial power resisting decolonization—hence the heavy emphasis on the convergence or merging (*sbliz-henie i sliianie*) of nations into a single Soviet nationality, the model for which is the Great-Russian Communist.

A particular effort is being made to Russify the Ukrainians. Intermarriage between Ukrainians and non-Ukrainians, mostly Russian, grew from only 3.4 percent in 1927 to over 18 percent of marriages involving Ukrainians in 1959. Hunt and Walker think that the gradual assimilation of Ukrainians is well under way and that cultural and economic differences between Ukrainians and the Russians are steadily diminishing (1974, p. 67). Weapons used to stifle Ukrainian nationalism include forced migration to Siberia, economic neglect, suppression of the Ukrainian language and cultural institutions, arrest and trial of Ukrainians who resist Russification, and Russian infiltration in the Ukrainian government (see Dushnyck, 1975b, p. 466). The obliteration of Jewish cultural and religious institutions in the USSR is another case of forced-draft assimilation. As Cornelia Gerstenmaier puts it:

Advanced assimilation has raised a wall of linguistic and cultural alienation between the synagogue and the Jews. A Jew who does not know his own language, or his history, who has grown up in the traditions of Russian culture and who, moreover, has no opportunity for assistance or guidance by the Jewish religious community, moves, like a blind man, by his sense of touch. Under these circumstances, it is not surprising that an intellectual of Jewish origin who is seeking religion not infrequently turns to Russian Orthodoxy which, in a final analysis, means one more step on the road to assimilation. (1972, p. 253)

D. Cultural Effects of Nonassimilation

Earlier in American history, many members of the nonwhite ethnic groups embraced the "melting pot" myth, hoping to become full-fledged Americans through cross-cultural assimilation. Instead, they were culturally deprived and superficially assimilated over a wide spectrum of social and cultural life, without being initiated into the primary relationships of the dominant white sociocultural groups. As Milton Gordon puts it: "Structural assimilation, then, has turned out to be the rock on which the ships of Anglo conformity and the melting pot have foundered" (1961, p. 283).

Many members of minority cultures chose to seek assimilation in what appeared to be the "mainstream," primarily to move upward in opportunity and reward. Most of the blacks were in this category. The experience of total or partial rejection was disenchanting. John J. Appel characterizes the situation:

Historians of American immigration and spokesmen for a pluralistic American society have not always agreed on the definition of what is, or should be, the degree of assimilation desired of newcomers. But both groups seem to have discarded the melting pot metaphor at the very time when Negro leaders, except for Black Muslim nationalists, vigorously espouse it. . . . They describe the *White* urban community as a conglomerate of coexisting groups divided on ethnic, religious, occupational and class lines. No White American, to be sure, moves exclusively in any one of these, but his allegiances are generally clear. Movement from group to group, especially from "out" to "in" groups, means partial assimilation, with elements of former identities being retained. Negroes, it would appear, cannot expect to be completely assimilated into any one of these groups, i.e. cease to be regarded as Negroes as the door to assimilation is opened for more of them. . . . Furthermore, the inevitable sense of separateness created by discrimination, heightens ethnic identity. Will the highly visible Negro American, his sense of solidarity developed by separateness and the struggle to achieve first-class citizenship, somehow avoid this paradoxical development? (1970, pp. 341–42)

Today, more than a decade after the beginning of the Civil Rights Movement, most blacks realize that their assimilation is still only marginal and that the vast majority of white

European Americans are not at all prepared to allow them full sociocultural integration—to say nothing of biological fusion. The Black Power Movement in the United States is a reaction to exclusion by the dominant white society as well as an attempt to fill a sociocultural vacuum.

Discrimination in the form of denial of assimilation is not, however, limited to the United States. In the United Kingdom, nonwhite immigrants find integration extremely superficial and highly selective. They often get a glimpse of the "holy land" of British white Anglo-Saxon society but, in general, are not allowed to enter it. These immigrants remain largely marginal, with the exception of individual sophisticates who are indeed fully assimilated. Biological amalgamation occurs only in isolated cases, at least where marriage is concerned. Non-white newcomers find the doors of churches, factories, government offices, public services, hotels, and restaurants opened to them, but not those of clubs, private dwellings, intimate friendship circles, or bedrooms.

In many respects the Coloureds of South Africa are experiencing the same resistance on the part of the whites to assimilation in general and to biological amalgamation in particular. Although a significant number of Coloureds oppose integration and prefer to be a distinctive people, the majority of the elite desire absorption in the white South African society. The majority of whites, on the other hand, particularly the Afrikaners, are still reluctant to permit assimilation for the Coloureds beyond public services and facilities and those areas of human activity that do not involve intimate, personal association. Coloured leaders perceive this limit on assimilation as discriminatory because it places a ceiling on their upward mobility.

The position of migrant laborer communities in Europe is also analogous. They have been mentioned in Chapters 13 and 15, and their economic situation is discussed in Chapters 21,A4. Concerning their cultural anomie, N. Peppard writes:

The first generation immigrant . . . has a hard time making the necessary adjustment. Yet, however great his difficulties, he can turn to the comfort of his own cultural roots. He may be homesick sometimes; he may frequently regret having migrated, but at least he is in no doubt as to who he is: he is basically an expatriate who must find a method of adaptation to a new country. The child of the immigrant, on the other hand, faces a much subtler, more severe problem. . . . He is poised uneasily with a foot in two separate worlds. His parents expect him to follow their culture and their traditions and to have a feeling for a "home country" he has never seen, while he desperately wants to belong to the only country he knows. At the same time the community of that country persists in regarding him as a stranger and he, a native, is sometimes told to "go back where he came from." (In Castles and Kosack, 1973, p. 366)

Switzerland is worried about alienation by its more than 600,000 migrants—35 percent of the labor force and more than 15 percent of the population. After defeat of two referenda calling for a major exodus of foreign workers (the latest in October 1974), the Swiss Government itself clamped a ceiling on their employment. Migrant workers in Switzerland will only come to "belong" in exceptional cases, both because of cultural exclusiveness and because Swiss citizenship is very difficult to acquire.

E. Educational Discrimination

There is a massive difference between the educational services offered in developed and lesser-developed countries. Educational progress in the Third World is often quantitative rather than qualitative. Charlotte Waterlow points to the problems of overcrowding, undertrained and underpaid teachers, lack of native-language text books, and malnutrition. She specifies:

An Englishman visiting a primary school in Tanzania found that at least half of a class of thirty-eight children had had no breakfast, and some only a cup of tea. . . .

The result of these conditions within the

classroom, together with other factors such as inability to pay school fees and failure in examinations, is that millions of children drop out before they have completed four or five years of schooling which are generally necessary to ensure that there is no fall-back into illiteracy. A UNESCO survey of 1969 showed, for example, a primary school dropout rate of 50 percent in India, Argentina and Libya, 60 percent in Brazil and Mexico and 80 percent in some African states. . . .

The quality of education is worse than weak. Secondary schools accept all candidates, even the most mediocre. I know teachers with 70 students or even more, who have become so discouraged that they have given up teaching their classes. University entrants have been so badly taught that I have seen students writing out their English language lessons phonetically in Arabic script. . . . [In India] large classes of half-comprehending students listen to lectures whose content is irrelevant to their real lives, and "examinitis" has become a common disease. In the northern half of India student unrest is now so serious that many universities are only teaching for about one hundred days a year. (1974, pp. 51–53)

The education offered is often unsuitable. Many Africans, Waterlow reports, think that practical and technical training condemns them to second-class citizenship—a carryover of tribal disdain for manual work. Massive illiteracy remains: in 1970 nearly half the adults in the world (74 percent in Africa, 47 percent in Asia, and 24 percent in Latin America) could neither read nor write. And the population explosion is increasing the number of illiterates.

1. ASSIMILATION AND CULTURAL AUTONOMY
   IN THE UNITED STATES

The Brown case of 1954, in which the U.S. Supreme Court abandoned the "separate but equal" principle that sanctioned segregated schools marked the beginning of progressive merger of white and black schools. But neither *de jure* educational integration nor "busing" black and white children for "racial balance" has brought the races closer together or overcome a persistent gap in achievement levels. In 1967, the U.S. Civil Rights Commission found

the reading level of Washington, D.C., blacks three years below that of whites at the 12th grade. Similar findings around the country have led to gloomy conclusions that it will take a generation or more to overcome the gap.

"Open admissions" policies proved insufficient to assure full black participation in American higher education. According to Alan Pifer, President of the Carnegie Corporation:

When one looks at the rate, in 1970, of participation of blacks at each level of the four-year undergraduate course, a disturbing pattern emerges. In the freshman year, blacks represented 8.3 percent of total enrolment; in the sophomore year, 6.8 percent; in the junior year, 5.4 percent; and in the senior year, less than 5 percent. . . .

Going farther up the ladder, one finds that in 1970 blacks constituted only 4.1 percent of the full-time enrolment in graduate and professional schools, including such vital fields as law and medicine. (1973, p. 23)

Except for strictly Negro colleges, Pifer continues, American higher education "showed little evidence, until relatively recently, of any sense of responsibility for the education of blacks."

Yet there is much to be registered on the positive side. According to the U.S. Bureau of the Census:

College enrollment has increased more rapidly for black students than for whites. Between 1970 and 1974, a 56-percent growth in college enrollment was noted for blacks, whereas white enrollment increased by only 15 percent. However, the proportion of young blacks (18 to 24 years old) enrolled in college was still below that of the comparable group of whites (28 versus 25 percent).

Enrollment has also increased for the very young black children—those 5 years old. By 1974, the enrollment rate for black children 5 years old (87 percent) was very close to that of whites (90 percent). The gains may be due, in part, to the increased availability of kindergarten to blacks, since more public school systems, especially those in the South, now include kindergarten.

Increased school enrollment by black teenagers and higher retention had resulted in rising educational attainment levels. By 1974, the proportion of blacks 20 to 24 years old completing high school reached 72 percent, rising faster than the proportion for the comparable group of whites. Yet, in 1974 an educational gap still remained between blacks and whites as 85 percent of the whites of this age group had completed high school. (*The Social and Economic Status of the Black Population in the United States*, 1974, pp. 3–4)

The success achieved by blacks has stimulated other ethnic minorities to seek restitution for the long history of educational deprivation. Susan Navarro Uranga catalogues the realities of Chicano educational deprivation:

Mexican Americans are grossly underrepresented among teachers in the Southwest, only about 12,000 or 4 percent, are Mexican American, while about 17 percent of the enrollment is Mexican American. Black teachers, although they are also under-represented, outnumber Mexican-American teachers by almost two to one.

Mexican Americans are also underrepresented on local boards of education. Of approximately 4,600 school board members in the Commission's survey area, only about 10 percent are Mexican American. . . . The Commission estimates that out of every 100 Mexican-American youngsters who enter first grade in the survey area, only 60 graduate from high school; only 67 of every 100 Black first graders graduate from high school. In contrast, 86 of every 100 Anglos receive high school diplomas.

Throughout the survey area, a disproportionately large number of Chicanos and other minority youngsters lack reading skills commensurate with age and grade level. At the fourth, eighth, and twelfth grades the proportion of Mexican-American and Black students reading below grade level is generally twice that of Anglos reading below grade level. . . . At the fourth grade, 51 percent of the Mexican Americans and 56 percent of the Blacks, compared with 25 percent of the Anglos, are reading below level. . . .

The suppression of the Spanish language is the most overt area of cultural exclusion. Schools have repressed languages other than English, regarding them as an educational handicap and a deterrent to Americanization. Nearly 50 percent of the Mexican-American first-graders do not speak English as well as the average Anglo first-grader. . . .

A second exclusionary practice is the omission of Mexican-American history, heritage, and folklore from the classrooms. . . . School and classroom activities, whenever they deal with Mexican-American culture, tend to stress only the superficial and exotic elements—the "fantasy heritage" of the Southwest. This reinforces existing stereotypes and denies the Mexican American student a full awareness and pride in his culture. (Uranga, 1973, pp. 164–67)

According to a more recent report of the National Committee on Mexican American Education of the US Office of Education:

In the Southwest the average Chicano child has only a 7th grade education. The drop out, or push-out, rate in Texas for Chicano high school students is 89%, while in California 50% of Chicano high school students leave school between the 10th and 11th grade.

Along the Rio Grande Valley of Texas four out of five Chicano children fall two years behind their Anglo classmates by the 5th grade. (The city manager of San Antonio estimates that 44.3% of the barrio residents are "functionally illiterate"; 20% never went to school at all.)

College enrollment is infinitesimal. In California, where 14% of public school students are Chicanos, less than 6.5% of college students at the seven campuses of the University of California are Chicanos (1973, p. 120).

The *Wall Street Journal* of December 15, 1972, reported that over 57 percent of the Spanish-speaking (largely Puerto Rican) students in New York City high schools drop out before graduation, compared with 46 percent of the black students and 29 percent of the Whites. Some 86 percent of the same city's Hispanic children read English below their grade and age level. Many such children have landed in classes for the mentally retarded because of the absence of mother-tongue education or adequate bilingual education.

Education is the single most important instrument for rising in America's power and reward system. An increasing number of minority leaders have therefore been demanding and obtaining the introduction of bilingual and ethnic programs in order to reverse the steady regression in minority education. The trend in American education is now in the direction of democratic cultural pluralism.

Yet bilingualism had to face some legal hurdles. Before 1968, 21 states, including California, New York, Pennsylvania, and Texas, had laws requiring that all public school instruction be in English. In seven states, including Texas, a teacher risked criminal penalties or the revocation of his license if he taught bilingually. Yet the US Office of Education estimates that 5 million children attending public schools "speak a language other than English in their homes and neighborhoods."

American Indians are not much better off. The Indian dropout rate is still more than twice the national average, and in some school districts it is 80 or 90 percent. In Minneapolis, where some 10,000 Indians live, the Indian dropout rate is more than 60 percent. In certain districts, Indian children are automatically retained an extra year in first grade or placed in slow-learner classes.

2. MINORITY EDUCATION IN THE USSR

The main victims of educational discrimination in the USSR are Jews, Muslims, and Buddhist Asians. While 211 Russian young people per 10,000 Great Russians were recently reported as university-level students, the ratio was only 150 for the Turkic peoples. The worst victims of educational deprivation, however, are the Jews. Yiddish as a school language was discontinued in 1959 and there is no instruction in Hebrew—although there are 45 languages of instruction in the Russian Republic (RSFSR) alone, while 59 languages are used for instruction in the USSR as a whole. This educational deprivation affects almost half a million Russian Jews, and is in direct violation of Article 21 of the Soviet constitution which guarantees "instruction in schools in the native language" (see Kochan, 1972, p. 39). Jews

today account for not quite 3 percent of all university-level students, compared with 13 percent in 1955. Since the Jews are the most highly urbanized of all population groups in the USSR, this decline, despite an expanding economy, can only be explained in terms of anti-Jewish discrimination (Dunner, 1975, p. 75).

3. UNEQUAL EDUCATION OF ETHNIC GROUPS

Educational discrimination against minority cultures occurs in virtually every African state. In the Republic of South Africa, for instance, the blacks, Asian Indians and Coloureds complain because the government budgets relatively far more funds for white than for nonwhite schools. They also charge that their education is inferior to that provided in white institutions and cite alarmingly high dropout rates in the first five grades. The white government claims that there are more graduate blacks in the RSA than in any other African state, but proportionately far fewer blacks than whites reach institutions of higher learning and a still smaller percentage of blacks complete their courses.

In Ghana, which has a relatively much smaller school population than non-white South Africa, certain ethnic groups evidently enjoy a distinct advantage in education. In the middle 1960s, for example, less than 45 percent of all males over the age of six years in five communities (Ga, Akyem, Akupem-Akwamu, Asanbe, and Ahamo) had never been to school, compared with 89 and 93 percent respectively of Gonja and Mole-Dagbani males in the same age group who had had no schooling whatever. In Kenya the majority of Kikuyu, Luhya, and Luo children have access to primary education, but less than 25 percent of the male Masai have ever been to school. There are 14 times as many children enrolled in primary schools in the Kikuyu-dominated Central Province as in the rural Northeastern Province. In Uganda, before General Amin assumed power, the Baganda accounted for nearly 34 percent of the students at Makerere College, although they represented less than 17 percent of the population of Uganda as a whole.

A somewhat lesser differentiation exists in Israel, at least in terms of the delivery of education. As a Minority Rights Group Report (No. 12, 1972, p. 11) observes, the settlement of Orientals *en bloc* combined with neighborhood schools has retarded integration and produced education that is separate and unequal. Teachers seek jobs in "good" schools and leave the deprived pupils whenever they can. "If teachers of Oriental descent were as well qualified academically as the Westerners, conditions in the *de facto* segregated schools would not be quite so bad—but obviously they are not." The latter factor contributes, no doubt, to a higher dropout rate among Orientals.

In New Zealand the Maoris lag seriously behind the whites at all levels of education. R. J. Walker writes:

There is a wide gap in educational achievement between Maori and European; many 13-year old Maori children may be retarded up to three or four years in reading . . . have no occupational goals . . . develop a hostility to school, and . . . see little relevance in school learning. . . . The Maori pass rate in the School Certificate Examination fluctuates between 19 and 23 percent, compared with the national average of 50 percent. . . . In 1965, 85.5 percent of pupils left school without any recognized educational qualifications . . . while Maori representation at universities is only 1:1541, compared with 1:185 for the Europeans. (1972, p. 401)

Educational discrimination is also rampant in Asia. Unequal school budgets were among the reasons why Bangladesh revolted from Pakistan. In Southeast Asia, Chinese and Indian minorities must struggle for educational rights. In Indonesia, for example, Mandarin is a school subject in some educational institutions, but Chinese-medium schools are prohibited. Deficient teaching facilities at government schools and Chinese quotas at state universities are compelling a growing number of Chinese parents to send their children to private institutions—at a cost which the average Indonesian cannot possibly pay. In Malaysia, the constitutional "special" position of the Malays results in various types of educational discrimination against the other ethnic groups.

In the United Kingdom, educational discrimination against nonwhite immigrants results mainly from the fact that they are usually concentrated in the poorer residential areas of the large urban-industrial centers, where educational standards and facilities do not meet middle-class standards. School authorities are introducing "compensatory education" in an effort to eliminate the cultural-linguistic disadvantage of immigrant children. But some experts object that this system stigmatizes the parents of the children concerned as socially and culturally inadequate. They would, apparently, like to solve the problem by pretending it does not exist.

The children of migrant workers in Western Europe suffer more from educational deprivation than is generally realized. In France, according to Castles and Kosack:

parents whose children are not legally in the country for one reason or another, hesitate to have them registered at school, for fear of discovery and expulsion of the children. Some families living in *bidonvilles* [shanty towns] in France "buy" an address in a more respectable area of the town in order to regularize their position. Their children can be refused by the schools near the *bidonvilles*, as they officially live elsewhere. If—as is not uncommon—such schools are overcrowded and make use of this regulation, a number of immigrant children are prevented from attending school. In Switzerland the Aliens Police have actually asked the schools to check with the appropriate authorities whether newly registered foreign children are in possession of resident's permits, so that children who entered the country as "visitors" but had stayed illegally, could be deported. (1973, p. 210)

"The split between indigenous and immigrant populations," Castles and Kosack conclude, "is widening" (*ibid.*, pp. 222–23).

4. INEQUALITY OF EDUCATIONAL STANDARDS

In the United States, the goal of integration has been interpreted in terms of racial mixing. When the children involved have radically different achievement levels, the mixing retards the education of and thus discriminates against the higher achievers, who are usually white. John Finley Scott and Lois Heyman Scott (1970, pp. 58–67) observe that parents desire to pass on to their children a status at least as good as their own, which makes the family the most conservative of all social institutions.

The behavior of professors as parents illustrates this well. . . . They generally do what they can to give their children an élite education of the kind their own occupation requires, and this proves difficult in class-heterogeneous schools. . . .

. . . Social change is the greatest enemy of familial inheritance and increases the burden of parental responsibility. Thus families concentrate on providing their offspring with training that will give them an advantage in the otherwise relatively open competition for valued positions in society.

The Scotts attribute the middle-class parent's fear of interracial education to a desire to maintain status in a stratified society. They note that a proposal to transport black children to the "hill" in Berkeley, California—the home of liberal professors—sparked a school-board recall campaign and caused a drop in property values. In Washington, D.C., school integration led to a massive exodus of whites; by 1970, 91 percent of the city's public-school pupils were black. In Boston, political liberals denounced the anti-integrationist Louise Day Hicks, but they voted for her with their feet—by moving to the suburbs, where lower-class blacks cannot afford to live. These facts suggest that "integration" cannot be pushed faster than public acceptance, despite the modern liberal theory that "the law is a teacher."

In American universities and colleges, "affirmative action" has resulted in a quota system that compensates for past discrimination but in turn produces a new variant—exclusion of brilliant students and teachers simply because their identity is White Anglo-Saxon. According to Richard A. Lester, a Princeton economist:

One effect of equal rights legislation: some women and minority instructors tend to fight back with complaints to federal agencies and discrimination suits even when they are passed over for tenure for such reasons as lack of drive or scholarship. In a number of fields, qualified scholars from minority groups are so scarce that the available talent shuttles from one faculty to another (usually with considerable pay increases at each move) in a kind of academic musical-chairs game. (Summarized in *Time*, July 15, 1974, p. 54)

Hillsdale College in Michigan is a small private liberal-arts college noted for its principled refusal of all federal aids and subsidies and the governmental controls that go with them. Its president, Dr. George C. Roche, an intellectual leader of American libertarianism, had this to say about the quota system:

Today, admission procedures in many schools are governed by a quota system which sets its own special double standards, unwritten but exercising great force in the lives of individual students. Such admission policies also have their effect on campus standards, compelling steadily lower requirements as the original applicants, often unqualified for admission, are retained on campus despite their poor performance. Such preferential treatment in admissions to undergraduate, graduate and professional schools has become increasingly common, penalizing both those qualified students who are thereby denied admission, and the standards of the schools themselves, which are eroded to maintain in residence those unqualified students who have been accepted. (Summarized in *U.S. News and World Report*, January 1, 1973)

Dr. Roche observed that the frenetic scurrying to recruit qualified minority faculty members would a few short years ago have been condemned as racist and discriminatory. But the octopus-like grip which the American Department of Health, Education and Welfare (HEW) has on the finances of many educational institutions makes it difficult for any school or university to avoid quotas, particularly since HEW answers complaints by claiming they do not exist.

The results of government pressure on colleges and universities to increase minority enrollments have been summarized by Dr. Thomas Sowell, Director of the Ethnic Minorities Research Project at the Urban Institute in Washington, D.C.:

there is a widespread problem of "underprepared" black students at many institutional levels, even though black student capabilities span the whole range by any standard used. The problem is not one of absolute ability level, but rather of widespread mismatching of individuals with institutions. . . . The schools which have most rapidly increased their enrollments of black students are those where the great majority of white American students could not qualify. However, since such schools typically do not admit underqualified white students, they have no "white problem" corresponding to the problem posed for them by underqualified black students.

The best-known program for placing and financing black students in law schools places an upper limit on the test scores students can achieve and still be eligible, a limit well below the average test score in the law schools where they are placed. Many government scholarships for minority undergraduates require academically substandard performances as well as lower socio-economic status. In some cases, such policies are explicitly defined legally; in others they simply exist in practice. Whatever the rationale for them in terms of retrospective justice, what they reward is a low performance level, whether or not a student is capable of more. Black high school students themselves have said that they refuse to perform at their best for fear of reducing their chances of getting the financial aid they need to go to college. (1974, pp. 179–85)

A similar problem, Dr. Sowell continues, was encountered in the USSR and other Warsaw Pact states in the early 1960s, when universities lowered standards to attract African students.

The results were also very similar to what has emerged with black American students. Both black

and white students bitterly resented these arrangements, and the resentment was directed at each other as well as at the administrations responsible for them. An observer of the pattern among African students in the early 1960's commented: "Many African students are uneasily aware that they are kept men. Often they take refuge from this reality in defiantly revolutionary verbiage."

Double standards, which exist widely though not uniformly, may in fact set a trap for the black student. Easily earned high grades in double-standard (or low-standard) courses give him a false sense of security. Then he encounters academic disaster in a rigid-standard course. Dr. Sowell continues:

Black academics tend to be especially severe in their criticisms of double standards for black students. The "benevolent paternalism" and "seemingly sympathetic" double standards of white faculty members, they say, tend to "generate feelings of inferiority in the students' hearts and minds in a way unlikely ever to be undone." (Ibid.)

The number of blacks on previously white campuses rose 173 percent, from 114,000 to 310,000, between 1964 and 1970 (Roche, 1976, p. 163), and this trend has continued. The cost, however, has been a differential lowering of admission standards for black students. As Martin Kilson and Thomas Sowell have pointed out, Scholastic Aptitude Test (SAT) and Graduate Record Examination (GRE) scores for most entering blacks (even at prestige universities) are now in the 25th percentile, whereas white applicants must reach the 90th percentile (in Ornstein, 1976, p. 361). In 1973, Northwestern Law School was admitting blacks scoring below the 10th percentile on the Law School Admission Test (LSAT), some from colleges with questionable accreditation, while rejecting whites in the 80th and 90th percentiles. A number of universities have established percentage quotas for minorities, knowing full well the later cost of higher dropout rates—which are already approaching 50 percent at the University of Michigan (Ornstein, 1976, p. 362; Roche, 1976, p. 156). Finding themselves academically outclassed, unsuccessful black students will turn to aggressive behavior rather than study. While blacks performing capably in responsible roles improve the black image, the visibility of substandard academic performance has a corresponding negative effect and may indeed spawn a revived racism. Hence "reverse discrimination" is counterproductive for blacks as well as whites. It even has bizarre aspects. According to Roche:

A young black woman with an I.Q. of 142 and comparable grades and recommendations was told by a national organization that she would be eligible to receive financial aid for legal studies if her scores were low enough. The scores were *too high*; the aid was denied. Another young black applied for a well-publicized doctoral fellowship specifically for black students. The fellowship was denied to this student, despite his brilliant academic record, because his social and political views were insufficiently militant. (*Ibid.*, pp. 162f., Roche's emphasis)

In the hiring of faculty, Affirmative Action has resulted in a de facto quota system, even though the Department of Health, Education, and Welfare (HEW) denies that intention. Roche (*passim.*) cites numerous job announcements calling for minorities and/or women, as well as cases in which scholars are refused employment or reappointment simply because of their race or sex. Since members of preferred minorities are given priority regardless of their individual social, educational, or economic status, additional minorities are pushing to find a place under the Affirmative Action umbrella. Portuguese-Americans, who are a formidable voting bloc in Massachusetts and Rhode Island, have recently secured the same privilege as their Spanish-surnamed compatriots; Italian-American groups are bringing intense and locally successful pressure for their own inclusion. The business manager of a large midwestern university has estimated that it will cost $1 million to convert to the records and procedures demanded by Affirmative Ac-

tion on his campus, but to date HEW has shown total indifference to expense. Americans learn slowly in matters of social policy, and it may take many years and many lawsuits by victims of reverse discrimination before Congress decides that Affirmative Action is not a feasible way to achieve equal opportunity. (For a fuller discussion of this topic, see Glazer, 1975.)

Members of European ethnic groups in the United States are beginning to ask why some groups need quotas, when Europeans were able to achieve their standing—high or low—in the American community without them. As David Brudnoy has written in *Human Events*:

Some will excel in one field or another. . . . Jews are indeed overly represented on the faculties of major universities, and Negroes are likewise overly represented on many athletic teams.

If quotas are not to push Jews down to their "proper" 2.8 per cent on faculties, shall quotas similarly push Negroes down to *their* "proper" 11 per cent on the Boston Celtics? [a professional basketball team] . . .

When people are appointed to impressive professorships at the great universities on the strength of mediocre achievements but the "right" (for the moment) race, then those Jews who have worked hard and developed their abilities and accomplished much are made the victims of racism. And there should be no doubt that racism in admissions and in university appointments has already cost the Jews a very considerable penalty (June 2, 1973, p. 21)

Jewish leaders have expressed concern at the policy by which the nation's leading medical schools allow only two or three Jews in every new class intake. "Just how many people have since died or been deprived of the best possible medical treatment because of this atrocious substitution of anti-Semitism for ability in criteria of admission to medical schools is an immeasurable tragedy" (*Ibid.*)

It should be evident by now that in the three main aspects of culture—language, religion, and education—discrimination is the rule rather than the exception. The remedy does not, however, lie in centralized and bureaucratic reform programs or judicial fiats, which tend to destroy communities and institutions without creating viable new ones. The problem is, rather, one that must be solved by people rather than governments: one of achieving mutual tolerance and respect and, above all, ability to accept differences without the compulsive need to remake others in one's own image. In public policy, the need is for decentralization of authority to the participants in and consumers of culture and education.

Parents should be able to *choose* between schools, curricula, and languages of instruction within available resources. People should be free to practice their religions, conduct religious education, and maintain theological schools of all faiths without state interference or preference. And the educational system—corresponding to the population it serves—should be differentiated, so that people of variant cultures, levels of preparation, and native abilities can find the schools and programs that best advance their personal development.

19

LEGAL DISCRIMINATION

Legal and political discrimination are two distinct though related areas, and are therefore considered in successive chapters. They have in common the need for theory to explain them, and much of that theory is applicable to both types of discrimination. What is said here and in section A thus applies to both chapters.

Meaningful comparisons require a common denominator, which can only be a body of theory by which social systems can be interpreted. Scholarship requires, however, that such a theory be more than a simple reassertion of the political or religious creed of any system, even if disguised in academic language. Otherwise, we might find ourselves agreeing with the mandarins of imperial China that Europeans are barbarians because they refuse to kowtow before the Emperor. Or we might have to agree with imperial and communist Chinese alike, that the denizens of the Middle Kingdom are superior to all other people. Any "social science" that asserts *a priori* the superiority of Europeans, Aryans, Jews, blacks, or any other particular group must therefore be rejected as invalid.

A. The Problem of Standards

If our comparison of societies with respect to legal or political discrimination is to make sense, we must begin by looking for universal standards—ideas that recur constantly in the philosophies of different cultures and thus represent the common experience of mankind. One such constant is the idea of justice.

Good rulers, among whom King Solomon comes to mind, are known for their dispensation of justice: a concept symbolized by the blindfolded goddess holding the scales and summed up in the motto "Equal Justice Under Law." Justice does not, however, mean the rigid or mechanical meting out of rewards and punishments. Three men might, for instance, be arrested for stealing jewelry of about the same value. One might turn out to be a professional thief; another an unemployed worker with a large family and no previous convictions; the third might be an escapee from a mental hospital. Justice would require that these men be treated in three different ways, even though objectively their offenses were the same. The idea of justice does not, therefore, imply rigid equality. Instead, it is expressed by the motto *suum cuique* (to each his own).

The concept of social justice admits many kinds of inequalities—in wealth, status and rank, and economic or political function—but it insists that differences be reasonable and purposeful rather than arbitrary. Justice does not, for instance, require that all workers draw the same pay or that all companies follow the same wage scales; these questions are decided by the market or by collective bargaining. But justice does require that a company pay equal wages for equal work at a given location. In proceedings of courts and public agencies, justice demands that decisions be based on objective evaluation of facts and not on the rank, status, or popularity of the parties. While rulers are permitted some leeway under the dictum of "reason of state," this principle has a narrow application in a free society—a fact demonstrated by the collapse of the Nixon Administration in the United States.

Closely related to the concept of justice is that of human dignity, which is reflected in the ban on "cruel and unusual punishment" in the British and American Bills of Rights. In criminal justice, human dignity requires that the accused, whatever the charge against him and even if convicted, be treated with the respect due a human being; he must not be made the victim of personal cruelty by those having custody of him. There is no agreement that human dignity forbids capital punishment, but there is agreement that it must be carried out with the least pain and that the condemned must be granted the last rites of his church.

Enforcement of human dignity is by no means universal in human history. In the ancient world political enemies were often drawn and quartered, while religious dissenters were thrown to the lions. The Holy Inquisition employed the rack as a means of enforcing orthodoxy, and various forms of cruelty persisted until the penal reforms of the nineteenth century. Today, respect for human dignity forbids torture either as punishment or as a means of extracting confessions—a confession so obtained is held worthless in the courts of the civilized world. Unfortunately, however, reports from countries such as Uganda, Rwanda, Burundi, Bangladesh, and Brazil show that tortures and massacres are by no means things of the past (see chapter 25).

The concept of human dignity reinforces that of social justice. It requires each society, within the limits of its resources, to assure its members and others in its care a subsistence level adequate to maintain health and the opportunity to better their condition through their own efforts. Justice and dignity do not, however, require a standard of welfare that defeats the incentive to work. Nor do they mandate the substitution of bureaucratic value judgments for the impersonal judgment of the market. Social justice and human dignity may, however, require control of internal migration in developing societies and those with large underdeveloped sectors. Rural people in such societies, moved by unrealistic expectations aroused by glimpses of the modern economy, crowd into metropolitan centers faster than the modern economy can provide jobs and housing. Failure to curb this tendency in Latin America and independent Africa gives rise to makeshift settlements (barrios, favellas, bidonvilles) that are hotbeds of crime, disease, and radicalism generated by the proximity of wealth and poverty.

1. JUSTICE AND HUMAN RIGHTS

Another concept closely linked to that of justice is the idea of *human rights*. Their classic formulation is found in Locke's *Second Treatise of Civil Government*, which enumerates the rights of life, liberty, and property. Locke's broad definition of property, paraphrased in the United States Declaration of Independence as "the pursuit of happiness," embraces the right of each person to pursue his or her self interest with due regard to the rights of others (Locke, 1690, *passim.*).

Human rights are given legal force by the dictum that no one should be deprived of life, liberty, or property without due process of law. This rule was stated in the Magna Carta of 1215 and repeated in the American Bill of Rights of 1789, as well as in most written constitutions. Due process means that no punitive action may be taken except after a full and fair trial before an impartial court, in which the accused is afforded opportunity for a full defense including the summoning of witnesses and cross-examining those of the prosecution. Evidence that a judge was biased against the defendant or that conviction met a political need rather than punishing a proven breach of law serves to invalidate the judgment.

In considering their effect on social justice and human rights, it should be kept in mind that government economic interventions do not create wealth but take it away from some to give others. Sometimes, as with United States urban renewal programs, the intended beneficiaries are victims. Tenants of old houses demolished cannot afford the new ones that replace them, and are therefore crowded into a decreasing number of old structures. Welfare programs that overstretch available resources or that prevent people from maximizing their gains through the market are violations of the human right of property, since they take away property and economic liberty without due process of law. The United States, Sweden, and most other countries with elaborate welfare programs contain a large class victimized in its human rights: people who, left to themselves, could have provided for themselves but whose property has been taxed or inflated away, leaving them impoverished wards of the state.

2. INDIVIDUAL AND GROUP RIGHTS

The human personality, in its social life, unfolds and expresses itself in two different dimensions. Hence there are two distinguishable dimensions of human dignity and human rights, and two corresponding dimensions of discrimination. These two dimensions are:

(a) The *individual dimension*, involving relations of individuals to one another, to each group to which they belong, and to the society or state as a whole. Within this individual dimension, discrimination may occur against an individual within a group, such as family discrimination against an unloved child, or neighborhood or school discrimination against a person "deviant" in appearance or manner.

Whenever discrimination is directed against a class of persons having a common characteristic or integrator, that class (as explained in chapter 6,B) becomes an externally determined group.

(b) The *group dimension*, involving the human personality as identified and formed by group membership, by intergroup relations, and by the status and fortunes of the group within the society or region as a whole.

It is thus necessary to distinguish between *individual rights* and *group rights*. Because much of the discrimination analyzed in this book is directed against ethnic groups, the concept of ethnic group rights (*Volksgruppenrecht*) plays a major role in these considerations.

Individual rights and group rights exhibit a dialectic relationship. Group rights often conflict with individual rights, in which case priorities must be set.

The twentieth century has seen a tendency to expand human rights to include such social rights as those to education, medical care, minimum wages, and security in old age. Such demands, however desirable their fulfillment, must be viewed in the light of limited resources. Extension of government-paid medical care to social insurance pensioners in the United States, for instance, was followed by increases in medical and hospital costs that placed severe economic burdens on the lower middle class and on workers not covered by employers' health schemes. Expansion of welfare programs in the United States and everywhere through deficit spending has wiped out resources of older people who have retired on fixed incomes. In many areas, inflation-generated property taxes are forcing retired people out of homes they paid for long ago, necessitating new laws to give them exemptions and shift the taxes to other people. However desirable an adequate wage, minimum wage laws do not assure anyone a job at the rate specified; instead, they force unemployment on people who are capable of working but whose marginal productivity is below what it would cost prospective employers to engage them at the legal minimum.

In South Africa, for instance, the Group Areas Act protects the right of ethnic-racial groups to live in homogeneous neighborhoods. This is done at the cost of denying to home-seekers of all groups the individual right to buy or rent any dwelling that takes their fancy. In the United States, on the other hand, the principle of "open housing" officially forbids an ethnic or racial group from maintaining a homogeneous neighborhood. Instead, it upholds the individual right to purchase or rent any dwelling on the market, overriding conflicting assertions of group rights.

Yet full enjoyment of individual rights is often impossible without respect for group rights. In Czecho-Slovakia, all citizens were theoretically granted equal access to the public service on the basis of individual abilities. But a law passed in 1923 required all state employees to be proficient in the "Czechoslovak language" even if employed in German-speaking districts. The result was wholesale dismissal of public servants belonging to the German and Magyar ethnic groups, who had been included in the Czecho-Slovak state against their will in the first place. Apologists for the first Czecho-Slovak Republic have pointed out, quite correctly, that all citizens enjoyed equal *individual rights*. But they were denied the *group right* to participate in public functions in their own languages.

World War II and its aftermath were marked by flagrant denials of group rights by both sides. Only a few will be mentioned here: the forcible repatriation of Baltic Germans under Hitler's *Heim ins Reich* policy; the German draft of several million civilians from occupied countries to work in factories; and the extermination of Jews in a number variously estimated as between 3 million and 6 million. On the Allied side, there were massacres of political leaders in Soviet-occupied territories; the seizure of private German property in the United States (deprivation of a class of people without

due process of law); the Russian murders of ten thousand Polish officers at Katyn and of many thousand Ukrainian leaders at Vinnitsa; President Roosevelt's concentration camps in which he incarcerated an entire ethnic group, the Nisei (Americans of Japanese descent); the expulsion of 18 million Germans from the Eastern Reich and East-Central Europe, to which Presidents Roosevelt and Truman gave consent if not approval; and finally the American-managed repatriation of Vlasovites and other Soviet citizens to the USSR (Operation Keelhaul) in the face of clear evidence they would not enjoy due process of law upon their return. In all these cases the denial of rights to groups extinguished the rights (and in many cases the lives) of individuals.

When individual and group rights interact, failure to distinguish between them results in confusion of public policy. The "open housing" policy written into United States law and intended to bring about "integrated" or "racially balanced" communities actually tends to change neighborhoods from solid white to solid black; it leads to multiracial communities only when limiting factors such as the cost of homes or unofficial quota systems curb black ingress. The contradiction of policy results from failure to recognize that while renting or buying a particular dwelling involves exercise of an individual right, living in an integrated or balanced community is a group right, since it involves a community defined as to ethnic composition. The only way to ensure an integrated community, if that is indeed the objective, is to let the group right prevail over the individual right, permitting a quota system reflecting the desired balance. But if all groups are to be accorded equal rights, then all-white groups, all-black groups, all-Hispanic groups, as well as all-German or all-Polish groups must be accorded the same privilege as mixed groups.

Perhaps as an echo of black success in achieving recognition of group rights, a number of smaller minorities with special problems and needs have appeared on the scene as organized interest blocs. Handicapped people, for instance, have secured the building of ramps in rapid transit stations and college buildings, and it will very likely become public policy that buses must have wheelchair lifts. Non-smokers enjoy special sections of airplanes and restaurants, and many cities ban smoking in elevators. Homosexuals, male and female, are waging a lengthy legal battle to end discrimination against them in government employment, especially in the Armed Services. Attention has recently been focused on problems of short people (*U.S. News and World Report*, March 28, 1977) as well as those of America's 100,000 dwarfs. The dwarfs have trouble with ordinary-size furniture, telephone booths, and plumbing and have an active special-interest organization, the Little People of America (Kleinfeld, 1975). People whose appearance deviates from the European somatic norm image find a champion in Uglies Unlimited, headquartered in Fort Worth, Texas, which concentrates on ending employment discrimination against the homely. And the National Association to Aid Fat Americans spreads the message that "fat is beautiful." All this goes to show that any group with a definable group interest will, all other things being equal, organize to defend that interest.

B. A Spectrum of Legal Discrimination

Legal discrimination may be classified in the order of its severity. The least severe type involves simple inequality of legal rights. In civil law, certain classes of persons may be limited or disqualified in their juristic capacity—that is, their power to make contracts, sue or be sued, and own or administer property. Such a disqualification is commonly imposed on infants and minors. In criminal law, simple legal discrimination might involve being subjected to more severe penalties than those imposed for analogous offenses on other classes of persons. Under the Salic Law, for instance, a Roman who plundered a Salian Frank had to pay 63 shillings, but a Frank who plundered a Roman was only fined 35 shillings (Henderson, 1912).

A special case of simple legal discrimination exists when variant systems of law apply to different groups within the same territory. In certain countries, tribal or customary laws—limited to members of the tribes, nationalities, or religions in which they have arisen—exist alongside a system of modern law applicable to the modern (typically European or partly European) community and to cases involving members of different groups. Such a dual system of law may afford members of traditional-law communities privileges (such as polygamy) denied to members of the modern society.

A more severe form of legal discrimination involves prohibiting those affected from working in certain occupations—or even from working for pay at all—from engaging in business, or from buying or leasing real property. A particular form of discrimination prohibits certain citizens of a state from entering or residing in certain areas and, in some cases, from even entering the metropolitan territory of that state at all. The ghettos of medieval Europe, the Jewish Pale of Czarist Russia, the British laws excluding "nonpatrial" subjects from the U.K., and South African pass laws are cases in point.

Still more extreme is the systematic denial of due process of law by means of rigged courts and controlled or intimidated defense attorneys. Such perversion of justice is a defensive weapon of totalitarian dictatorships, which accuse persons in unwanted categories—such as political opponents and leaders of subject peoples—of imaginary offenses, for which they are sentenced to labor or liquidation camps (Solzhenitsyn, 1974).

The worst form of legal discrimination is denial of the right to exist—usually the group right of an ethnic community to live in its traditional homeland and maintain its autonomous culture and political institutions. Such denial has frequently been expressed in mass expulsions (see chapter 22). In the least unfavorable case, the expelled group finds a territory where it can resettle. In other cases it is scattered across a continent, as in the *razvod* of objectionable minorities practiced by Russians since the days of Ivan the Terrible. Or those who purport to champion a group's cause may keep it indefinitely in refugee camps, since its permanent resettlement would defeat other purposes they have in mind.

The most extreme denial of the right to exist is genocide, the systematic extermination of nations, nationalities, or ethnic or racial groups. Genocide has been made a crime in international law through the United Nations Genocide Convention. Supplementing the Genocide Convention, German jurists have endeavored to secure international law recognition for the concept of *Heimatrecht:* the right of a people to be secure in its traditional homeland. While reaction in other countries has been mixed, there is no doubt that forcible deportation of a community jeopardizes its right to exist.

C. Inequality of Legal Rights

1. MEN VERSUS WOMEN

Women have suffered the most consistent inferiority of legal rights over the course of human history. The superiority of man is anchored in Biblical tradition. Eve was created from Adam's rib, and it was she who led him astray. Whereupon the Lord said to her: "I will greatly multiply thy sorrow and thy conception; in sorrow thou shalt bring forth children; and thy desire shall be to thy husband, and he shall rule over thee" (Genesis 3:16). The Decalogue places women in the same class with oxen and asses: that of property (Exodus 10:17). The day after the Romans had seized the Sabine women, Romulus is said to have lectured them on the Roman concept of marriage. According to Bullough,

A woman, he explained, was to be under the absolute power of her husband, and if she was unfaithful or took to drinking (an activity which might lead to unfaithfulness), she would be punished. The sole judges of her activities were to be her husband or her male relatives. (1973, p. 84)

As may be suspected, no such restrictions were imposed on the conduct of the husband.

The Twelve Tables, which formed the theoretical foundation of Roman common law, were equally explicit. Table IV, *Patria Potestas*, granted the father "absolute power over his legitimate children" (excluding any power on the part of the mother). A Roman father could imprison, scourge, or sell his son, or put him to death, even if the son held the highest offices of state. Under Table V, Inheritance and Tutelage all women (except vestal virgins) were under the authority of a guardian. A woman's property remained under control of her agnates (male relatives on her father's side), unless the husband should gain control through transfer or usucaption (acquisition of property through *de facto* possession) (Hunter, 1885).

Nor did things change much over the centuries. The laws of both France and England limited women's rights to administer their own property. It was not until 1964 that laws were passed in France enabling a woman, after marriage, to keep her own property, even though she and her husband had signed no private contract on the matter; gave women the right to open bank accounts in their own names, and to buy on credit; and granted women the legal right to take jobs without their husbands' approval or permission.

Birth control was not legalized in France until 1967. And it was as late as 1970 that ancient Napoleonic laws were wiped off the books—those prohibiting a French woman from taking her children outside the country without the husband's written agreement; allowing the husband to dictate where the family will live; and giving a divorced father entire control over minor children in their mother's custody (*France Actuelle*, June 1973).

Nor was the situation much better in England. As the *Encyclopedia Americana* summarizes the Common Law:

all real property which a wife held at the time of a marriage became a possession of her husband. He was entitled to the rent from the land and to any profit which might be made from operating the estate during the joint life of the spouses. As time passed, the English courts devised means to forbid a husband's transferring real property without the consent of his wife, but he still retained the right to manage it and to receive the money which it produced. As to a wife's personal property, the husband's power was complete. He had the right to spend it as he saw fit. (29:108)

It was not until a series of acts starting with the Married Women's Property Act of 1870 that married women achieved the right to own property and to enter contracts on a par with spinsters, widows, and divorcees (*Encyclopedia Britannica*, 1968, 23:624; Droubie, 1974).

The inability of women to control their own destinies was reinforced by laws treating birth control as obscene and the distribution of contraceptives as a crime. The status of American women was summarized in a declaration issued by feminists who met at Seneca Falls, New York, in 1848:

We hold these truths to be self-evident; that all men *and women* are created equal. . . . The history of mankind is the history of repeated injuries and usurpations on the part of man towards woman, having its direct object the establishment of absolute tyranny over her. (In Murphy, 1973, p. 5)

The Seneca Falls declaration claimed that man had made woman "if married, in the eye of the law civilly dead."

A number of American states have "community property" laws, supposedly to protect the interest of housewives without independent incomes. According to the *Yale Law Journal*, however, "in all the community states, except Texas and Washington the husband has power of attorney over the community property; and in some states he can assign, encumber or convey the property without his wife's consent" (80:946; in Murphy, p. 15). In the remaining 42 states, each partner owns whatever property he or she earns, but no credit is given for the value of a housewife's labor.

There are also discrepancies in criminal law. Several states have statutes like that of New Mexico, which exonerates a husband who kills his wife's lover *in flagrante delicto* but leaves punishable a similar crime of passion committed by a wife against her husband's mistress.

The situation of women in the German Federal Republic illustrates a phenomenon that seems to be recurrent: constitutional provisions and legislation purporting to grant equality do not succeed unless accompanied by social measures that assure real equality. Analyzing progress in "women's liberation" in Germany, Rudolph Krämer-Badoni (1974) points out that a "free" liaison, if it results in a child, discriminates against the woman, since a child born out of wedlock has no legal father. Women who desire to escape from the dependent role of housewife are frequently hampered in exercising "equal rights," since neither family nor divorce laws make any provision for their professional training or upgrading.

Whatever has been said during and since the Third Reich about the nobility of the German woman who devotes herself to *Kirche, Küche und Kinder*, the law of the Federal Republic, like that of the United States, does not recognize a housewife's work as a contribution to the Gross National Product. The occupation therefore lacks a financial basis: no wage is required or recognized and no provisions are made for mothers' stipends, invalidity insurance, or old-age pensions vested in the housewife. On the contrary, wives' benefits and survivors' annuities accrue to the *husband* as an appurtenance of his marriage. If a couple is divorced after a long marriage and the man remarries, the new wife obtains all the benefits, the first wife none. Finally, German income-tax law does not allow deductions for the automation of households needed to permit wives to pursue outside employment (Otzen, 1975, pp. 31–53).

Inequality of rights between men and women is even more pronounced in non-European societies. Among the Parsees of India, for instance, children of mixed marriages may only be brought up in the faith if the *man* is a Parsee—despite the fact that Parsee women have become prominent in Indian professional life ("Towers," 1974). The subjection of women appears in classical form in the Shari'a, the traditional Islamic law distilled from the Koran and the Hadith (sayings and daily acts of the Prophet Muhammad). It should, however, be kept in mind that Muslim law is an echo of Mosaic law in which women were property. (*Encyclopedia Biblica*, 3, p. 2942).

Insofar as Muslim women accept the role of housewife, the persistence of polygamy and arbitrary divorce makes their position unstable and insecure. Even in the upper and middle classes, Muslim women have two permanent worries: how to prevent their husbands from marrying additional wives and how to avoid sudden divorce. Various stratagems are used: spending the husband's money so fast he can afford neither an additional wife nor alimony; giving birth to as many children as possible; and hoarding money and possessions of the husband. Rivalry between wives and their children in polygamous marriages is said to cause disunity and hatred within basic social units and hence a lack of social cohesion in Arab society (Luca, 1975, pp. 224–25).

2. COURTS AND POOR PEOPLE

Even a legal system conceived in terms of equality may have different effects on different socioeconomic classes. As Anatole France once said: "The law, in all its majestic equality, forbids the rich as well as the poor to sleep under bridges on rainy nights, to beg on the streets and to streal bread." Judge J. Skelly Wright, of the District of Columbia Circuit Court, to illustrate the class bias that sometimes pervades the lower echelons of the U.S. judicial establishment, tells of an Eastern city where the local police court reacted promptly to a morning newspaper's editorial: "Get Bums Off Street and Into Prison Cells." That morning, 60 persons were tried and convicted of vagrancy by a single magistrate. In several cases, the magistrate simply called the defendant's name, looked at him, and pronounced sentence—usually three months in the city jail (Wright, 1969, pp. 431–32).

Police and magistrate courts—the kind with which poor people have most contact—sometimes ignore the presumption of innocence. If a defendant is ragged and unshaven and "looks guilty," an untutored magistrate is tempted to find him guilty. Vagrancy, defined in law as "having no visible means of support," is often involuntary: *the crime of poverty*. Few jails offer any work training, and having a "criminal record" makes it all the harder for a convicted vagrant to find a job.

Recent court decisions, the expansion of public defender systems and legal aid services, and the efforts of legal reformers have done much to strengthen the rights of defendants in criminal cases—so much so that criticism has arisen that American criminal law has now become too permissive. The civil courts, however, continue to function in a way prejudicial to poor people, mainly because they do not know the law can also be invoked on their side. Many states have established small-claims courts so the poor can prosecute and defend minor claims without counsel and at minimal cost. Yet these courts are in fact used mainly by businesses seeking to collect money from the poor. Wright cites a Federal Trade Commission report on retail practices in the District of Columbia:

In 1966, 11 ghetto retailers reported 2,690 court judgments, one for every $2,200 of sales. The report concluded that, while retailers generally may take legal action against delinquent customers only as a last resort, many of those who cater to the poor depend on such action as a normal order of business. And in many instances sales are made pursuant to unconscionable installment contracts with the expectation and hope that the goods sold will be repossessed so they can be resold. (Wright, 1969, p. 434)

An extreme case of victimization cited by Judge Wright was that of Mrs. Ora Lee Williams, a mother of seven living on welfare who bought about $1800 worth of appliances and furniture over a number of years on installment (hire purchase) contracts, and who had paid all except $170 by 1962, at which point the shop sold her a stereo set for $515. The manager knew of her financial straits, for he had noted on the reverse side of the contract the name of Mrs. Williams's social worker and the amount of her monthly welfare stipend— $218—which was all she had to feed, house, clothe, and support herself and seven children. When Mrs. Williams failed to make her payments on the stereo, the shop sought to repossess not only that article, but everything else it had sold her, most of which she had already paid for! The contracts "provided, in an obscure, almost unintelligible fine-print provision, that until the balance due on *every* item had been paid in full, the unpaid balance on a single item would be distributed among all the previous purchases. In other words, the debt incurred for each item was secured by the right to repossess all the items previously bought by the same purchaser." It was not until the case reached the District of Columbia Circuit Court that Mrs. Williams secured any relief from the order seizing all her possessions. As Judge Wright relates:

We pointed out that ordinarily one who signs an agreement without full knowledge of its terms might be held to them. But we felt that when a party of little bargaining power, and hence little real choice, signs a grossly unfair and commercially unreasonable contract with little or no knowledge of its terms his consent has not even been implied and the contract should not be enforced. (*Ibid.*, p. 435)

American law contains still other legal traps for the poor—and even the not-so-poor. One of them is the "holder in due course" doctrine under which a finance company can purchase installment contracts from dealers, without incurring the dealers' liability for defective or undelivered merchandise or services. A notorious St. Louis case involved a health club which sold hundreds of annual memberships on installment contracts and then sold the paper to a finance company. The club closed its doors, but the innocent members had to pay the rest of their fees for services they were no longer receiving. As the law stood they could prevail against the finance company only by showing that company *knew* the health club *intended* to defraud them, which could not be proved.

Another trap is the "confession of judgment" clause tucked away in the fine print of installment contracts. This language, seldom brought to the attention of poor debtors, provides that as soon as a payment is missed, the balance of the loan becomes immediately due and the creditor can obtain a repossession order without even notifying the purchaser. Since merchants who extend easy credit to poor people are inclined to sell shoddy goods, the repossessed articles are often resold for less than the balance due. In this case the creditor obtains a deficiency judgment, which entitles him to seize the debtor's remaining property or, if he is employed, to garnishee his wages. The employee often only learns about the latter when he receives a half-empty pay envelope. As Wright points out, many employers will dismiss a worker whose wages are garnisheed, because the withholding is too much bother. It is his contention that garnishments are a serious and unnecessary cause of unemployment (*ibid.*, pp. 437–38).

3. PLURAL LEGAL SYSTEMS

As noted earlier, there are plural societies in which different ethnic groups have their own distinctive legal systems based on tribal, religious, or national tradition. In South Africa, for instance, the Roman-Dutch law applicable to cases involving the white population is supplemented by Bantu law, administered by separate systems of "native courts" in cases involving members of black nations among themselves. Typical cases adjudicated under Bantu law involve usage of tribally owned land, payments and refunds of *lobola* or bride-money, as well as succession and inheritance. Male members of black nations retain the right to contract plural marriages under Bantu law, but such marriages are becoming infrequent among educated and urbanized blacks—partly because additional wives are no longer wanted for agricultural labor. Whites are governed by the Roman-Dutch law, which enjoins strict monogamy.

The situation is much the same in half-Christian, half-Muslim Lebanon. Its parliament, when functioning, has not attempted to legislate on domestic relations. The Muslims apply the Shari'a and each Christian church its own rules (Luca, 1975, pp. 221–22). Hence a Muslim man enjoys privileges of polygamy and instant divorce not available to his Christian compatriot, whereas the Muslim woman suffers the corresponding disabilities.

The Muslims of Israel enjoy a similar legal autonomy with their own Kadis, who enforce Islamic law in cases confined to the Muslim community. They also retain the right of polygamy, denied to Jewish Israelis. A few of the Oriental Jews who immigrate to Israel from Arab countries arrive with multiple wives, whom they are permitted to keep, but they may no longer contract plural marriages in Israel.

The situation in East Africa has been rather chaotic since the departure of the British. Because of the diversity of religious beliefs and customs, parliaments there have not been able to agree on new marriage laws—particularly insofar as polygamy and divorce are concerned. As a result, each religious community is left to follow its own customs and laws, sometimes with confusing results—especially where mixed marriages are involved.

Absurd consequences may result from the juxtaposition of traditional and modern legal systems. Following a complaint to President Tito, a commission investigated social conditions among the million ethnic Albanians in southeastern Yugoslavia and found that they still follow medieval Islamic customs including bride purchase. A nubile virgin costs between $7500 and $10,000, half of which must be paid in gold. Having bought his wife, the Albanian husband is entitled to treat her as a slave and in some cases even to kill her without interference by the local authorities, who likewise follow ancient Islamic customs. With increasing frequency, however, Muslim brides are running away with other men into the modern parts of Yugoslavia, where the courts refuse to return them to their husbands or to recognize any right of ownership. Tito's commission concluded that the Islamic tradition would have to be examined and its obsolete features set aside (Novak, 1974).

D. *Imposing of Disabilities: Aliens and Migratory Workers*

Moving along the scale toward more severe types of legal discrimination, we come to the imposition of disabilities: prohibitions and restrictions against particular groups of people, with their social effects. The most common type, which generally goes unnoticed because most people accept its legitimacy, is that imposed against aliens. The laws of most countries prohibit employment of aliens who lack work permits. Such permits are often refused because of the mistaken economic notion that an alien who works thereby deprives a native of a job. The Common Market provision opening employment in each member state to citizens of all members thus represents a major structural change in European society.

The right to decide who is a citizen and to impose legal disabilities on aliens is an attribute of sovereignty. The classification and treatment of aliens only involves international law to the extent that treaty rights or customary rights are at issue. The treatment of aliens is, however, a legitimate subject for social criticism, since the simplistic categories of "citizens" and "aliens" may not fully express the sometimes complex relationships between persons and groups concerned.

In the field of employment, the United States is noted for its restrictive policy toward aliens. Except for work permits granted to specialized personnel and to executives of foreign or international corporations, the right to pursue gainful employment is limited to aliens holding immigration visas—that is, to potential citizens. Foreign students, who are often unprepared for the inflationary prices they encounter in America, are specially hard hit by the ban the Immigration and Naturalization Service has imposed on off-campus employment. While the Service claims that it issues work permits in cases of serious need, they are often issued too late to do any good. Of 20,000 foreign students who sought summer employment in 1974, only 8000 were given permits, and these were issued when the summer was half over (Poddar, 1974).

In parts of the American Southwest, Mexican workers, including illegal immigrants or "wetbacks"—so called because of their reputation for wading or swimming across the Rio Grande—are an essential element of the rural labor force. For a number of years, the U.S. government authorized the temporary entry of migrant Mexican workers or *braceros*, who provided a ready source of cheap labor. Responding to pressure from churches, patriotic groups, and particularly trade unions, Congress ended the bracero program in 1964. The closure of legal immigration was, however, followed by a massive upsurge of illegal immigration.

The importance of Mexican migration to the United States is suggested by the statistics: between 1963 and 1972, 460,521 persons arrived legally from Mexico for permanent residence. Among the adult males, a majority had already lived in the United States illegally. At least a third of the immigrants had acquired a right to legal entry outside the quota by marrying a U.S. resident, siring a child born on American soil, or being the parent of a legal resident. The majority of the rest came as other close relatives of legally admitted Mexicans. The volume of illegal immigration is indicated by the fact that 430,213 deportable Mexican aliens were located in the United States and returned to Mexico in 1972—an increase of 24 percent over the preceding year. The Immigration Service recently acquired a fleet of 63 buses for transporting these people, and it also maintains 22 aircraft at the border to detect illegal crossings and provide additional transport for deportees. The consensus of observers of the immigration picture is that for each illegal entrant apprehended, another manages to establish residence in the United States. Estimates of the total annual number of illegal entries, detected and undetected, run as high as 1 million, so that the *net increase* in the Mexican population illegally in the United States would run about 500,000 each year (Portes, 1974).

The economic role of the "wetback" in the United States is closely linked to his illegal status. As Portes observes, he "fills the bottom of the occupational ladder since he is willing to take the marginal, minimum-pay jobs increasingly shunned by natives." Precisely because of his illegal status, he is the one worker who will never strike and will seldom complain about working or living conditions. His employer is free to violate federal and state laws on wages, hours, safety, and sanitary conditions, since the "wetback" who complains to the authorities will merely get himself deported. Curiously enough, it is not a crime to employ a "wetback" even though it is an offense to be one (Bustamente, 1972). The illegal Mexican workers in the United states are thus a class deprived of most of their legal rights. The Mexican government has been trying for some time to reach an agreement to regularize their status, and secure them wages and working conditions equal to those of U.S. workers in similar employment. Such an agreement has, however, been blocked by pressure from U.S. labor organizations ("Plantea," 1974).

Illegal aliens are natural targets for unscrupulous lawyers and "consultants." According to a report by the American Civil Liberties Union, thousands of aliens are swindled by "consultants" who charge large fees for "guaranteed results" and then respond to complaints or requests for refunds by telling the Immigration Service where their clients can be found. The Service itself is charged with abuses of power such as searches without warrants, mass arrests, and blackmailing aliens—who are ignorant of the many quirks in American immigration law that might permit them to stay in the United States—into waiving their right to due process (Walsh, 1974).

The "wetbacks" in the United States have their economic equivalent in the migratory workers of Europe and Southern Africa. Their legal situation may be described as a limitation rather than a denial of rights. The industrialized area of France, Germany, and the Benelux nations contained 7,750,510 foreigners in 1971. Those from other Common Market countries (the main contingent being 1,383,740 Italians) are the best off, since the Treaty of Rome guarantees them free movement and employment throughout the European Community. Legally recruited *Gastarbeiter* (literally "guest workers")—a majority of all migrants—come next. The worst off are the "illegals," estimated at 300,000 (mainly Turks and Moroccans) in West Germany alone. Lacking work permits, they arrive as "tourists" or are smuggled in, often through the machinations of private "arrangers" who charge what the traffic will bear.

In November 1972, the Federal Republic limited entry of job-seekers (except from within the Common Market) to holders of work permits issued by the foreign offices of the Federal Labor Institute. As a result, the husband of a Turkish female guest worker, having entered West Germany as a tourist, is administratively expelled at the end of three months, even if housing and employment are available. In response to the energy crisis, Europe has shifted toward more restrictive admission policies, curbing a trend that pointed toward a migrant population of 22 million by 1980 according to United Nations projections (Amelunxen, 1975a, Power, 1974).

The legal situation of migrant workers in Europe may be illustrated by that prevailing in West Germany. The sojourn permit, prerequisite for legal employment, can be granted before or after entry, but may be declared invalid at any time. It may be granted with or without time or area limitations; it may be shortened or prolonged or made subject to conditions and requirements. An alien can be deported if he endangers the security of the Federal Republic or violates tax law—but he may also be denied permission to leave West Germany for the same reasons. Sojourn in West Germany is thus treated as a privilege, not a right; the foreigner is at the mercy of the alien control authorities. He has a technical right to appeal to the Administrative Courts against arbitrary measures, but administrative "discretion" is difficult to probe through judicial control.

The *Gastarbeiter*—in contrast to many upper- and middle-class executives and professionals—are not granted permission to engage in independent business or trade. Their chance to stay in Germany thus depends on employment as well as housing, subjecting them to arbitrary treatment at the hands of employers, landlords, and the alien control officials. A guest worker who complains may be dismissed or evicted; he is then subject to deportation without a decision on the merits of his complaint.

The sojourn permit is usually limited to one year. When an extension is requested, the authorities must review the entire case, as they did in granting the original permit. A worker must wait one year before his family follows him, and even then permission is limited to the spouse and minor children; the admission of more distant relatives (to take care of the children, for instance) is not permitted. Although more than 1 million foreign workers, after five to eight years of good behavior, qualify under the law for permanent sojourn permits, only 7000 of these have achieved this more or less assured status. Non-European aliens are usually not given permanent sojourn permits, even after marriage with German women. This situation often causes the breakup of families. Other European countries, such as Sweden, Switzerland, and France, are somewhat more generous in granting unlimited sojourn permits (Amelunxen, 1975a).

Although guest workers from lesser developed regions face major problems of adjustment in the affluent society, they contribute less than their proportional share to West German crime statistics. Yet the lower criminal courts, despite admonitions from the Federal Supreme Court that foreigners are entitled to equal justice, often treat "abusing the hospitality of the Federal Republic" as a factor justifying more severe punishment than that given Germans for the same offenses. Once incarcerated, the guest worker may be unable to communicate with fellow-prisoners and guards, because they speak no Serbo-Croatian, Arabic, or Turkish. After serving his sentence, the guest worker is usually deported. But even minor offenses punished with fines may lead to nonextension of sojourn permits and hence to deportation (*ibid.*, pp. 118–19).

The industries and mines of the Republic of South Africa attract migratory workers from neighboring countries as well as from the black homelands within the Republic. Their status is based on the juridical presumption that each black African is a citizen of his or her land of origin and hence a nonresident in the white areas of the Republic. Homeland citizens are also South Africans for purposes of international travel, but that is subject to change as the homelands achieve independence. The rights and obligations of black Africans employed within the white areas are thus analogous to those of aliens in European states.

South African jurisprudence has always treated all persons coming before the courts as entitled to the same basic human rights of life, liberty, and due process of law. Chief Justice A. van de Sandt Centlivres declared in 1956 that the principles embodied in the American Bill of Rights "may be regarded as constitutional conventions in South Africa" (quoted, Dugard, 1972, p. 23). It is alleged that recent antisubversive legislation, such as the Terrorism Act of 1967, which permits detention without trial in certain cases, violates the rule of due process (*ibid.*, p. 29). But it will be seen on closer examination that the Terrorism Act applies only to revolutionary activity directed at overthrowing the state: a civil warfare situation in which military rather than civilian conventions govern. It is not invoked in cases involving personal, legal, or economic rights.

As in Europe, minority workers in Southern Africa are recruited on term contracts. Sojourn permits are conditional on employment and the availability of suitable housing. As in Europe, initially recruited workers are not permitted to bring their families, and family members who arrive without permission to stay are returned to their points of origin. Family housing is provided for employees of longer standing, some of whom have achieved quasi-permanent status as urban residents. Unlike migratory workers in Europe, however, those coming to the Republic of South Africa are provided with special machinery for the voicing and settlement of grievances, established under the Bantu Labour (Settlement of Disputes) Act of 1953. Those from within the Republic enjoy the aid of homeland government representatives assigned to residential townships, who serve as ombudsmen in dealings with the white authorities.

E. Systematic Denial of Legal Rights

The penultimate category of legal discrimination is that of serious or systematic denial of legal rights—sometimes with unintended or even intended lethal effects—though not reaching the scope or severity of deliberate denial of the right of entire groups to existence. The first two examples come from the United States. They are, the American authors of this book are glad to say, of minimal gravity within this category.

The first case involves what might be called a sin of bureaucratic obtuseness. In March 1974, Tirenne Deville, one of several hundred Haitians detained in Florida and Texas jails for illegal entry, hanged himself in the belief he would be returned to Haiti the following day. He was unaware that his deportation had been postponed from a Wednesday to the following Monday. Although the Miami homicide squad could find no motivation for the suicide, his priest was convinced that Deville had ended his life rather than return to the Duvalier dictatorship.

Several days later, attorneys representing more than 400 Haitians claiming to be political refugees pointed out that the United States admits automatically any Cubans who manage to escape from the Castro regime. Haitians arriving without visas, however, have been declared "deportable" by the Department of State, even though the Tonton Macoute, founded by the late "Papa Doc" Duvalier, continues its work of liquidating political opponents under his son and successor Jean-Claude, who has had himself "elected" president for life. The lawyers suggested that the fact that the Cubans are mostly white and middle class, whereas the Haitians are black and mostly unskilled workers, might have something to do with the differential treatment. Certain officials were said to have admitted privately that granting political asylum to Haitians would result in an influx of hundreds or thousands of illiterate blacks to the United States. The lawyers argued, however, that color and class should not be criteria when freedom and survival are at stake. The episode had a postscript a month later in the attempted suicide of a certain Jean Antonio, whose request for asylum had been refused by the Immigration Service because he had no documents to prove he was a persecutee—even though Papa Doc had executed both his father and his brother. Antonio was set free on $500 bail pending review of the deportation order by a federal court.

The second case of serious curtailment of legal rights in the United States is historical. It is included here because it illustrates an unresolved problem of American identity as well as the willingness of confirmed upholders of civil liberties to abandon legal norms when reason of state seems compelling. The case involves the Nisei, or Americans of Japanese descent, and their forced evacuation from the Pacific Coast in 1942.

1. AMERICA'S CONCENTRATION CAMPS: JAPANESE RELOCATION IN WORLD WAR II

Ever since Japanese workers had migrated to the American West Coast at the turn of the century—60,000 from 1899 to 1903—their assimilability had been hotly disputed by scholars as well as politicians. Josiah Royce and Sidney Luther Gulick, who accepted diversity within American society, argued for acceptance of the immigrants: the Japanese tradition of *giri*—"duty in spite in natural feelings"—would, Gulick argued, make Japanese-Americans loyal to the United States once allegiance had been transferred (Royce, 1908, and Gulick, 1915). Others, such as Edward A. Ross and Henry Pratt Fairchild, who visualized a homogenizing American society, argued that cultural and physical differences, breeding inevitable prejudice and reaction, would forever keep the Oriental in a category apart. Chester H. Rowell, California's leading Progressive journalist, complained that while the Chinese coolie was willing to remain "that perfect human ox," the Japanese set about rising in society. "Right or wrong our people will not live with those of a physically different race except on the basis of that race's inferiority. Since the Japanese are . . . in some respects superior, there is friction" (cited, Matthews, 1970, p. 279).

Further immigration of Japanese laborers was blocked by the 1907 "Gentlemen's Agreement," under which the Japanese government denied them exit visas. Immigration of all Japanese was cut off by the Immigration Act of 1924 and did not resume until U.S.–Japanese relations became cordial again after World War II.

The behavior to be expected of the Nisei in the event of hostilities between the United States and Japan was for some years a matter of conjecture, since some strategists considered such a war inevitable (see, for instance, Bywater, 1925). The judgment that prevailed was that of General John L. DeWitt, Commander of the Western Theater of Operations, who wrote the War Department early in 1942:

In the war in which we are now engaged racial affinities are not severed by migration. The Japanese race is an enemy race and while many second and third generation Japanese born on United States soil, possessed of United States citizenship, have become "Americanized," the racial strains are undiluted. (In App, 1967, p. 6)

Following General DeWitt's representations, orders were published April 1, 1942, ordering "all *Japanese* persons, *both alien and non-alien*" (emphasis added) to be evacuated from the entire coastal area, including the cities of San Francisco and Los Angeles and the farming areas in between, by noon, April 7. During the intervening five days, dealers rushed in to buy the possessions of the Japanese-Americans at panic prices (App, 1967). According to *Time* (February 17, 1967):

The loss to the internees, who had been allowed to take with them only what they could carry, was estimated at $400 million, a figure that includes the farms, businesses and personal possessions they were forced to leave behind. After the war, this loss was settled at approximately 10 cents on the dollar.

Professor Morton Grodzins called the episode "the first event in which danger to the na-tion's welfare was determined by group characteristics rather than individual guilt." He also pointed out: "No charges were ever filed against these persons and no guilt was ever attributed to them. The test was ancestry, applied with the greatest rigidity" (1949, pp. 146ff.). The 112,985 West Coast Nisei were moved en masse to "assembly centers" and later to more permanent relocation centers, a term that *Time* (August 11, 1961) called a euphemism for concentration camps. Here the internees were put to work at prison wages, with skilled workers receiving $12 and doctors or dentists $16 to $19 a month. In contrast to surviving concentration camp inmates in Germany, the Nisei never received compensation for salaries and wages lost. The best that can be said about the American camps is that no one was deliberately killed (App, 1967).

General DeWitt answered criticism of the evacuation by arguing that "it would be practically impossible to establish the loyalty of anyone of Japanese race. A Jap's a Jap. Once a Jap, always a Jap." This, of course, was turning both the Common Law and the American Constitution upside down, since both treat individuals as innocent unless they are proven guilty through due process of law. For the duration of World War II, West Coast Americans of Japanese descent (though not those living east of the coastal states and, curiously, not those in Hawaii) were denied their legal rights except for the bare rights to life and subsistence. A number of liberal scholars later denounced the wrong, but they waited until the war was over.

2. TERROR PREVAILS OVER THE RULE OF LAW IN ZAMBIA

Security in the enjoyment of both individual and group rights depends upon an independent judiciary free of executive or legislative interference. Progressive deterioration of the rule of law in Zambia is illustrated by several incidents from the legal history of that country. In December 1966, director of public prosecution Fitzpatrick Chuula withdrew charges against Matthew de Lux Nkoloma, a Kitwe city counselor, for alleged offences during race riots in the city. This action was criticized by several members of parliament and by Attorney General James Skinner. *The Star* (Johannesburg) commented on an apparent "reluctance to press home charges" against officials of the United National Independence Party (UNIP)—the sole legal political party.

In February 1967, Mrs. Reuben Kamanga, wife of the vice president, charged that Carlo Ottino, a Lusaka butcher, had sold her a rotten chicken. Mr. Ottino's shop was wrecked by youthful vandals the following day, his trading licence was withdrawn, and he was arrested under the immigration laws. The "rotten chicken" was actually a turkey, one of a number which Mr. Ottino gave away free to his best customers when he cleared his freezer; Mrs. Kamanga had failed to refrigerate her free turkey and it had gone bad.

Mr. Eustace Mumba, a UNIP youth secretary in Lusaka, was sentenced to 12 months imprisonment for contempt of court for public remarks about the "rotten chicken" affair. President Kaunda released him a week later—an action the *Times of Zambia* called "probably the most worrying event" since independence. That newspaper and the Johannesburg *Star* speculated that the UNIP had now attained a status "above the law."

Judicial independence in Zambia was most severely compromised in the Skinner affair of July and August 1969. Justice Ifor Evans quashed a magistrate's sentence of two years in prison for two Portuguese soldiers who had crossed the border to learn why a Zambian official was summoning them. His decision provoked the wrath of Bemba nationalists who demanded severe punishment. Chief justice James Skinner, the former attorney general, issued a statement in support of his colleague, saying that the duty of the judiciary to "share the hopes and aspirations of the nation does not mean that judges should impose sentences in

such a way as to please public opinion." President Kaunda, however, called Evans's decision politically motivated and used his presidential powers to keep the Portuguese soldiers detained despite the court order freeing them.

The UNIP Youth Brigade took its cue from Kaunda, and 500 youth raiders stormed the Supreme Court building, overturning benches, battering down doors, and strewing rotten eggs and rotten cabbages. Large demonstrations took place on the streets of Kitwe, Luanshia, and Lusaka; they soon took on an anti-white flavor. In Lusaka, a Czechoslovak diplomat was assaulted by a mob, apparently because he was white, and 2000 demonstrators paraded with placards reading: "The only good white man is a dead one." Although the ransacking of the Supreme Court was a planned UNIP operation, no arrests were made and no disciplinary action was taken.

Although a Zambian citizen, Chief Justice Skinner found it advisable to leave for London, where he resigned—as did two other senior judges. President Kaunda admitted publicly that he had made a mistake in handling the crisis and urged Skinner to return to his post. The judge, however, found an offer of the corresponding position in Malawi more attractive.

3. AGGRAVATED DENIAL OF LEGAL RIGHTS

When a modern regime sets out to deny the legal rights of entire classes of citizens it retains the apparatus of the law but perverts it to a wholly different purpose. The courts then become instruments, not for upholding individual and group rights, but for denying them and crushing anyone so bold as to assert them. This culminates in the paradox in which people are railroaded into labor camps for the "crime" of asserting that people are railroaded into labor camps.

Although Hitler's National Socialists were equally brutal in their treatment of unwanted minorities, the country where legal perversion has become a fine art is the USSR. The classic description of the gigantic mechanism its regime employs to extinguish freedom and dignity is Solzhenitsyn's *The Gulag Archipelago* (1974). After explaining the intricacies of Soviet legislation that provides criminal penalties not only for opposition or criticism but even for nonexistent offenses, Solzhenitsyn analyzes Bolshevik legal philosophy. The concepts of guilt and innocence, basic in Western criminal law, are dismissed as "rightist opportunism": *the heart of the matter is not personal guilt but social danger*. Since the regular courts were unable to handle the masses of "socially dangerous" persons who emerged at the close of World War II, they were supplemented by Special Boards of the MVD (Ministry of Internal Affairs) which could impose sentences up to 25 years without a trial, and with no appeal, for such crimes as

ASA—Anti-Soviet Agitation

KRD—Counter-Revolutionary Activity

PSh—Suspicion of Espionage (espionage beyond the bounds of suspicion was handed over to a tribunal)

SVPSh—Contacts Leading to Suspicion of Espionage

KRM—Counter-Revolutionary Thought

VAS—Dissemination of Anti-Soviet Sentiments

SOE—Socially Dangerous Element

PD—Criminal Activity (where no other charge could be trumped-up)

ChS—Member of a Family (of a person convicted under the above or other "letter" categories)

The Special Boards did not claim to be courts: they did not hand down sentences but only *administrative penalties*. Such a penalty, however, could be up to 25 years imprisonment and include:

deprivation of titles, ranks, and decorations;

confiscation of all property;

imprisonment, and

deprivation of the right to correspond.

The victim was therefore removed from society as effectively as though a court had convicted him (Solzhenitsyn, 1974, pp. 284–85).

The Special Boards were abolished in 1953 after Stalin's death. Why have courts at all, Solzhenitsyn asks, when the Special Boards were so much more efficient. The answer, of course, is that a "democratic" state is expected to have courts—to afford at least a pretense of due process. The function of Soviet courts was explained in some detail by the chief prosecutor and later People's Commissar of Justice, Nikolai V. Krylenko, whom Solzhenitsyn quotes as follows:

[The court is (K.G./S.P.)] at one and the same time both *the creator of the law* [Krylenko's italics, remaining italics are Solzhenitsyn's] . . . *and a political weapon* . . . don't tell me our criminal courts ought to act exclusively on the basis of existing written norms. We live in the process of Revolution. . . . A tribunal is an organ of the class struggle of the workers directed against their enemies [and must act (K.G./S.P.)] from the point of view of the interests of the Revolution . . . having in mind *the most desirable results* for the masses of workers and peasants. [People are not people, but (K.G./S.P.)] carriers of specific ideas. . . . No matter what the individual qualities [of the defendant (A.S.)], only one method of evaluating him is to be applied: evaluation from the point of view of *class expediency*. (Solzhenitsyn, 1974, pp. 307–8)

It is therefore only in occasional cases (where expedient, as in the Moscow doctors' trial) that Soviet courts deviate from predetermined verdicts on political defendants and permit the facts to guide their decisions.

Solzhenitsyn enumerates in some detail the groups whom Soviet dictators, from Lenin to Brezhnev, have thought expedient to funnel through the Soviet "sewage disposal system." They include the Mensheviks, the Left Social Revolutionaries, the Left Opposition (Trotskyites), the Right Opposition (Bukharin, Rykov, Tomsky, et al.), religious believers, kulaks, apparatchiks caught in the great purge, Volga Germans, Vlasovites, Ukrainians, Jews, and others too numerous to mention. They constitute a prison and labor-camp population that has varied between 6 and 12 million.

Since the "thaw" that followed Stalin's demise, the regime has turned increasingly to psychiatry and mental hospitals as weapons to paralyze opposition. Political dissenters, many of whose names and writings from captivity (Bukovsky, Grigorenko, Gorbanevskaya, Feinberg) are known in the West, are incarcerated in three types of mental hospitals: those of the ordinary kind, chronic hospitals, and the so-called Special Hospitals managed by the Ministry of Internal Affairs (MVD)—the police ministry. Violations of legal as well as human rights in these institutions are described by a former inmate in testimony for a United States Senate subcommittee:

In the Special Hospitals, all patients are rigorously isolated. Visits are permitted as a rule only from close relatives, and supervisors carefully observe the patients and their visitors to make sure that no manuscript or letter is transmitted. In these hospitals, patients are usually denied writing materials. They usually live from 2 to 15 people in a room and sometimes more. The rooms are a prison-cell type. Political prisoners are kept together with murderers and rapists. They are obliged to sleep with the electric light burning all night.

A great advantage for the authorities is the fact that they may sentence an imprisoned person to a psychiatric hospital in absentia. No procedural rights are granted to a person declared insane and, therefore, not responsible for his actions. Such rights are delegated to his assigned defense counsel who, as a matter of fact, is in no way obliged to even meet and talk to the accused.

In such cases, the question of guilt or innocence does not even arise, since this question is immaterial in the case of a person pronounced "not responsible" for his actions.

As a result, the arguments tending to justify the action of the accused are simply ignored. . . . there are many cases of the forcible use in Soviet psychiatric hospitals of medical preparations harmful to the mental and physical health of the patients. Among the preparations used are halaperidol, reserpin—25 tablets per day, sulfasil and others. (Yesenin-Volpin, 1972)

The functions of Stalin's Special Boards have to some extent been revived by the Psychiatric Commissions who render "expert" opinion to Soviet courts. Their task is eased by directives stating the medical reasons for compulsory hospitalization in deliberately vague and ambiguous terms, such as Directive (*Instrukcia*) 04–14 (32) published in 1963. It enumerates a number of morbid states, including:

incorrect behavior due to psychochemical disturbances (hallucinations, delirium, psychochemical automatism, syndromes of disturbed consciousness, pathologic impulsiveness) when accompanied by pronounced emotional stress and a desire for achievement; systematic delirium . . . if they indicate socially dangerous behavior on the part of the patient; hypochondriac delirious states producing incorrect and aggressive attitudes on the part of the patient toward individuals, organizations, or institutions.

The authors of the Directive evidently felt afterward that it was not broad enough; they added in a footnote that a patient might employ normal behavior to hide his illness, and that the list of "morbid states" was not exhaustive.

Special Decree 345–209 of May 15, 1969, signed jointly by the Ministers of Public Health and Internal Affairs leaves it to police departments, the procurator's office, and the psychiatrist to decide for themselves what is meant by "socially dangerous behavior" and "mental illness." The 1963 directive is henceforth to be used preventively: not only incorrect behavior, but even the *possibility* of incorrect behavior may be a reason for compulsory hospitalization. Medical reports include such "symptoms" of "mental illness" as: "a persistent mania for truth-seeking," "wears a beard," "meticulousness of thought and insufficient insight with regard to the existing situation," "considers the entry of Soviet troops into Czechoslovakia an act of aggression," and "shouted that he would fight for democracy and truth." Because of the political abuse of psychiatry, many Soviet citizens who really need psychiatric help are afraid to ask for it for fear they may be blackmailed (Medvedev, 1972).

Among a number of cases reported by the United States Senate Subcommittee on Internal Security (*Abuse of Psychiatry*, 1972), that of General Pyotr Grigorenko, a prominent military scholar with a long bibliography of technical writings, is typical. After becoming a critic of the regime in 1961, he was arrested in February 1964, declared mentally disturbed, and kept in an asylum fifteen months. While there, Grigorenko learned he had been expelled from the party, reduced to the ranks, and deprived of his pension.

Grigorenko was released after Khrushchev's fall from power, but never reinstated: the only job he could find was as a porter. He took part in protests against the trials of Sinyavsky and Daniel, of Vladimir Bukovsky, and of Yuri Galanskov and Alexander Ginzburg. He led a demonstration against the trial of the protesters against the invasion of Czecho-Slovakia. His popularity grew rapidly and the regime viewed him as a menace. As his arrest in Moscow would have caused considerable uproar, the KGB (security police) set a trap for him. With a false telegram, they lured him to Tashkent, Uzbekistan, to testify on behalf of arrested leaders of the Crimean Tartars. When he arrived, he found that the date of the trial had not even been fixed. He was arrested at the Tashkent airport and turned over to the Tashkent Committee of Forensic Psychiatry. When that body found him sane, he was flown to the senior institution of the MVD's hospital network: the Serbsky Institute of Forensic Psychiatry in Moscow. The head of the diagnosis department of this institute, Professor Daniil R. Lunts, is also a colonel of the KGB. Despite Grigorenko's protest that he preferred to face trial and possibly go to a labor camp, the Psychiatric Commission of the Serbsky Institute, in which Lunts played a leading role, made the required finding: that Grigorenko needed compulsory treatment in a special psychiatric hospital, as his "paranoid reformist ideas" were of obstinate character.

F. Denial of the Right to Exist

The ultimate form of legal discrimination is denial of the right to exist. Denial of existence to a group may leave to the individual the option of surviving by separating himself from the group, or it may involve the extinction of individuals because they belong to the persecuted group.

1. RECENT MASSACRES IN AFRICA

The best-known historical examples of denial of the right to exist are the Reigns of Terror in the French and Russian Revolutions, Hitler's "Night of the Long Knives" purge of 1934, and Stalin's purges in the late 1930s. A contemporary example is found in the actions of dictator Idi Amin of Uganda, who overthrew his predecessor, President Milton Obote, while the latter was attending a Commonwealth Conference.

Starting with an army of 6500 men, of whom 870 were killed during the January 1971 coup, Amin set about liquidating members of Obote's Lango tribe and the neighboring Acholi. During Amin's first 40 days, four of his trusted subordinates personally saw to the shooting of 1800 officers and enlisted men belonging to these groups. Further liquidations reduced the Uganda army to a strength of 2000 ("Inside," 1973). After the Israeli Military Aid Group had helped him train and equip a new army of 11,000—75 percent from his home province of West Nile—Amin suddenly broke with Israel and forced the entire mission to leave with hardly any notice (Mittelman, 1972). His Public Safety Unit, headed by Colonel Ali and Major Maliyamungu, has conducted a systematic elimination campaign against actual and potential opponents—including many who were prominent in the Obote administration. They have been secretly or publicly murdered. Chief Justice Kiwanuka of the Supreme Court, who had been organizing support for a restoration of tribal kings, was dragged at gunpoint from his courtroom. After Amin had uttered the fatal words, "Finish him," the Chief Justice was hacked to pieces while still alive (Martin, 1974a).

Individual as well as group existence is involved in the Tutsi–Hutu conflict in the former Belgian colonies of Rwanda and Burundi, the early phases of which have been described above. (see chapter 11,F2). In Hutu-ruled Rwanda, thousands of Tutsi who remained were massacred between 1959 and 1962 and their property looted or confiscated. An abortive Tutsi invasion from Burundi in 1963 triggered a renewed massacre in which 12,000 Tutsis were killed and practically all who remained fled across the borders (Lemarchand, 1974). It is quite understandable that for the Hutu the tall and highly visible Tutsi remain symbols of oppression. The fact is, however, that in Rwanda Tutsi do not enjoy the right to exist, individually or as a group.

In Tutsi-ruled Burundi, the Tutsis live in dread of Hutu reprisals, should the Hutu majority gain the levers of political and military power. What is involved is not merely a fear of being voted out of office: it is a fear of being exterminated. The Tutsi are boxed into a situation where they must rule in order to survive.

The Tutsi in Burundi have never attempted to exterminate the Hutu. They have, however, acted vigorously and violently to prevent the emergence of a Hutu elite that could lead a revolution. A 1965 coup attempt by Hutu military personnel, in which Prime Minister Biha was wounded, was defeated by loyalists under Captain Michel Micombero, who became Prime Minister himself on July 11, 1966, and President (having deposed the King) later that year. Micombero set about purging the army and the civil service. An alleged Hutu coup plan led to the arrest of 30 prominent Hutus, of whom 20 were executed in December 1966.

A Hutu revolt broke out on April 29, 1972; the core of rebel forces was said to have come from Tanzania. "Armed with small automatic weapons, machetes, and spears they proceeded to kill and mutilate every Tutsi in sight, in-cluding women and children. . . . They quickly overran the provincial capitals of Nyanza-Lac and Rumonge" (Lemarchand, 1974). After the Burundi army had suppressed the revolt, massive slaughter of Hutu ensued. In the capital city of Bujumbura, 4000 Hutu were loaded on trucks and taken to mass graves, and the massacre was extended to colleges and secondary schools. From April to June, a reported 80,000 Hutu were killed and another 100,000 fled into Tanzania, Zaire, and Rwanda (Martin, 1974b). Ironically, United Nations and UNICEF trucks were requisitioned as tumbrils to carry victims to their deaths. As things stand now, the Hutu in Burundi have a right to exist, but this right becomes increasingly tenuous as they attempt to rise in economic or educational status.

2. THE ULTIMATE LEVEL OF LEGAL DISCRIMINATION: THE BIHARIS AGAIN

A people whose right to exist is currently in serious jeopardy, more through a combination of circumstances than through the deliberate malice of persecutors, is that of the Biharis of Bangladesh, numbering between 700,000 and 1 million. As explained in chapter 11,D1, their misfortune was to be on the wrong side on the Pakistan civil war.

The West Pakistanis, who controlled the common government despite the greater population of East Pakistan, had appointed many Biharis to the civil service and had created an auxiliary force, the Razakars, containing a noticeable number of young Biharis. When the defeated Pakistani army and most of the West Pakistani civilians were evacuated in December 1971, the Biharis were left behind to face the rage of the Bengali masses—who thirsted for reprisals after the excesses committed by the Pakistanis. To protect the Biharis from slaughter, the Indian army grouped most of them in enclaves, where most are unemployed and dependent on relief. The withdrawal of the Indians on January 27, 1972, left them with no effective protection.

The Bangladeshi press treats the Biharis as collectively guilty of all the atrocities previously committed against the Bengalis. Their camps are raided from time to time by nationalist hooligans, with little interference by the police. Within the camps, the Biharis are living ten or more to a tent, with no protection from monsoon floods. In one camp, there are a single water tap and two latrines for 17,000 people: the outbreak of a major epidemic seems only a matter of time. The International Red Cross provides a daily ration of six ounces of food per adult and three per child. This provides 500 calories—less than the 1946 "starvation" ration of 1100 in Germany but more than many receive in Calcutta and elsewhere on the subcontinent.

The worst problem facing the Biharis is not their present condition but their apparent lack of a future: at least as a group. The Bengalis seem little disposed to tolerate anyone who speaks Urdu, while the prospects of resettlement in West Pakistan are poor. Nor is India able to absorb a large number of Bihari reimmigrants. The Biharis appear, indeed, to be "odd man out" in a Malthusian game.

As pointed out in chapter 11, the Minority Rights Group of London found itself forced to the conclusion that most individual Biharis could only survive through full integration into the Bangladeshi nation (Whitaker, 1972b). And since that nation defines itself linguistically, this means they will have to learn the Bengali language and bury all traces of their former cultural identity. The price of individual survival is abandonment of the right to group existence—that is, acquiescence to cultural genocide.

The case of the Biharis, although it also involves political, economic, and demographic elements, culminates and concludes our spectrum of legal discrimination. A nationality group of considerable size, without a livelihood in its present location and with no place to go, is effectively denied the right to exist.

20

POLITICAL DISCRIMINATION

Like legal discrimination, political discrimination can only be discussed meaningfully in terms of standards. Before we can decide whether someone is a victim of political discrimination, we must make an assumption as to the political rights he or she may properly claim. The word assumption is used deliberately, since political rights are norms based on political theory. And any theory, political or otherwise, must be *assumed*. It can be empirically validated—meaning that observed facts are found to agree with it—but it can never be proved.

The relation between political rights and political theory can be illustrated by quoting a dictator accepted in his time as the ultimate interpreter of Marxism-Leninism. Expounding Lenin's strictures against factionalism, Joseph Stalin told the 16th Congress of the Communist Party of the Soviet Union (Bolsheviks) (CPSU[B]) in June 1930:

The essence of Trotskyism is, lastly, denial of the necessity of iron discipline in the Party, recognition of freedom for factional groupings in the Party, recognition of the necessity of forming a Trotskyite party. According to Trotskyism, the *C.P.S.U.(B.)* must be not a single, united militant party, but a conglomeration of groups and factions, each with its own centre, its own discipline, its own press, and so forth. What does this mean? It means proclaiming freedom for political factions in the Party. It means

that freedom for political groupings in the Party must be followed by freedom for political parties in the country, i.e., bourgeois democracy. Thus, we have here recognition of freedom for factional groupings in the Party right up to permitting political parties in the land of the dictatorship of the proletariat, disguised by phrases like "inner-party democracy," "improving the regime" in the Party. That freedom for factional squabbling among groups of intellectuals is not inner-party democracy, that the wide self-criticism conducted by the Party and the colossal activity of the mass of the Party membership is real and genuine inner-party democracy—Trotskyism cannot understand. (Stalin, 1930, pp. 153f)

Interpreting the basic political rights to express opinions and to organize for political action in the light of Marxism-Leninism-Stalinism, we find them limited to opinions and activities confirming the Party Line as laid down by the leadership. The right to organize an opposition faction within the Communist Party simply does not exist—to say nothing of organizing a competing party.

Political rights, like legal rights, fall into two categories: rights of the individual as such and rights of groups and their members. As in the case of legal rights, the two kinds of political rights stand in dialectic relationship. Choices must sometimes be made; asserted individual rights must give way to group rights or vice-versa. Resolution of such issues depends on the political theory applied in the situation.

A. Individual and Group Political Rights

Individual political rights are those of the ruled vis-à-vis the rulers in a body politic conceived as unitary though not necessarily undifferentiated. As a member of the political community, each person has political rights and corresponding obligations: whether these are the same for all members depends on the prevailing political theory or ideology. In a medieval barony, for instance, the lord and his knights, the yeomen, and the serfs belonged to a single political system, but had very different rights and duties. The knights and yeomen owed obedience to the lord and were pledged to fight for him—the knights on horseback, the yeomen on foot. The serfs, who performed manual labor, were bound to the soil and forbidden to bear arms. With the advent of the armor-piercing crossbow, many local lords began arming their serfs, each of whom became a freeman the instant the lord placed a weapon in his hand (Wiefels, 1949). In Switzerland, the community of armed men became the foundation of an evolving democracy. The point for our purpose is that differentiation is not experienced as discrimination so long as each person enjoys the rights decreed by the prevailing ideology as appropriate to his function and status.

The concept of a right to participate in political decision-making—and hence of discrimination should such participation be denied—evolved as a feature of European forms of constitutional government. The first to achieve this right were the nobility, whose power over the public purse was confirmed in England by the Magna Carta of 1215. Representation in Parliament was progressively extended to the knights of the shires, the burgesses of the towns, and an increasing range of commoners. A parallel development took place in Germany, where the cities formed separate estates in the Reichstag of the Holy Roman Empire and in the diets of various kingdoms. As early as the fourteenth century, the direct democracy of the *Landsgemeinden* was established in the Alpine cantons of Switzerland; the cities of the plain became oligarchic republics governed by the guilds (Zurich, Basel) or the patrician families (Bern, Fribourg), who spoke French to emphasize their closeness to the court at Versailles (Thürer, 1948, ch. 1). In England and Germany, universal manhood suffrage was not achieved until the second half of the nineteenth century. The Prussian *Landtag* retained its three-class voting system until 1918. Voters were ranked by amounts of tax paid, and divided into three groups, each paying one-third of the taxes. The first group consisted of a few large landholders and industrial proprietors, the second embraced the relatively small upper middle class, and the third included the majority of petty bourgeois, small farmers, and workers (Article 71 of Prussian Constitution of 1850: Dennewitz, 1948, p. 81). This device assured a permanent majority representing the landlords and the upper middle class.

Is there a political right to equal representation? There is in the United States as a matter of positive law. In a series of cases beginning with *Baker v. Carr* (369 U.S. 166, 1962), the Supreme Court decreed that both houses of State legislatures as well as the Congressional delegation of each State must be based on districts equal in population, subject to variance within narrow limits. This dictum was based on the Fourteenth Amendment language: "No State shall . . . deny to any person within its jurisdiction the equal protection of the laws." Precisely here, however, a difficulty arises. If the right to vote confers a "protection," the latter must consist in the choice of representatives able to defend the interests of their electors and to achieve fair compromises with competing groups. In many American States, where the executive officials and the lower house were elected on the basis of population, the districting of the upper house to assure a majority from farm districts and small towns maintained a balance between city and country interests. Although the metropolitan areas had more voters, the regional interests of all were equally protected, since public policy was formed through compromise and tradeoff. This balance was overthrown in what many Americans feel was an orgy of unwarranted judicial activism. Insofar as legislators place their constituents' interests above those of the State as a whole, a metropolitan majority of 55 percent enjoys all the "protection," the small-town and rural minority of 45 percent none (Black, 1968). The rural people are clearly victims of discrimination in the name of nondiscrimination.

The difficulty, as with other American problems mentioned in this book, lies in the overemphasis of individual rights at the expense of group rights. The "one-man-one-vote" principle as an exclusive doctrine of representation, particularly when combined with single-member districts, implies the existence of a homogeneous body politic—which is exactly what the intellectual godfather of this principle, Jean Jacques Rousseau, intended to achieve. But the bodies politic of American States, and of most other countries, are composed of communities: geographic, economic, and in many cases ethnic. Communities of all types are notorious for refusing to fit into the standard sizes that arithmetic equality enjoins for parliamentary districts. Rousseauian jurisprudence in the United States has led to wholesale gerrymandering—the drawing of constituencies equal in number of voters, but resembling salamanders and other ungainly beasts in shape. The *quality* of representation is best when members are elected by communities with definable interests, even though unequal in size.

Numerical equality of districts does not, furthermore, assure representation of ethnic groups with definable interests or linguistic-cultural communities. It is only because discriminatory housing practices have concentrated American blacks in certain districts that they have been able to elect legislators, mayors, and Congressmen. Were "open housing" to scatter them across the landscape, blacks as a group could elect no one, though individual black candidates might gain office by winning the acceptance of white voters.

The content of individual political rights depends on prevailing ideology and its expression in political structure. In a state based on prescriptive differentiation (*Ständestaat*) political roles and hence rights depend on function and status—a cobbler could not claim a seat in the House of Peers. In a polity committed to mass democracy, each citizen has a right to an equal vote. But that right is deduced from the political theory of democracy, which is anchored neither in any of the major religions (except to a limited extent in the Puritan variant of Christianity) nor in natural law. The right to vote is instrumental, not basic or unalienable, and cannot be compared to the rights to life, liberty, and property. There are nondemocratic as well as democratic systems of representation, and there are societies where democratic representation will not (or will not yet) work. Indeed, citizens of the United States and the United Kingdom may sometimes wonder whether territorial representation is not yielding to functional representation through trade unions, business and associations, and interest groups, whose legislative agents (lobbyists) make legislatures into arenas for struggle, compromise, and tradeoff rather than rational debate.

The only individual political right that must be treated as basic, because it is a phase of liberty, is *freedom of speech*, including the right to print and publish. The right to organize political parties and associations of private character is a corollary individual right, though it overlaps into the area of group rights.

In a differentiated society, especially one

where ethnic, racial, caste, or class differences play a dominant role in shaping interpersonal relations, group rights take precedence over individual rights.

B. Group Political Rights in International Law

The essential political right enjoyed by groups—especially nations, nationalities, and ethnic groups that shape the culture and hence the personalities of their members—is the right to create political organs for defense of the group and fulfillment of its needs and aspirations. The exercise of this right ranges from the founding of private associations and clubs, through the forming of pressure groups and political parties, and creation of subordinate organs of government—perhaps with an ethnic rather than a territorial constituency—to self-determination at the highest level: the choice of national states, or the formation of a separate independent state.

The doctrine of self-determination was preached by Woodrow Wilson—much to the horror of his Secretary of State, Robert Lansing, who feared that the attempt to create national states in multinational areas would set the stage for further war (Baker, 1923, 1, pp. 15–16)—as it did in Central Europe and a generation later in Africa. Since World War II, efforts have been made to establish self-determination as a right vested by international law. On December 14, 1960, the General Assembly of the United Nations adopted Resolution 1514 (XV), which declared, among other things, that:

1) The subjection of peoples to alien subjugation, domination and exploitation constitutes a denial of fundamental human rights, is contrary to the Charter of the United Nations and is an impediment to the promotion of world peace and co-operation.
2) All peoples have the right to self-determination; by virtue of that right they freely determine their political status and freely pursue economic, social and cultural development.

3) Inadequacy of political, economic, social or educational preparedness should never serve as a pretext for delaying independence.

4) All armed action or repressive measures of all kinds directed against dependent peoples shall cease in order to enable them to exercise peacefully and freely their right to complete independence, and the integrity of their national territory shall be respected.

While these rights are couched in universal terms, they were asserted in the context of the wave of decolonization that followed World War II. It seems not to have occurred to anyone in the glass palace on the East River that they could also be claimed by peoples in East-Central Europe under communist regimes supported by Russian troops, or by minority nations within African states. Had the resolution been understood universally, it would have been defeated.

Resolutions of the General Assembly are advisory in character: they can, at best, express what *ought* to be the law. Two pieces of treaty legislation, therefore, were adopted by Resolution 2200 (XXI) on December 16, 1966. These documents, the International Covenant on Economic, Social and Cultural Rights and the International Covenant on Civil and Political Rights, contain identical first articles reading as follows:

1) All peoples have the right of self-determination. By virtue of that right they freely determine their political status and freely pursue their economic, social and cultural development.

2) All peoples may, for their own ends, freely dispose of their natural wealth and resources without prejudice to any obligations arising out of international economic co-operation, based upon the principle of mutual benefit, and international law. In no case may a people be deprived of its own means of subsistence.

3) The States Parties to the present Covenant, including those having responsibility for the administration of Non-Self-Governing and Trust Territories, shall promote the realization of the right of

self-determination, and shall respect that right, in conformity with the provisions of the Charter of the United Nations.

Here again the question of selective interpretation arises. Is not the USSR, which controls Czecho-Slovakia and other satellites through subservient parties backed by Soviet troops, a state "having responsibility for the administration of non-self-governing territories" if we consider substance rather than form? And are not the German expellees from the eastern regions of the Reich and from *Volksdeutsche* communities, who still seek international recognition of the right of homeland as an integral phase of self-determination, people who remain "deprived of their own means of subsistence"? The two Covenants go rather far in prescribing internal institutions and policies for participating states, which is perhaps why—after the euphoria of adoption had subsided—governments were slow in ratifying once they had read the fine print.

To commemorate the tenth anniversary of Resolution 1514 (XV), the General Assembly passed a "Programme of Action" for its "full implementation" (Resolution 2621 [XXV] of October 12, 1970, passed by a vote of 86 to 5, with 15 abstentions, with Australia, New Zealand, South Africa, the United Kingdom and the United States casting negative votes). This too was a recommendation, since the General Assembly cannot pass binding enactments. It was highly selective, condemning specifically the "illegal regime of Rhodesia" (without explaining why the United Nations should enforce the constitutional law of the United Kingdom when the latter fails to do so) but saying nothing about the long list of captive nations deprived of self-determination by the USSR.

To sum up, it would appear that group rights to political expression and self-determination remain undefined in international law. A right to found a state has never been established for any definable class or category of people: like a

revolution, the founding of a state is legal if it succeeds. This being the case, the tests for political discrimination are ideological rather than legal except insofar as rights can be deduced from natural law.

C. Political Discrimination in Constitutional-Democratic Systems

In judging which structures and practices observed in various political systems should be classed as discriminatory, we must return to the distinction between the *individual right* to participate in a political system taken as a given entity and the *group right* to create or maintain a system that expresses the specific character, traditions, needs, and aspirations of the group. The two kinds of right may be congruent, but in some cases—particularly those involving ethnic pluralism—they may clash. The way in which an individual, as a political subject, experiences freedom or discrimination depends not only on the characteristics of political institutions as such, but equally on the social, economic, and ethnic composition of the society in which they exist. It may be generalized that when political institutions reflect the social and ethnic composition of the peoples involved, maximum freedom is experienced by the most people. While democratic elections are a way of registering political consent, they are not the only way, and they are certainly not the same thing as consent itself.

1. INDIVIDUAL VERSUS GROUP RIGHTS IN CZECHO-SLOVAKIA

To illustrate this point, consider the first Czecho-Slovak Republic (1918–38), celebrated as a model democracy—thanks to superb public relations (including the buying of reporters and several entire newspapers) by the Foreign Minister and second President Dr. Eduard Beneš. The political system of Czecho-Slovakia, copied from the French Third Republic, was based on universal suffrage and equal formal rights of all citizens within a unitary and centralized structure. The constitution, however, was enacted by an assembly of the surviving Czech deputies in the old Austrian parliament plus appointed Czechs and Slovaks, with no representation of the 3.5 million Germans or the Magyar, Ukrainian, and Polish minorities whom the Paris Peace Conference had included in the Republic without their consent. Since the unitary state was in clear violation of the May 30, 1918, Pittsburgh Agreement, which called for autonomous government of Slovakia, and since the Sudeten Germans had seen their provincial governments overthrown by Czech troops and their demonstrators for self-determination massacred in the streets on March 4, 1919, there was danger that the peoples of Czecho-Slovakia might reject the constitution in a referendum. It was therefore placed in effect on February 29, 1920, without a popular vote, thus becoming a constitution without a legitimizing constituent power (Glaser, 1961, pp. 26–27). Since the Czecho-Slovak Republic, despite its multinational population, was conceived as an ethnic-linguistic state with the Czechs as *Staatsvolk* and the Slovaks as junior partners, the democratic constitution served as an instrument of discrimination by the Czech minority against the non-Czech minorities.

While individual rights reflecting citizenship in a territorial state were assured in Czecho-Slovakia, the right to function politically as a member of an ethnic group was granted fully only to Czechs and severely limited where other groups were concerned. Discrimination was amplified by laws transferring German farms to Czechs, requiring companies to employ a fixed percentage of Czech workers (but not German workers) if they wanted government contracts, and requiring all civil servants to speak Czech: a measure resulting in 33,000 dismissals. Advocacy of a federal reorganization of Czecho-Slovakia to match its multi-ethnic society was made a political crime. The

1923 "Law for the Protection of the Republic" prohibited, among other things:

§14. (1) Agitating, publicly or in the presence of several persons, against the state because of its origin, or against its independence, *constitutional unitary structure*, or democratic-republican form of government. . . .

§17. Founding a secret organization for the purpose of undermining the independence, the *constitutional unitary structure*, or the democratic-republican government of the state, or joining such an organization. (Emphasis supplied)

Under this law, members of the non-Czech nationalities were prevented from seeking a restructuring of the state permitting them fuller political expression. To create an artificial "majority," the myth of a "Czechoslovak nation" became a theme of official propaganda, and the hyphen in Czecho-Slovakia, which had been retained until the Slovaks were firmly incorporated in the new state, was quietly dropped by the Prague government and later by most commentators. To the dismay of the Slovaks, the "Czechoslovak language" turned out in many cases to be the Czech language used by Czech officials and teachers assigned to Slovakia (Vnuk, 1973, pp. 106–8 and *passim.*).

As a result, the Czecho-Slovak Republic succumbed to internal disaffection when it came under external pressure in 1938. Although the Sudeten Germans were never consulted about the Munich Agreement, it seems evident that most welcomed annexation by the Reich as a fulfillment of group rights, the Social Democrats being the main exception. By 1945, the Sudeten Germans were to regret this choice, the final outcome of which was expulsion of almost the entire ethnic group into Germany: a denial of group rights as well as individual rights.

2. DISCRIMINATION IN A TERRITORIAL DEMOCRACY: BLACKS IN THE UNITED STATES

A purely territorial system of representation favors the larger groups in a multiethnic society, especially if coupled with single-member districts. As Harold Baron observes (1971; p. 113), Blacks are seldom elected to city, State, or national legislative posts in the United States unless they represent mostly-black districts. Edward Banfield and James Q. Wilson have stated:

Not only are few Negroes elected to office, but those who are elected generally find it necessary to be politicians first and Negroes second. If they are to stay in office, they must soft-pedal the racial issues that are of the most concern to Negroes as Negroes." (ibid., p. 114.)

Because of the assimilationist ideology espoused by traditional black American leadership and its white liberal allies, the struggle for civil rights in the United States has emphasized individual rights to the practical exclusion of group rights. Black faith in the efficacy of individual rights as a means for achieving group goals is illustrated by these words of the late Dr. Martin Luther King, Jr., spoken May 17, 1957, on the steps of the Lincoln Memorial in Washington:

So our most urgent request to the President of the United States and every member of Congress is to give us the right to vote. Give us the ballot and we will no longer plead to the Federal Government for the passage of an anti-lynching law. We will by the power of our vote write the law on the statute books of the Southern States and bring to an end the dastardly acts of hooded perpetrators of violence.

. . . Give us the ballot and we will fill the legislative halls with men of good will and send to Congress men who will not sign a Southern Manifesto because their devotion is to the manifesto of justice.

Give us the ballot and we will place judges on the benches of the South who will do justly and love mercy and we will place at the head of the Southern States governors who have felt not only the pang of the human but also the glow of the divine. Give us the ballot and we will, quietly and nonviolently, implement the Supreme Court's decision of May 17, 1954. (In Andrew Young, 1974)

Although Dr. King's efforts led to passage of the Voting Rights Act of 1965, which enabled national intervention in voter registration, obstructions to black registration continue in the South on a reduced scale. In Hale County, Alabama, where black leaders demanded a purge of voting lists because 136 percent of the white population were registered compared to 68 percent of the blacks, registrars dropped 4000 names—of whom 90 percent were black voters (Young, ibid.). Yet despite chicanery here and there, black registration has stabilized at 64 percent of eligibles in the South and 67 percent in the North and West: a few points below the figures for white voters. The fraction of registered blacks who vote likewise lags a few points behind.

It is in the number of blacks elected to office that the continued discrepancy becomes visible. Between 1964 and 1974 the number of blacks holding elective office increased from 72 to 1307 in the South and reached 2991 in the United States as a whole. Yet the latter figure is only a little over .05 percent of the more than half a million elected officials in the country (Yinger, 1975, p. 56). Were blacks represented proportionally, they would have 11.4 percent of the elected officials—20 times what they actually have. In 1975, the United States had 108 black mayors, including those in Detroit, Los Angeles, Atlanta, and Newark, as well as 17 black Congressmen (of whom the proportional number would be 50). These, however, represent localized centers of black power created by the concentration of blacks in central cities—a result of centripetal migration combined with restrictive real estate and zoning practices in the suburbs. Many black political leaders seek to end these practices and achieve a dispersal of black populations over entire metropolitan areas (Sutton, 1971). Such a dispersal, however, would liquidate the base of black political representation except insofar as black candidates become acceptable to white voters. Several prominent black politicians have succeeded, but at the cost of abandoning distinctively black cultural styles and appealing to the community as a whole rather than merely the black sector.

The dilemma in which American blacks find themselves is suggested by a study of the Joint Center for Political Studies (JCPS), a Washington group that "provides research, information, education and supportive services for black and other minority group elected officials" (*Focus*, JCPS Newsletter, October, 1974). This study warns black leaders to be cautious in considering proposals for metropolitan or regional government, lest the power they now enjoy in central cities be diluted (Fox, 1974).

The contradiction between the black goals of "fair" representation and residential as well as educational integration has led several political scientists to propose that the single-member-district system be abandoned in favor of proportional representation in Congressional delegations and state legislatures. Such a change, however, would cause a total upheaval in American politics. It would abolish the traditional highly decentralized, locally oriented, non-ideological American political parties in favor of a plethora of ideological and ethnically based splinter parties. These would be highly unlikely to arrive at a consensus or compromise on any sensitive issue. Proportional representation, however it might appeal to an abstract sense of justice, might well mean the end of constitutional democracy in America.

. ETHNIC-LINGUISTIC DISCRIMINATION: CHINESE IN INDONESIA AND MALAYSIA

Citizenship is acquired at birth by being born within a state (*ius soli*) or by having its citizens as parents (*ius sanguinis*). But there is no natural right to join a political community; the granting of citizenship is a free act of the sovereign. The latter may, of course, predetermine who shall be citizens by limiting automatic eligibility to certain classes of people. As a result, a group living permanently in a country may find it difficult or impossible to become citizens and may therefore experience its situation as one of discrimination. A case in point is the status of the Chinese in Indonesia. There is considerable hostility against this group be-

cause of its business success and because, rightly or wrongly, it is identified with the communist subversion that came close to a takeover under the late President Sukarno. Chinese who lived in Indonesia when that state became independent were given automatic Indonesian citizenship unless they rejected it within two years. As there had been violence against Chinese during the revolution, almost 400,000 did so—many to their later regret. Those who did not had dual nationality, since the Republic of China's Nationality Act of 1929 recognized loss of nationality in special cases only. A treaty concluded with the Peking government in 1955, but not placed in effect until 1960, provided that Indonesian citizens of Chinese origin would have to reject their Chinese nationality within a definite period; otherwise they would be treated as Chinese citizens and aliens so far as Indonesia was concerned.

But in the meantime a 1958 law had changed the basis of citizenship by birth from *ius soli* to *ius sanguinis*, not retroactively. Children born to alien fathers after the law took effect would henceforth be aliens themselves. Alien Chinese, of whom there are over a million in Indonesia, can only become citizens through a cumbersome naturalization process, involving high fees as well as the bribes customary in many Asian countries. Thus a large population, permanently resident in Indonesia, finds itself excluded from the political process—except insofar as its members can wheedle or purchase the decisions they desire. Even ethnic Chinese who are Indonesian citizens are somewhat hampered in political activity, since the government regards any Chinese organization as at least potentially subversive and all people of Chinese culture as alien in spirit if not in law (Coppel, 1972).

Discrimination against the proportionally larger Chinese population in Malaysia takes a somewhat different form. Here it is relatively easy for a Chinese to acquire citizenship. But he may lose it if "he has shown himself by act or speech to be disloyal or disaffected towards the Federation." Such deprivation orders are not regularly open to review by the courts. Since interethnic rioting in 1971, the constitution has been changed to prohibit discussion of "sensitive issues" such as citizenship, national language, and the special position of the Malays (*ibid.*).

What is at issue in Malaysia, and to a lesser extent in Indonesia, is the right of a community to define itself in ethnic-linguistic terms— the right to have a state expressing the traditions and aspirations of the *Volk* rather than an ethnically neutral territorial state. Experience indicates that a *Staatsvolk* that has established an ethnic-linguistic state will grant political rights to "alien" groups only if they do not jeopardize the specific national character of the state. If a traditional religion is an important integrator of the *Staatsvolk*, adherents of other faiths desiring membership in the political community must accept the cultural content of the majority religion as essential to the national character, though they need not pretend to embrace its theology. In Lebanon, for instance, Christian Arabs accepted the *secular* history of Islam as part of their political tradition and Muhammad as a founder of the Arab nation—even if not the final interpreter of God's word (Milson, 1972, p. 26). This acceptance, however, appears to have been badly eroded by the recent civil war, since Christian Lebanese have now experienced Arab nationalism as hostile to their group existence.

The question then arises: What is to happen when an "alien" ethnic group within the state cannot be assimilated without endangering the essential character of the political community? Arab nationalists in Israeli-occupied territory and in Israel itself—as distinguished from Arab Israelis who accept cultural and religious autonomy within the Judaic state, thereby incurring the wrath of other Arabs—have classed themselves as unassimilable to Israel insofar as they demand it be abolished and replaced by a secular "Palestine Democratic State." Even that concept turns out, on closer inspection, to be a slogan designed for Western consumption,

cloaking the true intention to create an Arab state (Arab symposium reported in *Anwar*, Beirut, March 8, 1970). What rights can a *Staatsvolk* safely grant an ethnic group whose leaders have vowed destruction of the state without committing "national suicide"?

4. ETHNIC-CULTURAL VERSUS TERRITORIAL DEMOCRACY: THE PROBLEM OF COLOURED REPRESENTATION IN SOUTH AFRICA

In a constitutional-democratic system, an opposition party within the *Staatsvolk* may be tempted to strengthen its position by enfranchising and making an ally of a group alien to the ethnic mainstream. Such a maneuver, however, may destroy or render irrelevant the integrators that have enabled the nation to function as a political entity.

This is precisely the situation in South Africa. There, two former opposition parties, the United Party (UP) and the Progressives (the first since dissolved and the second merged into the Progressive Federal Party), proposed to restore a qualified franchise to non-whites: the UP by giving them a fixed number of seats in Parliament and the Progressives by requiring voters to meet an educational qualification (Suzman, 1972). The Afrikaner journalist Otto Krause comments on this score:

> It is significant that both these parties wish to open the door to the non-Whites only so far. . . . Neither relish the prospect of non-Whites flooding the electorate; in fact both parties (despite protestations) would resist any such flooding. Again it is a matter of the English–Afrikaner power struggle. The English-based parties would only allow in sufficient non-White votes to overturn Afrikaner political power: anything more would deprive them of their control. (1972, p. 536)

The South African nation, including its English-speaking as well as its Afrikaans component, has defined itself not as a territorial nation but as one of specific European ethnicity and culture. This definition became explicit after the National Party assumed power in 1948, but was already implicit in English policy. Definition of a nation in ethnic terms necessarily excludes those who do not meet the criteria for membership. Political rights, however, carry with them corresponding obligations, particularly to people "defined out" of a *Staatsvolk*. In South Africa the European nation, which has limited itself racially and culturally and which exercises territorial control over groups not belonging to the nation so defined, has the obligation to assure these groups equivalent opportunities for political expression. For the black African (Bantu-speaking) nations, this is being accomplished by granting self-government to the various homelands, each of which now has a distinctive citizenship. All blacks, including those in white areas, are entitled to vote in their homelands of origin. Transkei achieved its independence in October 1976, and Bophuthatswana followed in December 1977. Local political representation must still be provided for black Africans living in the townships—be it through local councils and school boards controlled by the homelands, where urban Africans' votes are counted, or through personal autonomy following the Austrian model.

Rigid segregation, which exhibited aspects of enforced stratification, has given way to separate development, a policy intended to afford each black ethnolinguistic nation the opportunity to create its own political, economic, and cultural institutions, while assuring the survival and self-determination of the white South African nation within a residual territory. Separate development is, however, reinforced within the white area by a mass of laws and rules designed to assure social separation and in some cases continued economic stratification. Their persistence is justified with the argument that they are "still necessary to prevent unnecessary friction between the different groups" (Mulder, 1972, p. 61). While some forms of segregation may prevent friction, others—in a day of growing insistence on equality and the dignity of all persons—may have the opposite effect.

The most essential structural aspect of separate development is the assignment of homeland citizenship to all blacks and its corollary, restriction of the franchise in white areas to South Africans classified as Europeans. Blacks who have lived on the fringes of white communities for a generation or more complain that this policy makes them "foreigners in their own country." The loudest protests are heard against the "Pass Laws" or influx control regulations, which make it very difficult for blacks to establish residence in white urban areas. Blacks not so qualified are hired on one-year contracts through labor bureaus in their homelands, to which they must return annually (Schlemmer, 1976, p. 308). Those found to be residing in white areas without permission are jailed or returned to their homelands. Difficulty in "shopping around" for a better job weakens the bargaining power of African workers.

In defense of influx control it may be argued that without it South Africa would experience the explosive and dysfunctional urbanization that characterizes the slums of Lagos, Caracas, and São Paulo or the rooftop shacks of Hong Kong. Even such a democratic country as Switzerland has for years practiced influx control to head off social problems caused by internal migration. Current controversies about Mexicans illegally in the United States and Commonwealth citizens in Britain suggest that no attractive country can do indefinitely without influx control. Curbing uncontrolled migration to cities is thus a social and economic, not a racial issue.

A phase of apartheid that seems unessential to the viability of a plural political system but essential to the psychological (and to a limited extent physical) security of White South Africans is found in the Group Areas Acts, under which cities and towns are divided into racial residential areas. As a rule, blacks and to some extent other nonwhites are settled on less desirable tracts farther from centers of work. The Acts have been employed to dispossess large numbers of Indian traders who catered to white as well as black customers. (Schlemmer, 1976, p. 314) and who certainly never threatened the fabric of white society.

The economic policies associated with apartheid were for the most part designed to shield the white work force from the competition of low-cost black labor. To the extent that they have blocked the upward mobility of black Africans, they have proved detrimental to the achievement of separate development—since the homelands need not only capital, but also skilled workers and managers. Job reservation, under which skilled and higher-paying jobs in a number of industries are reserved for whites (and in some cases for Coloured and Indians), affected somewhat less than 3 percent of South African blacks at its height, but is now being phased out. The situation a decade ago was pictured by a critic in terms of "the two basic South African commandments: Never shall a White man be subordinate to a Black man; and never shall a Black man get a job when a White man is available." (Hellmann, 1972, p. 25). These commandments, however, are rapidly falling into desuetude, especially in the homelands, where white technicians are supervised by black executives. In three universities, white professors serve under black or Coloured rectors.

The Industrial Conciliation Act, which authorizes job reservation, also excludes black Africans from the collective bargaining procedures enjoyed by white unions. Instead, they elect members of liaison committees and works committees, which may "communicate" the "wishes and aspirations" of African workers to management, but are not empowered to negotiate wages and working conditions. While unregistered African unions exist, and even conducted a series of successful strikes in 1973, they have no legal status. (For a discussion of the laws involved, see Schlemmer, 1976, pp. 303–13).

The lesser bargaining power of non-Whites is reflected in pay differentials. Schlemmer

Table 20.1. PAY DIFFERENTIALS BETWEEN RACIAL GROUPS IN SOUTH AFRICA

	White/Asian Diff.		White/Coloured Diff.		White/African Diff.	
	Absolute	Ratio	Absolute	Ratio	Absolute	Ratio
1960/1	R118	3.3·1	R121	3.5·1	R138	5.5·1
1970	R236	3.9·1	R242	4.2·1	R263	5.8·1
1972	R271	3.6·1	R276	3.8·1	R307	5.6·1

(*ibid.*, p. 312) gives the figures shown in table 20.1 for manufacturing. But another cause is probably more fundamental: the surplus of black labor, which leads to low market levels of wages as well as to persistence of labor-intensive methods that have long since disappeared in the United States and Europe. Since 1972, partly in response to moral pressure on employers to raise black wages (e.g. Klipin, 1973), percentage increases for South African blacks have been significantly higher than those for Whites. A bill has been introduced in Parliament granting black workers a statutory right to collective bargaining. More apprenticeship and vocational training opportunities have been opened to blacks, and the School of Business Leadership of the University of South Africa now conducts a 15-month course in small-business management designed specifically for black entrepreneurs and managers. Chairman Harry Oppenheimer of African Explosives and Chemical Industries (AECI), a leader in ameliorative measures for black Africans, recently reported that the company had moved 300 of its 8700 Black workers into skilled jobs formerly held by whites, while a further 1279 blacks were doing semiskilled work, some replacing whites. Between 1972 and 1977, the minimum black wage at AECI rose from R38 to R145 per month, while the average black wage reached R218.

The goal demanded by most urban black leaders and accepted as a target by many private and public employers is that of equal pay for equal work. It follows, however, that increasing wage costs will spur mechanization, so that only part of the potential black labor force can be accommodated within the white South African economy. This is why the "development" aspect of "separate development" is of the utmost urgency.

The legal framework of South African policy includes a number of laws designed to keep the races separated—some reaching far into the sphere of personal affairs. The effect of the Prohibition of Mixed Marriages Act is obvious from its title, but it is complemented by the Immorality Act, which makes sexual intercourse between whites and non-whites a criminal offense. A detailed system of so-called "petty apartheid" laws and regulations was created to enforce separation in hotels, restaurants, theaters, cinemas, trains, buses, and until recently even park benches, telephones, and lifts. As of this writing, however, petty apartheid is being dismantled—though too slowly to satisfy people strongly concerned with equality. An increasing number of hotels and restaurants in white areas are being licensed to serve all races, multiracial audiences are permitted under a permit system, and interracial sports are expanding. Blacks are now able to buy township houses they formerly only could rent, and increased amounts are being budgeted for non-white housing. The outcome of efforts by churches to integrate their schools remains to be seen. Since petty apartheid is irrelevant to the question of a unitary or differentiated political structure, and since the success of separate development depends to a large extent on black acceptance, the need for its early abolition is obvious.

The granting of political expression to the 2 million Coloured and 600,000 Indians in South Africa raises more difficult issues, since these groups lack compact settlement areas where they could exercise territorial autonomy. The Indians, most of whom live in Natal, in or near Durban, present the lesser problem, as they form a cohesive and relatively self-sufficient social body. Furthermore most Indians, though they dislike petty apartheid, feel a strong interest in maintaining the structural status quo. They are particularly anxious not to be governed by black Africans; they have observed from a distance the dispossession of Indians in Kenya and Zambia, and are distrustful of the liberal verbiage that accompanies arguments for territorial majority rule. There are some Indians who identify as "black" and urge unity of the "three black groups" (Africans, Indians, and Coloured) to achieve a racially integrated society, which is somehow—in defiance of political arithmetic—distinguished from black African domination (Meer, 1972, p. 455). More conservative Indians are willing to accept limited political autonomy and even a degree of apartheid as the price of security for their ethnic group (Joosub, 1972, pp. 424, 431).

Relations between the Coloured and the white South African nation present a quite different problem. In the Cape Province, where the majority of Coloured live, those meeting a property qualification were formerly eligible to vote for members of Parliament and for provincial and local councils on a common roll. They were deprived of this franchise through a series of laws sponsored by the National Party and passed between 1951 and 1970 as a phase of explicit self-definition of the South African nation. A Coloured Representative Council (CRC) was created and granted quasi-legislative powers in matters limited to the Coloured population. As of 1976 it had 40 elected members and 20 members appointed by the State President. There is an Executive of five, each member furnishing policy guidance to one of five Directorates of the Administration of Coloured Affairs: Finance and Auxiliary Services, Local Government, Rural Areas and Settlements, Education, and Community Welfare and Pensions. The Administration is headed by a Commissioner subordinate to the Minister of Coloured Affairs, and the extent to which the CRC has supervisory authority over the Directorates is ambiguous. Delegation of authority to the CRC appears to have moved the farthest in the field of education (Swartz, 1972, pp. 385–96; on the constitutional struggle over Coloured disenfranchisement, see Vosloo, 1972, pp. 368–70).

The Coloured in South Africa experience their political status as one of discrimination. They are excluded as a group from the white body politic and denied the franchise they once enjoyed. Creation of alternative political institutions is, however, hampered by two structural facts. Unlike the Bantu-speaking nations, which form coherent cultural-linguistic as well as racial entities, the Coloured are characterized by somatic as well as cultural diversity. They are registered as members of subgroups: Cape Coloured, Malay, Griqua, Chinese, Other Asiatic, and "Other Coloured"—a miscellaneous category with a connotation of nonidentity. Physical types vary from Khoisanid, Negroid, and Mongoloid to others hardly distinguishable from whites (Vosloo, 1972, p. 361). The Coloured share language and culture with the Whites: over 80 percent speak Afrikaans, though anti-National Party resentment has provoked some shift to English. While the experience of common discrimination has generated some feelings of *négritude*, typified by magazines such as *Drum*, the Coloured cling for the most part to their Afrikaner cultural heritage and are not anxious to merge with Black African groups (Small, 1971, pp. 5, 17).

The second structural fact that complicates political accommodation is the absence of a compact Coloured settlement area that could serve as a homeland. While most Coloured live in the Western Cape, that is also a region of dense white settlement. The Coloured are to a large extent integrated into the white economy, where they constitute almost the entire rural and much of the industrial labor force. While some *verkrampte* Nationalists advocate a "Colouredstan," that idea is rejected by all the Coloured parties and even the Government speaks of "parallel development" within a single territory. It is, however, Prime Minister Vorster's contention that the Coloured must be seen as a nation in the making—a "nation in its own right"—a statement confirmed by Tom Swartz of the Coloured People's Federal Party, who perceives an emerging Coloured nationalism (Vosloo, 1972, p. 381; Swartz, 1972, p. 397).

The Prime Minister's 1974 proposals to add Coloured members to statutory bodies such as the Group Areas Board, the Road Safety Council, and the Consumer Council and to create a Coloured "Consultative Cabinet" as well as a Coloured civil service, while continuing to deny Coloured representation in the white Parliament, met with a negative reception. Mr. Sonny Leon, leader of the Labour Party opposition in the CRC, said: "Mr. Vorster has merely confirmed that we will remain second-class citizens in the land of our birth . . ." (*Daily Telegraph*, London, November 11, 1974). The Prime Minister's 1977 proposals under which whites, Coloured, and Indians would each have their own parliaments, with a Council of Cabinets to coordinate common affairs, likewise met with initial rejection from leaders of the latter two groups (*South African Digest*, November 11, 1977, pp. 6, 15, 27–29).

The Coloured demand representation in the South African Parliament; maximalists call for a common roll based on universal adult suffrage. The extent to which this demand is justified is a question, not of morals, but of objective group characteristics and of ideology.

Where it is recognized, the right to equal parliamentary representation rests on two prior assumptions: commitment to an egalitarian as opposed to a class-differentiated political structure and a body politic homogenous enough or balanced enough to reach consensus on public policy. Each sovereign political community, exercising its right of self-definition, decides whom to admit and whom not to admit. And no community not afflicted with national masochism or a self-destructive impulse will knowingly admit a group judged unassimilable or whose inclusion would cause political convulsion. There is no moral imperative that decrees that all persons within a given territory form or must form a single body politic. To the contrary, there are countries where refusal to permit diverse ethnic groups to have autonomous social, cultural, and political institutions has led to oppression, chaos, and even warfare.

Many South African Coloured are largely of European descent; the Coloured intellectual and white-collar classes are for the most part European in manners, culture, and personal goals. It is these educated Coloured, whose assimilation as individuals would present no great problem, who most resent exclusion from white society and politics. But the Coloured category is highly diverse and contains a number of subcultures as well as large peasant and laboring masses, whose political behavior in a parliamentary democracy remains an unknown quantity. It would also be difficult to grant the vote to Coloured while denying it to urban Black Africans so long as the latter have not yet achieved satisfactory channels of political expression within their own systems. Yet there is a limit to the number of non-Europeans the South African nation can absorb into its political structure without losing control of its own destiny.

The Coloured have already figured as a disturbing factor in South African politics. Although their vote was never large, it was strategically placed; in the 1948 election, the last in which Coloured took part, they were influential in 25 constituencies and decisive in seven, more or less (Vosloo, 1972, p. 368). Because of the delicate balance between the Afrikaner and English-speaking segments of the South African nation and, under normal circumstances, between the National Party and the United Party or its successors, an ethnic voting group would not have to be very large to exercise critical leverage. With a very high birth rate, the Coloured today have a population more than half as large as the white nation, and outnumber the whites in the Cape Province. As current opinion among the Coloured demands rapid and radical changes in social and economic policy, it can be assumed that their members of Parliament would tend to function as a racially oriented coalition rather than in separate blocs affiliated with the opposing white parties. Even a partly proportional franchise would thus not only give the Coloured a voice in South African politics but would make their leaders the potential arbiters of South African national policy. White parliamentary politics would then become a competition to see which party could best placate the Coloured politicians—who in their turn would compete to see who could extract the greatest benefits from the whites. The latter might finally tire of competitive appeasement, whereupon the parliamentary scene would shift to one of Coloured–white confrontation. Both phases of this scenario would be disastrous, for the Coloured as well as for white South Africa.

Denial of admission to a body politic to a group that wants entry, in this case the South African Coloured, falls clearly in the category of political discrimination. But it is a less onerous form of discrimination than holding within a unitary political system a group that desires its own autonomous institutions, as happened to the Germans in Czecho-Slovakia between 1918 and 1938 and more recently to the Turkish Cypriots. In South Africa, discrimination is dictated by the imperative of national self-preservation, which forbids the transfer of political power to groups whose assimilation is doubtful. On the underlying philosophical issue, whether the South African nation is right in following its own interest, the American political scientist Hans Morgenthau, whose liberal credentials are beyond question, has this to say:

> The survival of a political unit, such as a nation, in its identity is the irreducible minimum, the necessary element of its interests vis-à-vis other units. Taken in isolation, the determination of its content in a concrete situation is relatively simple; for it encompasses the integrity of the nation's territory, of

its political institutions, and of its culture. . . .

The individual may say for himself: *"Fiat justitia, pereat mundus";* the state has no right to say so in the name of those who are in its care. Both individual and state must judge political action by universal moral principles, such as that of liberty. Yet while the individual has a moral right to sacrifice himself in defense of such a moral principle, the state has no moral right to let its moral disapprobation of the infringement of liberty get in the way of successful political action, itself inspired by the moral principle of national survival. (1952, pp. 973, 985–86)

Morgenthau's judgment is equally valid for the white South African nation and for each nonwhite nation and nationality.

The writings of responsible Coloured leaders suggest that they are more interested in raising the social and economic status of their people than with political power as a goal in itself (e.g. Swartz, 1972; Curry, and Small, 1971; *passim*.). Thus there are options open in the areas of social policy (such as accelerating the removal of petty apartheid, especially in theaters, concerts, and restaurants) and in economics (such as employment and training policies designed to bridge the white–Coloured wage and salary gaps). Such measures could be taken without structural risk, as could the strengthening of the CRC by vesting it with real legislative and budgetary powers in Coloured affairs, including the establishment and supervision of municipal councils (Vosloo, 1972, p. 382).

In Rhodesia, where the future of black–white political relations remains unsettled as of this writing, the 6.11 million blacks (as of 1976) constitute slightly over 95 percent of the population. The 278,000 whites account for about 4.3 percent, while the 30,900 Coloureds and Asians make up the remaining 0.5 percent. Among the blacks, 78.8 percent belong to the Shona language group, which is divided into a number of tribes; the second largest group is the Ndebele, who constitute 15.8 percent of the black population. The territory is divided into black and white areas of approximately equal size. The white area, held by right of conquest, contains much of the best agricultural land and land accessible to railways, all the larger towns and industrial areas, and most important mine workings. The rapidly growing black population cannot sustain itself on its remaining lands, and has thus become largely dependent on the white economy (Murphree and Baker, 1976, pp. 379, 381, and 391).

While the Rhodesian Front is as firmly dedicated to perpetuating White supremacy as is the National Party of South Africa, it lacks a clear political conception. While Rhodesian society is to a limited extent multiracial (there being, for instance, an integrated university and a few black Members of Parliament), the regime offers blacks neither equality nor self-determination.

Before independence, Rhodesian constitutions and laws were racially neutral in theory, stratification being maintained by the blocking of socioeconomic mobility. Voters were required to meet specific educational and financial requirements that were beyond the reach of all but a few blacks. As Murphree and Baker explain:

viewed historically, White society has restricted the development of economic resources and mobilization capabilities of Blacks, in four ways: first, by controlling and limiting the education of Blacks thereby assuring that Blacks have only limited skills for job opportunities and advancement; second, by restricting the types of jobs available to Blacks; third, by establishing wage scales for industries and other sectors, thereby assuring that various sectors do not compete for (and thereby increase the wages of) Black workers; and fourth by restricting the ability of Blacks to organize their own trade unions. . . .

Education played a crucial role. Earlier in the century, the government neglected Black education but did allow missionary groups to establish primary and secondary schools. Both government and White society saw little need for educating Blacks except in a vocational sense. Indeed, they criticized missionary schools that provided an academic rather than a vocational education to Blacks, for they argued that (a) Blacks should be trained for servitude and unskilled positions and (b) an academic education had the potential of turning Blacks into critics and opponents of the White dominance system. . . . (pp. 385–86)

While few blacks rose above the unskilled worker level and few met the financial qualifications for the franchise, white Rhodesians nevertheless feared that blacks might some day achieve a majority in Parliament. After independence was declared in 1965, therefore, a new constitution was adopted providing that the House of Assembly would consist of 50 Europeans and 16 blacks. When the black population pays at least 24 percent of the total income tax (as compared with the 0.5 percent they pay now), black representatives will be added until, at some future point, blacks achieve parity (though never a majority) in Parliament. The constitutional subordination of blacks is reinforced by a number of emergency laws under which the government restricts the convening of political meetings and rallies, has banned a number of black nationalist parties, and has censored publications written from the black nationalist point of view. Writing as early as 1968, former Chief Justice Sir Robert Tredgold declared: "The cumulative effect of the security laws was to turn Rhodesia into a police state . . ." (Ibid., pp. 389–90).

Many features of South African segregation are replicated in Rhodesia. There are separate public school systems; expenditures per pupil are $286.93 for whites and $18.75 for blacks in the primary schools, the corresponding secondary school figures being $493.05 and $185.67. The black secondary system is highly selective and takes in less than 5 percent of the black primary school enrollment. Yet those few blacks who pass the examinations (the same as for whites) find it difficult to obtain jobs: Only 11.6 percent of the blacks who completed secondary school in 1971 were employed in 1972, and many of these were underemployed in terms of their abilities. Very few blacks reach executive ranks in the civil service, and, as of 1976, there was not a single black magistrate or public prosecutor in Rhodesia, although a number of blacks have qualified as lawyers. While there are no national apartheid laws, the Municipal Amendment Act of 1967 empowers municipalities to maintain separate amenities on a racial basis, including parks, sport facilities, comfort stations, and swimming pools. Most bars, restaurants, and hotels are segregated by social convention, since proprietors are allowed though not required to bar customers because of race (ibid., p. 396). There is clearly a need for social as well as constitutional reform in Rhodesia, though it is beyond the scope of this book to prescribe what course it should take. The problem, briefly, is that of providing opportunities for social and economic development and the right of self-government to Rhodesian blacks—and in view of ethnic differences to the Shona and Ndebele as distinct nationalities—while at the same time assuring the survival and security of the white Rhodesian community. One possibility is the "cantonal" solution: Assigning to each of the three major ethnic groups a territorial base within which it would have final control. In any case, no policy is viable which requires a nation or nationality to commit social, economic, or political suicide—whatever their illiberality in the past.

D. How the Territorial Principle Works in Black Africa

Assertion of Coloured and black rights to elect members of a common South African Parliament is based on the ideological premise that all persons within a defined territory form or have the moral obligation to form a single political community: a concept that can be called *territorialism* for short. The idea originated in Western Europe, where vigorous rulers and ministers in France, England, and Spain—as we have seen in chapter 10—forged nations to match the dynastic states they had assembled (Lemberg, 1964, 1, pp. 165–71). Territorialism proved unworkable in Central Europe, which embraced Herder's concept of the ethnic-linguistic *Volk:* a people distinguished by language, culture, tradition, and in some cases racial type, whose area of settlement does not necessarily correspond to political boundaries. The awakening *Völker* of Central Europe demanded political structures to fit them; they refused to change identity to fit existing states. The choice in that region was and remains between multinational federalism and a disjointed cluster of small national states—so small as to invite domination by neighboring great powers. Since political boundaries could not be drawn to match settlement areas, each of the succession states turned out to have a *Staatsvolk* and a series of ethnic minorities. The latter became victims of political as well as cultural and economic discrimination despite the treaties adopted by the League of Nations for their protection (Jaksch, 1967, pp. 251–58).

The ethnic structure of Central and Southern Africa is more like that of Central Europe than that of Western Europe or the United States. African ethnic units have no structural relation to the colonial borders marked out by the European powers. Except for a few small countries such as Lesotho and Swaziland, the newly independent African states that emerged in the 1960s all inherited multiethnic populations. The territorial bias prevalent in Western Europe and even more in the United States, a country where "nationality" means citizenship and not ethnicity, has led administrators and social scientists to see African political development in terms of "nation building" and "detribalization" (Anderson et al., 1974, p. 29). In the African context, this type of modernization means loss of ethnic identity and culture.

South Africa is currently under pressure to grant independence to South West Africa, which the United Nations have christened

"Namibia." Choice of this name was a psychological coup, since most Americans and even some Europeans assume automatically that if there is a territory called Namibia, there must be a Namibian nation. Actually, South West Africa contains twelve distinct groups, of which the largest, the Ovambo with 342,455 members (1970), accounts for 46.2 percent of the population. The next largest groups are the whites (90,658: 12.0 percent), the Damara (64,973: 8.7 percent), the Okavango (49,577: 6.6 percent), and the Herero (49,203: 6.6 percent). The population as a whole lacks the integrators that hold a nation together; the principal independence organization, SWAPO (South West African People's Organization) is mainly an Ovambo group, though it makes efforts to cultivate "Namibian" nationalism.

Should South West Africa be granted independence as a unitary state—which means scrapping the present Odendaal Scheme for autonomous development of its nations—the Ovambo would then be the *Staatsvolk*, and the other black and Coloured groups, as well as the whites, would be at the mercy of whatever discrimination they saw fit to impose.

Since the principle of absolute territorial democracy, without built-in safeguards for ethnic groups, is invoked in demanding the end of white rule in South West Africa, Rhodesia, and South Africa itself, it is desirable to know how that principle works out in practice in the African situation. The *operational*, not the theoretical meaning of an idea is what counts.

1. SOUTH AFRICA'S "NEIGHBOR STATES"—
   BOTSWANA, LESOTHO, AND SWAZILAND

Of the three former High Commission territories: Botswana and Lesotho, independent since 1966, and Swaziland, granted independence in 1968, only Botswana has retained a system in which voters have a free choice among opposing candidates. Sir Seretse Khama's Botswana Democratic Party holds a comfortable majority, but opposition parties have been free to nominate candidates and have always won a few seats in the 32-member Parliament. Sir Seretse has declared that there would be no one-party rule in his lifetime (*The Guardian*, October 19, 1974).

Swaziland, on the other hand, had one-party government from the start, since the party led by King Sobhuza II, the Imbokodvo National Movement (INM), encountered no effective opposition. The King, furthermore, enjoyed the power to appoint half the Senators and one-fifth of the Deputies. In 1974, he set the constitution aside, since when he has ruled as an enlightened autocrat supported by a consensus of traditional chiefs and modern nationalists.

Of the three "BLS countries," Lesotho appears to have moved farthest toward a totalitarian state. Politics in the former Basutoland Protectorate, a mountainous enclave three-quarters the size of Switzerland, has centered around a perennial struggle between Prime Minister Chief Leabua Jonathan's Basuto National Party (BNP) and the Basutoland Congress Party (BCP), the largest of three opposition groups. When the BCP appeared to have gained a parliamentary majority in the election of January 30, 1970, Chief Jonathan set the results aside as falsified by bribery and intimidation. On February 16, the Prime Minister suspended the constitution and assumed emergency powers and in March he sent King Moshoeshoe II, who favored the opposition, into exile.

It has been alleged (typically by Maitland-Jones, 1973) that South Africa is the invisible power sustaining Chief Jonathan in office. But the authors' interviews with Lesothans have brought out the fact that South Africa has followed a policy of strict nonintervention; its citizens seconded to the Lesotho government have performed their technical functions and stayed out of Basuto politics.

King Moshoeshoe was allowed to return in December 1970, and a period of relative stability ensued. In December 1973, however, a group of churchmen and opposition leaders worked out a plan for an all-party national government. Chief Jonathan called this proposal "treason," and a struggle ensued, in which Jonathan's militia, euphemistically called the "Peace Corps," conducted a series of forays in which houses were burned, women raped, and between 50 and 100 opposition supporters killed in cold blood (*Rand Daily Mail*, March 28, 1974).

The government then rammed through parliament an Internal Security Act that makes it an offense for money to change hands "to commit any offence by way of protest against a law, or in support of any campaign against a law, or in support of any campaign for the repeal or modification of any law . . . or administration of any law." People can be arrested without warrant, held 60 days, and then rearrested. No one may visit them without permission of the Minister of Justice and no court may order their release. The new law further prohibits suits against public officials for acts committed under orders "in the interests of the state to discourage internal disorder, or maintain public safety or essential services" (*Rand Daily Mail*, March 7, 1974). Lesotho does not present a case of intertribal discrimination, since the Basuto are its only ethnic group. There is, however, clear and serious political discrimination against those who would compete with the present cabinet for political power. By blocking constitutional procedures, such discrimination forces democratic oppositionists into alliances with revolutionaries.

2. ZAMBIA—RESURGENT TRIBALISM IN PARTY GUISE

The Republic of Zambia, formerly Northern Rhodesia, has won liberal acclaim for its commitment to interracial democracy and for the humanism preached by its President, Kenneth Kaunda (see McKay, 1971). The reality behind this verbal idealism was reported by a

British political scientist who taught in Lusaka, Michael Wright, whose findings one of the present authors summed up in a review of Wright's 1972 book, *Zambia—I Changed My Mind:*

As in quite a few other African states, an ideology of "multi-racialism" is used in Zambia to cover up totalitarian domination by certain tribes which assume hegemony over others. Kaunda's party, the UNIP, is dominated by the Bemba tribes—about half the population of Zambia—who discriminate systematically against the Lozi of Barotseland in the west of the country, as well as several smaller tribes. Minority religious sects, such as the Lumpa and Jehovah's Witnesses, are the victims of downright persecution, including the burning of churches, the beating of entire congregations, and the destruction of crops. . . .

For several years, Kaunda has maintained a permanent "State of Emergency." This enables the president to detain people, seize their property, and amend or suspend any law by administrative fiat. After the 1968 elections, in which the opposition African National Congress increased its parliamentary seats from 1/7 to 1/4, the UNIP started a campaign of outright persecution: ANC civil servants were sacked, and merchants forced to change parties or lose their licenses. Non-Zambian merchants were put out of business altogether, resulting in a total breakdown of retail and then wholesale trade. (Glaser, 1973a, p. 412. UNIP = United National Independence Party)

There are, of course, extenuating factors. Black Zambians were long the victims of white arrogance, which continued several years after independence was achieved in October 1964. In April 1965, 2350 black rail workers went out on strike, because they were still required to carry the tool and lunch boxes of white railmen. Black frustration was also reflected in the 1966 copper strike: the social and economic gap between white and black was narrowing, but too slowly (Metrowich, 1974, pp. 9–10).

What followed was a wave of Black racism that had the effect of depriving whites of the elementary right to personal safety. A number of Europeans, including some who had lived many years in Zambia, were deported for trivial reasons—one because he absent-mindedly doodled red eyes into a newspaper photograph of President Kaunda. From 1965 to the present, whites have been victims of personal attacks, against which the police and courts give them little protection.

Serious riots broke out at Kitwe on the Copperbelt on October 30, 1966, after an explosion at an oil storage depot. There were indications that UNIP officials had organized the rioting; witnesses said they told black police to disobey orders to quell the riot and join in throwing stones at white vehicles. Mrs. Bridget Myburgh was stoned to death in her automobile while trying to protect her two small children from a screaming mob of about 200—three hours after the explosion. Although Vice-President Kamanga denounced the killing as "a blow against the country's policy of non-racialism," the murderers were never brought to trial. Only five of some 5000 rioters were arrested, and there was no public rebuke for the UNIP officials said to have incited the riot (Metrowich, 1974, pp. 14–15).

Loss of personal as well as economic security led to an exodus of whites from Zambia. Nearly 600 miners resigned after the Kitwe riots, leaving the mines with a shortfall of 800 skilled workers. The number of registered white farmers dropped from 1100 to 600 by August 1966, and has continued to decline. Altogether, the white population of Zambia fell from its pre-independence peak of 75,000 to 43,390 in 1969. The loss of white technicians faster than blacks could be trained to replace them is reflected in an almost static per capita GNP, while farm production was retrograde until 1971 (AID, 1972, pp. 17, 19).

The reduction of whites in Zambia to second-class political and civil status (though they continue to earn more, relative to blacks, than do whites in South Africa) is by no means the only form of political discrimination that exists in Zambia. President Kaunda's oratory about humanism and interracial society hid from the outside world for several years a fact obvious to those within the country: that Zambia's black population is rent by rampant tribalism. As early as September 9, 1966, the Johannesburg *Star* commented on the *Herrenvolk* complex prevalent among the Bemba. The UNIP Central Committee elections of August 1967, were fought along tribal lines, and the result upset the tribal and provincial balance Kaunda had constructed. The Bemba strengthened their position; their political leader, Simon Kapwepwe, became Vice-President at the expense of the Ngoni Reuben Kamanga, and two prominent Lozi ministers, Munukayumbwa Sipalo and Arthur Wina, were demoted to lesser posts. President Kaunda was so disgusted at the "spate of hate, based on tribe, province, race, colour, and religion" that he resigned—but, like his colleague Nasser of Egypt, was persuaded to return to office. Tribal enmity, which soon gave rise to noticeable secessionist movements (*Star*, February 8, 1968), finally permeated the entire civil service (*The Times*, London, May 10, 1971). Fights between Bemba and Lozi on the Copperbelt took place every weekend (*Star*, September 11, 1968).

In the December 1968, general election, three Cabinet Ministers and three Junior Ministers running on the UNIP ticket in Barotse Province were defeated because Lozi tribesmen refused to vote for that party—even for Lozi candidates. At this point President Kaunda forgot his commitment to rise above tribal differences and launched a campaign of intimidation against the Lozi. Claiming that the Ministers had been defeated through machinations, he declared he would "reorganize" Barotse Province and assure their reelection. On the Copperbelt, the intimidation took the form of attacks by UNIP gangs against Lozi miners (Metrowich, 1974, pp. 28–29).

Bemba leaders then resorted to the tactic of claiming that *their* tribe was being persecuted. Mr. Justin Chimba, a Bemba politician and Minister of Trade and Industry, alleged that Bemba were suffering constant persecution while members of minority tribes were coddled and not charged with offenses that brought dismissals, suspensions, and court trials for Bemba (*Zambia Mail*, January 25, 1971). His charges were echoed by ex-Minister John Chisata, and a judicial commission was appointed to look into the matter. Kaunda later used tribal dissension as a pretext for introducing a one-party state (Metrowich, 1974, pp. 29–30).

Tribal discrimination in Zambia has been reinforced by political party discrimination. Long before Zambia officially became a one-party state, the UNIP Youth Brigade set up blockades, preventing shoppers, bus passengers, and strollers from going about their business unless they could produce UNIP membership cards (*ibid.*, p. 31, reporting 1968 and 1969 episodes). On January 13, 1969, the *Times of Zambia* warned the people of the Choma district that their new governor, Jonathan Ntambo, planned to give police and civil servants three weeks to join the UNIP or quit. Mr. Ntambo told the newspaper he would "cut off the roots of [the African National] Congress" by evicting its members from their houses, denying them loans, and retarding development of their areas. "If they want houses, let Harry Nkumbula build them, if they want loans, let him provide them. They will not get one ngwee of Government money out of me." Merchants in the Lusaka area were told that only UNIP supporters would be granted trading licenses, while the Minister for the Western Province, H. D. Banda, told mines and other industries they could expect "severe action" if they failed to limit employment to UNIP loyalists (*Times of Zambia*, January 12 and 13, 1969). These measures followed the line laid down by President Kaunda, who in an angry speech after the 1968 election shouted to the Minister of Commerce and Industry: "If you renew these men's licenses you will be sacked yourself!" He was referring to businessmen elected to Parliament on the African National Congress (ANC) slate. Opposition civil servants, the President said, would be sacked: It would really be made to pay to belong to UNIP throughout the country. This speech, reported Christmas Eve, was followed by a Christmas Day message denouncing South Africa for discrimination.

The full force of political discrimination was felt by Kaunda's boyhood friend Simon Kapwepwe, who resigned from the UNIP in August 1971, and became leader of the largely Bemba-based United Progressive Party (UPP). UNIP immediately launched a terror campaign to block mass support for the UPP; houses were stoned and Molotov cocktails thrown. In September 1971, the Kaunda government arrested about 100 opposition politicians, comprising almost the entire UPP leadership—but not Kapwepwe himself. On January 12, 1972, Kapwepwe was attacked by youths in broad daylight, and three days later there were reports of petrol bomb attacks on UNIP offices, which were assumed to be UPP reprisals. Kapwepwe, who had won the Mufulira West seat in December 1971, was banned and detained and his UPP outlawed on February 3, 1972. That December, Kaunda proclaimed Zambia a one-party state—a principle embodied in the new constitution adopted August 24, 1973. Harry Nkumbula, the former leader of the ANC, had in the meantime accepted Kaunda's shrewd invitation to join the UNIP and take a top government post, while Kapwepwe—who had been released with 34 other UPP members in December 1972—announced his "temporary" retirement from politics. (Metrowich, 1974, pp. 33–34; Hitchcock, 1973).

3. TRIBALISM AND ONE-PARTY RULE IN EAST AFRICA

The principle of one-party government is likewise embedded in the Tanzanian constitution. Like Zambia, Tanzania has its political prisoners (*The Times*, London, December 9, 1974), and the local organization of President Julius Nyerere's Tanganyika African National Union (TANU) seems even more pervasive than that of UNIP in Zambia. TANU has its own flag, which flies over the TANU local office in every village. Like his colleague Dr. Kaunda, Dr. Nyerere is an ideologue— but with a difference. Kaunda's theoretical humanism and his political practice are worlds apart, whereas Nyerere's African Socialism is operationally specific and somewhat Spartan in its demands on the political activist.

TANU enjoys a political monopoly but individuals within it do not. After TANU had won 70 of 71 contested seats in 1960, Dr. Nyerere, who considers a one-party system compatible with democracy, felt the need to restore choice as an element of popular control. As recommended by a commission that reported in March 1965, TANU was established as the sole party, but nomination of parliamentary candidates was decentralized to constituency branches, each of which forwarded two names for endorsement by the central executive. Two junior ministers and six incumbent MP's failed to be renominated and two ministers and four junior ministers were defeated in the ensuing election (Hutchison, 1974). The pattern was repeated in the 1970 election, in which party endorsement was decentralized to district level, and in which three ministers and a number of MP's were defeated.

In the meantime, the Arusha Declaration of February 1967, drawn up by Nyerere himself, had provided a program for creating a socialist society. Banks, insurance, and some import-export houses were nationalized, and key manufacturing concerns placed under government control (Maitland-Jones, 1973, p. 50). More importantly, the Arusha Declaration provided a code intended to prevent the exploitation of political power for private gain. After a general salary cut in the higher levels, "leaders"— meaning all government or party officials who still earned more than £30 (about $75) a month—could not receive more than one salary, could not be a director of a company, or even own shares in a company. Such a political "vow of poverty" constitutes clear political discrimination against the business class, since all people with business interests are automatically excluded from political office.

Political processes in Tanzania include appreciable competition and even policy debate *within* TANU, whose central committee does not always accede to Dr. Nyerere's wishes (*ibid.*). But political freedom is limited to supporters of the Arusha Declaration and TANU; advocates of a radical shift in national policy—such as economic laissez-faire—become targets not only of discrimination but of direct oppression. A number of persons are held without trial under the Preventive Detention Act, including two brothers of former minister Oscar Kambona, who have (as of 1974) been held since 1967, except for a few months of freedom in 1972 (A.I. Report, 1974). Six MP's who disagreed with the leadership about carrying out the Arusha Declaration were expelled from TANU and thus automatically from Parliament in October 1968. Ms. Bibi Titi Mohamed, who had organized the women's section of TANU and had played a major role in building the party's mass base, was convicted of "treason" and only released from prison quite recently.

Conditions on the island of Zanzibar, over which the central government has little control, are somewhat worse. The overthrow of the Sultan's government in January 1964, which paved the way for unification with Tanganyika, was accompanied by many political arrests. A total of 545, including three former cabinet ministers, were held without trial ten years and finally released in a January 1974 amnesty. Three more Zanzibari ministers held since 1964 were among those released in mainland amnesties of December 1973 and May 1974. The trial of 81 persons accused of plotting the April 1972, fatal shooting of Zanzibari President Sheikh Abeid Karume proceeded amid charges of torture during pretrial investigations and without defense counsel;

President Nyerere refused to extradite 18 defendants held in mainland prisons for lack of guarantees they would have a fair trial (A.I. Report, 1974).

Dr. Nyerere's national policy and his use of the Swahili language in the attempt to forge a unified nation were discussed in Chapter 18, A3. His economic policy is evaluated in Chapter 21,D3.

In neighboring Kenya, one-party politics cloak a sometimes precarious balance among the major tribes. The four largest are the Kikuyu (1,642,065), the Luo (1,148,335), the Luhya (1,086,409), and the Kamba (993,219), within a total population of 8,636,263 (1967).

Kenyan nationalism was initially Kikuyu nationalism: the Mau Mau were bound by a Kikuyu tribal oath. The Kenya African Union headed by Jomo Kenyatta was mainly Kikuyu but contained a sizable Luo element. In 1960, the nationalist movement split into two parties: the Kenya African National Union (KANU) and the Kenya African Democratic Union (KADU). The first was dominated by the Kikuyu and Luo leadership, while the second was in essence a coalition of smaller tribes.

Reflecting the fears of the smaller tribes, KADU demanded a quasi-federal regional structure as the price of agreeing to proceed with independence in 1963. A year after Uhuru, however, the KANU government emasculated the regional assemblies by recentralizing most of their powers in the national government—a move that provoked little protest (Gertzel, 1969).

In the meanwhile KADU, after a brief alliance with the Kamba-based African People's Party, merged with KANU in November, 1964. The following month Kenya became a republic; Prime Minister Kenyatta became President and head of an executive cabinet, while former KADU leader Odinga became Vice President. Kenyatta had already indicated his preference for a one-party state and his rejection of the Westminster model of government-opposition dialogue (*Daily Nation,*

Nairobi, August 14, 1964). Mr. Odinga, for the time being, seconded his views. But factionalism soon became rampant, and in 1966 Odinga and 28 other MP's who also left KANU founded the Kenya People's Union (KPU) as an opposition party. The Kenyatta-controlled Parliament promptly passed an act requiring any member who crosses the floor voluntarily (though not if expelled by his party) to resign his seat and stand for reelection. In the ensuing "little general election," KANU won 21 House seats to KPU's seven, and eight Senate seats to KPU's two. KANU's power was further enhanced when the two houses voted in December 1966 to merge into a single National Assembly (Maitland-Jones, 1973, pp. 54f.; Gertzel et al., 1969, pp. 116–20, 142–58).

The 1966 "little general election" was followed by charges of intimidation of KPU supporters at the grass roots. A KPU member stated in Parliament that his party's chairman in North Ugenya had been called in by the District Officer and told he would be arrested if he did not switch to KANU. Cash rewards, on the other hand, would be paid for accusations against other KPU politicians. Similar threats of arrest were also reported from other districts. Merchants belonging to KPU were threatened with recall of their loans if they did not mend their political ways, while farm women who supported the KPU were told they would lose their plots. The government's reply was that it had not instructed administrative officers to engage in such repression (not that the repression did not exist!). (*Kenya Hansard*, September 28, 1966, cols. 158–68).

In June 1966, the KANU-controlled Parliament passed the Preservation of Public Security Act, authorizing preventive detention without trial. The regulations issued under the Act provided (Part III, 6, [1]):

If the Minister is satisfied that it is necessary for the preservation of public security to exercise control, beyond that afforded by a restriction order, over any person, he may order that that person shall be detained.

Any person so detained was to be "deemed to be in lawful custody"—a provision with the obvious effect of suspending the right of *habeas corpus* (Kenya PSR, 1966, Parts III and IV). Discussion in Parliament brought out the fact that parliamentary immunity was no protection against preventive detention. The government was not even obliged to tell the House why a member was being detained, since a statement of reasons would be, *ipso facto*, a breach of security (*Kenya Hansard*, November 21, 1967, cols. 2175–76). A number of trade union leaders and high officials of the KPU, including the General Secretary of that party, were detained under the Preservation of Public Security Act; several of them were still in custody in 1968. In September of that year, 20 KPU members in the National Assembly crossed the floor to join KANU, and by December the KPU had shrunk below the minimum of seven MP's required for recognition as a political party. In October 1969, several months after the mysterious slaying of Tom Mboya, the KPU was banned altogether and its leaders detained. With the restoration of KANU's *de facto* political monopoly, tribal and interest-group disputes assumed the form of intraparty maneuvering. Considerable competition developed in the KANU nominating conventions for the 1970 National Assembly elections. About half the sitting MP's, including five ministers and 14 junior ministers, were defeated by delegates representing the party rank and file (KANU Constitution, excerpted in Gertzel et al., pp. 215–17; Maitland-Jones, 1973, pp. 54f.).

Favoritism in the civil service was aired in a 1966 debate; three-quarters of the District Commissioners were Kikuyus, and they tended to import other Kikuyus into the home districts of smaller tribes. The Kikuyu were also the preferred tribe in the central ministries—except where the Minister happened to be a Luo. In that case, the entire staff down to the office boy was Luo, and business was conducted in the Luo language (*Kenya Hansard*, October 14, 1966, cols. 870–900). President

Kenyatta has not found it feasible to abolish tribalism in the central administration, but he has attempted to distribute patronage equitably among the various tribes (Breytenbach, 1974, p. 8).

To sum up: Tanzania and Kenya are both scenes of political discrimination despite theoretical commitment to democracy. Its bases are tribal membership in Kenya and compliance with a one-party system in both countries.

The situation in Uganda, the northernmost of the East African countries, has already been mentioned in chapter 19. Opponents of the current (1976) dictator, General Idi Amin, are shot out of hand or hacked to pieces (*The Observer*, London, December 22, 1974).

The central structural fact of Uganda politics is that of perennial struggle for power between the largest tribe, the Baganda, and shifting coalitions of smaller tribes. Led by their Kabaka, or king, the Baganda had originally sought separate independence for their kingdom of Buganda. They were persuaded, however, to remain within a federal Uganda, which became independent in 1962 with a central government of limited powers and four self-administering kingdoms: Buganda, Ankole, Toro, and Bunyoro. The government was a coalition of the Uganda People's Congress (UPC), led by the Lango tribesman Dr. Milton Obote, and the Kabaka's following, the Kabaka Yekka (KY). Uganda became a republic in October, 1963, with the Kabaka as President and Dr. Obote as Prime Minister (Maitland-Jones, 1973, 24, 52–53).

Conflict, however, was not long in appearing. In August 1964, Obote broke with the KY and the UPC governed alone. Later that year, tribesmen in border territory voted to leave Buganda and join Bunyoro. The Kabaka, as President of Uganda, refused to sign the Act of Parliament making the change, whereupon Obote signed it himself. Dissension then flared within the UPC. In February 1966, Parliament voted lack of confidence in Obote, who promptly dismissed five ministers he suspected of plotting against him, suspended the constitution, and assumed dictatorial powers. Obote framed a new constitution, but in May 1966, the Buganda diet rejected it and voted to secede from Uganda. Obote declared an emergency and forced the Kabaka to flee by bombarding his palace. A year later, Obote abolished all four kingdoms in favor of a unitary state. (Maitland-Jones, 1973, pp. 52–53.)

From his exile in Tanzania, Dr. Obote has protested against the slaughter under General Amin in tones suggestive of a civil libertarian (e.g. *Cape Times*, May 28, 1973). It should not be forgotten, however, that for several years he governed with the aid of the army and police, during which time the Baganda found themselves victims of political discrimination, since Obote's power rested on a Lango-Acholi military coalition (Breytenbach, 1974, p. 7). After the Kabaka's death in London in November 1969, which many Baganda suspected was murder, an attempt was made to assassinate Obote. The latter reacted by banning opposition parties, throwing political rivals (including MP's) into jail, and moving toward a one-party state.

General Amin, who found himself facing charges of misappropriating £2.5 million of army funds and of complicity in the murder of a high-ranking fellow-officer, acted "to save his own skin" by overthrowing Obote while the latter was attending the January 1971 Commonwealth Conference at Singapore. Amin's power base is a coalition of Lugbara, Mahdi, and his own Kakwa tribe, while the formerly ruling Lango and Acholi are now targets of oppression. Ben Otim, elected leader of the Lango, was shot and Simayo Oryem of the Acholi slain with an axe; both were dismembered. Although the Baganda were initially pleased by Amin's takeover and his appointment of some of their members to high positions (Rubin and Weinstein, 1974, p. 25), they are in no way immune from sudden death. Francis Walugembe, a leading Baganda Catholic, had his penis slashed off and was then murdered. An element of religious discrimination seems to have entered the picture, since Amin and most of his supporters are Muslims. The assassination squads that roam the country in search of victims under Amin's personal supervision consist entirely of Muslim Nubians imported from Sudan (Martin, 1974a).

Although Amin has appointed himself Chancellor of Makerere University, he is illiterate and hates education and intellectuals. Trained civil servants are sacked on flimsy pretexts to make room for uneducated people with whom Amin can talk, and university teachers are sent packing for no discernible reason. On one occasion Amin summoned his two personal physicians to give him a medical checkup, only to find he had expelled them two weeks before. A former minister reported he knew of a list of 2000 intellectuals, businessmen, church leaders and other prominent people marked for elimination. When this minister and two others fled for their lives early in 1973, Amin sent the whole cabinet on two months "vacation"—later extended to nine months (Martin, 1974a). On March 6, 1974, ex-Foreign Secretary Michael Ondoga was suddenly seized on the street by five men and bundled into a car; his badly mutilated body was found in the Nile a few days later. Amin is said to have been jealous of Ondoga's close friendship with Princess Elizabeth Bagaya, actress, lawyer, and model, whom Amin had appointed Foreign Secretary in Ondoga's place.* Amin's wife Kay, a Lugbara whose family was close to the Ondogas, intervened to save the former Secretary's life; when she learned he had been killed she left the General—who divorced her as well as his other two wives. On August 11, 1974, she went for treatment to the clinic of her family doctor Mbalu-Mukasa. The

doctor and his entire family were forced to take poison; he and two children died as a result. Kay's body was found in the trunk of the doctor's car, neatly dismembered and packed in a box. (Colin Legum in *The Observer*, November 3, 1974.)

While Dr. Obote's estimate of 80,000 killed under Amin may be high, there is no doubt that he has slain enough to make himself thousands of enemies. There was a troop revolt against him in Kampala in November 1974: it was crushed, but further anti-Amin violence seems a safe prediction. The Baganda, among whom separatism is still rife, remain a destabilizing element (Breytenbach, 1974, p. 8). With the Uganda treasury at such an ebb that soldiers' pay has become irregular, the possibility of overturn or even civil war is increasing.

4. TYRANNY IN FORMER FRENCH AND SPANISH COLONIES

The state of political freedom is not very different in several former French and Spanish possessions. In the Central African Empire, for instance, Marshal Jean Bedel Bokassa has reigned supreme for nine years; political opposition has been suppressed to the point where Bokassa felt it safe to promote himself from President to Emperor. The monarch has centralized power in his own hands to such a degree that when he travels abroad, the whole apparatus of government stops dead in its tracks. Businessmen and diplomats cannot obtain even the most trivial decisions from ministers or civil servants, who dare only to rubber-stamp the Emperor's acts. Bokassa must, to be sure, be given credit for a vigorous anti-crime policy; thieves are publicly tortured and the penalties for receiving stolen goods are first offense, left ear cut off; second offense, right ear; third offense, right hand amputated; fourth offense, public hanging (Jacobson, 1974a).

In the state of Mali, President Moussa Traore had a number of people arrested when he overthrew the last civilian government on

* Uganda political life is not without its bizarre aspects. Foreign Secretary Bagaya was sacked on November 28, 1974, on the charge (which she denied) of making love in a men's lavatory at the Paris airport. Having expelled 14 British diplomats in November, Amin telegraphed Queen Elizabeth in January 1975, announcing a state visit to give advice to British "liberation movements" and asking Her Majesty to assure "a steady and reliable supply of essential commodities."

November 19, 1968. More than 30 of them have been detained without charge or trial ever since, many at Kidal in the Sahara, where temperatures vary greatly from day to night. Groups of six occupy poorly ventilated cells measuring 2 by 3 meters (6½ x 10 feet), with only straw mats for sleeping. Several have died for lack of medical attention. Other groups have been arrested since 1968 and are still held as of this writing, including a number of intellectuals detained in June 1974, after they had circulated a pamphlet hostile to the ruling *Comité Militaire de Libération Nationale*. Ironically, that was the month in which 99 percent of the voters were counted in favor of a new constitution rededicating Mali to the Universal Declaration of Human Rights (*A.I. Newsletter*, December 1974).

Refugees from Equatorial Guinea, a small country (12,000 square miles; 290,000 population) that became independent from Spain in October 1968, have estimated that some 300 people were executed by order of President Francisco Macias Nguema during the five years ending in 1974. An African businessman named Elias told his story to Philip Jacobson (*Sunday Times*, London, December 29, 1974). Elias was hauled to the presidential palace and told he had been fined £7000. No reason was given; he had 24 hours to raise the money. Having a number of businesses, Elias produced the money, but was nevertheless jailed for two years, during which he was tortured regularly and witnessed the murder of friends, relatives, and business associates almost every week. As a so-called "political," Elias was brought to the ill-reputed jail at Bata, where his initiation consisted of having to stand 24 hours in filthy water and mud up to his neck. Twice a week two soldiers stood on his neck and feet while a third beat him with a bundle of sticks until they had broken them against his body. Some important "politicals" had their tendons cut to prevent escape; others were forced to fight each other with clubs to amuse the guards. In two months, Elias counted 69

prisoners who were hauled out of the cells to be killed, including a former governor of the Central Bank and a former governor of Rio Muni. Most of the victims belonged to the same tribe as Macias: the mainland Fangs. They included teachers, civil servants, and businessmen—almost the entire educated sector of the tribe. Elias was finally released and banned to his village; warned of impending rearrest and execution, he escaped to Cameroun.

Although Macias is turning for aid to China, Cuba, and the USSR, his executions have nothing to do with consolidating a political base for socialism. Macias has a paranoid fear of being overthrown—an event that would most likely culminate in his demise—and is determined to eliminate any possible competitors.

E. Political Discrimination Under Communist Rule

Communists within free societies take full advantage of freedom of speech and uphold John Stuart Mill's dictum that it is absolute (*On Liberty*, Mill, 1859, p. 111) rather than conditional on reciprocal assurance of free speech to others. Lenin instructed communists to seek election to "bourgeois" parliaments, not to join in rational debate about national interests, but to "blow them up from within" (Lenin, 1920, Part VIII). Carrying Leninism to its logical conclusion, Stalin preached a doctrine of deliberate political discrimination by the proletariat (in practice by its "vanguard," the Communist Party) against the bourgeoisie. He wrote in his *Foundations of Leninism:*

To put it briefly: the dictatorship of the proletariat is the domination of the proletariat over the bourgeoisie, untrammeled by law and based on violence and enjoying the sympathy and support of the toiling and exploited masses. (Stalin, 1924, Part IV [2]).

Although the entrepreneurial bourgeoisie has virtually disappeared in the USSR, Stalinism continues. Political dissidents of whatever ilk are given the treatment Lenin and Stalin prescribed for the bourgeoisie—though not necessarily in maximum dosage. Political prisoners are said to account for some 30 percent of the Russian labor force and are particularly concentrated in heavy industry (Shifrin, 1973).

The details of political discrimination as practiced in the USSR, mainland China, and the smaller communist states fall mainly in the categories of forced labor and brainwashing and are considered in chapters 24 and 26. Suffice it to say here that Stalin's successors have achieved a sophistication in the management of fear unknown in the days of the Great Purge. They have learned the principle of economy, which teaches that political power—including power based on terror—is expendable and can best be conserved by employing the minimum sanction that will achieve desired results. Because of continuous international scrutiny of the state of civil liberties in the USSR, aided by an efficient underground intelligence network which the secret police have been unable to suppress, executions or even disappearances may be counterproductive. A political dissident may often be effectively neutralized by cutting off his telephone and passing the word around that he is neither to be employed nor admitted as a degree candidate. The latter is a highly effective sanction in a society where the government is the only employer and the only educator. Such "disconnection" is what has happened to quite a number of Jews in the USSR who applied for exit visas to Israel.

For more intractable cases, the Kremlin disposes of a variety of intermediate measures, ranging up to the full *Gulag* treatment—including the notorious "general assignment" work in Arctic mines and forests (Solzhenitsyn, 1974, pp. 564, 604), which is usually fatal because of the lack of protective clothing and equipment. An informant told ex-Senator James Buckley

(Republican) of New York during his November 1974, visit in Moscow:

> Instead of the extermination camps of the Stalin years, there now exist camps dedicated to what might be called "protracted death," i.e. death on the installment plan, in little pieces of psychological pressure, of inhuman discipline and inhuman conditions, with the thread of life barely kept from snapping. (Buckley, 1975)

Concluding Observations

If a generalization may be drawn from the facts recited in this chapter, it is that political discrimination is virtually universal. It appears in liberal-constitutional, authoritarian, and totalitarian systems, and its impact varies from simple frustration to outright extermination. In the most favorable case, political discrimination results from structural problems. Single-member-district elections, for instance, may cause underrepresentation of salient minorities. Or a *Staatsvolk* may find it impossible to grant a large minority equal political expression within a unitary political system without jeopardizing its own political viability as it has defined itself. In the worst cases, discrimination stems from outright hostility and the compulsive need to deny other nations, nationality groups, or competitors for public office the right to political expression or even existence.

Territorial democracy, in the sense of a unitary political system embracing the whole population of a given territory, is no universal cure for political discrimination. To the contrary, it permits a numerical majority or plurality or an elite controlling the machinery of government to impose its political style, its values, and sometimes even its culture and language on those without access to the levers of political power. Yet the essential integrators of the *Staatsvolk* may be differentiators that exclude significant population groups within its territory. In that case, two structural solutions come to mind. In the first, the minority may be granted individual political rights within a unitary state, combined with group cultural rights assuring them their language and their autonomous schools and cultural facilities. This is the arrangement enjoyed by the 11 percent Swedish minority in Finland, whose situation is sometimes cited as a model for intergroup relations (Jaksch, p. 254). But it is not feasible where the minority is large and where survival of the *Staatsvolk* is linked to preservation of its specific ethnic character. Israel, for instance, could not absorb all the Palestine Arabs into a unitary state without ceasing to exist as Israel—which, incidentally, is what many Arabs want. In this second case, the only workable arrangement is political separation, usually but not necessarily accompanied by territorial separation. The only way in which two or more mutually nonassimilable groups can enjoy political expression without denial of group rights to self-definition is through the creation of parallel political institutions with consultative arrangements to deal with matters of common concern.

21

ECONOMIC DISCRIMINATION

Because political discussions of economic matters are notorious for their inexact usage of language, this chapter must begin by pointing out what is *not* economic discrimination. *Economic inequality, no matter how gross, does not constitute economic discrimination in itself.* It may, however, be wholly or partly *the result of such discrimination.*

The free market, were it left to operate spontaneously and without state interference—a theoretical construct since all governments do interfere with the market in varying degrees—would produce a degree of economic inequality, since some skills are rarer and more valued than others. A concert pianist who pleases the public will always earn more than a dustman, though one out of favor—because of unappreciated style or because he hits too many wrong notes—may earn considerably less. But a free market in labor as well as goods and land has a certain tendency toward equalization, since every economically rational person tends to maximize his or her advantage.

In a free market, everyone is free to sell his or her goods or services, so long as these are not prohibited by criminal statutes (e.g. hard drugs, dangerous toys, killing for hire, and in some jurisdictions prostitution or liquor), and to have these evaluated and bought on their merits. Buyers are likewise free to choose what they want to buy (within the same legal and moral limitations) and to buy them from the supplier who offers what they think the best combination of quality and price. The principle of the free market forbids government-operated or government-sponsored monopolies, as well as discriminatory taxes or subsidies that favor one business or type of business as against another. Government transport policies are economically discriminatory insofar as they regulate rates and subsidize certain forms of transport at public expense.

The free market is hampered by government interference. That interference may take the form of limiting access to a business, trade, or profession for reasons unrelated to technical competence or public safety; it may come in the guise of discriminatory taxation or credit policies; it may manifest itself in production quotas, subsidies, and price fixing. It is, for instance, compatible with the free market to require physicians and barbers to attend the appropriate schools and pass examinations, but it is not compatible to limit the number of medical practices or barber shops, or to regulate their fees. Government interference may reflect institutionalized racial, political, or religious discrimination. Examples of the first kind are British colonial laws that discouraged bank loans to Africans and present-day East African laws that force Asian merchants out of business (Tandon, 1973, pp. 10, 16–17), as well as South African laws reserving certain jobs for whites (a policy currently being phased out) and prohibiting racially mixed trade unions. Similar distortions of the free market, however, are caused by discrimination motivated by prejudices rooted in society—even prejudices condemned by official policy.

Insofar as people of different races, ethnic groups, and religions and of both sexes belong to the same body politic and pay the same taxes, they should all have equal access to public employment according to ability. Since public money is involved, governments can likewise insist that their contractors follow the same rule. In purely private transactions, however, the concept of the free market implies the right to make decisions for noneconomic as well as economic reasons: a person who is prejudiced has a right, *in administering his own property*, to discriminate according to his prejudice. The case of the publicly held corporation is marginal: there is no basis for assuming that the stockholders share management's prejudices unless they have so voted.

This leads up to a point made by Lord Lindsay of Birker (in *The Modern Democratic State*): that in a liberal political system the state does not attempt to legislate a complete code of morality. The effects of laws requiring universal love are described in Huxley's *Brave New World*. Most people would agree that discrimination in employment is morally wrong, but is passing a law the best way to overcome this wrong?

In short, there are cases where government interference in the market is justified for compelling reasons, including those of social justice. Such interference should be undertaken knowingly and sparingly, without disguising infringements of liberty and property with such euphemistic phrases as "new freedom," "new deal," or "great society," and in full awareness of the dangers involved in such policies.

A. Economic Inequality and Economic Discrimination

1. INEQUALITY RELATED TO OCCUPATIONAL STATUS

A major economic gap exists between those actively involved in economic life and those excluded from it, including people involuntarily retired for age, chronically ill and disabled persons, and the unemployed. In an age that glorifies youth, it is difficult for older people to obtain jobs, unless they have special skills not available in younger generations. In some countries, particularly in Europe, the pension system and other fringe benefits actually provide a disincentive for employers to hire older workers. While this is less true in the United States, there is nevertheless a differential related to age, as the following facts show:

1. In the 1960s, families with a head over 65 had a poverty rate 2.5 times that of the total population.
2. The percentage of the poor over 65 years of age has been increasing, not only because this group is growing faster than the total population, but also because fewer aged remain in the labor market. In 1890, 68.3 percent of men over 65 were in the labor market; only 27.6 were there in 1963.
3. People with the smallest incomes are least likely to continue working after 65. The Social Security Administration found that 69 percent of male professional and technical personnel continue working after 65, but only 57 percent of the male managers, officials, and proprietors, and less than 45 percent of craftsmen and service workers.
4. Leaving the labor market condemns most people over 65 to poverty. Figures released by the U.S. Department of Commerce showed that in 1973 those of age 65 and over had a median family income of only $6426, as compared with a median family income of $12,051 for all families in the United States (*U.S. News and World Report*, February 10, 1975, p. 49).

A causal analysis of poverty in the United

States cannot be undertaken here. The magnitude of the problem, however, is suggested by Michael Parenti in these terms:

Almost 80 million Americans live in the conditions of need on incomes that have been estimated as below minimum adequacy by the Department of Labor. Of these about half are designated as living in acute poverty and want. Of the 40 million who are very poor, only 5.4 million get either food stamps or free food. Of 6 million school children from rock-bottom poverty families, most attended substandard, overcrowded schools and fewer than 2 million receive either free or reduced-price school lunches. The majority of the poor are Whites, a fact which is not surprising in a country with a White population of more than 85 percent. Yet the non-White racial minorities are represented in disproportionate numbers. If Black people compose only about 12 percent of the population, they make up something closer to 45 percent of those below the officially designated poverty level (Parenti, 1974, pp. 10–11)

Parenti adds that American statistics tend to underestimate the number of poor and of blacks in particular. While many people described as "poor" in the United States would be considered fairly well-off in Third World nations, it is unfortunately true, as Parenti indicates, that extreme poverty resulting in hunger and infant mortality exists in certain places in America. As late as 1973, a Senate select committee reported that some 12 million Americans do not get enough to eat—despite the food-stamp program (*ibid.*, p. 11).

2. INCOME INEQUALITY IN BRITAIN

Unequal distribution of income in Britain was registered as early as 1688, when "temporal lords" had average yearly incomes of £3200, "freeholders of the better sort" earned an average of £91, while "vagrants, gipsies, thieves and prostitutes" were credited with only £2 a year" (Atkinson, 1975, p. 62). Income inequality has persisted, though it has decreased in recent years. In 1949 the 5 percent of Britons with the highest incomes received 23.8 percent of total personal income; by 1967 this percentage had declined to 18.4. The share received by the next 5 percent remained constant at 9.6 percent. While the top 40 percent showed a slight relative loss (from 68.1 to 66.9 percent), the share received by the poorest 30 percent declined from 12.7 percent in 1949 to 10.4 percent in 1967 (R. J. Nicholson, "The Distribution of Personal Income," cited, Atkinson, 1975). Inequality is not limited to wages and salaries but extends to conditions of employment and fringe benefits. A recent comparison of average earnings in Britain is given in table 21.1.

The profile of poverty in Great Britain is suggested by the following paragraphs from an article by John Downing:

the poor therefore are far more in number than just the elderly, the black, the disabled, and other minorities. They consist of something like the bottom nine-tenths of British society, who between them all, own only 17 per cent of the total personal wealth in Britain (the top tenth enjoys the other 83 per cent). By world standards, to label almost anyone in Britain "poor" is of course grotesque; but in terms of ending world poverty, the recognition of British poverty is very significant. For until the British poor overcome the inequalities internal to Britain, it is extremely doubtful that they will be able to recast their actions against international poverty.
. . . Should anyone be in any doubt that black people in Britain are overwhelmingly concentrated at the poorest end of the society, the data from the 1961 Census, the 1966 Sample Census and no doubt the 1971 Census reveal the tiny proportions in white-collar work, and the vast majority that is in semiskilled and unskilled work. This means low wages; and the very high proportion of women at work, especially in the Caribbean community, not only points to the low earnings of their men, but also involves them in being grossly underpaid simply as women workers. Furthermore, the general unemployment is hitting black workers extremely hard, most especially black school-leavers. (1973, pp. 23, 25)

Table 21.1. DISTRIBUTION OF EARNINGS BY INDUSTRY AND OCCUPATION,
APRIL 1970 (full-time men paid for a full week)

Selected Occupations	Median Earnings £ per Week	As Percentage of the Median			
		Lowest Decile	Lower Quartile	Upper Quartile	Highest Decile
Manufacturing industry					
Manual	28	69	83	120	142
Nonmanual	32	65	80	127	170
All industries and services					
Unskilled worker	22	69	82	123	149
Semiskilled worker	26	69	82	121	144
Skilled worker	27	71	83	121	145
Foreman or supervisor	31	72	85	118	137
Clerk—routine or junior	19	76	86	120	144
Clerk—intermediate	23	75	86	117	138
Technician—laboratory	26	67	80	128	156
Draftsman	31	74	87	116	131
Engineer—mechanical	37	61	78	125	154
Accountant	40	48	73	130	163
Works, production, manager	40	67	80	126	156
Marketing, advertising, sales manager	49	62	80	127	161

SOURCE: Department of Employment, "New Earnings Survey," 1970 (HMSO, 1971).

3. OCCUPATIONAL AND SOCIO-ECONOMIC INEQUALITY: AMERICAN BLACKS AND HARIJANS

Verba, et al. (1971) have established an interesting parallel between blacks in the United States and Harijans in India. In each country, occupations were divided into six strata according to income and prestige; 31 percent of American blacks and 53 percent of Harijans fell in the lowest stratum, which includes farm workers, unskilled labor, street vendors, sweepers, charpeople, etc. Only 7 percent of American whites and 13 percent of caste Hindus are employed in these low-status occupations. In the highest category of occupations, on the other hand, the percentage of dominant-group members is seven or eight times as high as that of the deprived group. Occupationally, therefore, American blacks suffer the same severe deprivation as the Untouchables of India.

In another phase of the analysis, Verba, Ahmed, and Bhatt compared the overall socioeconomic levels of blacks and Harijans in their respective societies. The index was a composite of education, income, occupation, and possessions; the range was in each case divided into six strata. It was found that only 13 percent of American whites but 48 percent of American blacks were in the bottom sixth; the comparable figures for caste Hindus and Harijans were 10 and 39. Conversely, only 2 percent of the blacks and Harijans, 18 percent of American whites, and 21 percent of caste Hindus enjoy socioeconomic status in the top sixth.

In absolute standard of living, blacks in America are better off than black people in any other country, and far better off than the Harijans, many of whom live on the verge of starvation. Relatively, however, American blacks are worse off since 48 percent are in the lowest sixth of their society, compared with only 39 percent of the Harijans.

4. EFFECTS OF ECONOMIC DISLOCATION

When an economic system fails to operate as theory claims it should, political and administrative leaders always manage to save their skins. The United States Congress, for instance, has had the effrontery to vote itself repeated salary increases in the face of rampant inflation and massive unemployment. Those who suffer are always the marginal people: those whose economic functions and rewards have been made insecure by structural factors.

One group of marginal people consists of displaced industrial workers and their families. In the United States, whites from Appalachia and rural areas and blacks as well as whites from the Deep South have for many decades been lured to northern industrial cities by prospects of employment: in times of economic expansion most in fact find jobs. But American factories, like those of many other countries, work on a rigid seniority system. When forces are cut, the last-hired are the first laid off. A depression also involves the lopping off of the least viable enterprises; it is the first stage in a process of reallocating resources, a later phase of which is the expansion of new enterprises. The workers, however, find themselves without jobs during the hiatus. When new businesses start, they may be located elsewhere or demand skills the redundant workers do not have.

To ease the hardships of economic change, most developed countries provide unemployment insurance, which provides emergency income for a limited time. In the case of low-paid workers, however, a problem of incentives arises. Since unemployment benefits are usually tax-free and the worker who stays home saves effort and expense, such workers may be inclined to "ask for the sack." It was brought out recently in the House of Commons that a married British man earning £55 a week would have more take-home pay for up to 14 weeks should he lose his job (*Daily Telegraph*, June 16, 1975). In most cases, however, loss of a job causes severe distress to workers and their families, especially after unemployment benefits run out. Prolonged joblessness in the United States has revived a depression phenomenon of the 1930s: mass migration in search of work, "unfolding countless stories of hardship and creating new problems for the public and private agencies that must deal with these wandering, often penniless families" (*U.S. News and World Report*, March 24, 1975, pp. 16–20).

The new migrants are not headed in any one direction. "They are pulling up stakes in areas hardest hit by unemployment and moving in desperation toward any area where rumor or instinct suggests that jobs might be found. . . . Involved are middle-income people as well as the poor, young and old, whole families and individuals, Blacks and Whites" (*ibid.*). Indicators of the volume of distress migration include a vast increase in the number of one-way trailer rentals, often with the destination left open, a growth in the case load of Travelers Aid offices, and a surge of unpaid bills referred to collection agencies when debtors have left town. Officials concerned with the mass movement of people are quoted by *U.S. News and World Report*) as follows:

Gerald Cornez, Director of Development for Travelers Aid—International Social Service of America, whose 80 offices handled about 1.3 million pleas for assistance last year:

"Basically what we're seeing is a surge in middle-class families who are unemployed and panicky. It's reminiscent of the movements back in the 1930's."
An official of the U.S. Bureau of the Census:

"The basis for staying put when you lose your job is the assumption that things will get better. But when people feel there is no hope, they start wandering."
The President of a Chicago-based bill-collection company with 160 offices throughout the United States:

"It has become a national problem. We've seen a definite increase in the number of middle-income 'skips.' I think it's because these people are the hardest hit. They don't use food stamps, don't have school-tuition subsidies and aren't welfare-oriented.

"There are a lot of people in their 40s today who are packing up and taking their families somewhere else, not necessarily intending never to pay their bills, but to buy a little time until they can find work." (*Ibid.*).

Middle-class migrants usually have serviceable vehicles (whether paid for or not), whereas migrants who were marginal in the first place move in "battered jalopies and decrepit trucks jammed with children and furniture. Often, old cars break down—and migrant families, without cash for repairs, throw themselves upon the mercy of relief agencies, wherever the breakdown occurs." While some migrants find jobs, others do not. In Odessa, Texas, a typical Mecca for job seekers because of an oil boom, the local employment office reports that almost all jobs still unfilled require skills the newcomers lack.

The foreign workers in Western Europe are economically marginal. As Amelunxen points out (1975a, pp. 119–21), those in Germany occupy the lowest paid and most disagreeable jobs on the occupational ladder, enabling Germans to rise to more skilled occupations and better paid positions. "Guest workers constitute the mobile shock absorber in the labour market, to be moved around as needed in times of boom and depression." Whenever industrial employment declines, recruitment in countries that send guest workers is stopped and expiring contracts are not renewed, often creating a hardship for Turks, North Africans, and Southern Europeans who have no job prospects at home. Amelunxen describes the economic role of *Gastarbeiter* in the Federal Republic in these terms:

In practice, guest workers perform the most menial and dirtiest tasks. They drag tar spreaders, carry pig iron, clean toilets, and cart away the garbage of affluence. The public service departments of most West German municipalities would collapse were the guest workers to disappear overnight. These people are classified in wage groups—for the women there are special "light wage groups"—for

which German workers can no longer be recruited. At least in the first year of their employment they are paid only what the wage standard calls for, while their German colleagues receive benefits over and above the standard. Aliens receive child allowances, but no separation allowances incident to split households.

Guest workers, who in the best case occupy places on the assembly lines of mass production, especially in automobile manufacture, suffer two and one-half times as many accidents on the job as their German colleagues. This is not only attributable to lack of knowledge of accident-prevention rules, but also to the higher objective danger of their particular jobs. Preventive health measures called for under the Federal Social Aid Law are not available to guest workers. (*Ibid.*, pp. 119–20)

Migrant workers in France likewise find themselves at wage levels considerably below those of French workers. This is particularly true of Turks, who are hampered by language problems, and of Africans, who are quite ready to accept wages that seem lavish by *African* standards, only to find themselves on the lowest level of purchasing power on the French market. The discrepancy between French workers is apparent from the statistics in table 21.2. Foreign workers in France hardly ever achieve promotion to executive ranks, and a considerable number never even have any contact with executive personnel (*ibid.*, pp. 66–67).

Table 21.2 DISTRIBUTION AMONG WAGE GROUPS OF FRENCH AND FOREIGN WORKERS IN RENAULT AUTOMOBILE PLANTS

Wage Groups	Percentage of Workers in Wage Groups	
	French (%)	Foreign (%)
1200 francs or less	43	74.5
1201 to 1500 francs per month	43	23.5
1501 francs or more per month	11.5	2

SOURCE: Valabrègue, 1973, p. 66.

The worst economic discrimination, however, is suffered by the rather large number of foreign workers illegally in France. Since they can be deported at a moment's notice, the employers can violate minimum wage laws and other social legislation with impunity—the workers dare not complain. Nor are they eligible for unemployment benefits, sick pay, or family allowances (N'Goumou and Power, 1974). The most unconscionable exploitation involves Africans, who are recruited by employment agencies in their home countries, brought illegally to France, and then farmed out to industrial firms. N'Goumou and Power found victims of this system at a number of construction sites in France, where the men were housed in huts and served mediocre food, denied association with women and the right to join trade unions, and forced to sleep "in huts on folding beds smaller than themselves and with no room to stand up." In some cases the employment agencies were charging the companies an estimated 1800 francs (about $360) per month, paying the men 760 francs, and pocketing the difference. The industrial accident rate for Africans is far higher than for French workers; the Commissariat au Plan has estimated it at 19.8 percent annually. The typical housing arrangement is a converted loft, often without windows, where the Africans sleep in double- or triple-decker beds, with less than two feet of aisle space and with only seven toilets to serve 541 inmates. Yet despite these hardships, immigration continues, since conditions are that much worse in tropical Africa. According to Papa Kane, a Soniké and Director of the École Supérieure d'Économie Appliqué at Dakar, a French embargo on African immigrants would cause economic collapse in the former French colonies (*ibid.*).

B. Discrimination Against Workers Through Labor-Market Distortion

Economic discrimination takes place whenever people are forced into economic behavior they would not exhibit under free-market conditions. A worker suffers discrimination when an employer who might otherwise have hired him or her is coerced into not doing so. This happens when wages are set above the market level at which all willing workers will be employed, either by union contract or by a minimum-wage law, when the marginal productivity of the worker—the incremental product the employer will gain from hiring her or him—is less than the employment cost (wages plus fringe benefits plus incremental overhead).

1. DISCRIMINATION THROUGH TRADE-UNION COERCION

An economically rational worker will accept the highest wage he can obtain, unless, of course, unemployment benefits or welfare are higher than that wage. Otherwise, a worker will normally not insist on an above-market wage unless he has some reasonable expectation of gaining it. That can only happen when the supply of available workers is reduced, either by excluding some workers from the labor market or by coercing the employer into accepting higher employment costs. In the latter case the employer will hire fewer workers, since with a given amount of capital the marginal productivity of each worker tends to be less than that of the worker hired before. A worker not barred from employment by coercion in one form or another will accept a job at the market wage, which is the wage at which all willing workers in a particular category will be employed. The market wage levels of similar jobs are interdependent insofar as the workers can shift from one job category to another.

While each particular worker would like to receive an above-market wage, the interest of workers as a whole demands that wages, which are simply the prices of various kinds of labor, be free to reach equilibrium at a market level. Classical economics holds that wages will move naturally toward the highest level that will support full employment (Kuhlman and Skinner, 1959, pp. 288–89). Even John Maynard Keynes, the father of interventionism, admitted that excessive real wages were the normal cause of extensive unemployment. But because he thought that lowering money wages was politically unfeasible—which is probably true so long as British and American trade unions exert their present political power—he proposed to lower real wages by lowering the value of money (Hayek, 1960, p. 280). This aspect of Keynesianism is kept under the carpet by its political practitioners.

For their members to reap the benefits of cost-push inflation in the form of above-market wages, unions must manage to keep "surplus" workers from employment in the trades concerned. This cannot be done without cercion. Friedrich Hayek describes in some detail how this coercion operates.

It cannot be stressed enough that the coercion which unions have been permitted to exercise contrary to all principles of freedom under the law is primarily the coercion of fellow workers. Whatever true coercive power unions may be able to wield over employers is a consequence of this primary power of coercing other workers; the coercion of employers would lose most of its objectionable character if unions were deprived of this power to exact unwilling support. . . .

It is true that any union effectively controlling all potential workers of a firm or industry can exercise almost unlimited pressure on the employer, and that, particularly where a great amount of capital has been invested in specialized equipment, such a union can practically expropriate the owner and command nearly the whole return of his enterprise. The decisive point, however, is that this will never be in the interest of all workers—except in the unlikely case where the total gain from such action is equally shared among them, irrespective of whether they are employed or not—and that, therefore, the union can achieve this only by coercing some workers against their interest to support such a concerted move.

The reason for this is that workers can raise real wages above the level that would prevail on a free market only by limiting the supply, that is, by withholding part of labor. The interest of those who will get employment at the higher wage will therefore always be opposed to the interest of those who, in consequence, will find employment only in the less highly paid jobs or who will not be employed at all.

The fact that unions will ordinarily first make the employer agree to a certain wage and then see to it that nobody will be employed for less makes little difference. Wage fixing is quite as effective a means as any other of keeping out those who could be employed only at a lower wage. The essential point is that the employer will agree to the wage only when he knows that the union has the power to keep out others. As a general rule, wage fixing (whether by unions or by authority) will make wages higher than they would otherwise be only if they are also higher than the wage at which all willing workers can be employed. (1960, pp. 269–70)

As Hayek further points out, unions cannot in the long run increase the real wages of all workers, though a powerful union can *increase the money wages of its own members at the expense of other people's real incomes.* When a number of unions do this, the result is mass unemployment. Dedicated to neo-Keynesian theories that automatically absolve trade unions of any responsibility for unemployment, the government then proceeds to "create purchasing power" through deficit spending. The resulting price increases discriminate most cruelly against those who lack coercive power to force increases in their money incomes: the aged, the poor, and minorities generally.

As Hayek indicates, the power of a union to bargain for above-market wages depends on its ability to exclude people from its particular sector of the labor force. A number of exclusionary devices are used. One of them is a high initiation fee, often beyond the reach of an unemployed person. Another is to require members to serve an apprenticeship while at the same time limiting rigidly and unreasonably the number of apprentices that may be hired. A related practice is that of persuading employers to reserve jobs for members' children—which introduces a phase of the caste system into Western countries.

2. TRADE UNION DISCRIMINATION AGAINST BLACKS

The easiest people to exclude from employment are those against whom social prejudice exists—unless public policy is invoked to protect them. Although the top leadership of the AFL-CIO, the principal American trade-union federation, has long been *verbally* opposed to discrimination, the U.S. Commission on Civil rights stated in its 1961 *Report on Employment:*

that the "efforts of the AFL-CIO have proved to be largely ineffective" in curbing discrimination and that the impact of union discrimination, especially in skilled craft occupations, was a basic factor in contributing to the concentration of Negroes in menial, unskilled jobs in industry, their virtual exclusion from construction and machinist crafts and accounted for the extreme vulnerability of Negro labor to long-term unemployment both of a cyclical and structural nature. The report urged passage of federal legislation for prohibiting discrimination by unions and stressed the inability of the AFL-CIO to take action on its own initiative against the broad pattern of union racist practices. (Summarized, Hill, 1965, p. 466)

Writing in 1965, Herbert Hill claimed that the earlier sensitivity of the CIO industrial unions to the problems of black wage earners "has now all but totally vanished."

Dr. Kenneth Clark wrote in the 1964 report of HARYOU (Harlem Youth Opportunities Unlimited):

The status of Negroes in the power councils of organized labor in New York City is most tenuous, if not nonexistent. The persistent pattern of racial discrimination in various unions, including some which still enjoy the reputation of being liberal, reflects the essential powerlessness of Negroes to af-

fect the conditions of their livelihood. HARYOU's difficulty in finding a suitable representative of labor for its Board of Directors highlighted the fact that there is no Negro who occupies a primary power position in organized labor in New York City. . . . Even in those unions where the bulk of all of the workers are Negroes and Puerto Ricans, the top overt or covert leadership is almost always white. There is evidence that under these circumstances the union leaders are not always above entering into sweetheart contracts, or other types of conspiracies with the bosses, to the disadvantage of the Negro and Puerto Rican workers. (*ibid.*, pp. 466–67)

A union accused of racial discrimination against Blacks is the International Ladies Garment Workers Union (ILGWU), whose leadership is given to liberal posturing. That union has two Italian locals which control some of the highest paying jobs in the women's wear industry. Despite a 1946 ruling by the New York State Commission Against Discrimination, not a single black or Spanish-speaking person held membership in either local in 1961. On April 4 of that year Ernest Holmes, a black worker, filed a complaint with the successor agency, the New York State Commission for Human Rights, alleging that he was denied promotion in the garment trade because of his race. As Hill reports:

The ILGWU was accused of discriminatory practices involving Negro workers. Later investigations revealed that nonwhites in the New York garment industry were concentrated in the lowest-paid job classifications with very little job mobility, because, with some few exceptions, they were denied admission into the union's skilled craft locals, that the virtually all-Negro and Puerto Rican "push boys" unit known as 60A is in practice a "jim crow" auxiliary, and that not a single Negro was an International Union officer, or on the 23-man executive board, or permitted to serve in any significant leadership position. (*Ibid.*, p. 467)

As the ILGWU refused for eight months to provide the Commission with data requested, the Commission issued a finding of "probable cause" on September 16, 1962. Eight months after that, the union finally agreed "to admit Mr. Holmes into the Cutter's [union] Local . . . to assist him in seeking employment, and to arrange for additional training as an apprentice cutter" (*ibid.*).

Under the Johnson and Nixon Administrations, steps were taken to correct the bias against blacks implicit in restrictive trade-union policies. In some cases, employers and unions were required to submit selection criteria and job-related tests for court approval, to add workers on an alternating black–white basis, or to achieve fixed ratios of non-whites to whites. Special attention was paid to enabling blacks and other minority workers to qualify as journeymen in skilled trades. Unions were ordered to admit them to apprenticeship classes and on-the-job training; in a number of cities federally aided apprenticeship courses were opened with union cooperation. (Equal Employment Opportunity Commission 7th Annual Report, p. 52.) It has been charged, however, that in many cases union instructors deliberately made the courses difficult, requiring arithmetic and writing skills blacks are not likely to acquire in ghetto schools and which are not actually needed on the job. Many training programs showed excessive dropout rates, with relatively few blacks attaining journeyman status and full union membership.

The *Monthly Labor Review* of May, 1972, "documents the exclusion of minorities from membership in local unions representing workers in the higher skilled trades" (*ibid.*, p. 31). In the trucking industry, the EEOC found that white men still had a near-monopoly of the better-paid assignments, especially over-the-road jobs. Because of seniority rules, which enjoy almost sacred status in trade-union thinking, minorities and women are particularly hard hit by any recession in employment. Between 1970 and 1971, 77 percent of the net decline of 600,000 employed represented minorities (mainly blacks) and women (*ibid.*, p. 27). The United States Bureau of the Census (1974) has reported that,

beginning in 1970, black incomes have slipped to a lower percentage of those received by white Americans. *Focus* (August, 1975, p. 6). summarizing the Census Bureau's study, cites two main causes: the recession and a greater number of families headed by women who cannot take regular jobs.

Young black couples with both husband and wife employed, who received 82 percent of the income of similar white families in 1970, advanced to 88 percent in 1973. But for American black families as a whole, the situation is retrograde. While their median income rose from 51 percent of equivalent white income in 1959 to 61 percent in 1970, it dropped back to 58 percent in 1973. Coincident with this slippage, the percentage of black families headed by women grew from 31 in 1970 to 35 in 1974. While the median income of black families with both spouses working was $12,982, black families headed by women realized a median income of only $4465—below the 1974 poverty live of $5038 for a family of four. Of the 974,000 Black female family heads, only 10 percent held full-time jobs (as of 1973), while 62 percent did not work outside the home at all. The Census Bureau mentioned the lack of adequate low-cost day care facilities as a factor hampering black women's ability to seek gainful employment.

As of the first quarter of 1975, the overall unemployment rate for black Americans was 13.7 percent, compared to 7.6 percent for whites (*Focus*, 1975, p. 6).

In a recent study, William J. Wilson (1976) has shown that urban blacks in America remain victims of structural problems that block their upward mobility. One of these is the recent dispersion of manufacturing and wholesaling from central cities to the suburbs. As the high cost of land, rising tax rates, traffic congestion, and mounting crime rates increased the operating costs of city industries, many firms began to rely more heavily on trucks and automobiles and therefore to locate in outlying areas near expressways and housing developments. Employment growth was concentrated in the suburbs; in the twelve largest metropolitan areas, the central city's share of manufacturing employment dropped from 66.1 percent in 1947 to less than 40 percent in 1970 (*ibid.*, p. 191). Black working-class and lower-class people, however, were for the most part left in the central cities. As of 1971, almost half of all blacks in metropolitan areas of 250,000 or more lived in poverty areas, in contrast to 10 percent of whites (*ibid.*, p. 186). Another problem is the existence of what is in substance a dual labor market consisting of a primary sector in which whites enjoy de facto preference and a secondary market in which blacks and other minorities predominate. As Wilson explains:

> Jobs in the primary labour market are distinguished by stable employment, high wages, good working conditions, advancement opportunities, and due process and equity in the administration of work rules. On the other hand, jobs in the secondary sector tend to be dead-end and to have high labour turnover, low wages, inadequate fringe benefits and capricious and arbitrary supervision. (p. 185)

Wilson cites research showing that blacks do not experience employment barriers in low-paid menial and casual jobs of the secondary labor market, but rather in the better, higher paying jobs in manufacturing, construction, and finance. While Affirmative Action has resulted in actual preference for blacks in government employment, the industries with the highest black employment are "dominated by a white elite labour force, who through effective unionization have solidified their hold on the higher paying and respectable blue-collar jobs in the primary sector." The unions have achieved "a protective private welfare state, financed by management," which makes it more economical for employers to pay their regular work force overtime than to hire additional employees. In addition to the structural factors

discussed by Wilson, mention may be made of the minimum wage law, the practical effect of which is to deny employment to increasing numbers of young people, black youth in particular.

3. "FEATHERBEDDING" AND ANALOGOUS PRACTICES

Another type of economic discrimination is the forcing or persuading of people into economic behavior they would not exhibit as a matter of free and informed choice, such as buying goods or services they do not need. The U.S. Federal Trade Commission (FTC) is currently looking into the practice of some funeral directors who tell persons arranging cremations that state laws require purchase of a casket—which is cremated along with the deceased—when such is actually not the case.

In the labor market, coercion to force the purchase of services having negative net utility takes the form of "featherbedding": requiring employers to hire workers they do not need. While this practice is normally associated with union contracts, it may be enforced as a matter of public policy, as in laws of certain American states requiring "full crews" on freight trains. A similar law in Venezuela, enacted to reduce unemployment, requires all public buildings to hire washroom attendants and lift operators—even where the lifts are automatic. "Elevator attendants in Caracas eat candy and ice cream and read comic books, while passengers push their own buttons. The head of a firm that owns one such building says that the attendants have to be paid even if they don't show up for work" (*U.S. News and World Report*, March 24, 1975, p. 49).

A practice analogous to featherbedding is the setting of production quotas enforced by union rules or customary practice. Local bricklayers' unions, for instance, frequently limit the number of bricks a member may lay in an eight-hour shift. Frederick Taylor, the pioneer of modern management engineering, served a stint as a bricklayer and incurred the undying wrath of his colleagues by prepositioning his materials and laying twice as many bricks per hour with no additional effort. The same effect is seen when rigid craft-union rules (e.g. that a carpenter or plumber may not touch electrical wiring) reduce efficiency on construction projects involving a number of crafts. Labor practices of this kind are intended to increase employment, but actually have the reverse effect, since they price the products—typically housing—above the ability of mass consumers to pay for them.

C. Economic Inequality in "Colonial" Context

1. SOUTH AFRICA AND HONG KONG

South Africa is sometimes charged with practicing "internal colonialism" toward its non-white subjects. It is uncritically assumed that wage discrepancies, which far exceed the skilled–unskilled differentials found in Europe or America, are the result of deliberate discrimination. Yet the fact remains that wages, like other prices, are always responsive to (free or distorted) market conditions. This point will be illustrated with reference to the South African Coloured: a group mainly of mixed European and Khoisanid (Bushman and Hottentot) descent, but containing other subgroups.

As it is government policy to remove black Africans from the Western Cape, the Coloured supply most of the unskilled farm and industrial labor in that region. While their upward mobility is steadily improving, per capita Coloured income was about one-fourth of white income in 1970. This discrepancy is only partly the result of salary differentials—such as those in the public sector where Coloured teachers, doctors, nurses, and clerks receive between 50 and 60 percent of the salary paid whites in identical jobs. The main reason lies in the fact that Coloured occupy lower-status positions: the 1960 census showed farm work

(29.45 percent) and unskilled labor (24.97 percent) as the two major occupations for Coloured males (Vosloo, 1972, pp. 371–72).

Deputy leader David M. Curry of the Coloured) Labour Party complains that the difference between wages paid to skilled and unskilled workers in South Africa is 400 percent, whereas in most overseas countries it is roughly 13 percent. In both these cases, however, wage differentials are not the result of deliberate discrimination or nondiscrimination but are determined by market conditions. Within any class of labor, they reflect the marginal productivity of the last worker employed. In South Africa, the salient fact is the coexistence of a modern industrial economy and preindustrial societies whose main export is the labor of superabundant manpower, which can only be fully used in labor-intensive (and therefore technologically inefficient) processes. While South African industry *could* employ unskilled Coloured and Africans at wages more nearly approximating European and American differentials, it could only do so at the cost of mechanizing and automating the majority of jobs out of existence. Labor-intensive processes in both industry and agriculture would have to give way to capital-intensive production methods. Those fortunate enough to avoid dismissal would enjoy a rapid increase in their standard of living, but the remainder of the labor force would probably remain unemployed for several decades until the capital plant could grow enough to provide jobs for them.

After an uproar about South African wages in the United Kingdom in 1973, various newspapers in the Republic retaliated by pointing to conditions in Hong Kong, one of the few remaining Crown Colonies—and likely to remain so, as this "anteroom" to mainland China is useful in several ways to the Peking government. Manufacturing in Hong Kong is concentrated in some 20,000 tiny factories employing intermediate technology. Martin Wollacott describes one of them:

The Lee Mon Metalworks, so grandly titled, consists in fact of a room no bigger than the average British sitting room in a tenement building in Kowloon. Into it are crammed seven machines, six workers, an overhead sleeping platform, a desk, and a television.

Bundles of brass and steel rods obstruct the entrance, and drying shirts and women's blouses flap in your face as you go in. Wong, a cheeky-faced boy who looks and might possibly be younger than his claim to 14 years, works eight hours a day, six days a week and gets 10 dollars (about $1.95) a day. (*Pretoria News*, November 1, 1973)

Crowded and unhealthy conditions and the employment of children—legally and illegally—have provoked charges that Hong Kong is a vast sweatshop.

British firms lag behind the American and Japanese in direct investment in Hong Kong, yet the British are responsible for governing it and have the power to intervene in the colony's economic affairs. Whether they could enforce a minimum-wage law without causing massive unemployment is, however, another question.

Of Hong Kong's 1.2 million full-time workers, over 600,000 (54 percent) are employed in manufacturing—the highest proportion in Asia. About one-fifth of Hong Kong workers are in firms with less than 20 employees. It has been estimated that the average family earned 500 Hong Kong dollars ($98 U.S.) per month in 1973. The government admitted that 15 percent of the people took in less than $9 HK ($1.74 U.S.) per day, and that only one-fifth of these received very meager social assistance. While families with several members working could afford color televisions and even cars, the illness of one would throw the entire family into crisis.

Although Hong Kong workers are the best paid in Asia, except in Japan, hours and working conditions are chaotic. Firms are not required to keep records of "mandatory" days off; therefore, while government surveys report work days of seven and a half to nine hours, critics such as Neil Carr of the University of Hong Kong claim that many are working days of 11 or 12 hours. Legally, children may begin factory work at 14, but there is evidence that thousands of younger children are employed, especially in home-work industries. While the Labor Department prosecutes some 200 or 300 child-labor cases a year, a source quoted by Wollacott comments: "Ironically those who are most against such industrial regulation are the poor themselves. As long as they receive meagre wages . . . they will want to work as many hours as possible and also send their children into the factories."

While wages of Chinese workers in Hong Kong are far lower than those paid in Europe, they are not starvation wages; real wages are reportedly rising 7 percent a year. Hong Kong is already out of the cheap labor market. As an American manager commented: "Hong Kong's remaining advantages are an educated and technically qualified labour force and a technological lead time over other Asian countries of maybe two years."

2. TAMIL TEA WORKERS IN SRI LANKA

The fact that independence is a nonsolution of social problems is illustrated by the plight of the Tamil tea workers who were brought from the Indian mainland to Ceylon by British companies in colonial days. The Hindu Tamils are now experiencing political as well as economic discrimination at the hands of the Buddhist Sinhalese majority in independent Sri Lanka. With wages too low to buy food for their families in a time of inflation, the Tamils on the tea estates have, for two years or so, been dying at a rate of at least 1000 people per month. By July 1974, their death rate had reached 22 per thousand—a figure comparable to famine areas like Bihar or Uttar Pradesh. Weights of children varied from 20 to 50 percent below the averages for Tamil children on the mainland (Michael Gillard in *The Guardian*, April 8, 1975). A large number were found to be victims of severe malnutrition.

Tea workers in Sri Lanka are generally paid

the government-approved minimum wage, which is 32p (78¢) for men and 24p (58¢) for women for an eight-hour day. This adds up to a maximum of £15 ($36) per month for a two-parent family. But a deduction is made from this sum for government-issued rice and flour, which only provides enough calories to meet the minimum need of a working adult for two or three days each week. According to a study by the Sri Lanka Medical Research Institute, adjusted for price increases through the autumn of 1974, it takes £26 a month to buy the basic minimum healthy diet for a family of five—the average on the tea estates. A Central Bank of Ceylon survey in 1973 estimated that 50 percent of tea workers earned less than £6 a month, compared with over £8 for farm hands and £14 for industrial workers. The average individual earnings were £6.90, compared with £14.50 for all workers in Sri Lanka. The British firm of Brooke Bond was, in 1973, paying its lowest-paid African factory workers six times the minimum wage on its Ceylon tea estates. The Sri Lanka government, today the largest tea grower, pays no more than its British competitors and has resisted proposals to raise the minimum wage. The situation is much the same in Tamil Nadu on the Indian mainland and even worse in Assam, where a man and wife take in 37p (89¢) per day or a *maximum* of £9.60 ($23.04) per month (*ibid.*). While there are many countries where cash incomes are lower, they are usually supplemented by home production, the possibilities for which on the Sri Lanka and Indian tea estates are minimal.

Paul Harrison, writing for the (London) Times News Service (*Pretoria News*, May 30, 1975), describes the tea estate as a "total institution," like a jail or mental hospital, where people are born, grow up, work, marry, and die. He describes conditions there:

Ninety percent of the estate workers live in rows of cells, usually about 3m by 4m. known as lines; 46 percent live in suffocating back-to-back lines, with no windows at all in the cramped inner room. Half of the hovels have only one room.

The worst hovels I saw . . . were at Walahanduwa, a collective estate taken over by the land reform from a Ceylonese: On one line about 100 people lived back-to-back in just 16 rooms, 3 m x 2.5 m which also had to house the smoky kitchen fires too.

Most families I met ate practically no protein, and were spending their entire income on food (though 60 percent even of the average Ceylon family's expenditures goes on food.)

On one estate a worker showed me what his wife and three young children had for their meals: In the morning a small piece of unleavened bread for each person, in the evening plain rice with, on special occasions, a vegetable curry.

In Kandy general hospital I saw a girl of 13 dying of advanced protein calorie malnutrition. She had had no solid food for three weeks, and had only a few days to live. Her father was dead and her mother crippled.

Deaths are most frequently caused by anemia, chest diseases (since laborers do not quit when it rains), and intestinal infections—all aggravated by malnutrition.

The political climate in Sri Lanka is hardly conducive to foreign investment. The Marxist parties in the Bandaranaike government spoke openly of "objective conditions for revolution" (*Daily Telegraph*, November 27, 1974) and even the leaders of the conservative United National Party, which defeated Mrs. Bandaranaike's Freedom Party in the July 1977 election, tried to outbid the United Front by promising to "smash capitalism" (*The Times*, July 25, 1975). Manufacturing jobs dropped from 124,000 in 1972 to 97,000 in 1974, the unemployment index is 19 percent, and the balance of payments has remained consistently in the red. Violence marked the aftermath of the 1977 election (see *To The Point International*, August 8, 1977, p. 13).

3. ECONOMIC DEPRIVATION IN INDIA

The anticapitalist bias of the government of India produces results that are not very different, since they discourage business development. They can be seen, typically, in the city of Madras. B. Kuppuswamy (1961) observed that 306 slums contained 20 percent of the city's population. A slum, as defined by the city council, lacks drinking water, sanitary facilities, and street lighting, and consists mainly of thatched huts. Even in the heart of the city, where the houses were built of masonry, living conditions were hardly better. As Kuppuswamy writes: "The per capita floor space was less than that in the slum and there was one lavatory for 12 to 15 persons. The household equipment of the people living in the slums consisted of mud pots, tins, bottles, and old mats. . . . Thirty-five per cent of the slum-dwellers earned below Rs. 50 and only 16 per cent above Rs. 100."

Conditions in Lucknow were even worse. As Kuppuswamy describes them:

Out of 516 localities in Lucknow, only two-thirds had water taps in their houses, and the remaining one-third were served by the public water taps. Only 41 per cent of the localities had electricity and 30 per cent of them were using kerosene public lamps. Out of 41,000 houses, less than 50 percent were pucca (masonry) and nearly 20 percent were in dilapidated condition. The survey found that 2.27 families were living in one house on the average. . . . Nearly one-third of the migrants were illiterate. . . . The bulk of the migrants came because of economic reasons—mostly unemployment and meagre income. Most of them go to their native places once a year (81 percent), but only 13 percent desire to go back and settle down in their home towns and villages.

The Anglo-Indians, cultural discrimination against whom was discussed in Chapter 17, B 1, are likewise victims of economic discrimination. Gist and Wright (1973, p. 68) describe their situation as follows:

Anglo-Indians interviewed in various cities were generally agreed that the men were seriously handicapped either in obtaining a job or advancement in the position held. One of the common complaints was the alleged discrimination in promotions. It was

repeatedly asserted that under the British regime Anglo-Indian personnel were seldom advanced to one of the higher ranks whatever their qualifications or work performance, and that this system is still widely followed in independent India. Said a retired railway officer in Bangalore: "There are many Anglo-Indians having the rank of a minor officer who are quite capable of performing the duties of higher officials. Unfortunately, these officers are never promoted to the higher grades. When promotions are made they find some non-Anglo-Indian officer and promote him. For this reason there is a lot of dissatisfaction among the Anglo-Indian workers who have been carrying out their duties for numbers of years."

D. Economic Discrimination in Independent Africa

Africans recruited into independence movements have sometimes believed that the day of *uhuru* would likewise be the millennium and that the economic gap between whites and blacks would instantly disappear. This did not happen, for the simple reason that the Europeans still needed for a variety of managerial and technical tasks command salaries far above those that would draw an overabundant supply of applicants from among the African elite, with whatever skills they possess.

The inevitable frustration of the "revolution of rising expectations" has provoked a series of irrational reactions, of which Amin's arbitrary arrests of Europeans who have criticized him are only the most extreme. An elaborate theory of "neocolonialism" has been propounded, according to which economic transactions between developed and lesser-developed states even though they are freely concluded by both sides and conform to world market conditions are somehow exploitative of the latter. This theory has culminated in the "Charter of Economic Rights and Duties of States" recently adopted by the UN General Assembly. This document proclaims the duty of rich states to channel both public and private investment into the lands of the poor, together with the right of poor states to confiscate these investments whenever they please, paying for them or not as they see fit (Bernard D. Nossiter in *St. Louis Globe-Democrat*, October 20, 1975).

The "New Order" that the Lesser Developed Countries (LDC's) would promote is derived from a model designed nearly 20 years ago by Paul Prebisch and elaborated by The United Nations Conference on Trade and Development (UNCTAD). It has three aspects: higher targets for foreign aid, protected prices for raw materials, and preferential tariffs for LDC's—which those in Africa already enjoy in the European Common Market. But, as Nossiter (*ibid.*) points out, foreign aid often spares poor nations the "politically painful task of breaking up large land holdings, ending caste and other discriminatory barriers that prevent the full use of their own labor, and taxing the huge accumulations of politicians, generals and other Third World beneficiaries of the present state of affairs. . . ."

1. SOCIAL OVERTURN AND ECONOMIC DISCRIMINATION IN ZAMBIA

Legal and political discrimination in Zambia since that state achieved independence in 1964 have been described in the two preceding chapters. Their economic effects were not slow in appearing: turnover of supervisory and technical personnel in the copper mines doubled and productivity declined, since new recruits lack the skills of the departed South Africans and Rhodesians (Metrowich, 1974).

If the black Zambians believed that anti-European excesses, as well as the "localization" of jobs and businesses, would close the economic gap between living standards of blacks and whites, they were doomed to be disappointed. In 1971—six years after independence, and despite the Zambian government's official nondiscrimination policy—the black–white industrial wage gap was still higher in Zambia than in South Africa. While black

earnings in South Africa averaged 19.88 percent of those of whites, the average black working in Zambia earned only 14.18 percent as much as the average white still remaining in the country. The reasons for the persistent wage gap are obvious: the jobs transferred from whites to blacks were those requiring lesser skills and commanding lesser pay, and life in Zambia has become so unattractive for whites that very high salaries have to be paid to induce them to go there at all. Nor has the "localization" of retail trade helped the black Zambians.

Discriminatory economic measures against Asians in Zambia, like similar measures in East Africa, appear to some extent motivated by Asian separatism—reflected in the fact that no black Zambian is known to have married an Asian girl. Any such girl who falls in love with a Zambian is sent back to India so she can forget about the whole affair. There are at the same time children with Zambian mothers and Asian fathers—evidence of a double standard on the part of the Indians (Daniel Mwale in *Times of Zambia*, March 1, 1973).

Specific measures against Asians began in April 1968, when President Kaunda decreed, as part of an economic reform program, that no expatriate would be allowed to trade in general goods after January 1, 1969, except in certain scheduled areas. It was later announced that no more wholesale licences would be issued to expatriates. Asian traders were the principal victims in both cases. Hundreds of shops closed as the deadline approached, as there were not enough Zambians with sufficient funds to take them over. Justin Chimba, minister of trade, stated in a press interview on January 1, 1969, that "not a single" Asian had sold his shop to a Zambian. In Luanshia 80 percent of the shops closed down, while there were 10 applications for the 50 shops available in Ndola. Two shops out of about 45 remained opened in Fort Jameson. Women with babies on their backs fought with men to buy provisions from the few shops still open.

The immediate result, according to General Secretary Joseph Musonda of the National Union of Commercial and Industrial Workers, was the unemployment of 6000 black workers. In Mufulira, alone, 300 employees of Asian businesses were laid off. By mid-January, 1969, only 11 out of some 100 Asian shops were open in Lusaka. By March 1973, a number of shops nationalized in 1968 had been repossessed by their former non-Zambian owners—who have been allowed to operate them so long as there are not Zambians able to do so, but who may be put out of their businesses again at any time. A United National Independence Party (UNIP) spokesman has accused Asian middlemen of selling their best goods to Asian and European shops and reserving poor-quality goods for Zambian traders—a charge that may have some truth since wholesalers normally give preference to their best customers.

More recent policies of the Zambian government have been contradictory. At a symposium in Botswana in May 1975, President Kaunda's personal advisor Mark Chona stated that his government regards whites in the area "as the moral responsibility of each and every Black man," and that "We understand fully the fears of Whites in Southern Africa and accept that they are here to stay." Zambia, he said, was prepared to act as a catalyst for meaningful change, but that would depend on changes within South Africa (*The Times*, London, May 27, 1975).

Later in the month, however, in connection with a cabinet shift, Dr. Kaunda announced that: "The revolution has no room for private enterprise"—a statement followed by a series of drastic measures. These included:

(a) Abolition of all freehold titles, with vacant lands reverting to public authorities; closing of all real-estate agencies and discontinuance of home loans to private persons including expatriates.

(b) Takeover of nursing homes by the Minister of Health, prohibition against part-time private practice by any expatriate doctor or other professional employed by the government.

(c) Nationalization of the *Times of Zambia*, the Printpak printing company, and of cinemas, all belonging to the (British) Lonrho concern.

(d) Drastic penalties for smuggling and corruption (*Keesing's Cont. Arch.*, July 7–13, 1975, p. 27213).

President Kaunda said that he wanted both papers in Zambia (the other had already been taken over) to reflect official party and government thinking. As for film theaters, "we cannot have cinemas reflecting the values which are contrary to Zambian values and interests." (*Facts on File*, July 12, 1975, p. 504). The blocking of copper exports by disturbances in Angola led to further austerity measures that bore most heavily on whites: foreign companies were permitted to take out only 10 percent of their profits instead of the previous 30 percent, while the vacation pay foreign workers could take with them out of Zambia was cut by two-thirds; vacation currency allowances for Zambians were cut out altogether (*ibid.*, October 11, 1975, p. 752). Whether President Kaunda's economic controls will prove enforceable, or whether they will promote corruption by overstepping the threshold of obedience, remains to be seen.

2. CONTRASTING POLICIES IN ZAÏRE AND KENYA

After the chaos attending the transfer of sovereignty from Belgium to the Congo (as it was called until recently) and the meteoric career of Patrice Lumumba, Zaïre settled down to a rather comfortable relation with the Europeans—the Belgians in particular. The Union Minière was compensated for its properties in Katanga and invited to stay on to manage them. Many Europeans who had fled the reign of terror in 1960 returned to resume business, and others joined them.

More recently, however, President Mobutu Sese Seko has invoked measures that discriminate heavily against smaller and intermediate

European business people while leaving larger international corporations—for the time being—untouched. On November 40, 1973, Mobutu announced that the entire economy, including plantations, farms, large and small businesses, industries, and hotels, would be "Zaïrianized" within 100 days. This step destroyed the businesses, homes, and lives of about 40,000 expatriate Portuguese, Greeks, Belgians, French, and Pakistanis, paralyzed retail trade, and opened the floodgates to a wave of corruption.

Between December 1, 1973, and February 28, 1974, thousands of expatriates in all parts of Zaïre were visited by Zaïrois waving chits of white paper announcing that the state had given their businesses to the bearer. According to the *Pretoria News*,

The new owners seized all assets, including stocks. The Government declared it illegal for the dispossessed expatriates to stop delivery of further stocks already ordered; the new owners repudiated responsibility for paying for them.

The expatriates were told they would not be allowed to leave Zaire until they had handed over their business in a satisfactory condition, trained the Zairois to run them and met all taxes, debts and other liabilities. (April 19, 1974)

It was ruled that the depossessed would be compensated within ten years by the new owners "provided the business made satisfactory progress." Interpreting this to mean no compensation at all, thousands of expatriates have fled illegally, taking only what they could carry with them. Many others remained "as economic prisoners, their embassies unable to help," while they waited for permission to leave.

Soon after his announcement, Mobutu left on a lengthy trip to the Middle East and Europe. When he returned in March 1974, he said he was "perturbed" at the way expatriate businesses had been allocated. "He had not intended, he said, that government officials and other leaders should have arranged to allocate seven or eight businesses to themselves, or that those allocated expatriate businesses should

merely sell the stocks and then close them." That, however, was precisely what took place throughout Zaïre; many towns suffered a total collapse of retail trade (*ibid.*).

Obtaining a possession chit was a matter of influence and graft. One Greek hotel owner was visited by three Zaïrois, each with a chit assigning ownership of the business. Finally an army general took possession and ordered the former proprietor to keep on running the hotel, without pay, until further notice. The effect of such measures on the economy was immediate. In December 1973, the cost of living in Kinshasa rose 10 percent, making a total of 25 percent for the year. It continued to rise steeply in 1974.

Curiously enough, Mobutu managed this property grab without turning off large-scale international investment. He declared he would honor the 1969 Investment Code under which an American power consortium, General Motors, and Goodyear, as well as a U.S.–Japanese–Belgian oil group, are building major projects. Belgium has stopped unilateral investments, but British and American investors have moved in to fill the gap. Since Mobutu's "respect" for property is expedient and selective, what will happen to their projects remains to be seen.

Development of a limited modern sector does not, however, solve problems of mass poverty. Unable to feed, clothe, or house the peoples of Zaïre adequately, Mobutu offered them the consolations of a secular religion. In the summer of 1974, the constitution was revised to give the President, "head of the great Zaïrese family and father of the nation," practically dictatorial powers. "Mobutism" was to become for Zaïre what Maoism is for "People's" China. As *Keesing's Contemporary Archive* reports:

Late in June it had been announced that, since Zaire as a state was "neutral towards religion", there would be no religious holidays, and Christmas would be an ordinary working day, though it was not forbidden for people to celebrate Christmas by going to church.

President Mobutu, drawing a parallel between Christianity and Mobutism in a speech on Aug. 15, said that the MPR [*Mouvement populaire de la révolution*] was for Mobutism what the Church was for Christianity, and that the role of the political commissars of Mobutism could be compared with that of the theologians of the Church.

On December 12 the Government announced the abolition of religious instruction in primary and secondary schools as from Jan. 1, 1975, and its replacement by courses in civics and politics. At the same time MPR militants began to replace crucifixes in public places by portraits of President Mobutu. (February 10–16, 1975, p. 26960)

A program of mind-changing was launched under the pretext that "colonization has alienated the minds of the Zaïrese by various means, among them religion, to suppress ancestral values and impose upon them an imported manner of interpreting man's relationship with God" (*ibid.*). All places connected with the life of the President were declared places of meditation, and his birthday became Youth Day.

Mobutu's political religion provided the ideological base for further drastic economic centralization. On January 1, 1975, the state took control of "all construction, production, distribution and transport companies, including companies producing building materials." All property in foreign countries owned by Zaïrois would have to be ceded to the state, and foreign bank deposits would have to be repatriated by September 30. Mobutu defined his policies in an "historic speech" on January 4, 1975, which Keesing's summarizes as follows:

Denying that he believed himself to be God, or wished to become God, or that the abolition of religious instruction in schools would lead to a "divine cult" of the head of state, he defended the measures taken as conforming to the country's constitution, under which Zaire had become a lay state. With regard to the display of his portrait he declared: "The children of Zaire must first know the man who sacrifices himself for them day and night, before they know the Pope or other foreign person-

alities." To those who accused him of Marxism, he replied: "In Zaire we know that we are not communists." At the same time, however, he confirmed the nationalization of all means of production and distribution, including those belonging to citizens of Zaire. He declared "war on the bourgeoisie," confirmed the "mobilization of the people" for the creation of agricultural communes and promised a new system of employment which would eliminate all work stoppages by the end of 1975. He added that Zaire supported all national liberation movements and had spared no expense for Angola, from which territory there were 1,000,000 refugees in Zaire (p. 26960).

These measures did not improve the economic situation nor did they prevent an abortive coup against Mobutu, which the President stylishly blamed on the American CIA (which is also accused of putting him in office in the first place). In July, the government was forced to adopt new pay scales, reducing all salaries of more than $300 a month except for teachers. The government had to sell two-thirds of its gold reserves to pay foreign creditors. It was hoped that the situation might improve after Zaïre Gulf Oil, in which the government has a 15 percent interest, had achieved full production (*Africa Report*, Vol. 20, No. 5, September–October, 1975, p. 32). Taken as a whole, however, Zaïre is a case study in economic self-destruction through economic discrimination. The dislocations caused by the invasion from Angola merely compounded the problem. Mobutu is reported to have asked that a U.S. plane dispatched to him be filled with $60,000 worth of Coca Cola (*To the Point International*, May 2, 1977, p. 22).

Whites in Kenya have, up to this writing at least, enjoyed a situation far more favorable than that recently experienced by foreign settlers in Zaïre. Having imprisoned Jomo Kenyatta, who seemed a dangerous radical in Mau Mau days, the British now wish that he would live forever since he is the main element of stability in an otherwise threatening situation. The 40,000 whites of Kenya are a test case as to whether a European community can survive in a black-ruled state. They have managed to retain much of their economic dominance, and their leisure time is typified by English-style fox hunts and garden parties. In addition to maintaining ownership of the largest farms and hotels in Kenya, as well as other profitable businesses, whites still hold key posts in the Kenyan civil service. About 4000 have taken citizenship in Kenya and many others are serving on long term contracts (Hoagland, 1973).

The Europeans in Kenya are aware that Kenyatta tolerates them as a matter of expediency and that he—or more likely his successors—could dispossess them if they decided to pay the price of economic dislocation and a cutoff of British aid. As Hoagland observes (*ibid.*): "Kenyatta appears to have convinced many of his people that the way to prosperity lies in allowing white capital to generate new development, with benefits trickling down to the masses from a growing black economic elite tied into the white community." As a result, British companies still control most of Kenya's major enterprises: breweries, tobacco processing, tea estates, banks, cement, insurance, soda-ash mining, foreign trade, and tourism. The United Kingdom has supported this system with more than $250 million in aid and loans since independence; there are about 2000 British technicians and teachers in Kenya, and a small number of British military officers hold direct line commands in the Kenyan army (*ibid.*).

The pressure for Africanization is increasing, however, and British and American companies can no longer employ one or two "front office blacks" and then rest on their laurels. A Kenyanization of Personnel Bureau was established some years ago to conduct what Americans would recognize as an "affirmative action" program. The Bureau has divided executive and managerial positions into four groups (listed from the top down), on which its policies are as follows:

(1) Directors and top level administrators: The Bureau does not press for Kenyanization of this group mainly because it consists of proprietors and/or key personnel in international companies. They stay on in Kenya until transferred elsewhere, and their work permit fees provide substantial revenue.

(2) Professionals: Although these positions are Kenyanizable, qualified citizens are rare and enforced Kenyanization might destroy entire enterprises. The Bureau investigates each such case carefully, since enterprises "have been known to place people in this category on blown-up job titles, job elements and remuneration to avert the pressures to Kenyanize."

(3) Executive and managerial: Kenyanization is extensive in this group, which consists mainly of personnel managers. A college degree is the normal entry requirement; companies find it expedient to have Kenyans in charge of personnel since most semi-skilled and unskilled employees are Kenyans.

(4) Technicians, works managers, shop foremen and other supervisors: Possibilities of Kenyanization vary. Technicians are rare, but shop foremen and other supervisors are not. (Summarized from a confidential report.)

Kenyans applying for professional and executive posts are often interviewed by precisely the people whose jobs they will take over. The incentive of such Europeans to raise the qualifications arbitrarily are obvious. Less obvious, but logical upon reflection and empirically verified, is that in a labor-surplus economy (which exists throughout Africa) Black Kenyans who have "made it" into the elite show no inclination to open executive suites to other blacks who may be their competitors. As the Kenyan source quoted above indicates:

After Kenya became independent, many employees with long service but considerably low qualifications moved up into managerial/executive job positions. These people, according to the majority of the college educated Africans interviewed, tend to see anyone with higher qualifications than they have as a threat. Consequently they tend to do what ever they can to keep the more qualified employees "down there" by not acknowledging their capability to hold more responsible jobs. Such practice is another great menace to the Africanization process.

Economic discrimination in Kenya, as in the rest of East Africa, is visited on the Asians, originally imported as laborers from former British India and Pakistan. They are the victims of the cultural discrimination described in chapter 17,B2. As the introduction of modern industry, mining, and agri-business led to a stratified society, the Asians moved into the middle class. Asians could not own land in the white highlands, but they had more members than the Africans on the Legislative Council. As Meisler observes, "The white man had the farmlands, the big trading firms and political power; the Asian had the small shops and some larger stores; the African had nothing" (1969, p. 174).

Once *uhuru* had been proclaimed, pressure to remove this alien monopoly was irresistible. The economy lacked the growth (especially in relation to rising population) to provide enough new jobs for Africans; to dispossess the Europeans would stop growth altogether. The Asians (in the middle) were the obvious victims. They were, in any case, the immediate targets of African wrath, since the popular stereotype of the Indian *dukawallah*, like that of the Jewish pawnbroker in Harlem, is that of an unprincipled exploiter who cheats his customers.

The two weapons levied against the Asians were work permits and trading licenses. A decree that all aliens must have work permits—which were then denied—triggered an exodus of clerks and salespeople in 1968. Beginning in 1969, the government began a policy of refusing trading licenses to Asian shopkeepers, as well as publishing a list of goods—including cigarettes, matches, sweets, biscuits, and nails—which only Kenyans could sell. Africanization by substitution is not without its pitfalls, however. As Meisler notes:

The government's program of Africanizing the jobs of Asians may run into trouble in at least one area. In business, the Kenya Government may find it easier to push Asians out than to move Africans in. Most Africans in Kenya have little education and less credit. Officials of the Ministry of Commerce and Industry say that small African businessmen often keep books badly, overestimate profits, and overspend. They usually dip into shop funds to give money to the many poor relatives who hang around a successful African. With little experience, they make elementary mistakes, stocking the wrong goods at the wrong time. Many fail to concentrate on their business, and many refuse to put any profits back into it. Unless the government mounts a huge training program, there is a danger that the departing Asian shopkeeper will be replaced by a bankrupt African shopkeeper. (1969, p. 175)

Kenyatta's economic policy is not without its critics. A team sent by the International Labor Office in 1972 found a widening abyss between rich and poor. While Kenya has sustained a growth rate of 6 or 7 percent annually, better than most LDCs in Africa or elsewhere, the poorer citizens have not benefited. After two years of independence, 6 million (half the population) have no jobs, another 2 million households have incomes less than $560 a year, a quarter of all children suffer from malnutrition, and illiteracy runs between 80 and 85 percent (Brenda Jones, 1973). The ILO recommended freezing wages and salaries of the top 25 percent on the earnings scale, deferring further capital-intensive investment in favor of intermediate labor-intensive technology, breaking up large farms into family-sized smallholdings, and stopping uncontrolled urbanization by putting a ceiling on spending in Nairobi (!). These proposals were rejected by the government, although the Minister of Finance and Planning indicated that large ranches would be bought up and subdivided as they became available. It may be observed that, since African smallholders have not achieved production levels reached by peasants in Japan and Taiwan under a very different culture, the rapid breakup of large estates would cause an immediate drop in food production (Ruthenberg, 1974, pp. 286–87).

3. TANZANIA: AFRICAN SOCIALISM AND UJAMAA

President Nyerere's African Socialism has had to proceed from a starting point of abject poverty. Tanzania's per capita GNP at independence (1964) was only $80, as compared with simultaneous figures of $292 for Ghana, $1134 for Kenya and $255 for Zambia (AID, 1972). The thrust has been utopian: the Arusha Declaration, with its stringent rules against personal enrichment by public officials, seems to have been designed for angels to administer. But Dr. Nyerere must work with human material. As Alan Hutchinson writes (*The Times*, December 9, 1974), "petty officialdom is still often bullying, inefficient, and corrupt" while there is a total lack of trained local administrators.

President Nyerere is probably correct in judging that development must be concentrated in the rural areas, where 80 percent of Tanzanians live, at the expense of city dwellers. His development strategy, however, is based on regrouping the entire rural population into "Ujamaa villages" of up to 3000 people. "Ujamaa" (togetherness) is intended to provide the rural population with the basic elements of economic development: education, health facilities, and running water. Regrouping was pressed throughout 1974, and it was estimated that the "Ujamaa villages" would contain 5 million people by the close of that year (interview with Michael Wolfers, *The Times*, December 9, 1974).

The regrouping action was discriminatory in its effects. People in locations judged "inaccessible" had to leave their farms, whereas those living in villages selected as nuclei remained undisturbed. Farmers located on arid or barren soil were helped by relocation, whereas others experienced it as the destruction of their life's work. According to Godfrey Morrison:

Although in some parts of the country the policy was carried out skillfully and the people involved were only too eager to move, in other parts of the country there has been great hardship and suffering with large numbers of people seeing their houses smashed down and being forcibly moved, sometimes to unsuitable locations. (Morrison, 1974)

In some areas, the peasants could not be persuaded to desert their traditional settlements, but could only be moved by brute force. "For wealthy tribes like the cattle-owning Sukumu and Chagga the collective policy was a straightforward invitation to give up their status and relative wealth to lesser and more indolent neighbours" (MacManus, 1974).

President Nyerere has declared that the entire rural population would have to be moved to Ujamaa villages by 1976. Obviously, this means abandoning any hope of achieving socialism through persuasion and example. The resort to compulsion, combined with the Stakhanovism fostered by the Tanzanian system of political competition, has produced results which those affected can hardly fail to find oppressive. As James MacManus writes:

The population shift led to brutalities. TANU officials in Tanzania's 22 districts competed with each other to get high percentages of the population into the new villages. Huts were burnt down in the bush and shambas, the cultivated strips around, were sometimes ploughed up to prevent the old inhabitants from returning. Families were often given only 24 hours to move and some cases villagers living only fractionally outside existing Ujamaa villages were compelled to make new homes only yards away. (*Ibid.*)

The economic efficiency of a rural program is reflected in farm production. Tanzanian grain output, the core of the country's food supply, is at an all-time low. While 1973 and 1974 were years of severe drought, informed opinion holds that forced resettlement was also a major contributing factor (Morrison, 1974, and MacManus, 1974).

The experience of Tanzania seems to support the generalization that the denial of economic rights, in this case the right of property including vested usufruct of tribal lands, exacts its own penalty in the reduction of national income. One of the immediate results of Ujamaa was an acute food emergency. The army took to requisitioning trucks carrying produce to Dar-es-Salaam, off-loading them, and sending them more than 1600 kilometers into Zambia to fetch grain for the starving population. There were also serious shortages of sugar, dairy products, cooking oil, rice, and other basic foods. Nyerere's government resorted to massive purchases on the international market (*Pretoria News*, May 6, 1974).

Internally, the government's response to the crisis is to create an "anticorruption squad" to deal draconically with food scandals rather than changing the socialist economics that have removed production incentives. Meanwhile, the white grain farmers on Mt. Kilimanjaro, who grow 40 percent of Tanzania's wheat, have curtailed planting because government price-fixing causes them a loss of $1.09 per bag: African grain and dairy farmers groan under the spread between farm and retail prices. Meanwhile, the government aggravates the crisis by printing more and more money, the supply of which increased by 7.5 percent in 1971 and by 19.2 percent in 1972.

Ujamaa demonstrates anew the thesis that the more radical a social change, the greater the violence needed to accomplish it. While the first stages of Ujamaa involved the poorest peasants, who had nothing to lose, established farmers objected when their permanent houses were smashed and they were forced to build mud and grass huts in collective villages. The warmest supporters of Ujamaa, the socialist students at Dar-es-Salaam University, began

labeling reluctant tribesmen "kulaks" and declaring they would be smashed like the kulaks of Russia. By the fall of 1974, hundreds of Tanzanians were fleeing into Uganda. General Amin's terror was something they had at most heard or read about, whereas Ujamaa they had felt directly (Reuters Dispatch, October 16, 1974).

A recent account (Reuters, December 4, 1974) described the Ujamaa process as follows:

> The Government tells entire communities that by a specified date they will have to move to a "planned village." It undertakes to provide the village with water and a school and the villagers with only one to three acres per family on which to grow their own food. That is all.
>
> Bulldozers and companies of "People's Militia," with rifles and fixed bayonets, move in. All the standing houses are demolished.
>
> Reluctant home-owners are ejected at bayonet-point. In some cases their crops have been destroyed. They are herded into prepared planned village sites where they build grass lean-tos as temporary shelters.
>
> They have no time to do more. They are told repeatedly, with truth, that the country is facing mass starvation; that if they don't get on with growing food, they will starve. . . .
>
> A villager tells of a young married woman with two babies who refused to leave the ruins of her bulldozed house until her husband returned. She went to sleep with her babies under a tree, only to be eaten in the night by hyenas.

Despite agricultural loans from the World Bank over the years totaling $100 million (of which American taxpayers contributed $40 million), per capita income in Tanzania has dropped from $84 at independence to $20 in 1974 (Reuters, October 16, 1974; *Human Events*, Washington, January 11, 1975). To avert starvation, the United States began massive food shipments under Public Law 480—the "Food for Peace" program. In the meantime, a new national capital costing hundreds of millions of dollars is rising from the bush at Dodoma in the interior, while the peasants in the surrounding dustbowl hover on the brink of starvation, as they cannot meet the increased food prices—up to 180 percent—announced in November 1974. Taken to task at a World Bank meeting in Paris in April 1975, Tanzanian Finance Minister C. D. Msuya admitted that "mistakes" had been made. In some cases new Ujamaa villages had been placed where there was no potential for production. The chairman, Stanley Please of the World Bank, commented that in spite of criticism of the farm scheme, in using development funds, Tanzania was "head and shoulders above the many other countries receiving aid" (*The Guardian*, Manchester, April 25, 1975). If this is true, the lowly taxpayer, American or otherwise, has cause to wonder about Robert McNamara's famous "cost effectiveness."

Henceforth, anyone living in a planned village will have to obtain written permission to leave it: a control more stringent than the Russian, which at least allows movement within the *oblast*. In the cities, the pass system so reviled in the case of South Africa is being introduced. All employed persons, of all races, are issued passes. Police conduct checks on city streets, and anyone without a pass is arrested forthwith (Reuters, December 4, 1974).

E. Housing and Residential Status

Housing discrimination in one form or another occurs in virtually every African state. Members of nonpreferred groups are usually segregated in poorer residential areas. This segregation can be either legally enforced or brought about by economic practices of the dominant group that have the same effect as legal segregation.

In the Republic of South Africa residential segregation of non-whites in the white regions of the country is sanctioned by law. The state spends proportionately far more on white housing than it does on non-white housing. Blacks in the white sector of South Africa are limited to townships reserved for them. Even

here, they are subject to "influx controls," which regulate the migration of rural blacks to the white urban-industrial areas. Blacks reject this system as a discriminatory device designed to prevent them from moving ahead economically. The black migrant laborers also complain that their housing is poor and that those who come without families must sometimes live 12 in a single room.

Whites, on the other hand, claim that residential segregation is a historical legacy that reflects different levels of development. They also point out that the blacks also segregate themselves by language and culture; that white–black residential segregation in the white sector of South Africa is largely applied to obviate friction among peoples very different in economic development, culture, lifestyles, values, historicity, descent, and physical appearance; and that in their homelands and independent countries (Kwa-Zulu and Transkei, for instance) the blacks are not subject to any residential segregation save the normal dispersal patterns determined by social and economic "market forces" operating in all societies.

In other African countries there is a close correlation between residential segregation and ethnic cleavages. Members of particular tribes are inclined to cluster in specific residential areas, often for protection against possible aggression or exploitation, but more usually to enjoy the feeling of security and belonging which living within their own group generates. Foreign-born people form separate "outsider" communities, such as the *Zongo* of Accra, capital of Ghana, who have lived in a ghetto for 60 years. In rural areas foreign-born farm laborers even establish their own separate villages. Fear of Africanization and a strong in-group solidarity have led to residential segregation of most Indians in Africa, especially in Malawi, Zambia, Kenya, and—until a few years ago when they were expelled—Uganda.

In some but not all Asian countries, Chinese are similarly separated. "Chinatowns," such as that in Manila, are a legacy of colonial segregation; most have a self-perpetuating momentum sustained by commercial convenience, anti-Chinese prejudice, and Chinese sociocultural "exclusiveness."

San Francisco's Chinatown is, however, by far the largest Chinese city outside mainland China, exceeding even Taipei. Most of the whites believe that the Chinese concentrate in Chinatown of their own accord, because they wish to preserve their traditional institutions and culture. This view is disputed by social scientists such as Russell D. Lee, who writes:

the origin and development of Chinatowns were in response to the economic and political activities of outside interest groups. The formation of China-towns, in other words, was less a "voluntary seg-regation" as some writers might argue, than a forced insulation from participation in the White society. Discrimination in housing and the racial "job ceil-ing" was initiated and continued to maintain the ghetto boundaries. The so-called "voluntary" sepa-ration of Chinese into ethnic ghettos has historically been nurtured by the unwillingness of a White soci-ety to allow the assimilation of an ethnic minority. (In Gelfand and Lee, 1973, p. 347)

The larger Chinatowns are also struggling to accommodate the large influx of Chinese immigrants from Hong Kong and Taiwan. Poor housing is the order of the day. One writer points out that

all Chinatowns are in parts of the oldest and most deteriorated sections of their cities. Over a third of the crumbling tenements in New York City's Chi-natown harbor rats; three-fourths are infested by roaches. Nearly two-thirds have not been painted for over three years as the code requires; indeed, the tenants often cannot find out where the landlords live. Rent control is regularly circumvented by the demand for "key money," which is usually paid in cash and not refundable. In San Francisco, 67 per-cent of Chinatown housing is substandard, as com-pared with 19 percent for the entire city. Recent im-migration has led to even more seriously overcrowded conditions (Odo, 1973, p. 376).

Two comments seem in order. First, the invisible landlords are quite likely to be Chinese themselves. Secondly, Chinese-Americans are sharing in the general wave of ethnic aware-ness, so that Chinatowns are increasingly held together by internal cohesion rather than ex-clusion from "mainstream" America.

Australian Aborigines have on the average twice as many persons per dwelling and three times as many per room as other Australians. Professor C. D. Rowley cites the popular ster-eotype: there is no use giving an Aboriginal a larger house—all his friends and relatives will move in. White property owners, like those in the United States, fear that black neighbors will depress property values—which is some-times a self-fulfilling prophecy. Aborigines are therefore often confined to slum areas, and are caught in a vicious circle of overcrowding, in-security, and inadequate equipment, causing and resulting from breakdown in household organization and family management (1972a, pp. 318, 322, 333).

Conditions of Aborigines on the reserves, where they are frequently used for cheap farm labor, are typical of unregulated peonage. Ac-cording to a 1973 report, the Aboriginal re-serve at Kununurra consisted of 12 galvanized iron houses, in each of which as many as 50 Aborigines were living. The houses contained three rooms without furniture, and a wood stove for cooking. There was no piped water inside the houses for bathing or sanitation, and insufficient power to permit use of electrical appliances. The average room measured less than 10 square meters and as many as four peo-ple were expected to sleep in them. This was so inadequate that the Aborigines usually used the houses for storage and slept outside in tents or under the trees. In the whole of Kununurra reserve, where the population varied from 200 to 500, there were only three ablution blocks with lavatories, and one laundry.

Other cases of residential segregation are found in the USSR, where non-Russians,

Turkic Muslims in particular, are often housed in "native quarters" containing the least desirable dwellings; and in Northern Ireland, where segregation is by religion and is to a great extent spontaneous, since interfaith social contact is nonexistent.

The social causes and effects of black ghettos in the United States were discussed at some length in chapter 15,C2–5, so that little more needs to be said about them here. Suffice it to note that the United States has experienced massive black migration northward, which reached 1,597,000 during the decade ending in 1950 and a peak of 400,000 a year in the early 1960s. Only 55 percent of black Americans live in the South today, compared with 91 percent in 1910.

Blacks have become more highly urbanized than whites: Black city population grew by 3.1 million during the 1960s, though the increase has slowed in favor of black suburbanization—following the earlier white movement and likewise motivated by a desire for better living conditions. The reasons why people leave ghetto areas whenever they can are made clear by Fred J. Cook's description of Newark, New Jersey:

Newark is a study in the evils, tensions and frustrations that beset the central cities of America. It is a city of 375,000, an estimated 61 percent Negro, 11 percent Puerto Rican. It is a city with an overall unemployment rate of 14 percent (25 to 30 percent among blacks and Puerto Ricans); around 25 percent of those who are employed work only part-time, and there are virtually no summer jobs and few programs for the city's 80,000 school children, who now roam the streets. As a result, one of every three Newarkers is getting some form of public assistance. There are, by conservative estimate, 20,000 drug addicts in the city, and only 7 percent of them are being treated. Newark has the highest crime rate of any city in the nation; the highest percentage of substandard housing; the highest rate of venereal disease, new tuberculosis cases and maternal mortality, and it is second in infant mortality. Most of these rates, like the crime rate, are still rising. In the Cen-

tral Ward, perhaps the worst ghetto in the East, decent black families live as virtual prisoners in housing-authority projects, afraid to let their children outside even to play. The city's first black Mayor, Kenneth A. Gibson, often says: "Wherever the central cities of America are going, Newark is going to get there first."

There are at least two Newarks, separate and distinct, divided from each other, existing in an atmosphere of mutual suspicion and racial tension. There is a white-dominated, business-oriented Newark, and there are the densely populated sections where blacks and Puerto Ricans live. (*New York Times Magazine*, July 25, 1971)

On one point, Mayor Gibson was happily wrong. Unlike far richer New York City, Newark is not bankrupt. Its books are balanced and it is paying its bills, because the New Jersey State Legislature insisted that services be reduced, employees be laid off, and taxes be raised so the city would remain solvent (*St. Louis Post-Dispatch*, November 23, 1975).

The mechanization of farming in the American South produced a phenomenon similar to that caused by the enclosure movement in late-eighteenth-century England: a temporary surplus of displaced farm labor. Unlike early English capitalism, however, Southern industry could not employ these people in labor-intensive (and hence low-wage) manufacturing, because federal wage and hour laws prohibited the employment of workers whose marginal utility for employers fell below the stated minimum. Meanwhile, however, there were rumors of better wages to be earned in the North and even relief rates exceeding incomes unskilled rural and small-town blacks could obtain locally. The compensating disadvantages of inner-city life were not so apparent from a distance. Not only is influx control almost unknown in the United States, but federal courts have overthrown state and local residency requirements for welfare, even for persons who admit moving to go on relief. The

influx of blacks into American central cities
has, therefore, been a response to socioeconomic incentives as perceived by the migrants.
If this concentration of black population is
deemed socially undesirable, then the economy of incentives must be shifted.

The need of urban blacks for more room
provides the opportunity for "block busting."
Unscrupulous real estate operators turn a
profit from racial fears and prejudices, not to
integrate, but to establish new patterns of segregation. Eunice and George Grier describe
"block busting" as follows:

> The *modus operandi* of the blockbuster is to turn
> over whole blocks of homes from white to Negro oc-
> cupancy—the quicker the better for his own profits,
> if not for neighborhood stability. Once one Negro
> family has entered a block, the speculator preys on
> the racial fears and prejudices of the whites in order
> to purchase their homes at prices as low as pos-
> sible—often considerably below fair market value.
> He then plays upon the pent-up housing needs of
> Negroes and resells the same houses at prices often
> well *above* their value in a free market situation.
> Often he makes a profit of several thousand dollars
> within a period of a few days. Studies have indi-
> cated that skillful blockbusters frequently double
> their investments in a brief interval. They can do
> this only because tight residential restrictions have
> "dammed up" the Negro need for housing to such a
> point that its sudden release can change the racial
> composition of a neighborhood within a matter of
> weeks or months. Apart from the damage done to
> both sellers and buyers and to the structure of the
> neighborhoods themselves, blockbusters have a far
> wider negative impact. By funneling Negro housing
> demand into limited sections of the city (usually
> around the edges of the Negro slums, since these
> neighborhoods are easier to throw into panic), the
> blockbusters relieve much of the pressure which
> might otherwise have encouraged the dispersion of
> Negroes throughout the metropolitan areas.

Technically speaking, blockbusters represent an
unscrupulous minority of the real estate industry—
"outlaws" in a moral if not a legal sense. However,
their activities would not prove profitable if racial
restrictions on place of residence were not accepted

and enforced by the large majority of builders, bro-
kers, and lenders, backed by the supporting opinion
of large segments of the white public (1972, pp.
452–53).

Alternately, it may be added, "block busting"
could be curbed by quota systems designed to
assure racial balance, such as has been under
consideration in Oak Park, Illinois (*St. Louis
Post-Dispatch*, February 17, 1974). But the
American courts, in their inscrutable wisdom,
have mandated racial balance in education but
seemingly forbidden it in housing.

American Indians and Mexican-Americans
have also had to put up with substandard housing and poor residential conditions. In the
Southwest, some Mexican neighborhoods have
disappeared as a result of compulsory urban
renewal, often over the objection of leaders.
Yet Chicano ghettos, internally integrated by
language, remain a marked characteristic of
Southwestern residential patterns.

An outsider community for whom inferior
housing has virtually become a permanent part
of the man-made environment is that of the
migrant workers of Western Europe. In Britain, for instance, the immigrant workers come
from Commonwealth countries, crowd into
the poorer residential areas already suffering
from congestion and all the social ills of urban
decay. Colored migrants and immigrants are
not segregated from all residential contact with
white people, but are forced to join the down-
and-outs of British society—those already classified as a problem (Rex, 1968, p. 1).

A study carried out by Political and Economic Planning (PEP) in 1966–67 showed a
high frequency of housing discrimination, particularly in renting from private landlords,
purchasing homes, and renting public housing—which was made available to less than 1
percent of the immigrants. More than half the
estate agents involved in the PEP study were
prepared to discriminate against non-white immigrants who wished to purchase houses.

These discriminatory practices can easily lead to the ghettoization of immigrant communities—a process already clearly in evidence in Sparkbrook (Birmingham). As *The Times* (London) observed: "Birmingham was approaching a situation in which large areas of decaying property near the city centre would be inhabited by Colored immigrants while newer housing would be solidly White" (in Bloom, 1971, p. 94). Colored immigrants, Rex and Moore point out, lack the power to influence local politics (cited, *ibid.*, p. 95). Birmingham City Council has earned for itself the disparaging soubriquet of the "biggest slum landlord" of the city.

Within the *Gastarbeiter* communities in EEC countries, the worst victimization and deprivation is found among workers who have no hope of a decent existence in their own homelands and are therefore forced by sheer economic destitution to accept inferior living conditions in the host country as the price of survival. In West Germany the magazine *Der Spiegel* reported (October 19, 1970) that foreign workers had to pay as much as 20 dollars a month for a bed in inferior boarding houses provided by employers, where there were only one bathroom and two toilets for every 36 workers. Two rooms in a cellar without daylight could cost a couple more than 50 dollars; and about 45 dollars was paid "for a hen-house of one and a half rooms, approached by a ladder, by a couple expecting a child . . . electricity and water not included" (Nikolinakos, p. 85). According to a survey of 2764 foreign worker families conducted by the Ministry of Labor of North Rhine–Westphalia in 1970, as many as 80 percent of the *Gastarbeiter* families were living in old houses; 40 percent of the houses had no kitchen; 64 percent had no toilet; and 67 percent of the households had less than one bed per person. Many single workers are cooped up in barrack-like quarters where it is common practice to put one bed on top of another. A sample survey carried out by the

Bundesanstalt für Arbeit in 1968 disclosed that 25 percent of all male foreign workers and 13 percent of all women were living in company-owned hostels. Castles and Kosack comment on this problem as follows:

> Discipline has become a fetish for many people dealing with immigrant workers, and regulations like those generally used in Germany are formulated and applied in a way more appropriate to a boarding school or a borstal [juvenile correctional school] than a workers' hostel. For instance, paragraph 2 of the German Regulations forbids entry to any person not employed in the works, in particular to women and children. It is not only single workers who are prevented from having normal social and sexual relationships in this way. Married men and women whose spouses are living in separate workers' hostels are only able to meet them in parks and cafés. Women have on occasion been expelled from hostels because their husbands stayed the night. . . . Further rules govern nearly every aspect of life, e.g. smoking is often prohibited except in the common room, lights must be off at a fixed time, personal possessions are regularly inspected under the pretext of checking tidyness of the wardrobe. (1973, pp. 260–61)

The same two authors, visiting Geneva in 1968, came upon two or three hundred Italian and Spanish seasonal workers housed in wooden huts, with three or four men to each room. Some of the rooms lacked even space for a bed for each man, so that mattresses had to be rolled out on the floor at night. All cooking was done in the rooms on two-burner bottled-gas stoves; heating was also by bottled-gas, but was inadequate. The windows were not windproof; roofs and walls allowed the damp to penetrate. For lack of wardrobes, the men's clothes, covered with mold, were hanging on lines fixed in the rooms. The workers suffered from complaints like influenza, colds, rheumatism—often forerunners of tuberculosis or bronchitis (*ibid.*, p. 251).

Similar housing conditions have been reported in France, particularly before a recent clampdown on the issuance of work permits to foreign labor. Castles and Kosack summarized the conditions of Algerians in Grenoble:

In a wider sample (838 persons), four percent were living in single rooms, 10 percent shared their room with one person, and 63 percent had to live with five other persons or more. Sixty percent of the Algerians had an area of less than four square meters each, and 17 percent had less than two square meters. One hundred and eleven out of 838 persons did not have beds and had to sleep on the floor. Altogether, 26 percent of the workers did not have running water either in their rooms or even in the building. Forty percent did not have a toilet within one hundred meters of their accommodation. Fifteen percent did not have any heating, and among those who had some form of heating, 40 percent said that it was insufficient or dangerous. (1973, p. 253)

In 1969, in an old chocolate factory owned by a private speculator at Ivry (a Paris suburb), 541 Black Africans were sharing eleven rooms. Some of the dormitories—including one in which seventy people were sleeping—had no windows. The ground floor boasted two taps with drinking water, the other floors two taps with nondrinking water. There were five WC's and one wash basin. The communal kitchen spread a revolting smell. No cleaning services for the rooms were arranged by the landlord. Each worker was entitled to one sheet which was changed every forty days. The blankets had not been cleaned once in the four years in which this "clandestine hostel" had existed (*ibid.*, p. 286).

In another privately owned "hostel" the electricity was cut off because the landlord had failed to pay the bill. As there was no other heating, the inmates were not only left in the dark, but also in the cold. To keep warm, the inhabitants of one room made a wood and coal fire in a makeshift stove. To conserve the little heat given by the fire, the windows and doors were kept shut. Five of the ten men living in the room died of carbon monoxide poisoning, and two were taken to the hospital, seriously ill (*ibid.*, p. 287). *Le Monde* of January 7, 1970,

carried a report of a hostel in Saint-Ouen in which 38 blacks were accommodated in three rooms, twenty of them sleeping on ten double-decker bunks. *Droit et liberté* of February, 1967, reported 80 North Africans living without lights or water in the basement of an unfinished house in Montpellier.

The worst form of housing in France is the *bidonville* (shantytown). In the Paris region alone there were fairly recently no fewer than 359 of them with a total population of almost 40,000 persons. In most of them one toilet for every ten "shacks" is nothing unusual. Nor is an occupation rate of four persons per 100 square feet. Adding insult to injury, the landlords expect the occupants to pay "rent" for accommodation in these hovels. Public outcry about the conditions of foreign workers was undoubtedly one of the factors that has motivated the French government to reduce radically the number of work permits granted non-EEC employees and laborers. Another factor, and perhaps the decisive one, was economic stringency induced by the oil crisis.

The ethnic ghettos, formed as a reaction to discrimination, are notorious for overcrowding. In Switzerland roughly every fourth overcrowded dwelling is occupied by an immigrant family. Discriminatory notices such as *Nur für Deutsche* (Germans only), *Gastarbeiter unerwünscht* (foreign workers not welcome), *Keine Italiener* (no Italians) often leave them very little choice. Workers with young children find househunting very difficult. Castles and Kosack tell of an Italian who had been working in the country for many years, living with his Greek wife in a single furnished room. When the woman had her first child, they were given notice. "A dog," the landlord said, "we might have tolerated, but a child, that is too much." When he found himself with his wife and the baby in the street, he sent her home to Greece (1973, p. 274). Castles and Kosack conclude:

In his search for housing on the private market, the immigrant is in direct competition with the indigenous population or at least its lower income groups. It is all too easy for him—a stranger singled out by his appearance and way of speaking—to be made the scapegoat for bad conditions and scarcity. The private housing market is the field where the immigrant is most likely to have his first experience of prejudice and discrimination. The freedom of the "free" housing market is often the freedom to reject or exploit the weakest social groups. (1973, pp. 266–67).

Throughout Europe, recent years have seen a growing awareness of the problems faced by *Gastarbeiter* in the matters of housing, social adjustment, and civil rights. Scholarly books have appeared, among which only four titles will be mentioned: *Foreigners in Our Community*, the report of a conference convened in Amsterdam in 1971 by the Anne Frank foundation (van Houte and Melgert, 1972); *L'Homme Déraciné* ("The Uprooted Man," Valabrègue, 1973); *Die Nigger Europas* ("Europe's Niggers," Klee, 1971) and *Die ungeliebten Gäste* ("The Unloved Guests," Uhlig, 1974). It would appear that the *Gastarbeiter* problem is moving toward a dual resolution. On the one hand, governments are responding to public pressure and are insisting that local authorities enforce housing codes and that adequate social services be provided: measures that will raise the relative cost of migrant labor. On the other hand, the number of such workers admitted is being radically reduced. Austria, where a report of substandard living conditions had caused a stir (*Die Presse*, May 25–26, 1974), expelled 100,000 of its 280,000 foreign workers in a year. In Germany, likewise, the number of *Gastarbeiter* has dropped from a September 1973 peak of 2.6 million to somewhat over 2 million, and the Labor Offices are refusing to renew foreigners' work permits when Germans are available for the jobs in question.

F. Hunger and Disease

Article 25 of the Universal Declaration of Human Rights, the programmatic part of which is recognized even within non-ratifying countries such as the United States, proclaims the right to an adequate standard of living. Clearly, someone's international right is someone else's international duty. The questions of sharing burdens and making best use of resources are, of course, political and to some extent ideological questions.

The argument is often heard: "We can't feed everybody." Authors such as the Paddocks, in *Famine 1975!* (1967) recommend *triage*, which is a policy of limiting food shipments to countries where the food–people imbalance is manageable and where self-sufficiency can be achieved with a rounded aid program. Countries that can survive without food imports would not receive them, whereas those whose population has passed the agricultural potential would be left to suffer a "Malthusian solution" of their population problem, since their catastrophes could at best be postponed, not averted. Admittedly, *triage* is blatant economic discrimination. But if we fail to discriminate, the Paddocks argue, more people will starve to death than would otherwise be the case.

In considering famines and epidemics, and the response of the "civilized" world, it is necessary to judge whether realistic solutions can be projected, or whether we are dealing with the kind John F. Kennedy once mentioned when in a pessimistic mood: problems that have no solutions.

1. DROUGHT AND FAMINE IN THE SAHEL

The Sahel is a wide band containing 4200 square kilometers (1615 sq. mi.) of arid steppe and savanna along the southern edge of the Sahara and containing the former French colonies of Senegal, Mauritania, Mali, Upper Volta, Niger, and Chad. With resources vastly inferior to those of other French African colonies, they were neglected both during French rule and afterward. By about 1960, while the countries of the Sahel were still in the process of becoming independent, "portents of the drought of 1972 were beginning to appear. It had become obvious to many that the cycles of the seasons were changing and that the annual rainy season . . . was not bringing enough rainfall for the crops and pasture lands to mature" (Kemp, 1975).

If the governments in the Sahel had demonstrated effective leadership, the drought would not necessarily have resulted in a catastrophe. But they were young and inexperienced, and had insisted on taking over their own affairs without a transitional training period. They had no personnel to carry out successful agricultural programs. Most importantly, however, they lacked the will to force a change in the traditional cattle-herding pattern, which had worked well enough in an era of sparser population and adequate rainfall, but became dysfunctional with overpopulation of the range combined with a secular shift to drier climate. The need for change was pointed out by a study group from the Massachusetts Institute of Technology, whose main recommendation has been summarized as follows: ". . . herdsmen probably could produce far more meat with half their present number of cattle. The tradition of measuring a man's wealth in terms of the number of cattle he possesses contributes to retention of old and worthless animals and gross overgrazing. One of the most effective ways to help the herdsmen would therefore be a programme to buy up their cattle" (Schmidt, 1974). As the drought worsened visibly from 1968 to 1972, the United Nations Food and Agriculture Organization (FAO) sent 100 or more officials into the area each year. These bureaucrats, however, never developed a master plan, but confronted the disaster with a series of improvisations (Morris, 1974).

As the Sahara moved into the grasslands, the herdsmen, with their tents of black goat's hair, were forced south into the higher grass, sparse woods, and millet and sorghum fields of the savanna (Schmidt, 1974). By the time the relief program was fully operational, 100,000 Africans had already perished. Even then, it did not always function properly. Nomad children suffering advanced malnutrition died in refugee camps because the special milk ration that might have reversed the process of edema failed to arrive. A measles epidemic killed others while vaccine was still being shipped (Morris, 1974). The drought reduced the Sahel's livestock population by 40 percent and forced one million or more, about 5 percent of all the people in the Sahel, to flee their homes in utter destitution. It then spread to Sudan and Ethiopia, and proved a major factor precipitating the revolution in the latter country. The extension of the Sahara by an estimated 650,000 square kilometers (250,000 sq. mi.) may prove to be irreversible damage which will affect Africa for many generations to come.

Although American and European aid (of which France contributed less than 10 percent) appears to have somewhat stabilized the situation temporarily, what is needed is a long-range economic plan for the 30 million people who live in the drought zone. They cannot possibly survive in the long run without a modernization of agriculture, which in turn requires some degree of industrialization to take surplus people off the land. Physically, the problem does not appear hopeless, since the area has large reserves of underground water as well as a number of minerals. Needed are a regional rather than country-by-country approach and a commitment to family planning, since the Sahel is already overpopulated in relation to its resources. Whether the Africans in the area are capable of creating the political conditions needed for their own survival is, however, extremely doubtful.

2. ON THE BRINK OF STARVATION IN INDIA

India has for many years been viewed as the classic example of a country where population has outstripped resources—a reputation now shared by Bangladesh. Major grain shipments under Public Law 480 ("Food for Peace") by the United States have made the difference between life and death for millions of Indians and Bangladeshi. The basic problem, as with cattle overgrazing in Africa, lies in a conflict between individual and social utility. Not only does the Hindu religion teach the virtue of large families, but a peasant with a small plot and primitive tools knows he can increase his output by having more children. In 1968 the government set a goal of reducing the birth rate from 41 per 1000 to 25 by 1976. But that goal has been postponed and family planning budgets have been cut. The birth rate is now 35 per 1000, and it is hoped to have it down to 30 or slightly less by 1980. Only 15 million of the 105 million couples in the reproductive age group (15–45 years), mostly literate, middle-class city people, are using birth control measures. The problem thus remains in the villages, where 80 pecent of the population lives and where birth rates are often as high as 45 or 50 per 1000 (Chutkow, 1975).

The "Green Revolution" that doubled yields in much of Asia and parts of Latin America during the 1960s made the need for population control seem less urgent. But by 1972 the euphoria had come to an end. Bad weather in Lesser Developed Countries (LDCs) combined with an economic boom in developed areas that expanded demand. The Russians, after their disastrous 1972 harvest, moved secretly into the market and bought 20 million tons of wheat and 10 million tons of coarse grains, mostly American. The U.S. Department of Agriculture clamped what amounted to an embargo on fertilizer exports, a policy duplicated by Japan. While Americans applied some 3 million tons of nutrients to lawns, gardens, cemeteries, and golf courses—more than used by all the farmers in India—the shortfall in the developing countries rose to 2 million tons. The FAO estimated the resulting loss in grain output at 20 million tons, enough to feed 100 million Asians or Africans for a year (Power, 1974).

As a result, 1974 was a year of unprecedented food shortage. By February, American export wheat cost almost four times what it had in June 1972. The poor of many LDCs began to find food priced out of their reach. Cereal prices doubled in Bangladesh between January and August 1974, marking a 400 percent rise in five years. In Thailand the price of rice doubled, while a kilo of pork rose from 16 to 25 bahts and a kilo of tuna fish from six to 22 bahts; yet the average factory worker earned only 16 bahts a day (*ibid.*). For people who spend three-fourths or more of their income on food, the result could only be malnutrition and, in time, a rising death rate.

In the meantime, the Indian government had compounded the difficulties arising from a poor 1972 harvest and the tight international market by intervening directly in grain marketing. The results were described by Michael Butterwick in the *Daily Telegraph* (London) of June 4, 1974, as follows:

> Over the past three or four months the staple food for most Indians, rice, wheat and other grains, has been difficult to obtain, and prices have moved erratically and generally upwards. Supplies of subsidised grains at Government shops have often run out. The consequence has been queues to buy food, frequent riots, black-marketeering and accusations of hoarding and profiteering by farmers and traders. . . .
>
> Needless to say, the new system was subjected to abuses from the outset. Farmers declined to collaborate, despite appeals from politicians, preferring to sell their grain whenever possible at free market prices, considerably higher than the procurement prices. It was ridiculous to expect them to behave otherwise. Why should they?

The net result was that the government obtained only about half as much wheat as planned. Over the longer run, Butterwick points out, India can be self-sufficient in food grains *if* the weather is always good and if farm supplies such as fuel oil and fertilizer are forthcoming in sufficient quantities. Unfortunately neither condition can be guaranteed.

Former Prime Minister Indira Gandhi's government persisted in trying to manage the crisis with crude measures of economic compulsion. A July 6, 1974, decree restricting dividend payments to 12 percent a year set off a Bombay stock market crash. Another decree froze half of cost-of-living raises. But instead of addressing itself to the economic diasaster at its 1974 All-India Congress Committee Meeting, the Congress Party launched into a lengthy debate as to whether members would still have to wear homespun cloth and eschew alcohol. Since energetic population policies, including the threat of mandatory sterilization which contributed to Mrs. Gandhi's downfall, are still in the talk stage in India, where there are 13 million more mouths to feed each year, it seems obvious that a major famine is just a matter of time.

Conditions in other Asian countries are not very different. To meet soaring prices, Sri Lanka and Indonesia have introduced subsidies of basic foods, while Singapore has relied on free trade and increased wages. Its Prime Minister Mr. Lee says: "To subsidise consumption is to pour money down a bottomless pit. Once the Government raises taxes to subsidise and sell rice cheap it will have embarked on an exercise in self-deception, in deficit budgeting that must end in bankruptcy" (*Pretoria News*, 13 September 1974). Should the bankruptcy predicted by Mr. Lee materialize, then famine will be the lot of the hapless Asians. This already seems to be the case in Bangladesh, where food prices are reportedly four times as high as in India (Ibrahim Noori in *Pretoria News*, September 13, 1974).

Health conditions in India are likewise retrogressive. A resurgence of malaria is attributed by the World Health Organization to "lagging governmental efforts and complacency, the oil price increase that has tripled the cost of DDT and insecticides, the increasing resistance of malaria-bearing mosquitos to DDT, and slackening funds to cope with malaria." The number of malaria cases climbed from 1.3 million in 1972 to 2.5 million in 1974, and was expected to reach 4 million in 1975 in India alone. Serious malaria problems also exist in Bangladesh, Burma, Indonesia, Thai-

land, Nepal, and Sri Lanka (*San Jose Mercury*, May 2, 1975, p. 14).

3. HUNGER AND DISEASE IN THE UNITED STATES

In an article significantly entitled "Going Hungry in America: Government's Failure," Elizabeth Drew (1968) quotes the report of a group of medical doctors who investigated reported malnutrition in Mississippi, and returned to tell the Senate Subcommittee on Poverty what they had seen:

In Delta counties . . . we saw children whose nutritional and medical condition we can only describe as shocking. . . . In child after child we saw: evidence of vitamin and mineral deficiencies; serious untreated skin infestation and ulcerations; eye and ear diseases, also unattended bone diseases secondary to poor food intake; the prevalence of bacterial and parasitic disease, as well as severe anemia . . . in boys and girls in every county we visited, obvious evidence of severe malnutrition, with injury to the body's tissues—its muscles, bones, and skin as well as its associated psychological state of fatigue, listlessness, and exhaustion. . . . We saw children who don't get to drink milk, don't get to eat fruit, green vegetables, or meat. They live on starches—grits, bread, Kool Aid. . . . In sum, we saw children who are hungry and who are sick—children for whom hunger is a daily fact of life and sickness, in many forms, an inevitability. . . . They are suffering from hunger and disease and directly or indirectly they are dying from them—which is exactly what "starvation" means. (Drew, 1968, p. 53)

A report in the Miami Spanish-language paper *Diario Las Americas* of January 25, 1974, describes the effect of rising food prices in the poorer areas of Dade County. Many families in these districts find themselves forced to spend 91 percent of their small income for food, and to borrow money to pay their other bills. A large number of poor persons have found themselves forced to reduce their food consumption, and most of these are buying less of any commodities. Poor families in general are required to pay more for their food than those having higher incomes, according to the Community Action Agency which investigated the situation. At least 80 percent of the people in the areas concerned and 95.7 percent of those in the district served by the CAA were having serious problems in reaching a minimum standard of essential nutrition. A few families, the report concludes, have been saved from hunger by the fact that they live in public housing or other low-rent projects.

It is possible to indicate some questions that should be asked in judging to what extent economic discrimination, direct or indirect, is a factor in these situations. A few of these questions are:

1. Does United States' agricultural policy, which has the effect of keeping food prices *high*, bear more heavily on poor people who spend greater percentages of their incomes for food?

2. Do large sales of wheat to the USSR measurably affect the retail prices of flour and bread?

3. Do traditional prejudices raise special barriers against black or Spanish-speaking workers seeking employment?

4. Does lack of adequate training opportunities impede black and Spanish-speaking workers in equal access to industrial work?

5. Do people in the rural areas of Mississippi and the Spanish-speaking poor of Miami have to pay more at retail for their food than urban and suburban dwellers with access to competitive supermarkets?

6. Does lack of training in basic dietetics *adapted to ethnic culture patterns* inhibit black and Spanish-speaking poor from making the best use of the small incomes they have?

7. Are the schools available to the rural blacks of Mississippi and to the Spanish-speaking in Florida inferior to those available to the population at large, with reference not only to instruction, but to school health programs, school lunches, and *adaptation of the curriculum to the specific cultural needs of the pupils?*

To the extent that any of these or similar questions, can be answered "yes," it is evident that not only impersonal economic causation but also economic discrimination, even if indirect, is a factor in the economic plight of Mississippi blacks and Spanish-speaking people in Florida.

G. Aggravated Forms of Economic Discrimination

The spectrum of aggravated forms of economic discrimination is rather broad. Two extreme forms, slavery and the extermination of primitive peoples, are dealt with in separate chapters. The discussion here will be limited to two cases. In the USSR economic discrimination is practiced for its direct benefits. In India, aggravated economic discrimination is used as a power device to suppress unruly ethnic groups and classes.

1. ECONOMICALLY MOTIVATED DISCRIMINATION: THE USSR

The rulers of the USSR discriminate against the non-Russian Union Republics—of which the Ukrainian SSR is typical—in two different ways. For one thing, all foreign trade is monopolized by the central Foreign Trade Agency in Moscow, and all payments are made through the State Bank and the Bank for Foreign Trade of the USSR for the account of the Russian-dominated central government. The Ukrainian authorities in Kiev are dependent on the central ministries in Moscow for any foreign exchange allocated to them, despite the fact that Ukrainian enterprises supply between 25 and 30 percent of Soviet foreign trade surpluses.

More importantly, Ukraine receives but a minuscule share of the economic resources apportioned under the periodic All-Union Five-Year Plans, except for those industries supplying raw or semifinished materials to Russian factories. Although the region was almost completely devastated after the German-

Soviet War of 1941–1945, reconstruction aid from Moscow was slow and inadequate. Yet Ukraine normally supplies over 60 percent of all Soviet raw materials: 63–69 percent of the coal, 70–77 percent of the iron, 83 percent of the coke, 75 percent of the manganese, 69 percent of the pig iron, 63 percent of the steel, 69 percent of the sugar, 60 percent of the preserved food, 76 percent of the vegetable oil, and 25 percent of the entire grain supply of the USSR (Dushnyck, 1975b, p. 480).

Discrimination on a wider scale is found in COMECON, the essential purpose of which is to gear the economies of the European satellites to the needs of the USSR. Consequently, a country such as Sovzone Germany (the so-called "German Democratic Republic") exports most of its finished industrial products to the USSR and is largely dependent on raw materials from that source. The prices in both cases are mostly less favorable than the "GDR" could realize on the free market. Within COMECON, only Rumania, and to a lesser extent Hungary, have been able to open freer trade channels with the West.

2. ECONOMIC DISCRIMINATION AS A POWER DEVICE—DEPRIVING DISSIDENTS OF THE MEANS OF SUBSISTENCE

The Nagas. Depriving people of their means of subsistence in order to establish political control is a method used by the supposedly democratic government of India in its efforts to "pacify" the Nagas, a group of twenty tribes of Sino-Tibetan origin whose homeland is in the jungle east of Bangladesh where the Burmese, Chinese, and Indian borders come together. Believing Gandhi's 1946 promise that Nagaland would not be forced to join the Indian Union, the Naga National Council proclaimed independence that year.

Nine years later, the army began a "pacification" drive, attempting to concentrate the Nagas in villages that could be protected and supplied by the army. Those who would not cooperate had their crops and food destroyed

until they did. This policy, needless to say, provoked armed resistance, which was answered with reprisals by the "pacifiers." According to Colonel Montgomery, secretary of the Anti-Slavery Society of London:

From 1956 to the present day, this policy has been applied with varying intensity. Villages have been burned and crops and granaries destroyed. Molestation has been used to deter the women from planting and harvesting the fields. Virtually every church in Nagaland—there are some 700—has been destroyed and rebuilt. Increasingly, it has seemed that their desecration by use for collective rape is intended to break the Nagas' will by showing them that they cannot defend what is most precious to them. If it should transpire that the intention is to breed out an inconvenient people, this would be nothing new even in modern times, nor peculiar to Asia. Whether as punishment for harbouring resistance fighters or to extract information, reports indicate a developing pattern of the public beating, torture and humiliation of village elders (*The Times*, London, November 14, 1973).

In 1958 the Nagas sought the help of the Reverend Michael Scott, whose fight for the rights of Indians in South Africa had made him a national hero in India. After several years' hesitation, Scott came in 1964 and for two years joined in a peace mission with two Indians, aiming to bring about a cease-fire and a subsequent settlement. When Scott appealed to the Indian government with massive evidence of persecution and infractions of the cease-fire, the Indian government deported him. A later visitor, Billy Graham, was permitted to meet only members of the puppet government installed by New Delhi.

After an attempt on the life of the puppet premier, Hokishe Sema, in August 1972, the Indian Government announced that Nagaland would now be "pacified for good." According to Colonel Montgomery:

A long-term road-building programme is far advanced; strong reinforcements have brought the Indian garrison to an estimated 100,000, and now large tracts of forest are being burned, presumably as a prelude to the destruction in detail of the Nagas who still resist. No wonder there are people who will not give money for famine relief in India while its Government can afford the luxury of a war of suppression.

Landless Indian Peasants. The "Green Revolution" in India has indeed produced bulkier and better crops, but at the cost of increased tension and violence. Unlike traditional village conflicts between rival landowning groups, the new conflicts have emerged along class lines, pitting the landless peasantry against a landlord class still clinging to its feudal privileges (Gough and Sharma, 1973, p. 80).

The story of the 1967 peasant uprising in Naxalbari is told by Sharma as follows:

From one harvest to the next, from one part of the country to another, the unrest spread. It took various forms: Ghandian satyagrahas (acts of non-violent civil disobedience), massive land-grab marches, forceful seizures of harvested crops, unionized demands for higher wages and, increasingly, the physical annihilation of landlords. The form varied, the content was the same; and in the process the line of demarcation became clearer. The other side—landlords, rich peasants, rentiers, paymasters—responded differently, depending on their strength and organization. Sometimes they fled to the cities, to return only when their allies in the state apparatus (the police, the army) made it safe for them to do so. At other times they retaliated with force. In the village of Venmani in East Thanjavur, for example, they attacked the landless laborers' hamlet at midnight. Shooting into the air, they forced everybody out of his or her house, pushed as many as they could into a single hut, and set fire to it. Forty-four people—men, women, and children—were burnt alive while the jubilant landlords stood guard to prevent anyone from escaping. (*Ibid.*, p. 81)

As Sharma points out, the Venmani incident was only the worst of many. As farm laborers have become organized and militant, landlords and moneylenders have stepped up their armed attack, often hiring thugs to assault the Harijans. In some areas the landlords do not even need to hire thugs: the local police, imbued with caste consciousness, are quite ready to take the offensive. Violent collisions have become so commonplace that the newspapers report them in small notices on the back pages (*ibid.*, pp. 81–82).

Underlying the rural violence that has become endemic in much of India is a pattern of inequality so gross as to constitute deprivation of the means of subsistence. Ten acres is considered the minimum economic family farm by Indian standards, but in 1951 more than 78 percent of the farmsteads fell below this level: they constituted 33 percent of the arable land. Fifty-nine percent of the farmers were trying to make a living on holdings of five acres each, which accounted for only 15.5 percent of the total cultivated area. Only 5.6 percent of the farms were over 25 acres each, but they took up 34.4 percent of the total farm land.

So far as ownership is concerned, 29 percent of the total agricultural population in 1951 were peasant proprietors, who owned between 40 and 45 percent of the farm land. The remaining 55 to 60 percent was controlled by feudal landlords and was cultivated for the most part by tenant farmers. Some land, mainly in the south, was owned by religious and charitable groups, but the priests who managed them behaved the same way as other feudal landlords (*Ibid.*, p. 83). About 42 percent of the agricultural population consisted of tenant farmers: occupancy tenants, who enjoyed fixed rents and heritable rights to the land they occupied, and tenants-at-will, who could be dismissed at any time and who were charged rents between one-half and two-thirds (sometimes as much as 75 or 80 percent) of the crop they produced. Both kinds of tenants had to perform unpaid labor for the landlord and to pay special levies whenever the landlord had extra expenses, such as a funeral, birth celebration, or marriage, purchase of a car or elephant, or sending a son to be educated in England—all except one of which were forbidden to the King of England by the Magna Carta. As Sharma summarizes:

The scene was thus one of pauperized peasantry, plundered by feudal landlords and moneylenders through rack-renting, illegal exactions, usury, and the applications of brute force. According to one estimate, in 1950–51 land rent and moneylenders' interest amounted to Rs. 14 billion, which was about a third of the value of the country's total farm produce that year. Under such circumstances, abject poverty, sporadic starvation, and periodic famines characterized rural India (*Ibid.*, p. 84)

Limited reform was achieved during the 1960s and some of the worst abuses eliminated. But the intention, if there ever was one, to convert the mass of Indian small farmers into landowners à la Stolypin never materialized: tenancy, high rents, and insecurity remain the main features of Indian farming. Statistics published in 1961 showed that 57 percent of rural households farmed no land or less than 2.5 acres each: their total holdings made up only 7 percent of the total cultivated area. Obviously, these people live on the edge of starvation if they are not already starving. A report of September 1974, indicated that about 3.5 million people in West Bengal were living on grass, as they had had no rice for months; their plight was typical of the condition of 250 million other Indians whose average daily income is 1 rupee (15 American cents) per day—with a purchasing power only one-fifth of its cash value. At this level, farm workers would rather receive food than cash, but in a time of rising food prices (caused in large part by the increased price of oil), employers of rural labor have turned to paying cash—and not enough of it for workers to feed their families.

With a given amount of land, larger farms means fewer farms. There is not enough land in rural India to provide more than half the population with economic family farms. Rural poverty in India cannot be overcome without transferring about 200 million people to the industrial sector—which is unlikely. The urgency of family planning is obvious, yet the government spends less than one rupee per child-bearing couple per year for that purpose (*Observer Review*, London, January 26, 1975).

PART FIVE

EXTREME FORMS OF DISCRIMINATION

22

MASS EXPULSIONS AND FORCED MIGRATIONS

Mass expulsions and forced migrations, both involving the movement of people against their will, must be distinguished clearly from voluntary migrations, even on a large scale. The latter have figured prominently in history, cases in point being the exodus of the Jews from Egypt, the incursions of East European "barbarians" during the dying days of the Roman Empire, the later eastward settlement of Germans recorded as the *Drang nach Osten*, and more recently the flow of Europeans into the New World and to Australia, New Zealand, and South Africa.

Lesser recent voluntary migrations include the movement of Latin Americans and Asians into the United States, the settlement of Indians within the confines of the British Commonwealth, the out-migration of Chinese into overseas territories, the large-scale movements of migrant workers after World War II into Western Europe, and the influx of Commonwealth citizens, mostly non-white, into the United Kingdom.

A. *Mass Expulsions Before World War II*

Mass expulsion is defined in the *Encyclopaedia of the Social Sciences* as "the forced evacuation of a certain region by large numbers of people upon order of the governing authority. The order may offer no alternative or one which is obviously unacceptable to most of the people affected" (Senturia, 1963, p. 186). A distinction should be made between mass expulsion in the strict sense, in which the victims are physically removed or forced at gunpoint to board outgoing trains, trucks, or boats, and forced migrations in which the price of staying put is religious conversion, acceptance of an unwanted citizenship, or perhaps even enslavement. When a government tramples upon the fundamental rights of a group, its migration is to be considered forced, "even when emigration is definitely prohibited, as in the case of the 400,000 Protestants who fled from France after the revocation of the Edict of Nantes in 1685 (*ibid.*)."

Like voluntary migrations, mass expulsions appear quite early in history. The Assyrian Empire, for instance, made a practice of transplanting subject peoples who had rebelled against Assyrian domination. The objective was forced cultural assimilation, for which purpose it normally sufficed to remove the rulers, leaders, artisans, and men capable of bearing arms. The remaining masses would merge into the cosmopolitan Assyrian population. This is quite likely what happened to the ten "lost tribes of Israel" deported from Samaria by Sargon II in 722 B.C. (*ibid.*, p. 186).

As a reaction to their religious and cultural separatism and their exemption from the medieval Christian taboo against lending money at interest, the Jews of Europe suffered repeated expulsions, notably from England in 1290 and from France in 1182, 1306, and 1394. At the close of the *reconquista*, the Spanish monarchy decreed forcible conversion to Catholicism and appointed royal offal inspectors to enforce conformity. Should repeated scrutiny reveal no pork bones in a family's dust bin, this was *prima facie* evidence that Judaism or Islam was still being practiced in secret. When enforced conversion failed, the Jews and *Moriscos* (Moors) were expelled. As they were the most skilled farmers, artisans, and merchants, this act of intolerance contributed to Spain's decline from world power status.

The czars of the growing Russian empire became adept in the use of mass expulsion as a political tool. It took two forms: *vyvod*, in which a group is moved in a body to a new location; and *razvod*, which is the scattering of a group—or in any case its leadership—across a wide area. Czar Yaroslav I used *vyvod* in 1031 when he moved large groups of Poles from northern Galicia to sparsely settled lands in central Russia. Ivan III, on the other hand, decreed the *razvod* of the German merchant class of Novgorod, after occupying that Hanseatic city in 1478. The city fathers opened the gates without a battle after the Czar's emissaries had assured them they would be left in peace. A few days later, however, wagons drew up before the doors of most important and many less important Germans. Russian soldiers supervised the loading of the merchants, their families, and whatever household goods would go in the wagons, which were then dispatched to destinations across a wide area of Russia. The Doukhobors, a dissenting sect believing in the "inner light" and rejecting the authority of the Orthodox Church, were subjected to *vyvod* in 1841 when land was pro-

vided for them in Transcaucasia. As they continued to make trouble for czarist authorities, their *razvod* was decreed in 1895. After Tolstoi had championed their cause, the Russian government consented to their emigration, while Canada agreed to allow them to settle in a compact body and to exempt them from military service. The main body of 7363 persons arrived in Canada in 1899 and were settled in British Columbia. Since then, however, they have been embroiled in periodic friction with the Canadian authorities, punctuated by nude protest marches on the part of the Doukhobors. *Razvod* was again employed during World War I, when the czarist government expropriated the descendants of old German colonists along a wide band of frontier territory, ostensibly because their loyalty was not assured but actually to provide land for Russian peasants (Senturia, 1963, p. 186).

Russia has also contributed its share of marginal cases of forced migration. Much of the Jewish emigration during the late nineteenth and early twentieth centuries, as well as the mass flights from Bolshevik Russia and from the Ukraine after 1917–18 and during World War II, were motivated by fear of genocide against proscribed racial, class, or national groups.

Turkey has likewise helped to fill the record of mass expulsion. After an initial policy of tolerant pluralism characterized by the inclusion of 60 Arabs and 73 other non-Turks (including 12 Armenians) among the 275 members of the parliament elected in 1908, the Young Turks embarked on a "nation building" policy based on the concept of a culturally and linguistically pure Turk nation. This doctrine found its main theoretician in Dr. Nazim Bey, who induced the Young Turk leaders to order the genocidal measures that are described in chapter 28,B (see Mandelstam, 1918, p. 32). Nazim's influence lasted until Turkey lost in World War I and he fled abroad. After his return he was executed by Kemal in 1926.

Nazim argued that in order to make Turkey

strong and prosperous "there exists a very simple method: expel the foreigners and replace them by Turks of pure race. We will call into Turkey every year half a million of (Turkish) emigrants whom we will settle next to our (Turkish) populations—Bosnians, Pomaks, the Turks and Tatars of Russia, Turkmen—Within twenty years we will have created an empire which essentially is Ottoman" (Mercérian, 1965, p. 37). Ironically, Nazim, who out-Turked the Turks, was a Dönme: a descendant of Sephardic Jews who during the seventeenth century were followers of the "Messiah of Smyrna," the well-known Sabbatai Zevi, and joined him in his forced conversion to Islam.

At first, the young Turks pursued Turkification by imposing the Turkish language. But the policy proved to be counterproductive. Hitherto loyal non-Turkish subjects of the Sultan, such as the Albanians, were alienated, while the Arabs rose in armed revolt. By the end of World War I Turkey had lost all its non-Turkish possessions.

The Turkish massacres of the Armenians and other non-Turks during and after World War I are classic cases of genocide and are considered as such in chapter 28. They and mass expulsions were the instruments of an ethnic purification policy that Senturia estimates "in a little over a decade removed over 2,000,000 members of alien minorities" (1963, p. 187). In 1913, after the First Balkan War, Turkey and Bulgaria agreed to exchange border populations—most of whom had already moved when the compact took effect. The Turks also expelled 150,000 Greeks from the Asia Minor coast to Greece and moved another 50,000 to inland Anatolia. Jews in Palestine also became a target in 1917 when they were ordered evacuated from Jaffa and Gaza, and subjected to pillaging and denial of food. It is not believed, however, that their losses were great. Renewed massacres of Greeks in 1920 set off a war between Greece and Turkey, and once again in 1922 the Greeks were subjected to a major

pogrom in Smyrna, where many Armenians also lost their lives.

Although defeated in World War I, Turkey succeeded in nullifying the Treaty of Neuilly imposed on it by the Peace Conference, and a new treaty was signed at Lausanne in 1923. It contained a Greco-Turk covenant explicitly sanctioning mutual forced expulsions. All Turkish nationals of the Greek Orthodox faith (except those living in Istanbul) were required to leave Turkey, while all Greek nationals of Muslim religion (except those in Western Thrace) were evicted from Greece. Although the convention was mainly a confirmation of a *fait accompli* for the Greeks in Turkey, almost 200,000 Greeks emigrated from Turkey under its terms. Greece reciprocated by expelling over 350,000 Muslims, thus obtaining lands upon which to resettle Greek expellees from Turkey. The League of Nations aided the transfer through its representative, Fridjhof Nansen (Senturia, 1963, p. 187).

The end of World War I also brought the first major forced migration of Germans. Large areas in the eastern part of the Reich were transferred to the new Polish Republic despite the warning of Lloyd George: "The proposal of the Polish commission to place 2,100,000 Germans under the tutelage of a people of a different religion, which has never demonstrated its capacity for self government throughout its history, must in my judgement lead to a new war in Eastern Europe sooner or later" (quoted, Müller-Sternberg, 1969, p. 78). Plebiscites in parts of East Prussia and four West Prussian counties brought overwhelming majorities for Germany, but the remainder of West Prussia and almost the entire province of Posen (Poznán) were given to Poland without a consultation of the people. Upper Silesia, where a plebiscite insisted upon by Lloyd George brought a 60 percent majority for Germany, was divided, with Poland receiving the industrial area (*ibid.*, p. 79). Persons living in the territories ceded to Poland were given the choice of moving to Germany or Austria as soon as they could wind up their affairs, or becoming Polish citizens. This presented no problem for the 2,300,131 persons of Polish ethnicity in former Prussian Poland or the 3,864,173 ethnic Poles in former Austrian Galicia. But the 1,363,019 ethnic Germans in Prussian territory and their 150,114 compatriots in ex-Austrian Poland—not to mention 675,550 ethnic Germans in former *Russian* Poland (1910 German and Austrian censuses and 1897 Russian census, cited by Bohmann, 1969a, pp. 40–41)—were faced with a difficult decision.

The number of Germans in Poland who opted to retain their German citizenship cannot be ascertained; Hermann Rauschning (1930, p. 121) estimated it at between 150,000 and 175,000. Taking the larger figure and adding another 25,000 for good measure, 1,988,683 of the 2,188,683 ethnic Germans (less war losses, plus births) should have been left in Poland. But the Polish census of September 30, 1921, showed only 1,036,000 persons of German language. The discrepancy is significant. Müller-Sternberg (1969, p. 84) estimates that 750,000 Germans, mainly in the cities, "found themselves forced to emigrate."

To protect its minorities from excesses of nationalist fervor, Poland was required to sign one of the minority treaties the Peace Conference imposed on all states awarded former enemy territory. As the Permanent Court of International Justice later explained, the purpose of these treaties was "to secure for certain elements incorporated in a State, the population of which differs from them in race, language, or religion, the possibility of living peaceably alongside that population and co-operating amicably with it, *while at the same time preserving the characteristics which distinguish them from the majority*, and satisfying the ensuing needs" (opinion of April 6, 1935, Series A/B Vol. 62, p. 17, quoted by Rabl, 1963, pp. 114–15; his emphasis). But the administration of minority protection by the League of Nations was notoriously inefficient (Jaksch, 1967,

pp. 252–58). For the Germans in Poland, in any case, the policy was laid down clearly by Wladislaw Grabski, twice Prime Minister (1920 and 1923–25), who declared on October 14, 1919, in Poznán:

There is one love for ethnic comrades and another for those of foreign ethnicity. Their percentage among us is decidedly too high. Poznán can show us a way in which their percentage can be reduced from 14 or even 20 to 1.5. The foreign element will have to look around to see whether it would not find things more comfortable somewhere else. The Polish land exclusively for Poles! (In Rabl, 1963, p. 126)

The German deputy Spickermann was not contradicted when he charged in the *Sejm* (Polish Parliament) on January 23, 1923: "The entire apparatus of internal administration has definitely been operating under the slogan: Leave no means untried to drive Polish citizens of German ethnicity out of the country, to de-Germanize and 'purify' the country. . . . Even the most brutal means are permitted for this purpose" (in Rabl, 1963, p. 126). It is hardly to be wondered that the German *Volksgruppe* became an unstable element in the Polish body politic, and susceptible to the lures of National Socialism.

B. Expulsions and Forced Migrations during and after World War II

1. "HEIM INS REICH" AND RENEWED RAZVOD

On August 23, 1939, Foreign ministers Ribbentrop and Molotov signed the German-Soviet nonaggression pact, signaling the Kremlin's advance approval for Hitler's invasion of Poland. Attached to the pact was a secret protocol dividing East-Central Europe into a German and a Soviet sphere of interest: the USSR was assigned the Baltic republics of Estonia, Latvia, and (later) Lithuania; Poland east of the Curzon line, and the Rumanian territories of Bessarabia (formerly Russian) and North Bu-

ovina (formerly Austrian). Anticipating So-
iet annexations of these areas, the Hitler gov-
rnment carried out the so-called *"Heim ins
eich"* movement, returning scattered ethnic
German communities in the region to German
overeignty. As these Germans were mostly
ndependent farmers and business people who
ould expect only short shrift from the communists, they accepted resettlement without
protest, even though many had lived in East
Europe for generations. The first contingents
f Baltic Germans were resettled in the so-
alled Warthegau, the erstwhile Polish Corri-
or which Germany had reannexed (Fircks,
962, p. 33; Müller-Sternberg, 1969, p. 88).

Between the latter part of 1939 and early
941 the following groups of ethnic Germans
ere resettled:

from Estonia	16,700
Latvia	64,000
Lithuania	52,900
Eastern Poland	159,000
Bessarabia	93,300
North Bukovina	43,600
	429,500

(SOURCE: Fircks, 1962, p. 33.)

urther resettlements continued during the
ar and involved ethnic Germans from remote
arts of the Balkans and finally, when the great
etreat began, some 350,000 Germans from the
USSR itself. Altogether, about 750,000 ethnic
Germans were moved in the *"Heim ins Reich"*
rogram. Most of them were settled in terri-
ory reannexed from Poland, and suffered a
econd mass expulsion when the *Wehrmacht*
ollapsed before the Russian invaders in 1945.

When the Russians occupied the Baltic Re-
ublics in 1940, they conducted a large-scale
azvod among the elites. Many years later,
hen Russian control was once more assured,
most of the deportees were allowed to return.

At various times during the war, the Soviet
overnment carried out the total deportation of
mall nationalities comprising an estimated
,332,436 persons in the Southern part of the

USSR, whom Stalin suspected of possible
sympathies with the Germans. These were:

In 1941, the Volga Germans (380,000)
In 1943, the Kalmyks (134,271), Chechens
(407,690), Ingush (92,074) Balkars (42,666), and
Karachais (75,735)
In 1944, the Crimean Tartars (200,000)

Solzhenitsyn describes the operation in these
words:

The military units gallantly surrounded the auls,
or settlements, and, within 24 hours; with the speed
of a parachute attack, those who had nested there for
centuries past found themselves removed to railroad
stations, loaded by the trainload, and rushed off to
Siberia, Kazakhstan, Central Asia, and the Russian
North. (1974, p. 84)

These nationalities were exiled on the basis of
ethnicity, without regard to individual behavior. They were not resettled in compact areas,
but scattered over the face of the continent, following the ancient Russian practice of *razvod*.

Khrushchev criticized the 1943 deportations
at the 20 Party Congress in February, 1956,
and the following year the president of the
Supreme Soviet declared that the Kalmyks,
Chechens, Ingush, and Balkars would be returned to their native areas. In 1964 the Supreme Soviet decided that the Volga Germans
had been unjustly accused, but no action was
taken with regard to the Crimean Tartars
(Dushnyck, 1974).

In 1968, a committee of the Crimean Tartars
in the USSR issued an "Appeal to the World
Public," which read in part:

In 1944 the whole of our people was slanderously
accused of betraying the Soviet motherland and was
forcibly deported from the Crimea.
All the adult men were at the front; able-bodied
older men were in the labor corps. In one single day,
May 18, about 200,000 women, children, and in-
firm persons were, without warning, driven out of
their homes by KGB troops, loaded on troop trains,
and removed under escort to reservations. The
operation was directed by Marshal Voroshilov. For
about three weeks they were transported in closed
trucks, almost without food or clothing, to Central

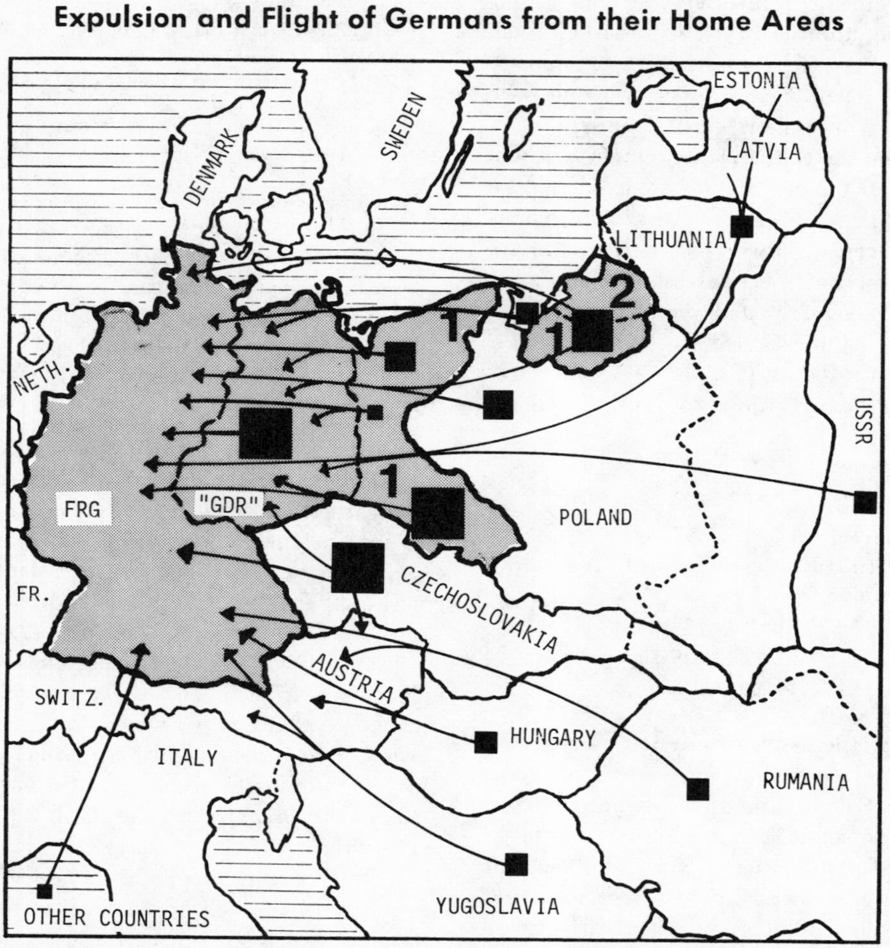

Expulsion and Flight of Germans from their Home Areas

FIGURE 22.1.   *Germany is shown in its 1937 boundaries, which remain legal until a peace treaty is concluded. FRG = Federal Republic of Germany; GDR = German Democratic Republic; 1 = under Polish administration; 2 = under USSR administration.*

Asia. After the war was over the men who returned from the front were sent to the same destination. As a result of the inhuman deportation and the intolerable conditions in which we found ourselves, more than half of all our people perished in these first years. Simultaneously, our national autonomy was extinguished, our national culture was completely destroyed, our monuments were pulled down and the graves of our ancestors were defiled and wiped off the face of the earth. (Reddaway, 1974, p. 249)

In June 1969, a group of Crimean Tartars demonstrated in Moscow for the return of their people to its homeland. The government arrested many demonstrators and then conducted a show trial of ten Tartar leaders in Tashkent (Uzbek SSR) for "anti-Soviet propaganda and agitation." The one prominent Soviet personality who took up the Tartar cause, General Grigorenko, was, as we have een, remanded to a psychiatric hospital Dushnyck, 1974, pp. 90–91). The Soviet regime evidently finds it inconvenient to have a Tartar ethnic group, related biologically and linguistically to the Turks, on the Southern seaboard of its empire. Its solution is therefore to treat the Crimean Tartars as an "un-people," denying their right to exist.

. EXPULSION OF GERMANS FROM THE EASTERN REICH

The greatest mass expulsion of the twentieth century was that of the Germans—both Reich citizens (*Reichsdeutsche*) and ethnic Germans *Volksdeutsche*)—from the eastern parts of the Reich (including territories reannexed from Poland), from Czecho-Slovakia, and from southeast Europe (fig. 22.1). In 1966, the German Federal Ministry for Expellees, Refugees, and War Victims summed up the statis-

tics in table 22.1. Although the expulsions and delayed resettlements, which still continue at a trickle, are parts of the same phenomenon, *Reichsdeutsche* will be considered in this subsection, *Volksdeutsche* in the following.

As the Russian forces advanced through Lithuania, Poland, and East Prussia, hundreds of thousands of German civilians fled before them. Some had horses and wagons, but most took only what they could carry on their backs. Those who stayed behind were sorry. When the Red Army arrived, its soldiers began a wholesale campaign of rape, plunder, and murder. Little girls and old women were ravished, men and women of all ages were shot or beaten to death, and many who survived were shipped to forced labor camps in the interior of the USSR. In Germany proper—east of the Oder and (western) Neisse Rivers—many survived the first onslaught. Here the Soviets

Table 22.1.   THE GERMAN POPULATION IN THE AREAS OF EXPULSION

Before Expulsion			*After Expulsion (1945–1950)*		
German population in 1939			Expelled		
Eastern areas of Germany		9,575,000	from the Eastern areas		
East Prussia	2,473,000		of Germany	6,944,000	
Eastern Pomerania	1,884,000		from Czecho-Slovakia	2,921,000	
Eastern Brandenburg	642,000		from other countries	1,865,000	
Silesia	4,577,000				
Czecho-Slovakia		3,477,000			11,730,000
Baltic States and District of			Remained in the home area		
Memel		250,000	in the Eastern areas		
Danzig		380,000	of Germany	1,101,000	
Poland		1,371,000	in Czecho-Slovakia	250,000	
Hungary		623,000	in other countries	1,294,000	
Yugoslavia		537,000			
Roumania		786,000			2,645,000
total*		16,999,000	Presumed still alive as prisoners	72,000	
Excess of births over deaths					
1939–1945		+659,000			14,447,000
			Dead and Missing during the expulsion (expulsion losses)		
		17,658,000	in the Eastern areas		
War losses 1939–1945		−1,100,000	of Germany	1,225,000	
German population at the end of the war		16,558,000	in Czecho-Slovakia	267,000	
			in other countries	619,000	
In addition in the Soviet Union 1½ to 2 million					
War losses		1,100,000			2,111,000
Expulsion losses		2,111,000			16,558,000
Total losses		3,211,000	Total number of German expellees in 1966 (estimated):		
			in the Federal Republic of Germany		10,6 million
			in the Soviet Zone of Germany		3,5 million
			in Austria and other western countries		0,5 million

This means that every fifth person of the Germans who had been residing in the expulsion areas in 1939 fell or perished.

turned over civilian administration to the Poles
and began shipping the German population in
freight cars, often without food or water, to the
remaining parts of the Reich.

The truncation of Germany along the Oder
and (western) Neisse rivers was decided in
principle by Stalin, Roosevelt, and Churchill
at Teheran in late November 1943, and confirmed at the February 1945 Yalta Conference. Only the briefest résumé of the pertinent
diplomacy can be given here.

Originally it had been thought that—having
recognized the Polish government in exile—the
USSR would be willing to restore Poland with
modest territorial adjustments. Foreign Ministers Anthony Eden of Great Britain and V. M.
Molotov of the USSR, and U.S. Secretary of
State Cordell Hull agreed on October 25,
1943, in Moscow that Germany would lose
East Prussia—which had been an exclave east
of the Polish Corridor since 1919—but would
otherwise return to her pre-1938 borders (Hull
Memoirs, 2, p. 1287). East Prussia would presumably be given to Poland in return for minor
cessions to the USSR.

These expectations were upset by Stalin,
who at the Teheran Conference insisted on retaining all the Polish territory the USSR had
occupied in September 1939, under the Rib-
bentrop-Molotov pact. Poland, as compensation, would be permitted to expand westward
as far as the Oder. The compensation proposal, which was wholly at odds with Article 2
of the August 14, 1941, Atlantic Charter (second, they desire to see no territorial changes
that do not accord with the freely expressed
wishes of the people concerned), had been
broached in 1942 by Soviet diplomats (Kulski,
1947, p. 679). The idea had been echoed by
pro-Soviet Poles but had been rejected by
Prime Minister Mikolajczyk and the exile government, who wanted to acquire East Prussia,
Danzig, and Upper Silesia—but not at the cost
of losing territories in the East (Mikolajczyk,
1948, p. 301).

Although a case could hardly be made for

Russian rule over the lands Stalin had seized
from Poland in 1939, there were good arguments for detaching most of them from Poland. The British and American delegations at
the 1919 Peace Conference favored a political
Poland corresponding rather closely to ethnic
Poland. But the new Warsaw regime reached
an agreement with the Ukrainian leader Pet-
lyura in Kiev, whereby Ukraine ceded Eastern
Galicia in return for Polish military support
against the Bolsheviks. This involvement led to
a Russo-Polish war. On July 11, 1920, when
Warsaw was hard-pressed by Trotsky's advancing Red Army, the British Foreign Minister, Lord Curzon, proposed a boundary along
the eastern edge of the area of solid Polish settlement. This boundary, later resurrected as
the German-Soviet demarcation line of 1939,
became known as the Curzon Line. The
August 1920, "miracle of the Vistula," however, changed the fortunes of war, and Polish
troops again penetrated deeply into the former
Russian Empire. By the Treaty of Riga (March
18, 1921), Soviet Russia yielded to Poland territories that were mainly Ukrainian and Byelo-
russian in population. In the meantime, Polish troops had seized the Lithuanian capital of
Vilnius, which Poland had annexed in 1922
after a questionable plebiscite.

Despite vigorous colonization efforts, Poland never succeeded in achieving an ethnic
Polish majority in its annexed eastern provinces. The 1931 census, which Ukrainians and
Byelorussians challenged for understating
their ethnic groups and inflating the Polish element, showed that only 36.5 percent of the
population were Polish by language, while the
Ukrainians accounted for 37.1 percent and the
Byelorussians for another 15.1 percent (Bohmann, 1969, p. 123). Of the 3.9 million Poles
in the regions the USSR annexed in 1939 and
reannexed in 1945, only 2.1 million had been
resettled in or had fled to postwar Poland by
1950, and the number of repatriations since
then has remained under 300,000 (*ibid.*, p.
148). Of these, only 1.75 million were resettled

in the parts of Germany placed under Polish administration. They were supplemented by 3.18 million resettlers from areas retained by Poland, but 600,000 of the latter returned to Poland proper. An additional 152,000 re-immigrants who responded to a postwar appeal for Poles abroad to return, were also resettled in the German eastern territories.

Consideration of these facts would suggest that—setting aside the question of the legitimacy of the Soviet government as the protector of non-Russian peoples (a question *never* considered during World War II)—the case for Polish retention of the territories annexed by the Treaty of Riga was weak to begin with. Even if the principle of territorial compensation were to be admitted—despite its manifest violation of self-determination—then there were no reasons for assigning Poland territory beyond that inhabited by 2 million Germans at most, such as East Prussia alone. Even then, international law contained no justification or firm precedent for wholesale removal of the inhabitants, despite the expulsions mentioned earlier in this chapter.

Churchill, nevertheless, agreed to the Curzon Line at Teheran, as well as to the Oder Line as compensation for Poland in the west (Churchill, 1954, 5, pp. 348–51). In so doing, he was motivated by an urgent practical consideration: that of assuring the return of the Polish government-in-exile to power rather than some Moscow-sponsored communist junta. Churchill was quite aware that Poland would be "liberated" and occupied by Soviet, not British troops; should Mikolajczyk refuse to concede the Curzon Line, Stalin would simply install a Polish government willing to do so.

Churchill decided to act firmly and harshly with the Poles in the hope that this would be the most successful method in forcing them to accept his point of view as to how to solve the Soviet-Polish dilemma. In a blunt manner Churchill stated that his Government considered the Curzon Line as a just frontier for Poland. The loss of territories east of that line would be compensated by pushing Poland westward to the Oder Line. (Rozek, 1958, p. 194)

Throughout 1944, Churchill continued his pressure on the Polish exile premier. But Mikolajczyk and his cabinet temporized, while Stalin's impatience mounted. On July 22, 1944, Radio Moscow announced that the Polish Committee of National Liberation (later known as the Lublin Committee) had been founded at Soviet-occupied Chelm. Under a Soviet-(Lublin) Polish agreement on July 27, it took administration of liberated territory. (For details, see Rozek, 1958, pp. 183–320.)

After a futile British-Polish-Soviet summit conference in Moscow in October 1944, Churchill—unable to wring any concessions from Stalin—turned his frustrated rage against Mikolajczyk. The latter agreed to convene his cabinet and to recommend acceptance of the Curzon Line and maximum compensation in the west. But the Polish parties in exile could not agree, and Mikolajczyk resigned. By the time the British and American delegations met in Malta on their way to the February 1945, Yalta Conference, the Lublin Committee had proclaimed itself the Provisional Government of Poland and had been recognized as such by the USSR and by Czecho-Slovakia (Malta, 1955, p. 509).

At the Yalta Conference, however, the Western allies agreed to recognize an expanded Lublin government as well as the Curzon Line. The "Big Three" agreed that Poland should receive "substantial accessions of territory in the North and West" but failed to settle a specific boundary. That would be determined at the Peace Conference (*ibid.*, pp. 938, 980).

As the war ended, Stalin created a *fait accompli* by turning over all territory east of the Oder and *western* Neisse rivers to the reorganized Polish regime and encouraging that regime to expel the German inhabitants. At the Potsdam Conference (July 23–August 2, 1945), President Truman and Prime Minister Attlee (who replaced Churchill after the Labour Party's electoral victory) yielded to Stalin, and the Potsdam Declaration recognized Polish *administration* of Germany east of the Oder-Neisse Line, though the three Heads of Government "reaffirm(ed) their opinion that the final delimitation of the Western frontier of Poland should await the peace settlement." They also agreed to a policy on expulsions, which read as follows:

XIII. Orderly Transfer of German Populations

The three Governments, having considered the question in all its aspects, recognise that the transfer to Germany of German populations, or elements thereof, remaining in Poland, Czechoslovakia and Hungary, will have to be undertaken. They agree that any transfers that take place should be effected in an orderly and humane manner.

Since the influx of a large number of Germans into Germany would increase the burden already resting on the occupying authorities, they consider that the Allied Control Council in Germany should in the first instance examine the problem with special regard to the question of the equitable distribution of these Germans among the several zones of occupation. They are accordingly instructing their respective representatives on the Control Council to report to their Governments as soon as possible the extent to which such persons have already entered Germany from Poland, Czechoslovakia and Hungary, and to submit an estimate of the time and rate at which further transfers could be carried out, having regard to the present situation in Germany.

The Czechoslovak Government, the Polish Provisional Government and the Control Council in Hungary are at the same time being informed of the above, and are being requested meanwhile to suspend further expulsions pending the examination by the Governments concerned of the report from their representatives on the Control Council. (Berlin, 1960, Vol. 2, Article XIII, pp. 1478–98)

As things turned out, the "transfer" was anything but "orderly and humane." Those who fled were in many cases harassed and robbed by Red Army troops and both regular and irregular Polish forces: a contemporary witness speaks of "the ravished land, the burned villages, plundered houses, heaps of corpses along the highways, women and girls whom a bestial lust had abused and then murdered" (Koenigswald, p. 20). A Dutch observer reported the condition of refugees in the Soviet Occupation Zone to British Military Government at Lübeck on July 17, 1945, in these words:

I have seen a large proportion of these people, numbering nearly a million, who are literally starving on the road. I saw children and babies lying dead in the ditch by the roadside, dead of hunger and epidemic disease, their arms and legs often not thicker than a man's thumb. The evacuees try to pick out of the refuse of the Russian field kitchens, often already in the state of decay, something suitable to satisfy their maddening hunger. Means of transportation do not exist or are absolutely inadequate, so they spend many weeks in rain and tempest and are exposed to all vicissitudes of the weather. (Quoted, Jaksch, 1963, p. 423.)

On July 30, the London *Times* published a report by its Berlin correspondent that diplomats attending the Potsdam Conference were receiving reports of unspeakable conditions on highways leading from Polish-occupied cities. "Women and children are said to be dying in the ditches, and similar things are reported to be happening in Frankfurt on the Oder and in Stettin" (Quoted, *ibid.*, p. 424).

During the winter of 1945–46, reports came across the desk of one of the authors, then an official of U.S. Military Government in Berlin, that Germans were being loaded into unheated freight cars in Silesia and other areas east of the Oder and Neisse, after which they were shipped cross-country in continuous journeys lasting 72 hours or more, with black bread and thin soup or water their only sustenance. British officers at Hannover, where the cars were unloaded, reported that large numbers of passengers, especially young children and the aged, were dead on arrival.

The magnitude of the expulsion of *Reichsdeutsche* as well as the lethal methods with which it was carried out are apparent from the statistics. The prewar population of the eastern areas of Germany was 9,575,000; addition of the excess of births over deaths and subtraction of direct war losses leaves an estimated postwar population of 9,350,000. According to the 1966 figures released by the Federal Ministry For Expellees, Refugees, and War Victims in Bonn, 6,944,000 people were expelled to Central and Western Germany, while 1,101,000 remained in their areas of origin—most of them persons of Polish or Masurian ethnicity. Simple subtraction would suggest that 1,307,000 people perished in the process of expulsion, a result that is fairly close to the Ministry's estimate of 1,225,000. Even the lower estimate is sufficient to characterize the expulsion as an exercise in genocide.

3. SUDETEN GERMANS AND OTHER VOLKSDEUTSCHE

Prior to World War II there were 7,224,000 *Volksdeutsche* living outside the 1937 borders of the Reich, not including an estimated 1.5 to 2 million Volga Germans and other ethnic Germans in the USSR. Of these *Volksdeutsche*, 4,786,000 were expelled to postwar Germany, while 1,544,000—the largest group being Transylvania Saxons in Rumania—remained in their regions of origin. The Ministry estimates that 886,000 of these Germans died during the process of expulsion.

Because of limitations of space, discussion will be limited to the largest group of *Volksdeutsche*: the Sudeten Germans expelled from Czecho-Slovakia. This nationality group of 3.3 million ethnic Germans (1930 census) consisted of former Austrian citizens incorporated against their will in the new Czecho-Slovak Republic established in October 1918. On the twenty-first of that month, when it was clear that the Austrian war effort was collapsing, the German-speaking members of the Imperial Parliament, including the deputies from Bohemia and Moravia-Silesia, met in Vienna as a provisional national assembly. Accepting President Wilson's principle of self-determination, the assembly claimed "the entire territory settled by German Austrians" with the exception of linguistic exclaves, for which international minority protection was demanded. The next day, the assembly resolved that Austria should seek to join the German Reich.

Upon receiving news that the Czecho-Slovak Republic had been proclaimed in Prague, the German deputies from northern and western Bohemia and from Moravia-Silesia organized the Austrian provinces of German Bohemia and Sudetenland, which the assembly in Vienna recognized on October 30, 1918. The new Czech government in Prague, however, obtained Allied approval for a military occupation of the German districts and overthrew the provincial governments by force of arms in December 1918. Trusting President Wilson and the Peace Conference (wrongly as it turned out), the Germans in these regions protested instead of fighting. "On March 4, 1919, the day on which Austria elected its new Constitutional Assembly, demonstrations for self-determination took place in many German cities in Bohemia and Moravia. While the demonstration in Teplitz, addressed by Josef Seliger, was permitted to proceed undisturbed, the Czech army crushed other demonstrations by force, wantonly killing 54 and injuring 107 unarmed demonstrators" (Glaser, 1961, pp. 22–23).

The story of the Munich Crisis of 1938 and the annexation of the Sudeten German districts by Hitler's Third Reich is too well known to require repeating here (for details, see Jaksch, 1967, pp. 303–44). It may be observed, however, that the transfer of the ethnic German regions from Czech to German sovereignty was regarded as an act in fulfillment of self-determination. Like the Saarländers, who had voted for Germany three years before, the Sudeten Germans had little idea of what life would be like under a totalitarian regime. There were, however, a goodly number, mostly but not all Social Democrats, who were so strongly opposed to Hitler and his concentration-camp system that they preferred continued Czech rule within an imperfect democracy.

As German forces advanced into the Sudeten districts in early October 1938, Social Democrats and other German opponents of Hitler fled into Central Bohemia. The Czech police began shipping them back into the Reich. Finally, after the British government, yielding to pressure, tardily produced an emigration scheme, some 3000 anti-fascist Sudeten Germans were enabled to escape. But a larger number, sometimes estimated as high as 20,000, were turned over to the Gestapo (Glaser, 1961, pp. 40–41).

President Eduard Beneš of Czecho-Slovakia, who had resigned after Munich and recognized his successor Dr. Emil Hacha, established an exile committee in Paris. As the Germans marched into France it moved to London, where—after lengthy negotiations and maneuvers—it was recognized as an exile government. The foreign and domestic policies of this government were based on the closest cooperation with the USSR. Dr. Hubert Ripka, Information Minister in the London exile government, wrote (1944, p. 58): "We Czechoslovaks make no secret of our satisfaction that Soviet Russia is beginning to participate in European and world politics as a strong world power." Soviet support was particularly required to achieve two extreme Czech national aims to which Beneš and Ripka had given top priority: The expulsion of the Sudeten Germans and the reestablishment of Czech domination over Slovakia, which had become an independent republic in 1939. As one of the present authors (Glaser, 1961, p. 78) wrote in his *Czecho-Slovakia: A Critical History:*

The "exile government" had planned from the beginning to reacquire for Czecho-Slovakia the territories which had been ceded to other states in 1938. If we are to believe Ripka, the plan to expel the Sudeten Germans was conceived in 1939 or earlier, but it was considered advisable to keep it under wraps temporarily. Dr. Beneš actually conducted extensive negotiations with Wenzel Jaksch, the leader of the anti-Nazi Sudeten German Social Democrats in London, finally breaking them off in 1943 with the excuse that Sudeten demands for political rights were incompatible with loyalty to the Czecho-Slovak state. A clue to the intentions of the London "government" had, however, been provided as early as August 29, 1941, when Foreign Minister Masaryk announced Czecho-Slovak reservations to the Atlantic Charter amounting to a rejection of its fundamental principles on the self-determination of peoples.

The maneuver employed by Dr. Beneš to secure Allied approval for expelling the Sudeten Germans has been summarized in the Göttingen Research Society's handbook (*Sudetenland* as follows:

December 5, 1942	Dr. Beneš discusses his proposal for an expulsion of the Sudeten Germans in a lecture at the University of Manchester.
May 12, 1943	In a conversation with President Roosevelt, Dr. Beneš asserts that he has already received Soviet approval of his proposal to expel the Sudeten Germans.
May 29, 1943	Dr. Ripka informs the Soviet Ambassador in London, Bogomolov, that the American Government agrees to an expulsion of the Sudeten Germans. Ripka expresses the expectation that the Soviet Government will now also agree. (Beneš had reported on May 13 that F.D.R. had agreed that "after the war the number of Germans in Czechoslovakia must be reduced by the transfer of as many as possible.")
June 6, 1943	Ripka informs Beneš, who is still in America, that Soviet agreement to the expulsion of the Sudeten Germans has now been received. (On June 7, Beneš reported that

December 12, 1943

F.D.R. had confirmed his approval of the "transfer.")

Beneš concludes a treaty of friendship and alliance with the U.S.S.R. in Moscow. While in Moscow, Beneš reaches agreement with the Czech Communists there on the complete expropriation and expulsion of the Sudeten Germans. (1954, p. 97)

Unlike the American and Soviet Governments, that of Great Britain withheld approval of the expulsion until it actually took place. A plan to expel all except 800,000 Sudeten Germans was rejected flatly by Foreign Minister Sir Anthony Eden as late as January 15, 1945. But the impotence of His Majesty's Government to influence the actual course of events has already been noted in the case of Poland.

Although it was a mortification to patriotic Czechs to see their country under German rule in the form of the Protectorate, the situation of Czechs at home during World War II was by no means unbearable. As the Czech author F. O. Miksche tells us:

The situation of the Czechs in the so-called Protectorate during the war was not unfavorable. In the first place they were exempt from military service, and worked quite willingly for Hitler's war machine in the Bohemian industries, which were greatly developed by the Germans. Thousands of tanks, airplanes and guns were produced in the factories, many more than could possibly have been destroyed by the Legions which were organized by Beneš in France, England and Russia. . . .

Statistics show that Bohemia's war-time industrial and agricultural production was proportionately equal to that of Germany, and food shortages were no worse there than in the Reich. In contrast to Poland active resistance and sabotage scarcely existed in Bohemia until the last days of the war, although arrests were made by the Gestapo in Bohemia and Moravia as in the other countries occupied by Germany, and in Germany itself. The assassination of Heydrich was planned and organized abroad, and the Beneš government in London cleverly exploited the severe reprisals that followed, and especially the shooting of the 168 male inhabitants of Lidice, to influence British and American public opinion in its favor. Care was taken, of course, to avoid mentioning the fact that the reprisals were not the responsibility of the Sudeten Germans but were carried out by German Nazis. (Miksche, 1953, p. 25)

Miksche's account is confirmed by Kenneth de Courcey, who wrote in 1944:

There is, in fact, almost no resistance movement at all in Ruthenia, Slovakia, Moravia and Bohemia. The Ruthenians are . . . anti-Russian. The masses in Slovakia are anti-Czech and anti-Russian. The attitude of the Czech population is curious. Quite a number are now actually serving in the German forces, viz., in the 5th and 8th Jaeger Divisions, the 18th Motorized Division, and the 81st, 122nd, 225th and 290th Infantry Divisions. Czech industry is most effectively supporting the German war effort and many workers seem very much to dislike the idea of risking the consequences of resistance. The Czech clergy is largely supporting President Hacha, partly because of its anti-Russian views and partly because it fears anti-clericalism from the radicals abroad. All these facts are everywhere well-known on the Continent, and it causes astonishment to many friends of the Allies that they should be so little known in Britain and America. *War-Time Rationing and Consumption*, published by the League of Nations, Geneva, 1942, states that the inhabitants of Bohemia had the same ration as Germany. (*Review of World Affairs*, London, April 28, 1944)

As World War II drew to a close, the German command in Bohemia began to withdraw its forces into Germany itself, and a Czech National Committee emerged from the underground and prepared to assume power. This committee instructed the Czech people not to attack the Germans, who were leaving in any case; an agreement for peaceful withdrawal was announced on the České Budějovice Radio on May 5. At the same time, a communist-dominated "Revolutionary Council" in the Prague area made preparations for an armed revolt, which was wholly unnecessary for ridding Bohemia of the German army. The

Beneš Government, which had in the meantime moved from London via Moscow (where
it was reorganized so that the communist contingent was doubled) to Košice in Eastern Slovakia, found itself in a dilemma. Should a conservative and anti-Russian Czech National
Committee assume power in Prague, the best
Beneš could hope for was a coalition, in which
his supporters might find themselves in a minority position. Secondly, the Czechs—unless
they should be stimulated by an intense dose of
agitprop—showed no inclination to begin the
expulsion of the Sudeten Germans that Dr.
Beneš and his associates had planned. (Glaser,
1961, pp. 102–4.) The converging political interests of Dr. Beneš and the communists made
it urgently necessary to provoke bloodshed between Czechs and Germans.

On May 1, 1945, Information Minister Dr.
Ripka, who was still in London, comman-
deered the BBC Czechoslovak Service and,
with the aid of the communist deputy Ho-
dinova-Spurna, harangued the people of
Prague to mount the barricades and help the
glorious Red Army which was coming to liberate them. But the attempt to make a revolution
by radio did not work. What then happened
can best be described by quoting again from
Czecho-Slovakia: A Critical History:

> Since a non-Communist Czech government,
> which did not even call itself "Czechoslovak," was
> coming into being without American assistance, the
> Russians intervened directly. Communist agents,
> strengthened by reinforcements dropped by para-
> chute, seized Radio Prague and proclaimed an upris-
> ing, shouting their slogan *Smrt nemeckym occupan-
> tum!* ("Kill the German occupiers!") over the loud
> speakers on the street corners. This time the people,
> who were in a high state of nervous tension, turned
> out *en masse* and attacked German installations. The
> departing Germans returned to rescue their rear
> guard, and an SS armored division, which was by-
> passing Prague, moved in to clear the city. Although
> Reich Protector Frank had been willing to turn over
> his powers to a conservative Czech government, he
> refused to surrender to the "Revolutionary Coun-
> cil." The Czech National Committee was not able to

> cope with the German *Wehrmacht*, nor with the
> Communists and their allies, who were operating
> under exact instructions. A renewed Czech appeal
> for American entry into Prague brought only nega-
> tive results. . . .
>
> During the course of May 6, the SS cleared the
> barricades in most of Prague at a cost of at least two
> thousand killed and some forty thousand wounded.
> While this was going on, the Communist-controlled
> radio broadcast appeals in Russian for reinforcement
> from NKVD head-quarters in Kiev, and appeals in
> English for American help, which the Communists
> were reasonably sure would not be forthcoming.
> . . . On May 7, the Russian Vlassov Army, which
> the Germans had organized from Soviet prisoners of
> war, turned against the *Wehrmacht:* the Germans
> resorted to aerial bombardment of partisan strong-
> holds, with heavy civilian casualties. By this time
> the Czech National Committee was thoroughly dis-
> organized, and the Communist-dominated "Czech-
> oslovak Revolutionary Council" had control of the
> situation. (In *ibid.*, pp. 105–7)

The Prague broadcasts that began on May 5,
1945, were not merely a call to armed revolution against the *Wehrmacht* and the *Reichspro-
tektor*—which as we have seen was not only
unnecessary but counterproductive—but an
incitement to mob violence against the defenseless German civilian population, most of
whom had lived in Prague since Austrian days.
The revolt was spearheaded by a "revolutionary guard," which included more than a
few of the rabble element that Prague shares
with other large cities, and which

began rounding up the Germans and herding
them into schools, cinemas, and barracks. Few were
permitted to take any food with them, and almost
none was provided in the internment centers. Conditions were worst in the cinemas, which in Prague
are mostly underground and which were packed far
beyond their normal capacity—men, women, and
children were forced to sit in artificial light for several days, almost suffocating from the lack of air.
From time to time, prisoners were ordered out to
remove the barricades—while working on the
streets they were beaten, whipped, tarred, and in
many cases murdered. Many committed suicide in
desperation. After the entry of the Red Army, the

Germans were transferred to large collection camps such as the Strahov Stadium where over ten thousand were housed, the Riding Academy, and the Slavia Stadium. Here they were kept on a starvation diet—with Russian soldiers admitted every night to rape the women and girls—until their further transfer to forced farm labor or concentration camps. (*Ibid.*, pp. 111–12)

The experiences of the victims of the carnage in Prague and the ensuing terror and "wild expulsion" in the Sudetenland have been recorded in *Documents on the Expulsion of the Sudeten Germans*, otherwise known as the "Sudeten German White Book" (Turnwald, 1951, 1953). The two personal accounts that follow are typical rather than extreme, and are excerpted from the sworn affidavits reprinted in the White Book.

Report of the physicist K.F.—Prague: "Partisans crowded in from the street and drove some 30 men to Weinberg Avenue to clear away the barricades. . . . After the first hour we were all covered with blood, as a result of kicks and blows upon the head and neck. Everything from shovels, iron bars and lead pipes up to poles was used on us.

"Our shoes were taken away from us and we had to walk barefoot over the glass splinters on the ground . . . and afterward were driven to work again, where everything started once more.

"[That evening] we were loaded in a lorry and driven to a former German college at Stefansgasse 22. All our belongings were left behind and we never saw any of them again. In the college we were forced to stand against the wall with our hands raised until one after another collapsed. We were then taken to another room where what they called the 'Gestapaci' were kept. There were about 50 of us. We were ordered to hit each other in the face and when that was not carried out to the full satisfaction of our jailers, we were shown how to do it properly. When I collapsed again, a burning match was held to my toes until I came to. Then I had to get up again. The second time I was allowed to lie a little longer. Then they trampled on my face, but since there was still no reaction on my part, I was left lying there. Anyone who put up the slightest resistance was shot dead.

"The afternoon of May 10th, a group of armed men came in and selected the six youngest and strongest men, I being one of them. . . . We reached the corner of Wassergasse and there we were confronted with our task: Three naked bodies, burned with petrol, were hanging by their feet from a large hoarding. The faces were mutilated beyond recognition with all the teeth knocked out. . . . The roasted skin stuck to our hands as we half carried and half dragged the bodies to the Stefansgasse.

"I had hardly washed the blood off when our guards entered, looking for the six of us; I suddenly realized what was bound to happen now. We had seen far too much to be allowed to live. . . . While being knocked about, we were asked our names and professions and then given the order: 'To the death cellar!'

"The first of us was done with and lying on the floor in his own blood. The second had his turn. I should have been fourth. But as the second victim was lying on the floor, the door opened and a Czech, who looked somewhat more intelligent and who, judging by the guards' manner, had a certain amount of authority, entered the cellar. Later I learned that he was a nephew of Minister Stransky. He asked who we were and after a good deal of hesitation, he had me and a boy of 17, a former member of the Hitler Youth, brought out of the room, because we were the only ones who could speak Czech. . . .

"When we passed the guard, he grinned and remarked that we were the first ones to leave the cellar alive."

Report of Helene Bugner—Prague: "My labor group consisted of 20 women, among them some 60 to 70 years old. We were in charge of Professor Zelenka. When we stepped out of the house, Professor Zelenka handed us over to the mob with the following words: 'Here are the German bitches for you.' Calling us German whores, the mob forced us to kneel down and then our hair was cut off with bayonets. Our shoes and stockings were taken off, so that we had to walk barefoot. With each step we were inhumanly beaten with sticks, rubber truncheons, etc. Whenever a woman sank to the ground, she was kicked, rolled in the mud, and stoned. I myself fainted several times; water was poured over me and I was forced to continue working. When I was quite unable to do any more work, I received a kick in the left side, by which two of my ribs were broken. During one of my fainting fits they cut a piece of about 0.6 square inches out of the sole of my foot. These tortures lasted the whole afternoon. Among us were women far advanced in pregnancy and nursing mothers, who were ill-treated in the same way . . . one of the women had a miscarriage.

"In the evening we went home. I was so disfigured from the maltreatment and tortures that my children no longer recognized me. My face was crusted with blood and my dress reduced to blood stained rags. Two women lying in our house committed suicide in despair; another woman became insane. . . .

"Three weeks later we were sent to the camp at Hagibor. There 1200 persons were lodged in four barracks. All fell sick with hunger dysentery, for the diet consisted of a cup of thin water gruel twice a day for the children and for the grown-ups a cup of black coffee with a thin slice of bread morning and evening and watery soup at noontime. . . . Each evening the forced labor groups returned to the camp badly beaten up. Medical care was completely lacking. . . . Epidemics of measles, scarlet fever, whooping cough, and diphtheria broke out, which could not be dealt with. . . .

"Every night the villagers sent groups of Russian soldiers to our lodgings, who raped the women."

On arriving in Prague, Klement Gottwald, Chairman of the Communist Party and Deputy Premier in the reorganized Czechoslovak Government, announced the deportation of the Sudeten Germans. On May 13, President Beneš arrived in Prague and "rows of Germans were set on fire as human torches in his honor" (Report of Dr. Hans Wagner, International Red Cross representative, quoted, Turnwald, 1953, p. 21). On May 16, Beneš proclaimed: "Our slogan will be that we must purge our country of everything which is German—culturally, economically, and politically" (quoted, Jaksch, 1967, p. 435).

Following Radio Prague's summons to violence, Czech units in Central Bohemia and Moravia began attacking German troops, resident ethnic Germans, and the many columns of refugees that were passing through the "Protektorat." Where German military units managed to defend themselves, the partisans reacted by taking all the more violent revenge on German civilians, particularly after the German forces had disbanded or surrendered. To quote again from the *Critical History* (Glaser, 1961, p. 117):

Gottwald's proclamation of May 11 was followed by the mass arrest of Germans in various "ethnic islands" such as Iglau-Stecken and areas near Vyskov (Wischau) and Olomouc (Olmütz), as well as the scattered German residents of Czech communities. The entire German population of Iglau was interned in the concentration camps of Altenberg, Obergoss, and Helenenthal, which were as overcrowded as the Prague camps. Inmates were roused at 0415 hours for a day of heavy labor without lunch and were beaten and tortured on their return to camp, women and girls were raped each night by Russian and Czech soldateska, and children and adults died of starvation and disease. The diet during the first week consisted of ¼ liter thin soup and ¼ liter "coffee," after which two to four ounces of bread or two potatoes were added. Margaret Zimmermann, an inmate of the Obergoss camp, reported that among 800–1500 inmates there were 10 to 15 deaths each day. At this rate the average length of survival was little more than three months. Some of the Iglau Germans were driven on foot to Austria in late June, 1945—during which trek many infants and aged died of exhaustion or exposure—while the remainder were held in the camps until their transfer to Germany in 1946.

One of the most gruesome episodes was the notorious Brno "Death March" of May 30–31, 1945, in which 25,000 Germans of that city were driven thirty miles on foot to the Austrian frontier. The Austrian government—which perhaps hoped to induce the Czechs to return the Germans to Brno—refused to admit the refugees, who were lodged for weeks in a grain elevator in the border town of Pohrlitz, where hundreds died in an epidemic. [For details, see Turnwald, 1953, Report No. 7 in English edition.]

To remove the Germans from the Sudetanland—that is, the area ceded to Germany in 1938—before the Western Allies could forbid the mass expulsion, Dr. Beneš resorted to the tactic of the *fait accompli*. To accomplish this, Revolutionary Guard units were sent to the

Sudetenland, where their members were promised public employment and confiscated German property. In some areas, groups of partisans were permitted to undertake punitive expeditions on their own initiative; they would move into a Sudeten town, beat and shoot victims denounced to them or selected at random, and plunder the houses and apartments. In many cases, the partisans held public executions, with the entire German population, including the families of the victims, as unwilling witnesses.

One of the early episodes of the "wild expulsion," at Landskron in the Eastern Sudetenland was described by an eyewitness as follows:

Report of Julius Friedel—Landskron: ". . . More than a thousand German men were rounded up in the market place in the early hours of the afternoon. They were ordered to fall in and they stood there with their hands above their heads, waiting for what would happen next.

"The men were forced to lie down on the pavement, to stand up quickly, and then to get in line again. The Czechs passed down the lines, kicked the men, preferably on the shins or in the genitals. They hit then with whatever lay convenient to their hands; they spat at them and fired wildly with their rifles.

"Many men were too badly wounded to get up again and lay in great pain. But this was not enough. There was a large water tank for air raids in front of the town hall. Into this the victims of this terrible madness were finally thrown one after the other. As they came to the surface, they were struck at with sticks and poles and kept under water. . . ."

While a variety of tortures were being conducted, a so-called People's Court established itself on the sidewalk in front of the town hall.

"One after the other, with their hands above the head, the Germans had to appear before the tribunal. . . . The last 20 or 30 paces up to the tribunal had to be made in a creeping position. Arriving there each one received his sentence, written on his back with a piece of chalk. About 170 to 200 feet distant from the tribunal, on the opposite side, was a gate; up to this the victims had literally to run the gauntlet. Many of them collapsed on their way, even before the sentence could be carried out. . . ." [The witness then describes various killings, giving a list of 24 victims and 25 suicides.] (Turnwald, 1953, condensed from Report 6 in English edition)

In Saaz, a city of 20,000 in the Western Sudetenland, the 5000 German males between 13 and 65 years of age were marched ten miles to the barracks at Postelberg, which became a concentration and liquidation camp. Here they were starved, beaten, and tortured for days, several hundred being arbitrarily shot and heaped into mass graves. On June 7, a total of 275 men were locked all night in a tightly closed room without windows; scores suffocated and others went insane in this "black hole of Calcutta." Mass murders also took place at Joachimsthal, Ober-Lipka, Totzau, and numerous other places.

In the Western part of Bohemia, which was occupied by the United States, American officers were forbidden to interfere with the brutality. One of them wrote home:

We came down here last week. Up there everybody got along fine with the Czechs and even liked them a lot. But here in the Sudetenland it's terrible. The Czech atrocities are outrageous, the Germans are being kicked around like dogs. About seventy-five per cent of the people here are German, but the few Czech soldiers and the burgomaster do as they please.

We are not allowed to interfere in any way in what the Czechs are doing, and are under orders from higher headquarters to approve all their actions. Germans are coming to me every day crying that the Czechs had taken their husbands and fathers away. Then, in most instances, the Czech soldiers had returned to "search the house for military items"—and looted the entire premises, carrying off every bit of food, silverware, dishes, furniture, and even the wash hanging on the line. That happens every day and I can't do a thing about it, because if I express as much as a doubt whether what the Czechs are doing is right, headquarters will squelch any inclination on my part to have sympathy, not to speak of Christian charity.

To-day I sent seventy-five "displaced" Germans back to Germany. They had all their baggage packed and I arranged for trucks for transportation. They got as far as the next town.

When they arrived there the Czechs conducted a search for military objects, ripped open the bundles with knives and took whatever of value they found. Our guards simply had to stand there and look on. . . . Interference with the Czech "authorities" is out of the question, because everything they do is right. It certainly burns me up. I was talking with the local priest the other day. He said, the future and particularly the coming winter will be the worst time the people here have ever gone through. The German occupation, he said, was terrible and he himself had been arrested by the Gestapo on several charges, but life since the Czechs took over is worse than any other former experience. . . .

This whole situation makes me furious. I thought I came over here and went through all that hell to stop this sort of thing. Where on God's earth do all our American ideals come in? . . . If the Czechs do go through with their super-plan and kick out the three million Germans, Czechoslovakia will dig its own grave. (*The Wanderer*, St. Paul, Minnesota, August 30, 1945)

The deportation of the Sudeten Germans was among the mass expulsions to which President Truman and Prime Minister Attlee agreed at Potsdam. It must be remembered, however, that 1945 marked the high point of anti-German "collective guilt" propaganda. The Western statesmen went to Potsdam without the backing of informed public opinion; they lacked the political conception necessary to resist the *fait accompli* that Soviet Russia and its satellites thrust upon them. As the American and British delegations saw the situation, there was nothing they could do to stop the expulsions from Czechoslovakia or from the Eastern Reich (Byrnes, 1947, pp. 79 ff.). It has been contended, however, that the helplessness of the Western Powers at Potsdam was largely self-imposed. The same has been said about Western helplessness in the face of more recent Communist aggression in Vietnam and Angola. To examine that question, however,

would be a distraction from the subject of this book.

C. *Mass Expulsions in the Postwar Era*

Mass deportations and mass flights to escape intolerable conditions have continued in various parts of the world since World War II. Space permits the reporting in some detail of only three such episodes, two of which are cases of genuine mass expulsion. In the third, as will be seen, the charge of forced expulsion and the claims of the "expellees" have been partly, though not entirely, fictionalized. Among episodes that will *not* be examined are the mass flights from the "German Demoratic Republic" into West Germany throughout the 1950s and until the building of the Berlin Wall in 1961, from Hungary after the 1956 revolution, and from Czecho-Slovakia after the Soviet occupation of 1968. There have also been continuing phenomena: practically the entire Cuban elite has migrated to Florida since Castro's accession to power. A steady flight of Chinese from the communist-ruled mainland continues. Although it involves only a small percentage of the Chinese population, it nevertheless adds up to millions.

1. POPULATION MOVEMENTS INCIDENT TO PARTITION OF INDIA

At the beginning of the twentieth century, most of the Muslims within the Indian Empire lived compactly in the western provinces and states, as well as in Bengal. Millions of additional Muslims were dispersed throughout the Hindu areas.

In 1909, the Minot-Morley reforms established separate electorates and consecrated the fact that the Muslim and Hindu communities were not politically compatible. The reforms were widely interpreted as a British *divide-et-impera* stratagem. But those divisions were not created by Britain; they were old and real, and they were preserved and accentuated by the Indians themselves. In 1911, however, Bengal was reunited upon Hindu pressure and against the strong protests of Muslim Bengalis.

The Muslim League originally assumed that India would remain undivided India but gradually came to view this concept as unrealistic. The idea of a large "Muslim nation" which would be free from Hindu domination gained prominence by several steps. In 1913, the League asked for self-government; in 1930 the concept of the "Muslim Nation" was born; in 1933 the concept of Pakistan was formulated; and in 1940, the League adopted the Pakistan concept—of a Muslim state in the northwest of India (Lévy, 1973, pp. 21–26). As the idea gained support, the Pakistan project was extended to include Bengal. Once it was clear that the Hindus were willing to grant proportional but not equal representation to the Islamic community—only a little more than one-third as large as the Hindu population—the Muslim League rejected federalism in all its forms and endorsed the solution of independent Muslim states.

According to the 1941 census, India had 389 million inhabitants, including 255 million Hindus and Scheduled Castes, 92 million Muslims, 6.3 million Christians, and 5.6 million Sikhs, plus 30 million of diverse small ethnic and religious groups and tribal societies. Thus, the Muslims, even if they could gain the support of the Christians and the small groups, had no chance of fending off Hindu domination through a one-man, one-vote system. Informed Congress Party leaders knew that aggressive Hindu groups were spreading the slogan of "Hindi, Hindu, Hindustan." They should have realized that the Muslims needed ironclad constitutional guarantees and that a unitary democracy is not feasible in a highly pluralistic society like India.

Each of the two major religious communities feared for the integrity of its way of life. These are so different that, despite minimal social interaction, interdining was infrequent and intermarriage hardly ever took place. Communal battles arose from minor incidents and accidents, and often enough from provocations by "Muslim mullahs, Hindu Priests, or fanatic laymen . . . raising the Muslim cry of Din ('Religion') or the Hindu charge of sacrilege" (W. N. Brown, 1966, p. 16). Each side feared *Umvolkung*, or forced ethnic transformation, and each side contained extremists who hoped to make its religion and lifestyle universal.

Communal tensions were acerbated by the hardships of World War II, including a famine in Bengal (1943) said to have cost 3 million lives. Toward the end of the war the British announced they would leave India, and in 1946 a plan was discussed for partitioning India into three parts: the Hindu provinces, the Muslim northwest, and Muslim Bengal and Assam. This approach was unacceptable to the Hindus, i.e. to Nehru's Congress Party, while the Muslim League wanted one instead of two Islamic states. Negotiations broke down.

The Muslim League proclaimed that it could no longer rely on democratic procedures and votes to reach its objectives. Mohammed Ali Jinnah, its leader, declared that Western democracy was totally unsuited to India and that, indeed, "its imposition on India was a disease in the body politic" (Quoted, Khosla, 1951, p. 42). Accordingly, on July 29, 1946, the Muslim League Council, meeting in Bombay, decided that the Moslems must resort to "direct action to achieve Pakistan . . . to get rid of the present slavery under the British and contemplated future caste Hindu domination." A Council of Action was created to prepare operational plans.

India was thus plunged into a two-year period of communal warfare. It began with a Muslim offensive between August 1946, and April 1947, which took place mainly in Calcutta, Bihar, Punjab, the northwest Frontier Province, and Sind. This was followed by a phase of Hindu retaliation which lasted from August to December 1947, and took place largely in the area later known as West Pakistan. Throughout 1947, and later, these hostilities were connected with mass migrations of Muslims moving into predominantly Muslim areas and of Hindus leaving for predominantly Hindu areas. The Sikhs were moving toward Hindu-dominated locations. A subsequent investigation by the Indian government detailed 591 separate incidents.

Calcutta was deliberately chosen by the Council of Action as their first target (*ibid.*, pp. 45–66). It was a good choice. There was a Muslim majority in Calcutta and in the Bengal countryside; Calcutta was economically the most important place in the country; and the incident was certain to be widely reported and to have maximum psychological shock effects. Furthermore, the city administration was in the hands of the Muslim League, which skillfully used the police to support the rioters.

The operation involved a general strike (*hartal*), the closing of shops, the removal of all means of transport, and the unleashing of the underworld, which is very numerous in Calcutta. Hindu shops and houses were attacked, robbed, and burned, as were Hindu temples. Acts of violence were directed against prominent as well as ordinary Hindus. The undertaking was presented as a sort of *riposte* to the appointment of Nehru as premier of an interim government in which Jinnah was not scheduled to participate. It also was presented as a *jihad* to build in India "the greatest Islamic kingdom in the world" (a Muslim killed in a holy war supposedly rises to heaven). When the Hindus struck back, the operation was halted.

With suitable variations this scheme was applied time and again. Essentially, it consisted of three parts: First, attacks were mounted where the local authorities were in the hands of the Muslim League. Second, there was unending and vicious hate propaganda which kept political passion and lust for violence at a very high pitch. Third, although rioters or pogromists were often recruited from the criminal underworld, organ-

ized combat groups or "storm troops" and in some instances semimilitary organizations were also engaged in the atrocities. Local leadership groups acted independently but usually under general directives issued from central leadership groups.

In all this, the Muslim intent of *Umvolkung* was very much in evidence. It took the form of forced conversions, especially of young women who were abducted, put under various forms of pressure (including serfdom), and were forced to convert and marry. Rapes also were organized to lower the resistance of Hindu women. Hindu temples were often destroyed, provoking further bloodshed. Finally, killings of businessmen, intellectuals, and political leaders had a strong aristocidal effect (*ibid.*, pp. 9, 43, 81, 107, 313f.).

Part of the violence was aimed at separating the Muslim and Hindu populations. Yet few wanted to leave their homes and abandon acquired rights and belongings. Hence violence was mounted to frighten the undesired elements away. When fear through terror did not work well enough, violence was employed to evict the "enemy" physically. This was done by means of expropriations, vandalism, systematic looting, blocking of income, and denial of food and water. Once the exodus was underway, the refugees and their caravans and trains were attacked once again; they were robbed, and killed. Those who carried money and valuables were in particular danger.

In the end, at least half a million Muslims and Hindus died, many directly from violence, others from the strain of the exodus and the hardship, deprivations and sickness it entailed. The fatalities were more or less evenly divided between the Muslims and Hindus. A minimum of 14 million people were uprooted through the population exchanges (Loshak, 1971, p. 6). While most of the damage took place in the northwest, the enormous loss of wealth affected the whole subcontinent.

In the political settlement, East and West Pakistan were split off from India as a single

Muslim state divided by 1200 miles of Hindu territory. Punjab, Bengal, and Assam, clearly defined historical entities, were partitioned into predominantly Muslim and predominantly Hindu parts. Paksitan emerged as the world's fifth most populous country.

The 40 million Muslims left in India continued to proliferate and there were 60 million of them by 1970. Pakistan, on the other hand, was down to four million Hindus. Yet it was by no means ethnically homogeneous. Some 56 percent of its inhabitants were Bengalis, 31 percent Punjabis, 7 percent Pakhtunis (Pathans), 5 percent Sindhis, and 1 percent Baluchis. In West Pakistan, the Punjabis had a clear majority of 70 percent, with the Pakhtunis, Sindhis and Baluchis accounting for 15, 12 and 3 percent respectively.

The India-Pakistan region adjoins the Central Asian areas of the USSR and China, and is hence geopolitically involved in the Sino-Soviet conflict. The ethnic problems of the Indian subcontinent thus remain part and parcel of one of the globe's most dangerous confrontations.

2. THE PALESTINIAN ARABS: A CASE OF CONFLICTING RIGHTS

The political leadership that has emerged among the displaced Arabs of Palestine, notably the Palestine Liberation Organization (PLO) headed by Yassir Arafat, has gained wide credence for the belief that a nation has been dispossessed of its rightful homeland. Many Europeans and Americans with only superficial knowledge of the Middle East accept the thesis that the Palestinian Arabs have political rights—the so-called "legitimate rights of the Palestinians in their homeland" (e.g. Hussein, 1975)—that would preclude the survival of Israel as an ethnic-linguistic state of the Jewish nation. The slogan used to gain Western support is that of a "Democratic and secular Palestinian state," in which Jews, Muslims, and Christians will supposedly enjoy equal rights.

The Palestinian Arabs have gained considerable tactical support for their goals, if not their methods, among the displaced *Reichsdeutsche* and *Volksdeutsche* in the Federal Republic of Germany. These *Heimatvertriebene* see an analogy between the situation of the Palestinian "expellees" and their own. This is particularly true in the case of the Sudeten Germans, whose *Landmannschaft* is party to the August 1950, Wiesbaden agreement calling for a bi-ethnic Bohemia. If Czechs and Germans can live together peacefully in the region where both have homeland rights, why not Arabs and Jews? A Sudeten German petition to the United Nations refers specifically to the "unalienable right of self-determination, national independence, the right of return to the traditional homeland and to retribution of property" recognized in the case of the Palestinian Arabs by General Assembly resolution No. 3236 of November 22, 1974 (*Sudetendeutsche Zeitung*, August 1, 1975).

Aside from the question whether the right to homeland (*Heimatrecht*) is in fact unalienable—which will be considered in the concluding section of this chapter—the analogy between displaced Germans and Palestinian Arabs is false and may eventually prove to be damaging to the German expellees. The apparent similarity rests both upon a semantic deception and upon inadequate knowledge of the demographic and economic history of Palestine.

The semantic error involves the notion that the Palestinian Arabs (who call themselves "Palestinians," thus implying the Jews are not) are a dispossessed nation. Arafat and his PLO claim to be and have been recognized by the United Nations (over U.S. objections) as spokesmen for "the Palestinian people." To Americans this term conjures up the analogy of the American people, whereas Germans think of *das deutsche Volk*. Both terms are, in this meaning, interchangeable with *nation*. Arab propagandists in the West take advantage of this identification.

When asked to retranslate the phrase "Palestinian people" back into Arabic, however, Arabs will always use the term *sha'ab*. A *sha'ab* is not a nation. The Arabic term closest to the Western concept of nation (or *Volk*) is *umma*, meaning the totality of the Muslim Arab nation united in devotion to Allah under the guidance of His Prophet (P.B.U.H.). A *sha'ab* is a regional or local people, such as those of the Anglo-Saxon Appalachians, the Pennsylvania Dutch, or the Bavarians, Suabians, Provençaux, or Sicilians. The Arab term *sha'ab* is closely translated by the German word *Stamm* (pl. *Stämme*), but there is no accurate English equivalent. The dictionary translation, "tribe," implies a primitive sociopolitical system, which may be but is not necessarily characteristic of a *sha'ab* or *Stamm*. A *sha'ab/Stamm* has a dialect but never a language; it may have a legitimate claim to local self-administration, but it does not meet the criteria of nationhood.

It is significant that the *Arabs* have never regarded their Palestinian *sha'ab* as a people with a claim to independence. As Yaniv points out:

Indeed, Haj Emin Al Husseini, the Grand Mufti of Jerusalem, and formerly the recognized leader of the Palestinian Arabs, explicitly opposed the British Mandate in Palestine on the grounds that it separated Palestine from Syria, while the representative of the Arab High Committee to the UN reminded the General Assembly in a formal statement submitted in May 1947, that "Palestine was part of the Province of Syria," and that "politically, the Arabs of Palestine were not independent in the sense of forming a separate political entity." And even as late as 31 May 1956, Ahmed Shukeiri, later the chairman of the PLO, told the Security Council that "it is common knowledge that Palestine is nothing but southern Syria." (1974, p. 5)

The desire for a separate national state was hardly evident among the Arabs in Palestine until the mid-1960s. A May 1964 Palestinian conference held by Shukeiri in the then Jordanian sector of Jerusalem, however, established a Palestinian National Council to coordinate all Palestinian Arab organizations. It also adopted

a National Covenant which, with minor amendments made in 1968, is still the basic programmatic statement of the PLO (Harkabi, 1974, pp. 49–50). By 1965, the PLO was already training thousands of Palestinians for an Egyptian-sponsored Arab Liberation Army centered in the Gaza strip. These preparations, the formation of several anti-Israeli sabotage groups, and the intensification of fedayeen attacks across the border doubtlessly contributed to the Israeli decision to launch the preventive war of June 1967.

Arab and Jewish Settlement. The historical homeland claims of the Palestinian Arabs, while not toally devoid of merit, are in no way comparable to those of the Germans who lived in regions such as East Prussia, Silesia, or Bohemia-Moravia before World War II. Palestine was badly neglected under Turkish rule. The British archaeologist Thomas Shaw described it in 1738 as "lacking in people to till its fertile soil," while the French historian and traveler Count Constantine François Volney called it a "ruined" and "desolate" country in 1785 (quoted, Aumann, 1974, p. 3). As Volney saw the Palestinian countryside in 1785:

The peasants are incessantly making inroads on each other's lands, destroying their corn, durra, sesame and olive-trees, and carrying off their sheep, goats and camels. The Turks, who are everywhere negligent in repressing similar disorders, are the less attentive to them here, since their authority is very precarious. The Bedouin, whose camps occupy the level country, are continually at open hostilities with them, of which the peasants avail themselves to resist their authority or do mischief to each other, according to the blind caprice of their ignorance or the interest of the moment. Hence arises an anarchy which is still more dreadful than the despotism that prevails elsewhere, while the mutual devastation of the contending parties renders the appearance of this part of Syria more wretched than that of any other. (In *ibid.*, pp. 3–4)

By mid-nineteenth century, Aumann relates in his brief *Land Ownership in Palestine, 1880–1948* (*ibid.*, p. 4), Turkish taxation and chronic indebtedness to moneylenders were forcing Arab farmers into tenancy or off the land altogether. Those who remained were involved in constant blood-feuds and were frequently raided by ferocious Bedouins, of whom H. B. Tristram wrote that they "have obtained their present possessions gradually and, in great measure, by driving out the fellahin (peasants), destroying their villages and reducing their rich cornfields to pasturage" (1865, p. 448; quoted in Aumann, 1974, p. 4). Tristram reported that the formerly cultivated Jordan Valley was now abandoned except for the slave-holding Bedouin: in the Sharon Plain, the Bedouins had wiped out twenty villages and extirpated the stationary population. Mark Twain wrote of the Holy Land in 1867 as: "Desolate country whose soil is rich enough but is given over wholly to weeds—a silent mournful expanse. . . . We reached Tabor safely. . . . We never saw a human being on the whole route" (1881, pp. 451, 180; in *ibid.*, p. 5). By the turn of the century, there were only 300,000 Arabs left in Palestine, including the West Bank and the Gaza strip. They were concentrated in the hilly regions, whereas Jewish land purchases and settlement, which had begun in 1880, involved mainly the largely uncultivated and thinly settled plains and valleys such as the Coastal Plain and, further north, the Jezreel, Jordan, Beisan, and Huleh Valleys (Aumann, 1974, p. 7). The lion's share of the arable land in Palestine had fallen into the hands of less than 200 absentee landowners; scattered parcels were worked by impoverished tenant farmers, but most of it was left unsettled and untended. As Aumann sums up:

This, then, was the picture of Palestine in the closing decades of the nineteenth century and the first quarter of the twentieth: a land that was overwhelmingly desert and swampland, with nomads continually encroaching on the settled areas and their farmers; a lack of elementary facilities and equipment; peasants wallowing in poverty, ignorance and disease, saddled with debts (interest rates

at times were as high as 60 percent) and threatened by warlike nomads or neighbouring clans. The result was a growing neglect of the soil and a flight from the villages, with a mounting concentration of lands in the hands of a small number of large landowners, frequently residing in such distant Arab capitals as Beirut and Damascus, Cairo and Kuwait. Here, in other words, was a social and economic order that had all the earmarks of a medieval feudal society. (*Ibid.*, pp. 8–9)

As Jewish settlement in Palestine proceeded during the last two decades of the nineteenth century and the first half of the twentieth century, the three large Jewish land-buying organizations made most of their purchases from large and usually absentee landowners. Of the 429,887 dunams of land purchased by PICA (Palestine Jewish Colonization Association) from private owners, almost 70 percent was in large tracts of mostly unfarmed land, often belonging to absentee landholders. The same was true of 90 percent of the land bought by the Palestine Land Development Company and by the Jewish National Fund from 1901 to 1930. Of the land bought by individual Jews, and by the JNF between 1931 and 1947, at least 50 percent was in large tracts either not cultivated or carrying only primitive agriculture. After 1922, however, the British Mandate Administration assigned vacant state lands almost entirely to Arabs—often in rather large tracts, which the Arab beneficiaries held without improvement and then sold to Jewish groups at a large profit. As Aumann points out: "In 1944, Jews paid between $1,000 and $1,100 per acre in Palestine, mostly for arid or semi-arid land; in the same year, rich black soil in the State of Iowa was selling for about $110 per acre (U.S. Department of Agriculture)."

The British required resettlement or other compensation of Arab farmers displaced by Jewish land purchases, but there were not many. Of 688 tenant farmers required to move between 1920 and 1930, 526 remained in agricultural occupations, some 400 of whom found other land. Of 3271 families registering as landless Arabs, only 664 were found to have valid claims; 347 of these were resettled and the remainder refused because they had found employment elsewhere or did not like the new areas.

The significant thing about Jewish settlement in and development of Palestine is that it reversed the net emigration of Arabs. Particularly after World War I, Arabs began immigrating to Palestine, precisely because there was employment to be had in Jewish enterprises and in trades catering to Jewish customers. While precise figures on Arab immigration between the two world wars are lacking, it is estimated between 60,000 and 100,000. The non-Jewish and non-Bedouin population of Palestine grew more than 75 percent between 1922 and 1929, leading a Royal Commission to comment in 1937: "The shortage of land is, we consider, due less to the amount of land acquired by the Jews than to the increase in the Arab population." While population growth in Arab-dominated towns such as Hebron and Bethlehem reflected the excess of births over deaths, the Arab population in Jewish cities soared. Between 1922 and 1943, Arab increases registered were 97 percent in Jerusalem, 134 percent on Jaffa, and 216 percent in Haifa. It is known that many Arabs entered Palestine during World War II to work on military projects and in the towns, but much of this immigration went unrecorded. The economic reason is clear from the comparative wage scales of the time (table 22.2).

Table 22.2.   DAILY WAGE SCALES, 1943
             (in mils)

	Unskilled Labor	Skilled Labor
Palestine	220–250	350–600
Egypt	30–50	70–200
Syria	80–100	150–300
Iraq	50	70–200

A mil is one-thousandth of a British pound.
SOURCE: A. Khoushy, *Brit Poalei Eretz-Israel* (1943), p. 25; cited, Aumann, 1974, p. 16.

By 1947, according to British figures, the Arab population of Palestine was 1.2 million. Only 750,000 at most lived in areas that became the State of Israel in 1949. And of these perhaps more than half represented immigration since the beginning of Jewish settlement: people whose *Heimatrecht* could hardly be senior to that of the Jews.

It is beyond the scope of this account to trace the history of political Zionism (for a concise account see Sachar, 1966, pp. 349 ff.). Suffice it to note that Theodore Herzl's vision began to be realized on a small scale in 1880 and that between 1882 and 1914 the Jewish population in Palestine was raised by *aliyah* from 24,000 to 85,000. World War I caused massive dislocations of Jews in Eastern Europe. As Sachar relates:

Through all of this violent fighting on the eastern front millions of Jews were caught between millstones of the invading and retreating armies. During the engagements in Russia and Poland they were harried by the advancing Russians; when the Russians retreated before the fury of Hindenburg's counter-offensive, hundreds of thousands of Jews were expelled at two or three days' notice and were brought to the interior provinces of Russia, lest they give up important military secrets. The deportations were conducted with an inhumanity unique even for brutalized soldiers. Whole communities were crowded like cattle into sealed box-cars, which were opened at infrequent intervals; it was a miracle that only half of the exiles perished. Other communities were driven afoot for hundreds of miles, the weakest succumbing by the roadside, only the strongest surviving to struggle for existence in strange, unfriendly worlds in the interior. The German advance was so rapid, however, that the Jews could not all be evacuated in time. Their homes were now subjected to the withering artillery of the German invaders and, after the conquest, to the brutalities of the war-drunk victors. As an appropriate accompaniment to the deportations and invasions, hundreds of Jews were executed as spies by both sides. (1966, p. 363)

Jews throughout the world strained their efforts to provide relief; the American Joint Distribution Committee raised large sums and managed to ship food, even after United States' entry into the war.

World War I marked both a setback and an advance for Zionism. In Palestine itself, expulsions and emigrations, disease, and famine brought the Jewish population down to some 57,000 (Harkabi, 1974, p. 5). On the diplomatic front, however, Justice Brandeis prevailed upon President Wilson to endorse the concept of a Jewish homeland, while Haym Weizmann, later Israel's first President, elicited from the British the famous Balfour Declaration of November 2, 1917: "His Majesty's Government view with favour the establishment in Palestine of a national home for the Jewish people, and will use their best endeavours to facilitate the achievement of this object, it being clearly understood that nothing shall be done which may prejudice the civil and religious rights of existing non-Jewish communities in Palestine or the rights and political status enjoyed by Jews in any other country."

Since the British—in return for services rendered against the Turks—had already committed themselves to an *Arab* state in Palestine, their reasons for issuing the Balfour Declaration remain a historical obscurity that cannot be explored here. The British military administration that controlled Palestine at the end of World War I was flatly opposed to any plan that would make the country, with ten times as many Arabs as Jews, a Jewish homeland. Despite the support of Colonel T. E. Lawrence, who declared that Zionism was "the only practical means of setting the new Semitic Near East in order in our own days," the prospect of a Jewish commonwealth remained in the balance throughout the Peace Conference. After an Arab coup in Syria had alarmed the West, however, the Balfour Declaration was finally incorporated in the Turkish treaty concluded on April 25, 1920 (Sachar, 1966, pp. 369–71).

It must be said that the British were less than enthusiastic executors of the Balfour Declaration. As Sachar points out (pp. 413–14), it was administratively "much easier to create one Arab state and to govern it in the hard-boiled tradition of the crown colony." He adds that British enthusiasm about building a Jewish homeland declined steadily, since even "the slightest concessions to the Jews brought violent protests from the Arab states that surrounded Palestine. And the British colonial office never relinquished the idea of a power life-line that would include the Arab states." When Arab extremists prevailed and attacks against Jews became serious in 1929, the British "instead of dealing with the aggressors, treated with maddening neutrality both those who attacked and those who defended, as if the Jews were equally responsible for the bloodshed" (*ibid.*, pp. 413–14). The future Israelis underwent their first, involuntary, training in guerrilla warfare.

The resettlement of Jews in Palestine was, however, by no means exclusively a Jewish or even a British idea. *Polonia Restituta*, the newly departitioned Polish Republic, had inherited 3 million Jews from the Czarist empire, and—despite special clauses in the Minority Treaties—continued the discriminatory policies of imperial Russia. Jews were confined to ghettos, where the houses were overcrowded, badly ventilated, and almost devoid of plumbing; they were denied public employment and their children were excluded from schools whenever these became overcrowded. When Poland was taken to task in Geneva because of pogroms that had broken out during the Depression, the Polish government replied that it was trying to suppress them but would nevertheless like to arrange for the emigration of at least 2.5 million Jews from Poland (Jaksch, 1967, pp. 256–57). An explicit endorsement of Zionism was adopted by the Polish State Party (the *Obóz Sjednoczenia Narodowego*, which enjoyed a political monopoly under the 1935 constitution) on May 21, 1938, in these terms:

1. The question of Jewish emigration is one of the most important problems of the Polish nation. The Polish state should make every effort to encour-

age emigration tendencies among the Jews, so as to reduce their number in Poland itself to a minimum. The main goal of emigration should be Palestine; but the Polish government should also endeavor to secure additional emigration areas for Jews through international co-operation.

2. The economic influence of the Jews is to be broken with all possible measures, in order to create sufficient freedom of movement for the natural development of the Polish ethnic nation in both cities and rural areas, and so as to free the Poles from dependency on Jewish capital.

3. The Jewish influence in Polish cultural and educational life is likewise to be eliminated with all possible means, and the excessive number of Jews in the press, in artistic activities, and particularly in the theater and film production is to be eliminated.

4. Through careful planning, an arrangement should be arrived at whereby the Jews will be segregated in all areas of education. The treatment of Jews, particularly at university-level institutions, shall no longer depend on the personal opinions of individual professors and rectors, but shall be regulated through procedures determined by the state. (In Rabl, 1963, pp. 127–28; our translation from German)

There is some justification for the claim that General Piłsudski's Polish government provided the training in practical anti-Semitism for Hitler's National Socialists.

When Jews began to flee from Germany in the early days of the Third Reich, the British restricted rather than facilitated immigration to Palestine. Despite all these obstacles, however, the Jewish population increased steadily throughout the mandatory period and reached approximately 650,000 on the eve of independence. Seventy-one percent of this growth was the result of *aliyah* and 29 percent produced by natural increase (Bachi, 1974, p. 5).

Establishment of the State of Israel led to the third wave of *aliyah* (1948–72) during which over 1.45 million Jews came to the new state. There was offsetting emigration of some 200,000, but natural increase brought the net Jewish population growth to approximately 2.02 million. As of May 1972, the Jewish pop-

ulation of Israel had reached 2.67 million and constituted 18 percent of world Jewry. It had passed the Jewish population of the USSR and was exceeded only by the Jewish community in the United States (*ibid.*, pp. 1,5).

Displacement of Arabs and Jews. Advocates of an Arab Palestinian state sometimes forget that such a state was proposed in the Peel Report of 1937, which the Zionist Congress accepted as a basis for negotiation, even though it left the Jews a territory much smaller than pre-1967 Israel. The Arab leaders, however, refused to negotiate but insisted on the whole of Palestine—emphasizing their point with a wave of anti-Jewish terror. An Arab Palestinian state was internationally sanctioned, however, after the British had announced early in 1947 that they were relinquishing their Mandate over Palestine. Against Arab opposition, the General Assembly of the United Nations passed with only three votes over the necessary two-thirds its resolution of November 29, 1947, authorizing independent Arab and Jewish states in a partitioned Palestine.

The British government, which had opposed partition, then announced it would lay down the Mandate as of May 15, 1948. But it began withdrawing British forces immediately, area by area, making no provision to transfer authority. The UN Security Council offered to send a commission to Palestine to bridge the gap, but the British refused to allow the commission to exercise authority, to recruit militia, or to form provisional governments until British forces were totally evacuated. British policy, which promised to frustrate the United Nations' decision, elicited from the American delegate the comment that it was not "entirely helpful" (Sachar, 1966, p. 434).

Instead of organizing their state in the territory allotted to them, however, the Arab leaders set their followers to attacking the Jews; guerrillas and mercenaries struck almost as soon as the partition resolution had been passed. Carrying out an openly announced plan of the Arab League "for the occupation of

Palestine and the forcible prevention of the establishment of the Jewish State," the seven surrounding states made ready to support the "Army of Liberation" (Prittie and Dineen, 1974, p. 3). The British continued to sell arms to the Arabs on the ground that contracts had to be fulfilled. But when the Jews demanded the right to defend themselves, the British refused to recognize the Haganah as a militia and disarmed its members when they came across them armed. The resulting bitterness strengthened extremist elements among the Jews (Sachar, 1966, p. 435).

It was during what turned out to be the Israeli War of independence that the major displacements of Arabs—accompanied by minor displacements of Jews—took place. Let it be emphasized at the start that *there was no deliberate mass expulsion* of Arabs comparable to the expulsions of Germans from the eastern Reich and from Czechoslovakia. The Jewish leaders had assumed that their state would contain as many Arabs as Jews, and they did not seek intercommunal warfare. On October 2, 1947, the Assembly of Palestinian Jewry (Vaad Leumi) declared that "the Jewish people extends the hand of sincere friendship and brotherhood to the Arab peoples and calls them to co-operate as free and equal allies for the sake of peace and progress" (In, Prittie and Dineen, 1974, p. 4.)

This appeal for "peaceful coexistence" did not, however, head off Arab attacks or the exodus of Arab civilians, which, as summed up by Prittie took place in three phases:

(1) In the weeks immediately after the announcement of the U.N. Partition Plan in November, 1947, an estimated 30,000 Arabs left their homes. They were mainly members of well-to-do families. They believed that war was imminent and that there would be a swift and sweeping Arab victory. Meanwhile the heads of these families were anxious to spare their relatives the temporary danger and discomfort that might have to be endured before the Jews were disposed of.

(2) Before the end of the British Mandate, after the early Jewish successes against guerrilla attacks, 200,000 or more Arabs left their homes, or were driven from them during the fighting. Most of them came from mixed urban areas which fell under complete Jewish control—as many as 70,000 Arabs fled from Jaffa and another 60,000 left Haifa. Many of these Arabs also believed that they were leaving their homes temporarily to spare their families from the bloody battles that would inevitably take place when Israel's neighbours launched their eagerly-anticipated invasion.

(3) Another 300,000 or more Arabs were displaced after May 15, 1948, when the armies of the neighbouring Arab states invaded Palestine, and fighting flared up in areas which had been relatively quiet until then. This third phase of the Arab exodus ended by November 1948. There was no large-scale fighting after that date. (*Ibid.*, p. 5)

Arab charges of deliberate expulsion or flight induced by threat of death center around episodes such as that of Deir Yassin, the principal "atrocity" charged to the Israelis. As Prittie tells the story:

This village lay to the south-west of Jerusalem, near the main route to the coast, in an area where there was much hot fighting. On April 8, 1948, patrols of the extreme para-military organisation, the Irgun Zvi Leumi, attacked the village; in the course of the action 254 Palestinian men, women and children were killed. Irgun apologists have claimed that the villagers first put out white flags and then opened fire on the Israeli force, killing eight and wounding another 57. The loud-speaker truck that was supposed to warn the Arab civilians to evacuate their homes fell into a ditch and never reached the village. When the Irgun forces charged into the village and began to quell resistance by lobbing hand grenades through doors and windows, there were many Arab families still in their homes. There can be no doubt that the killing constituted a horror-story which induced many Arabs to flee from their homes in other parts of Palestine. (*Ibid.*, p. 7)

In their operations in rural areas, the Israeli forces used loud speakers to warn the population to keep off the streets or to leave their homes temporarily where there was house-to-house fighting. The Arabs contend that the real purpose was to drive the villagers out permanently, and indeed—as the news of Deir Yassin spread—many did not come back. As Prittie observes, it was panic fear that induced the 70,000 Arabs of Jaffa to flee when the Israelis took this previously all-Arab city. He quotes the Jordan newspaper *Al Urdun* of April 9, 1953: "By spreading rumours of Jewish atrocities, killings of women and children, etc., [our leaders] instilled fear and terror into the hearts of the Arabs of Palestine, until they fled, leaving their homes and property to the enemy."

In the port city of Haifa, however, the Jewish authorities made a determined effort to induce the 62,000 Arabs to remain. On April 21, 1948, the British commander in Haifa informed Jewish and Arab leaders that his forces were evacuating their positions and would not involve themselves in fighting against "either the Jews or the Arabs over an issue of no great material importance." There followed a battle between Jewish and Arab forces of almost equal size, in which the Arabs were routed. The British then called a meeting of leading Arab and Jewish citizens to arrange a truce. The Jewish mayor, Shabetai Levi, begged the Arabs of Haifa to stay in their homes, and guaranteed their safety. The Arab National Committee in Haifa answered in a memorandum sent to the governments of Arab League states on April 27, 1948, from which Prittie quotes:

> The signing of a truce would be a disgrace to the Arab population of Haifa. . . . our delegation proudly refused to sign the truce and asked that the evacuation of the population and their transfer to the neighbouring Arab countries be facilitated. . . . The [British] military and civil authorities and the Jewish representatives expressed their profound regret at this grave decision. The Mayor adjourned the meeting with a passionate appeal to the [Arab] population to reconsider its decision. (*Ibid.*, p. 6)

A day later, the Workers Council of Haifa, a Jewish organization, published this appeal:

> For years we have lived together in our city, Haifa, in security and in mutual understanding and brotherhood. Thanks to this, our city flourished and developed for the good of both Jewish and Arab residents; thus did Haifa serve as an example to the other cities of Palestine. . . . Do not destroy your homes with your own hands; and do not bring tragedy upon yourselves by unnecessary evacuation and self-imposed burdens. By moving out you will be overtaken by poverty and humiliation. But in this city, yours and ours, Haifa, the gates are open for work, for life and for peace, for you and your families.

The same day, the British Superintendent of Police in Haifa reported: "There is no change in the situation in Haifa. The Jews are still making every effort to persuade the Arab populace to remain and settle back into their normal lives in the town."

The Haifa affair was later summed up by a special correspondent of the British weekly *The Economist* as follows:

> During subsequent days the Jewish authorities, who were now in complete control of Haifa (save for limited districts still held by the British troops) urged all Arabs to remain in Haifa and guaranteed them protection and security. As far as I know, most of the British civilian residents whose advice was asked by Arab friends told the latter that they would be wise to stay. However, of the 62,000 Arabs who formerly lived in Haifa, not more than 5,000 or 6,000 remained. Various factors influenced their decision to seek safety in flight. There is but little doubt that the most potent of these factors were the announcements made over the air by the Arab Higher Executive, urging all Arabs in Haifa to quit. The reason given was that upon the final withdrawal of the British, the combined armies of the Arab States would invade Palestine and drive the Jews into the sea, and it was clearly intimated that those Arabs who remained in Haifa and accepted Jewish protection would be regarded as renegades. (In *ibid.*, pp. 6–7)

The number of Arabs displaced during the Israeli War of Independence is a matter of some controversy. Prittie, whose concern for objectivity is clear, makes the following calculation: of the 1.2 million Arabs in Palestine, at least 450,000 lived in areas not in Israeli hands when the truce was concluded in 1949, so that the original Arab population of the state of Israel could not have been more than 750,000. About 160,000 Arabs remained in their homes in Israel, or were allowed to return soon after the fighting ended. At that time, Israel permitted refugees to return to rejoin families, most of whose members had remained at home. Subtraction of 160,000 from 750,000 indicates that the maximum number of Palestinian Arab refugees displaced in the 1947–48 fighting was 590,000. Higher Arab estimates are in part the result of propaganda, and partly the consequence of United Nations relief operations. The UNRWA (United Nations Relief and Works Agency for Palestine Refugees) provided food and supplies on the basis of the number of refugees registered—and there was every incentive for Arab camp administrators to inflate the rolls. Investigations at various times showed that about one-third of the "refugees" were ineligible or did not exist (*ibid.*, pp. 8–9).

The 1967 war produced a new crop of refugees. In addition to "old" refugees who fled for a second time, there were approximately 250,000 "new" refugees, most of them from the Israeli-occupied West Bank of the Kingdom of Jordan. Under a return program initiated by the Israeli government, about 50,000 of the 1967 refugees had returned to their homes by 1974. Prittie, who considers the UNRWA estimates high, assesses the net addition to the refugee population resulting from the 1967 war at between 130,000 and 160,000 (*ibid.*, p. 10). For the sake of fairness, it is perhaps advisable to accept the higher figure.

The 1948 war also caused the displacement of a few thousand Jews. When the walled Old City of central Jerusalem was captured by the Jordanian Arab Legion commanded by Glubb Pasha, the entire Jewish population had to seek refuge in West Jerusalem. At Etzion, between Bethlehem and Hebron, four Jewish settlements had to be evacuated. But, as Prittie observes (*ibid.*, pp. 4–5), "the Jewish exodus was relatively small, and for one main reason: Jewish settlers had nowhere else to go. They knew that they had to stand and fight or be driven into the sea."

The exodus of Arabs from Israel and its occupied territories, which adds up to a net figure of 750,000 at most, was more than balanced by the displacement of Jews living in Arab countries. There were approximately 837,000 of them in 1948, but by 1973 less than 50,000 were left—so that the net displacement was about 787,000. As they poured into Israel they changed its demographic structure radically. Only one Israeli in ten was Oriental in 1948; today the figure is one in two. Relations between Ashkenazim and Sephardim have already been mentioned in several chapters, notably in chapter 17,A2.

A rather detailed survey of Jewish emigration from Arab countries is given by Dineen (*ibid.*, pp. 20–31) in his part of *The Double Exodus*. Space limits our account to brief descriptions of the situation in three countries.

Upon the establishment of the State of Israel, all the Jews in Iraq were classed as enemy aliens. Jewish property and businesses were sequestered and emigration was banned. In March 1950, when the ban was lifted for one year, almost all of Iraq's 120,000 Jews fled, leaving 6000 in the country. Further anti-Jewish legislation followed, while the outflow of Jews continued. As of May 1967, the 2500 remaining Iraqi Jews faced sharp limitations in the areas of citizenship, travel, and property.

The Six-Day War brought on even more repressive measures: all Jewish homes were placed under surveillance; telephones were disconnected; personal property could not be sold; assets were frozen; licenses were cancelled; the dismissal of Jewish employees was ordered; and travel from their area of residence was forbidden. A complete ban on emigration made the discriminatory pressures under which Jews lived all the more burdensome.

Several Jews were publicly hanged in Baghdad, where the radio (January 27, 1969) called upon Iraqis to "come and enjoy the feast." Some 500,000 men, women, and children paraded and danced past the scaffolds where the grotesque bodies of the hanged Jews swung; the mob rhythmically chanted "Death to Israel" and "Death to all Traitors." The barbaric display brought a world-wide public outcry which President Bakr dismissed as "the barking of dogs." Another 18 Jews were hanged in secret between 1970 and 1972. Jews have been forced to house Palestinians and to raise money for Fatah and other guerrilla groups.

Even before the 1967 war, the 4000 Jews in Syria were terrorized by night arrest, interrogation, imprisonment, and torture. Jews were not permitted to leave the Damascus ghetto. After the war their situation deteriorated. An airport road was paved over the Jewish cemetery in Damascus; school examinations are scheduled on Saturdays to prevent Jewish participation; Jewish complaints against Muslims are automatically rejected; Jews are singled out as such (Musawi) on identity cards; Palestinian refugees are housed in the Jewish quarter to prey on residents. Jews are not permitted to leave the country, to go more than four kilometers from their place of business, to sell immovable property, to work for government and banks, to have telephones or drivers' licenses, or to bequeath property to heirs. Most Jews working for Arab merchants have been dismissed, and the state has confiscated the property of those who have escaped.

The Imams of Yemen always treated their Jewish subjects as infidels: Jews could not ride horseback, carry arms, own property or build houses taller than those of Muslim landlords. All the Yemeni Jews fled to Aden between June 1949, and June 1950; they were then flown to Israel in "Operation Magic Carpet."

Because the Jews in Arab countries moved to Israel to escape intolerable conditions, their exodus can properly be classed as a forced migration. Its results are summarized in table 22.3.

Table 22.3.   JEWISH POPULATION OF
ARAB COUNTRIES

	1948 Population	1973 Population
Aden	5,000	none
Algeria	150,000	900
Egypt	75,000	500
Iraq	125,000	300
Lebanon	20,000	2,000
Libya	40,000	40
Morocco	300,000	30,000
Syria	45,000	4,500
Tunisia	23,000	9,000
Yemen	54,000	none
Total	837,000	47,240

(SOURCE: Prittie and Dineen, 1974, p. 20.)

If Zionism is condemned by the Kremlin, it nevertheless remains very much on the operating agenda of its satellites in East-Central Europe. The postwar Polish regime has continued and even intensified the anti-Semitic discrimination practised by Piłsudski. The Jews of Poland who escaped Hitler's liquidation camps but did not succeed in emigrating have been barred from all gainful employment other than the most menial labor. "With their savings exhausted, their children mostly expelled from the universities and no sign of a decent job," Lendvai writes, "the purged Jews were left with no alternative but to apply to the emigration office." There they were advised that permission to emigrate would be granted, but they would have to repudiate their Polish citizenship, and exit permits would be valid only for Israel. Lendvai concludes, "this was forced expulsion. The emigrants became legal uncitizens with their exit permit merely stating that they are not of Polish nationality. The authorities do not care whether they really go to Israel or manage to get a residence permit in some other country" (Lendvai, 1971, p. 176). Lendvai projects the future of Polish Jewry as follows:

The Deputy Minister of Interior, Moczar's right hand in Jewish affairs, Franciszek Szlachcic, predicted in several lectures held in the summer of 1968 that if the present trend continued, only some ten thousand Jews would remain. But these too, he continued, were likely to depart by the end of 1970 with the exception of some two thousand old people and invalids. This "hard core" would be removed from the great urban centres, and the problem "will find a natural solution." In other words, what not even the Nazis could accomplish, the Communist regime seems likely to achieve: an irrevocable end to the thousand-year history of Polish Jewry. (*Ibid.*, p. 77.)

3. DISPLACEMENT OF GREEK AND TURKISH CYPRIOTS

Recent events in Cyprus have illustrated once again the dangers inherent in imposing a unitary state on a multinational population. Cyprus, the third largest island in the Mediterranean, is located 40 miles south of Turkey and 500 miles southeast of mainland Greece. Two-thirds of the island is mountainous; an agricultural plain containing the capital, Nicosia, is in the center. Of Cyprus's estimated population of 650,000, some 80 percent are ethnic Greeks of the Orthodox religion. About 18 percent are ethnic Turks and are Muslims; the remainder are largely Armenians and Maronites. With a 1973 per capita income of $1313, Cyprus was relatively well off; its problems have been political rather than economic.

Following conferences in Zurich and London, Cyprus became independent in 1960 under a constitution creating a unitary state with entrenched guarantees for the Greek and Turkish communities. It had, in effect, a dual executive, consisting of a Greek-Cypriot president and a Turkish-Cypriot vice-president, elected *separately* by the Greek-Cypriot and Turkish-Cypriot voters. In the absence or disability of the president his duties devolved, not on the vice-president but on the (Greek-Cypriot) president of the House of Representatives. A single Council of Ministers had seven Greek-Cypriot members and three

Turkish-Cypriot appointed and dismissed *separately* by the president and the vice-president—a device not conducive to the formation of interethnic coalitions. The president and the vice-president both enjoyed veto powers, which could be exercised jointly or separately. Either or both could veto a decision of the Council of Ministers concerning foreign affairs, defense, or security, or return any other decision for reconsideration. The executive right of final veto also applies to any law or decision of the House of Representatives concerning foreign affairs, defense, or security. Since it was unlikely that the president would veto a decision of the Greek-Cypriot majority in the Cabinet or the legislature, the veto power was in fact a prerogative of the Turkish-Cypriot vice-president, who could block any government policy in these three rather wide areas that was unacceptable to his ethnic community. Further provisions in the constitution established a 70:30 ratio for Greek-Cypriot and Turkish-Cypriot members of the House of Representatives, the civil service, the police, and the gendarmerie. The ratio in the armed forces was 6:4; the three heads of these forces were appointed by the president and vice-president jointly; one of them was a Turkish Cypriot and each had a deputy head from the other community. There were also separate systems of Greek-Cypriot and Turkish-Cypriot courts, as well as separate Communal Chambers exercising autonomous powers with regard to religion, education, culture, and family and other personal relations, including a separate taxing power to provide for Community functions (Polyviou, 1975, pp. 18–30).

Despite the statistical overrepresentation of the Turkish-Cypriots, the 1960 Constitution, the critical articles of which were unamendable, proved to be divisive rather than unifying. The entrenched officeholders, including the judges, tended to function as community spokesmen in an adversary relationship rather than as partners in a joint enterprise. A U.S.

Senate subcommittee headed by Senator Edward M. Kennedy commented that the Greek majority saw the constitution as a hindrance to their becoming masters in their own house and as legislating a state within a state, while the Turks feared that any erosion of their constitutional guarantees would leave them with no rights at all.

Given the peculiarities of the constitution, political conflict was probably inevitable. And such conflict intensified as the Greeks tried to show that only a unitary system of government would work on Cyprus, and as the Turks took every opportunity to block government business whenever they felt that their rights were infringed upon or their needs unmet. The two communities were soon deadlocked on a host of issues: civil service staffing, the Army, separation of municipalities, and the use of the Turkish veto on central government taxation, among other things. (*Crisis on Cyprus*, 1974, p. 11)

Proposals to strengthen the central government made on November 30, 1963, by the President, Archbishop Makarios, were rejected by Vice-President Kütchuk as leaving the Turks "at the absolute mercy of the Greeks" (Polyviou, 1975, p. 39.) A period of intercommunal violence followed, which continued throughout 1964 despite the presence of a United Nations force (UNFICYP) which became operational on March 27, 1964. During conciliation talks in Geneva, former U.S. Secretary of State Dean Acheson proposed that Cyprus be united with Greece, except for two Turkish cantons and a Turkish naval base—a proposal rejected out of hand by Archbishop Makarios. Dr. Kütchuk, representing the Turkish Cypriots at Geneva, countered with a proposal for territorial federation; the Turkish ethnic state would encompass the northern 38 percent of the land area and the boundary would divide the cities of Nicosia and Famagusta. The Greek Cypriots, however, rejected and to this date continue to reject federalist proposals (*ibid.*, pp. 108–19).

Appraisal of the Cyprus situation according to the criteria of national identity developed in chapter 10 suggests that Cyprus lacks the national integrators to support a unitary state. The primary loyalty of both Greek and Turkish Cypriots is not to any territorial or ideological entity called "Cyprus" but to the Greek and Turkish ethnic nations and secondarily to their ethnic communities on Cyprus. A territorial state of Cyprus can become viable only insofar as these ethnic communities accept it as guarantor of their security and self-determination—for which the Turkish Cypriots currently look to Turkey, while the Greek Cypriots seek international and particularly United States' support, since Greece cannot challenge Turkey that close to the Turkish mainland. It follows that if Cyprus can be reconstituted rather than partitioned, which is doubtful, it can only survive as a federation with limited central functions and powers.

The crisis of 1974 was precipitated on July 15 when the 650 Greek officers commanding the Greek Cypriot National Guard overthrew Archbishop Makarios on orders from the military junta in Athens. According to Senator Kennedy's subcommittee, "there is abundant evidence suggesting that the U.S. knew of the impending coup well in advance." Makarios was replaced by an ardent Greek nationalist, Nikos Sampson, which suggested a strong likelihood of *enosis* (union with Greece)—a development intolerable to Turks and Turkish Cypriots. Prime Minister Bulent Ecevit of Turkey flew to London, where he demanded recall of the Greek officers and a federal system of government on Cyprus. It seems likely, as suggested by the Kennedy subcommittee, that "clear-cut U.S. support of the Turkish *diplomatic* position would probably have significantly reduced the chances of Turkey opting for military action." Instead, the Department of State temporized in an effort to save face for the Greek military junta.

On July 20, 1974, Turkish forces began landing on Cyprus; within two days they had occupied a salient including a part of Nicosia. The UN Security Council passed a series of

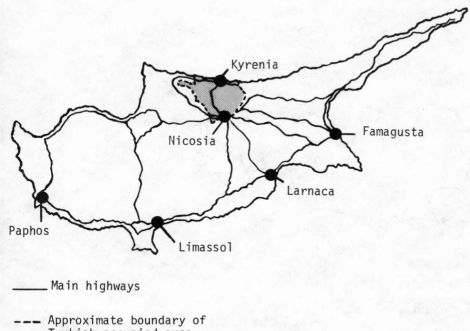

FIGURE 22.2.   *Cyprus. Approximate areas of Turkish occupation after first phase of invasion.*
Courtesy of American Hellenic Institute

resolutions calling for an immediate ceasefire, and there were a series of ceasefires, none of which lasted. The Greek junta fell on July 23, and was replaced by a civilian government under Constantine Karamanlis. The same day Glafkos Clerides, President of the House of Representatives, replaced Sampson as Acting President of Cyprus. The three guarantor powers, Britain, Greece, and Turkey, met in Geneva on July 26, and on the 30th signed a declaration agreeing to implement the UN ceasefire. Greek- and Turkish-Cypriot representatives arrived in Geneva for a new round of political talks that began on August 8. The following day, Greek, Turkish, British, and UN military observers agreed on a new ceasefire line, which ended the first phase of the Turkish invasion (see map). The negotiations reached an impasse, however, when Turkish proposals for a federal system giving the Turkish-Cypriots administration of a main zone and several smaller enclaves covering 38 percent of Cyprus (see map), were given a temporizing response by the Greek negotiators and Clerides, who requested 36 hours to discuss the proposals with their governments. On August 13, the U.S. Department of State issued a release indicating its support of the Turkish position, but *not* suggesting that the United States might react strongly to further military action (*Crisis on Cyprus*, 1974, p. 16). Before dawn on August 14, the Turkish army,

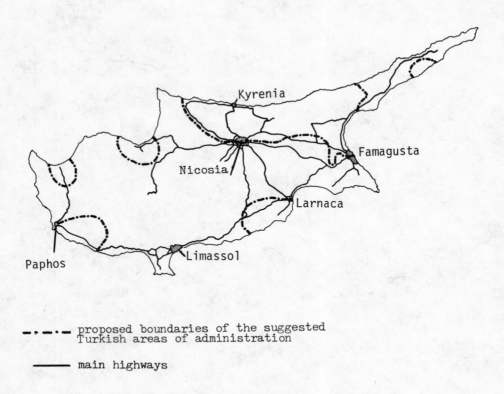

– · – · –   proposed boundaries of the suggested
              Turkish areas of administration

————   main highways

FIGURE 22.3.   *Cyprus. Proposal of Turkish Foreign Minister, August 1974.*
Courtesy of American Hellenic Institute

heavily reinforced with armor and enjoying complete air superiority, advanced again on a broad front. In three days, this massive military thrust sliced off at least 40 percent of Cyprus, slightly more than the Turks had demanded in the Geneva talks. This produced a new line of demarcation (see map) which represented the status quo as of October 1974, and still divides the Greek- and Turkish controlled areas at the time of this writing.

According to Greek-Cypriot sources:

The Turkish armed forces, after their . . . occupation, systematically looted and plundered the properties of the inhabitants, very frequently arrested all the men of villages they were capturing, taking many of them to detention camps in Turkey, brutally molested women, children and elderly people, and indulged in repeated rapes, arsons, cold-blooded murders of civilians and forced expulsion of the inhabitants from their homes. (Polyviou, 1975, p. 58).

The Senate subcommittee did not, however, seem to have enough hard evidence before it to confirm these charges except for "widespread looting" (*Crisis on Cyprus*, p. 54). It did, however, note a psychological effect similar to that caused by the Deir Yassin affair in Israel. According to its report:

Whether real or imagined—and it is probably real—the fear of what the Turkish military might do is widespread. Whenever and wherever the Study Mission talked with Greek Cypriot refugees, the story was basically the same: People moved the in

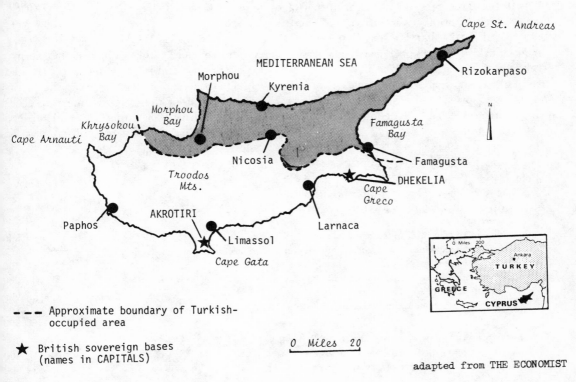

FIGURE 22.4. *Cyprus. Approximate areas of Turkish occupation, October 1974.*
Courtesy of American Hellenic Institute

stant they saw or thought the Turkish army was advancing towards their town or village. And they moved *instantly*—dropping everything, taking very little with them, and by foot, car, tractor, truck, bus, or wagon, moved to safety in Government controlled areas. The stories of rough and sometimes brutal treatment of civilians by Turkish forces in Kyrenia, after the first phase of the invasion, had spread over the island like wildfire. Thus, during the second phase of the invasion, Greek Cypriots fled the moment there was rumor or sight of military forces—creating a virtual vacuum into which the Turkish army could and did move without resistance and without the presence of people. (*Ibid.*, p. 27)

The Study Mission dispatched by Senator Kennedy observed "cars and trucks . . . moving down the road . . . loaded with people and whatever they could carry—clothes, baskets, mattresses, a few pots and pans—as well as the miserable conditions awaiting the refugees in their places of asylum."

Altogether, the Senate subcommittee found, some 282,000 Cypriots were displaced as a result of the invasion. The largest group consisted of 200,000 Greek Cypriots who fled or were expelled from Turkish-occupied areas to the Government-controlled south. Some 30,000 found shelter with relatives or friends, but the remainder have needed both shelter and general relief. The second largest group of refugees and persons in duress consisted of some 34,000 Turkish Cypriots in Government-controlled areas, including 10,000 in camps operated by the International Red Cross and the United Nations. In almost every way, the subcommittee found, "the plight and the needs of these refugees are identical to that of their Greek-Cypriot counterparts." There were also about 24,000 Turkish Cypriots isolated in Turkish villages or Turkish quarters of larger towns in the south (*ibid.*, p. 28). A revised estimate of displaced persons and others in need on Cyprus, as of November 1, 1974, as printed in the Senate subcommittee report (p. 19), is as follows:

D. The Problem of "Unalienable" Rights

As already noted, the leaders of the German expellees see—and hope to derive political advantage from—an analogy between their situation and that of the Palestinian Arabs. This analogy, however, is superficial and misleading. There are fundamental differences be-

DISPLACED PERSONS IN CYPRUS, NOVEMBER 1, 1974

I. Refugees:
1. Greek Cypriots in Government-controlled areas:

Satisfactorily sheltered with friends/relatives or in second homes rented	57,600
Living in public buildings, schools, etc.	5,800
Housed in permanent structures, but overcrowded conditions and will have to move	89,700
Living in shacks, garages, unfinished structures	11,000
Living in tents	9,000
Living in the open, under trees, in makeshift, open shelters	7,700
Total	180,800

2. Turkish Cypriots in Government-controlled areas:

Living in tents on British Sovereign Base areas	8,500
In isolated villages, cut off, or in controlled villages/enclaves	22,000
Total	30,500

3. Greek Cypriots in Turkish-occupied area:

Living in cut off villages, or displaced	9,000

4. Turkish Cypriot refugees in Turkish occupied areas:

Moved from the south to the north, and includes some refugees from 1963–64	8,500

II. Prisoners of war and detainees, both sides:

All have been released under U.N. auspices	6,000
Total	234,800

Since reunification of Cyprus as a unitary state—despite the arguments of Greek Cypriots, Greeks, and Greek-Americans—seems most unlikely, it is probable that most of the displaced Cypriots will have to be resettled. The problem could be eased by a combination of territorial and personal autonomy. But having experimented with one "sophisticated" solution, the Cypriots are hardly in a mood to try another.

tween the situations of the two displaced ethnic groups. They are cloaked by a misunderstanding of the term "unalienable," as popularized in the American Declaration of Independence.

The writings of German expellee scholars, and indeed of many other West German jurists, have tended to treat *Heimatrecht* as unalienable (see, for instance, Raschhofer in Fircks, 1962, pp. 39–40; for contrasting Polish and German views see Nasarski, 1963, *passim.*). This concept was endorsed by the German Federal Republic (see Bundestag, *Sitzungsprotokoll*, July 14, 1950). The analogy to the "life, liberty, and the pursuit of happiness" proclaimed as "unalienable" in 1776 is obvious. It would appear that "unalienable" is taken to mean *unalienable under any circumstances*.

If, however, Europeans and Americans believed that the rights to life and liberty could *never* be alienated, then there would be no prisons, let alone gibbets or guillotines. In actual fact, Western society is organized on the premise that "unalienable" rights *can* be alienated; the Bill of Rights clarifies the point by forbidding deprivation of life, liberty, or property *without due process of law*. In all civilized societies, a person who violates the rights of others may be deprived of his own to an appropriate degree; this is the root concept of "just punishment."

It thus follows that while *Heimatrecht* is a very real right, and indeed essential to self-determination and the enjoyment of political freedom, it can nevertheless be alienated by *denying it to others*. Application of this standard to displaced Germans and displaced Arabs leads to very different conclusions. Neither the German people nor its government ever undertook to expel the Poles from Poland or the Czechs from Bohemia and Moravia. While individual Germans commited atrocities, and many indeed have been convicted for them, the German populations in the Eastern Reich and in the Sudetenland did not alienate their *Heimatrecht*. Their claims today remain based on the universality of *Heimatrecht* and hence on respect for the *Heimatrecht* of others.

In the case of the Palestine Arabs, the greatest displacement—that of 1948—occurred in an operation intended to wipe out the nascent State of Israel. Had that succeeded there is little doubt that the Jews would have been expelled from Palestine—at least those who were not slaughtered on the spot.

But what of the "legitimate rights" claimed by the Palestinian Arabs? Even King Hussein of Jordan, the most moderate of all Arab rulers (at least until the emergence of President Sadat of Egypt in a peacemaking role), has said that Arab recognition of Israel would depend on (1) withdrawal to the pre-1967 borders and (2) recognition of "the legitimate rights of the Palestinians in their homeland." (Speech at the Citadel, Charleston, South Carolina, as reported in *The Times*, London, May 7, 1975.) The question has been answered repeatedly by Arabs. As quoted by Terence Prittie (Prittie and Dineen, 1974, p. 13):

*Dr. Mohammed Salah-ed-Din, Egyptian Foreign Minister, October 11, 1949:
"In demanding the restoration of the refugees to Palestine, the Arabs intend that they should return as the masters of their homeland, not as slaves. More explicitly, they intend to annihilate the State of Israel."

*Resolution, adopted by the Conference of Arab Refugees, at Homs in Syria, July 11–12, 1957:
"Any discussion aimed at a solution of the Palestine problem which will not be based on ensuring the refugees' right to annihilate Israel will be regarded as a desecration of the Arab people and an act of treason."

*President Nasser of Egypt, in interview with the Swiss newspaper, *Neue Zuercher Zeitung*, September 1, 1960, said:
"If the refugees return to Israel, Israel will cease to exist."

*Even the moderate Abdullah al-Yafi, when Prime Minister of Lebanon, said to the newspaper *Al-Hayat*, April 29, 1966:
"The day for the realisation of the Arab hope for the return of the refugees to Palestine means the liquidation of Israel."

Arab nationalists and their friends in the West operate with the slogan of a "democratic and secular Palestine state" in which Christians, Jews, and Muslims will live in equality and peace. But even in *The Link*, published by Americans for Middle East Understanding, an organization that advocates peaceful accomodation, a Palestinian professor calls for "a modern state which is integrated in the Arab world of which it is a part" (vol. 7, no. 4 [1974]: 3). Speaking among themselves, however, Palestinian Arabs are much franker. A report by the Popular Democratic Front on the Sixth Palestinian National Assembly in 1969 indicates alternate views: (1) that the slogan does not represent true Palestinian intentions but should be retained for its tactical or strategic propaganda value, and (2) that it should be abandoned, since it conflicts with the PLO Covenant and advocates peaceful settlement with the Jews (condensed from Harkabi, 1974, pp. 72–73). The Beirut daily *El Anwar* of March 8, 1970, reports a conference of *fedayeen* leaders in which the programmatic "incorrectness" and purely propaganda value of the "democratic state" slogan was likewise made clear.

The true intentions of the Palestinian Arabs are clearly stated in the Palestinian National Covenant. Adopted in 1964 and revised in 1968, the Covenant remains the basic manifesto of the Palestine Liberation Organization. The following articles are pertinent to the question of mass expulsion and *Heimatrecht*.

Article 1: Palestine is the homeland of the Palestinian Arab people and an integral part of the great Arab homeland, and the people of Palestine is a part of the Arab Nation.

Article 3: The Palestinian Arab people possesses the legal right to its homeland, and when the liberation of its homeland is completed it will exercise self-determination solely according to its own will and choice.

Article 5: The Palestinians are the Arab citizens who were living permanently in Palestine until 1947, whether they were expelled from there or remained. Whoever is born to a Palestinian Arab father after this date, within Palestine or outside it, is a Palestinian.

Article 6: Jews who were living permanently in Palestine until the beginning of the Zionist invasion will be considered Palestinians.

Article 14: The destiny of the Arab nation, indeed the very Arab existence, depends upon the destiny of the Palestine issue. The endeavor and effort of the Arab nation to liberate Palestine follows from this connection. The people of Palestine assumes its vanguard role in realizing this sacred national (Qawmî) aim.

Article 15: The liberation of Palestine, from an Arab viewpoint, is a national (Qawmî) duty to repulse the Zionist, imperialist invasion from the great Arab homeland and to purge the Zionist presence from Palestine. Its full responsibilities fall upon the Arab nation, peoples and governments, with the Palestinian Arab people at their head.

For this purpose, the Arab nation must mobilize its military, human, material and spiritual capabilities to participate actively with the people of Palestine. They must, especially in the present stage of armed Palestinian revolution, grant and offer the people of Palestine all possible help and every material and human support, and afford it every sure means and opportunity enabling it to continue to assume its vanguard role in pursuing its armed revolution until the liberation of its homeland.

Article 19: The partitioning of Palestine in 1947 and the establishment of Israel is fundamentally null and void, whatever time has elapsed, because it was contrary to the wish of the people of Palestine and its natural right to its homeland, and contradicts the principles embodied in the Charter of the United Nations, the first of which is the right of self-determination.

Article 20: The Balfour Declaration, the Mandate Document, and what has been based upon them are considered null and void. The claim of a historical or spiritual tie between Jews and Palestine does not tally with historical realities nor with the constituents of statehood in their true sense. Judaism, in its character as a religion of revelation, is not a nationality with an independent existence. Likewise, the Jews are not one people with an independent personality. They are rather citizens of the states to which they belong.

Articles 6 and 15, read in conjunction, indicate the goal of expelling the entire Jewish population of Israel except those present before 1917 and their descendants. Article 20, on the other hand, presumes to exercise external definition of the Jewish people. Clearly, the denial of *Heimatrecht* is central in the program of the PLO, and it can hardly claim the sympathy of anyone interested in civil liberties.

Certainly there are many individual Pales-nian Arabs who are not party to any scheme o liquidate Israel. Many thousands of these, fter screening, have been readmitted to the ccupied territories and to Israel itself. But so ong as the PLO and other militant organiza-ions persist in denying the right of the Israeli o their homeland and their right to govern hemselves as they see fit, they have alienated heir claim to *Heimatrecht* for themselves.

It sometimes happens that two parties have nore or less plausible rights to the same piece f real estate. When this happens, compassion nd common sense must prevail. The Jews were and still are persecuted in Russia and East-Central Europe; they were slaughtered by Hitler's SS; and they have recently been driven out of Arab states from Algeria to Yemen. The Israelis have no place else to go—adversity has forged them into a nation, and they are determined to hold their own. The Middle East, with vast open spaces, is large enough to accommodate Arabs *and* Jews: the techniques Israelis have used to make desert lands fertile will also work for Arabs. Surely it is the height of perversity to wish to add one more mass expulsion to the dismal catalogue.

23

SLAVERY

The United Nations Supplementary Convention on the Abolition of Slavery, the Slave Trade and Institutions and Practices Similar to Slavery (1956) defines a slave as someone "over whom any or all of the powers attaching to the right of ownership are exercised." Two simpler definitions proposed by the Anti-Slavery Society (1973, p.1) are: "one who, working for another, is not free to withhold his labour" or "one who is owned and thus has neither freedom nor rights." These definitions confirm that slavery is the ultimate form of economic discrimination, violating Locke's injunction that "no one ought to harm another in his life, health, liberty or possessions" (*Civ. Gov.* II, § 6) as well as the natural property of each individual in his own person and the fruits of his labours (*ibid.*, §§ 26, 27: Locke, 1690).

In addition to chattel slavery, or direct ownership of one person by another, the Supplementary Convention binds its signatories to forbid four practices identified as "similar to slavery." The lengthy definitions in the SC have been condensed by the Anti-Slavery Society (1973, p. 1) as follows:

DEBT BONDAGE is the state arising from a pledge by a debtor of his own personal services or of those of a person under his control as security for a debt, when the length and nature of the services is not defined nor does their value diminish th[e] debt.

SERFDOM is the condition of a tenant who mus[t] live and labour on the land of another person whether for reward or not, and who is not free t[o] change his status.

EXPLOITATION OF CHILDREN—any practic[e] whereby a person under 18 years old is delivere[d] by parent or guardian to another person, whethe[r] for reward or not, with a view to exploiting hi[m] or his labour.

SERVILE FORMS OF MARRIAGE—any institutio[n] whereby a woman, without the right to refuse, i[s] promised or given in marriage on payment of [a] consideration in money or in kind, or may b[e] transferred to another person or, on the death [of] her husband, may be inherited by another per[-]son.

According to the Anti-Slavery Society's se[c-]retary, Colonel Patrick Montgomery, "One o[r] more of these institutions survives at least ve[s-]tigially in at least forty countries and if these a[re] happen to be in the 'free' world it is onl[y] because they have been taken out of privat[e] ownership by the Communists, who in the S[o-]viet Union hold an estimated one million i[n] forced labour camps" (1973b, p. 1). As will b[e] seen in chapter 24, "corrective labor" and con[-]ditions on *kolkhoz* farms (which perpetuat[e] aspects of the medieval *corvée*) in the USS[R] constitute slavery and similar practices withi[n] the meaning of the UN Supplementary Co[n-] vention. The USSR, indeed, has by no means abolished slavery but has simply socialized its usufruct.

A. *International Measures to Abolish Slavery*

Concrete action against slavery dates back to 1792, when Denmark forbade its subjects to trade in slaves. France followed in 1794, Britain in 1807. The Webster-Ashburton Treaty of 1842 between the United States and Great Britain provided for the elimination of the Atlantic slave trade. Russia abolished serfdom in 1861; the United States freed its slaves in 1865 and Brazil did likewise in 1888. Ethiopia enacted the gradual abolition of slavery in 1924, and Saudi Arabia joined the movement in 1962, followed by the other states on the Arabian peninsula. The last state to end slavery was Muscat and Oman, where the despotic Sultan Said bin Taimur was deposed in 1972; his son Qabus freed the 500 palace slaves, some of whom could not speak because of enforced silence, while others could no longer raise their eyes from the ground (*The Times*, London, July 10, 1972). Today, no state still officially permits slavery, though the Anti-Slavery Society believes that some tens of thousands of chattel slaves still exist in various corners of the world.

The Geneva Convention of 1926, containing a general prohibition of slavery, left it to the signatories to operate as they saw fit within their own sovereignties. It made no provisions for inquiries to find out where slavery was still being practiced. The 1956 Supplementary Convention, which went into force on April 30, 1957, made a weak reference to forced or compulsory labor and stated that slavery "and practices similar to slavery have not yet been eliminated in all parts of the world."

In 1953, the International Labor Office, through an *ad hoc* Committee on Forced Labor, investigated allegations about practices similar

to slavery in both developed and lesser developed Latin-American countries, as well as South Africa, the colonies of several European countries, and even the USSR and the United States. The Committee circulated a questionnaire to all ILO members, solicited replies from states against which charges had been lodged, and heard representatives of a number of organizations in public hearings.

The charges were that Indian tribal populations were providing compulsory unpaid labor and services to landowners; that they were subjected to exploitive sharecropping practices; that Indians were forcibly recruited from tribes to work on estates; that the tribes provided cheap labor (*peonaje*) for agriculture and mining; and that Indians also were forced to do street cleaning and road repair. It was also charged that slave labor was performed on plantations in Colombia, Venezuela, Argentina, and Paraguay, and that blacks were used as slave labor in the West Indies.

The Committee's findings were evasive, but it averred that "indirect compulsion to work" probably occurred as a result of traditions and customs related to semifeudal land tenure. Since those institutions and practices did not "appear to be deliberately planned or tolerated by the governments concerned, they cannot be regarded as a system of forced labor within the meaning of the Committee's terms of reference" (ILO, 1953, p. 55). The Committee also concluded that compulsory labor for road building and maintenance in Paraguay was not "of appreciable importance to the economy of the country," but that Bolivia's law on compulsory labor, if extensively used, could result in an economically important system of forced labor.

The Committee found little evidence of practices similar to slavery, though it did not examine feudal tenancy practices in Latin America—including compulsory unpaid services to landowners. Such forced labor as was found was illegal under national laws and was managed by private persons and not by governments. Hence, the Committee felt, no action by the UN was indicated. The report skirted the issue of whether local authorities were supporting or enforcing "tenancy peonage." The Committee ignored the crucial problem: whether or not slavery and quasi-slavery exist and are tolerated, even if officially proscribed. Slave hunts in Paraguay are treated in chapter 27; suffice it to say here that peonage persists in many parts of Latin America.

In the form of tenancy peonage, slavery and quasi-slavery may permanently affect entire tribes. Additional tasks may be forced upon detribalized families or individuals, in which case forced labor rather than slavery may be involved. The vast area of domestic service, which on plantations may easily degenerate into serfdom and slavery, especially for female servants, was disregarded by the Committee. Nor did it investigate the equally urgent question of marriage customs that enslave the woman, such as child marriage, forced marriage, and *purdah*.

The ad hoc Committee did not investigate slavery and quasi-slavery in the Arab and Muslim world, even though slave trade across the Sahara and Sudan and slavery in Muslim African societies have involved many people and are not yet entirely eliminated (Fisher and Humphrey, 1971, chs. 1–3).

At the time of the investigation slavery was still legal in Saudi Arabia and other states on the Arabian Peninsula. It was also openly practiced in Ethiopia, while certain caste practices in India came fairly close to slavery or peonage.

B. Slavery and Similar Practices in the World Today

Various religious and tribal groups in Africa have been observed to indulge in practices close to slavery with other groups as victims. Relations between Muslims and Congoid non-Muslims are a case in point. Moreover, purchase of brides and marriage practices not far removed from slavery are widespread and still exist, albeit in mitigated form, even in Southeast Europe. The employment of children in factories (as mentioned in Chapters 19 and 21) also appears to be common in some parts of the world.

It must be conceded that thorough investigations of slavery and similar practices are most difficult, even in the rare cases when local governments cooperate fully and honestly with the investigators. Interpretations are equally difficult, since societies that function on different cultural levels require customs that are mutually unacceptable. Furthermore, tribal societies often have customs which, judged by modern European standards, show characteristics of slavery. Yet to enforce the instant abolition of such customs may tear apart the fabric of a primitive society.

The evidence does not indicate that slavery, in the strict sense of the word, still exists in significant magnitude, but neither can it be said that slavery and slavery-like practices are steadily declining and about to disappear.

Few governments have shown interest in the matter. The United Nations and the ILO have not pushed their investigations very hard and their concern has dwindled as "third world" countries gained control of their assemblies. Yet the need for UN action is self-evident, since slavery and quasi-slavery, where they persist, are closely tied to deprivation, corporal punishment, psychocide, short life-expectancy, and killings. Just as the slave must be kept alive to work, so his escape must be deterred—such deterrence always involves cruelty. As will be seen in chapter 27, some of the major surviving slave systems are genocidal.

1. FINDINGS OF THE ANTI-SLAVERY SOCIETY

In 1973 the Anti-Slavery Society reported chattel slavery and/or one or more of the four "similar" practices, either vestigial or customary, in at least 40 non-communist countries.

They lie in a belt between 30° north and 10° south of the Equator. The belt extends from the Philippines, through Southeast and Southern Asia and Asia Minor, the Persian Gulf and Southern Arabia, North, Central and West Africa to the Amazonas forests, the Andean Altiplano, and Central America.

Chattel slavery in the strict sense has declined markedly in recent years, a fact for which the Anti-Slavery Society takes some deserved credit. In Oman, for instance, slavery was abolished as a lawful institution in 1970. As the Society indicated in 1973 (p. 7):

As recently as 1966 Germaine Tillion, one of the best informed European ethnological authorities on the francophone Sahara, stated that slavery, though forbidden by both secular and Islamic law in eight named countries, was still widely practised and tolerated in all of them. In 1972 this is no longer true. There is no doubt that the action of newly independent governments to eliminate slavery has been encouraged both by publicity and by discussion at the UN.

As late as January 1975, Anne Balfour-Fraser reported (*Baptist Times*, January 9, 1975) that she had seen slaves in parts of the Sahara even though the government there denied that such slaves existed. They were owned by the Tuareg or Toubou tribes in Algeria, Niger, and Chad. Curiously enough, Ms. Balfour-Fraser observed, the slaves were in some cases better off than their masters, as they were sedentary artisans while the masters were only nomadic herdsmen. Quite often, she was offered female babies by their mothers—for obvious reasons.

The relations between masters and slaves in the southern Sahara are ambivalent. On the one hand, as Ms. Balfour-Fraser explains, the Tuareg and Toubou "are arrogant and as you would expect of slave owners they despise their slaves, though they share with them what little food, clothing, and shelter they possess." Mutual dependence, on the other hand, exchanging protection for service in the face of

enemies, including the harshest of climates, has evoked intense mutual loyalty. One slave, after finding his way to Paris in the 1960s to earn good money assembling cars, was sending half of it to his master in Mauretania (Montgomery, 1975a).

Chattel slavery can only persist clandestinely and its appearance in official statistics would be an admission that slavery is condoned or that the law cannot be enforced. The Anti-Slavery Society (1973, p. 2) estimates the number of chattel slaves in the strict sense as "some tens of thousands." Since the majority of the world's population live under conditions in which exploitation can flourish, the Society considers it "unreasonable to think of those embraced by the four 'institutions and practices similar to slavery' forbidden by the SC in terms of less than tens of millions."

At the United Nations in 1967, Colonel Montgomery, the secretary of the Anti-Slavery Society, was seeking sponsors for a resolution and approached the delegate of Pakistan. "I will not waste your time by reading it," the diplomat replied. "We have no slavery in Pakistan but we have neighbors who have slavery and I don't intend to embarrass them." The next week, however, newpaper headlines proclaimed: "Ayub orders slavery inquiry." It turned out that a thousand men and boys had been discovered by a foreign journalist working eighteen hours per day for their keep under contractors on government irrigation work on the Indus, 210 miles from Karachi. This had been going on for six years. Heavy sentences were subsequently announced (Montgomery, 1975b).

In 1970, the representative of the Anti-Slavery Society found serf labor being used throughout Badakshan, the northeasterly province of Afghanistan, to grow opium, most of which was traded illicitly to the West. The landowners' henchmen punished those who failed to produce their assigned quotas by flogging, branding, mutilation, and if all else failed eviction. In a society where no one dares employ an evicted peasant, eviction means starvation.

Some of the opium, as Colonel Montgomery relates, goes via Pakistan, some via Iran, where the penalty for carrying more than four pounds is death. It was usual for a peasant courier's wife to be held hostage until payment. In 1971 the Afghani government accepted a United Nations mission and set up ministerial committees to study remedies, but how much the situation has actually improved is a matter for conjecture.

2. SEXUAL EXPLOITATION OF WOMEN

Another persistent form of quasi-slavery is the traffic in women, including servile marriage. After noting the traffic in female children in the Sahara and countries to the south, Anne Balfour-Fraser (*Baptist Times*, January 9, 1975) reports that she visited some "very enlightened doctors in Ghana. . . . They had girls of ten and twelve who did the housework in return for being lodged and fed. They had been placed there by their parents. The doctors' attitude was that any child was lucky to be properly fed in a country where not every child could enjoy this privilege!" While the Ghana doctors may be credited with not taking advantage of the girls beyond requiring them to work for food only, such domestic bondage is, as Ms. Balfour-Fraser notes, usually connected with sexual activities in Arab countries. As late as 1973, a Ghana diplomat admitted to Colonel Montgomery that fifty schoolgirls in his own country had been sold into unpaid service in Lebanon.

Nor are African and Asian women the only victims of sexual exploitation. In his August, 1974, testimony before a UN subcommission, Colonel Montgomery summarized an article that had just appeared in the *Daily Telegraph Magazine* as follows:

Its subject is a sensational one, about which many irresponsible stories are written, the traffic in women. This one, by contrast, does not describe abduction and the outworn system—the breaking-in of the novice. It acknowledges that the women are willing recruits, whose ignorance, stupidity and lack of friends at home lead them to take the fatal first step of entering into a contract without advice to work in a foreign country. Only when they have been tricked, by an appearance of generous treatment, into losing their passports and having their contracts substituted by indigenous ones, do they discover that they are in danger. Only when they have been induced by trickery and the new contract to incur heavy debts and after seeking their consul's help do they discover that he is powerless to help them if this involves breaking a lawful contract they have signed. They have thus become, by their own apparently voluntary action, obliged to work very long hours, in conditions I need not describe, while their debt is progressively perpetuated. Until that debt is discharged no exit visa will be issued. Some thus become slaves, who are subsequently sold off to buyers from certain other countries where their presence will never be noticed.

Confirmation of Colonel Montgomery's charges was provided rather unexpectedly by a student of one of the authors who had served in the United States Army in Turkey. He told of a personal experience in class and, at the instructor's request, put the information in the form of a statement that reads as follows:

On the 5th day of August 1970, upon my arrival in Istanbul, Turkey from Karamusel, where I had been stationed for the past year and a half, I was approached by a Turk offering me a girl for sale. He stated that if I was interested, he could take me to a club where I could dance and drink with a variety of girls and have the pick of the lot for any amount of time from a twenty-four hour period to a year. The price would be determined by the seller after I had made my choice.

When I was a youngster I had read about the practice of buying and selling women, and I leaped at the opportunity of going with this man to his so-called club. This was about the tenth time I had been approached like this in my eighteen month stay in Turkey and since I would be leaving the next day, I decided that nothing would be hurt by going with him.

This club was located approximately ten blocks

from the Istanbul Hilton Hotel. The girls were Turkish, Arabian, French and German. It was just as the Turk had said. The men could come in, dance, drink and converse, and after some time would pay some well-dressed Turkish man and leave with their girl. The girls appeared to range from about 17 or 18 years of age to the early thirties.

At one point a girl of about twenty refused to go with an older man. An "enforcer" was called and he proceeded to beat the girl. He slapped her around, ripped her blouse and threw her on the floor. She got up sobbing, went into a backroom, changed, and walked out with the elderly gentleman.

After about two hours of drinking and watching, I decided to return to my hotel room and prepare for my flight to the U.S. the following day.

The Anti-Slavery Society has also directed considerable attention to servile marriage. That institution, particularly but not only in the less modernized Muslim societies, is usually associated with female circumcision. Ms. Balfour-Fraser (1975) describes this practice as follows:

To Western women, clitorectomy as practised in Sudan, East, Central and West Africa, seems horrifying. This practice is a form of female circumcision which entails the total or partial excision of the clitoris. The operation leaves the orifice of the vagina inelastic and reduced in diameter to half an inch so that childbirth and even penetration have normally to be surgically assisted.

The operation is always carried out by other women and it is the women who insist on maintaining this barbaric custom in the belief that no man will marry an uncircumcised woman and the only alternatives to marriage are slavery or prostitution or both.

I believe that when starvation as an alternative to bondage is removed, and with better education of women, when prostitution ceases to be the only alternative to marriage, most forms of actual slavery or bondage will disappear.

The Anti-Slavery Society has from time to time reported to the Human Rights Commission cases of forced marriage, including four that took place in Zanzibar in 1970.

The extreme case of forced marriage is the harem, which persists in certain Arab countries. Recognizing that the harem originally had an economic purpose—to provide maintenance for the widows of men lost in battle—and that the instant dissolution of harems would result in starvation for many of their inmates, the Anti-Slavery Society proposes a program for their gradual abolition. This would include repatriation and vocational training for inmates so desiring, and a freeze on any further additions to harems (Anti-Slavery Society, 1973, p.4). While it is often argued that women are happy in harems because they enjoy status, idleness, and ease, there are many whose only desire is to get out. As Montgomery (1975b) reports:

One such was Atajumba who, kidnapped on her wedding day as a gift to the Lamido of Ngaoundere, Cameroun, escaped over a twenty-foot wall after nine years inside. At the Norwegian Mission she told Pastor Endresen she would rather die than go back.

In 1919 the French recognised the domestic autonomy of Rei Bouba for the lifetimes of the Lamido and his son for war services. In 1969 the Cameroun Government persuaded the Lamido that he was no longer the owner of his 50,000 subjects. At that time the harem at Rei Bouba was believed to contain between 300 and 400 women.

It may be observed in passing that the Lamido acquired the title of *Hadji* by selling some of his slaves' children to pay the expenses of the flight to Mecca for himself and his court.

3. MOHAMED AWAD'S REPORT ON SLAVERY

The most recent United Nations investigation culminated in the *Report on Slavery* by Mohamed Awad, Special Rapporteur on Slavery (U.N. E/4168/Rev.1, New York 1966). Perceptively analyzed, this document will yield a certain amount of evidence, which is circumstantial rather than conclusive.

The main source of information was a questionnaire circulated to all members of the United Nations. Thirty-nine states made no response, including a number mentioned in reports or allegations of slavery or related practices. Among those in this category were: Bolivia, Brazil, Burundi, Central African Republic, Colombia, Ethiopia, Haiti, Lebanon, Liberia, Mauritania, Paraguay, Portugal, Saudi Arabia, Tanzania, and Upper Volta. The combination of non-response with a less-than-spotless reputation on the slavery issue suggests that at least some of these governments, despite antislavery laws on the books of most, did not, as of 1965, pursue eradication of slavery with crusading zeal. Allegations of slavery and quasi-slavery had recently been lodged against Ethiopia and Paraguay, and these practices had been reported earlier in such countries as Burundi, Central African Republic, Guinea, Mauritania, and Tanzania.

Altogether 82 states plus 11 British dependencies, 7 Trucial States and the Federation of South Arabia replied. Of these, 50 governments plus the Trucial Emirates either acknowledged the existence of *some* continuing form of slavery or answered evasively—or both.

The following governments submitted evasive replies: Afghanistan, Algeria, Bahrein, Bolivia, Brazil, Cameroon, Ceylon, Chad, Congo, Cuba, Dahomey, Dominican Republic, Ecuador, Gambia, Ghana, Guatemala, Iran, Iraq, Ivory Coast, Kuwait, Laos, Madagascar, Malawi, Malaysia, Maldive Islands, Mali, Nepal, Niger, Nigeria, Pakistan, Peru, Philippines, Rwanda, Saudi Arabia, Senegal, Sierra Leone, Somalia, South Arabia, Sudan, Surinam, Syria, Thailand, Togo, Trucial Emirates, Uganda, UAR (Egypt), Venezuela, (North) Yemen, and Zambia.

Evasiveness is often transparent—e.g. when Gambia asserted that "slavery no longer exists" and used less than 100 words to answer several questions. In contrast, Ecuador gave a lengthy legalistic reply and managed to say very little about real conditions.

Mali submitted a strong indictment of slavery in its feudal and colonial past and speculates, in one sentence, about the current possi-

bility that "particularly experienced criminals" might practice slavery by subterfuge. But since Mali has "no specific evidence to substantiate such a hypothesis," it can be accepted that "the slave trade and practices similar to slavery have now been eliminated from the Republic of Mali."

Saudi Arabia (which sent no formal reply) objected to a statement submitted by the Anti-Slavery Society which provided second-hand information about the size of the slave population (about 250,000) and the slave trade with the Trucial States. (The Society had acknowledged the 1962 decree abolishing slavery.) Saudi Arabia protested against alleged abuse of the Society's consultative status and declared that if such reports were admitted for consideration, the UN would "become the arena for engaging in vindictive and acrimonious allegations instead of initiating policies yielding constructive and fruitful results." Yet the fact of persisting slavery—three years after its official abolition—was hardly in doubt, and a progress report could have been expected. Saudi Arabia simply avoided the issue.

The Republic of China acknowledged specific problems and detailed its legislation and countermeasures. India also faced up to the problem, summarized its legislation, acknowledged the persistence of quasi-slavery, and explained the corrective measures it was taking (which appeared to be insufficient). Spain seems to have no serious residual slavery, yet its government went to considerable length to discuss its legislation and its policy toward white slavery, which it did not consider fully eliminated.

Governments may not always be aware of conditions in their countries, especially in remote districts. The Sudan government may have acted in good faith in stating "now there is no sign of slavery in the whole country," and that "servile status" was being "anxiously and vigorously" eradicated. Britain tried hard to provide realistic answers but made only a summary statement about 15 territories. It transmitted the reply of Bahrein as follows: "Neither the institution of slavery nor the slave trade exists in law or in fact." The answer by the Trucial States was evasive. In a statement of 1963 by the Supreme Council of the Federation of South Arabia, forwarded through Britain in reply to a factual statement by the Anti-Slavery Society, we read: "The absence of legislation specifically directed against slavery in some states is because the necessity for such legislation has never arisen. . . . the introduction of such legislation at this late date may be taken . . . as an admission that slavery does in fact exist within the Federation."

It is regrettable that France did not choose to present an adequate reply about its overseas territories.

The outstanding impression derived from the Awad report is that there is barely any enforcement anywhere; and that this lack of enforcement is advanced as "evidence" that slavery no longer exists. Yet Chad, in the Sub-Saharan Sahel, acknowledged that slavery in the form of "marriage, transfer of a women, inheritance" still existed because of tradition, that the government had taken no steps to eliminate the practice, and that no prosecutions had taken place. A similar answer was given by Uganda. Egypt admitted that "exploitation of women in prostitution" existed in its country but did not say anything about prosecution.

All in all Awad's report is just a collection of answers by governments to his questionnaire. Some of the answers appeared to have been written hastily and without research, while others repeated information given during earlier inquiries. The report suggests that (a) self-policing does not work, (b) that quite a few governments are cynical about the matter, and (c) that many developing countries simply do not have the resources and skill to do anything effective.

It would appear, however, that in a few cases the institution is allowed to "die out." Nothing much happens to the old slaves who are "legally" emancipated but remain at their old posts, having no better opportunities and

no share of their masters' lands. New enslavements, on the other hand, are prohibited.

If it is true that, as several submissions pointed out, economic progress takes care of most slavery problems, it would logically be true that economic trouble like the Sahel famine results in new slavery, especially for girls. This has indeed been reported for the Tuaregs, and it should be remembered that when a person faces the alternative of death-from-hunger or slavery, the survival instinct will make slavery "attractive."

In 1955, Hans Engen of Norway submitted a report (E/2673) which summarized statements by governments, a study by ILO on *Indigenous Peoples* (Geneva, 1953), and restricted memoranda by members of the Ad Hoc Committee on Slavery (E/AC.33/10–14). Since the governments were in most cases more responsive than to the later inquiry directed by Mr. Awad, and since the Ad Hoc Committee itself engaged in research, the Engen report contains much usable information. Pooling the information from the three sources—the 1953 ILO forced labor report, the 1955 Engen report, and the 1966 Awad report—it is possible to arrive at a tentative listing of countries where slavery and related practices have recently been observed. "Confirmed" cases are only those where the national governments admitted the existence of abuses. "Suspect" cases are those about which specific allegations were mentioned by responding governments or formulated by the ILO or committee members, and which have not been convincingly refuted. Evaluations of frequency (much, little, disappearing, etc.) have not been attempted. It should be noted that a number of countries listed as colonies have since become independent.

Recently Reported Cases of Slavery and Related Practices

Slavery, including domestic slavery, and slave trade:
CONFIRMED: Belgium (Congo and Ruanda-Urundi), France (Morocco), India, Saudi Ara-

bia (confirmed by official instruction of 1936), United Kingdom (Aden Protectorate and Persian Gulf States).

SUSPECT: Afghanistan, Colombia (with respect to Goajiro Indians), Ecuador, Netherlands (Aruba and Curaçao), Syria, Thailand, Venezuela (Goajiro), and Yemen. (On the basis of other information summarized in chapter 27, Paraguay may be added.)

Serfdom:
CONFIRMED: France (North Cameroon and French Equatorial Africa), and India.
SUSPECT: People's Republic of China, Guatemala, Indonesia, Nepal, and Thailand.

Unpaid or underpaid services exacted by landowners of their agents:
CONFIRMED: El Salvador, France (Morocco and French Equatorial Africa), India (Bihar, Madras, West Bengal and Punjab), Indonesia, Japan, Philippines, and U.K. (Persian Gulf States).
SUSPECT: Bolivia, Colombia, Ecuador, India (areas other than those mentioned above), Mexico, and Peru.

Debt Bondage:
CONFIRMED: France (Togoland), India, Japan, U.K. (Gold coast), U.K. (Nigeria), U.K. (Sierra Leone), U.K (Bahrain), U.K. (Quatar), U.K. (Trucial States), and U.S. (wetbacks).
SUSPECT: Belgium (Congo), Ceylon, China, Liberia, Nepal, Pakistan and Philippines.

Exploitation of Children:
CONFIRMED: Bolivia, El Salvador, France (Cameroons), Japan, Netherlands (Antilles), U.K. (Singapore-Malaya, Sarawak-Brunei, Hongkong), and Vietnam.
SUSPECT: Ceylon, China, Ecuador, Peru, and U.K. (Nigeria).

Purchase of Wives and Inheritance of Widows:
CONFIRMED: Australia (New Guinea), France (Black Africa), India, Netherlands (New Guinea), South Africa (Bantus), U.K. (Sudan), U.K. (South Rhodesia), and U.K. (Persian Gulf States).
SUSPECT: Afghanistan, Belgium (Congo), China, Colombia, and Japan.
Bondage in connection with prostitution was not examined in any of the reports used as sources here.

C. Slavery: A Dead Issue?

Slavery is incompatible with a modern industrial economy: it was efficiency more than Christianity that moved Czar Alexander II to free the serfs of Russia in 1861. It can be speculated that even had there been no Civil War, slavery would not have survived indefinitely in the American South.

But precisely because so many economies are not modern, conditions exist in which slavery and similar practices continue. In response to an inquiry, Colonel Montgomery, observing that conditions were perpetuated by unjust raw materials prices and a lack of population control, furnished the following list (*The Times*, October 10, 1970), which overlaps but is not identical with that given in the previous section:

Chattel Slavery: Algeria, Chad, Libya, Mali, Mauretania, Morocco, Niger, Pakistan, Philippines, Saudi Arabia, Senegal.

Serfdom: Afghanistan, Bolivia, Ecuador, Ethiopia, Peru.

Debt Bondage: Burma, India.

Sham Adoption and Exploitation of Children: Ghana and at least eight countries of West Africa, eight of South-East Asia, Lebanon, Syria, Turkey, and almost all of the 22 countries of Latin America. Colonel Montgomery praises Ghana for admitting the situation and helpfully describing the remedies applied.

Servile Forms of Marriage: All Islamic and part-Islamic countries, over 30 in number.

Lord Lugard, the greatest authority on slavery in his day, commented upon his 1933 appointment as Chairman of the League of Nations Standing Committee of Experts on Slavery that the international body had done nothing except to appoint "a temporary committee at intervals of several years with no means of obtaining the information necessary for its task or of following it up, and whose recommendations could be conveniently pigeonholed. Such committees are a mere waste of money and of the time and effort of the distinguished people who form them."

"The position in 1972," the Anti-Slavery Society declared (Background, 1972), "is strikingly similar to that in 1933, except that Lord Lugard and his Committee of Experts are lacking: the U.N. record of pigeon-holing and procrastination is worse than that of the League."

The Anti-Slavery Society has consistently urged that the United Nations establish machinery to police compliance with its conventions. Although the Economic and Social Council, in June 1972, passed a resolution listing a number of things that might be done to complete the abolition of slavery and similar practices (No. 1695 [LII] of June 2, 1972; 26 U.N. Yearbook 472–73), the Subcommission on Prevention of Discrimination and Protection of Minorities, which has jurisdiction, failed to call up the subject of slavery until the last day of its August 1972 meeting, and the debate took place "with one eye on the clock." Mr. Smirnov of the USSR observed that existing "communications" channels could be used and that slavery was in any case the domestic concern of governments, which were well able to cope with the matter themselves (Anti-Slavery Society, *Annual Report*, 1974). And that, to the date of this writing, is where the matter rests.

In the meantime, however, reports of slavery and related practices continue to appear. It was only in October 1975, for instance, that the government of India finally announced the abolition of debt bondage. And in March 1976, the Brazilian Foundation for Indians (FUNAI—see chapter 27,B4) reported that settlers in the rapidly developing Amazon valley were still forcing Indians into peonage and their women into prostitution (*Die Welt*, March 29, 1976). Conditions not very far from slavery have been reported on cut-rate freighters that sail under "convenience flags" (such as those of Cyprus, Lebanon, Liberia, and Panama) and are never subject to safety inspections—except those occasionally imposed by authorities at ports of call. Crews are recruited in Asia and Africa; their food ranges from poor to inedible, and it is the practice of many captains to withhold wages, except for small advances of pocket money, as a means of keeping the sailors from jumping ship (*Die Welt*, December 18, 1976). Nonenforcement of child-labor and school-attendance laws has been reported from Egypt, where illegally employed children receive as little as $7.50 per month (*Christian Science Monitor*, December 10, 1976), and from Italy, where children are actually sold into bondage in the poverty-stricken south (San Jose *Mercury News*, March 20, 1977). And the Anti-Slavery Society has reported the reintroduction of actual slavery in Equatorial Guinea, ruled by the bloody dictator Francisco Macias Nguema Biyogo (see chapter 20,D4). Following the exodus of some 45,000 Nigerians from the cocoa plantations of Fernando Po Island, in response to ill-treatment—including killings as well as attacks on Nigerian diplomats—Macias decreed compulsory manual labor for all over the age of 15 in "government plantations and mines" and called for recruitment of 60,000 forced laborers. Refugees told the London *Times* that "President Macias Nguema had ordered his guards to arrest between 2,000 and 2,500 people in each of the 20 districts of the mainland province of Rio Muni to be used as unpaid forced labor on the plantations of the island of Macias Nguema Biyogo (Fernando Po)" (*San Francisco Sunday Examiner-Chronicle*, November 20, 1976).

As in other areas of extreme oppression, there is still unfinished business under the heading of slavery.

24

FORCED LABOR

A. International Conventions on Forced Labor

Forced labor is treated by the Forced Labor Convention of 1930 and the Abolition of Forced Labor Convention of 1957. As of 1971, 105 states were parties to the 1930 instrument, while 89 states had agreed to abolish this barbarous practice—or prevent its arising where it did not exist—in the spirit of the 1957 convention. The 19 nonparticipating states and territories, as of 1962, included several, such as Luxembourg, South Africa, the United States, and Uruguay, where forced labor is not likely to exist.

The 1930 convention (printed in *ILO Official Supplement*, 1963) defines forced or compulsory labor as "all work or service which is exacted from any person under the menace of any penalty and for which the said person has not offered himself voluntarily." The term does not include work of a purely military character, "normal civic obligations of the citizens of a fully self-governing country," work resulting from sentence by a court of law, emergency work, and "minor communal services." Each signatory undertook "to suppress the use of forced or compulsory labor in all its forms and within the shortest possible period." The USSR is a party to the two forced labor conventions.

Work exacted through a conviction is to be carried out "under the supervision and control of a public authority" (Article 2/2c). A dilemma results from precisely this stipulation: since forced labor, wherever it is practiced consistently and on a large scale, is *necessarily* in the hands of "authority," the convention entrusts supervision to the perpetrator of the unlawful activity. For compulsory labor regarded as legal, Article 11/1 rules that "only adult able-bodied males . . . of an apparent age of not less than 18 and not more than 45 years may be called upon," and this only after medical examination and with due "respect for conjugal and family ties" (Article 11/1a and d).

Forced labor periods were limited by Article 12/1 to 60 days within twelve months. Normal working hours are to be the same as those of customary voluntary labor, with regular wages and overtime paid at locally prevailing rates (Articles 13/1 and 14/1). Article 21 prohibits the use of forced labor for underground work in mines, and Article 16 contains a number of protective stipulations about safety, health, and food. The main weakness of the Convention is the lack of provisions to ensure compliance.

The Abolition of Forced Labor Convention, which was concluded in 1957 and took effect in 1959, referred to the 1926 Slavery Convention with its proviso that "all necessary measures shall be taken to prevent compulsory or forced labor from developing into conditions analogous to slavery." Otherwise it made only one major new stipulation. This is contained in Article 1 which prohibits forced labor "as a means of *political coercion* or *education*, or as a *punishment* for holding or expressing *political views* or views *ideologically opposed* to the established political, social or economic system" (emphasis added).

B. *The ILO Report of 1953*

The ILO's ad hoc Committee on Forced Labor has conducted several intensive investigations. Its 1953 report presented extensive data on many areas, including much valuable information on Eastern Europe and the USSR. The Committee was unable to examine conditions in Albania and the People's Republic of China (see ILO, 1953).

1. GENERAL SCOPE OF INQUIRY

The Committee sent questionnaires to 81 governments, of which 33 did not respond. It investigated 24 countries and a number of dependent territories under the jurisdiction of incriminated governments. Only ten governments cooperated—a fact showing that politicians often do not feel obligated to live up to their rhetoric.

Aside from Latin America, a region given special consideration in chapter 27, the ILO Committee reached conclusions concerning 30 countries and territories. The allegations against 13 countries and territories were found to be without substance. In eight countries and territories a limited amount of forced labor was found to exist, or legislation and practices were identified which, the Committee felt, could be abused under certain conditions. Forced labor existed to a limited extent in Spain and in Portuguese territories, but was far more prevalent in Bulgaria, Czecho-Slovakia, the "German Democratic Republic," Hungary, Poland, Rumania, and the USSR.

Forced labor as a means of political coercion in South Africa had not been alleged and no such abuse was discovered there. Attention was diverted to racial barriers and the lower wages paid African labor. South Africa was criticized, but there was no finding that it was practicing forced labor.

Australia, Belgium and Britain did not get an entirely clean bill of health concerning some of their colonies and mandates. The Committee also suspected illegal forced labor of Mexican wetbacks, and possibly illegal peonage in the United States. American vagrancy laws were held to be too broadly defined.

The findings on the USSR were clear and devastating. They were based on Soviet legislation and made reference to copious testimony of persons subjected to the forced labor treatment. Much of the evidence has since been amply confirmed, even by texts published in the USSR and by admissions of Soviet leaders. The Committee's data on the communist-ruled countries of Eastern Europe showed that corrective labor camps existed in *all* of them and were meaningfully interrelated with the Soviet Gulag system. The fundamental evidence on forced labor in the Moscow-controlled bloc was presented to the UN in an official document (E/2431—cited here as ILO, 1953).

The ad hoc Committee investigated the Soviet *de facto* and *de jure* systems of forced labor as means of political coercion and education and of economic planning and development, as well as elements of judicial and administrative procedure. Pertinent allegations were submitted, *inter alia*, by the U.S. and U.K. governments, the International Confederation of Free Trade Unions, the International Federation of Free Journalists, and the International League for the Rights of Man. Much of the evidence consisted of legal codes and other documents promulgated by the communist governments, who were in no position to deny their authenticity.

In the case of the "German Democratic Republic," the UK representative testified that according to a British inquiry "the population of concentration camps was greater at the present time (1952–53) than it had been [under Hitler] in 1939. There was every reason to believe that 200,000 to 300,000 prisoners were interned in the six major or six or seven smaller camps." The Committee cited Article 137 of the "GDR" constitution of 1949, stating that "the execution of punishment is based on the conception of the educative influence of joint productive labor on those capable of improvement." Legal texts of 1952 referring to corrective labor were cited at length. Orders and ordinances of the Soviet Military Administration proved the existence of forced labor in the "GDR" up to the end of Stalin's regime.

A similar routine was followed in all cases, including the investigation of the USSR. In that inquiry, the British representative disclosed that "according to the most reliable information this government has been able to obtain, rather more than ten million people in the Soviet Union are at present subjected to forced labor." The U.K. government also stated that "political prisoners are more rigorously treated than common criminals." (ILO, 1953, pp. 441ff). The Committee adduced evidence proving that the corrective labor codes were applicable all over the USSR, and analyzed the *de jure* situation on the basis of the total *corpus juris* of the USSR, devoting no less than 40 pages (464–504) to this single task. The mass of evidence indicated that the USSR had violated its commitments under the 1930 Convention, including time limitation of labor service, age limit, medical fitness, health protection, normal working hours, adequate payment, shelter, clothing, food, and avoidance of harsh climates, as well as the general principles of due process of law.

A survey of the legal situation at the end of 1974 by one of the present authors showed that most of the provisions that existed in 1952 were still in force 22 years later. Although the

camp population in the USSR has been reduced since Stalin's death, forced labor as an institution has *not* been abolished (see Possony, 1975a). More is said about it in the concluding section of this chapter.

2. DETAILED FINDINGS OF THE AD HOC COMMITTEE: CZECHO-SLOVAKIA AND RUMANIA

The detailed findings of the ad hoc Committee are too voluminous to summarize in meaningful detail. It seems more informative to give information in some depth on two countries where the practice of forced labor was substantiated. All the quotations in this section are taken from the Report of the Ad Hoc Committee on Forced Labour, document E/2431 (Geneva: ILO, 1953).

In the case of Czecho-Slovakia the charges were levied by a representative of the United Kingdom in the Economic and Social Council (ECOSOC) (8th Session, 238th meeting: Official Records, p. 112) as follows:

In Czechoslovakia, no attempt was being made to disguise the fact that forced labour camps existed. Mr. Mayhew called the attention of the Council to Law 247 of 25 October 1948. Article 1, Section 3, of that Law stated that prisoners were employed in the national interest in fulfilment of the economic plan. Article 2, Section 1, stated that the prisoners were between 18 and 60 years of age and included persons who "menace the structure of the people's democratic order." Article 3, Section 2, stated that, officially, sentences varied from three months to two years. Article 5 specified that the execution of the sentence could not be delayed. Finally, Article 6 provided that the sentence could be shortened or prolonged at the suggestion of the camp administration. Before the adoption of that Law, some 170,000 Sudetens who had remained in Czechoslovakia had been sent to forced labour, mainly in the eastern part of the country. Some had been deported to Russia (p. 215).

Law 247 on forced labor camps was analyzed further by another ECOSOC member from the United Kingdom (11th Session, 413th meeting: Off. Rec., paragraph 21):

The authors of that Law had made no attempt to disguise such camps as educational institutions. Possibly the Czechoslovak forced labor camps were the least inhumane of such communist institutions, but they constituted a wholesale violation of human rights. The Law contained no provisions for a trial of any sort. Section 2 of the Law began with the words: "To the camp shall be sent: (a) Persons who have reached the age of 18 and are not older than 60 and are physically and mentally fit but shirk work or menace the structure of the people's democratic order or national economy . . . ; Section 3 with the words: "A commission of three, whose members and deputies shall be nominated by the regional national committees, shall decide upon sending persons to a camp, upon the duration of their term, etc. . . . "; and in Section 5 it was simply stated that: "An appeal lodged against a decision under Section 3 has no delaying effect." There was no suggestion in the Law that those condemned to forced labour should have legal advice or be heard in their own defence. Probably the first time they heard of the charge against them was when the police came to their house in the middle of the night and removed them to the camp. The United Kingdom delegation had circulated to delegations a specimen decree of the type issued through the security police, although paragraph 24 of the regulations showed that an arrest could be made in anticipation of the issue of a decree. It was true that the victim had the theoretical right to appeal against the arbitrary decision of the commission, but in the meantime he would be subjected to forced labour and his business might be taken over and his wife and family turned out of their house. The Law amounted to sheer terrorism and political oppression.

Since the United Kingdom was opposed to forced labor, it had concluded that there was a case for investigation by the United Nations. While he would not enter into a discussion of political systems, he wished to make it clear that the United Kingdom had not associated itself with the United States in the matter of forced labour on account of any similarity in their economic systems, but because both Governments were alarmed at the spread of forced labour in the countries dominated by the Soviet Union. (pp. 215–16)

The British government "regarded with the gravest concern" the spread of the system of forced and underpaid labor from the USSR to the Soviet-dominated states of Eastern Europe.

The United States representative cited articles from the New York Times, which Czecho-Slovak authorities had not denied, indicating that costs of internal security were greater than for defense, and that forced labor produced a considerable share of the income of the Czecho-Slovak Ministry of the Interior. He continued:

The information showed that forced labour had become an integral part of the Czechoslovak economy, as it was of the economy of the U.S.S.R. and other communist countries. On 11 August 1950, the information agency Reuter had despatched from Prague the following message: "The Czechoslovak Government today announced the setting up of labour camps where security offenders could be sent for periods of up to two years." That announcement was a clear admission by the Czechoslovak Government that it was its policy to send security offenders to labour camps.

As in Bulgaria, the offenses for which a person could be condemned to forced labour were drafted in very broad terms, the camps were under the authority of the Ministry of the Interior and people were condemned through administrative procedures. Under the new penal laws adopted on 12 July 1950, the authority to punish certain very broadly defined offenses was conferred entirely upon the people's committees, which were purely political bodies, and it was not even required to grant the accused hearing. (ECOSOC, 11th Session, 413th meeting; and 12th Session, 470th meeting: Official Records, paras. 26–27 and 12 respectively, p. 216 in E/2431).

A representative of the exile Council of Free Czechoslovakia observed that forced labor had two purposes: to supply cheap labor and to eliminate opposition to the Communist regime.

We call it forced labour and they call it re-education. All the forced labour camps, from their point of view, are for re-education purposes. . . . The kind of life that is led with the work [exacted from the forced labourers] is considered an education in itself, which will correct their previous wrong political opinions. That is the theory. . . . Yet, from the practice and the situation in the camps, that is not re-education but camouflage. . . . It is on the basis of suspicion, political unreliability that people are assigned to forced labour. (p. 217)

It was the opinion of this representative that the dividing line between free labor and serfdom had disappeared in Czecho-Slovakia. There were only varying degrees of coercion.

Violations of the Convention rule against employing forced labor in underground mining were pointed out by the International League for the Rights of Man and the International Federation of Free Journalists. According to the latter:

One of the largest concentrations of forced labour camps is in the region of the uranium mines near Jachymov, Western Bohemia.

The Jachymov region contains various camps lying to the north of Ostrov, near the Karlovy Vary-Jachymov highway, and in Vykmanov. . . . There are altogether about 65 individual camps accommodating some 25,000 prisoners. . . .

Another region of forced labour camps attached to uranium mines is in the vicinity of Pribram, in Central Bohemia, south of Prague. . . .

Among scores of other forced labour camps, these are the names of the worst: Svaty Jan Pod Skalou . . . , Central Bohemia—work in quarries; Krivoklat, Central Bohemia—work in quarries; Kutna Hora, east of Prague—work on a State farm; Budejovice, Southern Bohemia—construction of a large military airfield; Pardubice, Eastern Bohemia—production of explosives. (pp. 221–22)

The Federation estimated that there were about 240,000 people, men and women, in Czecho-Slovak labor camps. About 80 percent were political prisoners sentenced administratively by national committees, 12 percent were politicals sentenced by courts, and the remainder common criminals. Concerning working conditions, the Federation stated:

The prisoners in forced labour camps are made to work on jobs particularly dangerous to their lives or

health. Prisoners working in uranium mines are exposed to continuous serious internal diseases, and after a few years uninterrupted work comes certain death. Whilst ordinary workers in the uranium mines receive special food and additional milk, the prisoners have to live on ordinary malnutritive prison food. . . .

The working time is seldom shorter than 10 hours a day. . . . Cases of prisoners being beaten up by guards are reported from every camp. (p. 222)

The Committee also found that some 20,000 Czechs and Slovaks as well as a number of Sudeten Germans had been deported for forced labor in the USSR between 1945 and 1948.

In its reply to the ad hoc Committee's questionnaire the Czecho-Slovak delegation to the United Nations made no substantive answer to charges of forced labor. Instead, it registered a general objection to the inquiry:

The Government of Czechoslovakia is of the opinion that the *Ad Hoc* Committee on Forced Labour had been established for the purpose of spreading slander against Czechoslovakia and other countries which abolished exploitation of man by man and where work became really free. . . .

Therefore the Government of Czechoslovakia rejects this questionnaire as illegal. It aims at the spreading of a slander and interference into internal affairs of other countries and is contrary to the obligation of the Member States of the United Nations the purpose of which is to develop friendly relations among nations. (p. 223)

In the debates in the Economic and Social Council, the Czecho-Slovak delegate—with no reference to facts—simply asserted that the workers in countries that had overthrown capitalism had "acquired a new freedom" (ECOSOC, 12th Session, 472d meeting: *Official Records*, paragraphs 15–16, 23–24).

In the case of Rumania the American delegate made the following statement in the Economic and Social Council:

The Grand National Assembly of Romania, at its seventh ordinary session, had on 30 May 1950 approved, of course unanimously, after only one day's debate, a long new Labour Code, whose authors admitted that they had been inspired by corresponding instruments of the U.S.S.R.; the Code provided, *inter alia*, that "Romanian citizens, in exceptional cases such as calamities and important State projects, may be called for temporary compulsory labour." Those words might seem rather weak to those who were familiar with the daily arrests that were made in Romania. The words "in exceptional cases" and "temporary" were far from being precise; perhaps the latter denoted a temporary final period of life on earth. (p. 335)

The representative of the Rumanian National Committee, in his statement before the ad hoc Committee, stressed that, under the communist Penal Code of 1948, forced labor, formerly provided only for common criminals, had been extended to political offenders. He went on to state that,

The pool of available slave labour is constantly replenished with persons condemned for so-called economic sabotage. A Decree of August 1949 provides for punishment for a vast range of economic offences, all vaguely and elastically defined, including even acts of negligence. . . . In connection with the preparation of workers for the application of the Five-Year Plan, Decree No. 68 of 16 May 1951 . . . provides for the drafting of 45,000 to 55,000 workers each year from among young workers, which contingent is to be sent to certain professional and trade schools for two to three years and then to special schools for a period of six months. According to the Decree, graduates of such schools are to be assigned to sectors of activity in accordance with the plan approved by the Council of Ministers, and they must remain at least four years in the units to which they have been assigned. . . . The inevitable conclusion toward which one is led by this brief survey of prevailing conditions in Romania, is that between the communist political regime and the servitude of labour there is a direct relation of cause and effect. . . . First of all, they get cheap labour and they can obtain any amount of work. Any economic problems can be solved by obtaining this cheap labour. Secondly, it is a means of coercion and of keeping whole populations under control. It creates a state of terror. The idea that, at any moment, persons may

be sent to these labour camps makes them more subservient to the regime. (*Ibid.*)

Decree No. 68 means that a young boy or girl, once "recruited" by the Directorate-General of Labor Reserves, becomes available for a minimum of six-and-a-half years as bonded labor for the State. According to the representative of the International Federation of Free Journalists, forced labor in Rumania exhibited five main characteristics:

(1) It is regarded as a permanent economic institution; (2) it represents a second field of production as opposed to the free field . . . ; (3) even in this field, it is responsible only for the initial stage of the work, where no machinery or special skills are required . . . ; (4) it is of such economic importance to the State that a whole series of laws and regulations had to be enacted to provide a legal framework for it; (5) apart from the legal framework, considerable machinery was required to ensure that the flow of such labour was maintained. (p. 336)

A memorandum submitted by the Rumanian National Committee pointed out the large-scale use of forced labor for public works. The labor brigades consist of thousands sentenced for political offenses, as well as a large number held in administrative custody without formal arraignment, "usually on simple suspicion."

Not only do the courts have the widest latitude in sending people to labor camps, the Rumanian National Committee further stated, but—

The communist authorities can send people to forced labour on a simple administrative decision on the basis of a Decree of 19 August 1949 which is concerned with vagrants, beggars, prostitutes, etc. It is not a tribunal, but an administrative body which can send anybody to a centre of re-education, which in fact means that so-called vagrants can be sent to labour organisations. Vagrants are people without jobs. In a country where you can only get a job from the State, anybody can be made a vagrant at any moment if the State does not give him a job. (p. 338)

According to the International League for the Rights of Man, the population of the camps, administered by the Directorate-General of Labor Reserves, an arm of the Secret Police, consisted of:

(a) former members of the democratic parties, especially members of the Independent Socialist Democratic Party, Liberal Party, and National Peasant Party; (b) evacuated people from the frontier area (western border); (c) anticommunist workers; (d) former landowners, whose properties were expropriated; (e) former State employees, and army officers; (f) white-collar workers (civil employees); (g) economic saboteurs; (h) evacuated people from the houses where the Russians are billeted. (p. 338)

As of 1951–52, the figure of 500,000 was estimated as the probable number of forced laborers in Rumania. The largest projects at that time were the Danube–Black Sea Canal and the Lenin hydroelectric plant on the river Bistritza. Conditions in the camps were described as follows by the Rumanian National Committee (in a report referring to Camp U.M.2 at Cernavoda, containing 1500 male and female political prisoners):

The camp is surrounded with three rows of barbed wire, dominated by watchtowers with heavy guards and searchlights. . . . Prisoners are awakened at 4:30 A.M. for the roll-call, which is followed by a breakfast of *ersatz* coffee and a slice of black bread. They are then marched two miles to the actual working site, under heavy armed escort. Work lasts from 6 A.M. to 7 P.M., with half an hour off for the midday meal. Noon and evening, the meals are invariable, a soup of beans or potatoes and a dish of vegetables. On Wednesdays and Fridays—which are fast-days prescribed by the Church—a tiny portion of meat is added to the soup. The bread ration varies according to the nature of the individual prisoner's work: 350 to 750 grammes daily.

Labourers are divided into groups of 50 to 70, which must fulfil an ascribed "norm" that usually fails to take into account the state of the weather or other working conditions. The work consists mainly of excavation. Youngsters of 15 to 18 are required to carry at least 150 loads of stone a distance of 600 to 900 feet every day. In view of the poor food and general conditions, this is utterly exhausting. . . .

Each gang is guarded by two men with automatic weapons and police dogs. The guards fire without warning, and workers are severely punished if they attempt to make friends with the dogs or if they talk among themselves. . . .

The men go barefoot and their heads are shaved. Women, too, usually work barefoot. At the close of the working day, norms are verified. Those who fail to fulfil their assigned quotas are deprived of food and housed in the guardroom, without bedding of any sort. Those who worked well are given a postcard at the end of the week, which they may write to their family.

Every evening, following dinner, a programme of "political re-education" begins at 8 P.M. In the presence of political officers, prisoners must read brochures of Marxist doctrine, and study various themes, selected by the head of the "cultural agitation" unit of the camp. . . . At 10 P.M. the roll-call and searching of the prisoners take place. They are then locked up in their hutments, where lights burn the whole night. It is no rare occurrence for prisoners to be taken away during the night by the guard, and to disappear without trace.

Like the regime in Prague, the communist government of Rumania presented no evidence tending to contradict these allegations. It seems reasonable to suppose, however, that as in the USSR, forced labor in Rumania has also declined since 1952. One reason is that it is by no means as productive as free labor.

The forced labor practices of Poland cannot be discussed here. One feature of Polish communist policy requires mention, however: the extensive use of child labor on public projects. Dushnyck quotes a current report from Warsaw:

Polish parents are complaining that their children are being compelled to perform increasingly longer periods of "voluntary" unpaid labour for the state.

There have been no official statements on the subject, but children in Warsaw were reportedly told recently that they would be expected to perform 80 hours of unpaid labour a year from now on.

There have been reports that some children have been used to help bring in the potato crop. . . . Rumors are circulating that some school time will be cancelled to enable students to work on public service projects. . . .

Unpaid labour by office employees and others is especially encouraged on Sundays. Though Saturdays are still working days, the country is supposedly moving toward free Saturdays . . . but in many areas it seems to be making up for the free Saturdays with "voluntary" labour on Sundays. (1975a, p. 383)

The latter practice, as readers of Russian history will realize, is borrowed from the USSR where the *Subotnik*, or Saturday of "voluntary" labor, became an institution rather early in the Revolution.

C. *International Enquiries Since 1953*

In 1962, the ILO's Committee of Experts endorsed a report of 1961 which showed that "the use of forced labor has progressively diminished in a large number of countries, and even disappeared" under the influence of psychological and political pressures as well as economic and social progress." The experts noted "not inconsiderable progress" in various countries where the ad hoc Committee had found forced labor in 1953 (International Labor Conference, 46th Session, Report III, Geneva, ILO, 1962, p. 194).

But the experts also stated that forms of forced labor which the ILO and the UN "unreservedly condemned are still rife in some countries." Which countries was not specified. A number of states were criticized for some of their laws and regulations, including Brazil, Cameroon, Denmark, Finland, France, India, Israel, Japan, Liberia, New Zealand, Nigeria, Norway, Poland, Tanzania, Tunisia, United Kingdom, United States, Upper Volta, and a number of other LDC's and dependent territories (*ibid.*, pp. 223–42).

The USSR was cited for the vagueness of its legislation and for the obligation of its courts to "afford protection against any threat to the political and social system and the established economic order." But despite the documenta-

tion submitted by the ad hoc Committee of 1953, nothing was said about the USSR's corrective labor code, which provides explicitly and extensively for forced labor.

The matter was taken up again in 1968. There was a debate within the Committee as to whether its responsibility extended to compulsory labor performed "as a consequence of a conviction in a court of law" (ILO, 1968). The self-evident point was missed that the courts in a dictatorial state are an instrument of executive power, and hence cannot protect against forced labor. Their function is to legitimize it.

The Committee's 1968 report indicated that some 40 states had violated the rules against the use of forced labor for production or service. No less than 58 states had violated the rules concerning forced labor used for political coercion or education, or as a punishment. Eleven states were charged with violations on both counts. Communist China, Korea, and Vietnam were not discussed. The forced labor practices of the USSR and its union republics, and the East European communist states were touched upon only lightly. The Committee took note of

wide-ranging penal provisions which might permit the imposition of sanctions involving compulsory labor in circumstance falling within the scope of this clause. . . . In a number of cases problems . . . appear to arise from the wide discretionary powers of preventive control, not subject to any judicial review . . . by virtue of which individuals may find themselves exposed to the application of penal sanctions involving compulsory labor as a means of political coercion or as a punishment for expressing views. (ILO, 1968, p. 238)

The Committee concluded, in effect, that not much progress toward abolishing forced labor had been made.

A more recent review of the forced labor situation was undertaken by the Committee of Experts on the Application of Conventions and Recommendations as part of a survey of compliance with ratified Conventions generally (ILO, 1974). The Committee expressed—with respect to Convention No. 105: Abolition of Forced Labour, 1957—*satisfaction* at progress achieved by Argentina, Australia, Denmark, the Netherlands, Spain, and Sweden (*ibid.*, p. 22). Its observations about other countries (*ibid.*, pp. 171–87) may be summarized as follows (verbatim quotations in quotation marks):

Afghanistan (ratification: 1963)

"The Committee regrets to note that the Government has once more failed to supply the information and legislative texts requested by the Committee, relating to collective work in the public interest, compulsory military service, prison labour, penal legislation, freedom of assembly and association, and press legislation." Requests on these matters have been outstanding since 1968.

Cuba (ratification: 1958)

In view of a law of March 16, 1971, imposing security measures and imprisonment, involving compulsory labor, on able-bodied men between 17 and 60 years of age who are not connected with a work center or abandon their work without just cause, the Committee reserves further comment pending examination of subsequent legislation.

Central African Republic (ratification: 1964)

"Article 1 (a) of the Convention. In previous observations the Committee had noted that, by virtue of the provisions of Act No. 63-411 of 17 May 1963, every active citizen must belong to a designated National Movement and must respect its political line and the decisions of its executive bodies, and that the constitution or attempted constitution of any other group or association of a political character or the undertaking of political activities in any form outside the said National Movement was punishable with imprisonment (involving, by virtue of section 62 of Order No. 2772 of 18 August 1955, an obligation to perform compulsory labour).

"The Committee had pointed out that the imposition of forced or compulsory labour in these circumstances appeared to be contrary to Article 1 (a) of the Convention, and had expressed the hope that appropriate measures would be taken to ensure the observance of the Convention in this regard.

"In its latest report the Government states that certain matters, such as political matters, fall within the exclusive competence of the national authorities and cannot be subject to any intervention by international organisations, that it has repeatedly stated

that no form of forced labour exists on the national territory, and that therefore the Committee's observations appear not to be justified."

The Committee points out that the Convention requires "ratifying States to suppress and not make use of any form of forced or compulsory labour as a means of political coercion or education or as a punishment for holding or expressing political views or views ideologically opposed to the established political, social or economic system," and that the Central African Republic, having freely ratified the Convention, is bound thereby. . . . The Committee hopes the CAR will review its position and observe the Convention.

Egypt (ratification: 1958)

No report has been received. The Committee is bound to repeat its comments on earlier legislation indicating that compulsory labour could be imposed for "certain kinds of statements" or for participating in a strike.

El Salvador (ratification: 1958)

Referring to earlier laws including a 1952 decree "concerning the defence of the democratic and constitutional order, under which penalties involving compulsory labour might be imposed on persons advocating certain doctrines," the committee notes the Government's statement that a new 1973 Penal Code has repealed these provisions and requests that this Code be supplied.

Greece (ratification: 1962)

The Committee regrets that no report has been received in answer to previous observations and requests. Under a decree of November 17, 1973, a state of siege was again imposed and various constitutional guarantees were suspended, including freedom of expression and the press, the rights of association and meeting, protection against arbitrary arrest and detention and the right to trial by ordinary courts. The Committee emphasizes that measures contravening the Convention "could only be justified by the existence of circumstances of extreme gravity constituting an emergency" and requests the government of Greece to supply full information. (This was the government of the "Colonel's junta" which was overthrown in 1974.)

Guatemala (ratification: 1959)

The Committee had previously noted 1963 and 1965 decrees under which "persons who disseminate communist propaganda in any form or establish, support or take part in the activities of any group, association, party or entity of communist ideology are punishable with imprisonment (involving, by virtue of the Penal Code and legislation on the execution of sentences, an obligation to perform labour)." The Committee regrets that the new Penal Code of July 5, 1973, has in no way repealed the provisions previously criticized.

Guinea (ratification: 1961)

The Committee notes the Government's statement in its report that it had denounced this Convention. Under Article V, the Convention can only be denounced at ten-year intervals, the last of which ran from January 17, 1969 to January 17, 1970. Not having denounced during that time, Guinea remained bound by the Convention. The Committee had previously noted a decree of October 22, 1964, under which "all persons between 16 and 25 years are placed at the service of the Organization for Work Centres of the Revolution, which is aimed at insuring the rapid liquidation of the technical and economic underdevelopment of the Republic." This decree is in conflict with Article I (b) of the Convention providing for suppressing any form of forced or compulsory labor for purposes of economic development, and the Committee "trusts that the decree in question will be repealed at an early date." Guinea has also failed to supply requested legislative texts on such matters as prison labor, public order, the press and publications, meetings and associations, vagrancy and idle persons and the discipline of seamen.

Haiti (ratification: 1958)

Every year since 1960 a decree has granted full powers to the President of the Republic and suspended for periods of six to eight months a considerable number of constitutional guarantees essential to effective observance of the Convention. "Among the constitutional provisions suspended have been those guaranteeing individual liberty, trial by the courts established by the Constitution and the law and the right of peaceful assembly, reserving jurisdiction over cases involving civil or political rights to the courts of law, prohibiting the trial of political offences *in camera*, and requiring the courts to enforce orders and regulations made by the public authorities only to the extent that they conform to the . . . Constitution of 1971 . . ." and corresponding provisions of earlier constitutions.

The Committee notes that yearly suspensions of constitutional guarantees in Haiti have not been limited to the extreme emergencies contemplated by the Convention. It cites a number of laws and decrees under which forced labor might take place, and regrets the lack of progress.

Honduras (ratification: 1957)

The Committee had commented earlier on decrees appearing to contravene Article I (a) of the Convention, prohibiting imposition of forced or compulsory labor (including penal labor as a means of political coercion or as punishment for expressing political views or views ideologically opposed to the established political, social, or economic system. These included 1946 and 1956 decrees against various forms of communist activity; a decree of August, 1958, amended on July 1, 1966, "prohibiting doctrines which tend to sap the foundations of the State or of the family," as well as "insidious publications which tend to sap the prestige and dignity of the institutions which maintain the external and internal security of the State and the organs and officials of these institutions." . . . These offences, as well as criticism of public officials not "founded on facts," are punishable according to the Government of Honduras, by rigorous imprisonment. Explanations so far have not entirely satisfied the Committee that infractions of the Convention do not exist.

Jordan (ratification: 1958)

The Committee notes with regret the lack of information on the application of Article I (a) and (b) of the Convention, particularly involving compulsory labor for violating restrictions on freedom of expression and freedom of assembly.

Singapore (ratification: 1965)

The Committee had noted earlier that compulsory labor might result from violations of various restrictions on freedom of the press, including a prohibition against printing or publishing any newspaper except under a licence granted and revoked by the competent minister in his absolute discretion. Additional restrictions are imposed by the Undesirable Publications Act of 1967, which empowers the competent minister, in his absolute discretion, to prohibit particular publications; and the "Societies Act of 1966" that requires registration of every association of ten or more persons but excludes from registration ". . . any association whose registration is considered contrary to the national interest or which has affiliations or connections with any organisation outside Singapore considered to be contrary to the national interest, and making it an offence to act as a member of an unregistered society, to publish, sell or possess matter issued by or in behalf or in the interests of such a society, etc."

Despite the government's assurances "that there is no system of forced or compulsory labour of any kind or for any purposes in Singapore," the Committee, in view of the foregoing provisions, is not satisfied that violations of the Convention have been excluded.

Syrian Arab Republic (ratification: 1958)

The Committee referred to its previous comments on legislation "under which hard labour or imprisonment (which may, by virtue of sections 46 and 51 of the Penal Code, involve liability to compulsory labour) may be imposed as a punishment *inter alia* for any attempt to impede the implementation of socialist legislation and for any resistance to the Socialist regime, for the dissemination of certain kinds of information or statements, and as a punishment in connection with statutory restrictions on the press, in connection with the prohibition of political parties and certain kinds of associations and of political activity of any kind by students, and in relation to the holding of meetings; as a punishment for various breaches of labour discipline whether committed wilfully or by negligence, and for participation in certain kinds of strikes, including any strikes by agricultural workers." No report, however, has been received in response to the Committee's request for measures "to ensure that no form of forced or compulsory labour (including labour resulting from a sentence of imprisonment) might be imposed in circumstances falling within the Convention."

Turkey (ratification: 1961)

The Committee had noted earlier that forced labor in violation of Article I (a) of the Convention might be imposed under various statutory provisions restricting freedom of expression (which, because of their relevance to matters discussed in this book, are quoted in full from the Committee's report). The provisions are:

"(a) sections 141 and 142 of the Penal Code (which prohibit any form of propaganda with a view to the domination of one social class over another or the suppression of a social class, the disruption of any of the basic economic and social in-

stitutions of the country or the destruction of the political or legal order, as well as the creation, management or membership of any association having aims of this nature);

"(b) section 163 of the Penal Code (which prohibits propaganda aimed at adapting the fundamental social, economic, political or legal order, even in part, to religious principles and beliefs, as well as the creation, management or membership of any association pursuing aims of this nature);

"(c) section 241 of the Penal Code (which prohibits ministers of religion from publicly censuring state institutions, laws or official actions);

"(d) section 89 of Act No. 648 of 13 July 1965 concerning political parties (which prohibits political parties from asserting the existence in Turkey of any minorities based on nationality, culture, religion or language and from attempting to disturb national security by conserving, developing or propagating languages and cultures other than Turkish language or culture)."

There follows a lengthy and technical discussion, the essence of which is that the Committee is not yet satisfied that the Turkish government has excluded the possibility of violations of the Convention. Nor has it supplied information on the effects of recent amendments to the Turkish Constitution.

The Committee also fears that Act No. 1488 of September 20, 1972, "to provide for compulsory patriotic service to be performed either in the armed forces or in public services" may entail infractions of the Convention. Such infractions are also implicit in provisions of the Commercial Code providing that "seamen may be forcibly conveyed on board ship [shanghaied!] to perform their duties," and that various breaches of discipline by seamen are punishable with imprisonment involving forced labor. The same is true of legislation authorizing forced labor as a punishment for having participated in strikes. With regard to a state of siege proclaimed on April 26, 1971, and subsequently prolonged from time to time, the Turkish Government has not satisfied the Committee that no violations of the Convention on Forced Labor have occurred.

Uganda (ratification: 1963)

"The Committee regrets that the Government has supplied no report on this Convention, and that accordingly no reply has been furnished to its previous comments." The Committee then cites a number of enactments restricting freedom of expression, under which forced labor might be imposed, including a section of the Penal Code empowering "the competent Minister to declare any combination of two or more persons to be an unlawful society. . . ."

"In addition, requests regarding certain points are being addressed directly to the following States: Afghanistan, Algeria, Argentina, Australia, Austria, Canada, Central African Republic, Chad, Dahomey, Democratic Yemen (Aden), Ecuador, Egypt, Finland, France, Federal Republic of Germany, Ghana, Guatemala, Guinea, Guyana, Haiti, Honduras, Iceland, Iran, Iraq, Jamaica, Jordan, Kenya, Liberia, Malta, Mauritius, Netherlands, New Zealand, Nigeria, Norway, Pakistan, Panama, Paraguay, Peru, Philippines, Portugal, Sierra Leone, Singapore, Somalia, Spain, Sudan, Syrian Arab Republic, Tanzania, Trinidad and Tobago, Tunisia, United Kingdom, Uruguay, Zambia."

It may be concluded from the foregoing that, quite apart from the persistence of forced labor within the communist orbit, that pernicious institution has by no means abolished.

D. Forced Labor Today in the USSR

An extensive study of political punishment in the USSR has been made by one of the authors of this book (Possony, 1975a). The following account of the status of forced labor today in the USSR is quoted from this study with the kind permission of the Foundation for the Study of Plural Societies in The Hague.

1. CORRECTIVE LABOR LINKED TO DEPRIVATION OF FREEDOM

The so-called settlement colonies (kolonii poseleniya) are a mixture between freedom (soviet style) and non-freedom. The individual is not constantly watched by guards, instead he is under surveillance. He is not in jail, nor in a camp barrack, but he lives within a camp territory. His movements are not upon command, instead he is allowed to move freely within the camp during daytime, and he can obtain occasional authorization to go outside the area. Furthermore, he lives in private quarters and can have his family with him. Usually, this particular penalty is imposed upon persons who are liberated from labour camps as an additional punishment and as a method of keeping control. The settlement colonies or areas cluster around closed camps and are indispensable to sustain the logistics and the economic life of the camps.

Soviet legislation considers prison (tyuremnoye zaklyucheniye) as the most severe form of deprivation of freedom. Prison terms are given to felons, political criminals, repeaters or "recidivists," and to prisoners who behaved unlawfully in camp. The prisons are divided into those with general (obshchi) and strict or severe (strogi) regimes; in the latter the prisoners are isolated in cells (kartser). Since soviet prisons usually are over-crowded, isolation often is carried out in punishment cells (strafny isolator). Otherwise the regimes are differentiated in terms of "privileges" or lack of those, e.g. under the general regime the prisoner is allowed a daily walk of one hour, while under the strict regime he is allowed only half-an-hour daily. Similar discriminations are applied to food, money, correspondence, packages, etc.

Soviet practice has been to keep the majority of prisoners in corrective labour colonies where they are expected to correct themselves through labour (ispravitelny trud). A previous rule was to serve all sentences above three years in camps. To what extent this rule still holds is not known, but apparently more emphasis is now placed on prisons and on corrective labour indoors in workshops.

2. THE CAMP REGIMES

The colonies are divided into four main groups: the general, hard, strict, and special regime.

A first offender is assigned to the general regime, and a first offender felon to the hard regime. Recidivists and all convicted politicals are assigned to the strict (strogi) regime, and dangerous criminals and political recidivists, plus those whose death penalty has been commuted, are subjected to the special (*osoby*) regime. The rule of the old penal code, that delicts against the foundation of the soviet regime and counter-revolutionary activity are the worst crimes that can be committed in the USSR, still stands. The old practice of giving top penalties to about 60% of the politicals may also still be in force.

The differences between the various types of camps are not systematically spelled out; only a few points are mentioned in the legal sources. For example, with respect to visiting rights, the prisoner in the general regime can receive three short and two long visits, in the hard regime two short and two long visits, in the strict regime two short and one long visit, in the special regime one short and one long visit; and in prison he is only entitled to two or one short visit. Cases have been known when all visits were denied. (A short visit is defined as a four-hour meeting in the presence of guards, whereas a long visit is supposed to last three days.)

Similar gradations presumably extend to most factors which are important in the life of prisoners, such as money (earnings, remittances, and the right to spend), packages, and clothing, as well as living quarters and the choice of the camp itself. The statutes make it clear that the special (*osoby*) regime is, as a rule, one of hard labour. This stipulation, however, does not seem to exclude hard labour from the *strogi* or even the "lighter" regimes.

There are several types of special purpose prisons (*tyurma osobogo naznacheniya*), notably prisons for preliminary detention (i.e. interrogation), transit and distribution prisons. Those do not *per se* serve the purposes of punishment and correction but vitally affect the fate of the prisoners. The investigative prisons may house the prisoner for a long time. They are the place where he is most likely to be confronted by torture. If he is sentenced to death, that's where he dies. After sentencing he may stay in the investigative prison (*sledstvenny isolator*) for two to four months, or longer.

As to the transit and distribution prisons, the prisoners who are being moved about frequently spend much time there. From these prisons the individual may be sent to a better or worse camp. In those camps where mortality seems to be the highest he may become infected and die. Health hazards, often aggravated by lack of water, food, sleep, sanitation, etc., threaten the prisoner during transfer which is by rail and ship, and may last weeks or even months. The dangers of transit and transfer are proportionate to the number of prisoners transported.

Women prisoners are assigned to special camps and supposedly are completely segregated from male prisoners. In practice, this separation does not seem to be effective. Prostitution and related abuses appear to be widespread in the camps. In general, women are assigned to the first regime. However, they can be subjected to the stricter regimes, including the special regime. . . . Mothers are allowed to keep their children to the age of two, at which point the children are sent away. The mothers are forced to work, and since babysitting arrangements are deficient, the mortality of those children is high. However, quite a few children have been born in camps and were brought up by the MVD.

So-called educational labor colonies (*vospitatelnotrudovye kolonii*) exist for convicted or administratively confined juveniles between the ages of 12 and 18. The legislation on children dates from an *ukaz* of 7 April, 1935, and was preceded in the 1920s by genocidal operations against the *bezprisornyi*, i.e. free roaming bands of orphaned children. During the purges most of the children of purge victims were placed into "educational" camps. The fact that such camps still are being operated suggests that there remains a high rate of imprisonment for adults and that, furthermore, there is substantial criminality. The imprisoned youngsters are feared because of their especially vicious behaviour. Many of them grow up and form the criminal elements of the Archipelago (*blatnye*). The stipulations about the education which juvenile prisoners are to be given are extremely rudimentary.

Military offenders are assigned to punishment battalions which in time of war are mainly used for particularly dangerous missions frequently resulting in the death of the entire unit.

According to article 58 of the 1962 code, individuals can be subjected to compulsory medical measures. Persons selected for medical treatment may be assigned to a general or special psychiatric hospital. The latter type of establishment specializes in the handling of "socially dangerous persons" requiring special security.

Until 1937, the communists were content with sentences up to 10 years. After 2 October 1937, 10 to 25 year sentences were authorized, and during Stalin's later years, 25-year sentences to corrective labour camps were entirely commonplace. Usually they were handed out administratively: no need to bother the courts. At present, according to paragraph 24 of the 1962 criminal code, the court decides the punishment. It would seem that the maximum sentence is 15 years.

Under Stalin, the politicals usually got maximal punishment, while the criminals got off with lower comparative penalties. Whether, and to what extent, this dichotomy still prevails, is not known. Furthermore the matter of "maximal penalty" is not classified by the codes. A person can be punished for each of several crimes, and transgressions in prison or camp may be added to the original sentence. The legislative language is uninformative about consecutive terms but it would seem that the law can be bent easily to keep prisoners locked up indefinitely. Andrei Amalrik got a three-year sentence but before he completed it, he got still another three year sentence—in Anno Domini of 1973. The other practice exists that a basic delict is coupled with attempts and preparations for other delicts, and that conspiracy also may be used as a factor of aggravation. In any event, once a person is released from camp, he frequently is assigned to a settlement colony or to a *ssylka-vysylka* area and remains subjected to administrative surveillance by the police. Such surveillance lasts for a minimum of one year and involves regular reporting to the militia, travel and residence restrictions, curfews, etc. Violations entail administrative or criminal penalties and can return the person to the camp as a "recidivist."

3. THE DEATH PENALTY AND CAMP MORTALITY

Bolshevik propaganda was very critical of the death penalty as it was practiced by the tsarist regime and promised great reforms in penal law, such as the abolition of the "supreme punishment". Under the tsarist regime, between 1876 and 1904, there were 17 executions per annum. During the revolutionary period of 1905–1908, 2200 persons or 540 yearly were executed. The communists were indeed very progressive in that between June 1918 and October 1919 they attained an annual rate of 12,000 executions. The estimated number of those executed during 1937–1938, the peak period of the purges, ranges between 500,000 and 1.7 million plus 480,000 criminals (*blatnye*). This writer knows of no estimates concerning the number of executions under Brezhnev. It is clear that he has not matched Stalin's record by any means, but it is most unlikely that the number of executions is below the rate under the tsar. The USSR does not publish statistics on its current use of the death sentence.

The death penalty was abolished in 1917, restored in 1918, enshrined in article 21 of the 1919 criminal code for serious crimes threatening soviet power, abolished and restored again in 1920, and once again abolished in 1927, except for crimes under article 58, dealing with political delicts, and except also for military crimes and "banditry" (meaning rebellion). In

1932, in the course of the collectivization of agriculture, the so-called "wrecking" crimes were added. The new delicts were formulated in such a way that "theft" of an apple from the tree was potentially punishable by death. The death penalty was in force during 1937 and was made more broadly applicable in 1943. In 1947, after the military victory, the death penalty was replaced by 25 years of detention in special camps, but in 1950 the death penalty was reintroduced. Applicability was extended in 1954, i.e. *after* Stalin's death. Despite repeated "abolitions" the death penalty was always applied. In 1954, 1961, and 1962 further delicts were added which could be punished by death unless committed by juveniles below the age of 18 or by pregnant women. The death penalty is now stipulated in article 23 of the RSFSR code.

The new capital crimes falling under those revisions of the statute include rape, bribery, murder, theft of state property, counterfeiting, violations of currency laws, threatening the lives of policemen and of *druzhinniki* (communist activists), and terrorism at places of imprisonment (i.e. in the camps). The last provision has an obvious bearing on the question of "maximum penalty" discussed above.

It may be mentioned that, according to information obtained from defectors, Colonel Oleg Penkovsky was executed in a crematorium where he was burned alive. Yuri Galanskov died after he was denied the proper diet to control his ulcers and after the camp doctors had operated on him. . . .

The mortality of the soviet penal system is not chiefly derived from executions. Most of the fatalities occur in the corrective labour camps. Some of those deaths have been due to the general conditions of camp life. It is believed that after Stalin's demise orders were given to keep mortality below a certain undisclosed rate.

In the absence of deliberate liquidations, camp mortality is significantly affected by over-crowding. To the extent that, presum-

ably, overcrowding is avoided at present, mortality probably went down. But, according to Solzhenitsyn, "the main killer was camp labour." This is still true today, and it is necessarily true whenever the camp authorities and guards do refrain from suppressive actions of violence.

Solzhenitsyn dismissed the notion that there were good camps as "simply a delusion." However, he added that "the newcomer was not mistaken in thinking that there were whole camps which were death camps." This being the situation, and considering also that politicals are assigned to the strict regime anyway, there really is no need to pronounce death sentences and risk legal and political complications. If the Kremlin wants a person to perish, he can easily be made to die a "natural" death in camp.

4. EXTERMINATION CAMPS

It is easy to indicate the mechanism of extermination. First and foremost, assignment to a camp in an arctic climate is by itself enough to reduce the chances of survival *drastically*. In Lenin's time, the prisoners the bolsheviks wanted to eliminate inobtrusively were sent to the Solovietsky Islands which are located in the large bay west of Archangel known as the White Sea. This area is about two degrees south of the Arctic Circle. The climate of Solovietsky is a great deal better than that of the islands north of the Arctic Circle and in the Arctic Ocean, e.g. Novaya Zemlya, as well as of the mainland areas defined by the January isotherm of $-30C$ [$-22F$] which runs roughly from the Yenisei estuary through Bodaibo to 200 miles west from Komsomolsk and from there to a point southeast of Wrangel Island. About 500,000 square miles of Yakutia lie between the $-40C$ [$-40F$] and $-50C$ [$-58F$] January isotherms.

In 1958, *Kampfgruppe gegen Unmenschlichkeit* published a list of camps which was based upon information supplied by German military and civilian prisoners who had been repatriated from the Archipelago. This list identified the 125 most important "forced labour camps" as of 1948 and added 50 smaller local camps. Yakovlev listed 165 camp establishments. The two lists show overlaps and some differences.

The study from which this is quoted points out that many well-known camps were actually *clusters* of camps organized in districts. The safest 1948–1953 figures would seem to be 125–165 districts containing between 300 and 500 camps. As there were only 80 districts in 1941, the massive growth of the camp population is evident.

Although individual camps are moved, abolished and added, the overall geographic configuration of the Archipelago changed but little, to judge from recent defector information. The geographic distribution has been roughly as follows:

Area	% of Camp Districts
Eastern Siberia and Far East	34
Northwest Russia	16
Northeast Russia	9
Western Siberia	7
Urals	7
Central Asia	6
North Central Siberia	6
Central Russia	5
South Russia	5
East Russia	5
	100

Some 54 percent of those camp districts are located in what could be called acceptable climates; 46 percent are in zones of harsh climate. Of the total 6 percent are on islands in the Arctic Ocean, e.g. Franz Joseph Land, Novosibirsky Islands, Wrangel Island, Askold Island, and Vaigach Island in Kara Sea; and 12 percent in some of the world's coldest areas, including Chukotsk, Kamchatka, the North Siberian littoral, Kolyma, and Yakutia, where the "cold pole" is located near Verkhoyansk. Nearly one-fifth of the camp districts are situated in a zone of killing climate.

It is to be observed that zones with "killing climate" are part of the USSR and require settlers for diverse economic and strategic reasons. As such, no earth climate is bad enough to preclude settlement. However, if persons sent to such areas are not properly fed, equipped, and protected, they will inevitably die a tortured and early death. The USSR never yet set up its arctic camps in the way they could be organized and equipped to enable the inmates to survive and perform valuable work. Yet if the Kremlin really intended to reform its opponents, it would give them a chance—and it might develop its arctic possessions more effectively.

5. HARD LABOR

During the Stalinist period, two-thirds of the prisoners were in camp, and the rest in jail. The current proportion is probably different, but a large portion is still assigned to camps.

According to Solzhenitsyn, about 80 percent of the fatalities in Stalinist camps occurred in connection with "general assignment work." More specifically, Solzhenitsyn asserted that 80 percent of the prisoners are given this type of work, and that all of them die of it. General assignment work can be very hard in terms of physical exertion. It may be imposed for many more hours than the eight hours which are the legal norm, outside and inside the camps. There seems to be a six day week with only two or three holidays per year. This regime has been in existence, together with prolonged overtime as a prominent feature, since 1918.

The physical effort may take place under conditions of extended exposures to cold or wetness. And the work may be dangerous, such as in poorly constructed mines where accidents occur and where dust, poisonous fumes, radiation, and lack of oxygen may affect the miners' health and result in early death. Work detachments usually are limited to the eight-hour day, but there also are night shifts, and not infrequently the sleeping period is held down to 6:30 hours.

Hard labour is defined as work underground or involving heavy loads. Semi-hard labour can take the form of road building, for example. Normal industrial and agricultural labour is classified as "light." Sick people perform light work for four hours daily. Invalids are, theoretically, freed from work obligations. No limits are set on overtime.

Furthermore, every worker and every labour detachment must reach "norms" which during the Stalinist period were set so high that only 10 percent of the prisoners were able to attain them. In case of nonfulfilment, the workers in Stalinist camps either were forced to work as long as needed to complete their task or they were punished by reductions in their food ration. If groups were given a norm, they had to do the complete work regardless of whether they were at full strength or not. The norms exceeded those of tsarist institutions by a factor of 5 to 10. . . .

Whether this insane system which may be described as a spiral toward death still exists, is not known. Indications are that only alleviations were effected.

Forced labour is done in transportation (canal building and maintenance, railway, road, and airfield construction, loading and unloading), mining, timber cutting and moving, brick-making, fishing, and oil production (especially the preparation of oil fields). During the Stalin period, 85 percent of the prisoners were engaged in earth moving and forestry work and 7 percent worked in mines. At present, indications are that much work is performed on the Tyumen oilfields, as well as on the Baikal-Amur-Sea (BAM) railway. BAM-LAG camps have existed since before 1935, but at present BAM has become a high priority project. Unless elaborate precautions were taken, work on this railway which must be performed in the tundra—in swampy and permafrost areas and in mountains, and which involves the bridging of numerous large rivers—could entail large fatality rates.

According to articles 39 and 40 of the corrective labour code, the work performed in the camps carries a salary corresponding to the type of job that is being done. From this income costs for food and board are deducted, and so are taxes. The rest, which must be more than 10 percent of the gross income, is paid into a personal account. (The minimum deposit for invalids is 25 percent, for minors 45 percent, and for individuals in settlement camps 50 percent.) However, if the prisoner was given disciplinary punishment, his net earnings are cut. In brief, there is horrendous exploitation but the exploiter obtains little economic advantage from the arrangement.

The camps were formally established on 5 September 1918 when "red terror" was proclaimed after an attempt on Lenin's life. On 15 April 1919, *Izvestiya* published a decree legalizing forced labour camps (*lageri prinudityelnykh rabot*). . . . The corrective labour code of 1 August 1933 dropped the expression "forced labour", henceforth only the term "corrective labour" was employed. . . .

The soviets are entirely cynical about "correction"—all they care about is a signed "confession." The Chinese, by contrast, are most serious about coordinating punishment and supervision with reformulation of thought and of coupling work output with political education. This is the point where "brain washing" or "remoulding of thought" comes in as a unique feature of the Maoist penal system.

6. FOOD

Food is still another key factor of survival. Prisoners are supposed to receive rations which "assure normal vital activity of the organism." It is remarkable that soviet authorities never did manage to formulate a more satisfactory norm.

Through the history of the camps caloric intake was notoriously low, with some camps being worse off than others. Experience with soviet camp management in Germany showed that the soviets calculate too high a caloric content of the food they provided. The food is often spoiled. If so, it is never replaced. It is virtually always of poor quality.

Food supplies often break down so that meals are being missed. Quality foods with prophylactic effects are supplied only in minuscule quantities. Unless prisoners are allowed to purchase and receive food packages, their diet cannot assure the normal activity of the organism and results in avitaminoses and undernourishment. The normal fare is bread, dried fish, gruel, grits, soup, a little sugar, and barely *any* meat, fat, fruit, or even vegetables. The food rations which tsarist prisoners were receiving were substantially more healthful. According to information obtained by D. L. W. Ashton from inside the USSR a prisoner who is to be punished "can be put on the 'severe' intake of 1300 calories."

Prisoners pay for their food through deductions from their earnings. The packages they receive are limited in numbers and weight; and their purchases are limited to a few rubles. Both packages and purchases may be restricted as punishment. There is some clandestine storing of food and limited black market trading but there also is extensive theft within the camps.

The major abomination is this: prisoners who cannot fulfil the work norm receive lower rations. As they work overtime to reach the norm, they only get the normal ration. As they grow weaker, their rations go down further. Prisoners who are allowed to do minimal work and invalids who don't work at all receive the lowest rations, on the grounds that he who does not work, shall not eat. The logic of this system is that those who are weak and sick should not recover but die.

Food supply appears to have been improved somewhat but the basic system still operates. A 1973 report reflecting considerable research stated:

"In the strict and special regimes the worst factor is the constant hunger: prisoners are left on a starvation diet while being required to do hard physical labour. . . . As hunger is . . . used as a deliberate instrument to destroy the physical and psychological morale of the prisoner, the diet may be considered to be a form of torture."

It is believed that torture, in the technical sense of the word, is not regularly used in the camps, but physical coercion cannot be totally lacking. For example, the use of strait-jackets is permitted except on women and juveniles. Punishments in dark and small isolators, deprivation of sleep, and excessive overtime also have deleterious effects. Self-mutilations and hunger strikes are by no means rare. (Nor are suicides.) In addition, the prisoners are allowed only 2 square meters [22.2 sq ft.] of space and thus are subjected to crowding. They are not allowed to sleep with the lights turned off.

Readers interested in the documentary sources of the foregoing information are referred to the original publication (see Possony's notes, 1975a, pp. 33–38).

The findings of Professor Possony's study are confirmed by numerous other authorities. Avraham Shifrin, a prisoner released in the mid-1960s, told a United States Senate subcommittee that political prisoners formed a major part of the labor force in Soviet heavy industry. Those in Siberia were required to work ten hours a day, six days a week, in coal and gold mines and in lumbering operations —in sub-zero (Fahrenheit) temperatures in winter. He then told of his personal experiences:

The prisoners slept in poorly heated barracks on wooden bunks. They wore thin cotton underwear, quilted cotton outer jackets, boots crudely fashioned from truck tires, and footcloths in lieu of socks. Working prisoners received only 1,716 calories of food a day. Those who were too sick to work got barely half that.

Each camp contained about 2,000 prisoners, of whom 30 to 40 would die each night of starvation, frostbite, and other causes.

Prisoners who died during the winter were not buried, because the ground was too hard. They would be dragged naked into the forest and left in the snow. (Kelly, 1974)

The corpses left in the forest served an economic purpose, since they attracted bears, black foxes, sables, and other fur-bearing animals that were trapped by soldiers; their skins adorn the female contingent of *The Social Register* and *Burke's Peerage*. Labor under the conditions reported (and confirmed by Solzhenitsyn and other witnesses) is clearly of the lowest productivity, since the prisoners have neither the equipment nor the physical stamina to work effectively. More importantly, the Soviet slave camps, conditions in which are in striking contrast to the free-enterprise operations in Alaska and the Canadian Arctic, have preempted effective settlement of the low-isotherm area in the north of Russia and Siberia. There are both economic and strategic reasons for settling these areas, yet settlement in any effective sense is not taking place.

Not all involuntary labor in the USSR is performed by camp inmates. The mildest on the scale of punishments administered to political dissenters, as well as criminals, is "corrective labor without deprivation of freedom." The person thus "corrected" continues in his normal job, which he is forbidden to leave—or he may be assigned more onerous duties involving hard labor. Only a part of his wages, however, are paid to him; the remainder is confiscated. He earns no social security benefits and no vacation credits.

Another penalty frequently invoked is that of banishment, in the form of *vysylka* or *ssylka*. An individual sentenced to the *ssylka* is entitled to choose the *rayon* where he wants to live and pick his job within that *rayon;* except that certain towns and jobs are off limits. In *vysylka* the individual is assigned both residence and work for a period of two to five years. He can take his family along to the *vysylka* as well as the *ssylka*. (*Kodeks RSFSR*, articles 25, 26.)

A large volume of forced labor in the USSR, however, continues to be performed by camp inmates. The Committee for the Defence of Human Rights (Brussels) estimates their current number at 1 million, though there are higher estimates. Over the entire history of the *Gulag Archipelago*, under the normal USSR standards of productivity, slave labor should have created something like $700 billion of value. Despite several spectacular projects, such productivity has been conspicuously absent. It would even appear that the cash income the MGB receives from renting out the prisoners to industry is less than the cost of operating the camps—particularly since many inmates are too ill to work, or in the process of dying, and not all fit prisoners can always be rented out. Naum Yasny calculated that in 1941 the NKVD obtained 17 percent of the national investment and produced 1.2 percent of the national output (*Livre Blanc*, 1951, pp. 91, 108, and 207). Naftali Aronovich Frenkel, "the former capitalist" who sold Stalin on the utility of massive slave labor and who built the 140-mile White Sea Canal at a cost of 100,000 fatalities, including children and women, sold the *Vozhd* an economic white elephant (*Est et Ouest*, Paris, September, 16–30, 1974, p. 29). Since forced labor persists throughout the communist system, it must be concluded that political control takes a higher priority than economic efficiency.

25

TORTURE

Torture reappeared during the twentieth century, states Alec Mellor, a French writer. This statement is correct for Central and Western Europe, but it is hardly true for other parts of the world. Torture has never disappeared from some places. A vigorous fight against torture was waged in the advanced European countries during the eighteenth century. The practice was largely eliminated in the questioning of suspects and as court-ordered punishment. But it was revived by the twentieth-century totalitarian dictatorships, and has the disconcerting habit of reappearing, even in states that give lip service to human rights.

Torture was by no means uncommon in Russia, before or after the revolution, but it was contrary to regulation from 1918 to 1937. On January 20, 1939, the central committee of the CPSU, which Stalin controlled, in a coded circular telegram confirmed that "application of methods of physical pressure in NKVD practice is permissible from 1937 on, in accordance with permission of the party central committee."

Nikita Khrushchev deserves credit for disclosing in 1956 that through the application of physical methods persons were compelled to confess to crimes they did not commit. Physical methods of pressure and torture, Khrushchev said, were bringing a victim "to a state of unconsciousness, depriving him of his judgment, taking away his human dignity" (Conquest, 1968, p. 137). Yet that party secretary and his associates, having anything but clean hands in the matter, did not care to prosecute the torturers or to compensate the victims and their survivors. Torture was reduced but not eliminated in the USSR.

Torture is practiced not only by communists but by fascist and military dictatorships as well. Even a genuinely democratic country like France has at times resorted to physical pressure—mostly, but not exclusively, in connection with the war in Algeria.

Amnesty International has been diligent in collecting the evidence on torture throughout the contemporary world and in 1972 started a campaign for its abolition. There is, however, no evidence that the practice is on the decline, and it cannot be presumed that Amnesty International has succeeded in ferreting out even the major cases. In a recent history of torture (Lauréat and Lasierra, 1973), the major twentieth-century cases described are those of the Third Reich, the USSR, Algeria, Brazil, Greece, Turkey, the two Vietnams, and the terrorism of revolutionary wars. Alas, this list is by no means exhaustive.

A. *Torture in Ethical and Legal Theory*

Torture is a particular form of violence. It must be clearly distinguished from violence necessitated by the exigencies of warfare, including civil and revolutionary–antirevolutionary warfare. Since torture involves deliberate infliction of pain, the burden of proof is on the persons ordering and conducting the torture to prove it is *not* an atrocity.

1. MARXIST VIEWS ON VIOLENCE AND TORTURE

Karl Marx and Friedrich Engels, the foremost revolutionary theoreticians, contended that human emancipation can be accomplished by eliminating oppression, enlarging technological capabilities and productive output, and organizing property relationships rationally. The classical writers on violence, whether from the left or the right, did *not* confuse violence with cruelty, and they did not think that torture and human degradation would become a locomotive of progress. Many of them understood full well that such practices do not simply perpetuate the old oppression; they lead mankind back into barbarism. Marx saw the dictatorship of the proletariat as inevitable, and argued that it is impossible to achieve and conduct it without force. But he also thought it would bring a "higher" organization of labor. The German term *Gewalt*, which he usually employed, is wrongly translated as "violence," and carried no connotation of cruelty or torture. Nor did Georges Sorel, known as the high priest of violence, favor any kind of cruelty. Stalin, on the other hand, is probably correctly translated when his definition of the dictatorship of the proletariat is rendered as "the domination of the proletariat over the bourgeoisie, untrammelled by law and based on violence and enjoying the sympathy and support of the toiling and exploited masses" (Stalin, 1924).

If we disregard the Marquis de Sade, no theoretician of basic social change—at least no theoretician that we know of—has argued the necessity for cruelty in explicit language. But since the role of violence has been praised in various ways and with much extravagance, the practitioners of power have interpreted this literature in their own way, and torture in many different forms has been applied on a very large scale without arousing the conscience of mankind.

2. PUNISHMENT AND THE LEX TALIONIS

The view that punishment should be dispensed with entirely and be replaced by some sort of rehabilitory treatment was at one time fashionable but has lost popularity. Hence, it will be assumed here, without further discussion, that public policy will be based on the principle that serious and cruel crimes must be punished. The Western moralist par excellence, Immanuel Kant, and most of the various holy scriptures agree that the *lex talionis* provides the only concept of punishment which satisfies the sense of outraged justice. If criminals must be protected from unfair discrimination, the same protection must be extended to the victims of crime. If no retribution is exacted, the result is discrimination. Indemnification is one way of redressing the wrongs suffered by crime victims, yet it is only now emerging on legislative agenda in the United States and elsewhere.

That punishment *does* act as a deterrent is suggested by the fact that no government ever was willing to abolish all punishments; and that whenever justice breaks down, criminality rises. A problem beyond the scope of this book is how to "make the punishment fit the crime" and to enable the convicted criminal to contribute to the indemnification of the victim. In much of the Western world, prevailing systems of criminal justice clearly discriminate *against* the victims of crime and *for* the criminals; which, naturally, does not mean that con-

icts are protected against abuse (usually by
ther convicts).

In the application of the *lex talionis* to capital
rimes, all *verbal* political crimes should be
liminated from the catalogue of capital
rimes—no one should ever be executed for
omething he said or wrote. Yet political real-
sm demands that the state possess legal in-
truments to protect its own security. Where
ndividuals incite to or prepare armed rebellion
r even nonviolent protest of a disruptive char-
cter (such as a Ghandian *satyagraha** in the
egislative chamber), the law may properly
urb and punish such activity. A problem aris-
s, however, when dictatorial governments,
uch as that of the USSR, feel so insecure that
ney cannot permit what most Westerners
ould regard as wholly legitimate protest
gainst denials of justice.

If, under due process of law, harsh senten-
es, including the death penalty, may be im-
osed for cruel crimes, this must be done only
the evidence of guilt is very strong, so that
judicial murder" is avoided. The validity of
sanity as a defense, on which conventional
iews have been challenged by libertarians
uch as Dr. Thomas Szasz, will not be exam-
ed here.

The *lex talionis* does *not* require a sadistic
urderer to be executed through sadistic tor-
re. Whether the guillotine or the gas
namber is most humane or equitable need not
e decided in the present context (see Hibbert,
)63). Likewise the question whether corporal
unishments short of torture should be admis-
ble—through current American jurispru-
ence would tend to reject them as "cruel and
nusual."

Punishment by torture degrades the torturer
well as the victim. A government which
nowingly tolerates or practices torture is a
iminal government.

_iterally, truth force: a nonviolent protest, typically a sit-
wn or lie-down, that interrupts the activities of the
rget audience.

B. Torture as a Present-Day Reality

Execution after sentence is not the only way
people are publicly killed. Police often slay
dangerous criminals who resist arrest or fire at
the police—all too often with lethal effect—as
well as persons committing acts of rebellion,
sabotage, airplane hijacking, and the like. Few
would question the need for police organs to
defend themselves and the public effectively.

In many countries, however, police and
prison security forces use not only force but
torture as well to subdue resistance and to terrorize and punish prisoners. The tortures may
be carried out by means of special instruments;
but under modern conditions, care is taken to
resort to techniques which leave no obvious
traces—such as electric shock, submergence,
deprivation of sleep, cold or hot temperatures,
lights, "conveyor belts," dental "treatments"
and surgery without anesthesia, and forcible
administration of drugs—aside from more
"routine" methods like beatings and solitary
confinement in very small and dark cells. The
way police departments and prisons are organized, it is hard to protect prisoners against
abuse. They usually cannot prove that they
were tortured, and if they complain and accuse, they often are punished further.

1. TORTURE AS A MEANS OF EXTRACTING INTELLIGENCE

It is argued by some that torture by police or
security forces may have *one* legitimate purpose. This is to extract, rapidly, information
from a captive that can be used to forestall a
major crime or disaster. The classic case involves an individual who knows about a nuclear device which is to go off during rush hour
in the middle of town. He knows where the
bomb is, but he refuses to talk, and there is
little time to lose. Should the police sacrifice
the city or torture the prisoner?

This argument is rejected flatly by Amnesty

International, which contends that "just once" becomes once again—becomes a practice and finally an institution (*Report on Torture*, 1973, cited in *National Observer*, July 12, 1975). Confessions on the rack are notoriously unreliable. The use of thiopental or similar truth drugs may be more productive. The point is that under certain extreme conditions a case can be made for resort to physical coercion, *provided* it is done professionally without undue violations of human rights and without degradation. By the same token, resort to torture is illegitimate and to be prohibited under all *other* circumstances.

In war, the coercive extraction of information from prisoners is ruled out by international convention, but it is a widespread practice to apply pressure to prisoners who adhere to the rule of "name, rank and serial number." It is entirely unacceptable—and illegal—to have physicians give prisoners crippling treatments on the ground that they must be prevented from fighting again. (It has been reported, for example, that the Syrians destroyed the sense of balance of captured Israeli pilots.)

In the era of guerrilla war, both insurgents and counterinsurgents have been trained and used as torturers in many parts of the world. This practice cannot be excused with quotes from Marx and Engels; even communist theoreticians on guerrilla warfare divide over the utility of torture and terrorism. Ché Guevara, by and large, rejected them, whereas the North Vietnamese engaged in them with abandon. The South Vietnamese record was uneven. According to Amnesty International:

Although most of the prisons visited by the ICRC delegates during the period 1968 to 1972 were given satisfactory assessments by the international inspectors, two prisoner of war camps and the prisons of Chi Hoa and Tan Hiep were singled out in the reports because of the frequent use of torture. Ill treatment in these four facilities included shackling, beatings, caging prisoners in very small cells (the so-called "tiger cages") and exposure to the sun during the extreme heat of the Vietnamese summer. Serious diseases and inadequate medical care were commonplace.

These four facilities housed more than one third of the entire prison population, estimated by the ICRC at 70,000 civilians and prisoners of war. (*Amnesty Action*, September, 1975, p. 8)

While the Saigon government was extremely uncooperative, the North Vietnamese never let the ICRC in at all.

The point is that the current laws of war provide for the elimination of torture and unnecessary brutality. Now that guerrilla war has achieved a certain legitimacy, guerrilla and antiguerrilla forces should comply with those laws; and states supporting guerrilla forces should contribute their share to enforcing the rules. This point is not made in the expectation that guerrilla forces and their supporters will comply, but to emphasize the fragility of the human rights enactments of the UN.

2. RECENT CASES OF TORTURE

The use of torture by the SS in Hitler's concentration and extermination camps has been amply documented. One reference will suffice here: Eugen Kogon's *Der SS-Staat* (Munich, 1946) published in English as *The Theory and Practice of Hell: the German Concentration Camp and the System Behind Them* (Kogon, 1950). The present sampling will be limited to cases that have arisen *since* World War II.

A little-known fact is that after the "liberation" of Czecho-Slovakia and the installation of a supposedly democratic coalition under Dr Beneš, many formerly German-managed concentration camps were continued in operation with a not-quite-complete change of inmates—since Jews of German nationality were treated like other Germans—imprisoned, used for forced labor, or expelled. By 1953, the number of camps was estimated at 250, with a total of 380,000 inmates. The largest, at Jachymov (Joachimsthal), was administered by the Soviet KGB, which employed 30,000 prisoners a uranium miners. A typical "menu" for heavy laborers was:

Breakfast: Bitter black coffee
Bread
A small portion of jam *or* sugar for coffee,

Lunch: Weak soup
Potatoes
One piece of bread

Supper: Black coffee
Bread
Jam or margarine two days per week

Persons who "endangered public safety" were committed to these camps without trial or hearing (Glaser, 1961, pp. 127, 161).

Specific details of torture have been recorded in the affidavits of former inmates. Only one will be cited here, involving a camp at Moravské Ostrava. It is of interest because the Czech management appointed an ethnic German, one Glos, to preside over the torture of his fellow-Germans. The affidavit reads, in part:

Twenty-two prisoners were sitting there on the cement floor, and were forced to sing Czech songs. . . . Our room was 4 meters square; it had no windows, while the door to the courtyard was cemented shut with only a slit the width of two tiles. The light burned in our room days and night. We had to sing the entire day and were not allowed to stand up. . . .

. . . The hangman Glos enjoyed particularly sending Czech civilians in our room, who under the supervision of the guards beat us with steel bars and rubber truncheons until they were exhausted or almost all victims had fainted. When Glos was in a particularly good mood, he offered his Czech friends a special attraction. A prisoner was forced to lie on a bench about one and one-half meters long with his back to the ceiling, while another was forced to hold his hands under the bench. Glos stood at the victim's feet, the Czechs on both sides, and then they thrashed at the victim with rubber truncheons until they could do it no longer or the

victim died under their blows. When that happened, he was dumped off the bench and the next victim had his turn.

. . . Executions were always at night. . . . We always heard the screams and groans of the victims, for they were always beaten before being killed. . . . Up to 50 men were thus slaughtered in one night. The next morning the few survivors had to clean up the gallows room. The clothes and shoes of the hanged lay beside the gallows. Blood stood 3 to 4 centimeters deep in the gallows room and washroom. We had to sweep it into the sewer with shovels and then wash the cement floor with water. (*Sudetendeutsche Zeitung*, June 13, 1975, p. 5, our translation)

It would appear that the Greek colonels' regime that ruled from 1967 to 1974 brought torture to a fine art. There was a school for torturers in which the students were themselves tortured. At a trial in Athens in August, 1975, former military policemen testified that apprentice torturers had been "beaten daily and had to lick floors clean with their tongues as part of their training. They said that some candidates were left hanging upside down from trees and had to eat grass on all fours like grazing sheep" (*St. Louis Post-Dispatch*, August 28, 1975).

The Greek members of Amnesty International, some of them ex-prisoners and victims of torture, have mounted a campaign to bring ex-torturers to trial. But they are equally insistent that all those charged be given fair trials, since, as Virginia Tsouderous, a member of the Greek Parliament, declares, "A real democrat must be fair, even to his enemies" (*Amnesty Action*, September, 1975, p. 3).

Torture may be used as an instrument of political repression, as seems to be the case in Guatemala. Beginning with the story of a farmer named Efrain David Pineda, *Amnesty Action* (August, 1975, p. 7) reports as follows:

On May 23, 1975, after leaving the fields for lunch, two plainclothesmen called at his house. They produced military police credentials and took him away. After leaving him in a jail cell of another village for several hours, they took him to an isolated area by car. He was tied to a tree, beaten repeatedly, shot in the leg and chest, untied and left for dead. He managed to crawl to the village of Pecojate and was taken to a hospital.

Hundreds of unexplained deaths in the rural areas of Guatemala have been reported in the last several years, many of them apparently to intimidate peasants from beginning political mobilization. Of 683 political assassinations reported during 1973 in the Guatemalan press, 70% took place in the rural areas. Most of them were peasants dragged out of their houses and shot, many after having endured torture. In January 1975 at least 41 people died by violent means and for political reasons. In those cases in which assailants are even partially identified, they are often described as "well organized groups of heavily armed men who arrive in automobiles that have no registration plates." Some of these anonymous death squads are composed of men "dressed in olive-green uniforms."

According to an AI survey, 27 percent of the corpses of victims showed clear signs of torture or mutilation, including multiple fractures and severe burns.

Sophisticated methods are used in Argentina, where four French lawyers found in May 1975 that "detainees were subjected to various forms of torture during interrogation, such as the use of electric shocks and simulated executions. . . . The French lawyers heard allegations that the police have made some detainees wear stereophonic headphones through which high frequency signals were passed in order to break down their resistance without leaving any visible marks" (ibid.).

Across the Plata in Uruguay, the military government employs drastic methods against political dissenters, some of whom—like the terrorist Tupamaros—are admittedly not the most gentle people themselves. AI has stated its view that what began as repression of armed opposition has deteriorated into persecution of peaceful dissenters as well—since any criticism of the regime is treated as subversive. According to Amnesty Action,

The AI survey documents numerous such abuses, ranging from dismissal of teachers from their jobs on grounds of previous detention, however brief and for whatever reason, to torture that includes beatings all over the body, near drowning ("the submarine"), electric shocks, fake executions and other forms of psychological torture. Recent decrees not only violate Uruguay's constitution but also open a Pandora's box for police and military patrols, which have become accustomed to unrestricted powers of detention and treatment of detainees, who are completely at their mercy. (September 1975, p. 5)

A certain Pedro Cribari testified that after being tortured himself he was made to witness the torture of another detainee who eventually collapsed and died as a result of the submarine.

Another documented case is that of Walter Ramos, aged 21, who was arrested at dawn on May 3, 1975 at his house in Montevideo, immediately hooded and put in a van. His captors beat him and threatened to kill him, and at one point threw him out of the van, put a revolver to his head and fired three shots in the air. Another official told them not to kill Ramos "because he was not certain," and he was taken to a military barracks, where he was kept standing, handcuffed, for three days.

When on the third day he was given food for the first time, he was shown a photograph of his wife and told that, at that moment, she was being raped. He tried to attack the official but was too weak. He was then beaten up by five persons and later given electric shocks and the "submarine." A doctor ordered his transfer to the military hospital, where he remained for 11 days, during which time an official interrogated him once more and ended by saying that "everything had been clarified." He was again hooded, put in a van, and after a long ride, set free. At no time did any judicial authority intervene in his case. (Ibid., p. 6)

Probably the worst torture in the current wave is that reported from Brazil, where an American clergyman and free-lance reporter, Fred B. Morris, came in contact with people blacklisted by the regime and was given the "treatment" by Army Intelligence. One episode involved electrodes fastened to the foot, the breast nipple, and later the penis. The following is quoted from his account:

The first jolt was a light one, a sort of tickling and pulling at my breast. But then he increased the current and I began to jump around on the wet floor as though that might relieve the pain. I clamped my mouth shut as hard as I could, not wanting to scream and give him any satisfaction, but as the current increased, my mouth flew open with a great bellow of rage and pain. The current kept on increasing until I was thrown to the floor, doubled over in a vain attempt to diminish the pain. Then it stopped. "Get up," he yelled at me. My hands were handcuffed behind my back, and, as I slipped around trying to get up, he gave me light jolts, just to prod me on, like a steer being loaded into a truck. . . .

Then the same questions and some light jolts that made me dance from side to side. I was screaming, now almost in anticipation of the shocks, when he turned up the voltage hard, provoking spasms in both legs that caused them to fly out in front of me. I fell with all my weight on my back and hands, which were still manacled behind me. The current continued as I squirmed and wriggled on the wet floor. This must have seemed a pratfall, for the room filled with laughter from three or four men now gathered to watch the proceedings. (Morris, 1975, pp. 58–59)

On another occasion:

I was questioned with electric shock and more beatings for about another hour, then hung up again in my cell. Two or three times that afternoon, they repeated the procedure. Then I was taken into a different room. I was made to sit, the handcuffs were removed, and my arms and legs were firmly strapped to the chair. One electrode was placed on my breast and the other on my right ear. These were the worst shocks of all. I felt like the top of my head was actually going to burst. I screamed, jumped in the chair, tried to break the straps, and finally, on at least two occasions, was rendered unconscious. (*Ibid.*)

The "evidence" against Morris consisted mainly of allegations by people under torture themselves. Readers of *The Gulag Archipelago* will recognize the pattern, yet the episode recounted by Morris seems out of keeping with the many progressive and liberal aspects of Brazilian life. There is some reason to hope that the government in Brasilia will be more responsive to international criticism than the government in Moscow.

Cases are continually reported from Eastern Europe. The treatment of 13 Seventh-Day Adventists, who refused to work on Saturday, was said to include overcrowded cells, shackles, cold showers in the winter, and severe whippings (up to 30 strokes). Two of the 13 are reported to have died under these conditions (*Amnesty Action*, August, 1975, p. 8). The maltreatment of political prisoners in the Strzelce Opolskie prison in Poland is said to include "beatings with clubs and jailers' keys, sexual maltreatment, and subjection to the 'thermos cell,' which is allegedly designed to control sound and temperature. It is further alleged that two years ago two prisoners died because of suffocation in this 'thermos cell' " (*Amnesty Action*, September, 1975, p. 8).

C. Psychological Torture

There also are nonphysical types of torture. This particular form of suppressing human rights is extremely widespread and frequent, and often occurs without the tormentors being aware of what they are doing.

A great deal of psychological torture is inflicted when governments act on theories which turn out to be wrong—sometimes much later. Traffic jams on modern highways are attributable to inadequate budgets for road building, false forecasts of traffic trends, or fiscal policies that discourage alternate forms of transport. Such troubles bring harmful impacts on private lives and contribute to the psychological condition known as anomie.

1. THE SURFEIT OF DECIBELS AND THE LOSS OF MEANING

Noise pollution from vehicles, machinery, and amplifiers is a prominent phenomenon of modern life. Modern man must reconcile himself to living amid unwanted loud sounds, undesired music, and unsolicited messages. Noise pollution—including voluntary listening to excessively amplified rock music—seems to have led to a significant impairment of hearing among the younger American population. Furthermore, sustained high noise levels are "a health hazard to a significant number of workers." An estimated 1.7 million American workers "have a hearing handicap by retirement age from industrial noise . . . an estimate other experts consider very low" (*San José Mercury News*, May 18, 1975, p. 1f). Noise pollution may result in sleeplessness, fatigue, high blood pressure, changes in body chemistry, and stress. It also interrupts communication and concentration. Thus, a comparatively minor disturbance can have far-reaching negative psychological effects. These culminate in anomie. This is a syndrome resulting from psychological torture through conditions and actions that negate the individual as a self-determining entity and therefore, by implication, also negate his freedoms and rights.

A certain amount of manipulation is inevitable in human interaction: in politics, business, education, or social life. Trouble arises when the manipulation is overdone and tries to go beyond that which is manipulable and when the political power proceeds on the assumption that all human behavior must be managed to conform to prediction. The loss of meaning, and the contemporary fruitless search for meaning, is related to the substitution of animal, stimulus-response, electricity, biochemistry, matter, and machinery for man. Lack of purpose in life is the cause of about 20 percent of today's neuroses (Frankl, 1969, p. 400).

But worse, the urge for meaning has been put under a powerful taboo, which, according to J. R. Smythies, even extends to the concept of death. During the Freudian era, the repression of sex resulted in a high incidence of neuroses while, if we are to believe Frankl, repression of homosexuality led to much paranoia. Could the current taboo on the meaning of life and death be one of the causes of the high incidence of violence which marks our period? These problems are by no means purely theoretical, but have operational aspects.

2. STATISTICS AND THE "AVERAGE PERSON"

Modern statistics tend to put individuals in straitjackets: to treat different people as though they were all alike. Pupils with rare gifts or handicaps may be denied the special education they need, or a particular drug may be withheld from everybody, despite the fact that it could be very helpful to a particular type of individual.*

Any treatment given to the "average" person is mistaken, because an average is a statistical artifact and does not exist in real life. Naturally, by ignoring individual and typological differences, much hard work and expense can be avoided. But individuals, with their own flesh, blood, and minds, are erased and their individual rights violated. "Deviants," in particular, are sacrificed and their special problems ignored.

Personalities are "unimaginably unlike each other. Introvert and extrovert are like chalk and cheese; to group their behavior and reactions together by some process of averaging is as absurd as to average chalk and cheese" (Eysenck, 1972, pp. 105f). Such mixing is typical of public programs in the fields of health and education; it dominates the management of sex problems, and it prevails throughout the legal profession, with harmful impacts on society as a whole.

3. "PHYSICIAN, CURE THYSELF!"

Governmental control of pharmacological products is often based on improper statistical evaluations, at least in the United States. Psychiatrists and clinical psychologists, who divide into many different schools, each like to treat patients their own particular ways. Some fashionable types of psychological treatment were never properly validated and prolong rather than shorten the affliction (Eysenck, 1972, pp. 30, 115, and 358).

---

* Eysenck (1972) within his own context, discusses such irregularities in the application of statistics on p. 17f, and p. 117.

The creation of iatrogenic (doctor-caused) disease has been practiced as an art. The situation is not eased by the fact that "mentally ill physicians may harm their patients and go unattended, with alcoholism, depression, and drug addiction being primary special problems to the doctors," as three psychologists reported in the Journal of the American Medical Association (*San José Mercury*, May 19, 1975, p. 56). In other instances, validated therapeutic techniques are disregarded. Psychotics may be abandoned as incurables for whom death is the best hope. Mentally handicapped children may be victims of public indifference, as seems to be the case in West Germany, where they are said to account for about 5 percent of live births (Boxberg, 1975).

No blanket condemnation of psychiatric and psychological practice is intended. The profession is peculiar, however, in being disunited about its elementary concepts. Psychologists are by no means agreed on the limits of "normal" behavior, especially in response to abnormal environments. It is clear in any case that behavioral disorders affect millions of people through their relation to psychosomatic illnesses as well as to a large percentage of accidents, rape and other sex crimes, suicides, homicides, and politically motivated shootings and bombings.

Psychiatrists also prostitute their profession when they appear as highly paid "expert" witnesses in criminal cases. The customary spectacle of the prosecution psychiatrist at loggerheads with the defense psychiatrist is outrageous. Yet the phenomenon of the scientist exerting himself to help a lawyer's or client's case instead of presenting his knowledge objectively is by no means limited to psychiatry or medicine. Where psychology and psychiatry are relevant to criminal guilt and the possibilities of rehabilitation, such knowledge should be furnished to the judge by impartial professionals.

But what happens when a criminal is justly convicted and serves a fair sentence? If he has not been rehabilitated, it will prove impossible to reintegrate him into society; or else, if rehabilitation methods are poor, few employers will take their chances with a released criminal. Thus, he would be punished beyond his deserts and, in fact, might be given a sentence which makes it impossible for him ever to live a proper life again. Then, he might resume criminal activity, especially if crime pays and risks are low, thus punishing more innocent people. The root of the problem lies in determinist social philosophy, which holds that since a person is only the product of his environment, he is not really responsible for his acts. It should be made clear that human rights cannot be safeguarded without equal enforcement of human obligations.

Since the mid-1950s, the situation in mental hospitals has been improving, largely because of the discovery of analeptic drugs which have made it possible to reduce the excitement of patients and to achieve contact with psychotics. Drug treatment, however, is not enough and the hospitals have not yet been emptied. When Professor Eysenck supported a broad scientific attack, "a stone thrown into the slough of despond could not have caused less response." "No one cares; no one wants to know; no one is concerned. . . . Administrators ambulate in their predestined circles. Analysts cling to their outdated and useless theories. Patients go on suffering. The tax payer goes on paying" (p. 154).

Indeed, hospital patients are subjected to contraindicated treatment and their condition gets worse when they are handled with inappropriate "humaneness."

We have the cloud-cuckoo-land doctrine that patients are better off ill, incapable and incompetent than they are when capable of rational behavior, self-supporting, and able to live ordinary lives in the outside world. . . . Patients are thrust into an environment which abrogates [the] rules. They are attended to when they behave badly, they receive kindness when they are obstreperous, they are talked to when they are irrational. No wonder that often in this topsy-turvy world they get worse, not better. There is much evidence . . . that much of their "madness" is in fact hospital-produced. Now the kindly state, in its wisdom, ordains that a regime which makes patients madder shall continue, and that a regime which cures them and makes them able to take part in a world where contingencies govern behavior shall be outlawed—all in the name of kindness. (*Ibid.*, p. 374)

4. TORTURE THROUGH INAPPROPRIATE EDUCATION

Gifted children who remain undereducated are hampered in their careers and their losses and tribulations are damaging to society as a whole. Handicapped children who cannot be made self-supporting—unfortunately, many of them cannot under any circumstances—are condemned to a life of misery. The need for truly efficient education systems which sharpen the ability to think critically and enable each child to develop to his or her full potential is imperative. Yet skyrocketing educational budgets are not producing equivalent achievements. Recent studies in the United States indicate a decline in the performance of high school students, while the national education budget was running at a level of $108 billion in 1974–75, ten times higher than in 1951–52. In New York City schools there was a strong negative correlation between expenditures per pupil and pupil achievements, yet no extensive study of the relationship between expenditures and educational quality has been made (see Freeman, 1975, pp. 134–40).

Eysenck (1972) comments on the educational scene: "We are arbitrarily changing conditions, but not experimenting in the proper sense because there are no proper controls and no adequate measurements of effects to follow up."

Eysenck's criticism applies particularly to the situation of the many school children who suffer from misuse of statistical methodology as it is applied to teaching practices, to testing and selecting, and to the institutional structure of school systems. Once again individuality

and typology are systematically disregarded as are divergent cultural backgrounds in multi-ethnic schools. Furthermore, abuse of testing and misinterpretation of scores may condemn children to an education and a life that they do not desire. Even the U.S. Civil Service Commission, America's largest employer, has been charged with being "at least thirty years behind the time" in its testing techniques and using test scores in a discriminatory manner (*Wright Institute Report*, Berkeley, Cal., December 1974, p. 10).

Admittedly, tests of some kinds are useful guides in educational decision-making. The problem is that a standardized test, like Procrustes' famous bed, fails to account for the individuality of unstandardized people. All too often, tests are used for authoritarian decisions by teachers and "counsellors," who shirk personal responsibility by proclaiming the "objectivity" of the test. If Johnny—or more likely Pedro—shows a low IQ, "he's just dumb—that's all."

What test constructors and users fail to realize is that all tests are necessarily oriented to specific cultures and language patterns. They are inherently violative of the rights of children representing different cultures, as are monocultural and monolingual curricula based on majority cultures. Most American teachers, however, gain their degrees and certificates without more than the most superficial knowledge of the rich cultural resources of America's ethnic groups. Nor do many learn a foreign language—which is essential for a teacher who wishes to gain the sensitivity for cultural "gear shifting." The result of all this is that unusual children—and most are in one way or another—are unintentionally and unnecessarily tortured.

D. Conclusion

Torture did not disappear at the close of the Middle Ages, but remains a recurrent fact of modern life. In a survey article in *Skeptic* Ron Bernstein (1977) gives a catalog of countries where it is practiced, including the South American countries mentioned in B2, above, plus Venezuela, Colombia, and several others. Turning to Africa, Bernstein refers to allegations of torture of persons accused of subversive activities in South Africa. These charges are supported in particular cases by excerpts from court proceedings and newspaper articles compiled by the Christian Institute (Torture, 1977); its publication shows that in South Africa, as distinguished from some other countries, it is possible to bring the facts to light. Bernstein continues:

Authorized torture is common in Burundi, Cameroon, Ethiopia, Ghana, Morocco, Zanzibar, Tunisia, and Libya. In Malawi, torture is part of the terror campaign employed against Jehovah's Witnesses. In Togo, torture is merely a diversion of the army. Torture-for-fun, however, seems to be most in fashion in Idi Amin's Uganda. (1977, p. 26)

Indirect American involvement is suggested by several facts cited by Bernstein, such as a 1971 U.S. Navy contract for building 384 cages used in Vietnam's notorious "tiger cage" prison. The activities of AID's former Office of Public Safety would bear scrutiny. Whether or not its training activities became a laboratory for the CIA's "program to study possible means of controlling human behavior," including electric shock and psychological techniques, has yet to be explored. It is known, however, that AID provided massive training assistance for the police of Brazil, Uruguay, South Vietnam, Thailand, the Philippines, and Guatemala.

In the same issue of *Skeptic*, Patrick J. Buchanan argues that it is hypocritical to condemn flatly torture of individuals while condoning mass killings such as Churchill's bombardment of Dresden (February, 1945) and General LeMay's firebombing of Tokyo—to say nothing of Hiroshima. Buchanan considers that torture to extract information may be morally justified if (a) the matter is grave enough (innocent lives in jeopardy); (b) there is no less odious alternative (truth sera, etc.); and (c) it is almost certain that the torture victim has the vital information. The companion article by Ramsey Clark takes the position that torture is never justified for any reason. (*Skeptic*, January–February, 1977, pp. 16–23).

A group of Danish doctors working with Amnesty International are studying torture as a mass political syndrome. They fear that, despite growing awareness of human rights, a growing number of countries are subjecting people to highly sophisticated, medically supervised torture. Teams within the group work on different aspects of torture, such as the effects of shock treatment on the skin and hormone imbalance provoked by prolonged fear. One team studies psychiatric aspects and another the effects of torture on children. It is the group's hope to have the world medical profession condemn participation in torture as a violation of the Hippocratic Oath, even though doctors are often forced to assist or face punishment themselves (Colin Narborough, *St. Louis Post-Dispatch*, May 26, 1977).

A disturbing trend noticed recently in the United States is the production and distribution of pornographic photographs and movies involving children. New York police discovered in 1976 that one-third of their 2000 warehouse feet of pornography involved children. While some civil libertarians contend that the sale of such materials is protected by freedom of speech, it is the *making* of pornographic pictures and films involving children that constitutes the crime of torture, since it subjects young children to sexual experiences they cannot possibly digest. Inflicting psychological traumata on children in this way should be punished as severely as any other kind of torture. The United States Attorney in Philadelphia has announced his intention of prosecuting producers of child pornography and parents who make their children available for it, not under obscenity statutes, but under a

Federal law prescribing prison sentences to five years and fines up to $5000 for holding a child to involuntary servitude (See *St. Louis Post-Dispatch*, April 14, 1977).

The persistence of torture in the world, both physical and psychological, is largely attributable to indifference and negligence rather than evil intent. It is the professional intelligentsia, especially where they enjoy freedom of expression, who share with power-hungry and mad despots the responsibility for wholesale negations of human rights.

26

BRAINWASHING IN EAST AND WEST

An American boy who salutes his flag or pledges allegiance to the country "is being brainwashed as surely as . . . the Chinese boy who is made to carry Mao's *Thoughts* around in his pocket." This statement by Eysenck (1972), p. 325f.) seems shocking at first. But what he means is that any viable society is held together by socialization based on "some premises which are being taken for granted, and are never questioned." The problem is, therefore, to distinguish between non-oppressive and oppressive forms of socialization and mental conditioning.

There are fundamental differences between brainwashing as practiced by the Maoists in China and psychological abuses in Western countries. Even the major American effort to "re-educate" the Germans after 1945, ill-considered though it was, cannot be compared to Maoist brainwashing.

A. Nuremberg and the "Re-Education" of Germany

The prosecution of German war criminals was a part of the reeducative process. But they involved only a few hundred defendants, which meant that the thesis of national and collective guilt was dropped. Schrenck-Notzing (1965, pp. 119–26) has shown that the concept of reeducation originated in theories by psychologists and psychoanalysts influenced by Marxism. The underlying concept was that the "authoritarian personality," as defined by Erich Fromm in 1941, had achieved dominance in Germany.

Not every authoritarian personality, of course, is a potential fascist or concentration-camp commander. Leaders of totalitarian regimes always have additional characteristics. Furthermore, wartime studies on the authoritarian personality (e.g. by Adorno and Frenkel-Brunsvik) were not based on tests of Hitler and company but of middle- and working-class Americans. To apply such findings to a whole nation, despite the existence of competing psychological schools and concepts, and to use it as a basis for rewriting German history textbooks, is reductionism of a very evil kind.

1. WHO GOT BRAINWASHED?

The idea of "re-education," together with its intellectual preparation, was invalid because the bankruptcy of National Socialism had become apparent, and the Germans were quite able to handle the vestiges of that ideology themselves. Yet the effort enjoyed top-level support in the United States. The results were mainly in the nature of low comedy, with the Americans becoming the butt of ridicule.

There is another side to this event. Under the aegis of the so-called Morgenthau plan, Germany was to be transformed into a nation of small peasants and "pastoralists." The theory was that the Germans were incurable, but that without industry they would be unable to renew aggression. That pastoralization would result in starvation for tens of millions of people, and would seriously harm Europe and perhaps the entire world, was finally realized. The program was modified and then shelved altogether, but not until considerable dismantling had taken place in both the Soviet and Western Zones. Re-education was substituted—but Germany was partitioned, a measure that may yet have dire consequences.

What does the story show that is illustrative of brainwashing?

1. A genocidal program was approved by a liberal American President and a conservative British Prime Minister. It was supported warmly by the U.S. bureaucracy and half-heartedly by the British bureaucracy. It may have been invented and nursed to the decision-point by crypto-communist officials, but many non- and anticommunists endorsed the concept.

2. The democratic structure of the U.S. and the U.K. narrowly blocked implementation. Common sense and national self-interest were probably the decisive factors.

3. The program was based on questionable premises:

a. That the Germans were exclusively responsible for World Wars I and II and—still more ridiculously—that they had been especially aggressive throughout their entire history. This myth, first implanted by "devil" propaganda during World War I, was held firmly. The re-educators needed historical re-education more than their guinea-pigs.

b. That Hitler and the NSDAP were the logical emanation of the German character and represented the German national will. It was not realized that the National Socialist leadership was an unscrupulous clique which took advantage of an anomic situation to promote itself with a distorting ideology and skilled propaganda tactics—and which was helped by industrialists and foreign governments to seize power and stay in office.

c. That national character determined military aggressiveness, that it makes all members of a nation alike, that a nation cannot change itself but can be changed by an occupant's psychological engineering. This doctrine is an attenuated form of racism.

d. That the Germans could be transformed into peasants and that deindustrialization would tame the German spirit without provoking major resistance.

e. That the program could be continued for a long while without lengthy military occupation and without upsetting the world power balance. Roosevelt spoke of returning all American troops to the United States two years after the end of hostilities.

In retrospect, all these notions seem incredible. Yet false teachings on history, strategy, economics, and psychology were compounded into an amalgam that became the basis for American (and to some extent British and French) policy. Unfortunately, numerous scientists and academicians volunteered their intellectual services, confirming LeBon's contention that academicians are not more rational than factory workers. Few intellectuals rose in opposition and fewer still could make their voice heard.

2. COLLECTIVE GUILT THEORIES AND THEIR DANGERS

None of the theories exploited or abused for collective punishment of the Germans was explicitly corrected or disavowed. In brief, the structure of this oppressive and genocidal thought runs as follows: There are individuals, personality types, members of organizations and institutions, social classes, ethnic and religious groups, nations, elites, and governments who are necessarily and irrevocably diabolical. Some are mentally sick, while others are typologically destructive, ethnically and religiously obsessed with rapine and war, or possessed by a criminal and murderous lust for power. Since these groups are defined *a priori* as incurable, dangerous individuals, elites and leaders among them must be eliminated, while the lesser fry must be "transformed."

It is not to be denied that collectives and leadership groups may commit serious transgressions. Government policies may deny basic rights and thus be criminal in effect. A company or a trade union may violate the law and incur penalties. Members may be indirectly punished—e.g. if union members are assessed to pay a fine against their local or a penalized company skips a dividend. But it would be wrong to throw all a company's employees or stockholders or all the members of a union—or any other group—in prison; their guilt cannot be assumed because of association. Justice demands that a person, in accordance with established law, be punished only for the deeds he or she commits. If, as an official or member of an organization (which may be a government) a person commits or commands murder, he or she is guilty of homicide, and the same is true of lesser crimes. One who is mentally sick may be given punishment and treatment, or only treatment, as the case requires. But membership in a social class or even diagnosis as a personality type does not call for "transformation," which would be a gross violation of an individual's right to be himself. And membership in an unstructured group such as a nation (which never makes policy) can be cause for punishment only for those with genocide in mind. In any case, the International Military Tribunal operated on the principle of individual, not collective guilt.

It should be clear that blanket condemnation of any group—be it a class, a race, a nation, or a religious sect—is essentially a totalitarian attitude and carries within itself the seeds of aggressive and frequently criminal political behavior.

B. Medical Behavior Control and Maoist Brainwashing

Constitutional as well as totalitarian systems habitually influence thought and behavior through propaganda, agitation, information, and advertising, but they do not attempt to alter the personalities of or establish mental control over healthy individuals. Free societies forbid the use of psychiatric techniques to influence political thought or behavior. Criminals and insane persons may be forced to undergo treatment, but usually treatment is solicited by the patient himself or by his family. Mental disorders must be treated by a physician or psychologist in conformity with established professional standards. "Brainwashing" in free societies, insofar as the term is applicable, *is* an undertaking of medicine and vocational therapy, and Maoist brainwashing is *not*.

Although a viable social structure and a healthy political system depend on consensus on a body of norms to delineate permissible and desirable behavior, liberal theory does not hold that norms must never be questioned. Furthermore, premises regarded as basic, such as the rights to free speech and property, do not necessarily mean the same thing to all. A viable open society possesses and uses mechanisms for social and political change.

Maoist brainwashing techniques aim at obtaining unquestioned and total obedience to the point of total uniformity. That goal is utterly incompatible with a free society, and even with Mao's own ideas on nonantagonistic contradictions.

The Maoist system of brainwashing is an integral part of Mao's own psychology and is linked to his quest for "revolutionary immortality" (see Lifton, 1968, p. xiv). It is wholly foreign to the practices of a free society and even to anything like revolutionary rationality.

The point is fundamental. The quest for immortality, revolutionary or otherwise, involves an idea of human divinity and of the power of the political "God" to immortalize himself by creating a new and eternal order. Since such an order does not emerge spontaneously, the "immortal" politician must impose it by exacting complete discipline, unquestioning obedience, and imposing a new code of behavior.

Maoist brainwashing, which is basically a total negation of human rights except when permissiveness is deemed expedient, is aimed at achieving immediate and unconditional acceptance of any change in the norms and "lines" the leadership commands. This robot-omanic concept, if it were feasible, could only create a pseudo-order in which the individual is robbed of control over himself. Such a pseudo-order cannot be stable, because persons have no stable relationship to it. Order is characterized by security, predictability, consistency, clarity, and protection of rights, and by public policy accepted as reasonable. But those norms cannot be satisfied if men are so controlled that they lose one of the most essential and elementary aspects of their humanity—the capacity to form opinions and make judgments.

The fantasy of achieving immortality by imposing a tyrant's commonplace mortal thoughts is rooted in inability to distinguish between dreamlike imagination and reality, and is clearly pathological—Mommsen called it *Caesarenwahn*. Individuals are treated like grains of sand (or in the words of James I "like men at the Chesse") and have no other function than to serve as tools of history and society (reified concepts) and as servants of the omnipotent *Führer* or *Vozhd*.

Hegel called the ability to declare independence from reality the "freedom of emptiness" and ascribed to it

the fanaticism of smashing all established social order, of removing all individuals suspect of harboring order in their existence. . . . Only by destroying something has this negative will the feeling of its own existence. Even if it believes to will a positive state, as for instance the state of general equality

. . . it does not in fact want its realization. . . . What this freedom believes to will can be nothing but an abstract conception, and its realization must not go beyond the fury of destruction. (Hegel, 1955, p. 30; Eric Voegelin's translation; Voegelin, 1971, p. 34)

Voegelin added, " a human vacuum is . . . man's deformation of his humanity in its social and historical context." From this deformation results the inability to treat a person as a human being and a brother or sister.

The aberration of brainwashing must be understood in its full depth. In practice, it is law, psychology, psychiatry, sociology, and education turned upside down. Athough it cannot succeed, the attempts to remold man are utterly repressive and from time to time they must become paroxysmal. The purpose of brainwashing is to annihilate the person and re-create him as a living zombie with no trace of self-direction. "He who did not think himself, is not free—he who is not free, did not think himself" (Hegel, 1955, p. 308).

C. Chinese Techniques of Brainwashing

To understand these Chinese techniques, we must familiarize ourselves with five major elements: (1) Thought reform, more graphically referred to as "brainwashing" (*hsi-nao*); (2) The small group (*hsiao-tsu*); (3) Struggling and struggling against (*to-ts'un*); (4) The accusation process (*tou-cheng*); and (5) Self-confession (*t'an-pai*). (See bibliographical note at end of chapter.)

In 1942, Mao Tse-tung himself explained the purpose of thought reform as being to "punish the past, to warn the future," to "save men by curing their ills" and to expose errors. The object is like "curing a disease." The purpose is "to save the person, not to cure him to death" (Quoted, Lifton, 1968, pp. 13f). Mao and the Chinese Communist Party (CCP) took it upon themselves to define mental health and to diagnose mental disease in politics. The implication is that noncommunists and opponents within the party are afflicted by political disease and that nonconformist or new thoughts are pathological. To avert an epidemic of infectious political maladies which could devastate the country, thought reform is applied as a prophylaxis.

Brainwashing is carried out through interviews, interrogations, study classes, organized discussions, and group study of documents and writings. Repetition is endless, and enthusiastic participation is demanded. The operation aims at imposing a new moral code, at arousing predetermined emotions and motivations and at controlling behavior so as to achieve obedience and mass involvement. The subjects are encouraged to express their own views and praise is not withheld. Behavioral conformity is expected to entail conformist beliefs.

The main thrust of the discussions and debates is to "study" and assimilate the prescribed ideas, to "mobilize" the thoughts of the individual in the direction desired at the time, and to demand "progress in one's attitude." The techniques include criticism, self-criticism, and mutual criticism bearing on the person's past and present thoughts, ideological attitudes, work habits, and everything else personal—even the person's sex life. All this culminates in an admission of guilt and a promise to better oneself and to report progress continually, with every new confession gauging the progress of indoctrination. No criticism of the party or the government is tolerated and any such criticism, however faint, is promptly squelched.

To enable brainwashing to take full effect, the victim is made to bare his or her entire life story and abandon all privacy. Each is strongly conditioned against his or her past and aberrant thoughts, and is encouraged to "internalize" the various and often contradictory ideas which the government prescribes at successive moments. If the resulting confusion is distressing, suggestibility will be enhanced (Frank, 1973, p. 99.)

To eliminate errors and to provide full dossiers about each citizen, persons under treatment and others as well are forced to write down their biographies, thoughts, and self-criticisms. Since new thoughst are frequently handed down from the summit and "old" thoughts become forbidden, confusion may provoke neuroses like those that afflicted Pavlov's dogs.

1. SMALL GROUPS AND THEIR USES

The communists place great emphasis on small groups which, they find, allow them to mobilize the population more effectively than other elites have done so far. The impact of small groups on the personality has also been demonstrated in the West (see Mann, 1965, ch. 7). In China, small groups are maintained among peasants, workers, students, cadres, the military forces, urban neighborhoods, dormitories, and camps. Wherever people congregate on a regular basis, there a *hsiao-tsu* should be established. If the group is studying a new line or program, or has been reorganized or created anew, sessions may last a whole day; occasionally they are extended for several days. Normally, however, the group sessions vary from a maximum of two to four hours a day down to two to four hours a week, and they invariably cut into a person's free time.

The small group is the instrument through which thought reform takes place in "free life"—i.e., outside of jail and camp. Each small group is linked with other small groups and with larger organizations such as military units or factory crews, and it is used to select individuals for more responsible assignments. At the same time, it is used to detect nonconformists and threaten and punish them by demotion or expulsion.

The small group has the additional and crucial function of determining the wages for each member. Each group can choose between five different levels of wages, and as the individual shares in the group's work and reforms his thoughts, or fails to do so, he will be moved up and down the five steps of the wage ladder. Very often equivalent decisions are made with respect to food rations. The members grade each other by voting on performance in studies, production, work discipline, relations with other persons, and politics. The group also engages in mutual criticism and self-criticism. The group leader and his assistant usually are appointed by higher authority. They play a decisive role in the lives of group members and stimulate or ease "peer pressure."

2. "STRUGGLE" AND SLAVE LABOR

Group activities are influenced by denunciations received from the outside. All over China there are denunciation boxes which foreigners often mistake for mailboxes (Bao and Chelminski, 1973, p. 60). Thus, rumors, gossip, grudges, and mendacity are "mobilized" against the individual, who finds no place to hide.

Mao warned that the "target" should not be devastated. But in each small group certain members become scapegoats simply because they are weak or disliked. The *hsiao-tsu* is a structured group, not a haphazard one, and it is under steady pressure to identify and uproot, or else change, the "poisonous weeds." The security of the majority rests upon their finding or inventing a minority whose errors can be magnified and on whom all shortcomings and defects can be unloaded.

In the course of its work, the small group will inevitably discover persons within it who must be "struggled against." The party may select struggle targets belonging to the so-called "black classes"—landlords, rich peasants, counterrevolutionaries, property owners, capitalists, and their offspring—without reference to small groups. But members of the "red classes"—peasants and workers—are usually chosen by small groups.

Each *hsiao-tsu* member—and this means, in effect, each Chinese—is supposed to keep a diary and a record of his studies in addition to his biography and confessions. Those written materials may be inspected by the group leader and other party supervisors. Usually an outside party official determines whether a struggle meeting is desirable and picks the victim. Sometimes high party echelons order more frequent struggle sessions.

The person who is "struggled against" is placed before an audience which may be his own small group or a larger assembly. He is forced to kneel down and to keep his head bowed. He is then encircled, subjected to indignities and humiliations, spit upon, forced to acknowledge his guilt and to plead for mercy. Sometimes he is pushed, slapped, kicked and beaten. The session can go for a long time—to the complete exhaustion of the victim, whose every word or move gives rise to howls and protests, and often to violence. If he collapses, he may be revived or the meeting may be closed. Often the meeting is continued the next day; sometimes it goes on for weeks before changing audiences. In the end, a confession of guilt may be accepted and the victim may be released with a reprimand; or he may be forced to fulfill degrading chores in addition to his normal tasks. He may be sent to re-education or reform camp, or perhaps to prison, and in rare instances he may be executed.

At the beginning of the cultural revolution, high-school students were incited to struggle against their teachers. Numerous teachers were subjected to the ordeal, many not because they were disloyal to the regime, but because some students harbored grudges against them. With the help of quotations from Mao's little red book, the school bullies, who usually were not the best students, had a field day and numerous teachers were badly roughed up. Some were tied up, some were killed outright, and others committed suicide. These struggle sessions were accompanied by raids upon the teachers' homes, supposedly for the purpose of gathering evidence, but actually for the purpose of destroying the victims' belongings and plundering their valuables (Ling, 1972, *passim*.).

Landlords and capitalists—and their offspring—are called to task for exploitation, corruption, or "stealing," while communist bureaucrats are often charged with inefficiency and poor performance. Other crimes are purely *crimes of thought*—such as decadent philosophy, being "above politics," "above class," ideology of special privilege, etc.—and there is even a crime known as "dissatisfaction with reality." The struggle sessions usually serve as part of the punishment and as a demonstration of popular justice. There are no defense lawyers. There is no chance of an orderly defense, and any attempt by the victim to exculpate himself leads to additional torment. Wang Kuang-mei, the wife of Liu Shao-chi, was accused of being a "social butterfly," of having wormed her way into revolutionary ranks, of being an imperialist spy, and, to top it all, of having arranged an elaborate funeral with a stone monument for her reactionary father.

The system of thought reform is not just indoctrination plus forceful conditioning reinforced by rewards and punishments. Behind the entire effort has been the system of forced labor—that of "re-education" through labor and labor reform camps. These institutions may be camps in the normal meaning of the word, but frequently they are in the nature of agricultural communes and industrial factories. Often persons sentenced to "re-education" are in the same compound with those being "reformed," but they are housed in separate facilities and enjoy various privileges, such as better rations and "wages," and permission to go out for short periods of time. There are also camps for juvenile delinquents below the age of 17, detention houses, prisons, and "death farms" for expendable and very sick individuals where, to prevent waste, no medical treatment is provided.

There are also labor camps for "marginal people": the so-called *min-kung*, that is, persons with poor labor discipline and others not properly employable because of social origin or previous punishments and therefore limited to unskilled labor. Occasionally large numbers of people are recruited in corvées for jobs requiring many hands, such as dam building. It also has been customary to send youngsters and unemployed into the countryside, and to send "volunteers" to settle along the northern borders where persons who resisted communism were driven "into the desert" to perish.

An individual's self-accusation may be used as the sole basis of court and administrative judgments. The defendant is not heard, and the presence of a defense lawyer is considered unnecessary in view of the self-accusation. The procedure is exactly the opposite of Western "due process of law." On the other hand, "honest" confessions of guilt are said to help the accused or the prisoner because they bespeak improvement in the culprit's attitude. Those sentenced to labor reform camps usually are given long sentences but told they may be allowed time off for good behavior.

The inmates of prisons and camps are periodically subjected to struggle sessions either because they violate discipline or because their thoughts are not reforming fast enough. The latter is taken for granted when prisoners petition the government and thus "prove" that they doubt the leniency of the authorities. Disciplinary punishments, such as solitary confinement in chains or with hands tied behind the back, are usually preceded by struggle sessions in which the other prisoners are allowed to vent their frustrations and hatreds.

Each of the different types of camps has a specific wage and ration level, usually with five sublevels. The inmates get paid and fed according to their work and their attitude. The deductions for feeding and housing also vary with their performance, often as determined or co-determined by the *hsiao-tsu* of which the inmate is a member. If persons fall sick, their food rations are cut, so that they often become sicker and die.

When finally released, many prisoners are not reintegrated into Chinese society. Few find jobs above the unskilled and hard labor level, and many return to camp voluntarily as a better alternative. The wives and children of inmates are also seldom able to find suitable employment. Many wives, sooner or later, are compelled to divorce their husbands, who lose contact with their children.

3. THE ROLE OF TORTURE IN THE CHINESE SYSTEM

True-believing Chinese communists may be inclined to regard their system as chiefly one of mental and psychological pressure and to discount torture as a factor within it. But the living conditions of prisoners and forced laborers include lack of hygiene, incessant hunger, a low calorie diet without proteins and vitamins, inadequate clothing, disease, occasional medical experimentation, and punishments in chains and in solitary confinement. Escaped prisoners have reported no apparent intent to break their bodies, although medical assistance was minimal and the seriously sick and old inmates were often left to die, in gross violation of Chinese tradition. Specifically psychological tortures included threats to and stimulated worries about relatives, isolation from outside contacts, participation in and victimization by struggle sessions, poor sanitary and hygienic conditions, constantly provoked friction among prisoners, strains and stresses imposed by unrealistic work quotas, unending mutual supervision by inmates and reformers, frequent orders to write confessions, repeated assault by alternating Pavlovian signals leading to confusion, the virtual absence of free time, and, perhaps worst of all, crowding and complete deprivation of privacy. Do the communists really think that brainwashing can produce reliable and enthusiastic revolutionaries? It does create anxious, timid, and helpless individuals—dead souls who approach the point of non-identity. It is possible that the promoters of brainwashing are unaware of the actual re-

sults. Could it be that they deliberately close their eyes?

D. The Human Toll of Chinese Communism

Forced labor with and without connections to labor reform camps has played a major role in the economy of communist China. During the Great Leap Forward—which probably marked the peak in Maoist reliance on forced labor—about 100 million persons were drafted to help build irrigation canals and furnaces for iron smelting in back yards. Large areas in Manchuria and along China's northern frontiers in inner Asia are said to have been developed by inmates of reform and re-education camps. But the uneconomic character of such widespread use of forced labor seems demonstrated by the fact that it was abandoned.

1. THE CHINESE BODY COUNT

We do not know exactly what the human cost of Chinese communism has been and it seems probable that the real numbers are not known even in Peking. As indicated in chapter 5, the significance of a "body count" should not be overestimated. China, since 1949, has experienced numerous uprisings and battles, as well as civil and international wars which unavoidably entail human losses, not all of which can be charged to the communists.

But what has been the death toll? On April 7, 1969, Radio Moscow asserted that between 1949 and 1965 "26.4 million people in China were exterminated" (Walker, 1971, p. 13). Radio Moscow is not any more trustworthy than the information services of the PRC. But experience has shown that when the two main communist powers attack one another, they usually are quite factual. The Moscow figure is smaller than that issued by the Government Information Office in Taipei, which charged on September 18, 1970, that 37 million Chinese had been liquidated between 1949 and 1963. A further major bloodletting took place between 1967 and 1970, since when calmer times have prevailed.

Nevertheless, the camps were not abolished. On May 30, 1967, Radio Moscow asserted that there were 18 million political prisoners in about 10,000 camps throughout mainland China. A 1955 UN report, however, had mentioned 25 million people in "regular labor camps" (presumably re-education camps were meant), plus an additional 12.5 million in corrective labor camps (thought-reform camps) (Walker, 1971, p. 18).

Using the best available sources, Richard Walker summarized and integrated the various estimates in a conservative fashion and arrived at a "range of estimates" for the casualties of communism in China up to 1970. The low estimate was 44.3 million; and the high estimate, 63.8 million.

Actually, Walker's figures on the losses that occurred in various ways during the cultural revolution (250,000 to 500,000 people) are ultraconservative: 1 to 2 million would still be a conservative estimate. Furthermore, the Gulag Archipelago of China has been continuing to operate at full blast. If we assume that its population was held constant at 18 million, which once again is conservative, and that the annual casualty rate in the camps was 5 percent instead of 10 percent as assumed by Walker, the death toll exacted by CCP campaigns, thought reform, forced labor, and terrorism would lie somewhere between 38 and 67 million; it is not difficult to arrive at substantially higher estimates.

This blood toll means that about 100,000 to 200,000 Chinese were killed by the communists every *month* during the period from 1949 to about 1970. While exact statistics on recent political killings in China are lacking, a late 1977 report indicates that the overthrow of the "Gang of Four" was followed by a countrywide purge of "counterrevolutionaries" with executions running well into the thousands.

Republic of China intelligence sources report that remnants of the "Gang" faction have assassinated more the 100 communist cadres in an effort to stem the purge, including rector Chou Tsung-yun of Chekiang University and Chao Chiang, party secretary of the Chekiang Provincial Public Security Bureau (*To the Point International*, December 19, 1977, p. 12).

The psychological effects of this wholesale slaughter are aggravated by strains on relations with families and friends. Since, as we have seen, much of this killing arose from mutual criticism and struggle sessions between people who knew each other well and in many cases were neighbors, China's reservoir of mutual hostility and desire for revenge must be enormous. Resentments are intensified by the fact that people were condemned for thoughts which later became sanctified and that all groups in China have been struggling against one another in the name of Mao's thoughts. "The Red flag opposes the Red flag" was a *Maoist* formula used to describe events during the cultural revolution.

2. THE DESTRUCTION OF PERSONALITY

In Chinese society today, many actions of *purely private* life may get persons into trouble, such as pregnancies below the age of 25. No one is safe from denunciation by friends and close relatives who either are forced to denounce or who are anxious to save themselves from grief. Informers and spies are used systematically to break down the cohesiveness of primary and other groups, families and clans in particular (Frank, 1973, p. 95).

A new defense mechanism which Whyte (1974, p. 230) calls the "encapsulation of individuals" has made its appearance. The incessant interplay between assaults on the individual, overcrowding, defensive reactions, and carefully nurtured guilt feelings in an atmosphere of all-pervasive uncertainty and anxiety must result in serious personal and interpersonal stress. Such stress often leads to neurosis; and if "it exceeds . . . adaptive capacity," it may result in neuropysychiatric breakdowns (*ibid.*, p. 25). Wholesale stress and breakdown affect a whole country, perhaps in a fashion not altogether attractive to the rulers.

The Maoists were often able to win enemy soldiers to their side. In a country with widespread illiteracy, numerous languages, and (in earlier decades) lack of mass media, it was natural for them to merge propaganda with agitation, and both with group "study," and to link "teaching" to tension, detention, and terrorism. This led them inevitably to Pavlov, his controlled environment, his stimuli, and his second (verbal) signalling system. Chinese brainwashing is also reminiscent of religious practices involving ecstasy, hypnosis, and other abnormal psychological states.

Brainwashing (with its related features such as crowding, hunger, rhythmic chanting, speech in chorus, and work to exhaustion) puts the individual under stress. The effects depend on the strength of the person's nervous system and on the nature and intensity of the stress imposed. A superficial student of Pavlovism might assume that a conditioned reflex can be stabilized through the protracted application of a fairly strong and invariant stimulus, and this is quite correct; yet, the image of the dog hearing the bell and promptly salivating is too simple.

There is a tolerance to stress, as Pavlov's dog experiments showed. Once this threshold is passed, uncontrolled excitement intervenes which is followed by the brain's applying "protective inhibition," which has profound effects on behavior.

Cerebral inhibition comes in three phases: the equivalent phase, in which humans "display no more pleasure on receipt of a five pound note than on that of a sixpence"; the paradoxical phase, in which the sixpence might give greater pleasure than a thousand pounds; and the ultraparadoxical phase, in which "positive conditional patterns suddenly become negative, and *vice versa*," e.g., a person may smile

at an overwhelming disaster (Sargant, 1967, p. 114).

Sir Charles Sherrington, the outstanding physiologist of his time, observed one of Pavlov's experiments in which an ultraparadoxical phase was produced. Sherrington exclaimed that he now understood "how it was possible physiologically for the Christian martyrs to die happily, even when . . . being burnt at the stake, and sometimes without any apparent suffering" (Sargant, 1974, p. 72). If brainwashing results in a ultraparadoxical state, it may be followed by "sudden complete switch-overs from one strong human emotion, or doctrine, to a diametrically opposed one" (Sargant, 1967, 114).

Thus, carefully applied stress beyond the tolerance threshold can accomplish conversions and even transference, including even a positive attitude toward the persons practicing the conditioning, such as the Maoist brainwashers or the police in Kafka's *The Trial*.

> When a man's nervous system is subjected to such a degree of strain that his brain can no longer respond normally . . . he will become very much more suggestible than in his normal state of mind, far more open to ideas and people . . . and far less able to respond to them with caution, doubt, criticism and scepticism. . . . He may reach a condition in which he is as meekly obedient to commands and suggestions as someone under hypnosis, who can be made to behave in ways which, when in command of himself, he would reject as foolish or immoral and, by post-hypnotic suggestion, he can be made to act in these ways even after he has been brought out of trance and apparently restored to normal waking consciousness (Sargant, 1974, pp. 194f.).

The culmination and the goal of brainwashing are acceptance and obedience. The totalitarian regime thus achieves the uniformity of belief and complete responsiveness to government orders it considers essential for its own "immortality."

Self-identification of all fully conditioned individuals—their "I's," or egos, and their wills—would be quashed and self-expression and individual self-determination would be replaced by command behavior. "Alienation" would reach its peak, and psychological genocide would have been accomplished.

It is important to grasp this—implicit—goal of totalitarian brainwashing: once *psychological genocide* is understood, the true nature of totalitarianism and the torments it inflicts will become apparent. Totalitarianism must not be confused with authoritarian government which concentrates decision-making power but does not assert total control over the individual. A totalitarian government thinks of itself as being omnipresent, omnipotent, omniscient, and divinely wise, while its subjects are tools and robots. It does *not* aim at remaking the subject in the likeness of the deified leader—that would be dangerous. Instead, it seeks to suppress and ultimately extinguish individual personality.

E. Limits and Weaknesses of Totalitarianism

Totalitarianism carried to the extreme is destroyed by its own contradictions. Its breakdown has seven aspects.

(1) Not everybody can be brainwashed: there are not enough "washers," certainly not enough effective "washers," and few can devote enough time for a thorough job. Hence, only a low percentage of the population can be given the treatment. Among the ruling class, most of whose members are able to avoid the ordeal, the percentage is even smaller. Selection of victims is strongly influenced by personal enmities and grudges and is hence both haphazard and discriminatory.

Mass brainwashing devices—like parades, long marches, campaigns, and struggle meetings—impose a great deal of stress but they fall short of true brainwashing in that the ultraparadoxical phase is rarely reached.

(2) The vulnerability of individuals to the brainwash treatment varies with physical and nervous strength and with character or personality type. Quite a few people cannot be reconditioned. Many additional victims shake off the command suggestions even though they cannot always restore their thought processes to their former energy and efficiency levels.

(3) Benefits are nevertheless limited when treatment is effective and the command suggestions have taken root: persons under hypnosis or in a posthypnotic condition operate at a low mental tension. Complex tasks cannot be solved so long as mental energy is disrupted. True, the inner tension needed to oppose the tyranny would be lacking, too, and this would be an advantage to the despot. But persons in the condition of "other-directness" are suitable largely for unskilled jobs and they lack the capability, although they may possess the talent, for innovation and creativity. The more brainwashing is successful, the more the progress of society will be inhibited. The weight of effective brainpower thus shifts to the potential opposition: the "unwashed."

(4) Suppose, furthermore, that suggestibility is attained: the subsequent and more difficult problem is to find the commands suitable for exploiting the psychological opportunity. The difficulties are manifold:

(a) Slogans don't help much unless they are given concrete task-oriented meanings by individuals operating with the high inner tension of which brainwashing deprives them.

(b) The commands must be realistic and their execution feasible. This requires knowledge and prescience which is simply not available to the "washers" who must restrict themselves to generalities. The operation thus generates much ado about nothing.

(c) That slogans and commands are changed frequently to adjust to new and unexpected situations should come as no surprise. *If* brainwashing were effective, different groups of "brainwashees" must have been conditioned at different times to implement contemporary party lines. Insofar as command suggestions made lasting imprints, the social class struggle would be replaced by a struggle among groups of differently conditioned "Maoists." Yet switching of signals was the method Pavlov used to produce artificial neurosis. The constant switching by the Maoists cannot fail to spread neurosis throughout the population. Will this result immortalize the "People's Republic?"

(5) Whether or not suggestibility is attained and utilized, stress is produced strongly upon those who are left *outside* the camps and maximally upon those incarcerated in forced and corrective labor camps. Under conditions of Chinese brainwashing, stress is interrelated with crowding. The latter narrows the scope of individual privacy, thus aggravating anxiety and mutual hostility. The existence of universal stress provokes a "survival of the fittest" phenomenon reminiscent of Darwin rather than Marx.

(6) Stress has far-reaching medical effects, such as heart disease, hypertension, migraine, ulcers, colitis, diabetes, allergies, arthritis, etc. During World War II, Japanese PW camps imposed far heavier *psychological* stress than German camps. The mortality in German camps (which were by no means gentle) was less than one percent, while the mortality rate in Japanese camps was one in three (Wolff, 1953, quoted in McQuade and Aikman, 1974, pp. 12f). Stress also caused accident proneness and a high suicide rate—which were three and two times higher, respectively, in the Japanese camps.

(7) In the psychological sphere, stress leads to anxiety, often to neurosis, and to something Pavlov called "pan-phobia," which is little else than complete inhibition. Since stress also tends to produce disorders in the endocrine system, it can result in severe mental disease. The imposition of stress on a mass scale hardly contributes to the efficient functioning of society (see Selye, 1950, 1956a and 1956b).

1. PAVLOV REVISITED

Pavlov himself could hardly have believed that, as a tool to ensure political permanence, brainwashing would work. The whole *hsi nao* effort is, in fact, based upon a wildly reductionist reading of Pavlov's findings.

Pavlov dealt not only with conditioned but also with unconditioned reflexes, such as those involving food and sex. Superficial thinking about Pavlov tends to focus on the reflexes related to strictly physical survival. Since the target person can be expected to comply if submission is the price of continued eating and living, political conditioning by a coercive system appears feasible.

But Pavlov discovered reflexes which do *not* fit this pattern. In the first place, he was quite aware that not all animals can be conditioned easily or at all. He worked with dogs because he knew that cats, for example, would not play the game. Furthermore, he discovered that some dogs cannot be conditioned effectively and that there are differences in the "conditionability" of various breeds. He studied the strength of the nervous system and canine typology, and discovered defensive, inhibitory, self-curative, and aggressive reflexes which are more or less incompatible with conditioning.

Pavlov's single most important contribution was the discovery of the *freedom reflex*. This discovery was due to a dog which could not be conditioned because it "would not remain quiet so long as its movements were constrained." The dog's freedom reflex was finally overcome through the alimentary reflex. In other cases, the freedom reflex was extinguished through electric shocks, by switching signals to create neuroses, and through other shock and stress methods.

It turned out to be most difficult, and usually impossible, to restore the freedom reflex once it was strongly inhibited. It is not feasible to transform a docile dog into one with an active freedom reflex (Drabovich, 1934, p. 57). Nor can a freedom reflex be produced artificially.

Was Pavlov mixing politics with reflexology? Not at all. He regarded the freedom reflex as obviously "one of the most important reflexes or . . . reactions of any living being." "Without a reflex protest against restriction of an animal's movements, any insignificant obstacle in its way would interfere with the performance of certain of its important functions. . . . In some animals the freedom reflex is so strong that when placed in captivity they reject food, pine away and die" (Pavlov, 1955, p. 184).

Pavlov discussed the freedom reflex in connection with the investigative reflex—the "what-is-it?" reflex.

It also belongs to the fundamental reflexes and is responsible for the fact that given the slightest change in the surrounding world both man and animals immediately orientate their respective receptor organs towards the agent evoking the change. The biological significance of this reflex is enormous. If the animal were not provided with this reaction, its life, one may say, would always hang by a thread. In man this reflex is highly developed, manifesting itself in the form of an inquisitiveness which gives birth to scientific thought, ensuring for us a most reliable and unrestricted orientation in the surrounding world (*ibid.*, pp. 184f.).

The freedom reflex is not given much publicity by the communists, but Pavlov's discussion has not been censured and it does appear in his books printed and reprinted at Moscow. Paradoxically, the freedom reflex was ignored by leading Western psychologists of Pavlov's time, including Wundt, Ribot, Hoeffding, and Ebbinghaus. They also ignored its opposite, the servility reflex. Both reflexes are still kept buried by reductionists.

2. THE HUMAN FREEDOM REFLEX, PSYCHOTHERAPY, AND BRAINWASHING

Among humans the freedom reflex presumably occurs in varying intensities and manifests itself with different strengths against diverse forms of obstruction and coercion. If the freedom reflex were extinguished—which may be feasible, according to Pavlov's experiments—society as a whole would operate at a low level of nervous and cerebral energy. But it is not likely that the freedom reflex can be wholly eliminated. There will always be enough people who escape brainwashing or resist its impact. Others will manage to shake off the inhibitory effects of the treatment. Often, subjects will adapt by pretending compliance. Brainwashing, in brief, collides with human nature—that is, with unconditioned reflexes, as identified by Pavlov. The preordained failure of totalitarian systems constitutes the hope for humanity to survive the ordeal of oppression.

Psychotherapy has been practiced by all societies, in one form or the other, and is a legitimate branch of medicine and/or religion. Pavlov is not the only modern contributor whose insights need to be used if an effective program of societal psychotherapy is to be undertaken. For example, Jean Piaget has disproved the old empiricist-materialist view that the mind and knowledge acquired by it are a "passive copy of reality." Thinking is active discovery. It is now known that humans are far more autonomous and self-governing than was previously supposed (Maslow, 1970, p. 77). Precisely this finding would not have startled Pavlov, who knew so much about the freedom reflex.

There are, according to Maslow, seven kinds of psychotherapy, including suggestion by authority and catharsis, which with some license may be regarded as mild elements of brainwashing. Despite vast differences in approach, they all aim implicitly or explicitly at restoring "the person to the path of self-actualization and of development along the lines that his inner nature dictates" (*ibid.*, pp. 242–44, 270). Their goal is individuation and *not* collective directed behavior, let alone uniformization—even though a psychotherapist sometimes yields to his Pygmalion impulse.

Brainwashing, by definition, negates self-actualization, partly because it downgrades the unconditional reflexes (or needs) in favor of conditioned reflexes; partly because its conditioning suspends critical consciousness, judgment, volition, and self-generated thought; and partly because persons diminished by brainwashing and related inhibitors lose the desire for discovery and much of their motivation, initiative, and creativity. By rupturing human relationships, brainwashing frustrates vital and unextinguishable needs and therefore is pathogenic. It contributes to an accumulation of self-rejection, hatred, aggressiveness, and self-destruction.

A good society cannot be created by blocking and partly suppressing the higher mental functions. Psychological health requires that individuation and self-actualization not be frustrated by discriminatory denials of needs, by thwarting of satisfactory interpersonal relationships, and by the suppression of human diversity. If brainwashing really did work, it would freeze social and intellectual development.

Pathogenic psychological and intellectual treatment is not restricted to communist China but can be found all over the world. Wherever it occurs it must be classified as a major crime against humanity. Maslow wrote:

> The key concepts in the newer dynamic psychology are spontaneity, release, naturalness, self-choice, self-acceptance, impulse-awareness, gratification of basic needs. They *used* to be control, inhibition, discipline, training, shaping, on the principle that the depths of human nature were dangerous, evil, predatory, and ravenous. Education, family training, bringing up children, acculturation in general were all seen as a process of bringing the darker forces within us under control. (*Ibid.*, p. 279)

A warning is in order, however, that a total lack of discipline may be as psychologically destructive as too much discipline. The effects of modern reductionist educational methods in so-called affluent societies, where total permissiveness is the watchword, are surprisingly similar to those produced by brainwashing. Child and adolescent behavior is characterized by refusal to accept challenges, flat emotionality, poor communicatory ability, lack of solidarity, poor endurance in work, underdeveloped willingness to learn, weak self-discipline, brutality and aggressivity, pleasure in noise, rhythm, ecstasy, and intoxication. Their correlates—such as lassitude, lack of interest, indolence, inability to study, lack of orientation, weak critical sense, poor judgment, flabby self-direction, poor evaluation and contempt of self and others, and low creativity—combine to create a syndrome that is expressed in lower student performance in schools and colleges. (For a discussion of the same problem in West Germany, see Friedrich, 1975.)

Maslow may be too optimistic: dark forces do exist, and they are particularly rampant in an age when humankind has discovered all kinds of new techniques in the physical as well as behavioral sciences but has not yet created the institutions to assure their constructive use. But it is not unlikely that the perpetrators of massive political crime, such as genocide and menticide (including brainwashing), are moved by self-hatred, propelled to paroxysm through systematized and organized autistic ideas. Such people and their emissaries should not be regarded as socially acceptable in civilized society.

Bibliographical Note

For general information on Chinese and other brainwashing see Edward Hunter, *Brainwashing in Red China*, New York, Vanguard, 1951; Robert J. Lifton, *Thought Reform and the Psychology of Totalism, A Study of "Brainwashing" in China*, New York, Norton, 1961; Martin King

Whyte, *Small Groups and Political Rituals in China*, Berkeley, University of California Press, 1974. See also Joost A. M. Meerloo, *The Rape of the Mind*, New York, World Publishing Company, 1956; Theodor Reik, *The Compulsion to Confess*, New York, Farrar, Straus & Cudahy, 1959; Stefan T. Possony, *The Revolution of Madness*, Taipei, Institute of International Relations, 1971; and Bao Ruo-Wang (Jean Pasqualini) and Rudolph Chelminski, *Prisoner of Mao*, New York, Coward, McCann and Geohegan, 1973. Most of these writings present elaborate bibliographies. For the soviet technique, see F. Beck and W. Godin, *Russian Purge and the Extraction of Confession*, New York, Viking, 1951. On Vietnam consult Robert F. Turner, *Vietnamese Communism*, Stanford, Cal., Hoover Institution Press, 1975, pp. 76, 115–21, 144–46, 160. Concerning "struggle" in Red China, see Ken Ling, *The Revenge of Heaven: Journal of a Young Chinese*, New York, Putnam, 1972. This book resulted from interrogations of Chinese refugees and defectors undertaken by Ivan D. London and Miryam London; Ken Ling, who wrote a manuscript of 500,000 Chinese characters, is the pseudonym of a Chinese refugee. The English text was prepared on the basis of this manuscript by Miryam London and Ta-Ling Lee. The first chapter, entitled "Cow Ghosts and Snake Demons," and part of the second chapter report on struggle sessions against the teachers of a high school in Amoy.

For the Pavlovian aspect of totalitarianism, see W. Drabovitch, *Fragilité de la Liberté et Séduction des Dictatures*, Paris, Mercure de France, 1934, p. 57. Drabovitch worked for a long time in Pavlov's Institute of Experimental Medicine and combined the findings of Pavlov with those of Pierre Janet who wrote the preface to Drabovitch's book. Janet contributed the insights on psychological and mental energy and tension.

27

EXTERMINATION OF PRIMITIVE COMMUNITIES

An important item in the catalog of crimes against humanity is the extermination of primitive communities. Sometimes the disappearance of primitive tribes is the inevitable result of a clash between cultures millennia apart in relative time. All too often, however, it is at least in part the result of deliberate policy or neglect.

The decimation of American Indians reflected the universal tendency of high-density, developed cultures to crowd out lower-density, lesser developed cultures—without which the New World and the British overseas dominions would never have been Europeanized. The expanded high-density culture is, as Toynbee has pointed out (1949, ch. 11), subject to counterattack—which may be ideological as well as military. So far as the colonists in the Americas, Australia, New Zealand, and South Africa were concerned, the lands on which they settled were vacant, since the indigenes did not hold it as private property. The notion of a right to use based on non-ownership or common ownership—apart from the specifically demarcated commons of peasant villages—was foreign to European thinking. It is doubtful that the Indians knew what they were selling when they "sold" Manhattan Island to the Dutch for trinkets worth $24.

The Indians in the United States were treated as racial and cultural outsiders and subjected to complex discrimination, including forced sale or cession of Indian lands and a number of forced migrations. Alcohol contributed greatly to their downfall; despite strongly worded laws against selling liquor to Indians, they were able to obtain it easily in the chaotic society of a moving frontier. President Martin Van Buren (elected 1836), more charitable than his predecessor Andrew Jackson (*vide* the latter's refusal to enforce John Marshall's decision upholding the Cherokees), said that he thought the Indians' cause just but could not do anything about it.

A Bureau of Indian Affairs was established in the War Department in 1824; it presided over the removal of most eastern Indians to new "homes" west of the Mississippi. The "Indian threat" had largely subsided by 1849, and the Bureau was transferred to the Department of the Interior. But continued settlement west of the Mississippi led to the Plains Indian Wars of the 1850s and 1860s, and a demarcation of boundaries was needed to assure the separation that both sides desired. By the late 1860s, almost all western Indian tribes had made treaties with the United States, ceding vast tracts of land and receiving promises of food, clothing, health care, guarantees of reservation boundaries, and—most important—self-determination. But in 1871 the Indians were downgraded as the result of a House-Senate quarrel; the House wanted a voice in Indian affairs, which, being regulated by treaty, were the prerogative of the Senate alone. The Appropriations Act of that year contained a "rider" which read: "Hereafter, no Indian nation or tribe within the territory of the United States shall be acknowledged or recognized as an independent tribe or power with whom the United States may contract by treaty." From then on, the U.S. government legislated rather than negotiated on Indian affairs; Indian civil and property rights were often diminished without even consultation (Svensson, 1973, pp. 17–22).

It was not until the Hoover and F. D. Roosevelt Administrations that major corrective measures to assure the Indians their habitats and to some extent their own cultures were adopted. The present situation of American Indians remains far from satisfactory, but space does not permit an addition to the account already given in chapter 11,H4.

A. Extermination through Economic Extinction— the Aché of Paraguay

As pointed out in the final section of chapter 21, the worst form of economic discrimination against a nation, tribe, or ethnic group is to deprive it of its means of livelihood. If the victims are unable to find an alternative base of subsistence, they may submit to outright slavery or to peonage that is close to slavery. If economic deprivation is accompanied by cultural alienation—even though the latter be administered by well-meaning missionaries intent on stamping out paganism and saving souls—those affected may lose their will to live, succumbing all the more easily to the diseases of the "higher" culture.

Such a policy of economic extinction has been and is still being employed to "solve the Indian problem" in several Latin-American countries. An "Indian problem" exists because land wanted for settlement by modernizing societies is occupied by tribes with an economy and culture based on hunting or on swidden (slash and burn) crop raising. The "solution" therefore is to wipe out the Indian communities. If this process yields slaves or workers who can be held to subsistence or below-subsistence wages, the advance of "civilization" is thereby expedited.

A case in point is that of the Aché Indians of eastern Paraguay, whose fate has been observed on the spot and described in detail by the German anthropologist Mark Münzel (1973). Relations between the Aché and the Paraguayans (as well as European explorers and settlers) have been hostile from first contact. An account of an early Aché hunt reads as follows:

They had followed the traces of the Aché (in 1907), and they reached the Indians the very first evening of their journey. . . . They arrived at the camp of the Aché, slaughtered 7 women and children, and caught 7 small children. When leaving the next morning, they got into a dispute about the direction of their return. The captured children cried and lamented; their mothers, hidden in the forest, called for them. The manhunters felt threatened, although they had burnt all the bows and arrows left behind in the camp by the fleeing Achés. In his excitement and fear, Elijio Zarza, the (local) police chief, gave the order to cut the throats of all the children, so that their lamentations would not reveal to the Indians where the Paraguayans were. All his men except Rosario Mora obeyed. The latter brought to his home the little girl he had seized. But he was not allowed to keep her. She was brought up to the house of police sergeant Evangelista Hurtado in Jesús Trinidad. (H. Baldus, Anthropos 66 (3–4): 465–529; cited by Münzel, 1973, p. 5)

Although the Aché will fight to defend their forest, their families, and their freedom, they become very tame when captured, and are obedient laborers—perhaps because success in capturing invests the captors with a degree of authority. The hunting and selling of Aché became and remains an important branch of the economy in outlying eastern Paraguay. The Münzels interviewed an adult slave who had been captured as a small boy together with his sister by hunters who killed their father and raped their mother; both were sold. When his sister became pregnant, her owners put her out on the street and she could only reenter slavery (necessary to avoid starvation) by giving away her baby. One of the most aggressive slave hunters was a certain Pichín López, who, according to a 1959 UPI report, brought back 40 Aché in chains for public sale in the town of San Juan Nepomucano. As Münzel relates:

In 1961, the Italo-Paraguayan zoologist Dr. L. MIRAGLIA, who on his many research trips came to know the Paraguayan hinterland quite well, wrote: "In the villages near the Guayakí (Aché) area, there are slave traders who organize veritable manhunts for these aborigines. They catch a Guayakí (Aché) family by surprise, murder the parents, and carry off the children to sell them." How these hunts are executed, we are told by ALBOSPINO, then head of the Paraguayan Indigenist Association, a semi-official organization that includes national figures interested in Indian questions: "With the 'mboca-ñuhá,' a trap made of a firearm that is hidden in the woods and that fires automatically when the victim passes; with poisoned meals; with 'senuelos' (Aché Indians captured during childhood and sent into the forest as adults, in order to attract their brethren). . . . They put on their trail Indian scouts from other tribes or dogs." In 1960, the Paraguayan Indigenist Association declared that the Aché of the Villarica zone "are on their way to extinction, because of cruel persecution by the whites." (1973, pp. 7–8.)

Münzel quotes prominent Paraguayans, who in 1960 counted 22 Aché slaves in the Tavaí district and 51 in the Department of Guairá.

An office of Indian Protection was founded in 1950 under the leadership of the scientist León Cadogan, whose efforts led to 1957 and 1958 decrees intended to protect the Aché. Their legal rights as persons were recognized, and the hunting and selling of Indian children was declared a crime punishable under the penal code. Pichín López fled to avoid prosecution.

Yet the situation of the Aché did not improve. Indian affairs were placed under military control, and major highways cutting through the principal Aché territory were completed in 1965 and 1968. Settlers, cattle farmers, and speculators seized an increasing proportion of the land, which was treated as "vacant" since the Indians held no title from the Spaniards or the Creoles. Paraguayan land policy was following a precedent laid down a century earlier by U.S. Secretary of State John M. Clayton, who wrote in 1850:

We have never acknowledged, and can never acknowledge, the existence of any claim of sovereignty in . . . any . . . Indian in America. . . . Having always regarded an Indian title as a mere right of occupancy we can never agree that such a title should be treated otherwise than as a thing to be extinguished at the will of the discoverer of the country. (In Gorinsky, 1969)

Raids and massacres against the Aché continued into 1972, the year in which the Münzels gathered their data. "They are hunted; they are pursued like animals," the Paraguayan anthropologist Chase Sardi declared. "The parents are killed and the children sold . . . and there is no family of which a child has not been murdered." Aché children became a glut on the slave market, and the price of a five-year-old girl fell to aroung $5.00.

One of the largest raids was mounted from the "Naranjito" estate of a certain Mr. Parini in August 1971, shortly after that *haciendado* had been visited by Colonel Infanzón, head of the Native Affairs Department. Parini's foreman Marcial Enciso contracted some professional Aché killers and the party set forth armed with machetes. "There were between 12 and 20 killed, some of them most probably the mothers of kidnapped children. At least five small children were captured alive." Of these, at least two died within a few months after capture. (Münzel, 1973, p. 16)

The official solution to the "problem" found by the Paraguayan government was to create a reservation. The person placed in charge of this operation was Jesús Pereira, a slave trader and a junior partner of Pichín López. He acquired this function through a chain of circumstances. In 1959 a band of Ache, deprived of their hunting grounds and in fear of other slave traders, surrendered to Pereira on his farm at Torrín. Since the climate for selling slaves had become unhealthy, Pereira asked the Native Affairs Department for financial aid to support these Aché. The Department, apparently thinking the best way to control Pereira was to co-opt him, placed him on the payroll and his farm was renamed "Camp Blessed Roque Gonzalez of the Holy Ghost." Pereira proceeded to rob the inmates of all their weapons and ornaments and thereafter diverted part of the food sent from Asunción for the Indians, selling it for his private profit. Of the 100 Aché on the reservation in 1962, 25 died within a year of disease and malnutrition—there being no medical care whatever. Münzel attributes persistent decline in the reservation's population to nondistribution of available food.

The reservation was moved in 1970 to be closer to the remaining free Aché it was hoped to "attract." Its population statistics show a remarkable shortage of young girls, indicating that the sale of human beings continues. Several of the remaining girls live in Pereira's house and are available to him and his friends; others are taken away from their husbands and given to "tame" Aché men who participate in his manhunting expeditions. The only way the reservation population can be maintained is through capture, since no Aché in his right mind would go there.

After a raid of October 1970 had produced 47 new inmates, a newly founded Aid Commission—later called the Guayakí (Aché) Indian Aid Commission (GAIC)—conducted a fund-raising campaign in Asunción and claimed, at least, to have shipped important quantities of supplies. But a medical commission that visited the reservation in February 1971, after the Bishop of Coronel Oviedo had sent the President of Paraguay a report indicating that the Indians were not receiving the supplies donated for them, found that half of the October 1970 contingent were no longer there. Münzel concludes that at least some were victims of "the conscious withholding of food and medicine" (1973, p. 49).

In September and October 1971, Münzel recorded on tape the plans of "tame" Aché for a further manhunt. A portion reads:

First, we shall go far away by truck; then, far away from here, we'll descend to hunt the "Guayaki," and we'll take them with us, seizing them by the arms. We'll fall upon them in the night, we'll extinguish their fires, we'll knock them down. The damned women who will not like to be deported by truck, we'll make them run along until they collapse on the soil. It will be necessary to brutally fracture the arm of wild Krymbégi (the chief of the band these hunters were to capture), to make him come with us. Krymbégi will roar in pain; we'll have to strike him down with a machete. Krymbégi will roar in pain.

This hunt was unsuccessful, but the Münzels witnessed the departure of Pereira's party for another hunt which captured a band of some 80 Achés on March 6, 1972. They were able to interview a number of this group, despite Pereira's threat to kill anyone who talked. After the Münzels had collected further documentation and had launched a publicity campaign, the matter was brought before the United Nations Human Rights Commission. The scandal provoked an uproar in Paraguay, and Pereira was actually imprisoned—only to be set free after two weeks. He is said to have moved his "tame" Aché to a new site (*Observer*, London, March 25, 1973).

A disturbing aspect of this episode is the

participation of prominent German and American businessmen in the whitewashing operations of the GAIC. Those involved are the President of the Commission, Managing Director Milan Zeman of Hoechst del Paraguay; its Vice President, Managing Director Clemens von Thueman of the Paraguayan plastic company "r pppp"; and Thomas Holt, the American managing director of the Paraguay branch of the Bank of America. It was only after these three had visited the reservation after the March 6, 1972, raid and had given Pereira's operations a clean bill of health that the "arrival" of 80 Aché was publicly announced. As Herr Zeman mentioned to Dr. Münzel, Hoechst del Paraguay had a "scientific plan" of appearing in the Asunción newspapers at least once a week. His share in the GAIC whitewash appears to have been part of that plan.

B. Extermination of Indians in Central and Northern South America

The Aché of Paraguay are only one small tribe among a rather large population of South American Indians who retain their traditional cultures and who have faced, and to a large extent continue to face, extreme forms of oppression. These Indians, referred to as the Indigenos to distinguish them from people of Indian descent who have been to a greater or lesser extent Europeanized (such as the Aymaras and Quechuas of the Andes and the Guarani of Paraguay), have been estimated to number 800,000 and are located, for the most part, in the Amazon Basin and its various tributaries. Their social history has been summarized by Hugh O'Shaughnessy as follows:

Since the arrival of the Spaniards and the Portuguese at the beginning of the sixteenth century the response of the aborigine to European encroachment has primarily been one of helpless passivity.

Slaughtered gratuitously by conquerors, killed off slowly by slave labour, or ravaged by new diseases imported from Europe, the original inhabitants of both the advanced civilizations such as the Aztec and Inca empires and the more primitive societies . . . saw their populations fall drastically. Darcy Ribeiro in his book, *The Americas and Civilization* (Allen & Unwin, 1971), quotes figures to indicate that the original population of the more advanced civilizations fell from something between 70 million and 88 million at the time of Columbus to around 3½ million by the middle of the seventeenth century. . . . But even though many aboriginals escaped the direct domination of the European, only the most isolated and remote groups could escape the measles, influenza, smallpox, malaria and yellow fever brought from the Old World and against which they had no defense. (Today, the common cold, and the TB which frequently follows, is probably their worst health hazard). (1973, p. 9)

Despite their lack of modern weapons, the Indigenos met the incursions of the Spaniards and later of the Europeanized Latin-Americans with armed resistance from time to time. For the most part, however, the Indigenos retreated into the remote interior of South America, where for a long time penetration seemed unprofitable for the Europeans and Europeanized settlers (*ibid.*, p. 10).

Recently, however, population pressure and the drive to exploit natural resources have combined to raise new threats to the forest peoples. Reuters reported from Rio De Janeiro in December 1971 that experts on Indian affairs "consider a major clash almost inevitable following an attack by a 200-strong Indian war party on a jungle outpost of the National Indian Foundation (FUNAI) near the Brazilian border with Bolivia." FUNAI blamed this and similar incidents on the actions of tin and diamond prospectors and squatters, and Reuters quoted the *Jornal do Brasil* as saying there were 10,000 armed prospectors in the jungles of northern Brazil. Similar attacks against missionaries and explorers for minerals have been reported from the other countries sharing the Amazon Basin (O'Shaughnessy, p. 12).

Like the vanished original population of the West Indies, the Amerindians of South America have some immunity to local diseases, but none whatever to those brought in by outsiders. Experience indicates that the first contact with whites or Mestizos leads to a 50 percent mortality among the aborigines from viral infections alone (Gorinsky, 1969). The problem is aggravated by the insistence of missionaries that the Indians don clothing in the name of "decency." Left to their own devices, primitive tribes tend to adopt whatever costumes are most healthy—which in damp tropical climates is none at all or as little as possible. The near-total coverage demanded by a repressive "morality" inhibits natural ventilation and evaporation of sweat, thus increasing sensitivity to sudden temperature changes and the tendency to contract respiratory diseases. The common cold and tuberculosis are the greatest killers in the Amazon valley (O'Shaughnessy, p. 9). Bodley (1972, p. 7) found that measles was the greatest single cause of death among the Campa of eastern Peru.

The unhealthiness of European-style clothing is compounded by the fact that the second-hand garments contributed by well-meaning church members in Europe and America are seldom or never sterilized. The Amerindians thus acquire their wardrobes complete with germs against which they have no defenses and like the French literary heroine Virginie, who refused to leave her cabin during a shipwreck because too scantily clad, become unsung *sacrifices à la pudeur*. It is charged that the distribution of infected clothing is sometimes deliberate—or in any case undertaken without regard to consequences. The conservative Brazilian *Jornal da Tarde* has published photographs of Paracanan Indians in the Amazon forests receiving used clothing from a "pacification" expedition. Referring to the danger of infection, the paper comments: "by the end of the pacification work, some 50% of the tribe will have died." A Brazilian Ministry of the Interior report of 1968, after noting an attack on the

Cintas Largas Indians with sticks of dynamite dropped from airplanes, reports that two Patcho tribes were exterminated by giving them smallpox injections (Lennon, 1972).

1. DEMOGRAPHIC AND SOCIOECONOMIC FACTORS

The major surviving Amerindian groups may be enumerated roughly as follows (O'Shaughnessy, 1973, p. 11; Bodley, 1972; Arcand, 1972):

Bolivia: about 83,000, in tribes ranging from the 20,000 Chiquitanos to the seven remaining members of the Jora group.

Brazil: between 68,100 and 99,700 as estimated by Darcy Ribeiro in his *Fronteras indigenas de la civilización*, the largest linguistic groups being the Tupi (10,450 to 14,350), Arawak (11,000 to 16,150), and Carib (10,250 to 14,150). But in 1972 the Aborigines Protection Society found 77,000 Indians under the guardianship of FUNAI (discussed briefly below), with another possible 100,000 outside.

Colombia: 150,000 or possibly more—several government estimates are considerably higher. Among them may be mentioned the 70,000-odd Guambiana and Paez, who have become politically radicalized to the point where the Colombian Army deployed its antiguerrilla forces, and the hunting and food-gathering Cuiva, whose few remaining bands face extinction.

Ecuador: between 25,000 and 50,000—a very rough estimate in default of accurate statistics. The largest tribe in Ecuador are the Jivaros, who defend themselves with blowguns, spears, and rifles and discourage incursions by shrinking the heads of their slain enemies to keep as trophies (Crist, 1964, p. 5).

Guyana: an estimated 33,000, mostly in the southern parts of the country.

Peru: about 250,000, mostly located on reservations managed by the Native Forest Communities Division of the Ministry of

Agriculture. Among them are the 20,000 Campa, to be mentioned subsequently.

Paraguay: an estimated 58,877 in six linguistic families and 198 tribes. This figure does not include the largely Westernized Guarani, who form three quarters of Paraguay's population.

Venezuela: some 100,000 Indigenos, the largest group being Goajiros in the Maracaibo region (40,000) and the Orinoco Delta (12,000).

Smaller groups are to be found in the remoter areas of Argentina, Chile, and Panama.

The encounter between the Amerindians and the modernizing societies of South America could hardly have happened without a degree of economic conflict—reflecting in many ways the dispossession of North American Indians that attended the settlement of the United States. Conflicts of this kind have their roots in the fact that the land and resources of this planet are limited, whereas natural limitations to human fertility do not exist or have not been reached. The Indian societies of South America all follow extensive land-use patterns: hunting and gathering foods that grow without cultivation or slash-and-burn agriculture. Either of these two patterns—and especially the former—requires frequent migration over a rather large area. Population pressure and the need for intensive exploitation of resources to combat persistent poverty have forced the European-style societies of South America to expand into hitherto unpenetrated jungles. It would therefore be unrealistic to demand that all indigenous tribes—in South America or anywhere else in the world—be left in undisturbed possession of all the land they ever occupied. The problem is, rather, that of achieving a reasonable compromise of rights and interests. The point of departure for such a compromise is recognition that both sides have rights and that limited resources must be shared.

O'Shaughnessy (1973, p. 16) divides the countries he examines into three groups: "those who have effectively no policy (Bolivia, Ecuador, Paraguay and Venezuela): those whose policy is in course of formation or major change (Colombia and Peru): and those where policy is firmly established (Brazil)." In the absence of such a policy—and sometimes in spite of it—contacts of European-type societies with Amerindians tend to be economically discriminatory against the latter. This may even be true of contacts motivated by benevolence such as health and sanitation programs. A Edwin Brooks points out (1973) Europeans feel it a moral imperative to give antibiotics and inoculations to Indians. It is offensive to the whole spirit of the Hippocratic Oath to let a sick Indian child die when drugs could save it. Yet the result of Western medicine without corresponding cultural changes is an instant population explosion. Among the Xavante in the Mato Grosso, for instance, half the population is under the age of ten and the tribe is likely to double within ten years. As Brooks suggests, assistance to the Indian can unintentionally disrupt his balance with the local physical and social environment. Despite an expansion of the Xavante Reserve, Brooks sees conflict brought about by population pressure in the future.

In the matter of tribal land tenure, the situation of the Amerindians is in marked contrast to that of the African peoples in South Africa and South West Africa, whose tribal lands were demarcated when the Europeans settled and who enjoy security of possession, since Europeans may not acquire real estate in the Homelands. In South America, on the other hand, the forest tribes never held land grants or titles from the Spanish or national authorities; it never occurred to them to ask for any, since such documents are foreign to the indigenous culture. The rights of the Amerindians to their areas of hunting and peripatetic agriculture were never formally recognized until the belated establishment of reservations—limited fractions of the ranges over which Indians ormerly roamed. Encroaching settlers treat ndians lands as vacant and are encouraged to o so by the authorities, who grant them omestead rights to land they occupy and ence in. The result is that Indian tribes on heir periodic migrations find their hunting nd food-gathering grounds increasingly reempted by settlers, some of whom "ride hotgun," shooting at any Indian they see.

. DISPOSSESSION AND ENSLAVEMENT
IN COLOMBIA AND PERU

Deprivation of the economic base is particurly acute in the case of the Cuiva and Campa, rimitive tribes who live in the eastern districts f Colombia and Peru. Discussing economic onflict between the Cuiva Indians of Colombia and the proliferating cattle ranchers, Arand (1972, p. 16f.) suggests that a reasonable ompromise would be to provide the Cuiva with enough land and technical aid so they too ould become cattleraisers. To date, however, he Cuiva's adaptation to the Colombian conomy has been marginal. Arcand describes what happened to one band:

Since 1967, the band has visited Cravo Norte ore and more frequently: in 1970, some Cuiva ent as much as three months in the year living lose to the town. There they carry out menial tasks r which they are usually are given sugar, alcohol, lothes, or the leftovers from a slaughtered cow. When given money, the Cuiva spend it immediately the shops for food or clothes. . . . when in Cravo Norte the Cuiva eat much sweets and very little eat; the quantitative difference between the food onsumed when away from the settlers and when in Cravo Norte is enormous, and the qualitative difference . . . is probably just as great.

Within the next few years the whole band may ecide to settle close to Cravo Norte and serve as the own's chief labor force. This would repeat what appened in the town Arauca, where Guahibopeaking Indians live a short distance away from the own, providing it with water, firewood, and whatver unskilled work (including prostitution) is equired by the settlers. Without any formal educa-

tion and without expertise in the settler's way of life—not even knowing Spanish—the Cuiva could only be integrated into the lowest level of the Colombian lower class. (1972, p. 17)

Rather more deliberate economic exploitation is encountered by the Campa of the Peruvian Amazon. Among the estimated 21,000 members of this tribe, some 2500 still live in traditional forest communities, while another 10,750 are attempting and to some extent achieving integration into the Peruvian economy—sometimes by joining mission communities where work and education are available. In between is a population of 7750 Campa, whose breadwinners are more or less permanently employed by and in debt to particular settlers who act as their *patrones*, supplying them with manufactured goods in exchange for labor or forest products such as lumber or rubber. Economic exploitation is defined here to exclude transactions that correspond to true market prices—however onerous they may be for one party or the other. But many *patrones* capitalize on the Indians' ignorance of markets and monetary values and their craving for manufactured goods—for which they often have little practical use—to lure them into debt peonage. It is, Bodley writes (pp. 11–12), common practice for *patrones* to take advantage of the Campa's lack of experience by grossly overcharging for the cheap consumer goods they advance and undercrediting for the valuable labor and forest products they receive in return. For example, one Campa reported spending two years cutting mahogany to pay his *patron* for a $25 shotgun. A *patron* usually manages to keep his laborers in perpetual debt by urging them to accept new goods before the old are paid for. "The Campa are for the most part scrupulously honest with their *patrones* and rarely fail to deliver what is demanded of them." Deferred exchanges were an essential feature of traditional Campa economic life, and this pattern was readily transferred to a debt relationship which the Campa's ethics will not let him repudiate. When the Campa grows too old to work, however, the typical *patron* has no inhibitions about turning him out, and, as Bodley writes, "most Campa discover that they have traded their culture for a few ragged clothes, some battered metal kitchen utensils, and perhaps a broken flashlight."

Force as well as infection has served as a weapon of economic oppression. The killings and slave raids reported in Paraguay have, until very recently, had their counterparts further north. Slave raids or *correrías* to meet rising demands for cheap labor were formerly common throughout Campa territory, where the slave trade flourished as late as the 1940s. It has since been almost wholly suppressed, but Bodley's survey of the modern Campa community of Shahuaya in 1966 indicated that 20 of 68 adult members had either been captured as slaves themselves or had had a parent or grandparent captured (*ibid.*, p. 7). "It is certain," Bodley writes, "that slaving resulted in the removal of women and children, the killing of men, and the destruction and pillage of homes, as well as serious disturbance of surviving populations."

3. INDIANS ARE EXPENDABLE

Amerindians sometimes become innocent victims of economic struggles in which they are not directly involved. In January 1969, a revolt against the government headed by Prime Minister Forbes Burnham broke out in the Rupupuni region of Southern Guyana. It was started by two families of local landowners, allegedly with the connivance of Venezuela, which claims a large slice of Western Guyana. The two families feared that the government in Georgetown had designs on the land they ranched. They persuaded or forced local Amerindians, many of whom were their employees, to join the revolt. It was quickly crushed, however, and its ringleaders fled into Venezuela or Brazil.

While Prime Minister Burnham accepted that many Amerindians had acted under duress, mopping-up operations by the mostly Negro Guyana Defense Force gave rise to charges of massacre. The *Mirror* of Georgetown reported rumors of "Rupupuni residents being chopped to death and buried in unmarked graves by the security forces." The newspaper's request for permission to send a reporter and a photographer to the area was refused by the government. Guyana politics were also involved in the Rupupuni affair since the opposition United Force led by Peter d'Aguair had been actively soliciting the votes of Amerindians in the area (Hugh O'Shaughnessy in *The Observer*, London, January 19, 1969).

The Burnham government persisted in keeping journalists out of the Rupupuni area, and the entire affair seemed likely to slip into the memory hole. In the late spring, however, the Brazilian newspaper *O Globo* printed an eyewitness account by a Brazilian, Helio Magalhaes from the town of Boa Vista, across the frontier from Lethem, the capital of the Rupupuni region. His story, as quoted by Hugh O'Shaughnessy (*The Observer*, June 8, 1969), was as follows:

In Lethem . . . I saw houses destroyed by machinegun fire without the occupiers having the slightest chance of escape. . . . I saw the Guyanese police cut down eight people, three adults, and five children of seven and under.

Another time they captured two girls, one of 14 and the other of 15. The two of them stayed tied up naked for three days without anything to eat. Afterwards they were raped by the police and immediately thrown on the ground and crushed by a lorry.

I also saw police surround houses full of people in the middle of the night, throw petrol on the walls and set light to it, starting on the doors and windows, and the occupants inside screamed till they died.

I saw Indians swimming across the River Mau at the frontier with their children on their backs, and many corpses of fugitives blown up and floating along with marks of gunshots.

The Burnham government arrested ten teenagers, who obviously had played minor roles in he revolt, if any. Its ringleaders were cordially received by the Venezuelan government, which provided new ranches to replace their former properties in Guyana—which the government there seized. The Venezuelans also provided housing for several hundred Guyana refugees who had escaped across the border. The ranchers claimed that while Venezuela had encouraged their revolt, the United States had brought pressure for the withdrawal of such support, fearing that any weakening of the Burnham government would help its main opponent, the Marxist Dr. Cheddi Jagan. Obviously the massacred Amerindians had been victims of higher politics.

While Amerindians have from time to time burned ranches and missions and killed their occupants, the balance of violence has been on the side of the "civilized" people. In Colombia, according to Arcand:

Every dry season, expeditions of settlers are organized to track down and kill as many Indians as possible. In 1870, D. Pedro del Carmen Gutierres, the owner of a large ranch, invited some 250 Indians to a meal during which the settlers killed all but seven of the Indians. History has repeated itself many times; as recently as December 1967, 16 Cuiva from one of the bands living in Venzuela were killed after accepting an invitation to share a meal with the occupants of the La Rubiela ranch, near the border between Colombia and Venzuela (*El Espectador*, January 29, 1968). It is worth mentioning that during the trial which followed the 1967 massacre, the settlers frankly admitted their crime, as well as having killed about 40 Indians in other riads. They were acquitted because it was not deemed a crime for them to kill the Cuiva, whom they do not consider as human beings. During the first months of 1968 the Colombian press reported the numerous ways in which the Cuiva and the Guahibo are today still being hunted and murdered by settlers (see for example *El Tiempo*, Febrero 2/1968). Even today the settlers organize expeditions with the verb "cuiviar,"

colloquial term formed from "cuiva" and the Spanish verb ending "-ar," giving the meaning "to hunt Cuiva."

Even in Brazil, where a serious effort to safeguard the rights of Amerindians was begun

after the revelation of atrocities in 1968, the processes of extermination have not been entirely stopped. Kenneth Brecher, a social anthropologist from Oxford University who was in Brazil assisting the indigenes, witnessed an episode of genocide against an Indian tribe when a cattle company took a fancy to their land. It happened in 1970, while Brecher was conducting field work among the Waura tribe in the Xingu National Park, supposedly a model sanctuary for Indian tribes.

One day I was walking with a party of Waura to attend the funeral of a tribal chief, when we saw a plane coming in to land nearby. We decided to hide, and watched men in military uniforms carry bodies from the plane and dump them on the ground. When the plane had left, we saw that some of them were dead, and the others couldn't move or walk. We counted 41 of them.

Mr. Brecher subsequently learned from the survivors that they were the last of the Beiços de Pau (lips of wood) tribe, so called because they wear wooden lip disks. Their disks had been removed, so that their lips collapsed: they were naked and lacked strength to eat. In 1968, when the Beiços de Pau numbered about 400, they were discovered by a private expedition which offered them a feast. A white man sprinkled white powder over the food, whereupon a number of the Indians immediately fell sick and died. The Beiços de Pau were contacted again in 1969, this time by an official group from FUNAI, the National Indian Foundation. According to Brecher:

The following year, another official expedition arrived, and removed all their possessions and body ornaments. They were taken in open trucks, naked, in the middle of winter, across the interior on a journey in which they complained of being sexually molested, and some of them were to die. When I mentioned this to some Sioux Indians it struck a chord—their people remember another long march in the dead of winter.

The Beiços de Pau were then put on an unpressurised Government plane and dumped in the Xingu Park, where we found them. They insisted that some of the tribe, who fled during the cold epidemic, might still be alive near their homeland. In 1972 an expedition found their bones all in one place—they had all died together (In Stuart Wavell, 1974.)

Brecher's revelations, as reported by Stuart Wavell in *The Guardian*, provoked considerable controversy in the London press. Brecher then described the similar case of the Kreenakrore, a formerly self-sufficient tribe who had been deprived of their economic basis by the building of a superhighway through the jungle, and reduced to beggary and prostitution (Kenneth S. Brecher in *The Guardian*, Dec. 23, 1974). By the time this happened, the Villas Boas brothers, the Brazilian reformers who had led the fight to save the Indians and had founded the Xingu National Park, had requested early retirement—evidently because they felt it impossible to accomplish anything further. "We are leaving the life of backwoodsmen because we are convinced that every time we contact a tribe we are contributing to the destruction of the purest things that tribe possesses" (In O'Shaughnessy, 1973, p. 21n).

Occasionally, Amerindians find themselves targets of outright warfare. A case in point is the fate of the Guahibo tribe of east-central Colombia, whose 7000 surviving members are afflicted with tuberculosis (60 percent), venereal disease (80 percent), and malnutrition (100 percent). The story, told by Philip Knightley and Caelia Lambert (*Sunday Times*, London, January 15, 1971), began in 1965, when a government Malaria inspector named Rafael Jaramillo Ulloa visited the Planas region, where the Guahibo live, and was horrified at what he saw. White *colonos* had staked out farms up to 170,000 acres, and were forcing the Indians, who speak no Spanish and live on manioc (a tuberous root) to work for them at a wage of 2 cents per day or a little bag of salt. Jaramillo managed to get government loans to start a cooperative, a health station, and an electric plant. He obtained 35,000 acres (a quarter of the larger farms) as an Indian reser-

vation, and gained the confidence of the Indians. The authorities were pleased, and promoted Jaramillo to inspector of police.

In early 1970, however, Jaramillo had a fight with a planter about the latter's treatment of Indians, wounded him, and fled to the jungle with 200 loyal followers. Bogota reacted strongly: Castro had started with 12 men and Ché Guevara never had more than 40. While the government debated what to do, some outlying farms were attacked and 13 whites killed. The Colombian Army responded with a full offensive.

All 7000 Guahibo fled into the jungle. An enlightened officer, Major Andres Alvarez, started "Operation Friendship" to lure them back. Those who returned had suffered severely. Many were dying of hunger, and some children were ill from the pito mosquito whose bite causes the flesh to rot away to the bone. When the Indians returned to the reservation they found that the white settlers, in the throes of an oil rush, had burned their homes and destroyed their food crop. Major Alvarez was recalled and, on the settlers' petition, the Army launched a series of "Indian drives."

The Army made several sorties into the jungle but only once met Jaramillo's guerrilla band. On many other occasions it met and attacked unarmed Indian families who had returned to the jungle out of fear. Women were killed and children wounded. Men were strung up from trees, poked with electric cattle prods, burned with cigarettes, and tortured to tell where Jaramillo was hiding. When 35 Indians were imprisoned under foul conditions at Villavincencio, the Catholic Church launched an investigation. Father Gustavo Perez drew up a list of cases of torture and murder, which was signed by several academics and reached the World Council of Churches.

The situation of the Indians is complicated by the fact that Colombia contains Castroite and Maoist guerrilla groups, which enjoy some support among radical students. Groups such as Jaramillo's, however real their grievances are therefore treated as rebels to be given no quarter. A typical settler view of the matter is: "There will not be any peace in this region until the Indians are gone."

4. HESITANT REFORM IN BRAZIL

When complaints about massacres of Indians were at their peak in 1967 the Brazilian government appointed a commission to investigate the Indian Protection Service. On September 10, 1968, the commission reported that this Service was a complete failure and that crimes were indeed committed against the Indians, ranging from illegal destruction of the forest and seizure of territories belonging to the Indians to outright genocidal happenings. The government then in office disapproved of such crimes and abolished the Protection Service which, in large part, was responsible for the atrocities. Some of its functions were taken over by the newer National Indian Foundation (FUNAI).

In 1970, the President of Brazil signed a statute for the protection of Indians. In this statute, the Indians were recognized as individuals *as well as tribes*, and it was also recognized that they possess territories and have the right to their use. All territories, however, are legally the property of the national government of Brazil and the Indians were denied the mineral rights usually attached to land ownership. Furthermore, under exceptional circumstances, for reasons of national security, public health, and other reasons related to national development, the Indians can be removed from their territories, if it is deemed that no other alternative is available. The law does not make altogether clear whether Indians so evicted must be given new territories or under what conditions.

In addition, the intent of the 1970 statute is to promote the integration of the Indian communities into the "national community." That is to say, the Indian is not regarded as a member of a community with a right to preserve its own culture, but as a person in transi-

tion to becoming a Brazilian. The Indians were given no choice on the assimilation question. Up to then, Brazilian law had treated the Indian like a child: in need of tutelage. In an imprecise form, he was kept in this position by the 1970 decree (for text, see P. Crime, 1972).

Although there is a strong presumption in favor of leaving tribes, ethnic groups and nations in their areas of settlement, it cannot be contended that there is never a sufficient ground for the removal of a tribe or ethnic group from a given territory. In the case of primitive populations, medical necessities may be compelling, and so may be the need to put an end to intertribal warfare which often is quite murderous. But whether it is justifiable to remove tribes from their lands to make room for development in the "superior interests of the nation," as stated in Article 35/1 of the statute, is highly questionable. In fact, this formula places the Brazilian and the Indian peoples in opposition and subordinates the latter. Similarly, it well may be argued that mineral deposits should be exploited in the interest of all, and Article 46 suggests that the Indians would profit from such exploitation. But this sort of proviso is too vague to create *rights* which can be defended in court. In other words, the new statute incorporates discriminatory notions and reconfirms ancient legislation harmful to the Indians. The discrimination against Indians inherent in current Brazilian law has not been recognized.

C. Recognition of the Crime of Ethnocide

The 39th International Congress of Americanists, which met at Lima in 1970, issued a declaration against ethnocide in which it postulated a series of measures to protect endangered populations. These measures include effective self-protection, the allocation of full property rights to ethnic communities, the offering of new territories to groups which were chased away from their former habitats, and the recognition of local languages in addition to the official one (Jaulin, 1972, pp. 390–93). Apart from the question whether the proposals adopted were practical and sufficient for their purpose, the need for positive measures to prevent ethnocide was correctly recognized.

Actually, the proposals, though Latin American governments think them too revolutionary, were inadequate. Acquisitions or attributions of territory must be based on a solid legal foundation, physical protection must be provided against crime and aggression by local as well as foreign elements, while cultural autonomy and local self-government need stronger protection. Indian tribes must not be regarded as being in transit toward assimilation, but rather as ethnic entities of their own, entitled to live, prosper, grow, and succeed, and to merge with kindred tribes or not as they choose. Any other treatment would expose the smaller and weaker groups to gradual degeneration and ultimate dissolution. Though ethnic decay does not mean extinction of individuals, they would be deprived of the cultural and social prerequisites for their full and satisfactory development, as well as for the pursuit of their happiness as conceived according to their own traditions.

There are some who feel that the best policy for dealing with aboriginal tribes is to have no policy: to let contacts take place spontaneously, leaving cultural adaptation to individual free choice. The virtue of such a non-policy, however, is sharply contradicted by the recent experience of two young Belgian yachtsmen who cruised the canals of Tierra del Fuego, an area without navigation aids but with high winds and occasional underwater glaciers. The narrator, Patrick van Godtsenhoven (1975), describes their encounter with the Alakaluf, the only remaining Indians along the west coast of Tierra del Fuego. The first indication of the Indians was an abandoned camp, with the skeletons of huts stripped of their linings,

and tens of thousands of shells of the *cholga*, a large black mussel. The narrator continues:

We discovered them far on, leaving Paso de L'Abismo. The smiles were at first anxious, then widening in response to comical gestures. Wondering paupers, dressing in tattered pullovers, patched pants, skirts faded and torn, they generally prospect in two couples, accompanied by numerous dogs that help them in their hunting. When the weather is nice they spend hours, their arms in glacier water, collecting *cholgas*, which the women smoke over big fires before stringing them on short sticks. After two or three months, all the corners accessible by small boats having been cleaned of *cholgas*, they return to Puerto Eden to sell them and to relax, which to them means one thing: alcohol.

There are only 48 left.

We camped with them, ate *cholgas* with them. Unhappy? Certainly not. Happy? No, probably not. Resigned? Resignation supposes aspiration, a hope. No, they are born, gather *cholgas*, and die. To see their bloodshot eyes, the trembling of their hands, trembling which did not come from the cold, was a certitude that this race is soon to be extinct.

It is quite obvious that a policy of "benign neglect" is insufficient and indeed inhuman in its results. Where interaction between two cultures is uncontrolled, members of the more primitive culture are always exposed to and frequently victims of the *least desirable* aspects of the "higher" culture, long before they reap its benefits.

The treatment of ethnic groups as being in transition toward assimilation and having only partial rights in their territories constitutes discrimination, even though it may not be recognized as such by governments that practice such policies. Jean Poirier, a leading French ethnologist, complains that the ethnic problem is generally misunderstood and that it has been treated, by governments and academics alike, in a disappointing fashion (1972, pp. 15–20). He distinguishes genocide, an act of killing, from ethnocide which is a process of degradation and results in the loss of cultural identity. He explained that three problems are involved the disappearance of certain ethnic groups; the partition of ethnic groups which he calls *social vivisection;* and deculturation which arises in situations where different ethnic groups are interacting.

The phenomenon of ethnocide does not necessarily spring from colonialism. Many peoples have grown and have maintained their cultural cohesion under colonial rule, among them most of the African tribes in former British or French colonies. But other groups have been endangered. There are, according to Poirier, two types of disappearance: accidental and deliberate liquidation. In the cases of Indians in North America and Bushmen in South Africa, the latter took the form of hunting the natives like beasts. As victims of social or ethnic vivi-section, Poirier mentioned the Ewe and the Yoruba in West Africa, and he was particularly incensed about the plight of the Tuareg. This nomadic people enjoyed strong cultural unity but their territory was divided under French rule, and after decolonization was divided once again among Algeria, Mali, and Niger. Nobody took the trouble to grant to the Tuareg their right of self-determination. They were particular victims of the 1974 Sahel famine.

Considered as a whole, the protection of primitive communities is increasingly recognized as a problem. But it is one in which action, national and international, lags considerably behind the moral imperative.

28

GENOCIDE

A. A Typology of Genocide

Hervé Savon is a key member of the *Institut français de polémologie* (polemology = the study of war). His book *Du Cannibalisme au Génocide* (1972) is one of the most thoughtful and complete analyses of the latter phenomenon.

Savon sees a psychological and religious link between genocide and cannibalism, in both of which ritualized slaying plays an important symbolic role. The old myth that life is renewed through killing connects the two phenomena, Cannibalism, a practice found mainly among hunting-gathering and primitive agricultural peoples, may serve alimentary, punitive, and ritual (i.e. cultic and magical) purposes as well as initiation rites.

Genocide, Savon considers, stems from states of collective psychology caused by hunger, fear, and humiliation (pp. 245f). He also sees merit in Hobbes's idea that human conflict is rooted in competition for gain, defense to achieve security, and glory. According to Savon, glory is today felt necessary in order to impose one's image upon others—a compulsion Hans Morgenthau calls "nationalistic universalism." Savon is inclined, more or less implicitly, to correlate genocide with "democracy," by which he seems to mean mass movements. This insight reveals the element of "totalitarian democracy" inherent in both communism and national socialism, authoritarian rule within the respective political parties notwithstanding.

Savon quotes Horkheimer and Adorno, *Dialektik der Aufklärung* (1972, pp. 6, 42), to show the "enlightened" roots of genocide. They correlate de Sade with Nietzsche, who celebrated the cult of strength in epigrams like this (from *Umwertung aller Werte*): "The weak and unsuccessful must perish; this is the first proposition of our philanthropy." Nietzsche justified the cruelty of conquerors against "alien worlds" as "freedom from any social constraint. . . . return to the guiltlessness of a predatory conscience . . . a frightful sequence of murder, arson, rape, and torture, as if it were all no more than some student's prank, yet convinced that they have provided their bards with something to celebrate for ages to come" (*Genealogie der Moral*). In his essay significantly titled *Beyond Good and Evil*, Nietzsche extols "the terribly beauty of the deed." "If the aims are high," he wrote in a posthumously published paper, "then mankind has another yardstick and does not judge 'crime'—even the most frightful means—as such." (Quoted, Horkheimer and Adorno, pp. 97–100.) This sentence is strangely reminiscent of Rousseau's description of the General Will.

In his historical review, Savon cites the extinction of the Caribbean Indians and the near extermination of the Anuaks, Beirs, and Chilluks through slaving—these outcomes were *not* intended. Hence the definition of genocide should read: "any policy which has the objective *or the consequence* of decimating or destroying ethnic and social groups." He groups genocides in three classes: substitution, devastation, and elimination. Substitution genocide includes the replacement of the Bushmen of Southern Africa by Boers and Bantu-speaking blacks (he acknowledges that the white South Africans saved the Bushmen from extinction) and that of the Muslim population of Jerusalem by the crusaders when they captured that city in 1099. A similar substitution was conducted by the Vandal Genseric and his successors, Arian Christians, who slaughtered the Catholic clergy and much of the laity in Spain—an operation that proved fatal to the Vandal state.

Devastation included the subjugation of the Samnites who lived near Capua by Sulla after 91 B.C., various operations of the Assyrians, and the Roman destruction of Carthage. Savon makes the interesting point that Cato was a relentless enemy of the aristocrats as well as of trade-oriented and rich Carthage. Other cases of devastating genocide are the annihilation of the Jews in Palestine under Hadrian, and the twentieth-century operation against the Armenians which was largely the exploit of the reformist-democratic Young Turks. This and other recent genocides are mentioned again in the chronology that follows.

Savon also discusses the mass deportations in the USSR during World War II, which—at least in part—were intentionally genocidal. He shows that Volga German families were pulled apart to prevent procreation, a policy included in the crime of genocide as defined by the Convention (see chapter 4,C). Girls working in a factory at Kuibyshev were denied their labor books, without which they could not be hired elsewhere, and were not allowed to marry. Of the Crimean Tatars, Savon states that their death toll was officially estimated as 22 percent. Their probable loss was 46 percent but

persons using a figure above 22 percent were arrested. The genocide of the Kalmyks, Chechens, Ingush, Balkars, Karachai, Crimean Tatars, and Volga Germans cost the lives of at least 1.25 million persons (Savon, 1972, pp. 161, 166). Within the same category, Savon discusses the Sudan, where casualties between 1955 and 1966 were about 150,000. In Tanzania ethnocide was practiced against the Masai, who were forced to undergo deculturation. (This may also have occurred to some extent in Kenya.)

Under elimination, Savon mentions the forced emigration of 250,000 Huguenots from France after the revocation of the edict of Nantes in 1685, and he discusses Hitler's "final solution." Other cases of eliminatory genocide have been described in this book under various aspects, such as the slaughter of the Tutsi by the Hutu in Rwanda. Elimination also took place in Biafra; that in East Bengal will be described in Part C of this chapter. Between 200,000 and 500,000 communists and their relatives were killed in Indonesia in 1965, together with Chinese, foreigners, and atheists (and also, it should be added, anticommunists in the initial round). In Algeria, almost the entire French population of over 900,000 was eliminated, not entirely without loss of life.

Mass expulsions, in which the majority of deaths are likely to be the result of negligence, including failure to provide adequate food, accommodation, and medical care for persons in transit, are included in Savon's definition of genocide. They present aspects of substitution and elimination. Savon gives an extensive list of expulsions during the twentieth century (pp. 182f.), which will not be summarized here in view of the treatment in chapter 22.

Savon's oversights include the Cathars, the witches, the Jews and Marranos in Spain and Portugal, and the French revolution, including *la terreur*, *les noyades* and Babeuf's *système de dépopulation*. He gives only an incomplete account of genocides in the USSR and he fails to touch on mass killings in communist China.

Nor does he deal with genocide by ethnomorphosis: a nonlethal variety in which people are forced into an alien culture rather than
being exterminated (see Chapter 18,A6, also
Possony, 1976). But Savon does show that
genocide keeps on happening and is not just a
crime committed once by Hitler's SS.

B. A Chronology of Genocide

A number of authors have compiled records of
genocide and similar atrocities. Among them is
the late Wenzel Jaksch, before 1938 deputy
leader of the Sudeten German Social Democrats in the Czechoslovak parliament. During
the Second World War, Jaksch attempted to
dissuade Dr. Beneš from the mass expulsion
described in Chapter 22,B2—the cost of which
turned out to be the freedom of the Czech nation. The chronology that follows, which is
necessarily selective rather than exhaustive, is
based partly on Dr. Jaksch's listing (1963, pp.
464–78), partly on other sources.

1. *Armenians:* There were massacres of Armenians in Turkey in 1895–96; some 20,000
Christian Armenians were slaughtered in Cili-
cia in 1909 when they resisted conversion to
Islam. During World War I, which the Sultan
proclaimed as *jihad*—illegally, since only descendants of the Prophet have that right—the
Young Turks launched the great 1915–16 massacre, in which over one million Armenians
perished. In 1915, there was a mass deportation to Mesopotamia, during which all males
were killed. Of the 1,845,450 Christian Armenians in the Ottoman Empire in 1914, an estimated 1.4 million were slain during World
War I; 24,000 escaped and 204,000 were not
persecuted.

2. *Other Turkish Massacres During World War
I:* While they were about it, the Turks also
slaughtered most of the Nestorians, a small
people, a remnant of the Chaldeans living near
the Persian border. Young Turks under the direction of Djemal Pasha vented their spleen on

the Christians in Syria and Lebanon. Mass extermination was attempted through famine
coupled with the distribution of bread consisting mainly of sawdust. At least 100,000 Christians lost their lives. This particular tactic was
chosen because the Kurds who originally were
to be used as executioners were not available,
being subjected to some bloodletting themselves. Under Kemal Ataturk the Kurds were
driven out from Western Turkey.

3. *Deportation of Wolhynia Germans:* There
were about 200,000 of these Germans in Zhi-
tomir gubernia in 1914. The Duma decided in
February 1915, to expropriate and deport
them. About 60,000 returned in 1917; a few
emigrated to Germany, but the rest perished.

4. *Casualties Incident to Russian Revolution and
Civil War:* The Russian Revolution was accompanied by a massive exodus; Kulischer
(1944) estimates it at 1.5 million. Lorimer
(1946) estimates casualties of civil war and famine in the Volga area at 14 million in 1921 and
1922. He assesses the total population loss
from 1914 to 1926 as follows (quoted, Petersen, 1975, p. 675):

Military deaths	2 million
Civilian deaths	14 million
Net emigration	2 million
Birth deficit	10 million
total	28 million

5. *Forced Collectivization and Purges:* A
census of the USSR was taken in 1937, but
publication was suppressed, officially for inac-
curacies and ideological errors. The real reason, Petersen speculates (pp. 669–70), is that
the population figure would have suggested
how many millions had been killed in the
forced collectivization of agriculture during the
First Five-Year Plan. One of its results was the
1933–34 famine in Ukraine, reflected in a population drop from 31,195,000 in 1926 to
28,070,000 in 1939. Stalin later told Churchill
that 10 million peasants had been "processed"
during the four-year collectivization campaign—meaning that they had been sent to

forced labor camps, where annual mortality rose from 10 percent in 1933 to about 20 percent by 1965 (*ibid.*, pp. 680–81, 686). In Central Asia, 1.5 out of 4 million Kazakhs disappeared during forced "denomadization," when the Kazakhs' herds were depleted by about four-fifths (*ibid.*, p. 687).

6. *Aristocide Against Poles:* The attempted extermination of the Polish intellectual elite, begun in 1940 by the Soviets at Katyn, was continued by the SS, notably in the Lvov areas. (This episode was used as communist propaganda against West German Chancellor Adenauer and Professor Oberlaender, his refugee minister. Simon Wiesenthal, who exonerated Oberlaender, claims to have located the real culprit in Argentina.)

7. *Deportations in USSR During World War II:* The deportations of non-Russian nationalities in the USSR, described in chapter 22,B1, produced a considerable casualty list. Among the 400,000 Volga Germans and 1 million other ethnic Germans in the Russian imperium, some 300,000 deaths were reported (Jaksch, 1963, pp. 470ff.). About the Turkic peoples in the South, Petersen writes:

The strangest case is that of the "Meskhetians," various peoples listed in the censuses as Turkish or Azerbaidzhanian who were welded into a new people by their common fate. Since their land was never occupied by the German army, the removal was not punitive; rather, reflecting Soviet ambitions for Turkish territory, officials thought it better to move Turkic peoples from the border region and transport them to Central Asia and Kazakhstan. All told, they numbered some 200,000, of whom perhaps as many as 30,000 to 50,000 died from hunger and cold. Since no charge was ever made against them, they could not be rehabilitated. The world learned of their removal only in 1968, when they were given the right—on paper—to return home; but the very decree noted that they had "taken root" where they were. From the listing in the 1970 census it would seem that many "Meskhetians" have reverted to the designation "Turks," and in 1970 and 1971 a number of attempts were made to obtain permission to emigrate to Turkey, with no success.

Several leaders who addressed an appeal to the United Nations succeeded only in getting themselves sentenced to prison terms. (1975, p. 688)

Spokesmen for the Crimean Tartars contend, on the basis of a census they took in 1966, that 110,000 of 250,000 deported (44 percent), died in transit or within 18 months of reaching their destination. Soviet authorities say these figures are too high and that only 22 percent of 150,000 deportees, or 33,000 persons, died within that period. The Soviet figure does not, however, include deaths in the cattle cars from the desert heat of Kazakhstan. It may be added that of some 6000 Tartars who managed to return to the Crimea by 1967, all but a few were refused registration and redeported. As Petersen relates:

According to a protest addressed to the U.N. Human Rights Commission, members of eleven families who had been refused registration were seized in the middle of the night, put on trains leaving the Caucasus, and dumped at railroad stations, destitute except for a handful of possessions they were able to carry with them. They were all reduced to begging in order to keep alive. This incident took place not under Stalin but in 1969. Because of the publicity given to it and to similar brutalities, Crimean Tartars are now barred from Moscow hotels, in order to cut their communication with those who can be reached in the capital. (1975, p. 689)

8. *Genocide Against the Jews Under Hitler:* So much has been written about the holocaust that overwhelmed the Jews of Europe that a repetition at this point seems superfluous. The reader is referred to two standard accounts: Raul Hilberg, *The Destruction of the European Jews* (1961), and Gerald Reitlinger, *The Final Solution* (2d revised edition, 1968). As for the number of victims, the figure of 6 million has been widely used since the Nuremburg indictment of November 1945, mentioned a total of 5,700,000. Jaksch, however, concluded after some research that a more accurate figure would lie between 4,194,000 and 4,581,000 (1963, p. 472). Reitlinger likewise agrees that

Table 28.1.   SUMMARY OF EXTERMINATION ESTIMATES
(Revised 1966)

	Low	High	Anglo-American Committees Figures, April, 1946
Germany (1938 frontiers)	160,000	180,000	195,000
Austria	58,000	60,000	53,000
Czechoslovakia (1938)	241,000	251,000	255,000
Denmark	(less than 100)		(chiefly refugees in Sweden 1,500
France	60,000	65,000	140,000
Belgium	25,000	28,000	57,000
Luxembourg	3,000	3,000	3,000
Norway	700	700	1,000
Holland	102,700	102,700	120,000
Italy	8,000	8,000	20,000
Jugoslavia	55,000	58,000	64,000
Greece	57,000	60,000	64,000
Bulgaria (pre-1941 frontier)	—	—	5,000
Rumania (pre-1940 frontier)	204,000 [a]	209,000 [a]	530,000
Hungary (1938 frontiers)	180,000	200,000	200,000
Poland (1939 frontiers)	2,350,000 [a]	2,600,000 [a]	3,271,000
USSR (pre-139 frontiers), plus Baltic States	700,000 [a]	750,000 [a]	1,050,000
			6,029,500
		Less dispersed refugees	308,000
Sum Total	4,204,400 [a]	4,575,400 [a]	= 5,721,800

[a] Owing to the lack of reliable information at the time of writing, these figures must be regarded as conjectural.

the 6 million estimate is too high. His revised edition contains a detailed statistical appendix, which reviews the evidence country by country (1968, pp. 533–46). With the permission of his publishers (see Bibliography). Reitlinger's summary table is reproduced here:

9. *Genocidal Effects of Expulsion of Germans:* As already mentioned in chapter 22,B2, the mass expulsions of Reich and ethnic Germans at the close of World War II resulted in a death list estimated at 2,111,000. In Yugoslavia, however, genocide was a deliberate feature of the Tito regime's policy toward the Germans. A law passed by the People's Liberation Council deprived all ethnic Germans in Yugoslavia not only of their rights to vote and to hold property, but also of their right to life and liberty. At least 55,000 ethnic Germans were slaugh-

tered on the spot or died in concentration camps. About 300,000 *Volksdeutsche* were expelled to West Germay and Austria, and some 40,000 were drafted for forced labor in the USSR. The postwar Yugoslav census of 1948 showed only 55,328 members remaining of an ethnic group that had totaled 510,800 in 1944 (Schieder, 1961, pp. 119E–132E; Bohmann, 1969b, 2, pp. 273–77).

10. *Genocide Since World War II:* Probably the most flagrant case in which extermination of a rival group has been a primary objective has been the reciprocal genocide of Tutsi and Hutu in Rwanda and Burundi. Genocidal effects resulted from ethnic domination in the case of the Kurds, and from ethnic purification in the separation of India and Pakistan. The outstanding case of genocide led by rulers of a

country *against their own nation* is that of the Mao Tse-tung regime in mainland China. The Chinese communists actually boast of their prowess in this field. The following quotation is taken from an official Chinese Communist book distributed abroad in English in 1951:

With raised fists, the audience below shouted in one voice, "Down with reactionary landlords!" "We demand that Peng Ehr-hu be shot!" . . . "Long live the unity of the peasants!" . . .

By four o'clock over 20 peasants had poured out their grievances from the platform. Mass sentiment had surged to the boiling point. Over and above there was a curious hush of expectancy. Not one person left or took shelter in spite of the terrific downpour.

[Then the people's tribunal met to deliberate.]

"Peasant comrades!" The judge's voice was grave. "We have just heard some of the accusations made by local peasants. From these accusations, it ought to be clear to everyone how the landlord class has always worked hand in glove with the enemy of the peasants—whether it was Japanese imperialism or the KMT [Kuomintang]—to oppress the peasants themselves. The same motive has prompted them to act as fawning lackeys to American imperialism. . . .

"Our verdicts on the three criminal landlords are as follows: . . . Pen Yin-ting, age 49, native of Hsinlu Village, has caused the deaths of patriotic youths during the Resistance War. After liberation he organized superstitious societies and spread rumors to delude the public. Also he has hidden firearms with the intent to plan for an uprising. The sentence for him is—death. Do you all agree?"

The sound of applause that came from below the platform was deafening. . . .

With one arm sheltering his tear-stained face, Pen Yin-ting was hurried along. . . . When Grandma Li, with her bony fist clenched, edged her way through the crowds and tried to hit him on the shoulder, the guards immediately stopped her. A cordon was quickly formed by them around the prisoners as more blows were about to shower from all directions. . . .

The prisoners were escorted to the graveyard south of the temple. From the back of the graveyard came the sound of several shots.

The sound shrilly pierced through the thick, moist atmosphere enveloping Huiling hsiang. Sighs of relief were heaved as justice was meted out to the convicted.

"Down with the reactionary landlords!"
"Long live the emancipation of the peasants!"
"Long live the Communist Party!"
"Long live Chairman Mao Tse-tung!"

The masses, for the first time freed from their dread and restraints, let out these slogans with a voice stronger than ever. (In Walker, 1971, p. 12)

Table 28.2.   CASUALTIES TO COMMUNISM IN CHINA

		Range of Estimates	
1.	First Civil War (1927–36)	250,000	500,000
2.	Fighting during Sino-Japanese War (1937–45)	50,000	50,000
3.	Second Civil War (1945–49)	1,250,000	1,250,000
4.	Land reform prior to "Liberation"	500,000	1,000,000
5.	Political Liquidation Campaigns (1949–58)	15,000,000	30,000,000
6.	Korean War	500,000	1,234,000
7.	The "Great Leap Forward" and the Communes	1,000,000	2,000,000
8.	Struggles with minority nationalities, including Tibet	500,000	1,000,000
9.	The "Great Proletarian Cultural Revolution" and its aftermath	250,000	500,000
10.	Deaths in forced labor camps and frontier development	15,000,000	25,000,000
	Total	34,300,000	62,534,000

(Adapted from Richard L. Walker, *The Human Cost of Communism in China*, prepared for U.S. Senate, 92d Congress, 1st Session, Subcommittee on Internal Security, Washington: Government Printing Office, 1971, p. 16. For original sources see notes in publication cited.)

Professor Richard L. Walker, Director of the Institute of International Studies at the University of South Carolina and a specialist in Chinese affairs, has calculated the death toll of Chinese communism from 1927 to 1971 in table 28.2 (*ibid.*, p. 16).

C. A Case Study in Genocide— The Bengal Catastrophe

The most recent large-scale genocide was that incident to the Pakistan civil war, which ended in the secession of Bangladesh. It was precipitated by Bengali separatism, which in turn was provoked by economic discrimination. Bengali candidates were excluded from the public services, while investment and tax moneys were diverted to the more prosperous West. The government found enough resources to build two major dams in West Pakistan and a new and costly capital at Islamabad, even though East Pakistan was excessively vulnerable to flooding and urgently needed flood control dams and other installations. Major floods occurred during 1955 and 1968, and in each case caused a major shortage of rice. Yet a change of policy was not even considered.

Partition had deprived the Eastern Bengalis of their jute mills and their natural market and port, which was Calcutta. This had greatly damaged the prospects of jute cultivation and trade, which was the country's major and almost only resource. Pakistan's anti-Indian policy precluded sensible trade arrangements for the Eastern Bengalis.

Bengali sentiment for outright secession was growing very rapidly when, during August 1970, unusually heavy monsoon rains once again led to major floods, which destroyed some 350,000 homes and cost many human lives. In November 1970, a new disaster struck—a cyclone of exceptional violence. Winds of 150 miles per hour left some 500,000 people dead and 2 to 3 million homeless. The settlements which, because of Malthusian pressure, had grown up on the offshore islands and which were utterly unprotected against the waves whipped up by the storm, were devastated. The government had obtained timely warnings about the cyclone but failed to transmit the warnings to the threatened population. Subsequently, it took no real action to help the people in distress. Bengalis concluded that the Islamabad government was glad to see them immobilized by catastrophe.

The situation was worsened by the chauvinism of Pakistan's military leaders. Many of the top men were of Pathan origin and lived in the violent and cruel tradition of a warlike society. They despised the Hindus and thought them incapable of fighting; the Bengalis, they were convinced, did not like to work and could be ruled only by force.

Another disintegrating factor was the failure of the Bengalis to take what the Punjabis thought was a proper interest in Kashmir. That province was far from Bengal and the Kashmir war with India swallowed up resources East Pakistan could have used for its own development. The two Kashmir wars of 1947–1949 and 1965, as well as the permanent cold war about Kashmir, aggravated economic stringencies throughout Pakistan.

The disputes with India also included a territorial conflict about the Rann of Kutch, a big swamp near Bombay, troubles about enclaves and exclaves, disagreements about water rights, and an unending list of economic difficulties resulting from the *de facto* interdependence of the two countries. There also were recurrent population movements in both directions, provoked by communal rioting and causing tension between the two governments. Most of these movements occurred in the Bengal area, and on the Indian side were particularly harmful to Calcutta. Attempts at accommodation failed, and the mutual distrust between India and Pakistan precluded constructive cooperation.

Yahya Khan understood that he needed consent, and for this reason he agreed to elections and promised to establish a democratic (or semidemocratic) regime. But the experiment in democracy was the wrong choice. In a multiethnic situation with incompatible ethnic groups, democracy practiced through a single multiethnic electorate cannot work; especially if one ethnic group accounts for more than half of the total population.

The Debacle. Negotiations between the West Pakistani leaders Yahya Khan and Zulfikar Ali Bhutto and the charismatic Bengali Sheik Mujibur Rahman broke down on March 24, 1971. At that time unrest, mostly stirred up by Mujibur's Awami League, had been going on for about three weeks. Yet Mujibur, whom the government charged with planning an armed uprising for March 26, had a resolute and highly unified people behind him. Yahya, in contrast, was finding out that the "Pak nation" was entirely fictitious: the breakup was inevitable.

Pakistan could only be held together with force, and repression had in fact been under preparation for weeks. A large army contingent stood ready for action in East Pakistan, additional forces were en route, and others were still being assembled. On March 25, Yahya told the population to stay in their homes and ordered the army to crush the autonomy movement. The uprising was supposedly being prepared in university buildings, in Awami League headquarters, and in the Revolutionary Councils, which had been established all over the country. These were the targets, together with government and press buildings.

The army struck in the early hours of March 26. Reports agree that a large number of students were shot down. The East Bengal Regiment and the East Pakistan Rifles mutinied and started to fight back. Thus, about 60,000 soldiers loyal to Yahya were opposed by 15,000 soldiers loyal to Mujibur. Still, there were not enough clearly defined targets to suppress the autonomy movement—actually to suppress almost the entire people. So in addition to fighting for army posts, mowing down students, and occupying government, transport and service installations, the army simply attacked the civilian population—workers, strikers, traders, city dwellers, and peasants, as well as women and children. The slaughter, in which civilian terror squads participated, lasted for nearly two months, until General Tikka Khan announced on May 16 that all resistance had been broken. Large numbers of Bengalis fled or were driven to India. By mid-July, their number had reached more than 7 million, or about 10 percent of the East Pakistani population. Before the disaster was over, the stream of refugees swelled to 10 or 12 million. This incredible mass of people which scarcely could be fed and housed suffered a large variety of sicknesses, including a cholera epidemic. Yet with all the agony, the Pakistan army did not succeed in "cleansing" the Bengal population.

On the contrary, the Bengali spirit was unbroken and their loyalty to Bangladesh—their own country whose independence was proclaimed formally on April 10—grew steadily as the vain fury of the enemy rose, reached a climax, and gradually subsided. Resistance was spreading across the country. By August the Bengali guerrillas were well organized and struck back with growing effectiveness.

Although India supported Bengali independence from the start, and state governments, such as that of Bihar, gave overt support, the Indian government denied for some time that it was intervening in Pakistan. Yet in the long run the Indians had no choice but support the Bengalis in their fight against the Punjabis.

Whatever their original intentions may have been, by April the Indians were confronted by three developments requiring positive actions on their part: the mass flight of Bengalis into India attended by frequent military border violations on both sides; the establishment of Bangla independence; and the discernible danger that the guerrillas might be taken over by the Maoists, who would spread guerrilla war to India.

On May 14, the Indian government castigated Pakistan for its campaign of terror.
There was heated talk about genocide. Ten
days later, Pakistan accused India of intervening massively. New Delhi denied the allega-
tion. If these denials were accurate, it would
have to be explained how the Bangla forces, in
the face of control and terror by the Pakistan
army, and Pak control of Bangla ports, could
become organized and launch, at the time of
heavy monsoon rains and severe hunger, most
effective operations some three months after
Awami resistance was declared by General
Tikka to have been suppressed. There was
only one place whence the weapons, supplies,
and military leadership could have come:
India.

Yahya threatened war on July 14, for the
first time; and both Pakistan and India stepped
up open war preparations. As the number of
refugees rose dramatically, relations deteriorated amidst complaints of cross-border shell-
ings and troop movements, as well as ceasefire
violations in Kashmir. UN Secretary General
U Thant offered to mediate. Yahya welcomed
this offer, but Mrs. Gandhi replied *inter alia:*
"The root of the problem is the fate of 75
million people of East Bengal and their inalienable rights. This is what must be kept in mind,
instead of the present attempt to save the military regime."

Yahya proclaimed a state of emergency on
November 23, declaring that "Pakistan is faced
with external aggression." Attacks on Pakistan
forces were reported from almost all sectors of
East Pakistan between November 1 and December 2, 1971, and fighting along the border
with India intensified rapidly. The Pakistanis
blamed the Indians. The Indians, in turn, attributed the assaults to the Mukti Bahini (the
Bangla guerrillas), whom their parliament had
decided to support.

On December 2, the Indians crossed the
border near Tripara (east of Dacca). The Pakistanis replied with ineffective air attacks. Radio
Islamabad talked about a *jihad*, while Mrs.

Gandhi denounced this "false and pernicious
cry of a religious war." Finally, on December
4, the Indian army launched "an integrated
ground, air and naval attack against East Pakistan," which was entered from five main directions, with the army linking up with the Mukti
Bahini. This operation clearly had been prepared for many months and was predicated on
advanced joint planning with the guerrillas.

India recognized Bangladesh on December
6. Fighting stopped on December 17, and by
December 23 all Pakistani forces in Bangladesh
had surrendered (Keesing's Archive, pp.
118–22).

"Killing defenseless people became a habit
like smoking cigarettes or drinking wine. Before they had finished, they had killed three
million people. Not since Hitler invaded Russia had there been so vast a massacre" (Payne,
1973, p. 29). "Kill three million of them,"
Yahya reportedly told a military conference in
February 1971, "and the rest will eat out of our
hands." But the Banglas were not subdued,
while Yahya and his forces bit the dust. Nor is
the figure of three million killed substantiated
by concrete evidence.

An April 18, 1971, the acting prime minister
of Bangladesh, Tajuddin Ahmed (reported
slain in jail during the military coup of November 1975), asserted that 30,000 persons had
been killed in Dacca during the first few days
of the massacre. The Pakistani *White Paper*
gives figures which suggest that up to April 10,
some 50,000 persons were killed *outside* Dacca.
The two figures can be added, for a total of
80,000 during the initial two weeks, which
were the worst. Assume the carnage continued
at this level for 10 weeks, and for the remaining
20 weeks at half this level: the killings during
the entire period would have been about
950,000. No one will ever know the exact figure, and Bangladesh's population records provide no real basis for a meaningful estimate.
The crime of genocide, however, lies in the act
and its purpose, not in the number killed.
Genocide is murder of a group; the crime can

be perpetrated against a small as well as a large group. Furthermore, genocide statistics are, in the nature of things, inaccurate: figures tend to be inflated and to grow as propaganda mills grind.

Genocide, the case study shows, is more than mass murder—it has enormous indirect effects. One of them is that of aristocide—the disproportionately high elimination of a nation's leadership, elites, professional, artistic, technical, educational, and student groups. Aristocide inevitably and severely harms a nation's progress, development, and security. The events of 1971 were partly planned as an exercise in aristocide (although this nomenclature was not used), and they hit Bangladesh's qualified population hardest.

Bangladesh's history during the first three years of independence remained unhappy, and its policies, even if the effects of the genocide catastrophe are taken into account, were not successful. Close relations with India and the USSR did not prove to be profitable, and stability was not achieved despite U.S. assistance totalling about one billion dollars. Mujibur Rahman, his family, and some 200 of his associates were killed in a mini-aristocide during August 1975. In November 1975, there followed a military coup which involved further assassinations and led to the installation of a new government—proving, once again, that political revolutions, even entire series of political upheavals, aggravate but do not solve social problems.

29

CONCLUSION:
WHAT THE FACTS TELL US

Ending a book such as this is not easy. As the manuscript undergoes final editing, new information arrives that might have been included in one chapter or another. While one of the authors was writing of the near-extinction of the Alakaluf Indians of Tierra del Fuego, the other was perusing a report (in *Die Welt* of February 25, 1975) of two neighboring tribes that had actually become extinct. As the result of genocidal practices dating back to 1880, the last of the Yamana tribe died in southern Argentina in 1974, while the last Ona Indian died near the Chilean town of Punta Arenas early in 1975.

When Cambodia fell to the Communists in April 1975, the predicted bloodbath was limited to relatively few higher officials of the Lon Nol regime. The news blackout was practically total, and it was not until a column of European diplomats and newsmen reached Thailand in early May that the outside world learned what had actually happened: the Khmer Rouge had launched a "peasant revolution," throwing the entire country into upheaval. "Perhaps four million people, most of them on foot, have been forced out of the cities into the countryside where, the Communists say, they will have to become peasants and till the soil" (*The Times*, London, May 9, 1975). The very day the Communists took over the capital city of Phnom Penh (April 17), they began moving its 2 million people "out of the city *en masse* in stunned silence; walking, cycling, pushing cars that had run out of petrol, covering the roads like a human carpet, bent under sacks of belongings hastily thrown together when the heavily armed peasant soldiers came and told them to leave immediately" (*ibid.*). Even the hospitals jammed with the wounded as well as the seriously ill were emptied to the last patient; surgeons and nurses were dragged from operating rooms, leaving the patients to die on the operating tables. Non-ambulatory patients were "expedited" through the windows.

It soon became apparent that the evacuation was not limited to Phnom Penh. As Jon Swain wrote in the *Sunday Times* (London) of May 11, 1975, the diplomats and newsmen traveling to Thailand found that almost every other city, town, or village that had resisted the communists had likewise been emptied into the countryside. It seemed that the greater part of the Cambodian nation of 7 million had been uprooted; furthermore that the Khmer Rouge had ordered the mass evacuation not so much to *punish* the people as to *revolutionize* their ways and thoughts. This form of "instant brainwashing" was certain to cause thousands of casualties. When the column reached the provincial capital of Kompong Chhnang, they found it emptied of its 500,000 people. Swain talked with a male nurse, Tong San, from the municipal hospital, who said that on April 20 the Khmer Rouge had "carried away all the hospital patients in lorries and dumped them 18 miles in the forest without food or water." (An ironical sidelight: the worst behaved people in the column were the Russians, who had brought food with them from the USSR embassy, but then demanded their share of the meager soup and rice the Cambodians were able to provide.)

Europeans and Americans shuddered with horror for a few days, and then Cambodia was forgotten. The news blackout after the takeover was almost complete, not so much for lack of news but because the Western press—motivated no doubt by at least subconscious guilt feelings about the abandonment of entire nations to tyranny—has been extremely reluctant to publish anything about conditions in Indochina. Almost a year later, there was a flurry of news about a series of measures that involve both cultural and physical genocide. Dr. Otto von Habsburg (1976) describes the Cambodian program of disidentification as follows:

In August the second step for the transformation of the country was taken. All people were deprived of their names and given new ones by the ruling bureaucracy without regard for family ties. At the same time it was decreed that people who mentioned their previous name were to be sentenced to 25 years hard labour.

At the end of September all the nation's records covering births, marriages, deaths and land or house ownership were burnt to destroy evidence of families. The systematic levelling of cemeteries began last November to wipe out memories of previous generations.

The purpose is to create a malleable mass of humans deprived of any sense of dignity and hence transformable according to the will and whim of those in power. Thus a new man should be created of whom all Marxists dream. To that end, one is ready to destroy the morale of all living beings.

In April 1976, Cambodia's chief delegate to the Law of the Sea Conference, Thiounn Prasith, denied recent press reports setting the total revolutionary death toll at 500,000 or more, and explained why the Khmer Rouge had evacuated the cities. The main reason was to bring the people to the food: a secondary reason was to forestall a CIA plot for an urban counterrevolution. Prasith also attempted to rewrite history by asserting that the evacuation was accomplished with "explanation" rather than military compulsion—a story contradicted by all witnesses (Richard Dudman in *St. Louis Post-Dispatch*, April 25, 1976).

In the meantime, however, testimony had accumulated showing that whatever the total casualties might be, the fact of deliberate wholesale massacre was not to be contradicted. Ith Thaim, the local Khmer Rouge commander at Mongkol Borei, had ten former civil servants and their families, 60 people altogether, trucked into a banana plantation. One by one, the men were forced to kneel between two soldiers, who bayonetted them to death through the chest and the back. The wives were then made to kneel by the corpses of their husbands and the procedure was repeated. The children were bayonetted where they stood; six small children were literally torn apart. The witness was one Ith Thaim, who had been forced to drive the truck, but who escaped into the jungle (*Die Welt*, Hamburg, April 22, 1976).

Similar episodes are reported by *Paris-Match* in an article, "Terreur au Cambodge," published April 24, 1976. Some 80 officers who had escaped to Thailand imprudently accepted an offer to return to Cambodia "to rejoin their families." After proceeding 30 kilometers, they were mowed down by machinegun fire; only four escaped and returned to Thailand. A similar ambush decimated a group of 350 officers who had been ordered to don their uniforms and medals to "meet Prince Sihanouk."

As for the progress of "re-education" in the resettlement camps, *Paris-Match* reports:

Each family has a machete, a pickaxe, and a plow, and is allotted about three square meters as living space. Children and adolescents are re-grouped in squads. . . . from the age of eight, boys and girls are taken away from their family. Their education is entrusted to the Angkar (Party). . . . In order to mix the population so as to eradicate any trace of the past, the Khmer Rouge decrees forced marriages. Young girls of bourgeois origin and former female students are required to marry peasants or are joined to ex-soldiers or mutilated veterans.

The number who have fled Cambodia is estimated at 70,000; even Vietnam under Communist rule is a "paradise" compared to what they left (*ibid.*). What is most unusual is that this genocidal program was perpetrated by political leaders *on their own people*, not on a minority of "foreign" ethnicity.

Cambodia, however, does not monopolize the news on the brainwashing front. A study of alcohol consumption in the USSR by Vladimir Treml, Professor of Economics of Duke University, indicates that the Soviet government actually promotes alcohol addiction among its subject nationalities so as to have a ready source of slave labor. Blue collar addicts are sentenced to forced labor on their third conviction for drunkenness, whereas professionals in essential jobs are given curative treatment à la Pavlov (Nassif, 1976). And from England comes a report that scientists seeking an acoustical device to keep drivers awake on long trips discovered a sound so penetrating that it wipes the brain entirely clean of any content and renders the subject helpless to resist any suggestion that may be made. The tape containing the sound has been locked up in a vault, but its demonstrated effect of total control indicates a frightening weapon.

This catalog of horrors could be continued *ad infinitum*. In February 1976, the Indian government headed by Mrs. Gandhi, after dissolving the legislature of Tamil Nadu and placing that state under federal rule, had arrested some 700 members of the Dravida Munetra Tasagam Party, the former governing party that had enjoyed majority support among the Tamils. Suppression of civil liberties in India continued unabated until shortly before the March 1977 general election in which Mrs. Gandhi and the Congress Party were defeated. In Lebanon, after shortages of ammunition had forced a temporary lull in the civil war in early 1976, both Christians and Muslims replenished their stocks and "hard fighting" resumed (*St. Louis Globe-Democrat*, February 2, 1976). Since then, the war has continued. The only favorable aspect is that dissensions among the Arab forces have, for much of the time, eased the pressure on Israel.

There is no point in lengthening the enumeration: however long, it would lead us back to the point discussed in chapter 1: The Human Condition. Even though we like to think of the "normal" condition of humankind as one of accommodation if not love, the fact remains that most of human history is a chronicle of struggle, conflict, and killing.

A. *The Pragmatic Questions of Responsibility*

It is beyond the scope of this book to attempt a philosophical, let alone a theological, explanation of the human condition. One thing that can be done here is to ask the question "Who Is Responsible?" as an *empirical* question. It has two interrelated aspects: active and passive responsibility. We need, in other words, to ask what kind of people perpetrate the injustices and atrocities recounted in this book, and what kind of people condone them—making themselves co-responsible by refusing to join in active protest or in corrective and preventive measures that do not cause greater misery. (War, it should be obvious, is not usually a feasible way of correcting human injustice.)

1. THE PSYCHOLOGY OF MASS CRIMES

Perpetrators of mass crimes must necessarily occupy top governmental positions in which they exercise, at least temporarily, dictatorial power. But both before and after they have seized the reins of power, they have a social and psychological history that can be examined with psychoanalytic techniques—even though there is no "patient on the couch." Temper tantrums, violent and sadistic behavior, destructiveness, and narcissism leave early and long tracks; home conditions, school experiences, and social relationships can be reconstructed, sometimes even from public relations photographs. The task is to hunt for traumas and to determine whether the dictatorial criminal suffered brain dysfunction or brain damage through parental beatings, especially by a hated father, accidents, fights, military service, or illness. (On the significance of brain troubles see Mark and Ervin, *Violence and the Brain*, 1972.) The histories of Lenin, Hitler, and Stalin contain facts suggesting that these men had significant brain disorders. An autopsy revealed that Lenin's brain was physically abnormal. Yet not all extreme-criminal types are medically and especially cerebrally impaired, and such impairment is rarely the sole cause of criminal behavior. Increases and decreases in the rate of violence can be more realistically ascribed to social changes and the flow of ideas with criminal consequences, such as the notion that only society, not the criminal, is guilty.

Nations are sometimes seized by fits of collective madness that might be called "mental epidemics." It could even be argued that a democracy needs a purposefully stimulated "mental epidemic" to fight a successful war—consider, for instance, the excesses of propaganda in World Wars I and II and the lack of such propaganda (except by the enemy) in the Vietnam War. Mental epidemics, such as that which seized Germany under Hitler, never arise without political or environmental stimulus, and contagion is fanned by the purely psychological urge to imitate. War and natural catastrophes, and other types of stress, are accompanied and followed by large-scale mental and behavioral disturbances, as well as sadism, which is subject to "learning" and feeds upon itself like a chain reaction.

It is usually possible to identify empirically the perpetrators of political crimes, ranging from deprivation of life or liberty in individual cases to genocide. It is also possible to point to statesmen who, without criminal intent, have made decisions resulting in mass deaths or political convulsions that, in the light of history, might have been avoided. President Wilson's decision to lead the United States into World War I, and President Truman's decision to drop the atomic bomb on Hiroshima have been so classified by certain historians. Identifying mistakes in statesmanship, however, always involves historical and geopolitical judgment, and therefore can never be truly "final" in the scholarly sense.

2. RESPONSIBILITY THROUGH COMPLICITY OR INACTION

The list of statesmen and governments that share passive responsibility for acts of extreme discrimination or oppression because they failed to take realistic action to prevent or protest such acts is longer than the list of perpetrators and, for most readers of this book, will come closer to home. Implication of British and Americans in Hitler's crimes may seem preposterous to some, yet it has been historically documented that both countries failed to carry out massive resettlements of German Jews, which was possible in 1937 and 1938, while an influential clique in England actively favored the National Socialists. For the sake of brevity, our narrative of passive responsibility will be limited to episodes in the closing months of World War II and in the postwar era.

It was common knowledge that the Bolshevik government of Russia engaged in genocide against the Don and Kuban Cossacks, who—insofar as within the USSR—were reportedly annihilated between 1928 and 1930 (Genocide Convention, 1950, p. 325). Yet at the close of World War II, the Western Allies carried out the forcible repatriation of numerous Cossacks who had escaped and were naturalized in other countries; they were almost invariably either sent to the Gulags or executed (Glaskow, 1958, pp. 242–53). Other Cossacks who fought on the German side were forcibly repatriated by the British in a shameful operation that engulfed not only USSR citizens and former Red Army soldiers, but also persons who never had held Soviet citizenship.

The arguments adduced to justify the handing over of these people as "traitors" may or may not be valid—the *true* reason was that the British and U.S. governments had yielded to Kremlin demands. In any case, the British authorities were clearly remiss in failing (a) to screen each individual to determine whether he had to be surrendered and (b) to require a Soviet commitment that the repatriates be treated humanely and in accordance with international law. Of the six Cossack leaders whose execution was publically announced by Moscow, one was a German, four had not lived in the USSR since its creation, and only one was a USSR citizen "and liable to trial as a traitor" (Bethell, 1974, p. 164). At least 35,000 Cossacks—possibly close to 50,000—among some 250,000 who had fled from the USSR or were fighting communism, were turned over to Soviet authorities. Of those 35,000, including many women and children who could hardly be guilty of "treason," more than 7000 died during the first year in the Gulag meat grinder (*ibid.*, pp. 158, 163). The Cossacks have ceased to be listed as a nationality in the Soviet census and only a few seem to be surviving in the USSR.

On October 1, 1945, a Soviet Army spokesman disclosed that 5.2 million USSR citizens had been repatriated of whom 1.6 million had found employment, while 750,000 were waiting for jobs (Huxley-Blythe, 1964, p. 169). This leaves nearly 3 million persons unaccounted for. In the early phase of forced repatriation, which lasted for nearly three years, Bethell estimated that over 2 million individ-uals were "delivered," including the Vlassov soldiers, who had volunteered to liberate their country from communism. United States Military Government in Germany played an active role in this repatriation—given the code name "Operation Keelhaul"—knowing full well that every Vlassov officer and any Russian or non-Russian from the USSR who had actively opposed communism was a candidate for summary execution. Juergen Thorwald has estimated that altogether 6 to 7 million nationals were repatriated, most of them against their will. This is consistent with the Soviet announcement of 1945. (For the full story, see Epstein, 1973, *passim*.)

Croatia seceded from Serb-dominated Yugoslavia during World War II; its army fought on the German side. There was a similar forced repatriation of that army to Tito, who had most of the 200,000 to 300,000 men slaughtered, some still within view of British observers in Austria.

The United States bears a share of guilt for its part in the forced repatriation, even from American soil, of persons who did not want to go "home." By the time of the Korean war, however, it had learned its lesson. It insisted successfully that Chinese war prisoners be given a free choice of going to Communist China or Taiwan; the vast majority chose the latter. Responding to public pressure, Washington rejected forced repatriation from Austria, which the USSR wanted to accomplish through the Austrian State Treaty of 1955. The United States has likewise refused to recognize the conquest of the three Baltic states by the USSR—a refusal conforming to United Nations principles. Should an American administration weaken and extend such recognition for the sake of détente, the implication would be that the United States had no real objections against the measures of political subjugation and cultural alienation the Kremlin has been practicing to reduce Estonia, Latvia, and Lithuania to the status of Russian provinces.

Somewhat inconsistently, the United States has accepted Russian domination of Ukraine, and has even agreed to admitting the non-sovereign Ukrainian SSR as a voting member of the United Nations. This complaisance has continued despite a spectrum of oppression that has been genocidal in its total effect and has included artificial famines and outright massacres such as that at Vinnitsa. The 1970 Soviet census showed approximately 42 million Ukrainians in the USSR, 36 million of them living in Ukraine. Census projections of normal growth would indicate 50 million Ukrainians.

Granted, some form of diplomatic communication is necessary—there is business that must be transacted even with criminal regimes. But does it have to be accompanied by the kind of socializing and exchange of platitudes that convey a sense of approval? If our highest officials would conduct themselves so as to register national disapproval of gross violations of human rights by governments on which we have little or no influence, it would enable them to exercise influence where we do have it more credibly on behalf of human beings.

B. Reasons for Indifference to Injustice

The perceptive reader who has perused the accounts of discrimination and oppression throughout the world in this book must have asked himself or herself more than once: "How can it be that people are so indifferent? What are the psychological or behavioral causes of this 'deafening silence'?" The reasons for seeming indifference to human suffering, which can only be suggested here, would seem to fall into two categories. First, there are motivations of interest, including group and national survival, which make it impossible to be "one's brother's keeper" all over the world and on all occasions. There is also the psychological protective mechanism that leads us to close our eyes and minds to problems (like the inevitability of

death) we can do nothing about. Secondly, there is a widespread tendency to deal with social problems, international problems in particular, in terms of categories that fail to do justice to the groups or persons involved.

The dilemma of the religious person who would like to live in today's brutal world according to the Sermon on the Mount or the teachings of Buddha, but is forced to admit that it would be suicidal to do so, is illustrated by Reinhold Niebuhr's contribution to a 1955 conference on theories of international politics. "Political morality," the noted theologian asserted, "contains an inevitable ambiguity because the factors of interest and power, which are regarded as an irrelevance in pure morality, must be at least tentatively admitted to the realm of social morality." Niebuhr is willing to bridge the gap between moral ideals and reality with a tempered hypocrisy. While "it is important not to claim too much for the moral quality of our policies," hypocrisy is inevitable if we have moral principles and do not fully live up to them. "The price of eliminating those hypocrisies entirely is to sink into a consistent cynicism in which moral principles are not operative at all" (Niebuhr, 1955; quoted by K. W. Thompson, 1955, pp. 741–42). Precisely this hypocrisy, however, and the resultant tendency—once drastic action can no longer be avoided—to grasp for absolute political solutions (such as "unconditional surrender") has propelled the United States and the world at large into the political chaos of the twentieth century. It is far better to seek values that may sound less high-flown, but that recognize the realities of group behavior and that we *can* observe in practice. This is what Aristotle would advise us to do (Nicomachean Ethics, Book II).

1. INJUSTICE AND DOMINANT GROUP INTEREST

Concern for the oppressed may play a significant role in motivating action to reform or abolish a social or political system judged discriminatory or tyrannical. But political motives are seldom pure. When reform or revolutionary change becomes the policy of a politically dominant group, we may rest assured that the self-interest of that group is at least a contributing factor and that its real objective is not liberation or uplift of the oppressed but rather a tangential institutional change that will consolidate its own power. Once that change has occurred, the dominant group will adopt a new set of goals, in the pursuit of which further action to promote the welfare of the partly liberated minority may be irrelevant or actually dysfunctional. A group that has been the object of pity, moral outrage, and indeed heroism may suddenly become a nuisance, to be ignored and downgraded— perhaps to be revived at a later date when interests and goals shift again.

This phenomenon can best be illustrated by a practical example. A suitable one is found in the history of attitudes toward blacks in the United States, especially Southern blacks, that have been assumed by the Northeastern political establishment, including its liberal as well as its conservative wing.

The late Frank S. Meyer pointed out that President Lincoln, whatever his image as a folk-hero, was a ruthless centralizer and one of the "major architects of emerging liberal collectivism"—occupying a position midway between Andrew Jackson and F. D. Roosevelt. Lincoln as well as most of his defenders, Meyer writes, "deny that the abolition of slavery was ever Lincoln's intent." His real goal was to abolish the balance of the American federal system, to "consolidate central power and render nugatory the autonomy of the states" (1969, pp. 471, 474). Lincoln's structural objectives were implicit in his war policy, which Meyer describes as follows:

Nor, once battle was engaged, did Lincoln wage the war in a manner calculated to bring about the conditions of reconciliation. He waged it to win *at any cost*—and by winning he meant the permanent destruction of the autonomy of the states. We all know his gentle words, "With malice toward none, with charity for all," but his actions belie this rhetoric (*ibid.*, p. 472).

It may well be that Lincoln, whom Meyer classifies as an "ideologue," was moved by disinterested reason of state having some affinity with Plato's Republic. But since his war depended on Congress, where support for subjugation of the South was not only forthcoming but assumed exaggerated forms during the Johnson and Grant Administrations, we are entitled to ask the perennial political question: *cui bono?*

The majority in Congress, including the radical Republicans who overrode Johnson's veto of the Reconstruction Acts and came within one vote in the Senate of convicting him after impeachment by the House, represented a coalition of Northeastern business and Northwestern agricultural interests which evidently felt it advantageous to keep the South in a state of political and economic turmoil. The instant citizenship the Reconstructionists sought to confer on the blacks thus became not only a means for political education of the latter—though it may have so served to a limited extent—but, more importantly, an instrument for keeping the Southern white establishment from resurrection as a political power ready to exploit any difference that might arise within the Northern coalition. The blacks, whatever temporary gains Reconstruction may have brought them, were used as a political tool—to be discarded when no longer needed.

Abandonment of the blacks came when a majority within the Northeastern establishment, alarmed by the near loss of the presidency to the Democrats in 1876, decided that accommodation with the South would be more profitable than the attempt to continue tutelage. The Reconstruction forces were withdrawn and the Southern white establishment reasserted its supremacy. As C. Vann Woodward observes, the Compromise of 1877 "defined the beginning, but not the ultimate extent, of the liberal retreat on the race issue." Since the Negro now emerged as the symbol of sectional strife, Northern liberals shied away from his cause and began to embrace Southern racial views. Magazines such as the *Nation*, *Harper's Weekly*, the *North American Review*, and the *Atlantic Monthly* frequently contained articles by Northern liberals and former abolitionists proclaiming "the Negroes' innate inferiority, shiftlessness, and hopeless unfitness for full participation in the White man's civilization." The Northern establishment thus achieved reconciliation with its Southern counterpart at the expense of the blacks, who were subjected, up to the turn of the century, to increasingly harsh Jim Crow laws—all sanctioned by the United States Supreme Court (Woodward, 1966).

When the United States turned to overseas imperialism in 1898, it suddenly acquired some 8 million nonwhite subjects. Since the Constitution was not to follow the Flag, a doctrine to justify the White Man's Burden was needed. This took the form of the Anglo-Saxon superiority preached by Professor Burgess of Columbia University, Captain Mahan of the United States Navy, and Senator Albert Beveridge of Indiana. Newspapers such as the Boston *Transcript* and *The New York Times* admitted that the nation had now adopted Southern racial attitudes and policies. The junior senator from South Carolina, John J. McLaurin, thanked his colleague George F. Hoar of Massachusetts "for his complete announcement of the divine right of the Caucasian to govern the inferior races." This racism persisted throughout a wide spectrum of American liberalism until World War I, and was implicit if not explicit in many political utterances of the Progressives. Its persistence was made evident by the discriminatory treatment to which Americans of Japanese descent were subjected during World War II.

2. THINKING IN POLITICAL ABSTRACTIONS

Members of European cultures, Anglo-Saxons in particular, tend to universalize rules and categories originally propounded in specific situations and with mainly situational validity. Thus the Fifth Commandment, "Thou

shalt not commit murder" in the Hebrew Bible—meaning thou shalt kill *only* when authorized or commanded by Scripture—comes out "Thou shalt not kill" in the King James translation.

Americans in particular are inclined to apply abstract and standardized categories to international and interethnic problems. Since the United States emerged as a territorial nation with ideological and legal rather than linguistic, cultural, or racial integrators, it is automatically assumed that each defined political territory must contain a territorial nation to match. Thus untutored Americans speak of "Czechoslovaks" or "Czechoslovakians," terms encouraged by nationalist Czechs whose *Staatsvolk* aspirations are strengthened thereby—but anathema to Slovaks, Sudeten Germans, and the smaller ethnic groups within Professor Masaryk's republic. The same is true of "Yugoslavs"—a term having the *operational effect* of supporting Serb hegemony over a multinational area. Such blanket categories obscure the facts of multiethnicity and, in many cases, of political, cultural, or economic discrimination against ethnic minorities.

The territorial assumption is most pernicious in the case of Africa, where basic loyalties are to tribal groups united by heredity, culture, and language. Yet American and many European political scientists conceive of African development in terms of "nation building." Their model is the monolingual, monocultural European-type nation state which, on closer analysis, turns out to be a rarity even in Europe. If the necessary unitary nation does not exist in the African state, a compulsion arises to create it; the social scientist is charged with clearing the way for *modernization* defined as *overcoming tribalism*. When that model is applied to African reality, what happens is that the most aggressive tribe assumes—or competing tribes and coalitions try to seize—the role of *Staatsvolk*. The results are abuse of power, arson, murder, and sometimes outright civil war.

It is this abstractionism that makes it difficult for Americans to understand the conflict that began in late 1975 in Angola. Western news media have emphasized the ideological orientation of the three competing independence movements and their external backers but have said nothing about their differing tribal roots—and the latter remain the mainsprings of political loyalty regardless of imported ideologies. Thus the possibility of a partition or federalization of Angola along tribal borders—with the Ovambo in the south being joined to their brothers in South West Africa (who are on the road to independence)—is not even considered. More blood must therefore be shed over the destiny of a multitribal territory which, without the mediating and developing functions of the Portuguese, is of doubtful viability as a state. While Western journalists are restricted in their movements, available information seems to indicate that the MPLA (Luanda) forces control only the highways and major towns in much of eastern and southern Angola, while the villages and jungles are open territory for guerrillas associated with UNITA and other dissident movements. As these guerrillas enjoy the sympathy of the local inhabitants they have the tactical advantages explained in the writings of Lin Piao and Regis Debray. In late summer 1976, the Luanda government dispatched a number of "search and destroy" missions under Cuban command. Pastor Kornelius Njoba, Chief Minister of the Owambo homeland in South West Africa, estimated the number killed at 1000. Another 3000 had fled to SWA and were being fed by the South Africans. Although the Ambadjo tribe, the victims of the raids, are closely related to the Ovambo, guerrillas of the South West Africa People's Organization (SWAPO) took part in mass killings. The willingness of the Ovambo-dominated SWAPO to slaughter its own people for political advantage places the legitimacy of its claim to represent the "Namibian nation" in proper perspective. It has already been pointed out (in chapter 20,D) that South West Africa is utterly lacking in national integrators. The attempt of an American Secretary of State to endow it with "self-determination" can only lead to chaos.

The same uncritical territorialism prevents Americans, and to a lesser extent Western Europeans, from coming to grips with the multinational reality of the USSR. Unfortunately the English language, not the best instrument for political science, contains no noun designating the collectivity of the USSR's subjects that does not also *imply their loyalty to and the speaker's endorsement of the communist status quo.* American politicians and even scholars—who should know better—fall constantly into this semantic trap when they mouth such phrases as "Soviet people(s)," "Soviets" (accurate only in referring to *functionaries* of the regime) or—even worse—"Russians" or "Russian people" in reference to the Kremlin's subjects as a whole. A terminology closer to the actual state of affairs would be:

Persons holding USSR citizenship:
USSR citizens or *subjects*
Russian or Muscovite nation and its members:
Russia or *Russia proper* (does not include entire RSFSR)—*Russians*
Other nations in the USSR and their members:
Non-Russian nations in (not of) *the USSR* or *captive nations in the USSR: non-Russians, members of captive nations*
Totality of nations in the USSR and their members:
Nations (or *peoples*) *in the USSR.* If a singular term is needed, use *"population,"* not "people." *USSR inhabitants*

The semantic trap from which an escape has been suggested causes Europeans and Americans alike to close their eyes to an immense amount of human suffering. "If they're Russians (Soviets), why should they object to being Russified (Sovietized)?"

Another communist semantic weapon that need be mentioned only in passing, since recent events have made its falsity so obvious, is the identification of imperialism with capitalism.

A further abstraction that derails American and, again to a lesser extent, European political thought is the notion of the inviolability of the state—*any* state. International law requires sovereigns and states to respect one another's sovereignty—a principle written into the Charter of the United Nations. What is forgotten, however, is that modern international law emerged as a law of convenience among *civilized* states. Its benefits were not extended to "barbarian" kingdoms until they accepted the obligations of civilized intercourse. Since public international law has to do with relations among *states*, its moral authority cannot exceed that of the states concerned. John Locke, who provided the political theory for the American Declaration of Independence, explains that rulers lose their legitimacy when they trample upon the basic rights of the people. In that case power devolves to the people, who have the right to establish such new government as they see fit (*Civil Government*, ch. 19). Applying Locke's standard, it should seem obvious that a number of governments whose crimes have been discussed in this book have lost their legitimacy—certainly the Russian-dominated communist regime in Moscow has long since lost every right to govern the *non-Russian* nations in the USSR—and for many Russians the government is likewise intolerable.

There is nothing in the main current of Western political theory that forbids assisting the subjects of a tyrannical *foreign* government in exercising their right of revolution. The communists have specifically proclaimed the legitimacy of "wars of national liberation," and they are theoretically correct on this point; it is their *standards* of freedom and democracy that are upside down. But for some reason Western liberals, Americans in particular, have been seized by the notion that it is morally wrong to subvert or conspire to overthrow *any* foreign government, no matter how tyrannical it becomes. Let an Amin butcher his subjects by the thousands; let a Castro maintain a concentration-camp regime and grant the greatest imperialist power a submarine base within 100 miles of America's shores. There is nothing to be done about it, since each is sovereign in his own right. Modern liberals have come full circle and embraced Bodin's "The King can do no Wrong"—at least for foreign and particularly communist rulers. United States Senators have agonized over CIA complicity in the overthrow of President Allende: an operation that saved Chile from a Marxist dictatorship and set it on an (admittedly tortuous) road back to freedom.

Obviously, we need to revise our political theory so that it will place *people* first and abstract principles in a lower priority.

C. Reconciling Ethics and Realism

The concrete evidence of the human condition amassed in this book, even if read selectively, can hardly fail to be depressing. The authors admit freely that *they* were depressed at times while compiling the facts. Some readers may conclude that the condition of humankind is inevitably depraved, and that nothing can be done about it until the Messiah appears—or reappears. Others may feel a personal urge to do something and yet a sense of frustration at how little one person—or a political party—or even a nation unified for action—can do. They may even ask: "How can I maintain my ethical integrity and my sanity in a world where people do to one another the things they do?"

Some readers may already have a religion, philosophy, or *Weltanschauung* that integrates all the facts of human unkindness, particularly in the form of group behavior, and that indicates a course of action. Others, however, may take some comfort in the stoic philosophy, expounded most fully by the Roman slave

Epictetus and the Dutch Jew Spinoza, which addresses itself to the art of enduring adversity. According to Dean Leys of Roosevelt University, who summarizes the essence of stoicism in his *Ethics for Policy Decisions*, the stoic asks four questions:

"What is not within our power?"
"What is a true knowledge of life?"
"What must be accepted as external conditions, and what is intolerable because it destroys personal integrity?"
"What is the true good without which life is worthless?" (1952, pp. 78–100)

Expressed most succinctly, the stoic philosophy tells us to learn to accept and understand the world as it is, rather than pretending it is as we should like it to be. It also tells us not to attempt the impossible, to "adjust our desires to our resources," as Dean Leys puts it (*ibid.*, p. 84).

Stoicism is *not*, however, a philosophy of abject resignation to whatever happens, as though it were inevitable. Nor does the stoic flee to the ivory tower, a behavior more typical of Epicureans. Stoicism adjures men to face their moral duty, however unpleasant it may be—it only insists that this duty be defined in terms of the possible. As Leys points out, the man who flatly declares that nothing can be done about a bad situation, when *something* could be done to effect *partial* improvement, is a "pseudo-stoic" who abuses the principle to hide laziness or cowardice (*ibid.*, pp. 88–89).

Finally, the stoic fixes his line of final retreat—the barrier at which he will turn to fight even a hopeless battle, risking his life rather than submitting to injustice which would destroy his personal integrity. It would seem that there are entire national groups, such as the Kurds and the Kabyls, who have earned the title of stoic.

Epictetus and Spinoza admonish us to look at things as they are, and to acquire intellectual understanding of them. Spinoza tells us that "human power is considerably limited and infinitely surpassed by the power of external causes"—which may, of course, include other combinations of human beings. We cannot hope to control every situation to our own advantage. We can, however, bear a disadvantageous situation "with equanimity" if we have done our duty and know that we lack power to control the course of events. We need not pretend that we like the situation, but we can face it without panic or neurosis. "For in so far as we understand, we can desire nothing save that which is necessary." (*Ethics*, 1910, 4th Part, App. XXXII.) On the process of controlling our emotions, Spinoza tells us:

An emotion which is a passion ceases to be a passion as soon as we form a clear and distinct idea of it. . . . Therefore, the more an emotion becomes known to us, the more it is within our power and the less the mind is passive to it" (*ibid.*, 5th Part, Proposition III).

When the stoic philosophy is applied, a series of propositions emerges:

1. WE CANNOT ACHIEVE PERFECTION IN EVERYTHING

As a political principle, the pursuit of perfection is self-defeating. You cannot have perfect freedom, perfect order, perfect democracy, perfect justice, perfect sovereignty, and perfect peace all at once. You have to choose. Rational choice involves formulating a system of priorities, indicating in general terms the extent to which we will sacrifice one value for another when we cannot have both. (On the problem of choice among values, see Willmoore Kendall in *National Review*, November 16, 1957, p. 449.)

What happens when people attempt the impossible is illustrated by the experience of the Weimar Republic, when the Germans attempted to combine nearly perfect freedom (no restrictions on extremist parties) with nearly perfect democracy (absolute proportional representation). Communists and National Socialists combined to form a "negative majority" in the Reichstag, defeating every attempt at orderly government by the moderate center. The resulting chaos opened the way for Hitler's coup, and freedom and democracy were lost altogether.

2. ANY VALUE CARRIED TO EXCESS REACHES A POINT OF SELF-CONTRADICTION

While this proposition, which may be called the principle of the paradox, would be hard to prove through abstract logic, it is amply demonstrated by experience. The classic case in point is the French Revolution, in which the all-powerful Assembly was a nearly perfect example of representative democracy. What happened was the terrorization of the Assembly and the nation by successive committees of deputies, the last one being Robespierre's Committee of Public Safety. Then Thermidor, the confusion of the Directorate, and the "democratic caesarism" of Napoleon. (For a factual account, see Prélot, 1948, pp. 52–113.)

Recent world affairs have demonstrated this second proposition anew. Absolute self-determination for the Czechs in 1918 resulted in denial of self-rule to the Sudeten Germans and Slovaks and thus became an indirect cause of World War II. Attempts to exercise total self-determination by the Hellenic majority on Cyprus caused discrimination against the Turkish minority and provoked the Turkish invasion of 1974—thereby leaving the Greek Cypriots with less freedom than would have resulted from compromise in the first place. And the contradiction between "absolute" rights for the Palestinian Arabs and the Israelis is too obvious to require repeating here.

3. THE VALUE OF A NORM IS DETERMINED BY ITS OPERATIVE RESULTS

To illustrate: Gandhi's *Satyagraha* (literally "truth force": civil disobedience or nonviolent resistance), which Richard Gregg calls "moral jiujitsu," worked effectively in India. However annoying British officers may find demonstrators who lie down in the middle of the street, they will not order their troops to drive tanks over them. Officers steeped in totalitarian ideology will give such an order without a second thought (the probability of obedience being a further variable).

While the law exists as a guide to right conduct and to jurisprudence it is no substitute for moral judgment. To judge is more than the mere application of laws or rules: it is to weigh facts and to reach an ethically and practically acceptable decision. The judge who insists on applying a law when the result violates common sense is often accused of "judicial crime."

Freedom to make decisions necessarily includes freedom to make mistakes. To *decide*—as distinguished from mere ascertainment of facts and from drawing conclusions from pure casuistry—means to choose between right and wrong. Moral choice is the recognition and willing of what is right. Liberty rests on the premise that people are intellectually free and morally responsible for their actions, notwithstanding the current tendency to charge human failings to glands or environment.

D. Re-Examination of Political Norms

Since the foreign policies of civilized states are based on a reconciliation of principle and self-interest, the search for policies to tide us through the current world crisis requires that we reexamine the norms which have served as guidelines in the past. One by one, traditional concepts of liberty, equality, democracy, self-determination, and anticolonialism—all our slogans and battle cries—must be run through the wringer of operational analysis. Do not ask: "What does this principle mean in theory?" Ask: "When this principle is applied to the existing situation, what are the results?"

Since we desire survival as an ethical community, the evaluation of operational results is more complex than in a state dedicated to pure *Machtpolitik*. We cannot ask merely: "How does the principle affect the relative power of the United States and its allies?" We must also ask: "What does this principle do for and to human beings?"

There are obviously certain practices in which civilized governments cannot and will not indulge. Measures such as genocide, police terror, and psychological torture would, to use the stoic formulation, destroy our own integrity. Usually, however, the shoe is on the other foot. The United States has repeatedly insisted on principles that have weakened its own position and those of its allies because of a feeling that these principles were essentially right. If operational analysis shows them to be of trivial or even negative moral content, we can rid ourselves of useless baggage, with no injury to our national conscience.

One thing is immediately evident: the operative moral value of a norm is not a constant, but varies from case to case. Sovereignty, for instance, means one thing to the citizens of Denmark, who enjoy a constitutional government which they can remove at pleasure, and something quite different to the forsaken Kurds, the starving and persecuted Biharis of Bangladesh, the Jews in the USSR and in Arab states, and the many still condemned to forced labor for political unorthodoxy or because they belong to the wrong tribe. Likewise, the operative value of liberty and the extent to which it is possible are conditioned by its employment or abuse in the particular case. As Willmoore Kendall suggests, every society has a range of tolerable discourse with definite limits, transgression of which jeopardizes the body politic. In a sophisticated constitutional state these limits are very broad, but they exist nonetheless: contrary to Mill's abstractionist view, it is not always truth which emerges the victor (Kendall, 1955).

It follows from what has been said that the necessities of survival may require the abandonment of certain traditional principles and the modification of others. Even more: there is need for greater *flexibility* in applying principles which survive the operational test. This is

a matter of discomfort for liberal purists who join with Mill in distrusting human judgment because it is not infallible, but who repose absolute faith in dogma and casuistry. We may, however, take solace in the thoughts of Locke who, realizing that no government is infallible, was willing to repose authority in the consensus of reasonable men with a *limitation* on governmental power as a protection against tyranny (*Civil Government*, pp. 183–90). Similar thoughts are expressed by the modern Jesuit writer Viktor Cathrein, who tells us (1914): "The certainty required for action need not be absolutely infallible. It is sufficient to have moral certainty in the broader sense, such as normally satisfies sensible people. Such certainty usually achieves the truth, though occasionally an error may occur."

1. OPERATIONAL VALUES OF DEMOCRACY AND MAJORITY RULE

Anticolonialism, a dominant concept since the end of World War II, is essentially a feedback of Western political and ethical ideas. When black politicians in Rhodesia or South West Africa, for instance, demand "majority rule," they are borrowing a component of liberal constitutional systems that has little meaning apart from such systems. When a 99-percent "majority" of USSR voters, or 99.5 percent in the German "Democratic" Republic, endorse the communist ticket, that is not majority rule as Europeans and Americans would understand it. The demand for equality is likewise a feedback of an idea once elaborated by Aristotle and propagated in different ways by the American and French revolutions: equality is manifestly not a feature of Asian or African social and political systems.

Because the populations of Northern Europe, the United States, and the older British Dominions are—with the partial exception of *Gastarbeiter* in Europe and certain U.S. minorities—universally literate, we sometimes forget that the workability of democracy as a system of *periodic choice* depends on the ability of the voters to make informed and reasoned political decisions. Supporters of democracy count on ethical indoctrination, rational leadership, and the necessities of compromise to keep democratic politics on an even keel. A symposium on "Cultural Prerequisites to a Successfully Functioning Democracy" published in the *American Political Science Review* (Griffith et al., 1956) made it clear that European-style democracy will only work in modernized, literate societies. Even in these it is dependent on social stratification and on devices such as single-member districts, decentralized parties, and home rule, which help to keep the masses divided into manageable fragments; but the existence and centralized control of mass communications media (especially radio and television) poses the danger that a demagogue may polarize them into a lemming-like flight into tyranny.

Analysis of the cultural prerequisites of democracy, based on the comparative study of countries where it works successfully and where it does not work, suggests several conclusions:

1. *Democracy is made workable by its own imperfections.* Practical politics is the art of compromise, and compromise is only possible when power is dispersed among various interest groups, whose leaders can enter into bargains. Conversely, pure or plebiscitary democracy, as projected by J. J. Rousseau, has always led to instability and ultimately to "democratic caesarism." This perception is based on the principle of the paradox stated in C2, above.
2. *Majority rule requires a unified body politic.* As a principle assuring the human rights of *all*, it can only work within a community commanding the higher loyalty of its members, over and above loyalties to partial and particular groups. If this overarching loyalty is lacking, which is likely to be the case in multiethnic or multiracial or multireligious societies, the larger or more powerful group will use majority rule as a device to persecute or eliminate minorities. It is also essential that majority rule be limited, so that the basic rights of minorities are protected.
3. *Democracy creates legal equality; it cannot work without substantial homogeneity in political behavior.* Where formal democracy is introduced in a society with a small literate elite and vast illiterate masses, the result is a manipulated system, of which one-party states like Tanzania, Zambia, and Uganda under Dr. Milton Obote are typical. Frequently, illiterate soldiers or demagogues seize the controls, and the result is bloody tyranny, as in the cases of Amin's Uganda, the Central African Empire, and Equatorial Guinea. "Instant democracy" is a chimera. Progress toward democracy in Africa, Asia, and Latin America must be slow, as it was in Europe and North America. It must *begin* with the education of literate masses so they can make the rational choices democracy requires.
4. *Interest must prevail over ideology.* The essential compromises that keep a society at peace require that groups act in terms of their enlightened self-interest. In order to do this they must be free to speak without fear of persecution.

African and Asian politicians have learned how to mobilize for their own purposes American belief in the inherent goodness of democracy. But American- or European-style democracy is not what most of them want. Preying on the ignorance of the European and American publics—itself the result of defective political science for which our fraternity must take the blame—*they have learned how to manipulate the symbols of human rights and democracy to achieve goals in absolute contradiction to the principles concerned.* A case in point is Mozambique, the "liberation" of which was supported by Western public opinion, and where Samora Machel has presided over a total denial of due process of law and political freedom.

2. THE PROBLEM OF DOUBLE STANDARDS

"Decolonization" in the name of freedom is followed more often than not in a decline of the most basic human rights: freedom and personal security. This paradox was pointed out by Ambassador John Scali, Chief of the United States Mission to the United Nations, who told a model United Nations of students on March 6, 1975:

In no other area (the subject of human rights) is the contrast between what nations say and what they do so stark and so vivid. On no other issue is the gap between the ideally desirable and the practically attainable so frustratingly wide. . . .

. . . It is difficult . . . to demonstrate that the boundaries of genuine human freedom have been significantly extended during this same period. Admittedly the chains of colonialism have almost everywhere been broken and this is a momentous accomplishment. But the hopes of the United Nations founders for a world genuinely free from fear—fear of want, fear of oppression, fear of injustice, such a world remains to be achieved.

. . . Not only have the United Nations members remained divided over how far the organization is permitted to go in promoting human rights, but there is also no consensus on the very definition of the term—human rights. Thus, from the earliest days of the United Nations representatives of East and West found themselves using the same words—freedom, justice, rights and dignity—but sharply disagreeing on their meaning.

. . . Today Americans still tend to accept their own view of man's relationship to society unquestioningly and we assume that the rest of the world does too. We sometimes forget that the vast majority of the world's peoples have not been raised in this Western tradition, that they do not automatically share our values and that they, therefore, view human rights issues from a different perspective. . . . No doubt this view of human rights serves as a rationalization, a shield behind which some governments perpetuate their authoritarian regimes and seek to deprive their citizens of political liberties.

We should realize, however, that this view has a strong appeal throughout the Third World. Personal liberties are fine, is the attitude of many, but you can't eat them. You can't wear them, nor will they build a roof over your head. Many Third World leaders feel that the extension of civil liberties must take second place to economic development. . . .

Many nations of the Third World also tend to share the Soviet bloc's very restrictive interpretation of the United Nations human rights mandate, at least as it applies to them. Having only recently achieved independence, it is understandable, if regrettable, that these new nations guard their sovereign prerogatives with fierce intensity and that they join together with others as a bloc in resisting international inquiries into what they regard as the domestic affairs of any of their number.

A malaise that has become epidemic since World War II is the tendency to apply double standards in assessing human rights problems. European countries and those settled by Europeans are held to the strictest standards and castigated for noncompliance, whereas massive denials of human rights and even genocides in the Third World are tolerated or passed over in silence. Ambassador Scali said on this score.

Because all nations are reluctant to embarrass their friends, the United Nations tends to confine its critical spotlight to states which for one reason or another find themselves relatively friendless in the international community. All too often this leads to one-sided investigations of human rights abuses—what United States Ambassador Thomas Melady has called selective outrage.

The concern of the United Nations for human rights is, strictly speaking, a departure from the noninterference rule stated in Article 2 (7) of the Charter. That departure, however, is most pronounced in the cases of South Africa and Rhodesia, whereas it is hardly noticeable when wholesale killings and systematic torture in countries such as Uganda, Cambodia, Brazil, and Uruguay are on the agenda.

In a UN committee meeting in November 1975, United States Ambassador Daniel

Moynihan had this to say about "selective outrage":

A draft resolution in the Social, Cultural and Humanitarian committee, entitled "Protection of Human Rights in Chile," called for the government there to ensure "the rights of all persons to liberty and security of person, in particular those who have been detained without charge or in prison solely for political reasons." The United States voted for this resolution. Is there, however, any reason to stop there, to limit our concerns to only two members of the United Nations, when there are all together 142 members? . . .

[T]he selective morality of the United Nations in matters of human rights threatens the integrity not merely of the United Nations, but of human rights themselves. There is no mystery in this matter. Unless standards of human rights are seen to be applied uniformly and neutrally to all nations, regardless of the nature of their regimes or the size of their armaments; unless this is done, it will quickly be seen that it is not human rights at all which are invoked when selective applications are called for, but simply arbitrary political standards dressed up in the guise of human rights. From this perception it is no great distance to the conclusion that in truth there are no human rights recognized by the international community.

. . . the language of human rights is increasingly being turned in United Nations forums against precisely those regimes which acknowledge some or all of its validity and they are not, I fear, a majority of the regimes in this United Nations. More and more the United Nations seems only to know of violations of human rights in countries where it is still possible to protest such violations.

What is obviously needed is a reexamination of the standards by which human rights and their observance (or nonobservance) are judged in the United Nations and by civilized public opinion. Whatever standards are set should then be applied, impartially and objectively, to countries as divergent as the USSR and South Africa, Burundi and the United States. While backward development may explain deficiencies in respect for human rights, *it can never excuse them.*

E. The Future of Human Rights

The moral basis for human rights is present in the doctrines of the higher religions, including Judaism, Christianity, Islam, Hinduism, and Buddhism, as well as in the teachings of Confucius and the Greek and Roman philosophers. They achieved their fullest intellectual development, in the form recognized by nearly world-wide consensus today and embodied in the United Nations conventions discussed in part I of this book, within the framework of European culture. Human rights emerged as the basis for political systems in the wake of the Puritan Revolution in England. They were given concrete form by John Locke and by writers of the enlightenment, among whom Voltaire, Burke, Schiller, and Jefferson may be mentioned. Significantly, however, they were rejected by some philosophers of the technocratic school. "The only right we have is to perform our duty," wrote Auguste Comte in his *Politique Positive* (quoted, de la Presa, 1974).

At first, human rights appeared as abstract ideals cherished by a small stratum of individuals. But with the spread of mass education and mass literacy, they became enshrined in the traditions of entire nations, and were incorporated in the American, French, and other constitutions. So enshrined, they are accepted as universal values. Wisely or unwisely, the United States and the United Kingdom have at times gone to war on behalf of the human rights of *foreign peoples;* while national interests were also involved, they might not alone have provided a *casus belli.*

The United Nations Commission On Human Rights (UNCHR) was founded in 1946; its first chairperson was Eleanor Roosevelt. But efforts to mobilize world opinion were soon obscured by politics. Two former United States delegates to the Commission charged that the Department of State silenced criticism of U.S. allies, while a House of Representatives subcommittee charged that Washington had "discarded human rights for the sake of other assumed interests" (Bria and Kramer, 1974). For years, UNCHR spent much time and effort castigating South Africa, Rhodesia, and Portugal, while ignoring oppression in communist countries, including persistent slave labor and the persecution of intellectuals and Jews in the USSR. At its 1974 meeting it refused to consider documented files compiled by a subcommission that found "a consistent pattern of gross violations" of human rights in Brazil, Northern Ireland, Indonesia, Burundi, Iran, Guyana, Tanzania, and Portugal. "We play the game somewhat as the Russians play the game," said Morris Abram, U.S. delegate to the Commission from 1965 to 1968, "If a country is your friend or allied with you . . . we don't lower the boom." When Abram moved a resolution to study human rights violations in Greece and Haiti, the "State Department apparatus descended on me because Greece was our NATO ally . . . all hell broke loose and I had to withdraw the resolution" (quoted, *ibid.*). In the same year, Cuban exiles noted that Castro's delegates were the most energetic prosecutors of the Chilean Junta, while their own complaints of political imprisonments, tortures, and executions in Cuba were ignored (Martinez, 1974).

Two years later Prince Sadruddin Aga Khan, the United Nations High Commissioner for Refugees, felt obliged to tell the General Assembly that the Human Rights pact was being treated with "ridicule" and to condemn "the levity with which international humanitarian principles are transgressed." While Prince Sadruddin was mainly concerned with Rhodesian and Chilean refugees, he also deplored the denial of aid to Vietnamese fleeing in leaky boats and the forced repatriation of a Russian pilot by Iran. As is well known, Secretary of State Kissinger appears to have acted on the assumption that public attention to human rights would jeopardize United States foreign policy, détente with the USSR in particular. That is why he forestalled a visit to President Ford by the Russian writer Solzhenitsyn. Kissinger refused to comply with a law requiring a country-by-country report on human rights violations as a means of judging whether foreign aid should be granted (*St. Louis Post-Dispatch*, January 4, 1977).

President Carter's active interest in human rights has cast a new light across an otherwise gloomy perspective. While the President's power to take direct action is limited by traditional international law forbidding interference in the internal affairs of sovereign states and by a traditional reluctance of Congress to countenance foreign interventions, there is no doubt that an American chief of state possesses strong leverage and powers of persuasion. Carter's hand is strengthened by a new law requiring that reports on human rights conditions in countries receiving U.S. aid accompany the administration's requests for funds. Publication of these reports was followed by the rejection of military aid by Brazil and a cutoff of such aid to Ethiopia, Argentina, and Uruguay (*Los Angeles Times*, March 13, 1977). In other cases, including Indonesia, Iran, South Korea, and the Philippines, the Department of State recommended continuance of aid despite deficiencies in human rights observance.

Cynical observers speculate that President Carter may see political advantage in verbalizing about human rights. Yet there is little doubt that the President is sincerely and deeply committed on the issue (James Deakin in *St. Louis Post-Dispatch*, March 24, 1977). The effect of his leadership may well be to broaden a trend toward modifying a traditional doctrine of absolute sovereignty: a trend already seen in UN pronouncements on South Africa and Rhodesia. In his first major foreign policy speech, the President said that since the UN Charter contained a pledge to observe and respect basic human rights, "no member of the United Nations can claim that mistreatment of its citizens is solely its own business. Equally, no member can avoid its responsibilities . . . to speak when torture or unwarranted deprivation of freedom occurs in any part of the world." The seriousness of the President's intentions was made clear when the U.S. delegate to UNCHR, former Congressman Allard Lowenstein, raised the subject of human rights violations in the USSR and in Uganda, and opposed a one-sided resolution criticizing Israel (*San Jose Mercury*, March 17, 1977).

What is both innovative and realistic in President Carter's new policy is his insistence on basic human rights rather than any particular system of government or economics. Carter's approach is vastly superior to the ill-conceived Wilsonian tradition of confusing morality with democracy and of insisting on elections and plebiscites where they are neither understood nor workable. The globe is not inhabited by Americans who happen to speak foreign languages. The American political system, while it has features that can be used on all continents, is specifically adapted to conditions in the United States. Since Americans uphold the right to self-government, they must concede that each country should select its own system.

The degrees and kinds of democracy that are practical in particular countries depend on circumstances of time and place. By contrast, the observation of human rights is a universally valid moral command.

In principle, all forms of government, including autocracy and even dictatorship, are compatible with human rights. Frederick the Great, known as a classical autocrat, was also the protector of the Prussian *Rechtsstaat* that assured all citizens due process of law, although some of his contemporaries, notably in France and Russia, were less scrupulous in that regard. Only when a regime is governing badly does preservation of the state require abridgement or denial of human rights. It must be admitted that this is most likely to happen in autocracies and dictatorships, including party dictatorships, since they are not subject to effective public control. Regimes which violate human rights consistently and brutally always lose their flexibility and eventually their power, despite the massive police organizations and armies at their disposal.

For a human rights policy to succeed, it must be skillfully executed and must not become the instrument of publicity coups. It must be applied to friend and foe alike, and to human rights abuses in the United States as well as elsewhere. There must be no double or multiple standards. The policy must concentrate on consistent violations rather than occasional lapses. It must not be aimed to arouse hatred or aggression, but must be a low-key, consistent, and polite exercise in persuasion. The objective is not to pillory those who are disliked but to construct a common future in which there is only one world of human rights—even without a world government.

The effectiveness of a human rights policy will vary with the broadness of consensus recognizing the rights protected as universal and morally binding. There is need, therefore, for scholarly as well as diplomatic review of the whole catalog of human rights, to sort out those that are universally valid from those limited to particular systems and cultures. The right to operate a business, however much Americans cherish it, implies an economic market system and may be limited in constitutional as well as dictatorial socialist states. The kinds of property a person may have vary from society to society; in modern complex societies property is defined by law. Conversely, certain rights asserted in the United Nations conventions seem to imply interventionist economic policies or nondifferentiated territorial democracies. There is also the question of conflicting rights. Some who organized to defeat Indira Gandhi appeared to feel that she violated the right of Indians to have as many children as they please regardless of the country's food supply, as well as the right of free religious observance. But do we have a right to bring children into the world when this means that they, or someone else's children, are certain or likely to starve to death? Rights, in other words, must be reconciled with necessity. Pending further study and perhaps a new international convention, therefore, it would be best to concentrate on universally recognized rights such as life, liberty, the right to earn a living, and the right of nations and ethnic groups to their cultures and their traditional homes (*Heimatrecht*). Attention should be focused on major violations such as genocides and mass executions, forced and cruelly executed expulsions and deportations, slavery and slave labor, torture, including forced administration of drugs, denial of due process, withholding of food and medical treatment, and imposition of unhealthful living conditions. It should, of course, be kept in mind that people are often the victims of catastrophes both natural and human, which governments are powerless to prevent.

A policy of upholding human rights is easy to understand. It is far more comprehensible than insistence on particular ideologies or political structures. A human rights policy should, needless to say, contain its own guarantee of due process. It should require complaints to be specific, to indicate the right alleged to be violated, and to give the fullest factual description of the violation—analogous to that required in a criminal case. The government criticized should be given a full opportunity to provide verifiable evidence refuting the accusation. Once proved, however, the facts of human rights violations should be given the widest publicity.

So far, the American human rights initiative has been confused. Chile and the USSR have been targets of particular criticism, apparently in the belief that moves against right and left must be parallel. South Africa continues to be attacked, even though the main charge against it is insistence on separate political development rather than undifferentiated territorial democracy. At the same time, black African states whose leaders are responsible for genocides and massacres benefit from a policy of sympathetic silence—Uganda being a notable exception. Cambodia is committing extensive genocide—almost unique in being directed against majority Khmers rather than minorities or foreigners. On this outrage, too, the U.S. Government remains silent. Only Congress has registered complaints about mainland China, which during 27 years of Mao Tsetung's rule violated human rights more massively than any other country. Nor has the United States taken any initiative to secure the repeal of United Nations declarations in favor of guerrilla warfare—which necessarily involves repeated savage violations of human rights.

While the historical record shows that oppression derived from discrimination has occurred at all times and under all types of political systems, President Carter has committed his administration to an area in which progress is possible. People will never become angels, but most are fundamentally rational, and ready to recognize the rights of others if their own are respected. Much of the delay in abolishing discrimination, mass expulsions, slavery-like practices, torture, and genocide simply reflects the fact that comparatively little is said or written about these inhumane practices. As public consciousness is awakened—a development for which nongovernmental organizations such as Amnesty International, the Anti-Slavery Society, and the Minority Rights Group deserve much credit—demand for effective policies will be an automatic response.

It is important that the quest for individual human rights not be conducted so as to deny group rights—particularly the rights of ethnic groups to preserve their languages and cultures and manage their own affairs. Groups are more or less compatible: to force a minority under the unrestricted rule of a discordant majority means to oppress it. But the right of self-government does not stand in splendid isolation. It is limited by and linked to other principles, and it clashes with the criterion that any group must achieve certain capabilities before it can be entitled to govern itself. Applied uncritically, absolute self-determination may spawn too many dwarf states incapable of political or economic survival. Self-determination may at times conflict with *Heimatrecht*.

If variant ethnic groups are merged within a unitary state, they may suffer discrimination against their freedom of choice and may be prevented from moving to areas where their economic prospects would be better. There is no cut-and-dried solution applicable to all cases; political structure must correspond to ethnic reality. Practical nondogmatic arrangements can be worked out, keeping incompatible groups apart and allowing others to intermingle—but even the best arrangements need plenty of time to stabilize.

While limitations of individual freedom are undesirable, no viable society can be constructed where compulsion is ruled out completely. Its disadvantages should, however, be compensated, and compulsion itself kept to a minimum. It must be kept in mind that history is dynamic: groups grow and decline, mutual hostilities are aggravated or softened, and stratification rankings are constantly being modified.

In most complex cases, an ideological policy of imposed nondiscrimination results in new discrimination. Since the state is in charge of the program, nonoppressive intentions may produce oppression. For this reason, state action should be mainly restricted to the prevention of conflict, and should seldom if ever attempt to produce social changes by force. What is important is to give to all groups means of representation and political expression and to bring them together in joint planning and problem-solving efforts.

There are two major forms of protection against discrimination in the sense of denial of inalienable rights. The first is explicit recognition that discrimination is harmful in that, at least in the long run, it is economically costly and deleterious, results in political oppression and dictatorship, often leads to war, and frequently ends in widespread destruction and genocide. The second form of protection consists in the progressive development of resources, which provide to each group the means of its existence and prosperity. The notion that to survive one group needs to deprive other groups of their means and rights of sur-

vival must be rejected. In most economic situations, groups can survive better in cooperation than in conflict.

Similarly, there are two phenomena that cause discrimination rather than genuine nondiscrimination. One is extremist egalitarianism which sees nondiscrimination as an absolute regardless of social, political, and cultural compatibility; which attempts enforcement beyond the practicable; which aims for utopian perfectionism; which disregards time needed for progress and seeks instant optimization; which cavils at trivial troubles but often remains blind to grave injustices—which, in brief, escalates a good idea to absurdity. The second disturbing factor is criminal-pathological government, as exemplified by Cambyses, Nero, Torquemada, Hitler, Stalin, Amin, Macias Nguema, and many others. Should rulers of this type come to power once again, catastrophe would be repeated, and mass oppression and genocide would be elements of that catastrophe. Protection against this danger requires a viable, properly constructed, and effectively defended state, the selection of good rulers, mature political consciousness on the part of the citizens, and international cooperation to limit the threat.

Criminal political behavior is not, of course, limited to governments. Terrorism, in the form of assassinations, airplane hijackings, seizure of trains, schools, and office buildings, and guerrilla attacks on farms and villages, has recently become highly visible. A March 2, 1977, report by the Task Force on Disorders and Terrorism predicts more to come (William Morrissey in *St. Louis Post-Dispatch*, March 10, 1977)—and indeed it has. Terrorism in its modern forms is made possible by advanced technology. Its specific *modus operandi* is the denial of human rights, usually those of people not directly involved in the matter at stake. Their lives are placed in danger, and often they are killed out of hand. Terrorism could not be treated at length in the present context, but the authors would like to register their views

Endangering or extinguishing the lives of innocent people is *never* justified, whatever the cause or pretext. Conversely, action to rescue victims of terrorism is justified, even at the cost of offending the sovereignty of a state that, in effect, aids and abets the terrorists. It should be kept in mind that supposedly "free lance" terrorist groups are often secretly and indirectly supported by governments.

We do not know how to change man. Even if we did, we doubt that the planned transformation of man is a legitimate undertaking of free government. The prevention of policies which deny human rights requires, above all, constitutions and legislation which define the rights of individuals and groups in a sensible manner, as well as the loyalty of the populations concerned to their constitutions. Only constitutions which are reasonable and workable achieve protracted loyalty.

The task of creating good government remains as uncompleted as the task of preparing the citizen for rational political behavior. But the labor continues, and human resourcefulness is growing. Although our period is marked by political illiteracy and unprecedented barbarity, the road toward greater realization of human rights remains open. It is long and strenuous but progress can be made step by step.

BIBLIOGRAPHY

Abadan-Unat, Nermin, 1976. *Turkish Workers in Europe, 1960–1975*. Leiden: E. J. Brill.

Abernathy, Ralph David, 1971. "The Non-Violent Movement: the Past, the Present, and the Future." In Goldstein, ed., 1971 (q.v.), pp. 180–209.

Abramson, Harold J., 1973. *Ethnic Diversity in Catholic America*. Rotterdam: Martinus Nijhoff.

Abuse of Psychiatry, 1972. *Abuse of Psychiatry for Political Repression in the Soviet Union*. Hearing before the Subcommittee to Investigate the Administration of the Internal Security Act and Other Internal Security Laws of the Committee on the Judiciary, United States Senate. 92d Congress, second session, September 26. Washington: Government Printing Office.

Adams, Brooks, 1900. *America's Economic Supremacy*. New York: Macmillan, esp. pp. 9–26.

Adams, T. W., 1966. "The First Republic of Cyprus: A Review of an Unworkable Constitution." *The Western Political Quarterly* 19, no. 3 (September): 475–90.

Adorno, Theodor W. and Max Horkheimer, 1972. *Dialectic of Englightenment*. New York: Herder and Herder.

AID, 1972. *Africa: Economic Growth Trends*. Washington: Agency for International Development, Office of Statistics and Reports. May.

A. I. Newsletter, *Amnesty International Newsletter*. Published monthly by Amnesty International Publications, 53 Theobald's Road, London, WC 1, England. Obtainable in the U.S. from *Amnesty International*, 200 W. 72 St. New York, N.Y. 10023.

A. I. Report, 1974. *Amnesty International Annual Report 1973–74*. London: Amnesty International Publications.

Akpan, Ntyieyong U., 1971. *The Struggle for Secession, 1966–1970: A Personal Account of the Nigerian Civil War*. London: Frank Cass.

Albino, Oliver, 1973–74. *The Sudan: A Southern Viewpoint*. London: Oxford University Press.

Alier, Abel, 1973. "The Southern Sudan Question." In Wai, 1973 (q.v.), pp. 11–28.

Alland, Alexander, Jr., 1973. *Human Diversity*. New York: Feffer and Simons, Inc.

Allport, Gordon W., 1952. "Resolving Intergroup Tensions." In Allen Lloyd Cook, ed., *Toward Better Human Relations*. Detroit: Wayne State University Press.

—— 1954. *The Nature of Prejudice*. Cambridge, Mass.: Addison-Wesley Publishing Co.

Allworth, Edward, ed., 1973. *The Nationality Question in Soviet Central Asia*. Publ. in cooperation with the Program on Soviet Nationality Problems, Columbia University. New York-Washington-London: Praeger Publishers.

Amelunxen, Clemens, 1975a. "Foreign Workers in West Germany." In Veenhoven, 1975 (q.v.) 1: 113–32.

—— 1975b. "Marriage and Women in Islamic Countries." In Veenhoven, 1975 (q.v.) 2: 83–99.

Amnesty International, 1973. *Report on Torture*. Liverpool: Duckworth.

Amsden, John, 1972. *Collective Bargaining and Class Conflict in Spain*. London: Weidenfeld and Nicolson.

Anber, Paul, 1967. "Modernization and Political

Disintegration: Nigeria and the Ibos." *Journal of Modern African Studies* 5, no. 2 (September): 163–79.

Anders, Wilhelm, ed., 1975. *Verbrechen der Sieger, Das Schicksal der deutschen Kriegsgefangenen in Osteuropa: Berichte und Dokumente.* Leoni am Starnbergersee: Druffel-Verlag.

Anderson, Charles, Fred R. von der Mehden, and Crawford Young, 1974. *Issues of Political Development,* 2nd ed. Englewood Cliffs, N.J.: Prentice-Hall, Inc.

Anderson, David D. and Robert L. Wright, eds., 1971. *The Dark and Tangled Path: Race in America.* Boston: Houghton Mifflin Company.

Anti-Slavery Society, Background, 1972. "Background to the Present Situation at the United Nations Concerning Slavery." London: Anti-Slavery Society, 5 pp., mimeographed.

—— 1973. "Some Common Questions Answered" (about the Anti-Slavery Society for the Protection of Human Rights, in which is incorporated the Aborigines Protection Society). London: 9 pp., mimeographed.

—— 1974. *Annual Report.* London: Anti-Slavery Society.

App, Austin J., 1967. "The Rooseveltian Concentration Camps for Japanese-Americans, 1942—46." A pamphlet. Philadelphia: Boniface Press.

Appel, John J., 1970. "American Negro and Immigrant Experience: Similarities and Differences." In Dinnerstein and Jaher, 1970 (q.v.), pp. 339–47.

Arasaratnam, Sinnappah, 1970. *Indians in Malaysia and Singapore.* Bombay, Oxford University Press; London, Oxford University Press, 1974.

Arcand, Bernard, 1972. *The Urgent Situation of the Cuiva Indians of Colombia.* Copenhagen: International Work Group for Indigenous Affairs, Pub. No. 7.

Archer, Margaret Scotford, and Salvador Giner, eds., 1971. *Contemporary Europe: Class, Status and Power.* London: Weidenfeld and Nicolson.

Arnold, Walter, 1971. Review of B. F. Skinner, *Beyond Freedom and Dignity. Saturday Review,* October 9, 1971, pp. 47–49.

Arraes, Miguel, 1972. *Brazil: The People and the Power,* translated by Lancelot Sheppard. Harmondsworth, England: Penguin Books.

Aswad, Barbara C., 1974. *Arabic Speaking Communities in American Cities.* New York: Center for Migration Studies.

Atkinson, Anthony B., 1975. *The Economics of Inequality.* Oxford: Clarendon Press.

Aumann, Moshe, 1974. *Land Ownership in Palestine 1880–1948.* Jerusalem: Israel Academic Committee on the Middle East.

Awad, Mohamed, 1966. *Report on Slavery.* New York: United Nations E/4168/REV.1.

Bachi, Roberto, 1974. "The Jewish Population." In *Society,* Israel Pocket Library. Jerusalem: Keter Publishing House, pp. 1–28.

Background, 1972. *See* Anti-Slavery Society.

Baer, Ed, 1973. *Heredity and Society: Readings in Social Genetics.* New York: Macmillan.

Bagley, Christopher, 1973. *The Dutch Plural Society: A Comparative Study in Race Relations.* London: Oxford University Press, published for the Institute of Race Relations.

Bailey, Harry A., Jr., and Elise Katz, eds., 1969. *Ethnic Group Politics.* Columbus, Ohio: Charles E. Merrill Publishing Co.

Baker, Donald G., 1975. *Politics of Race.* London: Lexington Books.

Baker, John R., 1974. *Race.* London: Oxford University Press.

Baker, Ray Stannard, 1923. *Woodrow Wilson and World Settlement.* Two volumes. Garden City, N.Y.: Doubleday, Page.

Banfield, Edward C., 1970. *The Unheavenly City: The Nature and Future of Our Urban Crisis.* Boston: Little, Brown.

—— 1974. *The Unheavenly City Revisited.* Revised and updated edition of *The Unheavenly City.* Boston: Little, Brown.

Banton, Michael, 1967. *Race Relations.* London: Tavistock Publications.

—— 1972. *Racial Minorities.* London: Fontana Collins.

Bao Ruo-wang (Jean Pasqualini) and Rudolph Chelminski, 1973. *Prisoner of Mao.* New York: Coward, McCann and Geoghegon.

Barghoorn, Frederick C., 1974. "Soviet Dissenters on Soviet Nationality Policy." In Bell and Freeman, 1974 (q.v.), pp. 117–33.

Baron, Harold, 1971. "Black Powerlessness in Chicago." In Edward S. Greenberg, Neal Milner and David J. Olson, eds. *Black Politics: the Inevitability of Conflict—Readings.* New York: Holt, Rinehart and Winston, pp. 105–17.

Barratt et al., eds. 1974. *Accelerated Development in Southern Africa*. John Barratt, Simon Brand, David S. Collier, and Kurt Glaser, eds. London: Macmillan.

Barron, Milton L., ed., 1967. *Minorities in a Changing World*. New York: Alfred A. Knopf.

Barzun, Jacques, 1965. *Race: A Study in Superstition*. New York: Harper and Row.

Baucic, Ivo, 1972. *The Effects of Emigration from Yugoslavia and the Problems of Returning Emigrant Workers*. The Hague: Martinus Nijhoff.

Baxter, Paul and Basil Sansom, eds., 1972. *Race and Social Difference*. Harmondsworth: Penguin.

Bebler, Anton, 1973. *Military Rule in Africa: Dahomey, Ghana, Sierra Leone and Mali*. London: Pall Mall; New York: Praeger.

Beilenson, Laurence W., 1972. *Power Through Subversion*. Washington: Public Affairs Press.

Bell, Wendell, and Walter Freeman, eds., 1974. *Ethnicity and Nation-Building: International and Historical Perspectives*. London: Sage Publications, Ltd.

Ben-Dasan, Issiah, 1972. *The Japanese and the Jews*, translated by Richard L. Gage. New York: Weatherill.

Bendix, Gabrielle, 1973. Dem Bitteren Erwachen im Lande der Träume durch Beratung und Hilfeleistung zuvorkommen, interview with Director Heppert of Advisory Office for Emigrants. *Sudetendeutsche Zeitung*, October 12, 1973.

Benedict, Burton, 1962. "Stratification in Plural Societies." *American Anthropologist* 64, no. 6 (December): 1235–46.

Benedict, Ruth, 1945. *Race, Science and Politics*. New York: Viking Press.

Bergel, Egon Ernest, 1962. *Social Stratification*. New York: McGraw-Hill Book Co.

Berger, John, and Jean Mahr, 1975. *A Seventh Man: The Story of a Migrant Worker in Europe*. London: Penguin Books.

Berlin, 1960. *Foreign Relations of the United States, Diplomatic Papers: The Conference of Berlin* (Potsdam Conference), 1945. Vols. 1 and 2, Department of State Publications Nos. 7015 and 7163. Washington: Government Printing Office, 1960.

Bernard, Jessie, 1971. *Women and the Public Interest*. Chicago: Aldine Atherton.

Bernstein, Ron, 1977. "Chamber of Horror." *Skeptic*, No. 17 (January–February 1977), pp. 24–29.

Berreman, Gerald D., 1967. "Stratification, Pluralism and Interaction: A Comparative Analysis of Caste." In De Reuck and Knight, 1967 (q.v.), pp. 45–73.

—— 1973. "Caste as Social Process." In Gelfand and Lee, 1973 (q.v.), pp. 33–47.

Berry, B., 1965. *Race and Ethnic Relations*. Boston: Houghton Mifflin.

Beshir, Mohamed Omer, 1965. *The Southern Sudan: Background to Conflict*. New York: Frederick A. Praeger.

Béteille, André, 1969. *Castes: Old and New Essays in Social Structure and Social Stratification*. New York: Asia Publishing House.

—— ed., 1972a. *Social Inequality*. Harmondsworth, England: Penguin.

—— 1972b. "Pollution and Poverty." In Mahar, 1972 (q.v.) pp. 411–20.

Bethell, Nicholas, 1974. *The Last Secret*. New York: Basic Books.

Bhatia, Prem, 1973. *Indian Ordeal in Africa*. London: Vikas.

Biegel, L. C., 1972. *Minderheden in het Midden-Osten: Hun betekenis als politieke fact in de Arabische wereld*. Deventer, Netherlands: Van Loghum Slaterus.

Binder, Leonard, 1964. "National Integration and Political Development." *American Political Science Review* 58, no. 3 (September): 622–31.

—— 1966. *Politics in Lebanon*. New York: John Wiley and Sons.

Black, Henry Campbell, 1968. *Black's Law Dictionary*, 4th edition. St. Paul: West Publishing Company.

Blackburn, Robin, ed., 1975. *Explosion in a Subcontinent: India, Pakistan, Bangladesh and Ceylon*. London: Penguin Books.

Blair, Philip M., 1973. *Job Discrimination and Education: A Case Study of Mexican-Americans in Santa Clara County*, London: Pall Mall Press.

Blau, Peter M., and Duncan Otis Dudley, 1969. "Sponsored and Contest Mobility and the School System." In Heller, 1969 (q.v.).

Blauner, Robert, 1972. "Black Culture: Myth or Reality?" In Bromley and Longino, 1972 (q.v.).

Bloom, Leonard, 1971. *The Social Psychology of Race Relations*. London: George Allen and Unwin.

Boas, Franz, 1911. Introduction to *Handbook of American Indian Languages*, orig. pub. 1911, reprinted with Powell, 1891 (q.v.), 1966. Lincoln: University of Nebraska Press.

Bodley, John H., 1972. *Tribal Survival in the Amazon: The Campa Case*, Copenhagen: International Work Group for Indigenous Affairs, Pub. No. 5.

Bogardus, E. S., 1933. "A Social Distance Scale." *Sociology and Social Research* 17, no. 3 (January-February): 265–71.

Bohmann, Alfred, 1969a. *Menschen und Grenzen: Vol. I—Strukturwandel der deutschen Bevölkerung im polnischen Staats- und Verwaltungsbereich.* Cologne: Verlag Wissenschaft und Politik.

—— 1969b. *Menschen und Grenzen,* Vol. II—*Bevölkerung und Nationalitäten in Südosteuropa.* Cologne: Verlag Wissenschaft und Politik.

—— 1970. *Menschen und Grenzen,* Vol. III —*Strukturwandel der deutschen Bevölkerung im sowjetischen Staats- und Verwaltungsbereich.* Cologne: Verlag Wissenschaft und Politik.

Böhning, W. Roger, 1972. *The Migration of Workers in the United Kingdom and the European Community.* London: Oxford University Press.

Borer, Mary Cathcart, 1963. *Africa: A Short History of the Peoples of Africa.* London: Museum Press.

Bose, Nirmal Kumar, 1965. "Calcutta: A Premature Metropolis." *Scientific American* 213 (September).

—— 1967. *Culture and Society in India.* Bombay: Asia Publishing House.

Boskin, Joseph, 1972. "Sambo: The National Jester in the Popular Culture." In Baxter and Sansom, 1972 (q.v.), pp. 152–64.

Bottomore, T. B., 1969. "Classes in Modern Society." (Extract from book of same title. London: Allen & Unwin, 1965.) In Heller, 1969 (q.v.), pp. 524–31.

—— 1971. "Class Structure in Western Europe." In Archer and Giner, 1971 (q.v.), pp. 388–408.

Bourdeaux, Michael et al., 1973. *Religious Minorities in the Soviet Union.* London: Minority Rights Group Report No. 1, revised edition.

Bouvard, Marguerite, 1973. *Labour Movements in the Common Market Countries.* London: Pall Mall Press.

Boxberg, Katharina von, 1975. "Rettung vor dem Spiegel." (New Methods of Early Diagnosis of Mentally Handicapped Children.) *Die Welt,* May 3, 1975, part 4, p. 5.

Bracher, Karl Dietrich, 1970. *The German Dictatorship,* trans. Jean Steinberg. New York and Washington: Praeger.

Brass, Paul R., 1974. *Language, Religion and Politics in North India.* Cambridge, England: Cambridge University Press.

Bretton, Henry L., 1973. *Power and Politics in Africa.* Chicago: Aldine.

Breytenbach, W. J., 1974. *The Role of Ethnicity in Determining Social Distance and Differentiation in Some African Countries.* Pretoria: Research Paper, Africa Institute of South Africa. Reproduced as manuscript.

Bria, George, and Gene Kramer, 1974. "Human Rights—An Area Where UN Has Slipped." *Pretoria News,* April 24, 1974.

Bromley, David G., and Charles F. Longino, eds., 1972. *White Racism and Black Americans.* Cambridge, Massachusetts: Schenkman.

Brooks, Dennis, 1973, 1975. *Race and Labour in London Transport.* London, Blackwell's (1973); London: Oxford University Press (1975).

Brooks, Edwin, 1973. "Prospects of Integration for the Indians of Brazil." *Patterns of Prejudice* (March-April).

Brown, Ina Corinne, 1973. *Understanding Race Relations.* Englewood Cliffs, N.J.: Prentice-Hall.

Brown, Leon Carl, 1967. "Color in Northern Africa." *Daedalus* 96 (Winter-Spring): 464–82.

Brown, Susan Love et al., 1974. *The Incredible Bread Machine.* San Diego: World Research, Inc., Campus Studies Institute Division.

Brown, W. Norman, 1966. "Hindu-Muslim Differences." In T. Walter Wallbank, ed., *The Partition of India, Causes and Responsibilities.* Boston: Heath.

Brownlie, Ian, 1971. *Basic Documents on Human Rights.* Oxford: Clarendon Press.

Brudnoy, David, 1973. "A Closer Look at Egalitarianism." *Human Events,* June 2, 1973.

Bryant, Clifton D., ed., 1971. *Social Problems Today: Dilemmas and Dissensus.* Philadelphia: Lippincott.

Buckley, James L., 1975. "Soviet Minorities, Dissidents Beg for U.S. Recognition and Aid." *Human Events,* January 18, 1975, pp. 18–20.

Bullock, Charles S., and Harrel R. Rodgers, Jr., 1975. *Racial Equality in America: In Search of an Unfulfilled Goal.* Pacific Palisades, Cal.: Goodyear Pub. Co.

Bullough, Bonnie, and Vern L. Bullough, 1972. *Poverty, Ethnic Identity and Health Care.* New York: Appleton-Century-Crofts.

Bullough, Vern L., 1973. *The Subordinate Sex: A His-*

tory of Attitudes Toward Women. Urbana: University of Illinois Press; reprinted, Baltimore: Penguin Books, 1974. References are to reprint.

Bunge, William, 1971. *Fitzgerald: Geography of a Revolution*. Cambridge, England: Schenkman Publishing Co.

Burkey, Richard M., 1971. *Racial Discrimination and Public Policy in the United States*. London: Heath Lexington Books.

Burton, Benedict, 1965. *Mauritius: Problems of a Plural Society*. London: Pall Mall Press.

Busch, Peter A., 1974. *Legitimacy and Ethnicity*. London: Lexington Books.

Bustamente, Jorge A., 1972. "The Wetback as Deviate: An Application of Labelling Theory." *American Journal of Sociology* (January).

Butterwick, Michael, 1974. "India Dithers as Grain Runs Out." *Daily Telegraph*. London, June 4, 1974.

Byrnes, James F., 1947. *Speaking Frankly*. New York: Harper. Reprint 1974, Westport, Conn.: Greenwood Press.

Bywater, Hector C., 1925. *The Great Pacific War: a History of the American-Japanese Campaign of 1931–33*. Boston: Houghton Mifflin.

Campbell, A., and H. Schuman, 1970a. "Black Views of Racial Issues." In Goldschmid, 1970 (q.v.), pp. 346–65.

—— 1970b. "The Uses of Violence." In *ibid.*, pp. 401–18.

—— "White Beliefs About Negroes." In *ibid.*, pp. 270–84.

Campbell, Angus, 1971. *White Attitudes toward Black People*. Ann Arbor, Michigan: Institute for Social Research.

Campbell, Byram, 1952. *American Race Theorists*. Boston: Chapman and Grimes.

Cardinal, Harold, 1971. "The Unjust Society: The Tragedy of Canada's Indians." In Elliott, 1971 (q.v.), pp. 134–49.

Carmichael, Stokely, and Charles Hamilton, 1967. *Black Power: The Politics of Liberation in America*. New York: Vintage Books.

—— 1973. "Black Power: Its Need and Substance." In Hill et al., 1973 (q.v.), pp. 279–93.

Casavantes, Edward J., and Richard S. Leiva, 1973. "The Mexican American." In Spiegel and Keith-Spiegel, 1973 (q.v.), pp. 408–34.

Castberg, Frede, 1974. *The European Convention on Human Rights*. Leiden, Netherlands: Sijthoff.

Castles, Stephen, and Godula Kosack, 1973. *Immigrant Workers and Class Structure in Western Europe*. London: Oxford University Press, published for the Institute of Race Relations.

Cathrein, Viktor, 1914. *Die Grundbegriffe des Strafrechts* (Fundamentals of Criminal Law). Freiburg, 1914.

Chakravarti, N. R., 1971. *The Indian Minority in Burma: The Rise and Decline of an Immigrant Community*. London: Oxford University Press, published for the Institute of Race Relations.

Chandra, Kananur V., 1973. *Racial Discrimination in Canada: Asian Minorities*. San Francisco: R. and E. Research Associates.

Chaudhuri, Joyotpaul, and Jean Chaudhuri, 1972. "Emerging American Indian Politics: The Problem of Powerlessness." In de la Garza et al, 1972 (q.v.), pp. 103–12.

Cherne, Leo, 1975. "Into A Dark, Bottomless Hole." *Freedom at Issue*, no. 32 (September-October): 10–13.

Chornovil, Vyacheslav, 1970. *The Chornovil Papers*. New York: McGraw-Hill.

Choudhary, Rahmat Ali, 1947. "The Idea of Pakistan." Reprinted in Elie Kedourie, ed., *Nationalism in Asia and Africa*. New York: Meridian, 1970, pp. 245–49.

Choudhury, G. W., 1974. *The Last Days of United Pakistan*. London: C. Hurst and Company.

Churchill, Winston S., 1954. *The Second World War*. Boston: Houghton Mifflin.

Chutkow, Paul, 1975. "No Damming India's Human Tide." *St. Louis Post-Dispatch*, Everyday Magazine, November 18, 1975.

Clark, K. B., 1955. *Prejudice and Your Child*. Boston: Beacon.

Cleaver, Eldridge, 1966. "Letters from Prison." *Ramparts* (August): 16–26. Excerpt in Dinnerstein and Jaher, 1970 (q.v.), pp. 299–312.

—— 1968. *Soul on Ice*. New York: McGraw-Hill. Paperback reprint, Dell, 1969.

Clutterbuck, Richard, 1973. *Riot and Revolution In Singapore and Malaya, 1945–1963*. London: Faber and Faber.

Cohen, Abner, 1969. *Custom and Politics in Urban Africa: A Study of Hausa Migrants in Yoruba Towns*. Berkeley and Los Angeles: University of California Press.

—— 1974. *Urban Ethnicity*. London: Associated Book Publishers Ltd.

Cohen, John and Dov Weintraub, 1975. *Land and Peasants in Imperial Ethiopia*. Assen, Netherlands: Van Gorcum and Company.

Conference on Ethnic Problems in the Contemporary World, 1972. Boston: American Academy of Arts and Sciences.

Conflict Regulation in Divided Societies, 1972. Cambridge, Mass.: Center for International Affairs, Harvard University.

Conflict Studies, No. 30, 1972. *Ethnic Pressures in the Soviet Union*, containing essential background and articles by Victor Swoboda and Ann Sheehy (q.v.). London: Institute for the Study of Conflict, December.

Connor, Walker, 1967. "Self-Determination." *World Politics* (October).

Conquest, Robert, 1968. *The Great Terror: Stalin's Purges of the Thirties*. New York: Macmillan.

—— 1970. *The Nation Killers*. London: Macmillan.

—— 1971. Staff Consultation, *The Human Cost of Soviet Communism*. 92nd Congress, 1st Session (July), Subcommittee on Internal Security. Washington: Government Printing Office.

Constant, Benjamin, 1814. *De l'Esprit de Conquête et de l'Usurpation, dans leurs rapports avec la civilisation européene*. Göttingen, 1814.

Cooley, Charles Horton, 1912. *Social Organization: A Study of the Larger Mind*. New York: Scribner and Sons.

Cooley, John K., 1973. *Green March, Black September: The Story of the Palestinian Arabs*. London: Frank Cass.

Coon, Carleton S., 1963. *The Origin of Races*. New York: Knopf.

Coppel, Charles, 1972. "The Position of the Chinese in the Philippines, Malaysia, and Indonesia," Part II in *The Chinese in Indonesia, the Philippines and Malaysia*. London, Minority Rights Group, Report No. 10.

Coppieters, Franz, 1971. *The Community Problem in Belgium*. Brussels: Belgian Information and Documentation Institute.

Cousins, Jane, 1973. *Turkey: Torture and Political Persecution*. London: Blackwell's.

Cox, Barry, 1975. *Civil Liberties in Britain*. London: Penguin Books.

Cox, Kevin et al, 1974. *Locational Approaches To Power and Conflict*. London: Sage Publications Ltd.

Crain, Robert L., and Carol Sachs Weisman, 1972. *Discrimination, Personality and Achievement*. New York: Seminar Press.

Cranston, Maurice, 1973. *What Are Human Rights?* London: Bodley Head.

Crewe, Ivor, ed., 1973. *Elites in Western Democracy, British Political Sociology Yearbook*, Vol. 1. London: Blackwell's.

Crime, Paul, 1972. "Le Nouveau Statut de l'Indien au Brésil." In Jaulin, 1972 (q.v.), pp. 50–67.

Crisis on Cyprus, 1974. United States Senate, Committee on the Judiciary, Subcommittee to Investigate Problems Connected with Refugees and Escapees, *Crisis on Cyprus*, a report prepared for the Subcommittee, with preface by Senator Edward M. Kennedy, chairman. Washington: Government Printing Office, 1974; reprinted by American Hellenic Institute, 1974, 1975.

Crist, Raymond E., 1964. *Andean America: Some Aspects of Human Migration and Settlement*. Occasional Paper No. 3, Graduate Center for Latin-American Studies, Vanderbilt University. Nashville, Tennessee.

Cross, Malcolm, 1972. *The East Indians of Guyana and Trinidad*. London: Minority Rights Group, Report No. 13.

Crozier, Brian, ed., 1973. *Annual of Power and Conflict 1972–73: A Survey of Poli-Violence and International Influence*. London: Institute for the Study of Conflict.

—— 1974. *Annual of Power and Conflict*. London, Institute for the Study of Conflict.

Crum Ewing, Winifred, 1975. Discrimination in Great Britain. In Veenhoven, 1975 (q.v.), 1: 509–78.

Cumming, Peter, and N. Mickenberg, eds., 1971. *Native Rights in Canada*. Toronto: General Publishing.

Curry, David, 1972. "The Frustration of Being Coloured." In N. J. Rhoodie, ed., 1972 (q.v.), pp. 400–417.

Curtis, Lynn A., 1975. *Violence, Race and Culture*. London: Lexington Books.

Czaplicka, Marie Antoinette, 1973. *The Turks of Central Asia in History and at the Present Day*. London: Blackwell's.

Dahl, Robert, 1967. *Pluralist Democracy in the United States*. Chicago: Rand McNally.

Dahrendorf, Ralf, 1959. *Class and Class Conflict in Industrial Society*. Stanford, Cal.: Stanford University Press; London, Routledge and Kegan Paul.

—— 1972. "On the Origin of Inequality Among Men." In Béteille, 1972 (q.v.), pp. 16–44.

—— 1973. *Homo Sociologicus*. London: Blackwell's.

Dalwai, Hamid, 1969. *Muslim Politics in India*. Bombay: Nachiketa Publications.

Daniel, Pete, 1973. *The Shadow of Slavery: Peonage in the South 1901–1969*. New York: Oxford University Press.

Dashefsky, Arnold, ed., 1976. *Ethnic Identity in Society*. Chicago: Rand McNally College Publishing Co.

Davidson, Basil, 1971. "Pluralism in Colonial African Societies: Northern Rhodesia/Zambia." In Leo Kuper and M. G. Smith, eds., *Pluralism in Africa*. Berkeley and Los Angeles: University of California Press, 1971, pp. 211–45.

Davies, James Chowning, 1971. *When Men Revolt and Why: Reader in Political Violence and Revolution*. New York: Free Press.

Dawidowicz, Lucy S., and Leon J. Goldstein, 1963. *Politics in a Pluralistic Democracy: Studies of Voting in the 1960 Election*. New York: Institute of Human Relations Press.

Dawson, Frank Griffith and Ivan L. Head, 1971. *International Law, National Tribunals and the Rights of Aliens*. Syracuse, N.Y.: Syracuse University Press.

Decalo, Samuel, 1976. *Coups and Army Rule in Africa*. New Haven and London: Yale University Press.

de la Garza, R. O., A. Kruszewski, and T. A. Arciniega, eds., 1973. *Chicanos and Native Americans: The Territorial Minorities*. Englewood Cliffs, N.J.: Prentice-Hall.

de la Presa, 1974. "Pero, ¿Tiene Derechos el Hombre?" *Diario Las Americas*, Miami, May 17, 1974.

Deloria, Vine, 1970. *We Talk, You Listen: New Tribes, New Turf*. New York: Macmillan.

Dennewitz, Bodo, 1948. *Die Verfassungen der Modernen Staaten*, Vol. III (consisting mainly of texts of German constitutions). Hamburg: Hansischer Gildenverlag.

den Ouden, J. H. B., 1975. *De Onaanraakbaren van Konkunad*. A Study of Status Change of the Scheduled Castes in a Village of the Coimbatore District, India. Part I, The Social Position of the Scheduled Castes. Wageningen, Netherlands: Landbouwhogenschool.

De Reuck, Anthony and Julie Knight, eds., 1967. *Caste and Race: Comparative Approaches*. London: J. & A. Churchill, Ltd.

Despres, Leo A., 1967. *Cultural Pluralism and Nationalist Politics in British Guiana*. Chicago: Rand McNally and Co.

—— 1975. *Ethnicity and Resource Competition in Plural Societies*. Paris: Mouton Publishers.

De St. Jorre, John, 1972. *The Nigerian Civil War*. London: Hodder and Stoughton.

Deutsch, Karl W., 1966. *Nationalism and Social Communication: An Inquiry Into the Foundations of Nationality*. Cambridge, Mass.: The M.I.T. Press.

—— 1970. *Politics and Government: How People Decide Their Fate*. Boston: Houghton Mifflin Co.

Deutsch, Martin et al, eds., 1968. *Social Class, Race and Psychological Development*. New York: Holt.

De Villiers, Cas, 1976. "Colour Discrimination and Policy Evolution in South Africa." In Veenhoven, 1976 (q.v.), 5: 327–46.

DeVise, Pierre et al., 1969. *Slum Medicine: Chicago's Apartheid Health System*. Chicago: University of Chicago Press.

DeVos, George A., 1971, 1972. *Japan's Outcastes: The Problem of the Burakumin*. London: Minority Rights Group Report No. 3, 1971. Reprinted in Whitaker, 1972 (q.v.). Page references are to Whitaker. A revised report, including Koreans and Ainu, was published in 1974.

DeVos, George, and Lola Romanucci-Ross, 1974. *Ethnic Identity*. San Diego: National Press Books, University of California.

——, eds., 1975. *Ethnic Identity: Cultural Continuities and Change*. Palo Alto, Calif.: Mayfield Publishing Co.

DeVos, George and Hiroshi Wagatsuma, eds., 1966. *Japan's Invisible Race: Caste in Culture and Personality*. Berkeley: University of California Press.

Dietze, Gottfried, 1972. *Bedeutungswandel der Menschenrechte*. Karlsruhe: Juristische Studiengesellschaft Karlsruhe.

Dinnerstein, Leonard and Frederic Cople Jaher, eds., 1970. *The Aliens: A History of Ethnic Minorities in America*. New York: Appleton-Century Crofts.

Djilas, Milovan, 1972. *The Unperfect Society: Beyond the New Class*. Trans. Dorian Coocke. London: Unwin Books.

Dodge, Peter, 1966. "Ethnic Fragmentation and Politics: The Case of Surinam." *Political Science Quarterly* 81, no. 4 (December 1966): 593–601.

Donoghue, John D., 1973. "The Social Persistence

of an Outcaste Group, Japan." In Tumin, 1973 (q.v.), pp. 108–23.

Downing, John, 1973. "Equal Opportunity for Inequality: Racism and Poverty in Britain." In Henderson, 1973 (q.v.), pp. 17–38.

Drabovitch, W., 1934. *Fragilité de la liberté et séduction des dictatures.* Paris: Mercure de France.

Drake, St. Clair, 1971. "The Social and Economic Status of the Negro in the United States." In Greenberg, Milner, and Olson, 1971 (q.v.), pp. 16–54.

Drew, Elizabeth B., 1968. "Going Hungry in America: Government's Failure." *The Atlantic Monthly* 222 (December): 53–61.

Droubie, E. 1974. "The Status of Women in Islam." Pamphlet. London: Minaret House.

Drummond, Stuart, and David Hawkins, 1970. "The Malaysian Elections of 1969: An Analysis of the Campaign and the Results." *Asian Survey* 10, no. 4 (April): 320–35.

DuBois, W. E. B., 1897. "Striving of the Negro People." *The Atlantic Monthly,* (August).

Duchaček, Ivo D., 1973a. *Power Maps: Comparative Politics of Constitutions.* Santa Barbara: University of California.

—— 1973b. *Rights and Liberties in the World Today: Constitutional Promise and Reality.* Santa Barbara: University of California.

Dugard, John, 1972. "South African Lawyers and the Liberal Heritage of the Law." Ch. 4 in Peter Randall, ed., *Law, Justice and Society.* Report of the Legal Commission of the Study Project on Christianity in Apartheid Society. Johannesburg: Christian Institute, 1972.

Dumont, Louis, 1970. *Homo Hierarchicus: An Essay on the Caste System,* trans. Mark Sainsbury. Chicago: University of Chicago Press.

Duncan, Otis D., 1972. "Patterns of Occupational Mobility Among Negro Men." In Richmond, 1972 (q.v.), p. 220.

Dunn, James A., 1970. "Social Cleavages, Party Systems and Political Integration: a Comparison of the Belgian and Swiss Experiences." Ph.D. dissertation, University of Pennsylvania.

Dunn, John, 1973. *Modern Revolutions: An Introduction to the Analysis of a Political Phenomenon.* Cambridge, England: Cambridge University Press.

Dunner, Joseph, 1975. "Anti-Jewish Discrimination Since the End of World War II." In Veenhoven, 1975 (q.v.) 2: 65–110.

Duran, Livie Isauro, and H. Russel Bernard, 1973. *Introduction to Chicano Studies.* New York: Macmillan.

Dushkin, Lelah, 1972. "Scheduled Caste Politics." In Mahar, 1972 (q.v.), pp. 165–226.

Dushnyck, Walter, 1975a. "Human Rights in Communist-Ruled East-Central Europe." In Veenhoven, 1975 (q.v.) 1:377–443.

—— 1975b. "Discrimination and Abuse of Power in the USSR." In *ibid.,* 2: 445–555.

Duverger, Maurice, 1955. *The Political Role of Women.* Paris: UNESCO.

Dzidienyo, Anani, 1972. *The Position of Blacks in Brazilian Society.* London: Minority Rights Group Report No. 7.

Eckhoff, T. ed., 1973–74. *Justice: Its Determinants in Interaction.* Leiden: A. W. Sijthoff.

Edmondson, Locksley, 1974. "Caribbean Nation-Building and the Internationalization of Race: Issues and Perspectives." In Bell and Freeman, 1974 (q.v.).

Eickstedt, E. von, 1937. "Geschichte der anthropologischen Namengebung und Klassifikation (unter Betonung der Erforschung von Südasien). II Teil, 2. Hälfte, B. Die jüngere Erforschungsgeschichte der Südasiaten." *Zeitschrift für Rassenkunde* 6: 151–210.

Eisenstadt, S. N., 1969. "The Emerging Pattern of Israeli Stratification." In Heller, 1969 (q.v.), pp. 438–52.

Eitzen, D. Stanley, 1968. "Two Minorities: The Jews of Poland and the Chinese of the Philippines." *Jewish Journal of Sociology* 10, no. 2 (December); reprinted in Gelfand and Lee, 1973 (q.v.), pp. 140–56.

Elliot, Gil, 1972. *Twentieth-Century Book of the Dead.* New York: Scribner's.

Elliott, Jean Leonard, ed., 1971. *Minority Canadians.* Vol. 1, *Native Peoples;* Vol. 2, *Immigrant Groups.* Englewood Cliffs, New Jersey, and Scarborough, Ontario: Prentice Hall.

Elon, Amos, 1973. "The Black Panthers of Israel." In Gelfand and Lee, 1973 (q.v.), pp. 173–78.

Engels, Friedrich, 1886. *Der Ursprung der Familie, des Privateigentums und des Staats.* Stuttgart, 1886.

Engen, Hans, 1955. *Report on Slavery to International Labor Office.* Geneva: ILO, e/2673. (Summarizes ILO study on *Indigenous Peoples,* 1953).

Enloe, Cynthia H., 1974. "Foreign Policy and Ethnicity in 'Soft States': Prospects for Southeast

Asia." In Bell and Freeman, 1974 (q.v.), pp. 223–30.

Epp, Frank H., and John Goddard, eds., 1974. "The Palestinians Speak." Special issue of *The Link*. New York: Americans for Middle East Understanding, September–October.

Epps, Edgar G., ed., 1973. *Race Relations: Current Perspectives*. Cambridge, Mass.: Winthrop.

Epstein, Cynthia Fuchs, 1972. "Woman's Place: Options and Limits in Professional Careers." In Thielbar and Feldman, 1972 (q.v.), pp. 597–609.

Epstein, Julius, 1973. *Operation Keelhaul: The Story of Forced Repatriation from 1944 to the Present*. Old Greenwich, Connecticut: Devin-Adair.

Ermacora, Felix, 1971. *Diskriminierungsschutz und Diskriminierungsverbot in den Vereinten Nationen*. Vienna, Stuttgart: Wilhelm Braumüller.

Ethnic Heritage, 1970. *Ethnic Heritage Studies Centers:* Hearings before the General Subcommittee on Education of the Committee on Education and Labor, U.S. House of Representatives, 91st Congress, 2d Session, on HR 14910, February 16 to May 6, 1970. Washington: U.S. Government Printing Office, 1970.

Expellee Facts, 1960. "Facts Concerning the Problem of the German Expellees and Refugees." 5th edition. Bonn: Federal Ministry for Expellees, Refugees and War Victims.

Eysenck, H. J., 1972. *Psychology Is About People*. New York: Library Press.

Faber, George Sebastian. *See* Alfred Schmid, 1933.

Fainsod, Merle, 1963. *How Russia Is Ruled*, revised edition. Cambridge, Mass.: Harvard University Press.

Fawcett, James T., ed., 1973. *Psychological Perspectives on Population*. New York: Basic Books.

Feaver, George, 1975. The American Indians, 5 articles appearing in *Encounter*. London, 44 (2–5, 10): I, "Wounded Knee and the New Tribalism," February, pp. 28–35; II, "Wounded Knee and the New Tribalism," continued, March, pp. 16–24; III, "Vine Deloria, Jr.," April, pp. 33–46; IV, "An Indian Melodrama," May, pp. 23–34; V, Epilogue, October, pp. 25–32.

Feinstein, Otto, 1971. *Ethnic Groups in the City*. Lexington, Mass.: Heath Lexington Books.

Feldman, Saul D., ed., 1972. *Life Styles: Diversity in American Society*. Boston: Little Brown and Co.

Ferguson, Jack, 1971. "Eskimos in a Satellite Society." In Elliott, 1971 (q.v.), pp. 15–28.

Ferry, W. H., 1968. "Farewell to Integration." *The Center Magazine*, March, 35–40. Excerpt reprinted in Samuel Hendel, ed., *The Politics of Confrontation*. New York: Appleton-Century Crofts, 1971, pp. 51–57.

Feuer, Lewis Samuel, 1969. *The Conflict of Generations: The Character and Significance of Student Movements*. New York, London: Basic Books.

Fidell, Linda S. and Patricia Keith-Spiegel, 1973. "The Woman." In Spiegel and Keith-Spiegel, 1973 (q.v.), pp. 435–69.

Field, F. and P. Haiken, 1971. *Black Britons: Readings in General Studies*. London: Oxford University Press.

Fircks, Otto Freiherr von, 1962. *Fibel zur Deutschlandfrage*, herausgegeben im Auftrag des Bundes der Vertriebenen. Berlin, Hannover, Darmstadt: Hermann Schroedel Verlag.

Fisher, Allan G. B. and J. Humphrey, 1971. *Slavery and the Muslim Society in Africa*. New York: Doubleday.

Fisher, Jack C., 1966. *Yugoslavia—A Multinational State*. San Francisco: Chandler Publishing Company.

Fitzgerald, C. P., 1973. *China and South-East Asia Since 1945*. London: Blackwell's.

Fleming, G. James, 1960. "An All-Negro Ticket in Baltimore." Monograph in *Case Studies in Practical Politics*. New York: Holt, Rinehart and Winston.

Fogelson, Robert M., and Robert B. Hill, 1968. "Who Riots? A Study of Participation in the 1967 Riots." In *Supplemental Studies for the National Advisory Commission on Civil Disorders*. Washington: Government Printing Office, July, 1968.

Foltz, William J., 1974. "Ethnicity, Status and Conflict." In Bell and Freeman (q.v.), pp. 103–16.

Foucault, Michel, 1965. *Madness and Civilization*. New York: Random House.

Fougeyrollas, Pierre, 1968. *Pour une France fédérale, vers l'unité européene par la révolution régionale*. Paris: Denoël.

Fox, Jeanne, 1974. "Regionalism and Minority Participation." Washington: Joint Center for Political Studies Public Policy Series.

Fraggomen, Austin T., 1972. *The Illegal Alien: Economic Refugee or Criminal?* New York: CMS Publications, Center for Migration Studies.

France Actuelle, A monthly report, in English, on modern France, published by the Comité France Actuelle, Paris. The June 1973 issue is largely devoted to an article on the economic and social progress of French women, entitled: Women Are Working Partners in France.

Frank, Jerome D., 1973. *Persuasion and Healing*, revised edition. Baltimore: Johns Hopkins University Press.

Frankl, Viktor E., 1969. "Reductionism and Nihilism." In Arthur Koestler and J. R. Smythies, eds., *Beyond Reductionism*. Boston: Beacon, 1969.

Freedman, S., 1969. "How Is Racism Maintained?" *Radical Sociology*, no. 2.

Freedman, Morris, and Carolyn Banks, eds., 1972. *American Mix: The Minority Experience in America*. Philadelphia, J. B. Lippincott.

Freeman, H.E. et al., 1966. "Color Gradation and Attitudes among Middle-Income Negroes." *American Sociological Review*, no. 31, pp. 365–74. Reprinted in Richmond, 1972 (q.v.), to which page references apply.

Freeman, Roger A., 1975. *The Growth of American Government*. Stanford, California: Hoover Institution Press.

Freyre, Gilberto, 1946. *The Masters and the Slaves*. New York: Knopf.

Friedrich, Carl J., 1972. *The Pathology of Politics*. New York: Harper and Row.

Friedrich, Hans, 1975. "Leben aus zweiter Hand? Freizeitprobleme von jungen Leuten." *Rheinischer Merkur*, June 6, 1975, p. 24.

Friendly, Alfred, 1972. *Israel's Oriental Immigrants and Druzes*. London: Minority Rights Group, Report No. 12.

Gamio, Manuel, 1971a. *Mexican Immigrant: His Life Story*. New York: Dover Publications, Inc.

—— 1971b. *Mexican Immigration to the United States: A Study of Human Migration and Adjustment*. New York: Dover.

Garn, Stanley M., 1971. *Human Races*, 3rd ed. Springfield, Ill.: Charles C. Thomas.

Gehlen, Arnold, 1950. *Der Mensch: seine Natur und seine Stellung in der Welt*. Bonn: Athenäum-Verlag, 1950.

—— 1953. *Sozialpsychologische Probleme einer Industriellen Gesellschaft*, No. 2 in Schriftenreihe der Akademie Speyer. Tübingen, J. C. B. Mohr.

Gelfand, Donald E. and Russell D. Lee, eds., 1973. *Ethnic Conflicts and Power: A Cross-National Perspective*. New York: John Wiley and Sons.

Genocide Convention, 1950. United States Senate, 81st Congress, 2nd Session, Committee on Foreign Relations. *The Genocide Convention*. Washington: Government Printing Office.

Gergen, Kenneth J., 1968. "The Significance of Skin Color in Human Relations." In John Hope Franklin, ed., *Color and Race*. Boston: Houghton-Mifflin, 1968, pp. 112–28.

Gerson, Louis L., 1964. *The Hyphenate in Recent American Politics and Diplomacy*. Lawrence, Kansas: The University of Kansas Press.

Gerstenmaier, Cornelia, 1972. *The Voices of the Silent*, trans. Susan Hecker. New York: Hart Pub. Co.

Cherry Gertzel, Maure Goldschmidt, and Donald Rothchild, eds., 1969. *Government and Politics in Kenya*. Nairobi: East African Publishing House, 1969, reprinted 1972. (See esp. introductory chapter by Cherry Gertzel.)

Ghai, Dharam P. and Yash P. Ghai, 1970. *Portrait of a Minority: Asians in East Africa*. London: Oxford University Press.

Ghurye, G. S., 1968. *Social Tensions in India*. Bombay: Popular Prakashan.

Giddens, Anthony, 1974. *The Class Structure of the Advanced Societies*. London: Hutchinson University Library.

Giddings, Franklin H., 1922. *Studies in the Theory of Human Society*. New York: Macmillan.

Gilbert, Rodney, ed., 1959. *Genocide in Tibet*. New York: American-Asian Educational Exchange.

Gist, Noel P. and Roy Dean Wright, 1973. *Marginality and Identity: Anglo Indians as a Racially-Mixed Minority in India*. Leiden, Netherlands: E. J. Brill.

Glasenapp, Igor O., 1969. "Recent Developments in Soviet Policy Towards Israel." *Institute for the Study of the USSR Bulletin*, 16 (May): 27–36.

Glaser, Kurt, 1953. *The Iron Curtain and American Policy*. Washington: Public Affairs Press.

—— 1961. *Czecho-Slovakia: A Critical History*. Caldwell, Idaho: The Caxton Printers, Ltd.

—— 1971. "World War II and the War Guilt Question." *Modern Age* 15, no. 1 (Winter): 57–69.

—— 1972. "National States versus Federalism in the Future of Central Europe." *Plural Societies* 3, no. 1 (Spring): 3–18.

—— 1973a. Review of Michael Wright, *Zambia—I Changed My Mind*. *Ukrainian Quarterly* 29, no. 4 (Winter): 411–13.

—— 1973b. "Nineteenth-Century Messianism and

Twentieth-Century Interventionism." *Modern Age* 17, no. 1 (Winter): 16–32.

—— 1973c. "Does America Have (or Need) a *Staatsvolk?*" Review of Wilmot Robertson, *The Dispossessed Majority* (Cape Canaveral, Fla.: Howard Allen, 1972, 1973) and Michael Novak, *The Rise of the Unmeltable Ethnics* (New York: Macmillan, 1972). *Modern Age* 17, no. 4 (Fall): 414–19.

—— 1973d. "National States Versus Federalism in the Future of Central Europe." In Joseph M. Kirschbaum, ed., *Slovakia in the 19th and 20th Centuries*. Proceedings of the Conference of the Slovak World Congress on June 17–18, 1971, in Toronto. Toronto: Slovak World Congress, 1973.

Glaskow, W. G., 1958. "The Cossacks as a Group." In Nikolai K. Deker and Andrei Lebed, eds., *Genocide in the USSR, Studies in Group Destruction*. Munich: Institute for the Study of the USSR; New York: Scarecrow Press.

Glazer, Nathan, 1975. *Affirmative Discrimination: Ethnic Inequality and Public Policy*. New York: Basic Books.

Glazer, Nathan, and Daniel P. Moynihan, 1963. *Beyond the Melting Pot*. Cambridge, Mass.: M.I.T. Press.

Glazer-Malbin, Nona, and Helen Youngelson-Waehrer, 1972. *Woman in A Man-Made World*. Chicago: Rand McNally.

Gleason, Philip, 1968. *Conservative Reformers: German-American Catholics and the Social Order*. Notre Dame, Ind.: University of Notre Dame Press.

Goldhagen, Erich, 1968. *Ethnic Minorities in the Soviet Union*. New York: Praeger.

Goldschmid, Marcel L., ed., 1970. *Black Americans and White Racism: Theory and Research*. New York: Holt, Rinehart and Winston.

Goldstein, Rhoda L., ed., 1969. *Black Life and Culture in the United States*. New York: Crowell, 1969.

Goldthorpe, J. E., 1974. *An Introduction to Sociology*, 2nd Edition. Cambridge, England: Cambridge University Press.

Goldthorpe, John H., 1973. "Social Inequality and Social Integration in Modern Britain." In Wedderburn, 1973 (q.v.), pp. 217–38.

Goodman, M. E., 1964. *Racial Awareness in Young Children*. Cambridge, Mass.: Addison-Wesley.

Gordon, Milton, M., 1971. "Assimilation in America: Theory and Reality." *Daedalus* 90, no. 2 (Spring): 263–85. Reprinted in Yetman and Steele, 1971 (q.v.), pp. 261–83. Page references are to Yetman and Steele.

Gorer, Geoffrey, 1948. *The American People*. New York: Norton.

Gorinsky, Conrad, 1969. "The Annihilation of the Amerindians." In *Venture*, September, 7ff.

Gotlieb, Allan, ed., 1970. *Human Rights, Federalism and Minorities*. Toronto: Canadian Institute of International Affairs.

Gough, Kathleen, and Hari P. Sharma, 1973. *Imperialism and Revolution in South Asia*. New York: Monthly Review Press.

Gould, J., and W. L. Kolb, 1964. *A Dictionary of the Social Sciences*. London: Tavistock.

Greeley, Andrew, 1971. *Ethnicity as an Influence on Behavior*. In Feinstein, 1971 (q.v.), pp. 3–16.

Greenberg, Edward S., Neal Milner, and David J. Olson, eds., 1971. *Black Politics: the Inevitability of Conflict: Readings*. New York: Holt, Rinehart and Winston.

Griffith, Ernest S., John Plamenatz, and J. Roland Pennock, 1956. "Cultural Prerequisites to a Successfully Functioning Democracy: A Symposium." *American Political Science Review* 50, no. 1 (March): 101–37.

Grier, George and Eunice Grier, 1972. "Equality and Beyond: Housing Segregation in the Great Society." In Yetman and Steele, 1972 (q.v.), pp. 443–53.

Grigorenko, Pyotr, 1972. Excerpts from the diary of General Pyotr Grigorenko, included in appendix III, *Abuse of Psychiatry*. See that entry.

Grigsby, J. Eugene, 1971. "An Interpretative Analysis of Recent Work." In Orleans and Ellis, 1971 (q.v.), pp. 577–602.

Grobbelaar, J. S., 1972. "Race and Labour Relations." In Rhoodie, 1972. (q.v.), pp. 297–312.

Grodzins, Morton, 1949. *Americans Betrayed: Politics and the Japanese evacuation*. Chicago: University of Chicago Press.

—— 1958. *The Metropolitan Area as a Racial Problem*. Pittsburgh: University of Pittsburgh Press. Excerpt in Terrence P. Goggin and John M. Sidel, eds., *Politics, American Style: Race, Environment, and Central Cities*. Englewood Cliffs, N.J.: Prentice-Hall, 1972, pp. 146ff.

Grulich, Rudolf, 1973. "Ohne Russisch kein sozialer Aufstieg." *Sudetendeutsche Zeitung*. Munich, January 12.

Gulick, Sidney L., 1915. *Hawaii's American-Japanese Problem: A Description of the Conditions, a Statement of the Problems, and Suggestions for Their Solution.* Honolulu: Pamphlet published by Honolulu Star Bulletin, 42 pp.

Gutkind, Peter C. W., 1970. *The Passing of the Tribal Man in Africa.* Leiden, Netherlands: E. J. Brill.

Habel, Fritz Peter, 1962. *Dokumentensammlung zur Sudetenfrage.* Munich: Verlag Robert Lerche. Publication of the Sudetendeutsches Archiv.

Habsburg, Dr. Otto von, 1976. "How Reds Destroy Human Beings." *To the Point,* January 16.

Haddox, John H., 1972. "American Indian Values." In de la Garza et al, 1972 (q.v.), pp. 61–77.

Hanbury-Tenison, Robin, 1973. *A Question of Survival for the Indian of Brazil.* London: Angus and Robertson.

Hantsch, Hugo, 1953. *Die Nationalitätenfrage im alten Österreich,* Vol. 1 of Vienna Historical Studies. Vienna: Verlag Herold.

Harding, J. et al, 1954. "Prejudice and Ethnic Relations." In G. Lindzey, ed., *Handbook of Social Psychology,* vol. 2. Cambridge, Mass.: Addison-Wesley.

Hare, Nathan, 1965. *The Black Anglo-Saxons.* New York: Marzanni and Munzel.

Harkabi, Y., 1974. *Palestinians and Israel.* Jerusalem: Keter Publishing House.

Harper, Edward B., 1964. Ritual Pollution as an Integrator of Caste and Religion. In Harper, ed., *Religion in South Asia.* Seattle: University of Washington Press, pp. 151–96.

Harris, M., 1968. "Race." In *International Encyclopaedia of the Social Sciences,* vol. 13.

Harris, Marvin, 1974. *Cows, Pigs, Wars and Witches: The Riddles of Culture.* New York: Random House.

Hatem, M. Abdel-Kader, 1974. *Information and the Arab Cause.* London: Longmans.

Hayek, Friedrich A., 1960. *The Constitution of Liberty.* Chicago: University of Chicago Press.

Hegel, G. W. F., 1955. *Grundlinien der Philosophie des Rechts,* 4th edition. Hamburg, Meiner.

Heineman, Benjamin W., 1972. *The Politics of the Powerless: a Study of the Campaign Against Race Discrimination.* London: Oxford University Press.

Heller, Celia S., 1966. *Mexican-American Youth: Forgotten Youth at the Crossroads.* New York: Random House.

—— ed. 1969. *Structural Social Inequality.* New York: Macmillan.

Hellmann, Ellen, 1972. "The Crux of the Race Problem in South Africa." In Rhoodie, 1972 (q.v.), pp. 14–33.

Henderson, Ernest F., ed., 1912. "The Salic Law," in *Select Historical Documents of the Middle Ages.* London: G. Bell & Sons, Ltd., pp. 176–89. Reprinted in William S. Carpenter and Paul Tutt Stafford, eds., *Readings in Early Legal Institutions.* New York: Crofts, 1932, pp. 118–29.

Henderson, Ian, ed., 1973. *The New Poor: Anatomy of Underprivilege.* London: Owen.

Hernandez, Jose, 1974. *People, Power and Policy: A New View of Population.* Palo Alto, Calif.: National Press Books.

Herskovits, Melville J., 1941. *The Myth of the Negro Past.* New York: Harper.

Hertz, Frederick, 1947. *The Economic Problem of the Danubian States.* London: Gollancz.

Hewsen, Robert H., 1966. "The Armenians in the Middle East." *Viewpoints,* no. 6 (August-September): 3–10.

Heye, Jürgen B., 1975. *A Sociolinguistic Investigation of Multilingualism in the Canton of Ticino, Switzerland.* Paris: Mouton Publishing Company.

Hibbert, Christopher, 1963. *The Roots of Evil: A Social History of Crime and Punishment.* Boston: Little Brown.

Hilberg, Raul, 1961. *The Destruction of European Jews.* Chicago: Quadrangle Books.

Hill, A. David et al., eds., 1973. *The Quality of Life in America: Pollution, Poverty, Power and Fear.* New York: Holt, Rinehart and Winston.

Hill, Herbert, 1965. "Racial Inequality in Employment: The Patterns of Discrimination." *The Annals of the American Academy of Political and Social Science,* January. Excerpt reprinted in Yetman and Steele, 1971 (q.v.), pp. 454–70. Page references are to Yetman and Steele.

Hinds, Lennox S., 1971. "The Relevance of the Past to the Present: A Political Interpretation." In Goldstein, ed., 1971 (q.v.), pp. 360–79.

Hirsch, Herbert, 1973. "Political Scientists and Other Comrades: Academic Myth-Making and Racial Stereotypes." In de la Garza et al, 1973 (q.v.), pp. 10–22.

Hitchcock, Bob, 1973. "Leaving Democracy Behind." *Rand Daily Mail,* Aug. 28, 1973, p. 17.

Hoagland, Jim, 1973. "Whites Prosper under Kenyatta, but Brood about Future." *Washington Post,* January 8, 1973.

Hoetink, Harmannus, 1962. *De gespleten samenleving in het Caribisch Gebied; bijdrage tot de sociologie der rasrelaties in gesegmenteerde maatschappijen.* Assen, Netherlands: Van Gorcum.

—— 1967. *The Two Variants in Carribean Race Relations: A Contribution to the Sociology of Segmented Societies.* trans. Eva Hooykaas. London and New York: Oxford University Press, for the Institute of Race Relations.

—— 1971. *El pueblo dominicano: 1850–1900; Apuntes para su sociologia.* trans. Ligia Espinol de Hoetink. Santiago, Dominican Republic: U.C.M.M.

—— 1974. National Identity and Somatic Norm Image. In Bell and Freeman, 1974 (q.v.), pp. 29–44.

Hofstätter, P. R., 1954. *Einführung in die Sozialpsychologie.* Stuttgart: Kroner.

Holland, Sekai, 1972. "Australia, Rhodesia and South Africa: A Comparison." In Stevens, 1972 (q.v.), 3: 187–212. (This article is omitted in American edition.)

Hollingshead, August de B., 1949. *Elmtown's Youth: The Impact of Social Classes on Adolescents.* New York: Wiley.

Holmen, Milton G., and Richard S. Docter, 1974. "Criticism of Standardized Testing." *Today's Education,* (Journal of the National Education Association) 63, no. 1 (January-February): 50–52, 58, 60.

Holzach, Michael, 1974. "Die Polen im Ruhrgebiet." *Das Parlament,* Bonn, August 24, 1974, p. 18.

Horkheimer, Max, and Theodor W. Adorno, 1972. *Dialectic of Englightenment,* transl. of *Dialektik der Aufklärung,* 1947. New York: Herder and Herder.

Hudson, G. F., 1973. *Reform and Revolution in Asia.* London: Allen and Unwin for St. Anthony's College, Oxford.

Hüfner, Klaus, 1972. "Problems of Education and Vocational Training of Migrant Workers and Their Children." In Van Houte and Melgert, 1972 (q.v.), pp. 139–44.

Hughes, David R., and Evelyn Kallen, 1974. *The Anatomy of Racism: Canadian Dimensions.* Montreal: Harvest House.

Hull, Cordell, 1948. *The Memoirs of Cordell Hull,* 2 volumes. New York: Macmillan.

Human Cost, 1971. 92nd Congress, 1st Session, United States Senate, Committee on the Judiciary, Internal Security Subcommittee, *The Human Cost of Communism in China.* Prepared by Professor Richard L. Walker. Subcommittee Print. Washington, Government Printing Office.

Hunt, Chester, and Lewis Walker, 1974. *Ethnic Dynamics: Patterns of Intergroup Relations in Various Societies.* Homewood, Illinois: Dorsey Press.

Hunter, Guy, 1973–74. *South-East Asia: Race, Culture and Nation.* London: Oxford University Press.

Hunter, W. A., 1885. *Roman Law.* London: William Maxwell & Sons. Pages 17–22 contain a reconstruction of the Twelve Tables, which is reprinted in Carpenter and Stafford (see entry for Henderson), pp. 74–82.

Hussein, 1975. Speech of King Hussein of Jordan at The Citadel, Charleston, South Carolina, May 6, 1975. Our source: Report in London *Times,* May 7, 1975.

Hutchinson, Alan, 1974. "Upholding Democracy in One-Party System," "Discipline Needed to Hold Hard Won Gains," and other articles in *The Times,* London, special report commemorating tenth anniversary of Tanzanian independence, December 9 and 10.

Hutson, H. W., 1973. *Majority Rule—Why? Cooperation Not Confrontation in Southern Africa.* London: Johnson.

Hutton, J. H., 1946. *Caste in India.* London: Oxford University Press.

Huxley-Blythe, Peter J., 1964. *The East Came West.* Caldwell, Idaho: Caxton.

Hyer, Paul, 1974. "The Basis and Nature of Discrimination against the Mongolian Nation within the People's Republic of China." Manuscript prepared for Foundation for the Study of Plural Societies. The Hague.

ILO, 1953. United Nations, E/2431, International Labor Office, *Report of Ad Hoc Committee on Forced Labor.* Geneva.

—— 1962a. International Labor Conference, 46th Session, *Report III.* Geneva.

—— 1962b. International Labor Conference, 46th Session, *Report III, Part IV, Report of the Committee of Experts on the Application of Conventions and Recommendations.* Geneva.

—— 1963. *Official Supplement.* Vol. 36, no. 2, Supplement II (April): 45–62.

—— 1968. *Report of the Committee on Forced Labor.* Geneva.

—— 1973a. *Migration of Workers as an Element in Employment Policy*. Geneva.

—— 1973b. *Report of the Committee of Experts on the Application of Conventions and Recommendations*. Geneva.

Inkeles, Alex, and Kent Geiger, eds., 1961. *Soviet Society*. Boston: Houghton Mifflin.

Inside, 1973. "Inside Amin's Uganda: More Africans Murdered," by an African in Uganda. 1973. *Munger Africana Library Notes*, no. 18 (March). Pasadena: California Institute of Technology.

IRR, 1968. "Colour and Immigration in the U.K." IRR Fact Paper. London: Institute of Race Relations.

Irvine, Keith, 1972. *The Rise of the Coloured Races*. London: Allen and Unwin.

Isaacs, Harold R., 1962. *Images of Asia: American views of China and India*. New York: Capricorn Books.

—— 1972a. "Blackness and Whiteness." In Baxter and Sansom, 1972 (q.v.), pp. 145–51.

—— 1972b. "The Ex-Untouchables." In Mahar, 1972 (q.v.), pp. 375–410.

Isajiw, Wsevolod, W., 1974. Definitions of Ethnicity. In *Ethnicity*, No. I.

Israel Yearbook on Human Rights. Volume 2, 1972. New York: Anti-Defamation League of B'Nai B'Rith.

Jackson, Harold, 1972. *The Two Irelands: The Double Minority—a Study of Intergroup Tensions*. London: Minority Rights Group Report No. 2, rev. edition. Reprinted in Whitaker, 1972a (q.v.), pp. 187–216. Page references are to Whitaker.

Jacobs, Paul, 1972. "Health and Medical Care." In Bromley and Longino, 1972 (q.v.).

Jacobson, Phillip, 1974a. "Meanwhile in Bangui The President (for Life) Is Unrivalled." *Sunday Times*, London, December 8.

—— 1974b. "The Man the Churches Call the Caligula of Africa." President Francisco Macias Nguema of Equatorial Guinea. *Sunday Times*, London, December 29.

Jaksch, Wenzel, 1963. *Europe's Road to Potsdam*, trans. and ed. by Kurt Glaser. New York: Praeger.

—— 1967. *Europas Weg nach Potsdam: Schuld und Schicksal im Donauraum*. Neu bearbeitet und ergänzte Ausgabe (newly revised). Cologne: Verlag Wissenschaft und Politik.

Jaulin, Robert, 1972. *De l'Ethnocide, Recueil de Textes*.

Paris: 10–18. (10–18 is the imprint of the Union Générale d'Éditions, Paris.)

Jenness, R. A., 1974. "Canadian Migration and Immigration: Patterns and Government Policy." *International Migration Review* (Spring).

Johnston, Edward, E., 1975. "Micronesia Trusteeship Is Considered To be 'Strategic.' " *The Commonwealth* 69, no. 12 (March 24): 86–88.

Jones, Brenda, 1973. "Kenya Today needs a Revolution." *Pretoria News*, September 4, 1973.

Joosub, H. E., 1972. "The Future of the Indian Community." In N. J. Rhoodie, ed., 1972 (q.v.), pp. 418–34.

Kabara, J., 1971. "Sudanese Strife." *Bulletin of the Africa Institute*, Pretoria, no. 6.

Kahn, Herman, 1970. *The Emerging Japanese Superstate: Challenge and Response*. Englewood Cliffs, N.J.: Prentice-Hall, Spectrum Paperback.

Kalijarvi, Thorsten V., ed., 1954. *Modern World Politics*. New York: Crowell.

Kanitkar, Helen, 1973. "Equal Opportunities for Men and Women." *New Community*, no. 4 (Autumn).

Kantrowitz, N., 1973. *Ethnic and Racial Segregation Patterns in the New York Metropolis*. London: Pall Mall.

Katz, D. and K. Braly, 1933. Racial Stereotypes of One Hundred College Students. *Journal of Abnormal and Social Psychology*, 28: 280–91.

Kedourie, Elie, 1970. *The Chatham House Version and Other Middle Eastern Studies*. New York: Praeger.

Kelly, Mike, 1974. "Soviet Refugee Confirms Existence of USSR Penal Camps." Article summarizing testimony of Avraham Shifrin before Senate Internal Security Subcommittee. *Human Events* (September 7): 8. See also Shifrin, 1973.

Kemp, Maida Springer, 1975. "When the Sahara Moved South." *Free Trade Union News*, AFL-CIO (February): 10–11.

Kendall, Willmoore, 1955. Unpublished paper read at conference at Buck Hill Falls, Pennsylvania, June.

Kenya PSR, 1966, Public Security (Detained and Restricted Persons) Regulations 1966. Legal Notice No. 212, July 25, 1966, Kenya Gazette Supplement No. 67. Legislative Supplement No. 41.

Kerr, Malcolm H., 1964. "Political Decision Making in a Confessional Democracy." Reprinted in Binder, 1966 (q.v.), pp. 187–212.

Khosla, Gopal Das, 1951. *Stern Reckoning*. A survey of events leading up to and following the partition in India (no publisher). Based on the findings of the Indian Government's agency which interrogated "thousands of refugees."

Kilian, Lewis M., 1972. "The Negro Revolution: Possible or Impossible?" in Yetman and Steele, 1972 (q.v.), pp. 577–98.

Killingsworth, Charles C., 1969. "Jobs and Income for Negroes." In Irwin Katz and Patricia Gurin, eds., *Race and the Social Sciences*. New York: Basic Books, pp. 231–32.

Kimball, Penn, 1972. *The Disconnected*. New York: Columbia University Press.

King, Robert R., 1973. *Minorities Under Communism: Nationalities as a Source of Tension among Balkan Communist States*. Cambridge, Mass.: Harvard University Press.

Kinski, Ferdinand Graf, 1974. "Im Aostatal Spricht Man Französisch: um Erhaltung der kulturellen Eigenart bemüht." *Das Parlament*, August 24, 1974, p. 18.

Klee, Ernst, 1971. *Die Nigger Europas, zur Lage der Gastarbeiter: eine Dokumentation*, 2nd edition with new material. Düsseldorf: Patmos-Verlag.

Kleinfeld, Sonny, 1975. "Dwarfs." *The Atlantic Monthly* 236, no. 3 (September): 62–66.

Klineberg, P., 1968. "Prejudice: The Concept." *International Encyclopaedia of the Social Sciences*, vol. 12.

Knabe, Erika, 1974. "Afghan Women: Does Their Role Change?" In *Afghanistan in the 1970's*. Praeger Special Studies in International Economics and Development. New York: Praeger, pp. 144–64.

Kobrick, Jeffrey W., 1972. "The Compelling Case for Bilingual Education." *Saturday Review*, April 29, 54–58.

Kochan, Lionel, ed., 1972. *The Jews in Soviet Russia Since 1917*, 2nd ed. London: Oxford University Press.

Kodeks RSFSR. 1962. RSFSR Ministry of Justice, *Ugolovnyi Kodeks RSFSR*, Moscow.

Kodesia, Krishna, 1969. *The Problems of Linguistic States in India*. Delhi: Sterling Publishers.

Koenigswald, Harold von, 1954. *Der unabsehbare Strom*. Bonn: Federal Ministry for All-German Questions. Bundesministerium für gesamtdeutsche Fragen.

Kogon, Eugen, 1950. *The Theory and Practice of Hell: The German Concentration Camps and the System Behind Them*, translation of *Der SS-Staat*, Munich, 1946. New York: Farrar Straus; London, Secker & Warburg.

Kolm, Richard, 1971. "Ethnicity in Society and Community." In Feinstein, 1971 (q.v.), pp. 57–78.

Komisar, Lucy, 1971. "The Feminist Perspective." In Bryant, 1971 (q.v.), pp. 420–30.

Konfliktforschung, 1971. *Beiträge zur Konfliktforschung*. Cologne: Markus-Verlagsgesellschaft.

Korey, William, 1972. "The Legal Position of Soviet Jewry: A Historical Enquiry." In Kochan, 1972 (q.v.), pp. 76–98.

—— ed., 1973. *The Soviet Cage: Anti-Semitism in Russia*. New York: Anti-Defamation League of B'nai B'rith.

Korson, J. Henry, ed., 1974. *Contemporary Problems of Pakistan*. Leiden, Netherlands: E. J. Brill.

Kothari, Rajni, ed., 1970. *Caste in Indian Politics*. New York: Gordon and Breach.

Kovel, Joel, 1971. *White Racism: A Psychohistory*. New York: Vintage Books.

Kramer, Judith R., 1970. *The American Minority Community*. New York: Thomas Y. Crowell Company.

Krämer-Badoni, Rudolf, 1974. "Zuletzt zieht die Frau immer den Kürzeren." *Die Welt*. Hamburg, July 13, 1974.

Krause, Otto, 1972. "Trends in Afrikaner Race Attitudes." In Rhoodie, 1972 (q.v.), pp. 532–39.

Kroeber, A. L., 1948. *Anthropology*. New York: Harcourt-Brace.

Kuhlman, John M., and Gordon S. Skinner, 1959. *The Economic System*. Homewood, Illinois: Richard D. Irwin, Inc.

Kulischer, Eugene M., 1948. *Europe on the Move: War and Population Changes, 1917–1947*. New York: Columbia University Press.

Kulski, Wladislaw W., 1947. "The Lost Opportunity for Russian-Polish Friendship." *Foreign Affairs* 25, no. 3 (July): 667–84.

Kunstadter, Peter, ed., 1967. *Southeast Asian Tribes, Minorities and Nations*, Volume 1. Princeton, Princeton University Press.

Kuper, Leo, 1973. "Theories of Revolution and Race Relations." In Gelfand and Lee, 1973 (q.v.), pp. 48–65.

Kuppuswamy, B., 1961. *An Introduction to Social Psychology*. Bombay: Asia Publishing House.

—— 1972. *Social Change in India*. Delhi, Bombay, and London: Vikas Publications.

Laffin, John, 1975. *The Arab Mind: A Need for Understanding*. London: Cassell; also publ. New York: Taplinger, under the title *The Arab Mind Considered*.

Lamacchia, G. A., 1974. *Collision* (short stories). Newark, N.J.: Washington Irving Publishing Co.

Lambiri-Dimake, Jane, 1972. "Dowry in Modern Greece: An Institution at the Crossroads between Persistence and Decline." In Safilios-Rothschild, 1972 (q.v.), pp. 73–81.

Landau, Jacob M., 1972. *Man, State and Society in the Contemporary Middle East*. London: Pall Mall.

Landis, Joseph B., 1973. "Racial Attitudes of Africans and Indians in Guyana." *Social and Economic Studies*, no. 4 (December).

Landsberger, Henry A., 1969. *Latin American Peasant Movements*. Ithaca and London: Cornell University Press.

Lane, David, 1971. *The End of Inequality? Stratification under State Socialism*. Harmondsworth, England: Penguin.

Lane, David, and George Kolankiewicz, eds., 1973. *Social Groups in Polish Society*. London: Macmillan.

Lane, Robert E., 1969. "The Way of the Ethnic in Politics." In Harry A. Bailey, Jr., and Ellis Katz, eds. *Ethnic Group Politics*. Columbus, Ohio: Merrill, pp. 85–109.

Lasswell, Harold D., 1936. *Politics: Who Gets What, When, How?* New York: McGraw-Hill.

Lauréat, Jean-Claude, and Raymond Lasierra, 1973. *La torture et les pouvoirs*. Paris: Balland.

Leach, Edmund, 1967. "Caste, Class and Slavery." In de Renck and Knight, 1967 (q.v.), pp. 5–16.

Legum, Colin, 1970. "Tribal Survival in the Modern African Political System." In Gutkind, ed., 1970 (q.v.), 102–12.

—— 1973. *Africa Contemporary Record: Annual Survey and Documents 1972–73*. London: Rex Collings, Ltd.

Lemarchand, René, 1970. *Rwanda and Burundi*. London: Pall Mall Press.

—— 1974. *Selective Genocide in Burundi*, part I. Report No. 20 of Minority Rights Group. London, July.

Lemberg, Eugen, 1964. *Nationalismus*, 2 vols. Hamburg: *Rowohlts deutsche Enzyklopädie*.

—— 1974. "Ideology and Minority Conflict." *Plural Societies* 5, no. 3 (Autumn): 43–52.

Lendvai, Paul, 1971. *Anti-Semitism in Eastern Europe*. London: Macdonald.

Lenin, V. I., 1918. *The Proletarian Revolution and The Renegade Kautsky*. New York: International Publishers, Little Lenin Library, No. 21.

—— 1920. *Left-Wing Communism, an Infantile Disorder*. Reprinted, New York, International Publishers, 1940.

Lennon, Peter, 1972. "How the 'Dying' Tribes Die." *The Guardian*, June 4.

Le Page, R. B., 1973–74. *The National Language Question: Linguistic Problems of Newly Independent States*. London: Oxford University Press.

Lesser, Alexander, 1972. "Education and the Future of Tribalism in the United States: The Case of the American Indian." In Yetman and Steele, 1972 (q.v.), pp. 333–42.

Levenberg, S., 1972. "Soviet Jewry: Some Problems and Perspectives." In Kochan, 1972 (q.v.), pp. 29–43.

Levine, Edward M., 1966. *The Irish and Irish Politicians: A Study of Cultural and Social Alienation*. Notre Dame, Ind.: University of Notre Dame Press.

LeVine, R. A., and D. T. Campbell, 1972. *Ethnocentrism: Theories of Conflict: Ethnic Attitudes and Group Behavior*. New York: Wiley.

Levitin, R., et al., 1971. "Sex Discrimination Against the American Working Woman." *American Behavioral Scientist* 15(2): 237–54.

Lévy, Bernard-Henri, 1973. *Bangladesh, nationalisme dans la révolution*. Paris: Maspero.

Levy, Marvin R., and Michael S. Kramer, 1972. *The Ethnic Factor: How America's Minorities Decide Elections*. New York: Simon and Schuster. Especially chapters 6 and 7.

Lewis, W. Arthur, 1970. "The Road to the Top Is Through Higher Education—Not Black Studies." In Mack, 1970 (q.v.), pp. 242–54.

Lewis, Bernard, 1971. *Race and Color in Islam*. New York: Harper and Row.

Lewis, Philippa, 1972. "The 'Jewish Question' in the Open, 1968–71." In Kochan, 1972 (q.v.).

Leys, Wayne A. R., 1952. *Ethics for Policy Decisions*. New York: Prentice-Hall.

Lifton, Robert J., 1968. *Revolutionary Immortality, Mao Tse-tung and the Chinese Cultural Revolution*. New York: Vintage Books.

Lijhart, Arend, 1969. "Consociational Democracy." *World Politics* 21, no. 2 (January 1969): 207–25.

Lincoln, Eric C., 1964. *My Face Is Black*. Boston: Beacon Press.

Ling, Ken, 1972. *The Revenge of Heaven: Journal of a Young Chinese*. New York: Putnam. See bibliographical note following chapter 26.

Lippman, Lorna, 1972. "Aboriginal-White Attitudes: A Syndrome of Race Prejudice." In Stevens, 1972 (q.v.), pp. 25–34.

Lippmann, Walter, 1944. *Public Opinion*. New York: Macmillan.

Littlejohn, James, 1972. *Social Stratification*. London: George Allen and Unwin.

Livre Blanc, 1951. Rapport de la Commission d'Instruction, *Livre Blanc sur les Camps de Concentration Soviétiques*. Brussels: Commission Internationale Contre le Régime Concentrationnaire.

Lloyd George, David, 1938. *The Truth About the Peace Treaties*. London.

Locke, John, 1690. *Of Civil Government*, two treatises. London, Toronto, and New York: J. M. Dent & Sons; E. P. Dutton, 1924, Everyman's Library No. 751.

Lockwood, William G., 1975. *European Moslems: Economy and Ethnicity in Western Bosnia*. New York: Academic Press.

Lofchie, Michael F., 1965. *Zanzibar: Background to Revolution*. Princeton: Princeton University Press.

Lorenz, Konrad, 1966. *On Aggression* (esp. chapter entitled "Bonding, Aggression, and Territory"), trans. Marjorie K. Wilson. New York: Harcourt, Brace and World; paperback, Bantam Books, 1969.

Lorimer, Frank, 1946. *The Population of the Soviet Union: History and Prospects*, League of Nations. Princeton, N.J.: Princeton Univ. Press.

Lorwin, Val R., 1966. "Belgium: Religion, Class, Language in National Politics." In Robert A. Dahl, ed., *Political Opposition in Western Democracies*. New Haven: Yale University Press.

—— 1971. "Segmented Pluralism: Ideological Cleavages and Political Cohesion in the Smaller European Democracies." *Comparative Politics*, 3 (January): 141–75.

Loshak, David, 1971. *Pakistan Crisis*. New York: McGraw-Hill.

Love, Joseph L., 1969. "La Raza: Mexican Americans in Rebellion." *Trans-Action*, No. 4 (February): 35–41.

Lowenthal, David, 1969. "Race and Color in the West Indies." In Tumin, 1969 (q.v.), pp. 293–312.

—— 1972. *West Indian Societies*, published for the Institute of Race Relations and the American Geographic Society. London and New York: Oxford University Press.

Luca, Costa, 1975. "Discrimination in the Arab Countries of the Middle East." In Veenhoven, 1975 (q.v.), 2: 211–40.

Lyon, Patricia, 1974. *Indians of South America: Natives of the Least Known Continent*. New York: Feffer and Simons.

Mabbett, Hugh, and Ping-Ching Mabbett, 1972. *The Chinese Community in Indonesia*. Part I of Minority Rights Group, Report No. 10. London.

Mabbett and Coppel, 1972. *The Chinese in Indonesia, the Philippines and Malaysia*, containing "The Chinese Community in Indonesia" by Hugh and Ping-Ching Mabbett, and "The Position of the Chinese in the Philippines, Malaysia and Indonesia," by Charles Coppel. London: Minority Rights Group, Report No. 10.

Macdonald, Dwight, 1962. "Masscult and Midcult." In *Against the American Grain*. New York: Random House, Vintage Books, pp. 3–75.

Mack, Raymond W., ed., 1970. *Prejudice and Race Relations*. Chicago: Quadrangle Books.

Mackie, J. A. C., 1973. *Confrontation: the Indonesia-Malaysia Dispute*. London: Blackwell's.

MacManus, James, 1974. "Rising Price of Principles." *The Guardian*. Manchester, December 3, 1974.

Mahar, J. Michael, ed., 1972. *The Untouchables in Contemporary India*. Tucson: The University of Arizona Press.

Maier, Erich, 1975. "Parallelitäten gleichen Schicksals erörtert." *Sudetendeutsche Zeitung*, January 17, 1975.

Maier, Georg, 1975. "Peru: Portrait of a Fragmented Society." In Veenhoven, 1975 (q.v.), 1: 155–75.

Maitland-Jones, J. F., 1973. *Politics in Africa: The Former British Territories*. New York: Norton.

Majumdar, Dn, 1961. *Races and Cultures of India*, 4th Edition, Bombay: Asia Publishing House.

Makielski, S. J., ed., 1973. *Beleaguered Minorities: Cultural Politics in America*. Reading, England: W. H. Freeman and Company, Ltd., and New Orleans, Loyola University Press.

Malik, Yogendra K., 1973–74. *East Indians in Trini-*

dad: A Study in Minority Politics. London: Oxford University Press.

Mallinson, Vernon, 1970. *Belgium.* New York: Praeger.

Malta, 1955. *Foreign Relations of the United States, Diplomatic Papers: the Conferences at Malta and Yalta, 1945.* Department of State Publication 6199. Washington: Government Printing Office.

Mandelbaum, David G., 1972. *Society in India,* 2 vols. Berkeley: University of California Press.

Mandelstam, André, 1918. *La Turquie.* Paris: Flinikowski.

Manheim, Harold, and Melanie Wallace, 1974. *Political Violence in the United States, 1875–1974: A Bibliography.* London: Garland Publishing Company.

Mann, John, 1965. *Changing Human Behavior.* New York: Scribners.

Mann, Michael, 1973. *Workers on the Move: The Sociology of Relocation.* London: Cambridge University Press.

Marden, Charles F. and Gladys Meyer, 1968. *Minorities in American Society.* New York: Van Nostrand Reinhold.

Mark, Vernon H., and Frank R. Ervin, 1972. *Violence and the Brain.* New York: Harper and Row, Medical Department.

Marshall, Adriana, 1973. *The Import of Labour: The Case of the Netherlands.* Rotterdam: Martinus Nijhoff.

Martens, M. F. de, 1883. *Traité de Droit International.* Paris.

Martin, David, 1974a. "Amin Massacres and Messages from God." *Observer Review.* London, June 30. Extracted from *General Amin,* by the same author. London: Faber and Faber.

—— 1974b. Part Two in *Selective Genocide in Burundi.* Report no. 20 of Minority Rights Group, London.

—— 1974c. *General Amin.* London: Faber and Faber.

Martin, David, and Colin Crouch, 1971. "England." In Archer, M. S., and S. Giner, eds., 1971 (q.v.), pp. 241–78.

Martindale, Don, 1972. "The Theory of Stratification." In Thielbar and Feldman, 1972 (q.v.), pp. 209–26.

Martínez Márquez, Guillermo, 1974. "Denuncias y Violaciones de los Derechos Humanos." *Diario Las Americas.* Miami, February 19.

Masaryk, Thomas G., 1927. *Die Weltrevolution, Erinnerungen und Betrachtungen 1914–1918.* Berlin.

Mascarenhas, Anthony, 1971. *The Rape of Bangla Desh.* Delhi: Vikas Publications.

Maslow, Abraham H., 1970. *Motivation and Personality.* New York: Harper and Row.

Mason, Philip, 1970a. *Patterns of Dominance.* London: Oxford University Press.

—— 1970b. *Race Relations.* London: Oxford University Press.

—— ed., 1974. *India and Ceylon: Unity and Diversity: A Symposium.* London: Oxford University Press.

Masotti, Louis H., K. Jeffrey Hadden, Kenneth Seminatore, and Jerome Corsi, 1969. *A Time to Burn? A Critical Evaluation of the Present American Race Relations Crisis.* Chicago: Rand McNally.

Mathews, Anthony S., 1972. *Law, Order and Liberty in South Africa.* London: University of California Press.

Matthews, Fred H., 1970. "White Community and 'Yellow Peril.'" In Dinnerstein and Jaher, 1970 (q.v.), pp. 268–84.

Matthews, Mervyn, 1972. *Class and Society in Soviet Russia.* London: Allen Lane.

Maxwell, Neville, 1973. *India and the Nagas.* London: Minority Rights Group, Report No. 17.

Mayer, Kurt B., 1951. "Cultural Pluralism and Linguistic Equilibrium in Switzerland." *American Sociological Review* 16 (April): 157–63.

—— 1967. "Migration, Cultural Tensions and Foreign Relations." *Journal of Conflict Resolution* 11 (January): 139–52.

—— 1968. "The Jura Problem: Ethnic Conflict in Switzerland." *Social Research* 35, no. 4 (Winter): 707–41.

Maykovich, Minako K., 1972. *Japanese American Identity Dilemma.* Tokyo: Waseda University Press.

Mazrui, Alì, 1969. "Pluralism and National Integration." In Leo Kuper and M. G. Smith, eds., *Pluralism in Africa.* Berkeley: University of California Press, pp. 333–49.

—— 1973. "The Black Arabs in Comparative Perspective: The Political Sociology of Race Mixture." In Wai, 1973 (q.v.), pp. 29–46.

Mbiti, John S., 1970. *African Religion and Philosophy.* New York: Anchor Books (Doubleday).

Mboya, Tom, 1963. *Freedom and After.* Boston: Little, Brown.

McConnochie, Keith R., 1973. *Realities of Race: An*

Analysis of the Concepts of Race and Racism and Their Relevance to Australian Society. Sydney: Australia and New Zealand Book Co.

McDonagh, Edward C., and Eugene S. Richards, 1953. *Ethnic Relations in the United States.* New York: Appleton-Century-Crofts, Inc.

McDonald, Gordan C., et al., 1969. *Area Handbook for Burundi.* Washington: U.S. Government Printing Office.

McGuinness, Bruce, 1972. "Black Power in Australia." In Stevens, 1972 (q.v.), 2: 150–58.

McKay, Vernon, 1971. "The Propaganda Battle for Zambia." *Africa Today,* April (reprint).

McLellan, David, 1971. *Marx Before Marxism.* New York: Harper Torchbooks.

McNamara, Robert S., 1973. *One Hundred Countries, Two Billion People.* London: Pall Mall.

McQuade, Walter, and Ann Aikman, 1974. *Stress.* New York: Dutton.

Means, Gordon P., 1970. *Malaysian Politics.* New York: New York University Press.

Medding, P. Y., ed., 1973. *Jews in Australian Society.* London: Macmillan.

Medina, Manuel, 1975. "Spain: Regional Linguistic and Ideological Conflict." In Veenhoven, 1975 (q.v.), 1: 133–55.

Medvedev, Jaurès, 1972. "Compulsory Psychiatric Hospitalization for Political Reasons." Report to the Committee on Human Rights. Excerpts reprinted as appendix I to *Abuse of Psychiatry,* q.v.

Meer, Fatima, 1972. "An Indian's Views on Apartheid." In N. J. Rhoodie, ed., *South African Dialogue* (q.v.), pp. 435–56.

Meisel, John, 1974. *Cleavages, Parties and Values in Canada.* London: Sage Professional Papers in Contemporary Political Sociology.

Meisler, Stanley, 1969. "Kenya's Asian Outcasts." *The Nation,* September 1, 173–76.

Mercérian, Jean, S.J., 1965. *Le Génocide du peuple Arménian, le sort de la population arméniènne de l'empire Ottoman.* Beirut: Imprimerie Catholique.

Merkx, Gilbert W. and Richard J. Griego, 1972. "Crisis in New Mexico." In Yetman and Steele, 1972 (q.v.), pp. 599–609.

Merton, Robert K., 1957. *Social Theory and Social Structure,* revised edition. Glencoe, Illinois: The Free Press.

Metrowich, F. R., 1974. *Discrimination in Zambia.* Manuscript compiled for Foundation for the Study of Plural Societies. The Hague, July.

Meyer, Frank S., 1969. *The Conservative Mainstream.* New Rochelle, N.Y.: Arlington House.

Mhina, George A., 1974. "The Role of Kiswahili in the Development of Tanzania." Seminar presentation. *Munger Africana Library Notes,* no. 25, August.

Mikolajczyk, Stanislaw, 1948. *The Pattern of Soviet Domination.* London: S. Low. Also published in New York, Whittlesey House, 1948, under title: *The Rape of Poland; Pattern of Soviet Aggression.*

Miksche, Ferdinand O., 1953. *Danubian Federation.* Camberley, Surrey: published by the author.

Mill, John Stuart, 1859. *On Liberty.* In *Utilitarianism, Liberty, and Representative Government.* London: Everyman's Library, J. M. Dent and Sons, 1910 (reprinted 1929), pp. 65–170.

—— 1861. *Representative Government.* In *ibid.,* pp. 173–393.

Miller, D. B., ed., 1975. *From Hierarchy to Stratification: Changing Patterns of Social Inequality in a North-Indian Village.* London: Oxford University Press.

Miller, Herman P., 1970. "The Job Gap." In Mack, 1970 (q.v.), pp. 116–25.

Miller, S. C., 1969. *The Unwelcome Immigrant: The American Image of the Chinese.* Berkeley: University of California Press.

Milson, Menahem, 1972. "Medieval and Modern Intellectual Traditions in the Arab World." *Daedalus* (Summer): 17–37.

Mittelman, James H., 1972. "The Uganda Coup and the Internationalization of Political Violence." *Munger Africana Library Notes,* no. 14, September.

Mohan Das, S. R., 1975. "Discrimination in India." In Veenhoven, 1975 (q.v.), 2: 157–77.

Molnar, Thomas, 1972. "The God-Problem and the Philosophers," *Modern Age* 16, no. 1 (Winter): 48–58.

Montagu, Ashley, 1963. *Race, Science and Humanity* Princeton: Van Nostrand.

—— 1973. *Man and Aggression,* 2d ed. New York: Oxford University Press.

Montgomery, J. R. P., 1973a. "The Work of the Anti-Slavery Society Today." *Journal of the Royal Society of Arts* (May). Reprint issue by Anti-Slavery Society, London.

—— 1973b. "The Anti-Slavery Society 1973." *Contemporary Review,* Vol. 223, No. 1291 (August 1973). Reprint issued by Anti-Slavery Society.

—— 1975a. "Why Can't the U.N. Guard Human Rights?" *Baptist Times*, January 9, 1975, p. 6.

—— 1975b. "Kidnapped on Her Wedding Day." *Baptist Times*, Jan. 9, 1975, p. 7.

Montseny, Federica, 1950. *Pasion y muerte de los Españoles en Francia*. Toulouse: Universo.

Moon, Henry Lee, 1948. *Balance of Power: The Negro Vote*. Garden City, New York: Doubleday and Company.

Moore, Joan W., 1973. "Colonialism: The Case of the Mexican-Americans." In Gelfand and Lee, 1973 (q.v.), pp. 302–10.

Moquin, Wayne, and Charles Van Doren, 1971. *A Documentary History of the Mexican Americans*. New York: Praeger Publishers.

Morgenthau, Henry J., 1952. "Another 'Great Debate': The National Interest of the United States." *American Political Science Review* 44, no. 4 (December): 961–88.

Mörner, Magnus, ed., 1970. *Race and Class in Latin America*. New York: Columbia University Press.

Morris, Fred R., 1975. "In the Presence of Mine Enemies, Faith and Torture in Brazil." *Harper's* 251 (October): 57–70.

Morris, Roger, 1974. *Disaster in the Desert*. Report on drought relief in African Sahel. New York: Carnegie Endowment for International Peace.

Morrison, Donald George, 1973. *Black Africa: A Comparative Handbook*. New York: The Free Press.

Morrison, Godfrey, 1974. "Blows to Foreign Trade Balance," In *The Times*, London, Special report on Tanzania, December 9, 1974.

Mouzelis, Nikos, and Michael Attalides, 1971. "Greece." In Archer and Giner, 1971 (q.v.), pp. 162–97.

Mphahlele, Ezechiel, 1974. *The African Image*. Revised edition, New York: Praeger.

Mulder, C. P., 1972. "The Rationale of Separate Development." In Rhoodie, 1972 (q.v.), pp. 49–63.

Mullard, Chris, 1974. *Black Britain*. London: George Allen & Unwin.

Müller-Sternberg, Robert, 1969. *Deutsche Ostsiedlung—eine Bilanz für Europa*. Bielefeld, Gieseking.

Multinational, 1965. *Seminar on the Multinational Society*. Ljubljana, Yugoslavia, June 8 to 21, 1965. Organized by the United Nations in cooperation with the Government of Yugoslavia. New York United Nations 1965, Document No ST/TAO/HR/23.

Munger, Edwin S., 1973. Introduction to "Inside Amin's Uganda," q.v.

—— 1974. Introduction to Mhina, 1974, q.v.

Münzel, Mark, 1973. *The Aché Indians: Genocide in Paraguay*. Copenhagen: International Work Group for Indigenous Affairs, Pub. No. 11.

Murphree, Marshall W., and Donald G. Baker, 1976 "Racial Discrimination in Rhodesia." In Veenhoven, 1976 (q.v.), V, pp. 375–413.

Murphy, Irene L., 1973. *Public Policy on the Status of Women: Agenda and Strategy for the 1970's*. Lexington, Mass.: Heath.

Mustafa, Zaki, 1971. *The Common Law in the Sudan. An Account of the "Justice, Equity and Good Conscience" Provision*. London: Clarendon Press.

Nassif, Doug, 1976. "Soviets make Slaves with Alcohol; Addicts Placed in Labor Camps." *Twin Circle*, March 21, 1976, p. 15.

National Commission on the Causes and Prevention of Violence, 1969. *Report*, Washington: Government Printing Office.

Nava, Julian, ed., 1970. *Mexican Americans: A Brief Look at Their History*. New York: Anti-Defamation League of B'Nai B'Rith.

Nehru, Jawaharlal, 1961. *The Discovery of India*. Bombay: Asia Publishing House.

N'Goumou, Edima, and Jonathan Power, 1974 "The Clandestine Traffic." *The Times*. London June 15, p. 8.

Nicholls, David G., 1971. "East Indians and Black Power in Trinidad." *Race* 12, no. 4 (April) 443–59.

Niebuhr, Reinhold, 1955. Unpublished paper. "The Moral Issue in International Relations.' Cited by Thompson, 1955 (q.v.), pp. 741–42.

Nieburg, H. L., 1972. *Culture Storm: Politics and the Ritual Order*. New York: St. Martin's Press.

Nikolinakos, Marios, 1972. "Economic Foundations of Discrimination in the Federal Republic of Germany." In Van Houte and Melgert, 1972 (q.v.). pp. 78–97.

Noel, Donald L., 1968. "A Theory of the Origin of Ethnic Stratification." *Social Problems*, no. 16 (Fall): 157–71.

Nordlinger, Eric A., ed., 1970. *Politics and Society*. Englewood Cliffs, New Jersey: Prentice-Hall.

—— 1972. *Conflict Regulation in Divided Societies.* Cambridge, Mass.: Center for International Affairs, Harvard University.

Novak, Leopold, 1974. "Woman Mädchen wie Vieh verkauft" (Where Maidens are Sold like Cattle). *Sudetendeutsche Zeitung,* August 9, 1974.

Novak, Michael, 1973. *The Rise of the Unmeltable Ethnics: Politics and Culture in the Seventies.* New York: Macmillan, 1971. Citations are from 1973 paperback edition.

Nove, Alec, 1961. "The Worker and His Livelihood." Originally published in *Soviet Survey,* no. 26 (October–December) 1958. Reprinted in Inkeles and Geiger, 1961 (q.v.), pp. 382–88. Citations are from 1961 edition.

Nyquist, Thomas E., 1965. "The Sudan: Prelude to Elections." *Middle East Journal* 19, no. 3 (Summer): 263–72.

Nyrop, Richard F., et al., 1969. *Area Handbook for Rwanda.* Washington: U.S. Government Printing Office.

Nzomo, D., 1971. *Occupational Kenyanization in the Private Sector.* Institute of Development Studies, University of Nairobi, Staff Paper No. 108.

Oberschall, Anthony, 1973. *Social Conflict and Social Movements.* Englewood Cliffs, New Jersey: Prentice-Hall.

Odo, Franklin S., 1973. "The Asian American." In Spiegel and Keith-Spiegel, 1973 (q.v.), pp. 371–90.

Okpaku, Joseph, ed., 1972. *Nigeria; Dilemma of Nationhood: An African Analysis of the Biafran Conflict.* New York: Third Press.

Olorunsola, Victor A., 1972. "Nigeria." In Olorunsola, ed., 1972 (q.v.), pp. 5–46.

Olorunsola, Victor, A., ed., 1972. *The Politics of Cultural Sub-Nationalism in Africa.* New York: Doubleday.

Opler, Morris E., 1972. North Indian Themes— Caste and Untouchability. In J. Michael Mahar, 1972 (q.v.).

Opper, Frederick B., 1973. "Slavery Is Still with Us." *San Jose Mercury,* August 12, 1973, p. 14.

Orleans, Peter and William Russell Ellis, Jr. eds., 1971. *Race, Change and Urban Society.* Beverly Hills: Sage Publications.

Ornstein, Allan C., 1976. "Affirmative Action and American Universities." In Veenhoven, 1976 (q.v.), 5:347–73.

Osborn, Robert J., 1970. *Soviet Social Policies: Welfare, Equality, and Community.* Homewood, Illinois: The Dorsey Press.

Osborne, Milton, 1973. *Politics and Power in Cambodia: The Sihanouk Years.* London: Blackwell's.

O'Shaughnessy, Hugh, 1973. *What Future for the Amerindians of South America?* London: Minority Rights Group, Report No. 15.

Otzen, Katharina, 1975. "Discrimination and Preferment in the Federal Republic of Germany." In Veenhoven, 1975 (q.v.), 2:31–53.

Paddock, William, and Paul Paddock, 1967. *Famine—1975: America's Decision: Who Will Survive?* Boston: Little, Brown.

Pakistan White Paper, 1971. Government of Pakistan, *White Paper on the Crisis in East Pakistan.* Islamabad, August 5.

Palfreeman, A. C., 1971. "The White Australia Policy." In Stevens, 1971 (q.v.), 1:136–45.

Palmer, Howard, 1972. "Land of the Second Chance." *The Lethbridge* (Alberta) *Herald.*

Palmer, N., and H. Perkins, 1957. *International Relations.* 2nd edition, Boston: Houghton Mifflin.

Palmore, Erdman B., 1967. "Ethnophaulisms and Ethnocentrism." In Barron, 1967 (q.v.), pp. 205–10.

Parenti, Michael, 1967. "Ethnic Politics and the Persistence of Ethnic Identification." *American Political Science Review* 61, no. 3 (June): 717–26.

—— 1974. *Democracy for the Few.* New York: St. Martin's Press.

Pareto, Vilfredo, 1923. *Trattato di sociologia generale.* Florence: G. Barbéra.

—— 1972. "Circulation of Elites." Extract from *The Mind and Society.* New York: Dover Publications, 1935. In Thielbar and Feldman, 1972 (q.v.), pp. 156–60.

Parkin, Frank, 1971a. *Class, Inequality and Political Order: Social Stratification in Capitalist and Communist Societies.* London: MacGibbon & Kee.

—— 1971b. "Yugoslavia." In Archer and Giner, 1971 (q.v.), pp. 197–317.

Parry, Albert, 1976. *Terrorism from Robespierre to Arafat.* New York: Vanguard Press.

Patterson, Sheila, 1968. *Immigrants in Industry.* London: Oxford University Press for Institute of Race Relations.

Paul, Richard, 1974. "Jure Libre, 23. Schweizer Kanton?" *Das Parlament,* Bonn, August 24, p. 11.

Pavlov, I. P., 1955. *Selected Works*, edited by Kh. S. Koshtoyants. Moscow: Foreign Languages Publishing House.

Payne, Robert, 1973. *Massacre, The Tragedy of Bangladesh and the Phenomenon of Mass Slaughter throughout History.* New York: Macmillan.

Peacock, James L., 1973. *Indonesia: An Anthropological Perspective.* Pacific Palisades, Cal.: Goodyear Publishing Co.

Peck, Cornelius J., 1967. "Nationalism, 'Race,' and Developments in the Philippine Law of Citizenship." *Journal of Asian and African Studies*, 2 (January and April 1967), pp. 128–43.

Peirce, Neal R., 1972. *The Megastates of America: People, Politics, and Power in the Ten Great States.* New York: W. W. Norton and Company, Inc.

Pelikán, Jiří, 1970. *Das Unterdrückte Dossier.* Vienna-Frankfurt-Zurich: Europa-Verlag.

Penchef, Esther, ed., 1971. *Four Horsemen: Pollution, Poverty, Famine, Violence.* San Francisco: Canfield Press.

Peters, H. B., 1937. Die wissenschaftlichen Namen der menschlichen Körperformgruppen. Eine Zusammenstellung nach den internationalen Nomenklaturregeln. *Zeitschrift für Rassenkunde*, 6:211–41.

Petersen, William, 1975. *Population*, 3rd ed. New York: Macmillan.

Petrov, Victor P., 1971. *Mongolia: A Profile.* London: Pall Mall.

Pifer, Alan, 1973. *The Higher Education of Blacks in the United States.* Johannesburg: South African Institute of Race Relations.

Pious, Richard M., ed., 1970. *Civil Rights and Liberties in the 1970's.* New York: Random House.

Pittock, A. Barrie, 1972. "Aboriginal Land Rights." In Stevens, 1972 (q.v.), 2, pp. 188–208.

Pitt-Rivers, Julian, 1969. "Race, Color and Class in Central America and the Andes." *Daedalus* (Spring 1967); extract in Heller, 1969 (q.v.), pp. 380–87.

Plantea, 1974. "Plantea México Problema de Braceros." *Diario Las Americas*, Miami, March 24, 1974.

Plumb, J. H., 1973. *In the Light of History.* Boston: Houghton Mifflin.

Plunkett, Thomas J., 1968. *Urban Canada and Its Government: A Study of Municipal Organization.* Toronto: Macmillan of Canada.

Poddar, Shrikumer, 1974. Statement to New York Times News Service. *Fall River* (Mass.) *Herald*, August 6.

Poirier, Jean, 1972. Ethnies et Cultures. In Poirier, ed., *Ethnologie Régionale*, vol. 1, *Encyclopédie de la Pléiade.* Paris: Gallimard, pp. 15–20.

Polk, Barbara Bovee, and Robert B. Stein, 1972. "Is the Grass Greener on the Other Side?" In Safilios-Rothschild, 1972 (q.v.), pp. 14–23.

Polyviou, Polyvios G., 1975. *Cyprus: the Tragedy and the Challenge.* Washington: American Hellenic Institute.

Portes, Alejandro, 1974. "Return of the Wetback." *Society* 11, no. 3 (March–April): 40–46.

Portisch, Hugo, 1967. *Eyewitness in Vietnam*, transl. from German by Michael Glenny. London and Sydney: The Bodley Head.

Possony, Stefan T., 1968. *Zur Bewältigung der Kriegsschuldfrage, Völkerrecht und Strategie bei der Auslösung zweier Weltkriege.* Cologne: Westdeutscher Verlag.

—— 1975a. "From Gulag to Guitk: Political Prisons in the USSR Today." In Veenhoven, 1975 (q.v.), 1:1–38.

—— 1975b. "Anti-Semitism in the Russian Orbit." In *ibid.*, 2:405–44.

—— 1976. "Ethnomorphosis: Invisible Catastrophic Crime." *Plural Societies*, no. 3 (Autumn): 3–36.

Possony, Stefan T., and Lynn Bouchey, 1978. *International Terrorism, the Communist Connection.* Washington: American Council for World Freedom.

Powell, J. W., 1891. *Indian Linguistic Families of America North of Mexico:* reprinted with Boas, 1911 (q.v.), 1966. Lincoln: University of Nebraska Press.

Powell, John Duncan, 1971. *Political Mobilization of the Venezuelan Peasant.* Cambridge, Mass.: Harvard University Press.

Power, Jonathan, 1974. "The New Proletariat." *Encounter* (London) 43, no. 3 (September): 8–22.

Prago, Albert, 1973. *Strangers in Their Own Land: A History of Mexican Americans.* New York: Four Winds Press.

Pratt, Henry J., 1974. *Ethno-Religious Politics.* Cambridge: Schenkman Publishing Company.

Prélot, Marcel, 1948. *Précis du droit constitutionnel.* Paris: Dalloz.

Prittie, Terence, and Joseph Dineen, 1974. *The Double Exodus: A Study of Arab and Jewish Refugees In the Middle East* London: The Goodhart Press.

Pritzel, Konstantin, 1974. Die DDR: Die Stellung der Frau in der sozialistischen Gesellschaft. *Ost-Kurier* (Munich), No. 8 (August, 1974).

Prothro, E. T. and Melikian, L. H., 1954. "Studies in Stereotypes: III. Arab Student in the Near East." *Journal of Social Psychology* 40: 237–44.

Protocols, 1957. *Protocols of the Elders of Zion*, Political Books, No. 5. Cairo: United Arab Republic Ministry of Information.

Puxon, Grattan, 1973. *Rom: Europe's Gypsies*. London: Minority Rights Group, Report No. 14.

Puxon, Grattan and Kenrick, Donald, 1972. *The Destiny of Europe's Gypsies*. London: Chatto-Heinemann.

Quandt, William B., Fuad Jabber, and Mosely Lesch, 1973. *The Politics of Palestinian Nationalism*. Berkeley: University of California Press.

Rabl, Kurt, 1963. *Das Selbstbestimmungsrecht der Völker*. Munich: Bergstadt-Verlag Wilh. Gottlieb Korn.

Rabushka, Alvin, 1970. "The Manipulation of Ethnic Politics in Malaya." *Polity* 2, no. 3 (Spring, 1970): 345–56.

Rabuschka, Alvin and Kenneth A. Shepsle, 1972. *Politics in Plural Societies: A Theory of Democratic Instability*. Columbus, Ohio: Charles E. Merrill.

al-Rahman al-Darbandi, Abd, 1970. *The Contemporary Iraqi Woman*. Bagdad, Dar al Basri Press.

Rainwater, L. 1965. "Crucible of Identity: The Negro Lower-Class Family." In Talcott Parsons, ed., *The Negro American*. Boston: Beacon Press.

Ramsaur, E. E., 1957. *The Young Turks, Prelude to the Revolution of 1908*. Princeton: Princeton University Press.

Randall, Peter, ed., 1972. *Law, Justice and Society*. Report of the legal commission of the study project on Christianity in an Apartheid society. Johannesburg, Spro-cas.

Rauschning, Hermann, 1930. *Die Entstehung West-Preussens und Posens: Zehn Jahre polnischer Politik*. Berlin: 1930.

Raveau, F. H. M., 1975. "Role of Color in Identification Processes." In De Vos and Romanucci-Ross, 1975 (q.v.)

Ray, Lovelle, 1972. "The American Woman in Mass Media: How Much Emancipation and What Does It Mean?" In Safilios-Rothschild, 1972 (q.v.), pp. 41–62.

Red Papers, 1974. *How Capitalism Has Been Restored in the Soviet Union and What This Means for the World Struggle, The Red Papers*. Chicago: Revolutionary Union (October).

Reddaway, Peter, editor and translator, 1973. *Uncensored Russia: Protest and Dissent in the Soviet Union. The Unofficial Moscow Journal: A Chronicle of Current Events*, with a foreword by Julius Telesin. New York: American Heritage Press, a division of McGraw-Hill Book Company.

Reichling, G. and F. H. Betz, 1949. *Die Heimatvertriebenen: Glied oder Aussenseiter der Deutschen Gemeinschaft?* Kleine Schriften für den Staatsbürger No. 5. Frankfurt/Main: Institut zur Förderung öffentlicher Angelegenheiten.

Reissman, Leonard, 1973. *Inequality in American Society: Social Stratification*. Glenview, Ill.: Scott, Foresman & Co.

Reitlinger, Gerald, 1968. *The Final Solution*. London: Vallentine Mitchell; originally published 1953, 2nd rev. edition, 1968.

Rendon, Armando B., 1971. *Chicano Manifesto*. New York: Macmillan.

Report on Torture, 1973. (See Amnesty International.)

Reynolds, Hubert, 1968. "Overseas Chinese College Students in the Philippines: A Case Study." *Philippine Sociological Review*, 5 (July–October): 132–34.

Rex, John, 1968. *The Formation of Ghettoes in Britain's Cities*. London: Institute of Race Relations.

—— 1973. *Race, Colonialism, and the City*. London: Routledge & Kegan Paul.

Rex, John, and Robert Moore, 1967. *Race, Community and Conflict*. London: Oxford University Press for Institute of Race Relations.

Rhoodie, N. J., ed., 1972. *South African Dialogue: Contrasts in South African Thinking on Basic Race Issues*. Philadelphia: Westminster Press.

Richmond, Anthony H., 1972. *Readings in Race and Ethnic Relations*. Oxford: Pergamon Press.

—— 1973. *Migration and Race Relations in an English City: A Study in Bristol*. London: Oxford University Press.

Rivera, Julius, 1971. *Latin America*. New York: Appleton-Century-Crofts.

Roberts, Hew, 1972. *Australia's Immigration Policy*. Perth: University of Western Australia Press.

Robertson, A. H., ed., 1973. *Privacy and Human Rights*. Manchester, England: Manchester University Press.

Robertson, Wilmot, 1972. *The Dispossessed Majority.* Cape Canaveral, Florida: Howard Allen.

Roby, Pamela, ed., 1974. *The Poverty Establishment.* Englewood Cliffs, N.J.: Prentice-Hall.

Roche, George, 1976. "The Balancing Act: Quota Hiring in Higher Education." In Veenhoven, 1976 (q.v.), 4:135–92.

Rodgers, Harrell R. Jr., ed., 1975. *Racism and Inequality: The Policy Alternatives.* San Francisco: W. H. Freeman and Company.

Rohrlich-Leavitt, Ruby, ed., 1975. *Women Cross-Culturally: Change and Challenge.* Paris: Mouton Publishers.

Rokeach, M., 1960. *The Open and the Closed Mind.* New York: Basic Books.

Rosaldo, Robert, Robert A. Calvert, and Gustav L. Seligman, eds., 1973. *Chicano: The Evolution of a People.* California: Rinehart Press.

Rose, Arnold M. and Caroline B. Rose, eds., 1972. *Minority Problems.* New York and London: Harper and Row; 2d ed.

Rose, Jerry D., 1976. *Peoples: The Ethnic Dimension in Human Relations.* Chicago: Rand McNally.

Rose, Peter I., 1968. *The Subject Is Race.* New York: Oxford University Press.

Rose, Richard, 1971. *Governing without Consensus: An Irish Perspective.* Boston: Beacon Press.

Rothchild, Donald, 1973. *Racial Bargaining in Independent Kenya.* London: Oxford University Press.

Rothenberg, J., 1972. "Jewish Religion in the Soviet Union." In Kochan, 1972 (q.v.), pp. 159–87.

Rothman, David J., ed., 1972. *On Their Own: The Poor in Modern America.* Reading, Penna.: Addison-Wesley.

Roumani, Maurice M., 1975. *The Case of the Jews from Arab Countries: The Neglected Issue.* New York: World Organization of Jews from Arab Countries.

Rousseau, Jean Jacques, 1762. *The Social Contract* and *Discourses.* Translated with an introduction by G. D. H. Cole. London and New York: Everyman's Library, 1913, 1950.

Rowley, C. D., 1972a. *Outcasts in White Australia.* Harmondsworth, England: Penguin.

—— 1972b. *The Destruction of Aboriginal Society.* Harmondsworth, England: Penguin.

Royce, Josiah, 1908. *Race Questions, Provincialism and other American Problems.* New York.

Rozek, Edward J., 1958. *Allied Wartime Diplomacy: A Pattern in Poland.* New York: Wiley.

Rubin, Leslie, and Brian Weinstein, 1974. *Introduction to African Politics: A Continental Approach* New York: Praeger.

Rudner, Martin, 1970. "The Malaysian General Election of 1969: A Political Analysis." *Modern Asian Studies,* 4, no. 1 (January): 1–21.

Runciman, W. G., 1972. *Relative Deprivation and Social Justice.* Harmondsworth: Penguin.

Ruo-Wang, Bao (Jean Pasqualini) and Rudolph Chelminski, 1973. *Prisoner of Mao.* New York: Coward, McCann and Geoghegan.

Rushing, William A., 1972. *Class, Culture, and Alienation: A Study of Farmers and Farmworkers.* Lexington, Massachusetts: D. C. Heath and Co.

Russell, Peter, and Storrs McCall, 1973. "Can Secession Be Justified? The Case of the Southern Sudan." In Wai, 1973 (q.v.), pp. 93–102.

Russett, Bruce M., 1974. *Power and Community in World Politics.* New Haven: Yale University Press.

Rustin, Bayard, 1971. *Down the Line: the Collected Writings of Bayard Rustin.* Chicago: Quadrangle Books.

Ruthenberg, Hans, 1974. "A Decade of Agricultural Development in Tanzania and Kenya." In Barratt et al, 1974 (q.v.), pp. 279–92.

Ryan, William, 1971. *Blaming the Victim.* New York: Random House, Vintage Books. Extract in Roby, 1974 (q.v.), pp. 171–81. Page references are to Roby.

Sachar, Abram, 1966. *A History of the Jews.* New York: Knopf.

al-Sádāwī, Nawāl, 1972. *al-Khayt wa-al-jidār.* Cairo: 1972.

Safilios-Rothschild, Constantina, ed., 1972. *Toward a Sociology of Women.* Lexington, Mass.: Xerox Corporation.

—— 1974. *Women and Social Policy.* Englewood Cliffs, New Jersey: Prentice-Hall.

Samora, Julian, 1971. *Los Majados: The Wetback Story.* Notre Dame, Indiana: University of Notre Dame Press.

Sandford, Jeremy, 1973. "Britain's Gypsies and Travellers." In Henderson, 1973 (q.v.), pp. 75–98.

Sargent, William, 1967. *The Unquiet Mind.* Boston: Little, Brown.

—— 1974. *The Mind Possessed.* Philadelphia: Lippincott.

Savon, Hervé, 1972. *Du Cannibalisme au Génocide.* Paris: Hachette.

Schaufelberger, Alfred, 1973. *Blacks and the Trial by Jury: The Black Man's Experience in the Courts.* Frankfurt: Herbert Lang.

Schermerhorn, R. A., 1949. *These Our People.* Boston: D.C. Heath.

—— 1967. "Minorities: European and American." In Barron, 1967 (q.v.), pp. 5–14.

Schieder, Theodor, ed., 1961. *Das Schicksal der Deutschen in Jugoslawien,* Vol. 5 in *Dokumentation der Vertreibung der Deutschen aus Ost-Mitteleuropa.* Bonn: Federal Ministry for Expellees, Refugees, and War Victims.

Schlemmer, Lawrence, 1976. "Institutionalised Inequality and Differentiation: An Evaluation of Race Discrimination in South Africa." In Veenhoven, 1976 (q.v.), 5: 291–326.

Schlochauer, H. J., 1962. *Wörterbuch des Völkerrechts.* Berlin: Gruyter.

Schmid, Alfred, 1933. *Der Erzkönig: eine Kampfschrift.* Published under pseudonym Georg Sebastian Faber. Berlin: Der graue Verlag. (Our translation.)

Schmidt, Dana Adams, 1974. "New Ways to Combat Africa's Drought." *The Christian Science Monitor,* April 4.

Schmitter, Phillipe C., 1971. *Interest, Conflict and Political Change in Brazil.* Stanford: Stanford University Press.

Schöndube, Claus, 1974. "Die Südtirolfrage: ein Vertrag zwischen Italien und Österreich zur Lösung des Problems." *Das Parlament,* Bonn. no. 34–35 (August 24), pp. 5–6. (Interview with Peter Brugger, member of Italian Senate, and Dr. Walter Weiss, director of German-language middle school in Latsch, both members of Südtiroler Volkspartei [SVP].)

Schrag, Peter, 1970. *The Decline of the WASP.* New York: Simon & Schuster.

Schrenk-Notzing, Caspar, 1965. *Charakterwäsche.* Stuttgart: Seewald.

Schulenberg, Wolfgang, 1957. *Ansatz und Wirksamkeit der Erwachsenenbildung.* Vol. 1 in *Göttinger Abhandlungen zur Soziologie,* Stuttgart.

Schuman, Howard, 1972. "Free Will and Determinism in Public Beliefs about Race." In Yetman and Steele, 1972 (q.v.), pp. 382–90.

Scott, John Finley, and Lois Heyman Scott, 1970. "They Are Not So Much Anti-Negro as Pro-Middle Class." In Mack, 1970 (q.v.), pp. 56–70.

Scott, Stanley, and John C. Bollens, 1968. *Governing a Metropolitan Region: The San Francisco Bay Area.* Berkeley: University of California, Institute of Governmental Studies.

Segal, David R., 1974. *Society and Politics: Uniformity and Diversity in Modern Democracy.* Glenview, Illinois: Scott, Foresman and Co.

Segal, Ronald, 1965. *The Anguish of India.* New York: Stein and Day.

Selye, Hans, 1950. *The Physiology and Pathology of Exposure to Stress.* Montreal: Acta.

—— 1956a. *The Stress of Life.* New York: McGraw-Hill.

—— 1956b. "Stress and Psychiatry." *American Journal of Psychiatry,* 113:423.

Selzer, Michael, 1972. *Kike!* New York: World Publishing Co.

Selznick, Gertrude J., and Stephen Steinberg, 1971. *The Tenacity of Prejudice: Anti-Semitism in Contemporary America.* New York: Harper and Row.

Senturia, Joseph J., 1963. "Mass Expulsion." *Encyclopedia of the Social Sciences,* Vol. 10. 15th ed., New York: Macmillan.

Shannon, Lyle, and Magdaline Shannon, 1973. *Minority Migrants in the Urban Community: Mexican-American and Negro Adjustments to Industrial Societies.* London: Sage Publications Ltd.

Shapiro, Harry L., 1958. "Races of Mankind." In *National Encyclopedia.* Washington: Educational Enterprises, Inc. Vol. 8.

Sharma, B. S., 1966. "The 1965 Elections in the Sudan." *The Political Quarterly* 37, no. 4 (October-December): 441–452.

—— 1967. "Failure of Local-Government-Democracy in the Sudan." *Political Studies* 15, no. 1 (February): 62–71.

Sharma, Surya P., 1971. *India's Boundary and Territorial Disputes.* London: Vikas.

Sheehy, Ann, 1972. "The Central Asian Republics." Part 2 in *Conflict Studies,* no. 30 (q.v.), pp. 19–27.

—— 1973. *The Crimean Tartars, Volga Germans and Meskhetians: Soviet Treatment of Two National Minorities.* London: Minority Rights Group Report No. 6, revised edition.

Shibutani, Tamotsu, and Kian M. Kwan, 1965. *Ethnic Stratification: A Comparative Approach.* New York: Macmillan.

Shifrin, Avraham, 1973. *U.S.S.R. Labor Camps.* Testimony Before the Subcommittee to Investigate the Administration of the Internal Security Act and Other Internal Security Laws, Committee on the Judiciary, United States Senate. 93d Congress, 1st Session, February 1 and 2. Washington: Government Printing Office.

Shils, Edward, 1966. "The Prospects for Lebanese Civility." In Binder, 1966 (q.v.), pp. 1–11.

Shostak, A. B., J. Van Til, and S. B. Van Til, 1973. *Privilege in America: An End to Inequality.* Englewood Cliffs, New Jersey: Prentice-Hall.

Shrinivas, M. N., 1972. "The Caste System of India." In Béteille, 1972 (q.v.) pp. 265–72.

Siddiqui, Kalim, 1972. *Conflict, Crisis and War in Pakistan.* London: Macmillan.

Sigmund, P. E., ed., 1961. *The Ideology of the Developing Nations.* New York: Praeger.

Simon, Gerhard, 1974. *Church, State and Opposition in the U.S.S.R.* London: C. Hurst and Company.

Simon, Paul, and Arthur Simon, 1973. *The Politics of World Hunger.* New York: Harper's Magazine Press.

Simpson, George E., and J. Milton Yinger, 1972. *Racial and Cultural Minorities: An Analysis of Prejudice and Discrimination*, 4th edition. New York: Harper and Row.

Singh, Charan, 1964. *India's Poverty and its Solution.* Bombay: Asia Publishing House. (When writing this book, Mr. Singh was Minister of Agriculture of the Indian state of Uttar Pradesh.)

Singham, A. W., 1972. "The Political Socialization of Marginal Groups." In Yetman and Steele, 1972 (q.v.), pp. 102–16.

Sinha, Surajit, 1967. "Caste in India: Its Essential Pattern of Socio-Cultural Integration." In De Reuck and Knight, 1967 (q.v.), pp. 92–105.

—— 1970a. *Science, Technology and Culture: A Study of the Traditions and Institutions of India and Ceylon in Relation to Science and Technology.* New Delhi: Research Council for Cultural Studies, India International Center.

—— 1970b. *Research Programmes on Cultural Anthropology and Allied Disciplines.* Calcutta: Anthropological Survey of India.

Sivan, Emmanuel, 1975a. "The Kurds: Another Perspective." In Veenhoven, 1975 (q.v.), 2: 137–156.

—— 1975b. "The Kabyls: An Oppressed Minority in North Africa." In Veenhoven, 1975 (q.v.), 1: 261–79.

Skidmore, Thomas E., 1974. *Black Into White: Race and Nationality in Brazilian Thought.* New York: Oxford University Press.

Skinner, B. F., 1971. *Beyond Freedom and Dignity.* New York: Knopf.

Skolnick, Jerome H., 1972. "Black Militancy, National Violence Commission Staff Report." In Yetman and Steele, 1972 (q.v.), pp. 529–76.

Small, Adam, 1971. *A Brown Afrikaner Speaks: A Coloured Poet and Philosopher Looks Ahead.* Pasadena, California: No. 8 of *Munger Africana Library Notes.*

Smith, William L., 1973. "The Melting-Pot Theory: Demise of Euphemism." In Stent et al., 1973 (q.v.).

Solaun, Mauricio, and Sidney Kronus, 1973. *Discrimination Without Violence: Miscegenation and Racial Conflict in Latin America.* New York: John Wiley and Sons.

Solzhenitsyn, Alexandr I., 1974. *The Gulag Archipelago, 1918–1956.* New York: Harper and Row. Esp. chapters 2, 8–10.

Sosnowsky, Michael, 1972. "Nations, People, Humanity: Official Program of Genocide in the USSR." *Ukrainian Quarterly* 28, no. 3 (Autumn): 247–65.

Sowell, Thomas, 1974. "The Plight of Black Students in the United States." *Daedalus,* no. 103(2) (Spring): 179–96.

Spengler, Oswald, 1923. *Der Untergang des Abendlandes.* 2 vols. Munich: C. H. Beck'sche Verlagsbuchhandlung. (*Decline of the West.* C. F. Atkinson, trans. London: Allen and Unwin, 1932.)

Spiegel, Don and Patricia Keith-Spiegel, eds., 1973. *Outsiders U.S.A.: Original Essays on Twenty-Four Outgroups in American Society.* San Francisco, Rheinhart.

Spinoza, Baruch, 1910. *Ethics.* New York: Dutton.

Stalin, Joseph V., 1924. *Foundations of Leninism.* Originally published 1924. 10th Anniversary Edition, New York: International Publishers, 1934.

—— 1930. *Political Report of the Central Committee to the 16th Congress of the Communist Party of the Soviet Union (Bolshevik),* June 27. Moscow: Foreign Languages Publishing House, 1951.

Steiner, Kurt, 1965. *Local Government in Japan.* Stanford: Stanford Univ. Press.

Stent, M. D. et al., 1973. *Cultural Pluralism in Education.* New York: Appleton-Century-Crofts.

Stevens, F. S., ed., 1971, 1972. *Racism: The Australian Experience,* Vol. 1, *Prejudice and Exnophobia;* Vol. 2, *Black Versus White;* Vol. 3, *Colonialism.*

Sydney: Australia and New Zealand Book Company.

Stoll, Clarice Stasz, ed., 1973. *Sexism: Scientific Debates*. Reading: Addison-Wesley.

Stone, Carl, 1973. *Class, Race and Political Behavior in Urban Jamaica*. Kingston: Institute of Social and Economic Research, University of the West Indies.

Stone, Chuck, 1970. *Black Political Power in America*. New York: Dell Publishing Co.

Strauss, Joseph H. and Lawrence Clinton, 1972. "The Bureau of Indian Affairs, Adult Vocational Training Program: Success By Whose Criteria?" In de la Garza et al., 1972 (q.v.), pp. 153–60.

Strizower, Schifra, 1971. *The Bene Israel of Bombay: A Study of a Jewish Community*. New York: Schocken.

Sudetenland, 1954. Göttinger Arbeitskreis (Göttingen Research Society), *Sudetenland*. (Reference book on all areas of German settlement in Bohemia, Moravia, and Silesia.) Kitzingen/Main: Holzner-Verlag.

Suelzle, Marijean, 1973. "Women in Labor." *Transaction* (November/December, 1970): 50–58. Reprinted in Stoll, 1973 (q.v.), pp. 87–106.

Suleiman, Michael W., 1967. *Political Parties in Lebanon: The Challenge of a Fragmented Political Culture*. Ithaca: Cornell University Press.

Sumner, William Graham, 1906. Address at dinner of the Committee on Tariff Reform of the Reform Club in the city of New York, June 2.

Sutton, Percy E. (Former Pres. of the Borough of Manhattan, New York), 1971. "The Urban Poor." In Mervyn M. Dymally, ed., *The Black Politician: His Struggle for Power*. Belmont, California: Duxbury Press, pp. 26–32.

Suzman, Helen, 1972. "The Progressive Party's Programme for a Multiracial South Africa." In Rhoodie, 1972 (q.v.), pp. 227–44.

Suzuki, Jiro, and Mickey Sakamoto, 1975. "Discrimination Against Foreigners of Japanese Descent in Japan." In Veenhoven, 1975, (q.v.), 2: 247–84.

Svalastoga, Kaare and Gosta Carlsson, 1971. "Scandinavia." In Archer and Giner, 1971 (q.v.), pp. 358–87.

Svensson, Frances, 1973. *The Ethnics in American Politics: American Indians*. Minneapolis: Burgess Publishing Co.

Swartz, Tom, 1972. "Coloured Progress Under Separate Development." In Rhoodie, 1972 (q.v.), pp. 383–99.

Szaszy, Istvan, 1974. *Conflict of Laws in the Western Socialist Developing Countries*. Leiden, Netherlands: A. W. Sijthoff.

Taft, Ronald et al., 1970. *Attitudes and Social Conditions*. Canberra: Australian National University Press.

Tamarin, Georges R., 1973. *The Israeli Dilemma: Essays on a Warfare State*. Rotterdam: Rotterdam University Press.

—— 1975. "Israeli Society: Authoritarian Traditionalism Versus Pluralist Democracy." In Veenhoven, 1975 (q.v.), 2: 101–36.

Tandon, Yash, 1973. *Problems of a Displaced Minority: The New Position of East Africa's Asians*. London, Minority Rights Group, Report No. 16.

Tatz, C. M., 1972. "Education and Land Rights: Australian and South African Ideologies." In Stevens, 1972 (q.v.), 2: 253–66.

Taubinger, L. M. von, 1975. "Suffering and Struggle of the Kurds." In Veenhoven, 1975 (q.v.), 1: 243–59.

Taylor, Ronald B., 1973. *Child Labor on the Farm*. Boston: Beacon Press.

Theodorson, George A., and Achilles G. Theodorson, 1969. *A Modern Dictionary of Sociology*. London: Methuen and Co.

Thernstrom, Stephan, 1973. *The Other Bostonians: Poverty and Progress in the American Metropolis, 1880–1970*. Cambridge: Harvard University Press.

Theunis, Sjef, 1972. "Political Rights and Foreign Workers." In van Houte and Melgert, 1972 (q.v.), pp. 162–65.

Thielbar, Gerald W., and Saul D. Feldman, 1972. *Issues in Social Inequality*. Boston: Little, Brown.

Thompson, Kenneth W., 1955. "Toward a Theory of International Politics." *American Political Science Review* (September): 733–46.

Thompson, Richard, 1969. "Race in New Zealand." In Tumin, 1969 (q.v.), pp. 178–96.

Thürer, Georg, 1948. *Bundesspiegel: Werdegang und Verfassung der Schweizerischen Eidgenossenschaft*. Zurich: Artemis-Verlag.

Tiger, Lionel, and Robin Fox, 1971. *The Imperial Animal*. New York: Holt, Rinehart and Winston.

Tinker, Hugh, 1972. "Manifestations of Discrimination in Great Britain." In van Houte and Melgert, 1972 (q.v.), pp. 66–70.

Tökes, Rudolf L., 1975. *Dissent in the U.S.S.R.: Politics, Ideology and People.* Baltimore and London: Johns Hopkins University Press.

Tomasi, Lydia F., 1972. *The Ethnic Factor in the Future of Inequality.* New York: Center for Migration Studies.

Toplin, Robert Brent, ed., 1974. *Slavery and Race Relations in Latin America.* London: Greenwood Press.

Torture, 1977. *Torture in South Africa.* Johannesburg, The Christian Institute of South Africa, April 1977 (brochure).

Towers, 1974. "Towers in Bombay Criticized." Article referring to towers on which Indian Parsees leave their dead to be eaten by vultures, and dealing with the social conditions of the Parsees generally. *Washington Post*, September 11, p. 9.

Townsend, Peter, 1973. *The Social Minority.* London: Lane.

Toynbee, Arnold J., 1949. *Kultur am Scheidewege.* Transl. of *Civilization on Trial.* London: Oxford University Press. Zürich and Vienna: Europa-Verlag.

Tristram, H. B., 1865. *The Land of Israel: A Journal of Travels in Palestine.* London: Society for Promoting Christian Knowledge.

Tsuchigane, Robert, and Morton Dodge, 1974. *Economic Discrimination Against Women in the United States.* London: Lexington Books.

Tucker, Robert W., 1960. *The Just War.* Baltimore: Johns Hopkins Press.

Tumin, Melvin M., 1967. *Social Stratification: The Forms and Functions of Inequality.* Englewood Cliffs, New Jersey: Prentice-Hall.

—— 1969. *Comparative Perspectives on Race Relations.* Boston: Little, Brown.

—— 1973. *Patterns of Society: Identities, Roles, Resources.* Boston: Little, Brown.

Turnwald, W. K., ed., 1951 and 1953. *Documents on the Expulsion of the Sudeten Germans.* Munich: Arbeitsgemeinschaft zur Wahrung sudetendeutscher Interessen. German edition 1951. Condensed English edition 1953.

Twain, Mark, 1881. *The Innocents Abroad.* British Edition, London.

Ugly, 1976. "Now, A Drive To End Discrimination Against 'Ugly' People." *USN & WR* (August 23, 1976), p. 50. "When Authority Looks Into The Problem of Ugliness." Interview with research psychologist Leonard Saxbe. *Ibid.*, pp. 51–52.

Uhlig, Otto, 1974. *Die ungeliebten Gäste: ausländische Arbeitnehmer in Deutschland.* Munich: Praeger.

Ulč, Otto, 1969. "Communist National Minority Policy: The Case of the Gypsies in Czechoslovakia." *Soviet Studies,* 20 (April): 421–43; reprinted in Yetman and Steele, 1971 (q.v.), pp. 138–46. Page references are to this reprint.

Ullendorff, Edward, ed., 1973. *The Ethiopians: An Introduction to Country and People.* London: Oxford University Press.

Uranga, Susan Navarro, 1972. "The Study of Mexican-American Education in the Southwest: Implications of Research by the Civil Rights Commission." In de la Garza et al, 1972 (q.v.), pp. 161–72.

Urban America, Inc. and Urban Coalition, 1969. *One Year Later.* New York: Praeger.

Urwin, Derek W., 1970. "Social Cleavages and Political Parties in Belgium: Problems of Institutionalization." *Political Studies* 18, no. 3 (September): 320–40.

U.S. News and World Report, weekly news magazine, Washington, D.C.

Utley, Freda, 1969. "Upside-Down Victory in the Holy Land." *Arab World,* 15 (*January/February*). 3–6.

Uwechue, Raph, 1971. *Reflections on the Nigerian Civil War: Facing the Future.* New York: Africana Publishing Corp.

Valabrègue, Catherine, 1973. *L'Homme Déraciné: Le Livre Noir des Travailleurs Étrangers.* Paris: Mercure de France.

Vallat, Francis (Sir), 1972. *An Introduction to the Study of Human Rights.* Based on a Series of Lectures delivered at King's College. London: Europa.

Van den Berghe, Pierre, 1972. "Race as a Special Case of Differentiation and Stratification." Extract from *Race and Racism* (New York: Wiley). In Thielbar and Feldman, 1972 (q.v.) pp. 256–59.

Van der Veen, Klaas W., 1972. *I Give Thee My Daughter: A Study of Marriage and Hierarchy Among the Anavil Brahmins of South Gujarat.* Trans. Nanette Jockin. Assen, Netherlands: Van Gorcum.

Van Godtsenhoven, Patrick, 1975. "Inexplorado!" *Yachting.* New York, June, 45, 118–121; at p. 120.

Van Haegendoren, Maurits, 1971. *Nationalisme en Federalisme, Politieke Bedenkingen.* Antwerp: Uitgeverij De Nederlandsche Boekhandel.

—— 1975. "Ethno-Linguistic Cleavage in Belgium." In Veenhoven, 1975 (q.v.), 2: 3–29.

van Houte, Hans and Willy Melgert, eds., 1972. *Foreigners in Our Country*. Amsterdam and Antwerp: Keesing Publishers.

Vansertima, Ivan, 1971. "African Linguistic and Mythological Structures in the New World." In Rhoda L. Goldstein, ed., *Black Life and Culture in the United States*. New York: Crowell, pp. 12–35.

Vasil, R. K., 1971. *Politics in a Plural Society: A Study of Non-Communal Political Parties in West Malaysia*. London: Oxford University Press.

Vasijev, Y., 1969. "A Just and Stable Peace is Urgently Needed." Transl. in *Current Digest of the Soviet Press*, 21 (February 21): 9–10.

Vaughan, Michalina, 1971. "Poland." In Archer and Giner, 1971 (q.v.), pp. 318–57.

Vecoli, Rudolph J., 1972. *Ethnic Studies and Higher Education: A Comment*. Presented at the meeting of the Upper Midwest Ethnic Studies Association, St. Olaf College, U.S.A., October 14.

Veenhoven, Willem A., ed., 1975 and 1976. *Case Studies on Human Rights and Fundamental Freedoms: A World Survey*. 5 vols. The Hague: Martinus Nijhoff. (Willem A. Veenhoven, Editor-in chief; Winifred Crum Ewing, assistant to the Editor-in-chief; Clemens Amelunxen, Kurt Glaser, Stefan T. Possony, Jan Prins, Nic Rhoodie, Jiro Suzuki, and L. P. Vidyarthi, associate editors.)

Verba, Sidney, et al., 1971. *Caste, Race and Politics: A Comparative Study of India and the United States*. Beverly Hills: Sage Publications.

Verbunt, Gilles, 1969. "Intégration et Désintégration de la Famille." *Hommes et Migration Documents*, no. 771 (July 15).

Vnuk, František, 1973. "Slovakia in pre-Munich Czecho-Slovakia." In Joseph M. Kirschbaum, ed., *Slovakia in the 19th and 20th Centuries*. Toronto, 1973, Slovak World Congress, pp. 97, 123.

Voegelin, Eric, 1971. "On Paradise and Revolution." *The Southern Review*, January, 39ff.

—— 1975. *From Enlightenment to Revolution*. Durham, N.C.: Duke University Press.

Voronel, A. and Viktor Yakhot, eds., undated. *I Am A Jew: Essays on Jewish Identity in the Soviet Union*. New York: Anti-Defamation League of B'nai B'rith.

Vosloo, W. B., 1972. "The Coloured Policy of the National Party." In Rhoodie, 1972 (q.v.), pp. 359–82.

Wachtel, Howard M. 1974. "Looking at Poverty from Radical, Conservative and Liberal Perspectives." In Roby, 1974 (q.v.), pp. 180ff.

Wagatsuma, Hiroshi, 1967. "The Pariah Caste in Japan: History and Present Self-Image." In de Reuck and Knight, 1967 (q.v.), pp. 118–40.

Wagley, Charles and Marvin Harris, 1958. *Minorities in the New World*. New York: Columbia University Press.

Wagner, P. L., 1958. "Remarks on the Geography of Language." *Geographical Review*, no. 48, pp. 86–98.

Wai, Dunston, M., ed., 1973. *The Southern Sudan: The Problem of National Integration*. London: Frank Cass.

Waiguchu, Julius M., 1971. "Black Heritage: Of Genetics, Environment, and Continuity." In Rhoda L. Goldstein, ed., *Black Life and Culture in the United States*. New York: Crowell, pp. 64–86.

Wakin, Edward, 1961. "The Copts in Egypt." *Middle Eastern Affairs* 12 (August/September).

—— 1963. *A Lonely Minority: The Modern Story of the Egyptian Copts*. New York: William Morrow.

Walker, R. J., 1972. "Urbanism and the Cultural Continuity of an Ethnic Minority: The Maori Case." In Baxter and Sansom, 1972 (q.v.), pp. 399–410.

Walker, Richard L., 1971. *The Human Cost of Communism in China*. Washington: Government Printing Office. *See also* Human Cost, 1971.

Wallerstein, Immanuel Maurice, 1970. "Ethnicity and National Integration in West Africa." In M. E. Doro and N. W. Stultz, eds., *Governing in Black Africa*. Englewood Cliffs, N.J.: Prentice-Hall, 1970.

—— 1973. *Conflict Social en Afrique Noire Indépendante*. Brussels: Centre d'Étude et de Deocumentation Africaines.

Walsh, Annmarie Hauck, 1968. *Urban Government for the Paris Region*. New York: Frederick A. Praeger.

Walsh, Denny, 1974. "Illegal Aliens Called Duped by Lawyers." *New York Times* (July 7).

Warren, Max, 1964. "Christian Minorities in Muslim Countries." *Race* 6 (July): 41–51.

Waterlow, C., 1974. *Superpowers and Victims: The Outlook for the Poor Countries*. Englewood Cliffs, N.J.: Prentice-Hall.

Watson, Peter, ed., 1973. *Psychology and Race*. Harmondsworth, England: Penguin.

Wavell, Stuart, 1974. "Indian File." (Dealing with criticism of Brazilian Indian policy.) *The Guardian* (December, 21).

Wax, Murray L., and Robert W. Buchanan, eds., 1975. Solving *"The Indian Problem": The White Man's Burdensome Business*. New York: New Viewpoints.

Weber, Max, 1968. *Economy and Society*, edited by Guenther Roth and Claus Wittich, 3 vols. New York: Bedminster Press.

Wedderburn, Dorothy, 1973. *Poverty, Inequality, and Class Structure*. London: Cambridge University Press.

Wedderburn, D., and C. Craig, 1969. "Relative Deprivation in Work." Paper presented at the British Association for the Advancement of Science, Exeter.

Weeks, David R., ed., 1972. *A Glossary of Sociological Concepts*. Bletchley, Bucks, England: Open University Press.

Weil, Gordon L., 1970. *Benelux Nations: The Politics of Small-Country Democracies*. New York: Holt, Rinehart, and Winston.

Weinryb, B. D., 1972. "Antisemitism in Soviet Russia." In Kochan, 1972 (q.v.), pp. 288–320.

Weltsch, Robert, 1974. "The Cyprus Tragedy." *New Outlook*, October. Reprinted in *Crisis on Cyprus*, Part II, Appendix III, pp. 65–66.

Wenk, Michael G., S. M. Tomasi, and Geno Baroni, eds., 1972. *Pieces of a Dream: The Ethnic Worker's Crisis in America*. New York: C.M.S. Publications, Center for Migration Studies.

Western, John S., 1975. "Discrimination in Australia and New Zealand." In Veenhoven, 1975 (q.v.), 2: 302–42.

Wetherall, William and DeVos, George A., 1975. "Ethnic Minorities in Japan." In Veenhoven, 1975 (q.v.), 1: 333–75.

Wheeler, Geoffrey, 1973–74. *Racial Problems in Soviet Muslim Asia*. London: Oxford University Press.

Whitaker, Ben, ed., 1972a. *The Fourth World: Victims of Group Oppression*. Eight Reports from the Field Work of the Minority Rights Group. London: Sidgwick and Jackson, Ltd.

—— 1972b. "The Biharis in Bangladesh." Report No. 11 of the Minority Rights Group. London.

Whyte, Martin King, 1974. *Small Groups and Political Rituals in China*. Berkeley: University of California Press.

Wickramanayake, D., 1975. "The Caste System in Sri Lanka." In Veenhoven, 1975 (q.v.), 2: 179–89.

Wiefels, J., 1949. *Deutsche Verfassungsgeschichte*. Stuttgart: W. Kohlhammer-Verlag.

Wierer, Rudolf, 1960. *Der Föderalismus im Donauraum*. Graz and Cologne, Böhlau-Verlag.

Wilkinson, Paul, 1975. *Political Terrorism*. Studies in Comparative Politics Series. Basingstoke, Hampshire, England: Macmillan.

Willems, Fredericus, 1972. "Manifestations of Discrimination in the Netherlands." In van Houte and Melgert, 1972 (q.v.), pp. 71–77.

Williams, Frederick, 1973. *Language and Poverty: Perspectives on a Theme*. Chicago: Rand McNally.

Williams, Robin M., 1973. "Strangers Next Door: Ethnic Relations in American Communities." In Hill et al., 1973 (q.v.), pp. 472–91.

Wilpert, Friedrich von, 1964. *The Oder-Neisse Problem*. Bonn and Brussels: Atlantic Forum.

Wilson, A. Jeyaratnam, 1974. *Politics in Sri Lanka, 1947–1973*. London: Macmillan Press.

Wilson, James, 1974. *Canada's Indians*. London: Minority Rights Group, Report No. 21.

Wilson, William J., 1973. *Power, Racism, and Privilege*. New York: Macmillan.

—— 1976. "The Changing Context of American Race Relations: Urban Blacks and Structural Shifts in the Economy." In Veenhoven, 1976 (q.v.), 5: 175–96.

Wirth, Louis, 1945. "The Problem of Minority Groups." In Ralph Linton, ed., *The Science of Man in the World Crisis*. New York: Columbia University Press, 1945.

Wolff, Harold, 1953. *Stress and Disease*. Springfield, Ill.: Charles C Thomas.

Wolfinger, Raymond E., 1965. "The Development and Persistence of Ethnic Voting." *American Political Science Review* 59, no. 4 (December): 896–908.

Wolman, Harold L. and Norman C. Thomas, 1970. "Black Interests, Black Groups, and Black Influence in the Federal Policy Progress: The Cases of Housing and Education." *Journal of Politics* 32, no. 4 (November): 875–97.

Wolstenholme, Gordon T. and Maeve O'Connor, eds., 1965. *Man in Africa*. London: Churchill.

Woodward, C. Vann, 1966. *The Strange Career of Jim Crow*, 2nd rev. ed. New York: Oxford University Press.

Wright, D., 1972. "Sex Differences." In P. Barker,

ed., *A Sociological Portrait*. Harmondsworth, England: Penguin Books, 1972.

Wright, J. Skelly, 1969. "The Courts Have Failed the Poor." *New York Times Magazine*, March 9. Reprinted in Bryant, 1971 (q.v.), pp. 300–312; and in Yetman and Steele, 1971 (q.v.), pp. 430–43. Page references are to Yetman and Steele.

Wright, Michael, 1972. *Zambia: I Changed My Mind*. London: Johnson Publications, Ltd.

Wright, David E., Esteban Salinas, and William P. Kuvlesky, 1973. "Opportunities for Social Mobility for Mexican-American Youth." In de la Garza et al, 1973 (q.v.), pp. 43–60.

Wrong, Dennis H., 1972. "Social Inequality Without Social Stratification." In Thielbar and Feldman, 1972 (q.v.), pp. 91–104.

Yaari, Ehud, 1968. "Al-Fatah's Political Thinking." *New Outlook* 11 (November–December): 20–33.

Yaniv, A., 1974. *P.L.O.* (Palestine Liberation Organization): *A Profile*. Jerusalem: Israel Universities Study Group for Middle Eastern Affairs (August).

Yee, Albert H., 1973. "Myopic Perceptions and Textbooks: Chinese Americans' Search for Identity." *The Journal of Social Issues* 29 (2): 99–113.

Yesenin-Volpin, Dr. A. S., 1972. Testimony before U.S. Senate Internal Security Subcommittee. Printed in *Abuse of Psychiatry* (See that entry).

Yetman, Norman R. and C. Hoy Steele, eds., 1972. *Majority and Minority: The Dynamics of Racial and Ethnic Relations*. Boston: Allyn and Bacon.

Yinger, J. Milton, 1965. *A Minority Group in American Society*. New York: McGraw-Hill.

—— 1968. "Social Discrimination." In *International Encyclopaedia of the Social Sciences*, Vol. 12.

—— 1975. "Discrimination Against American Blacks." In Veenhoven, 1975 (q.v.), 1: 39–64.

Young, Andrew, 1974. "The Voting Rights Struggle Continues." *Focus*, 2, no. 12 (October): 4–5. Washington, Joint Center for Political Studies.

Young, Donald, 1932. *American Minority Peoples*. New York: Harpers.

Young, Ian, 1974. *The Private Life of Islam*. London: Allen Lane.

Zangwill, Israel, 1909. *The Melting Pot* (a play). New York: Macmillan.

Zimmerman, Joseph F., 1973. *The Federated City: Community Control in Large Cities*. New York: St. Martin's.

INDEXES

GENERAL NOTE: There are three indexes: an index of persons; an index of places, peoples, and languages; and an index of subjects. Generally, subjects and names are indexed wherever substantial, even if brief, statements are made about them. Enumerations or lists, such as a list of countries where practices similar to slavery have been reported, are not indexed in detail. Events or documents associated with places, such as the Treaty of Versailles, will be found in the subject index.

INDEX OF PERSONS

NOTE: No attempt has been made to list all the people mentioned in this book, or all the authors cited. This index is limited to people who figure prominently in the Human Rights story, whether "on the side of the angels" or otherwise, as well as important political, historical, and cultural personages.

INDEX OF PLACES, PEOPLES, AND LANGUAGES

NOTE: Combined entries are used insofar as countries or regions, peoples or ethnic groups, and languages have the same names and are contiguous. Thus, the entries for "Denmark, Danes" and "Turkey, Turks" would include references to the Danish and Turkish languages, respectively. References to France and Spain, however, are separated from those to the French and Spanish languages, since the latter are spoken far beyond their countries of origin. Likewise, entries are separate when a people and its country have different names. "Zulu," for instance, refers to the Zulu nation and its language; the Zulu homeland, however, is listed as KwaZulu. This index contains references to religions only insofar as their adherents tend to form political communities. Other references to religions will be found in the Subject Index.

SUBJECT INDEX

NOTE: Subjects are grouped under main heads. For chattel slavery, for instance, see Slavery, chattel. For a subject in a particular country, such as forced labor in the USSR, see also under that country in the places, peoples, and languages index. Where there is no specific negative entry (such as Freedom, Deprivation of), an entry indicating a right may refer to cases in which that right is violated rather than upheld. Thus, Freedom of assembly and association refers to page 537, where mention is made of mass arrests of opposition party members—a violation of freedom of association.

EAST ORANGE PUBLIC LIBRARY
Victims of politics : the state of hum
323.4 G548   / Glaser, Kurt,

3 2665 0001 5071 6

323.4 - G548 cop.1   OCLC

There is a penalty for removing either the book
card or the control card from this pocket.
EAST ORANGE PUBLIC LIBRARY
21 So. Arlington
Branches—Ampere, 89 Ampere Plaza—Franklin, 192 Dodd Street
Elmwood, 317 South Clinton Street
EAST ORANGE, NEW JERSEY
DISCARD